CW00751321

MACMIL

Chinese Character

DICTIONARY

汉语学习字典

Macmillan Education
Between Towns Road, Oxford, OX4 3PP
A division of Macmillan Publishers Limited
Companies and representatives throughout the world

ISBN 9780230405943

Text © Foreign Language Teaching and Research Press 2010
Cover design © Macmillan Publishers Limited 2010
First published by the Foreign Language Teaching and Research Press 2009
This edition published by Macmillan Publishers Limited 2010
CharGuide software © Changzhou SinoType Technology Co., Ltd. 2010

All rights reserved; no part of this publication may be reproduced, stored in a
retrieval system, transmitted in any form, or by any means, electronic,
mechanical, photocopying, recording, or otherwise, without the prior written
permission of the publishers.

This dictionary includes words on the basis of their use in the Mandarin
Chinese language today. Some words are identified as being trademarks or
service marks. Neither the presence nor absence of such identification in this
Dictionary is to be regarded as affecting in any way, or expressing a judgment
on, the validity or legal status of any trademark, service mark, or other
proprietary rights anywhere in the world.

The publishers have tried to trace and contact copyright holders before
publication, but if they have inadvertently overlooked any, they will be pleased
to make the necessary arrangements at the first opportunity.

Printed and bound in China

2014   2013   2012   2011   2010

10 9 8 7 6 5 4 3 2 1

Contents

Foreword

This dictionary is mainly intended for non-native Chinese learners. Two distinguishing features render the dictionary innovative.

First, special attention is paid to the selection of characters and words. About 3,000 characters are collected in the dictionary. Among them, 2,500 commonly used characters are chosen from the official *List of Commonly Used Characters in Contemporary Chinese.* In addition, some 500 more characters are selected from this list in accordance to the principle of "high frequency in word building and high frequency of use in daily life". The 32,000 or so words and expressions almost cover the words in the *Syllabus of Graded Words and Characters for Chinese Proficiency*, as tested in the HSK examination. In short, the entry words in this dictionary are the most likely to occur in everyday Chinese communication and are therefore most useful for non-native learners.

Second, the dictionary lays emphasis on some of the most prominent features of the relationships between Chinese characters and Chinese language. These include 1) an individual character consists of form, sound and meaning, and as a result, many characters are also monosyllable words; 2) when a character (or a morpheme) forms a word, its position is not fixed; and 3) a commonly used Chinese character is often multisemantic. The meaning of a compound word is often related to one of the meanings of the constituent character(s). It is not uncommon that the meanings of words can be inferred from the constituent characters.

The structure of the entries in the dictionary is based on the above features of Chinese characters and words.

Targeted towards non-native learners, this dictionary helps learners to read and write Chinese characters correctly and to get acquainted with basic knowledge about Chinese characters. Therefore, each character has Pinyin to show its pronunciation. The order and number of strokes, and the radical of each character are also clearly indicated. Moreover, Pinyin is added to all the words and illustrative sentences.

Another prominent innovation of the dictionary is its inclusion of backward-sequence words under head characters. For example, under the head character 单, the learner can find the word 床单 (bed sheet), which carries one of the meanings of 单, i.e. sheet. In this way, the learner will find more words to illustrate the meanings of a character, and learn more connections between characters and words. This can be highly inductive to enlarging the learner's vocabulary.

A learner's dictionary should be seen as an integral part of relevant textbooks. The compilers believe that frequent reference to this dictionary will enable learners to master Chinese more rapidly and more efficiently.

Zheng Shupu
Chief Editor

How to Use this Dictionary

担（擔）dān ····· 8画 扌部 ··········· traditional form
········· pronunciation,
number of strokes and radicals

担 担担担担担担担担 ·········· stroke order

❶[动]用肩挑：carry on a shoulder pole ｜ ～水 dānshuǐ *carry water (with a shoulder pole and buckets)* / ～柴 dānchái *carry firewood with a shoulder pole* ········ part of speech

❷[动]负起；承当：take on; undertake ········· definition
｜ ～责任 dān zérèn *shoulder responsibility* / ～风险 dān fēngxiǎn *run risks; take risks* ········· example phrases and collocations

担负 dānfù bear; shoulder; take on; be charged with

担任 dānrèn assume the office; hold the post

担心 dānxīn worry; feel anxious ········· words and phrases containing the character

担忧 dānyōu worry; be anxious

承担 chéngdān　负担 fùdān
See dàn. ················· homonym

单（單）dān ···· 8画 丷部

单 单单单单单单单单

❶ [形]一个：one; single ｜ ～身 ········· example words in Pinyin
dānshēn *unmarried; single* / ～扇门 dānshànmén *single-leaf door*
单词 dāncí word

1a

单项 dānxiàng (sports) individual event

单一 dānyī single; unitary

单元 dānyuán unit

孤单 gūdān

❷ [形]薄弱：thin; weak ┊ ～薄 dānbó thin; frail / 你的身体太～了。Nǐ de shēntǐ tài dān le. *You are too thin and weak.*

❸ [形]不复杂；纯一：simple

单纯 dānchún ① simple; pure ② alone; purely; merely

单调 dāndiào monotonous; dull; drab

简单 jiǎndān

❹ [形]只有一层的：unlined ┊ ～衣 dānyī *unlined garment* / ～裤 dānkù *unlined trousers* / 这件大衣是～的还是夹层的? Zhè jiàn dàyī shì dān de háishì jiācéng de? *Is this coat unlined or lined?*

❺ [名]覆盖用的纺织品：sheet ┊

被～bèidān *sheet*

床单 chuángdān

❻ [名]记事用的纸片：bill; list ┊ 账～zhàngdān *bill; check* / 价目～jiàmùdān *price list*

❼ [形]奇数的（跟"双shuāng"相对）：odd (the opposite of "双 shuāng") ┊ ～号 dānhào *odd number* / ～数 dānshù *singular number*

单方面 dānfāngmiàn one-sided; unilateral

◇单位 dānwèi unit

head character in an example is represented by "～"

"/" used to separate examples

example sentences

"┊" used to keep definitions and examples apart

antonyms

words without example sentences are separated with "◇"

Listing of Entries

1. The entries are classified into single-character and multi-character categories. Single-character entries are enlarged. The Pinyin, the number of strokes, and their radicals are clearly indicated, and the sequence of writing strokes is shown in red.

2. For entries with multiple meanings, the sequence of meanings is shown in black numerals.

3. Immediately below most single-character entries are multi-character entries that begin with the head character, listed in alphabetical order according to the pronunciation of the second character. Words which do not have example sentences are marked by "◇", and listed after other multi-character entries.

4. Backward-sequence words, i.e. words that do not begin with the head character, are listed after relevant regular entries.

5. Single-character entries are listed in the alphabetical order of Chinese Pinyin. Homonyms are arranged according to their number of strokes from fewer to more; those with the same number of strokes are listed in order of the horizontal stroke (—), the vertical stroke (|), the downward stroke to the left (丿), the dot (、) and the horizontal stroke with a bending tip (﹁).

6. Single-character entries with the same forms but different pronunciations and meanings, such as 好(hǎo) and 好(hào), 当(dāng) and 当(dàng), are listed as separate entries. Those with identical forms and with similar meanings but different in pronunciation and usage, such as 剥(bāo) and 剥(bō), are also listed as separate entries.

7. Multi-character entries (including backward-sequence words) are arranged in order of the number of their component characters. Two-

character words come before three-character words, which come before four-character words. Words formed with the same number of characters are listed in order of the Pinyin alphabet of the second character, or the third character if the second character pronounced the same, etc. Multi-character words similar in pronunciation but different in form are arranged in order of their strokes, from fewer to more.

Written Forms of Characters

8. The dictionary follows the official standard of simplified Chinese characters. Traditional forms of corresponding single-character entries are put in brackets. The traditional forms of multi-character entries are not provided.

9. The dictionary does not provide variant forms of characters.

10. Words that may or may not be inflected with the character 儿 in written Chinese but which must be spoken with the inflection are indicated by 儿, such as 小孩儿，大伙儿；words that are not normally inflected in written form but that are usually inflected in spoken form are not indicated by 儿.

Pronunciation

11. All entries (including backward-sequence words) are provided with Pinyin. All examples (phrases and sentences) are also provided with Pinyin. Tones are indicated in their original pronunciation, whereas tone changes in certain combination of words are not marked.

12. All the phonetic transcriptions follow the *Basic Rules for Hanyu Pinyin Orthography*.

13. Regarding the 儿 inflection, all entries with 儿 inflection have the consonant "r" at the end of their basic Pinyin transcription, e.g. 纽

扣儿 (niǔkòur).

14. An apostrophe "'" is used in transcribing multi-character entries in order to avoid possible confusion among syllables, such as 平安(píng'ān).

Part of speech

15. The part of speech is given only in single-character entries, not in multi-character entries.

16. For single-character entries with a number of meanings, each of the meanings is given its part of speech.

17. The part of speech is concisely given in square brackets [ ], such as [名], [动], [形].

18. Parts of speech fall into the following categories:

[名]名词 noun   [动]动词 verb   [形]形容词 adjective
[副]副词 adverb   [量]量词 classifier [连]连词 conjunction
[代]代词 pronoun   [数]数词 numeral [助]助词 auxiliary word
[介]介词 preposition[叹]叹词 interjection[象声]象声词 onomatopoeia
[词尾]词尾 end morpheme [词头]词头 head morpheme

Definitions

19. Definitions are based on contemporary Chinese.

20. Definitions of single-character entries are given both in Chinese and English. For multi-character entries only their English equivalents are given.

21. For some nouns denoting names of things, their English equivalents are immediately given, with their Chinese definitions omitted, such as:

肠（腸）cháng 7画 月部

肠　肠肠肠肠肠肠肠

[名] intestine

香肠 xiāngcháng

22. For some single-character entries that have no meaning by themselves and can only be used together with another character to denote meaning, "See..." is used to indicate that the learner should read the example words for reference.

23. Some single-character entries have certain senses with antonyms. In such cases, the antonym is put in brackets at the end of the definition. "The opposite of ..." is used.

24. Usage illustrations are given after the definition of each single-character entry (with the exception of pure morphemes). Between each definition and example, a vertical line "｜" is used to keep them apart.

25. Usage examples include word collocations, phrases and sentences. A left slash "/" is used to keep two or more examples apart.

26. If a head character is used in an example sentence, it is substituted by the symbol "～".

Phonetic Index
音序检字表

The number to the right of each character indicates the page number in the dictionary.

Radical Index
部首检字表

Introduction

1. The list of radicals is largely the same as those in other Chinese dictionaries. Radicals are listed from fewer to more strokes; those with the same number of strokes are listed in the order of their beginning stroke, i.e. horizontal stroke (一), vertical stroke (丨), downward stroke to the left (丿), dot (丶), horizontal stroke with a bending tip (乛), and so on.

2. First, look up the page number of the radical in the List of Radicals. Then look up the page number of the character in the Radical Index.

3. Variants of radicals are listed after the last entry under the normal radical and are indicated with the symbol "△", or annotated in brackets immediately after the normal radicals.

4. In the Radical Index, traditional forms of characters are listed in brackets under the relevant entries. Non-standard radical variants of characters are not included.

5. Some characters are listed under two or more different radicals, such as 杰 , which is listed under both the radicals of 木 and 灬.

I. Radical List

The number to the right of each radical indicates the page number in the Character List by Radical beginning on page 4c.

一画		亠	8c	尢(兀)	13c	尸	19c	止	22c
一	4c	冫	8c	弋	13c	己(已巳)	19c	(⺌)	17c
丨	4c	冖	8c	小	13c	弓	19c	日(曰曰)	22c
丿	4c	讠	8c	△⺌	13c	子	19c	贝	22c
、	5c	△言	9c	口	13c	屮	19c	(水)	17c
乛(乚乙)	5c	凵	9c	囗	14c	女	19c	见	23c
二画		卩(⼞)	9c	山	14c	飞	20c	牛(牜)	23c
十	5c	阝(左)	9c	巾	14c	马	20c	(手扌)	12c
厂(厂)	5c	阝(右)	9c	彳	15c	纟	20c	毛	23c
匚	5c	(刀)	6c	彡	15c	△糸	20c	气	23c
(卜)	6c	力	9c	犭	15c	幺	20c	攵(攴)	23c
刂	5c	厶	10c	△犬	15c	巛	20c	长	23c
△刀	6c	又	10c	夕	15c	**四画**		片	23c
△⺈	6c	廴	10c	夂	15c	王	20c	斤	23c
△卜(⼘)	6c	(巳)	9c	饣	15c	△玉	20c	爪(爫)	23c
冂(⺆)	6c	**三画**		△食	15c	无(旡)	20c	父	23c
亻	6c	干	10c	爿	15c	(耂)	28c	月(⺼)	23c
△人	7c	工	10c	广	15c	木	21c	氏	24c
△入	7c	土	10c	门	16c	支	21c	欠	24c
八(丷)	7c	△士	11c	氵	16c	(犬)	15c	风	24c
(⺈)	6c	扌	11c	△水	17c	歹	21c	殳	24c
(冂)	6c	△手扌	12c	△氺	17c	车	21c	文	24c
勹	7c	艹	12c	忄	17c	牙	22c	方	24c
儿	7c	寸	13c	△心⺗	17c	戈	22c	火	24c
匕	8c	廾	13c	宀	18c	比	22c	△灬	24c
几(⺇)	8c	大	13c	辶	18c	瓦	22c	斗	25c
				彐(彑)	19c			户	25c

II. Character List by Radical

The number to the right of each character indicates the page number in the dictionary.

23c

A a

阿   ā   7画 阝(左)部

阿 阿阿阿阿阿阿阿

❶[词头] 用在兄弟姐妹等称谓和小名、姓氏的前面：used before terms of address such as brother and sister, pet names and surnames | ～哥 āgē *elder brother* / ～妹 āmèi *younger sister* / ～宝 Ā Bǎo *A Bao* / ～张 Ā Zhāng *A Zhang*

❷[词头] 用在某些亲属名称的前面：used before terms of address for some relatives

阿舅 ājiù uncle (mother's brother)

阿姨 āyí aunt

◇阿拉伯语 Ālābóyǔ Arabic (language)

啊   ā   10画 口部

啊 啊啊啊啊啊啊啊啊啊啊

[叹]表示惊讶或赞叹：expressing admiration or surprise | ～，下雪了! Ā, xiàxuě le! *Oh, it's snowing!* / ～，风景太美了! Ā, fēngjing tài měi le! *Oh, the view is so beautiful!* / ～，这幅画真好看哪! Ā, zhè fú huà zhēn hǎokàn na! *Oh, what a beautiful picture!*

See á; ǎ; à; a.

啊   á   10画 口部

啊 啊啊啊啊啊啊啊啊啊啊

[叹]表示追问或要求重复：pressing for an answer or asking for a repetition | ～，真的吗? Á, zhēn de ma? *Oh, is it true?* / ～，你说什么? Á, nǐ shuō shénme? *Ah, what did you say?*

See ā; ǎ; à; a.

啊   ǎ   10画 口部

啊 啊啊啊啊啊啊啊啊啊啊

[叹]表示惊疑：expressing surprise or puzzlement | ～，我的帽子呢? Ǎ, wǒ de màozi ne? *Well, where is my hat?* / ～，这怎么可能呢? Ǎ, zhè zěnme kěnéng ne? *Well, how can this be true?*

See ā; á; à; a.

啊   à   10画 口部

啊 啊啊啊啊啊啊啊啊啊啊

❶[叹]表示应诺：expressing compliance or agreement | ～，就这样办吧! À, jiù zhèyàng bàn ba! *OK. Let's do it this way.*

❷[叹]表示醒悟：expressing sudden realization | ～，原来是你呀! À, yuánlái shì nǐ ya! *Ah, so it's you.*

❸[叹]表示赞叹或惊异：expressing admiration or amazement | ～，家乡的变化真大呀! À, jiāxiāng de biànhuà zhēn dà ya! *What great changes have taken place in our hometown!* / ～，你说得真好! À, nǐ shuō de zhēn hǎo! *Mm, well said!*

　　See ā; á; ǎ; a.

啊　　　　a　　10画 口部

啊 啊啊啊啊啊啊啊啊啊
啊啊

❶[助]用在句子末尾，加重语气：used at the end of a sentence for emphasis | 你可真行～! Nǐ kě zhēn xíng a! *Oh, you are so great!* / 你找谁～? Nǐ zhǎo shéi a? *Whom are you looking for?*

❷[助]用在句中停顿处，表示强调或列举：used at the pauses of sentences to emphasize or to enumerate items | 这个孩子～，可真可爱。Zhège háizi a, kě

zhēn kě'ài. *Oh, how lovely the child is!* / 那里的山～，水～，一切都很美。Nàli de shān a, shuǐ a, yīqiè dōu hěn měi. *Everything there — mountains and rivers — is so beautiful.*

❸[叹]表示劝导或轻度提示：expressing advice or suggestion | 你在家等着～! Nǐ zài jiā děngzhe a! *You'd better wait at home.*

　　See ā; á; ǎ; a.

哎　　　　āi　　8画 口部

哎 哎哎哎哎哎哎哎哎

❶[叹]表示惊讶或不满意：expressing surprise or dissatisfaction | ～!真想不到你也来了! Āi! Zhēn xiǎngbudào nǐ yě lái le! *Hey, I didn't expect you to come here too!* / ～，真怪啊! Āi, zhēn guài a! *Why, how strange it is!* / ～，你怎么能这样说呢! Āi, nǐ zěnme néng zhèyàng shuō ne! *Hey, how can you talk like this?* / ～，你怎么在这儿吸烟? Āi, nǐ zěnme zài zhèr xīyān? *Hey, how can you smoke here?* / ～，你怎么搞的! Āi, nǐ zěnme gǎo de! *See what you have done!*

哎呀　āiyā　① expressing astonishment or pain, used as "ah" or "my god", etc. ② expressing complaint or showing impatience, used as "goodness" or "oh dear", etc.

哎哟 āiyō expressing surprise and agony

❷[叹]表示提醒：reminding somebody of something ｜～，要迟到了! Āi,yào chídào le! *Oh, I'm going to be late.* ／～，我想起来了。Āi, wǒ xiǎng qǐlai le. *Ah, now I remember it.*

哀　　　　āi　　9画 一部

哀哀哀哀哀哀哀哀哀

❶[形]难过；悲伤；悲痛：grief, sorrow ｜喜怒～乐 xǐ-nù-āi-lè *happiness, anger, grief and joy* 悲哀 bēi'āi

❷[动]对死去的人表示悼念：mourn 哀悼 āidào grieve over sb.'s death; mourn

❸[副]苦苦地：piteously 哀求 āiqiú entreat; implore

埃　　　　āi　　10画 土部

埃埃埃埃埃埃埃埃埃埃

[名]灰尘；尘土：dust 尘埃 chén'āi

挨　　　　āi　　10画 扌部

挨　挨挨挨挨挨挨挨挨挨挨

❶[动]顺次，逐一：follow a regular order or sequence ｜～家赠送礼品 āi jiā zèngsòng lǐpǐn *distribute gifts from door to door* ／～着号叫 āizhe hào jiào *call the roll* ／把这些东西～着次序放好。Bǎ zhèxiē dōngxi āizhe cìxù fànghǎo. *Arrange these things in order.*
挨个 āigè in turn; one by one

❷[动]靠近；接触；紧接着：get close to; be next or near to ｜一个～着一个 yī gè āizhe yī gè *next to one another* ／他家～着图书馆。Tā jiā āizhe túshūguǎn. *His house is next to the library.* ／我们俩的座位紧～在一起。Wǒmen liǎ de zuòwèi jǐn āi zài yīqǐ. *Our seats are next to each other.*
挨近 āijìn be near to; get close to
挨着 āizhe be next to; get close to
See ái.

唉　　　　āi　　10画 口部

唉唉唉唉唉唉唉唉唉

❶[叹]表示应答：a sound used as an answering voice ｜～，我这就去。Āi,wǒ zhè jiù qù. *Yes, I'm going right away.*

❷[叹]叹息声：a sighing sound | ～!真拿他没办法!Āi! Zhēn ná tā méi bànfǎ! *Oh, there's no way to deal with him.* / ～，这下完了!Āi, zhè xià wán le! *Alas, it's finished!* / ～，太累了! Āi,tài lēi le! *Oh, I'm so tired.*

挨 ái 10画 扌部

挨挨挨挨挨挨挨挨挨挨

❶[动]遭受：suffer; endure | ～冻 āidòng *suffer from cold* / ～饿 āi'è *go hungry* / ～骂 āimà *be scolded; get a dressing-down* / 他没带伞，这下要～淋了。Tā méi dài sǎn, zhè xià yào āilín le. *He forgot his umbrella and would be caught in the rain.* / ～批评 āi pīpíng *be criticized sharply* / 他～了一个耳光。Tā āile yī gè ěrguāng. *He was given a slap in the face.*

❷[动]拖延：delay; put off | ～时间 āi shíjiān *play for time*

❸[动]困难地度过（时间）：struggle to pull through (hard times) | 总算～过了这段苦日子。Zǒngsuàn āiguo le zhè duàn kǔ rìzi. *In the end we struggled to pull through that miserable time.* / 老人的病恐怕～不过三个月。Lǎorén de bìng kǒngpà āibuguò sān gè yuè.

The old man is so ill that he is not likely to last another three months.

    See āi.

癌 ái 17画 疒部

癌癌癌癌癌癌癌癌
癌癌癌癌癌癌癌癌
癌

[名]恶性肿瘤：malignant tumour 癌症 áizhèng *cancer*

矮 ǎi 13画 矢部

矮矮矮矮矮矮矮矮
矮矮矮矮矮

❶[形]身材短：short of stature | ～个子 ǎi gèzi *a short person* / 弟弟比哥哥～。Dìdi bǐ gēge ǎi. *The younger brother is shorter than the elder brother.*

❷[形]高度小的；低：short in height or low | 这几棵小树很～。Zhè jǐ kē xiǎoshù hěn ǎi. *These small trees are very short.* / 院子四周有一道～墙。Yuànzi sìzhōu yǒu yī dào ǎi qiáng. *There is a low wall around the courtyard.*

❸[形]等级、地位低：low in grade or position | 他比我～一个年级。Tā bǐ wǒ ǎi yī gè niánjí. *He is one year lower than me.*

蔼 (藹) ǎi　14画 艹部

蔼 蔼蔼蔼蔼蔼蔼蔼蔼
蔼蔼蔼蔼蔼蔼

[形]和气；态度温和：kindly and friendly

和蔼 hé'ǎi

艾 ài　5画 艹部

艾 艾艾艾艾艾

[名]一种药用植物：Chinese mugwort

◇艾滋病 àizībìng AIDS (acquired immune deficiency syndrome)

爱 (愛) ài　10画 爫部

爱 爱爱爱爱爱爱爱爱
爱爱

❶[动]对人或事物有深厚的感情：love; have deep feelings for people or things | 他很~自己的妻子。Tā hěn ài zìjǐ de qīzi. *He loves his wife devotedly.* / 她最~花儿。Tā zuì ài huār. *She loves flowers most.*

爱戴 àidài love and esteem
爱国 àiguó love one's country; be patriotic
爱心 àixīn love; compassion;

sympathy
爱面子 àimiànzi be concerned about saving face; be sensitive about one's reputation

慈爱 cí'ài　　关爱 guān'ài
敬爱 jìng'ài　　亲爱 qīn'ài
热爱 rè'ài　　友爱 yǒu'ài

❷[动]喜好；喜欢：like; be fond of | 老李从小~唱歌。Lǎo Lǐ cóng xiǎo ài chànggē. *Lao Li has been fond of singing since childhood.* / 年轻人~热闹。Niánqīngrén ài rènao. *Young people enjoy being boisterous.*

爱好 àihào like; love; be fond of; be keen on

喜爱 xǐ'ài　　　　心爱 xīn'ài

❸[动]怜惜；爱护：cherish; treasure, hold dear; take good care of | ~公物 ài gōngwù *Cherish public property*

爱护 àihù cherish; take good care of; treasure
爱惜 àixī cherish; treasure; use sparingly

❹[动]容易发生某种行为(或变化)：be apt to; be in the habit of; tend to | 弟弟~哭。Dìdi ài kū. *The younger brother is apt to cry.* / 铁~生锈。Tiě ài shēngxiù. *Iron rusts easily.*

❺[名]特指男女间爱恋的感情：love between a man and a woman

爱情 àiqíng love (between sexes)
爱人 àirén ①husband or wife ②

sweetheart; lover
恋爱 liàn'ài　　相爱 xiāng'ài

隘　　　　ài　12画 阝(左)部

隘 隘隘隘隘隘隘隘隘隘
隘隘隘隘

❶[形]狭窄；狭小：narrow
狭隘 xiá'ài
❷[名]关口；险要的地方：narrow way over or through mountains │ 要～yào'ài a narrow pass

碍 (礙)　ài　13画 石部

碍 碍碍碍碍碍碍碍碍
碍碍碍碍碍

[动]妨害；阻挡：hinder; obstruct; be in the way of
碍事 àishì ① be in the way; be a hindrance ② be of consequence; matter
妨碍 fáng'ài　　障碍 zhàng'ài
阻碍 zǔ'ài

安　　　　ān　6画 宀部

安 安安安安安安

❶[形]平安，没有事故或危险：safe and sound
安全 ānquán safe; secure
安全带 ānquándài safety belt; seat belt

安全套 ānquántào condom; sheath
保安 bǎo'ān　　公安 gōng'ān
平安 píng'ān　　晚安 wǎn'ān
治安 zhì'ān
天安门 Tiān'ānmén
一路平安 yīlù-píng'ān
❷[形]平静；稳定：calm, stable │ 心神不～xīnshén-bù'ān feel uneasy / 这孩子坐立不～。Zhè háizi zuòlì-bù'ān. The child fidgets whether sitting or standing.
安定 āndìng ① stable; quiet; settled ② stabilize; maintain
安静 ānjìng quiet; peaceful
安宁 ānníng peaceful; tranquil
安稳 ānwěn firm and secure
安详 ānxiáng composed; serene; unruffled
安心 ānxīn ① feel at ease; be relieved; set one's mind at rest ② harbour an ulterior motive
不安 bù'ān
❸[动]使安定；使稳定：stabilize; settle down │ 他到这里后一直没有～下心来。Tā dào zhèlǐ hòu yīzhí méiyǒu ānxià xīn lai. He has not felt at ease yet since he came here.
安慰 ānwèi comfort; console
❹[动]安置；使人或物有适当的位置：find a place for │ 把他～到了重要部门。Bǎ tā āndàole zhòngyào bùmén. He was placed in an important de-

partment.

安排 ānpái arrange; fix up; plan

安置 ānzhì arrange for; find a
place for; help settle down

❺[动]装设：install; assemble ｜ ～
电灯 ān diàndēng *install electric lights* / ～空调 ān kōngtiáo
install an air conditioner

安装 ānzhuāng install; fix;
mount

❻[动]存着；怀着：harbour an
intention ｜你～的什么心，我
全知道。Nǐ ān de shénme
xīn, wǒ quán zhīdào. *I
know all about what you are
up to.*

   岸   àn   8画 山部

岸 岸 岸 岸 岸 岸 岸 岸

[名]江、河、湖、海等水域边缘的陆
地：bank; shore; coast ｜ 小河
两～种了许多柳树。Xiǎohé
liǎng'àn zhòngle xǔduō
liǔshù. *A lot of willows are
planted on both banks of the
river.* / 船马上就靠～了。Chuán
mǎshàng jiù kào àn le. *The
ship is nearing the shore.*

对岸 duì'àn   海岸 hǎi'àn

口岸 kǒu'àn   沿岸 yán'àn

   按   àn   9画 扌部

 按 按 按 按 按 按 按 按
按

❶[动]用手或指尖压：press or push
down with hand or fingers ｜ ～
门铃 àn ménlíng *ring the door
bell* / ～图钉 àn túdīng *stick a
drawing pin*

按摩 ànmó massage

❷[动]经过考核研究后下论断：
draw a conclusion after investigation and research

编者按 biānzhě'àn

❸[动]依照：according to; on the
basis of ｜～人数计算 àn rénshù jìsuàn *make calculations
according to the number of
people* / ～理说你应该去。Ànlǐshuō nǐ yīnggāi qù. *Realistically speaking, you should go.*

按揭 ànjiē mortage

按期 ànqī on time; on schedule

按时 ànshí on time; on schedule

按照 ànzhào according to; in
accordance with; in the light of;
on the basis of

按劳分配 ànláo fēnpèi distribute to each according to his
work

案   àn   10画 木部

案 案 案 案 案 案 案 案
案 案

❶[名]长方形的桌子：a long narrow

desk | 书～上摆满了书。Shū'àn shang bǎimǎn le shū. *Books are all over the long narrow desk.*

❷[名]记录事件或处理公务的文书: documents of institutions or organizations | 记录在～jìlù zài'àn *be recorded*

档案 dàng'àn

❸[名]有关计划、建议的文件: a plan or proposal submitted for consideration

草案 cǎo'àn　　答案 dá'àn
方案 fāng'àn　　提案 tí'àn
议案 yì'àn

❹[名]涉及法律或政治的事件: law case or political event | 破～ pò'àn *clear up a criminal case* / 办～bàn'àn *handle a case*

案件 ànjiàn law case; legal case
案例 ànlì case
案情 ànqíng case; details of a case
案子 ànzi law case; case

报案 bào'àn　　法案 fǎ'àn
个案 gè'àn　　立案 lì'àn
作案 zuò'àn

暗　àn　13画 日部

暗 暗暗暗暗暗暗暗暗 暗暗暗暗暗

❶[形]光线不足;不明亮: not bright; dim; dark | 灯光太～。Dēngguāng tài àn. *The light*

is too dim. / 这个房间比较～,开开灯吧。Zhège fángjiān bǐjiào àn, kāikai dēng ba. *This room is dark. Turn on the light.* / 天色渐渐～下来了。Tiānsè jiànjiàn àn xiàlai le. *It's getting dark.* / 不要在光线～的地方看书。Bùyào zài guāngxiàn àn de dìfang kànshū. *Don't read books in dim light.*

暗淡 àndàn dim; dismal; faint; gloomy

黑暗 hēi'àn　　阴暗 yīn'àn

❷[形]隐藏的;不外露的: secret; hidden | 他虽然不说,心里却～自高兴。Tā suīrán bù shuō, xīnli què àn zì gāoxìng. *He didn't say anything, but felt pleased in his heart.* / 明人不做～事。Míng rén bù zuò ànshì. *One who is above board does nothing on the sly.*

❸[副]偷偷地;私下里: secretly

暗暗 àn'àn secretly; inwardly; to oneself

暗恋 ànliàn love secretly; fall in love with sb. secretly

暗杀 ànshā assassinate

暗示 ànshì drop a hint; hint; suggest

暗中 ànzhōng in secret; on the sly

昂　áng　8画 日部

昂 昂昂昂昂昂昂昂昂

❶[动]仰着(头)：hold high｜～头挺胸 ángtóu tǐngxiōng *hold up one's head and throw out one's chest*

❷[形]价钱高：(of price) high, expensive

昂贵 ángguì *expensive; costly*

❸[形]精神振奋，情绪高涨：high-spirited

昂扬 ángyáng *high-spirited*

高昂 gāo'áng

凹　　　āo　　5画｜部

凹 凹凹凹凹凹

❶[形]中间低，四周高：sunken｜～凸不平 āotū bù píng *full of bumps and holes; uneven*

❷[动]由周围向中心陷下：hollow; sunken｜他的脸颊已经瘦得～进去了。Tā de liǎnjiá yǐjīng shòu de āo jìnqu le. *His cheeks are sunken in.*

熬　　　āo　　14画｜灬部

熬 熬熬熬熬熬熬熬熬熬熬熬熬熬熬

❶[动]久煮：stew; boil｜～粥 āozhōu *cook gruel* ／～药 āoyào *decoct medicinal herbs*

❷[动]忍受；勉强支撑：endure; hold out｜～夜 áoyè *stay up late or all night* ／～白了头 áobáile tóu *suffer so much that one's hair turns grey*

袄 (襖)　āo　　9画 衤部

袄 袄袄袄袄袄袄袄袄袄

[名]有衬里的中式上衣：lined Chinese-style coat or jacket｜棉～ mián'ǎo *cotton-padded jacket*

傲　　　ào　　12画 亻部

傲 傲傲傲傲傲傲傲傲傲傲傲傲

[形]自高自大，看不起别人：proud; haughty｜这个人很～。Zhège rén hěn ào. *This person is quite arrogant.*

骄傲 jiāo'ào

奥　　　ào　　12画 大部

奥 奥奥奥奥奥奥奥奥奥奥奥奥

[形]含义深，不容易懂：profound and difficult to understand

奥秘 àomì *profound mystery*

深奥 shēn'ào

◇奥运会 Àoyùnhuì the Olympic Games

奥林匹克 Àolínpǐkè the Olympics

 ào   15画 氵部

澳澳澳澳澳澳澳澳
澳澳澳澳澳澳澳

❶[名]指澳门：Macao
❷[名]指澳大利亚：Australia
澳洲 Àozhōu Australia (the continent)

B b

bā　　2画 八部

　八 八八

[数]数字：eight | 7加1等于～。Qī jiā yī děngyú bā. *Seven plus one equals eight.*

乱七八糟 luànqībāzāo

七嘴八舌 qīzuǐ-bāshé

四面八方 sìmiàn-bāfāng

五花八门 wǔhuā-bāmén

◇丑八怪 chǒubāguài

bā　　4画 一部

巴 巴巴巴巴

❶[动]盼望；期望：look forward to; earnestly wish | ～望 bāwàng *hope; look forward to*

❷[动]讨好：curry favour with; fawn on

巴结 bājie *curry favour with; fawn on; make up to*

❸[词尾] as a suffix

尾巴 wěiba　　下巴 xiàba

嘴巴 zuǐba

◇巴士 bāshì bus (a transliteration)

bā　　5画 扌部

扒 扒扒扒扒扒

❶[动]抓住(可依附的东西)：cling to; hold on to | ～着栏杆 bāzhe lángān *hold on to the railing* / ～着窗户 bāzhe chuānghu *hold on to the window*

❷[动]刨开；挖：dig up | ～房子 bā fángzi *pull down the house*

❸[动]拨动：push aside | ～开草丛 bākāi cǎocóng *push aside a thick growth of grass* / ～开众人 bākāi zhòngrén *push aside the crowd of people*

❹[动]剥下；脱掉：strip off; take off | 他把鞋一～，趟水过河了。Tā bǎ xié yī bā,tāngshuǐ guòhé le. *Taking off his shoes, he waded across the river.* / ～下衣裳 bāxià yīshang *take off the clothes*

See pá.

bā　　5画 口部

叭 叭叭叭叭叭

[拟声] crack | ～的一声枪响 bā de yī shēng qiāng xiǎng *the crack of a gunshot*

喇叭 lǎba

芭　　bā　　7画　艹部

芭 芭芭芭芭芭芭芭

See 芭蕾舞

芭蕾舞 bālěiwǔ ballet

吧　　bā　　7画　口部

吧 吧吧吧吧吧吧吧

[拟声] crack｜～的一声，树枝折断了。Bā de yī shēng, shùzhī zhéduàn le. *The branch broke with a snap.* ／大门～的一下关上了。Dàmén bā de yīxià guānshang le. *The door shut with a slam.*

◇吧台 bātái bar; pub counter

　酒吧 jiǔbā　　网吧 wǎngbā
　See ba.

疤　　bā　　9画　疒部

疤 疤疤疤疤疤疤疤疤疤

❶ [名] 疮口或伤口长好后留下的痕迹：scar｜他腿上有块～。Tā tuǐshang yǒu kuāi bā. *There's a scar on his leg.*

❷ [名] 器物上像疤的痕迹：a scar-like mark on a utensil｜这个茶杯上有个～。Zhège chábēi shang yǒu ge bā. *There is a*

scratch on the cup.

捌　　bā　　10画　扌部

捌 捌捌捌捌捌捌捌捌
捌捌

[数]"八"的大写：complicated form of the numeral "八" (eight)

笆　　bā　　10画　竹部

笆 笆笆笆笆笆笆笆笆
笆笆

[名] 用竹片或树枝等编成的东西：sth. made of bamboo or twigs

　篱笆 líba

拔　　bá　　8画　扌部

拔 拔拔拔拔拔拔拔拔

❶ [动]（连根）拉出：pull; pull out; uproot｜～剑 bá jiàn *draw one's sword* ／～草 bá cǎo *pull up weeds* ／～牙 bá yá *pull out a tooth* ／把钉子～出来。Bǎ dīngzi bá chūlai. *Pull out the nail.*

　拔河 báhé tug-of-war
　一毛不拔 yīmáo-bùbá

❷ [动]超出；高出：surpass
　海拔 hǎibá

❸ [动]挑取；提升：choose; select;

promote
提拔 tíbá　　选拔 xuǎnbá

把

bǎ　　7画 扌部

把 把把把把把把把

❶[动]拿；握住：hold; grasp｜两手～着栏杆 liǎng shǒu bǎzhe lángān hold on to railings with both hands／他紧紧地～着我的手。Tā jǐnjǐn de bǎzhe wǒ de shǒu. He held my hand tightly.
把柄 bǎbǐng handle; mistake that can be used against oneself
把脉 bǎmài feel the pulse
把手 bǎshǒu handle
把握 bǎwò ① grasp; hold ② assurance; certainty
❷[动]控制；掌握：grasp; control｜～握时机 bǎwò shíjī seize the opportunity; seize the right time
❸[动]看守；管：guard; watch｜～门 bǎmén guard a gate
把关 bǎguān check on; guard a pass; strictly check against criteria to prevent errors
❹[名]器物上的柄：handle
❺[量]用于有把手的器具：used for sth. with a handle｜一～扇子 yī bǎ shānzi a fan／一～刀 yī bǎ dāo a knife
❻[量]用于一只手可以托住或抓起来的数量：used for sth. that one hand can hold｜一～糖 yī bǎ táng a handful of candies／一～米 yī bǎ mǐ a handful of rice／两～花 liǎng bǎ huā two bunches of flowers
❼[量]用于某些抽象事物：used for some abstract things｜一～力气 yī bǎ lìqi be quite strong／加～劲 jiā bǎ jìn make an extra effort／我都一大～年纪了。Wǒ dōu yī dà bǎ niánjì le. I'm getting on in years.
❽[介]表示致使：used to shift the object in front of the verb｜～房间收拾一下 bǎ fángjiān shōushi yīxià tidy the room／～他累坏了。Bǎ tā lèihuài le. He was tired out.／请～门带上。Qǐng bǎ mén dàishang. Shut the door, please.
❾[数]约略估计：about; or so｜个～月 gè bǎ yuè about a month／他只有千～块钱。Tā zhǐyǒu qiān bǎ kuài qián. He has only about a thousand yuan.
◇把戏 bǎxì ① acrobatics; juggling ② trick; deceit
一把手 yībǎshǒu

坝 (壩) bà　　7画 土部

坝 坝坝坝坝坝坝坝

[名]拦水的建筑物：a barrier preventing the flow of water｜水～ shuǐbà *dam* ／堤～dībà *dykes and dams*

爸 bà 8画 父部

爸 爸爸爸爸爸爸爸爸

[名]父亲：father
爸爸 bàba *papa; dad; father*

罢 (罷) bà 10画 四部

罢 罢罢罢罢罢罢罢罢
罢罢

❶ [动]停止：stop; rest; cease｜～课 bàkè *students' strike*
罢工 bàgōng *strike; go on strike*

❷ [动]免去；解除：dismiss from office｜～去官职 bàqù guānzhí *remove sb. from office* ／～职 bàzhí *remove from office; dismiss*

❸ [动]完了；完毕：finish｜吃～饭 chībà fàn *finish one's meal* ／他说～就走了。Tā shuōbà jiù zǒu le. *With these words he left.* ／说～，他站了起来。Shuōbà, tā zhànle qǐlai. *With these words he stood up.*

霸 bà 21画 雨部

霸 霸霸霸霸霸霸霸霸
霸霸霸霸霸霸霸霸
霸霸霸霸霸

❶ [名]古代诸侯联盟的首领：the leader of an alliance of feudal lords
霸王 bàwáng *overlord; despot*

❷ [名]依靠权势蛮横无理欺压他人的人：tyrant; bully｜恶～èbà *local tyrant (or despot)*

❸ [动]依仗权势强行占有或占据：forcibly occupy; seize
霸道 bàdào *high-handed; overbearing*
霸权 bàquán *hegemony; supremacy*
霸占 bàzhàn *forcibly occupy; seize*

吧 ba 7画 口部

吧 吧吧吧吧吧吧吧

❶ [助]用于句尾，表示商量、建议、命令、请求：used at the end of a sentence to indicate suggestion, command or request｜帮帮我的忙～! Bāngbāng wǒ de máng ba! *Give me a hand!* ／还是你自己去～。Háishì nǐ zìjǐ qù ba. *It would be better to go yourself.* ／别说了～! Bié shuōle ba! *Say no more!*

❷ [助]用于句尾，表示估计、推测、不敢肯定的语气：used at the end of a sentence to indicate estimation, inference, doubt or conjecture | 今天不会下雨～。Jīntiān bù huì xiàyǔ ba. *It is not likely to rain today.* / 大概是前天～，他来过这儿。Dàgài shì qiántiān ba,tā láiguo zhèr. *It was probably the day before yesterday that he came here.*

❸ [助]用于句尾，表示同意：used at the end of a sentence to indicate agreement or approval | 好～，我明天去。Hǎo ba, wǒ míngtiān qù. *All right, I'll go tomorrow.* / 好～，就这么办～。Hǎo ba, jiù zhème bàn ba. *OK, let's do it this way.* / 好～，我答应你。Hǎo ba, wǒ dāying nǐ. *All right. You can have my consent.*

❹ [助]用于句中停顿处，有两难之意：used to indicate a pause in a sentence, suggesting a dilemma | 走～，不好；不走～，也不好。Zǒu ba, bù hǎo; bù zǒu ba, yě bù hǎo. *To go or not to go, neither is appropriate.*

See bā.

bāi　12画 手部

掰 掰 掰 掰 掰 掰 掰 掰 掰 掰 掰

[动]用手把东西分开或折断：break apart with hands | ～两半 bāi liǎngbàn *break in two* / 把这个东西～开。Bǎ zhège dōngxi bāikāi. *Break it apart.*

掰开 bāikāi break off with fingers and thumbs

白

bái　5画 白部

白 白 白 白 白 白

❶ [形]像雪或霜那样的颜色：white; colour of snow or frost | ～手帕 bái shǒupà *a white handkerchief* / 他的头发全～了。Tā de tóufa quán bái le. *All his hair has turned grey.*

白宫 Báigōng the White House

白酒 báijiǔ spirit usu. distilled from sorghum or maize; white spirit

白领 báilǐng white collar

白人 báirén white man or woman

白色 báisè white (colour)

白头 báitóu hoary head; old age

苍白 cāngbái　　黑白 hēibái

雪白 xuěbái

❷ [形]明亮：bright

白天 báitiān daytime; day

白日梦 báirìmèng daydream;

wishful thinking

❸ [形]清楚；明白：clear; make clear; plain

白话文 báihuàwén vernacular Chinese (as against classical Chinese)

明白 míngbai

❹ [形]没有加上什么东西的；空的：blank; pure | ～开水 bái kāishuǐ *plain boiled water* / 交～卷 jiāo báijuàn *hand in a blank examination paper*

空白 kòngbái

❺ [副]无效果地：in vain; to no effect | ～去一回 bái qù yī huí *run a fruitless errand* / ～费力气 bái fèi lìqi *make an effort for nothing*

白白 báibái in vain; for nothing

❻ [副]不付代价地：free of charge | ～吃 báichī *eat sth. without paying for it* / ～送我都不要。Báisòng wǒ dōu bù yào. *I wouldn't have it even if it was free.*

❼ [形]读音或字形错误：(of words) wrongly pronounced or written | 写～字 xiě báizì *write a character wrongly*

◇ 白菜 báicài Chinese cabbage

白血病 báixuěbìng leukaemia

大白菜 dàbáicài

蛋白质 dànbáizhì

开场白 kāichǎngbái

百   bǎi   6画 白部

百 | 百百百百百百

❶ [数]数目：hundred | 五～个学生 wǔ bǎi gè xuésheng *five hundred students*

百分比 bǎifēnbǐ percentage

百分点 bǎifēndiǎn one percentage point

❷ [数]形容很多：numerous

百倍 bǎibèi hundredfold; a hundred times

百货 bǎihuò general merchandise

百姓 bǎixìng common people

百花齐放 bǎihuā-qífàng a hundred flowers in bloom

百家争鸣 bǎijiā-zhēngmíng let a hundred schools of thought contend

老百姓 lǎobǎixìng

千方百计 qiānfāng-bǎijì

身价百倍 shēnjià-bǎibèi

◇ 百合 bǎihé lily

柏   bǎi   9画 木部

柏 | 柏柏柏柏柏柏柏柏柏

See 柏树

柏树 bǎishù cypress

摆 (擺❶-❺襬❻) bǎi 13画 扌部

摆 | 摆摆摆摆摆摆摆摆摆摆摆

❶[动]安放；排列：display; exhibit; arrange｜桌子上~着许多书。Zhuōzi shang bǎizhe xǔduō shū. *There are a lot of books on the desk.* / 把东西~好。Bǎ dōngxi bǎihǎo. *Put the things in order.*

摆放 bǎifàng put; place; lay

摆设 bǎishe ① ornaments; decorations ② objects or articles merely for show

❷[动]列举；陈述：enumerate; state clearly｜~事实，讲道理 bǎi shìshí, jiǎng dàolǐ *present the facts and reason things out*

❸[动]显示；炫耀：show; display; flaunt｜~阔 bǎikuò *display or flaunt one's wealth* / ~威风 bǎiwēifēng *put on airs; give oneself airs*

摆架子 bǎijiàzi put on airs; give oneself airs

❹[动]摇动：sway; wave｜~尾巴 bǎi wěiba *wag tail* / 他向我直~手。Tā xiàng wǒ zhí bǎishǒu. *He waved his hand to me continuously.*

摆动 bǎidòng swing; sway

摆脱 bǎituō cast off; shake off; break away from; free oneself from

摇摆 yáobǎi

❺[名]钟表或仪器上能往复摇动的机械装置：pendulum｜钟~ zhōngbǎi *pendulum*

❻[名]衣裙的下边：the lower hem of a gown, jacket or shirt｜下~ xiàbǎi *the lower hem of a gown, jacket or shirt*

败（敗）bài　8画 贝部

败 败败败败败败败败

❶[动]毁坏；把事情搞坏：ruin; spoil｜~家 bàijiā *ruin the family* / 他~了我的名声。Tā bàile wǒ de míngshēng. *He spoiled my reputation.*

败坏 bàihuài ruin; corrupt; undermine

❷[动]输；失利；不成功：be defeated; fail｜惨~ cǎnbài *a crushing defeat; disastrously defeated* / 主队以二比三~于客队。Zhǔduì yǐ èr bǐ sān bàiyú kèduì. *The host team lost to the visiting team 3 to 2.*

败诉 bàisù lose a lawsuit

成败 chéngbài

❸[动]打败；使失败：defeat; beat; cause to fail｜击~敌军 jībài díjūn *defeat the enemy troops* / 打~对手 dǎbài duìshǒu *beat the opponent*

打败 dǎbài　　　击败 jībài

❹[形]破旧；腐烂；衰落；凋谢：decay; wither｜这些花没开几天就~了。Zhèxiē huā méi kāi jǐ tiān jiù bài le. *These flowers withered in a few days.*

腐败 fǔbài

拜 bài 9画 手部

拜拜拜拜拜拜拜拜拜
拜

❶ [动]表示敬意的礼节、仪式：an old etiquette to show one's respect for others
礼拜 lǐbài
礼拜天 lǐbàitiān

❷ [动]尊崇；敬仰：respect; admire
崇拜 chóngbài

❸ [动]行礼祝贺：show obeisance to; congratulate ｜~寿 bàishòu congratulate an elderly person on their birthday; offer birthday felicitations
拜年 bàinián pay a New Year call

❹ [动]以礼会见：make a polite visit
拜访 bàifǎng pay a visit; call on
拜会 bàihuì pay an official call; call on

❺ [动]通过一定的仪式结成某种关系：form a certain relationship with sb. ceremoniously ｜~他为师 bài tā wéi shī take him as one's teacher
◇拜托 bàituō request a favour

扳 bān 7画 扌部

扳扳扳扳扳扳扳

[动]用力使一端固定的东西改变方向或转动：pull sth. that is fixed at one end to change its direction ｜~动开关 bāndòng kāiguān turn on a switch / ~着指头算 bānzhe zhǐtou suàn count on one's fingers

班 bān 10画 王部

班班班班班班班班
班班

❶ [名]工作或学习的组织：groups organized for the sake of study or work ｜我们这个年级有六个~。Wǒmen zhège niánjí yǒu liù gè bān. There are six classes in our grade.
班长 bānzhǎng class monitor; squad leader; team leader
班子 bānzi group; team
班主任 bānzhǔrèn teacher in charge of a class
培训班 péixùnbān

❷ [名]工作按时间分成的段落：shift; duty ｜你今天上什么~? Nǐ jīntiān shàng shénme bān? Which shift are you on today?
加班 jiābān   接班 jiēbān
上班 shàngbān   下班 xiàbān
夜班 yèbān   值班 zhíbān

❸ [名]定时开行的(交通工具)：regularly-run; scheduled

班机 bānjī airliner; regular air service

航班 hángbān

❹[名]军队编制中的基层单位：squad (basic unit in the military establishment)

❺[量]用于定时开行的交通运输工具：used to refer to means of transportation that are regularly run | 你搭下一一飞机走吧。Nǐ dā xiàyībān fēijī zǒu ba. *Why don't you take the next flight?*

般 bān 10画 舟部

般般般般般般般般般般

❶[名]种；样：kind; way | 百~bǎibān *in every possible way* / 这~zhèbān *such; this kind of*

❷[助]一样，似的：same as; just like | 暴风雨~的掌声 bàofēngyǔ bān de zhǎngshēng *thunderous applause* / 兄弟~的情谊 xiōngdi bān de qíngyì *brotherly affection*

颁 (頒) bān 10画 页部

颁颁颁颁颁颁颁颁颁颁

[动]发布；公布：promulgate; issue

颁布 bānbù promulgate; issue; publish

颁发 bānfā award

颁奖 bānjiǎng award medal, certificate or merit, or trophy, etc.

斑 bān 12画 王部

斑斑斑斑斑斑斑斑斑斑斑斑

❶[名]杂色的点子或条纹：spot; speck; speckle | 红~hóngbān *red spot* / 黑~hēibān *black speck* / 脸上有块~。Liǎnshang yǒu kuài bān. *There is a speck on your face.*

❷[形]有斑点或条纹的：spotted; striped | ~马 bānmǎ *zebra*

搬 bān 13画 扌部

搬搬搬搬搬搬搬搬搬搬搬搬搬

❶[动]移动较重的物体：move; remove | ~家具 bān jiājù *move the furniture* / 这些东西我~不动。Zhèxiē dōngxi wǒ bānbudòng. *I can't move these things by myself.*

❷[动]迁移：move | 他家早就~走了。Tā jiā zǎo jiù bānzǒu le. *His family moved away long ago.*

搬迁 bānqiān move; transfer

搬运 bānyùn carry; transport

板 bǎn 8画 木部

板 板板板板板板板板

❶ [名]片状的较硬的物体：sth. flat, thin and comparatively hard | 玻璃~ bōlibǎn *glass plate*
板凳 bǎndèng wooden bench or stool
地板 dìbǎn   黑板 hēibǎn
❷ [形]不灵活；少变化：stiff; lack of change | ~正 bǎnzhèng *stiff; unnatural*
❸ [动]使面部表情严肃：look serious | 他~着脸不说话。Tā bǎnzhe liǎn bù shuōhuà. *He kept a straight face without a word.*

版 bǎn 8画 片部

版 版版版版版版版版

❶ [名]上面有文字或图形的供印刷的底子：a printing plate with words or pictures on it | 排~ páibǎn *composing; typesetting* / 底~ dìbǎn *photographic plate*
版权 bǎnquán copyright
出版 chūbǎn   盗版 dàobǎn
正版 zhèngbǎn
出版社 chūbǎnshè
❷ [名]印刷物排印的次数：edition; the number of times something is printed | 再~ zàibǎn *second edition* / 修订~ xiūdìngbǎn *revised edition* / 绝~ juébǎn *out of print*
版本 bǎnběn edition
❸ [名]报纸的一面叫一版：a page of a newspaper | 头~头条 tóubǎn tóutiáo *front-page headline* / 今天的日报共十四~。Jīntiān de rìbào gòng shísì bǎn. *There are fourteen pages in today's newspaper.*
版面 bǎnmiàn ① space of a whole page ② layout of a printed sheet
◇版图 bǎntú domain; territory

办 (辦) bàn 4画 力部

办 办办办办办

❶ [动]处理：handle | ~手续 bàn shǒuxù *go through the forma-lities* / 这件事到现在还没有~呢。Zhè jiàn shì dào xiànzài hái méiyǒu bàn ne. *This matter has not been done yet.*
办案 bàn'àn ① handle a legal case ② apprehend (a suspect)
办法 bànfǎ way; means; measure
办公 bàngōng handle official business; work
办理 bànlǐ handle; conduct;

transact

办事 bànshì handle affairs; work

办公室 bàngōngshì office

办事处 bànshìchù office; agency

包办 bāobàn　承办 chéngbàn

代办 dàibàn　主办 zhǔbàn

❷[动]置备；采购：purchase; get sth. ready | ～年货 bàn niánhuò *do New Year shopping; do shopping for the Spring Festival* / 筹～展览会 chóu bàn zhǎnlǎnhuì *prepare an exhibition* / ～酒席 bàn jiǔxí *prepare a feast; give a banquet*

❸[动]处罚：punish (by law) | 法～fǎbàn *punish by law*

惩办 chéngbàn

❹[动]创立；经营：set up; run | ～工厂 bàn gōngchǎng *run a factory* / 村里新～了一所中学。Cūn li xīn bànle yī suǒ zhōngxué. *A new middle school has been set up in the village.*

办学 bànxué conduct a school; run a school

创办 chuàngbàn　举办 jǔbàn

开办 kāibàn　兴办 xīngbàn

半 bàn　5画　丶部

半 半半半半半

❶[数]二分之一；一半：half; semi- | ～个月 bàn gè yuè *half a month* / 一天～yī tiān bàn *one and a half days* / 减～jiǎnbàn *reduce by half*

半截 bànjié half

半径 bànjìng radius

半拉 bànlǎ half

半数 bànshù half the number; half

半天 bàntiān ① half of the day ② a long time; quite a while

半夜 bànyè midnight

半边天 bànbiāntiān ① half of the sky ② women of the new society (from Mao Zedong's saying)

半决赛 bànjuésài (sports) semi-finals

半真半假 bànzhēn-bànjiǎ be half genuine and half forged; be partly true and partly false

大半 dàbàn

北半球 běibànqiú

东半球 dōngbànqiú

南半球 nánbànqiú

西半球 xībànqiú

❷[形]中间：middle

半路 bànlù halfway; midway; on the way

半途而废 bàntú'érfèi stop halfway

❸[形]不完全：partly; not completely | ～透明 bàntòumíng *translucent* / ～自动 bànzìdòng *semi-automatic* / 他的房

门~掩着。Tā de fángmén bàn yǎnzhe. *The door of his room was half closed.*

半岛 bàndǎo peninsula

半导体 bàndǎotǐ semiconductor

❹ [数]比喻很少: very little; the least bit | 一星~点 yīxīng-bàndiǎn *a tiny bit; a very small amount* / 他一句话都没说就走了。Tā bànjùhuà dōu méi shuō jiù zǒu le. *He left without saying a word.* / 等了一上午, ~点消息都没有。Děngle yī shàngwǔ, bàn diǎn xiāoxi dōu méiyǒu. *We waited the whole morning but there was no news whatsoever.*

扮 扮扮扮扮扮扮扮   bàn   7画 扌部

❶ [动]化装成(某种角色): play the part of; disguise oneself as | 小周在这出戏里~主角。Xiǎo Zhōu zài zhè chū xì li bàn zhǔjué. *Xiao Zhou acted the leading role in the play.*

打扮 dǎbàn

❷ [动]装成(某种样子): put on (an expression) | ~鬼脸 bàn guǐliǎn *make grimaces; make faces* / 他在表演中男~女装。Tā zài biǎoyǎn zhōng nánbàn-nǚzhuāng. *He disguised himself as*

a woman in the show.

扮演 bànyǎn play the part of; act

伴 伴伴伴伴伴伴伴   bàn   7画 亻部

❶ [名]同在一起工作或生活的人: companion; partner | 搭个~儿 dā ge bànr *join sb. on a trip; travel together* / 让我来跟你做个~儿吧。Ràng wǒ lái gēn nǐ zuò ge bànr ba. *Let me keep you company.* / 结~ jiébàn *have sb. for company*

伴侣 bànlǚ spouse; companion; mate; partner

老伴 lǎobàn   同伴 tóngbàn

❷ [动]陪着: accompany | 有他陪~我, 你放心吧。Yǒu tā péibàn wǒ, nǐ fàngxīn ba. *Do set your mind at rest since I am with him.*

伴随 bànsuí accompany; follow

陪伴 péibàn

❸ [动]从旁配合: accompany

伴郎 bànláng groomsman; best man

伴娘 bànniáng bridesmaid

伴奏 bànzòu (of music) accompany

拌   bàn   8画 扌部

拌 拌拌拌拌拌拌拌拌

[动]搅和：mix ｜ ～糖 bàn táng
mix sugar
搅拌 jiǎobàn

绊 (絆) bàn 8画 纟部

绊 绊绊绊绊绊绊绊绊

[动] 行走中腿脚被缠住或挡住：
stumble over or be tangled up
by sth. while walking ｜ ～手～
脚 bàn shǒu bàn jiǎo *be in the
way* ／ ～了一跤 bànle yī jiāo
trip and fall
绊脚石 bànjiǎoshí stumbling
block; obstacle

瓣 bàn 19画 辛部

瓣 瓣瓣瓣瓣瓣瓣瓣瓣
瓣瓣瓣瓣瓣瓣瓣
瓣瓣瓣

❶ [名]花冠的分片或草木的叶片：
petal; pieces that form the
corolla ｜ 花～huābàn *petal*
❷ [名]植物的种子、果实等可以分
开的小块：segment or section
(of a tangerine, etc.); clove (of
garlic, etc.) ｜ 橘子～儿 júzibànr
tangerine slices
❸ [量]用于计算片状物：used for a
petal, a leaf or a fragment of fruit
｜ 他把苹果切成四～。Tā bǎ

píngguǒ qiēchéng sì bàn.
He cut the apple into four pieces.

邦 bāng 6画 阝(右)部

邦 邦邦邦邦邦邦

[名]国：state; country
联邦 liánbāng

帮 (幫) bāng 9画 巾部

帮 帮帮帮帮帮帮帮帮
帮

❶ [名]物体两旁或周围的部分：the
side of sth.; the outer leaf ｜ 鞋～
xiébāng *uppers (of a shoe)* ／
船～chuánbāng *the side of a
ship*
❷ [动]相助：help; assist ｜ 我做不
好，请～～我。Wǒ zuòbuhǎo,
qǐng bāngbāng wǒ. *I can't do
it well all by myself. Please help
me.* ／ ～他一把 bāng tā yī bǎ
give him a hand; help him
帮忙 bāngmáng help; give a
hand; lend a hand
帮助 bāngzhù help; assist
帮倒忙 bāngdàománg be
more of a hindrance than a help;
do sb. a disservice
❸ [动]从事雇佣劳动：work ｜ ～短
工 bāng duǎngōng *work as a
casual labourer*
❹ [名]群；伙；为某种目的组合在一

起的集体：clique; gang; band | 匪～ fěibāng *bandit gang*

❺ [量]用于一群人：a group; a gang; a band | 一～中学生 yī bāng zhōngxuéshēng *a group of middle school students* / 一～人围在那儿看热闹。Yī bāng rén wéi zài nàr kàn rènao. *A crowd of people were there watching the bustling scene.*

绑 (綁) bǎng 9画 纟部

绑 绑绑绑绑绑绑绑绑

[动]捆；缠绕：bind; tie | 把两根棍子～在一起 bǎ liǎng gēn gùnzi bǎng zài yīqǐ *tie two sticks together* / ～紧 bǎng jǐn *tie up tight*

绑架 bǎngjià kidnap
捆绑 kǔnbǎng

榜 bǎng 14画 木部

榜 榜榜榜榜榜榜榜榜榜榜榜榜榜

[名]张贴的文告或名单：a notice or a list of names posted up | ～上有名 bǎng shang yǒu míng *with one's name on the list of successful candidates* / 他等着看～。Tā děngzhe kàn bǎng. *He is waiting to see the list of successful candidates.*

排行榜 páihángbǎng

◇榜样 bǎngyàng example; model

 膀 bǎng 14画 月部

膀 膀膀膀膀膀膀膀膀膀膀膀膀膀膀

❶ [名]肩膀：shoulder
❷ [名]翅膀：wing

棒 bàng 12画 木部

棒 棒棒棒棒棒棒棒棒棒棒棒棒

❶ [名]棍子：rod; stick | ～球～ bàngqiúbàng *baseball bat* 棒球 bàngqiú baseball
❷ [形]好，多指体力、能力、成绩：(of one's body) strong, (of ability and achievement) excellent | 画得好～! Huà de hǎobàng! *The painting is excellent.* / 这小伙子身体真～! Zhè xiǎohuǒzi shēntǐ zhēn bàng! *This young fellow is really strong!*

 傍 bàng 12画 亻部

傍 傍傍傍傍傍傍傍傍傍傍傍傍

❶ [动]靠近；依靠：be close to | ～近 bàngjìn *be close to; near*

❷ [动]时间临近： draw near; be close to
傍晚 bàngwǎn toward evening; at nightfall; at dusk

谤 (謗) bàng 12画 讠部

谤谤谤谤谤谤谤谤谤谤谤谤

[动]恶意地说人坏话：slander; defame
诽谤 fěibàng

磅 bàng 15画 石部

磅磅磅磅磅磅磅磅磅磅磅磅磅磅磅

[名] pound | 一～牛奶 yī bàng niúnǎi *one pound of milk* / 两～肉 liǎng bàng ròu *two pounds of meat* / 他的体重大约有150～。Tā de tǐzhòng dàyuē yǒu yībǎi wǔshí bàng. *He weighs about 150 pounds.*

包 bāo 5画 勹部

包包包包包

❶ [动]裹起来：wrap | 把糖果～起来。Bǎ tángguǒ bāo qǐlai. *Wrap up the sweets.* / 用布把伤口～好。Yòng bù bǎ shāngkǒu bāohǎo. *Wrap up the wound with some cloth.*
包围 bāowéi surround; encircle
包装 bāozhuāng pack; package

❷ [名]裹起来的东西：sth. wrapped up | 这一大～你拿不动。Zhè yī dà bāo nǐ nábudòng. *You can hardly carry such a big bundle.*
包袱 bāofu ① a bundle wrapped in cloth ②millstone round one's neck; load; weight; burden
包裹 bāoguǒ bundle; package; parcel
红包 hóngbāo   邮包 yóubāo

❸ [名]装东西的口袋：bag | 请你把书装进～里。Qǐng nǐ bǎ shū zhuāngjìn bāo li. *Please put the books in the bag.*
背包 bēibāo   钱包 qiánbāo
书包 shūbāo   提包 tíbāo
掏腰包 tāoyāobāo

❹ [名]凸出的包状物：protuberance; swelling | 头上碰了个～tóushang pèngle gè bāo *have (get) a bump on one's head* / 树干上有个大鼓～。Shùgàn shang yǒu gè dà gǔbāo. *There is a big protuberance on the tree trunk.*

❺ [名]有馅的面制食品：steamed bun with stuffing
包子 bāozi steamed stuffed bun

❻ [量]用于成包的东西：used for a

bundle or a pack of things │ 两～糖果 liǎng bāo tángguǒ *two packets of sweets* ／一～花生米 yī bāo huāshēngmǐ *a pack of shelled peanuts* ／一～火柴 yī bāo huǒchái *a box of matches*

❼[动]容纳；总括：include; contain
包含 bāohán contain; embody; include
包括 bāokuò include; contain; consist of; comprise; incorporate

❽[动]把整个任务承担下来，全面负责：undertake the whole thing; take full responsibility │ ～销 bāoxiāo *have exclusive selling rights* / ～教～会 bāojiāo bāohuì *undertake to help sb. master certain skill, etc. with guarantee* / 这件事～在我身上。Zhè jiàn shì bāo zài wǒ shēn shang. *I shall take full charge of the matter.*
包办 bāobàn take care of everything; run the whole show; monopolize everything
承包 chéngbāo

❾[动]担保：guarantee; assure │ ～你满意。Bāo nǐ mǎnyì. *You'll like it, I assure you.*

❿[动]约定专用：reserve; charter │ 这场电影是我们公司～的。Zhè chǎng diànyǐng shì wǒmen gōngsī bāo de. *This film*

showing is reserved for our company. / 我们～的车还没到。Wǒmen bāo de chē hái méi dào. *The car we hired hasn't arrived yet.*

芭 bāo 8画 艹部

芭芭芭芭芭芭芭芭

[名]花未开时包着花朵底部的小叶片：bud │ 含～待放 hánbāodàifàng *be in bud and ready to burst*

胞 bāo 9画 月部

胞胞胞胞胞胞胞胞胞

❶[名]同父母的；嫡亲的：born of the same parents │ ～兄 bāoxiōng *full older brother* / ～妹 bāomèi *full younger sister*

❷[名]同一国家或民族的人：fellow countryman
侨胞 qiáobāo 同胞 tóngbāo
◇干细胞 gànxìbāo

剥 bāo 10画 刂部

剥剥剥剥剥剥剥剥剥剥

[动]去掉（外面的皮或壳）：shell;

peel; get rid of (the shell or skin) | ～花生 bāo huāshēng *shell peanuts* / ～橘子 bāo júzi *peel a tangerine*

See bō.

雹 bāo 13画 雨部

[名]hail | 冰～bīngbáo *hail; hailstone*
雹子 báozi hail

薄 báo 16画 艹部

薄薄薄薄薄薄薄薄
薄薄薄薄薄薄薄薄

❶[形]厚度小：thin | 这块布太～。Zhè kuài bù tài báo. *The cloth is too flimsy.* / 地上结了一层～～的冰。Dìshang jiéle yī céng báobao de bīng. *The ground is covered with a thin layer of ice.*

❷[形]不肥沃：infertile; poor | 这一带的土地很～。Zhè yī dài de tǔdì hěn báo. *The soil of this area is infertile.*

❸[形]冷淡：cold; indifferent | 我待她不～，可她始终不喜欢我。Wǒ dāi tā bù báo,kě tā shǐzhōng bù xǐhuan wǒ. *I*

treated her quite well, but she never liked me.

❹[形]不浓；淡：(of taste) weak; light | 酒味很～。Jiǔ wèi hěn báo. *This is a light wine.*

See bō.

饱 (飽) bǎo 8画 饣部

饱饱饱饱饱饱饱饱

❶[形]吃足：have eaten one's fill; be full | 不能吃得过～。Bù néng chī de guò bǎo. *Don't fill yourself to the point of bursting.*

❷[形]足；充分：full; plump | 谷粒儿很～。Gǔlìr hěn bǎo. *The grains are quite plump.*
饱和 bǎohé saturation
饱满 bǎomǎn full; plump

❸[动]满足：satisfy | 大～眼福 dàbǎo-yǎnfú *feast one's eyes on a certain scene*

宝 (寶) bǎo 8画 宀部

宝宝宝宝宝宝宝宝

❶[名]珍贵的东西：sth. precious | 粮食是个～。Liángshi shì gè bǎo. *Grain is a treasure.* / 那幅画是无价之～。Nà fú huà shì wújiàzhībǎo. *That painting is a priceless treasure.*

宝库 bǎokù treasure-house; mine

法宝 fǎbǎo   珠宝 zhūbǎo

传家宝 chuánjiābǎo

❷ [形]珍贵的: precious

宝贝 bǎobèi ① treasured object; treasure ② darling; baby

宝贵 bǎoguì valuable; precious

宝剑 bǎojiàn double-edged sword

宝石 bǎoshí precious stone; gem

◇宝宝 bǎobao (a pet name for a child) darling; baby

保   bǎo   9画 亻部

保 保保保保保保保保保

❶ [动]保护；守卫: defend; protect from damage or loss | ~家卫国 bǎojiā-wèiguó *protect our homes and defend our country*

保安 bǎo'ān ensure public security

保存 bǎocún preserve; conserve; keep

保单 bǎodān ① warranty ② insurance policy

保管 bǎoguǎn take care of

保护 bǎohù protect; safeguard

保健 bǎojiàn health protection; health care

保姆 bǎomǔ nurse; babysitter

保卫 bǎowèi defend; safe-guard

保养 bǎoyǎng ① take good care of one's health ② maintain; keep in good condition

保障 bǎozhàng ensure; guarantee; safeguard

保重 bǎozhòng take care of oneself

❷ [动]保持，维持住: guard; keep | ~平衡 bǎo pínghéng *keep one's balance*

保持 bǎochí keep; maintain; preserve

保留 bǎoliú ①continue to have; retain ② hold back; keep back; reserve

保密 bǎomì maintain secrecy; keep sth. secret

保守 bǎoshǒu ① guard; keep ② conservative

保温 bǎowēn heat preservation; keep warm

保鲜 bǎoxiān keep something fresh; preserve freshness

保值 bǎozhí maintain the original value of something

❸ [动]负责；担保: take responsibility; guarantee | ~质~量 bǎozhì-bǎoliàng *guarantee both quality and quantity*

保险 bǎoxiǎn insurance

保证 bǎozhèng pledge; guarantee; assure; ensure

保险柜 bǎoxiǎnguì strongbox; safe

保证金 bǎozhèngjīn ① cash

deposit ② (leg.) bail

担保 dānbǎo 确保 quèbǎo

准保 zhǔnbǎo

堡 bǎo 12画 土部

堡 堡堡堡堡堡堡堡堡
堡堡堡堡

[名]土筑的小城，也泛指军事上构筑的工事：fort; fortress │ ～垒 bǎolěi fort; fortress; stronghold; blockhouse

报 (報) bǎo 7画 扌部

报 报报报报报报报

❶[动]告诉；通知：announce; report │ ～火警 bǎo huǒjǐng *report a fire* / ～捷 bǎojié *announce a victory; report a success* / 电台每个小时～时一次。Diàntái měi gè xiǎoshí bǎoshí yī cì. *The radio station gives the correct time every hour.*

报案 bǎo'àn report a case to the security authorities

报到 bǎodào report for duty; check in; register

报道 bǎodào report (news); cover

报告 bǎogào ① report; make known ② speech; lecture

报价 bǎojià quoted price

报警 bǎojǐng ① report (an incident) to the police ② give an alarm

报考 bǎokǎo register for examination; enter oneself for an examination

报名 bǎomíng register one's name; sign up

报销 bǎoxiāo submit an expense account; apply for reimbursement

播报 bōbào 汇报 huìbào
上报 shàngbào 申报 shēnbào
通报 tōngbào

❷[名]报纸：newspaper │ 今天～上登了一条重要新闻。Jīntiān bǎo shang dēngle yī tiáo zhòngyào xīnwén. *An important piece of news has been published in the newspaper today.*

报刊 bǎokān newspapers and periodicals

报社 bǎoshè newspaper office

报纸 bǎozhǐ newspaper

晨报 chénbào 日报 rìbào
晚报 wǎnbào 周报 zhōubào

❸[名]某些刊物：periodical; journal

画报 huàbào

❹[名]传达消息、言论的文字或信号：telegram; cable; bulletin; report

电报 diànbào 公报 gōngbào
海报 hǎibào 警报 jǐngbào
情报 qíngbào

❺[动]回答大家：respond │ ～以热

豹
暴

bào

烈的掌声 bàoyǐ rèliè de zhǎngshēng respond with warm applause

❻[动]报答：repay; pay back

报仇 bàochóu revenge; avenge

报酬 bàochou reward; remuneration; pay

报答 bàodá repay; pay back

报复 bàofù make reprisals; retaliate; get one's revenge

报国 bàoguó dedicate oneself to the service of one's country

报应 bàoyìng retribution; judgment

回报 huíbào

抱 bào 8画 扌部

抱 抱抱抱抱抱抱抱抱

❶[动]心里存着：harbour; cherish | 我对这件事的成功不~什么幻想。Wǒ duì zhè jiàn shì de chénggōng bù bào shénme huànxiǎng. *I harbour no illusions about the accomplishment of this task.* / 你对这件事~什么态度？Nǐ duì zhè jiàn shì bào shénme tàidu? *What's your attitude towards it?*

抱负 bàofù aspiration; ambition

抱歉 bàoqiàn be sorry; feel apologetic; regret

抱怨 bàoyuàn complain; grumble

❷[动]用手臂围住：hold or carry in the arms | 她激动得紧紧~住妈妈。Tā jīdòng de jǐnjǐn bàozhù māma. *She was so excited that she embraced her mother tightly.* / 他~着很多参考书走进了教室。Tā bàozhe hěn duō cānkǎoshū zǒujìnle jiàoshì. *He entered the classroom with many reference books in his arms.*

拥抱 yōngbào

❸[动]初次得到（儿孙）：have one's first child or grandchild | 听说他已经~孙子了。Tīngshuō tā yǐjīng bào sūnzi le. *I hear that he has become a grandfather.*

豹 bào 10画 豸部

豹 豹豹豹豹豹豹豹豹豹豹

[名] panther; leopard

暴 bào 15画 日部

暴 暴暴暴暴暴暴暴暴暴暴暴暴暴暴暴

❶[动]显现：expose

暴露 bàolù expose

❷[形]突然而且猛烈：sudden and violent

暴动 bàodòng insurrection; rebellion

暴发 bàofā ① break out ② suddenly become rich or important; get rich quick

暴利 bàolì sudden huge profits

暴雨 bàoyǔ torrential rain; rainstorm

暴涨 bàozhǎng (of flood, prices, etc.) rise suddenly and sharply

暴风骤雨 bàofēng-zhòuyǔ violent storm; hurricane; tempest

风暴 fēngbào

❸[形]凶狠：fierce; cruel

暴力 bàolì violence; force

残暴 cánbào   强暴 qiángbào

❹[形]急躁：short-tempered; irritable ｜这人脾气很～。Zhè rén píqi hěn bào. *This person has a very hot temper.*

粗暴 cūbào

爆 bào   19画 火部

爆 爆爆爆爆爆爆爆爆
爆爆爆爆爆爆爆
爆爆爆

[动]猛然破裂或迸出：burst violently ｜气球～了。Qìqiú bào le. *The balloon has burst.* ／汽车轮胎～了。Qìchē lúntāi bào le. *The tyre has burst.*

爆发 bàofā erupt; burst out; break out

爆破 bàopò blow up; demolish; dynamite; blast

爆炸 bàozhà explode; blow up;

detonate

爆竹 bàozhú firecracker

引爆 yǐnbào

◇火爆 huǒbào

杯 bēi   8画 木部

杯 杯杯杯杯杯杯杯杯

❶[名]杯子，盛液体的器具：cup; glass; a vessel used to contain wine, water, tea, etc. ｜～子 bēizi *cup; glass*／酒～jiǔbēi *wineglass*

杯子 bēizi cup; glass

干杯 gānbēi

❷[名]杯状的奖品：(prize) cup, trophy ｜奖～jiǎngbēi *cup (as a prize)*／金～jīnbēi *gold cup*

❸[量]用于杯子：used for a cup, glass, etc. ｜一～茶 yī bēi chá *a cup of tea* ／一～啤酒 yī bēi píjiǔ *a mug of beer* ／再喝一一～吧。Zài hē yī bēi ba. *Have another cup (or glass).*

卑 bēi   8画 丿部

卑 卑卑卑卑卑卑卑卑

❶[形]低下：low ｜～贱 bēijiàn *lowly; humble*

自卑 zìbēi

❷[形]品质低劣：mean

卑鄙 bēibǐ base; mean; contemptible; despicable

背　bēi　9画 月部

背背背背背背背背
背

❶[动]用背驮：carry sth. on one's back | ～行李 bēi xíngli *carry luggage* / ～着孩子 bēizhe hǎizi *carry a baby on one's back* 背包 bēibāo　rucksack; knapsack

背黑锅　bēihēiguō（inf.）be made a scapegoat; be unjustly blamed

❷[动]承受；负担：bear; shoulder | 为了治好父亲的病，他～了一身债。Wèile zhìhǎo fùqīn de bìng, tā bēile yī shēn zhài. *In order to cure his father's disease, he was saddled with debts.* / 这个责任我～得起。Zhège zérèn wǒ bēideqǐ. *I presume I am up to this responsibility.*
　　See bèi.

悲　bēi　12画 非部

悲悲悲悲悲悲悲悲
悲悲悲悲

[形]伤心；哀痛：sorrowful; sad
　　悲哀 bēi'āi sad
　　悲惨 bēicǎn miserable; tragic
　　悲愤 bēifèn grief and indigna-

tion
　　悲观 bēiguān pessimistic
　　悲剧 bēijù tragedy
　　悲伤 bēishāng sad; sorrowful; melancholy
　　悲痛 bēitòng grieved; sorrowful

碑　bēi　13画 石部

碑碑碑碑碑碑碑碑
碑碑碑碑碑

[名]刻有文字或图画作为纪念或标记的石头：stele (stela); an upright stone tablet bearing a commemorative inscription or design | 这块～立于 1931 年 2 月。Zhè kuài bēi lìyú yī-jiǔsānyī nián èr yuè. *The stele was erected in February 1931.*
　　纪念碑 jìniànbēi
　　里程碑 lǐchéngbēi

北　běi　5画 匕部

北北北北北

[名]north | 往～去 wǎng běi qù *go northward* / 这屋子朝～，冬天很冷。Zhè wūzi cháo běi, dōngtiān hěn lěng. *This house faces north, so it is very cold in winter.*
　　北边 běibian north; the northern part

北部 běibù north; the northern part

北侧 běicè north; the northern side

北方 běifāng north; the northern part of a country or certain area

北京 Běijīng Beijing (Peking)

北面 běimian north; the northern side

北半球 běibànqiú the Northern Hemisphere

北冰洋 Běibīngyáng the Arctic (Ocean)

北美洲 Běiměizhōu North America

东北 dōngběi   西北 xīběi

贝 (貝) bèi   4画 贝部

贝 贝 贝 贝 贝

❶ [名] shellfish; clam; pearl oyster; cowrie

贝壳 bèiké shell

❷ [名] shell

宝贝 bǎobèi

狈 (狽) bèi   7画 犭部

狈 狈 狈 狈 狈 狈 狈

[名]传说中的一种野兽，前腿短，行动时趴在狼身上：a legendary animal with such short forelegs that it moves about by crouching over a wolf

狼狈 lángbèi

备 (備) bèi   8画 夂部

备 备 备 备 备 备 备 备

❶[形]齐全：complete

责备 zébèi

❷[动]具备；具有：be equipped with; have ｜德才兼～ décáijiānbèi *have both ability and integrity*

具备 jùbèi   配备 pèibèi

完备 wánbèi

❸[动]准备；防备：prepare; provide against; take precautions against

备用 bèiyòng reserve; spare; alternate

备战 bèizhàn ① prepare for war ② be prepared against war

备忘录 bèiwànglù ① (diplomacy) memorandum ② memorandum book

筹备 chóubèi   储备 chǔbèi

防备 fángbèi   预备 yùbè

准备 zhǔnbèi

❹[名]设备：equipment

军备 jūnbèi   装备 zhuāngbèi

背   bèi   9画 月部

背 背 背 背 背 背 背 背 背

❶[名]脊背，躯干的一部分：the back of the body｜马~mǎbèi the back of a horse / 他把~靠在墙上。Tā bǎ bèi kào zài qiáng shang. He leans his back against the wall. /立正时~要挺直。Lìzhèng shí bèi yào tǐngzhí. One should keep his back upright when standing at attention.

背后 bèihòu behind sb.'s back; at the back; in the rear

背心 bèixīn waistcoat; vest

❷[名]物体的反面或后部：the back or reverse side of an object｜手~ shǒubèi the back of a hand / 刀~dāobèi the back of a knife

背景 bèijǐng background; backdrop

背面 bèimiàn the back; the reverse side; the wrong side

❸[动]用背部对着：sit, stand, etc., with the back towards｜他~着太阳站在那里。Tā bèizhe tàiyáng zhàn zài nàli. He stands there with his back to the sun. / 不要~着光线写字。Búyào bèizhe guāng-xiàn xiězì. Do not write with your back to the light.

❹[动]违反；不遵守：act contrary to; violate｜~约bèiyuē break an agreement

背叛 bèipàn betray; forsake

违背 wéibèi

❺[形]倒霉；不顺利：unlucky｜手气~shǒuqì bèi unlucky at gambling, card playing, etc.

❻[动]躲避；瞒着：hide sth. from view; do sth. behind sb's back｜我没做什么~着人的事。Wǒ méi zuò shénme bèi zhe rén de shì. I have nothing to hide from anyone.

❼[动]凭记忆读出：recite from memory; learn by heart｜~诗bèi shī recite a poem from memory / ~数学公式bèi shù-xué gōngshì learn a math-ematics formula by heart

背诵 bèisòng recite; repeat from memory

❽[形]听觉不灵：poor hearing｜奶奶的耳朵有些~。Nǎinai de ěrduo yǒu xiē bèi. Grand-ma has poor hearing.

❾[形]偏僻：out-of-the-way｜~街bèijiē back street; side street / 这地方太~了。Zhè dìfang tài bèi le. This place is rather out of the way.

See bēi.

倍 bēi 10画 亻部

倍 倍倍倍倍倍倍倍倍倍倍

[量] times; fold; be multiplied by｜8是4的2~。Bā shì sì de èr bèi. Eight is twice as much as *four.* / 他的水平比我不知高出多少～。Tā de shuǐpíng bǐ wǒ bù zhī gāochū duōshǎo bèi. *His ability is much stronger than mine.*

倍数 bèishù (math.) multiple

百倍 bǎibèi

身价百倍 shēnjià-bǎibèi

被 bèi 10画 衤部

被 被被被被被被被被被被

❶ [名]被子：quilt | 盖～gài bèi *cover oneself with a quilt* / 床上只有一条～。Chuáng shang zhǐyǒu yī tiáo bèi. *There is only one quilt on the bed.*

被子 bèizi quilt

❷ [助]用在动词前，表示该动作是被动的：used before verbs as a symbol of passiveness | 树枝～压弯了。Shùzhī bèi yāwān le. *The branches were weighed down.* / 他～选为会议主席。Tā bèi xuǎn wéi huìyì zhǔxí. *He was elected chairman of the conference.*

被捕 bèibǔ be arrested; under arrest

被动 bèidòng passive

被告 bèigào defendant; the accused

被迫 bèipò be forced; be compelled

被告人 bèigàorén (leg.) defendant; the accused

被害人 bèihàirén (leg.) the injured party; the victim

❸ [介]用在名词前，表示名词所指的人或事物是主动者：used before a noun, which is the doer of an action in a passive sentence | 这本书～人借走了。Zhè běn shū bèi rén jièzǒu le. *The book was borrowed by someone.* / 帽子～风刮掉了。Màozi bèi fēng guādiào le. *The cap was blown off.*

辈 (輩) bèi 12画 非部

辈 辈辈辈辈辈辈辈辈辈辈辈辈

❶ [名]辈分：generation in a family | 长～zhǎngbèi *elder members of a family; one's seniors* / 晚～wǎnbèi *the younger generation; one's juniors* / 我们是同～人。Wǒmen shì tóngbèi rén. *We belong to the same generation.*

老一辈 lǎoyībèi

❷ [名]一生：lifetime | 一～子 yībèizi *all one's life*

惫 (憊) bèi 12画 心部

惫 惫惫惫惫惫惫惫惫惫惫惫惫

[形]疲乏：tired; exhausted
疲惫 píbèi

 臂 bei　17画 月部

臂 臂臂臂臂臂臂臂臂
臂臂臂臂臂臂臂臂
臂

[名]上臂：arm
胳臂 gēbei
　　See bì.

 奔 bēn　8画 大部

奔 奔奔奔奔奔奔奔奔

❶[动]跑；急走：walk quickly; run | 他急忙～向药店。Tā jímáng bēnxiàng yàodiàn. *He walked quickly to the drugstore.* / 孩子见爸爸回来了，连忙～了过去。Háizi jiàn bàba huílai le, liánmáng bēnle guòqu. *On seeing his father back home, the child quickly ran over to him.*
奔驰 bēnchí run quickly; speed
奔跑 bēnpǎo run
奔腾 bēnténg ① gallop ② surge forward; roll on in waves
东奔西走 dōngbēn-xīzǒu

❷[动]赶忙去做：hurry | ～命 bēnmìng *rush about on errands; be kept on the run*
奔波 bēnbō rush about; be busy running about

奔赴 bēnfù hurry to (a place); rush to
　　See bēn.

 本 běn　5画 木部

本 本本本本本

❶[名]草木的茎干或根；事物的根源：the root or stem of a plant; the origin of sth. | 你这样说可真是忘了～了! Nǐ zhèyàng shuō kě zhēn shì wàngle běn le! *You forget your past by saying so.*
根本 gēnběn　基本 jīběn
基本上 jīběnshàng

❷[形]重要的；中心的：central; principal
本质 běnzhì essence; true nature; origin

❸[形]本来；原来：original
本领 běnlǐng skill; ability; capability
本能 běnnéng instinct
本事 běnshi skill; ability; capability
本性 běnxìng natural instinct; natural character; nature; inherent quality
原本 yuánběn

❹[形]现今的：current | ～世纪 běn shìjì *the present century* / ～次列车 běn cì lièchē *this train*

❺[代]自己或自己方面的：one's

own | ～工厂 běn gōngchǎng *our factory* / ～合同 běn hé-tong *this contract* / ～公司 běn gōngsī *our company* / ～校 běn xiào *our school*

本地 běndì this locality; local

本人 běnrén I; me; myself; oneself; in person

本身 běnshēn itself; in itself

本土 běntǔ one's native country (or land)

本命年 běnmìngnián every 12th year after the year of one's birth

❻[副]本来：originally | 他～姓李。Tā běn xìng Lǐ. *His original surname was Li.* / 我～以为她会来的。Wǒ běn yǐwéi tā huì lái de. *I thought she would come.* / 他～是广东人。Tā běn shì Guǎngdōngrén. *He comes from Guangdong originally.*

本来 běnlái ① original ② originally; at first ③ it goes without saying; of course

本色 běnsè natural colour

❼[名]本钱：capital; principal | 够～儿 gòuběnr *make enough money to cover the cost; break even* / 连～带利都还给你。Lián běn dài lì dōu huángěi nǐ. *Pay back the capital (or principal) plus interest to you.*

本金 běnjīn capital; principal

本钱 běnqián ① capital; principal ② (fig.) qualification; abil-ity; asset

成本 chéngběn   赔本 péiběn

资本 zīběn   资本家 zīběnjiā

资本主义 zīběn zhǔyì

❽[名]本子；书册：book; notebook | 笔记～bǐjìběn *notebook* / 练习～liànxíběn *exercise book*

版本 bǎnběn   车本 chēběn

剧本 jùběn   课本 kèběn

书本 shūběn   样本 yàngběn

正本 zhèngběn

❾[量]用于书籍、簿、册等：used for books, albums, etc. | 四～书 sì běn shū *four books* / 我向他借了三～杂志。Wǒ xiàng tā jièle sān běn zázhì. *I borrowed three magazines from him.*

◇ 本科 běnkē regular under-graduate course

本着 běnzhe in line with; in conformity with; in light of

本科生 běnkēshēng under-graduate

奔 bēn   8画 大部

奔 奔奔奔奔奔奔奔奔

❶[动]径直（向目的地）走去：go straight towards; head for | 直～车站 zhí bēn chēzhàn *head straight for the station* / ～向远方 bēnxiàng yuǎn-fāng *go to a distant place* / 他一下火车就直～学校报到。Tā yī xià huǒchē jiù zhí bēn xuéxiào bàodào. *After getting off the train, he went straight to school to register.*

各奔前程 gèbēnqiánchéng

❷ [动]为某事奔走：try one's best for a certain purpose | 需要什么？我去～。Xūyào shénme? Wǒ qù bèn. *What do you need? I'll go and get it.*

❸ [动]年岁接近：(of age) approaching | 这位老大爷都～80 了。Zhè wèi lǎodàye dōu bèn bāshí le. *The grandpa is getting on for eighty.*

See bēn.

笨

笨 bèn 11画 竹部

笨笨笨笨笨笨笨笨笨笨笨

❶ [形]不聪明；不灵巧：foolish; unintelligent; clumsy | ～手～脚 bènshǒu-bènjiǎo *clumsy; all thumbs* / 愚～ yúbèn *stupid* / 脑子～nǎozi bèn *stupid; slow-witted*

笨蛋 bèndàn *fool; idiot*

笨拙 bènzhuō *clumsy; awkward; stupid*

❷ [形]庞大；沉重：large in size; heavy | 这个衣柜样子太～。Zhège yīguì yàngzi tài bèn. *The wardrobe looks too heavy.* / 穿上那么～的靴子，还怎么走路? Chuānshàng nàme bèn de xuēzi, hái zěnme zǒu lù? *Wearing such heavy boots, how can I walk?*

笨重 bènzhòng *heavy; unwieldy*

崩

崩 bēng 11画 山部

崩崩崩崩崩崩崩崩崩崩崩

❶ [动]倒塌：collapse | 雪～ xuěbēng *avalanche* / 山～地裂 shānbēng-dìliè *land sliding and ground cracking*

❷ [动]破裂：burst | 他把气球吹了。Tā bǎ qìqiú chuībēng le. *He filled the balloon with so much air that it burst.* / 俩人谈～了。Liǎ rén tánbēng le. *The negotiations between the two broke down.*

绷 (繃)

绷 (繃) bēng 11画 纟部

绷绷绷绷绷绷绷绷绷绷绷

❶ [动]拉紧；张紧：stretch (or draw) tight | 把绳子～直了bǎ shéngzi bēngzhí le *pull the string straight* / 衣服紧～在身上。Yīfu jǐnbēng zài shēn shang. *The clothes are tight on her.*

❷[动]猛然弹起：spring; bounce | 她把橡皮筋～断了。Tā bǎ xiāngpíjīn bēngduàn le. *She stretched the rubber band until it snapped.*

❸[动]粗粗地缝上或用别针别上：stitch loosely | ～被面 bēng bèimiàn *stitch up the quilt cover*

◇绷带 bēngdài bandage

甭 běng 9画 一部

甭 甭甭甭甭甭甭甭甭甭

〈方〉"不用"的合音，表示不需要：don't; needn't | ～着急 běng zháojí *don't worry* / 您～客气。Nín béng kèqi. *Please don't stand on ceremony.* / ～管他。Béng guǎn tā. *Leave him alone.*

蹦 bèng 18画 足部

蹦 蹦蹦蹦蹦蹦蹦蹦蹦蹦蹦蹦蹦蹦蹦蹦蹦蹦

[动]跳：jump | ～跳 bèngtiào *skip and jump* / 他高兴得～起来。Tā gāoxìng de bèng qǐlai. *He jumped for joy.*

逼 bī 12画 辶部

逼 逼逼逼逼逼逼逼逼逼逼逼逼

❶[动]靠近；迫近：close in on; press on towards; press up to | 直～城下 zhí bī chéngxià *advance to the city wall*
逼近 bījìn press on towards; close in on; approach; draw near

❷[动]威胁；强迫：force; compel | 寒气～人 hánqì-bīrén *there is a nip in the air* / 他们～我开口。Tāmen bī wǒ kāikǒu. *They forced me to talk.*
逼迫 bīpò force; compel; coerce

鼻 bí 14画 鼻部

鼻 鼻鼻鼻鼻鼻鼻鼻鼻鼻鼻鼻鼻鼻鼻

[名]鼻子：nose
鼻涕 bítì nasal mucus; snivel
鼻子 bízi nose

比 bǐ 4画 比部

比 比比比比

❶[动]比较；较量：compare; compete | ～本领 bǐ běnlǐng *compare one's ability (or skill) with other people* / 你俩～一～，看谁跑得快。Nǐ liǎ bǐyibǐ, kàn shéi pǎodekuài. *You two can compete with each other to see who runs faster.*

比较 bǐjiào ① compare; contrast ② fairly; comparatively; relatively; quite; rather

比赛 bǐsài match; competition

对比 duìbǐ 评比 píngbǐ

无比 wúbǐ 相比 xiāngbǐ

❷ [动]表示比赛双方得分的对比：used to indicate the different scores of two contestants or contesting teams | 北京队以二～一胜了广州队。Běijīngduì yǐ èr bǐ yī shèngle Guǎngzhōuduì. *Beijing beat Guangzhou by two to one.*

比分 bǐfēn score

❸ [动]仿照：copy; model after | 请你～着这张图样再画一张。Qǐng nǐ bǐzhe zhè zhāng túyàng zài huà yī zhāng. *Please draw a new picture after this one.*

❹ [动]比方：compare to; draw an analogy; liken to | 人们常把儿童～作花朵。Rénmen cháng bǎ értóng bǐzuò huāduǒ. *People often compare children to flowers.*

比方 bǐfang ① analogy; instance ② suppose ③ for example; such as

比如 bǐrú for example; for instance; such as

比喻 bǐyù metaphor; analogy; figure of speech

好比 hǎobǐ

打比方 dǎbǐfang

❺ [名]同类事物数量的比较关系：ratio; proportion

比价 bǐjià price relations; rate of exchange

比例 bǐlì proportion

比率 bǐlǜ ratio; rate

比重 bǐzhòng ① specific gravity ② proportion; amount of sth. in its entirety

正比 zhèngbǐ 反比 fǎnbǐ

百分比 bǎifēnbǐ

❻ [介]比较性质、状态和程度的差别，引进比较的对象：used to compare the difference in degree or properties between two things or people | 妹妹～弟弟更喜欢唱歌。Mèimei bǐ dìdi gèng xǐhuan chànggē. *The younger sister likes singing more than the younger brother.* ／他英语说得～我好一点儿。Tā Yīngyǔ shuō de bǐ wǒ hǎo yīdiǎnr. *His oral English is a bit better than mine.* ／我每天～他早来十分钟。Wǒ měi tiān bǐ tā zǎo lái shí fēnzhōng. *I come 10 minutes earlier than he does every day.*

bǐ 8画 彳部

彼 彼彼彼彼彼彼彼彼

❶ [代]那；那个：that; that one | 此

起~伏 cǐqǐ-bǐfú *as one falls, another rises; rise here and subside there*

彼此 bǐcǐ each other; one another

❷[代]他；对方：the other party｜知己知~ zhījǐ-zhībǐ *know both your opponent and yourself*

 笔 (筆) bǐ　10画 竹部

笔 笔笔笔笔笔笔笔笔 笔笔

❶[名]写字、绘画的工具：writing or painting tool｜一支~ yī zhī bǐ *a pen*
粉笔 fěnbǐ　　钢笔 gāngbǐ
毛笔 máobǐ　　铅笔 qiānbǐ
大手笔 dàshǒubǐ
圆珠笔 yuánzhūbǐ

❷[动]写：write
笔记 bǐjì notes
笔迹 bǐjì handwriting
笔试 bǐshì written examination
笔友 bǐyǒu pen friend; pen pal
笔者 bǐzhě the present writer; the author
笔记本 bǐjìběn notebook

❸[名]笔画：stroke; touch｜这个字你少写了一~。Zhège zì nǐ shǎo xiěle yī bǐ. *You missed a stroke in this character.* ／再添几~ zài tiān jǐ bǐ *add a few touches*

❹[量]用于一定数额的钱款：(of money) amount｜一~款子 yī bǐ kuǎnzi *a sum of money* ／他的父亲留下了一~遗产。Tā de fùqīn liúxiàle yī bǐ yíchǎn. *His father bequeathed a legacy to him.*

◇笔直 bǐzhí perfectly straight; straight as a ramrod

 鄙 bǐ　13画 阝(右)部

鄙 鄙鄙鄙鄙鄙鄙鄙鄙 鄙鄙鄙鄙鄙

❶[形]粗俗；恶劣：low; mean; vulgar
卑鄙 bēibǐ

❷[动]看不起：look down upon; despise
鄙视 bǐshì despise; disdain; look down upon

 币 (幣) bì　4画 丿部

币 币币币币

[名]钱；货币：money; currency
港币 gǎngbì　　货币 huòbì
外币 wàibì
人民币 rénmínbì

 必 bì　5画 丶部

必 必必必必必

[副]必然；一定要：surely; certainly

| 分秒～争 fēnmiǎo-bìzhēng *seize every minute and second; make every second count; not a second is to be lost* / ～不可少 bìbùkěshǎo *absolutely necessary; indispensable*

必定 bìdìng *be bound to; be sure to*

必将 bìjiāng *will certainly; surely will*

必然 bìrán *inevitable; certain*

必修 bìxiū *(of a course) required; obligatory*

必须 bìxū *must; have to*

必需 bìxū *essential; indispensable*

必要 bìyào *necessary; essential; indispensable*

不必 búbì　何必 hébì

势必 shìbì　未必 wèibì

务必 wùbì

 毕 (畢) bì　6画 比部

毕 毕毕毕毕毕毕

[动]结束；完成：finish; accomplish | 完～wánbì *finish; complete; end* / 阅～请放回原处。Yuèbì qǐng fànghuí yuánchù. *Please replace it after reading.*

毕业 bìyè *graduate; finish school*

毕业生 bìyèshēng *graduate*

◇毕竟 bìjìng *after all; all in all*

闭 (閉) bì　6画 门部

闭 闭闭闭闭闭闭

❶ [动]合；关：shut; close | ～着眼睛bìzhe yǎnjing *with one's eyes closed* / 每天晚上10点～灯。Měi tiān wǎnshang shí diǎn bì dēng. *The light is turned off at 10:00 every night.*

倒闭 dǎobì　封闭 fēngbì

关闭 guānbì

❷ [动]堵塞：obstruct; block up | 他～住气又游了十米。Tā bìzhù qì yòu yóule shí mǐ. *He held his breath and swam another 10 metres.*

闭塞 bìsè ① stop up; close up ② hard to get to; out-of-the-way; inaccessible

❸ [动]结束：stop; draw to a close

闭幕 bìmù ① the curtain falls; lower the curtain ② close; conclude

闭幕式 bìmùshì *closing ceremony*

 毙 (斃) bì　10画 比部

毙 毙毙毙毙毙毙毙毙 毙毙

[动]死：die

枪毙 qiāngbì

痹 bì　13画 疒部

痹 痹痹痹痹痹痹痹
痹痹痹痹痹

[名]中医指由于风、寒、湿等引起的肢体疼痛或麻木的病症：t h e disease of ache or numbness in the limbs, usu. caused by wind, cold, dampness, etc.
麻痹 mábì

辟 bì　13画 辛部

辟 辟辟辟辟辟辟辟辟
辟辟辟辟辟

[名]君主：monarch; sovereign
复辟 fùbì

碧 bì　14画 石部

碧 碧碧碧碧碧碧碧碧
碧碧碧碧碧碧

[名]青绿色：bluish green
碧绿 bìlǜ dark green

蔽 bì　14画 艹部

蔽 蔽蔽蔽蔽蔽蔽蔽蔽
蔽蔽蔽蔽蔽蔽

[动]遮盖；挡住：cover; shelter; hide
隐蔽 yǐnbì

弊 bì　14画 廾部

弊 弊弊弊弊弊弊弊弊
弊弊弊弊弊弊

❶ [名]害处；毛病：disadvantage; harm
弊病 bìbìng ① malady; evil; malpractice ② drawback; disadvantage
弊端 bìduān malpractice; abuse; corrupt practice
利弊 lìbì
❷ [名]欺蒙人的行为：fraud; abuse; malpractice
作弊 zuòbì

壁 bì　16画 土部

壁 壁壁壁壁壁壁壁壁
壁壁壁壁壁壁壁壁

❶ [名]墙：wall | 四~sìbì the four walls of the room
隔壁 gébì　　碰壁 pèngbì
墙壁 qiángbì
❷ [名]直立的山崖：cliff | 陡~dǒubì sheer cliff

避 bì　16画 辶部

避 避避避避避避避避
避避避避避避避避

❶ [动]躲开：avoid; manage to keep away from | ~风 bìfēng seek

shelter from the wind / ~暑 bìshǔ *be away for summer holidays; go somewhere or do sth. to escape the summer heat* / 咱们在这里~~雨吧。Zánmen zài zhèlǐ bìbì yǔ ba. *Let's take shelter from the rain here.*

避开 bìkāi *keep clear of; avoid*

躲避 duǒbì　　　回避 huíbì

逃避 táobì

❷[动]防止：*prevent*

避免 bìmiǎn　*avoid; refrain from; avert*

不可避免 bùkěbìmiǎn

臂 bì　17画 月部

臂 臂臂臂臂臂臂臂臂 臂臂臂臂臂臂臂臂 臂

[名]胳膊：*arm* | 左~zuǒbì *the left arm* / 他~上有一块伤疤。Tā bì shang yǒu yī kuài shāngbā. *There is a scar on his arm.*

手臂 shǒubì

See bei.

边（邊）biān　5画 辶部

边 边边边边边

❶[名]边缘；界限：*side; border* | 海~hǎibiān *seaside* /河~ hébiān *riverside* / 他们坐在床~儿

上。Tā zuò zài chuángbiānr shang. *He sat on the edge of the bed.*

边缘 biānyuán *edge; brink*

两边 liǎngbiān　周边 zhōubiān

❷[名]近旁；靠近物体的地方：*near; close by (an object)* | 手~ shǒubiān *on hand; at hand* / 马路~mǎlùbiān *on the side of a street*

旁边 pángbiān　身边 shēnbiān

❸[名]两个地区交界处：*border between countries or regions*

边防 biānfáng *frontier defence; border defence*

边疆 biānjiāng *border area; borderland; frontier; frontier region*

边界 biānjiè *boundary; border*

边境 biānjìng *border; frontier*

❹[名]方面：*sides; parties*

单边 dānbiān　　那边 nàbiān

双边 shuāngbiān

这边 zhèbiān

半边天 bànbiāntiān

❺[副]两个"边"字分别与动词连用，表示同时动作：*used before verbs, indicating the simultaneous progression or development of two actions* | ~走~唱 biān zǒu biān chàng *go along singing; sings as one goes along* / ~学~干 biān xué biān gàn *learn while working; learn on the job; learn by doing* / 他们~喝茶~闲谈。Tāmen biān hēchá biān xiántán. *They had a chat over a cup of tea.*

边···边··· biān ... biān ... used with two verbs to indicate the simultaneous progression or development of two actions 一边···一边··· yī biān... yībiān...

❻[名]几何学术语，线段；side of a geometrical figure | 三角形有三条～。Sānjiǎoxíng yǒu sān tiáo biān. *A triangle has three sides.*

❼方位词词尾：suffix of nouns of locality

北边 běibian　东边 dōngbian
后边 hòubian　里边 lǐbian
南边 nánbian　前边 qiánbian
上边 shàngbian 外边 wàibian
西边 xībian　下边 xiàbian
右边 yòubian　左边 zuǒbian

编 (編) biān　12画 纟部

编 编编编编编编编编编
编编编编

❶[动]把细长条的东西交织起来：weave; plait | ～草帽 biān cǎomào *weave a straw hat*

❷[动]组织；排列：organize; arrange | ～组 biān zǔ *organize into groups* / 这本书已经～过号了。Zhè běn shū yǐjīng biānguo hào le. *This book has already been given a serial number.*

编号 biānhào give numbers (to)
编制 biānzhì ① weave; plait; braid ② work out; draw up ③ authorized strength; establishment

❸[动]编辑；创作：edit; compile; write; compose | ～杂志 biān zázhì *edit a magazine* / ～字典 biān zìdiǎn *compile a dictionary* / 他特别会～写故事。Tā tèbié huì biānxiě gùshi. *He is particularly good at writing stories.*

编辑 biānjí ① edit ② editor
编剧 biānjù ① write a play, scenario, etc. ② screenwriter; scenarist
编写 biānxiě ① compile ② write; compose
改编 gǎibiān

❹[动]虚构；捏造：fabricate; invent; make up | ～谎话 biān huǎnghuà *make up a lie* / 这个故事也～得太离奇了。Zhège gùshi yě biān de tài líqí le. *This story is too far-fetched.*

◇邮编 yóubiān

鞭 biān　18画 革部

鞭 鞭鞭鞭鞭鞭鞭鞭鞭
鞭鞭鞭鞭鞭鞭鞭
鞭鞭

❶[名]鞭子，驱赶牲畜的用具：

whip; sth. used to drive live-stock | 皮~pí biān *leather-thonged whip* / 马~mǎbiān *horse-whip*

鞭子 biānzi whip

❷[动]用鞭子打：lash with a whip | ~策 biāncè *spur on; urge on; encourage*

❸[名]成串的爆竹：small firecrackers woven into strings | 一挂~ yī guà biān *a string of fire-crackers*

鞭炮 biānpào firecrackers

 贬 (貶) biǎn 8画 贝部

贬 贬贬贬贬贬贬贬贬

❶[动]减低；降低：reduce; devalue

贬值 biǎnzhí devalue

❷[动]给予低的、不好的评价：depreciate; play down | 你不该把他~得那么低。Nǐ bù gāi bǎ tā biǎn de nàme dī. *You shouldn't put him down so much.*

贬低 biǎndī degrade; play down

贬义 biǎnyì derogatory sense

 扁 biǎn 9画 户部

扁 扁扁扁扁扁扁扁扁扁

[形]物体宽平而较薄：flat and thin | 鸭子的嘴很~。Yāzi de zuǐ hěn biǎn. *The bill of the duck is quite flat.* / 纸盒压~了。Zhǐhé yābiǎn le. *The cardboard box was crushed flat.*

扁豆 biǎndōu hyacinth bean

 变 (變) biàn 8画 又部

变 变变变变变变变变

❶[动]改变；性质、状态或情况跟原来不同：change; become different in quality, state, or situation | 天气~了。Tiānqì biàn le. *The weather has changed.* / 这地方~得认不出来了。Zhè dìfang biàn de rèn bù chūlái le. *The place has changed beyond recogni-tion.*

变成 biànchéng change into; turn into; become

变动 biàndòng change; alter-ation

变革 biàngé transform; change

变更 biàngēng change; alter; modify

变化 biànhuà change; vary

变换 biànhuàn vary; alternate

变脸 biànliǎn suddenly turn hostile

变迁 biànqiān change

变数 biànshù (math.) variable

变相 biànxiàng in disguised form; covert

变形 biànxíng be out of shape; become deformed

变质 biànzhì go bad; deteriorate

改变 gǎibiàn 转变 zhuǎnbiàn 千变万化 qiānbiàn-wànhuà

❷[动]使改变：transform; change; turn | 现在少数～成了多数。Xiànzài shǎoshù biànchéng le duōshù. *The minority now has become the majority.*

变为 biànwéi change into; turn into

❸[动]表演戏法或魔术：perform conjuring tricks; conjure | 他的魔术～得真好!Tā de móshù biàn de zhēn hǎo! *His magic was performed so well!*

便 biàn 9画 亻部

便 便便便便便便便便便

❶[形]方便；便利：convenient; handy | ～利 biànlì *handy; convenience*

便道 biàndào shortcut; sidewalk

便捷 biànjié ① convenient ② quick

便民 biànmín for the convenience of the people

便于 biànyú be easy to; be convenient for

不便 búbiàn   简便 jiǎnbiàn

轻便 qīngbiàn   随便 suíbiàn

以便 yǐbiàn

❷[形]简单的；非正式的：simple; informal

便饭 biànfàn an ordinary meal; a simple meal

便条 biàntiáo a brief note

❸[名]小便；大便：urine or excrement

小便 xiǎobiàn

❹[副]就：then; in that case; just; simply | 这～是我的家。Zhè biànshì wǒ de jiā. *This is my house.* / 这几天不是刮风，～是下雨。Zhè jǐ tiān bùshì guāfēng, biànshì xiàyǔ. *It has been either windy or rainy these last few days.*

See pián.

遍 biàn 12画 辶部

遍 遍遍遍遍遍遍遍遍遍遍遍遍

❶[形]全：all over; everywhere | ～野 biànyě *all over the fields* / 我们的朋友～天下。Wǒmen de péngyou biàn tiānxià. *We have friends all over the world.* / 他走～了书店，就是没有买到这本书。Tā zǒubiànle shūdiàn, jiùshì méiyǒu mǎidào zhè běn shū. *He went from bookshop to bookshop but still failed to get this book.*

遍布 biànbù be found everywhere; spread all over

遍地 biàndì everywhere; all around

普遍 pǔbiàn

❷[量]指动作从开始到结束的整个过程: used to indicate the process of an action from beginning to end | 看了一～ kànle yī biàn *read sth. once* / 这首曲子我听过好几～。Zhè shǒu qǔzi wǒ tīngguo hǎo jǐ biàn. *I have heard the melody several times.* / 请你再说一～，我没听清楚。Qǐng nǐ zài shuō yī biàn, wǒ méi tīng qīngchu. *I couldn't catch what you said. Please repeat it.*

 辨 biàn 16画 辛部

辨 辨 辨 辨 辨 辨 辨 辨 辨 辨 辨 辨 辨 辨

[动]区别; 识别: distinguish; differentiate | 明～是非 míngbiàn-shìfēi *make a clear distinction between right and wrong*

辨别 biànbié differentiate; distinguish; discriminate

辨认 biànrèn distinguish

分辨 fēnbiàn

 辩 (辯) biàn 16画 辛部

辩 辩 辩 辩 辩 辩 辩 辩 辩 辩 辩 辩 辩 辩 辩 辩

[动]争论; 说明是非或真假: argue; make clear what is right or wrong, what is true or false | 善～ shànbiàn *have the gift of the gab* / 两个人～来～去, 谁也说不服谁。Liǎng gè rén biàn lái biàn qù, shéi yě shuōbufú shéi. *The two of them kept arguing and neither of them could convince the other.*

辩护 biànhù defend; plead

辩解 biànjiě exculpate

辩论 biànlùn argue; debate

辩证 biànzhèng investigate and authenticate

辩证法 biànzhèngfǎ dialectics

分辩 fēnbiàn

辫 (辮) biàn 17画 辛部

辫 辫 辫 辫 辫 辫 辫 辫 辫 辫 辫 辫 辫 辫 辫 辫 辫

[名]把头发分股编成的条状物: plait; braid; pigtail | 梳小～儿 shū xiǎobiànr *wear pigtails*

辫子 biànzi plait; braid; pigtail

 标 (標) biāo 9画 木部

标 标 标 标 标 标 标 标 标

❶[名]非根本的或非主要的事物(跟"本běn"相对)：external sign; symptom (the opposite of "本běn") | 治～不如治本 zhì biāo bùrú zhì běn *cure the disease rather than merely relieve the symptoms*

❷[名]标志；记号；符号：mark; sign | 路～lùbiāo *road sign*

标本 biāoběn specimen; sample

标点 biāodiǎn punctuation

标签 biāoqiān label; tag

标示 biāoshì mark; indicate

标志 biāozhì ① sign; mark; symbol; hallmark ② indicate; mark; symbolize

标准 biāozhǔn standard; criterion

标准化 biāozhǔnhuà standardize; standardization

超标 chāobiāo　达标 dábiāo

光标 guāngbiāo　目标 mùbiāo

商标 shāngbiāo　鼠标 shǔbiāo

指标 zhǐbiāo

❸[动]用文字或其他事物表明：mark sth. with words or other things | ～上号码 biāoshàng hàomǎ *put a number on* / 文章的重点部分已用红线～出。Wénzhāng de zhòngdiǎn bùfen yǐ yòng hóngxiàn biāochū. *The important parts in the article have been marked with red lines.* / 商品都～了价格。Shāngpǐn dōu biāole jiàgé. *There is a price tag on each item.*

标价 biāojià ① mark a price ② marked price

标题 biāotí title; heading; headline; caption

标语 biāoyǔ slogan; poster

标枪 biāoqiāng javelin

标致 biāozhì (usu. of women) beautiful; handsome

竞标 jìngbiāo

中标 zhòngbiāo

锦标赛 jǐnbiāosài

表（錶❺）biǎo　8画 一部

表表表表表表表表表

❶[名]外面；外部；外貌：surface; outside; external | ～里一致 biǎolǐ-yīzhì *think and act in one and the same way*

表面 biǎomiàn surface; face; outside appearance

外表 wàibiǎo　　　仪表 yíbiǎo

❷[动]表示；显示：show; indicate

表达 biǎodá express; show; voice; convey

表明 biǎomíng make known; make clear; state

表情 biǎoqíng expression; countenance; look

表示 biǎoshì show; express; indicate

表述 biǎoshù explain; state

表态 biǎotài make known one's position; declare where

one stands

表现 biǎoxiàn show; express; display; manifest

表演 biǎoyǎn perform; act; play; demonstrate

表扬 biǎoyáng praise; commend

表彰 biǎozhāng cite (in dispatches); commend

代表 dàibiǎo   发表 fābiǎo

代表团 dàibiǎotuán

❸ [名]分类分项记录事物的书籍或表格：table; form｜课程~kèchéngbiǎo school timetable／请在这张~上填上你的名字。Qǐng zài zhè zhāng biǎo shàng tiānshang nǐ de míngzi. Please fill your name in this form.

表格 biǎogé form; table

图表 túbiǎo

时间表 shíjiānbiǎo

❹ [名]称呼父亲、祖父的兄弟姊妹所生的子女，或者母亲、祖母的兄弟姊妹所生的子女。表示亲戚关系：cousin; cousinship; the relationship between the children or grandchildren of brothers or of sisters｜~哥 biǎogē cousin／~兄弟 biǎoxiōngdi cousins

表弟 biǎodì younger male cousin; cousin

表姐 biǎojiě elder female cousin; cousin

表妹 biǎomèi younger female

cousin; cousin

❺ [名]计时器具：watch｜你的~停了，该上弦了。Nǐ de biǎo tíng le, gāi shàng xián le. Your watch has stopped and it needs winding.

手表 shǒubiǎo 钟表 zhōngbiǎo

❻ [名]测量某种量的器具：metre; gauge｜温度~wēndùbiǎo thermometer／体温~tǐwēnbiǎo (clinical) thermometer

biē 15画 心部

憋 憋憋憋憋憋憋憋
憋憋憋憋憋憋憋

❶ [动]气不通：suffocate; feel oppressed｜气压低，~得人透不过气来。Qìyā dī, biē de rén tòubuguò qì lái. The atmospheric pressure was so low that one could hardly breathe.／她心里~得慌，想出去走走。Tā xīnli biēdehuang, xiǎng chūqu zǒuzou. As she felt pressured, she wanted to go out for a walk.

❷ [动]抑制或忍住：suppress, hold back｜~着一口气 biēzhe yī kǒu qì hold one's breath／他们~足了劲儿，要踢赢这场球。Tāmen biēzúle jìnr, yào tīyíng zhè chǎng qiú. They are bursting with energy to win this game.

别 bié 7画 刂部

别 别 别 别 别 别 别 别

❶[动]分离：leave | 久～重逢jiǔbié-
chóngféng *meet again after a
long separation* / 一～二十多
年，今天又相见了。Yī bié èrshí
duō nián, jīntiān yòu
xiāngjiàn le. *Today, they met
again at last after a separation
of more than twenty years.* /
久～故乡 jiǔbié gùxiāng *leave
one's native place for years*
　分别 fēnbié　　告别 gàobié
　离别 líbié
　不辞而别 bùcí'érbié

❷[动]区分；分辨：distinguish;
differentiate
　辨别 biànbié　　鉴别 jiànbié
　区别 qūbié　　识别 shíbié

❸[名]差别：difference; distinction
　差别 chābié　　个别 gèbié
　特别 tèbié

❹[名]类别：category; kind
　级别 jíbié　　类别 lèibié
　派别 pàibié　　性别 xìngbié

❺[代]另外的：other
　别处 biéchù　another place;
　elsewhere
　别人 biérén　other people; oth-
　ers; people
　别字 biézì　wrongly written or
　mispronounced character

❻[动]用针等附着或固定：fasten

or pin | 把两张发票～在一起bǎ
liǎng zhāng fāpiào bié zài
yìqǐ *clip the two receipts
together* / 他胸前～着一朵小白
花。Tā xiōng qián biézhe yī
duǒ xiǎo báihuā. *He has a
little white flower pinned on his
chest.*

❼[副]不要，表示禁止或劝阻：
don't; had better not (used in
giving commands or advice
against doing sth.) | 在公共场
所～抽烟。Zài gōnggòng
chǎngsuǒ bié chōuyān.
Don't smoke in public places.
/ ～走了，就在这儿住下吧。Bié
zǒu le, jiù zài zhèr zhùxià ba.
Don't leave. Just stay here. / ～
忙，这事得商量商量。Bié máng,
zhè shì děi shāngliang
shāngliang. *Don't hurry. We'd
better talk it over.*

　　See biè.

别 (彆) biè 7画 刂部

别 别 别 别 别 别 别 别

See 别扭
　别扭 bièniu awkward; difficult
　　See bié.

宾 (賓) bīn 10画 宀部

宾 宾宾宾宾宾宾宾宾
宾宾

[名]客人：guest
宾馆 bīnguǎn guest-house;
hotel
贵宾 guìbīn　来宾 láibīn
外宾 wàibīn
◇宾语 bīnyǔ (gram.) object

滨 (濱) bīn 13画 氵部

滨滨滨滨滨滨滨滨
滨滨滨滨滨

[名]靠近水边的地方：bank; shore
| ～海 bīnhǎi by the sea / 长江
之～Cháng Jiāng zhī bīn on
the bank of the Yangtze River

冰 bīng 6画 氵部

冰 冰冰冰冰冰冰

❶ [名] ice | 河里的～已经化了。Hé
li de bīng yǐjīng huà le. The
ice in the river has melted.
冰棍儿 bīnggùnr popsicle; ice
lolly
冰淇淋 bīngqílín ice cream
滑冰 huábīng
❷ [动]使人感到寒冷：make one
feel very cold | 这水很～手。
Zhè shuǐ hěn bīngshǒu. The
water is very icy. / 河水～冷。
Héshuǐ bīnglěng. The river
water is freezing cold.
❸ [动]用冰使食物变凉：ice; cool
food with ice | 把汽水～一下。
Bǎ qìshuǐ bīng yī xià. Ice the
soda water for a while.
冰箱 bīngxiāng refrigerator;
freezer
冰镇 bīngzhèn iced
电冰箱 diànbīngxiāng
◇冰毒 bīngdú ice (a highly ad-
dictive stimulant that works on
the central and sympathetic nervous system, used as a narcotic
drug); crystal meth

兵 bīng 7画 八部

兵 兵兵兵兵兵兵兵

❶ [名]战士；军队：soldier; army |
他是一个～。Tā shì yī gè
bīng. He is a soldier.
步兵 bùbīng　练兵 liànbīng
民兵 mínbīng　哨兵 shàobīng
士兵 shìbīng
❷ [名]军事或战争：military | 纸
上谈～zhǐshàng-tánbīng
be an armchair strategist

丙 bǐng 5画 一部

丙 丙丙丙丙丙

[名]天干的第三位，也表示次序第
三：the third of the ten Heav-
enly Stems; third in order | 他

在甲班，我在～班。Tā zài jiǎ bān,wǒ zài bǐng bān. *He is in class A and I am in class C.*

秉 bǐng 8画 丿部

秉 秉秉秉秉秉秉秉秉

❶[动]拿着；握着：(in old written language) grasp; hold ｜ ～烛 bǐngzhú *(in written) carry a candle*

❷[动]掌握；主持：control; preside over

◇秉性 bǐngxìng nature; disposition; natural instincts

柄 bǐng 9画 木部

柄 柄柄柄柄柄柄柄柄 柄

❶[名]器物的把手：handle of sth. ｜ 刀～dāobǐng *the handle of a knife* / 伞～sǎnbǐng *the shaft of an umbrella*

❷[名]喻指在言行上被人抓住的材料：handle; target ｜ 话～huà- bǐng *subject for ridicule* 把柄 bǎbǐng

❸[名]花、叶、果实同枝丫或茎相连的部分：(of a flower, leaf or fruit) the part that combines with the twig or stem ｜ 别把花～弄断了。Bié bǎ huābǐng nòng- duàn le. *Don't break the small*

stem of the flower.

饼 (餅) bǐng 9画 饣部

饼 饼饼饼饼饼饼饼饼 饼

❶[名]扁圆形的面制食品：round flat cake

饼干 bǐnggān biscuit; cracker 烧饼 shāobing 月饼 yuèbing

❷[名]形状像饼的东西：sth. shaped like a cake ｜ 柿～shì- bǐng *dried persimmon* 铁饼 tiěbǐng

禀 bǐng 13画 一部

禀 禀禀禀禀禀禀禀禀 禀禀禀禀禀

[动]向上级或长辈报告：report to one's superior or senior 禀告 bǐnggào report (to one's superior or senior)

并 bìng 6画 丷部

并 并并并并并并

❶[动]合在一起：combine together ｜ 把这两张桌子～在一起。Bǎ zhè liǎng zhāng zhuōzi bìng zài yīqǐ. *Put the two desks together.* ／把几个小厂～成一个大厂。Bǎ jǐ gè xiǎo chǎng bìngchéng yī gè dà chǎng. *Combine several small factories into a big one.*

兼并 jiānbìng　合并 hébìng

❷ [动]并排;挨着: side by side | 肩～着肩 jiān bìngzhe jiān *(walk or act, etc.) side by side*

❸ [副]一齐;同时: simultaneously; side by side

并存 bìngcún exist side by side; coexist

❹ [副]放在否定词前,加强否定的语气,带有反驳的意味: (not) at all (used before a negative for emphasis) | 天气～不冷。Tiānqì bìng bù lěng. *It is by no means cold.* / 他～不糊涂。Tā bìng bù hútu. *He is not muddle-headed at all.*

并非 bìngfēi really not

❺ [连]表示进一层的意思: and (indicating increased degree) | 同意～拥护 tóngyì bìng yōnghù *agree with and support sth.* / 会议讨论～通过了这个方案。Huìyì tǎolùn bìng tōngguòle zhège fāng'àn. *This proposal was discussed and approved at the meeting.*

并且 bìngqiě and; besides; moreover; furthermore

病　bìng　10画 疒部

病 | 病病病病病病病病病病

❶ [名]生理上或心理上出现的不健康、不正常的状态: disease; ailment | 害了一场～ hàile yī chǎng bìng *fall seriously ill* / 有了～,应该及时医治。Yǒule bìng, yīnggāi jíshí yīzhì. *Once you fall ill, you should get timely treatment.* / 他的～已经好了。Tā de bìng yǐjīng hǎo le. *He has already recovered from illness.*

病毒 bìngdú virus

病菌 bìngjūn pathogenic bacteria; germs

病例 bìnglì case (of illness)

病情 bìngqíng patient's condition

得病 débìng　　发病 fābìng
患病 huànbìng　疾病 jíbìng
看病 kànbìng
生病 shēngbìng
胃病 wèibìng 艾滋病 àizībìng
白血病 báixuèbìng
糖尿病 tángniàobìng
心脏病 xīnzàngbìng

❷ [动]生病: be sick; be taken ill | 孩子～得很厉害。Háizi bìng de hěn lìhai. *The child was seriously ill.* / 她～了三天。Tā bìngle sān tiān. *She has been ill for three days.*

病床 bìngchuáng hospital bed; sickbed

病房 bìngfáng ward; sickroom

病号 bìnghào sick person; patient

病人 bìngrén patient; invalid

❸ [名]弊害：malady; evil

弊病 bìbìng

❹ [名]缺点；错误：fault; defect | 通~tōngbìng common failing / 请找出语~。Qǐng zhǎochū yǔbìng. *Please find the grammatical error.*

毛病 máobìng

 拨 (撥) bō　8画 扌部

拨 拨拨拨拨拨拨拨拨

❶ [动]用手脚或棍棒等横向用力，使东西移动或分开：turn, move with one's hand, foot, or a stick | ~电话号码bō diànhuà hàomǎ *dial a telephone number* / ~好闹钟 bōhǎo nàozhōng *set the alarm clock*

拨打 bōdǎ dial; call

挑拨 tiǎobō

❷ [动]分给；调配：allocate; assign; set aside | ~一笔款子bō yī bǐ kuǎnzi *allocate a sum of money* / ~两个人给我 bō liǎng gè rén gěi wǒ *assign two people to me*

拨款 bōkuǎn ① appropriate fund; allocate funds ② appropriation

❸ [量]用于成批的、分组的人或物：

batch; group | 分两~儿干活fēn liǎng bōr gānhuó *work in two groups* / 一~年轻工人到工地来了。Yī bō niánqīng gōngrén dào gōngdì lái le. *A group of young workers came to the construction site.* / 你们班50个同学分~儿去参观。Nǐmen bān wǔshí gè tóngxué fēnbōr qù cānguān. *The 50 students of your class will go to visit in groups.*

 波 bō　8画 氵部

波 波波波波波波波波

[名]一起一伏的浪纹：wave; ripple | 水 ~shuǐbō *wave*

波动 bōdòng undulate; fluctuate; rise and fall

波及 bōjí spread to; involve; affect

波浪 bōlàng wave

波涛 bōtāo great waves; billows

◇ 奔波 bēnbō　　风波 fēngbō

微波炉 wēibōlú

玻 bō　9画 王部

玻 玻玻玻玻玻玻玻玻玻

See 玻璃

玻璃 bōli glass

剥

bō   10画 刂部

剥 剥剥剥剥剥剥剥剥
剥剥

[动]强行夺去：deprive by force
剥夺 bōduó deprive; expropriate; strip
剥削 bōxuē exploit
See bāo.

菝

bō   11画 艹部

菝 菝菝菝菝菝菝菝菝
菝菝菝

See below
菝菜 bōcài spinach
菝萝 bōluó pineapple

播

bō   15画 扌部

播 播播播播播播播
播播播播播播播

❶ [动]撒；撒种：sow | 种子已经全
部~到田里去了。Zhǒngzi yǐ-
jīng quánbù bōdào tiān li qù
le. All the seeds have been sown
in the fields.
播种 bōzhǒng sow seeds
❷ [动]散布；传扬：broadcast | 这
条新闻在今天中午又~了一遍。
Zhè tiáo xīnwén zài jīntiān
zhōngwǔ yòu bōle yī biàn.

*The news was broadcast again
this noon.*
播报 bōbào broadcast
播放 bōfàng broadcast
播送 bōsòng broadcast; transmit
播音 bōyīn broadcast
重播 chóngbō 传播 chuánbō
点播 diǎnbō 广播 guǎngbō
直播 zhíbō 转播 zhuǎnbō

伯

bó   7画 亻部

伯 伯伯伯伯伯伯伯

❶ [名]父亲的哥哥：father's elder
brother | ~伯 bóbo *father's
elder brother*
❷ [名]尊称年龄大、辈分高的人：a
respectful form of address for
someone older than one's father
伯伯 bóbo ① father's elder
brother; uncle ② a term of address for a man of one's father's
generation who is older than
one's father; uncle
伯父 bófù father's elder brother;
uncle
伯母 bómǔ aunt; wife of
father's elder brother
◇阿拉伯语 Ālābóyǔ

驳 (駁) bó   7画 马部

驳 驳驳驳驳驳驳驳

[动]说明理由，否定对方意见：state one's own opinions to refute other's points | 真理是～不倒的。Zhēnlǐ shì bōbudǎo de. *Truth fears no refutation.* / 这种说法不值一～。Zhè zhǒng shuōfa bùzhí-yībó. *Such remarks are not worth refuting.*
驳斥 bóchì refute; denounce
驳回 bóhuí reject (an appeal, request, proposal, etc.); turn down; overrule
反驳 fǎnbó

泊　　bó　　8画 氵部

泊 泊泊泊泊泊泊泊泊

❶ [动]船靠岸：anchor alongside the shore
停泊 tíngbó
❷ [动]停留：stop; stay for a time
漂泊 piāobó

勃　　bó　　9画 力部

勃 勃勃勃勃勃勃勃勃勃

❶ [形]旺盛：vigorous; thriving | 生机～～ shēngjī-bóbó *full of vigour*
朝气蓬勃 zhāoqì-péngbó
❷ [形]突然；忽然：(in written) sudden | ～发 bófā *break out*

舶　　bó　　11画 舟部

舶 舶舶舶舶舶舶舶舶舶舶

[名]大海船：oceangoing ship
船舶 chuánbó

脖　　bó　　11画 月部

脖 脖脖脖脖脖脖脖脖脖脖脖

❶ [名]头同身躯相连接的部分：neck
脖子 bózi neck
❷ [名]身体上或器物上像脖子的部分：sth. like (or function as) a neck | 脚～子 jiǎobózi *ankle*

博　　bó　　12画 十部

博 博博博博博博博博博博博博

❶ [形]广；多：abundant; plentiful
博物馆 bówùguǎn museum
❷ [形]见识广：well-informed | ～古通今 bógǔ-tōngjīn *possess a wide knowledge of things both ancient and modern*
博士 bóshì (of academic degree) doctor
博士后 bóshìhòu ① postdoctoral student of researcher ② postdoctoral study of research ③ postdoctoral; postdoctorate

博士生 bóshìshēng student who studies for a doctorate

博览会 bólǎnhuì (international) fair; trade fair

❸[动]以某种言行获取同情或欢心：win; gain | ～取信任 bóqǔ xìnrèn *win the confidence* / ～得同情 bódé tóngqíng *win sympathy*

博彩 bócǎi gambling in the form of a tombola, or lottery

赌博 dǔbó

搏　bó　13画 扌部

搏搏搏搏搏搏搏搏搏搏搏搏搏

❶[动]对打：wrestle; combat

搏斗 bódòu wrestle; fight; struggle

❷[动]跳动：beat; pulsate

脉搏 màibó

膊　bó　14画 月部

膊膊膊膊膊膊膊膊膊膊膊膊膊膊

[名]上身近肩的部分：upper arm | 赤～ chìbó *stripped to the waist*

胳膊 gēbo

薄　bó　16画 艹部

薄薄薄薄薄薄薄薄薄薄薄薄薄薄薄薄

❶[形]轻微；少：slight; meagre; small

薄弱 bóruò weak; frail

❷[动]看不起；轻视：look down upon; despise

❸[形]不庄重；不厚道：frivolous; ungenerous; unkind; mean | 我待你不～。Wǒ dài nǐ bù bó. *I have never treated you unkindly.*

薄膜 bómó ① membrane ② film

　　See bāo.

簸　bǒ　19画 竹部

簸簸簸簸簸簸簸簸簸簸簸簸簸簸簸簸簸簸

❶[动]用簸箕颠动食物，扬去其中的杂物：winnow with a fan to get rid of chaff and dust | ～稻谷 bǒ dàogǔ *winnow away the chaff*

❷[动]上下颠动：quiver; shake

颠簸 diānbǒ

卜　bǔ　2画 卜部

卜卜卜

❶[动]占卜：divine | ～卦 bǔguà

a system of divination

❷[动]预测；推测：foretell; predict | 吉凶难～jíxiōng-nánbǔ *It's difficult to predict how it will turn out.* / 胜败可～ shēngbài-kěbǔ *victory or defeat can be predicted; one can forecast the outcome*

补 (補) bǔ   7画 衤部

补 补补补补补补补

❶[动]加上材料，修理破损的东西：mend; repair | ～衣服 bǔ yīfu *mend clothes* / ～过的鞋子 bǔguo de xiézi *mended shoes*

❷[动]把不足或缺少的填上；使齐全：supply; make up for | 把作业～齐 bǎ zuòyè bǔqí *make up the unfinished assignment* / 弥～赤字 míbǔ chìzì *make up a deficit* / 我们还得～三个人。Wǒmen hái děi bǔ sān gè rén. *We have three vacancies to be filled; We need three more people.* / 把漏了的字～上 bǎ lòule de zì bǔshang *fill in the missing words*

补偿 bǔcháng compensate; make up

补充 bǔchōng ① replenish; supplement; complement ②additional; complementary; supplementary

补救 bǔjiù remedy

补课 bǔkè make up missed lessons

补贴 bǔtiē subsidy; allowance

补习 bǔxí take lessons after school or work

补语 bǔyǔ (gram.) complement

补助 bǔzhù subsidy; allowance

候补 hòubǔ   互补 hùbǔ

弥补 míbǔ   替补 tìbǔ

填补 tiánbǔ

取长补短 qǔcháng-bǔduǎn

❸[动]滋养：nourish | ～身体 bǔ shēntǐ *take nutritious food to build up one's health* / ～元气 bǔ yuánqì *help restore vitality*

捕 bǔ   10画 扌部

捕 捕捕捕捕捕捕捕捕

[动]捉；逮：catch; seize | ～鱼 bǔ yú *catch fish* / ～老鼠 bǔ lǎoshǔ *catch the mouse*

捕捞 bǔlāo fish for; catch

捕捉 bǔzhuō catch; seize

被捕 bèibǔ   逮捕 dàibǔ

抓捕 zhuābǔ   追捕 zhuībǔ

哺 bǔ   10画 口部

哺哺哺哺哺哺哺哺
哺哺

[动]喂：feed | ~养 bǔyǎng *feed; rear*

哺乳 bǔrǔ breast-feed; nurse

 bù 4画 一部
. . . .

不 不不不不

❶ [副]用在动词、形容词、助动词或其他副词前，表示否定；没有：(used before verbs, adjectives, auxiliary and some adverbs to indicate negation) not; no | 这件衣服~干净。Zhè jiàn yīfu bù gānjìng. *This coat is a dirty one.* / 今天下雨，我就~回家了。Jīntiān xiàyǔ, wǒ jiù bù huíjiā le. *I will not go home today as it is raining.* / 他~常来。Tā bù cháng lái. *He does not come here often.* / 天气~怎么冷。Tiānqì bù zěnme lěng. *It's not very cold.*

不安 bù'ān ① turbulent; unstable ② uneasy; disturbed; worried

不比 bùbǐ unlike

不必 bùbì need not; not have to

不便 bùbiàn inconvenient; inappropriate; unsuitable

不曾 bùcéng never (have done sth.)

不错 bùcuò ① correct; right ②

not bad; pretty good

不但 bùdàn not only

不当 bùdàng unsuitable; improper; inappropriate

不得 bùdé (used after a verb to indicate disallowance or forbiddance) must not; not be allowed

不等 bùděng vary; differ

不定 bùdìng not sure; indefinite

不断 bùduàn unceasing; uninterrupted; continuous; constant

不对 bùduì incorrect; wrong

不法 bùfǎ lawless; illegal; unlawful

不妨 bùfáng there is no harm in; might as well

不服 bùfú refuse to obey (or comply); remain unconvinced by; not give in to

不符 bùfú not agree (or square) with; be inconsistent with

不公 bùgōng unjust; unfair

不顾 bùgù in spite of; regardless of

不管 bùguǎn no matter (what, how, etc.); regardless of

不光 bùguāng ① not the only one ② (conj.) not only

不过 bùguò ① used as an intensifier after an adjective ② only; merely; no more than

不见 bùjiàn not see; not meet

不解 bùjiě not understand

不禁 bùjīn can't help (doing sth.); can't refrain from

不仅 bùjǐn ① not the only one ② not only

不久 bùjiǔ ① soon; before long ② not long after; soon after

不堪 bùkān ① cannot bear; cannot stand ② utterly; extremely

不可 bùkě ① cannot; should not; must not ② used in "非 fēi…不可" to indicate what one is set to do

不愧 bùkuì be worthy of

不利 bùlì unfavourable; disadvantageous; harmful; detrimental

不良 bùliáng bad; harmful; unhealthy

不料 bùliào happen unexpectedly

不论 bùlùn no matter (what, how, who, etc.)

不满 bùmǎn resentful; discontented; dissatisfied

不免 bùmiǎn unavoidable

不明 bùmíng ① not clear; unknown ② fail to understand

不平 bùpíng ① injustice; unfairness; wrong ② grievance

不然 bùrán ① not so ② if not so; or else; otherwise (used at the beginning of a sentence to indicate disagreement)

不容 bùróng not tolerate; not allow; not brook

不如 bùrú ① not as good as; inferior to ② had better; would rather

不少 bùshǎo many

不时 bùshí from time to time

不是 bùshi fault; blame

不停 bùtíng without stop

不同 bùtóng different from; distinct from

不惜 bùxī ① not stint; regardless of; not spare ② not scruple (to do sth.)

不行 bùxíng ① won't do; be out of the question ② be no good; won't work

不幸 bùxìng ① misfortune; adversity ② unfortunate; sad

不朽 bùxiǔ immortal

不许 bùxǔ not allow; must not

不要 bùyào don't

不宜 bùyí unsuitable; inadvisable

不易 bùyì not easy; difficult

不用 bùyòng need not

不再 bùzài no more; no longer; not any longer

不止 bùzhǐ ① incessant; without end ② more than; not limited to

不只 bùzhǐ not only; not merely

不住 bùzhù ceaselessly; continuously

不足 bùzú less than; insufficient

不得不 bùdébù have no choice / option but to; cannot but; have

to

不得了 bùdéliǎo desperately serious; disastrous

不得已 bùdéyǐ act against one's will; have no alternative but to; cannot help but

不动产 bùdòngchǎn real estate; property

不敢当 bùgǎndāng I'm flattered; it's too much of an honour

不见得 bùjiàndé not necessarily; not likely

不景气 bùjǐngqì ① (econ.) depression; recession ② in a depressed state

不买账 bùmǎizhàng not willing to accept sth.; to think nothing of sb.

不起眼 bùqǐyǎn (dial.) not attract attention; not be noticeable; not be attractive

不像话 bùxiànghuà ① unreasonable ② shocking ; outrageous

不要紧 bùyàojǐn it doesn't matter; never mind; it's not serious

不要脸 bùyàoliǎn (offens.) have no sense of shame; shameless

不一定 bùyīdìng uncertain; not sure; not necessarily so

不由得 bùyóude can't help

不至于 bùzhìyú not as far as; unlikely

不卑不亢 bùbēi-bùkàng neither humble nor disrespectful

不辞而别 bùcí'érbié leave without saying goodbye

不法分子 bùfǎ fēnzǐ a lawless person

不顾一切 bùgù-yīqiè fling caution to the winds; regardlessness

不好意思 bùhǎoyìsi ① feel bashful; be shy; be ill at ease ② find it embarrassing (to do sth.)

不慌不忙 bùhuāng-bùmáng unhurried; calm; leisurely

不可避免 bùkě-bìmiǎn inevitably; inescapability; ineluctability

不可思议 bùkě-sīyì inconceivable; unimaginable

不劳而获 bùláo'érhuò gains without pains

不同寻常 bùtóng-xúncháng outstanding; out of the ordinary; above the common run

不相上下 bùxiāng-shàngxià equally matched; roughly the same

不言而喻 bùyán'éryù it goes without saying; it is self-evident

不由自主 bùyóu-zìzhǔ can't help; involuntarily

不正之风 bùzhèngzhīfēng malpractice; unhealthy tendency

不知不觉 bùzhī-bùjué unconsciously; unwittingly; without being aware of sth.

从不 cóngbù   绝不 juébù

差不多 chàbuduō

恨不得 hènbudé

可不是 kěbushì

前不久 qiánbujiǔ

说不定 shuōbudìng

想不到 xiǎngbudào

要不然 yàoburán

要不是 yàobushì

哭笑不得 kūxiào-bùdé

❷ [助]用在动补结构中间，表示不能达到某种结果：used between a verb and its complement, indicating a certain result that cannot be achieved | 做～好 zuòbuhǎo *can not do sth. well* / 天太黑，看～清楚。Tiān tài hēi, kàn bù qīngchu. *It's too dark to identify it clearly.* / 太重了，我拿～动。Tài zhòng le, wǒ nábudòng. *It's too heavy to lift by myself.*

对不起 duìbuqǐ

顾不得 gùbudé

怪不得 guàibudé

来不及 láibují

看不起 kànbuqǐ

忍不住 rěnbuzhù

舍不得 shěbudé

用不着 yòngbuzháo

❸ [副]单用，表示否定性的回答：used by itself as a negative answer | "他知道吧?" —— "～, 他不知道。"Tā zhīdào ba?" —— "Bù, tā bù zhīdào." *Does he know? — No, he doesn't.*

◇ 了不起 liǎobuqǐ

布 bù 5画 巾部

布 布布布布布

❶ [名]棉、麻等织物的统称：cloth | 花～ huābù *cotton print* / 这块～的颜色不太好看。Zhè kuài bù de yánsè bù tài hǎokàn. *The colour of this cloth is not so good.*

布鞋 bùxié cloth shoe

布艺 bùyì fabric art

抹布 mābù

❷ [动]分散到各处；广泛传播：spread

遍布 biànbù   分布 fēnbù

散布 sànbù   纱布 shābù

❸ [动]设置：arrange

布局 bùjú overall arrangement; layout; distribution

布置 bùzhì ① fix up; arrange; decorate ② make arrangement for; give instructions about

❹ [动]宣告；陈述：declare; announce; state to the public

布告 bùgào notice; bulletin; proclamation

颁布 bānbù   发布 fābù

公布 gōngbù   宣布 xuānbù

步 bù 7画 止部

步 步步步步步步步

❶ [动]走：walk; go on foot | ～入会场 bùrù huìchǎng *walk into*

the meeting place
步兵 bùbīng infantry
步入 bùrù step in; pace in
步行 bùxíng go on foot; walk
❷[名]脚步：step; pace │ 这孩子刚学迈～。Zhè háizi gāng xué màibù. *The child has just begun to learn to walk.* / 每天跑跑～，对身体有好处。Měi tiān pǎopao bù, duì shēntǐ yǒu hǎochu. *Jogging every day is good for one's health.* / 邮局离这儿只有几～路。Yóujú lí zhèr zhǐyǒu jǐ bù lù. *The post office is only a few steps away.*
步伐 bùfá step; pace
步子 bùzi step; pace

进步 jìnbù	跑步 pǎobù
起步 qǐbù	让步 ràngbù
散步 sànbù	同步 tóngbù
退步 tuìbù	稳步 wěnbù

❸[名]程度；阶段：stage; step │ 事情一～比一～顺利。Shìqing yī bù bǐ yī bù shùnlì. *Things are getting easier and easier.* / 下一～怎么办？Xià yī bù zěnme bàn? *What's the next step?*
步骤 bùzhòu step; move
初步 chūbù　　逐步 zhúbù
进一步 jìnyībù
❹[名]地步；境地：state; situation │ 没想到他竟会落到这样的地～。Méi xiǎngdào tā jìng huì luòdào zhèyàng de dìbù. *We never expected that he would come to such a pass.*

地步 dìbù

怖　　bù　　8画 忄部
怖 怖怖怖怖怖怖怖怖

[动]惧怕：fear
恐怖 kǒngbù

部　　bù　　10画 阝(右)部
部 部部部部部部部部
部部

❶[名]全体中的一份：part; section │ 胸～xiōngbù chest; thorax
部分 bùfen part; section; portion
部件 bùjiàn parts; components; assembly
部位 bùwèi position; place; part; section

北部 běibù	底部 dǐbù
东部 dōngbù	腹部 fùbù
局部 júbù	面部 miànbù
南部 nánbù	内部 nèibù
全部 quánbù	头部 tóubù
外部 wàibù	中部 zhōngbù

❷[名]某些机关、军队、企业中单位的名称：unit; department; ministry │ 教育～jiàoyùbù *the Ministry of Education* / 编辑～biānjíbù *editorial board*
部队 bùduì army; forces; troops
部门 bùmén department;

branch

部长 bùzhǎng minister

干部 gànbù　　　支部 zhībù

俱乐部 jùlèbù

司令部 sīlìngbù

❸[动]安排：dispose; deploy

❹[量]用于书籍、影片等：used for books, films, etc. ｜三～小说 sān bù xiǎoshuō *three novels* ／一～电影 yī bù diànyǐng *a film*

◇部落 bùluò tribe

埠　　　bù　　11画 土部

埠　埠埠埠埠埠埠埠
　埠埠埠

[名]停船的码头；也指有码头的城镇：wharf; a town with a wharf ｜本～běnbù *this port; this locality*

C c

擦 cā 17画 扌部

擦擦擦擦擦擦擦擦擦擦擦擦擦擦擦擦擦

❶ [动] 摩擦；接触：rub; scrape | ~根火柴 cā gēn huǒchái *strike a match* / 手上~破一点皮。Shǒu shang cāpò yīdiǎn pí. *Just a slight scratch on the hand.*

❷ [动] 贴近：very close to | 他从我身边~过。Tā cóng wǒ shēnbiān cāguò. *He brushed past me.*

❸ [动] 用手、布等揩拭：clean; wipe | ~黑板 cā hēibǎn *clean the blackboard* / ~脸 cā liǎn *dry one's face* / ~汗 cā hàn *wipe the sweat away*

❹ [动] 涂抹：smear; put on | 这药只能~，不能口服。Zhè yào zhǐnéng cā, bùnéng kǒufú. *This medicine is to be used on the skin only, not to be taken orally.* / 她淡淡地~了一点儿口红。Tā dàndàn de cāle yīdiǎnr kǒuhóng. *She applied lipstick lightly.* / 这种鞋油一~就亮。Zhè zhǒng xiéyóu yī cā jiù liàng. *This*

polish puts a good shine on shoes easily.

猜 cāi 11画 犭部

猜猜猜猜猜猜猜猜猜猜

❶ [动] 怀疑：doubt; suspect | 我~他说的不是真话。Wǒ cāi tā shuō de bù shì zhēnhuà. *I think he told us a lie.* / 我~他和这件事有点牵连。Wǒ cāi tā hé zhè jiàn shì yǒudiǎn qiānlián. *I suspect that he is more or less involved in the affair.*

❷ [动] 推测：guess | ~谜语 cāi míyǔ *guess a riddle* / 你~他是谁？Nǐ cāi tā shì shéi? *Guess who he is?* / 你~他有多大年纪。Nǐ cāi tā yǒu duō dà niánjì. *Guess how old he is.* / 我们都~不出他的心思。Wǒmen dōu cāibuchū tā de xīnsi. *None of us know what he thinks about.*

猜测 cāicè guess; conjecture; surmise

猜想 cāixiǎng suppose; guess; suspect

才 (繁 ❸-❼) cāi 3画 一部

才才才

❶ [名] 能力：ability; capacity; capability | 德~兼备 décāijiānbèi *have both ability and integrity* / 多～多艺 duōcái duōyì *be gifted in many ways* / 这个人很有～。Zhège rén hěn yǒu cái. *This person is very talented.*

才干 cáigàn ability; competence; talent

才华 cáihuá literary or artistic talent

才能 cáinéng talent

才智 cáizhì ability and wisdom

❷[名]从才能方面指称某类人：used to address a capable person

人才 réncái　　天才 tiāncái

❸[副]刚刚，表示事情发生不久：a moment ago; just; just now | 他～走。Tā cái zǒu. *He has just left.* / 节目～开始。Jiémù cái kāishǐ. *The performance has just started.* / 这首歌我是～学会 的。Zhè shǒu gē wǒ shì cái xuéhuì de. *I have just learned to sing this song.*

刚才 gāngcái

❹[副]表示事情发生或结束得晚：(used to indicate that sth. happens or ends late) not until; only | 他晚上～能到。Tā wǎnshang cáinéng dào. *He won't arrive until the evening.* / 会议一直开 到深夜～结束。Huìyì yīzhí kāi-dào shēnyè cái jiéshù. *The meeting didn't finish until late at night.* / 大雨到清晨～停。Dà-yǔ dào qīngchén cái

tíng. *The heavy rain didn't let up until early morning.*

❺[副]表示范围小、数量少、程度低 等：used to indicate a small scale, amount or low level | 我 们公司～二十来个人。Wǒmen gōngsī cái èrshí lai gè rén. *There are only about 20 employees in our company.* / 他刚来中 国，～会说几句汉语。Tā gāng lái Zhōngguó, cái huì shuō jǐ jù Hànyǔ. *He has just arrived in China and speaks only a bit of Chinese.* / 当时他～五岁。Dāngshí tā cái wǔ suì. *He was only five years old then.*

❻[副]表示限于某个范围：within the limit | 因为过节，他～穿了 件新衣服。Yīnwèi guòjié, tā cái chuānle jiàn xīn yīfu. *He wears a new coat for the festival.* / 只有肯努力，～能得到好的 学习成绩。Zhǐyǒu kěn nǔlì, cáinéng dédào hǎo de xuéxí chéngjì. *Only by studying harder will you get good results.*

❼[副]表示强调确定语气：used to indicate an emphatic tone | 这～是我想听的。Zhè cái shì wǒ xiǎng tīng de. *This is what I expect to hear.* / 那场球赛～精 彩呢！Nà chǎng qiúsài cái jīngcǎi ne! *What an exciting game it was!*

cái 7画 木部

材 材材材材材材材

❶ [名]木料，泛指原料：wood; timber; materials in a broad sense
材料 cáiliào material; facts for reference
材质 cáizhì ① quality or texture of timber ② quality of material
钢材 gāngcái　棺材 guāncai
建材 jiàncái　木材 mùcái
器材 qìcái　药材 yàocái
原材料 yuáncáiliào
❷ [名]资料：material
教材 jiàocái　题材 tícái

 (財) **cái** 7画 贝部

财 财财财财财财财

[名]金钱和物资的总称：general term for money and property |
发~fācái get rich / 理~lǐcái manage money matters
财产 cáichǎn property
财富 cáifù wealth; riches
财经 cáijīng finance and economics
财会 cáikuài finance and accounting
财力 cáilì financial resources; financial capacity
财务 cáiwù financial affairs
财物 cáiwù belongings

财政 cáizhèng (public) finance
钱财 qiáncái

 cái 12画 衣部

裁 裁裁裁裁裁裁裁裁
裁裁裁裁

❶ [动]用剪子铰或用刀割开：cut sth. into parts | 把纸~开 bǎ zhǐ cáikāi cut the paper into parts / 衣服~得很合适。Yīfu cái de hěn héshì. The garment is well cut.
裁缝 cáifeng tailor; dressmaker
❷ [动]削减；去掉不用的或多余的：cut; reduce; slash | ~减人员 cáijiǎn rényuán reduce (cut down) the staff / 国家~减了军费开支。Guójiā cáijiǎn le jūnfèi kāizhī. The government has cut down the military expenditure. / 工厂~了18名工人。Gōngchǎng cáile shíbā míng gōngrén. The factory dismissed 18 workers.
裁军 cáijūn disarmament
裁员 cáiyuán cut down the number of persons employed; reduce the staff
❸ [动]控制：control; command; dominate
独裁 dúcái　制裁 zhìcái
总裁 zǒngcái
❹ [动]判断：judge | ~夺 cáiduó

give an opinion; appraise critically

裁定 cáidìng (leg.) decide or declare judicially; rule

裁决 cáijué ruling; adjudication

裁判 cáipàn ① judgment ② act as referee

裁判员 cáipànyuán (sports) referee; judge; umpire

仲裁 zhòngcái

采 cǎi 8画 爫部

采 采采采采采采采采

❶ [动]摘：pick; take off | ~茶 cǎichá *pick tea* / 她~了一朵花。Tā cǎile yī duǒ huā. *She picked a flower.*

❷ [动]选取：select; choose
采购 cǎigòu make purchases; purchase
采纳 cǎinà accept; adopt
采取 cǎiqǔ adopt; take
采用 cǎiyòng put to use; adopt; employ

❸ [动]搜集：gather; collect | ~标本 cǎi biāoběn *collect specimens*
采访 cǎifǎng cover (news); gather material; interview
采集 cǎijí gather; collect

❹ [动]挖掘矿藏：mine; tap mineral ore | ~煤 cǎiméi *mine coal* / 这里的金矿已经被~完了。

Zhèli de jīnkuàng yǐjīng bèi cǎiwán le. *This gold mine has been fully exploited.*

开采 kāicǎi

◇ 风采 fēngcǎi

兴高采烈 xìnggāo-cǎiliè

彩 cǎi 11画 彡部

彩 彩彩彩彩彩彩彩彩彩 彩彩彩

❶ [名]各种颜色：different colours | ~虹 cǎihóng *rainbow* / ~旗 cǎiqí *colourful flag; bunting*
彩电 cǎidiàn colour television set; colour TV
彩色 cǎisè multicolour; colour
光彩 guāngcǎi   色彩 sècǎi
云彩 yúncai
丰富多彩 fēngfù-duōcǎi

❷ [名]彩色的丝绸：coloured silk | 张灯结~ zhāngdēng-jiécǎi *decorate with lanterns and colourful ribbons*
剪彩 jiǎncǎi

❸ [形]光荣；完美：glorious, perfect
精彩 jīngcǎi

◇ 彩票 cǎipiào lottery ticket
博彩 bócǎi

睬 cǎi 13画 目部

睬 睬睬睬睬睬睬睬睬 睬睬睬睬睬

[动]答理；理会：pay attention to; give heed to | 不要～他。Bùyào cǎi tā. *Take no notice of him.*; *Ignore him.*

理睬 lǐcǎi

踩 cǎi 15画 足部

踩踩踩踩踩踩踩踩踩
踩踩踩踩踩踩踩踩

[动]脚接触地面或物体：step on; trample | 小心，别～着地上的花草。Xiǎoxīn, bié cǎizháo dìshang de huācǎo. *Be careful not to trample the grass and flowers on the ground.* / 对不起! 我～你脚了吧? Duìbuqǐ! Wǒ cǎi nǐ jiǎo le ba? *Sorry! Did I step on your foot?*

菜 cǎi 11画 艹部

菜菜菜菜菜菜菜菜
菜菜菜

❶ [名]蔬菜，供做副食品的植物：vegetables; greens | 种～ zhòngcǎi *grow vegetables* / 鲜～xiāncǎi *fresh vegetables* / 夏季上市的～很多。Xiàjì shàngshì de cǎi hěn duō. *Plenty of vegetables appear on the market in summer.*

白菜 báicài   菠菜 bōcài
凉菜 liángcài   芹菜 qíncài

青菜 qīngcài   蔬菜 shūcài
香菜 xiāngcài   油菜 yóucài
大白菜 dàbáicài
大头菜 dàtóucài

❷ [名]经过烹调的蔬菜、肉类等副食品的统称：cooked vegetables and meat | 烧～shāo cài *cook dishes; prepare dishes* / 她做的～特别好吃。Tā zuò de cài tèbié hǎochī. *The dishes she prepares are very tasty.*

菜单 cǎidān menu
菜谱 cǎipǔ ① menu ② cookery book
川菜 chuāncài   点菜 diǎncài
素菜 sùcài   咸菜 xiáncài

 参 (參) cān 8画 厶部

参参参参参参参参

❶ [动]加入：join; take part in
参观 cānguān visit; look around
参加 cānjiā join; attend; take part in
参军 cānjūn join the army
参谋 cānmóu ①staff officer ② give advice
参赛 cānsài participate in a match or contest
参与 cānyù participate in; have a hand in
参议院 cānyìyuàn senate

❷ [动] 对照别的材料加以考察：contrast; compare

参考 cānkǎo ① consult; refer to ② reference
参阅 cānyuè consult; refer to
参照 cānzhào consult; refer to

餐 cān　16画 食部

餐餐餐餐餐餐餐餐餐
餐餐餐餐餐餐餐餐

❶[动] 吃；吃饭：eat | 聚～jùcān *dine together* / 野～yěcān *go on a picnic; picnic*
餐车 cānchē restaurant car
餐馆 cānguǎn restaurant
餐厅 cāntīng dining room; restaurant
餐饮 cānyǐn food and drink

❷[名]饭食：meal | 快～kuàicān *snack* / 一顿美～yī dùn měicān *a delicious meal*
大餐 dàcān　套餐 tàocān
午餐 wǔcān　西餐 xīcān
中餐 zhōngcān

残 (殘) cán　9画 歹部

残残残残残残残残残

❶[动]伤害，破坏：hurt; injure | ～害 cánhài *cruelly injure or kill*
摧残 cuīcán

❷[形]凶狠的；凶恶的：fierce; malicious; malevolent
残暴 cánbào cruel and fero-

cious; ruthless; brutal; savage
残酷 cánkù cruel; brutal; ruthless
残忍 cánrěn cruel; ruthless

❸[形]剩余的；快完的：surplus; remainder | ～冬 cándōng *the last days of winter* / ～汤剩饭 cántāng-shèngfàn *remains of a meal; leftovers; crumbs from the table*
残余 cányú remnants; remains; vestiges

❹[形]不完整的，有缺损的：incomplete | ～稿 cángǎo *an incomplete manuscript* / ～缺 cánquē *incomplete; with parts missing*
残疾 cánjí deformity; handicap
残障 cánzhàng deformity; handicap; physical disability
残疾人 cánjírén a disabled (or handicapped) person

蚕 (蠶) cán　10画 虫部

蚕蚕蚕蚕蚕蚕蚕蚕
蚕蚕

[名]家蚕，柞蚕等的统称：silkworm | 养～yǎng cán *silkworm breeding; sericulture* / ～丝 cánsī *natural silk*

惭 (慚) cán　11画 忄部

惭惭惭惭惭惭惭惭
惭惭惭

[副]羞愧：ashamed; shameful
惭愧 cánkuì feel ashamed

 惨 (慘) **cǎn** 11画 忄部

惨 惨惨惨惨惨惨惨惨
惨惨惨

❶[形]表示程度严重：to a serious
degree; disastrous | 这盘棋输得
真～! Zhè pán qí shū de zhēn
cǎn! *What a disastrous defeat
suffered in the chess game!* / 今
天可把我累～了。Jīntiān kě
bǎ wǒ lèicǎn le. *I was tired out
today.*
惨败 cǎnbài be crushingly defeated
惨重 cǎnzhòng heavy; griev-
ous; disastrous
❷[形]令人难受；悲惨：feel ill; feel
unhappy | 孩子哭得真～! Háizi
kū de zhēn cǎn! *How bitterly
the child cried!*
悲惨 bēicǎn   凄惨 qīcǎn

 灿 (燦) **càn** 7画 火部

灿 灿灿灿灿灿灿灿

[形]光彩耀眼：very brightly
coloured and dazzling
灿烂 cànlàn splendid; resplendent; bright

 仓 (倉) **cāng** 4画 人部

仓 仓仓仓仓

[名]储存谷物等的建筑物：store-
house | 粮～liángcāng *barn;
granary* / 货～huòcāng *warehouse*
仓库 cāngkù warehouse; storehouse
◇仓促 cāngcù hurriedly; hastily;
all of a sudden

苍 (蒼) **cāng** 7画 艹部

苍 苍苍苍苍苍苍苍

❶[形]青色：blue or green | ～天
cāngtiān *the blue sky; Heaven*
苍蝇 cāngying fly
❷[形]灰白色：greyish white
苍白 cāngbái pale; pallid; wan

舱 (艙) **cāng** 10画 舟部

舱 舱舱舱舱舱舱舱舱
舱舱

[名]船或飞机中载人或装东西的空
间：cabin; module | 客～kè-
cāng *passenger cabin* / ～里装
满了货物。Cāng li zhuāng-
mǎnle huòwù. *The hold is full
of cargo.*

藏 cáng 17画 艹部

藏藏藏藏藏藏藏藏
藏藏藏藏藏藏藏藏
藏

❶ [动]躲藏：hide | 东西被～起来
了。Dōngxi bèi cáng qǐlai le.
Things have been hidden. / 他～
在树后。Tā cáng zài shù hòu.
He hid behind the tree.
躲藏 duǒcáng　隐藏 yǐncáng
❷ [动]储存；存放：keep in reserve;
store up | 贵重物品应该～好。
Guìzhòng wùpǐn yīnggāi
cánghǎo. *Valuables should be
stored securely.* / 这些名画一直
完好地～到今天。Zhèxiē
míng- huà yīzhí wánhǎo de
cáng- dào jīntiān. *These famous paintings have been well
preserved until today.*
储藏 chǔcáng
矿藏 kuàngcáng
收藏 shōucáng
蕴藏 yùncáng

操 cāo 16画 扌部

操操操操操操操操
操操操操操操操操

❶ [动]拿着；掌握：grasp; hold | ～
刀 cāodāo *hold a knife*
操纵 cāozòng ① control; operate ② manipulate; rig

❷ [动]从事：be engaged (occu-
pied) in | 重～旧业 chóng-
cāo-jiùyè *resume one's old profession; take up one's old trade
again*
操劳 cāoláo work hard
操作 cāozuò operate; manipulate
❸ [动]使用（某种语言或方言）：
master | 他～一口流利的英语。
Tā cāo yī kǒu liúlì de Yīngyǔ.
He speaks fluent English.
❹ [名]有规定动作的运动：drill;
exercise | 广播～guǎngbō-
cāo *setting-up exercises to radio music* / 做～zuòcāo *do exercises*
操场 cāochǎng sports ground
操练 cāoliàn drill; exercise
体操 tǐcāo
◇操心 cāoxīn worry about;
trouble about; take pains to do sth.

糙 cāo 16画 米部

糙糙糙糙糙糙糙糙
糙糙糙糙糙糙糙糙

[形]不细致；不光滑：coarse; crude;
rough | 这活儿做得很～。Zhè
huór zuò de hěn cāo. *This is
a rough piece of work.*

槽 cáo 15画 木部

槽 槽槽槽槽槽槽槽槽
槽槽槽槽槽槽槽

❶[名]一种盛饲料或液体等的器具：manger (for water or animal feeding) | 马~mǎcáo manger / 水~shuǐcáo water trough; kitchen sink
跳槽 tiàocáo

❷[名]物体上两边高起，中间凹下的部分：groove; slot | 在木板上挖个~。Zài mùbǎn shang wā gè cáo. Cut a groove in the plank.

草 cǎo 9画 艹部
草 草草草草草草草草
草

❶[名] grass | 拔~bácǎo pull weeds; weed / 院子里的~长得太高了。Yuànzi li de cǎo zhǎng de tài gāo le. The grass in the courtyard has grown too high.
草地 cǎodì grassland; meadow
草垛 cǎoduǒ haystack
草原 cǎoyuán grasslands; steppe
烟草 yāncǎo
奇花异草 qíhuā-yìcǎo

❷[名]特指作燃料或饲料的稻、麦类茎叶：straw | ~帽 cǎomào straw hat / ~鞋 cǎoxié straw sandals / ~绳cǎoshéng straw rope

❸[形]不仔细；马虎：careless;

casual | 字写得很~。Zì xiě de hěn cǎo. *The characters are written very carelessly.*
草书 cǎoshū (in Chinese calligraphy) cursive script
草率 cǎoshuài careless; perfunctory; rash
潦草 liáocǎo

❹[名]没最后确定的(文稿、文件等)：draft
草案 cǎo'àn draft (of a plan, law, etc.)
起草 qǐcǎo
◇皮草 pícǎo

册 cè 5画 丿部
册 册册册册册

❶[名]装订好的本子：volume; book | 画~huàcè picture album; album of paintings / 纪念~jìniàncè autograph book; autograph album; commemorative album

❷[量]用于书籍：(used for books) copy; volume | 全套书共有五~。Quán tào shū gòng yǒu wǔ cè. *The whole set of books has five volumes.* / 每~书都有精美的插图。Měi cè shū dōu yǒu jīngměi de chātú. *Each book has exquisite illustrations.*

厕 (厠) cè 8画 厂部

| 厕 | 厕厕厕厕厕厕厕厕 |

See below

厕所 cèsuǒ lavatory; toilet
公厕 gōngcè

側 (侧) cè　8画 亻部

| 侧 | 侧侧侧侧侧侧侧侧 |

❶[名]旁边：side | 左~zuǒcè *the left side* / 街道两~种了许多花。Jiēdào liǎngcè zhòngle xǔduō huā. *Many flowers are planted on both sides of the street.*

侧面 cèmiàn side; aspect; flank; profile; side face
北侧 běicè　　东侧 dōngcè
右侧 yòucè

❷[动]向旁边扭或转：lean to one side | ~耳细听 cè'ěr xìtīng *incline the head and listen attentively; prick up one's ears* / ~着身子睡 cèzhe shēnzi shuì *sleep on one's side* / 他~过头来听我们说话。Tā cèguò tóu lai tīng wǒmen shuōhuà. *He inclined his head to listen to us.*

測 (测) cè　9画 氵部

| 测 | 测测测测测测测测测 |

❶[动]量：measure; survey | ~体

重 cè tǐzhòng *measure the weight* / ~身高 cè shēngāo *measure the height* / 用这种仪器能~出人体内的某些疾病。Yòng zhè zhǒng yíqì néng cèchū réntǐ nèi de mǒuxiē jíbìng. *With this equipment, certain diseases in a human body can be detected.*

测定 cèdìng determine
测量 cèliáng survey; measure; gauge
测试 cèshì test
测算 cèsuàn measure and calculate
测验 cèyàn test
观测 guāncè　　监测 jiāncè
检测 jiǎncè　　探测 tàncè

❷[动]料想；推测：guess; infer
猜测 cāicè　　推测 tuīcè
预测 yùcè

策 cè　12画 竹部

| 策 | 策策策策策策策策 策策策策 |

❶[动]计划；谋划：scheme; plan
策划 cèhuà plan; plot; scheme; engineer

❷[动]用马鞭子赶马：spur a horse | ~马前进 cèmǎ qiánjìn *spur a horse on*
鞭策 biāncè

❸[名]计谋；办法：scheme; plan | 计~jìcè *stratagem; plan* / 良~

liǎngcè *good (the best) plan*
策略 cèlüè ① tactics ② tactful
对策 duìcè   决策 juécè
政策 zhèngcè

层 (層) céng　7画 尸部

层 层层层层层层层

❶ [名]重叠的东西中的一部分；层次：layer; level; component part in a sequence
层次 céngcì ① arrangement of ideas (in writing or speech) ② administrative levels ③ (photog.) gradation
层级 céngjí level; layer
层面 céngmiàn ① scope; range ② aspect; field
高层 gāocéng   基层 jīcéng
阶层 jiēcéng
上层 shàngcéng
深层 shēncéng

❷ [量]用于重叠或累积的事物：(of anything that consists of several layers or stratums) tier; stratum | 五～大楼 wǔ céng dà lóu *a five-storey building* / 前边出了什么事，围了好几～人？Qiánbian chūle shénme shì, wéile hǎo jǐ céng rén? *A big crowd is gathering. What's going on over there?* / 这块糖包着两～纸。Zhè kuài táng bāozhe liǎng céng zhǐ. *The candy is wrapped up with two layers of paper.*

❸ [量]用于覆盖在物体表面上的东西：(of anything that can be spread over sth. else) layer | 涂了一～油漆 túle yī céng yóuqī *coated with a layer of paint* / 河面上结了一～厚厚的冰。Hé miàn shang jiéle yī céng hòuhòu de bīng. *The river is covered with a thick layer of ice.*

❹ [量]用于可以分项、分步骤的事物，主要是表示思想、含义、理由等抽象意思：a component part in a sequence (indicating abstract conceptions, such as thoughts, meanings, reasons, etc.) | 这段话有两～意思。Zhè duàn huà yǒu liǎng céng yìsi. *This remark has a double meaning.* / 你能做到这一～我就放心了。Nǐ néng zuòdào zhè yī céng wǒ jiù fàngxīn le. *I feel relieved as you have achieved this point.*

❺ [副]一次又一次地：repeatedly; time and again; again and again
层出不穷 céngchū-bùqióng occur frequently; appear repeatedly; emerge in an endless stream

曾 céng　12画 丷部

曾 曾曾曾曾曾曾曾曾
曾曾曾曾

[副]表示以前有过某种行为或情况：(used to indicate that an action once happened or a state once existed) once; formerly | 他~说过这句话。Tā céng shuō-guo zhè jù huà. *He once said this.* / 我不~去过长城。Wǒ bùcéng qùguo Cháng-chéng. *I have never been to the Great Wall.* / 几年前我~见过她一面。Jǐ nián qián wǒ céng jiànguo tā yī miàn. *I met her once several years ago.*

曾经 céngjīng once
不曾 bùcéng

蹭 **cèng** 19画 足部

蹭蹭蹭蹭蹭蹭蹭蹭
蹭蹭蹭蹭蹭蹭蹭
蹭蹭蹭

❶[动]摩擦：rub; scrape | ~了一身泥 cèngle yīshēn ní *the clothes were all stained with mud* / 把手~破了 bǎ shǒu cèngpò le *graze one's hand* / 桌面上的漆都~没了。Zhuōmiàn shang de qī dōu cèngméi le. *The paint on the surface of the table has worn off.*

❷[动]擦过并沾上：rub against sth. and get stained | 小心~上油漆。Xiǎoxīn cèngshang yóuqī. *Mind the fresh paint.*

❸[动]慢吞吞地行动：be slow in

moving | 磨~móceng *dilly-dally* / 你走得这么慢，什么时候才能~到家! Nǐ zǒu de zhème màn, shénme shíhou cái néng cèngdào jiā! *You'll never get home if you drag along like this all the way!*

叉 **chā** 3画 又部

叉叉叉

❶[名] fork | 吃西餐要用~。Chī xīcān yào yòng chā. *People eat Western food with forks.*
叉子 chāzi fork
刀叉 dāochā

❷[动]用叉子挑或扎：work with a fork | ~鱼 chāyú *spear fish* / 他喜欢把苹果切成块儿~着吃。Tā xǐhuan bǎ píngguǒ qiēchéng kuàir chāzhe chī. *He likes cutting apples in pieces and eating them with a fork.*

❸[动]交错：crisscross; interlock
交叉 jiāochā

差 **chā** 9画 羊部

差差差差差差差差
差

❶[形]不相合；不同：different; dissimilar
差别 chābié difference; disparity

差距 chājù gap; disparity

差异 chāyì difference; divergence; discrepancy; diversity

反差 fǎnchā　误差 wùchā

偏差 piānchā　时差 shíchā

❷ [名]失误；错误：fault; mistake

差错 chācuò mistake; error; slip

❸ [名]两数相减所得的数：difference | 15减8的～是7。Shí wǔ jiǎn bā de chā shì qī. Take 8 from 15 and the remainder is 7.

差价 chājià price difference

See chà; chāi.

 插　chā　12画 扌部

插插插插插插插插插插插插

❶ [动]扎入；把细长或薄的东西挤入：prick; stab | ～蜡烛 chā làzhú stick in a candle / 她头上～了一朵花。Tā tóushang chāle yī duǒ huā. She had a flower stuck in her hair.

插秧 chāyāng transplant rice seedlings (shoots)

❷ [动]加入进去：stick in; insert | 他在这篇文章中间～进了一段话。Tā zài zhè piān wénzhāng zhōngjiān chājìnle yī duàn huà. He inserted a paragraph into the article. / 他说个没完，别人半句话也～不进。Tā shuōge méi-

wán, biérén bànjùhuà yě chābujìn. He talked on and on and nobody else could get a word in edgeways.

插嘴 chāzuǐ interrupt; chip in

 茶　chá　9画 艹部

茶茶茶茶茶茶茶茶茶

❶ [名]tea plant | 这～怎么样，我品不出来。Zhè chá zěnmeyàng, wǒ pǐn bù chūlái. I cannot tell the quality of the tea.; I am not a good judge of tea.

茶叶 cháyè tea

花茶 huāchá　绿茶 lǜchá

❷ [名]茶叶沏成的饮料：tea | 沏～ qīchá make tea / 喝杯～吧。Hē bēi chá ba. Have a cup of tea.

茶馆 cháguǎn teahouse

茶几 chájī tea table; side table

❸ [名]某些饮料的名称：certain kinds of drink or liquid food | 面～miànchá seasoned millet mush / 奶～nǎichá tea with milk / 杏仁儿～xìngrénrchá almond tea

---

查　chá　9画 木部

查查查查查查查查查

❶ [动]检查；仔细验看：check;

examine | ～卫生 chá wèi-shēng *make a public health and sanitation check* / 请你～一下出席人数。Qǐng nǐ chá yīxià chūxí rénshù. *Please find out how many people are present.* / 无论谁进门都得～一下出入证。Wúlùn shéi jìnmén dōu děi chá yīxià chūrùzhèng. *Whoever enters must have their entry pass checked.*

查封 cháfēng seal up; close down

查获 cháhuò hunt down and seize; ferret out; track down

查看 chákàn look over; examine

查询 cháxún inquire about

查找 cházhǎo look for

抽查 chōuchá　核查 héchá

检查 jiǎnchá　　清查 qīngchá

审查 shěnchá　　搜查 sōuchá

❷[动]调查；仔细了解：investigate | ～一一事故的原因 chá yichá shìgù de yuányīn *find out the cause of an accident* / 要好好儿～～这个事故是谁的责任。Yào hǎohǎor cháchá zhège shìgù shì shéi de zérèn. *We must find out who is to blame for the accident.*

查处 cháchǔ investigate and prosecute

查明 chámíng prove through investigation

调查 diàochá　　普查 pǔchá

追查 zhuīchá

❸[动]翻检；看看：look up | ～字典 chá zìdiǎn *look up a word in the dictionary; consult a dictionary* / ～资料 chá zīliào *consult the reference material (on a special subject)* / 我在电话簿里～到他的电话号码了。Wǒ zài diànhuàbù li chádào tā de diànhuà hàomǎ le. *I found his phone number in a telephone book.*

查阅 cháyuè consult; look up

查号台 cháhàotái (at a telephone exchange) directory inquiries; information desk

碴　chá　14画 石部

碴碴碴碴碴碴碴碴
碴碴碴碴碴碴

❶[名]东西上的破口：sharp edge of broken things | 碗上有一道破～儿。Wǎn shang yǒu yī dào pō chár. *There is a sharp edge on the bowl.*

❷[名]引起争吵的事由：the cause of a quarrel | 找～打架 zhǎochá dǎjià *pick a quarrel (with sb.)*

❸[名]小碎块：broken pieces | 玻璃～子 bōli cházi *fragments of glass* / 冰～儿 bīngchár *small pieces of ice*

察　chá　14画 宀部

察 察察察察察察察
察察察察察察

[动]仔细看；调查：look into; check carefully
观察 guānchá　监察 jiānchá
检察 jiǎnchá　警察 jǐngchá
觉察 juéchá　考察 kǎochá
视察 shìchá　侦察 zhēnchá
检察官 jiǎncháguān

岔　　chà　7画 山部

岔 岔岔岔岔岔岔岔

❶[名]由干道分出的山、水流或道路：branch; fork｜~路 chàlù branch road / ~道 chàdào side road

❷[动]转移话题：change the topic｜请你别把话~远了。Qǐng nǐ bié bǎ huà chàyuǎn le. Please don't digress from the topic.

❸[动]错开时间，防止冲突：stagger; space out｜两个会议的时间最好~开。Liǎng gè huìyì de shíjiān zuì hǎo chàkāi. It would be better to have the two meetings staggered.

❹[动]离开原来的方向而偏到一边：turn off｜汽车~上那条小路开走了。Qìchē chàshang nà tiáo xiǎolù kāizǒu le. The car turned off into a path.

诧 (詫) chà　8画 讠部

诧 诧诧诧诧诧诧诧诧

[形]惊讶：surprised
诧异 chàyì surprised; amazed; astonished

差　　chà　9画 羊部

差 差差差差差差差差
差

❶[形]不相同：different; dissimilar｜虽然是兄弟俩，但性格~远了。Suīrán shì xiōngdì liǎ, dàn xìnggé chàyuǎn le. Though brothers, they are worlds apart in character.
差不多 chàbuduō just the same; similar; almost; just about; nearly; just about right; just about enough; not far off

❷[动]欠缺；短少：be short of; be deficient in｜~两个人 chà liǎng gè rén two people short
差点儿 chàdiǎnr ① not quite up to the mark; not good enough ② almost; nearly; on the verge of

❸[形]不好；不够标准：bad; not up to the standard｜质量~ zhìliàng chà poor quality / 学习成绩~ xuéxí chéngjì chà poor academic record

❹[形]错误：wrong; mistaken｜

弄～了 nòngchà le *make a mistake* / 说～了 shuōchà le *be wrongly spoken* / 这件事我可能记～了。Zhè jiàn shì wǒ kěnéng jìchà le. *Perhaps my poor memory deceived me.*

See chā; chāi.

拆 chāi 8画 扌部

拆 拆拆拆拆拆拆拆拆

❶[动]把合在一起的东西打开；卸下来：take apart; strip | ～信 chāi xìn *open a letter* / ～机器 chāi jīqì *disassemble a machine; take a machine apart*
拆散 chāisàn break up (a marriage, family, group, etc.)

❷[动]拆毁：pull down | ～房子 chāi fángzi *pull down a house* / 北京的古城墙几乎全～光了。Běijīng de gǔ chéngqiáng jīhū quán chāiguāng le. *The ancient walls of Beijing have been almost completely pulled down.*
拆除 chāichú dismantle; tear down; demolish

差 chāi 9画 羊部

差 差差差差差差差差
差

❶[动]派去做事：assign sb. to do

sth. | 他～人去请大夫。Tā chāi rén qù qǐng dàifu. *He sent someone for a doctor.* / 这件事可以～他去。Zhè jiàn shì kěyǐ chāi tā qù. *He is the appropriate candidate for this job.*

❷[名]公务；职务：被派遣去做的事情：job; errand; official post | 上个月我出了一趟～。Shàng gè yuè wǒ chūle yī tàng chāi. *I went on an official (or business) trip last month.* / 他兼了好几个～。Tā jiānle hǎo jǐ gè chāi. *He held more than one job (or post) concurrently.*
差事 chāishi errand; assignment
出差 chūchāi 公差 gōngchāi
See chā; chà.

柴 chāi 10画 木部

柴 柴柴柴柴柴柴柴柴
柴柴

[名]firewood | 砍～ kǎnchái *cut firewood*
火柴 huǒchái
◇柴油 cháiyóu diesel oil

掺 (掺) chān 11画 扌部

掺 掺掺掺掺掺掺掺掺
掺掺掺

[动]把一种东西混合到另一种东西里去：mix | 这牛奶里～了水。

Zhē niúnǎi li chānle shuǐ. *The milk has been adulterated with water.*

掺假 chānjiǎ adulterate
掺杂 chānzá mix; mingle

搀(攙) chān 12画 扌部

搀 搀搀搀搀搀搀搀搀搀 搀搀搀搀

❶ [动] 用手轻轻架着别人的手或胳膊：support sb. gently by the arm | 他~着老大娘过马路。Tā chānzhe lǎodàniáng guò mǎlù. *He helped the old woman across the street.* / 护士把病人~到床上。Hùshi bǎ bìngrén chāndào chuáng shang. *The nurse helped the patient to the bed.*

❷ [动] 同"掺 chān"，把两种东西混合在一起：mix | 咖啡里多~点儿奶。Kāfēi li duō chān diǎnr nǎi. *Add some more milk to the coffee.* / 牛奶里~了一些糖。Niúnǎi li chānle yīxiē táng. *Some sugar was added to the milk.*

馋(饞) chán 12画 饣部

馋 馋馋馋馋馋馋馋馋 馋馋馋馋

❶ [形] 贪吃；专爱吃好的：greedy | 这孩子的嘴~得很。Zhè háizi de zuǐ chándehěn. *The child is greedy for food.* / 这是只小~猫，每天都要吃鱼。Zhè shì zhī xiǎo chán māo, měi tiān dōu yào chī yú. *This little cat is greedy. It eats fish every day.*

❷ [形] 羡慕：admire | 他看见那个孩子钢琴弹得那么好，真~得命。Tā kànjiàn nàge háizi gāngqín tán de nàme hǎo, zhēn chán de yàomìng. *That child played the piano so well. It filled him with admiration.*

缠(纏) chán 13画 纟部

缠 缠缠缠缠缠缠缠缠 缠缠缠缠缠

❶ [动] 绕；围绕：twine; wind | 再多~上两道绳子就结实多了。Zài duō chānshang liǎng dào shéngzi jiù jiēshi duō le. *It would be more solid if two more cords were wound round it.* / 他手上~着一块纱布。Tā shǒu shang chánzhe yī kuài shābù. *His hand was bandaged with gauze.* / 她把长辫子~在头上。Tā bǎ cháng biànzi chán zài tóushang. *She wound her long plait on her head.*

❷ [动] 搅扰；纠缠：nag; pester | 孩子~着我要买玩具。Háizi chánzhe wǒ yào mǎi wánjù. *The child kept pestering me to buy him toys.* / 他最近特别忙，别总去～他。Tā zuìjìn tèbié máng, bié zǒng qù chán tā. *He has been especially busy these days. Don't always nag him.* / 他被事情～住了没能来。Tā bèi shìqing chánzhùle méi néng lái. *He couldn't come because he was too busy to get away.*

 产 (產) chǎn 6画 一部

产 产 产 产 产 产 产

❶ [动]人或动物生子：give birth to | 她顺利地～下了一个女婴。Tā shùnlì de chǎnxiàle yī gè nǚyīng. *She gave birth to a girl smoothly.*

❷ [动]生产；出产：produce; manufacture | 奶牛～奶。Nǎiniú chǎn nǎi. *Dairy cows yield milk.* / 这里～鱼和虾。Zhèli chǎn yú hé xiā. *Fish and shrimp are the local products.* /今年这块地～了很多粮食。Jīnnián zhè kuài dì chǎn le hěn duō liángshi. *This farmland has produced a bumper crop this year.*

产出 chǎnchū output; yield
产地 chǎndì place of production; place of origin
产区 chǎnqū production area
产生 chǎnshēng bring about; give rise to; emerge; come into being

产物 chǎnwù outcome; result; product

超产 chāochǎn 出产 chūchǎn
丰产 fēngchǎn 高产 gāochǎn
国产 guóchǎn 减产 jiǎnchǎn
生产 shēngchǎn
盛产 shèngchǎn
投产 tóuchǎn
增产 zēngchǎn
生产力 shēngchǎnlì
生产率 shēngchǎnlǜ
生产线 shēngchǎnxiàn

❸ [名]生产出来的东西；出产的东西：product; produce
产量 chǎnliàng output; yield
产品 chǎnpǐn product; produce
产值 chǎnzhí value of output; output value
矿产 kuàngchǎn 水产 shuǐchǎn
特产 tèchǎn
农产品 nóngchǎnpǐn
畜产品 xùchǎnpǐn

❹ [名]物质财富；财产：property; estate | 他的动～不动～合起来有几百万美元。Tā de dòngchǎn bùdòngchǎn hé qǐlai yǒu jǐ bǎiwàn měiyuán. *The total of his possessions and property is worth millions of US dollars.*

产权 chǎnquán property right
产业 chǎnyè ① estate; property ② industry
财产 cáichǎn 房产 fángchǎn
破产 pòchǎn 遗产 yíchǎn

资产 zīchǎn
不动产 bùdòngchǎn
共产党 gòngchǎndǎng
房地产 fángdìchǎn
共产主义 gòngchǎn zhǔyì
无产阶级 wúchǎn jiējí
资产阶级 zīchǎn jiējí

铲 (鏟) chǎn 11画 钅部

铲铲铲铲铲铲铲铲
铲铲铲

❶ [名]用来削平或撮取东西的工具：
shovel; spade | 煤~ méichǎn
coal shovel / 铁~ tiěchǎn *iron
spade*

❷ [动]用铲子削平或撮取东西: lift
or move sth. with a shovel | 快
把门口的垃圾~走。Kuài bǎ
ménkǒu de lājī chǎnzǒu.
*Move away the rubbish by the
door with a spade at once.* / 我~
土，你种花。Wǒ chǎn tǔ, nǐ
zhòng huā. *I shovel earth while
you plant flowers.*

阐 (闡) chǎn 11画 门部

阐阐阐阐阐阐阐
阐阐阐

[动]说明；表明: explain; clarify
阐明 chǎnmíng expound;
clarify
阐述 chǎnshù expound; elabo-

rate; set forth

颤 (顫) chàn 19画 页部

颤颤颤颤颤颤颤颤
颤颤颤颤颤颤颤颤
颤颤颤

[动]短促而频繁地震动；发抖:
vibrate | 他兴奋得声音发~。Tā
xīngfèn de shēngyīn fā
chàn. *His voice trembled with
excitement.* / 天真冷啊，我们冻
得直~。Tiān zhēn lěng a,
wǒmen dòng de zhí chàn.
*What a cold day! We were shiv-
ering all over.*
颤动 chàndòng vibrate; quiver
颤抖 chàndǒu shake; tremble;
quiver; shiver

昌 chāng 8画 日部

昌昌昌昌昌昌昌昌

[形]兴旺；发达: prosperous;
flourishing
昌盛 chāngshèng prosper;
thrive

猖 chāng 11画 犭部

猖猖猖猖猖猖猖猖
猖猖猖

[形]凶猛；狂妄: ferocious; savage

猖狂 chāngkuáng savage; furious; outrageous

 长（長）cháng 4画 长部

长 长长长长

❶ [形] 距离大（兼指时间和空间）: distant; long (referring to time and space) | 夏季昼~夜短。Xiàjì zhòucháng yèduǎn. *In summer, days are long and nights are short.* / 他在中国住的时间不~。Tā zài Zhōngguó zhù de shíjiān bù cháng. *He has not lived in China for a long time.* / 这条河真~。Zhè tiáo hé zhēn cháng. *This river is very long.* / 这部小说写得很~。Zhè bù xiǎoshuō xiě de hěn cháng. *This novel is very long.*

长城 Chángchéng ① the Great Wall ② impregnable bulwark
长假 chángjià long leave of absence; resignation
长江 Cháng Jiāng the Changjiang (Yangtze) River
长久 chángjiǔ for a long time; permanently
长期 chángqī over a long period of time; long term
长寿 chángshòu long life; longevity
长途 chángtú long-distance

长项 chángxiàng good qualities; strong points
长效 chángxiào enduring effect
长远 chángyuǎn long-term; long-range
长征 chángzhēng long march
长方体 chángfāngtǐ cuboid
长方形 chángfāngxíng rectangle
长颈鹿 chángjǐnglù giraffe
长舌妇 chángshéfù a gossipy woman
长筒袜 chángtǒngwà stockings
长年累月 chángnián-lěiyuè year in year out; over the years
漫长 màncháng
延长 yáncháng
天长地久 tiāncháng-dìjiǔ
❷ [名] 长度: length; footage | 这条公路全~700千米。Zhè tiáo gōnglù quáncháng qībǎi qiānmǐ. *The total length of the highway is 700 km.*
长度 chángdù length
长短 chángduǎn length
❸ [名] 长处; 优点: strong point
长处 chángchu forte; merit
擅长 shàncháng
特长 tècháng
专长 zhuāncháng
一技之长 yījìzhīcháng
　　See zhǎng.

肠（腸）cháng 7画 月部

肠 肠肠肠肠肠肠肠

[名] intestine
香肠 xiāngcháng

尝（嘗）cháng 9画 ⺌部

尝 尝尝尝尝尝尝尝尝
尝

❶[动]吃一点试试；辨别滋味：taste
| ~~汤的味道 chángcháng
tāng de wèidào *taste the soup*
/ 请你~一下菜的味道。Qǐng
nǐ cháng yīxià cài de
wèidào. *Please have a taste of
this dish.*

❷[动]试：try
尝试 chángshì attempt; try

❸[动]经历；体验：experience;
come to know | 他开始~到了
生活的甘苦。Tā kāishǐ
chángdàole shēnghuó de
gānkǔ. *He began to taste the
hardship of life.*

常 cháng 11画 ⺌部

常 常常常常常常常常
常常常

❶[形]一般；普通；平常：general;
ordinary; common
常规 chángguī convention;

rule; common practice; routine
常识 chángshí common sense;
general knowledge; elementary
knowledge
常务 chángwù day-to-day
business; routine
反常 fǎncháng 非常 fēicháng
家常 jiācháng
平常 píngcháng
日常 rìcháng
通常 tōngcháng
往常 wǎngcháng
寻常 xúncháng 异常 yìcháng
照常 zhàocháng
正常 zhèngcháng
家常饭 jiāchángfàn
拉家常 lājiācháng
不同寻常 bùtóng xúncháng

❷[形]不变的；经常的：frequent;
constant | 柏树四季~青。Bǎi-
shù sìjì cháng qīng. *Cypress
stays green throughout the year.*
常年 chángnián throughout the
year; year in year out
常委 chángwěi member of the
standing committee

❸[副]时常；常常：frequently;
often; usually | 他~参加体育锻
炼。Tā cháng cānjiā tǐyù
duànliàn. *He often goes for
sports.* / 希望你~给我们写信。
Xīwàng nǐ cháng gěi wǒ-
men xiěxìn. *Hope you write to
us often.* / 他身体不好，~生病。
Tā shēntǐ bù hǎo, cháng
shēngbìng. *He is weak and*

often gets ill.

常常 chángcháng frequently; often; usually

常见 chángjiàn common; everyday

常用 chángyòng in common use

经常 jīngcháng

 偿 (償) cháng 11画 亻部

偿 偿偿偿偿偿偿偿偿 偿偿偿

[动] 归还；抵补：repay; compensate for｜~债 chángzhài *pay (discharge) a debt*

偿还 chánghuán repay; pay back

补偿 bǔcháng 赔偿 péicháng

无偿 wúcháng

有偿 yǒucháng

得不偿失 débùchángshī

 厂 (廠) chǎng 2画 厂部

厂 厂厂

[名] 工厂：factory; plant; mill｜这家~主要生产服装。Zhè jiā chǎng zhǔyào shēngchǎn fúzhuāng. *Clothing is the main product of this factory.*

厂房 chǎngfáng factory building

厂家 chǎngjiā manufacturer; firm

厂商 chǎngshāng manufacturer; firm

厂长 chǎngzhǎng factory director

工厂 gōngchǎng

 场 (場) chǎng 6画 土部

场 场场场场场场

❶ [名] 适应某种需要的较大的地方；事情发生的地方：large place where people gather for a specific purpose; yard; site; field

场地 chǎngdì space; place; site

场馆 chǎngguǎn sports grounds or gymnasiums and stadiums

场合 chǎnghé occasion; situation

场景 chǎngjǐng ① scene in theatre, film and TV ② sight; scene; picture

场所 chǎngsuǒ place; arena

操场 cāochǎng

出场 chūchǎng

当场 dāngchǎng

到场 dàochǎng

赌场 dǔchǎng

广场 guǎngchǎng

会场 huìchǎng 机场 jīchǎng

剧场 jùchǎng

考场 kǎochǎng

林场 línchǎng 牧场 mùchǎng

农场 nóngchǎng

球场 qiúchǎng 入场 rùchǎng

商场 shāngchǎng

市场 shìchǎng

现场 xiànchǎng

刑场 xíngchǎng

战场 zhànchǎng

主场 zhǔchǎng

体育场 tǐyùchǎng

公共场所 gōnggòng chǎngsuǒ

农贸市场 nóngmào shìchǎng

❷ [名]舞台：stage; arena | 快，该你上～了，怎么还不化装? Kuài, gāi nǐ shàngchǎng le, zěnme hái bù huàzhuāng? *Be quick! You are the next to come on stage. Why haven't you put on your make-up?* |～上正在表演舞蹈。Chǎng shang zhèng zài biǎoyǎn wǔdǎo. *A dance is being performed on the stage.*

登场 dēngchǎng

上场 shàngchǎng

下场 xiàchǎng

❸ [量]用于文娱、体育活动：used for entertainment and sports activities | 两～球赛 liǎng chǎng qiúsài *two ball games* / 一～电影 yī chǎng diànyǐng *a film show*

场次 chǎngcì the number of showing of a film, play, etc.

场面 chǎngmiàn scene; spectacle; occasion

一场空 yīchǎngkōng

◇ 开场白 kāichǎngbái

敞 **chǎng** 12画 攵部

敞 敞敞敞敞敞敞敞敞 敞敞敞敞

❶ [形]宽阔；没有遮拦：spacious; open

宽敞 kuānchǎng

❷ [动]张开；打开：open |～着门 chǎngzhe mén *leave the door open; with the door open*

敞开 chǎngkāi open wide; unlimited; unrestricted

畅（暢）**chàng** 8画 丨部

畅 畅畅畅畅畅畅畅畅

❶ [形]没有阻碍：smooth; unimpeded | 流～liúchàng *easy and smooth; fluent*

畅通 chàngtōng unimpeded; unblocked

畅销 chàngxiāo be in good demand; sell well; have a ready market

顺畅 shùnchàng

❷ [形]痛快；尽情：joyful; carefree |～饮 chàngyǐn *drink one's fill*

畅谈 chàngtán talk freely and to one's heart's content

舒畅 shūchàng

倡 **chàng** 10画 亻部

倡倡倡倡倡倡倡倡倡
倡倡

[动]首先提出；带头发起：promote;
initiate; advocate | 提~tí-
chàng advocate; promote; encourage; recommend
倡导 chàngdǎo initiate; advocate
倡议 chàngyì propose; sponsor

唱 chàng 11画 口部
唱 唱唱唱唱唱唱唱唱
唱唱唱

❶[动]唱出乐音：sing | 他~了一
首抒情歌曲。Tā chàngle yī
shǒu shūqíng gēqǔ. He sang
a lyric song. / 他激动得~不下
去了。Tā jīdòng de chàng bù
xiàqù le. He is too excited to go
on singing.
唱歌 chànggē sing (a song)
唱片 chàngpiàn phonograph
(or gramophone) record; disc
唱反调 chàngfǎndiào a different tune; speak or act contrary to
唱高调 chànggāodiào mouth
high-sounding words; say fine-
sounding things
唱对台戏 chàng duìtáixì put
on a rival show; enter into rivalry with sb.
歌唱 gēchàng 合唱 héchàng
演唱 yǎnchàng
演唱会 yǎnchànghuì

❷[动]高声叫、念：call in a loud
voice | ~票 chàngpiào call
out the names of candidates on
a vote while counting ballot-slips

 chāo 7画 扌部
抄 抄抄抄抄抄抄抄

❶[动]照原文或底稿写：copy | ~生
词 chāo shēngcí copy the new
words / 请把稿件~一下。Qǐng
bǎ gǎojiàn chāo yīxià. Please
make a fair copy of the manuscript.
抄写 chāoxiě copy
❷[动]抄别人的作品当自己的：
plagiarize | 这一段是作者从别
人的作品中~来的。Zhè yī
duàn shì zuòzhě cóng biérén
de zuòpǐn zhōng chāolai de.
The author lifted the paragraph
from the work of someone else.
❸[动]搜查并没收：search out and
confiscate | 公安机关~了一家
赌场。Gōng'ān jīguān chāo
le yī jiā dǔchǎng. The public
security bodies raided a gambling house and confiscated its
property.
❹[动]从侧面走捷径：take a short
cut; outflank | 我们还是~小道
走吧。Wǒmen háishì chāo
xiǎodào zǒu ba. We'd better
take a short cut.

钞 (鈔) chāo 9画 钅部

钞 钞钞钞钞钞钞钞钞钞
钞

[名]纸币：banknote; paper money
钞票 chāopiào banknote; paper money

超 chāo 12画 走部

超 超超超超超超超超超
超超超超

❶[动]超出；越过：surpass; exceed | 我在学习上总也～不过他。Wǒ zài xuéxí shang zǒng yě chāobuguo tā. *I have never surpassed him in study.* / 我的假期已经～了，一定得回去了。Wǒ de jiàqī yǐjīng chāo le, yīdìng děi huíqu le. *I have exceeded my period of leave and must go back.*
超标 chāobiāo surpass the set standard; exceed the quota
超产 chāochǎn overfulfil a production target
超出 chāochū overstep; go beyond; exceed
超额 chāo'é exceed the quota
超过 chāoguò outstrip; surpass; exceed
超越 chāoyuè surmount; overstep; transcend; surpass
超载 chāozài (transportation) overload

❷[形]超过一般的：extraordinary; above average
超级 chāojí super
超市 chāoshì supermarket
高超 gāochāo

巢 chāo 11画 巛部

巢 巢巢巢巢巢巢巢巢
巢巢巢

[名]鸟窝；蜂、蚁的窝：nest; comb | 鸟～niǎochāo *bird's nest* / 蜂～fēngcháo *honeycomb* / 蚁～yǐcháo *ant's nest*

朝 chāo 12画 十部

朝 朝朝朝朝朝朝朝朝
朝朝朝朝

❶[名]朝代；一姓君主世代相传的整个统治时期：dynasty | 唐～tángcháo *the Tang Dynasty*
朝代 chāodài dynasty
王朝 wángcháo

❷[动]面对着；向着：face; look | 仰面～天yǎngmiàn cháo tiān *lie on one's back* / 孩子转脸～着我。Háizi zhuǎn liǎn chāozhe wǒ. *The child turned his face to me.*

❸[介]向：toward; in the direction of | 大门～南开。Dàmén cháo nán kāi. *The gate faces south.* /

他们 ～ 着河边慢慢走去。Tāmen cháozhe hébiān mànmàn zǒuqù. *They walked slowly toward the river bank.* / 他～大家点点头表示同意。Tā cháo dàjiā diǎndiǎn tóu biǎoshì tóngyì le. *He gave a nod of assent to all.*

See zhāo.

嘲 cháo 15画 口部

嘲 嘲嘲嘲嘲嘲嘲嘲
嘲嘲嘲嘲嘲嘲嘲

[动]讽刺；讥笑：satirize; mock | 冷～热讽 lěngcháo-rèfěng *freezing irony and burning satire*
嘲笑 cháoxiào ridicule; deride; jeer at; laugh at

潮 cháo 15画 氵部

潮 潮潮潮潮潮潮潮
潮潮潮潮潮潮潮

❶ [名]tide | 涨～zhǎngcháo *flood tide* / 落～luòcháo *ebb tide* / ～水 cháoshuǐ *tide water; tidal water*
潮流 cháoliú ① tide; tidal current ② trend
浪潮 làngcháo
❷ [名]比喻像潮水那样起伏的事物：large-scale social upheaval; rise and fall of a campaign | 学～

xuécháo *student strike; campus upheaval*
高潮 gāocháo   热潮 rècháo
思潮 sīcháo
❸ [形]微湿：moist; damp | 这房间有点儿～。Zhè fángjiān yǒudiǎnr cháo. *It is a bit damp in this room.* / 火柴受～了。Huǒchái shòu cháo le. *The matches have got damp.*
潮湿 cháoshī moist; damp

吵 cháo 7画 口部

吵 吵吵吵吵吵吵吵

❶ [动]声音杂乱扰人：disturb sb. by making noises | 别～他！Bié chǎo tā! *Don't disturb him!* / 他被收音机～醒了。Tā bèi shōuyīnjī chǎoxǐng le. *He was awakened by the radio.*
❷ [动]争吵；拌嘴：quarrel; squabble; have words with | 不要为一点儿小事就～起来。Bùyào wèi yìdiǎnr xiǎoshì jiù chǎo qǐlai. *Don't squabble over trifles.* / 你们别～，有话慢慢讲。Nǐmen bié chǎo, yǒu huà mànmàn jiǎng. *Stop quarreling. Speak calmly to each other.*
吵架 chǎojià quarrel; wrangle; have a row
吵闹 chǎonào ① wrangle; kick up a row ② din; hubbub
吵嘴 chǎozuǐ quarrel; bicker

争吵 zhēngchǎo

炒 chǎo 8画 火部

炒 炒炒炒炒炒炒炒炒

[动]把食物放在锅里边加热边翻动使熟：stir-fry | ～花生 chǎo huāshēng *roasted peanuts* / 他～的菜很好吃。Tā chǎo de cài hěn hǎochī. *The dishes he cooks taste good.*

◇炒股 chǎogǔ speculate in stocks and shares

炒作 chǎozuò publicity hype; persistent media promotion; publicizing a person or an event; hype

车 (車) chē 4画 车部

车 车车车车

❶[名]陆地上有轮子的交通工具：vehicle | 他买了一辆新～。Tā mǎile yī liàng xīn chē. *He bought a new car.* / ～已经开走了。Chē yǐjīng kāizǒu le. *The bus (car) has already left.*

车本 chēběn driving licence

车程 chēchéng (used to describe the distance of a journey, usu. of an automobile) distance covered in a certain amount of time

车道 chēdào (traffic) lane; roadway

车队 chēduì motorcade

车祸 chēhuò traffic accident; road accident

车辆 chēliàng vehicle; car

车轮 chēlún wheel (of a vehicle)

车门 chēmén door (of a vehicle)

车牌 chēpái licence plate

车票 chēpiào train or bus ticket; ticket

车身 chēshēn the body of a vehicle

车速 chēsù speed of a motor vehicle

车头 chētóu ① the front of a vehicle ② engine (of a train); locomotive

车位 chēwèi parking spot; parking space

车厢 chēxiāng railway carriage

车型 chēxíng model (or type) of a vehicle

车站 chēzhàn station; depot; stop

车子 chēzi ① a small vehicle (such as a car, pushcart, etc.) ② (dial.) bicycle

餐车 cānchē	打车 dǎchē
倒车 dàochē	电车 diànchē
火车 huǒchē	机车 jīchē
轿车 jiàochē	警车 jǐngchē
卡车 kǎchē	客车 kèchē
列车 lièchē	马车 mǎchē
跑车 pǎochē	汽车 qìchē
赛车 sàichē	刹车 shāchē
停车 tíngchē	通车 tōngchē
小车 xiǎochē	

出租车 chūzūchē
公交车 gōngjiāochē
机动车 jīdòngchē
吉普车 jípǔchē
开夜车 kāiyèchē
面包车 miànbāochē
摩托车 mótuōchē
三轮车 sānlúnchē
停车场 tíngchēchǎng
自行车 zìxíngchē
公共汽车 gōnggòng qìchē

❷[名]利用轮轴转动来工作的生产器械：lathe
车床 chēchuáng lathe

❸[名]泛指机器：machine (in a general sense)
车间 chējiān workshop

扯 chě 7画 扌部

扯 扯扯扯扯扯扯扯

❶[动]拉：drag; pull｜孩子～住妈妈的衣服不放。Háizi chězhù māma de yīfu bù fàng. *The child pulled at his mother's dress and wouldn't let go.*｜他把绳子～断了。Tā bǎ shéngzi chěduàn le. *He pulled apart the rope.*

牵扯 qiānchě

❷[动]撕：tear; tear off｜他把墙上的广告～下来了。Tā bǎ qiáng shang de guǎnggào chě xiàlai le. *He tore down the advertisement from the wall.*｜他

看过信后就把信～了。Tā kàn guo xìn hòu jiù bǎ xìn chě le. *Having read the letter, he tore it up.*

❸[动]随便谈：talk freely｜请别把问题～远了。Qǐng bié bǎ wèntí chěyuǎn le. *Don't drift away from the topic.*｜这两个好朋友一见面，就～个没完。Zhè liǎng gè hǎo péngyou yī jiànmiàn, jiù chě ge méiwán. *The two friends have been talking since the moment they met.*

彻 (徹) chě 7画 彳部

彻 彻彻彻彻彻彻彻

[副]通；透：thorough; penetrating
彻底 chèdǐ thorough; thoroughgoing
贯彻 guànchè　透彻 tòuchè

撤 chě 15画 扌部

撤 撤撤撤撤撤撤撤撤撤撤撤撤撤撤撤

❶[动]除去；取消：remove; take away; withdraw｜这些空盘子可以～走了。Zhèxiē kōng pánzi kěyǐ chēzǒu le. *These empty plates can be cleared away.*｜前面的岗哨已经～了。Qiánmian de gǎngshào yǐjīng chě le. *The front sentry has already been withdrawn.*

撤出 chēchū withdraw; evacuate

撤销 chēxiāo cancel; rescind; revoke

❷[动]退：retreat | 向后~xiàng hòu chē *withdraw; retreat* / 我们的军队有计划地往南~。Wǒmen de jūnduì yǒu jìhuà de wǎng nán chē. *Our troops withdrew southward as planned.*

撤军 chējūn withdraw troops

撤离 chēlí withdraw from; leave; evacuate

撤退 chētuì withdraw; pull out

 chén 6画 臣部

臣 臣臣臣臣臣臣

[名]君主制时代的官吏：officials in feudal society; subject

大臣 dàchén

 (塵) chén 6画 小部

尘 尘尘尘尘尘尘

[名]飞扬的极细的灰土：dust; dirt in the air

尘埃 chén'āi dust

尘土 chéntǔ dust

灰尘 huīchén

 chén 7画 辰部

 辰 辰辰辰辰辰辰辰

❶[名]地支的第五位，也用作次序第五：the fifth of the twelve Earthly Branches

❷[名]日、月、星的总称：the general name for celestial bodies

星辰 xīngchén

❸[名]日子；时间：time of the day

诞辰 dànchén

生辰 shēngchén

沉 chén 7画 氵部

沉 沉沉沉沉沉沉沉

❶[动]没入水里：sink into water | 船~了。Chuán chén le. *The boat (ship) has sunk.* / 石头~到水底。Shítou chéndào shuǐdǐ. *The rock sank to the bottom of the water.* / 她不会游泳，很快就~下去了。Tā bù huì yóuyǒng, hěn kuài jiù chén xiàqu le. *She sank into the water quickly as she couldn't swim.*

沉淀 chéndiàn sediment; precipitate

❷[动]往下陷落；降落：sink; keep down; go down | 太阳已经西~。Tàiyáng yǐjīng xī chén. *The sun has set in the west.*

❸[动]情绪等低落：be upset; be unhappy; be depressed | 把脸

陈
晨

chén

一~bǎ liǎn yī chén *put on a grave expression; pull a long face* / 听到这个消息，大家的心一一。Tīngdào zhège xiāoxi, dàjiā de xīn yī chén. *Our heart sank at the news.*

沉闷 chénmèn ① oppressive; depressing ② depressed; in low spirits

❹ [形] 镇定；稳重：calm; able to hold back one's feelings | 她~下心来，又仔细研究了一遍。Tā chénxiā xīn lai, yòu zǐxì yánjiūle yī biàn. *She calmed down and examined it carefully once again.* / 别紧张，要~住气。Bié jǐnzhāng, yào chénzhù qì. *Don't be nervous. Keep calm.*

沉静 chénjìng quiet; calm; serene; placid

沉着 chénzhuó cool-headed; composed; steady

深沉 shēnchén

❺ [形] 程度深：deep; profound; sound | 他睡得很~。Tā shuì de hěn chén. *He slept soundly.*

沉默 chénmò ① reticent; taciturn; uncommunicative ② silent

沉思 chénsī ponder; meditate; be lost in thought

沉痛 chéntòng ① deeply grieved ② deeply felt; bitter

❻ [形] 重；分量大：heavy | 这件行李真~。Zhè jiàn xíngli zhēn chén. *This piece of luggage is really heavy.* / 这么多书，多~啊! Zhème duō shū, duō chén a! *So many books, how heavy they are!*

沉重 chénzhòng ① heavy ② serious; critical

❼ [形] 感到沉重、不舒服：feel heavy or uncomfortable | 胳膊~得抬不起来。Gēbo chén de tái bù qǐlái. *My arm is too stiff to be raised.* / 我的头有点发~。Wǒ de tóu yǒudiǎn fā chén. *My head feels a bit heavy.*

 (陳) chén 7画 阝(左)部

陈 陈陈陈陈陈陈陈

❶ [动] 安放；摆设：lay out; put on display

陈列 chénliè display; set out; exhibit

❷ [动] 叙说：state; recite; chat

陈述 chénshù state

陈述句 chénshùjù (gram.) declarative sentence

❸ [形] 旧的；时间很久的：old; stale | ~酒 chénjiǔ *old wine; aged spirits*

陈旧 chénjiù outmoded; obsolete; old-fashioned; out-of-date

新陈代谢 xīnchén-dàixiè

 chén 11画 日部

晨 晨晨晨晨晨晨晨晨
晨晨晨

[名] morning
晨报 chénbào morning edition
(of a newspaper)
晨练 chénliàn do morning exercises
凌晨 língchén 清晨 qīngchén
早晨 zǎochén

衬 (襯) chèn 8画 衤部
衬衬衬衬衬衬衬衬

❶ [形] 贴身的 (衣服)：(of clothes)
underneath
衬衫 chènshān shirt; blouse
衬衣 chènyī underclothes; shirt
❷ [动] 在里面托上一层：place sth.
underneath ｜ ~上一层布 chèn-
shang yī céng bù *put a piece
of cloth underneath*

称 (稱) chèn 10画 禾部
称称称称称称称称
称称

[动] 适合；相当：fit; match; suit ｜
颜色相~ yánsè xiāngchèn *be
well matched in colour*
称心 chènxīn feel sth. satisfactory; be gratified
对称 duìchèn
　　See chēng.

趁
chèn 12画 走部
趁趁趁趁趁趁趁趁
趁趁趁趁

[介] 利用 (时间、机会)：take advantage of (time, opportunity)
｜ ~热打铁 chènrè-dǎtiě
strike the iron while it is hot / ~
天不黑，你快走吧。Chèn tiān
bù hēi, nǐ kuài zǒu ba. *You'd
better leave while it is still light.*
/ 我想~这个机会讲几句话。Wǒ
xiǎng chèn zhège jīhuì jiǎng
jǐ jù huà. *I'd like to take this opportunity to say a few words.* /
~着年轻多学点儿知识。Chèn-
zhe niánqīng duō xué diǎnr
zhīshi. *Learn more while you
are still young.*

称 (稱) chēng 10画 禾部
称称称称称称称称
称称

❶ [动] 测重量：weigh ｜ ~体重
chēng tǐzhòng *(body) weight
weighing* / 请你给我~1公斤梨。
Qǐng nǐ gěi wǒ chēng yī
gōngjīn lí. *I'd like one kilogram of pears, please.*
❷ [动] 赞扬：praise
称赞 chēngzàn praise; acclaim;
commend

❸[动]说：say; speak｜大家连声～好。Dàjiā liánshēng chēng hǎo. *Everybody said repeatedly in praise: "Well done!"*
宣称 xuānchēng

❹[动]叫；叫做：call｜我们都～他老师傅。Wǒmen dōu chēng tā lǎoshīfu. *We all call him master craftsman.* / 他的所作所为～得起"人民英雄"这个称号。Tā de suǒzuò-suǒwéi chēngdeqǐ "rénmín yīngxióng" zhège chēnghào. *What he has done is worthy of the honourable title of "People's Hero".*
称呼 chēnghu call; address
称为 chēngwéi call or be called; be known as
称作 chēngzuò call or be called; be known as
称得上 chēngdeshàng deserve to be called; be worthy of the name of
号称 hàochēng 自称 zìchēng

❺[名]名称：name; title
称号 chēnghào title; name; designation
简称 jiǎnchēng
职称 zhíchēng
尊称 zūnchēng
See chèn.

撑 chēng 15画 扌部
撑撑撑撑撑撑撑撑
撑撑撑撑撑撑

❶[动]用力抵住：support; prop up｜她手～着下巴沉思。Tā shǒu chēngzhe xiàba chénsī. *She was lost in thought, with her chin propped up in her hands.*

❷[动]支持；支撑：support; prop up｜一家人的生活，他一人～着。Yī jiā rén de shēnghuó, tā yī rén chēngzhe. *He supported his family all by himself.*
支撑 zhīchēng

❸[动]用篙抵住河床使船行进：punt; move a boat forward by setting a bamboo pole against the river bottom and pushing｜他把船～到了河对岸。Tā bǎ chuán chēngdàole hé duì'àn. *He poled the boat to the opposite bank.* / 你～船，我掌舵。Nǐ chēng chuán, wǒ zhǎngduò. *You pole the boat while I am at the helm.*

❹[动]张开：open; unfurl｜请你把伞～开。Qǐng nǐ bǎ sǎn chēngkāi. *Please open the umbrella.* / 你把口袋～大一点儿！Nǐ bǎ kǒudai chēngdà yīdiǎnr! *Hold the sack wide open.*

❺[动]装得过满；吃得过饱：fill up｜你少装一点儿，这口袋都～破了。Nǐ shǎo zhuāng yīdiǎnr, zhè kǒudai dōu chēngpò le. *Pack no more or the sack will burst.* / 我肚子有点儿～。Wǒ dùzi yǒu diǎnr chēng. *I'm rather full.*

成 chéng 6画 戈部

 成成成成成成

❶ [动]完成；成功：finish; succeed; accomplish | 事情已经～了。Shìqing yǐjīng chéng le. *We've done it.* / 这笔买卖谈～了。Zhè bǐ mǎimai tánchéng le. *We have made the deal.*

成败 chéngbài success or failure

成功 chénggōng succeed; success

成交 chéngjiāo strike a bargain; conclude a transaction

成立 chénglì ①found; establish; set up ② be tenable; hold water

成名 chéngmíng become famous; make a name for oneself

促成 cùchéng 达成 dáchéng

合成 héchéng 速成 sùchéng

完成 wánchéng

养成 yǎngchéng

组成 zǔchéng

❷ [动]成为：become; turn into | 他俩～了好朋友。Tā liǎ chéngle hǎo péngyou. *The two of them have become good friends.* / 雪化～水。Xuě huàchéng shuǐ. *Snow melts into water.* / 她～了一名独唱演员。Tā chéngle yī míng dúchàng yǎnyuán. *She became a soloist.*

成为 chéngwéi become

变成 biànchéng

当成 dàngchéng

构成 gòuchéng 合成 héchéng

落成 luòchéng

形成 xíngchéng

❸ [动]成熟：be ripe; be mature

成熟 chéngshú mature; ripen

成长 chéngzhǎng grow up; grow to maturity

老成 lǎochéng

❹ [形]发育成熟的：ripe; mature

成年 chéngnián grow up; come of age

成人 chéngrén ① grow up; become full-grown ② adult; grown-up

成年人 chéngniánrén grown-up; adult

未成年人 wèichéngniánrén

❺ [形]已定的；定型的；现成的：ready-made

成品 chéngpǐn end product; finished product

成药 chéngyào pharmacist-prepared medicine; patent medicine

成语 chéngyǔ set phrase; idiom; idioms and allusions

现成 xiànchéng

❻ [名]成就；成果：achievement; accomplishment; success

成果 chéngguǒ achievement

成绩 chéngjì result; achievement; success

成就 chéngjiù ① achievement; success; attainment ② achieve;

accomplish

成效 chéngxiào effect; result

收成 shōucheng

❼ [动]表示同意；许可：agree; approve | ～，就这么办吧。Chéng, jiù zhème bàn ba. *All right. Let's do it this way.*

赞成 zànchéng

❽ [动]表示达到了一定的数量：in a considerable number or amount

成套 chéngtào a complete set

成天 chéngtiān all day long

成千上万 chéngqiān-shàngwàn tens of thousands of; thousands and thousands of

❾ [量]十分之一叫一成：one tenth | 今年的产量又提高了一～。Jīnnián de chǎnliàng yòu tígāole yī chéng. *The output of this year has increased by 10 percent.*

分成 fēnchéng

◇成本 chéngběn cost

成分 chéngfèn ① composition; component; part; ingredient ② one's profession or economic status

成心 chéngxīn intentionally; on purpose

成员 chéngyuán member

 chéng 7画 口部

呈 呈 呈 呈 呈 呈 呈

❶ [动]恭敬地送上去：respectfully present | 公文～上去了。Gōng-

wén chéng shàngqu le. *The official paper has been presented to the higher authorities for approval.* / 他双手～上贺信。Tā shuāngshǒu chéngshang hèxìn. *He presented the letter of congratulation with both hands.*

❷ [动]显露出：display; reveal | 这种叶子～椭圆形。Zhè zhǒng yèzi chéng tuǒyuánxíng. *This kind of leaf is oval in shape.* / 梨树的花一般～白色。Líshù de huā yībān chéng báisè. *Pear flowers are white in general.*

呈现 chéngxiàn present; appear; emerge

◇辞呈 cíchéng

 (誠) chéng 8画 讠部

诚 诚 诚 诚 诚 诚 诚 诚

[形]真实的：honest; sincere

诚恳 chéngkěn sincere

诚实 chéngshí honest

诚信 chéngxìn honest; keep or live up to one's promise; credit

诚意 chéngyì good faith; sincerity

诚挚 chéngzhì sincere; cordial

诚心诚意 chéngxīn-chéngyì with all one's heart; earnestly and sincerely

真诚 zhēnchéng

忠诚 zhōngchéng

chéng 8画 一部

承 承承承承承承承承

❶ [动]担当；接受：undertake; contract (to do a job)

承办 chéngbàn undertake

承包 chéngbāo contract

承担 chéngdān bear; undertake; assume

承接 chéngjiē ① continue; carry on ② undertake the task of; contract to accept

承诺 chéngnuò promise to undertake; undertake to do sth.

承认 chéngrèn ① admit; acknowledge ② give diplomatic recognition; recognize

承受 chéngshòu bear; support; endure

承载 chéngzài bear the weight of

❷ [动]继续：carry on; continue

继承 jìchéng

城

chéng 9画 土部

城 城城城城城城城城城

❶ [名]城墙：city wall | 颐和园在北京～外。Yíhéyuán zài Běijīng chéng wài. *The Summer Palace is on the outskirts of Beijing city.*

城墙 chéngqiáng city wall

长城 Chángchéng

❷ [名]城墙以内的地方：city; capital | 东～dōng chéng *east of a city* / 我家以前住在西～。Wǒ jiā yǐqián zhù zài xī chéng. *My family used to live in the west of the city.*

城区 chéngqū the city proper

❸ [名]城市：city | 北京是中国历史文化名～。Běijīng shì Zhōngguó lìshǐ wénhuà míngchéng. *Beijing is a famous historical and cultural city of China.* / 这是一个小～，人口不多。Zhè shì yī gè xiǎochéng, rénkǒu bù duō. *This is a small city with a small population.*

城市 chéngshì city

城镇 chéngzhèn cities and towns

乘

chéng 10画 丿部

乘 乘乘乘乘乘乘乘乘乘乘

❶ [动]搭坐交通工具：ride | ～飞机 chéng fēijī *travel by plane* / 我每天～公共汽车上班。Wǒ měi tiān chéng gōnggòng qìchē shàngbān. *I go to work by bus every day.*

乘客 chéngkè passenger

乘坐 chéngzuò take a ride (in a car, ship, etc.)

乘务员 chéngwùyuán crew

member; attendant on a train
搭乘 dāchéng

❷[动]趁；利用：take advantage of
乘机 chéngjī seize the opportunity

❸[动]算术上指求一个数的若干倍的运算方法：multiply ｜ 3~5等于15。Sān chéng wǔ děngyú shíwǔ. *Five times three is fifteen.*
乘法 chéngfǎ (math.) multiplication
乘方 chéngfāng involution; power

盛　　　chéng 11画 皿部

盛 盛盛盛盛盛盛盛盛
盛盛盛

❶[动]把东西放在容器里：put sth. into a container ｜ 你们坐着，我来~饭。Nǐmen zuòzhe, wǒ lái chéng fàn. *Stay seated. I'll fill the bowls with rice for you.* / 我把鱼~在盘子里。Wǒ bǎ yú chéng zài pánzi li. *I put the fish on the plate.* / 这碗汤是~给客人的。Zhè wǎn tāng shì chénggěi kèrén de. *This bowl of soup is for the guest.*

❷[动]容纳：contain; hold ｜ 箱子太小，~不了这么多东西。Xiāngzi tài xiǎo, chéngbuliǎo zhème duō dōngxi. *The box is*

too small to hold so many things. See shèng.

chéng 12画 禾部

程 程程程程程程程程
程程程程

❶[名]规矩；法则：rule; regulation ｜ 规~guīchéng *rules*
章程 zhāngchéng

❷[名]距离：distance
单程 dānchéng 里程 lǐchéng
路程 lùchéng
行程 xíngchéng
远程 yuǎnchéng

❸[名]道路：journey; stage of a journey
车程 chēchéng 历程 lìchéng
启程 qǐchéng
前程 qiánchéng
全程 quánchéng
专程 zhuānchéng
各奔前程 gèbēnqiánchéng

❹[名]进度；程序；过程：course; procedure; sequence
程度 chéngdù level; degree
程序 chéngxù order; procedure; course; sequence
工程 gōngchéng
过程 guòchéng 进程 jìnchéng
课程 kèchéng 日程 rìchéng
议程 yìchéng
工程师 gōngchéngshī
课程表 kèchéngbiǎo

惩 (懲) chéng 12画 心部

惩 惩惩惩惩惩惩惩惩惩惩惩惩

[动]处罚：punish; penalize | ～前毖后 chéngqián-bìhòu *learn from past mistakes to avoid future ones*

惩办 chéngbàn punish; chastise; punishment; chastisement

惩罚 chéngfá punish; penalize

澄 chéng 15画 氵部

澄 澄澄澄澄澄澄澄澄澄澄澄澄澄澄澄

❶[形]水很清：clear; limpid
❷[动]使清楚：clarify; make clear

澄清 chéngqīng ① clear; transparent ② clear up; clarify

橙 chéng 16画 木部

橙 橙橙橙橙橙橙橙橙橙橙橙橙橙橙橙

❶[名]常绿乔木，果实为橙子：orange

橙汁 chéngzhī orange juice
橙子 chéngzi orange

❷[形]红和黄合成的颜色：orange | ～色 chéngsè *orange (colour)*

秤 chèng 10画 禾部

秤 秤秤秤秤秤秤秤秤秤秤

[名]balance; scales | 请过一下～。Qǐng guò yīxià chèng. *Weigh it, please.* / 用～称一下有多重。Yòng chèng chēng yīxià yǒu duō zhòng. *Use the scales to see how heavy it is.*

吃 chī 6画 口部

吃 吃吃吃吃吃吃

❶[动]eat; take | 一天～三顿饭 yī tiān chī sān dùn fàn *have three meals a day*
吃饭 chīfàn have a meal
大吃大喝 dàchī-dàhē

❷[动]吸收：absorb | 这种纸不～水。Zhè zhǒng zhǐ bù chī shuǐ. *This kind of paper doesn't absorb water.*

❸[动]消灭（用于军事或下棋等）：wipe out | ～掉一个卒子 chīdiào yī gè zúzi *take a pawn (in chess)* / 这次战斗中，我军～掉敌人一个团。Zhè cì zhàndòu zhōng, wǒ jūn chīdiào dírén yī gè tuán. *Our troops wiped out an enemy regiment in the battle.*

102

❹[动]承受；感受：suffer; bear; withstand | 他~尽了没有文化的苦头。Tā chījìnle méiyǒu wénhuà de kǔtou. *He suffered a great deal due to his illiteracy.*/我可不~这一套。Wǒ kě bù chī zhè yī tào. *I am not willing to accept this.*

吃惊 chījīng be startled; be shocked; be amazed; be taken aback

吃苦 chīkǔ bear hardships

吃亏 chīkuī ① suffer losses; get the worst of it ② at a disadvantage; in an unfavourable situation

吃力 chīlì strenuous; painstaking; be a strain

吃苦头 chīkǔtou suffer loss; endure hardships; come to grief

吃老本 chīlǎoběn live off one's past gains; rest on one's laurels

痴 chī 13画 疒部

痴 痴痴痴痴痴痴痴痴痴痴痴痴痴

❶[形]傻：foolish; stupid | 白~báichī *idiot*
痴呆 chīdāi dull-witted; mentally retarded

❷[形]形容极度迷恋：crazy; infatuated; obsessed
痴迷 chīmí infatuated

痴情 chīqíng passionate love

池 chí 6画 氵部

池 池池池池池池池

[名]水塘（多指人工挖的）：pool; pond | 游泳~yóuyǒngchí *swimming pool* / ~里的鱼真不少。Chí li de yú zhēn bù shǎo. *There are quite a lot of fish in the pond.*
池塘 chítáng pool; pond

驰 (馳) chí 6画 马部

驰 驰驰驰驰驰驰

[动]快跑（多指车马）：speed; gallop | 飞~fēichí *speed along* / 那辆汽车奔~而过。Nà liàng qìchē bēnchí ér guò. *The car sped away.*
奔驰 bēnchí

迟 (遲) chí 7画 辶部

迟 迟迟迟迟迟迟迟

❶[形]慢：slow; tardy | 延~yánchí *delay; defer; postpone* / 这事为何至今仍然~~不解决？Zhè shì wèihé zhìjīn réngrán chíchí bù jiějué? *Why does this problem take so long to solve?* / 大家等了一个多小时，

他~~不来。Dàjiā děngle yī gè duō xiǎoshí, tā chíchí bù lái. *We've been waiting for over an hour. There is still no sign of him.*

迟缓 chíhuǎn slow; tardy; sluggish

迟疑 chíyí hesitate

❷[形]比规定的或合适的时间晚：delayed | 时间太~了，来不及了。Shíjiān tài chí le, láibují le. *It is too late to do it.* / 会议已经开始，他来~了。Huìyì yǐjīng kāishǐ, tā láichí le. *He did not show up until the meeting had started.*

迟到 chídào be late; come late; arrive late

推迟 tuīchí

持 chí 9画 扌部

持持持持持持持持持

❶[动]拿着；握着：hold | ~枪 chí qiāng *hold a gun*

持有 chíyǒu hold; own

❷[动]掌管；料理：manage; handle | 勤俭~家 qínjiǎn-chíjiā *be industrious and thrifty in managing a household*

主持 zhǔchí

主持人 zhǔchírén

❸[动]守住不变：hold; keep | 我依然~过去的看法。Wǒ yīrán chí

guòqù de kànfǎ. *I still stick to my old opinion.*

持久 chíjiǔ lasting; enduring; protracted

持平 chípíng unbiased; fair

持续 chíxù continued; sustained

保持 bǎochí   坚持 jiānchí

维持 wéichí   支持 zhīchí

❹[动]控制；挟制：control; take advantage of sb.'s weakness and control them

劫持 jiéchí   挟持 xiéchí

匙 chí 11画 匕部

匙匙匙匙匙匙匙匙匙匙匙

[名]舀东西的小勺：spoon | 汤~ tāngchí *tablespoon; soup spoon*

尺 chǐ 4画 尸部

尺尺尺尺

❶[量]市制长度单位，十寸为一尺，十尺为一丈：a traditional Chinese unit of length. One "*chi*" is equal to 10 "*cun*". And ten "*chi*" is equal to one "*zhang*". One metre is equal to three "*chi*". | 妹妹买了三~花布。Mèimei mǎile sān chǐ huā bù. *The younger sister bought 3 chi of cotton print.*

尺寸 chǐcùn measurement; dimension; size

尺度 chǐdù yardstick; measure; scale

公尺 gōngchǐ 英尺 yīngchǐ

❷[名]量长度或画图的用具：ruler

尺子 chǐzi ruler

齿 (齒) chǐ 8画 齿部

齿 齿齿齿齿齿齿齿齿齿

❶[名]牙齿：tooth

咬牙切齿 yǎoyá-qièchǐ

❷[名]像牙齿那样排列的东西：tooth-like object | 这把梳子的～儿很密。Zhè bǎ shūzi de chǐr hěn mì. *The teeth of the comb are closely set.*

齿轮 chǐlún gear wheel; gear

侈 chǐ 8画 亻部

侈 侈侈侈侈侈侈侈侈

[形]浪费：waste; squander

奢侈 shēchǐ

耻 chǐ 10画 耳部

耻 耻耻耻耻耻耻耻耻
耻耻

[动]羞愧：shame; disgrace

无耻 wúchǐ 羞耻 xiūchǐ

斥 chì 5画 斤部

斥 斥斥斥斥斥

❶[动]责备：blame; reproach | ～责 chìzé *reprimand; rebuke; denounce*

驳斥 bóchì

❷[动]使离开：repel; dismiss

排斥 páichì

赤 chì 7画 赤部

赤 赤赤赤赤赤赤赤

❶[形]比红稍暗的颜色：泛指红色：dark red; red | ～色 chìsè *red colour*

❷[形]空：empty; bare | ～手空拳 chìshǒu-kōngquán *be empty-handed*

赤字 chìzì deficit

❸[动]光着；露着：naked; bare | ～脚 chìjiǎo *barefoot*

◇赤道 chìdào equator

翅 chì 10画 支部

翅 翅翅翅翅翅翅翅翅
翅翅

See 翅膀

翅膀 chìbǎng wing

chōng 6画 儿部

充 充充充充充充

❶[形]满；足：sufficient; full

充分 chōngfèn full; ample; abundant

充满 chōngmǎn full of; brimming with; permeated with; imbued with

充沛 chōngpèi plentiful

充实 chōngshí ① substantial; rich ② substantiate; enrich; replenish

充足 chōngzú adequate; sufficient; abundant; ample

❷[动]填满；装：fill; fill up; pack up | 他给汽车的电池~了电。Tā gěi qìchē de diànchí chōng le diàn. *He charged the battery of his car.*

充电 chōngdiàn charge (a battery)

补充 bǔchōng 扩充 kuòchōng

❸[动]担任：assume the office of; serve as

充当 chōngdāng serve as; act as; play the part of

❹[动]假冒：disguise as; pretend to be | ~内行 chōng nèiháng *pretend to be an expert*

冒充 màochōng

冲 (衝) **chōng** 6画 冫部

冲 冲冲冲冲冲冲

❶[动]很快地向前闯；猛烈撞击：charge forward quickly | 他们迅速~出敌人重围。Tāmen xùnsù chōngchū dírén chōngwéi. *They quickly broke through the close siege of the enemy.*

冲刺 chōngcì (sports) spurt; sprint

冲动 chōngdòng ① impulse ② get excited; be impetuous

冲锋 chōngfēng charge; assault

冲浪 chōnglàng (sports) surfing; surfboarding

冲破 chōngpò break through; breach

❷[动]用开水等浇：pour boiling water on | ~茶 chōngchá *make tea* / 我给你~一杯浓咖啡。Wǒ gěi nǐ chōng yī bēi nóng kāfēi. *I'll make a cup of strong coffee for you.* / 这种奶粉用热水一~就化。Zhè zhǒng nǎifěn yòng rèshuǐ yī chōng jiù huà. *This kind of milk powder dissolves instantly in hot water.*

❸[动]冲洗，冲击：wash; rinse | 把盘子~一~ bǎ pánzi chōng-yichōng *rinse the plates*

冲击 chōngjī lash; pound; break against

◇冲突 chōngtū conflict

See chǒng.

虫 (蟲) chóng 6画 虫部

虫 | 虫虫虫虫虫虫

[名]昆虫或某些动物：worm; insect | 害~ hàichóng *pest* / 益~ yìchóng *useful insect*

虫子 chóngzi insect; worm

重 chóng 9画 丿部

重 | 重重重重重重重重重

❶[动]重复：repeat; duplicate | 你举的两个例子~了。Nǐ jǔ de liǎng gè lìzi chóng le. *The two examples you gave are the same.* / 这本书买~了。Zhè běn shū mǎichóng le. *Two copies of the same book were bought by mistake.*

重叠 chóngdié one on top of another; overlapping

重阳节 Chóngyángjié the Double Ninth Festival (the 9th day of the 9th lunar month)

❷[副]再；重新：again; once more | ~写一遍 chóng xiě yī biàn *write it once more* / 请你~说一遍。Qǐng nǐ chóng shuō yī biàn. *Please say it again.*

重播 chóngbō ① rebroadcast a programme (from the same sta-

tion) ② resow (the same field)

重复 chóngfù repeat; duplicate

重建 chóngjiàn rebuild; reestablish; restoration

重申 chóngshēn reaffirm; reiterate; restate

重现 chóngxiàn recur; reappear

重新 chóngxīn again; anew; afresh

❸[量]层：layer; tier | 再翻过两~山就到了。Zài fānguo liǎng chóng shān jiù dào le. *We'll arrive there after climbing over two more mountains.* / 他们克服了一~又一~的困难。Tāmen kèfúle yī chóng yòu yī chóng de kùnnan. *They overcame one difficulty after another.*

双重 shuāngchóng

See zhòng.

崇 chóng 11画 山部

崇 | 崇崇崇崇崇崇崇崇崇崇崇

❶[形]高：lofty; high

崇高 chónggāo sublime; lofty; noble

❷[动]尊重；重视：attach importance to; respect; esteem | 推~ tuīchóng *hold in esteem; praise highly*

崇拜 chóngbài worship; adore

崇敬 chóngjìng esteem; respect; revere

宠（寵） chǒng 8画 宀部

宠 宠宠宠宠宠宠宠宠

[动]偏爱；过分地爱：dote on; bestow favour on | 你把孩子~坏了。Nǐ bǎ háizi chǒnghuài le. *You've spoiled the child.*

宠物 chǒngwù pet (e.g. a cat or a dog)

冲（衝） chōng 6画 冫部

冲 冲冲冲冲冲冲

❶[动]对着；向着：towards; facing | 大门是~南的。Dàmén shì chōng nán de. *The gate faces south. /* 他的桌子~着窗户。Tā de zhuōzi chōngzhe chuānghu. *His desk faces the window.*

❷[介]对着；向着：at; towards | 他~着我笑。Tā chōngzhe wǒ xiào. *He smiled at me.*

❸[介]凭；根据：because of; on the basis of; according to | ~他的聪明才干，准能胜任这个工作。Chōng tā de cōngmíng cáigàn, zhǔn néng shèngrèn zhège gōngzuò. *He is surely qualified for the work with his ability and wisdom. /* ~你这句话，我也要帮你一把。Chōng nǐ zhè jù huà, wǒ yě yào bāng nǐ yī bǎ. *I'll give you a hand on account of your kindly remarks.*

❹[形]猛烈：strong and pungent | 这药味很~。Zhè yào wèi hěn chōng. *This medicine has a strong smell.*

See chōng.

抽 chōu 8画 扌部

抽 抽抽抽抽抽抽抽抽

❶[动]把夹在中间的东西取出：take sth. out from in between | 他把信纸从信封中~了出来。Tā bǎ xìnzhǐ cóng xìnfēng zhōng chōule chūlai. *He took the letter out of the envelope. /* 我从书架上~出一本书。Wǒ cóng shūjià shang chōuchū yī běn shū. *I took a book from the bookshelf.*

抽屉 chōuti drawer

❷[动]从总体中取出一部分：take a part from a whole | 这篇文章请您~时间看看。Zhè piān wénzhāng qǐng nín chōu shíjiān kànkan. *Please manage to find time to read the article. /* 他被~到国家队去参加国际比赛。Tā bèi chōudào guójiāduì qù cānjiā guójì bǐsài. *He has been transferred to the national team for inter-*

national competitions.

抽查 chōuchá carry out selective examinations; make spot checks; spot-check

抽检 chōujiǎn inspect or examine sth. through samplings

抽奖 chōujiǎng draw lots to determine the prize-winners; draw a winning number (in a lottery or raffle)

抽空 chōukòng manage to find time

抽签 chōuqiān draw (or cast) lots

抽象 chōuxiàng abstract

❸ [动]长出：grow | 春天到了，树枝上～出了新芽。Chūntiān dào le, shùzhī shang chōuchūle xīn yá. *Spring has come and the trees are in bud.*

❹ [动]收缩：shrink | 这种布一下水就～。Zhè zhǒng bù yī xià shuǐ jiù chōu. *This cloth shrinks when washed.*

❺ [动]吸：inhale | ～烟 chōu yān smoke (a cigarette, a cigar, etc.) / 他们已经把河里的水～干了。Tāmen yǐjīng bǎ hé li de shuǐ chōugān le. *They have pumped the river dry.*

❻ [动]用长条形东西打：lash; whip | 马被～了一鞭子。Mǎ bèi chōule yī biānzi. *The horse was given a lash.*

抽打 chōudǎ lash; whip; thrash

 chóu 4画 亻部

仇 仇仇仇仇

❶ [名]强烈的怨恨：hatred; enmity | 深～大恨 shēnchóu-dàhèn *profound hatred* / 你跟他有什么～？Nǐ gēn tā yǒu shénme chóu? *Why do you hate him so much?*

仇恨 chóuhèn hatred; enmity; hostility

报仇 bàochóu   复仇 fùchóu

❷ [名]敌人：enemy; foe | ～敌 chóudí *enemy; foe*

 (綢) chóu 11画 纟部

绸 绸绸绸绸绸绸绸绸绸绸

See below

绸子 chóuzi silk fabric; silk

丝绸 sīchóu

 (疇) chóu 12画 田部

畴 畴畴畴畴畴畴畴畴畴畴畴畴

[名]种类：category

范畴 fànchóu

酬 chóu 13画 酉部

酬 酬 酬 酬 酬 酬 酬 酬 酬 酬 酬 酬 酬

❶[名]报酬；为报答别人的劳动等而付给的钱物：reward; payment | ～谢 chóuxiè *thank sb. with gift, money, etc.*
报酬 bàochou 薪酬 xīnchóu

❷[动]交际往来：have social interaction with
应酬 yìngchou

稠 chóu 13画 禾部

稠 稠 稠 稠 稠 稠 稠 稠 稠 稠 稠 稠 稠

❶[形]多而密：dense
稠密 chóumì dense

❷[形]液体的浓度大：dense; thick | 粥太～了。Zhōu tài chóu le. *The porridge is too thick.*

愁 chóu 13画 心部

愁 愁 愁 愁 愁 愁 愁 愁 愁 愁 愁 愁

[动]忧虑；苦闷：worry | 这件事可把我～坏了。Zhè jiàn shì kě bǎ wǒ chóuhuài le. *I was extremely worried about this.* | 他～找不到一个好工作。Tā

chóu zhǎobudào yī gè hǎo gōngzuò. *He is worried about being unable to get a good job.*
发愁 fāchóu

筹 (籌) chóu 13画 竹部

筹 筹 筹 筹 筹 筹 筹 筹 筹 筹 筹 筹 筹

[动]想办法；谋划：prepare; plan; raise | ～款 chóukuǎn *raise funds*
筹备 chóubèi prepare; arrange
筹集 chóují accumulate; raise (money)
筹建 chóujiàn prepare to construct or establish sth.
统筹 tǒngchóu
◇筹码 chóumǎ chip; counter

踌 (躊) chóu 14画 足部

踌 踌 踌 踌 踌 踌 踌 踌 踌 踌 踌 踌 踌 踌

See 踌躇
踌躇 chóuchú hesitate; shillyshally

丑 (醜 ❷❸) chǒu 4画 一部

丑 丑 丑 丑 丑

❶[名]地支的第二位：the second of the twelve Earthly Branches

❷ [形]相貌难看：ugly; unpleasant to look at | 她长得并不～。Tā zhǎng de bìng bù chǒu. *She is not ugly.*

丑八怪 chǒubāguài (inf.) a very ugly person

❸ [形]可耻的；讨厌的：shameful; detestable | 说这些脏话真～！Shuō zhèxiē zānghuà zhēn chǒu! *It's a shame to say such obscene words!*

丑恶 chǒu'è ugly; repulsive; hideous

丑闻 chǒuwén scandal

❹ [名]戏剧里的滑稽的角色：clown; buffoon

小丑 xiǎochǒu

 chǒu 10画 自部

 臭臭臭臭臭臭臭臭
臭臭

❶ [形]气味难闻：foul; smelly; stinking | 这条鱼～了。Zhè tiáo yú chǒu le. *This fish smells foul.* / 气味好～呀！Qìwèi hǎo chǒu ya! *How stinking the smell is!*

❷ [形]令人厌恶的；可耻的：shameful; disgraceful | 他总是摆出一副教训别人的～架子。Tā zǒngshì bǎichū yī fù jiàoxùn biérén de chǒujiàzi. *He always acts like a critic, finding fault with people* / 他的名声很～。Tā de míng-shēng hěn chǒu.

He is notor-ious.

❸ [副]狠狠地：severely; relentlessly | ～骂 chǒumà *a tongue-lashing*

 chū 5画 凵部

出 出出出出出

❶ [动]由里到外：go out | 从屋里～来 cóng wūli chūlai *get out of the room* / ～了这条街你就看见那座楼了。Chūle zhè tiáo jiē nǐ jiù kànjiàn nà zuò lóu le. *Getting out of the street, you'll see that building.*

出差 chūchāi be away on business; go on a business (or official) trip

出场 chūchǎng ① come on the stage; appear on the scene ② enter the arena

出动 chūdòng set out; start off

出发 chūfā set out; start off; leave; proceed from

出访 chūfǎng visit a foreign country

出国 chūguó go abroad

出击 chūjī ① launch an attack; hit out; make a sally ② fight against (evil, crime, etc.)

出境 chūjìng leave the country

出局 chūjú out (in baseball, softball, etc.)

出口 chūkǒu ① speak; utter ② exit; way out ③ export

111

出来 chūlái(lai) come out; emerge

出路 chūlù way out

出门 chūmén ① go out ② leave home; be away from home; go on a journey

出去 chūqù(qu) go out; get out

出入 chūrù ① come in and go out; go out and come in ② discrepancy; divergence; inconsistency

出院 chūyuàn leave hospital

出征 chūzhēng go on an expedition; go out to battle

出走 chūzǒu leave one's home or country under compulsion; run away

出发点 chūfādiǎn purpose

输出 shūchū   退出 tuìchū

外出 wàichū

❷ [动] 显露，出现：appear; show; reveal | 雨过天晴，天空～了一道彩虹。Yǔ guò tiān qíng, tiānkōng chūle yī dào cǎihóng. *After the rain, the sky cleared up and a rainbow appeared.* | 夜晚的天空～了好多星星。Yèwǎn de tiānkōng chūle hǎo duō xīngxing. *Numerous stars appeared in the night sky.*

出面 chūmiàn act in one's own capacity or on behalf of sb.; appear personally; come forth

出名 chūmíng famous; well-known

出示 chūshì ① show; produce

② (formal) put up a notice

出台 chūtái make a public appearance

出庭 chūtíng appear in court

出现 chūxiàn appear; arise; emerge; turn up

出风头 chūfēngtou seek or be in the limelight; enjoy being the centre of attention

出洋相 chūyángxiàng make a laughing stock of oneself; make an exhibition of oneself

提出 tíchū   突出 tūchū

演出 yǎnchū   指出 zhǐchū

展出 zhǎnchū

层出不穷 céngchū-bùqióng

❸ [动] 来到：come

出世 chūshì be born

出席 chūxí attend; be present

❹ [动] 拿出；支付：give; prepare; put forth | 你给我～个主意吧。Nǐ gěi wǒ chū ge zhǔyi ba. *Think of a way for me, please.* | 谁～钱？Shéi chū qián? *Who'll pay for it?* | 晚会上你～什么节目？Wǎnhuì shang nǐ chū shénme jiémù? *What are you going to perform at the party?*

出卖 chūmài ① offer for sale; sell ② sell out; betray; barter away

出让 chūràng sell (one's own things)

出手 chūshǒu get (hoarded goods, etc.) off one's hands; dispose of; sell

出售 chūshòu offer for sale; sell

出资 chūzī provide funding

出租 chūzū hire; let; rent out

出点子 chūdiǎnzi offer advice; make suggestions

出难题 chūnántí pose a difficult problem; set sb. a very difficult task

出租车 chūzūchē taxi; taxi cab

付出 fùchū   支出 zhīchū

❺[动]超出: exceed | 考试内容～不了这个范围。Kǎoshì nèiróng chūbuliǎo zhège fànwéi. *The examination questions are within the given range.* / 球～了边线。Qiú chūle biānxiàn. *The ball went beyond the sideline.*

出界 chūjiè (sports) out-of-bounds; outside; out

出色 chūsè outstanding; remarkable; splendid

出线 chūxiàn (sports) qualify for the next round of competitions

出众 chūzhòng be out of the ordinary; be outstanding

出人意料 chūrén-yìliào exceeding all expectations; beyond all expectations

杰出 jiéchū   超出 chāochū

❻[动]产生; 发生; 出产: produce; turn out | ～成果 chū chéngguǒ *bear fruit* / 他又～了一本书。Tā yòu chūle yī běn shū. *He has published another book.* / 我

的家乡～茶叶。Wǒ de jiāxiāng chū cháyè. *Tea is the speciality of my hometown.*

出版 chūbǎn come off the press; publish; come out

出产 chūchǎn produce; manufacture

出处 chūchù source (of a quotation or allusion)

出品 chūpǐn ① produce; manufacture; make ② product

出身 chūshēn class origin; family background

出生 chūshēng be born

出事 chūshì meet with a mishap; have an accident

出自 chūzì come from; originate from

出版社 chūbǎnshè publishing house

产出 chǎnchū   得出 déchū

有出息 yǒuchūxi

❼[动]发出: send out; give out | ～汗 chūhàn *perspire; sweat* / 别～声, 大家都休息了。Bié chūshēng, dàjiā dōu xiūxi le. *Be quiet. Everyone is taking a rest.* / 他吓得气也不敢～。Tā xià de qì yě bù gǎn chū. *He was so scared that he almost did not dare to breathe.*

出血 chūxiě ① bleed; shed blood ② (dial.) give out money or things

❽[动]放在动词后, 表示向外或完成: used after a verb to indicate

an outward movement or completion of an action | 他把客人送～门外。Tā bǎ kèrén sòngchū mén wài. *He saw the guest out of the door.* / 他在工作中作～了很大成绩。Tā zài gōngzuò zhōng zuòchū le hěn dà chéngjì. *He made a remarkable achievement in his work.*

撤出 chèchū　　露出 lùchū
推出 tuīchū

◇ 出神 chūshén be spellbound; be in a trance; be lost in thought
出息 chūxi prospects; a bright future

初　　chū　　7画 衤部

初 初初初初初初初

❶[形]开始的：beginning; initial part | 年～niánchū *at the beginning of the year*
初步 chūbù initial; preliminary; tentative
初次 chūcì the first time
初期 chūqī initial stage; early days
初衷 chūzhōng one's original intention
当初 dāngchū　　起初 qǐchū
月初 yuèchū　　最初 zuìchū
❷[副]第一次；刚刚：first time; only a short time ago; just | ～次 chūcì *first time* / ～学

外语时，要特别注意打好语音基础。Chū xué wàiyǔ shí, yào tèbié zhùyì dǎhǎo yǔyīn jīchǔ. *When starting to learn a foreign language, pay particular attention to building a solid pronunciation base.*
❸[形]最低的：on the initial stage of | ～等 chūděng *elementary; primary*
初级 chūjí elementary; primary; junior
初中 chūzhōng junior middle school

除　　chú　　9画 阝(左)部

除 除除除除除除除除
除

❶[动]去掉：eliminate; get rid of | ～害虫 chú hàichóng *get rid of pests*
拆除 chāichú　　废除 fèichú
解除 jiěchú　　开除 kāichú
扣除 kòuchú　　免除 miǎnchú
排除 páichú　　破除 pòchú
清除 qīngchú　　扫除 sǎochú
❷[介]不计算在内：except | ～了一张床，屋里都是书。Chúle yī zhāng chuáng, wūli dōu shì shū. *Except for a bed the room is completely full of books.* / ～他以外，我们都去了。Chú tā yǐwài, wǒmen dōu qù le. *We*

all went except him.

除了 chúle (prep.) ① except ② besides; in addition to

除外 chúwài except; except for; but

除此之外 chúcǐzhīwài with the exception of this; excepting this

❸ [名]算术中的除法：division in arithmetic | 3～12 得 4。Sān chú shí'èr dé sì. *12 divided by 3 is 4.* / 加减乘～四则运算 jiā-jiǎn-chéng-chú sìzé yùnsuàn *the four fundamental operations of arithmetic—addition, subtraction, multiplication and division*

除法 chúfǎ (math.) division

◇ 除非 chúfēi ① only if; only when ② unless

除夕 chúxī New Year's Eve

厨 chú 12画 厂部

 厨厨厨厨厨厨厨厨 厨厨厨厨

❶ [名]kitchen | 她妈妈亲自下～做菜。Tā māma qīnzì xiàchú zuòcài. *Her mother did the cooking herself in the kitchen.*

厨房 chúfáng kitchen

❷ [名]以烹调为职业的人：a professional cook

厨师 chúshī cook; chef

锄 (鋤) chú 12画 钅部

锄 锄锄锄锄锄锄锄锄 锄锄锄锄

❶ [名]松土、除草的用具：hoe, a tool used to loosen the soil or dig up weeds | 这把～很好用。Zhè bǎ chútou hěn hǎo yòng. *This hoe works very well.*

❷ [动]用锄松土、除草：dig soil and weed with a hoe | ～草 chúcǎo *hoe up weeds; weed with a hoe* / ～地 chúdì *hoe the fields*

橱 chú 16画 木部

橱 橱橱橱橱橱橱橱橱 橱橱橱橱橱橱橱橱

[名]放置衣服等物件的家具：furniture for keeping clothes or other stuff | 书～shūchú *bookcase* / 衣～yīchú *wardrobe*

处 (處) chǔ 5画 夂部

处 处处处处处

❶ [动]居于(某种位置、条件、情况等)：be situated in | 灾民正～在十分困难的境地。Zāimín zhèng chǔzài shífēn kùnnan de jìngdì. *The victims of this natural calamity are in a very difficult situation.* / 我要是~在他的地位，就不会这么做。Wǒ yào shì chǔzài tā de dìwèi, jiù bú huì zhème zuò. *If I were in his place, I would not do it.*

处境 chǔjìng (usu. refer to) unfavourable situation; plight

处于 chǔyú be (in a certain situation)

❷[动]同在一起生活；交往：get along with; live together | 他俩~得很好。Tā liǎ chǔ de hěn hǎo. *The two of them are getting along well with each other.* / 他们在一起~了好几十年。Tāmen zài yìqǐ chǔle hǎo jǐshí nián. *They have been living together for decades.*

难处 nánchǔ   相处 xiāngchǔ
和平共处 hépíng gòngchǔ

❸[动]办理：deal with; handle | 这小伙子~事挺老练的。Zhè xiǎo huǒzi chǔshì tǐng lǎoliàn de. *This young man is experienced in dealing with matters.*

处方 chǔfāng ① write out a prescription; prescribe ② prescription; recipe

处决 chǔjué put to death; execute

处理 chǔlǐ ① handle; deal with; dispose of; manage; settle ② sell at reduced prices ③ treatment; treat by a special process

处置 chǔzhì ① handle; deal with; manage; dispose of ②

punish

处方药 chǔfāngyào prescription drug; prescription medicine

处理器 chǔlǐqì processor

❹[动]惩罚：punish | 他被~三年徒刑。Tā bèi chǔ sān nián túxíng. *He was sentenced to three years' imprisonment.*

处罚 chǔfá punish; penalize

处分 chǔfèn take disciplinary action against; punish

查处 cháchǔ   判处 pànchǔ
See chū.

础 (礎) chǔ   10画 石部

础础础础础础础础
础础

[名]置于房柱下的石块叫础石：plinth

基础 jīchǔ

储 (儲) chǔ   12画 亻部

储储储储储储储储
储储储储

[动]积蓄；存放：store up; keep in reserve

储备 chǔbèi store for future use; lay in; lay up; reserve

储藏 chǔcáng save and preserve; store; keep

储存 chǔcún lay in; lay up; store up; keep in reserve; stockpile

储蓄 chǔxù save; deposit
存储 cúnchǔ

 (處) chū　5画 夂部

处 处处处处处

❶[名]地方：place; locality |
住～zhùchù *residence; lodging*
/ 故事说到伤心，听众也都落
下眼泪。Gùshi shuōdào
shāngxīn chù, tīngzhòng yě
dōu luòxià yǎnlèi. *The audience shed tears when the story
came to a climax.*
处处 chùchù everywhere; in all
respects
处所 chùsuǒ location
别处 biéchù　　出处 chūchù
四处 sìchù　　深处 shēnchù
办事处 bànshìchù

❷[名]部分：点：part of; centre
长处 chángchu
短处 duǎnchu　害处 hàichu
好处 hǎochu　坏处 huàichu
难处 nánchu
用处 yòngchu
恰到好处 qiàdào-hǎochù

❸[名]单位或单位里的一个部门：
department; office | 教育～
jiāoyùchù *educational department* / 财务～cáiwùchù
financial department / 人事～
rénshìchù *personnel division*

See chǔ.

 chū　10画 田部

畜 畜畜畜畜畜畜畜畜
畜畜

[名]禽兽；多指家畜：birds and
beasts; domestic animal; livestock
家畜 jiāchù　　牲畜 shēngchù
See xù.

触 (觸) chū　13画 角部

触 触触触触触触触触
触触触触触

❶[动]接触；碰；撞：touch | ～电
chūdiàn *get an electric shock* /
他用手～了一下我的肩膀。Tā
yòng shǒu chùle yīxià wǒ de
jiānbǎng. *He touched my
shoulder with his hand.*
接触 jiēchù

❷[动]触动；感动：touch; move
| ～动 chùdòng *touch sth.;
move sb.* / 这封信～起了他对往
事的回忆。Zhè fēng xìn
chùqǐle tā duì wǎngshì de
huíyì. *The letter awakened his
recollection of the past.*
触犯 chùfàn offend; go against;
violate

川 chuān 3画 丿部

川 川川川

❶[名]河流：river｜高山大～ gāoshān dàchuān *high mountains and big rivers* 川流不息 chuānliú-bùxī *flow past in an endless stream*

❷[名]平地，平原：plain

❸[名]指四川省：abbreviation for Sichuan Province 川菜 chuāncài Sichuan food; Sichuan cuisine

穿 chuān 9画 穴部

穿 穿穿穿穿穿穿穿穿穿

❶[动]破；透：bore (punch) a hole｜他在门上～了个小孔。Tā zài mén shang chuān le ge xiǎo kǒng. *He punched a hole through the door.* / 衣服上烧～了两个洞。Yīfu shang shāochuānle liǎng gè dòng. *Two holes are burnt in the coat.*

❷[动]从空隙里通过：go through｜～过这片小树林就看见海了。Chuānguo zhè piàn xiǎo shùlín jiù kànjiàn hǎi le. *Going through the woods, we'll come in sight of the sea.* / 行人迅速～过马路。Xíngrén xùnsù chuānguo mǎlù. *The pedestrians crossed the street quickly.* 穿越 chuānyuè pass through; cut across

❸[动]把物体串连起来：string together｜这是用贝壳～成的项链。Zhè shì yòng bèiké chuānchéng de xiàngliàn. *This is a necklace strung with shells.*

❹[动]把衣服、鞋袜等套在身上：put on dress, shoes, socks, etc.｜～衣服 chuān yīfu *put on clothes* 穿着 chuānzhuó dress; apparel

传（傳）chuān 6画 亻部

传 传传传传传传

❶[动]传递：deliver; transmit｜这些家产是他祖父～下来的。Zhèxiē jiāchǎn shì tā zǔfù chuán xiàlai de. *The family property is bequeathed from his grandfather.* / 这张纸条请往前～。Zhè zhāng zhǐtiáo qǐng wǎng qián chuán. *Please pass this slip of paper forward.* / 他～球～得又准又快。Tā chuánqiú chuán de yòu zhǔn yòu kuài. *He passed the ball fast and accurately.* 传达 chuándá ① pass on (information, etc.); transmit; relay; communicate ② reception and registration of callers at a public establishment

传递 chuándì transmit; deliver; transfer

传说 chuánshuō ① legend; tradition ② it is said; they say

传送 chuánsòng convey; deliver

传统 chuántǒng tradition

传奇 chuánqí legend; romance

传家宝 chuánjiābǎo ① family heirloom ② a cherished tradition or heritage

流传 liúchuán 遗传 yíchuán

❷ [动]传授；教给：pass on knowledge, skill, etc. to; teach | ~手艺 chuán shǒuyì *pass on craftsmanship* / 他年纪大了，想赶快把这些经验~下去。Tā niánjì dà le, xiǎng gǎnkuài bǎ zhèxiē jīngyàn chuán xiàqu. *As he is getting old, he wishes to pass on his experience (or skills) without delay.*

传授 chuánshòu pass on (knowledge, skill, etc.); impart; teach

❸ [动]传播；散布：disseminate; spread | 这个喜讯很快在全校~开了。Zhège xǐxùn hěn kuài zài quán xiào chuánkāi le. *The good news spread all over the school quickly.*

传播 chuánbō disseminate; propagate; spread

传单 chuándān leaflet; handbill; propaganda sheet

传媒 chuánméi media

传染 chuánrǎn infect; be contagious

传闻 chuánwén ① it is said; they say ② hearsay; rumour; talk

传言 chuányán hearsay; rumour

传染病 chuánrǎnbìng infectious disease

宣传 xuānchuán

❹ [动]表达：express; show | ~神 chuánshén *vivid; lifelike*

❺ [动]叫来：subpoena or summon people related to a case | 法院~他去一趟。Fǎyuàn chuán tā qù yī tàng. *He was summoned to court.*

❻ [动]传导：conduct; propagate | ~电 chuándiàn *conduct electricity* / 电波能~到很远的地方。Diànbō néng chuándào hěn yuǎn de dìfang. *Electrical current can be conducted over a long distance.*

传真 chuánzhēn fax

传真机 chuánzhēnjī fax machine

　See zhuàn.

船 chuán 11画 舟部

船船船船船船船船船船船

[名]ship; boat | 坐~zuòchuán *go*

by ship / 划~huáchuán *paddle (row) a boat; go boating*
船舶 chuánbó *shipping; boats and ships*
船员 chuányuán *(ship's) crew*
船只 chuánzhī *shipping; vessels*
渡船 dùchuán 帆船 fānchuán
轮船 lúnchuán 汽船 qìchuán
游船 yóuchuán 渔船 yúchuán

 喘 chuǎn 12画 口部

喘 喘喘喘喘喘喘喘喘喘 喘喘喘喘

[动]呼吸急促：breathe heavily; pant; puff | 等我~一口气再跟你说。Děng wǒ chuǎn yī kǒu qì zài gēn nǐ shuō. *Let me take a breath before I go on.* / 他一走快就~。Tā yī zǒukuài jiù chuǎn. *He pants whenever he walks fast.* / 屋子里闷得人都~不过气来。Wūzi li mēn de rén dōu chuǎnbuguò qì lái. *It is too stuffy to breathe in this room.*
气喘 qìchuǎn

串 chuàn 7画 丨部

串 串串串串串串串

❶[量]用于连贯在一起的东西：a string of | 一~钥匙 yī chuàn yàoshi *a bunch of keys* / 一~葡

萄 yī chuàn pútao *a cluster of grapes* / 这~葡萄有多重?Zhè chuàn pútao yǒu duō zhòng? *How much does this cluster of grapes weigh?*
❷[动]互相勾结：conspire; gang up
❸[动]往来；走动：go from one place to another | ~门儿 chuànménr *call at sb.'s home; drop in; stop by* / ~亲戚chuàn qīnqi *go visiting one's relatives*
❹[动]错乱地连接：connect wrongly | 他的电话经常~到我这里来。Tā de diànhuà jīngcháng chuàndào wǒ zhèli lai. *His phone calls are often misconnected with mine.* / 他念~行了，自己都没发现。Tā niàn chuànháng le, zìjǐ dōu méi fāxiàn. *He read the wrong line without being aware of it.*

 疮 (瘡) chuāng 9画 疒部

疮 疮疮疮疮疮疮疮疮 疮

[名]skin ulcer; boil | 腿上长了个~。Tuǐ shang zhǎngle ge chuāng. *There is a boil on my leg.*

窗 chuāng 12画 穴部

窗 窗窗窗窗窗窗窗窗 窗窗窗窗

[名]window | 关～guānchuāng *close the window* / 他喜欢开着～睡觉。Tā xǐhuan kāizhe chuāng shuìjiào. *He likes to sleep with the windows open.*
窗户 chuānghu window
窗花 chuānghuā paper-cut for window decoration
窗口 chuāngkǒu window
窗帘 chuānglián (window) curtain
窗台 chuāngtái windowsill

床 chuāng 7画 广部

床 床床床床床床床

❶[名]bed | 木～mùchuáng *wooden bed* / 这张～没人睡。Zhè zhāng chuáng méi rén shuì. *Nobody sleeps on this bed.*
床单 chuángdān sheet
床铺 chuángpù sleeping bunk
床位 chuángwèi berth; bunk; bed
病床 bìngchuáng
临床 línchuáng
起床 qǐchuáng
❷[名]像床的东西：sth. like a bed
车床 chēchuáng
机床 jīchuáng
❸[量]用于被子等：used for quilt, bunk, etc. | 一～被 yī chuáng bèi *a quilt*

闯 (闖) chuǎng 6画 门部

闯 闯闯闯闯闯闯

❶[动]猛冲：dash, charge | 突然外边～进一个人来。Tūrán wàibian chuǎngjìn yī gè rén lai. *Suddenly a man rushed in from the outside.*
❷[动]惹下：incur; get into trouble | 这个乱子是他～的。Zhège luànzi shì tā chuǎng de. *It was he who caused the trouble.*
闯祸 chuǎnghuò get into trouble; bring disaster
❸[动]经历，锻炼：experience; train oneself | 真不简单,他在外边居然～出名了。Zhēn bù jiǎndān, tā zài wàibian jūrán chuǎngchū míng le. *It is a wonder that he has become famous in the outside world.* / 年轻人应该到社会上去～一～。Niánqīngrén yīnggāi dào shèhuì shang qù chuǎngyichuǎng. *Young people should experience being a part of society.*

创 (創) chuàng 6画 刂部

创 创创创创创创

[动]开始做，初次做：begin to do sth.; do sth. for the first time | ～纪录 chuàng jìlù *make a new record* / 这份家业是他祖父～下的。Zhè fèn jiāyè shì tā zǔfù chuàngxià de. *The family property was built up by his grandfather.* / 他决心在这方面～出一番事业来。Tā juéxīn zài zhè fāngmiàn chuàngchū yī fān shìyè lai. *He was determined to start an undertaking in this field.*

创办 chuàngbàn establish; set up; found

创建 chuàngjiàn found; establish; set up

创立 chuànglì found; originate

创设 chuàngshè ① found; create; set up ② create (conditions, etc.)

创新 chuàngxīn innovate; create sth.

创业 chuàngyè start an undertaking; do pioneering work; found an undertaking

创意 chuàngyì original idea

创造 chuàngzào create; produce; bring about

创作 chuàngzuò ① create; produce; write ② creative work; creation

创始人 chuàngshǐrén founder; originator; initiator

创造性 chuàngzàoxìng creative power (or ability)

开创 kāichuàng

首创 shǒuchuàng

原创 yuánchuàng

吹 chuī 7画 口部

吹 吹吹吹吹吹吹吹

❶ [动] 合拢嘴唇用力吐气：blow with force | ～口哨 chuī kǒushào whistle / 他～了～手上的灰。Tā chuīlechuī shǒu shang de huī. *He blew the dust off his hand.* / 他把蜡烛～灭了。Tā bǎ làzhú chuīmiè le. *He blew out the candle.*

❷ [动] 吹气演奏：play (a wind instrument) | 他的笛子～得特别好。Tā de dízi chuī de tèbié hǎo. *He played the flute extremely well.*

❸ [动] 说大话；夸张：brag; boast | 别听他～，他根本干不了。Bié tīng tā chuī, tā gēnběn gànbuliǎo. *Don't believe his bragging. He can't do the job at all.* / 这个人做了一点儿事就到处～。Zhège rén zuòle yīdiǎnr shì jiù dàochū chuī. *This chap does little but boasts a lot.*

吹牛 chuīniú boast; brag; talk big

吹捧 chuīpěng flatter; laud to the skies; lavish praise on; extol

鼓吹 gǔchuī

❹ [动] 不成功：fall through; break off | 小王出国的事已经～了。Xiǎo Wáng chūguó de shì yǐjīng chuī le. *Xiao Wang's plan of going abroad has fallen through.*

❺[动]空气流动：blow｜那张纸被风～走了。Nà zhāng zhǐ bèi fēng chuīzǒu le. *That piece of paper was blown away by the wind.* / 北风呼呼地～着。Běifēng hūhū de chuīzhe. *The north wind was whistling.*

炊 chuī 8画 火部

炊 炊炊炊炊炊炊炊炊

[动]烧火做饭菜：cook a meal
炊事员 chuīshìyuán cook; kitchen staff

垂 chuí 8画 丿部

垂 垂垂垂垂垂垂垂垂

❶[动]挂下；低下：hang down; let fall｜～下头 chuíxià tóu *lower one's head*
垂直 chuízhí perpendicular; vertical
❷[动]流传：hand down
永垂不朽 yǒngchuí-bùxiǔ

捶 chuí 11画 扌部

捶 捶捶捶捶捶捶捶捶捶捶捶

[动]敲打：beat with a stick or fist｜你给我～～腰。Nǐ gěi wǒ chuí chui yāo. *I would like you to pound (massage) my waist.*

锤 (錘) chuí 13画 钅部

锤 锤锤锤锤锤锤锤锤锤锤锤锤锤

❶[名]hammer｜拿把～来敲钉子。Ná bǎ chuí lái qiāo dīngzi. *Go and get a hammer to drive in the nail.*
锤子 chuízi hammer
❷[动]用锤子打：beat with a hammer｜你把这根钉子～进去。Nǐ bǎ zhè gēn dīngzi chuí jìnqu. *Hammer in the nail, please.*

春 chūn 9画 日部

春 春春春春春春春春春

❶[名]春季：spring｜～夏秋冬 chūn-xià-qiū-dōng *spring, summer, autumn and winter*
春风 chūnfēng ① spring breeze ② a kindly and pleasant countenance
春耕 chūngēng spring ploughing
春季 chūnjì spring
春联 chūnlián Spring Festival couplets (pasted on gateposts or door panels conveying one's best wishes for the year); New Year couplets

123

春节 Chūnjié Spring Festival
春天 chūntiān spring
❷[名]生机；活力：life; vitality
青春 qīngchūn

 纯 (純) chún 7画 纟部

纯 纯纯纯纯纯纯纯

❶[形]单一；不杂：pure | 这块金子很～。Zhè kuài jīnzi hěn chún. *This bar of gold is of pure quality.* | 他的英语发音很～。Tā de Yīngyǔ fāyīn hěn chún. *He speaks standard English.*
纯粹 chúncuì ① pure; unadulterated ② solely; purely; only
纯洁 chúnjié ① pure; clean and honest ② purify
纯属 chúnshǔ purely belong to; be part of
单纯 dānchún
❷[形]熟练：skilled; proficient | 你的功夫还不～，还得练。Nǐ de gōngfu hái bù chún, hái děi liàn. *You are not skilful enough. Keep on practising.*

 唇 chún 10画 辰部

唇 唇唇唇唇唇唇唇唇
唇唇

[名] lip
嘴唇 zuǐchún

 醇 chún 15画 酉部

醇 醇醇醇醇醇醇醇醇
醇醇醇醇醇醇醇

[形]酒味浓厚：(of wine) mellow | ～酒 chúnjiǔ *mellow wine or spirit; rich wine*

 蠢 chún 21画 虫部

蠢 蠢蠢蠢蠢蠢蠢蠢蠢
蠢蠢蠢蠢蠢蠢蠢蠢
蠢蠢蠢蠢蠢

❶[形]愚笨；stupid; clumsy | 这件事你做得太～了。Zhè jiàn shì nǐ zuò de tài chǔn le. *You did a stupid thing.* / 这个人真～，这么简单的问题也不明白! Zhège rén zhēn chǔn, zhème jiǎndān de wèntí yě bù míngbai! *The man is so stupid that he cannot understand such a simple question!*
愚蠢 yúchǔn
❷[形]笨拙；clumsy; awkward | 他胖得都有些～了。Tā pàng de dōu yǒuxiē chǔn le. *He is so fat that he always appears clumsy.*

 词 (詞) cí 7画 讠部

词 词词词词词词词

❶ [名]语言里能独立运用的最小单位：word; term | 这些～他一个也不懂。Zhèxiē cí tā yī gè yě bū dǒng. *He knows none of these words.* / 你知道这个～的词性吗？Nǐ zhīdāo zhège cí de cíxìng ma? *Can you tell the part of speech of this word?*

词典 cídiǎn dictionary
词汇 cíhuì vocabulary; words and phrases
词句 cíjù words and phrases; expressions

代词 dàicí	单词 dāncí
动词 dòngcí	副词 fùcí
歌词 gēcí	介词 jiècí
连词 liáncí	量词 liàngcí
名词 míngcí	生词 shēngcí
实词 shící	叹词 tāncí
虚词 xūcí	组词 zǔcí

❷ [名]说话或诗歌、文章、戏剧中的语句：words in speeches, poems, articles, or plays | 他在台上一着急，忘～儿了。Tā zài tái shang yī zháojí, wàng cír le. *He was so nervous on stage that he forgot his lines.*

贺词 hècí 致词 zhìcí

❸ [名]古代一种诗歌体裁，句子有长有短：a kind of Chinese poetry written in fixed numbers of lines and words | 这位老先生填了一首～。Zhè wèi lǎo xiānsheng tiánle yī shǒu cí. *This old gentleman composed a piece of ci poetry.*

瓷 cí 10画 瓦部

瓷瓷瓷瓷瓷瓷瓷瓷瓷瓷

[名] porcelain | 这些碗碟都是～的。Zhèxiē wǎndié dōu shì cí de. *These bowls and plates are all made of porcelain.*

瓷瓶 cípíng ① china vase ② popular name of insulator
瓷器 cíqì porcelain; chinaware

辞 (辭) cí 13画 舌部

辞辞辞辞辞辞辞辞辞辞辞辞辞

❶ [动]不接受，请求离去：resign; bid farewell; say goodbye | 你还是～了工作吧。Nǐ háishì cíle gōngzuò ba. *You'd better resign from this job.* / 你怎么能这样随意地把工作～了？Nǐ zěnme néng zhèyàng suíyì de bǎ gōngzuò cí le? *How could you quit the job so casually?*

辞呈 cíchéng (written) resignation
辞去 cíqù decline; resign (one's post, duty, etc.)
辞职 cízhí resign; hand in one's resignation

❷[动]逃避；推却：decline
推辞 tuīcí

❸[动]解雇：dismiss; discharge |
他上班老迟到，最后被老板~
了。Tā shàngbān lǎo
chídào, zuìhòu bèi lǎobǎn
cí le. *At last, he got dismissed
by the boss for being always late
for work.*

❹[动]告别：take leave
告辞 gàocí
不辞而别 bùcí'érbié

慈　　cí　　13画 心部

慈慈慈慈慈慈慈慈
慈慈慈慈慈

[形]和善；怜惜：kind; loving
慈爱 cí'ài love; affection; kindness
慈善 císhàn charitable; benevolent; philanthropic
慈祥 cíxiáng kindly
仁慈 réncí

磁　　cí　　14画 石部

磁磁磁磁磁磁磁磁
磁磁磁磁磁磁

[名]magnetism | ~力 cílì *mag-
netic force*
磁带 cídài tape
磁卡 cíkǎ magnetic card
磁盘 cípán (computer) mag-
netic disk

磁铁 cítiě magnet; ferromagnet

雌　　cí　　14画 隹部

雌雌雌雌雌雌雌雌
雌雌雌雌雌雌

[形]母的；阴性的：female | ~性
cíxìng *female*

此　　cǐ　　6画 止部

此　此此此此此此

❶[代] 这；这个：this | ~人是这家
公司的经理。Cǐ rén shì zhèjiā
gōngsī de jīnglǐ. *This person
is the manager of this company.* /
~书的作者是位农民。Cǐ shū de
zuòzhě shì wèi nóngmín. *The
author of this book is a farmer.*
此后 cǐhòu from now on;
henceforward
此刻 cǐkè at present; now
此人 cǐrén this person
此时 cǐshí this moment; now
此事 cǐshì this matter
此外 cǐwài besides; in addition
彼此 bǐcǐ　　　　特此 tècǐ
因此 yīncǐ
由此可见 yóucǐ-kějiàn
❷[代]此地；此时：this place; here
| 在~集合 zài cǐ jíhé *assemble
here* / 谈话到~结束。Tánhuà
dào cǐ jiéshù. *The conversation
stops here.*

从此 cóngcǐ
岂有此理 qǐyǒu-cǐlǐ
与此同时 yǔcǐ-tóngshí
诸如此类 zhūrú-cǐlèi
❸[代] 这样：like this; such
如此 rúcǐ

 次　cì　6画 冫部

次 次次次次次次

❶[形]第二：second | ~日 cìrì the next day
❷[形]质量较差的；等级较低的：poor in quality; inferior | 你的成绩太~了! Nǐ de chéngjì tài cì le! Your score is too poor! / 这种布料很~。Zhè zhǒng bùliào hěn cì. This cloth is of poor quality.
次品 cìpǐn substandard goods
次要 cìyào less important; secondary; subordinate
其次 qícì
❸[名]顺序：order
次序 cìxù order; sequence
层次 céngcì　场次 chǎngcì
档次 dàngcì　名次 míngcì
依次 yīcì
❹[量]用于反复出现或可能反复出现的事情：occurrence; time | 无数~试验 wúshù cì shìyàn countless experiments / 我去过两~美国。Wǒ qùguo liǎng cì Měiguó. I have been to America twice. / 这个月我参加了三~会

议。Zhège yuè wǒ cānjiāle sān cì huìyì. I have attended three meetings this month.
次数 cìshù times
初次 chūcì　屡次 lǚcì
再次 zàicì　一次性 yīcìxìng
三番五次 sānfān-wǔcì

 伺　cì　7画 亻部

伺 伺伺伺伺伺伺伺

See 伺候
伺候 cìhou wait upon; serve

 刺　cì　8画 刂部

刺 刺刺刺刺刺刺刺刺

❶[动]尖的东西扎入或穿透：stab with sth. pointed | 我的手被鱼刺~了。Wǒ de shǒu bèi yúcì cì le. My hand was pricked by a fishbone. / 蜜蜂~了我一下。Mìfēng cìle wǒ yīxià. I was stung by a bee.
刺绣 cìxiù ① embroider ② embroidery
冲刺 chōngcì
❷[动]挖苦；嘲讽：ridicule; satirize
讽刺 fěngcì
❸[名]尖锐像针的东西：sth. like a pin; thorn; prickle | 手上扎了个~儿。Shǒu shang zhāle ge cìr. My hand got pricked by a thorn. / 这种鱼好吃，但是~多。

Zhē zhǒng yú hǎo chī, dànshì cì duō. *This kind of fish tastes good, but it has too many bones.*

❹ [动]刺激：stimulate; irritate | 阳光～得人睁不开眼。Yángguāng cì de rén zhēngbu-kāi yǎn. *Dazzled by the sun, I cannot open my eyes.* / 我故意用话～他。Wǒ gùyì yòng huà cì tā. *I said this to irritate him.*
刺激 cìjī stimulate

匆 cōng 5画 勹部
匆 匆匆匆匆匆

[形]急促：hastily; hurriedly
匆匆 cōngcōng hurriedly; in a rush; in haste
匆忙 cōngmáng hastily; in a hurry; in haste

葱 cōng 12画 艹部
葱 葱葱葱葱葱葱葱葱 葱葱葱葱

[名] 一种用作蔬菜或调味品的草本植物：spring onion
大葱 dàcōng 洋葱 yángcōng

聪 (聰) cōng 15画 耳部
聪 聪聪聪聪聪聪聪聪 聪聪聪聪聪聪聪

[形]智力强：bright; intelligent
聪明 cōngmíng clever; bright

从 (從) cóng 4画 人部
从 从从从从

❶ [动]听从；依顺：obey
服从 fúcóng 盲从 mángcóng
❷ [动]做；参与：participate
从事 cóngshì ① go in for; be engaged in ② deal with
从业 cóngyè obtain employment
❸ [介]表示时间、处所或范围的起点：from (a time, a place, a point of view, etc.) | ～明天起开始上课。Cóng míngtiān qǐ kāishǐ shàngkè. *Class will begin tomorrow.* / 我刚～学校回来。Wǒ gāng cóng xuéxiào huílai. *I've just come back from school.* / ～不懂到懂，他付出了很大的努力。Cóng bù dǒng dào dǒng, tā fùchūle hěn dà de nǔlì. *He has built up his knowledge from scratch through strenuous effort.*
从…出发 cóng...chūfā from (a time, a place, or a point of view)
从此 cóngcǐ from now on
从而 cóng'ér thus; thereby
从前 cóngqián before; in the past
从头 cóngtóu from the begin-

ning

从小 cóngxiǎo from childhood; as a child

从中 cóngzhōng out of; from among; therefrom

从⋯到⋯ cóng... dào... from... to...

从⋯看来 cóng... kànlái view from...; observe from...

从⋯起 cóng... qǐ from... (certain time, certain thing, etc.) onwards

从头到尾 cóngtóu dàowěi from the very beginning to the very end; from top to bottom

无从 wúcóng   自从 zìcóng

❹ [介]表示经过的路线：route; line | ~小路走 cóng xiǎolù zǒu *walk along a path* / 我每天都~这个商场门前经过。Wǒ měi tiān dōu cóng zhège shāngchǎng ménqián jīngguò. *I walk past this store every day.* / 火车~大桥上驶过。Huǒchē cóng dàqiáo shang shǐguò. *The train runs along the bridge.*

❺ [介]表示凭借、根据：base on; go by | ~小事做起 cóng xiǎoshì zuòqǐ *start from doing sth. small* / 作决策要~实际出发。Zuò juécè yào cóng shíjì chūfā. *Decision making should be based on the actual situation.*

❻ [副]一向；向来：earlier on; lately

| ~不计较 cóngbù jìjiào *never give any consideration to* / ~没听说过这件事。Cóngméi tīngshuōguo zhè jiàn shì. *I've never heard of it.*

从不 cóngbù never

从来 cónglái at all times; always

从没 cóngméi ⇒从不

从未 cóngwèi never

◇从容 cóngróng calm; unhurried; leisurely

从容不迫 cóngróng-bùpò take it leisurely; go easy; calm and unhurried

 丛 (叢) cóng   5画 一部

丛 丛丛丛丛丛

[名]聚集在一起的人或东西：gather; crowd together | ~书 cóngshū *a series of books; collection* / 我看着他消失在树~中。Wǒ kànzhe tā xiāoshī zài shùcóng zhōng. *I saw him disappearing into the woods.*

 凑 còu   11画 冫部

凑 凑凑凑凑凑凑凑凑 凑凑凑

❶ [动]聚集：crowd together | 几个人~在一起说说笑笑。Jǐ gè rén còu zài yīqǐ shuōshuo-xiāoxiào. *Several people got together, talking and laughing.* / 再加一个学生就可以～一个班。Zài jiā yī ge xuésheng jiù kěyǐ còu yī ge bān. *Add one more student to form a class.*

❷ [动]接近：approach; move close to | ～近点儿。Còu jìn diǎnr. *Come closer, please.* / 小黄～上来跟他打招呼。Xiǎo Huáng còu shànglai gēn tā dǎ zhāohu. *Xiao Huang went up to greet him.* / 他拿起一束鲜花～着鼻子闻。Tā náqǐ yī shù xiānhuā còuzhe bízi wén. *He picked up a bunch of flowers and pressed it to his nose to smell it.*

凑热闹 còurènao join in the fun

❸ [动]碰上；赶：happen to | 正～上是个星期天。Zhèng còushang shì ge xīngqītiān. *It happened to be a Sunday.*

粗粗粗粗粗粗粗粗粗粗粗

cū　11画　米部

❶ [形]不精致：coarse; crude | 这手工活儿真～。Zhè shǒugōnghuór zhēn cū. *The workmanship of this is very coarse.* / 他的手艺～得很。Tā de shǒuyì cūdehěn. *His craftsmanship is quite poor.*

粗粮 cūliáng coarse food grains

❷ [形]疏忽；不周密：careless | 这个人就是心太～。Zhège rén jiù shì xīn tài cū. *This person is rather careless.*

粗心 cūxīn careless; thoughtless

粗心大意 cūxīn-dàyì negligent; careless

❸ [形]粗大：wide; thick | 这棵树真～。Zhè kē shù zhēn cū. *This tree has a thick trunk.*

粗细 cūxì (degree of) thickness

❹ [形]声音低而响：(of sound) low and resonant | 他说话声音真～。Tā shuōhuà shēngyīn zhēn cū. *He has a husky voice.*

❺ [形]鲁莽；没礼貌：rude; rough | 他满口～话，真没修养。Tā mǎnkǒu cūhuà, zhēn méi xiūyǎng. *He always speaks rudely. What a poorly-bred man he is!*

粗暴 cūbào rude; rough; crude; brutal

粗鲁 cūlǔ rough; rude; boorish

❻ [副]略微：slightly; a little | ～略 cūlüè rough; sketchy

促促促促促促促促促

cù　9画　亻部

❶ [形]急迫；时间紧：in a hurry; in haste

仓促 cāngcù　短促 duǎncù

❷ [动]催促；推动：promote; advance

促成 cùchéng help to bring about; facilitate

促进 cùjìn promote; advance; accelerate

促使 cùshǐ impel; urge; spur

促销 cùxiāo promote

督促 dūcù

醋　cù　15画 酉部

醋醋醋醋醋醋醋醋醋醋醋醋醋醋醋

[名]vinegar | 这~真够酸的。Zhè cù zhēn gòu suān de. *This vinegar is really sour.*

醋坛子cùtánzi a jealous woman

簇　cù　17画 竹部

簇簇簇簇簇簇簇簇簇簇簇簇簇簇簇簇簇

[量]用于聚集成团或成堆的东西：cluster | 一~鲜花 yī cù xiānhuā *a bunch of flowers* / 一~人群 yī cù rénqún *a group of people*

窜（竄）cuàn　12画 穴部

窜窜窜窜窜窜窜窜窜窜窜窜窜

[动]奔逃；乱跑：flee; scurry | 一群小鹿被狼追赶得在林中乱~。Yī qún xiǎolù bèi láng zhuīgǎn de zài lín zhōng luàncuàn. *Chased by wolves, a group of deer fled in all directions in the forest.* / 在阅览室，别~来~去的。Zài yuèlǎnshì, bié cuān lái cuān qù de. *Don't rush around in the reading room.* / 老鼠一下子~到洞里去了。Lǎoshǔ yīxiàzi cuàndào dòng li qù le. *The mouse scurried into the hole.*

催　cuī　13画 亻部

催催催催催催催催催催催催催

❶ [动]叫人赶快行动：urge; press | 学校~我回去。Xuéxiào cuī wǒ huíqu. *The school urged me to return.* / 妈妈~女儿快起床。Māma cuī nǚ'ér kuài qǐchuáng. *The mother hurried her daughter to get up.* / 他又来电话~了。Tā yòu lái diànhuà cuī le. *He called again to urge us on.*

❷ [动]使事物的产生和变化加快：hasten or speed up the production or development of certain things | 这种药可以~你很快入

睡。Zhè zhǒng yào kěyǐ cuī nǐ hěn kuài rùshuì. *This medicine can help you fall asleep very quickly.*

摧 **cuī** 14画 扌部

摧摧摧摧摧摧摧摧摧摧摧摧摧摧

[动]折断；毁坏：break; destroy; ruin

摧残 cuīcán wreck; destroy; devastate

摧毁 cuīhuǐ destroy; smash; wreck

脆 **cuì** 10画 月部

脆脆脆脆脆脆脆脆脆脆

❶[形]容易断或碎：fragile; brittle | 玻璃很～。Bōli hěn cuì. *Glass is very brittle.* / 这种金属管比较～，容易断。Zhè zhǒng jīnshǔguǎn bǐjiào cuì, róngyì duàn. *This kind of metal tube is rather brittle and easy to break.*

脆弱 cuìruò fragile; frail; weak

❷[形]声音清亮：clear; crisp | 他说话的声音很～。Tā shuōhuà de shēngyīn hěn cuì. *He has a very clear voice.* / 她的嗓音又～又甜。Tā de sǎngyīn yòu cuì yòu tián. *Her voice is clear and sweet.*

❸[形]说话做事爽利痛快：be crisp; be clean-cut; be frank

干脆 gāncuì

粹 **cuì** 14画 米部

粹粹粹粹粹粹粹粹粹粹粹粹粹粹

[形]纯；不杂：pure

纯粹 chúncuì

◇纳粹 Nàcuì

翠 **cuì** 14画 羽部

翠翠翠翠翠翠翠翠翠翠翠翠翠翠

[形]青绿色：emerald green

翠绿 cuìlǜ emerald green; jade green

村 **cūn** 7画 木部

村村村村村村村

[名]村庄：village

村民 cūnmín villager; village people

村庄 cūnzhuāng village

村子 cūnzi village

农村 nóngcūn 乡村 xiāngcūn

存 cún 6画 子部

存 存存存存存存

❶[动]存在；活着：alive | 这位老人六十多了，父母俱~。Zhè wèi lǎorén liùshí duō le, fùmǔ jù cún. *This old man is over sixty years old, yet his parents are still alive.*
存在 cúnzài exist; be
并存 bìngcún　生存 shēngcún

❷[动]积聚；保存：keep in store; preserve | 冰箱里~了好多肉和菜。Bīngxiāng li cúnle hǎo duō ròu hé cài. *A lot of meat and vegetables are kept in the refrigerator.*
存储 cúnchǔ (electron.) memory; storage
存款 cúnkuǎn savings
存盘 cúnpán (computer) save
存折 cúnzhé deposit book; bankbook
保存 bǎocún　储存 chǔcún
库存 kùcún　内存 nèicún

❸[动]寄放：leave with | 把自行车~在寄车处。Bǎ zìxíngchē cún zài jìchēchù. *Leave your bicycle in the bicycle park.* / 这些东西暂时在你这儿~一下行吗? Zhèxiē dōngxi zànshí zài nǐ zhèr cún yīxià xíng ma? *May I leave these things temporarily in your care?*

存放 cúnfàng leave with; leave in sb.'s care
❹[动]心中怀有：keep in mind | 不~幻想 bù cún huànxiǎng *harbour no illusions* / 我对他~有很大希望。Wǒ duì tā cúnyǒu hěn dà xīwàng. *I have high hopes for him.*
❺[动]保留：reserve; retain | 有话快说，别~在肚子里。Yǒu huà kuài shuō, bié cún zài dùzi li. *Speak up. Don't hold your tongue.*

寸 cùn 3画 寸部

寸 寸寸寸

[量]长度单位，市寸的通称：*cun*, a traditional unit of length, equal to one tenth of one *chi*
尺寸 chǐcùn　分寸 fēncun
英寸 yīngcùn

搓 cuō 12画 扌部

搓 搓搓搓搓搓搓搓搓 搓搓搓搓

[动]两手相对摩擦或用手来回揉擦别的东西：rub with one's hands on sth. repeatedly | 衣服太脏了，得用手~洗。Yīfu tài zāng le, děi yòng shǒu cuōxǐ. *The clothes are so dirty that you must wash them by hand.* / 天

气冷得他直～双手。Tiān qì lěng de tā zhí cuō shuāngshǒu. *It is so cold that he has to rub his hands to keep warm.*

磋　　cuō　14画 石部

See 磋商

磋商 cuōshāng consult; exchange views

撮　　cuō　15画 扌部

❶[动]用手指捏取（细碎的东西）：take up with fingers｜～了一点儿盐。Cuōle yīdiǎnr yán. *Take a pinch of salt.*

❷[量]用于可用手撮的东西，借指极小的量：used to indicate a tiny amount｜一～盐 yī cuō yán *a pinch of salt* / 一～茶叶 yī cuō cháyè *a pinch of tea*

蹉　　cuō　16画 𧾷部

See 蹉跎

蹉跎 cuōtuó waste time

挫　　cuō　10画 扌部

[动]事情进行得不顺利；失败：defeat; frustrate

挫折 cuòzhé setback; frustration

措　　cuò　11画 扌部

See 措施

措施 cuòshī measure; step

错（錯）cuò　13画 钅部

❶[动]交叉；杂乱：interlocked and jagged; complex

交错 jiāocuò

❷[形]不正确；与事实不符：wrong; mistaken｜别把东西放～了地方。Bié bǎ dōngxi fàngcuòle dìfang. *Do not put your things in the wrong place.* / 这道题目我做～了。Zhè dào tímù wǒ zuòcuò le. *I got this question wrong.* / 她～把我当成她妈妈了。Tā cuò bǎ wǒ dàngchéng tā māma le. *She mistook me for her mother.*

错过 cuòguò miss; let slip

错误 cuòwù ① wrong; mistaken; erroneous ②mistake; error; blunder

错字 cuòzì misprint; wrongly written character

差错 chācuò

❸ [名] 过失：fault | 这是我的～。 Zhè shì wǒ de cuò. *This is my fault.* / 我向你认个～。Wǒ xiàng nǐ rèn ge cuò. *I must apologize to you.*

过错 guòcuò

❹ [形]坏；差(用于否定式)：bad; poor (used in negative sentences) | 这幅画儿画得不～。 Zhè fú huàr huà de bùcuò. *This painting is not bad.* / 她们俩的关系不～。Tāmen liǎ de guānxi bùcuò. *They are on good terms with each other.* / 菜的味道不～。Cài de wèidào bùcuò. *The dish tastes good.*

不错 bùcuò

❺ [动]避开，使不碰上或不冲突：avoid; evade | ～开会议时间 cuòkāi huìyì shíjiān *stagger the time for the meeting*

错位cuòwèi (med.) dislocation

D d

搭 dā 12画 扌部

搭搭搭搭搭搭搭搭搭搭搭搭搭

❶ [动]轻放；附挂：put over; hang over | 毛巾～在肩上 máojīn dā zài jiān shang *put a towel over one's shoulder* / 衣服～在竹竿上 yīfu dā zài zhúgān shang *hang the washing on a bamboo pole*

❷ [动]乘；坐：take (a ship, plane, train, etc.); travel by | ～车 dāchē *take a bus* / ～船 dāchuán *travel by ship* / 他总算～上了最后一班飞机。Tā zǒngsuàn dāshangle zuìhòu yī bān fēijī. *He caught the last flight in the end.*

搭乘 dāchéng travel by (plane, car, ship, etc.)

搭载 dāzài (of trucks, freighters, etc.) pick up extra passengers or freight

❸ [动]支架起来：put up; build | ～桥 dā qiáo *build a bridge* / ～棚子 dā péngzi *put up a shed* / 喜鹊在树上～了一个窝。Xǐquè zài shù shang dāle yī gè wō. *The magpie built a nest in the tree.*

搭建 dājiàn put up (a shed, etc.)

❹ [动]配合：arrange in pairs or groups

搭配 dāpèi ① arrange in pairs or groups ② collocation

搭档 dādàng ① partner ② co-operate; work together

❺ [动]附加上：add | 卖大的～小的 mài dà de dā xiǎo de *sell big ones together with small ones* / 为了帮助她学习，我～进去很多时间。Wèile bāngzhù tā xuéxí, wǒ dā jìnqù hěn duō shíjiān. *I spent a lot of time helping her with her studies.*

❻ [动]连接：come into contact; join | 前言不～后语 qiányán bù dā hòuyǔ *speak incoherently; mumble disconnected phrases* / 两根电线～在一起。Liǎng gēn diànxiàn dā zài yīqǐ. *The two wires are joined.*

答 dā 12画 竹部

答答答答答答答答答答答答

[动]用于口语表示"答应""答理"等：used in spoken language as 答应(dāying) and 答理(dāli)

答理 dāli respond

答应 dāying ① answer; reply; respond ② promise; agree

See dá.

达（達）**dá** 6画 辶部

达 达达达达达达

❶[动]通；到：reach; get to｜四通八~sìtōng-bādá *extend in all directions* / 这列火车直~北京。Zhè liè huǒchē zhídá Běijīng. *This is a through train to Beijing.*
到达 dàodá　　抵达 dǐdá

❷[动]实现：realize; attain｜~成协议 dáchéng xiéyì *reach an agreement* / 我们不~目的决不罢休。Wǒmen bù dá mùdì juébù bàxiū. *We will never give up until we achieve our goal.*
达标 dábiāo reach a set standard
达成 dáchéng reach (agreement, etc.)
达到 dádào achieve; attain; reach

❸[动]通晓明白：understand thoroughly｜通情~理 tōngqíng-dálǐ *be understanding and reasonable*

❹[动]告知；表达：express; communicate; convey｜词不~意 cíbùdáyì *the words fail to convey the idea*
表达 biǎodá　传达 chuándá
下达 xiàdá　　转达 zhuǎndá

❺[形]显贵：distinguished; eminent｜显~xiǎndá *eminent; distinguished*

答 **dá** 12画 竹部

答 答答答答答答答答答答答答

❶[动]回答；回复：answer; reply; respond｜一问一~ yī wèn yī dá *question and answer* / 老师提的问题我都~对了。Lǎoshī tí de wèntí wǒ dōu dáduì le. *I answered all the teacher's questions correctly.* / 他想了半天也~不出来。Tā xiǎngle bàntiān yě dá bù chūlái. *After thinking for a long time, he still couldn't answer the question.*
答案 dá'àn　answer; solution
答辩 dábiàn reply (to a charge, query, or an argument)
答复 dáfù　answer; reply
答卷 dájuàn examination paper
答谢 dáxiè express appreciation (for sb.'s kindness or hospitality)
解答 jiědá　　　问答 wèndá

❷[动]回报别人给自己的好处：return; reciprocate
报答 bàodá
See dā.

 打 **dǎ** 5画 扌部

打 打打打打打

❶[动]击；敲：strike; hit; beat｜~钟 dǎzhōng *ring the bell* / 趁

热～铁 chènrè-dǎtiě *strike while the iron is hot*

打鼓 dǎgǔ beat a drum

抽打 chōudǎ

敲锣打鼓 qiāoluó-dǎgǔ

❷[动]物体因受撞击而破碎：break; smash ｜ 别把玻璃杯～了。Biè bǎ bōlibēi dǎ le. *Be careful not to break the glass.* / 花瓶～得粉碎。Huāpíng dǎ de fěnsuì. *The vase was smashed to pieces.*

❸[动]攻打；殴打：fight; attack ｜ ～成一团 dǎchéng yī tuán *fight together* / 这两个男孩又～起来了。Zhè liǎng gè nánhái yōu dǎ qǐlai le. *The two boys are fighting again.*

打败 dǎbài defeat; beat

打倒 dǎdǎo overthrow

打击 dǎjī hit; strike; attack

打架 dǎjià come to blows; fight; scuffle

打破 dǎpō break; smash

打人 dǎrén beat a person

打仗 dǎzhàng fight; go to war; make war

打嘴仗 dǎzuǐzhàng quarrel; bicker; wrangle

❹[动]放射；发出：send; dispatch ｜ ～电话 dǎ diànhuà *make a telephone call*

打雷 dǎléi thunder

拨打 bōdǎ

❺[动]发生与人交涉的行为：negotiate; make representations ｜ ～官司 dǎguānsi *go to court (against sb.)*

打交道 dǎjiāodǎo come into contact with

❻[动]建筑；制造：construct; build ｜ ～墙 dǎ qiáng *build a wall* / ～地基 dǎ dìjī *lay a foundation* / ～首饰 dǎ shǒushi *make jewellery* / ～家具 dǎ jiājù *make furniture*

打造 dǎzào make (metal work); forge

❼[动]捆；收拾：tie up; pack ｜ ～包 dǎbāo *tie up in a bundle* / 行李已经～好了。Xíngli yǐjīng dǎhǎo le. *The luggage has been packed.*

❽[动]编织：knit; weave ｜ ～毛衣 dǎ máoyī *knit a sweater* / ～草鞋 dǎ cǎoxié *weave straw sandals*

❾[动]翻动，开启：open ｜ 请大家把书～开。Qǐng dàjiā bǎ shū dǎkāi. *Please open your books.* / ～开箱子 dǎkāi xiāngzi *open the chest (trunk)*

打开 dǎkāi ① open; unfold ② turn on; switch on

打通 dǎtōng get through; open up

❿[动]涂抹；写画；印：make a mark on; draw ｜ ～鞋油 dǎ xiéyóu *polish one's shoes with shoe polish* / ～图样 dǎ túyàng *draw a pattern* / ～分数 dǎ fēnshù *give a mark* / ～手印 dǎ shǒuyìn *put one's fingerprint on (a*

document)

打卡 dǎkǎ punch the clock

打印 dǎyìn typing and print-ing

打印机 dǎyìnjī printer

⓫ [动]举；提：raise; hoist | ~灯笼 dǎ dēnglong *carry a lantern* / ~起精神来 dǎqǐ jīngshen lái *raise one's spirits; cheer up*

打伞 dǎsǎn hold up an um-brella

打旗 dǎqí hold up a flag

⓬ [动]舀取：draw, fetch | 从井里~水 cóng jǐng li dǎshuǐ *draw water from a well*

打水 dǎshuǐ draw water

⓭ [动]割取：collect; reap | ~粮食 dǎ liángshi *gather in grain*

打草 dǎcǎo mow down the hay

打柴 dǎchái gather firewood

⓮ [动]捉(鱼、禽、兽等)：catch; hunt | ~鱼 dǎyú *catch fish*

⓯ [动]注入：inject

打针 dǎzhēn give or receive an injection

⓰ [动]盘算；计划：work out; draw | ~草稿 dǎ cǎogǎo *work out a draft* / ~主意 dǎ zhǔyi *think up an idea*

打算 dǎsuan intend; plan; think; mean

精打细算 jīngdǎ-xìsuàn

⓱ [动]表示身体上的某些动作：used to indicate certain body move-ments | ~手势 dǎ shǒushì *make a gesture* / ~哆嗦 dǎ

duōsuo *tremble; shiver* / ~瞌睡 dǎ kēshuì *doze off; nod*

⓲ [动]做；从事：do; engage in | ~夜班 dǎ yèbān *go on night shift*

打工 dǎgōng work for others; be employed

打下手 dǎxiàshǒu act as an assistant; be a helper

打杂儿 dǎzár do odds and ends

⓳ [动]进行某些球类活动或游戏：play | ~秋千 dǎ qiūqiān *play on a swing* / ~篮球 dǎ lánqiú *play basketball* / ~扑克 dǎ pūkè *play poker; play cards*

打球 dǎqiú play a ball game

单打 dāndǎ

⓴ [动]采取某种行为或方法：adopt; use

打比方 dǎbǐfang draw an anal-ogy

打官腔 dǎguānqiāng speak in a bureaucratic tone; confuse with official jargon

打招呼 dǎzhāohu greet; say hello; tip one's hat; give a pre-vious notice; warn

㉑ [动]购买：buy (using one's own container) | ~酒 dǎjiǔ *buy some wine (using one's own container)*

打票 dǎpiào buy a ticket

㉒ [动]与其他动词结合成一个动词：used with other verbs to form a new verb

打扮 dǎban dress up; make up;

deck out

打发 dǎfa ① send; dispatch ② dismiss; send away ③ while away (one's time)

打量 dǎliang ① measure with one's eyes; look sb. up and down; size up ②think; suppose; reckon

打猎 dǎliè go hunting

打扰 dǎrǎo disturb; trouble

打扫 dǎsǎo sweep; clean

打听 dǎting ask about; inquire about

❷ [介]自；从：from; since | ~今天起 dǎ jīntiān qǐ *from now on* / ~这儿走。Dǎ zhèr zǒu. *This way, please.* / 他~门缝里往外看。Tā dǎ ménfèng li wǎng wài kàn. *He looked out through the crack between the door and its frame.*

◇ 打车 dǎchē call a taxi; take a taxi

打动 dǎdòng move; touch

大 dà 3画 大部

大 大大大

❶ [形]面积超过一般或所比较的对象：big; large | ~城市 dà chéngshì *a big city* / 这间房比那间~。Zhè jiān fáng bǐ nà jiān dà. *This room is bigger than that one.*

大地 dàdì the earth

大陆 dàlù continent; mainland

大海 dàhǎi sea; ocean

大西洋 Dàxīyáng the Atlantic (Ocean)

大洋洲 Dàyángzhōu Oceania; Australasia

大自然 dàzìrán nature

广大 guǎngdà

❷ [形]宽度超过一般或所比较的对象：wide; main

大道 dàdào wide road; main road

大街 dàjiē main street; street

大街小巷 dàjiē-xiǎoxiàng streets and lanes

❸ [形]形体、形制超过一般或所比较的对象：big; large; great

大葱 dàcōng green Chinese onion

大豆 dàdòu soybean; soya bean

大风 dàfēng ① gale; strong wind ② (meteorol.) fresh gale

大楼 dàlóu multi-storied building

大门 dàmén entrance (or front) door; gate

大米 dàmǐ rice

大脑 dànǎo cerebrum; brain

大炮 dàpào artillery; big gun; cannon

大厦 dàshà large building

大腿 dàtuǐ thigh

大象 dàxiàng elephant

大小 dàxiǎo ① size ② big or small

大型 dàxíng large-scale; large

大衣 dàyī overcoat

大白菜 dàbáicài Chinese cabbage

大肚子 dàdùzi (inf.) ① pregnant ② big eater ③ pot belly

大头菜 dàtóucài (bot.) rutabaga; swede

大拇指 dàmǔzhǐ thumb

大手大脚 dàshǒu-dàjiǎo wasteful; extravagant

高大 gāodà   巨大 jùdà

宽大 kuāndà   庞大 pángdà

❹ [形] 规模超过一般或所比较的对象: main; major | ~手术 dàshǒu-shù *major operation*

大餐 dàcān ① a sumptuous meal ② Western-style food

大幅 dàfú by a wide margin

大会 dàhuì ① plenary session ② mass meeting; mass rally

大奖 dàjiǎng award at the highest level or with large prize

大举 dàjǔ carry out (a military operation) on a large scale

大赛 dàsài match on a large scale and high level

大选 dàxuǎn general election

大吃大喝 dàchī-dàhē eat and drink to one's heart's content; eat and drink extravagantly

夸大 kuādà   宏大 hóngdà

盛大 shèngdà

❺ [形] 重要的; 主要的: important; great | ~人物 dà rénwù *important person; great personage*

大臣 dàchén minister (of a monarchy)

大概 dàgài general; rough; approximate

大局 dàjú overall situation

大师 dàshī ① great master; master ② Great Master, a courtesy title used to address a Buddhist monk

大事 dàshì major event; important matter; major issue

大体 dàtǐ ① on the whole; by and large; roughly ② general interest; fundamental principle

大王 dàwáng ① king; magnate ② a person of the highest class or skill in sth.; ace

大意 dàyì ① general idea; main points; gist; tenor ② careless; negligent; inattentive

大致 dàzhì generally; roughly; approximately; more or less

大手笔 dàshǒubǐ ① the work of a well-known writer ② a well-known writer

大同小异 dàtóng-xiǎoyì much the same but with minor differences; alike except for slight differences; very much the same

重大 zhòngdà

顾全大局 gùquán-dàjú

❻ [形] 数量多: in great number

大半 dàbàn ① more than half ② very likely; most probably

大都 dàdū for the most part; mostly

141

大队 dàduì a military unit corresponding to a battalion or regiment

大多 dàduō for the most part; mostly

大家 dàjiā all; everybody

大量 dàliàng a large number; a great quantity

大批 dàpī large quantity or number; large amount of

大众 dàzhòng the masses; the public; the broad masses of the people

大多数 dàduōshù great (vast) majority; the bulk

大伙儿 dàhuǒr we all; all of us

广大 guǎngdà

发扬光大 fāyáng-guāngdà

❼ [形]某方面的能力超过一般或所比较的对象：great

大胆 dàdǎn bold; daring; audacious

大方 dàfang ① generous; liberal ② natural and poised; easy; unaffected

伟大 wěidà

❽ [形]职位、等级较高的：of higher rank or class

大使 dàshǐ ambassador

大学 dàxué college; university

大使馆 dàshǐguǎn embassy

大学生 dàxuéshēng university (or college) student

❾ [形]超过实际情况，不真实的：not true

大话 dàhuà big talk; boast;

bragging

说大话 shuōdàhuà

❿ [形]用的力量超过一般或所比较的对象：strong; heavy

大力 dàlì energetically; vigorously

大声 dàshēng loud voice

大肆 dàsì without restraint; wantonly

大喊大叫 dàhǎn-dàjiào shout at the top of one's voice

⓫ [副]程度深：greatly; fully｜～吃一惊 dàchīyījīng *be greatly surprised; be quite taken aback* ／～有问题 dà yǒu wèntí *very problematic* ／天已经～亮了。Tiān yǐjīng dàliàng le. *It is already broad daylight.*

大大 dàdà greatly; enormously

大有可为 dàyǒu-kěwéi be well worth doing

粗心大意 cūxīn-dàyì

恍然大悟 huǎngrán-dàwù

⓬ [形]范围较广：vast in range

放大 fàngdà 扩大 kuòdà

远大 yuǎndà 壮大 zhuàngdà

⓭ [形]年长；排行第一：eldest｜～哥 dàgē *eldest brother* ／～嫂 dàsǎo *eldest sister-in-law*

大姐 dàjiě ① eldest sister ② elder sister (a polite form of address for a woman about one's own age)

大妈 dàmā ① father's elder brother's wife; aunt ② aunt (an

affectionate or respectful form of address for an elderly woman)

大娘 dàniáng aunt (a respectful form of address for an elderly woman)

大爷 dàye (inf.) ① father's elder brother; uncle ② uncle (a respectful form of address for an elderly man)

老大爷 lǎodàye

⑭ [形] 再；时间更远：earlier in time

大后年 dàhòunián three years from now

大后天 dàhòutiān three days from now

大前天 dàqiántiān three days ago

⑮ [形] 敬词，称与对方有关的事物：term of respect | ~作 dàzuò *your work; your writing* / 尊姓~名? Zūnxìng dàmíng? *May I have your name?*

⑯ [形] 年纪大小：of age | 你的孩子多~了?Nǐ de háizi duō dà le? *How old is your child?* / 他比我三岁。Tā bǐ wǒ dà sān suì. *He is three years older than me.*

大人 dàrén ① adult; grown-up ② Your (His) Excellency

⑰ [副] 跟 "不bù" 连用，表示程度浅或次数少：used after "不bù" to indicate low degree or frequency | 不~清楚 bùdà qīngchu *not too clear* / 他对这个工作不~满意。Tā duì zhè-

ge gōngzuò bùdà mǎnyì. *He is not very satisfied with this job.* / 他不~看电影。Tā bùdà kàn diànyǐng. *He seldom goes to the cinema.*

◇大便 dàbiàn defecate; have a bowel movement

大气 dàqì ① (meteorol.) atmosphere; air ② heavy breathing

大蒜 dàsuàn garlic

大雁 dàyàn wild goose

大约 dàyuē approximately; about

大理石 dàlǐshí marble

大气压 dàqìyā atmospheric pressure; atmosphere

大舌头 dàshétou thick-tongued person; one who lisps

马大哈 mǎdàhā

呆 dāi 7画 口部

呆 呆呆呆呆呆呆呆

❶ [形] 傻；愚蠢 stupid; silly

❷ [形] 不灵活；死板：slow-witted; dull | ~头~脑 dāitóu-dāinǎo *dull-looking* / ~~地望着 dāidāi de wàngzhe *stare at sth. blankly* / 这个人有些~。Zhè gè rén yǒuxiē dāi. *This person is slow-witted.*

书呆子 shūdāizi

❸ [动] 停留；迟延：stay | 他在北京~了几天。Tā zài Běijīng dāile jǐ tiān. *He stayed in*

Beijing for several days.

歹 dǎi 4画 歹部

歹 歹 歹 歹 歹

[形]坏；恶：bad; evil; vicious | 好~不分 hǎodǎi-bùfēn *unable to tell good from bad* / 为非作~ wéifēi-zuòdǎi *do evil* 歹徒 dǎitú hoodlum; ruffian; evildoer

逮 dǎi 11画 辶部

逮 逮 逮 逮 逮 逮 逮 逮 逮 逮

[动]捉，捕：catch; hunt | 猫会~老鼠。Māo huì dǎi lǎoshǔ. *Cats can catch mice.* / 小偷被~住了。Xiǎotōu bèi dǎizhù le. *The thief has been caught.*

See dài.

代 dài 5画 亻部

代 代 代 代 代

❶ [动]代替：replace; take the place of; act for (or on behalf of) others | 请你~我写一份报告。Qǐng nǐ dài wǒ xiě yī fēn bàogào. *Please write a report on my behalf.* / 张老师在替李老师~课。Zhāng lǎoshī zài tì

Lǐ lǎoshī dàikè. *Teacher Zhang has taken over teacher Li's classes.* / 请~我向他致意。Qǐng dài wǒ xiàng tā zhìyì. *Please give him my regards.*

代办 dàibàn ①do sth. for sb.; act on sb.'s behalf ②chargé d'affaires

代表 dàibiǎo ① deputy; delegate; representative ② represent; stand for ③ on behalf of; in the name of

代词 dàicí (gram.) pronoun

代号 dàihào code name

代价 dàijià price; cost

代理 dàilǐ act on behalf of; act as agent

代数 dàishù algebra

代替 dàitì replace; substitute for; take the place of

代表团 dàibiǎotuán delegation; mission; deputation

代理人 dàilǐrén ① agent; deputy; proxy ② (leg.) procurator; attorney

代理商 dàilǐshāng agent; procurator; surrogate

代言人 dàiyánrén spokesperson; mouthpiece

取代 qǔdài   替代 tìdài

新陈代谢 xīnchén-dàixiè

❷ [名]历史上的分期：historical period

朝代 cháodài   当代 dāngdài

古代 gǔdài   近代 jìndài

历代 lìdài   年代 niándài

时代 shídài   现代 xiàndài
现代化 xiàndàihuà

❸ [名]世系的辈分：generation |
后～hòudài posterity; descendants / 下一～xiàyīdài the next
generation / 祖孙三～ zǔsūn
sān dài three generations
世代 shìdài

带 (帶) dài   9画 中部

带 带带带带带带带带
带

❶ [名]带子或像带子的长条物：belt;
girdle; ribbon; band; tape | 领～
lǐngdài necktie / 鞋～xiédài
shoelaces
带儿 dàir belt; girdle; ribbon;
band
绷带 bēngdài   磁带 cídài
皮带 pídài   腰带 yāodài
安全带 ānquándài
录像带 lùxiàngdài

❷ [名]地带；区域：zone; area; belt
| 黄河一～dài Huáng Hé yīdài the
Yellow River region
地带 dìdài   寒带 hándài
热带 rèdài   温带 wēndài
副热带 fùrèdài

❸ [动]随身拿着：take; bring; carry
| ～行李 dài xíngli bring lug-
gage / ～雨具 dài yǔjù take rain
gear / 我的包儿忘～了。Wǒ de
bāor wàng dài le. I forgot to
carry my bag.

带来 dàilái bring along
携带 xiédài

❹ [动]领；引导：lead; take | 他把
我～进会客室。Tā bǎ wǒ
dàijìn huìkèshì. He led me into
the reception room. / 老师～着
学生参观展览。Lǎoshī dàizhe
xuésheng cānguān zhǎnlǎn.
The teacher took the students to
the exhibition. / 李教授～了三个
研究生。Lǐ jiàoshòu dàile sān
gè yánjiūshēng. There are
three graduate students under
Professor Li's guidance.
带动 dàidòng drive; spur on;
bring along; boost
带领 dàilǐng lead; guide
带头 dàitóu take the lead; be the
first; take the initiative; set an
example

❺ [动]连带；附带：have sth. at-
tached; (do sth.) simultaneously |
连枝～叶 liánzhī-dàiyè with
branches and leaves on / 连说～
笑地走进来 liánshuō-dàixiào
de zǒu jìnlai enter laughing
and talking / 这些～叶的桃子真
新鲜。Zhèxiē dài yè de táozi
zhēn xīnxiān. The peaches with
leaves on are very fresh.
附带 fùdài
连滚带爬 liángǔn-dàipá

❻ [动]顺便做：do sth. incidentally
| 你出去请把门～上。Nǐ chūqù
qǐng bǎ mén dàishang. Please
close the door when you go out.

145

/ 上街时给我～点儿茶叶来。Shàngjiē shí gěi wǒ dài diǎnr cháyè lái. *When you go out, please buy some tea for me.*

❼[动]呈现；含有：bear; have; with | 面～笑容miàn dài xiàoróng *wear a smile* / 这梨～点儿酸味。Zhè lí dài diǎnr suānwèi. *This pear tastes a bit sour.*

带劲儿 dàijìnr energetic; wonderful

贷（貸）dài   9画 贝部

贷 贷贷贷贷贷贷贷贷贷
贷

[动]借出；借入：borrow or lend | 向银行～款 xiàng yínháng dàikuǎn *get a bank loan* / 银行～给这家公司大量款项。Yínháng dàigěi zhè jiā gōngsī dàliàng kuǎnxiàng. *The bank granted a huge loan to this company.*

贷款 dàikuǎn provide a loan; extend credit; credit
还贷 huándài

待   dài   9画 彳部

待 待待待待待待待待
待

❶[动]等；等候：wait for; await | 整装～发 zhěngzhuāng-dàifā *get ready and wait* / 有～改进 yǒudài

gǎijìn *have yet to be improved*
待业 dàiyè be unemployed
等待 děngdài   期待 qīdài
有待 yǒudài

❷[动]要；打算：be going to; be about to | 我正～出门，他来了。Wǒ zhèng dài chūmén, tā lái le. *He came as I was about to go out.*

❸[动]对待：treat; deal with | 平等～人píngděng dàirén *treat others as equals* / 你应该～他更客气些。Nǐ yīnggāi dài tā gèng kèqi xiē. *You should treat him more politely.*

待遇 dàiyù ① treatment ② remuneration; pay; wages; salary
看待 kàndài   亏待 kuīdài
善待 shàndài

❹[动]招待：treat; entertain | ～客周到 dàikè zhōudào *entertain guests thoughtfully* / 她～客很慷慨。Tā dàikè hěn kāngkǎi. *She entertained her guests lavishly.*

接待 jiēdài   款待 kuǎndài
招待 zhāodài
招待会 zhāodàihuì

怠   dài   9画 心部

怠 怠怠怠怠怠怠怠怠
怠

❶[形]轻慢；不恭敬：neglect; disrespect

怠慢 dàimàn cold-shoulder; slight

❷[形] 懒惰；松垮：idle; slack
| 怠工 dàigōng work with less efficiency; slow down on purpose

dài   11画 衣部

袋 袋袋袋袋袋袋袋袋袋
袋袋袋

❶[名]用布、纸、皮、塑料等制成的有口盛器：bag; sack | 衣~yīdài *pocket* / 旅行~lǚxíngdài *travelling bag* / 文件~wénjiàndài *document pouch; dispatch case* | 口袋 kǒudài 麻袋 mádài 手袋 shǒudài

❷ [量]用于袋装的东西：bag | 一~糖果 yī dài tángguǒ *a sack of candy* / 两~米 liǎng dài mǐ *two sacks of rice* / 三~水泥 sān dài shuǐní *three sacks of cement*

dài   11画 辶部

逮 逮逮逮逮逮逮逮逮
逮逮逮

[动]捉拿：capture; catch
| 逮捕 dàibǔ arrest; take into custody
　　　　See dǎi.

dài   17画 戈部

戴 戴戴戴戴戴戴戴戴戴
戴戴戴戴戴戴戴戴
戴

❶[动]把东西加在头、脸、颈、胸、臂、手等处：put sth. on (one's head, face, neck, chest, arm, hand, etc.) | ~帽子 dài màozi *wear a hat* / ~眼镜 dài yǎnjìng *wear glasses* / ~红花 dài hónghuā *wear a red flower* / ~手表 dài shǒubiǎo *wear a watch*

❷[动]拥护；尊敬：respect; honour | 爱~àidài *love and respect* / 拥~yōngdài *support (sb. as a leader)*

丹 dān   4画 丿部

丹 丹丹丹丹

❶[形]红色：red | ~顶鹤 dāndǐnghè *red-crowned crane*

❷ [名]依成方配制成的、颗粒状或粉末状的中药：a kind of traditional Chinese medicine, usually pellets or powder, prepared according to a certain set of prescriptions | 清凉~qīngliángdān *cooling pellets*

担 (擔) dān   8画 扌部

担 担担担担担担担担

❶[动]用肩挑：carry on a shoulder

pole | ～水 dānshuǐ *carry water (with a shoulder pole and buckets)* / ～柴 dānchái *carry firewood with a shoulder pole*

❷[动]负起；承当：take on; undertake | ～责任 dān zérèn *shoulder responsibility* / ～风险 dān fēngxiǎn *run risks; take risks*

担保 dānbǎo assure; guarantee; vouch for

担当 dāndāng take on; undertake; assume

担负 dānfù bear; shoulder; take on; be charged with

担任 dānrèn assume the office; hold the post

担心 dānxīn worry; feel anxious

担忧 dānyōu worry; be anxious

承担 chéngdān　负担 fùdān See dàn.

单 (單) dān 8画 ˙部

单 单单单单单单单

❶[形]一个：one; single | ～身 dānshēn *unmarried; single* / ～扇门 dānshànmén *single-leaf door*

单边 dānbiān (econ.) unilateral

单程 dānchéng one way

单词 dāncí word

单独 dāndú alone; by oneself; on one's own; single-handed; independently

单项 dānxiàng (sports) individual event

单一 dānyī single; unitary

单元 dānyuán unit

孤单 gūdān

❷ [形]薄弱：thin; weak | ～薄 dānbó *thin; frail* / 你的身体太～了。Nǐ de shēntǐ tài dān le. *You are too thin and weak.*

❸[形]不复杂；纯一：simple

单纯 dānchún ① simple; pure ② alone; purely; merely

单调 dāndiào monotonous; dull; drab

简单 jiǎndān

❹[形]只有一层的：unlined | ～衣 dānyī *unlined garment* / ～裤 dānkù *unlined trousers* / 这件大衣是～的还是夹层的？Zhè jiàn dàyī shì dān de háishì jiācéng de? *Is this coat unlined or lined?*

❺[名]覆盖用的纺织品：sheet | 被～bèidān *sheet*

床单 chuángdān

❻[名]记事用的纸片：bill; list | 账～zhàngdān *bill; check* / 价目～jiàmùdān *price list*

保单 bǎodān　菜单 càidān

传单 chuándān 订单 dìngdān

罚单 fádān　　名单 míngdān

清单 qīngdān

黑名单 hēimíngdān

❼[形]奇数的（跟"双shuāng"相对）：odd (the opposite of "双shuāng") | ～号 dānhào *odd number* / ～数 dānshù *singular number*

单打 dāndǎ *(sports) singles*

单方面 dānfāngmiàn *one-sided; unilateral*

❽[副]只；仅：*only; solely; alone* | 不能～凭经验 bùnéng dān píng jīngyàn *can not rely on experience alone* / ～靠书本知识是不够的。Dān kào shūběn zhīshi shì bù gòu de. *Merely depending on book learning is not enough.*

◇单位 dānwèi *unit*

 耽 dān 10画 耳部

耽 耽耽耽耽耽耽耽耽耽耽

[动]迟延：delay | ～搁 dānge *stop over; delay*

耽误 dānwu *delay; hold up*

胆（膽）dǎn 9画 月部

胆 胆胆胆胆胆胆胆胆胆

❶[名]胆囊：*gallbladder*
❷[名]胆量；勇气：*courage; guts; bravery* | 壮～zhuàngdǎn *boost sb.'s courage* / 浑身是～húnshēn shì dǎn *be every inch a hero; be the very embodiment of valour* / 他从小～就大，什么也不怕。Tā cóngxiǎo dǎn jiù dà, shénme yě bù pà. *Being dauntless since he was a child, he is never afraid of anything.*

胆量 dǎnliàng *courage*
胆怯 dǎnqiè *timid; coward*
胆子 dǎnzi *courage; guts; bravery*

大胆 dàdǎn

❸[名]某些器物内部装气或水的东西：*inner container* | 暖瓶～nuǎnpíngdǎn *the glass liner of a Thermos flask*

旦 dàn 5画 日部

旦 旦旦旦旦旦

❶[名]早晨；天亮的时候：*dawn; daybreak*
❷[名]某一天：*day; daytime* | 元～yuándàn *New Year's Day*
❸[名]传统戏曲中扮演妇女的角色：*the female role in traditional opera* | 花～huādàn *the female role of girls* / 老～lǎodàn *the female role of old ladies*

 但 dàn 7画 亻部

但 但但但但但但但

❶[副]只；仅：*only; merely* | ～愿如此 dànyuàn rúcǐ *I wish it*

were true!; We hope so.

不但 bùdàn

❷ [连] 不过；可是：but; yet; nevertheless | 他们都去了，～我没去。Tāmen dōu qù le, dàn wǒ méi qù. *They all went except me.*

但是 dànshì but; yet; still; nevertheless

 (擔) dàn   8画 扌部

担 担担担担担担担担

❶ [名] a carrying pole with loads

担子 dànzi a carrying pole with loads

❷ [量] 用于可挑的东西：shoulder-pole load | 一～水 yī dàn shuǐ *two buckets of water (carried with a shoulder pole)*

挑重担 tiāozhòngdàn

See dān.

诞 (誕) dàn   8画 讠部

诞 诞诞诞诞诞诞诞诞

❶ [形] 荒唐的；不合情理的：absurd; fantastic | 怪～guàidàn *weird; strange* / 荒～huāngdàn *fantastic*

❷ [动] 出生：be born

诞生 dànshēng be born; come into being; emerge

圣诞 shèngdàn

圣诞节 Shèngdànjié

❸ [名] 生日：birthday | 寿～shòudàn *birthday celebration for elderly people*

诞辰 dànchén birthday

 dàn   11画 氵部

淡 淡淡淡淡淡淡淡淡淡 淡淡淡

❶ [形] 味道不浓：tasteless; weak; light | ～而无味 dàn ér wú wèi *tasteless; insipid* / 这个菜太～了。Zhège cài tài dàn le. *The flavour of this dish is too bland.*

淡水 dànshuǐ fresh water

❷ [形] 所含的某种成分少：稀薄(跟"浓nóng"相对)：thin; light (the opposite of "浓nóng") | 一杯～酒 yī bēi dànjiǔ *a glass of light wine*

❸ [形] 颜色浅：light; faint; pale | 这幅画颜色上得太～了。Zhè fú huà yánsè shàng de tài dàn le. *The colouring of this painting is too pale.*

淡化 dànhuà desalinate

暗淡 àndàn

❹ [形] 不热心：indifferent; apathetic | ～～地答应了一声 dàndàn de dāyingle yī shēng *reply drily* / 他对人向来就很～。Tā duì rén xiànglái jiù hěn dàn. *He is always indifferent to people.*

冷淡 lěngdàn

❺ [形] 营业不旺盛：slack; dull |

清～qīngdàn *slack*
淡季 dànjì *slack season*

 弹（彈）dàn　11画 弓部

弹 弹弹弹弹弹弹弹弹
弹弹弹

❶[名] 小丸：ball; pellet｜泥～
ní dàn *mud ball* / 铁～tiědàn
iron ball

❷[名] 内装爆炸物，具有破坏、杀伤
能力的东西：bullet; bomb｜
枪～qiāngdàn *cartridge; bullet*
弹药 dànyào *ammunition*
导弹 dǎodàn　炮弹 pàodàn
炸弹 zhàdàn　子弹 zǐdàn
手榴弹 shǒuliúdàn
原子弹 yuánzǐdàn
　　See tán.

 蛋　dàn　11画 虫部

蛋 蛋蛋蛋蛋蛋蛋蛋蛋
蛋蛋蛋

❶[名] egg｜下～xiàdàn *lay eggs*
蛋糕 dàngāo *cake*
蛋白 dànbái ① egg white; al-
bumen ② protein
蛋白质 dànbáizhì *protein*
鸡蛋 jīdàn

❷[名] 形状像蛋的东西：an egg-
shaped thing｜泥～儿 ní dànr
mud ball

❸[名] 指具有某种特点的人：a
person of certain character (often negative)
笨蛋 bèndàn　坏蛋 huàidàn
穷光蛋 qióngguāngdàn
◇完蛋 wándàn

 氮　dàn　12画 气部

氮 氮氮氮氮氮氮氮氮
氮氮氮氮

[名] nitrogen (N)

 当（當嘗❸）dāng　6画 小部

当 当当当当当当

❶[动] 相配；相称：be equal; match
with｜实力相～shílì-xiāng-
dāng *well-matched in strength*
相当 xiāngdāng
相当于 xiāngdāngyú
门当户对 méndāng-hùduì

❷[动] 主持；掌管：run; manage
当家 dāngjiā *manage* (household) affairs
当局 dāngjú *the authorities*

❸[动] 承担；承受：bear; accept;
deserve｜敢做敢～gǎnzuò-
gǎndāng *dare to do sth. and take
responsibility for it* / 我可～不起
这样的夸奖。Wǒ kě dāngbuqǐ
zhèyàng de kuājiǎng. *I don't deserve such praise.* / 一人做事一
人～。Yī rén zuòshì yī rén

dāng. *One should answer for what he does.*

当事人 dāngshìrén litigant; person involved

担当 dāndāng

不敢当 bùgǎndāng

❹ [动] 充当；担任：serve (act) as ｜ ～翻译 dāng fānyì *act as an interpreter* / 选他～组长 xuǎn tā dāng zǔzhǎng *elect him as group leader* / 他在一家银行～办事员。Tā zài yī jiā yínháng dāng bànshìyuán. *He works as a clerk in a bank.*

当选 dāngxuǎn be elected

充当 chōngdāng

❺ [介] 对着；向着：in sb.'s presence; to sb.'s face ｜ ～着大家谈 dāngzhe dàjiā tán *speak out in the presence of everyone*

当面 dāngmiàn to sb.'s face; in sb.'s presence

❻ [介] 正在(那时候或那地方)：just at (a certain time or place)

当场 dāngchǎng on the spot; then and there

当初 dāngchū originally; in the beginning; in the first place

当代 dāngdài the present age; the contemporary time

当地 dāngdì at the place in question; in the locality; local

当红 dānghóng (performers) be at the height of one's popularity

当即 dāngjí at once; right away

当今 dāngjīn now; at present; nowadays

当年 dāngnián ① in those years; in those days ② the prime of life

当前 dāngqián ① (sth. is) before one; (sth. is) facing one ② present; current

当日 dāngrì at that time; back then

当时 dāngshí at that time; then

当中 dāngzhōng ① in the middle; in the centre ② among

当…的时候 dāng... de shíhou when...; as...; while...

正当 zhèngdāng

❼ [动] 应该：should; ought to ｜ 理～如此 lǐ dāng-rúcǐ *that's just as it should be* / 能省的就省，～用的就要用。Néng shěng de jiù shěng, dāng yòng de jiù yào yòng. *Save what you can, but use what you must.*

当然 dāngrán ① as it should be; only natural ② without doubt; certainly; of course; to be sure

理所当然 lǐsuǒdāngrán

❽ [拟声] 撞击金属器物的声音：clank; clang, the sound of a gong or a bell ｜ ～～的钟声 dāng-dāng de zhōngshēng *the tolling of a bell; the ding-dong of bells*

◇当心 dāngxīn take care; be

careful; look out
See dǎng.

挡 (擋) dǎng 9画 扌部

挡 挡挡挡挡挡挡挡挡
挡

❶ [动]阻拦;抵抗: block; keep off
| ～道 dǎngdào *block the
road* / ～住去路 dǎngzhù qùlù
get in the way
阻挡 zǔdǎng

❷ [动]遮住:shelter from; keep out
| ～雨 dǎng yǔ *keep off the
rain* / ～太阳 dǎng tàiyáng
shelter from the sun / 窗户～得
严严实实。Chuānghu dǎng
de yányán-shíshí. *The window is covered completely.*
挡箭牌 dǎngjiānpái ① shield
② excuse; pretext

党 (黨) dǎng 10画 儿部

党 党党党党党党党党
党党

❶[名]由私人利害关系而结成的集
团: a gang of people getting
together for private interests

❷[名] 政党: political party
党派 dǎngpài political parties
and groups
党委 dǎngwěi party committee
党性 dǎngxìng party spirit

党员 dǎngyuán party member
党章 dǎngzhāng party constitution
党中央 dǎngzhōngyāng the
Party Central Committee
政党 zhèngdǎng
共产党 gòngchǎndǎng
国民党 guómíndǎng

当 (當) dàng 6画 ⺌部

当 当当当当当当

❶ [形]适合: proper | 用词不～
yòng cí bùdàng *inappropriate choice of words*
不当 bùdàng   恰当 qiàdàng
适当 shìdàng   妥当 tuǒdàng
稳当 wěndàng

❷ [动]抵得上; 等于: equal; match
| 以一～十 yǐ yī dàng shí *pit
one against ten* / 一个人～两个
人用 yī gè rén dàng liǎng gè
rén yòng *one person does the
work of two*

❸ [动]看作; 作为: regard as; serve
as; treat as; take for | 把公众的
事～自己的事 bǎ gōngzhòng
de shì dàng zìjǐ de shì *treat
public affairs as one's own*
当成 dàngchéng regard as;
treat as; take for
当做 dàngzuò regard as; treat
as; take for

❹[动]以为; 认为: think | 我～是
谁, 原来是你! Wǒ dàng shì

shéi, yuánlái shì nǐ! *Oh, it's you! I thought it was someone else at first.*

❺[动]指用实物作抵押向当铺借钱；也指押出实物：pawn | 家里实在没东西可~了。Jiāli shízài méi dōngxi kě dàng le. *There is really nothing at home to be pawned.*

❻[介]指事情发生的那个时候：when ... ; at the time... | ~日 dàngrì *the same day*

当天 dàngtiān the same day; that very day

当晚 dàngwǎn at the same evening

See dāng.

荡 (蕩) dàng 9画 艹部

荡 荡荡荡荡荡荡荡荡荡

❶[动]洗刷：wash; rinse | 用开水把杯子~~~。Yòng kāishuǐ bǎ bēizi dàngyidàng. *Rinse the cup with boiled water.*

❷[动]摇动：swing; sway | ~秋千 dàng qiūqiān *play on a swing*

动荡 dòngdàng 震荡 zhèndàng

❸[动]没有目的地来走去；闲逛：loaf about; wander; roam; loiter | 东游西~ dōngyóu-xīdàng *loaf about here and there*

档 (檔) dàng 10画 木部

档 档档档档档档档档档档

❶[名]存放公文、案卷的橱架：shelves for documents, files | 存~ cúndàng *keep in the archives;* / 归~ guīdàng *place on file; file*

❷[名]分类保存的文件、材料等：files; archives

档案 dàng'àn files; archives; record; dossier

❸[名]等级：grade

档次 dàngcì grade

高档 gāodàng

◇档期 dàngqī (of films or television programmes) slot; time or season to be shown

搭档 dādàng

刀 dāo 2画 刀部

刀 刀刀

❶[名] knife; sword | 用~切菜 yòng dāo qiēcài *cut up vegetables*

刀叉 dāochā (of tableware) knife and fork

刀刃 dāorèn the edge of a knife

刀子 dāozi knife; sword

剪刀 jiǎndāo   开刀 kāidāo

镰刀 liándāo

❷[名]形状像刀的东西：sth. shaped like a knife | 冰~ bīngdāo *ice skates*

叨

叨 dāo 5画 口部

叨 叨叨叨叨叨

See 叨唠
叨唠 dāolao talk on and on;
chatter away

导

导 (導) dǎo 6画 已部

导 导导导导导导

❶[动] 引；带领：lead; guide
导读 dǎodú give guidance to
readers; guide to reading
导航 dǎoháng navigation
导游 dǎoyóu ① conduct a sightseeing tour ② tour guide
导致 dǎozhì lead to; bring
about; result in; cause
导火线 dǎohuǒxiàn ① (blast-
ing) fuse ② a small incident that
touches off a big one
倡导 chāngdǎo领导 lǐngdǎo
误导 wùdǎo   向导 xiàngdǎo
引导 yǐndǎo   主导 zhǔdǎo
❷[动] 启发；教育：instruct; give
guidance to
导师 dǎoshī tutor; teacher; supervisor
导演 dǎoyǎn director
辅导 fǔdǎo   教导 jiāodǎo
指导 zhǐdǎo
❸[动] 传导：transmit; conduct
| ~热 dǎorè heat conduction /

~电 dǎodiàn transmit electric
current; conduct electricity
导体 dǎotǐ conductor
半导体 bàndǎotǐ
◇导弹 dǎodàn missile

岛

岛 (島) dǎo 7画 山部

岛 岛岛岛岛岛岛岛

[名]island | ~上没有居民。Dǎo
shang méiyǒu jūmín. *There
are no inhabitants on this island.*
岛屿 dǎoyǔ islands
半岛 bàndǎo   群岛 qúndǎo

捣

捣 (搗) dǎo 10画 扌部

捣 捣捣捣捣捣捣捣捣
捣捣

❶ [动]用棍棒等工具的头撞击：pound
with a pestle, etc.; smash; crush
| ~蒜 dǎosuàn *crush garlic*
❷ [动]搅乱：disturb
捣蛋 dǎodàn make trouble
捣乱 dǎoluàn make trouble;
create a disturbance

倒

倒 dǎo 10画 亻部

倒 倒倒倒倒倒倒倒倒
倒倒

❶[动] 由直立变成横卧：fall; topple
| 跌~ diēdǎo *fall; tumble* /

155

墙～了。Qiáng dǎo le. *The wall collapsed.*

倒塌 dǎotā collapse; topple down

倾倒 qīngdǎo

❷[动]失败；垮台：collapse; be overthrown; close down | 商店经营得不好，没过两月就～了。Shāngdiàn jīngyíng de bù hǎo, méi guò liǎng yuè jiù dǎo le. *The store was poorly managed and closed down within two months.*

倒闭 dǎobì close down; go bankrupt; go into liquidation

打倒 dǎdǎo

❸[动]（人的某些器官）受到损伤或刺激致使功能变坏：(of organs of the body) be harmed; lose voice | 他的嗓子～了。Tā de sǎngzi dǎo le. *He has lost his voice.*

❹[动]转换；更换：change | ～班 dǎobān *work on shifts* / ～车 dǎochē *change trains or buses*

倒腾 dǎoteng ① turn upside down; turn over and over ②engage in buying and selling

❺[动]买卖：resell at a profit | 他～水果赚了不少钱。Tā dǎo shuǐguǒ zhuànle bù shǎo qián. *He sold fruit and made a lot of money.*

倒爷 dǎoyé profiteer

投机倒把 tóujī-dǎobǎ

◇倒霉 dǎoméi have bad luck; be out of luck; be down on one's luck

See dào.

蹈 dǎo　17画 足部

蹈蹈蹈蹈蹈蹈蹈蹈蹈蹈蹈蹈蹈蹈蹈蹈蹈

❶[动]踩；践踏：tread; step | 赴汤～火 fùtāng-dǎohuǒ *go through fire and water; defy all difficulties and dangers*

❷[动]跳动：skip; jump | 手舞足～ shǒuwǔ-zúdǎo *dance for joy*

舞蹈 wǔdǎo

到 dào　8画 刂部

到 到 到 到 到 到 到 到

❶[动]达到；到达：arrive; reach | 春天～了。Chūntiān dào le. *Spring has come.* / 火车～上海了。Huǒchē dào Shànghǎi le. *The train has arrived in Shanghai.*

到场 dàochǎng be present; show up; turn up

到处 dàochù at all places; everywhere

到达 dàodá arrive; get to; reach

到底 dàodǐ ①to the end; to the finish ② at last; in the end; finally ③ (used in questions for emphasis) on earth

到来 dàolái arrival; advent

到期 dàoqī become due; mature; (what) expire

到位 dàowèi be in place or position; reach the designated place

到…为止 dào... wéizhǐ until (certain time); close (by a specified time)

报到 bàodào   迟到 chídào
直到 zhídào
从头到尾 cóngtóu-dàowěi
归根到底 guīgēn-dàodǐ
恰到好处 qiàdào-hǎochù

❷ [动]往；去：go to; leave for | ~北京 dào Běijīng *go to Beijing*

❸ [形]周密；周到：thoughtful; considerate | 面面俱~ miànmiàn-jùdào *attend to every aspect (of certain matter)* / 有照顾不~的地方请原谅。Yǒu zhàogù bù dào de dìfang qǐng yuánliàng. *Please excuse me if I am inconsiderate in any respect.*
周到 zhōudào

❹ [动]用作动词的补语，表示动作有结果：used after a verb as a complement to indicate achievement of certain thing | 想不~ xiǎngbudào *do not expect* / 办得~ bàndedào *capable of doing sth.* / 报名参加考试的学生已增加~800人。Bàomíng cānjiā kǎoshì de xuésheng yǐ zēngjiā dào bābǎi rén. *The number of students who signed up to take the exam has reached 800.*

达到 dádào   得到 dédào
等到 děngdào   感到 gǎndào
受到 shòudào   提到 tídào
遇到 yùdào   遭到 zāodào

倒   dào   10画 亻部

倒 倒倒倒倒倒倒倒倒 倒倒

❶ [动]上下或前后的位置相反：turn upside down; reverse; invert | 你把书摆~了。Nǐ bǎ shū bǎidào le. *You have put the book upside down.*

❷ [形](位置、次序、方向等)相反的；反过来的：upside down; backward; reversed | ~数第一 dàoshǔ dì-yī *the last one* / 次序~了。Cìxù dào le. *The order is reversed.*
倒数 dàoshǔ (math.) reciprocal
倒计时 dàojìshí countdown
帮倒忙 bāngdàománg

❸ [动]向后；向相反的方向移动：move backward | ~车 dàochē *back the car* / 你再往后~一~，我们就过去了。Nǐ zài wǎng hòu dàoyidào, wǒmen jiù guòqu le. *Back your car a little farther, and we'll go through.*
倒退 dàotuì go backwards

❹ [动]倾斜或反转容器，使里面的

倒

dào

157

东西出来：pour; tip; dump | ～水 dàoshuǐ *pour water* / ～茶 dàochá *pour tea* / ～垃圾 dào lājī *dump rubbish*

倾倒 qīngdǎo

❺ [副]表示跟预料的相反：(contrast to one's expection) but; yet | 都春天了，～下起雪了。Dōu chūntiān le, dào xià qǐ xuě le. *Although it's spring already, it is snowing.* / 房间不算大，～还干净。Fángjiān bù suàn dà, dào hái gānjing. *The room is not big, but it is clean.*

❻ [副]表示催促、追问、不满意等语气：used to indicate urge, impatience or dissatisfaction | 你～说句话呀! Nǐ dào shuō jù huà ya! *Say something please!* / 你～去不去呀?Nǐ dào qùbuqù ya? *Do you want to go or not?*

❼ [副]表示让步：used to denote a concession | 我去～去了，但他们都不在。Wǒ qù dào qù le, dàn tāmen dōu bù zài. *I did go there, but none of them were there.*

❽ [副]表示舒缓的语气：used to indicate a mild tone | 你说她聪明，那～不见得。Nǐ shuō tā cōngmíng, nà dào bùjiànde. *You say she is smart, but I don't quite see that.* / 咱俩一起走，那～挺好。Zán liǎ yīqǐ zǒu, nà dào tǐnghǎo. *So we*

both shall go together. That's good.

See dǎo.

盗 dào 11画 皿部

盗盗盗盗盗盗盗盗盗盗盗盗

❶ [动]偷：steal; rob
盗版 dàobǎn illegally copy; pirate
盗窃 dàoqiè steal
盗印 dàoyìn print illegally; pirate

❷ [名]偷窃、抢劫财物的人：thief; robber
强盗 qiángdào

悼 dào 11画 忄部

悼悼悼悼悼悼悼悼悼悼悼

[动]悲伤、哀念：mourn; grieve
悼念 dàoniàn mourn;grieve over
哀悼 āidào

道 dào 12画 辶部

道道道道道道道道道道道道

❶ [名]路：road; way; path | 林阴小～línyīn xiǎodào *a shady path* / 从这条～走比较近。Cóng zhè tiáo dào zǒu bǐjiào jìn. *It's nearer if we take this route.*

道路 dàolù road; way; path

便道 biàndào	车道 chēdào
大道 dàdào	地道 dìdào
轨道 guǐdào	国道 guódào
航道 hángdào	街道 jiēdào
楼道 lóudào	跑道 pǎodào
频道 píndào	隧道 suìdào
铁道 tiědào	通道 tōngdào
一道 yīdào	走道 zǒudào
人行道 rénxíngdào	

❷ [名]水、气通行的途径：channel, course (for the passage of water or gas)

管道 guǎndào　河道 hédào
渠道 qúdào
呼吸道 hūxīdào

❸ [名]方向；途径：way; method | 养生之~ yǎngshēng zhī dào *the way to keep fit* / 生财之~ shēngcái zhī dào *ways to develop financial resources; ways to make money*

柔道 róudào

❹ [名] 道理：doctrine; principle | 志同~合 zhìtóng-dàohé *cherish the same ideals and follow the same path; have a common goal* / 他讲得头头是~。Tā jiǎng de tóutóushìdào. *What he said was very clear and logical.*

道理 dàolǐ principle; reason
霸道 bàdào　公道 gōngdào

❺ [名]道德；正义：moral; moral-ity

道德 dàodé morals; morality; ethics
人道主义 réndào zhǔyì

❻ [名]道教的简称：Taoist; Taoism | ~士 dàoshi *Taoist priest*

道家 Dàojiā Taoist school; Taoists
道教 Dàojiào the Taoist religion; Taoism

❼ [名]线条：line | 画了一条横~ huàle yī tiáo héngdào *draw a horizontal line*

❽ [动]说；用语言表示：say; speak; talk | 能说会~ néngshuō-huìdào *have the gift of the gab* / "我明白了。"他回答~。"Wǒ míngbaile." Tā huídá dào. *"I see." He replied.*

道歉 dàoqiàn apologize; make an apology
报道 bàodào
微不足道 wēibùzúdào

❾ [量]用于条形的东西：used for anything in the form of a line | 一~彩虹 yī dào cǎihóng *a rainbow* / 裂了一一缝 lièle yī dào fèng *have a crack*

❿ [量]用于门、关口等阻拦的事物：used for doors, walls, etc. | 三~门 sān dào mén *three successive doors* / 院子中间隔着一~墙。Yuànzi zhōngjiān gézhe yī dào qiáng. *A wall stood in the middle of the yard.*

⓫ [量] 用于题目、命令等：used for

orders or questions | 一～命令 yī dào mìnglìng *an order* / 两～算术题 liǎng dào suànshùtí *two arithmetic questions*

⓬ [量]用于连续事物中的一次：a step or stage in procedures; time | 省一～手续 shěng yī dào shǒuxù *eliminate one step from the process*

◇打交道 dǎjiāodào
东道主 dōngdàozhǔ

稻 **dào** 15画 禾部

稻 稻稻稻稻稻稻稻稻 稻稻稻稻稻稻稻

[名] rice; paddy
稻米 dàomǐ rice
稻子 dàozi rice; paddy

得 **dé** 11画 彳部

得 得得得得得得得得 得得得

❶ [动]（获取）到（跟"失 shī"相对）：get; gain; obtain (the opposite of "失 shī") | 多劳多～ duōláo-duōdé *more pay for more work* / ～了两次冠军 déle liǎng cì guànjūn *won the championship twice* / 他在国外～了博士学位。Tā zài guówài déle bóshì xuéwèi. *He has obtained a doctoral degree abroad.*

得病 débìng fall ill
得出 déchū reach (a conclusion); obtain (a result)
得到 dédào get; gain
得分 défēn score
得手 déshǒu come off; do fine; succeed
得知 dézhī have learned of sth.; have heard of sth.
得主 dézhǔ winner of a cup or a medal in a game or competition
得罪 dézuì offend; displease

夺得 duódé   获得 huòdé
难得 nándé   求得 qiúdé
取得 qǔdé   使得 shǐdé
所得 suǒdé   心得 xīndé
赢得 yíngdé   值得 zhídé
舍不得 shěbudé

❷ [动]可以；容许：permit; allow | 阅览室的书一律不～带出室外。Yuèlǎnshì de shū yīlù bùdé dàichū shìwài. *The books cannot be taken outside the reading room.* / 这笔钱不～动用。Zhè bǐ qián bùdé dòngyòng. *This sum of money is not allowed to be used.*

❸ [动]适合：fit; proper
得力 délì capable; competent

❹ [形]满意：satisfied; pleased
得意 déyì proud of oneself; pleased with oneself; complacent

❺ [动]完成：be finished; be ready | 菜做～了就开饭。Cài zuò dé le jiù kāifàn. *The meal will be served as soon it is ready.*

❻ [动]演算产生结果：(of a calculation) result in | 二四～八。Èr sì dé bā. *Two times four is eight.*

得以 déyǐ *so that...can...; so that...may...*

不得不 bùdébù

不由得 bùyóude

不得了 bùdéliǎo

不得已 bùdéyǐ

不见得 bùjiàndé

　　See de; děi.

德 dé　15画 彳部

德 德德德德德德德 德德德德德德德

❶ [名]品行；道德：virtue; morals | 品～pǐndé *moral character* / ～才兼备décái-jiānbèi *have both ability and moral integrity; be both capable and noble-minded*

德行 déxíng *moral integrity; moral conduct*

德育 déyù *moral education; education in ethics*

道德 dàodé　　美德 měidé

❷ [名]恩惠；好处：favour; benefit | 恩～ēndé *kindness; benevolence*

◇ 德文 Déwén *German (language)*

德语 Déyǔ *German (language)*

地　de　6画 土部

地　地地地地地地

[助]表示它前面的词或词组是状语：used to indicate the word or phrase in front of it is an adverbial | 天气渐渐～冷了。Tiānqì jiànjiàn de lěng le. *The weather is getting cold.* / 她愉快～笑了。Tā yúkuài de xiào le. *She laughed cheerfully.*

　　See dì.

的　de　8画 白部

的　的的的的的的的

❶ [助]表示它前面的词或词组是定语：used to indicate the word or phrase in front of it is an attribute | 伟大～祖国 wěidà de zǔguó *great motherland* / 勤劳～人民 qínláo de rénmín *hardworking people*

❷ [助]附在部分词语后面构成词组，代替跟这些词语有关的人或物：used after words to form a noun phrase or nominal expression as a substitute for certain people or certain thing | 开车～kāichē de *a driver* / 爱吃甜～àichī tián de *someone who has a sweet tooth*

❸ [助] 用在句末，表示肯定的语气，常跟"是"相应：used at the end of a declarative sentence for emphasis, often used corre-spondingly with "是shì" | 太阳是从东方升起~。Tàiyáng shì cóng dōngfāng shēngqǐ de. *The sun rises in the east.*

See dí; dì.

得 .... de 11画 亻部

得 得得得得得得得得 得得得

❶[助]用在动词后面表示可能或可以：used after certain verbs to indicate possibility or per-mission | 这东西晒不~。Zhè dōngxi shàibude. *It cannot be exposed to the sun.* / 我为什么就去不~? Wǒ wèishénme jiù qùbude? *Why can't I go?*
恨不得 hènbude

❷[助]用在动词或形容词后连接表示程度或结果的补语：used af-ter a verb or an adjective as a complement to indicate result or degree | 写~清楚 xiě de qīng-chu *be clearly written* / 讲~不快 jiǎng de bù kuài *not speak quickly* / 他汉语说~非常流利。Tā Hànyǔ shuō de fēicháng liúlì. *He speaks fluent Chinese.* / 雪下~很大。Xuě xià de hěn dà. *It's snowing heavily.*
不由得 bùyóude
称得上 chēngdeshàng
懂得 dǒngde 对得起 duìdeqǐ

记得 jìde   觉得 juéde
来得及 láidejí 认得 rènde
舍得 shěde   省得 shěngde
显得 xiǎnde 晓得 xiǎode
    See dé; děi.

得 .... děi 11画 亻部

得 得得得得得得得得 得得得

❶[动]必须；需要；应该：must; need; have to | 你~好好想想。Nǐ děi hǎohǎo xiǎngxiang. *You must think it over.* / 我~亲自去一次。Wǒ děi qīnzì qù yī cì. *I have to go myself.*
❷[动]表示估计揣测：probably; certainly will | 看天色，今天~下雨。Kàn tiānsè, jīntiān děi xiàyǔ. *It looks like it will rain.* / 爸爸准~来。Bàba zhǔn děi lái. *Papa is sure to come.*
    See dé; de.

灯 (燈) dēng 6画 火部

灯 灯灯灯灯灯灯

[名]照明或作其他用途的发光器具：lamp; light | 开~kāi dēng *turn on the light* / 关~guān dēng *turn off the light*
灯火 dēnghuǒ lights
灯光 dēngguāng ① the light of a lamp; lamplight ② (stage)

lighting

灯笼 dēnglong lantern

灯泡 dēngpào electric (light) bulb

灯饰 dēngshì decoration lamps

电灯 diàndēng

红灯 hóngdēng

幻灯 huàndēng　路灯 lùdēng

开绿灯 kāilùdēng

登　dēng　12画　癶部

登登登登登登登登登
登登登登

❶ [动] 由低处往高处行进：ascend, mount │ ~山 dēngshān *climb a mountain* / ~车 dēngchē *get on a bus* / ~上讲台 dēngshang jiǎngtái mount the platform (prepared for instructors)

登场 dēngchǎng come on stage

登机 dēngjī board a plane

登陆 dēnglù land; disembark

登录 dēnglù register; enter; log on (to certain Internet websites)

❷ [动] 刊载；记载：publish; record; enter │ ~在报纸上 dēng zài bàozhǐ shang *publish in the newspaper* / 这条消息~在头版头条。Zhè tiáo xiāoxi dēng zài tóubǎn tóutiáo. *This news made the headlines.*

登记 dēngjì register; check in;

enter one's name

刊登 kāndēng

蹬　dēng　19画　足部

蹬蹬蹬蹬蹬蹬蹬蹬
蹬蹬蹬蹬蹬蹬蹬蹬
蹬蹬蹬

❶ [动] 踩；踏：step on; tread │ 脚~在门槛上 jiǎo dēng zài ménkǎn shang *step on the threshold* / 他~着梯子上去了。Tā dēngzhe tīzi shàngqu le. *He got up by a ladder.*

❷ [动] 腿和脚向脚底方向用力：pedal; press down with the foot │ ~自行车 dēng zìxíngchē *pedal a bicycle* / ~被子 dēng bèizi *kick off the quilt*

蹬车 dēngchē pedal a bike

等　děng　12画　竹部

等等等等等等等等
等等等等

❶ [形] 程度、数量相同：equal in quantity or degree │ 大小不~ dàxiǎo-bùděng *not equal in size; vary in size*

等于 děngyú ① be equal to; be equivalent to ② be the same as; amount to

不等 bùděng　平等 píngděng

相等 xiāngděng

❷ [名]等级：grade; class; rank |
一～品 yīděngpǐn *top quality
goods* / 优～生 yōuděngshēng
top students / 产品质量共分三～。
Chǎnpǐn zhìliàng gōng fēn
sān děng. *The quality of products
is classified into three
grades.*

等级 děngjí ① grade; rank ②
order and degree; social estate
高等 gāoděng 上等 shàngděng
同等 tóngděng 中等 zhōngděng

❸ [助]表示列举未尽：and so on;
etc. | 我去过日本、美国、加拿
大～国。Wǒ qùguo Rìběn,
Měiguó, Jiānádà děng guó. *I
have been to Japan, the US,
Canada, and so on.* / 李明、张
海～人 Lǐ Míng, Zhāng Hǎi
děng rén *Li Ming, Zhang Hai
and other people*

❹ [助]列举后煞尾：used to end an
enumeration | 五金通常是指金、
银、铜、铁、锡～五种金属。Wǔjīn
tōngcháng shì zhǐ jīn, yín,
tóng, tiě, xī děng wǔ zhǒng
jīnshǔ. *The five metals usually
refer to gold, silver, copper, iron
and tin.*

❺ [动]等候：wait; await | ～一会
儿 děng yīhuìr *wait a moment*
/ ～得心急了 děng de xīnjí le
*become impatient after waiting
for a long time* / 你先走，我～
她一起走。Nǐ xiān zǒu, wǒ
děng tā yīqǐ zǒu. *You go first*

and I'll wait for her to go together.

等待 děngdài wait; await
等到 děngdào by the time;
when
等候 děnghòu wait; await; expect

❻ [动]等到：by the time; when

dēng 14画 几部

凳凳凳凳凳凳凳凳
凳凳凳凳凳凳

[名]stool; bench | 方～fāngdèng
square stool / 圆～yuándèng
round stool

凳子 dèngzi stool
板凳 bǎndèng

dèng 17画 目部

瞪瞪瞪瞪瞪瞪瞪瞪
瞪瞪瞪瞪瞪瞪瞪瞪
瞪

❶ [动]（因生气或不满）睁大眼睛直
视：(due to anger or resentment)
stare; glare | 老张～了他
一眼。Lǎo Zhāng dèngle tā yī
yǎn. *Lao Zhang gave him an
angry glare.*

❷ [动]睁大眼睛：open one's eyes
wide | 她～着一双大眼睛发呆。
Tā dèngzhe yī shuāng dà
yǎnjing fādāi. *She stared*

blankly with wide open eyes. / 她～着眼看我。Tā dèngzhe yǎn kàn wǒ. *She stared at me.*

低 dī 7画 亻部

低 低低低低低低低

❶[形]从下到上的距离小；离地面近(跟"高gāo"相对)：low (the opposite of "高gāo") | 飞机飞得很～。Fēijī fēi de hěn dī. *The plane flies at a low altitude.* 高低 gāodī

❷[动]向下垂：let droop; hang down | ～着头走路 dīzhe tóu zǒulù *walk with one's head bowed* | ～头弯腰 dītóu wānyāo *lower one's head and crouch one's back* | 姑娘不好意思地～下了头。Gūniang bùhǎoyìsi de dīxiàle tóu. *The girl lowered her head coyly.*

❸[形]在一般标准或平均程度之下：lower than the average standard or degree | 声音～ shēngyīn dī *in a low voice* | 水平～ shuǐpíng dī *of a low level* | 我的英语水平很～。Wǒ de Yīngyǔ shuǐpíng hěn dī. *My English is not good.*
低调 dīdiào ① low-key ② (photog.) low tone
低估 dīgū underestimate; underrate
低谷 dīgǔ all-time low

低廉 dīlián cheap; low
低劣 dīliè inferior; low-grade
低迷 dīmí (oft. of an economic depression) sluggish; slumping
低温 dīwēn low temperature; microtherm
低下 dīxià low; lowly
贬低 biǎndī 　　减低 jiǎndī
降低 jiàngdī

❹[形]等级在下的(跟"高gāo"相对)：low in grade (the opposite of "高gāo") | ～档 dīdàng *low-grade* | ～年级 dī niánjí *(of students) the junior years or lower grades* | 我比他～一年级。Wǒ bǐ tā dī yī niánjí. *I am one grade below him.*
低级 dījí elementary; rudimentary; lower; vulgar

堤 dī 12画 土部

堤 堤堤堤堤堤堤堤堤堤堤堤堤

[名]dyke; embankment | 河～ hédī *river embankment* / 海～ hǎidī *sea embankment*

嘀 dī 14画 口部

嘀 嘀嘀嘀嘀嘀嘀嘀嘀嘀嘀嘀嘀嘀嘀

See 嘀嗒
嘀嗒 dīdā tick; tick-tack
See dí.

滴 dī 14画 氵部

滴滴滴滴滴滴滴滴
滴滴滴滴滴滴

❶ [动](使)液体一点点落下来：drip | ～眼药水 dī yǎnyàoshuǐ *put eye drops into one's eyes* / 汗水直往下～。Hànshuǐ zhí wǎng xià dī. *Sweat kept dripping.*

❷ [名]落下的少量液体：drop of liquid | 雨～yǔdī *raindrops* / 汗～直往下落。Hàndī zhí wǎng xià luò. *Beads of sweat kept dripping.*

❸ [量]用于滴下的液体的数量：drop | 一～汗 yī dī hàn *a bead of sweat* / 两～眼泪 liǎng dī yǎnlèi *two drops of tears* / 几～油 jǐ dī yóu *several drops of oil*

的 dí 8画 白部

的 的的的的的的的的

[副]确实；实在：indeed; trully 的确 díquè *indeed; really*
◇ 的士 díshì (transliteration) taxi See de; dì.

敌 (敵) dí 10画 攵部

敌 敌敌敌敌敌敌敌敌
敌敌

❶ [名]对手；敌人：enemy; foe |

化～为友 huàdí wéiyǒu *turn an enemy into an ally* / 你怎么～我不分呢？Nǐ zěnme dí wǒ bù fēn ne? *How could you fail to distinguish between enemies and allies?*
敌人 dírén enemy; foe
敌视 díshì be hostile to; be antagonistic to; adopt a hostile attitude towards

❷ [动]抵挡；对抗：fight; resist; withstand | 北京队不～国家队，以一比二告负。Běijīng duì bù dí guójiāduì, yǐ yī bǐ èr gàofù. *The Beijing team was beaten by the national team 2:1.* / 你一个人～不过他们。Nǐ yī gè rén dí bù guò tāmen. *You alone are no rival to them.*
敌对 díduì hostile; antagonistic

涤 (滌) dí 10画 氵部

涤 涤涤涤涤涤涤涤涤
涤涤

[动]洗；清除：wash; cleanse 洗涤 xǐdí

笛 dí 11画 竹部

笛 笛笛笛笛笛笛笛笛
笛笛笛

❶ [名] bamboo flute | 竹 ~zhúdí *bamboo flute* / 长 ~chángdí *flute*

笛子 dízi flute; bamboo flute

❷ [名] 响声尖厉的发音器: whistle | 汽 ~qìdí *steam whistle* / 警 ~jǐngdí *police whistle; siren*

嘀 dí 14画 口部

嘀嘀嘀嘀嘀嘀嘀嘀
嘀嘀嘀嘀嘀嘀

See 嘀咕

嘀咕 dígu ① talk in whispers; talk in a very low voice ② have misgivings about sth.

See dī.

抵 dǐ 8画 扌部

抵抵抵抵抵抵抵抵

❶ [动] 支撑: support; sustain | 把门 ~上 bǎ mén dǐshang *prop sth. against the door* / 他双手 ~着下巴沉思。Tā shuāngshǒu dǐzhe xiàba chénsī. *He was thinking, with his chin propped in his hands.*

❷ [动] 挡; 抗拒: resist; withstand | 坚决 ~住 jiānjué dǐzhù *withstand firmly*

抵抗 dǐkàng resist; stand up to
抵制 dǐzhì resist; boycott

❸ [动] 相当; 能代替: be equal to |

一个人 ~两个人用。Yī gè rén dǐ liǎng gè rén yòng. *He can do the work of two men.*

❹ [动] 到达: arrive; reach | 平安 ~京 píng'ān dǐ jīng *arrive in Beijing safe and sound*

抵达 dǐdá arrive; reach

❺ [动] 抵押: mortgage | 贷款要拿房产作 ~。Dàikuǎn yào ná fángchǎn zuò dǐ. *To get a loan you need to mortgage the house.*

抵押 dǐyā mortgage

底 dǐ 8画 广部

底底底底底底底底

❶ [名] 最下面的部分: bottom; base | 海 ~hǎidǐ *the bottom of a sea* / 鞋 ~xiédǐ *sole (of a shoe)*

底部 dǐbù bottom; base
底盘 dǐpán chassis (of a car)
底下 dǐxià ① under; below; beneath ② next; later; afterwards
彻底 chèdǐ   到底 dàodǐ
井底之蛙 jǐngdǐzhīwā

❷ [名] 根源; 内情; 基础: base; basis; foundation

底线 dǐxiàn ① (sports) baseline of a football field, or a basketball or tennis court ② principle; base line

归根到底 guīgēn-dàodǐ

❸ [名] 做根据的底子: a copy or duplicate kept as a record | 留个 ~儿 liú gè dǐr *keep a copy on file;*

duplicate and file (a letter, etc.)
/ ～稿 dǐgǎo *draft; manuscript*
底片 dǐpiàn *negative; photographic plate*

❹[名]（时间的）末了；end｜年～ niándǐ *the end of a year* / 月～ yuèdǐ *the end of a month*

地 dì　6画 土部

地　地地地地地地

❶[名] 地球；陆地；土地：the earth; land; soil

地板 dìbǎn floor board

地道 dìdào tunnel

地道 dìdao authentic

地理 dìlǐ ① geographical features of a place ② geography

地面 dìmiàn the earth's surface; ground

地球 dìqiú the earth; the globe

地势 dìshì physical features of a place; terrain

地毯 dìtǎn carpet; rug

地铁 dìtiě metro; subway; underground

地图 dìtú map

地下 dìxià underground; subterranean

地下 dìxia on the ground

地形 dìxíng topography; terrain

地震 dìzhèn earthquake; seism

地质 dìzhì geology

地主 dìzhǔ landlord

地下水 dìxiàshuǐ groundwater

遍地 biàndì　　草地 cǎodì

大地 dàdì　　耕地 gēngdì

荒地 huāngdì　　陆地 lùdì

落地 luòdì　　绿地 lùdì

盆地 péndì　　山地 shāndì

天地 tiāndì　　田地 tiándì

土地 tǔdì　　种地 zhòngdì

房地产 fángdìchǎn

天昏地暗 tiānhūn-dì'àn

❷[名] 地区；地点：a certain area; place; locality｜目的～ mùdìdì *destination* / 这里是省会的所在～。Zhèlǐ shì shěnghuì de suǒzàidì. *This is the provincial capital.* / 请在原～等我。Qǐng zài yuándì děng wǒ. *Please stay where you are and wait for me.*

地带 dìdài district; region; zone; belt

地点 dìdiǎn place; site; locale

地段 dìduàn sector of a town, etc.; area

地方 dìfang ① place; space; room ② part; respect

地区 dìqū area; district; region

地址 dìzhǐ address

地方戏 dìfāngxì local opera; local drama

本地 běndì　　产地 chǎndì

场地 chǎngdì　　当地 dāngdì

各地 gèdì　　工地 gōngdì

基地 jīdì　　就地 jiùdì

内地 nèidì　　外地 wàidì

阵地 zhèndì

殖民地 zhímíndì

随时随地 suíshí-suídì

❸[名]处境;地位：position; situation | 留有余～liúyǒu-yúdì *allow for unforeseen circumstances; leave some leeway*
地步 dìbù extent; degree
地位 dìwèi position; standing; place; status
余地 yúdì
❹[名]衬托花纹图案的底子：background | 白～黑字 báidì hēizì *black characters on a white background*
　　See de.

 弟 dì 7画 ⺉部

弟 弟弟弟弟弟弟弟

❶[名]称同父母或同辈亲戚中年纪比自己小的男子：younger brother
弟弟 dìdi younger brother
弟兄 dìxiong brothers
表弟 biǎodì
❷[名]男性朋友间的谦称;称比自己年纪小的男性朋友：a modest form of address between men who are friends; used to address a younger man of one's same generation
◇弟子 dìzǐ disciple; pupil; follower

 的 dì 8画 白部

的 的的的的的的的的

[名]箭靶的中心：target; bull's-eye
目的 mùdì
　　See de; dí.

 帝 dì 9画 巾部

帝 帝帝帝帝帝帝帝帝帝

❶[名]上帝：the Supreme Being; God
❷[名]君主：emperor
帝国 dìguó empire
帝国主义 dìguó zhǔyì imperialism
皇帝 huángdì　黄帝 Huángdì
炎帝 Yándì

 递 (遞) dì 10画 辶部

递 递递递递递递递递递递

❶[动]传送：hand over; pass | ～支烟给他。Dì zhī yān gěi tā. *Hand him a cigarette.* / 请把报纸～给我。Qǐng bǎ bàozhǐ dìgěi wǒ. *Hand me the newspaper, please.*
递交 dìjiāo hand over; present; submit
传递 chuándì　快递 kuàidì
❷[副]顺次：successively; in the proper order
递增 dìzēng increase progre-

169

ssively

第 **dì** 11画 竹部

第 第第第第第第第第第
第第第第

[助]表示次序的词头：used before numerals to form ordinal numbers | 考试他得了全班～一名。Kǎoshì tā déle quánbān dì-yī míng. *He tops his class in the exam.* / 请把书翻到～3页。Qǐng bǎ shū fāndào dì-sān yè. *Please turn to page 3.*

第一 dì-yī first; primary; foremost

第二 dì-èr second

第三者 dìsānzhě third party (of disputes, divorce proceedings, etc.)

蒂 **dì** 12画 艹部

蒂 蒂蒂蒂蒂蒂蒂蒂蒂
蒂蒂蒂蒂

[名]the base of a fruit | 瓜熟～落 guāshú-dìluò *when a melon is ripe, it falls off its stem; things will be easily settled when conditions are ripe*

缔 (締) **dì** 12画 纟部

缔 缔缔缔缔缔缔缔缔
缔缔缔缔

[名]结合；订立：combine; unite | ～约 dìyuē *conclude a treaty*

缔结 dìjié conclude; establish

掂 **diān** 11画 扌部

掂 掂掂掂掂掂掂掂掂
掂掂掂

[动]用手托着东西上下抖动估量轻重：weigh sth. in the hand | 这个包～着不轻。Zhège bāo diānzhe bù qīng. *This bag feels heavy in the hand.* / ～～分量有多重。Diān diān fēnliàng yǒu duō zhòng. *Weigh this in your hand.*

颠 (顛) **diān** 16画 页部

颠 颠颠颠颠颠颠颠颠
颠颠颠颠颠颠颠颠

❶ [名]顶端：top; summit | 山～ shāndiān *the top of a mountain*

❷ [动]跌落；倒下：totter; tumble
颠倒 diāndǎo ① put upside down; turn upside down; transpose; reverse; invert ② confused; disordered
颠覆 diānfù overturn; subvert

❸ [动]摇动；震荡：jolt; bump | 车子～得厉害。Chēzi diān de lìhai. *The car jolted badly.*

颠簸 diānbǒ jolt; bump; toss

典　diǎn　8画 八部

典 典典典典典典典典

❶ [名] 可以作为标准、典范的书籍：classical works
词典 cídiǎn　　古典 gǔdiǎn
经典 jīngdiǎn　　字典 zìdiǎn

❷ [名] 标准；法则：standard; law
典范 diǎnfàn model; example; paragon
典型 diǎnxíng ① typical case (example); model; type ② typical; representative

❸ [名] 郑重举行的礼节、仪式等：ceremony
典礼 diǎnlǐ ceremony; celebrations
庆典 qìngdiǎn
◇典故 diǎngù allusion

点 (點) diǎn　9画 灬部

点 点点点点点点点点
点

❶ [名] 液体的小滴：spot; dot; speck; drop
水点 shuǐdiǎn　　污点 wūdiǎn
雨点 yǔdiǎn

❷ [名] 小的痕迹：spot; dot; speck | 斑~bāndiǎn spot; stain / 黑~hēidiǎn a black spot
墨点 mòdiǎn　　油点 yóudiǎn

❸ [名] 汉字的笔画，形状是"、"：dot stroke (、) in Chinese characters | 这个字少写了一~。Zhège zì shǎoxiěle yī diǎn. This character is missing a dot stroke.

❹ [名] 时间单位，相当于"时shí"：(used to indicate time) o'clock | 飞机9~到京。Fēijī jiǔ diǎn dào jīng. The plane will arrive in Beijing at 9:00. / 现在是下午两~。Xiànzài shì xiàwǔ liǎng diǎn. It's two o'clock in the afternoon.

❺ [名] 钟点；规定的时间：o'clock; appointed time | 到~了。Dào diǎn le. It's time.
钟点 zhōngdiǎn
钟点工 zhōngdiǎngōng

❻ [名] 一定的位置或程度的标志：point (indicating locality or degree) | 起~qǐdiǎn starting point / 沸~fēidiǎn boiling point
点球 diǎnqiú (football) penalty kick
景点 jǐngdiǎn　　热点 rèdiǎn
出发点 chūfādiǎn

❼ [名] 事物的方面或部分：part; point; aspect | 从这~来看 cóng zhè diǎn lái kàn view from this point (aspect)
焦点 jiāodiǎn　　论点 lùndiǎn
难点 nándiǎn　　缺点 quēdiǎn
弱点 ruòdiǎn　　视点 shìdiǎn
特点 tèdiǎn　　要点 yàodiǎn
疑点 yídiǎn　　优点 yōudiǎn
重点 zhòngdiǎn

典
点

diǎn

❽[名]小数点：point | 3.2 读作三点二。3.2 dúzuò sān diǎn èr. *3.2 is read as three point two.*
小数点 xiǎoshùdiǎn

❾[名]数学中指没有长、宽、高而只有位置的几何图形交点：point, a geometric figure

❿[名]点心；食品：pastry | 茶～ chádiǎn *tea and pastries; refreshments* / 糕～ gāodiǎn *cake; pastry*
点心 diǎnxin refreshments
早点 zǎodiǎn

⓫[动]用笔加上点子：put a dot | 他在字下面～了一个点儿。Tā zài zì xiàmian diǎnle yī gē diǎnr. *He put a dot under the character.* / 老师告诉我们怎样～标点符号。Lǎoshī gàosu wǒmen zěnyàng diǎn biāodiǎn fúhào. *The teacher taught us how to use punctuation marks.*
标点 biāodiǎn

⓬[动]装饰：embellish; ornament; adorn
点缀 diǎnzhuì ① embellish; ornament; adorn ② use sth. merely for decoration

⓭[动]一落一起的动作：move up and down; touch on briefly | ～了下头 diǎnle xià tóu *nod one's head* / 用手指～了点 yòng shǒuzhǐ diǎnle diǎn *point at sth. with one's finger*
点播 diǎnbō request a pro-

gramme from a radio station, etc.

⓮[动]使液体一点点落下：drip | ～眼药水 diǎn yǎnyàoshuǐ *put in eye drops*

⓯[动]逐个查对：check one by one | ～货品 diǎn huòpǐn *check over goods; take stock*
点名 diǎnmíng ① make a roll-call; call the roll; call out names ② mention by name; name
盘点 pándiǎn

⓰[动]指定：select; choose | ～歌 diǎngē *song requested by a listener; request a song to be played on the radio, TV, etc.* / ～菜 diǎncài *order dishes (in a restaurant)*
点击 diǎnjī click; hit

⓱[动]指明；启示：instruct; hint | 一～就明白 yī diǎn jiù míngbai *take the hint quickly* / ～破真相 diǎnpò zhēnxiàng *throw light on the truth* / ～到了要害 diǎndàole yàohài *come to the point; hit the point*
点评 diǎnpíng ① make comments on; discuss ② comment (spoken or written)
指点 zhǐdiǎn

⓲[动]燃火：light; burn; kindle | ～灯 diǎndēng *light a lamp* / ～蜡烛 diǎn làzhú *light a candle*
点火 diǎnhuǒ ① light a fire ② ignition
点燃 diǎnrán light; kindle; ig-

nite

❶ [量]表示少量的：a little | 喝～儿水 hē diǎnr shuǐ *drink some water* / 多做一～儿工作 duō zuò yīdiǎnr gōngzuò *do a little more work*

差点儿 chàdiǎnr

一点儿 yīdiǎnr

有点儿 yǒudiǎnr

❷ [量]用于事项：item; part | 三～意见 sān diǎn yìjiàn *three suggestions* / 内容有四～。Nèiróng yǒu sì diǎn. *The content consists of four points.*

◇点子 diǎnzi ① key point ② idea; pointer

出点子 chūdiǎnzi

百分点 bǎifēndiǎn

 电（電）diàn 5画 | 部

电 电电电电电

❶ [名] electricity

电车 diànchē trolleybus

电池 diànchí (electric) cell; battery

电灯 diàndēng electric lamp; electric bulb

电动 diàndòng (of machinery) power-driven

电话 diànhuà telephone; phone

电力 diànlì electric power; power

电铃 diànlíng electric bell

电流 diànliú electric current

电炉 diànlú ① electric stove; hot plate ② electric furnace

电路 diànlù electric circuit

电脑 diànnǎo computer

电气 diànqì electric

电器 diànqì electrical appliance; electrical equipment

电扇 diànshàn electric fan

电视 diànshì television

电台 diàntái ① transmitter-receiver; transceiver ② radio station

电梯 diàntī lift; elevator

电网 diànwǎng electrified wire netting; live wire entanglement

电线 diànxiàn electric wires

电信 diànxìn telecommunications

电压 diànyā voltage

电影 diànyǐng film; movie; motion picture

电源 diànyuán electricity supply

电子 diànzǐ electron

电冰箱 diànbīngxiāng refrigerator; fridge; freezer

电风扇 diànfēngshàn electric fan

电话卡 diànhuàkǎ telephone card

电话亭 diànhuàtíng telephone booth; telephone kiosk; call box

电视机 diànshìjī television; TV

电视剧 diànshìjù TV drama; TV play

电视台 diànshìtái TV station

电影院 diànyǐngyuàn cinema

充电 chōngdiàn　发电 fādiàn
闪电 shǎndiàn　水电 shuǐdiàn
停电 tíngdiàn
手电筒 shǒudiàntǒng
公用电话 gōngyòng diànhuà
❷ [动]电流打击；触电：give or get an electric shock｜别~着了。Bié diànzháo le. *Be careful of the strong electric current.*
❸ [名]电报：telegram｜贺~hèdiàn *message of congratulation; congratulatory telegram*
外电 wàidiàn　　邮电 yóudiàn
致电 zhìdiàn
◇彩电 cǎidiàn
无线电 wúxiàndiàn

店　　diàn　8画 广部
店 店店店店店店店店

❶ [名] 商店：store; shop｜花~ huādiàn *florist shop* / 新开了一个~ xīn kāile yī gè diàn *a shop is newly opened*
店铺 diànpù shop; store
店员 diànyuán salesman or saleswoman; shop assistant
店主 diànzhǔ ① shopkeeper ② innkeeper; restaurateur
饭店 fàndiàn　　酒店 jiǔdiàn
商店 shāngdiàn　书店 shūdiàn
药店 yàodiàn
专卖店 zhuānmàidiàn
❷ [名] 旅店：inn

垫 (墊) diàn　9画 土部
垫 垫垫垫垫垫垫垫垫
垫

❶ [动]用东西支、铺或衬：put sth. under sth. else to raise it or make it level; cushion; pad｜把桌子~高 bǎ zhuōzi diàngāo *put sth. under the legs of the table to increase its height* / 床不平，需要~一~。Chuáng bù píng, xūyào diànyidiàn. *You need to put sth. under the bed to make it level.*
❷ [名]垫在下面的东西：pad; cushion; mat｜~子 diànzi *mat; pad; cushion* / 床~chuángdiàn *mattress*
垫圈 diànquān (mech.) washer
气垫 qìdiàn
❸ [动]暂时替人付钱：pay for sb. (and expect to be repaid later)｜我先给你~上。Wǒ xiān gěi nǐ diànshang. *I will pay for you for the time being (and you can pay me back later).*

淀 (澱) diàn　11画 氵部
淀 淀淀淀淀淀淀淀淀
淀淀淀

[动]液体里沉下来东西：form sediment

174

淀粉 diànfěn starch
沉淀 chéndiàn

惦 diàn 11画 忄部

惦 掂掂掂掂掂掂掂掂
掂掂掂

[动]挂念：be concerned about; keep thinking about | ～念 diànniàn keep thinking about / ～记 diànjì remember with concern / 她心里只～着孩子。Tā xīnli zhǐ diànzhe háizi. She is only concerned about her child.

奠 diàn 12画 大部

奠 奠奠奠奠奠奠奠奠
奠奠奠奠

❶ [动] 陈列祭品向死者致祭：make offerings to the spirit of the dead | 祭～jìdiàn hold a memorial ceremony
❷ [动] 安置；建立：establish; settle 奠定diàndìng establish; settle

殿 diàn 13画 殳部

殿 殿殿殿殿殿殿殿殿
殿殿殿殿殿

[名]高大的建筑物；特指封建帝王受理朝事或宗教徒供奉神佛的房屋：hall; palace, esp. imperial palace (where the emperors handle state affairs, or the followers of a religion make offerings to the god, buddha, etc.) | 太和～Tàihédiàn the Hall of Supreme Harmony

习 diāo 2画 乛部

习 习习

[形]狡诈；无赖：tricky; artful; sly | 做人不能太～，要宽厚一些。Zuòrén bùnéng tài diāo, yào kuānhòu yī xiē. One shouldn't be deceitful to others. It's better to be honest and broad-minded instead.

叼 diāo 5画 口部

叼 叼叼叼叼叼

[动]用嘴夹住：hold in the mouth | 嘴里～着一支烟 zuǐ li diāozhe yī zhī yān bite a cigarette between one's teeth / 狼把一只羊羔～走了。Láng bǎ yī zhī yánggāo diāozǒu le. The wolf ran off with a lamb in its mouth.

雕 diāo 16画 隹部

雕 雕雕雕雕雕雕雕雕
雕雕雕雕雕雕雕

❶ [名]vulture

❷[动]雕刻：carve; engrave
雕刻 diāokè carve; engrave
雕塑 diāosù sculpture
❸[名]雕刻成的器物：carving |
木～mùdiāo wood carving
浮雕 fúdiāo

吊　　　diāo　6画 口部

吊 吊吊吊吊吊吊吊

❶[动]祭奠死者,或向死者家属、有
关团体表示慰问：offer condo-
lence; hold a memorial ceremony for the dead or offer con-
dolences to the family or related
group of the deceased |～丧
diāosāng pay a condolence visit
❷[动]悬挂：hang; suspend | 门前～
着两盏灯。Ménqián diāozhe
liǎng zhǎn dēng. There are two
lights hanging over the door.
❸[动]用绳子向上提或向下放：lift
up or let down with a rope |～
水 diāoshuǐ draw water / 把楼
板～上去。Bǎ lóubǎn diāo
shàngqu. Hoist up the floor slab.

钓（釣）diāo　8画 钅部

钓 钓钓钓钓钓钓钓钓

[动]fish |～鱼 diāoyú angle; go
fishing

调（調）diāo　10画 讠部

调 调调调调调调调调调
调调

❶[动]调动; 分派：transfer; shift
|～工作 diāo gōngzuò trans-
fer to another post / 他是从外
地～来的。Tā shì cóng wàidì
diāolái de. He was transferred
from other parts of the country.
/ 老师想把他～到二年级去。
Lǎoshī xiǎng bǎ tā diāodào
èr niánjí qù. The teacher wants
to transfer him to the second
grade.
调动 diāodòng ① transfer;
shift ②move (troops); manoeuvre; muster ③ bring into play;
arouse; mobilize
调度 diāodù ①dispatch (trains,
buses, etc.) ②dispatcher ③man-
age; control
调换 diāohuàn exchange; change;
swap
❷[动]考查; 了解：investigate
调查 diāochá investigate; inquire into; look into; survey
❸[名]戏曲或歌曲的调子：(of an
opera or a song) melody; tune
| 这个～儿很好听。Zhège
diāor hěn hǎotīng. The tune
is melodious.
唱反调 chàngfǎndiāo
唱高调 chànggāodiāo

❹[名]说话的声音、语气等：tone; tune | 他说话的～儿有点儿特别。Tā shuōhuà de diàor yǒudiǎnr tèbié. *His tone of speaking is a bit unusual.*

低调 dīdiào 高调 gāodiào
声调 shēngdiào 语调 yǔdiào
See tiáo.

掉 diào 11画 扌部

掉掉掉掉掉掉掉掉
掉掉掉

❶[动]回转：turn | ～过脸来diào-guò liǎn lai *turn one's face*
掉头 diàotóu turn round; turn about

❷[动]对换：exchange; change | ～个座位 diào ge zuòwèi *exchange seats; swap places with sb.*
掉换 diàohuàn change; exchange

❸[动]落下：fall; drop | ～头发diào tóufa *lose one's hair* / ～眼泪 diào yǎnlèi *shed tears* / 帽子～在地上了。Màozi diào zài dìshang le. *The cap fell on the ground.*
老掉牙 lǎodiàoyá

❹[动]落在后面：fall behind
掉队 diàoduì drop out; drop off; fall behind

❺[动]遗失；遗漏：lose; be missing | 钢笔～了。Gāngbǐ diào le. *The pen is lost.* / 帽子不知～在什么地方了。Màozi bùzhī diào-zài shénme dìfang le. *The hat has been left somewhere.*
丢掉 diūdiào

❻[动]减损；降低：reduce | 鸡蛋的价格一直～不下来。Jī dàn de jiàgé yīzhí diào bù xiàlái. *The price of eggs hasn't fallen recently.*
掉价 diàojià fall in price; devalue

❼[动]在动词后表示去除或离开：used after certain verbs to indicate to get rid of or to leave from | 把东西吃～bǎ dōngxi chī-diào *eat sth. up* / 改～了坏习气 gǎidiàole huài xíqì *have abandoned bad habits*

爹 diē 10画 父部

爹爹爹爹爹爹爹爹
爹爹

[名]父亲：father

跌 diē 12画 𧾷部

跌跌跌跌跌跌跌
跌跌跌跌

❶[动]摔倒：fall; stumble | ～了个跟头 diēle ge gēntou *have a fall* / 他～伤了。Tā diēshāng le. *He fell down and got injured.*

下跌 xiàdiē

❷[动] 下降：drop; fall | 这几天股票~得厉害。Zhè jǐ tiān gǔpiào diē de lìhai. *These days stock prices are dropping sharply.* / 物价~下来了。Wùjià diē xiàlai le. *The prices of consumer goods have dropped.*

谍 (諜) dié　11画 讠部

谍谍谍谍谍谍谍谍谍谍谍

[名] espionage | 间~jiàndié *spy*

叠 dié　13画 又部

叠叠叠叠叠叠叠叠叠叠叠叠叠

❶[动] 一层一层往上加；累积：pile up; overlap | 把书一摞一摞~好。Bǎ shū yī luò yī luò diéhǎo. *Pile up the books.*
重叠 chóngdié

❷[动] 折叠：fold | ~衣服 dié yīfu *fold up clothes* / ~报纸 dié bàozhǐ *fold the newspaper*

碟 dié　14画 石部

碟碟碟碟碟碟碟碟碟碟碟碟碟碟

[名] 盛食物等的小盘子：small plate

| 菜~儿 càidiér *a small dish plate*
碟子 diézi small plate
飞碟 fēidié　光碟 guāngdié

蝶 dié　15画 虫部

蝶蝶蝶蝶蝶蝶蝶蝶蝶蝶蝶蝶蝶蝶蝶

[名] butterfly
蝴蝶 húdié

丁 dīng　2画 一部

丁丁丁

❶[名] 天干的第四位，也用作次序第四：the fourth of the ten Heavenly Stems; the fourth in a sequence | 他在甲班，我在~班。Tā zài jiǎbān, wǒ zài dīngbān. *He is in Class A and I am in Class D.*

❷[名] 成年男子；从事某种劳动的人：man; a person engaged in a certain occupation (usu. manual work)
园丁 yuándīng

❸[名] 蔬菜、肉类切成的小块：small cube of meat or vegetable; cube | 肉~儿 ròudīngr *cubes of meat* / 鸡~儿 jīdīngr *cubes of chicken*

叮 dīng 5画 口部

叮 叮叮叮叮叮

❶ [动] 蚊子等咬人：sting; bite | 腿上被蚊子~了一口 tuǐshang bèi wénzi dīngle yī kǒu *get a mosquito bite on the leg*

❷ [动] 再三嘱咐：urge again and again; remind repeatedly
叮嘱 dīngzhǔ remind repeatedly; exhort

盯 dīng 7画 目部

盯 盯盯盯盯盯盯盯

[动] 把视线集中在一点上；注视：gaze at; stare at; fix one's eyes on | 两眼~着她看 liǎngyǎn dīngzhe tā kàn *fix one's eyes on her* / 他~着墙上的照片，回忆着往事。Tā dīngzhe qiáng shang de zhàopiàn, huíyìzhe wǎngshì. *Staring at the picture on the wall, he recalled the past.*

钉 (釘) dīng 7画 钅部

钉 钉钉钉钉钉钉钉

❶ [名] nail; tack
钉子 dīngzi nail
螺丝钉 luósīdīng

❷ [动] 紧跟着：follow closely; tail

| 小李~住了对方的前锋。Xiǎo Lǐ dīngzhùle duìfāng de qiánfēng. *Xiao Li is guarding the forward of the opposite team.* / 有人一直在~我的梢。Yǒu rén yīzhí zài dīng wǒ de shāo. *Someone has been tailing me.*

❸ [动] 督促；催：urge; press | 你要经常~着他吃药。Nǐ yào jīngcháng dīngzhe tā chīyào. *You must remind him regularly to take his medicine.*
碰钉子 pèngdīngzi
See dìng.

顶 (頂) dǐng 8画 页部

顶 顶顶顶顶顶顶顶顶

❶ [名] 最高最上的部分：top; peak; summit; crown | 头~tóudǐng *the crown of the head* / 山~shāndǐng *the top of a mountain*
顶点 dǐngdiǎn apex; zenith; acme; pinnacle
顶端 dǐngduān top; peak; apex
顶尖 dǐngjiān ① top-class ② tip
顶头上司 dǐngtóu shàngsi (inf.) one's immediate (or direct) superior
屋顶 wūdǐng

❷ [副] 最；极：very, most, extremely

179

| ～好 **dǐnghǎo** *the best* | ～多再有两个星期就放假了。**Dǐngduō zài yǒu liǎng gè xīngqī jiù fàngjià le.** *The holiday is coming in two weeks.*

❸ [量]用于有顶的东西：used for sth. with a top | 两～帽子 **liǎng dǐng màozi** *two caps*

❹ [动]用头支着：support with one's head | 她用头～着一罐水。**Tā yòng tóu dǐngzhe yī guàn shuǐ.** *She carried a pitcher of water on her head.* / 这么重的东西，我可～不动。**Zhème zhòng de dōngxi, wǒ kě dǐngbudòng.** *I can't carry such a heavy thing on my head.*

❺ [动]用东西支撑或抵住：prop up | 把门～好 **bǎ mén dǐnghǎo** *prop sth. against the door*

❻ [副]相当；抵得上：equal; be equivalent to | 他干活儿一个人～两个人。**Tā gànhuór yī gè rén dǐng liǎng gè rén.** *He did the work of two men.*

❼ [动]代替：take the place of; substitute; replace | 拿次货～好货 **ná cìhuò dǐng hǎohuò** *substitute goods of superior quality with goods of inferior quality*

顶替 **dǐngtì** take sb.'s place; replace

❽ [动]用头撞击：gore; butt | ～球 **dǐngqiú** head a ball | 这头牛～人。**Zhè tóu niú dǐng rén.** *This bull gores people.*

❾ [动]迎着：go against; brave | ～风冒雪 **dǐngfēng-màoxuě** *brave wind and snow*

❿ [动]顶撞，强硬地反驳别人：contradict; retort | 妻子～了他几句。**Qīzi dǐngle tā jǐ jù.** *His wife said a few words to him in retort.*

⓫ [动]从下面拱起：push from below; prop up | 蒸汽把锅盖～起来了。**Zhēngqì bǎ guōgài dǐng qǐlai le.** *Steam has pushed up the lid of the cooking pot.*

订 (訂) dìng 4画 讠部

订 订订订订

❶ [动]改正；核定：make corrections; revise
修订 **xiūdìng**

❷ [动]经过商量而立下条约、计划、章程等：draw up; conclude; agree on (a treaty, a plan, regulations, etc.) | ～条约 **dìng tiáoyuē** *conclude a treaty* / ～计划 **dìng jìhuà** *draw up a plan* / ～规章制度 **dìng guīzhāng zhìdù** *lay down rules and regulations*

订婚 **dìnghūn** be engaged; be betrothed

签订 **qiāndìng** 制订 **zhìdìng**

❸ [动]预订：subscribe to; book; order | ～报纸 **dìng bàozhǐ**

subscribe to a newspaper | ~了
两桌酒席 dìngle liǎng zhuō
jiǔxí *order two tables for a feast*
订单 dìngdān *order for goods;
order form*
订购 dìnggòu *order (goods)*
订货 dìnghuò *order goods*
订阅 dìngyuè *subscribe*
预订 yùdìng

❹[动] 把书页等穿连成册: *staple
together* | ~书机 dìngshūjī
stapler; stapling machine
装订 zhuāngdìng

钉 (釘) dìng 7画 钅部

钉 钉钉钉钉钉钉钉

❶[动] 用钉子把东西固定起来: *nail* |
~钉子 dìng dīngzi *drive in a
nail*
❷[动] 缝合在一起: *sew on* | ~扣
子 dìng kòuzi *sew a button on*
See dīng.

定 dìng 8画 宀部

定 定定定定定定定定

❶[形] (使)平静; 安稳: *calm down*
| 心神不~ xīnshén-búdìng *be
ill at ease; feel restless* | ~下心
来 dìngxià xīn lai *pull oneself
together*
安定 āndìng   不定 búdìng
稳定 wěndìng   镇定 zhèndìng

❷[动] 使确定; 决定: *decide; fix; set*
| ~计划 dìng jìhuà *make a
plan* | 会议~在明天上午开。
Huìyì dìng zài míngtiān
shàngwǔ kāi. *The meeting is
scheduled for tomorrow morning.*
定点 dìngdiǎn *fixed point; designated place*
定金 dìngjīn *deposit (put down
on sth. for future purchase)*
定居 dìngjū *settle down*
定位 dìngwèi ① *fixed posi-
tion; location; orientation* ② *ori-
entate; position*
定性 dìngxìng *determine the
nature of sth.*

裁定 cáidìng   测定 cèdìng
奠定 diàndìng   断定 duàndìng
否定 fǒudìng   假定 jiǎdìng
界定 jièdìng   决定 juédìng
肯定 kěndìng   拟定 nǐdìng
判定 pàndìng   评定 píngdìng
确定 quèdìng   设定 shèdìng
审定 shěndìng   锁定 suǒdìng
协定 xiédìng   选定 xuǎndìng
预定 yùdìng   约定 yuēdìng
指定 zhǐdìng   制定 zhìdìng
注定 zhùdìng

❸[形] 不可改变的, 已经确定的:
fixed; established; settled
定理 dìnglǐ *theorem*
定律 dìnglǜ *law*
定义 dìngyì *definition*
必定 bìdìng   法定 fǎdìng
固定 gùdìng   坚定 jiāndìng
限定 xiàndìng   议定 yìdìng

181

不一定 bùyīdìng

议定书 yìdìngshū

❹ [动]预先约好：subscribe to; order | ~票 dìngpiào *book a ticket* / ~货 dìnghuò *order goods; place an order for goods*

定购 dìnggòu order

❺ [形]规定的：fixed, established

定额 dìng'é quota; norm

定价 dìngjià ① fix a price ② fixed price; price

定量 dìngliàng ration; fixed quantity

定期 dìngqī ① fix a date ② regular; at regular intervals; periodical

定向 dìngxiàng ① directional ②orient ③orientation; sense of orientation

规定 guīdìng　特定 tèdìng

◇定语 dìngyǔ (gram.) attribute

丢　diū　6画 厶部

丢　丢丢丢丢丢丢

❶ [动]失去：lose; be missing | 手表~了。Shǒubiǎo diū le. *The watch is lost.*

丢人 diūrén lose face; be disgraced

丢失 diūshī lose

❷ [动]扔；抛弃：throw; cast; toss | 不要随地~纸屑。Bùyào suídì diū zhǐxiè. *Don't litter scraps of paper.* / 把钥匙~过来 bǎ yàoshi diū guòlai *toss me the keys*

❸ [动]搁置；放：put aside; dismiss (from one's mind) | 这件事情不能~开不管。Zhè jiàn shìqing bùnéng diūkāi bù guǎn. *This matter cannot be completely ignored.*

东 (東) dōng　5画 一部

东　东东东东东东

❶ [名] east | 由西向~ yóu xī xiàng dōng *from west to east* / 往~走一点儿，就到邮局了。Wǎng dōng zǒu yīdiǎnr, jiù dào yóujú le. *Go eastwards a little further and there is the post office.*

东北 dōngběi ① northeast ② northeast China; the Northeast

东边 dōngbian the east side

东部 dōngbù the eastern area

东侧 dōngcè east side

东方 dōngfāng ① east ② the East; the Orient

东风 dōngfēng ① east wind; spring wind ② driving force of revolution

东海 Dōng Hǎi the Donghai Sea; the East China Sea

东面 dōngmian ① face east ② the east

东南 dōngnán ① southeast ② southeast China; the Southeast

东半球 dōngbànqiú the Eastern Hemisphere

东奔西走 dōngbēn-xīzǒu run to and fro; run about busily (for sth.)

中东 Zhōngdōng

❷[名] 主人；请客的人：host | 这次请客谁做~? Zhècì qǐngkè shéi zuòdōng? *Who will be the host this time?*

东道主 dōngdàozhǔ one who treats sb. (to a meal, etc.); host

房东 fángdōng 股东 gǔdōng

◇东西 dōngxi thing; creature

冬 dōng 5画 夂部

冬 冬冬冬冬冬

[名] 一年四季中的第四季：winter | 寒~腊月 hándōng làyuè *a severe winter; a hard winter* / ~去春来 dōng qù chūn lái *spring follows winter*

冬季 dōngjì winter

冬青 dōngqīng (bot.) Chinese ilex

冬天 dōngtiān winter

越冬 yuèdōng

◇冬瓜 dōngguā wax gourd; white gourd

董 dǒng 12画 艹部

董 董董董董董董董董 董董董董

[动]监督管理：direct; supervise

董事 dǒngshì director; trustee

董事会 dǒngshìhuì board of directors (in an enterprise); board of trustees (in an educational institution)

董事长 dǒngshìzhǎng chairman (or president) of the board of directors

懂 dǒng 15画 忄部

懂 懂懂懂懂懂懂懂懂 懂懂懂懂懂懂懂

[动]明白；了解：understand; know | 他~俄语。Tā dǒng Éyǔ. *He knows Russian.* / 你的话我听不~。Nǐ de huà wǒ tīngbudǒng. *I don't understand what you are saying.*

懂得 dǒngde understand; know; grasp

懂事 dǒngshì sensible; perceptive

动 (動) dòng 6画 力部

动 动动动动动动

❶[动]改变原来的位置或状态（跟"静jìng"相对）：move; stir (the opposite of "静jìng") | 微风吹~树叶。Wēifēng chuī dòng shùyè. *A breeze stirred the leaves.* / 桌子上的书~过了。Zhuōzi shang de shū dòngguo le. *The book on the table has been moved.*

动词 dòngcí (gram.) verb

动荡 dòngdàng turbulence; upheaval; unrest

动感 dònggǎn (of images in paintings, sculpture, literature, etc.) dynamic; vibrant with life; lively; vivid

动画 dònghuà animated cartoon; cartoon; motion picture

动力 dònglì ① motive power; power ② motive force; driving force; impetus

动乱 dòngluàn turmoil; disturbance; upheaval; turbulence

动脉 dòngmài artery

动身 dòngshēn go on a journey; set out on a journey

动态 dòngtài trends; developments

动向 dòngxiàng trend; tendency

动摇 dòngyáo shake; vacillate; waver

摆动 bǎidòng	变动 biàndòng
波动 bōdòng	颤动 chàndòng
打动 dǎdòng	电动 diàndòng
浮动 fúdòng	滚动 gǔndòng
活动 huódòng	流动 liúdòng
跳动 tiàodòng	移动 yídòng
运动 yùndòng	振动 zhèndòng
震动 zhèndòng	
转动 zhuǎndòng	
自动 zìdòng	

不动产 bùdòngchǎn

机动车 jīdòngchē

运动会 yùndònghuì

运动员 yùndòngyuán

❷[动] 使用: use | ~脑筋 dòng nǎojīn *use one's brain*

动手 dòngshǒu ① start work; get to work ② touch; handle

动用 dòngyòng put to use; employ; draw on

机动 jīdòng

❸[动] 活动; 行动: act; get moving | 只要大家都~起来, 事情就好办了。Zhǐyào dàjiā dōu dòng qǐlai, shìqing jiù hǎobàn le. *It will be easier if everybody puts in the effort.*

动工 dònggōng ① begin construction; start building ② construct

动机 dòngjī motive; intention

动静 dòngjing movement; activity

动作 dòngzuò movement; motion; action

暴动 bàodòng	被动 bèidòng
出动 chūdòng	带动 dàidòng
发动 fādòng	反动 fǎndòng
互动 hùdòng	开动 kāidòng
劳动 láodòng	启动 qǐdòng
推动 tuīdòng	行动 xíngdòng
主动 zhǔdòng	
发动机 fādòngjī	
劳动力 láodònglì	

❹[动] 使人情感受触动: touch (one's heart); arouse | ~感情

dōng gǎnqíng *be carried away by emotion; get worked up*
动人 dòngrén *moving; touching*
动员 dòngyuán *mobilize; arouse*
冲动 chōngdòng
调动 diàodòng 感动 gǎndòng
鼓动 gǔdòng 轰动 hōngdòng
激动 jīdòng 惊动 jīngdòng
❺[动] 作动词的补语：(used as a complement after a verb) *be moved* | 拿得～ nádedòng *be able to carry* | 走不～ zǒubudòng *be unable to walk* | 箱子太重，你一个人拿不～. Xiāngzi tài zhòng, nǐ yī gè rén ná-budòng. *The trunk is too heavy, you can't carry it alone.*
◇动物 dòngwù *animal*
动物园 dòngwùyuán *zoo*

冻（凍）dòng 7画 冫部

冻 冻冻冻冻冻冻冻

❶[动] 液体遇冷凝结：*freeze* | 水～成冰了. Shuǐ dòngchéng bīng le. *Water is frozen into ice.*
冻结 dòngjié *freeze; congeal*
❷[动] 受冷; 感到冷：*feel cold* | 多穿点儿衣服，别～着. Duō chuān diǎnr yīfu, bié dòngzháo. *Put on more clothes to keep warm.* | 孩子的脚～了. Háizi de jiǎo dòng le. *The child's feet are frostbitten.*

栋（棟）dòng 9画 木部

栋 栋栋栋栋栋栋栋栋栋栋

[量] 用于房屋：*used for buildings* | 五～楼房 wǔ dòng lóufáng *five buildings*

洞 dòng 9画 氵部

洞 洞洞洞洞洞洞洞洞洞洞

[名] 物体上穿通的或凹入很深的部分：*hole; cavity; cave* | 这个～很深. Zhège dòng hěn shēn. *This cave is quite deep.* | 衣服上破了一个～. Yīfu shang pòle yī gè dòng. *There is a hole in the clothes.*
漏洞 lòudòng

都 dōu 10画 阝(右)部

都 都都都都都都都都都都都

❶[副] 表示总括全部：*all; both* | 大家～来了. Dàjiā dōu lái le. *Everybody is here.* | 人人～说好. Rénrén dōu shuō hǎo. *Everybody agrees with it.*
❷[副] 甚至：*even* | 他的事连我～不知道. Tā de shì lián wǒ dōu bù zhīdào. *Even I know noth-*

ing about his matter.

❸[副] 已经：already ｜ 天～黑了,
快走吧! Tiān dōu hēi le, kuài
zǒu ba! *It's already dark. Hurry
up!* / 饭～凉了, 快吃吧! Fàn
dōu liáng le, kuài chī ba! *The
meal is already cold. Eat quickly!*
/ ～半夜了, 快睡吧! Dōu bànyè
le, kuài shuì ba! *It's already midnight. Go to bed quickly.*

See **dū**.

dōu　11画 儿部

兜兜兜兜兜兜兜兜
兜兜兜

❶[动] 做成口袋形把东西拢住：wrap
up in a piece of cloth folded like a
bag, etc. ｜ 用头巾～着几个鸡蛋
yòng tóujīn dōuzhe jǐ gè
jīdàn *carry several eggs wrapped
up with a scarf*

❷[名] 口袋一类的东西：pocket;
bag ｜ 衣～儿 yīdōur *pocket* /
网～儿 wǎngdōur *string bag*
兜儿 dōur *pocket; bag*

抖

dǒu　7画 扌部

抖抖抖抖抖抖抖

❶[动] 颤动；哆嗦：tremble; shiver;
quiver ｜ 浑身直～húnshēn zhí
dǒu *tremble all over*
颤抖 chàndǒu　　发抖 fādǒu

❷[动] 振动；甩动：shake ｜ 把身上
的雪～掉 bǎ shēnshang de
xuě dǒudiào *shake off the
snow on one's body*

❸[动] 振作：rouse; stir up ｜ ～起
精神来 dǒuqǐ jīngshen lai
pluck up one's spirits

❹[动] 全部倒出：shake off; shake
out of sth. ｜ 他把抽屉里的东西
全～出来了。Tā bǎ chōuti li de
dōngxi quán dǒu chūlai le. *He
dumped everything out of the drawer.*

❺[动] 彻底揭穿：expose; bring to
light ｜ 老底～出来了。Lǎodǐ
dǒu chūlai le. *The unsavoury
past has been exposed.* / 在警察
面前, 他把知道的事全～出来
了。Zài jǐngchá miànqián, tā
bǎ zhīdào de shì quán dǒu
chūlai le. *He told the policemen
everything he knew.*

陡

dǒu　9画 阝(左)部

陡陡陡陡陡陡陡陡
陡

[形] 斜度很大：steep; precipitous ｜
这个坡真～。Zhège pō zhēn
dǒu. *This slope is really steep.* /
山～路险 shāndǒu-lùxiǎn *the
hill is steep and the route is dangerous*

(鬥) **dōu**　4画 斗部

斗斗斗斗

❶[动]对打：fight; struggle against
搏斗 bódòu 　　战斗 zhàndòu
❷[动]斗争：struggle; combat; fight
｜我们要坚决和坏人坏事～到
底。Wǒmen yào jiānjué hé
huàirén huàishì dòu dào dǐ.
*We should struggle resolutely
against evil-doers and evil
deeds.*
斗争 dòuzhēng struggle; combat; fight
斗志 dòuzhì will to fight; morale
奋斗 fèndòu
艰苦奋斗 jiānkǔ-fèndòu
❸[动]争胜：contest with; contend
with ｜ ～智 dòuzhì *duel of wits*
我～不过你。Wǒ dòubuguò
nǐ. *I'm no match for you.*
❹[动]使动物对打：make animals
fight (as a game or show) ｜ ～
牛 dòuniú *bullfight* / ～鸡 dòujī
cockfight

豆 **dòu** 7画 豆部
. . . .
豆 豆豆豆豆豆豆豆

❶[名]豆类植物的统称；这些植物
的种子：a general term for legumes (such as soybeans, peas
and broad beans), also indicates
their seeds
豆腐 dòufu bean curd; tofu
豆浆 dòujiāng soya-bean milk

豆角 dòujiǎo fresh kidney beans
豆奶 dòunǎi soya-bean milk
豆芽 dòuyá bean sprouts
豆子 dòuzi beans; peas; legumes
扁豆 biǎndòu 　　大豆 dàdòu
豌豆 wāndòu
荷兰豆 hélándòu
❷[名]形状像豆的东西：a bean-
shaped thing ｜ 花生～ huā-
shēngdòu *shelled peanut; peanut kernel*
土豆 tǔdòu

逗 **dōu** 10画 辶部

逗 逗逗逗逗逗逗逗逗
逗逗

❶[动]停留：stay; stop ｜ ～留
dōuliú *stay; stop*
❷[动]招引，惹：play with; tease;
tantalize ｜ 你别～了。Nǐ bié
dōu le. *Stop teasing me.* / 孩子
有一双～人喜爱的大眼睛。Háizi
yǒu yī shuāng dōu rén xǐ'ài
de dà yǎnjing. *The child has a
pair of charming big eyes.*

 dū 10画 阝(右)部

都 都都都都都都都都都
都都

❶[名]大城市：big city
都市 dūshì city; metropolis
❷[名]首都：capital
See dòu.

督

督 dū 13画 目部

督督督督督督督督
督督督督督

[动]监管; 察看：superintend and direct
督促 dūcù supervise and urge
◇基督教 Jīdūjiào

毒

毒 dú 9画 母部

毒毒毒毒毒毒毒毒
毒

❶ [名]对其他生物体有害的物质：poison; toxin | 蝎子有～。Xiēzi yǒu dú. *Scorpions are poisonous.*
病毒 bìngdú　　杀毒 shādú
消毒 xiāodú

❷ [名]对思想意识有害的事物：sth. that is harmful to one's mind | 他看黄色小说中了～。Tā kàn huángsè xiǎoshuō zhòngle dú. *Those pornographic novels have brought about a corrosive influence on him.* | 不要看这种书，小心中～。Bùyào kàn zhè zhǒng shū, xiǎoxīn zhòngdú. *Don't read this kind of book. Be careful not to be poisoned.*

❸ [形]凶狠; 残酷：malicious; cruel; fierce | 他的心肠真～! Tā de xīncháng zhēn dú! *How cruel he is!* | 太阳正～，把地都晒裂了。Tàiyáng zhèng dú, bǎ dì dōu shàiliè le. *The heat of the sun was so fierce that the land was dry and cracked.*
恶毒 èdú　　狠毒 hěndú

❹ [动]用有毒的东西杀害：kill with poison | 用药～老鼠 yòng yào dú lǎoshǔ *poison rats*
毒害 dúhài poison

❺ [形]有毒的：poisonous; noxious | 这是一条～蛇，千万小心。Zhè shì yī tiáo dúshé, qiānwàn xiǎoxīn. *This is a poisonous snake. You must be careful.*
毒品 dúpǐn narcotic drugs; narcotics
毒性 dúxìng poisonousness; toxicity

❻ [名]毒品：narcotics
毒贩 dúfàn drug trafficker
冰毒 bīngdú　　贩毒 fàndú
戒毒 jièdú

独

独 (獨) dú 9画 犭部

独独独独独独独独
独

❶ [形]单一; 只有一个：only; sole | ～子 dúzǐ *the only son* | ～木桥 dúmùqiáo *single plank (single-log) bridge*
独家 dújiā sole; the only one; exclusive
独特 dútè unique; distinctive

独有 **dúyǒu** have sth. all to oneself; monopolize

独生子女 **dúshēng zǐnǚ** only child

独一无二 **dúyī-wú'èr** unique; unparalleled; unmatched

❷[副]单独; 独自: alone | ~唱 **dúchàng** *solo* / ~坐 **dúzuò** *sit alone*

独立自主 **dúlì-zìzhǔ** maintain independence and keep the initiative; act independently and with the initiative in one's own hands

❸[形]自私; 容不得人: stand-offish | 这人很~, 从不跟人来往。**Zhè rén hěn dú, cóngbù gēn rén láiwǎng.** *He is rather stand-offish and has never had any dealings with other people.* / 一个人生活了二十多年, ~惯了。**Yī gè rén shēnghuóle èrshí duō nián, dú guàn le.** *I have lived by myself for more than 20 years and have been used to being alone.*

读 (讀) **dú** 10画 讠部

读 读读读读读读读读读 读读

❶[动] 照文字念出声来: read aloud | ~报 **dú bào** *read the newspaper aloud* / ~文章 **dú wénzhāng** *read the article aloud* /

请你把这封信~一~。**Qǐng nǐ bǎ zhè fēng xìn dúyidú.** *Please read this letter.*

读书 **dúshū** ① read; study ② attend school

朗读 **lǎngdú**　　宣读 **xuāndú**

重读 **zhòngdú**

❷[动] 阅读; 看: read | 这本书很容易~。**Zhè běn shū hěn róngyì dú.** *This book is easy to read.* / 这部小说值得一~。**Zhè bù xiǎoshuō zhíde yī dú.** *This novel is worth reading.*

读物 **dúwù** readings; reading material

读者 **dúzhě** reader

导读 **dǎodú**　　阅读 **yuèdú**

❸[动] 上学: go to school or college | 他在~大学。**Tā zài dú dàxué.** *He is studying at university.* / 他~完高中就参加了工作。**Tā dúwán gāozhōng jiù cānjiāle gōngzuò.** *He went to work after he graduated from high school.*

复读 **fùdú**　　攻读 **gōngdú**

堵 **dǔ** 11画 土部

堵 堵堵堵堵堵堵堵堵 堵堵堵

❶[动] 塞住: block up; stop up | 把洞~上 **bǎ dòng dǔshang** *block up the hole* / 别~着门! **Bié dǔzhe mén!** *Don't stand in the* doorway!

堵车 dǔchē traffic jam; traffic congestion

堵塞 dǔsè stop up; block up

❷ [形]心中不畅快：suffocated; oppressed | 心里~得慌 xīnli dǔdehuang *feel suffocated; feel tight in the chest*

❸ [量]用于墙壁：used for walls | 一~墙 yī dǔ qiáng *a wall*

赌 (賭) dǔ   12画 贝部

赌 | 赌赌赌赌赌赌赌赌赌赌赌赌

❶ [动]用财物作注来争输赢：gamble | 他~输了。Tā dǔshū le. *He lost at gambling.*

赌博 dǔbó gamble

赌场 dǔchǎng gambling house

❷ [动]泛指争输赢：bet | 我提出与他打~。Wǒ tíchū yǔ tā dǎdǔ. *I offered to bet with him.* / 咱俩打个~，看谁说的对。Zán liǎ dǎ ge dǔ, kàn shéi shuōdeduì. *Let's make a bet and see who is right.*

睹 dǔ   13画 目部

睹 | 睹睹睹睹睹睹睹睹睹睹睹睹睹

[动]看见：see | 有目共~ yǒumù-gòngdǔ *be there for all to see;*

be obvious to all

目睹 mùdǔ

杜 dù   7画 木部

杜 | 杜杜杜杜杜杜杜

[动]堵塞；防止：prevent; eradicate

杜绝 dùjué stop; put an end to

肚 dù   7画 月部

肚 | 肚肚肚肚肚肚肚

❶ [名] belly | ~里难受 dùli nánshòu *feel ill in the stomach* / 一口吞下~去 yīkǒu tūnxià dù qu *gobble up in one gulp*

肚子 dùzi belly; abdomen; stomach

大肚子 dàdùzi

❷ [名] 物体圆而凸起或中间鼓出的部分：(of certain object) a belly-shaped part

妒 dù   7画 女部

妒 | 妒妒妒妒妒妒妒

[动]因为别人比自己强而忌恨：be jealous (or envious) of; envy | 嫉~jídù *be envious of*

度 dù   9画 广部

190

度 度度度度度度度度
度

❶ [名]按一定计量标准规定的单位：(unit of measurement) degree, level

季度 jìdù   角度 jiǎodù
年度 niándù

❷ [名]程度；限度：limit; extent; degree | 劳累过~láolèi guòdù be overworked

长度 chángdù   程度 chéngdù
尺度 chǐdù   幅度 fúdù
高度 gāodù   过度 guòdù
宽度 kuāndù   厚度 hòudù
力度 lìdù   密度 mìdù
难度 nándù   浓度 nóngdù
强度 qiángdù   深度 shēndù
湿度 shīdù   速度 sùdù
温度 wēndù   限度 xiàndù
透明度 tòumíngdù
温度计 wēndùjì

❸ [名]法则，应遵守执行的标准：law; regulation
制度 zhìdù

❹ [动]经过；经历：spend; pass | 欢~佳节 huāndù jiājié joyously celebrate a festival
度过 dùguò tide over; go through
度假 dùjià spend one's holidays (or vacation); go on holiday

❺ [量]次：occasion; time | 一年一~yī nián yī dù once a year / 再~声明 zàidù shēngmíng state sth. for a second time
一度 yīdù

◇印度洋 Yìndùyáng

渡 dù 12画 氵部
渡 渡渡渡渡渡渡渡渡渡
渡渡渡渡

[动]由一岸到另一岸：cross (a river, the sea, etc.) | ~河 dùhé cross a river / 远~重洋 yuǎndù-chóngyáng travel across the vast oceans
渡船 dùchuán ferryboat; ferry
渡口 dùkǒu ferry
过渡 guòdù

镀 (鍍) dù 14画 钅部
镀 镀镀镀镀镀镀镀镀
镀镀镀镀镀镀

[动]用化学方法使一种金属附着到别的金属或器物的表面：plate | 这块铁皮上~了一层锌。Zhè kuài tiěpí shang dùle yī céng xīn. This iron-sheet has been plated with a layer of zinc.

端 duān 14画 立部
端 端端端端端端端端
端端端端端端

❶ [形]正；直：upright; proper | 品行不~pǐnxíng bù duān improper behaviour (or moral conduct); misconduct

端详 duānxiáng look sb. up and down

端正 duānzhèng ① upright; regular ② proper; correct

❷ [动]平举着拿：hold sth. level with both hands; carry | ～茶 duānchá *serve tea* / ～饭上菜 duānfàn shàngcài *serve a meal*

❸ [动]把事情、问题、困难等全摆出来：come out (with issues, problems, difficulties, etc.) | 有什么想法都～出来。Yǒu shénme xiǎngfǎ dōu duān chūlai. *Whatever you think, come out with it.* / 把问题全～出来，大家一起研究。Bǎ wèntí quán duān chūlai, dàjiā yìqǐ yánjiū. *Let's set forth all the problems and discuss them together.*

❹ [名]东西的一头：end; extremity | 从这一～到另一～cóng zhè yīduān dào lìng yīduān *from this end to that end* / 岛的南～dǎo de nánduān *the southern tip (end) of the island* 顶端 dǐngduān 高端 gāoduān 极端 jíduān 尖端 jiānduān 终端 zhōngduān

❺ [名]开头：beginning | 开～kāiduān *beginning*

❻ [名]项目；方面：item; point | 变化多～biànhuà duōduān *very changeable; always changing* / 举其一～jǔ qí yīduān *for instance; just to mention one example*

弊端 bìduān

◇ 端午节 Duānwǔjié the Dragon Boat Festival (the fifth day of the fifth lunar month)

duǎn 12画 矢部

短 短短短短短短短短短短短短

❶ [形]空间或时间的距离小：short; brief | ～距离 duǎn jùlí *a short distance* / 时间～shíjiān duǎn *a short time* / 发言要～。Fāyán yào duǎn. *Make your speech brief.* / 昼长夜～zhòu cháng yè duǎn *the day is long and the night is short* / 这条路最～。Zhè tiáo lù zuì duǎn. *This is the shortest route.*

短促 duǎncù of very short duration; very brief

短期 duǎnqī short-term

短信 duǎnxìn message; note

短语 duǎnyǔ (gram.) phrase

短暂 duǎnzàn of short duration; transient

长短 chángduǎn 简短 jiǎnduǎn 缩短 suōduǎn

❷ [名]不足；缺点：weak point; fault | 取长补～qǔcháng-bǔduǎn *learn from others' strong points to offset one's weakness* / 不要揭人的～。Bùyào jiē rén de duǎn. *Do not pick on others' faults.*

短处 duǎnchu shortcoming; failing; fault; weakness
◇短缺 duǎnquē shortage
寻短见 xúnduǎnjiàn

段 duǎn 9画 殳部

段 段段段段段段段段段段

❶ [名]时间、事物的一部分：section; part; segment
阶段 jiēduàn

❷ [量]用于条状物分成的若干部分：used for sections, segments, or parts | 两~木头 liǎng duàn mùtou *two blocks of wood* / 一~铁路 yī duàn tiělù *a section of railway*

❸ [量]用于时间或空间的一定距离：used for a period or distance | 一~时间 yī duàn shíjiān *a period of time* / 一~路 yī duàn lù *a certain distance* / 再往前走一~就到了。Zài wǎng qián zǒu yī duàn jiù dào le. *Go forward farther and we will be there.*
地段 dìduàn

❹ [量]用于事物的一部分：used of a paragraph or passage | 一~故事 yī duàn gùshi *a passage of a story* / 一~话 yī duàn huà *part of a speech* / 这支曲子分三~。Zhè zhī qǔzi fēn sān duàn. *The song can be divided into three parts.*

◇手段 shǒuduàn

断（斷）duàn 11画 斤部

断 断断断断断断断断断断断

❶ [动]长形的东西分成两段或几段：break; snap; cut | 绳子~了。Shéngzi duàn le. *The rope snapped.* / 粉笔掉到地上~成几节。Fěnbǐ diàodào dìshang duànchéng jǐ jié. *The chalk fell to the floor and broke into pieces.*
断裂 duànliè ① split; crack ② (geol.) rift

❷ [动]隔绝；不继续：break off; cut off | ~电 duàndiàn *cut off electricity* / 他俩已~了联系。Tā liǎ yǐ duànle liánxi. *They have lost contact with each other.*
断绝 duànjué break out; cut off; sever
断断续续 duànduàn-xùxù intermittently
不断 búduàn　隔断 géduàn
中断 zhōngduàn

❸ [动]判定；决定：judge; decide | 当机立~ dāngjī-lìduàn *decide promptly and opportunely; make a prompt decision* / 我可~不清你们的事。Wǒ kě duànbuqīng nǐmen de shì. *I cannot make a clear judgement about your business.* / 法院~这个案子~

得很公平。Fǎyuàn duàn zhège ànzi duàn de hěn gōngpíng. *The court judged this case fairly.*

断定 duàndìng conclude; form a judgment; decide; determine
果断 guǒduàn 判断 pànduàn
诊断 zhěnduàn

❹[动]戒除：give up; abstain from | ~烟 duànyān *give up smoking; quit (stop) smoking* / 他心脏不好，大家都劝他把酒~了。Tā xīnzàng bù hǎo, dàjiā dōu quàn tā bǎ jiǔ duàn le. *People encourage him to give up drinking for the sake of his heart.*

缎 (緞) duàn 12画 纟部

缎 缎缎缎缎缎缎缎缎缎缎缎缎

[名]satin | 绸~ chóuduàn *silks and satins*
缎子 duànzi satin

锻 (鍛) duàn 14画 钅部

锻 锻锻锻锻锻锻锻锻锻锻锻锻锻锻

[动]把金属加热后锤打：forge | ~铁 duàntiě *wrought iron*
锻炼 duànliàn ① temper; steel; toughen ② take exercise; have physical training

堆 duī 11画 土部

堆 堆堆堆堆堆堆堆堆堆堆堆

❶[动]累积聚集在一起：pile; stack | 路边~了很多沙子。Lùbiān duīle hěn duō shāzi. *Sand was piled beside the road.* | 粮食~了一仓。Liángshi duīle yī cāng. *The storehouse is heaped with grain.*
堆积 duījī pile up; heap up
❷[名]堆积在一起的东西：heap; pile; stack | 雪~ xuěduī *snow drift; snowbank* / 草~ cǎoduī *haystack* / 土~ tǔduī *mound*
❸[量]用于成堆的物或人：heap; pile; crowd | 一~衣服 yī duī yīfu *a heap of clothes* / 一~人 yī duī rén *a crowd of people*

队 (隊) duì 4画 阝(左)部

队 队队队队

❶[名]行列：row (or line) of people | 列~欢迎 lièduì huānyíng *line up to welcome sb.* / 排成两~ páichéng liǎng duì *fall into two lines*
队伍 duìwu ① troops ② ranks; procession; parade
车队 chēduì   排队 páiduì

❷ [名] 集体；具有某种性质的群体：team; group | 消防～xiāofáng-duì *fire brigade* / 篮球～lánqiúduì *basketball team*

队员 duìyuán team member
队长 duìzhǎng group leader; team leader

部队 bùduì	分队 fēnduì
军队 jūnduì	连队 liánduì
领队 lǐngduì	球队 qiúduì
团队 tuánduì	乐队 yuèduì
中队 zhōngduì	

 对 (對) duì   5画 又部

对 对 对 对 对 对

❶ [动] 回答：answer; reply | ～话 duìhuà *dialogue; conversation*

❷ [动] 朝着；向着：face | 门口～着小河。Ménkǒu duìzhe xiǎohé. *The door faces the small river.* / 她的话不是～着你的。Tā de huà bù shì duìzhe nǐ de. *What she said was not directed at you.*

面对 miànduì
面对面 miànduìmiàn
门当户对 méndāng-hùduì

❸ [介] 向；跟：with; to | 他～我笑了笑。Tā duì wǒ xiàole xiào. *He smiled at me.*

对…来说 duì... láishuō to... ; as to... ; in respect of...

❹ [动] 对待；对付：treat; counter | ～事不～人 duì shì bù duì

rén *direct at facts and not at individuals* / 她～我很好。Tā duì wǒ hěn hǎo. *She treats me well.* / 上海队～北京队 Shànghǎiduì duì Běijīngduì *the Shanghai team versus the Beijing team*

对策 duìcè the way to deal with the situation; countermeasure; countermove

对待 duìdài treat; approach; handle

对付 duìfu ① deal with; cope with; counter; tackle ② make do

对不起 duìbuqǐ ① pardon me; I beg your pardon ② let sb. down; be unworthy of; do a disservice to; be unfair to

对得起 duìdeqǐ not let sb. down; treat sb. fairly; be worthy of

❺ [介] 对于：concerning; with regard to

相对 xiāngduì 针对 zhēnduì

❻ [形] 对面的；对立的：opposing; opposite

对岸 duì'àn the opposite bank; the other side of the river

对称 duìchèn symmetry

对方 duìfāng the other side; the other party; the opposite side

对话 duìhuà dialogue

对抗 duìkàng ① antagonism; confrontation ② resist; oppose

对立 duìlì oppose; set sth.

against; be antagonistic to
对门 duìmén the house opposite
对面 duìmiàn opposite
对手 duìshǒu ① opponent; adversary ② match; equal
对头 duìtou enemy; opponent
对象 duìxiàng ① target; object ② boy / girl friend
死对头 sǐduìtou
唱对台戏 chàngduìtáixì

❼[副]互相：mutually
对应 duìyìng corresponding
敌对 díduì　　反对 fǎnduì

❽[名]双；成对的：pair; couple
对联 duìlián antithetical couplet
对仗 duìzhàng (in poetry, etc.) a matching of both sound and sense in two lines, sentences, etc., usu. with the matching words in the same part of speech; antithesis

❾[动]把两个东西放在一起比较看是否相符：check against; compare; identify | ～笔迹 duì bǐjì *identify the handwriting* / ～号码 duì hàomǎ *check numbers*
对比 duìbǐ ①contrast; balance ② ratio
对照 duìzhào contrast; compare

❿[形]正确：correct; right | 说得～。Shuōdeduì. *What you said is correct.* / 数目不～。Shùmù bù duì. *It does not match with the original number.* / ～,

就这么办。Duì, jiù zhème bàn. *Fine, just go ahead.*

⓫[动]掺和液体：mix; add | ～点开水 duì diǎn kāishuǐ *add some boiled water* / 牛奶里～水了。Niúnǎi li duìshuǐ le. *The milk has been adulterated with water.*

⓬[量]pair; couple | 一～花瓶 yī duì huāpíng *a pair of vases* / 一～夫妇 yī duì fūfù *a married couple* / 一～选手 yī duì xuǎnshǒu *a couple of players*

兑 duì　7画 ..部

兑 兑兑兑兑兑兑兑

[动]交换：exchange | ～款 duìkuǎn *change money* / 请将这张支票～成现金。Qǐng jiāng zhè zhāng zhīpiào duìchéng xiànjīn. *I'd like to cash this cheque please.*
兑换 duìhuàn exchange; convert
兑现 duìxiàn ①cash (a cheque, etc.) ② honour (a commitment, etc.); fulfil; make good
兑换率 duìhuànlǜ rate of exchange (between two currencies)

吨 (噸) dūn　7画 口部

吨 吨吨吨吨吨吨吨

[量]ton

蹲 dūn 19画 足部

蹲蹲蹲蹲蹲蹲蹲蹲蹲蹲蹲蹲蹲蹲蹲蹲蹲蹲蹲

❶ [动] squat | ～在火边 dūn zài huǒ biān *squat about (by) the fire*

❷ [动] 比喻呆着或闲居：stay or enjoy one's leisure | ～在家里看书 dūn zài jiāli kànshū *stay at home to read books* / 毕业后，他一直在家～着。Bìyè hòu, tā yīzhí zài jiā dūnzhe. *He has stayed at home since he graduated from school.*

❸ [动] 较长时间地留在某地工作：stay somewhere for a long time for work | 他在实验室里一～就是好几个小时。Tā zài shíyànshì li yī dūn jiùshì hǎo jǐ gè xiǎoshí. *He would stay for hours at a stretch in the laboratory.*

盾 dùn 9画 厂部

盾盾盾盾盾盾盾盾盾

[名]shield
矛盾 máodùn
自相矛盾 zìxiāng-máodùn

顿 (頓) dùn 10画 页部

顿顿顿顿顿顿顿顿顿顿

❶ [动]稍停：pause | 他～了一下，接着又往下说。Tā dùnle yīxià, jiēzhe yòu wǎng xià shuō. *After a short pause, he went on talking.*
停顿 tíngdùn

❷ [动]安排；处理：arrange; settle
整顿 zhěngdùn

❸ [量]表示次数：time | 一天三～饭 yī tiān sān dùn fàn *three meals a day* | 批评了一～ pīpíngle yī dùn *give (sb.) a dressing-down*

◇顿时 dùnshí immediately; at once

多 duō 6画 夕部

多多多多多多多

❶ [形]数量大(跟"少shǎo"相对)：many; much (the opposite of "少shǎo") | 书很～shū hěn duō *a lot of books* / ～种～样 duōzhǒng-duōyàng *(of species, types, etc.) varied; manifold* / 家里来了很～客人。Jiāli láile hěn duō kèrén. *Many guests come to visit our home.*

多少 duōshǎo ① number; amount ② somewhat; more or less

多少 duōshao ① an unspecified number or amount ② how much; how many

多数 duōshù majority; most

多样 duōyàng diversified

多功能 duōgōngnéng multi-functional; multi-purpose

多媒体 duōméitǐ multimedia

多劳多得 duōláo-duōdé more pay for more work

大多 dàduō　　繁多 fánduō

好多 hǎoduō　　许多 xǔduō

至多 zhìduō　　众多 zhòngduō

诸多 zhūduō

丰富多彩 fēngfù-duōcǎi

或多或少 huòduō-huòshǎo

❷ [动]有余，比原来的或应有的数量有所超过或增加：more; too many or too much｜~了两个人 duōle liǎng gè rén *two extra persons* / 这里你~写了一个字。Zhèli nǐ duōxiěle yī gè zì. *You have written an extra character here.* / 他~喝了一点儿。Tā duōhēle yīdiǎnr. *He's had a few too many glasses of wine.*

多半 duōbàn ① the greater part; most; mostly ② probably; most likely

多余 duōyú ① extra; surplus ② unnecessary; superfluous

❸ [形]过分的；不必要的：excessive; unnecessary｜~疑 duōyí *oversensitive; oversuspicious; given to suspicion*

❹ [形]表示相差的程度大：much

more; far more｜他比我强~了。Tā bǐ wǒ qiángduō le. *He is much better than me.* / 今年冬天比去年冷~了。Jīnnián dōngtiān bǐ qùnián lěngduō le. *This winter is much colder than the last.*

差不多 chàbuduō

❺ [形]表示疑问：(used in questions) how, what｜这孩子~大了? Zhè háizi duō dà le? *How old is this child?*

❻ [副]多么，表示赞叹：(used in exclamations) to what an extent｜这叶子~绿啊! Zhè yèzi duō lǜ a! *How green the leaves are!* / 看她~精神! Kàn tā duō jīngshen! *How energetic she is!*

❼ [副]虚指某种程度：to an unspecified extent｜有~大劲使~大劲。Yǒu duō dà jìn shǐ duō dà jìn. *Use all your strength.* / 无论困难~大，他都不怕。Wúlùn kùnnan duō dà, tā dōu bù pà. *No matter how great the difficulty is, he has no fear.*

多么 duōme ① (used in questions) to what extent ② (used in exclamations) to what extent

❽ [数]表示整数后的零头：odd; over; more than｜五十~岁 wǔshí duō suì *over fifty years old* / 我每天工作十~个小时。Wǒ měitiān gōngzuò shí duō gè xiǎoshí. *I work more than ten hours every day.*

◇ 多亏 duōkuī thanks to; luckily

哆 duō 9画 口部

哆 哆哆哆哆哆哆哆哆
哆

See 哆嗦
哆嗦 duōsuo tremble; shiver

夺 (奪) duó 6画 大部

夺 夺夺夺夺夺夺

❶[动] 强取；抢：take by force;
seize ｜他从我手里把书~去了。
Tā cóng wǒ shǒuli bǎ shū
duóqù le. *He wrested the book
out of my hands.*
夺取 duóqǔ ① capture; seize;
wrest ② strive for
剥夺 bōduó 　　掠夺 lüèduó
抢夺 qiǎngduó
❷[动] 争先取得：strive for ｜~得
冠军 duódé guànjūn *carry off
the championship* ｜我们有信心
把失去的奖杯再~回来。Wǒ-
men yǒu xìnxīn bǎ shīqù de
jiǎngbēi zài duó huílai. *We are
sure to win the cup back.*
夺得 duódé take; seize; win;
carry off
争夺 zhēngduó

踱 duó 16画 足部

踱 踱踱踱踱踱踱踱踱
踱踱踱踱踱踱踱踱

[动]慢慢地走：pace; stroll ｜~方
步 duó fāngbù *walk with mea-
sured tread* / ~来~去 duólái-
duóqù *pace to and fro; pace up
and down*

朵 duǒ 6画 木部

朵 朵朵朵朵朵朵

❶ [名]植物的花或苞：flower or
bud of a plant
花朵 huāduǒ
❷ [量]计算花朵、云彩或类似东西
的单位：used for flowers,
clouds or sth. in a cluster ｜一一~
花 yī duǒ huā *a flower* / 两~云
liǎng duǒ yún *two clouds*

垛 duǒ 9画 土部

垛 垛垛垛垛垛垛垛垛
垛

[名]用泥土、砖、石等建成的掩蔽物：
crenel; battlement ｜城~
chéngduǒ *battlement on a city
wall*

See duò.

躲 duǒ 13画 身部

躲 躲躲躲躲躲躲躲
躲躲躲躲躲

[动]避开；隐藏：avoid; hide; dodge ｜ ~雨 duǒyǔ *take shelter from the rain* ｜ 你怎么老~着他? Nǐ zěnme lǎo duǒzhe tā? *Why do you always avoid meeting him?* ｜ 有车，快~开! Yǒu chē, kuài duǒkāi! *A car is coming! Get out of the way!* ｜ 老鼠~在洞里。Lǎoshǔ duǒ zài dòng li. *The mouse hid in its hole.*

躲避 duǒbì dodge; avoid; elude
躲藏 duǒcáng hide oneself; conceal oneself; go into hiding

垛 duǒ　9画 土部
垛 垛垛垛垛垛垛垛垛垛垛

❶ [动]把分散的东西整齐地堆积起来：pile up neatly; stack ｜ 把晒干的稻草~起来bǎ shàigān de dàocǎo duǒ qǐlai *pile up the dried hay*
❷ [名]成堆的东西：pile; stack
草垛 cǎoduǒ
See duǒ.

舵 duǒ　11画 舟部
舵 舵舵舵舵舵舵舵舵舵舵舵

[名]rudder; helm ｜ 掌~zhǎngduò

operate the rudder; be at the helm ｜ 你划桨，我把~。Nǐ huájiǎng, wǒ bǎduò. *You pull the oars and I steer the rudder.*

堕 (墮) duò　11画 土部
堕 堕堕堕堕堕堕堕堕 堕堕堕

[动]落下：fall; sink
堕落 duòluò degenerate; sink low

惰 duò　12画 忄部
惰 惰惰惰惰惰惰惰惰 惰惰惰惰

[形]懒：lazy; indolent ｜ 懒~lǎnduò *lazy* ｜ ~性 duòxìng *inertia*

跺 duò　13画 足部
跺 跺跺跺跺跺跺跺跺 跺跺跺跺跺

[动]用力踏地：stamp (one's foot) ｜ 他急得直~脚。Tā jí de zhí duòjiǎo. *He stamped his foot with anxiety.* ｜ 他用力~去脚上的土。Tā yònglì duòqù jiǎoshang de tǔ. *He stamped his foot to get the dirt off.*

E e

讹 (訛) é   6画 讠部

讹 讹讹讹讹讹讹讹

❶ [名]错误: error (written) | ~字 ézì *incorrect character*

❷ [动] 敲诈: blackmail | ~诈 ézhà *extort under false pretences; blackmail* / ~人 érén *blackmail sb.*

俄 é   9画 亻部

俄 俄俄俄俄俄俄俄俄俄

[名] 俄罗斯的略称: short for Russia
俄文 Éwén Russian (language)
俄语 Éyǔ Russian (language)

鹅 (鵝) é   12画 鸟部

鹅 鹅鹅鹅鹅鹅鹅鹅鹅鹅鹅鹅鹅鹅

[名]goose | 一群~yī qún é *a drove (flock) of geese* /~的羽毛可用来做羽绒服。É de yǔmáo kě yōnglái zuò yǔróngfú. *Goose feathers can be used to make down jackets.*
◇ 企鹅 qǐ'é

蛾 é   13画 虫部

蛾 蛾蛾蛾蛾蛾蛾蛾蛾蛾蛾蛾蛾蛾

See 蛾子
蛾子 ézi moth

额 (額) é   15画 页部

额 额额额额额额额额额额额额额额额

❶ [名]头部眉毛以上头发以下的部位: forehead | 前 ~qián'é *forehead*

❷ [名]规定的数量: quota; a fixed number or amount
额外 éwài extra; additional; added
超额 chāo'é   定额 dìng'é
份额 fèn'é   金额 jīn'é
名额 míng'é   数额 shù'é
余额 yú'é   总额 zǒng'é

恶 (惡噁) è   10画 心部

恶 恶恶恶恶恶恶恶恶恶恶

See 恶心
恶心 èxin ① feel sick; nauseate; disgust ② disgusting; nauseating

201

See ě; wū.

恶（惡）è　10画 心部

恶恶恶恶恶恶恶恶
恶恶

❶ [名] 极坏的行为（跟"善shàn"相对）：evil; vice; wickedness (the opposite of "善shàn") | 作∼zuò'è *do evil*

❷ [形] 凶狠；凶猛：vicious; ferocious; fierce | ∼人 èrén *evil person; vile creature; villain* | ∼心肠 è xīncháng *evil-minded*
恶毒 èdú vicious; malicious; venomous
凶恶 xiōng'è

❸ [形] 极坏的；不好的：evil; wicked | ∼势力 è shìlì *evil force*
恶化 èhuà worsen; deteriorate; take a turn for the worse
恶劣 èliè odious; abominable; disgusting; very bad; mean
恶性 èxìng malignant; pernicious; vicious
恶意 èyì evil (or ill) intention; ill will; malice
恶作剧 èzuòjù a practical joke; a mischievous prank; mischief
丑恶 chǒu'è
See ě; wū.

饿（餓）è　10画 饣部

饿 饿饿饿饿饿饿饿饿饿饿饿
饿饿

❶ [形] 肚子空，想吃东西（跟"饱bǎo"相对）：hungry; feel like eating (the opposite of "饱bǎo") | 挨∼āi'è *go hungry; starve* / 我肚子∼了。Wǒ dùzi è le. *I'm hungry.*

❷ [动] 使挨饿：starve | 别∼着小猫。Bié èzhe xiǎomāo. *Don't starve the kitten.* / 家里没人做饭，让孩子∼了一整天。Jiāli méi rén zuòfàn, ràng háizi è le yī zhěng tiān. *There was nobody to cook at home, so the child was hungry the whole day.*

恩　ēn　10画 心部

恩 恩恩恩恩恩恩恩恩
恩恩

[名] 给予或得到的好处：kindness, favour; grace | 救命之∼jiùmìng-zhī'ēn *owe one's life to sb.* / 报∼bào'ēn *requite benevolence; pay a debt of gratitude*
恩爱 ēn'ài (of a married couple) be deeply in love with each other
恩情 ēnqíng loving kindness; love; kindness
恩人 ēnrén benefactor
感恩节 Gǎn'ēnjié
小恩小惠 xiǎo'ēn-xiǎohuì

儿（兒）ér　2画 儿部

儿　儿儿

❶[名] 小孩子：child ｜ 婴~ yīng'ér *baby; infant*
儿童 értóng *children*
托儿所 tuō'érsuǒ
幼儿园 yòu'éryuán

❷[名] 儿子：son ｜ 生~育女 shēng'ér-yùnǚ *raise children* / 他有一~一女。Tā yǒu yī ér yī nǚ. *He has a son and a daughter.*
儿女 érnǚ *sons and daughters; children*
儿子 érzi *son*

❸[名]年轻人：youngster; youth ｜ 男~nán'ér *man* / 健~jiàn'ér *valiant fighter; good athlete*

❹[词尾]同前一字连成一个卷舌音：retroflex ending ｜ 盆~pénr *(small) basin*/ 小猫~xiǎomāor *kitten* / 他火~了。Tā huǒr le. *He got angry.*
哪儿 nǎr
差点儿 chàdiǎnr
大伙儿 dàhuǒr
干活儿 gànhuór
老头儿 lǎotóur
聊天儿 liáotiānr
墨水儿 mòshuǐr
男孩儿 nánháir
纽扣儿 niǔkòur
女孩儿 nǚháir

玩意儿 wányìr
小孩儿 xiǎoháir
心眼儿 xīnyǎnr
烟卷儿 yānjuǎnr
药水儿 yàoshuǐr
一点儿 yīdiǎnr
一会儿 yīhuìr
一块儿 yīkuàir
有点儿 yǒudiǎnr
这会儿 zhèhuìr
闹着玩儿 nàozhewánr
偏心眼儿 piānxīnyǎnr
小心眼儿 xiǎoxīnyǎnr
走后门儿 zǒuhòuménr

 而　ér　6画 而部

而　而而而而而而

❶[连] 表示前后意思互相补充：used to indicate coordination ｜ 少~精 shǎo ér jīng *small in quantity but good in quality* / 有名~无实 yǒu míng ér wú shí *own sth. in name but not in reality*
而且 érqiě *and also; but also*
时而 shí'ér

❷[连] 表示转折：and yet; but ｜ 不谋~合 bùmóu'érhé *agree without prior consultation* / 地少~人多 dì shǎo ér rén duō *a small territory with a large population*
反而 fǎn'ér
半途而废 bàntú'érfèi
不辞而别 bùcí'érbié

不劳而获 bùláo'érhuò

不言而喻 bùyán'éryù

似是而非 sìshì'érfēi

❸[连] 表示前面的话是后面话的目的、原因、依据方式、状态等；used to connect cause and effect | 为未来的事业～努力学习。Wèi wèilái de shìyè ér nǔlì xuéxí. *Study hard for your future career.*

而后 érhòu after that; then

从而 cóng'ér   进而 jìn'ér

因而 yīn'ér

敬而远之 jìng'éryuǎnzhī

可想而知 kěxiǎng'érzhī

显而易见 xiǎn'éryìjiàn

一概而论 yīgài'érlùn

一哄而散 yīhòng'érsàn

总而言之 zǒng'éryánzhī

❹[连] 表示由一种状态过渡到另一种状态；used to indicate change from one state to another | 自上～下 zìshàng'érxià *from top to bottom*

而已 éryǐ *that is all; nothing more*

 尔 (爾) ěr   5画 小部

尔 尔尔尔尔尔

❶[代] 如此；这样：like that; so | 不过～～bùguò-ěr'ěr *(written) just middling*

❷[代] 你；你的：you; your | ～等 ěrděng *(in old Chinese) you*

people

偶尔 ǒu'ěr

 耳 ěr   6画 耳部

耳 耳耳耳耳耳耳

❶[名] ear | 我亲～听他这么说的。Wǒ qīn'ěr tīng tā zhème shuō de. *I heard him say so with my own ears.*/ 这音乐很刺～。Zhè yīnyuè hěn cì'ěr. *The music is ear-piercing.*

耳朵 ěrduo ear

❷[名] 形状像耳朵的东西：any ear-like thing | 银～yín'ěr *tremella*

 二 èr   2画 一部

二 二二

❶[数] 数目字：two | ～两茶叶 èr liǎng cháyè *two liang of tea*/ ～路公共汽车 èr lù gōnggòng qìchē *No. 2 bus*

二胡 èrhú *erhu, a two-stringed bowed instrument with a lower register than jinghu.*

二手 èrshǒu second-hand

二战 Èrzhàn the Second World War

二氧化碳 èryǎnghuàtàn (chem.) carbon dioxide

独一无二 dúyī-wú'èr

接二连三 jiē'èr-liánsān

一分为二 yīfēnwéi'èr

E

一干二净 yīgān-èrjìng

❷[数] 次等的：second; inferior | 这件衣服是～等品。Zhè jiàn yīfu shì èrděngpǐn. *The quality of this garment is second-class.* / 他得了～等奖。Tā déle èrděngjiǎng. *He won the second prize.*

◇二百五 èrbǎiwǔ ① (inf.) a stupid person ② (dial.) dabbler; smatterer

 (貳) èr　9画 弋部

 貳貳貳貳貳貳貳貳貳

[数] "二 èr" 的大写：two (the corresponding character of the numeral "二 èr", used on cheques, banknotes, etc. to avoid mistakes or alterations) | 填写汇款单时，"二" 这个数要大写，写成 "～"。Tián xiě huìkuǎndān shí, "二" zhège shù yào dàxiě, xiěchéng "貳". *When filling in a money order, you should write "貳" in place of "二".*

E

F f

发(發) fā   5画 又部

发 发发发发发

❶ [动] 放射：launch; fire; radiate | ~炮 fāpào *discharge a gun-shot* / 百~百中 bǎifā-bǎizhòng *shoot with unfailing accuracy* / ~光~热 fāguāng fārè *emit light and heat*

发球 fāqiú serve a ball

发射 fāshè launch; emit; fire; shoot; discharge

❷ [动] 产生；发生：occur; take place | ~芽 fāyá *sprout* / 旧病复~ jiùbìng fùfā *have an attack of a recurrent sickness; have a recurrence of an old illness*

发病 fābìng (of a disease) come on; attack

发电 fādiàn generate electricity; furnish power; power generation

发热 fārè generate heat; have a fever

发烧 fāshāo have (run) a fever (temperature)

发生 fāshēng happen; occur; take place; arise; crop up

发炎 fāyán inflame; inflamma-tion; fire

暴发 bàofā   爆发 bàofā
突发 tūfā

❸ [动] 引起；开始行动：cause; give rise to

发动 fādòng start; launch; call into action; mobilize; arouse

发起 fāqǐ initiate; sponsor; start; launch

发动机 fādòngjī engine; motor

发愤图强 fāfèn-túqiáng strive for progress (prosperity) with determination

激发 jīfā   引发 yǐnfā

❹ [动] 显现；感到：show; feel | ~黄 fāhuáng *turn yellow* / 脸色~白 liǎnsè fābái *lose colour; become pale* / ~苦 fākǔ *have a bitter taste* / ~酸 fāsuān *have a sour taste* / 有点儿~冷 yǒudiǎnr fālěng *feel a bit chilly*

发愁 fāchóu worry; be anxious

发抖 fādǒu shiver; shake; tremble

发火 fāhuǒ ignite; go off; get angry; lose one's temper

发蒙 fāmēng (inf.) get confused; get into a muddle

发作 fāzuò ① break out; show effect ② have a fit of anger; flare up

发脾气 fāpíqi lose one's temper; get angry

❺ [动] 财势兴旺：prosperous both in wealth and power | ~家 fājiā *build up a prosperous family*

发财 fācái get rich; make a fortune; make a pile

❻ [动] 开展；兴起：rise; spring up

发达 fādá developed; flourishing

发扬 fāyáng ① develop; carry on (forward) ② make the most of; make full use of

发育 fāyù growth; development

发展 fāzhǎn ① develop; expand; grow; burgeon ② recruit; admit

发扬光大 fāyáng-guāngdà enhance; develop; carry forward

❼ [动] 特指食物由于发酵或水泡而体积增大：(of food stuffs) rise or expand when fermented or soaked | ~面 fāmiàn leaven dough / 面~起来了。Miàn fā qǐlai le. The dough has risen.

❽ [动] 离开；起程：leave; set out | 车船齐~。Chēchuán qí fā. All the boats and vehicles started off at the same time. / 早上8点钟~车。Zǎoshang bā diǎn zhōng fāchē. The train departs at 8:00 in the morning.

出发 chūfā

出发点 chūfādiǎn

从···出发 cóng...chūfā

❾ [动] 揭露；打开：discover; unfold

发觉 fājué find; discover; detect

发掘 fājué excavate; unearth; explore

发明 fāmíng invent; invention

发现 fāxiàn find; discover

揭发 jiēfā   开发 kāifā

启发 qǐfā

❿ [动] 散发；散开：send out; diffuse | 挥~ huīfā evaporate / ~散 fāsàn diverge

蒸发 zhēngfā

⓫ [动] 说出；表达：express; convey | ~命令 fā mìnglìng give out orders / 他这个人就好~议论。Tā zhège rén jiù hào fā yìlùn. He likes to make comments on whatever.

发表 fābiǎo publish; issue; deliver; report; project; announce

发布 fābù announce; issue; release

发挥 fāhuī ① bring into play; give play to; give free rein to ② develop; elaborate

发声 fāshēng produce a sound

发誓 fāshì vow; swear

发言 fāyán speak; make a statement (speech)

发音 fāyīn pronounce; enunciate

发言人 fāyánrén spokesman; spokeswoman

⓬ [动] 送出；派出：transmit; dispatch | ~电报 fā diànbào send a telegram / ~奖金 fā jiǎngjīn distribute bonus / 作业还没~下来。Zuòyè háiméi fā xiàlai. The assignment papers have not been given back.

F

发出fāchū issue; send out; give out; emit

发放fāfàng provide; grant; extend

发售 fāshòu sell; put on sale

发行fāxíng issue; publish; distribute; put on sale

颁发 bānfā 　　　打发 dǎfā

批发 pīfā 　　　签发 qiānfā

散发 sānfā

⓭ [量] used for ammunition | 一～子弹 yī fā zǐdàn a bullet

◇发票 fāpiào bill; receipt
See fà.

乏 　　　fá 　　　4画 丿部

乏 乏乏乏乏

❶ [动] 缺少：lack | ～味fáwèi dull / 不～其人 bùfáqírén there's no lack of such people

贫乏 pínfá 　　　缺乏 quēfá

❷ [形] 疲劳：tired | 走～了 zǒufá le be tired from a long walk / 人困马～rénkùn-mǎfá dog-tired; exhausted

疲乏 pífá

伐 　　　fá 　　　6画 亻部

伐 伐伐伐伐伐伐

❶[动] 砍：cut down; chop | 砍～kǎnfá cut; chop; hack / ～树 fá shù cut down trees

❷[动] 攻打；攻击：strike; attack | 讨～tǎofá send a punitive expedition

◇步伐 bùfá

罚 (罰) fá 　　　9画 四部

罚 罚罚罚罚罚罚罚罚罚

[动] 处分；惩处：punish | 赏～分明shǎngfá-fēnmíng be fair in meting out rewards or punishments / 他被～了不少钱。Tā bèi fále bùshǎo qián. He has been heavily fined. / 他因多次犯规被判红牌～下。Tā yīn duōcì fànguī bèi pàn hóngpái fáxià. Having fouled time and time again, he was ordered off the field with a red card.

罚单 fádān slip of penalty

罚款 fákuǎn impose a fine (forfeit); fine; forfeit; penalty

罚球 fáqiú (in basketball) foul shot; free throw; (in football) penalty kick

惩罚 chéngfá 　　　处罚 chǔfá

阀 (閥) fá 　　　9画 门部

阀 阀阀阀阀阀阀阀阀阀

❶[名]在某一方面有势力的人、家族或集团：a powerful person,

family or group
军阀 jūnfá

❷[名]管道或机器上的活门：valve |
~门 fámén *valve* / 水~shuǐfá
water valve / 安全~ānquánfá
safety valve

 法 fǎ   8画 氵部

法 法法法法法法法法

❶[名]指国家立法机关制定的一切
法规：law, a general term for
the rules and regulations made
and enforced by the legislative
body of a state | 无论谁犯了~，
都要受法律制裁。Wúlùn shéi
fànle fǎ, dōu yào shòu fǎlǜ
zhìcái. *Whoever violates the
law must be punished by legal
sanctions.*

法案 fǎ'àn proposed law; bill
法定 fǎdìng legal; statutory
法官 fǎguān judge; justice
法规 fǎguī laws and regulations
法令 fǎlìng laws and decrees;
decree
法律 fǎlǜ law; statute
法人 fǎrén legal person; juridi-
cal person
法庭 fǎtíng court; tribunal
法网 fǎwǎng the net of justice;
the arm of the law
法学 fǎxué the science of law;
law
法医 fǎyī legal medical expert

法院 fǎyuàn court of justice;
law court; court
法制 fǎzhì legal system; legal
institution; legality

不法 bùfǎ   犯法 fànfǎ
非法 fēifǎ   国法 guófǎ
合法 héfǎ   立法 lìfǎ
守法 shǒufǎ   司法 sīfǎ
违法 wéifǎ   宪法 xiànfǎ
刑法 xíngfǎ   执法 zhífǎ
国际法 guójìfǎ
不法分子 bùfǎ fènzǐ

❷[名]标准；模式：pattern; stan-
dard | 效~xiàofǎ *take as model*
法则 fǎzé rule; law
书法 shūfǎ   语法 yǔfǎ

❸[名]方法；办法：way; mode |
表达~biǎodáfǎ *mode of ex-
pression*
法宝 fǎbǎo ① (Buddhism) the
Sutras ② a magic weapon or
formula
法子 fǎzi way; method

办法 bànfǎ   乘法 chéngfǎ
除法 chúfǎ   方法 fāngfǎ
加法 jiāfǎ   减法 jiǎnfǎ
看法 kànfǎ   疗法 liáofǎ
设法 shèfǎ   手法 shǒufǎ
书法 shūfǎ   说法 shuōfa
想法 xiǎngfǎ   写法 xiěfǎ
用法 yòngfǎ   作法 zuòfǎ
做法 zuòfǎ
辩证法 biànzhèngfǎ
书法家 shūfǎjiā

❹[名]法国的简称：short for
France

法郎 fǎláng franc
法文 Fǎwén French (language)
法语 Fǎyǔ French (language)
◇法西斯 fǎxīsī fascist

 发 (髮) fā　　5画　又部

发 发发发发发

[名] 头发: hair | 毛～ máofà hair
/ 短～ duǎnfà short hair / 理～
lǐfà have one's hair cut

理发师 lǐfàshī

See fā.

 帆 fān　　6画　巾部

帆 帆帆帆帆帆帆

[名]sail | 扬起风～ yángqǐ fēng-
fān hoist sail / 一～风顺 yīfān-
fēngshùn plain sailing

帆船 fānchuán sailing boat

 番 fān　　12画　釆部

番 番番番番番番番番
番番番番

❶[量] 次；回: a turn; time | 嘱
咐了一～ zhǔfùle yī fān exhort
sb. to do a certain thing in a certain way, etc. / 他思考了一～才
作决定。Tā sīkǎole yī fān cái
zuò juédìng. He considered it
carefully before making his

decision.

三番五次 sānfān-wǔcì

❷[量] 倍: times; -fold | 产量翻了
两～ chǎnliàng fānle liǎng fān
redouble the output

❸[量] 种: kind; sort | 一～好意 yī
fān hǎoyì a show of hospitality / 别有一～天地 bié yǒu yī
fān tiāndì an entirely different
world

◇番茄 fānqié tomato

 翻 fān　　18画　羽部

翻 翻翻翻翻翻翻翻翻
翻翻翻翻翻翻翻翻
翻翻

❶[动] 上下或里外位置变换；歪倒:
turn upside down or inside out;
turn over | ～跟头 fān gēntou
turn a somersault / 车～了。Chē
fān le. The truck turned over. /
孩子～了一下身子，又睡着了。
Háizi fānle yīxià shēnzi, yòu
shuìzháo le. The child turned
over and fell asleep again.

翻身 fānshēn turn one's body
over

推翻 tuīfān

❷[动] 变换；改变: reverse; overturn
| 他的后代把这个案子～了过
来。Tā de hòudài bǎ zhège
ànzi fānle guòlai. His descendants reversed the original verdict through legal procedures.

❸ [动] 翻译：translate | 英文～中文 Yīngwén fān Zhōngwén *translate English into Chinese* / 这篇日文稿请你～一下。Zhè piān Rìwéngǎo qǐng nǐ fān yīxià. *Please translate this Japanese article.*

翻译 fānyì translate; (口头 oral) interpret

❹ [动] 态度突然变坏：suddenly turn hostile | 他俩闹～了。Tā liǎ nàofān le. *They fell out with each other.* / 你怎么跟人家一起脸来了？Nǐ zěnme gēn rénjia fānqǐ liǎn lai le? *How did you fall out with him (or her)?*

❺ [动] 数量成倍地增长：multiply | 生产～一番 shēngchǎn fān yī fān *double the output* / 老师的工作量～了一倍。Lǎoshī de gōngzuòliàng fānle yī bèi. *The teacher's workload doubled.*

❻ [动] 越过：get over; climb over | ～山越岭 fānshān-yuèlǐng *climb over hills and mountains* / ～墙而过 fān qiáng ér guò *get over the wall*

凡　　　　fán　　3画 几部

凡　凡凡凡

❶ [名] 大概；要略：general idea; outline | 大～ dàfān *in most cases*

❷ [副] 凡是；所有的：all; any; every | ～在这方面犯有错误的人，都要受批评。Fán zài zhè fāngmiàn fànyǒu cuòwù de rén, dōu yào shòu pīpíng. *People who made mistakes in this respect should be criticized.* / ～到过的地方，他都拍了照片。Fán dàoguo de dìfang, tā dōu pāile zhàopiàn. *He took pictures wherever he went.*

凡是 fánshì all; every; any

❸ [形] 平常的；寻常：common; ordinary | ～人 fánrén *mortal*

非凡 fēifán 　　平凡 píngfán

❹ [名] 指尘世：this mortal world | ～间 fánjiān *this mortal world*

 烦 (煩)　fán　10画 火部

烦　烦烦烦烦烦烦烦烦烦烦

❶ [形] 苦闷：restless; irritable; depressed | 真～人! Zhēn fán rén! *How annoying!* / 这几天心里特别～。Zhè jǐ tiān xīnli tèbié fán. *I have been very annoyed these few days.*

烦闷 fánmèn be unhappy; be worried; moody

烦恼 fánnǎo vexed; fretted; worried

烦躁 fánzào fidgety; agitated; fretful; restless

❷ [动] 厌烦；使厌烦：be tired of;

annoy | 我特别~他。Wǒ tèbié fán tā. *I quite dislike him.* / 我今天心情不好，别来~我。Wǒ jīntiān xīnqíng bù hǎo, bié lái fán wǒ. *Leave me alone. I am in low spirits today.* / 这些话我都听~了。Zhèxiē huà wǒ dōu tīngfán le. *I'm tired of such remarks.*

耐烦 nàifán

❸ [动] 烦劳，表示请人帮忙：trouble; request | ~你捎个信。Fán nǐ shāo ge xìn. *Could you please pass on a message for me?*

麻烦 máfan

fán   17画 糸部

繁 繁 繁 繁 繁 繁 繁 繁 繁 繁 繁 繁 繁 繁 繁

❶ [形] 多；复杂：numerous and complicated | ~星 fánxīng *an array of stars* / 枝叶~茂 zhīyè fánmào *luxuriant branches and leaves* / 手续太~，应该尽量简化。Shǒuxù tài fán, yīnggāi jìnliàng jiǎnhuà. *The procedures are too complicated and should be simplified.*

繁多 fánduō various; numerous

繁华 fánhuá flourishing; bustling

繁忙 fánmáng busy; occupied

繁荣 fánróng flourishing; pros-

perous; booming

繁体 fántǐ the original complex form of simplified Chinese character

繁重 fánzhòng heavy

繁体字 fántǐzì unsimplified Chinese character

频繁 pínfán

❷ [动] 生殖：reproduce

繁殖 fánzhí breed; multiply; propagate

反   fǎn   4画 厂部

反 反 反 反 反

❶ [动] 转换；翻转：turn over | ~败为胜 fǎnbài-wéishèng *turn failure to success*

反常 fǎncháng unusual; abnormal; perverse; strange

反复 fǎnfù ① repeatedly; again and again; over and over again; time and again; time and time again ② reversal; relapse; changeable; fickle

❷ [形] 颠倒的；方向相背的：upside down; reverse | ~方向 fǎnfāngxiàng *in the opposite direction* / 袜子穿~了。Wàzi chuānfǎn le. *He has his socks on inside out.* / 你把我的意思弄~了。Nǐ bǎ wǒ de yìsi nòngfǎn le. *What you understand is the opposite of my idea.*

反比 fǎnbǐ inverse ratio

反差 fǎnchā ① (photog.) contrast ② contrast between good and bad, and the beautiful and the ugly in people or things

反讽 fǎnfěng irony

反馈 fǎnkuì feedback

反面 fǎnmiàn ① reverse side; wrong side; back ② opposite; negative side

反射 fǎnshè reflex; reflection

反思 fǎnsī introspection; reflect over the past

反弹 fǎntán ① bounce off; rebound in the opposite direction after meeting an obstacle ② (fig.) (of price or market conditions) rebound (after a fall)

反问 fǎnwèn ask (a question) in reply; ask in retort

反响 fǎnxiǎng repercussion; echo; reverberation

反省 fǎnxǐng engage in introspection, self-examination or soul-searching

反应 fǎnyìng ① reaction ② response; repercussion

反映 fǎnyìng ① reflect; mirror ② report; make known

反之 fǎnzhī conversely; on the contrary; otherwise

相反 xiāngfǎn

唱反调 chàngfǎndiào

❸ [动] 对抗；背叛：rebel; revolt | 你简直~了! Nǐ jiǎnzhí fǎn le! *How dare you!*

反驳 fǎnbó refute; retort

反动 fǎndòng reactionary

反对 fǎnduì oppose

反感 fǎngǎn repugnance; loathing; abhorrence; be disgusted with; be averse to; dislike

反攻 fǎngōng counteroffensive; counterattack

反击 fǎnjī strike back; beat back; counterattack

反抗 fǎnkàng revolt; resist

❹ [副] 反而：on the contrary; instead | 近来身体~不如以前。Jìnlái shēntǐ fǎn bùrú yǐqián. *On the contrary, my health is worse than before.* / 解释了半天，~让人听不懂了。Jiěshìle bàntiān, fǎn ràng rén tīngbudǒng le. *Many explanations had been given; nevertheless, nobody understood what they meant.*

反倒 fǎndào on the contrary; instead

反而 fǎn'ér conversely

◇反正 fǎnzhèng anyway; anyhow; all the same; in any case

返 fǎn 7画 辶部

返 返返返返返返返

[动] 回：return | ~家 fǎnjiā *return home* / 往~ wǎngfǎn *go to and fro; go (somewhere) and come back* / 一去不复~ yī qù bù fù-

F

fǎn *gone forever; leaving (going) without returning*

返还 fǎnhuán return; give or sent back

返回 fǎnhuí return; come or go back

犯 fàn   5画 犭部

犯 犯犯犯犯犯

❶ [动] 侵害；进攻：violate; encroach on

侵犯 qīnfàn

❷ [动] 违反；抵触：violate; run counter to | ～纪律 fàn jìlǜ *violate discipline* / 他～了法，自己还不知道。Tā fànle fǎ, zìjǐ hái bù zhīdào. *Without realizing it, he has violated the law.*

犯法 fànfǎ break (violate; transgress) the law; be against the law

犯规 fànguī ① break the rules ② (sports) foul

触犯 chùfàn   违犯 wéifàn

❸ [动] 发生；发作：break out; take effect | ～错误 fàn cuòwù *commit a mistake* / 最近他的旧病又～了。Zuìjìn tā de jiùbìng yòu fàn le. *His old illness came again recently.* / 他的胃病又～了。Tā de wèibìng yòu fàn le. *He suffered a relapse of stomach trouble.*

犯浑 fànhún be unreasonable

犯罪 fànzuì   commit (perpetrate) a crime (an offence)

❹ [名] 有罪的人：offender; criminal

犯人 fànrén criminal; convict; prisoner

嫌犯 xiánfàn   战犯 zhànfàn

罪犯 zuìfàn

饭 (飯) fàn   7画 饣部

饭 饭饭饭饭饭饭饭

❶ [名] 粮食做成的熟食；特指米饭：cooked rice or other cereals, usu. cooked rice | 蛋炒～ dànchǎofàn *cooked rice fried with eggs* / 今天的～做得有点儿硬。Jīntiān de fàn zuò de yǒudiǎnr yìng. *Today's cooked rice is a bit hard.*

便饭 biànfàn   米饭 mǐfàn

稀饭 xīfàn

❷ [名] 每天定时吃的主食：meal | 一天三顿～ yī tiān sān dùn fàn *three meals a day* / ～前洗手。Fàn qián xǐshǒu. *Wash your hands before the meal.* / 我喜欢吃妈妈做的～。Wǒ xǐhuan chī māma zuò de fàn. *I like the meals prepared by my mother.*

饭店 fàndiàn restaurant

饭馆 fànguǎn restaurant

饭碗 fànwǎn ① rice bowl ②

job; means of livelihood

吃饭 chīfàn 开饭 kāifàn
晚饭 wǎnfàn 午饭 wǔfàn
早饭 zǎofàn 做饭 zuòfàn
家常饭 jiāchángfàn
年夜饭 niányèfàn
铁饭碗 tiěfànwǎn

泛 fàn 7画 氵部

泛 泛泛泛泛泛泛泛泛

❶ [动] 透出；浮现出：appear; show | ～出香味 fànchū xiāngwèi *smell aromatic (sweet-smelling)* / 脸上～红 liǎnshang fànhóng *one's cheeks suffused with blushes*

❷ [形] 不切实；不深入：superficial; unrealistic | 空～kōngfàn *vague and general*

❸ [形] 普遍；一般：ordinary; general
广泛 guǎngfàn

❹ [动] 水向四处溢出：flood; overflow
泛滥 fànlàn be in flood; overflow; spread unchecked

范 (範) fàn 8画 艹部

范 范范范范范范范范

❶ [名] 榜样：example; model | 典～diǎnfàn *example*

风范 fēngfàn 规范 guīfàn
模范 mófàn 师范 shīfàn
示范 shìfàn

❷ [名] 一定的界限：limit; range; scope
范畴 fànchóu category; domain; scope
范围 fànwéi scope; limits; range

❸ [动] 限制：place restrictions on; confine | 防～fángfàn *be on guard; keep a lookout*

贩 (販) fàn 8画 贝部

贩 贩贩贩贩贩贩贩贩

❶ [名] 买进货物后再卖出以获取利润的行商或小商人：trader; monger | 小～xiǎofàn *pedlar*
贩卖 fànmài peddle; sell
毒贩 dúfàn

❷ [动] 购进货物再卖出：buy to resell | 他从外地刚刚～来这些货物。Tā cóng wàidì gānggāng fànlai zhèxiē huòwù. *He has just transported these goods from other place for resale.* / 从南方～来一批货。Cóng nánfāng fànlai yī pī huò. *A batch of goods has been bought from the south.*
贩毒 fàndú traffic in narcotics

方 fāng 4画 方部

方 | 方方方方

❶ [形] square | 这块玻璃是~的。Zhè kuài bōli shì fāng de. *The shape of the glass is square.*
长方体 chángfāngtǐ
长方形 chángfāngxíng
正方体 zhèngfāngtǐ

❷ [名] 地区；地方：area; region
地方 dìfāng   远方 yuǎnfāng

❸ [名] 方向：direction | 四面八~ sìmiàn-bāfāng *in all directions*/前~ qiánfāng *ahead; front*
方向 fāngxiàng direction; orientation
方针 fāngzhēn policy; guiding principle; orientation
方向盘 fāngxiàngpán steering wheel
北方 běifāng   东方 dōngfāng
后方 hòufāng   南方 nánfāng
四方 sìfāng   西方 xīfāng

❹ [名] 方面：side; party | 责任在 A~，不在 B~。Zérèn zài A fāng, bù zài B fāng. *It's party A who should assume the responsibility instead of party B.*
方面 fāngmiàn respect; aspect; side; field
对方 duìfāng 官方 guānfāng
双方 shuāngfāng
单方面 dānfāngmiàn

❺ [名] 方法：method; way; means | 教导有~ jiàodǎo-yǒufāng *exercise good instruction* / 张先生教子有~。Zhāng xiānsheng

jiāo zǐ yǒufāng. *Mr Zhang always guides his children in the proper way.*
方案 fāng'àn scheme; plan; programme; proposal; suggestion; formula
方法 fāngfǎ method; way; means
方式 fāngshì way; fashion; mode; pattern
千方百计 qiānfāng-bǎijì
想方设法 xiǎngfāng-shèfǎ

❻ [名] 配药的单子：(of medicine) prescription | 验~ yànfāng *proved recipe* / 偏~儿 piānfāngr *folk prescription*
处方 chǔfāng   配方 pèifāng
药方 yàofāng
处方药 chǔfāngyào

❼ [名] 乘方：power; involution | 2 的 3 次~是 8。Èr de sān cì fāng shì bā. *The third power of 2 is 8.*
方程 fāngchéng equation
乘方 chéngfāng
立方 lìfāng
立方米 lìfāngmǐ
平方米 píngfāngmǐ
平方公里 píngfāng gōnglǐ
◇方便 fāngbiàn convenient
比方 bǐfāng
打比方 dǎbǐfāng

坊 ...... fāng 7画 土部

216

坊坊坊坊坊坊坊

[名]城镇中的小街小巷：lane (usu. as part of a street name)
街坊 jiēfang
See fāng.

 fāng　7画 艹部

芳芳芳芳芳芳芳

[形]香：fragrant; scented | ～香 fāngxiāng *fragrant*
芬芳 fēnfāng

防 fāng　6画 阝(左)部

防防防防防防

❶[名]挡水的建筑物：dyke; embankment | 堤～dīfāng *dyke*
❷[动]防备；戒备；守卫：guard against | ～身 fāngshēn *defend oneself* / 以～万一 yǐfāngwànyī *be prepared for all contingencies; be ready for any eventuality*
防备 fāngbèi guard against
防范 fāngfàn be on guard; keep a lookout
防护 fānghù protect; shelter
防空 fāngkōng air defence
防守 fāngshǒu defend; guard
防伪 fāngwěi counterfeit prevention
防线 fāngxiàn line of defence
防汛 fāngxùn flood prevention

or control
防疫 fāngyì epidemic prevention
防御 fāngyù defend; guard
防止 fāngzhǐ prevent; guard against; forestall
防治 fāngzhì prevention and cure
边防 biānfāng　国防 guófáng
消防 xiāofáng　预防 yùfáng

 fāng　7画 土部

坊坊坊坊坊坊坊

[名]小手工业者的工作场所和某些店铺的名称：workshop; mill | 磨～mòfāng *mill* / 油～yóufāng *oil mill* / 染～rǎnfāng *dyer's workshop*
See fāng.

 fāng　7画 女部

妨妨妨妨妨妨妨

[动]阻碍：hinder; obstruct | 不～同他再谈一次。Bùfáng tóng tā zài tán yī cì. *We might as well have another talk with him.* / 不～早点儿动身。Bùfáng zǎodiǎnr dòngshēn. *We'd better leave a little earlier.*
妨碍 fáng'ài hinder; hamper; impede; obstruct; interfere with

肪 fáng 8画 月部

肪 肪肪肪肪肪肪肪肪

See 脂肪
脂肪 zhīfáng

房 fáng 8画 户部

房 房房房房房房房房

❶ [名] 房子：house ｜ 瓦~wǎfáng *tile-roofed house* ｜ 草~cǎofáng *thatched cottage*
房产 fángchǎn house property
房东 fángdōng landlord or landlady
房屋 fángwū house; building
房子 fángzi house or building; room; apartment
房租 fángzū rent; rental
房地产 fángdìchǎn real estate
厂房 chǎngfáng 楼房 lóufáng
现房 xiànfáng 住房 zhùfáng
❷ [名] 房间：room ｜ 卧~wòfáng *bedroom* ｜ 书~shūfáng *study*
房间 fángjiān room
病房 bìngfáng 厨房 chúfáng
库房 kùfáng 牢房 láofáng
票房 piàofáng 新房 xīnfáng
❸ [名] 指家族的一支：a branch of a clan ｜ 远~yuǎnfáng *(of kinship) distantly related*
◇ 乳房 rǔfáng

仿 fǎng 6画 亻部

仿 仿仿仿仿仿仿

❶ [动] 类似；像：be more or less the same; resemble ｜ 相~xiāngfǎng *be similar; be like*
仿佛 fǎngfú ①seemingly; as if; as though ②be more or less the same; be similar
❷ [动] 照样子做：imitate ｜ ~照 fǎngzhào *imitate* ｜ ~制 fǎngzhì *copy*
仿造 fǎngzào copy; be modelled on
仿真 fǎngzhēn ① emulate; experiment with a model that simulates the real thing ② simulation; have or take on the external appearance
模仿 mófǎng

访（訪）fǎng 6画 讠部

访 访访访访访访

❶ [动] 调查；寻求：seek by enquiry or search ｜ 寻~xúnfáng *seek by enquiry or search*
采访 cǎifǎng
❷ [动] 拜访；探望：pay a visit; call on ｜ 来~láifáng *come to visit* ｜ 家~jiāfáng *(officially) visit somebody's family* ｜ ~友 fǎngyǒu *call on a friend*

访谈 fǎngtán interview
访问 fǎngwèn visit; call on; interview; pay a call
拜访 bàifǎng

 纺 (紡) fǎng 7画 丝部

纺 纺 纺 纺 纺 纺 纺

[动] spin | ～线 fǎngxiàn *spin into thread*

纺织 fǎngzhī spinning and weaving

纺织品 fǎngzhīpǐn textile; fabric

放 fàng 8画 方部

放 放 放 放 放 放 放 放

❶ [动] 不加约束：give way to | ～声大笑 fàngshēng dàxiào *laugh a hearty laugh* / ～声歌唱 fàngshēng gēchàng *sing heartily*

❷ [动] 解除约束：release; let go; set free | ～开手脚 fàngkāi shǒujiǎo *give sb. a free hand; unrestrained* / 不要～他走。Bùyào fàng tā zǒu. *Don't let him go.* / 女儿把关在笼子里的鸟儿～了。Nǚ'ér bǎ guān zài lóngzi li de niǎor fàng le. *My daughter released the bird from the cage.* / 游泳池的水全～干净了。Yóuyǒngchí de shuǐ quán fàng gānjìng le. *All the water has been let out of the swimming pool.*

放弃 fàngqì give up; abandon; renounce; abstain from
放手 fàngshǒu let go; release; have a free hand
放心 fàngxīn set one's mind at rest; be at ease; rest assured; feel relieved
解放 jiěfàng 排放 páifàng
释放 shìfàng

❸ [动] 带牲畜到野外去活动、吃草：put out to pasture; herd | ～羊 fàng yáng *herd sheep* / ～牛 fàng niú *pasture cattle*

❹ [动] 暂时停止工作或学习，使自由活动：dismiss; let out
放假 fàngjià have a day off; have a holiday
放学 fàngxué dismiss school

❺ [动] 点燃：light | ～爆竹 fàng bàozhú *light firecrackers* / ～火 fànghuǒ *set on fire* / 国庆节的夜晚，广场上～了两个小时的礼花。Guóqìngjié de yèwǎn, guǎngchǎng shang fàngle liǎng gè xiǎoshí de lǐhuā. *On the night of the National Day, fireworks were displayed on the square for two hours.*
燃放 ránfàng

❻ [动] 发出：let off | ～炮 fàngpào *fire guns* / ～风筝 fàng fēngzheng *fly a kite* / 今天学校礼堂～电影。Jīntiān xuéxiào lǐtáng fàng diànyǐng. *The school auditorium has a film show today.*

放射 fàngshè radiate; emit; shoot; emission

放映 fàngyìng show; project

播放 bōfàng　　发放 fāfàng

❼[动] 开：come into bloom | 鲜花开~。Xiānhuā kāifàng. *Flowers blossom.* / 心花怒~ xīnhuā-nùfàng be wild with joy

开放 kāifàng

百花齐放 bǎihuā-qífàng

❽[动] 扩展；加大：enlarge; widen | ~宽一寸 fàngkuān yī cùn *let out an inch* / ~松一点 fàngsōng yīdiǎn *loosen a little* / 照片~得太大了。Zhàopiàn fàng de tài dà le. *The photograph is enlarged too much.*

放大 fàngdà enlarge; magnify; amplify

放松 fàngsōng relax

❾[动] 搁；置：lay aside; shelve | 这件事暂且~一~。Zhè jiàn shì zànqiě fàngyifàng. *Lay this matter aside for the moment.*

放下 fàngxià lay down; put down; drop

放置 fàngzhì lay up; lay aside

摆放 bǎifàng　　存放 cúnfàng

投放 tóufàng

❿[动] 加进去：put in | 我喝牛奶不~糖。Wǒ hē niúnǎi bù fàng táng. *I prefer to drink milk without adding sugar.*

⓫[动] 控制(行动、态度等)：control; manage | 声音~大点儿。Shēngyīn fàngdà diǎnr. *Speak louder.* / 脚步~轻些。Jiǎobù fàngqīng xiē. *Step more softly.* / 把速度~慢点儿。Bǎ sùdù fàngmàn diǎnr. *Slow down a little.*

 (飛) fēi　　3画 飞部

飞 飞 飞 飞

❶[动] (鸟、虫等)拍动翅膀在空中行动：fly | 小鸟~了。Xiǎoniǎo fēi le. *The bird flew away.* / 老鹰在天上~来~去。Lǎoyīng zài tiānshang fēi lái fēi qù. *The eagle hovers back and forth in the sky.* / 蜻蜓在水面上~。Qīngtíng zài shuǐmiàn shang fēi. *The dragonflies skim on the surface of the water.*

飞快 fēikuài ① very fast ② extremely sharp

飞舞 fēiwǔ dance in the air; flutter

飞翔 fēixiáng flight; circle in the air; hover

飞跃 fēiyuè leap

❷[动] (物体)在空中飘动或行驶：drift; flutter | ~雪花了。Fēi xuěhuā le. *Snowflakes flutter in the air.* / 这架飞机已经累计~了一千多个小时。Zhè jià fēijī yǐjīng lěijì fēile yīqiān duō ge xiǎoshí. *The flight time of this plane has totalled more than 1, 000 hours.*

飞船 fēichuán airship; spaceship

飞碟 fēidié ① (sports) skeet shooting; skeet trapshooting ② flying saucer; UFO

飞机 fēijī airplane; plane; aeroplane; aircraft

飞速 fēisù at full speed

飞行 fēixíng flight; flying; aviate

飞行员 fēixíngyuán pilot; aviator; flyer

起飞 qǐfēi

❸ [动] 挥发：evaporate | 香味儿~光了。Xiāngwèir fēi guāng le. *The sweet scent all disappeared.*

 fēi   8画 非部

非 非 非 非 非 非 非 非

❶ [动] 不合于；违背：run counter to; go against; violate | ~礼 fēilǐ *a breach of etiquette; impolite; take liberties with (a woman)* | 那些~人道的做法受到了公众的谴责。Nàxiē fēiréndào de zuòfǎ shòudàole gōngzhòng de qiǎnzé. *Those inhuman ways of acting are condemned by the public.*

非常 fēicháng extraordinary; unusual; special; extremely

非法 fēifǎ illegal; unlawful; illicit

❷ [名] 错误；坏事：mistake; wrong; error | 招惹是~zhāorě-shìfēi *ask for trouble* / 明辨是~míngbiàn-shìfēi *make a clear distinction between right and wrong*

是非 shìfēi

❸ [动] 不是：be wrong; be not | 答~所问dáfēisuǒwèn *give an irrelevant answer*

非凡 fēifán outstanding; extraordinary; uncommon

并非 bìngfēi   绝非 juéfēi

似是而非 sìshì'érfēi

似笑非笑 sìxiào-fēixiào

❹ [副] 跟"不"呼应，表示必须：used in cooperation with "不bù", expressing necessity | 学外语，~下苦功不可。Xué wàiyǔ, fēi xià kǔgōng bùkě. *One cannot master a foreign language without great effort.* / 今天的会议很重要，你~参加不可。Jīntiān de huìyì hěn zhòngyào, nǐ fēi cānjiā bùkě. *You must attend today's meeting as it is very important.* / 你这病~动手术不可。Nǐ zhè bìng fēi dòng shǒushù bùkě. *An operation must be undertaken due to the condition of your illness.*

非…不可 fēi... bùkě ① must;

have to ② will inevitably; be bound to

无非 wúfēi

❺ [名] 非洲的简称：short for Africa

非洲 Fēizhōu Africa

◇除非 chúfēi

肥 fēi 8画 月部

肥 肥肥肥肥肥肥肥肥

❶ [形] 胖；含脂肪多的：fat; oily | ～肉 fēiròu *fat meat* / ～胖 fēipàng *fat; corpulent* / 鸡养得很～。Jī yǎng de hěn fēi. *Those fat chickens are well fed.*

减肥 jiǎnfēi

❷ [形] 土质好：fertile; rich | 土质～ tǔzhì fēi *rich soil* / 这里的土地很～。Zhèli de tǔdì hěn fēi. *The soil of this area is very fertile.*

肥沃 fēiwò fertile; rich

❸ [名] 肥料：fertilizer; manure

肥料 fēiliào fertilizer

化肥 huàfēi 施肥 shīfēi

❹ [形] 宽大(指衣服、鞋袜等)：(of clothes, shoes, socks, etc.) large; big; loose | 裤腰太～了。Kùyāo tài fēi le. *The waist of the trousers is too large.* / 这衣服稍微～了点儿。Zhè yīfu shāowēi fēile diǎnr. *The coat is a bit too loose.*

◇肥皂 fēizào soap

匪 fēi 10画 匚部

匪 匪匪匪匪匪匪匪匪匪匪

[名] 强盗：bandit; robber | 盗～ dàofēi *brigand*

匪徒 fěitú gangster; bandit; outlaw; robber

劫匪 jiéfēi

诽 (誹) fēi 10画 讠部

诽 诽诽诽诽诽诽诽诽诽

See 诽谤

诽谤 fěibàng slander; libel; defame

肺 fēi 8画 月部

肺 肺肺肺肺肺肺肺肺

[名] lung | 妈妈的～一直不好。Mā-ma de fēi yīzhí bù hǎo. *My mother has been suffering from lung problems.* / 老师做了～切除手术。Lǎoshī zuòle fēi-qiēchú shǒushù. *The teacher underwent a pneumonectomy.*

肺炎 fēiyán pneumonia

excitement

 废（廢）fèi　　8画 广部

废 废废废废废废废废

❶ [动] 取消；停止；不用：abandon; abolish; abrogate

废除 fèichú abolish; abrogate; annul; repeal

作废 zuòfèi

半途而废 bàntú'érfèi

❷ [形] 没用的：useless | ～报纸 fèi bàozhǐ *back copies of a newspaper* / ～铁 fèitiě *scrap iron*

废话 fèihuà nonsense; rubbish; superfluous words

废旧 fèijiù (of things) old and useless

废品 fèipǐn waste product; reject; scrap; waste

废气 fèiqì waste gas; exhaust gas

废物 fèiwù ① waste material; trash ② good-for-nothing

废墟 fèixū ruins

沸 fèi　　8画 氵部

沸 沸沸沸沸沸沸沸沸

[动] 液体受热到一定程度，产生气泡而翻腾：boil; bubble up | 水～了。Shuǐ fèi le. *The water is boiling.*

沸腾 fèiténg ① boiling; ebullition ② boil over; seethe with

 费（費）fèi　　9画 贝部

费 费费费费费费费费费

❶ [动] 消耗：consume; spend | ～脑筋 fèi nǎojīn *rack one's brains* / ～功夫 fèi gōngfu *be time-consuming* / ～时间 fèi shíjiān *take time* / ～力气 fèi lìqi *need or use great effort* / 这样花钱太～了。Zhèyàng huāqián tài fèi le. *It is too extravagant to squander money in this way.*

费力 fèilì need or exert great effort; be strenuous

费心 fèixīn ① give a lot of care; take a lot of trouble ② (pol.) (used in making a request or giving thanks) may I trouble you (to do sth.); would you mind (doing sth.)

❷ [名] 费用：cost; expenses | 电～diànfèi *charges for electricity* / 水～shuǐfèi *water rates* / 生活～shēnghuófèi *living expenses* / 住院～zhùyuànfèi *hospitalization expenses*

费用 fèiyòng cost; expenses

付费 fùfèi　　公费 gōngfèi

话费 huàfèi　　经费 jīngfèi

免费 miǎnfèi　　收费 shōufèi

税费 shuìfèi　　邮费 yóufèi

学费 xuéfèi　　资费 zīfèi

自费 zìfèi
消费品 xiāofèipǐn
消费者 xiāofèizhě

分 fēn　4画 八部

分 分分分分

❶ [动] 分开；使整体变成若干部
分：divide; separate | ～成两半
fēnchéng liǎngbàn *divide
into two* / 这些东西我们～了吧。
Zhèxiē dōngxi wǒmen fēnle
ba. *Let's share out these things.*
/ 一年～四季 yī nián fēn sìjì
*the year is divided into four
seasons*
分别 fēnbié ① part; leave each
other ② distinguish; differentiate ③separately; individually;
respectively
分布 fēnbù be distributed over
an area; be dispersed; be scattered; spread
分成 fēnchéng (money, prop-
erty, goods, etc.) share; divide
by tenths
分割 fēngē cut apart; break up;
carve up; decollate
分化 fēnhuà become divided;
break up; split up
分解 fēnjiě ① resolve; decompose; disintegrate; break down;
break up ② explain; disclose
分开 fēnkāi ① be apart; part ②
(cause to) separate or part

分类 fēnlèi classify
分离 fēnlí separate; sever; leave;
part
分裂 fēnliè fission; split; divide;
break up
分流 fēnliú ① distributary; split-
flow ② diversion; (of crowds
and vehicles) split flow
分批 fēnpī in batches; in turn
分期 fēnqī by stages
分散 fēnsàn disperse; scatter;
decentralize
分手 fēnshǒu part company; say
good-bye
分析 fēnxī analyze; analysis
瓜分 guāfēn　　划分 huàfēn
一分为二 yīfēn-wéi'èr
❷ [动] 分配；分给：distribute;
allot | 他～了一间单人宿舍。Tā
fēnle yījiān dānrén sùshè. *He
was allotted a one-room apartment.* / 这个月每人～了300元奖
金。Zhège yuè měi rén fēnle
sānbǎi yuán jiǎngjīn. *Each
person was awarded a bonus of
300 yuan this month.*
分工 fēngōng division of labor
分红 fēnhóng draw dividends;
share profits
分配 fēnpèi distribute; allot;
assign; distribution
分享 fēnxiǎng share (joy, rights,
etc.); partake of
按劳分配 ànláo fēnpèi
❸[名]从主体中分出来的：division

or subdivision of organization, etc. | ~店 fēndiàn *branch store* / ~公司 fēngōngsī *branch company*

分队 fēnduì contingent; detachment

分机 fēnjī (telephone) extension

分支 fēnzhī subdivision; branch

❹ [动] 辨别；区别：distinguish | 他是非不~。Tā shìfēi bù fēn. *He couldn't distinguish right from wrong.* / 我总是~不清他和他的弟弟。Wǒ zǒngshì fēnbuqīng tā hé tā de dìdi. *I can never tell him from his younger brother.*

分辨 fēnbiàn distinguish; tell apart; make out; identify

分辩 fēnbiàn defend oneslf (against a charge); offer an explanation

分明 fēnmíng clearly demarcated; obviously; evidently

分歧 fēnqí differ; difference; divergence

分清 fēnqīng distinguish; draw a clear distinction between

区分 qūfēn

❺ [量] 表示成绩的计数单位：point; mark

总分 zǒngfēn

❻ [量] 表示分数：portion; part | 三~之一 sān fēn zhī yī *one-third*

分母 fēnmǔ denominator

分子 fēnzǐ numerator

百分比 bǎifēnbǐ

百分点 bǎifēndiǎn

❼ [量] 十分之一；成数：percentage

十分 shífēn　　万分 wànfēn

❽ [名] 成绩或比赛胜负的分数：marks or points one gets in an exam or contest | 他英语考了 95~。Tā Yīngyǔ kǎole jiǔshíwǔ fēn. *He scored 95 in the English examination.* / 排球比赛我队以 1~之差败了。Páiqiú bǐsài wǒ duì yǐ yī fēn zhī chā bài le. *We lost by one point in the volleyball match.* / 他的体操项目在运动会上得了满~。Tā de tǐcāo xiàngmù zài yùndònghuì shang déle mǎnfēn. *His gymnastics won full marks at the sports meet.*

分数 fēnshù ① fraction; fractional number ② mark; grade; point

分数线 fēnshùxiàn bottom or floor mark for enrolment eligibility

比分 bǐfēn

❾ [量] 时间单位，1小时的六十分之一：minute | 6点20~ liù diǎn èrshí fēn *twenty past six* / 现在是几点几~?Xiànzài shì jǐ diǎn jǐ fēn? *What's the time to the minute now?*

分钟 fēnzhōng minute

❿ [量] 我国货币单位，1角钱的十分之一：cent; *fen* (a unit of RMB, equal to 0.1 *jiao*)

225

◇分寸 fēncun proper limits for speech or action; sense of propriety; sense of proportion

分泌 fēnmì secrete

分子 fēnzǐ ① (math.) numerator (in a fraction) ② (chem.) molecule

See fèn.

芬　fēn　7画 艹部

芬芬芬芬芬芬芬

[名]香气：fragrance; perfume

芬芳 fēnfāng sweet smell; frgrance

吩　fēn　7画 口部

吩吩吩吩吩吩吩

See 吩咐

吩咐 fēnfù tell; instruct

纷（紛）fēn　7画 纟部

纷纷纷纷纷纷纷

❶ [形] 多；杂乱：numerous; confused; disorderly ｜ ~杂 fēnzá numerous and disorderly / 雪片 ~ 飞 xuěpiàn fēnfēi snowflakes flutter about

纷纷 fēnfēn ① numerous and confused ②one after another; in succession

❷ [名] 争执：dispute

纠纷 jiūfēn

氛　fēn　8画 气部

氛氛氛氛氛氛氛氛

[名]情景；状况：atmosphere

气氛 qìfēn

坟（坟）fén　7画 土部

坟坟坟坟坟坟坟

See 坟墓

坟墓 fénmù grave; tomb

粉　fěn　10画 米部

粉粉粉粉粉粉粉粉粉粉

❶ [名] 特指化妆用的香粉：(of cosmetics) face powder ｜ 涂脂抹 ~ túzhī-mǒfěn apply powder and paint / 这种 ~ 真香。Zhè zhǒng fěn zhēn xiāng. This brand of powder is so fragrant!

❷ [名] 细末状的东西：powder-like thing ｜ 米 ~ mǐfěn rice flour / 洗衣 ~ xǐyīfěn detergent powder

粉末 fěnmò powder

淀粉 diànfěn　　面粉 miànfěn

奶粉 nǎifěn

❸ [动] 变成或使变成粉末：turn into

powder

粉碎fěnsuì ① broken to pieces ② smash; shatter; crush

❹ [名] 用淀粉等制成的食品：meals made from starch | 凉~liángfěn *bean jelly* / ~丝 fěnsī *noodles made from bean starch*

❺ [形] 红和白合成的颜色：pink; pale-red colour | ~红fěnhóng *pink* / 这块绸子是~的。Zhè kuài chōuzi shì fěn de. *The colour of this silk fabric is pink.*

◇粉笔 fěnbǐ chalk

fēn　　4画 八部
. . . .

分 分分分分

❶[名] 成分；构成事物的不同的物质或因素：element; content | 水~shuǐfèn *moisture content*

分量 fènliàng weight
分子 fēnzǐ member; element
部分 bùfèn　　成分 chéngfèn
充分 chōngfèn 养分 yǎngfèn
缘分 yuánfèn
不法分子 bùfǎ fēnzǐ
知识分子 zhīshi fēnzǐ

❷[名] 职责和权利的限度：limits of powers or rights | 本~ běnfèn *one's duty; honest* / 恰如其~qiàrúqí fèn *appropriate; just right*

分外 fènwài beyond one's duty
◇过分 guòfèn

See fēn.

fèn　　6画 亻部
. . . .

份 份份份份份份

❶ [名] 整体里的一部分：share; part; portion

份额 fèn'é share; portion
成分 chéngfèn　　股份 gǔfèn
股份制 gǔfènzhì

❷ [量] 用于整体分成的部分或组成整体的部分：share；part；portion | 一~礼yī fèn lǐ *a gift* / 每人都有一~。Měi rén dōu yǒu yī fèn. *Everyone has his share.*

❸ [量] 用于报刊、文件等：used for newspaper, document, etc. | 一~报纸 yī fèn bàozhǐ *a copy of the newspaper* / 一~文件 yī fèn wénjiàn *a copy of document* / 合同一式两~。Hétong yī shì liǎng fèn. *The contract has been done in duplicate.*

❹ [量] 用于餐厅、商店为单人搭配的食物量：set meal | 中午买了一~米饭。Zhōngwǔ mǎile yī fèn mǐfàn. *I bought a portion of cooked rice at noon.* / 快餐六块钱一~。Kuàicān liù kuài qián yī fèn. *Quick meals are sold at 6 yuan a set.*

❺ [名] 用在"省、县、年、月"后面，表示划分的单位：used after

"省 shěng" "县 xiàn" "年 nián" "月 yuè" to indicate units of differentiation | 省～shěng-fēn *province*
月份 yuèfēn
身份证 shēnfènzhèng

奋 (奮) fèn 8画 大部

奋 奋奋奋奋奋奋奋奋

[动] 振作；鼓劲：exert oneself; act vigorously
奋斗 fèndòu struggle; fight; strive
奋力 fènlì do all one can; spare no effort
奋勇 fènyǒng summon up all one's courage and energy
奋战 fènzhàn fight bravely; work strenuously
勤奋 qínfèn   兴奋 xīngfèn
振奋 zhènfèn
兴奋剂 xīngfènjì

 (粪) fèn 12画 米部

粪 粪粪粪粪粪粪粪粪
粪粪粪粪

[名] 屎：excrement | 鸟～niǎofèn *bird droppings* | ～是最好的有机肥料。Fèn shì zuìhǎo de yǒujī féiliào. *Excrement is the best organic fertilizer.*

愤 (憤) fèn 12画 忄部

愤 愤愤愤愤愤愤愤愤
愤愤愤愤

[动] 因为不满意而激动；发怒：get angry; resent
愤恨 fènhèn indignantly resent; detest
愤怒 fènnù indignation; anger; wrath; fury
悲愤 bēifèn   气愤 qìfèn
发愤图强 fāfèn-túqiáng

丰 (豐) fēng 4画 一部

丰 丰丰丰丰

[形] 丰富：rich; abundant | ～盛 fēngshèng *rich* | ～年 fēngnián *a bumper harvest year*
丰产 fēngchǎn high yield; bumper crop
丰富 fēngfù abundant; ample; rich; plentiful
丰厚 fēnghòu ① thick ② rich and generous
丰满 fēngmǎn plentiful; full and round; plump
丰收 fēngshōu yield abundantly; abundant harvests
丰富多彩 fēngfù-duōcǎi rich and varied; rich and colourful

风 (風) fēng 4画风部

风 风风风风

❶ [名] wind | ～把树吹得哗哗响。Fēng bǎ shù chuī de huāhuā xiǎng. *The leaves are rustling in the wind.* / 北京春天～多。Běijīng chūntiān fēng duō. *During the spring, it's rather windy in Beijing.*

风暴 fēngbào windstorm; storm; tempest; a violent commotion

风波 fēngbō ① wind and waves ② (fig.) disturbance; storm

风浪 fēnglàng stormy waves; storm

风力 fēnglì wind-force

风沙 fēngshā sand blown by the wind

风衣 fēngyī windcheater; windbreaker; windjacket

风雨 fēngyǔ wind and rain; trials and hardships

风云 fēngyún wind and cloud; a stormy or unstable situation

风筝 fēngzheng kite

风和日丽 fēnghé-rìlì a bright sun and a gentle breeze; warm and sunny weather

风调雨顺 fēngtiáo-yǔshùn good weather for the crops; favourable weather

春风 chūnfēng 大风 dàfēng

东风 dōngfēng

狂风 kuángfēng

台风 táifēng

通风 tōngfēng 微风 wēifēng

❷ [名] 风气；习俗：practice; custom; atmosphere | 学～ xuéfēng *academic atmosphere; academic discipline* / 文～ wénfēng *style of writing*

风貌 fēngmào ① style and features ② elegant appearance and bearing

风气 fēngqì general mood; atmosphere; common practice

风情 fēngqíng ① (formal) bearing; demeanour ② amorous feelings; flirtatious expressions ③ local conditions and customs

风尚 fēngshàng prevailing custom (practice, habit)

风俗 fēngsú custom

风味 fēngwèi special flavour; local colours (flavours)

风土人情 fēngtǔ-rénqíng local conditions and customs

不正之风 bùzhèngzhīfēng

❸ [名] 外在的姿态；作风：gesture; style

风采 fēngcǎi ① (formal) elegant demeanour; graceful bearing ② (formal) literary grace

风度 fēngdù demeanour; bearing

风范 fēngfàn (formal) ① demeanour; bearing; poise ② style; manner; air

风格 fēnggé style; manner;

mode

风趣 fēngqù humour; wit

整风 zhěngfēng 作风 zuòfēng

❹ [名] 消息；风声：word; news; rumour | 闻～而逃 wénfēng'értāo *flee at the news* / 最近没听到什么～声? Zuìjìn méi tīngdào shénme fēngshēng? *Have you had any news recently?*

❺ [名] 景象：scene; picture; sight

风光 fēngguāng scenery; scene; view; sight

风光 fēngguang grand; impressive; in style

风景 fēngjǐng scenery; landscape

◇风琴 fēngqín organ

风险 fēngxiǎn risk; hazard

风云人物 fēngyún rénwù man of the hour

担风险 dānfēngxiǎn

封 fēng 9画 寸部

封封封封封封封封封

❶ [动] 古代帝王把爵位、土地或称号赐给臣子：(of ancient kings) grant title or territories to their family members or subordinates

封建 fēngjiàn the system of enfeoffment; feudalism

❷ [动] 封闭：seal; cap | 把瓶口住 bǎ píngkǒu fēngzhù *seal the bottle* / 这个出口被～了。

Zhège chūkǒu bèi fēng le. *The entrance was blocked.* / 大雪～山了。Dàxuě fēngshān le. *The mountains are blocked by heavy snow.*

封闭 fēngbì seal; close; seal off

封锁 fēngsuǒ block or seal off; blockade

查封 cháfēng 密封 mìfēng

❸ [名] 用来封东西的物品：envelope; package

封面 fēngmiàn front cover; the front and back cover of a book

信封 xìnfēng

❹ [量] 用于封着的东西：used for sth. packed or sealed | 一～信 yī fēng xìn *a letter* / 两～电报 liǎng fēng diànbào *two telegrams*

疯 (瘋) fēng 9画 疒部

疯疯疯疯疯疯疯疯疯

❶ [形] mad; crazy | 发～fāfēng *become crazy* / 他完全～了。Tā wánquán fēng le. *He was stark raving mad.*

疯狂 fēngkuáng frenzied; unbridled; insane

疯子 fēngzi lunatic; madman

❷ [形] 野性的，不受拘束的：unbridled; wild | 孩子都玩～了，连饭都顾不上吃。Háizi dōu wánfēng le, lián fàn dōu gūbushang chī. *The children are having so much fun that they have forgotten to eat.*

峰 fēng 10画 山部

峰峰峰峰峰峰峰峰
峰峰

[名]高而尖的山顶：summit; peak
峰会 fēnghuì summit; summit meeting; meeting of heads of states
顶峰 dǐngfēng
山峰 shānfēng

锋 (鋒) fēng 12画 钅部

锋 锋锋锋锋锋锋锋锋
锋锋锋锋

❶[名]刀、剑等兵器的锐利部分；器物的尖端部分：a sharp point or cutting edge of a knife, etc. | 剑~jiànfēng *the cutting edge of a sword* | 针~相对zhēnfēng-xiāngduì *give tit for tat*
锋利 fēnglì sharp; keen; incisive; poignant
交锋 jiāofēng

❷[名]带头在前的人：vanguard | 前~qiánfēng *spearhead of army*
先锋 xiānfēng
中锋 zhōngfēng

蜂 fēng 13画 虫部

蜂 蜂蜂蜂蜂蜂蜂蜂蜂
蜂蜂蜂蜂蜂

[名]bee; wasp
蜂蜜 fēngmì honey
黄蜂 huángfēng 蜜蜂 mìfēng
一窝蜂 yīwōfēng

逢 fēng 10画 辶部

逢 逢逢逢逢逢逢逢
逢逢

[动]遇到；遇见：meet; encounter; come across | 重~chóngfēng *meet again* | 每~星期日他都去看电影。Měi fēng xīngqīrì tā dōu qù kàn diànyǐng. *He goes to the cinema every Sunday.*
逢年过节 féngnián-guòjié on New Year's Day or other festivals
萍水相逢 píngshuǐ-xiāngféng

缝 (縫) fēng 13画 纟部

缝 缝缝缝缝缝缝缝缝
缝缝缝缝缝

[动]用针线连缀：sew; stitch | ~衣服 féng yīfu *sew a dress* | ~伤口 féng shāngkǒu *sew up a wound*
See fèng.

讽 (諷) fěng 6画 讠部

讽 讽讽讽讽讽讽

[动] 用含蓄的话指责、劝告或讥笑：criticize a person or thing with implicit remarks | 讥~jīfěng *ridicule; mock* / 冷嘲热~lěngchāo-rěfěng *with biting sarcasm*

讽刺 fěngcì satirize; mock; ridicule; sarcasm

反讽 fǎnfěng

凤 (鳳) fèng 4画 几部

凤 凤凤凤凤

[名] 传说中的百鸟之王。雄的叫 "凤"，雌的叫 "凰"：phoenix, a legendary bird king. A male is called "凤fèng", while the female one is called "凰huáng" | 百鸟朝~bǎiniǎo cháofèng *all kinds of birds pay respects to the phoenix*

凤凰 fènghuáng phoenix

奉 fèng 8画 一部

奉 奉奉奉奉奉奉奉奉

❶ [动] 恭敬地献上；送：present with respect | ~送 fèngsòng *offer as a gift* / ~上新茶一盒，

请收下。Fèngshang xīn chá yī hé, qǐng shōuxia. *(in polite writing) Please kindly accept a box of newly picked and processed tea I herewith send you.*

奉献 fèngxiàn offer as a tribute; present with all respect

❷ [动] 遵照；遵照执行：obey; act in accordance with | ~命 fèngmìng *receive orders*

奉行 fèngxíng pursue (a policy, etc.)

❸ [副] 敬词，用于自己的举动涉及对方时：term used to show respect to the one concerned | ~劝 fèngquàn *offer a piece of advice* / ~陪 fèngpéi *keep company*

无可奉告 wúkěfènggào

缝 (縫) féng 13画 纟部

缝 缝缝缝缝缝缝缝缝 缝缝缝缝缝

❶ [名] 接合的地方：seam | 门~ ménfèng *the crack between the door and its frame* / 无~钢管 wúfèng gāngguǎn *seamless steel tube*

❷ [名] 间隙：crack | 墙壁裂了一道~。Qiángbì lièle yī dào fèng. *There is a crack in the wall.*

See féng.

佛 fó 7画 亻部

佛 佛佛佛佛佛佛佛

❶[名] 指佛教创始人释迦牟尼：the founder of Buddhism—Sakyamuni; the Buddha

❷[名] 修成佛道的人：real Buddhist

❸[名] 佛教：Buddhism
佛教 fójiào Buddhism

❹[名] 佛像：figure of the Buddha | 大殿上塑着三尊～。Dàdiàn shang sùzhe sān zūn fó. *There are three statues of Buddha in the main hall of the temple.*

See fú.

否 fǒu 7画 口部

否 否否否否否否否

❶[副] 否定；不同意：vote down; deny | 我的建议被他～了。Wǒ de jiànyì bèi tā fǒu le. *My suggestion was voted down by him.*
否定 fǒudìng negate; deny; refute; contradict; reject
否决 fǒujué vote down; veto; overrule; reject; vote against
否认 fǒurèn deny; repudiate

❷[副] 表示疑问：used in an interrogative sentence | 你能～帮我一下？Nǐ néngfǒu bāng wǒ yīxià? *Could you help me?* | 我们能～按时到达北京？Wǒmen néngfǒu ànshí dàodá Běijīng? *Can we arrive in Beijing on time?*
是否 shìfǒu
◇否则 fǒuzé otherwise; if not; or else

夫 fū 4画 一部

夫 夫夫夫夫

❶[名] 丈夫，女子的配偶：husband | ～妇 fūfù *husband and wife*
夫妻 fūqī husband and wife
姑夫 gūfu   姨夫 yífu
丈夫 zhàngfu

❷[名] 称从事某种体力劳动的人：manual worker; labourer | 农～ nóngfū *farmer* / 渔～ yúfū *fisherman* / 车～ chēfū *driver*

❸[名] 成年男子的通称：man
◇夫人 fūrén a lady of high rank; the wife of a feudal lord; Lady; madam; Mrs
下功夫 xiàgōngfu
高尔夫球 gāo'ěrfūqiú

肤 (膚) fū 8画 月部

肤 肤肤肤肤肤肤肤肤

❶[名] 身体表面包在肌肉外面的组织：skin | 肌～ jīfū *skin* / ～色 fūsè *colour (of skin)*

233

皮肤 pí fū

❷ [形] 表面的；浅薄的：shallow; superficial

肤浅 fūqiǎn superficial; shallow

敷 fū　15画 攵部

敷敷敷敷敷敷敷敷敷敷敷敷敷敷敷

[动] 搽；涂：apply | ～药 fūyào apply medical ointment or powder | 护士给孩子～上了药。Hùshi gěi háizi fūshang le yào. *The nurse applied the plaster for the child.*

热敷 rèfū

◇敷衍 fūyǎn act in a perfunctory manner; muddle through one's work

伏 fú　6画 亻部

伏伏伏伏伏伏

❶ [动] 身体向前靠在物体上；趴：bend over or lean over sth. | ～在桌子上 fú zài zhuōzi shang *bend over one's desk* / 她～在我的肩上哭起来。Tā fú zài wǒ de jiān shang kū qǐlai. *She leant over my shoulder crying.*

❷ [动] 隐藏：conceal; remain under cover | 潜～ qiǎnfú hide

埋伏 máifú

❸ [动] 低下去：lower

起伏 qǐfú

❹ [动] 屈服，低头顺服：yield; surrender | 在事实面前他只有～罪。Zài shìshí miànqián tā zhǐyǒu fúzuì. *In face of the facts, he had no alternative but to admit his guilt.*

扶 fú　7画 扌部

扶扶扶扶扶扶扶

❶ [动] 用手支持使起来或不倒：support with the hand | ～老携幼 fúlǎo-xiéyòu *bring along the old and the young* / ～着孩子点儿，别让他摔着。Fúzhe háizi diǎnr, bié ràng tā shuāizháo. *Hold the child, don't let him fall.*

❷ [动] 帮助；援助：help | ～助 fúzhù *help; aid* / 护士～着病人坐起来。Hùshi fúzhe bìngrén zuò qǐlai. *The nurse helped the patient to sit up.*

佛 fú　7画 亻部

佛佛佛佛佛佛佛

See 仿佛

仿佛 fǎngfú

See fó.

拂 fú 8画 扌部

拂 拂拂拂拂拂拂拂拂

❶ [动] 轻轻擦过: touch lightly; stroke | 春风~面 chūnfēng fú miàn *a spring breeze gently blowing on one's face*

❷ [动] 掸去: brush off; flick | ~袖而去 fúxiù'érqù *leave in anger*

服 fú 8画 月部

服 服服服服服服服服

❶ [动] 担任；承当: serve | ~役 fúyì *be on active service; enlist in the army*

服务 fúwù give service to; be in the service of; serve

服刑 fúxíng serve a sentence

服务器 fúwùqì server

服务台 fúwùtái service desk (or counter); information and reception desk

服务员 fúwùyuán attendant; waiter; waitress; porter; server

❷ [动] 听从；信服: obey; be convinced | 心~口~xīnfú-kǒufú *be sincerely convinced* / 大家对张师傅的技术没有不~的。Dàjiā duì Zhāng shīfu de jìshù méiyǒu bùfú de. *Everyone submits willingly to Master Zhang's consummate skills.* / 你有道理，我自然~你。Nǐ yǒu dàolǐ, wǒ zìrán fú nǐ. *Since what you said is reasonable, I am convinced.*

服从 fúcóng obey; submit oneself to; be subordinated to; subject; succumb

服气 fúqì be convinced; be won over

服输 fúshū admit defeat

不服 bùfú　　克服 kèfú

佩服 pèifú　　屈服 qūfú

说服 shuōfú　　征服 zhēngfú

❸ [动] 习惯；适应: suit; fit; accustom | 水土不~shuǐtǔ bùfú *not accustomed to the climate (of a new place)*

❹ [动] 吃: eat; have; take | ~药 fúyào *take medicine* / ~毒fúdú *take poison* / 这种药片每次~三片。Zhè zhǒng yàopiàn měicì fú sān piàn. *Take three tablets each time.*

服用 fúyòng take (medicine)

❺ [名] 衣服: clothes; garments | 工作~gōngzuòfú *work uniform*

服饰 fúshì dress and personal adornment; dress

服装 fúzhuāng dress; clothing; costume; garment; apparel

西服 xīfú　　　衣服 yīfú

制服 zhìfú　　　羽绒服 yǔróngfú

俘

fú   9画 亻部

俘 俘俘俘俘俘俘俘俘俘

❶ [动] 作战时把对方捉住：capture | 被~ bèifú be captured
俘虏 fúlǔ capture; take prisoner
❷ [名] 作战时被对方捉住的人：prisoner | 战~ zhànfú prisoner of war
俘虏 fúlǔ captive; captured personnel

浮

fú   10画 氵部

浮 浮浮浮浮浮浮浮浮浮浮

❶ [动] 停留在液体表面上：float | 油~在水面上。Yóu fú zài shuǐmiàn shang. Oil floats on the surface of the water. / 沉船终于~上来了。Chénchuán zhōngyú fú shànglai le. The shipwreck floated off at last.
❷ [动] 在水里游：swim | 他一口气能~到对岸。Tā yīkǒuqì néng fúdào duì'àn. He can swim across the river in one go.
浮动 fúdòng ① drift ② be unsteady
◇浮雕 fúdiāo relief sculpture

符

fú   11画 竹部

符 符符符符符符符符 符符符

❶ [名] 记号；标记：symbol; mark | 音~ yīnfú musical notes
符号 fúhào symbol; mark
❷ [动] 相合：accord with; conform to | 他所说的与事实不~。Tā suǒ shuō de yǔ shìshí bùfú. What he said is inconsistent with the facts.
符合 fúhé accord with; tally with; conform to; be in keeping with
不符 bùfú   相符 xiāngfú

袱

fú   11画 衤部

袱 袱袱袱袱袱袱袱袱 袱袱袱

[名] 包裹或覆盖东西用的布单：cloth-wrapper
包袱 bāofu

幅

fú   12画 巾部

幅 幅幅幅幅幅幅幅幅 幅幅幅幅

❶ [名] 泛指宽度：width; size
幅度 fúdù range; scope; extent
大幅 dàfú   增幅 zēngfú
涨幅 zhǎngfú
❷ [量] 用于布匹、字画等：used for cloth, picture, etc. | 两~布 liǎng fú bù two sheets of cloth /

一～画 yī fú huà *a painting*

輻 (輻) fú　　13画 车部

辐 辐辐辐辐辐辐辐辐
辐辐辐辐辐

[名] 车轮上连接轮边到轮中心的一
条条细金属杆：spoke of a wheel
辐条 fútiáo spoke
◇ 辐射 fúshè radiation; exposure;
beaming

福 fú　　13画 礻部

福 福福福福福福福福
福福福福福

❶[名] 幸福：happiness; blessing
| 植树造林是造～子孙的事。
Zhíshù zàolín shì zào fú zǐsūn
de shì. *Afforestation is an undertaking benefiting our future
generations.*
福利 fúlì welfare; well-being;
material benefits
享福 xiǎngfú　　幸福 xìngfú
祝福 zhùfú
❷[名] 福气：good luck; a happy
lot | 他是个有～的人。Tā shì
ge yǒu fú de rén. *He is a man
of good luck.*
福气 fúqi good luck; good fortune; a happy lot

抚 (撫) fú　　7画 扌部

抚 抚抚抚抚抚抚抚

❶[动] 用手轻触摸：stroke; soothe
by hand | ～琴 fúqín *play the
zither*
抚摸 fúmō stroke; fondle
❷[动] 慰问：comfort; console |
安～ānfǔ *pacify* / ～慰 fúwèi
comfort
❸[动] 扶持；保护：support with
the hand; give aid to
抚养 fúyǎng foster; raise; bring
up
抚育 fúyù foster; nurture; tend

斧 fú　　8画 父部

斧 斧斧斧斧斧斧斧斧

See 斧子
斧子 fúzi axe; hatchet

府 fú　　8画 广部

府 府府府府府府府府

See 政府
政府 zhèngfǔ

俯 fú　　10画 亻部

俯 俯俯俯俯俯俯俯俯
俯俯

[动]低头；向下：bow one's head; bend forward or down | ～视 fǔshì *look down at* / ～冲 fǔchōng *dive* / 她～下身亲了亲孩子。Tā fǔxià shēn qīnle qīn háizi. *She bent down and kissed the child.*

辅 (輔) fǔ　　11画 车部

辅 辅辅辅辅辅辅辅辅 辅辅辅

[动]帮助：assist; help
辅导 fǔdǎo give guidance in study or training; coach
辅路 fǔlù auxiliary lane; narrow roads used to alleviate traffic congestion
辅修 fǔxiū minor; selected subject
辅助 fǔzhù assist; assistance; subsidiary; auxiliary; supplementary

腐 fǔ　　14画 广部

腐 腐腐腐腐腐腐腐腐 腐腐腐腐腐腐

❶ [动]烂；变坏：become rotten; go bad; decay | 陈～ chénfǔ *stale* / 流水不～ liúshuǐ-bùfǔ *running water is never stagnant*
腐败 fǔbài rotten; putrid; decayed; corruption
腐化 fǔhuà degenerate; become corrupt; dissolute or depraved; rot; decay
腐烂 fǔlàn decompose; become putrid; become rotten
腐蚀 fǔshí corrode; corrosion; rot; eat off
腐朽 fǔxiǔ rotten; decayed; decadent; degenerate
❷ [名]豆制食品：bean products
豆腐 dòufu

父 fù　　4画 父部

父 父父父父

❶ [名]父亲：father | ～子 fùzǐ *father and son*
父母 fùmǔ father and mother; parents
父亲 fùqīn father
❷ [名]对男性长辈的称呼：address for male seniors
伯父 bófù　　　祖父 zǔfù
外祖父 wàizǔfù

付 fù　　5画 亻部

 付 付付付付付

[动]交给：hand or turn over; pay | ～电费 fù diànfèi *pay for electricity* / 我们商店不欠账，要～现钱。Wǒmen shāngdiàn bù qiànzhàng, yào fù xiànqián. *We do not sell on credit. You can only pay cash.*

付出 fùchū pay; expend

付费 fùfèi pay a sum of money

付款 fùkuǎn pay a sum of money

交付 jiāofù　　　　赔付 péifù

◇对付 duìfu　　　　应付 yīngfù

 负（負）fù　　6画 ⼓部

负 负负负负负负

❶[动] 背：shoulder; carry on the back or shoulder | 他每天~重跑步。Tā měi tiān fùzhòng pǎobù. *He goes for a loaded run every day.*

❷[名] 担任；承担：bear; undertake; assume | 身~重任 shēn fù zhòngrèn *shoulder an important task* / ~责任 fù zérèn *be responsible*

负担 fùdān bear; shoulder; burden; load; encumbrance

负责 fùzé be responsible for; be in charge of; take charge of

负责人 fùzérén person in charge; leading cadre

抱负 bàofù　　　　担负 dānfù

自负盈亏 zìfù yíngkuī

❸[动] 遭受：suffer; sustain

负伤 fùshāng be wounded (injured)

❹[动] 欠：owe | 你~了债要还的。Nǐ fùle zhài yào huán de. *You should pay your debts.*

负债 fùzhài ① be in debt; incur debts ② liabilities

❺[动] 背弃；违背：betray; break; violate | ~心 fùxīn *unfaithful* / 宁可别人~我，我决不~人。Nìngkě biérén fù wǒ, wǒ juébù fù rén. *I'd rather be betrayed than betray others.*

辜负 gūfù　　　　欺负 qīfù

❻[动] 输；失败：be defeated, lose | 不分胜~ bù fēn shèngfù *end in a draw* / 甲队以两分之差~于乙队。Jiǎduì yǐ liǎng fēn zhī chā fùyú yǐduì. *Team A lost by two points to team B.*

胜负 shèngfù

❼[形] 小于零的（跟"正 zhèng"相对）：minus; negative (the opposite of "正 zhèng") | ~数 fùshù *negative number*

负面 fùmiàn negative; downside

负增长 fùzēngzhǎng negative growth; decrease; reduction or drop in scale, amount, etc.

 妇（婦）fù　　6画 女部

妇 妇妇妇妇妇妇

❶[名] 妇女：woman; matron; lady

妇女 fùnǚ woman; matron; lady

孕妇 yùnfù

长舌妇 chángshéfù

❷[名] 已婚的女子。引申为女性的通称：married woman; a general term for women

239

妇人 fùrén married woman; lady

寡妇 guǎfu   媳妇 xífu

❸[名] 妻子：wife

夫妇 fūfù

附   fù   7画 阝(左)部

附 附 附 附 附 附 附

❶[动] 依从；依附：comply with; yield to | ~议 fùyì *second a motion*

附和 fùhè echo; chime in with; repeat what others say

附属 fùshǔ subsidiary; auxiliary; attached; affiliated

❷[动] 靠近；贴近：approach; near; be close by | 她~在他的耳边低声说话。Tā fù zài tā de ěrbiān dīshēng shuōhuà. *She whispers in his ear.*

附近 fùjìn nearby; neighbouring; neighbourhood

❸[动] 附带；外加：attach; appendix | ~寄一张照片 fù jì yī zhāng zhàopiàn *enclose herewith a photo* / 你写信请代我~上一笔。Nǐ xiěxìn qǐng dài wǒ fùshàng yī bǐ. *Please add a few words for me in your letter.*

附带 fùdài in passing; attach; subsidiary; supplementary

附加 fùjiā add; attach; additional; attached; appended

赴   fù   9画 走部

赴 赴 赴 赴 赴 赴 赴 赴 赴

❶[动] 前往：go to; attend | ~约会 fù yuēhuì *keep an appointment* / ~宴 fùyàn *attend a banquet*

奔赴 bēnfù

❷[动] 参加；投入：take part in; join | 全力以~ quánlìyǐfù *spare no effort*

复 (復)   fù   9画 夂部

复 复 复 复 复 复 复 复 复

❶[动] 转过来或转过去：turn around; turn over | 翻来~去 fānlái-fùqù *toss in bed; over and over again* / 反~无常 fǎnfù-wúcháng *changeable; capricious*

反复 fǎnfù

❷[动] 回答；回报：answer | 收到我的电邮后，请~。Shōudào wǒ de diànyóu hòu, qǐng fù. *Please reply after receiving my e-mail.*

答复 dáfù   批复 pīfù

❸[动] 恢复：resume; return to | ~学 fùxué *go back to school*

复辟 fùbì restore; restoration of the old order or a dethroned monarch

复活 fùhuó bring back to life;

revive; resurrection

复苏 fùsū ① come back to life or consciousness; resuscitate ② recovery; resurgence

复兴 fùxīng revive; resurge; rejuvenate; resuscitate

复活节 Fùhuójié Easter; Easter Sunday

恢复 huīfù   康复 kāngfù

收复 shōufù   修复 xiūfù

❹ [动] 重复: repeat; duplicate

复读 fùdú re-taking of a year or grade

复述 fùshù repeat; retell

复习 fùxí review; revise; go over

复印 fùyìn duplicate; replication; photocopy; xerox

复制 fùzhì duplicate; reproduce; copy; make a copy of; reproduction; dubbing

复印机 fùyìnjī Xerox (machine); duplicator

重复 chóngfù

❺ [动] 报复: make reprisal

复仇 fùchóu revenge; avenge

报复 bàofù

❻ [形] 繁多的；不单一的: compound; complicated

复合 fùhé compound; complex; composite

复杂 fùzá complicated; complex; sophisticated; intricate

副

fù   11画 刂部

副 副 副 副 副 副 副 副 副 副

❶ [形] 第二位的；起辅助作用的: deputy; vice; assistant | ～市长 fùshìzhǎng deputy mayor / ～经理 fùjīnglǐ deputy manager

❷ [形] 次等的；次要的；附带的: secondary; auxiliary

副刊 fùkān supplement

副食 fùshí non-staple food

副业 fùyè sideline; side occupation

副热带 fùrèdài subtropical zone; subtropics; semitropics

副作用 fùzuòyòng side effect; by-effect

❸ [动] 符合: accord with

名副其实 míngfùqíshí

❹ [量] 用于成对成套的东西: used for a set or pair of objects | 两～手套 liǎng fù shǒutào two pairs of gloves / 一～眼镜 yī fù yǎnjìng a pair of glasses

❺ [量] 用于面部表情: used for facial expressions | 一～笑脸 yī fù xiàoliǎn a smiling face / 一～严肃的面孔 yī fù yánsù de miànkǒng a grave face

◇ 副词 fùcí ① (Chin. gram.) adverbial word, any of a class of words that are used mainly to modify a verb or an adjective ② (Eng. gram.) adverb

赋 (賦) fù   12画 贝部

赋 赋赋赋赋赋赋赋赋赋赋
赋赋赋赋

[动]交给：bestow on; endow with
赋予 fùyǔ give; endow; entrust
天赋 tiānfù

富　fù　12画 宀部

富 富富富富富富富富
富富富富

❶ [形] 丰富：rich; abundant |
年~力强 niánfù-lìqiáng *in
one's prime* / ~于创造性 fùyú
chuàngzàoxìng *be highly creative* / 这种食品~含维生素。
Zhè zhǒng shípǐn fù hán wēi-
shēngsù. *This food is rich in vi-
tamins.* / 青少年总是~于幻想。
Qīng-shàonián zǒngshì fùyú
huànxiǎng. *Young people are
always full of imagination.*
富强 fùqiáng prosperous and
strong; thriving and powerful;
rich and mighty
富余 fùyú have more than needed; surplus
丰富 fēngfù
丰富多彩 fēngfù-duōcǎi
❷ [形] 财产多：rich | 这户人家
很~。Zhè hù rénjiā hěn fù. *This
family is very rich.* / 现在他~了。
Xiànzài tā fù le. *Now he has become rich.*
富豪 fùháo rich and powerful

people
富翁 fùwēng man of wealth;
moneybags
富有 fùyǒu rich; wealthy; full of
富裕 fùyù prosperous; well-to-
do; well-off
❸ [名] 资源、财产的总称：wealth
财富 cáifù　　　　致富 zhìfù

腹　fù　13画 月部

腹 腹腹腹腹腹腹腹腹
腹腹腹腹腹

[名]肚子：abdomen; stomach | 这
种药应该空~吃。Zhè zhǒng
yào yīnggāi kōngfù chī. *The
medicine should be taken on an
empty stomach.* / 做体操时注意
收~。Zuò tǐcāo shí zhùyì
shōufù. *Remember to contract
your abdominal muscle while
doing exercises.*
腹部 fùbù belly (of the body);
abdomen; stomach
腹泻 fùxiè diarrhoea

缚 (縛) fù　13画 纟部

缚 缚缚缚缚缚缚缚缚
缚缚缚缚缚

[动]捆绑；缠束：bind; tie up
束缚 shùfù

覆 fù 18画 西部

覆覆覆覆覆覆覆覆
覆 覆覆覆覆覆覆覆覆
覆覆

[动]遮盖: cover
　覆盖 fùgài cover; plant cover

G g

该（該）gāi　8画 讠部

该 该该该该该该该该

❶ [动] 应当是：ought to; should | 这件事～我去做。Zhè jiàn shì gāi wǒ qù zuò. *It's my responsibility to handle this matter.* / 今天～你值班了。Jīntiān gāi nǐ zhíbān le. *It's your turn to be on duty today.* / ～你表演节目了。Gāi nǐ biǎoyǎn jiémù le. *It is your turn to give a performance.*

❷ [动] 活该；不委屈：serve sb. right; not feel wronged | ～! 谁让你不听劝告。Gāi! Shéi ràng nǐ bù tīng quàngào. *It served you right! Why didn't you take my advice?*

❸ [助] 表示理应如此；应当：ought to be; should | 我～走了。Wǒ gāi zǒu le. *It's time for me to go.* / 你不～听他的话。Nǐ bù gāi tīng tā de huà. *You shouldn't obey him.* / ～做的一定要做。Gāi zuò de yīdìng yào zuò. *What ought to be done must be done.*

❹ [助] 估计情况应当如此：suppose | 火车～到站了。Huǒchē gāi dàozhàn le. *The train is supposed to be arriving.*

❺ [动] 欠：owe | 我～他几块钱。Wǒ gāi tā jǐ kuài qián. *I owe him a few yuan.*

❻ [代] 指上面说过的人或事：used to refer to the above-mentioned person or thing | ～书 gāi shū *this book* / ～地 gāi dì *this (or the mentioned) place* / ～生表现良好。Gāi shēng biǎoxiàn liánghǎo. *The student behaved well.*

改 gǎi　7画 己部

改 改改改改改改改

❶ [动] 改变：change | ～日期 gǎi rìqī *change a date* / ～名字 gǎi míngzi *change a name* / 开会的时间～在明天了。Kāihuì de shíjiān gǎi zài míngtiān le. *The date of the meeting was changed to tomorrow.*

改变 gǎibiàn change

改革 gǎigé reform

改建 gǎijiàn reconstruct; rebuild

改进 gǎijìn improve; modify

改良 gǎiliáng ① improve; ameliorate ② reform

改期 gǎiqī change the date; postpone

改善 gǎishàn improve; ameliorate

改造 gǎizào transform; reform;

remould; remake

改组 gǎizǔ reorganize; reshuffle

更改 gēnggǎi

❷[动]纠正：correct; rectify | 知过必~ zhī guò bì gǎi *always correct an error whenever one becomes aware of it* / 请把写错的字~过来。Qǐng bǎ xiěcuò de zì gǎi guòlai. *Please correct the wrong characters.*

改正 gǎizhèng correct; amend; put right

改邪归正 gǎixié-guīzhèng give up evil and return to good; turn over a new leaf

悔改 huǐgǎi

❸[动]修改：revise; alter | ~文章 gǎi wénzhāng *revise an article* / ~衣服 gǎi yīfu *alter a dress*

改编 gǎibiān ① adapt; rearrange; revise ② reorganize; redesignate

改写 gǎixiě rewrite; adapt

批改 pīgǎi   修改 xiūgǎi

钙 (鈣) gài   9画 钅部

钙 钙钙钙钙钙钙钙钙钙

[名]calcium | 牛奶中含有丰富的~。Niúnǎi zhōng hányǒu fēngfù de gài. *Milk contains plenty of calcium.* / 中老年人应补~。Zhōng-lǎonián rén yīng bǔ gài. *Middle-aged and old-aged*

people should take extra calcium.*

盖 (蓋) gài   11画 丷部

盖 盖盖盖盖盖盖盖盖
盖盖盖

❶[名](~儿)覆盖器物的东西：lid; cover | 瓶~儿 pínggàir *a bottle top* / 锅~儿 guōgàir *lid of a cooking pot*

盖子 gàizi lid; cover; cap; top

❷[动]由上而下地遮掩；蒙上：put a cover on; cover | ~被子 gài bèizi *cover oneself (someone) with a quilt* / 用纸把书上的字~住。Yòng zhǐ bǎ shū shang de zì gàizhu. *Cover the words on the page with a piece of paper.*

覆盖 fùgài   铺盖 pūgài
铺盖 pūgai   掩盖 yǎngài
卷铺盖 juǎnpūgai

❸[动]印上去：affix; stamp; seal | ~图章 gài túzhāng *affix a seal* / ~钢印 gài gāngyìn *affix a steel seal*

❹[动]压倒；超过：overwhelm; surpass; exceed | ~世无双 gàishì-wúshuāng *unparalleled anywhere on earth; matchless throughout the world* / 欢呼声~过了他的叫声。Huānhūshēng gàiguole tā de jiàoshēng. *Cheers drowned out his shouting.* / 他游泳的本领已经~过我了。Tā yóuyǒng de běnlǐng yǐjīng gàiguo wǒ le. *He has already surpassed me in swimming.*

❺ [动] 建筑；build; put up | ~房子 gài fángzi build a house / 图书馆~好了。Túshūguǎn gài-hǎo le. *The library has been built.*

 溉 gài 12画 氵部

溉 溉溉溉溉溉溉溉溉溉溉溉溉

[动]浇灌：irrigate
灌溉 guàngài

 概 gài 13画 木部

概 概概概概概概概概概概概概概

❶ [名] 气度：bearing; tolerance
气概 qìgài

❷ [名] 大略：general idea
概况 gàikuàng general situation; survey
概括 gàikuò ①summarize; generalize; epitomize ② briefly; in broad outline
概率 gàilǜ (math.) probability
概念 gàiniàn concept; conception; notion
大概 dàgài

❸ [副] 一律：all; without exception

| ~不外借 gài bù wài jiè *cannot to be lent out* / 这些货物售出，~不退换。Zhèxiē huòwù shōuchū, gài bù tuìhuàn. *Once these commodities are sold, they are not to be returned or exchanged.*

一概 yīgài
一概而论 yīgài'érlùn

 干 (乾❹~❿) gān 3画 干部

干 干干干

❶ [动] 扰乱：harass; disturb
干扰 gānrǎo disturb; interfere; obstruct

❷ [动] 牵连，涉及：involve; concern | 不相~bù xiānggān *have nothing to do with*
干涉 gānshè interfere; intervene; meddle
干预 gānyù intervene; interpose; meddle

❸ [名] 天干，历法中用的"甲、乙、丙、丁、戊、己、庚、辛、壬、癸" 十个字，也作编排次序用：*tiangan,* the heavenly stems, used as the ten serial numbers and also used to arrange order

❹ [形] 没有水分或水分很少：dry | 油漆未~yóuqī wèi gān *wet paint* / 衣服晒~了。Yīfu shàigān le. *The washing has dried off in the sun.*

干旱 gānhàn (of weather or soil) arid; dry

干燥 gānzào ① dry; arid ② dull; uninteresting

❺ [形] 净尽；枯竭；空虚：completely or utterly dried up; exhausted; spiritually empty | ～一杯 gān yī bēi *drink a toast* / 大河没水小河～。Dàhé méi shuǐ xiǎohé gān. *When the main stream is low, the small streams run dry.* / 酒瓶～了。Jiǔpíng gān le. *The wine bottle is empty.*

干杯 gānbēi cheers; drink a toast

干净 gānjìng ① clean; neat and tidy ② complete; total

一干二净 yīgān-èrjìng

❻ [副] 徒然；白白地：in vain; to no purpose | ～着急 gān zhāojí *be anxious but unable to do anything about it* / 我～等了他半天。Wǒ gān děngle tā bàntiān. *I wasted a lot of time waiting for him (and he didn't turn up).*

❼ [形] 拜认的（亲属）：nominally acknowledge sb. as one's kinsfolk | ～妈 gānmā *godmother; adoptive mother* / ～女儿 gānnǚ'ér *adoptive daughter*

❽ [形] 只有形式的：only in form | ～哭 gānkū *cry tearlessly* / ～笑 gānxiào *hollow laugh*

❾ [形] 不用水的：clean (without using water) | ～洗 gānxǐ *dry-clean; dry cleaning*

❿ [名] 干的食品：dried or dehydrated food | 葡萄～pútaogān *raisins* / 豆腐～dòufugān *dried bean curd*

饼干 bǐnggān

◇干脆 gāncuì ① clear-cut; straightforward ② simply; just; altogether

See gàn.

甘　　　　gān　5画 甘部

甘 甘甘甘甘甘

❶ [形] 甜；美好：sweet; fine; happy | 苦尽～来 kǔjìn-gānlái *the hardship ends and the happiness begins* / 同～共苦 tónggān-gòngkǔ *share weal and woe; share comforts and hardships*

甘薯 gānshǔ sweet potato

甘蔗 gānzhe sugarcane

❷ [动] 情愿：be willing | 不～落后 bùgān-luòhòu *unwilling to lag behind* / ～心情愿 gānxīn-qíngyuàn *willingly and gladly*

甘心 gānxīn ① willingly; readily ② be reconciled to; resign oneself to

杆　　　　gān　7画 木部

甘
杆

gān

gān

G

247

杆 杆杆杆杆杆杆杆

[名]较长的棍状物：a lengthy rod or stick | 电线~子 diànxiàn gānzi wire pole / 把衣服搭在~上 bǎ yīfu dā zài gān shang hang the clothes on the pole (to dry in the air)
栏杆 lángān   桅杆 wéigān
See gǎn.

 肝   gān   7画 月部

肝 肝肝肝肝肝肝肝

[名] liver
肝炎 gānyán hepatitis
乙肝 yǐgān

 竿   gān   9画 竹部

竿 竿竿竿竿竿竿竿竿竿

[名]截取竹子的主干而成的杆子：the main stalk of the bamboo plant | 钓鱼~ diàoyúgān fishing rod / 竹~ zhúgān bamboo pole

杆   gān   7画 木部

杆 杆杆杆杆杆杆杆

[名]器物上细长的棍状部分：the shaft or arm of sth. | 笔~ bǐgǎn penholder / 枪~ qiānggǎn the barrel of a rifle
See gān.

 秆   gǎn   8画 禾部

秆 秆秆秆秆秆秆秆秆

[名]某些植物的茎：the stalk of certain plants | 高粱~儿 gāolianggǎnr sorghum stalk

赶 (趕)   gǎn   10画 走部

赶 赶赶赶赶赶赶赶赶赶赶

❶ [动] 追：try to catch; hurry; rush | 你追我~ nǐzhuī-wǒgǎn emulate one another
赶上 gǎnshàng ① overtake; catch up with; keep pace with ② be in time for; run into (certain situation)
赶时髦 gǎnshímáo follow the fashion; try to be in style
追赶 zhuīgǎn
❷ [动] 加快行动，使不误时间：quicken paces so as to avoid delay | ~火车 gǎn huǒchē catch a train / ~任务 gǎn rènwù rush through one's job / ~写文章 gǎn xiě wénzhāng dash off an article
赶紧 gǎnjǐn lose no time; hasten; hurry
赶快 gǎnkuài at once; quickly

赶忙 gǎnmáng make haste

❸ [动] 驱逐：drive away | ～羊 gǎn yáng *herd the sheep* / ～苍蝇 gǎn cāngying *whisk flies off*

❹ [动] 驾驭：drive; control | ～大车 gǎn dàchē *drive a cart*

❺ [动] 碰上：happen to; chance to | ～上好运气 gǎnshang hǎo yùnqi *as luck would have it* / 正～上他没在家。Zhèng gǎnshang tā méi zài jiā. *He happened to be out at that moment.*

敢 gǎn 11画 攵部

敢敢敢敢敢敢敢敢敢敢敢

❶ [形] 有胆量；有勇气：bold; courageous; daring | ～想～干 gǎnxiǎng gǎngàn *dare to have a dream and dare to realize it* / ～负责任 gǎn fù zérèn *dare to take responsibility* / 我不～再往前走一步。Wǒ bùgǎn zài wǎng qián zǒu yī bù. *I dare not venture a step further.*

敢于 gǎnyú dare to; be bold in; have the courage to

勇敢 yǒnggǎn

不敢当 bùgǎndāng

❷ [助] 表示有把握作某种判断：have confidence to; be certain | 医生也不～保证他的病马上就好。Yīshēng yě bùgǎn bǎo-

zhèng tā de bìng mǎshàng jiū hǎo. *The doctor cannot guarantee the quick recovery of his illness.* / 我～说他一定会来。Wǒ gǎn shuō tā yīdìng huì lái. *I am sure that he will come.*

感 gǎn 13画 心部

感感感感感感感感感感感感感

❶ [动] 受到外界影响而引起思想情绪变化：feel; sense

感动 gǎndòng move; touch

感化 gǎnhuà convert; influence

感慨 gǎnkǎi sigh with emotion

感情 gǎnqíng ① emotion; feeling; sentiment ② affection; attachment; love

感染 gǎnrǎn ① infect ② influence; affect; contagion

感人 gǎnrén touching; moving

感受 gǎnshòu ① be affected by ② feel; experience

感叹 gǎntàn sigh with feeling

感想 gǎnxiǎng impressions; reflections; thoughts

灵感 línggǎn

❷ [名] 感觉；情感；感想：feeling; emotion; impression | 自豪～zìháogǎn *a sense of pride* / 他的责任～很强。Tā de zérèngǎn hěn qiáng. *He has a strong sense of responsibility.*

感觉 gǎnjué sense; feeling

动感 dònggǎn　反感 fǎngǎn
好感 hǎogǎn　敏感 mǐngǎn
情感 qínggǎn　性感 xìnggǎn
安全感 ānquángǎn
真情实感 zhēnqíng-shígǎn

❸ [动] 觉得：feel ｜深~内疚 shēn gǎn nèijiù *deeply feel guilty*
感到 gǎndào　feel; sense; find
感兴趣 gǎnxìngqù　be interested

❹ [动] 怀有谢意：be grateful ｜深~厚谊 shēn gǎn hòuyì *profound sentiments of friendship*
感激 gǎnjī　feel grateful; be thankful; feel indebted
感谢 gǎnxiè　thank; be grateful
感恩节 Gǎn'ēnjié Thanksgiving Day

◇感冒 gǎnmào cold

干 (幹) gàn　3画 干部

干 干 干 干

❶ [名] 事物的主体或重要部分：trunk or main part of a thing or object ｜躯~ qūgàn *trunk; torso*
干线 gànxiàn main line; trunk line
干细胞 gànxìbāo stem cell
骨干 gǔgàn　树干 shùgàn

❷ [动] 做(事)：work; work on a job ｜~工作 gàn gōngzuò *work; have a job* / 埋头苦~ máitóu-kǔgàn *quietly immerse oneself in hard work* / 你在~什么? Nǐ

zài gàn shénme? *What are you doing?*
干劲 gànjìn drive; vigour; enthusiasm
干事 gànshi a secretary (or clerical worker) in charge of sth.
干活儿 gànhuór work; work on a job

❸ [名] 办事能力：ability; capability ｜真能~ zhēn néng gàn *really capable*
才干 cáigàn
能干 nénggàn

❹ [动] 担任(某种职务)；从事(某种工作)：work as; serve as; go in for; be engaged in ｜~导游 gàn dǎoyóu *be a tour guide* / ~翻译 gàn fānyì *be a translator* / 他~过队长。Tā gànguo duìzhǎng. *He used to be a team leader.* / 这活儿他~过。Zhè huór tā gànguo. *He engaged in this kind of work before.*

See gān.

冈 (岡) gāng　4画 冂部

 冈 冈 冈 冈

[名] 较低的山脊：ridge (of a low hill) ｜山~ shāngāng *low hill; hillock*

刚 (剛) gāng　6画 刂部

刚 刚刚刚刚刚刚

❶ [形] 坚强；硬：firm; strong; indomitable; hard | 性情～正 xìngqíng gāngzhèng *upright; honorable* / 这人性子太～。Zhè rén xìngzi tāi gāng. *He has a tough character.*

❷ [副] 表示发生在不久前；才；方才：(happened) not long ago; just; just now | ～下过一场雨。Gāng xiàguo yī chǎng yǔ. *It has just rained.* / 电影～开始。Diànyǐng gāng kāishǐ. *The film has just started.* / 他～从北京回来。Tā gāng cóng Běijīng huílai. *He has just returned from Beijing.*

刚才 gāngcái just now; a moment ago

刚刚 gānggāng ① just; only; exactly ② a moment ago; just now

❸ [副] 表示勉强达到某种程度；仅仅：only; barely; simply | 声音很小，～可以听到。Shēngyīn hěn xiǎo, gāng kěyǐ tīngdào. *The voice was so low that it could barely be heard.*

❹ [副] 正好：just; exactly | 这顶帽子不大不小，～好适合你。Zhè dǐng màozi bù dà bù xiǎo, gānghǎo shìhé nǐ. *The size of the hat fits you nicely.* / ～达到标准 gāng dádào biāozhǔn *just come up to a certain standard*

刚好 gānghǎo ① just; exactly ② by chance; by coincidence

纲 (綱) gāng 7画 纟部

纲 纲纲纲纲纲纲纲

[名] 网上的总绳；比喻事物最主要的部分：the head of a fishing net; key part of sth.; key link | 大～ dàgāng *the general programme; outline*

纲领 gānglǐng programme; guiding principle

纲要 gāngyào ① outline; sketch ② essentials; compendium

提纲 tígāng

钢 (鋼) gāng 9画 钅部

钢 钢钢钢钢钢钢钢钢钢

[名] steel | ～铁 gāngtiě *iron and steel; steel* / 不锈～ bùxiùgāng *stainless steel*

钢笔 gāngbǐ pen; fountain pen

钢材 gāngcái steel products; steels

钢琴 gāngqín piano

 gāng 9画 缶部

缸缸缸缸缸缸缸缸
缸

❶[名]用陶瓷、玻璃等制作的盛东西的器物，一般底小口大：a pottery or glass container with a big mouth and a small bottom; vat; jar; crock｜水～shuǐgāng *water vat* /鱼～yúgāng *fish tank* /～里装满了水。Gāng li zhuāng-mǎnle shuǐ. *The vat is filled with water.*

❷[名]像缸的东西：vat-like vessel｜汽～qìgāng *cylinder*

（岗）gǎng　　7画 山部

岗岗岗岗岗岗岗岗

❶[名]高起的土坡：hillock; mound｜黄土～儿 huángtǔgǎngr *loess hills*

❷[名]守卫的位置：place where a guard is stationed｜站～zhàn-gǎng *be on sentry*
岗位 gǎngwèi post; station

港
gǎng　　12画 氵部

港港港港港港港港
港港港港

❶[名]水运和空运线上供上下旅客、装卸货物的地方：place where passengers embark and disem-bark, and cargo is loaded and unloaded｜船一到～，你就会看

到接你的人。Chuán yī dào gǎng, nǐ jiù huì kàndào jiē nǐ de rén. *When the boat arrives at the harbour, you will see the person who is to pick you up.*
港口 gǎngkǒu port; harbour
海港 hǎigǎng

❷[名]指香港：Hong Kong
港币 gǎngbì Hong Kong dol-lar

gǎng　　7画 木部

杠杠杠杠杠杠杠

[名]较粗的棍子：thick stick｜木～mùgāng *a wooden bar* /铁～tiěgāng *a thick iron stick*
杠杆 gànggǎn lever
敲竹杠 qiāozhúgàng

gāo　　10画 高部

高高高高高高高高
高高

❶[形]由下至上的距离大；离地面远：high; tall｜～山 gāoshān *a high mountain* /飞机飞得真～。Fēijī fēi de zhēn gāo. *The plane is flying very high in the sky.*
高大 gāodà ①tall and big; tall ② lofty
高低 gāodī ① height ② sense of propriety; discretion

高度 gāodù ① altitude; height ② a high degree of; highly

高峰 gāofēng peak; summit; height

高空 gāokōng high altitude; upper air

高原 gāoyuán plateau; highland; tableland

提高 tígāo　　跳高 tiàogāo

❷ [名] 高度；height | 他俩一样~。Tā liǎ yīyàng gāo. *The two of them are of the same height.* / 这棵小树长得有三层楼那么~了。Zhè kē xiǎoshù zhǎng de yǒu sān céng lóu nàme gāo le. *The small tree has reached as high as a three-storey building.*

身高 shēngāo

❸ [形] 地位、等级在上的：high rank and status | 地位~dìwèi gāo *superior position* / ~年级 gāo niánjí *higher grades*

高层 gāocéng senior; high-ranking; high-level; high

高档 gāodàng top grade; superior quality

高等 gāoděng higher; advanced

高官 gāoguān senior cadre; high-ranking official

高贵 gāoguì ① noble; high ② highly privileged; elitist

高级 gāojí ① senior; high-ranking; high-level; high ② high-grade; high quality; advanced

高考 gāokǎo college entrance examination

高手 gāoshǒu past master; master-hand; ace

高中 gāozhōng senior middle school

高等教育 gāoděng jiàoyù higher education

高等学校 gāoděng xuéxiào institutions of higher learning; colleges and universities

❹ [形] 在一般标准或平均程度之上：above the average degree | 质量~zhìliàng gāo *of good quality* / ~速度 gāo sùdù *high speed* / 他的汉语水平特别~。Tā de Hànyǔ shuǐpíng tèbié gāo. *He has a very high proficiency in Chinese.*

高昂 gāo'áng ① hold high (one's head, etc.) ② high; elated ③ dear; expensive

高产 gāochǎn ① high yield; high production ② productive; prolific

高超 gāochāo superb; excellent

高潮 gāocháo ① tide; high water ② upsurge; high tide; climax

高调 gāodiào ① lofty tone; high-sounding words ② (photog.) high tone

高端 gāoduān high; high-grade; high-quality; advanced

高价 gāojià high price

高龄 gāolíng advanced age

(usu. over 60); venerable age

高明 gāomíng brilliant; wise

高尚 gāoshàng noble; lofty

高烧 gāoshāo high fever

高速 gāosù high speed

高危 gāowēi be liable to; be susceptible to (sth. undesirable or threatening)

高温 gāowēn high temperature

高效 gāoxiào high efficiency; highly active

高兴 gāoxìng ① glad; happy; cheerful ② be willing to; be happy to

高压 gāoyā ① high pressure ② high tension; high voltage ③ high-handed

高涨 gāozhǎng rise; upsurge; run high

高血压 gāoxuèyā hypertension; high blood pressure

高速公路 gāosù gōnglù expressway; freeway

崇高 chónggāo

兴高采烈 xìnggāo-cǎiliè

❺ [形] 敬词，称别人的事物：term of respect, used to address other people | ~见 gāojiàn (your) brilliant idea; insightful opinion

◇高粱 gāoliang kaoliang; Chinese sorghum

高尔夫球 gāo'ěrfūqiú golf; golf ball

羔 gāo　10画 羊部

羔 羔羔羔羔羔羔羔羔羔羔

[名] 小羊；泛指幼小的动物：lamb; fawn; a general term for baby animals | 羊~ yánggāo lamb; kid

膏 gāo　14画 高部

膏 膏膏膏膏膏膏膏膏膏膏膏膏膏膏

[名] 很稠的糊状物：paste; cream; ointment | ~药 gāoyào plaster; medicated plaster 牙膏 yágāo

篙 gāo　16画 竹部

篙 篙篙篙篙篙篙篙篙篙篙篙篙篙篙篙篙

[名] 撑船的竹竿或木杆：bamboo or wood pole used to move a boat | 用一把船撑出去 yòng gāo bǎ chuán chēng chūqu punt the boat off with a pole

糕 gāo　16画 米部

糕 糕糕糕糕糕糕糕糕糕糕糕糕糕糕糕糕

[名] 用米、面、豆等制成的块状食品 cakes made from rice, wheat and bean

蛋糕 dàngāo　　年糕 niángāo

搞
gǎo　13画 扌部

搞 搞搞搞搞搞搞搞搞
搞搞搞搞搞

❶[动] 做；弄；干；办：do; carry on; be engaged in | ～工作 gǎo gōngzuò *carry on one's work* / ～教学 gǎo jiāoxué *engage in teaching* / 清问题 gǎoqīng wèntí *obtain a clear understanding of the question (or problem); clear up the matter* / 这事儿不太好～。 Zhè shìr bù tài hǎo gǎo. *It is not easy to do.* / 他在学校～了一个美术展览。 Tā zài xuéxiào gǎole yī gè měishù zhǎnlǎn. *He set up an art exhibition in the school.*

搞鬼 gǎoguǐ play tricks; be up to some mischief

搞活 gǎohuó enliven; vitalize; invigorate

搞笑 gǎoxiào provoke laughter; amuse

❷[动] 设法得到：manage to get | ～两张电影票 gǎo liǎng zhāng diànyǐngpiào *manage to get two film tickets* / 咱们先给他们～点儿东西吃。 Zánmen xiān gěi tāmen gǎo diǎnr dōngxi chī. *Let's get them something to eat first.*

稿
gǎo　15画 禾部

稿 稿稿稿稿稿稿稿稿
稿稿稿稿稿稿稿

❶[名] 文章或图画的底子：draft of an article or rough sketch of a drawing | 底～dǐgǎo *draft; manuscript* / 初～chūgǎo *the first draft*

❷[名] 写或画成的文章、图画作品：article or drawing that has been finished

稿件 gǎojiàn manuscript; contribution

稿纸 gǎozhǐ squared or lined paper for making drafts or copying manuscripts

稿子 gǎozi ① draft; sketch ② manuscript; contribution

告
gǎo　7画 口部

 告 告告告告告告告

❶[动] 把事情、意见等说给别人听：tell; notify | 忠～zhōnggào *sincere advice* / 胜利的消息传来，大家奔走相～。 Shènglì de xiāoxi chuánlái, dàjiā bēnzǒu-xiānggào. *When the news of victory came, people ran around spreading it.*

告诫 gàojiè warn; admonish; exhort

告诉 gàosu tell; let know

报告 bàogào 广告 guǎnggào

警告 jǐnggào 劝告 quàngào

转告 zhuǎngào

无可奉告 wúkěfènggào

❷[动]请求：request; ask for | ~假 gàojiǎ ask for leave / ~饶 gàoráo beg for mercy; ask for pardon

❸[动]宣布或说明某种情况的实现或完成：announce the completion of sth. | 大功~成 dàgōng-gàochéng be crowned with success / 事情已~结束。Shìqing yǐ gào jiéshù. The matter has come to an end.

❹[动]表明；表示；declare; announce | ~辞 gàocí take leave (of one's host)

告别 gàobié ① take leave of; part from ②bid farewell to; say good-bye to

布告 bùgào   公告 gōnggào

通告 tōnggào 宣告 xuāngào

预告 yùgào

❺[动]揭发；提出诉讼：report an offender; inform against; go to law against | 有人~他贪污。Yǒu rén gào tā tānwū. He was accused of corruption. / 你可以去法院~他。Nǐ kěyǐ qù fǎyuàn gào tā. You can go to the court to sue him.

告状 gàozhuàng ① go to law against sb.; bring a lawsuit against sb. ②lodge a complaint against sb.; tell on sb.

被告 bèigào 原告 yuángào

被告人 bèigàorén

疙 gē 8画 疒部

疙疙疙疙疙疙疙疙

See 疙瘩

疙瘩 gēda ① pimple; lump; a swelling on the skin ② lump; knot (in one's mind); misunderstanding (among people)

哥 gē 10画 口部

哥哥哥哥哥哥哥哥哥

❶[名] 同父母或同辈亲戚中比自己年龄大的男子：elder brother | 大~ dàgē the eldest brother / 表~biǎogē older male cousin 哥哥 gēge (elder) brother

❷[名] 称呼年龄跟自己差不多的男子：term of address for elder males of one's own generation | 张大~Zhāng dàgē Brother Zhang

胳 gē 10画 月部

胳胳胳胳胳胳胳胳胳胳

See below

胳臂 gēbei arm
胳膊 gēbo arm

鸽 (鴿) gē　11画 鸟部

鸽 鸽鸽鸽鸽鸽鸽鸽鸽 鸽鸽鸽

[名] pigeon; dove | 信~xìngē *carrier pigeon; homing pigeon* / 和平~hépínggē *peace dove*
鸽子 gēzi pigeon; dove

搁 (擱) gē　12画 扌部

搁 搁搁搁搁搁搁搁搁 搁搁搁搁

❶[动] 放；使处于一定的位置：put or lay sth. in a certain position | 把书~在桌子上吧。Bǎ shū gē zài zhuōzi shang ba. *Put the book on the table.* / 把衣服~进箱子里。Bǎ yīfu gējìn xiāngzi li. *Pack the clothes in the case.*

❷[动] 放着；暂缓进行：put aside; leave on the shelf | 这事~了一个月。Zhè shì gēle yī gè yuè. *The matter was put aside for a month.* / 这问题咱们先~一~。Zhè wèntí zánmen xiān gēyigē. *Let's put (lay) the problem aside for a while.*

❸[动] 加进去：add | 盐~在水里就化了。Yán gē zài shuǐ li jiù huà le. *Salt melts in water.*

割 gē　12画 刂部

割 割割割割割割割割 割割割割

[动] 截断；放弃：cut off; give up | ~草 gē cǎo *cut grass; mow* / 手~破了。Shǒu gēpò le. *The hand was cut.*

歌 gē　14画 欠部

歌 歌歌歌歌歌歌歌歌 歌歌歌歌歌歌

❶[动] 唱：sing | 高~gāogē *sing heartily* / 能~善舞 nénggē-shànwǔ *good at both singing and dancing*
歌唱 gēchàng sing (usu. in praise)
歌迷 gēmí people who love listening to songs or are engrossed by singing
歌声 gēshēng sound of singing
歌手 gēshǒu singer; vocalist
歌颂 gēsòng sing the praise of; extol; eulogize
歌厅 gētīng karaoke hall
歌舞 gēwǔ song and dance
歌星 gēxīng famous singer; vocalist
歌咏 gēyǒng singing
可歌可泣 kěgē-kěqì
❷[名] 歌曲：song | 请老师教我

们唱中文~儿。Qǐng lǎoshī jiāo wǒmen chàng Zhōngwén-ēr. *Ask the teacher to teach us Chinese songs.* / 这首~曲调很优美。Zhè shǒu gē qǔdiào hěn yōuměi. *The melody of this song is very beautiful.*

歌词 gēcí lyric; word of a song
歌剧 gējù opera
歌曲 gēqǔ song
唱歌 chànggē　　民歌 míngē
诗歌 shīgē

革 gé 9画 革部

革革革革革革革革革

❶ [名] 去毛加工后的兽皮：leather; hide that has been processed | 制~ zhìgé *process hides; tan* 皮革 pígé

❷ [动] 改变；更换：change; reform | 洗心一面 xǐxīn-gémiàn *turn over a new leaf; thoroughly reform oneself*
革新 géxīn innovation
变革 biàngé　　改革 gǎigé

❸ [动] 撤除；去掉：eliminate; get rid of | ~除 géchú *abolish; get rid of* / ~职 gézhí *remove sb. from office; cashier*

◇ 革命 gémìng revolution

阁 (閣) gé 9画 门部

阁阁阁阁阁阁阁阁阁阁

❶ [名] 旧指女子的卧房：(arch.) chamber for an unmarried woman

❷ [名] 一种类似楼房的建筑物 (风景区或庭院里供人休息、远视的建筑物，多为两层)：pavilion; a structure like a storeyed building in a scenic spot or in a yard attached to a private house for people to have a rest, or do some sightseeing

❸ [名] 指内阁，某些国家的最高行政机关：cabinet, the highest administrative organ of some countries

格 gé 10画 木部

格格格格格格格格格格

❶ [名] 隔成的方形空栏或框子：squares formed by crossed lines | 打~子 dǎ gézi *square off the paper* / 这个书架有四层~儿。Zhège shūjià yǒu sì céng gér. *This bookshelf has four levels of shelves.*
表格 biǎogé

❷ [名] 标准；式样：standard; model; style; type
格局 géjú layout
格式 géshì pattern; format
规格 guīgé　　合格 hégé
及格 jígé　　价格 jiàgé

严格 yángé　　　资格 zīgé

❸[名] 品质；风度：character; quality; demeanour; bearing

风格 fēnggé　　　人格 réngé

性格 xìnggé

◇格外 géwài especially; all the more

格格不入 gégé-bùrù incompatible with; out of tune with; out of one's element; like a square peg in a round hole

隔 gé 12画 阝(左)部

隔 隔隔隔隔隔隔隔隔 隔隔隔隔

❶[动]拦断；阻隔：cut off; separate | ～着一堵墙 gézhe yī dǔ qiáng wall off / 这间屋子很大，可以～成两间。Zhè jiān wūzi hěn dà, kěyǐ géchéng liǎng jiān. The room is big enough to be partitioned into two.

隔壁 gébì next door (neighbour)

隔断 géduàn cut off; separate; obstruct

隔阂 géhé communications gap; barrier

隔绝 géjué completely cut off; isolated

隔离 gélí keep apart; isolate; segregate

❷[动]间隔；距离：separate; space; be apart from | 我和他～得很

远。Wǒ hé tā gé de hěn yuǎn. *I was far away from him.* / 我们～两天再去。Wǒmen gé liǎng tiān zài qù. *We'll go again in two days.*

间隔 jiàngé

个（個）gè 3画 人部

个 个个个

❶[量] 用于没有专用量词的事物，也可以用于某些有专用量词的事物：used before a noun without a fixed measure word or to replace certain measure words | 一～地方 yī gè dìfang *a place* / 两～苹果 liǎng gè píngguǒ *two apples* / 三～星期 sān gè xīngqī *three weeks* / 一～故事 yī gè gùshi *a story* / 一～理想 yī gè lǐxiǎng *an ideal*

个个 gègè each and every one; all

各个 gègè

❷[量] 用于约数的前面，显得语气轻快、随便：used before an approximate number to make the tone mild and casual | 每星期来～一两趟 měi xīngqī lái ge yī liǎng tàng *come once or twice a week* / 差～两三岁 chà ge liǎng sān suì *about two or three years too young*/ 这本书我得看～三遍五遍的。Zhè běn shū wǒ děi kàn ge sān biàn wǔ biàn de. *For me, this book is worth reading several times.*

❸ [量] 用于带宾语的动词后，有表示动量的作用，使整个语句显得轻松、随便：used between a verb and its object to make the tone mild and casual | 见～面 jiàn ge miàn *meet a person* / 说～话 shuō ge huà *have a talk* / 洗～澡 xǐ ge zǎo *have a bath*

❹ [动] 用在动词和补语中间，表示程度或持续：used between a verb and its complement to denote the degree or continuity of an action | 笑～不停 xiào ge bù tíng *keep on laughing* / 问～明白 wèn ge míngbai *keep asking until everything is clear* / 明天我们要玩～痛快。Míngtiān wǒmen yào wán ge tòngkuài. *We are sure to have a wonderful time tomorrow.*

❺ [动] 前面加"一"跟少数名词、动词结合，用在谓语动词前，表示快速或突然：used after "一" in combination with certain nouns or verbs to express fastness or abruptness | 一～跟头栽了下来 yī ge gēntou zāile xiàlai *have a sudden fall*

❻ [名] 单独的；单独的事物：individual; things taken singly
个案 ge'àn case; individual case; exceptional case
个别 gèbié ① individual; indi-

vidually; separately ② very few; one or two; exceptional; specific
个人 gèrén ① individual (person) ② oneself; in one's opinion
个体 gètǐ individual
个性 gèxìng individual character; individuality; personality
个体户 gètǐhù petty entrepreneur; self-employed labourer
某个 mǒugè   哪个 nǎge
那个 nàge   这个 zhège
整个 zhěnggè

❼ [名] 人的身材或物体的大小：size (height; stature) of a person or thing | 高～子 gāo gèzi *a tall person* / 馒头～儿不小。Mántou gèr bù xiǎo. *The buns are quite big.*
个儿 gèr ① size; height; stature ② persons or things taken singly
个子 gèzi height; stature; build

各 gè   6画 夂部

各 各各各各各各

❶ [代] 指某个范围内的所有个体：each; different | 世界～国 shìjiè gè guó *all countries of the world* / 他～门功课都不错。Tā gè mén gōngkè dōu bùcuò. *He is doing well in all subjects at school.* / 他们～订一份报纸。Tāmen gè dìng yī fèn *bāozhǐ. Each of them sub-scribes to a newspaper.*

各别 gèbié ① distinct; different ② out of the ordinary; peculiar ③ odd; eccentric; funny

各地 gèdì different places (or areas)

各个 gègè ① each; every; various ② one by one

各界 gèjiè all walks of life; all circles

各位 gèwèi ① everybody (a term of address) ② every

各种 gèzhǒng various kinds (species, categories)

各自 gèzì each; respective

各行各业 gèháng-gèyè the various walks of life; all trades and professions

各式各样 gèshì-gèyàng a variety of

各种各样 gèzhǒng-gèyàng all kinds of

❷ [副] 表示分别做或分别具有：used to indicate that each thing or person does or possesses sth. | ~有特点 gè yǒu tèdiǎn *Each has its own characteristics.* / ~占一半 gè zhàn yībàn *each takes up a half*

各奔前程 gèbēnqiánchéng each pursues his own course; each goes his own way

给 (給) gěi 9画 纟部

给 给给给给给给给给给

❶ [动] 使对方得到或受到：give sth. to sb. | 老师~了我一张话剧票。Lǎoshī gěile wǒ yī zhāng huàjùpiào. *The teacher gave me a drama ticket.* / 请把钢笔~我。Qǐng bǎ gāngbǐ gěi wǒ. *Please hand me the pen.* / ~他一顿批评 gěi tā yī dùn pīpíng *give him a dressing-down*

给以 gěiyǐ give; grant

❷ [介] 被：used in passive sentences | 玻璃杯~我打碎了。Bōlibēi gěi wǒ dǎsuì le. *I have broken the glass.* / 羊~狼吃了。Yáng gěi láng chī le. *The sheep was eaten by the wolf.* / 衣服~雨淋湿了。Yīfu gěi yǔ línshī le. *The clothes have got soaked with rain.*

❸ [介] 表示行为的对象；为：used to denote the object of an action | 他~我们当翻译。Tā gěi wǒmen dāng fānyì. *He is our interpreter.* / 他~她送去一束花。Tā gěi tā sòngqu yī shù huā. *He sent her a bunch of flowers.* / 医生~他看病。Yīshēng gěi tā kànbìng. *The doctor examined him.*

❹ [动] 引进动作的接受者；朝；向：used to introduce the receiver of an action; in the direction of; toward | ~老师行个礼 gěi lǎoshī xíng ge lǐ *salute the teacher* /

261

~他道歉 gěi tā dàoqiàn *make an apology to him* / 他~我使了个眼色。Tā gěi wǒ shǐle ge yǎnsè. *He tipped me the wink.*

❺ [介] 引进交付、传递的接受者：used to introduce the receiver | ~我来封信 gěi wǒ lái fēng xìn *write me a letter* / 家里~他寄来几件衣服。Jiāli gěi tā jìlai jǐ jiàn yīfu. *He received some clothes from his family by mail.* /这本词典留~你用吧。Zhè běn cídiǎn liúgěi nǐ yòng ba. *I leave this dictionary to you.*

交给 jiāogěi

❻ [介] 加强语气，表示说话人的意志，用于命令句，常说 "给我⋯⋯"：used to lay emphasis, expressing the will of the speaker in an imperative tone | 你~我小心点儿! Nǐ gěi wǒ xiǎoxīn diǎnr! *Be cautious, and mind what you do!* / ~我下来! Gěi wǒ xiàlai! *Come down now!*

根 gēn 10画 木部

根根根根根根根根根根

❶ [名] 植物茎干下部长在土里的部分：root, the lower part of the stem that grows beneath the soil | 树~ shùgēn *the roots of a tree* / 这棵小树已经扎~了。Zhè

kē xiǎoshù yǐjīng zhāgēn le. *The young tree has taken root.*

根深蒂固 gēnshēn-dìgù deep-rooted; ingrained; inveterate

斩草除根 zhǎncǎo-chúgēn

❷ [名] 物体的下部或同其他东西连着的部分：the lower part of sth. or the part connected with the other part | 耳~ ěrgēn *the base of an ear* / 牙~ yágēn *the root of a tooth* / 墙~ qiánggēn *the foot of a wall*

命根子 mìnggēnzi

❸ [名] 事物的本源：origin of sth. | 祸~ huògēn *the root of trouble or disaster* / 知~知底 zhīgēn-zhīdǐ *know (sb. or sth.) to the very root or source*

根本 gēnběn ① basic; fundamental; essential; cardinal ② at all; simply ③ radically; thoroughly

根源 gēnyuán source; origin; root

归根到底 guīgēn-dàodǐ

❹ [名] 依据：basis

根据 gēnjù on the basis of; according to; in the light of; in line with

根据地 gēnjùdì base area; base

❺ [副] 从根本上；彻底地：fundamentally; thoroughly; once for all | ~除 gēnchú *completely do away with*

❻ [量] 用于条形物：used for things of long and cylindrical shape |

262

几～铅笔 jǐ gēn qiānbǐ *several pencils* / 两～绳子 liǎng gēn shéngzi *two lengths of rope*

❼ [名] 代数方程式内未知数的解：root of an unknown number in an algebraic equation | 立方～ lìfānggēn *cube root*

跟 gēn 13画 足部

跟跟跟跟跟跟跟跟
跟跟跟跟跟

❶ [名] 脚或鞋、袜的后部：rear part of a foot, shoe, sock | 脚后～ jiǎohòugēn *heel* / 高～儿鞋 gāogēnrxié *high-heeled shoes*

❷ [动] 随；紧接着向同一方向行动：follow; move immediately in the same direction | 你走慢点儿，我～不上。Nǐ zǒumàn diǎnr, wǒ gēnbushàng. *Walk slowly, please. I can't keep up with you.* / 他唱一句，我也～着唱一句。Tā chàng yī jù, wǒ yě gēnzhe chàng yī jù. *He sang a line at a time, and I followed him right away.* / 开完会～着就参观。Kāiwán huì gēnzhe jiù cānguān. *A visit has been arranged right after the meeting.*

跟随 gēnsuí follow
跟踪 gēnzōng follow the tracks of

❸ [介] 引进动作的对象：introduc-

ing the object of an action 同 with | 有事～我们商量。Yǒu shì gēn wǒmen shāngliang. *If there is any problem, please consult with us.* / 我的看法～他差不多。Wǒ de kànfǎ gēn tā chàbuduō. *My opinion is not much different from his.* / 我～你一起去。Wǒ gēn nǐ yīqǐ qù. *I will go with you.* / 这本书是～朋友借的。Zhè běn shū shì gēn péngyou jiè de. *I borrowed this book from my friend.* / 你～大家说说。Nǐ gēn dàjiā shuōshuo. *Tell us about it.*

❹ [介] 引进比较异同的对象：introducing a different object or opposite view | 我的意见～你的相反。Wǒ de yìjiàn gēn nǐ de xiāngfǎn. *My opinion is the opposite of yours.* / 她待我～亲人一样。Tā dài wǒ gēn qīnrén yīyàng. *She treated me as her own family.* / 我～你不同。Wǒ gēn nǐ bùtóng. *I am different from you.*

◇跟前 gēnqián ① in front of; close to; near ② nearby; near at hand
跟头 gēntou ① fall ② somersault

更 gēng 7画 一部

更更更更更更更

[动]改变；改换：replace; change; alter

更改 gēnggǎi change; alter

更换 gēnghuàn change; replace

更名 gēngmíng rename; change one's name

更新 gēngxīn renew; replace

更正 gēngzhèng make corrections

更衣室 gēngyī shì changing room; dressing room

变更 biàngēng

自力更生 zìlì-gēngshēng

See gèng.

耕　gēng　10画 耒部

耕耕耕耕耕耕耕耕
耕耕

[动]用犁翻松土：loosen the soil with a plough │ 精～细作 jīnggēng-xìzuò intensive cultivation

耕地 gēngdì ① till the land (fields) ② cultivated land

耕种 gēngzhòng till; cultivate

春耕 chūngēng

耿　gěng　10画 耳部

耿耿耿耿耿耿耿耿
耿耿

[形]正直：honest and just; upright

耿直 gěngzhí honest and frank; upright

梗　gěng　11画 木部

梗梗梗梗梗梗梗梗
梗梗梗

[名]某些植物的枝或茎：stem or stalk of certain plants │ 菠菜～儿 bōcàigěngr spinach stem / 茶叶～儿 cháyègěngr tea leaf stalks

更　gèng　7画 一部

更更更更更更更

[副]表示程度增高；愈加；越发：indicating a higher degree; more; still more; all the more │ 北风一吹就～冷了。Běifēng yī chuī jiù gèng lěng le. *With the north wind blowing, it is even colder.* / 问题～复杂了。Wèntí gèng fùzá le. *The situation has become even more complicated.*

更加 gèngjiā more; still more; even more

See gēng.

工　gōng　3画 工部

工 工 工

❶[名] 工人和工人阶级：worker; working class │ 车～chē- gōng

turner; lathe operator / 技~ jìgōng *skilled worker* / 女~ nǚgōng *woman worker*

工会 gōnghuì trade union; labour union

工人 gōngrén worker; workman

工人阶级 gōngrén jiējí the working class

矿工 kuànggōng

民工 míngōng

职工 zhígōng

❷[名]工作；生产劳动：work; productive labour | 周末他常出去打~。Zhōumò tā cháng chūqù dǎgōng. *On weekends he often goes out to do temporary jobs.* / 这事很费~。Zhè shì hěn fèigōng. *This is a time-consuming job.*

工厂 gōngchǎng factory; mill; plant

工地 gōngdì building site; construction site

工具 gōngjù tool; means; instrument; implement

工龄 gōnglíng length of service; standing; seniority

工钱 gōngqián ① money paid for odd jobs; charge for a service ② wages; pay

工序 gōngxù working procedure; process

工资 gōngzī wages; pay; salary

工作 gōngzuò work; job

工具书 gōngjùshū reference books

工作日 gōngzuòrì workday; working day

罢工 bàgōng 怠工 dàigōng

动工 dònggōng 分工 fēngōng

加工 jiāgōng 旷工 kuànggōng

人工 réngōng 手工 shǒugōng

完工 wángōng 义工 yìgōng

员工 yuángōng 做工 zuògōng

磨洋工 móyánggōng

小时工 xiǎoshígōng

钟点工 zhōngdiǎngōng

❸[名]一个劳动力干一天的工作量：man-day; work done by one worker in one day | 这项工作需要多少个~?Zhè xiàng gōngzuò xūyào duōshǎo ge gōng? *How many workdays will it take to complete this project?*

❹[名]工程：engineering; project | 竣~ jùngōng *complete a project* / 体育馆下半年动~兴建。Tǐyùguǎn xiàbànnián dònggōng xīngjiàn. *The gymnasium will be under construction in the latter half of the year.*

工程 gōngchéng engineering; project

工程师 gōngchéngshī engineer

❺[名]工业：industry

工业 gōngyè industry

工业化 gōngyèhuà industrialization

化工 huàgōng

轻工业 qīnggōngyè

重工业 zhònggōngyè

◇工夫 gōngfu ① time ② leisure time ③ at that time

工事 gōngshì fortifications; defence works

工艺 gōngyì technology; craft

工艺品 gōngyìpǐn handicraft article; handiwork; handicraft

弓 gōng 3画 弓部

弓 弓 弓 弓

❶[名] 射箭或发弹丸的器械：bow | ～箭 gōngjiàn *bow and arrow* / 一张～yī zhāng gōng *a bow*

❷[名] 弯着：bend | ～着腰 gōng zhe yāo *with one's back bent forward*

公 gōng 4画 八部

公 公 公 公

❶[形] 属于群众、集体的或国家的；公事：belonging to the public, collective or the state; public; official

公差 gōngchāi public errand; go on official business

公费 gōngfèi at public (state) expense

公款 gōngkuǎn public money (or fund)

公立 gōnglì established and maintained by the government; public

公路 gōnglù highway; road

公民 gōngmín citizen

公社 gōngshè ① primitive commune ② commune ③ people's commune

公司 gōngsī firm; company

公诉 gōngsù (leg.) public prosecution

公务 gōngwù public affairs; official business

公债 gōngzhài (government) bonds

公职 gōngzhí public office; public employment

公务员 gōngwùyuán government office worker; civil servant

子公司 zǐgōngsī

高速公路 gāosù gōnglù

❷ [名] 属于群众、集体或国家的事务：public affairs; official business | 因～出差 yīn gōng chūchāi *go on a business trip*

办公 bàngōng

办公室 bàngōngshì

❸ [形] 公正合理：just; fair; impartial; reasonable | 大～无私 dàgōng-wúsī *selfless; unselfish*

公道 gōngdào fair; just; reasonable; impartial

公平 gōngpíng fair; just; impartial; equitable

公正 gōngzhèng just; fair; impartial; fair-minded

❹[形] 共同的；大家承认的：common; public; universally acknowledged｜每逢～休日，他常常和家人逛～园。Měi féng gōngxiūrì, tā chángcháng hé jiārén guàng gōngyuán. *On public holidays, he often takes a stroll with his family in the park.*

公安 gōng'ān public security

公厕 gōngcè toilet (for public); W. C.

公共 gōnggòng public; common; communal

公认 gōngrèn generally ackowledged (recognized); (universally) accepted; established

公式 gōngshì formula

公益 gōngyì public good; public welfare

公用 gōngyòng for public use; public; communal

公有 gōngyǒu publicly-owned; public

公寓 gōngyù ① lodging houses for long-term boarders paying by the month, mainly for working people or students ② apartment buildings; complex housing shared by many families, usually with suites of rooms and well equipped

公园 gōngyuán park

公众 gōngzhòng public

公积金 gōngjījīn accumulation fund (of a socialist economic collective)

公交车 gōngjiāochē bus; public bus having a regular route and fixed stops

公有制 gōngyǒuzhì public ownership (of means of production)

公共场所 gōnggòng chǎngsuǒ public places

公共汽车 gōnggòng qìchē bus

公用电话 gōngyòng diànhuà public telephone

❺ [形] 国际通用的：internationally acknowledged

公尺 gōngchǐ metre (m.)

公分 gōngfēn ① centimetre (cm.) ② gram (g.)

公斤 gōngjīn kilogram (kg.); kilo

公里 gōnglǐ kilometre (km.)

公顷 gōngqǐng hectare (ha.)

公元 gōngyuán the Christian era

公约 gōngyuē ① convention; pact ② joint pledge

平方公里 píngfāng gōnglǐ

❻ [形] 公开的：open; public; known to the public

公报 gōngbào communique; bulletin

公布 gōngbù announce; publish; make public

公告 gōnggào announcement; proclamation

公开 gōngkāi open; make public

公然 gōngrán openly; undisguisedly; brazenly

公证 gōngzhèng acknowledge; notarize

❼ [名] 对上了年纪的男子的尊称：(old) a reverent form of address to a male senior citizen | 张～ Zhāng gōng the revered Mr. Zhang

❽ [名] 丈夫的父亲：father of a woman's husband

公公 gōnggong ① husband's father; father-in-law ② grandpa; grandad

❾ [形] 雄性的：male | ～牛 gōngniú bull / ～鸡 gōngjī cock; rooster

◇公主 gōngzhǔ princess

老公 lǎogōng　外公 wàigōng

主人公 zhǔréngōng

花花公子 huāhuā gōngzǐ

功 gōng 5画 工部

功 功功功功功

❶ [名] 作出的贡献；较大的成绩：contribution made; outstanding achievement | 立～ lìgōng do a deed of merit / 记大一次 jì dàgōng yī cì award sb. a citation for merit of first class

功绩 gōngjì merits and achievements; contribution

功劳 gōngláo contribution; meritorious service; credit

❷ [名] 成效；效果：result; effect | 徒劳无～ túláo-wúgōng make a fruitless effort / 这个地区经济的发展，教育～不可没。Zhège

dìqū jīngjì de fāzhǎn, jiàoyù gōng bù kě mò. It is education that has made great contributions to the economic development of this area.

功率 gōnglǜ power; rate of work in unit time

功能 gōngnéng function

功效 gōngxiào efficacy; effect

成功 chénggōng

多功能 duōgōngnéng

❸ [名] 技术和技术修养：technique and skills | 唱～ chànggōng art of singing; singing / 下苦～ xiàkǔgōng exert painstaking efforts / 基本～ jīběngōng basic training; basic skill

功夫 gōngfu ① skill; attainment ② same as 工夫

功课 gōngkè schoolwork; homework

气功 qìgōng　用功 yònggōng

下功夫 xiàgōngfu

攻 gōng 7画 工部

攻 攻攻攻攻攻攻攻

❶ [动] 主动打击敌人：attack; take the offence | 能～能守 nénggōng-néngshǒu be equally good at attacking and defending

攻关 gōngguān ① storm a strategic pass ② tackle key problems

攻击 gōngjī ① attack; assault;

launch an offensive ② accuse; charge; vilify

攻克 gōngkè capture; take

反攻 fǎngōng　进攻 jìngōng

围攻 wéigōng

❷[动] 致力研究；学习：devote oneself to the study of sth.; specialize in | 专～医学 zhuān gōng yīxué *major in medicine* / 努力三年，他终于～下了英语。Nǔlì sān nián, tā zhōngyú gōngxiàle Yīngyǔ. *He eventually mastered English as the result of three years' hard work.*

攻读 gōngdú study; major in; specialize in

供　gōng　8画 亻部

供供供供供供供供

❶[动] 拿出物资或钱财给需要者应用：supply sth. needed or useful (usu. money or goods) | ～养 gōngyǎng *provide for; support* / 姐姐～他上的大学。Jiějie gōng tā shàng de dàxué. *It was his elder sister who gave him full financial support during his college years.*

供给 gōngjǐ supply; provide; furnish

供销 gōngxiāo supply and marketing

供养 gōngyǎng provide for (one's parents or elders); support

供应 gōngyìng supply

供不应求 gōngbùyìngqiú supply falls short of demand; demand exceeds supply

❷[动] 提供某种东西让使用：offer sth. for use | 仅～参考 jǐn gōng cānkǎo *for your reference only* / 这儿有个小亭子～游客休息。Zhèr yǒu ge xiǎo tíngzi gōng yóukè xiūxi. *Here is a pavilion for tourists to have a rest.* / 这本字典～小学生使用。Zhè běn zìdiǎn gōng xiǎoxuéshēng shǐyòng. *This dictionary is compiled for elementary school pupils.*

提供 tígōng

宫　gōng　9画 宀部

宫宫宫宫宫宫宫宫宫

❶[名] 指古代帝王的住所：residence of an ancient emperor | 皇～ huánggōng *(imperial) palace*

宫殿 gōngdiàn palace

故宫 Gùgōng　王宫 wánggōng

❷[名] 神话中神仙的住所：house or temple in which supernatural beings live | 天～ tiāngōng *the Palace of Heaven*

❸[名] 一些文化娱乐场所的名称：a

place for cultural activities and recreation | 少年～shàonián-gōng *the Children's Palace* / 文化～wénhuàgōng *the Cultural Palace*

◇ 白宫 Báigōng

恭 gōng 10画 忄部

恭 恭恭恭恭恭恭恭恭恭恭

[形]严肃而有礼貌：serious and courteous

恭候 gōnghòu (pol.) await respectfully

恭敬 gōngjìng respectful; reverent

恭喜 gōngxǐ congratulations

躬 gōng 10画 身部

躬 躬躬躬躬躬躬躬躬躬躬

[动]弯下身子：bend one's body | ～身行礼 gōngshēn xínglǐ *bend one's body to bow (or salute)*

巩 (鞏) gǒng 6画 工部

巩 巩巩巩巩巩巩

[形]牢固：firm; secure

巩固 gǒnggù ① consolidate; strengthen; solidify ② consoli-dated

汞 gǒng 7画 工部

汞 汞汞汞汞汞汞汞

[名]mercury | ～是银白色的。Gǒng shì yínbáisè de. *Mercury is silver in colour.*

拱 gǒng 9画 扌部

拱 拱拱拱拱拱拱拱拱拱

❶ [动] 两手在胸前合抱，表示敬意：(Chinese traditional form of etiquette, for males) cup one hand in the other before one's chest to make an obeisance | ～手 gǒngshǒu *make an obeisance by cupping one hand in the other before one's chest*

❷ [形] 弧形的 (建筑物)：arched; curved | ～门 gǒngmén *arched door* / ～桥 gǒngqiáo *arch bridge*

❸ [动] (肢体) 向上耸或向前弯成弧形：arch; hunch up | ～肩膀 gǒng jiānbǎng *hunch up one's shoulders* / 小猫～了～腰，从桌子上跳了下来。Xiǎomāo gǒngle gǒng yāo, cóng zhuōzi shang tiàole xiàlai. *The little cat arched its back and jumped down from the table.*

❹ [动] 向前或向上顶；向里或向外钻：forward; push upward or wriggle one's way outside or inside | 猪用嘴~地。Zhū yòng zuǐ gǒng dì. *Pigs dig up earth with their snouts.* / 麦苗~出土了。Màimiáo gǒngchū tǔ le. *The wheat seedlings sprang up from the soil.*

❺ [动] 环绕：surround; encircle | 众星~月 zhòngxīng-gǒngyuè *a myriad of stars surround the moon; enjoy respect and support from a host of people*

共 **gòng** 6画 八部

共 共共共共共共

❶ [副] 一起；一块儿：together; jointly | 同甘~苦 tónggān-gòngkǔ *share weal and woe; share comforts and hardships* / 宾主~进晚餐。Bīnzhǔ gòngjìn wǎncān. *The hosts and guests had dinner together.*
共有 gòngyǒu in common; pool; communion; intercommunity
共产党 gòngchǎndǎng the Communist Party
共和国 gònghéguó republic
共青团 gòngqīngtuán the Communist Youth League
共产主义 gòngchǎn zhǔyì communism
和平共处 hépíng gòngchǔ

❷ [形] 相同的：similar; identical; the same
共鸣 gòngmíng sympathetic response
共识 gòngshí common understanding; consensus; to concur on
共同 gòngtóng ① common ② together; jointly
共性 gòngxìng commonplace; general character; generality

❸ [形] 共同：common
共享 gòngxiǎng enjoy together; share
公共 gōnggòng
公共场所 gōnggòng chǎngsuǒ

❹ [副] 表示总计：in total | 这本书~有12篇课文。Zhè běn shū gòng yǒu shí'èr piān kèwén. *There are 12 texts in the book altogether.* / 我们班~有20名学生。Wǒmen bān gòng yǒu èrshí míng xuésheng. *There are 20 students in our class.*
共计 gòngjì altogether; in all; all told
一共 yīgòng 总共 zǒnggòng

❺ [名] 共产党的简称：short form for the Communist Party

贡 (貢) **gòng** 7画 工部

贡 贡贡贡贡贡贡贡

[动] 古代臣子或属国向帝王进献物品：articles of tribute presented

to the emperor in ancient times by a vassal state or a subject | 进~jìngòng *pay tribute to (an imperial court)*

贡献 gòngxiàn ① contribute ② contribution

 勾 gōu 4画 勹部

勾 勾勾勾勾

❶ [动] 用笔画出符号，表示重点或删除：draw signs under words to show emphasis or deletion | 把优美的文句~出来 bǎ yōuměi de wénjù gōu chūlai *underline the beautiful sentences* / ~掉这笔账 gōudiào zhè bǐ zhàng *write off the debt* / 一笔~销 yībǐ-gōuxiāo *liquidate; tick off*

❷ [动] 描画：draw; delineate | 他只几笔就把这座建筑的轮廓~出来了。Tā zhǐ jǐ bǐ jiù bǎ zhè zuò jiànzhù de lúnkuò gōu chūlai le. *He drew the outline of the building with only a few strokes.*

❸ [动] 串通：work hand in glove with

勾结 gōujié collude with; collaborate with; gang up with

❹ [动] 招引：induce; evoke; call to mind | 他的话~起了我的回忆。Tā de huà gōuqǐle wǒ de huíyì. *What he said evoked my memories.* / 这一问~起他的话

来了。Zhè yī wèn gōuqǐ tā de huà lai le. *The question touches off his remarks.*

❺ [动] 用灰、水泥等涂抹砖石建筑物的缝儿：fill up the joints of brickwork with mortar or cement | ~墙缝儿 gōu qiángfèngr *point a brick wall*

See gòu.

沟 (溝) gōu 7画 氵部

沟 沟沟沟沟沟沟沟

❶ [名] 水道：water course; water route | 排水~pāishuǐgōu *drainage ditch; drain* / 这条~又陡又深。Zhè tiáo gōu yòu dǒu yòu shēn. *The ditch is deep.*

山沟 shāngōu

❷ [名] 沟状的防御工事：ditch-like defensive work | 地~dìgōu *sewer* / 暗~àngōu *underground passage*

❸ [名] 像沟的浅槽：shallow trough shaped like a ditch | 车~chē-gōu *rut*

◇ 沟通 gōutōng link up; communicate

钩 (鈎) gōu 9画 钅部

钩 钩钩钩钩钩钩钩钩
钩

272

❶ [名] hook│钓鱼~diàoyúgōu *fishhook* / 挂~儿guàgōur *hook* 钩子 gōuzi *hook*

❷ [动]用钩状物搭、挂或探取：secure, explore or probe with a hook│~住gōuzhù *get hooked* / 把床底下那本书~出来。Bǎ chuáng dǐxia nà běn shū gōu chūlai. *Try to fish the book out from under the bed.* / 我把水桶从井里~上来了。Wǒ bǎ shuǐtǒng cóng jǐng li gōu shànglai le. *I have fished the bucket up from the well.*

❸ [动]用带钩的针编织、缝：use a hooked needle to knit, sew│~毛衣 gōu máoyī *crochet a sweater* / 这块桌布全是手工~成的。Zhè kuài zhuōbù quán shì shǒugōng gōuchéng de. *This tablecloth is manually made with a hooked needle.*

苟 gǒu 8画 艹部

苟 苟苟苟苟苟苟苟苟

[形]随便、马虎：careless; casual
一丝不苟 yīsī-bùgǒu

狗 gǒu 8画 犭部

狗 狗狗狗狗狗狗狗狗

[名]dog│他养了一只可爱的小~。

Tā yǎngle yī zhī kě'ài de xiǎo gǒu. *He has a lovely little dog.*
◇热狗 règǒu

勾 gōu 4画 勹部

勾 勾勾勾勾

See 勾当
勾当 gōudàng (derog.) business; deal
See gōu.

构 (構) gōu 8画 木部

构 构构构构构构构构

❶ [动] 把各个组成部分安排、结合起来：construct; form; compose│~图gōutú *composition (of a picture)* / ~词gōucí *form a word*
构成 gōuchéng constitute; form; compose; make up
构建 gōujiàn (mostly in abstracts) build; construct
构造 gōuzào construct
机构 jīgōu　　　结构 jiégōu
❷ [名] 结成(用于抽象事物)：form (sth. abstract)│虚~ xūgòu *fabrication*
构思 gōusī ①(of writers or artists) work out the plot of a literary work or the composition of a painting ② conception
构想 gōuxiǎng conception

购 (購) gōu 8画 贝部

购 购购购购购购购购

[动] 买; buy | 我们研究所最近~进几台很高级的电脑。Wǒmen yánjiūsuǒ zuìjìn gōujìn jǐ tái hěn gāojí de diànnǎo. *Recently our research institute purchased several advanced computers.*

购买 gōumǎi purchase; buy

购物 gōuwù go shopping; shopping for sth.

购置 gōuzhì buy; purchase (oft. durable goods)

购买力 gōumǎilì purchasing power

采购 cǎigōu   订购 dìnggòu

定购 dìnggòu 收购 shōugōu

选购 xuǎngòu

够 gōu 11画 勹部

够 够够够够够够够够 够够够

❶ [动] 足; 满足需要的数量标准、程度等: be enough; be up to standard in quantity and degree | 这些书~你读的。Zhèxiē shū gōu nǐ dú de. *It will take you enough time to read through these books.* / 这些铅笔~你一年用的。Zhèxiē qiānbǐ gōu nǐ yī nián yòng de. *These pencils are enough for you for one*

year. / 她昨晚没睡~。Tā zuówǎn méi shuìgòu. *She didn't have enough sleep last night.*

不够 bùgòu   足够 zúgòu

❷ [副] 修饰形容词, 表示达到某个标准或某种程度: used to modify adjectives, to indicate reaching a certain standard or degree | 他汉语说得~好的了。Tā Hànyǔ shuō de gōu hǎo de le. *His Chinese is good enough.* / 这个孩子~结实的。zhège háizi gōu jiēshi de. *The child is very strong.*

能够 nénggòu

❸ [副] 修饰形容词, 表示程度很高: used to modify an adjective to indicate a very high degree | 天气~冷的。Tiānqì gōu lěng de. *It's rather cold.*

❹ [动] 伸直了胳膊或用长形的工具取东西: reach out one's hand or use a lengthy tool to get sth. | 东西挂得太高了, 我~不着。Dōngxi guà de tài gāo le, wǒ gōubuzháo. *It was hung too high for me to reach.* / 他伸手到架子上~东西。Tā shēnshǒu dào jiàzi shang gōu dōngxi. *He reached out his hand for something on the shelf.*

估 gū 7画 亻部

估估估估估估估

[动] 揣测；大致推算：estimate; appraise ｜～一～价钱 gūyigū jiāqián *evaluate the price of sth.* / 这楼房的造价你～得出来吗？ Zhè lóufáng de zàojià nǐ gū de chūlái ma? *Could you calculate the construction cost of the building?*

估计 gūjì estimate; appraise; reckon

估算 gūsuàn estimate; appraise; reckon

低估 dīgū

 gū   8画 口部

咕 咕咕咕咕咕咕咕咕

[拟声] coo ｜～～叫 gūgu jiào *coo*

 gū   8画 子部

孤 孤孤孤孤孤孤孤孤

❶[形] 幼年丧父或父、母双亡的：fatherless; parentless; orphaned

孤儿 gū'ér orphan

❷[形] 单独：lonely; solitary ｜～雁 gūyàn *a solitary wild goose*

孤单 gūdān alone; lonely; friendless

孤独 gūdú lonely; solitary

孤立 gūlì ① isolated ② isolate

 gū   8画 女部

姑 姑姑姑姑姑姑姑姑

❶[名] 父亲的姐妹：sister of one's father; aunt

姑夫 gūfu husband of father's sister; uncle

姑姑 gūgu father's sister; aunt

❷[副] 暂且：for the time being

姑且 gūqiě tentatively; for the moment

◇姑娘 gūniang ① girl ② daughter

 gū   11画 艹部

菇 菇菇菇菇菇菇菇菇
菇菇菇

[名] 蘑菇：mushroom ｜香～xiānggū *fragrant mushroom*

辜 gū   12画 辛部

辜 辜辜辜辜辜辜辜辜
辜辜辜辜

[动] 负；违背：let down; fail to live up to

辜负 gūfù let down; fail to live up to; be unworthy of; disappoint

古 gǔ 5画 十部

古 古古古古古

❶ [名] 过去已久的年代；很久以前：in the remote past; ancient times; long ago | ～为今用 gǔwéijīnyòng *make the past serve the present*

古今中外 gǔjīn-zhōngwài ancient and modern, Chinese and foreign; at all times and in all countries

自古 zìgǔ

万古长青 wàngǔ-chángqīng

❷ [名] 古代的事物：ancient things; antiquities

考古 kǎogǔ

❸ [形] 时代久远的：age-old; ancient | ～书 gǔshū *ancient books* | ～画 gǔhuà *ancient painting* | ～建筑 gǔjiànzhù *ancient building*

古城 gǔchéng ancient city

古代 gǔdài ancient times; antiquity

古典 gǔdiǎn classical allusion; classical

古迹 gǔjì historic site; place of historic interest

古老 gǔlǎo ancient; age-old

古琴 gǔqín ancient Chinese stringed instrument made of parasol wood with five strings and later seven strings

古人 gǔrén the ancients; forefathers

古文 gǔwén prose written in the classical literary style; ancient Chinese prose

古体诗 gǔtǐshī ancient Chinese poems

名胜古迹 míngshèng-gǔjì

◇古怪 gǔguài odd; eccentric

谷 (穀❷) gǔ 7画 谷部

谷 谷谷谷谷谷谷谷

❶ [名] gully; ravine | 峡～xiágǔ *gorge; canyon*

低谷 dīgǔ   山谷 shāngǔ

❷ [名] 一种粮食作物：a kind of grain

谷子 gǔzi ①millet ②unhusked rice

股 gǔ 8画 月部

股 股股股股股股股股

❶ [量] 用于条形的东西：used for sth. lengthy | 一～泉水 yī gǔ quánshuǐ *a stream of spring water* | 一～线 yī gǔ xiàn *a piece of thread*

❷ [量] 用于气体、气味、气力等：used for things such as gas, smell, strength, etc. | 一～热气 yī gǔ rèqì *a stream of hot air* | 一～香味 yī gǔ xiāngwèi *a whiff of fragrance* | 一～劲儿 yī gǔ jìnr *a burst of energy* | 一～力量 yī gǔ lìliàng *a burst of strength*

❸ [量] 用于成批的人：used to refer to groups of people | 两～敌人 liǎng gǔ dírén *two groups of enemy*

❹ [名] 股票：share; stock | 每个职工都可以入～。Měi gè zhígōng dōu kěyǐ rùgǔ. *All staff members can be shareholders of the company.*

股东 gǔdōng shareholder; stockholder

股份 gǔfèn share; stock

股价 gǔjià prices of stocks

股民 gǔmín shareholder; stockholder

股票 gǔpiào share certificate; share; stock

股市 gǔshì ① stock market ② stock market quotations; current prices of stocks

股份制 gǔfènzhì joint-stock system; organizational form of enterprise property management and profit distribution

炒股 chǎogǔ

骨   gǔ   9画 骨部

骨骨骨骨骨骨骨骨骨

❶ [名] bone | 脊椎～ jǐzhuīgǔ *spine* / 我的脚～扭伤了。Wǒ de jiǎogǔ niǔshāng le. *I had my ankle sprained.*

骨干 gǔgàn backbone; mainstay

骨肉 gǔròu flesh and blood; kindred

骨头 gǔtou bone

骨折 gǔzhé bone fracture; break

甲骨文 jiǎgǔwén

懒骨头 lǎngǔtou

❷ [名] 物体内部支撑的架子：frame used to support the inside of an object | 钢～ gānggǔ *steel framework*

❸ [名] 品质；气概：character; quality; lofty quality

骨气 gǔqì strength of character; moral integrity; backbone

鼓 (皷)   gǔ   13画 鼓部

鼓鼓鼓鼓鼓鼓鼓鼓鼓鼓鼓鼓鼓

❶ [名] drum | 敲锣打～，真热闹! Qiāoluó dǎgǔ, zhēn rènao! *There is a deafening sound of drums and gongs everywhere. How noisy and lively!*

敲锣打鼓 qiāoluó-dǎgǔ

❷ [动] 使某些乐器或东西发声：play or beat (some musical instruments, etc.) | ～琴 gǔqín *(written) play the zither*

鼓掌 gǔzhǎng clap one's hands; applaud

❸ [动] 发动；振奋：rouse; agitate; rise with spirit; stimulate; inspire

277

| ～足干劲 gǔzú gànjìn *pluck up one's enthusiasm* / 老师的话使他又～起了勇气。Lǎoshī de huà shǐ tā yòu gǔqǐ le yǒngqì. *What the teacher said gave him courage.*

鼓吹 gǔchuī ① advocate ② preach; advertise; play up

鼓动 gǔdòng ① agitate; arouse ② egg on; incite; instigate

鼓励 gǔlì encourage; urge

鼓舞 gǔwǔ inspire; hearten

❹ [动] 凸起；涨大：protrude; go up ｜ 他～着嘴半天没出声。Tā gǔzhe zuǐ bàntiān méi chūshēng. *He pouted and kept silent for a long time.*

固　固固固固固固固固

❶ [形] 结实；牢靠：firm; fast ｜ 稳～wěngù *stable; steady*

固定 gùdìng ① fixed; regular ② fix; regularize

巩固 gǒnggù　　　坚固 jiāngù

牢固 láogù

根深蒂固 gēnshēn-dìgù

❷ [形] 坚硬：hard; solid

固体 gùtǐ solid body; solid

凝固 nínggù

❸ [形] 坚定；坚决：firm; staunch; steadfast; firm; resolute; determined

固守 gùshǒu defend tena-

ciously; be firmly entrenched in

固执 gùzhí ① obstinate; stubborn ② persist in; cling to

顽固 wángù

❹ [副] 原来；本来：originally; at first ｜ ～当如此 gù dāng rúcǐ *it is just as it should be*

固然 gùrán no doubt; it is true; of course; admittedly

固有 gùyǒu intrinsic; inherent; innate

gù　　9画 攵部

故　故故故故故故故故故

❶ [名] 原因：cause ｜ 不知何～ bùzhī hégù *out of unknown reason* / 开会时，他常常无～缺席。Kāihuì shí, tā chángcháng wúgù quēxí. *He is always absent from meetings without any reason.*

缘故 yuángù

❷ [名] 意外的或不幸的事情：accident; sth. unfortunate

故障 gùzhàng hitch; breakdown; stoppage; trouble; malfunction

事故 shìgù

❸ [副] 故意；有意地：on purpose; intentionally; deliberately ｜ 明知～犯 míngzhī-gùfàn *knowingly violate; deliberately break (a rule, etc.)* / ～作镇静 gùzuò-zhènjìng *pretend to be calm*

故意 gùyì intentionally; wilfully

❹ [形] 原来的；过去的；旧有的：original; former; past; old | ～人 gùrén *old friends* / ～居 gùjū *former residence*

故宫 Gùgōng palace of a former dynasty, esp. refers to the Imperial Palace of the Qing Dynasty in Beijing

故乡 gùxiāng native place; hometown; birthplace

❺ [连] 所以；因此：so; therefore | 因有急事，～不能前往。Yīn yǒu jíshì, gù bùnéng qiánwǎng. *I can't go there because of an urgent matter.* / 他有坚强的意志，～能克服困难。Tā yǒu jiānqiáng de yìzhì, gù néng kèfú kùnnan. *It's his strong will that enabled him to overcome the difficulty.*

◇故事 gùshi ① story; tale ② plot

世故 shìgù

顾（顧）gù   10画 页部

顾 顾顾顾顾顾顾顾顾顾顾

❶ [动] 回头看；看：turn round and look; look back | 环～huángù *look around*

回顾 huígù

❷ [动] 照看；注意：look after; notice | 他只～别人，不～自己。

Tā zhǐ gù biérén, bùgù zìjǐ. *He always cares for others, without thinking about himself.*

顾虑 gùlǜ misgiving; apprehension; worry

顾问 gùwèn adviser; consultant

顾不得 gùbudé can't take into account; can't give consideration to; have no time to attend to

顾全大局 gùquán-dàjú take the interests of the whole into account

不顾 bùgù   照顾 zhàogù

只顾 zhǐgù

不顾一切 bùgù-yīqiè

◇顾客 gùkè customer; shopper; client

gù   12画 户部

雇 雇雇雇雇雇雇雇雇 雇雇雇雇

❶ [动] 出钱叫人做事：hire; employ | ～保姆 gù bǎomǔ *hire a housemaid* / 他的公司～了四个职员。Tā de gōngsī gùle sì gè zhíyuán. *His company employs 4 clerks.*

雇佣 gùyōng employ; hire

雇员 gùyuán employee

雇主 gùzhǔ employer; person who employs

❷ [动] 租赁交通工具：hire a vehicle | 我想～一辆出租车。

279

Wǒ xiǎng gù yī liàng chūzūchē. *I need to hire a car.*

 瓜 guā 5画 瓜部

瓜 瓜瓜瓜瓜瓜

[名] 果实可吃的葫芦科植物：general
term for water melon, pumpkin,
white gourd, cucumber, etc. |
种~ zhòng guā *plant melons* /
摘~ zhāi guā *pick melons*
瓜分 guāfēn carve up; divide
up; partition
瓜子 guāzǐ melon seeds
冬瓜 dōngguā　黄瓜 huángguā
苦瓜 kǔguā　木瓜 mùguā
南瓜 nánguā　甜瓜 tiánguā
西瓜 xīguā
哈密瓜 hāmìguā

刮 (颳❷) guā 8画 舌部

刮 刮刮刮刮刮刮刮刮

❶ [动] 用刀等在物体的表面移动，除
去物体表面的东西：s c r a p e;
shave | ~铁锈 guā tiěxiù
scrape off rust / ~胡子 guā húzi
shave the beard
❷ [动] (风) 吹：blow | 大风把树叶
全都~下来了。Dàfēng bǎ
shùyè quán dōu guā xiàlai le.
*The strong wind blew all the
leaves off the tree.*

 寡 guǎ 14画 宀部

寡 寡寡寡寡寡寡寡寡
寡寡寡寡寡寡

[形] 死了丈夫的：widowed | 守了
几年~ shǒule jǐ nián guǎ *live in
widowhood for several years*
寡妇 guǎfu widow

挂 guà 9画 扌部

挂 挂挂挂挂挂挂挂挂
挂

❶ [动] 用钩子、钉子等使物体悬在
某个地方：hang; put up (with a
hook, nail, etc.) | ~衣服 guà
yīfu *hang up clothes* / 请你帮我
把地图~起来。Qǐng nǐ bāng
wǒ bǎ dìtú guà qǐlai. *Please
help me put up the map.*
悬挂 xuánguà
❷ [动] 惦记：remember; keep in
mind | 你让他办的事，他会~在
心上的。Nǐ ràng tā bàn de
shì, tā huì guà zài xīnshang
de. *It's certain he will remember what you ask him to do.*
挂念 guàniàn worry about sb.
who is absent; miss
❸ [动] 连接上或切断电话；钩上：
connect or disconnect the phone;
hook | 把电话~上。Bǎ diàn-
huà guàshang. *Hang up.* / 请

你～外事处。Qǐng nǐ guà wàishìchù. *Please put me through to the Foreign Affairs Section.* / 钉子把衣服～住了。Dīngzi bǎ yīfu guàzhù le. *The garment got caught on a nail.*

挂钩 guàgōu ① couple (two railway coaches); articulate ② link up with; establish contact with; get in touch with

❹ [动] 登记：record; register; check in | ～失 guàshī *report the loss of sth.*

挂号 guàhào ① register (at a hospital etc.) ② send by registered mail

乖 guāi 8画 丿部

乖 乖 乖 乖 乖 乖 乖 乖

❶ [形] (小孩儿) 听话；不淘气：(of children) obedient; not naughty | ～孩子 guāi háizi *good boy (or girl)* / 小宝宝很～。Xiǎobǎobǎo hěn guāi. *The little one is well-behaved.*

❷ [形] 机灵：clever; smart; intelligent | 这孩子嘴～。Zhè háizi zuǐ guāi. *The child is cute with words.* / 上了一次当，他也学～了。Shàngle yī cì dàng, tā yě xuéguāi le. *He became cleverer after being taken in once.*

拐 guǎi 8画 扌部

拐 拐 拐 拐 拐 拐 拐 拐

❶ [名] 走路时帮助支持身体的棍子：walking stick; crutch | ～棍儿 guǎigùnr *walking stick* / 一位老人在拄着～走路。Yī wèi lǎorén zài zhǔzhe guǎi zǒulù. *An old man was walking with a cane.*

❷ [形] 走路不稳；瘸：walk unsteadily; limp | 他一瘸一～地走到学校去。Tā yī qué yī guǎi de zǒudào xuéxiào qù. *He limped toward the school.* / 他的腿～得很厉害。Tā de tuǐ guǎi de hěn lìhai. *His leg is very lame.*

❸ [动] 转弯；改变方向：turn round; change direction | 向右～xiàng yòu guǎi *turn to the right* / 那人～进胡同里去了。Nà rén guǎijìn hútong li qù le. *That man turned into a lane.*

拐弯儿 guǎiwānr ① turn a corner; turn ② turn round; pursue a new course

❹ [动] 用诱骗手段弄走：kidnap; abduct | 骗子～了他的钱就逃走了。Piànzi guǎile tā de qián jiù táozǒu le. *The swindler made off with all his money.* / 那孩子被人～走了。Nà háizi bèi rén guǎizǒu le. *That child was abducted.*

怪 guài 8画 忄部

怪 怪怪怪怪怪怪怪怪

❶ [形] 奇异的；不平常的：strange; unusual | ~现象 guài xiànxiāng *something quite unusual* / ~样子 guài yàngzi *odd-looking* / 这件事真是有点儿~。Zhè jiàn shì zhēn shì yǒudiǎnr guài. *It is really a bit odd.*

古怪 gǔguài   奇怪 qíguài

❷ [名] 传说中的妖魔：monster in legend

妖怪 yāoguài

丑八怪 chǒubāguài

❸ [副] 很；非常：very; quite; rather | ~不好意思的 guài bù-hǎoyìsi de *feel rather embarrassed* / 这只小猫~可爱的!Zhè zhī xiǎo māo guài kě'ài de! *How cute the little cat is!*

❹ [动] 责备；埋怨：blame; reproach | 自己做错了事，不能~别人。Zìjǐ zuòcuò le shì, bùnéng guài biérén. *Don't blame others for what you have done wrong.* / 这事不能~他。Zhè shì bùnéng guài tā. *He's not to blame for this.*

怪不得 guàibude ① no wonder; so that's why; that explains why ② not to blame

难怪 nánguài   责怪 zéguài

关（關） guān 6画 丷部

关 关关关关关关

❶ [动] 闭；使开着的物体合上：close; shut | ~窗子 guān chuāngzi *close (shut) the window* / ~上箱子 guānshang xiāngzi *close the case* / 他把我~在门外边了。Tā bǎ wǒ guān zài mén wàibian le. *He shut me out.*

关闭 guānbì ① close; shut ② (of a shop or factory) close down; shut down

开关 kāiguān

❷ [动] 放在里面不使出来：confine; lock up | 笼子里~着一只鸟。Lóngzi li guānzhe yī zhī niǎo. *A bird was confined in the cage.* / 他把宠物~在家里了。Tā bǎ chǒngwù guān zài jiāli le. *He left the pet shut up at home.*

关押 guānyā lock up; imprison; put under detention

❸ [动] 使开动的机器、电气设备等停止工作：switch off (machines, electric appliances, etc.) | ~机 guānjī *stop (turn off) the machine*

❹ [动] 停止营业：suspend business; close down | 商店~了。Shāngdiàn guān le. *The shop has closed down.* / 他们决定把那个分公司~了。Tāmen jué-dìng bǎ nàge fēngōngsī guān le. *They have decided to close down the branch company.*

❺ [名] 古代在险要的地方或交通要道设置的防守处所：mountain pass or guarded passage at the strategic place or on the border | 边~biānguān *border checkpoint* / ~口 guānkǒu *strategic pass*

❻ [名] 货物进出口征税的地方：government organization established to collect taxes when goods leave or enter a country
关税 guānshuì customs duty; customs; tariff
海关 hǎiguān

❼ [名] 重要的转折点或不易度过的一段时间：time that has a transformational function; a critical juncture | 他有信心过好这一~。Tā yǒu xìnxīn guòhǎo zhè yī guān. *He is confident of being able to get through this critical moment.*
关头 guāntóu juncture; moment
把关 bǎguān 攻关 gōngguān
难关 nánguān
鬼门关 guǐménguān

❽ [名] 起转折关联作用的部分：joint; a key link
关键 guānjiàn hinge; key; crux
关联 guānlián interrelation among different things; be related; be connected
关节炎 guānjiéyán arthritis

机关 jīguān 卖关子 màiguānzi

❾ [动] 牵连；关系：involve; concern | 这不~他的事。Zhè bù guān tā de shì. *It doesn't concern him.* / 事~成败，你一定要小心。Shì guān chéngbài, nǐ yīdìng yào xiǎoxīn. *Success or failure hinges on it. Do handle the matter with caution.* / 你的意见已经反映到有~部门了。Nǐ de yìjiàn yǐjīng fǎnyìng dào yǒuguān bùmén le. *Your suggestion has been transferred to the department concerned.*

关爱 guān'ài express solicitude for the well-being of
关怀 guānhuái show loving care for; show solicitude for
关切 guānqiè be deeply concerned; show one's concern over
关系 guānxi ① relation; relationship ② bearing; impact; significance
关心 guānxīn be concerned with; show solicitude for; be interested in; care for
关于 guānyú about; on; with regard to; concerning
关照 guānzhào ① look after; keep an eye on ② notify by word of mouth
关注 guānzhù follow with interest; pay close attention to; show solicitude for
公关 gōngguān 无关 wúguān
相关 xiāngguān 有关 yǒuguān

没关系 méiguānxi

观 (觀) guān 6画 又部

观 观观观观观观

❶ [动] 看：look | 走马~花 zǒumǎ-guānhuā *look at flowers while riding a horse; gain a shallow understanding from a fleeting glance*

观测 guāncè observe

观察 guānchá observe; watch; survey

观光 guānguāng go sightseeing; visit; tour

观看 guānkàn watch; view

观赏 guānshǎng view and admire; enjoy the sight of

观望 guānwàng ① wait and see ② look around

观众 guānzhòng spectator; viewer; audience

参观 cānguān

坐井观天 zuòjǐng-guāntiān

❷ [名] 景象；样子：scene; appearance

宏观 hóngguān 景观 jǐngguān

美观 měiguān 奇观 qíguān

外观 wàiguān

微观 wēiguān

壮观 zhuàngguān

❸ [名] 对事物的认识或态度：view; concept; attitude

观点 guāndiǎn point of view; viewpoint; standpoint

观念 guānniàn sense; idea; concept

悲观 bēiguān 客观 kèguān

乐观 lèguān 主观 zhǔguān

价值观 jiàzhíguān

世界观 shìjièguān

官 guān 8画 宀部

官 官官官官官官官官

❶ [名] 属于国家或政府的：pertaining to state or government; official

官方 guānfāng of or by the government; official

官司 guānsi (oral) lawsuit

打官腔 dǎguānqiāng

打官司 dǎguānsi

❷ [名] 在国家机构中，担任一定公职的人员：one who serves as a public officer | 听说他最近升~了。Tīngshuō tā zuìjìn shēngguān le. *It was said that he has been promoted recently.* / 他是一位外交~。Tā shì yī wèi wàijiāoguān. *He is a diplomat.*

官僚 guānliáo bureaucrat

官员 guānyuán official

官僚主义 guānliáo zhǔyì bureaucracy

法官 fǎguān 警官 jǐngguān

军官 jūnguān 贪官 tānguān

检察官 jiǎncháguān

外交官 wàijiāoguān

❸ [名] 生物体上有特定功能的部分：

organ; part of the human body with a specific function | 五～ wǔguān *five sense organs*

棺 guān 12画 木部

棺 棺棺棺棺棺棺棺棺 棺棺棺棺

See 棺材
棺材 guāncai coffin

馆 (館) guǎn 11画 饣部

馆 馆馆馆馆馆馆馆馆 馆馆馆

❶[名]招待宾客或旅客居住的房屋: place where accommodation is provided for guests
宾馆 bīnguǎn   旅馆 lǚguǎn

❷[名]一个国家在另一个国家办理外交事务的人员办公的处所: residence in a country where diplomats from another country deal with diplomatic affairs | 领事～lǐngshìguǎn *consulate*
使馆 shǐguǎn
大使馆 dàshǐguǎn

❸[名]某些服务性店铺的名称: shop; store | 照相～zhàoxiàngguǎn *photo studio* / 理发～lǐfàguǎn *barbershop; hairdresser's*
餐馆 cānguǎn 茶馆 cháguǎn
场馆 chǎngguǎn
饭馆 fànguǎn

❹[名]某些陈列文物或进行文化体育活动的场所: place of cultural activities
博物馆 bówùguǎn
纪念馆 jìniànguǎn
体育馆 tǐyùguǎn
图书馆 túshūguǎn

管 guǎn 14画 竹部

管 管管管管管管管管 管管管管管管

❶[名]细长中空的圆筒: pipe; tube | 钢～gāngguǎn *steel tube* / 水～shuǐguǎn *waterpipe*
管道 guǎndào pipeline; piping; conduit; tubing
管子 guǎnzi tube; pipe
血管 xuèguǎn
气管炎 qìguǎnyán

❷[动]管理；负责: manage; be in charge of | ～家务 guǎn jiāwù *run the house; keep house* / ～吃～住 guǎnchī guǎnzhù *provide meal and accommodation (by host)* / 这些工作都由他来～。Zhèxiē gōngzuò dōu yóu tā lái guǎn. *He is in charge of all these works.*
管理 guǎnlǐ manage; run; administer; supervise
管辖 guǎnxiá administer
管制 guǎnzhì ① control ② put (a criminal, etc.) under surveillance

保管 bǎoguǎn 　 接管 jiēguǎn
托管 tuōguǎn
掌管 zhǎngguǎn 　 主管 zhǔguǎn

❸ [动] 约束；照料：practise rigid discipline; take care of | ～孩子 guǎn háizi *discipline the child* / 这件事你们得好好儿～～。Zhè jiàn shì nǐmen děi hǎohāor guǎnguǎn. *You should take good care of this matter.*

❹ [动] 过问；参与：attend to; involve; look after; interfere | ～闲事 guǎn xiánshì *poke one's nose into other people's business* / 不该你～的事，你不要～。Bù gāi nǐ guǎn de shì, nǐ bùyào guǎn. *Don't involve yourself in things that don't concern you.* / 这事我们不能不～。Zhè shì wǒmen bùnéng bù guǎn. *We cannot leave this matter alone.*

不管 bùguǎn 　 尽管 jǐnguǎn
只管 zhǐguǎn

贯（貫） guàn 8画 贝部

贯 贯贯贯贯贯贯贯贯

❶ [动] 穿透；连通：penetrate; connect; pass through | 铁路～通 tiělù guàntōng *the railway line has been linked up*
贯彻 guànchè carry out (through); implement; put into effect

❷ [名] 世代居住的地方；出生地：place where people live generation after generation; birthplace
籍贯 jíguàn

冠 guàn 9画 冖部

冠 冠冠冠冠冠冠冠冠 冠

[动] 超出众人，居第一位：surpass all others and rank first | 名～世界 míng guàn shìjiē *be known as the best in the world*
冠军 guànjūn champion

惯（慣） guàn 11画 忄部

惯 惯惯惯惯惯惯惯惯 惯惯惯

❶ [形] 习以为常的：be used to; be in the habit of | 她任性～了。Tā rènxìng guàn le. *She has been used to having her own way.* / 他已经～了，每天都睡得很晚。Tā yǐjīng guàn le, měi tiān dōu shuì de hěn wǎn. *He is used to staying up late.* / 他过～了这种平静的生活。Tā guòguànle zhè zhǒng píngjìng de shēnghuó. *He has been accustomed to this tranquil life.*

惯例 guànlì convention; usual practice

惯用语 guànyòngyǔ word and phrase commonly and habitually used

习惯 xíguàn

❷ [动] 纵容；过分宠爱：spoil; indulge | 不要把孩子~坏了。Bùyào bǎ háizi guànhuài le. *Don't spoil the child.* / 她爱孩子，但从来不~着他们。Tā ài háizi, dàn cónglái bù guànzhe tāmen. *Though she is attached to her children, she never spoils them.*

娇惯 jiāoguàn

娇生惯养 jiāoshēng-guànyǎng

灌 guàn 20画 氵部

灌灌灌灌灌灌灌灌
灌灌灌灌灌灌灌
灌灌灌灌

❶[动] 浇水：irrigate; sprinkle water | 引水~田 yǐnshuǐ guàntián *channel water into the fields*

灌溉 guàngài irrigate

浇灌 jiāoguàn

❷[动] 倒进去或装进去：pour; fill | ~一瓶水 guàn yī píng shuǐ *fill a bottle with water* / 那响亮的声音直往他耳朵里~。Nà xiǎngliàng de shēngyīn zhí wǎng tā ěrduo li guàn. *His ears were filling with the loud and clear sound.* / 这个歌曲已经~了唱片了。Zhège gēqǔ

yǐjīng guànle chàngpiàn le. *The song has been made into a record.*

◇灌木 guànmù bush; shrub

罐 guàn 23画 缶部

罐罐罐罐罐罐罐罐
罐罐罐罐罐罐罐
罐罐罐罐罐罐罐

[名]盛东西用的大口的圆筒形器具：container with a big mouth | 铁~儿 tiěguànr *an iron jar* / 把茶叶装进~里。Bǎ cháyè zhuāngjìn guàn li. *Put the tea into the tin.*

罐头 guàntou tin; can

光 guāng 6画 小部

光光光光光光光

❶ [名] light | 没有~，屋里一片漆黑。Méiyǒu guāng, wū li yī piàn qīhēi. *Without any light, it is pitch dark in the house.*

光标 guāngbiāo (computer) cursor

光碟 guāngdié compact disc; CD

光辉 guānghuī ① radiance; brilliance; glory ② brilliant; magnificent; glorious

光芒 guāngmáng rays of light; brilliant rays; radiance

光盘 guāngpán compact disc; CD

光线 guāngxiàn light; ray

灯光 dēngguāng

激光 jīguāng

亮光 liàngguāng

日光 rìguāng

眼光 yǎnguāng

阳光 yángguāng

月光 yuèguāng

❷ [形] 明亮: bright | 地板擦得～～的。Dìbǎn cā de guāngguāng de. *The shining floor is well polished.*

光亮 guāngliàng ① bright; shiny; luminous ② light

光明 guāngmíng ① light ② bright; promising

❸ [名] 光荣; 荣誉: honour; glory; credit | 为国增～ wèi guó zēngguāng *bring honour to one's country* / 她特别得意, 感到脸上有～。Tā tèbié déyì, gǎndào liǎnshang yǒu guāng. *Her face is radiant with complacence.*

光彩 guāngcǎi ① lustre; splendour ② honourable; glorious

光荣 guāngróng honour; glory; credit

赏光 shǎngguāng

发扬光大 fāyáng-guāngdà

❹ [名] 时间; 日子: time; days

光阴 guāngyīn time

时光 shíguāng

❺ [名] 景色; 景物: scene; scen-ery; view; landscape

风光 fēngguāng

观光 guānguāng

❻ [形] 物体表面平滑: smooth; glossy; polished | 地板很～。Dìbǎn hěn guāng. *The floor is very smooth.*

光滑 guānghuá smooth; glossy; sleek

❼ [形] 净; 尽; 一点儿不剩: clean; complete; without anything left | 喝～了 hēguāng le *drink up* / 他把整块蛋糕都吃～了。Tā bǎ zhěng kuài dàngāo dōu chī le. *He has eaten up the whole cake.* / 纸都用～了。Zhǐ dōu yòngguāng le. *The paper has been used up.*

❽ [动] 露着(身体): bare | ～着膀子 guāngzhe bǎngzi *be stripped to the waist* / ～着头 guāngzhe tóu *be bare-headed* / ～着脚 guāngzhe jiǎo *be bare-footed*

❾ [副] 只; 单: only; merely; just; alone | 今天我们～谈学习。Jīntiān wǒmen guāng tán xuéxí. *Today we'll confine our discussion to study only.* / 不要～凭热情干事。Bùyào guāng píng rèqíng gànshì. *Doing things cannot rely on enthusiasm alone.* / 不～他一个人, 还有别人去。Bùguāng tā yī gè rén, hái yǒu biérén qù. *He is not alone, there are others going too.*

不光 bùguāng

◇光棍儿 guānggùnr unmarried man; bachelor

光临 guānglín presence (of a guest etc.)

穷光蛋 qióngguāngdàn

 广 (廣) guǎng 3画 广部

广 广 广 广

❶ [形] (面积、范围)宽阔：(of area, scope) wide | 他的知识面很~。Tā de zhīshimiàn hěn guǎng. *He has a wide range of knowledge.*/这个动人的故事流传很~。Zhège dòngrén de gùshi liúchuán hěn guǎng. *This moving story is widely spread.*

广场 guǎngchǎng public square; square

广大 guǎngdà ① vast; wide; extensive ② large-scale; widespread

广阔 guǎngkuò vast; wide; broad

宽广 kuānguǎng

❷ [动] 扩大：spread; extend | 好人好事应该~为宣传。Hǎo rén hǎo shì yīnggāi guǎng wéi xuānchuán. *Good people and their good deeds should be propagated extensively.*

广播 guǎngbō broadcast; be on the air

广告 guǎnggào advertisement

推广 tuīguǎng

❸ [形] 多：numerous; a lot of | 此人阅历很~。Cǐ rén yuèlì hěn guǎng. *He has plenty of experience.*

广泛 guǎngfàn extensive; wide-ranging; widespread

 逛 guàng 10画 辶部

逛 逛 逛 逛 逛 逛 逛 逛 逛 逛

[动]闲游；游览：go out for an airing; stroll; wander | ~公园 guàng gōngyuán *stroll in the park; have a stroll in the park* / ~商店 guàng shāngdiàn *go shopping*

 归 (歸) guī 5画 彐部

归 归 归 归 归 归

❶[动] 返回：go back; return | 早出晚~ zǎochū-wǎnguī *leave home early and return late* / 他整天不~家。Tā zhěngtiān bù guī jiā. *He's not at home all day long.*

归来 guīlái be back to one's original place; return; come back

回归 huíguī

改邪归正 gǎixié-guīzhèng

❷[动] 还给：return | 物~原主 wù guī yuánzhǔ *return sth. to its*

rightful owner

归还 guīhuán return; revert

❸[动] 集中到一起；把性质相同的
问题归为一类：gather; assemble; call together; concentrate |
把两支队伍～在一起。Bǎ liǎng
zhī duìwu guī zài yīqǐ. *Join
the two armies together.* / 千条
河流～大海。Qiān tiáo héliú
guī dàhǎi. *A thousand rivers
find their ways to the sea.*

归结 guījié ① sum up; put in a
nutshell ② end (of a story etc.)

归纳 guīnà induce; conclude;
sum up

归根到底 guīgēn-dàodǐ in the
final analysis

❹[动] 归；属于 (谁所有)：go to;
belong to | 这个荣誉不～我个
人，是大家的。Zhège róngyù
bù guī wǒ gèrén, shì dàjiā
de. *The honour does not belong
to myself, but to all of us.* / 这些
东西应该～他。Zhèxiē dōngxi
yīnggāi guī tā. *These things
should belong to him.*

归属 guīshǔ belong to; come
under the jurisdiction of; be affiliated to

❺[动] 由 (谁负责)：be in charge of
| 这些工具～我管。Zhèxiē
gōngjù guī wǒ guǎn. *I'm in
charge of these tools.* / 这件事～
我处理。Zhè jiàn shì guī wǒ
chǔlǐ. *I'm in charge of this matter.*

龟 (龜) guī   7画 龟部

龟 龟龟龟龟龟龟龟

[名] tortoise | 海～hǎiguī marine
(sea) turtle
乌龟 wūguī

规 (規) guī   8画 见部

规 规规规规规规规规

❶ [名] 法则；惯例：law; rule;
convention; usual practice |
校～xiàoguī *school regulations*
/ 法～fǎguī *laws and regulations*

规范 guīfàn standard; norm

规格 guīgé specifications; stan-
dards; norms

规矩 guīju ① established practice; custom ② well-behaved;
law-abiding

规律 guīlǜ law; regular pattern

规模 guīmó scale; scope; di-
mensions

规则 guīzé ① rule; regulation
② regular

规章 guīzhāng rules; regulations

常规 chángguī 犯规 fànguī
正规 zhèngguī

❷ [动] 打算；谋划：intend; plot

规定 guīdìng ① stipulate; provide ② stipulation; prescript

规划 guīhuà programme; plan

闺 (閨) guī 　9画 门部

闺 闺闺闺闺闺闺闺闺
　　闺

[名] 旧指未婚女子的卧室：(in former times) unmarried lady's chamber
闺女 guīnü daughter

瑰 guī 　13画 王部

瑰 瑰瑰瑰瑰瑰瑰瑰瑰
　　瑰瑰瑰瑰瑰

See 玫瑰
玫瑰 méigui

轨 (軌) guǐ 　6画 车部

轨 轨轨轨轨轨轨

[名] 本指车子两轮之间的距离，后指车轮碾过的痕迹：originally used to refer to the distance between two wheels, later also used to indicate the deep narrow track left in soft ground by a wheel | 钢～ gāngguǐ rail
轨道 guǐdào ① track ② orbit; trajectory
轨迹 guǐjì ① locus ② orbit ③ (fig.) track; path along which a person goes through his or her life, or along with which sth. develops

诡 (詭) guǐ 　8画 讠部

诡 诡诡诡诡诡诡诡诡

[形] 狡诈；奸滑：deceitful; cunning; slick; sleek
诡计 guǐjì crafty plot; cunning scheme; trick; ruse

鬼 guǐ 　9画 鬼部

鬼 鬼鬼鬼鬼鬼鬼鬼鬼
　　鬼

❶ [名] 迷信的人指人死后的灵魂：ghost | ～神 guǐshén *ghosts and spirits; supernatural beings* / 我从小爱听～故事。Wǒ cóngxiǎo ài tīng guǐ gùshi. *I have enjoyed listening to ghost stories since I was a child.*
鬼门关 guǐménguān (superstition) gates of hell; jaws of death; (fig.) dangerous place
魔鬼 móguǐ
做鬼脸 zuòguǐliǎn
❷ [名] 对人表示轻蔑、憎恨的称呼：address of contempt or dislike for sb. | 胆小～dǎnxiǎoguǐ *coward* / 酒～jiǔguǐ *drunkard*
鬼子 guǐzi devil (term of abuse for foreign invaders)
冒失鬼 màoshiguǐ
小气鬼 xiǎoqìguǐ

❸ [名] 不可告人的勾当、打算：sinister design; dark scheme ｜ 他不回答你的问题，准是心里有～。Tā bù huídá nǐ de wèntí, zhǔn shì xīnli yǒu guǐ. *He didn't answer your question—he's definitely up to something.*

搞鬼 gǎoguǐ

❹ [形] 恶劣；糟糕：nasty; terrible; lousy ｜ ～天气 guǐ tiānqì *terrible weather*

❺ [形] 机灵；smart; clever ｜ 这孩子真～。Zhè háizi zhēn guǐ. *This kid is really smart.*

◇ 机灵鬼 jīlingguǐ

柜 (櫃) guì 8画 木部

柜 柜柜柜柜柜柜柜柜

[名] cupboard ｜ 橱～ chúguì *kitchen cabinet* / 衣～ yīguì *wardrobe*

柜台 guìtái counter; bar

柜子 guìzi cupboard; cabinet

保险柜 bǎoxiǎnguì

贵 (貴) guì 9画 贝部

贵 贵贵贵贵贵贵贵贵贵

❶ [形] 价钱或价值高：expensive; dear ｜ 这地方东西很～。Zhè dìfang dōngxi hěn guì. *The things here are very expensive.* /

这本书不～。Zhè běn shū bù guì. *This book is not expensive.* / 钢比铁～。Gāng bǐ tiě guì. *Steel is more expensive than iron.*

贵重 guìzhòng valuable; precious

昂贵 ángguì

❷ [形] 地位高：high in status ｜ ～妇人 guìfūrén *noble woman*

贵宾 guìbīn honoured guest; distinguished guest

贵族 guìzú noble; aristocrat

高贵 gāoguì

❸ [形] 值得珍视或重视：highly valued; valuable ｜ 物以稀为～ wù yǐ xī wéi guì *when a thing is scarce, it is precious*

宝贵 bǎoguì   可贵 kěguì

名贵 míngguì   珍贵 zhēnguì

❹ [形] 敬词，称与对方有关的事物：term of respect, used to address things related to the other party ｜ ～国 guìguó *your country* / ～校 guìxiào *your school*

贵姓 guìxìng your surname

桂 guì 10画 木部

桂 桂桂桂桂桂桂桂桂桂桂

[名] 桂花树，常绿乔木，花白色或黄色，极香：cassia-bark tree, evergreen, sweet scented, with yellow or white flowers ｜ ～花 guìhuā

sweet-scented osmanthus

◇桂冠 guìguān laurel (as an emblem of victory or distinction)

 跪 guì 13画 足部

跪 跪跪跪跪跪跪跪跪 跪跪跪跪跪

[动]两膝弯曲，使一个或两个膝盖着地：kneel | 下～xiàguì *kneel upon one's knees; kneel down (before sb.)*

 滚 gǔn 13画 氵部

滚 滚滚滚滚滚滚滚滚 滚滚滚滚滚

❶[动] 旋转着移动；使翻转：roll; trundle | ～铁环 gǔn tiěhuán *trundle an iron hoop* / 荷叶上～着水珠。Héyè shang gǔnzhe shuǐzhū. *Water beads rolled on the lotus leaves.* / 石头从山顶上～下来。Shítou cóng shāndǐng shang gǔn xiàlai. *Rocks rolled down from the mountain top.*

滚动 gǔndòng roll
摇滚 yáogǔn
连滚带爬 liángǔn-dàipá

❷[动] 液体达到沸点而翻腾：boil | 水～了。Shuǐ gǔn le. *The water is boiling.* / 油锅烧～了。

Yóuguō shāogǔn le. *The oil in the pot is boiling.*

❸[动]走开；离开(用于辱骂或斥责)：get away; leave here (used when reprimanding sb.) | ～出去！Gǔn chūqu! *Get out of here!*

 棍 gùn 12画 木部

棍 棍棍棍棍棍棍棍棍 棍棍棍棍

[名]用树枝、竹子截成或用金属制成的圆长条：rod; stick | 木～mùgùn *wooden rod* / 铜～tónggùn *brass rod*
棍子 gùnzi rod
冰棍儿 bīnggùnr
曲棍球 qūgùnqiú
◇光棍儿 guānggùnr

 郭 guō 10画 阝(右)部

郭 郭郭郭郭郭郭郭郭 郭郭

[名]古代在城的外围加筑的城墙：(in ancient times) the outer wall of a city | 城～chéngguō *the inner and outer city walls*

锅（鍋）guō 12画 钅部

锅 锅锅锅锅锅锅锅锅 锅锅锅锅

❶[名] pot; pan | 饭～fànguō *a*

rice pot / 火 ~huǒguō *hot pot*
背黑锅 bēihēiguō
❷[名]某些装液体加热用的器具：utensils used to heat water or other liquids
锅炉 guōlú boiler

国 (國) guó 8画 口部

国国国国国国国国

❶ [名] 国家：country | 他一直在~外学习。Tā yīzhí zài guówài xuéxí. *He has been studying abroad all along.* / 中国是个大~。Zhōngguó shì ge dà guó. *China is a big country.*
国法 guófǎ the law of the land; national law; law
国防 guófáng national defence
国会 guóhuì parliament
国籍 guójí nationality
国际 guójì international
国家 guójiā country; state; nation
国力 guólì national power (or strength, might)
国民 guómín national; citizen
国内 guónèi internal; domestic; home
国情 guóqíng the condition (or state) of a country; national conditions
国庆 guóqìng National Day
国土 guótǔ territory; land

国外 guówài external; overseas; abroad
国王 guówáng king
国营 guóyíng state-operated; state-run
国有 guóyǒu state-owned
国际法 guójìfǎ (public) international law; law of nations
国民党 guómíndǎng the Kuomintang (KMT)
国庆节 guóqìngjié National Day (October 1, in China)
国务院 guówùyuàn the State Council
国际象棋 guójì xiàngqí chess (a board game for 2 players, each with 16 pieces in 6 kinds)
爱国 àiguó 报国 bàoguó
出国 chūguó 帝国 dìguó
邻国 língguó 卖国 màiguó
全国 quánguó 三国 Sān Guó
外国 wàiguó 王国 wángguó
战国 Zhànguó 中国 Zhōngguó
祖国 zǔguó
联合国 Liánhéguó
外国语 wàiguóyǔ
异国他乡 yìguó-tāxiāng
❷ [形] 代表国家的：national | ~歌 guógē *national anthem*
国旗 guóqí national flag
❸ [形] 属于本国的：of the state; of our country | ~画 guóhuà *traditional Chinese painting*
国产 guóchǎn domestic produced; made in one's own country

国道 guódào state highway; national road; national highway

国语 guóyǔ Mandarin (former term for *putonghua* or standard Chinese); official national language of a country

国债 guózhài national debt; treasury bond

国库券 guókùquàn treasury bond (TB); treasury bill; treasury stock

果　　　guǒ　8画 |部

果 果果果果果果果果

❶[名]果实，植物花落后含有种子的部分：fruit | 水~shuǐguǒ *fruit*
果实 guǒshí ① fruit ② gain; fruit
果树 guǒshù fruit tree
苹果 píngguǒ

❷[名]事情的最后；结局：result; consequence; ending; conclusion | 前因后~qiányīn-hòuguǒ *cause and effect; the entire process*
成果 chéngguǒ　后果 hòuguǒ
结果 jiéguǒ　　效果 xiàoguǒ

❸[副]确实；真的：indeed; really | 他~真来了吗？Tā guǒzhēn lái le ma? *Has he really come?*
果然 guǒrán really; as expected; sure enough
如果 rúguǒ

❹[形]坚决：determined; resolute
果断 guǒduàn resolute; decisive

裹　　　guǒ　14画 一部

裹 裹裹裹裹裹裹裹裹
裹裹裹裹裹裹裹

❶[动]包；缠绕：wrap; bind | ~伤口 guǒ shāngkǒu *bind up the wound* / 用纸~上 yòng zhǐ guǒ shang *wrap it with paper*

❷[动]卷进去：be carried along; be drawn along | 他们干的是违法的事，你可别~进去。Tāmen gàn de shì wéifǎ de shì, nǐ kě bié guǒ jìnqu. *What they are doing is against the law. Don't get involved in it.*

过（過）guò　6画 辶部

过 过过过过过过

❶[动]经过(处所)：pass through | ~马路 guò mǎlù *cross the street* / ~河 guò hé *cross a river*
过程 guòchéng course; process
过渡 guòdù transition; interim
过户 guòhù (of property, vehicles, stocks and bonds, etc.) transfer of ownership from one person to another in conformity with certain legal procedures;

transfer of names

过来 guòlái(lai) come over; come up

过去 guòqu go over; pass by

经过 jīngguò　　路过 lùguò

通过 tōngguò

❷ [动] 经过或度过(某段时间): pass, spend (a period of time) | ~年 guònián *celebrate the New Year* / ~节 guòjié *celebrate a festival* / 我~两天再来。Wǒ guò liǎng tiān zài lái. *I'll come again in a few days.* / 日子越~越好。Rìzi yuè guò yuè hǎo. *Our life is becoming better and better.*

过后 guòhòu afterwards; later

过去 guòqù in or of the past; formerly; previously

过日子 guòrìzi lead a life; get by; get along; live

逢年过节 féngnián-guòjié

❸ [动] 使经过(某种处理): go through (a certain process) | 他常常说话不~脑子。Tā chángcháng shuōhuà bù guò nǎozi. *He seldom uses his head when making a statement.* / 把这批货~~数吧。Bǎ zhè pī huò guòguò shù ba. *Please count this batch of goods.*

❹ [动] 超出(某种范围或限度): surpass; exceed (certain range or limit) | 探望病人的时间已~。Tānwàng bìngrén de shíjiān yǐ guò. *Visiting hours*

are over. / 这罐头已~了保质期。Zhè guàntou yǐ guòle bǎozhìqī. *The expiry date of this canned food has passed.* / 投票已~半数。Tóupiào yǐ guò bànshù. *The votes cast have already exceeded half of the total.*

过度 guòdù excessive; undue; over

过分 guòfèn excessive; undue; over

过奖 guòjiǎng (in response to a compliment) overpraise; lay it on thick

过敏 guòmǐn ① allergy; allergic reaction ② oversensitive

过期 guòqī exceed the time limit; be overdue

过于 guòyú too; unduly; excessively

超过 chāoguò　　越过 yuèguò

❺ [名] 错误: mistake; error | 知~必改 zhīguò-bìgǎi *always correct the error when you become aware of it* / 功大于~ gōng dàyú guò *one's achievements outweigh one's errors* / 学校决定给他记一次。Xuéxiào juédìng gěi tā jìguò yī cì. *The school has decided to give him a demerit record.*

过错 guòcuò fault; error; blame; offence

过剩 guòshèng excess; surplus; oversupply

过失 guòshī fault; slip; error
See guo.

 (過) guo 6画 辶部

过 过过过过过过

❶[助] 用在动词后，表示动作完毕：used after a verb to indicate the completion of an action | 我已经吃～饭了。Wǒ yǐjīng chīguo fàn le. *I have already had my meal.*

❷[助] 用在动词后，表示过去曾经有这样的事情：used after a verb to denote sth. that happened in the past already | 我们曾经谈～这个问题。Wǒmen céngjīng tánguo zhège wèntí. *We discussed this question before.* / 他去年来～北京。Tā qù-nián láiguo Běijīng. *He came to Beijing last year.* / 这个地方三年前我曾经来～。Zhège dìfang sān nián qián wǒ céngjīng láiguo. *I was here three years ago.*

❸[助] 用在形容词后，表示曾经有过某种性质或状态：used after an adjective to denote a certain quality or condition existing in the past | 上星期冷～几天，现在又热起来了。Shàng xīngqī lěngguo jǐ tiān, xiànzài yòu rè qǐlai le. *It was cold for a couple of days last week, and now it is getting hot again.* / 他从没这么高兴～。Tā cóngméi zhème gāoxìngguo. *He has never been so happy.*

◇ 错过 cuòguò
    See guò.

H h

真有这种怪事。Hāi! Zhēn yǒu zhè zhǒng guàishì. *What? That's really strange!*
See kě.

哈 hā   9画 口部

哈 哈哈哈哈哈哈哈哈 哈

❶[动]张口呼气；blow one's breath; breathe out | 他～了一口气。Tā hāle yī kǒu qì. *He breathed out with his mouth open.*

❷[拟声]模拟笑声（大多叠用）：sound of laughing (usu. in reduplicated form) | 他～～地笑个不停。Tā hāhā de xiào ge bù tíng. *He kept on roaring with laughter.*

哈哈 hāhā ha-ha
◇哈密瓜 hāmìguā Hami melon; saccharinus
马大哈 mǎdàhā

咳 hāi   9画 口部

咳 咳咳咳咳咳咳咳咳 咳

[叹]表示伤感、后悔或惊异：used to express sentimentality, regret or surprise | ～!我怎么这么糊涂! Hāi! Wǒ zěnme zhème hútu! *Damn! How stupid I was!* / ～!

还（還） hái   7画 辶部

还 还还还还还还还

❶[副]表示动作或状态持续不变；仍然：used to indicate a continuous action or state; still | 十年过去了，她～是那么年轻。Shí nián guòqu le, tā háishì nàme niánqīng. *Ten years have passed, but she still looks so young.* / 过两天我～会来的。Guò liǎng tiān wǒ hái huì lái de. *I'll come again in a couple of days.*

还是 háishì ① still; nevertheless; all the same ② had better ③ or

❷[副]表示在某种程度之上有所增加；更加：used to indicate an increase of a certain degree; all the more | 今天比昨天～冷。Jīntiān bǐ zuótiān hái lěng. *Today is even colder than yesterday.*

❸[副]表示项目、数量增加，范围扩大：used to indicate an expansion of a project or an increase of a number | 他们参观了学校，～参观了工厂和医院。Tāmen cānguānle xuéxiào, hái cānguānle gōngchǎng hé yīyuàn. *They visited factories, hospitals as well as schools.* ／孩子们～想再玩一次这个游戏。Háizimen hái xiǎng zài wán yī cì zhège yóuxì. *Children want to play this game again.* 还有 háiyǒu (still) have; have (more)

❹[副]用在形容词前，表示程度上勉强过得去：used before an adjective to indicate that something is passable to certain extent｜菜的味道～可以。Cài de wèidào hái kěyǐ. *The taste of the dish is not bad.* ／你现在走～来得及。Nǐ xiànzài zǒu hái láidejí. *It is not too late if you leave now.*

❺[副]表示数量小，时间不到：used to indicate that a number is small, that it is not yet time to...

❻[副]用在上半句里，作为陪衬，下半句作推论；尚且：used to form a contrast in the first part of the sentence and introduce a deduction in the latter part of the sentence｜连你～不知道，我怎么可能知道呢? Lián nǐ hái bù zhīdào, wǒ zěnme kěnéng zhīdào ne? *Even you don't know that. How could I?*

❼[副]表示超出预料，有赞叹的语气：used to indicate a happening beyond expectation with a tone of praise and admiration｜他～真有办法。Tā hái zhēn

yǒu bànfǎ. *He is really resourceful.*

❽[副]表示应该怎样而不怎样，有责备或讥讽的语气：used to express a tone of reproach or irony｜你～说得出!Nǐ hái shuōdechū! *And you have the nerve to say that!*

❾[副]表示加强语气，用于反问：used to lay emphasis in a rhetorical question｜那～用说!Nà hái yòng shuō! *That goes without saying!*

See huán.

 hái　9画　子部

孩 孩孩孩孩孩孩孩孩孩

[名]儿童：child
孩子 háizi ① child ② son or daughter; children
男孩儿 nánháir
小孩子 xiǎoháizi

 hǎi　10画　氵部

海 海海海海海海海海海海

❶[名]sea｜南～Nán Hǎi *the South China Sea* ／他常去一边游泳。Tā cháng qù hǎibiān yóuyǒng. *He often goes swimming at the beach.*

海岸 hǎi'àn seacoast; coast; seashore

海拔 hǎibá height above sea level; elevation

海滨 hǎibīn seashore; seaside

海港 hǎigǎng seaport; harbour

海关 hǎiguān custom house; customs

海军 hǎijūn navy

海面 hǎimiàn sea level

海水 hǎishuǐ seawater; brine; the sea

海滩 hǎitān seabeach; beach

海外 hǎiwài overseas; abroad

海峡 hǎixiá strait; channel

海鲜 hǎixiān seafood

海啸 hǎixiào tsunami; seismic sea wave

海洋 hǎiyáng seas and oceans; ocean

大海 dàhǎi   东海 Dōng Hǎi

航海 hánghǎi   沿海 yánhǎi

山珍海味 shānzhēn-hǎiwèi

❷[名]比喻聚集成一大片的人或事物：used figuratively to indicate myriads of people or things | 林~línhǎi *a vast stretch of forest* / 火~huǒhǎi *a sea of fire* / 人~rénhǎi *crowds of people*

❸[形]大：big; vast | ~碗 hǎiwǎn *big bowl* / 夸下~口 kuāxià hǎikǒu *boast; talk big*

◇海报 hǎibào playbill; poster; notice

hǎi   10画 宀部

害害害害害害害害 害害

❶[动]使受损害：do harm to; make sb. suffer from | 你~我白跑了一趟。Nǐ hài wǒ báipǎole yī tàng. *You made me go all that way for nothing.* / 你这样做既~了别人，又~了自己。Nǐ zhèyàng zuò jì hàile biérén, yòu hàile zìjǐ. *In doing so, you have done harm both to others and to yourself.*

受害 shòuhài

❷[名]祸患；坏处：disaster; scourge; harm | 大家一齐动手消灭虫~。Dàjiā yīqí dòngshǒu xiāomiè chónghài. *Let's work together to get rid of the insects (pests).* / 吸烟对身体有~。Xīyān duì shēntǐ yǒu hài. *Smoking is harmful to health.*

❸[形]有害的（跟"益 yì"相对）：harmful; destructive (the opposite of "益 yì")

害虫 hàichóng destructive insect

害处 hàichu harm; damage

❹[动]杀；杀死：kill; murder | 他被~了。Tā bèi hài le. *He was murdered.*

遇害 yùhài

被害人 bèihàirén

❺[动]发生（疾病）：contract (a disease)：| ~眼病 hài yǎnbìng *suffer from eye disease* / 我不

久前～了一场重病。Wǒ bùjiǔ qián hàile yī chǎng zhòngbìng. *I have just recovered from a serious attack of illness.*

❻[动]产生不安的感觉或情绪：feel uneasy or ashamed | 我实在为你感到～臊。Wǒ shízài wèi nǐ gǎndào hàisào. *I am utterly ashamed of you.*

害怕hàipà be afraid; be scared
害羞hàixiū bashful; be shy

◇厉害lìhai

酣 hān 12画 酉部

酣酣酣酣酣酣酣酣
酣酣酣酣

[形]尽兴；畅快：to one's heart's content; heartily | ～畅 hānchàng *merry and lively* / ～睡 hānshuì *sleep soundly; be fast asleep*

憨 hān 15画 心部

憨憨憨憨憨憨憨
憨憨憨憨憨憨憨

❶[形]傻；呆：slow-witted; foolish | 这人有点儿～。Zhè rén yǒudiǎnr hān. *He is a little slow-witted.*

❷[形]朴实；天真：simple; plain; innocent | ～态 hāntài *naive manner*

含 hān 7画 口部

含含含含含含含

❶[动]嘴里放着东西，不吐也不咽：keep in the mouth | 你一～片药，嗓子就不痛了。Nǐ hán yī piàn yào, sǎngzi jiù bù tòng le. *Keep a tablet in the mouth and your sore throat will be relieved.* / 孩子嘴里～着一块糖。Háizi zuǐli hánzhe yī kuài táng. *The child kept a sweet in his mouth.*

❷[动]藏在（里面）；包括：contain | ～水分 hán shuǐfèn *containing water or moisture* / 这种蔬菜～维生素比较多。Zhè zhǒng shūcài hán wéishēng sù bǐjiào duō. *This vegetable contains a lot of vitamins.*

含量 hánliàng content
含义 hányì meaning; implication
含有 hányǒu contain; include
包含 bāohán

❸[动]怀着某种意思、情感：nurse; harbour; cherish | 他～笑对我点头。Tā hánxiào duì wǒ diǎntóu. *He nodded to me with a smile.*

含糊 hánhu ① ambiguous; vague ② careless; perfunctory

函 hān 8画 凵部

函函函函函函函函

[名]信件：letter; correspondence | 来~已经收到。Láihán yǐjīng shōudào. *I have received your letter.*

函授 hánshòu teach by correspondence; give a correspondence course

寒 hán 12画 宀部

寒寒寒寒寒寒寒寒
寒寒寒寒

❶ [形]冷：cold | 天~tiān hán *the weather is cold*

寒带 hándài frigid zone; cold zone

寒冷 hánlěng cold; frigid; chilly

寒暄 hánxuān exchange greetings

饥寒交迫 jīhán-jiāopò

❷ [名]寒冷的季节（跟"暑shǔ"相对）：cold season (the opposite of "暑shǔ") | ~来暑往 hánláishǔwǎng *summer goes and winter comes; with the passage of time*

寒假 hánjià winter vacation

❸ [形]灰心；害怕：disheartening; discouraging; afraid; scared | 心~ xīnhán *be bitterly disappointed*

罕 hǎn 7画 宀部

罕罕罕罕罕罕罕

[形]稀少：rare | ~闻 hǎnwén *seldom heard* / 稀~xīhǎn *rare* / 这真是世间~有的事。Zhè zhēn shì shìjiān hǎn yǒu de shì. *It's really a rare event in this world.*

罕见 hǎnjiàn seldom seen; rare

喊 hǎn 12画 口部

喊喊喊喊喊喊喊喊
喊喊喊喊

❶ [动]大声叫：shout; cry; holler | ~口号 hǎn kǒuhào *shout slogans* / 别大声~，人家都休息了。Bié dàshēng hǎn, rénjia dōu xiūxi le. *Stop shouting. People are having a rest.*

喊叫 hǎnjiào shout; cry out

叫喊 jiàohǎn

大喊大叫 dàhǎn-dàjiào

❷ [动]招呼；叫（人）：call; hail; greet; call sb. | 你~谁？Nǐ hǎn shéi? *Who are you calling?* / 你走时~他一声。Nǐ zǒu shí hǎn tā yī shēng. *Call him when you leave.*

汉（漢） hàn 5画 氵部

汉

汉汉汉汉汉

❶[名]朝代，公元前206—公元220年：the Han Dynasty (206 BC—220 AD)

❷[名]汉族：the Han nationality
汉奸 hànjiān traitor (to China); collaborator
汉学 hànxué the Han school of classical philology; Sinology
汉语 Hànyǔ Chinese (language)
汉字 Hànzì Chinese character
汉族 Hànzú the Han nationality

❸[名]男子：man
好汉 hǎohàn   老汉 lǎohàn

◇门外汉 ménwàihàn

汗

hàn   6画 氵部

汗 汗汗汗汗汗汗

[名]从皮肤表面排出的液体：sweat; perspiration | 他出了一身～。Tā chūle yī shēn hàn. *He sweated all over.*
汗水 hànshuǐ sweat; perspiration

旱

hàn   7画 日部

旱 旱旱旱旱旱旱旱

❶[形]长时间不下雨、雪或雨量太小（跟"涝lào"相对）：drought (the opposite of "涝lào") | 抗～kànghàn *combat drought; fight*

against drought / 防～fánghàn *drought prevention* / 总不下雨，庄稼都～了。Zǒng bù xiàyǔ, zhuāngjia dōu hàn le. *There hasn't been any rain for a long time and the crops are suffering from the drought.*
旱灾 hànzāi drought
干旱 gānhàn

❷[形]跟水无关的：unrelated to water | ～田 hàntián *non-irrigated farmland* / ～地 hàndì *non-irrigated farmland; dry farmland* / ～路 hànlù *overland route*

捍

hàn   10画 扌部

捍 捍捍捍捍捍捍捍捍捍

[动]保卫：defend
捍卫 hànwèi defend; guard

焊

hàn   11画 火部

焊 焊焊焊焊焊焊焊焊焊焊焊

[动]用熔化的金属连接或修补金属器物：weld; solder | 这个接头断了，要一一下。Zhège jiētóu duàn le, yào hàn yīxià. *The joint is disconnected and needs to be soldered.*

撼 hàn 16画 扌部

撼撼撼撼撼撼撼撼
撼撼撼撼撼撼撼撼

[动]摇；摇动：shake; vibrate ｜～
动 hàndòng *shake*
震撼 zhènhàn

憾 hàn 16画 忄部

憾憾憾憾憾憾憾
憾憾憾憾憾憾憾

[动]失望；不满意：disappoint;
dissatisfy ｜～事 hànshì *a matter
for regret* ／缺～quēhàn *regret*
遗憾 yíhàn

行 háng 6画 彳部

行行行行行行

❶[名]行列：line; row ｜单～
dānháng *single line* ／柳树
成～liǔshù chéng háng *lined
with rows of willows*
行列 hángliè ranks
排行榜 páihángbǎng

❷[名]行业；职业：line; profession;
occupation ｜他热爱教师这
一～。Tā rè'ài jiàoshī zhè yī
háng. *He has a deep love for
teaching.* ／咱们是同～。Zán
men shì tóngháng. *We are in

the same trade.* ／他在这一～干
得很出色。Tā zài zhè yī háng
gàn de hěn chūsè. *He is doing very well in this trade.*
行情 hángqíng quotations (on
the market); prices
行业 hángyè trade; profession;
industry
内行 nèiháng 同行 tóngháng
外行 wàiháng
各行各业 gèháng-gèyè

❸[量]用于成行的东西：used for
things shaped into a line ｜两～
眼泪 liǎng háng yǎnlèi *two
streams of tears* ／一～字 yī
háng zì *a line of words*
◇银行 yínháng
See xíng.

航 háng 10画 舟部

航航航航航航航航
航航

[动](船)行驶；(飞行器)飞行：navigate;
navigate by water; fly; navigate
by air
航班 hángbān flight; flight
number
航道 hángdào channel; lane;
course
航海 hánghǎi navigation
航空 hángkōng aviation
航天 hángtiān spaceflight; aero-
space
航线 hángxiàn air or shipping

line; route; course

航行 hángxíng ① navigate by water; sail ② navigate by air

航运 hángyùn shipping

导航 dǎoháng　民航 mínháng

通航 tōngháng

宇航员 yǔhángyuán

毫 háo　11画 毛部

毫毫毫毫毫毫毫毫
毫毫毫

❶[量]计量单位名称，10毫等于1厘：unit of weight (10 *hao* equals 1 *li*)

毫米 háomǐ millimetre; mm.

丝毫 sīháo

❷[副]数量极少；一点：very little in amount; in the least | ～无诚意 háowú chéngyì *without the least sincerity*

毫不 háobù not in the least; not at all

毫无 háowú not at all; without

豪 háo　14画 豕部

豪豪豪豪豪豪豪豪
豪豪豪豪豪豪

[形]气魄大：forthright; unrestrained | ～放 háofàng *bold and unconstrained* / ～爽 háoshuǎng *straightforward; forthright*

◇豪华 háohuá luxurious; sumptuous

好 hǎo　6画 女部

好 好好好好好好

❶[形]优点多的；使人满意的（跟"坏huài"相对）：good; virtuous; satisfying; nice; (the opposite of "坏huài") | ～消息 hǎo xiāoxi *good news* / ～主意 hǎo zhǔyi *a good idea* / 我们的生活越过越～。Wǒmen de shēnghuó yuè guò yuè hǎo. *Our living standard is getting better and better.*

好处 hǎochu ① good; benefit; advantage ② gain; profit

好坏 hǎohuài good and bad; mishap; anyway

好评 hǎopíng favourable comment; high opinion

好运 hǎoyùn good luck

好转 hǎozhuǎn take a turn for the better; take a favourable turn; improve

好好儿 hǎohāor ① in perfectly good condition; when everything is all right ② all out; to one's heart's content

好好先生 hǎohǎo xiānsheng one who tries not to offend anybody

刚好 gānghǎo　良好 liánghǎo

美好 měihǎo　恰好 qiàhǎo

幸好 xìnghǎo

正好 zhènghǎo 最好 zuìhǎo
恰到好处 qiàdào-hǎochù

❷[形]友爱；和睦；相好，好感：
friendly; kind; good; affinitive
| ～朋友 hǎo péngyou *great
(good) friend* / 她一直对我
很～。Tā yīzhí duì wǒ hěn
hǎo. *She has always been kind
to me.*

好感 hǎogǎn good opinion
好友 hǎoyǒu good friend
要好 yàohǎo 友好 yǒuhǎo

❸[形]用在动词后，作结果补语，表
示完成或达到完善的地步：used
after a verb as a complement to
indicate completion or a perfect
condition of sth. | 计划订～了。
Jìhuà dìnghǎo le. *The plan
has been drawn up.* / 文章已经
写～了。Wénzhāng yǐjīng
xiěhǎo le. *The article has been
finished.*

❹[形]健康；痊愈：in good health;
recovered | 他的病完全～了。
Tā de bìng wánquán hǎo le.
*He recovered completely from
illness.* / 他身体一直很～。Tā
shēntǐ yīzhí hěn hǎo. *He has
always been in good health.*

❺[副]用在形容词、动词前，表示程
度深：used before an adjective
or verb to denote a high degree
| ～冷啊!Hǎo lěng a! *It's so
cold!* / 街上～热闹!Jiēshang
hǎo rènao! *The street is really
bustling!* / ～险哪!Hǎo xiǎn na!

That was so close!

❻[副]用在数量词、时间词或形容
词"多"、"久"前，强调多或久：
used before a quantity word, time
word or adjectives such as
"many", "long" for emphasis
| ～半天 hǎo bàntiān *quite a
while* / 他学过～几年英语。Tā
xuéguo hǎo jǐ nián Yīngyǔ.
*He has studied English for sev-
eral years.*

好多 hǎoduō a good many; a
good deal; a lot of
好久 hǎojiǔ long; for a long time
好些 hǎoxiē quite a lot; a good
deal of; many

❼[形]表示赞成、同意、结束或不满
等语气：used to express ap-
proval, agreement, completion
or dissatisfaction | ～，干得漂
亮。Hǎo, gàn de piàoliang.
Great. It's well done. / ～了，不
要再说了。Hǎole, bùyào zài
shuō le. *All right. There's no
need to say any more.*

好说 hǎoshuō a polite response
used to express gratitude or
compliments; a polite response
used to express possible agreement

❽[形]容易(跟"难 nán"相对)：easy
(the opposite of "难 nán") |
那篇文章～懂。Nà piān wén-
zhāng hǎo dǒng. *The article
is easy to understand.* / 这个问
题很～解决。Zhège wèntí hěn

hǎo jiějué. *The problem is very easy to solve.*

好说话 hǎoshuōhuà good-natured; open to persuasion; easy to deal with

❾ [形] 表示效果(形象、声音、气味、味道、感觉等)好：used to indicate the effect (image, voice, smell, feeling, etc.) is good

好吃 hǎochī tasty; delicious

好看 hǎokàn ① good-looking; nice ② honoured; proud

好听 hǎotīng pleasant to hear

好像 hǎoxiàng seem; be like

好在 hǎozài fortunately; luckily

好玩儿 hǎowánr amusing; interesting

◇ 好比 hǎobǐ can be compared to; may be likened to; be just like

不好意思 bùhǎoyìsi

See hào.

号 (號) hào 5画 口部

号 号号号号号

❶ [名] 命令：command; order
号召 hàozhào call; appeal
口号 kǒuhào

❷ [名] 军队或乐队中使用的西式喇叭：bugle | 长~chánghào *trombone* / 军~jūnhào *bugle*

❸ [名] 用号吹出的表示一定意义的声音：bugle call; any call made on a bugle to convey a certain meaning | 起床~qǐchuánghào *rev-*

---

eille / 熄灯~xīdēnghào *taps*

❹ [名] 名称：name | 外~wàihào *nickname* / 国~guóhào *the name of a dynasty*

号称 hàochēng ① be known as ② claim to be

称号 chēnghào 旗号 qíhào

字号 zìhao

❺ [名] 标志; 信号：sign; signal | 信~灯 xìnhàodēng *signal lamp* / 做记~zuò jìhao *mark; make a mark*

代号 dàihào 符号 fúhào

句号 jùhào 信号 xìnhào

❻ [名] 表示次第; 等级; 规格：order; sequence; grade; specifications; standards; norms：| 第一~dì-yī hào *number one* / 中~zhōnghào *medium size*

号码 hàomǎ number; size

编号 biānhào 挂号 guàhào

型号 xínghào

账号 zhànghào

查号台 cháhàotái

◇ 号脉 hàomài (traditional Chinese medicine) feel the pulse

好 hǎo 6画 女部

好 好好好好好好

❶ [动] 喜爱(跟"恶 wù"相对)：like (the opposite of "恶 wù") | ~下棋 hào xiàqí *like playing chess* / ~喝酒 hào hējiǔ *like drinking alcohol* / 这个人~说

笑话。Zhège rén hǎo shuō xiǎohua. *The man likes to tell jokes.*

好客hǎokè be hospitable; keep open house

好奇hǎoqí be curious; be full of curiosity

爱好 àihào

❷ [动]常容易(发生某种状态或行为)：having a tendency to be a certain situation or to do sth.; be liable to｜～发脾气 hào fā píqi *apt to lose one's temper* / 这孩子～哭。Zhè háizi hào kū. *The child often cries.*

See hǎo.

耗 hào 10画 耒部

耗 耗耗耗耗耗耗耗耗 耗耗

❶ [动]减损；消费：wear; spend; consume｜锅里的水都快～干了。Guō li de shuǐ dōu kuài hàogān le. *The pot is nearly boiling dry.*

耗费 hàofèi consume; expend

消耗 xiāohào

❷ [动]拖延：delay｜～时间 hào shíjiān *waste time; dawdle* / 别～着了，快干吧。Bié hàozhe le, kuài gàn ba. *Stop idling and take action quickly.*

浩 hào 10画 氵部

浩 浩浩浩浩浩浩浩浩 浩浩

[形](气势、规模等)大：great; vast; grand (in momentum or size)｜声势～大 shēngshì-hàodà *great in strength and impetus; powerful and dynamic*

浩浩荡荡 hàohào-dàngdàng vast and mighty

呵 hē 8画 口部

呵 呵呵呵呵呵呵呵呵

[叹]表示惊讶：expressing surprise｜～，你来了。Hē, nǐ lái le. *Oh, you have come.* / ～，你真漂亮! Hē, nǐ zhēn piàoliang! *Wow, how pretty you are!* / ～，这小伙子真了不起! Hē, zhè xiǎohuǒzi zhēn liǎobuqǐ! *Wow, this young guy is terrific!*

喝 hē 12画 口部

喝 喝喝喝喝喝喝喝喝 喝喝喝喝

❶ [动]吸食液体或流质食物：drink; take in liquid food or be on a liquid diet｜～茶 hē chá *drink tea* / ～咖啡 hē kāfēi *drink cof-*

fee / ～粥 hē zhōu *have gruel*

❷[动]特指喝酒：like drinking | 这个人就是爱～两口。Zhège rén jiùshì ài hē liǎng kǒu. *This person likes a drink of liquor most.*

大吃大喝 dàchī-dàhē

hé   5画 禾部

禾 禾 禾 禾 禾 禾

[名]谷类作物的幼苗，特指水稻：standing grain (esp. rice)

禾苗 hémiáo seedlings of cereal crops

hé   6画 人部

合 合 合 合 合 合

❶[动]关闭；合拢：close; shut | ～眼 héyǎn *close the eyes; sleep* / 把书～起来 bǎ shū hé qǐlai *close the book*

❷[动]聚集在一起(跟"分 fēn"相对)：gather (the opposite of "分 fēn")

合并 hébìng merge; amalgamate

合成 héchéng ① compose; compound ②synthetize; synthesize

合伙 héhuǒ form a partnership

合计 héjì amount to; add up to; total

合金 héjīn alloy

合同 hétong contract

合资 hézī pool capital; enter into partnership; joint

合作 hézuò cooperate; collaborate; work together

凑合 cōuhe   复合 fùhé

化合 huàhé   磨合 móhé

配合 pèihé   融合 rónghé

整合 zhěnghé   组合 zǔhé

综合 zōnghé   混合物 hùnhéwù

❸[副]共同；一起：together; jointly

合唱 héchàng chorus

合营 héyíng jointly owned; jointly operated

合影 héyǐng group photo (or picture)

❹[动]符合；适合：suit | 他说的话正～我的心意。Tā shuō de huà zhèng hé wǒ de xīnyì. *What he said suits my mind exactly.*

合法 héfǎ legal; lawful; legitimate; rightful

合格 hégé qualified; up to standard

合乎 héhū conform with (to); correspond to; accord with; tally with

合理 hélǐ rational; reasonable; equitable

合适 héshì suitable; appropriate; becoming; right

合算 hésuàn ① paying; worthwhile ② reckon up

合情合理 héqíng-hélǐ fair and reasonable; fair and sensible

符合 fúhé 　　　　巧合 qiǎohé

适合 shìhé 　　　　吻合 wěnhé

迎合 yínghé

❺[动]折算；相当于：convert into; amount to ｜一米～多少尺? Yī mǐ hé duōshǎo chǐ? *How many chi is one metre equal to?*

折合 zhéhé

◇合约 héyuē (esp. one with simple clauses) contract

百合 bǎihé 　　　　回合 huíhé

汇合 huìhé

何 hé 7画 亻部

何 何何何何何何何

❶[代]表示疑问，有"什么""哪""哪里""为什么"的意思：used to indicate queries such as "what" "where" "why" ｜有～困难? Yǒu hé kùnnan? *Is there any problem?* / 从～说起 cóng hé shuōqǐ *where to start the story*

任何 rènhé 　　　　如何 rúhé

为何 wèihé

无可奈何 wúkěnàihé

无论如何 wúlùn-rúhé

❷[代]表示反问：used to indicate a rhetorical question ｜～足挂齿 hézúguàchǐ *not worth mentioning* / 谈～容易 tán hé róngyì *not easy at all*

何必 hébì there is no need; why

何等 héděng ① what kind ② how; what (used in exclamations)

何况 hékuàng much less; let alone

 和 hé 8画 禾部

和 和和和和和和和和

❶[形]协调；相处得好：harmonious; (be) on good terms with

和解 héjiě become reconciled

和睦 hémù harmony; concord; amity

和平 hépíng ① peace ② mild ③ peaceful; tranquil

和谐 héxié harmonious

和约 héyuē peace treaty

和平共处 hépíng gòngchǔ peaceful coexistence

缓和 huǎnhé 　　　　柔和 róuhé

调和 tiáohé 　　　　温和 wēnhé

共和国 gònghéguó

风和日丽 fēnghé-rìlì

❷[形]温和；不激烈；不粗暴：gentle; mild; kind

和蔼 hé'ǎi kind; affable; amiable

和气 héqi gentle; kind; polite; amiable

平和 pínghé

❸[形]不分胜负：ending in a draw ｜这盘棋～了。Zhè pán qí hé le. *The game of chess ended in a draw.*

❹[介]表示共同、协同；跟：together with ｜有事要～大伙儿商量。

Yǒu shì yāo hé dàhuǒr shāngliang. *You should discuss things with the others.*

❺ [介]指示动作的对象；向；对；跟：to; toward | 你~大家谈谈自己的看法。Nǐ hé dàjiā tántán zìjǐ de kànfǎ. *Please tell us your own opinions.* / 林老师有话~你讲。Lín lǎoshī yǒu huà hé nǐ jiǎng. *Teacher Lin wants to talk to you.*

❻ [介] 表示与某事有联系：i n; with | 这件事~他有关。Zhè jiàn shì hé tā yǒuguān. *He is involved in this matter.* / 我去不去~你不相干。Wǒ qùbuqù hé nǐ bù xiānggān. *It's none of your business whether I shall go or not.*

❼ [介]引进用来比较的对象；跟：used to introduce the object for comparison | 他讲的~他做的不一致。Tā jiǎng de hé tā zuò de bù yīzhì. *What he said does not agree with what he did.*

❽ [连]表示平等的联合关系：and | 哥哥~姐姐 gēge hé jiějie *brothers and sisters* / 工业~农业 gōngyè hé nóngyè *industry and agriculture*

❾ [连]表示选择，相当于"或huò"：or

❿ [名]加起来的总数：sum; total | 两数之~liǎng shù zhī hé *the sum of two numbers*

总和 zǒnghé
◇和尚 héshang Buddhist monk

河　　　hé　　8画 氵部

河河河河河河河河

❶ [名]特指黄河：specifically referring to the Yellow River
黄河 Huáng Hé

❷ [名]水道的通称：general term for waterways | 这条~全长20千米。Zhè tiáo hé quáncháng èrshí qiānmǐ. *The river is 20 kilometres long.*
河道 hédào river course
河流 héliú rivers
山河 shānhé　　运河 yùnhé
◇河马 hémǎ hippopotamus; hippo
拔河 báhé　　银河 yínhé

荷　　　hé　　10画 艹部

荷荷荷荷荷荷荷荷荷荷

[名]lotus | ~叶 héyè *lotus leaf*
荷花 héhuā lotus
◇荷兰豆 hélándòu mangetout; snow pea

核　　　hé　　10画 木部

核核核核核核核核核核

❶ [名]pit, stone | 这是一种无~葡

萄。Zhè shì yī zhǒng wúhé pútao. *This is a kind of seedless grape.* / 桃子的～通常很大。Táozi de hé tōngcháng hěn dà. *The peach-pit is usually big.*

核桃 hétao walnut

❷[名]物体中像核的部分：core-like part in an object | 细胞～ xìbāohé *cell nucleus*

❸[名]原子核：atomic nucleus | ～战争 hézhànzhēng *nuclear war*

核弹 hédàn common name for nuclear weapons such as the atomic bomb and hydrogen bomb

核武器 héwǔqì nuclear weapons

❹[动]仔细地对照考察：examine; check | ～算 hésuàn *assess; check; calculate*

核查 héchá check; exam and verify

核实 héshí verify; check

考核 kǎohé　　审核 shěnhé

◇核心 héxīn nucleus; core; kernel

盒　　hé　　11画 皿部

盒 盒盒盒盒盒盒盒盒 盒盒盒

[名]box | 纸～ zhǐhé *paper box* / 文具～ wénjùhé *pencil box* / 火柴～ huǒcháihé *match box*

墨盒 mòhé

贺（賀）hè　　9画 贝部

贺 贺贺贺贺贺贺贺贺 贺

[动]庆祝；道喜：celebrate; congratulate | ～喜 hèxǐ *congratulate on a happy occasion*

贺词 hècí speech (message) of congratulation; congratulations; greetings

贺岁 hèsuì extend New Year greetings

庆贺 qìnghè　　祝贺 zhùhè

赫　　hè　　14画 赤部

赫 赫赫赫赫赫赫赫赫 赫赫赫赫赫赫

[形]显耀；盛大：conspicuous; grand; very impressive | 声势～ ～shēngshì hèhè *grand in strength and impetus; powerful and dynamic*

赫赫有名 hèhè-yǒumíng prominent; noted

显赫 xiǎnhè

褐　　hè　　14画 衤部

褐 褐褐褐褐褐褐褐 褐褐褐褐褐褐

[形]黄黑色：brown

黑 hēi　12画 黑部

黑 黑 黑 黑 黑 黑 黑 黑 黑
黑 黑 黑 黑

❶ [形]像煤的颜色（跟"白bái"相对）：black (the opposite of "白bái") | ～皮鞋 hēi píxié *black shoes* / ～头发 hēi tóufa *black hair*

黑白 hēibái ① black and white ② right and wrong

黑板 hēibǎn blackboard

黑人 hēirén black people; black; negro

黑色 hēisè black

黑龙江 Hēilóng Jiāng ① the Heilongjiang River ② Heilongjiang (Province)

背黑锅 bēihēiguō

❷ [形]光线昏暗：dark | 天～了。Tiān hēi le. *It's dark.* / 屋子里很～。Wūzi li hěn hēi. *It's dark in the room.*

黑暗 hēi'àn dark

黑夜 hēiyè dark night

漆黑 qīhēi

❸ [形]坏；狠毒：wicked; sinister | ～心 hēixīn *black-hearted; evil-minded* / 这个人心真～。Zhège rén xīn zhēn hēi. *This person is really evil.*

❹ [形]秘密的；非法的：secret; shady; illegal | ～名单 hēimíngdān *blacklist* / ～社会 hēishèhuì *underworld; criminal clique*

黑幕 hēimù inside story of a plot; shady deal, etc.

嘿 hēi　15画 口部

嘿 嘿 嘿 嘿 嘿 嘿 嘿 嘿
嘿 嘿 嘿 嘿 嘿 嘿 嘿

❶ [叹]表示得意或赞叹：expressing complacence, pleasure, praise | ～，我总算找到你了。Hēi, wǒ zǒngsuàn zhǎodào nǐ le. *Hey, I have found you at last.* / ～，这个真好!Hēi, zhège zhēn hǎo! *Oh, how nice this is!*

❷ [叹]表示招呼或提醒：expressing a greeting or reminder | ～，你来啦。Hēi, nǐ lái la. *Hey, you are here.* / ～!当心点! Hēi! Dāngxīn diǎn! *Hey! Be careful!*

❸ [叹]表示惊异：expressing surprise | ～，下雪了!Hēi, xiàxuě le! *Why, it's snowing!*

痕 hén　11画 疒部

痕 痕 痕 痕 痕 痕 痕 痕
痕 痕 痕

[名]事物留下的印迹：mark; trace | 泪～lèihén *tear stains* / 伤～ shānghén *scar from a wound* / 裂～lièhén *rift; crack; fissure*

313

痕迹 hénjì mark; trace; vestige

很 hěn 9画 彳部

很很很很很很很很

[副]表示程度相当高：used to indicate quite a high degree | 好得～ hǎodehěn *very good* / ～可能 hěn kěnéng *very likely* / ～满意 hěn mǎnyì *feel very satisfied; feel quite pleased*

狠 hěn 9画 犭部

狠狠狠狠狠狠狠狠

❶ [形]残忍；凶恶：ruthless; relentless; fierce; ferocious; fiendish | 他的心真～。Tā de xīn zhēn hěn. *He is such a cruel man.* 狠毒 hěndú vicious; venomous 狠心 hěnxīn cruel-hearted; heartless; merciless 凶狠 xiōnghěn

❷ [形]严厉；坚决：stern; severe; firm; resolute; determined | ～抓服务质量 hěn zhuā fúwù zhìliàng *vigorously promote the quality of service*

恨 hěn 9画 忄部

恨 恨恨恨恨恨恨恨恨 恨

❶ [动]仇视；怨；hate; resent; be hostile to; blame; complain | ～之入骨 hènzhīrùgǔ *hate sb. to the marrow of one's bones* / 他因为这件事～我。Tā yīnwéi zhè jiàn shì hèn wǒ. *He hates me for it.* / 我对他～不起来。Wǒ duì tā hèn bù qǐlái. *I can't hate him.* 仇恨 chóuhèn 愤恨 fènhèn 痛恨 tònghèn

❷ [动]遗憾；懊悔：regret; be sorry that; feel remorse; repent | ～铁不成钢 hèn tiě bù chéng gāng *feel disappointed that sb. does not live up to one's expectations* 悔恨 huǐhèn

◇ 恨不得 hènbudé how one wish one could; one would if one could; itch to

哼 hēng 10画 口部

哼 哼哼哼哼哼哼哼哼 哼哼

❶ [动]鼻子发出声音：groan | 那个病人昨天～了一整夜。Nàge bìngrén zuótiān hēngle yī zhěngyè. *The patient groaned for a whole night last night.*

❷ [动]低声唱：sing in a low voice | 他边走边～着小调。Tā biān zǒu biān hēngzhe xiǎodiào. *He hummed a tune as he walked along.*

See hèng.

恒 héng 9画 忄部

恒 恒恒恒恒恒恒恒恒
恒

[形]长久；固定不变的：permanent;
lasting; solid; fixed; constant
恒星 héngxīng star
永恒 yǒnghéng

横 héng 15画 木部

横 横横横横横横横横
横横横横横横横

❶[形]（跟"竖shù""直zhí""纵
zòng"相对）：horizontal (the
opposite of "竖shù""直zhí"
or "纵zòng")｜～梁héngliáng
crossbeam ／人行～道 rénxíng
héngdào *pedestrian crossing;
zebra crossing*
纵横 zònghéng

❷[形]蛮不讲理：impervious; per-
sistent in being unreasonable
｜～加阻拦 héngjiā zǔlán *wil-
fully obstruct*
横行 héngxíng run wild; run
amuck; be on a rampage

❸[动]使物体变成横向：move cross-
wise; traverse｜这条铁路～贯全
国。Zhè tiáo tiělù héngguàn
quánguó. *The railway traverses*

the country.｜把扁担～过来放。
Bǎ biǎndan héng guòlai
fàng. *Put the carrying pole in a
horizontal position.*

❹[动]下定决心，不顾一切：resolve
to do sth. despite any obstacle｜
他～下一条心，决定与她分手。
Tā héngxia yī tiáo xīn,
juédìng yǔ tā fēnshǒu. *He has
decided to break up with her.*

❺[名]汉字的笔画，平着从左向右，
形状是"一"：a stroke in Chinese
characters written from left to
right
See hèng.

衡 héng 16画 彳部

衡 衡衡衡衡衡衡衡衡
衡衡衡衡衡衡衡衡

❶[动]掂量；比较：weigh; compare
｜权～quánhéng *weigh*
衡量 héngliáng weigh; mea-
sure; judge

❷[形]平：flat; level; even; smooth
平衡 pínghéng

哼 hèng 10画 口部

哼 哼哼哼哼哼哼哼哼
哼哼

[叹]表示不满、瞧不起或气愤：ex-
pressing dissatisfaction, contempt or anger｜～，没这么便

315

宜！Hēng, méi zhème piányi! *Humph, I won't let him off so lightly.*

See hēng.

横 hēng 15画 木部

横横横横横横横横横横横横横横横

❶[形]粗暴；凶狠的：rough; fierce and malicious; malevolent ｜ 蛮～mánhēng *rude and unreasonable* / 专～zhuānhēng *imperious; peremptory; domineering*

❷[形]意外的：unexpected ｜ ～财 hèngcái *ill-gotten wealth* / ～祸 hènghuò *unexpected calamity*

See hēng.

轰（轟）hōng 8画 车部

轰轰轰轰轰轰轰轰

❶[拟声]表示巨大的声响：bang; boom ｜ ～的一声巨响，震得地动山摇。Hōng de yī shēng jùxiǎng, zhèn de dìdòngshānyáo. *The explosion shook the earth with a big bang.*

❷[动]打雷、爆炸或炮击：rumble; bombard; explode ｜ ～击 hōngjī *bombard*
轰炸 hōngzhà bomb

❸[动]驱赶：drive out ｜ 把猫～出去。Bǎ māo hōng chūqu. *Drive away the cat.; Shoo the cat away.*

◇轰动 hōngdòng cause a sensation; make a stir
轰轰烈烈 hōnghōng-lièliè on a grand and spectacular scale; vigorous

烘 hōng 10画 火部

烘烘烘烘烘烘烘烘烘烘

[动]烤：bake; roast; toast

红（紅）hóng 6画 纟部

红红红红红红

❶[形]red ｜ ～玫瑰 hóng méigui *red rose* / 万紫千～wànzǐqiānhóng *a riot of colours* / 山上的枫叶都～了。Shānshang de fēngyè dōu hóng le. *All the maple leaves have turned red over hill and dale.*

红包 hóngbāo red paper envelope containing money as a gift, tip, or bonus
红茶 hóngchá black tea
红灯 hóngdēng red light
红牌 hóngpái red card (warning card used in some ball games

by the referee to punish players who commit flagrant fouls)

红旗 hóngqí red flag or banner

红色 hóngsè red colour

红烧 hóngshāo braised in soy sauce

红领巾 hónglǐngjīn ① red scarf (worn by Chinese Young Pioneers) ② Young Pioneer

红楼梦 Hónglóumèng *Dream of the Red Chamber* (a Chinese classic)

通红 tōnghóng 鲜红 xiānhóng 西红柿 xīhóngshì

❷ [形] 象征喜庆、顺利、成功或受人重视、欢迎等: symbolizing a happy event or occasion, success, etc. | 开门~ kāiménhóng *get off to a good start* / 满堂~ mǎntánghóng *success in every field* / 她唱戏唱~了。Tā chàngxì chànghóng le. *She has won success as a Chinese traditional opera singer.*

红火 hónghuǒ (dial.) flourishing; prosperous

当红 dānghóng

❸ [形] 象征革命或政治觉悟高的: symbolizing revolutionariness, high political consciousness | ~军 hóngjūn *the Red Army*

◇ 红利 hónglì bonus; extra dividend

宏 hóng 7画 宀部

宏 宏宏宏宏宏宏宏

[形] 广大: great; grand; magnificent | ~观 hóngguān *macroscopic*

宏大 hóngdà grand; great

宏伟 hóngwěi magnificent; grand

虹 hóng 9画 虫部

虹 虹虹虹虹虹虹虹虹虹

[名] rainbow | 彩~ cǎihóng *rainbow*

洪 hóng 9画 氵部

洪 洪洪洪洪洪洪洪洪洪

❶ [名] 大水: flood | 防~ fánghóng *flood control* / 抗~ kànghóng *fight (combat) a flood*

❷ [形] 大: big; vast

洪水 hóngshuǐ flood; floodwater

哄 hǒng 9画 口部

哄 哄哄哄哄哄哄哄哄哄

❶ [动] 用假话骗人: fool; humbug | 你不要~我。Nǐ bùyào hǒng wǒ. *Don't kid me.*

❷ [动]用言语或行动引人高兴，特指照顾小孩儿：coax; humour, especially referring to attending children | 他很会～小孩儿。Tā hěn huì hǒng xiǎohái'r. *He knows how to handle children.; He has a way with children.* / 妈妈～孩子睡觉。Māma hǒng háizi shuìjiào. *The mother coaxed her child to sleep.*

    See hǒng.

 hōng 9画 口部

哄哄哄哄哄哄哄哄哄

[动]吵闹；开玩笑：be in an uproar; horseplay | 起～qǐhōng *(of a crowd of people) intentionally create a disturbance; boo and hoot*

    一哄而散 yīhōng'érsàn

    See hǒng.

 hóu 9画 亻部

侯侯侯侯侯侯侯侯侯

[名]古代贵族的一种爵位：a nobleman or a high official in ancient times | 王～wánghóu *aristocrats*

 hóu 12画 口部

喉喉喉喉喉喉喉喉喉喉喉喉

See 喉咙

    喉咙 hóulóng throat

 hóu 12画 犭部

猴猴猴猴猴猴猴猴猴猴猴猴

See 猴子

    猴子 hóuzi monkey

 hǒu 7画 口部

吼吼吼吼吼吼吼

❶ [动]猛兽大声叫：(of animals) roar; howl | 狮子～shīzi hǒu *the roar of a lion*

❷ [动]发怒或情绪激动时大声喊叫：shout out of anger or excitement | 不要对我大～大叫。Bùyào duì wǒ dà hǒu dà jiào. *Don't yell at me.*

    怒吼 nùhǒu

❸ [动]泛指发出巨大的响声：roar; howl | 汽笛一声长～qìdí yī shēng cháng hǒu *the long howl of the steam whistle*

 (後 ❷–❻) hòu 6画 厂部

后后后后后后

❶ [名]帝王的妻子；empress; queen
皇后 huánghòu
王后 wánghòu
❷ [形]时间上较晚的；未来的（跟"先xiān""前qián"相对）：later in time; coming; approaching; future (the opposite of "先xiān" or "前qián") | 先来～到xiānlái-hòudào *in the order of arrival; first come, first served* / 不久以～bùjiǔ yǐhòu *soon after*
后代 hòudài ① later periods (in history); later ages ② later generations; descendants; posterity
后果 hòuguǒ consequence; aftermath
后患 hòuhuàn future trouble
后悔 hòuhuǐ regret; repent
后来 hòulái afterwards; later
后年 hòunián the year after next
后期 hòuqī later stage; later period
后天 hòutiān ① the day after tomorrow ② postnatal; acquired
大后年 dàhòunián
大后天 dàhòutiān
思前想后 sīqián-xiǎnghòu
❸ [名]空间位置在背面的（跟"前qián"相对）：rear; behind; back (the opposite of "前qián") | 向～转xiàng hòu zhuǎn *about-turn* / 他朝～看了一眼。Tā cháo hòu kànle yī yǎn. *He looked back.*
后边 hòubian behind

后方 hòufāng rear
后面 hòumian ① at the back; in the rear; behind ② later
后勤 hòuqín rear service; logistics
后台 hòutái ① backstage ② backstage supporter; behind-the-scenes backer
后头 hòutou at the back; in the rear
后退 hòutuì draw back; fall back; retreat
开后门 kāihòumén
拖后腿 tuōhòutuǐ
走后门儿 zǒuhòuménr
❹ [形]次序靠近末尾的：last; back (in sequence) | ～排 hòupái *back row* / ～十名 hòu shí míng *the last ten (persons)*
后者 hòuzhě the latter
前赴后继 qiánfù-hòujì
争先恐后 zhēngxiān-kǒnghòu
❺ [词尾]指在某事或某时间以后：(of time) later; (of an event) yet to come
博士后 bóshìhòu
❻ [名]子孙，后代：offspring; posterity | ～人 hòurén ① *later generations* ② *posterity; descendants*
◇善后 shànhòu

hòu   9画 厂部

厚 厚厚厚厚厚厚厚厚厚

❶[形]扁平物上下两面的距离较大（跟"薄 báo"相对）：thick (the opposite of "薄 báo")｜～棉被 hòu miánbèi *a thick quilt* ∕ ～木板 hòu mùbǎn *a thick plank*

❷[名]厚度；扁平物体上下两面间的距离：thickness｜昨夜雪落得很～。Zuóyè xuě luò de hěn hòu. *It snowed heavily last night.*
厚度 hòudù thickness

❸[形]（利润）大；（礼物）重；（味道）浓：(of profit) big; (of gifts) large; (of taste) rich or strong｜这礼太～了。Zhè lǐ tài hòu le. *The gifts are too generous.* ∕ 酒味很～。Jiǔwèi hěn hòu. *The wine tastes pure and strong.*
丰厚 fēnghòu　浓厚 nónghòu
雄厚 xiónghòu

❹[动]优待；重视；推崇：favour; stress｜～待 hòudài *treat sb. kindly*

❺[形]（感情）深：deep; profound｜深情～意 shēnqíng-hòuyì *profound affection*
深厚 shēnhòu

候
候候候候候候候候候
候候

hòu　10画　亻部

❶[动]看望、问安：visit and inquire after; send one's regards
伺候 cìhou　　侍候 shìhòu

问候 wènhòu

❷[动]等待：wait｜稍～片刻。Shāo hòu piànkè. *Wait a minute.*
候补 hòubǔ be a candidate (for a vacancy)
候选人 hòuxuǎnrén candidate
等候 děnghòu　恭候 gōnghòu
守候 shǒuhòu

❸[名]时间、季节：time; season｜气～ qìhòu *climate*
候鸟 hòuniǎo migratory bird; migrant
时候 shíhou

乎
乎乎乎乎乎乎

hū　5画　丿部

[助]用在文言文的句子末尾，表示疑问、反问等语气，相当于"吗 ma"：used at the end of a sentence in classical Chinese as a question or rhetorical question, same as "吗 ma" in Chinese vernacular

呼
呼呼呼呼呼呼呼呼

hū　8画　口部

❶[动]往外出气（跟"吸 xī"相对）：breathe out (the opposite of "吸 xī")｜他深深地～了一口气。Tā shēnshēn de hūle yī kǒu qì.

He exhaled a deep breath.

呼吸 hūxī breathe; respire

呼吸道 hūxīdào respiratory tract

❷[动]大喊；shout out; call out | ～口号 hū kǒuhào *shout slogans* / 大声疾～dàshēng-jíhū *shout loudly; call for*

呼唤 hūhuàn call; shout to

呼声 hūshēng cry; voice

呼啸 hūxiào whistle; scream; whiz

呼吁 hūyù appeal; call on

欢呼 huānhū

❸[动]唤；叫(人来)：call out; summon; call sb. | 直～姓名zhí hū xìngmíng *address sb. by name*

称呼 chēnghu　招呼 zhāohu

打招呼 dǎzhāohu

❹[拟声]模拟刮风、吹气等的声音：imitating the blowing of wind and the exhaling of breath | 北风～～。Běifēng hūhū. *The north wind is whistling.*

呼呼 hūhū onomatopoeia, imitating the sound of the wind

 hū　8画 心部

忽忽忽忽忽忽忽忽忽

❶[动]不注意；粗心：neglect; overlook; ignore

忽略 hūlüè neglect; overlook; lose sight of

忽视 hūshì ignore; overlook; neglect

疏忽 shūhu

❷[副]表示情况发生得迅速而又出人意料：used to indicate sth. happens rapidly and out of one's expectation | ～冷～热 hūlěng-hūrè *cold one minute and hot the next* / ～高～低 hūgāo-hūdī *sudden shifts of mood; in high spirits one moment and in low spirits the next* / ～明～暗 hūmíng-hū'àn *flash and die by turns; flicker*

忽然 hūrán suddenly; all of a sudden

 hú　8画 犭部

狐狐狐狐狐狐狐狐

See 狐狸

狐狸 húli fox

 hú　8画 弓部

弧弧弧弧弧弧弧弧

[名]圆周上的任意一段：part of a curved line or circle | ～形 húxíng *arc* / 圆～yuánhú *arc*

 (鬍 ❷) hú　9画 月部

胡胡胡胡胡胡胡胡胡

❶[副]不认真；随意乱来：in a messy manner; carelessly; at will | ~来 húlái ① mess things up; fool with sth. ② run wild; make trouble / 你在书上~写些什么呀！Nǐ zài shū shang húxiě xiē shénme ya! *What are you scribbling on the book?*

胡乱 húluǎn carelessly; casually; at random

胡说 húshuō ① talk nonsense; drivel ② nonsense

❷[名]胡子：beard; moustache or whiskers | ~须 húxū *beard*

胡子 húzi beard; moustache or whiskers

◇胡同 hútòng lane; alley

胡琴 húqin *huqin*, a general term for certain two-stringed bowed instruments, such as *erhu*, *jinghu*, etc.

胡萝卜 húluóbo carrot

二胡 èrhú

壶（壺）hú　10画 士部

壶 壶 壶 壶 壶 壶 壶 壶 壶 壶

[名]盛液体的用具，一般有嘴儿和把儿：kettle, pot, vessel with handle and spout for holding liquid | 铜~ tónghú *copper kettle* / 水~ shuǐhú *kettle* / ~里有水。Hú li yǒu shuǐ. *There is some water in the kettle.*

葫　hú　12画 艹部

葫 葫 葫 葫 葫 葫 葫 葫 葫 葫 葫 葫

See 葫芦

葫芦 húlu bottle gourd; calabash

湖　hú　12画 氵部

湖 湖 湖 湖 湖 湖 湖 湖 湖 湖 湖 湖

[名]lake | ~光山色 húguāngshānsè *the landscape of lakes and mountains* / ~里养了许多鱼。Hú li yǎngle xǔduō yú. *A lot of fish are raised in the lake.*

湖泊 húpō lakes

西湖 Xī Hú

蝴　hú　15画 虫部

蝴 蝴 蝴 蝴 蝴 蝴 蝴 蝴 蝴 蝴 蝴 蝴 蝴 蝴 蝴

See 蝴蝶

蝴蝶 húdié butterfly

糊　hú　15画 米部

糊 糊 糊 糊 糊 糊 糊 糊 糊 糊 糊 糊 糊 糊 糊

[动]粘贴：paste | ~窗户 hú chuāng-

hu *paste a piece of paper over a lattice window* / 你的书皮破了，我替你～好。Nǐ de shūpí pò le, wǒ tì nǐ húhǎo. *This book cover of yours has been worn out. Let me mend it for you.*
◇糊涂 hútu muddled; confused; bewildered

hǔ   8画 虎部
虎 虎虎虎虎虎虎虎虎

[名]tiger | 驯～xùn hǔ *train a tiger*
◇ 马马虎虎 mǎmǎhūhū

hù   4画 一部
互 互互互互

[副]表示彼此进行相同的动作或具有相同的关系：mutually; each other / ～教～学 hùjiāo-hùxué *teach and learn from each other* / ～不干涉 hù bù gānshè *mutual noninterference*
互补 hùbǔ ① be at a supplementary angle to each other ② mutually complement
互动 hùdòng interact; interaction
互利 hùlì mutually beneficial
互相 hùxiāng mutual; each other
互助 hùzhù help each other

互联网 hùliánwǎng Internet
相互 xiānghù

hù   4画 户部
户 户户户户

❶[名]门：door | 门～ménhù *door; important passageway*
户外 hùwài outdoors; open air; the wild
❷[名]住户；人家：household; family | 千家万～qiānjiā-wànhù *innumerable households or families; every family*
户籍 hùjí ① census register; household register ② registered permanent residence
户口 hùkǒu ①number of households and total population ② registered permanent residence
客户 kèhù   农户 nónghù
用户 yònghù   住户 zhùhù
家家户户 jiājiā-hùhù
家喻户晓 jiāyù-hùxiǎo
❸[名]门第：family status
门当户对 méndāng-hùduì
❹[名]指建立了正式财物往来关系的个人或团体：individual or group which has opened an account with a bank | 账～zhànghù *account* / 开～kāihù *open an account*
过户 guòhù
◇个体户 gètǐhù
专业户 zhuānyèhù

（護）hù　　7画 扌部

护 护护护护护护护

❶ [动]保卫; 照顾: guard; care for | 看～kānhù *look after* / ～航 hùháng *escort; convoy*

护栏 hùlán ① iron railing by the roadside or between a roadway and the sidewalk ② guardrail; protective railing (fence)

护理 hùlǐ nurse; tend and protect

护士 hùshi (hospital) nurse

爱护 àihù　　保护 bǎohù
辩护 biànhù　　防护 fánghù
维护 wéihù　　掩护 yǎnhù
拥护 yōnghù
救护车 jiùhùchē

❷ [动]偏袒; 包庇: be partial to; shield; harbour; cover up | ～短 hùduǎn *shield a shortcoming or fault* / 不要总是～着他。Būyào zǒngshì hùzhe tā. *Don't be partial to him all the time.*

◇护照 hùzhào passport

huā　　7画 艹部

花 花花花花花花花

❶ [名] flower | 开～kāihuā *come into bloom* / 一束～儿 yī shù huār *a bunch of flowers*

花茶 huāchá scented tea
花朵 huāduǒ flower
荷花 héhuā　　菊花 júhuā
葵花 kuíhuā　　兰花 lánhuā
梅花 méihuā　　棉花 miánhua
桃花 táohuā　　樱花 yīnghuā
牵牛花 qiānniúhuā
水仙花 shuǐxiānhuā

❷ [名]可供观赏的植物: ornamentary plant | 栽～zāihuā *cultivate flowers* / 赏～shǎnghuā *admire flowers*

花园 huāyuán flower garden; garden

鲜花 xiānhuā
百花齐放 bǎihuā-qífàng
奇花异草 qíhuā-yìcǎo

❸ [名]像花朵的东西: sth. like a flower in shape | 雪～xuěhuā *snowflakes* / 火～huǒhuā *spark*

窗花 chuānghuā

❹ [名]烟火的一种: a kind of fireworks | 礼～lǐhuā *fireworks* / 放～fànghuā *set off fireworks*

烟花 yānhuā

❺ [名]花纹; 图案: decorative pattern; figure; pattern; design | 她织的～儿真好看。Tā zhī de huār zhēn hǎokàn. *The patterns she knitted are really beautiful.*

花轿 huājiào (old) bridal sedan chair

花色 huāsè ①design and colour

②(merchandise) a variety of designs, sizes, and colours

花纹 huāwén pattern; design

花样 huāyàng pattern; variety

绣花 xiùhuā

❻[形]有花纹的; 颜色或种类错杂的: multicoloured; variegated | 头发～白 tóufa huābái *grey-haired* / ～边 huābiān *decorative border; lace* / 那只猫是～的。Nà zhī māo shì huā de. *The cat is variegated.*

五花八门 wǔhuā-bāmén

❼[形](看东西)模糊: not clear; confusing | ～眼 huāyǎn *presbyopia; be dazzled* / 眼～了。Yǎn huā le. *The eyes are blurred.*

❽[形]用来迷惑人的; 不真实或不真诚的: tending to confuse or puzzle; false; dishonest | 耍～招 shuǎ huāzhāo *play tricks* / ～言巧语 huāyán-qiǎoyǔ *fancy words and fine promises; sweet talk; flattery*

❾[名]作战时受的外伤: wound received in action | 挂～ guàhuā *be wounded (in action)*

❿[动]耗费; 用: spend; expend; use | ～钱 huāqián *spend money* / ～功夫 huā gōngfu *spend time* / 我～了不少时间查对资料。Wǒ huāle bùshǎo shíjiān cháduì zīliào. *I have spent a lot of time checking the data.*

花费 huāfèi money spent; expenditure; expenses

◇花卷 huājuǎn steamed twisted roll

花生 huāshēng peanut; groundnut

花花公子 huāhuā gōngzǐ dandy; coxcomb; fop

 哗 (嘩) huā 9画 口部

哗哗哗哗哗哗哗哗哗

[拟声]模拟流水、下雨等的声音: imitating the sound of flowing water and downpouring rain | 水～～地流。Shuǐ huāhuā de liú. *The water went gurgling.* / 铁门～的一声打开了。Tiěmén huā de yī shēng dǎkāi le. *The iron gate was pulled open with a clang.* / 风吹得树叶～～直响。Fēng chuī de shùyè huāhuā zhí xiǎng. *The leaves rustled in the wind.*

哗哗 huāhuā gurgle

 划 (劃❸) huá 6画 戈部

划划划划划划

❶[动]拨水前进: paddle (a boat) forward | ～船 huá chuán *paddle (row) a boat; go boating* / 船从对岸～过来了。Chuán cóng duì'àn huá guòlai le. *A boat came from the opposite bank.*

皮划艇 pí huá tǐng

❷[形]合算：to one's advantage; to one's profit | ~得来 huádelái *be worth it*

❸[动]用尖锐的东西割开或擦过物体表面：scratch; cut sth. with a knife or sth. else | ~玻璃 huá bōli *cut a piece of glass* / ~火柴 huá huǒchái *strike a match* / 他的手~破了。Tā de shǒu huápò le. *His hands were scratched.*

See huà.

华 (華) huá 6画 十部

华 华华华华华华

❶[形]繁荣：prosperous; flourishing | 荣~富贵 rónghuá-fùguì *high rank and great wealth*
繁华 fánhuá

❷[形]光彩好看：lustrous; splendid; radiant; pleasing to the eye
华丽 huálì magnificent; resplendent; gorgeous
豪华 háohuá   奢华 shēhuá

❸[名]事物最美好的部分：best part; cream; essence
才华 cáihuá   精华 jīnghuá

❹[名]指中国：China | ~夏 Huá-xià *China*
华侨 huáqiáo overseas Chinese
华人 huárén Chinese people

中华 Zhōnghuá
◇嘉年华 jiāniánhuá

猾 huá 12画 犭部

猾 猾猾猾猾猾猾猾猾猾 猾猾猾猾

[形]奸诈；不诚实：cunning; dishonest
狡猾 jiǎohuá

滑 huá 12画 氵部

滑 滑滑滑滑滑滑滑滑 滑滑滑滑

❶[形]smooth | 下雨天路~。Xiàyǔ tiān lù huá. *The road is slippery when it rains.* / 桌面很光~。Zhuōmiàn hěn guānghuá. *The tabletop is very smooth.*
光滑 guānghuá

❷[动]在光滑的物体表面迅速移动：slip; slide | 他冰~得很好。Tā bīng huá de hěn hǎo. *He is good at skating.*
滑冰 huábīng ice-skating; skating
滑坡 huápō (geol.) landslide; landslip
滑雪 huáxuě skiing

❸[形]不诚实；狡诈：cunning; crafty; slippery | 这人很~。Zhè rén hěn huá. *This person is very crafty.*

油腔滑调 yóuqiāng-huádiào

化 huà 4画 亻部

化 化化化化

❶[动]改变原来的性质或状态：change; turn; transform | ~整为零 huàzhěng-wéilíng *break up the whole into parts*
化名 huàmíng (use an) assumed name; alias
化妆 huàzhuāng put on makeup; make up
化妆品 huàzhuāngpǐn cosmetics, including rouge, powder, lipstick, perfume, etc.
变化 biànhuà
造化 zàohua
转化 zhuǎnhuà
千变万化 qiānbiàn-wànhuà
❷[动]用言语行动影响人，使人转变：convert; influence | 教~ jiàohuà *educate* / 开~ kāihuà *become civilized*
感化 gǎnhuà
❸[动]融解；消散：melt; thaw | 冰~了。Bīng huà le. *The ice has melted.*
熔化 rónghuà 融化 rónghuà
❹[动]消除；消化：digest | ~食 huàshí *help digestion*
消化 xiāohuà
❺[名]化学的简称：short form for chemistry
化肥 huàféi chemical fertilizer
化工 huàgōng chemical industry
化合 huàhé chemical combination
化纤 huàxiān chemical fibre
化学 huàxué chemistry
化验 huàyàn chemical examination; laboratory test
❻[词尾]附在名词或形容词后，表示转变成某种性质或状态：suffix attached to a noun or adjective to indicate transforming to a certain property or state | 现代~ xiàndàihuà *modernization* / 科学~ kēxuéhuà *resort to science; apply scientific knowledge to sth.*

淡化 dànhuà	恶化 èhuà
分化 fēnhuà	腐化 fǔhuà
简化 jiǎnhuà	进化 jìnhuà
净化 jìnghuà	开化 kāihuà
绿化 lǜhuà	美化 měihuà
强化 qiánghuà	
氧化 yǎnghuà	优化 yōuhuà
标准化 biāozhǔnhuà	
工业化 gōngyèhuà	
数字化 shùzìhuà	

◇二氧化碳 èryǎnghuàtàn

划 (劃) huà 6画 戈部

 划 划划划划划划

❶[动]把整体分开：divide; carve out | ~清界限 huàqīng jièxiàn *draw a clear line of de-*

marcation / ~分区域 huàfēn qūyù *divide a region into certain areas*

划分 huàfēn ① *divide* ② *differentiate*

❷[动]计划、拟定做事的办法和步骤等：*make plans to do sth.* | 筹~chóuhuà *plan and prepare*

策划 cèhuà　规划 guīhuà　计划 jìhuà

❸[动](把账目或钱物)分出来拨给：*appropriate; transfer (funds on account or money)* | ~款 huàkuǎn *transfer money; (of money) distribute and hand out* / ~拨 huàbō *transfer*

See huà.

画 (畫) huà　8画 凵部

 画 画 画 画 画 画 画 画

❶[动]draw; paint | ~个圈 huà ge quān *draw a circle* / ~地图 huà dìtú *draw a map*

画家 huàjiā *painter; artist*

画像 huàxiàng ① *draw a portrait; portray* ② *portrait; portrayal*

画蛇添足 huàshé-tiānzú *draw a snake and add feet to it; ruin the overall effect by adding sth. superfluous*

绘画 huìhuà

❷[名]绘出的图画：*painting* | 一张~儿 yī zhāng huàr *a picture*

/ 风景~fēngjǐnghuà *landscape painting*

画报 huàbào *illustrated magazine or newspaper; pictorial*

画面 huàmiàn ① *general appearance of a picture; tableau* ② *(movie) frame*

动画 dònghuà　漫画 mànhuà

书画 shūhuà　图画 túhuà

油画 yóuhuà　字画 zìhuà

诗情画意 shīqíng-huàyì

话 (話) huà　8画 讠部

话 话 话 话 话 话 话 话 话

❶[名]说出或写出的语言：*spoken or written word* | 普通~ pǔtōnghuà *Putonghua; standard Chinese pronunciation* / 无~可说 wúhuà-kěshuō *have nothing to say* / 这些~很有道理。Zhèxiē huà hěn yǒu dàolǐ. *These words are reasonable.* / 这些~说得太好了。Zhèxiē huà shuō de tài hǎo le. *These remarks are wonderful.*

废话 fèihuà　讲话 jiǎnghuà

空话 kōnghuà　梦话 mènghuà

神话 shénhuà　实话 shíhuà

说话 shuōhuà　俗话 súhuà

听话 tīnghuà　通话 tōnghuà

童话 tónghuà　闲话 xiánhuà

笑话 xiàohuà

好说话 hǎoshuōhuà

客套话 kètàohuà

闹笑话 nàoxiàohuà
说大话 shuōdàhuà
说闲话 shuōxiánhuà

❷ [动]说；谈：say; speak ｜～别 huàbié *say good-bye* ／～家常 huà jiācháng *chitchat*

话费 huàfèi payment for telephone service

话剧 huàjù modern drama; stage play

话题 huàtí subject of a talk; topic of a conversation

话筒 huàtǒng ① microphone ② telephone transmitter ③ megaphone

电话 diànhuà   对话 duìhuà
会话 huìhuà   谈话 tánhuà
电话卡 diànhuàkǎ
电话亭 diànhuàtíng
公用电话 gōngyòng diànhuà
◇不像话 bùxiànghuà

 怀（懷）huái   7画 忄部

怀 怀怀怀怀怀怀怀

❶ [名]胸部；胸前：thorax; chest; bosom ｜把小孩儿抱在～里 bǎ xiǎoháir bào zài huáili *hold a child in one's arms (or to one's bosom)*

❷ [动]想念：miss; cherish ｜～乡 huáixiāng *be homesick*

怀念 huáiniàn cherish the memory of; think of

关怀 guānhuái

❸ [动]心中存有：harbour; entertain; cherish ｜不～好意 bù huái hǎoyì *harbour evil designs* ／胸～壮志 xiōnghuái-zhuàngzhì *harbour great ambitions; have lofty aspirations*

怀疑 huáiyí doubt; suspect
满怀 mǎnhuái
◇怀孕 huáiyùn pregnant

 槐 huái   13画 木部

槐 槐槐槐槐槐槐槐槐 槐槐槐槐槐

See 槐树
槐树 huáishù pagoda tree; Chinese scholar tree

 坏（壞）huái   7画 土部

坏 坏坏坏坏坏坏坏

❶ [形]东西受到损伤变成无用、有害的：broken and useless; bad ｜自行车～了。Zìxíngchē huài le. *The bicycle is broken.* ／苹果都～了。Píngguǒ dōu huài le. *The apples are all rotten.*

❷ [形]用在一些动词后，作补语表示导致损坏：used after some verbs to serve as a complement indicating the result of ruining ｜摔～shuāihuài *cause to fall*

and break / 弄～nònghuài
ruin; break

❸[动]使人不满意的; 恶劣的(跟"好
hǎo"相对): *dissatisfying; foul;*
bad (the opposite of "好 hǎo")
| ～脾气 huài píqi *bad temper*
/ ～主意 huài zhǔyì *bad idea*
/ ～天气 huài tiānqì *bad (foul)*
weather
坏处 huàichu *harm; disadvan-*
tage
坏蛋 huàidàn *scoundrel; bas-*
tard
❹[形]表示程度深: *expressing a*
high degree | 累～了 lèihuài le
be extremely tired; be exhausted
/ 气～了 qìhuài le *be beside*
oneself with rage / 真把我忙～
了。Zhēn bǎ wǒ mánghuài le.
I was extremely busy.

 (歡) huān 6画又部

欢 欢欢欢欢欢欢

[形]快乐; 高兴: joyous; merry;
jubilant
欢呼 huānhū *hail; cheer; ac-*
claim
欢乐 huānlè *happy; joyous; gay*
欢送 huānsòng *see off; send off*
欢喜 huānxǐ ① *joyful; happy;*
delighted ②*like; be fond of; de-*
light in
欢笑 huānxiào *laugh heartily*
欢迎 huānyíng *welcome; greet*

联欢 liánhuān　　喜欢 xǐhuan

 (還) huán 7画辶部

还 还还还还还还还

❶[动]返回; 恢复原状: *return; go*
back; return to the original shape
| ～乡 huánxiāng *return to one's*
native place / 生～ shēnghuán
return alive
还原 huányuán *restore (return)*
to the original condition
❷[动]归还: give back | ～钱
huánqián *pay back money* /
把它～给我。Bǎ tā huángěi
wǒ. *Give it back to me.*
还贷 huándài *pay one's loan*
偿还 chánghuán　返还 fǎnhuán
归还 guīhuán　　退还 tuìhuán
❸[动]回报; 回敬: give back; re-
turn; return a compliment | ～
手 huánshǒu *hit back* / ～礼
huánlǐ *present a gift in return*
讨价还价 tǎojià-huánjià
　　See hái.

 (環) huán 8画王部

环 环环环环环环环环

❶[名]圆圈形的东西: ring; loop |
耳～ěrhuán　*earring* / 花～
huāhuán *garland*
❷[动]围绕: surround | ～绕
huánrào *surround* / ～球

huánqiú *round the world* / ～视 huánshì *look around*
环境 huánjìng environment; surroundings; circumstances
循环 xúnhuán
❸[名]指互相关联的许多事物中的一个：used to indicate one of the many interrelated things | 重要一～zhòngyào yī huán *an important link* / 一～扣一～yī huán kòu yī huán *closely linked*
环节 huánjié link

缓(緩) huǎn 12画 纟部

缓 缓缓缓缓缓缓缓缓 缓缓缓缓

❶[形]不紧张；不剧烈：not tense; relaxed; not violent; not fierce | 轻重～急 qīngzhòng huǎnjí *relative importance or urgency* / ～冲 huǎnchōng *buffer*
缓和 huǎnhé relax; ease up; mitigate; alleviate
❷[形]慢（跟"急jí"相对）：slow (the opposite of "急jí") / ～步 huǎnbù *walk unhurriedly*
缓缓 huǎnhuǎn slow; unhurried; in an easy manner
缓慢 huǎnmàn slow
迟缓 chíhuǎn
❸[动]推迟；延迟：put off; defer; postpone; delay | ～兵之计 huǎnbīngzhījì *measures to stave off*

an attack; stalling tactics / ～两天再办 huǎn liǎng tiān zài bàn *postpone sth. for one or two days; do sth. a couple of days later*
缓解 huǎnjiě relieve; alleviate; ease
延缓 yánhuǎn
❹[动]恢复正常的生理状态：come to; revive | 让我～一口气再走吧。Ràng wǒ huǎn yī kǒu qì zài zǒu ba. *Let me have a respite before going on.* / 过了好一阵他才～过来。Guòle hǎo yī zhèn tā cái huǎn guòlai. *He revived after a long time.*

幻 huàn 4画 幺部

幻 幻幻幻幻

❶[形]不可能实现的；不真实的：imaginary rather than existent; unreal; illusory | 梦～ mènghuàn *dream* / 虚～ xūhuàn *unreal; imaginary*
幻想 huànxiǎng illusion; fancy; fantasy
❷[动]不寻常的变化：change magically | 变～ biànhuàn *change irregularly*
幻灯 huàndēng slide show

换 huàn 10画 扌部

换 换换换换换换换换 换换

❶[动]change; alter ｜互～huàhuàn *exchange* ／以物～物 yǐ wù huàn wù *barter*
换取 huànqǔ exchange (barter) sth. for sth.; get in return
兑换 duìhuàn　交换 jiāohuàn
兑换率 duìhuànlǜ
❷[动]变换; 以一种代替另一种: change; convert; replace; swap ｜～衣服 huàn yīfu *change one's clothes* ／你愿意和我～座位吗? Nǐ yuànyì hé wǒ huàn zuòwei ma? *Will you change seats with me?*

huàn　10画　口部

唤唤唤唤唤唤唤唤
唤唤

[动]叫; 呼喊: call; shout ｜呼～ hūhuàn *call* ／～醒 huànxǐng *wake up*

huàn　11画　心部

患患患患患患患患
患患患

❶[名]灾祸; 灾难: trouble; calamity; disaster; misfortune ｜免除水～miǎnchú shuǐhuàn *prevent floods*
后患 hòuhuàn　隐患 yǐnhuàn
有备无患 yǒubèi-wúhuàn
❷[动]生病; 害病: fall ill; suffer from an illness; contract a disease ｜他最近～了一场大病。Tā zuìjìn huànle yī chǎng dàbìng. *He has been seriously ill recently.*
患病 huànbìng suffer from an illness; fall ill
患者 huànzhě sufferer; patient

huāng　9画　艹部

荒荒荒荒荒荒荒荒
荒

❶[形]长满野草的、无人耕种的: waste; uncultivated ｜开～ kāihuāng *open up wasteland* ／地～了。Dì huāng le. *The land lies waste (uncultivated).*
荒地 huāngdì wasteland; uncultivated (undeveloped) land
❷[名]因欠收或无粮引起的灾难: famine; crop failure ｜饥～ jīhuāng *famine*
逃荒 táohuāng　灾荒 zāihuāng
❸[形]人烟稀少; 偏僻: sparsely populated; remote; out-of-the-way; far off ｜～郊 huāngjiāo *wilderness* ／～野 huāngyě *wilderness*
荒凉 huāngliáng bleak and desolate; wild
❹[形]极不合情理的:unreasonable
荒谬 huāngmiù absurd; preposterous
荒唐 huāngtáng ① absurd; fantastic; preposterous ② dissi-

pated; loose; intemperate

慌 huāng 12画 忄部

慌慌慌慌慌慌慌慌慌慌慌慌慌

❶[形]不沉着；忙乱：alarmed; disturbed; agitated; flustered; alarmed and bewildered | ～里～张 huāngli-huāngzhāng hurried and confused / 他做事太～。Tā zuòshì tài huāng. He does things too hurriedly.

慌乱 huāngluàn flurried; flustered; confused

慌忙 huāngmáng in a great rush; in a flurry; hurriedly

慌张 huāngzhāng nervous; flustered; confused

不慌不忙 bùhuāng-bùmáng

❷[动]由慌张而造成某种状态：mental condition caused by agitation | 心里发～xīnli fāhuāng feel nervous / ～了手脚 huāngle shǒujiǎo be panic-stricken; get into a panic / 你要沉住气，不要～。Nǐ yào chénzhù qì, búyào huāng. Be calm. Don't be flustered.

恐慌 kǒnghuāng

❸[形]放在动词或形容词后作补语（读轻声），表示情况或状态达到较高的程度：used after a verb or adjective as a complement to indicate a higher degree of certain condition | 累得～lèidehuang be tired out / 闷得～mèndehuang bored beyond endurance; too stuffy

皇 huáng 9画 白部

皇皇皇皇皇皇皇皇皇

[名]皇帝；君主：emperor; monarch

皇帝 huángdì emperor

皇宫 huánggōng imperial palace

皇冠 huángguān imperial crown, symbolizing imperial power

皇后 huánghòu empress

黄 huáng 11画 黄部

黄黄黄黄黄黄黄黄黄黄黄

❶[形]yellow | ～土地 huángtǔdì yellow soil / 树叶变～了。Shùyè biànhuáng le. Leaves have turned yellow.

黄蜂 huángfēng wasp

黄瓜 huánggua cucumber

黄昏 huánghūn dusk

黄金 huángjīn gold

黄酒 huángjiǔ yellow rice or millet wine; Shaoxing wine

黄牌 huángpái (sports) yellow card

黄色 huángsè ① yellow ② obscene; pornographic
黄油 huángyóu butter
金黄 jīnhuáng
❷ [动]事情失败、计划落空:(of a plan, etc.) fail; fizzle out | 这件事～不了。Zhè jiàn shì huángbuliǎo. *This project will not fail.*
◇黄帝 Huángdì Xuan Yuan, also known as the Yellow Emperor, a legendary ruler of China in remote antiquity; ancestor of Chinese
黄河 Huáng Hé the Huanghe River; the Yellow River
黄山 Huáng Shān Huang-shan Mountain

煌

huáng   13画 火部

煌煌煌煌煌煌煌煌煌煌煌煌煌

[形]明亮: bright; brilliant | 星火～～ xīnghuǒ huánghuáng *bright with sparks*
辉煌 huīhuáng

蝗

huáng   15画 虫部

蝗蝗蝗蝗蝗蝗蝗蝗蝗蝗蝗蝗蝗蝗蝗

See 蝗虫
蝗虫 huángchóng locust

恍

huǎng   9画 忄部

恍恍恍恍恍恍恍恍恍

❶ [形]模糊；不清楚: dim; unable to see clearly
恍惚 huǎnghū absent-minded; faintly
❷ [副]忽然: suddenly; abruptly
恍然大悟 huǎngrán-dàwù suddenly see the light; suddenly realize what has happened

晃

huǎng   10画 日部

晃晃晃晃晃晃晃晃晃晃

❶ [形](亮光)闪耀: dazzling | ～眼 huǎngyǎn *dazzle; make (sb.) unable to see clearly because of too much light* / 明～～ mínghuǎnghuáng *shining; gleaming*
❷ [动]很快地闪过: pass quickly; flash past | 一～半个月过去了。Yī huǎng bàn gè yuè guòqù le. *A fortnight passed in a flash.* / 窗户上有个人影，一～就不见了。Chuānghu shang yǒu ge rényǐng, yī huǎng jiù bùjiàn le. *At the window, a man's shadow flashed past.*
See huàng.

谎（謊）huǎng 11画 讠部

谎 谎谎谎谎谎谎谎谎谎谎谎谎谎

❶[名]假话；不真实的话：lie ǀ 说～
shuōhuǎng *tell lies* / 撒～
sāhuǎng *tell lies*
❷[形]假的；不真实的：false

晃 huǎng 10画 日部

晃 晃晃晃晃晃晃晃晃晃晃

[动]摇动；摆动：shake；sway；
swing；shake from side to side
ǀ 摇头～脑 yáotóu-huǎngnǎo
wag one's head / 树枝来回～。
Shùzhī láihuí huǎng. *The
branches are swaying to and fro.*
摇晃 yáohuàng
See huàng.

灰 huī 6画 火部

灰 灰灰灰灰灰灰

❶[名]物体燃烧后剩下的粉末：ash
ǀ 炉～lúhuī *stove ashes* / 烟～
yānhuī *tobacco or cigarette ash*
❷[名]尘土；(某些)粉末状的东西：
dust；stuff in powder form ǀ
屋里蒙上了一层～。Wū li
méngshàngle yī céng huī.
*Everything in the room is cov-
ered with dust.*
灰尘 huīchén dust；dirt
❸[形]介于黑色和白色之间的颜色：
grey ǀ ～布 huībù *grey cloth* /
天色变～了，大概要下雨了。
Tiānsè biànhuī le, dàgài yào
xiàyǔ le. *The sky is turning
murky grey and looks like it's
going to rain.*
❹[形]消沉；失望：downhearted；
dejected；disappointed；disap-
pointing
灰心 huīxīn lose heart；be discouraged
心灰意懒 xīnhuī-yìlǎn

挥（揮）huī 9画 扌部

挥 挥挥挥挥挥挥挥挥挥

❶[动]举起手臂摆动：raise and
wave one's arm(s) ǀ ～手告别
huīshǒu gàobié *wave farewell*
/ 大笔一～dà bǐ yī huī *with
one stroke of the writing brush*
指挥 zhǐhuī
❷[动]抹去或甩掉(泪、水等)：wipe
away (tears, sweat, etc.) ǀ ～汗
huīhàn *drip with sweat* / ～泪
huīlèi *wipe away tears；shed
tears*
❸[动]散出；散发：sprinkle；scat-
ter；disperse ǀ ～洒 huīsǎ *shed*
/ ～发 huīfā *evaporate*

挥霍 huīhuò spend freely; squander

发挥 fāhuī

恢 huī 9画 忄部

恢 恢恢恢恢恢恢恢恢恢
恢

See 恢复

恢复 huīfù ① resume; renew ② recover; regain

辉 (輝) huī 12画 小部

辉 辉辉辉辉辉辉辉辉辉
辉辉辉辉

[名] 闪耀的光: brightness; shining rays | 余 ~ yúhuī afterglow

辉煌 huīhuáng brilliant; splendid; glorious

光辉 guānghuī

徽 huī 17画 彳部

徽 徽徽徽徽徽徽徽徽徽
徽徽徽徽徽徽徽徽
徽

[名] 标志; 符号: sign; symbol | 国 ~ guóhuī national emblem / 校 ~ xiàohuī school badge

 回 (迴❶❷) huí 6画 口部

回 回回回回回回

❶ [动] 掉转: turn | ~过身来 huíguò shēn lai turn back / 他头也不~就走了。Tā tóu yě bù huí jiū zǒule. He left without turning his head.

回顾 huígù look back; review

回头 huítóu ①turn one's head; turn around ② repent ③ some other time; later

❷ [动] 返回到原来的地方: return to where one came from | ~家 huíjiā go back home / ~国 huíguó return to one's country / ~到原地 huídào yuándì return to where one came from

回归 huíguī ① return ② draw back; fall back; retreat ③ (statistics) regression

回来 huílái(lai) return; come back; be back

回去 huíqù(qu) ① return; go back; come back ② back

回收 huíshōu retrieve; recover; reclaim

回想 huíxiǎng think back; recollect; recall

回忆 huíyì call to mind; recollect; recall

驳回 bóhuí   返回 fǎnhuí
收回 shōuhuí   退回 tuìhuí
挽回 wǎnhuí

❸ [动] 回报; 答复: repay; reciprocate; reply | ~敬 huíjìng do or give sth. in return; return a compliment / 我只~过他一封

信。Wǒ zhǐ huí guo tā yī fēng xìn. *I have only sent him one letter in reply.*

回报 huíbào ① report back on what has been done ② repay; requite; reciprocate ③ retaliate; get one's own back

回答 huídá answer; reply; response

回击 huíjī fight back; return fire; counterattack

回扣 huíkòu sales commission

回信 huíxìn ① write in reply; write back ② a letter in reply

回应 huíyìng answer; respond

回执 huízhí a short note; acknowledging receipt of sth.; receipt

❹[量]指事情、动作的次数：time; occasion | 两~liǎng huí *twice* / 他来过一~。Tā láiguo yī huí. *He has been here once.*

回合 huíhé round; bout

❺[量]用于事情。有 "件" 的意思：a; one | 是这么~事。Shì zhème huí shì. *It's like this.* / 这是怎么~事? Zhè shì zěnme huí shì? *What's the matter?* / 咱俩说的不是一~事。Zánliǎ shuō de bùshì yī huí shì. *We were not talking about the same thing.*

❻[量]章回小说或评书所分的章节：chapter of a Chinese novel or *pingshu* | 第十~ dì shí huí *Chapter 10*

◇回避 huíbì evade; dodge; avoid (meeting sb.)

悔 huǐ 10画 忄部

悔悔悔悔悔悔悔悔悔悔

[动]做错事或说错话后心里责怪自己：regret | 懊~àohuǐ *repent*
悔改 huǐgǎi repent and mend one's ways
悔恨 huǐhèn regret deeply; be bitterly remorseful
后悔 hòuhuǐ

毁 huǐ 13画 殳部

毁毁毁毁毁毁毁毁毁毁毁毁毁

[动]破坏；损坏：destroy; ruin; damage | 好好儿的一个玩具，让你给~了。Hǎohāor de yī gè wánjù, ràng nǐ gěi huǐ le. *What a nice toy, but you have ruined it.*
毁坏 huǐhuài destroy; damage
毁灭 huǐmiè destroy; exterminate
摧毁 cuīhuǐ 烧毁 shāohuǐ
销毁 xiāohuǐ

汇 (匯彙 ❶❷)huì 5画 氵部

汇汇汇汇汇

❶[动]聚集; 综合: come or flow together; synthesize | ～成巨流 huìchéng jùliú *converge into a mighty current*

汇报 huìbào report; give an account of

汇合 huìhé converge; join

汇集 huìjí ①collect; compile ② come together; converge; assemble

❷[名]聚集而成的事物: things collected | ～编 huìbiān *compile*

词汇 cíhuì

❸[动]通过银行或邮局把钱由一地拨付到另一地: remit money from one place to another | 货款已经～出。Huòkuǎn yǐjīng huìchū. *The payment for the goods has been remitted.*

汇款 huìkuǎn ① remit money; make a remittance ②remittance

◇汇率 huìlǜ exchange rate

会（會） huì   6画 人部

会 会会会会会会

❶[动]聚集在一起: get together; assemble; meet | 在哪儿～合? Zài nǎr huìhé? *Where shall we meet?*

会谈 huìtán talks

会同 huìtóng (of handling an affair) jointly with (other organizations concerned)

聚精会神 jùjīng-huìshén

❷[动]见面: meet; see | 我要～一～他。Wǒ yào huìyihuì tā. *I want to meet him.* / 我们偶然相～。Wǒmen ǒurán xiānghuì. *We met by chance.*

会见 huìjiàn (formally) meet with

会客 huìkè receive a visitor (guest)

会面 huìmiàn meet

会晤 huìwù meet

拜会 bàihuì   约会 yuēhuì

再会 zàihuì   照会 zhàohuì

❸[名]有一定目的的集会: meeting | 纪念～jìniànhuì *commemoration meeting* / 这个～一定要开。Zhège huì yīdìng yào kāi. *This meeting must be held.*

会场 huìchǎng meeting place; conference hall

会议 huìyì meeting; conference

会议室 huìyìshì meeting (or conference) room; council chamber

大会 dàhuì   峰会 fēnghuì

集会 jíhuì   酒会 jiǔhuì

聚会 jùhuì   开会 kāihuì

庙会 miàohuì   全会 quánhuì

散会 sànhuì   晚会 wǎnhuì

舞会 wǔhuì   宴会 yànhuì

奥运会 Àoyùnhuì

博览会 bólǎnhuì

演唱会 yǎnchànghuì

音乐会 yīnyuèhuì

展览会 zhǎnlǎnhuì

招待会 zhāodàihuì

座谈会 zuòtánhuì

❹[名]为一定目的而成立的团体、组织：union or association ｜学生～xuéshēnghuì *student union; student association* ／校友～xiàoyǒuhuì *society of alumni*

会员 huìyuán member

工会 gōnghuì　　教会 jiàohuì

团会 tuánhuì　　协会 xiéhuì

学会 xuéhuì　　议会 yìhuì

董事会 dǒngshìhuì

基金会 jījīnhuì

居委会 jūwěihuì

理事会 lǐshìhuì

委员会 wěiyuánhuì

❺[名]中心城市：central city

省会 shěnghuì

❻[名]时机：opportunity; an opportune moment

机会 jīhuì

❼[动]理解；领悟：understand; grasp ｜领～lǐnghuì *understand; grasp*

理会 lǐhuì　　　　体会 tǐhuì

误会 wùhuì

❽[动]熟悉；通晓：know ｜他～法语。Tā huì Fǎyǔ. *He knows French.*

❾[动]擅长：be good at; be skilful ｜你真～说话。Nǐ zhēn huì shuōhuà. *You are so eloquent.*

❿[动]懂得怎样做或有能力做某事：can; be able to ｜他～游泳。Tā huì yóuyǒng. *He can swim.*

⓫[助]表示有可能：expressing possibility ｜今天不～下雨。Jīntiān bù huì xiàyǔ. *It's not likely to rain today.* ／我想他不～不懂。Wǒ xiǎng tā bù huì bù dǒng. *I don't think he may not understand it.*

◇会话 huìhuà conversation (as in a language course)

社会 shèhuì　　　一会儿 yīhuìr

这会儿 zhèhuìr

社会主义 shèhuì zhǔyì

　　See kuài.

绘 (繪)　huì　　9画 纟部

绘 绘绘绘绘绘绘绘绘绘

[动]画出图形：draw; paint ｜～图 huìtú *mapping; charting* ／～制 huìzhì *draw*

绘画 huìhuà drawing; painting

描绘 miáohuì

贿 (賄)　huì　　10画 贝部

贿 贿贿贿贿贿贿贿贿贿贿

❶[动]用财物买通别人替自己做事：buy over; bribe ｜行～xínghuì *practise bribery*

贿赂 huìlù bribe; bribery

❷[名]买通别人所用的财物：bribery

受贿 shòuhuì

秽（穢）huì　11画 禾部

秽秽秽秽秽秽秽秽
秽秽秽

❶[形]肮脏：dirty｜污～wūhuì *filthy*

❷[形]丑恶的；下流的：ugly; abominable; low-down; mean; dirty｜淫～yínhuì *obscene*

惠　huì　12画 心部

惠惠惠惠惠惠惠惠
惠惠惠惠

[名]给予或受到的好处：favour; benefit｜实～shíhuì *material benefit* / 优～yōuhuì *favourable; preferential*
小恩小惠 xiǎo'ēn-xiǎohuì

慧　huì　15画 心部

慧慧慧慧慧慧慧慧
慧慧慧慧慧慧慧

[形]聪明；有才智：clever; talented｜～眼 huìyǎn *insight; mental discernment*
智慧 zhìhuì

昏　hūn　8画 氏部

昏昏昏昏昏昏昏昏

❶[名]天刚黑的时候：dusk｜晨～chénhūn *dawn and dusk*
黄昏 huánghūn

❷[形]黑暗；模糊不清：dark; unclear; murky
天昏地暗 tiānhūn-dì'àn

❸[形]神志不清；糊涂：insane; muddleheaded｜发～fāhūn *feel giddy (or dizzy)*
昏头昏脑 hūntóu-hūnnǎo addle-brained
头昏脑胀 tóuhūn-nǎozhàng

❹[动]失去知觉：lose consciousness｜他～过去了。Tā hūn guòqu le. *He fainted.*
昏迷 hūnmí stupor; coma

婚　hūn　11画 女部

婚婚婚婚婚婚婚婚
婚婚婚

❶[动]男女双方经过合法手续结为夫妻：wed; marry｜已～yǐhūn *married* / 新～xīnhūn *newly-married*

❷[名]婚姻：marriage
婚礼 hūnlǐ wedding ceremony; wedding
婚姻 hūnyīn marriage; matrimony
订婚 dìnghūn　　结婚 jiéhūn

浑（渾）hún　9画 氵部

浑 浑浑浑浑浑浑浑浑
浑

❶ [形]水不清；污浊：(of water) muddy; turbid ｜ ～水坑 húnshuǐkēng *a muddy water pool* 浑浊 húnzhuó muddy; turbid

❷ [形]整个的；满：whole; all over 浑身 húnshēn from head to foot; all over

 魂 hún 13画 鬼部

魂 魂魂魂魂魂魂魂魂
魂魂魂魂魂

[名]迷信的人指能离开肉体而单独存在的精神：soul; spiritual part of a person believed to be able to be existent apart from the human body ｜ 鬼～guǐhún *ghost; spirit* 灵魂 línghún

 混 hún 11画 氵部

混 混混混混混混混混
混混混

❶ [动](不同的东西)掺杂在一起：mix; confuse; mingle ｜ 这两件事不能～在一起。 Zhè liǎng jiàn shì bùnéng hùn zài yīqǐ. *These two matters should not be mixed up.*
混纺 hùnfǎng (text.) blending
混合 hùnhé mix; blend; mingle
混乱 hùnluàn confusion; chaos

混淆 hùnxiáo obscure; confound
混合物 hùnhéwù mixture
混凝土 hùnníngtǔ concrete

❷ [动]用欺骗的手段使人相信假的东西：pass for; pass off as ｜ 你别想～过去。 Nǐ bié xiǎng hùn guòqu. *You can't get by under false pretences.*

❸ [形]不清洁：unclean
混浊 hùnzhuó muddy; turbid

❹ [动]将就过日子：drift along aimlessly ｜ ～日子 hùn rìzi *fool away one's time*

 豁 huō 17画 谷部

豁 豁豁豁豁豁豁豁豁
豁豁豁豁豁豁豁豁
豁

❶ [动]裂开：fissure; crack ｜ ～口 huōkǒu *opening; break* ／这块木板～开了。 Zhè kuài mùbǎn huōkāi le. *There is a crack in the plank.*

❷ [动]狠心舍弃；舍弃：sacrifice; give up ｜ ～出性命 huōchu xìngmìng *risk one's life; go all out regardless of danger to one's life* ／～出几天时间 huōchu jǐ tiān shíjiān *spare several days to do sth.*

 活 huó 9画 氵部

活

活活活活活活活活
活

❶[动]生存；有生命(跟"死 sǐ"相对)：survive; live (the opposite of "死 sǐ") | 通常鱼在水里才能～。Tōngcháng yú zài shuǐ li cái néng huó. *Generally speaking, fish can only live in water.* / 新栽的这棵树～了。Xīn zāi de zhè kē shù huó le. *The newly planted tree is alive.*

活力 huólì vigour; vitality; energy

复活 fùhuó　　搞活 gǎohuó
激活 jīhuó　　生活 shēnghuó
养活 yǎnghuó

❷[名]工作：job; chore | 做～儿 zuòhuór *do some work* / 零～ línghuó *odd jobs* / 重～儿 zhònghuór *heavy work* / 干活儿 gànhuór

❸[名]产品；制成的东西：product; finished work | 这～儿做得真好。Zhè huór zuò de zhēn hǎo. *This job is well done.*

❹[形]生动自然：lively and natural; resourceful | 脑子很～nǎozi hěn huó *have a quick mind*

活泼 huópo lively; vivacious; vivid

活跃 huóyuè ① brisk; active; dynamic ② enliven; animate; invigorate

❺[形]有生命的；在活的状态下的：living; when alive | ～捉 huózhuō *capture alive* / ～字典 huó zìdiǎn *a walking dictionary* / 在他～着的时候 zài tā huózhe de shíhou *during his lifetime (when he was alive)*

❻[形]不固定的；可移动的：not fixed; movable; mobile | 这扇门是～的。Zhè shàn mén shì huó de. *This door can be moved (opened and closed).*

活动 huódòng ① move about; exercise ② shaky; unsteady ③ movable; mobile ④ activity ⑤ use personal influence or irregular means (to achieve certain purpose)

活塞 huósāi (mech.) piston

灵活 línghuó

◇活该 huógāi serve sb. right

活受罪 huóshòuzuì (inf.) suffer a living hell; have a hell of a life

火

huǒ　　4画 火部

火 火火火火

❶[名]物体燃烧时发出的光和焰：fire; flame | 用～取暖 yòng huǒ qǔnuǎn *warm by fire* / ～烧得很旺。Huǒ shāo de hěn wàng. *The fire was roaring.*

火柴 huǒchái match

火车 huǒchē train

火锅 huǒguō hot pot

火花 huǒhuā spark

火箭 huǒjiàn rocket

火力 huǒlì firepower; fire

火热 huǒrè ① burning hot; fervent; fiery ② intimate

火山 huǒshān volcano

火星 huǒxīng ①Mars ② spark

火焰 huǒyàn flame

火灾 huǒzāi fire (as a disaster); conflagration

灯火 dēnghuǒ 点火 diǎnhuǒ

烈火 lièhuǒ

❷[动]指怒气：be angry; be furious ｜ 他～儿了。Tā huǒr le. *He flared up.*

火爆 huǒbào ① (dial.) fiery; irritable ② vigorous; exuberant; lively

发火 fāhuǒ 恼火 nǎohuǒ

怒火 nùhuǒ

❸[名]中医指引起发炎、红肿、烦躁等症状的病因：(in traditional Chinese medicine) internal heat, a cause that leads to inflammation, red swelling, fidgets and other symptoms ｜ 上～shànghuǒ *suffer from excessive internal heat* / 清～qīnghuǒ *reduce the internal heat*

退火 tuìhuǒ

❹[名]指枪炮弹药：firearms; ammunition ｜ 军～jūnhuǒ *munitions*

火药 huǒyào gunpowder; powder

炮火 pàohuǒ

导火线 dǎohuǒxiàn

伙 (夥 ❶-❸) huǒ 6画亻部

伙 伙伙伙伙伙伙

❶[名]同伴：companion; fellow ｜ 同～儿 tónghuǒr *partner; companion; pal*

伙伴 huǒbàn partner; companion

❷[名]由同伴组成的集体：partnership; company ｜ 入～rùhuǒ *join in a partnership or team*

合伙 héhuǒ 团伙 tuánhuǒ

大伙儿 dàhuǒr

❸[量]用于人群：group; crowd ｜ 一～人 yī huǒ rén *a group of people* / 三个一群，五个一～ sān gè yī qún,wǔ gè yī huǒ *in twos and threes*

❹[名]伙食：mess; food ｜ 起～ qǐhuǒ *cook meals* / 包～ bāohuǒ *board*

伙食 huǒshí mess; food; meals

◇伙计 huǒji ① partner ② guy; mate ③ salesman; salesclerk

小伙子 xiǎohuǒzi

或 huǒ 8画 戈部

或 或或或或或或或或

❶[连]表示选择关系：or ｜ 同意～反对 tóngyì huǒ fǎnduì *for or against*

或是 huǒshì or

或者 huòzhě ①perhaps; maybe ② or; either...or...

❷[连]表示几种交替的情况：either...or... | ～去～留 huò qù huò liú *either stay or leave*

或多或少 huòduō-huòshǎo more or less; to a greater or lesser extent; in varying degrees

◇或许 huòxǔ perhaps; maybe

货 (貨) huò　8画 贝部

货货货货货货货货货

❶[名]商品；供出售的商品：goods; commodity; commodity for sale | ～真价实 huòzhēn-jiàshí *genuine goods at a fair price* / 这个店里的～很便宜。Zhège diàn li de huò hěn piányi. *The goods of this shop are very cheap.* / 明天店里来新～。Míngtiān diàn li lái xīnhuò. *We'll have some new goods delivered to our store tomorrow.*

货物 huòwù　goods; commodity; merchandise

百货 bǎihuò　　订货 dìnghuò
定货 dìnghuò　期货 qīhuò
售货 shòuhuò
冒牌货 màopáihuò

❷[名]钱：money
货币 huòbì　money; currency

获 (獲❶❷ 穫❸)huò 10画 艹部

获 获获获获获获获获 获获

❶[动]捉住；抓住：capture; get hold of | 捕～bǔhuò *catch* / 缴～jiǎohuò *capture*
查获 cháhuò　　破获 pòhuò
抓获 zhuāhuò

❷[动]得到；取得：get; obtain; achieve | ～奖 huòjiǎng *win a prize* / ～胜 huòshèng *win victory*
获得 huòdé gain; obtain; acquire; win; achieve
获取 huòqǔ obtain; gain; procure
荣获 rónghuò
不劳而获 bùláo'érhuò

❸[动]收割庄稼：gather (bring) in the crops
收获 shōuhuò

祸 (禍) huò　11画 礻部

祸 祸祸祸祸祸祸祸 祸祸祸

❶[名]危害性大的事情；灾难（跟"福fú"相对）：misfortune; disaster (the opposite of "福fú") | 闯～chuǎnghuò *get into trouble; bring disaster* / 大～临头 dàhuò-líntóu *disaster is imminent*
车祸 chēhuò

❷[动]损害；危害：harm; damage; endanger; imperil | ～国殃民

huòguó-yāngmín *bring calamity to the country and the people*

祸害 huòhai ① disaster; curse; scourge ② damage; destroy

惑 huò 12画 心部

❶ [形]不明白：be puzzled; be bewildered ｜ 大～不解 dàhuò-bùjiě *be extremely puzzled*

困惑 kùnhuò　迷惑 míhuò
疑惑 yíhuò

❷ [动]使迷惑：puzzle; confuse ｜ 妖言～众 yāoyán-huòzhòng *spread fallacies to deceive people*

诱惑 yòuhuò

霍 huò 16画 雨部

霍霍霍霍霍霍霍霍
霍霍霍霍霍霍霍霍

[形]迅速；快：quickly; fast ｜ ～然 huòrán *suddenly; quickly* ／ ～地站起来 huò de zhàn qǐlái *stand up suddenly*

J j

几 (幾) jī　　2画　几部

几 几几

[副]差一点儿；将近：nearly; almost | 到会者～近三千人。Dàohuìzhě jījìn sānqiān rén. *Nearly 3,000 people came to the meeting.*

几乎 jīhū nearly; almost; practically

◇茶几 chájī
　　See jǐ.

讥 (譏) jī　　4画　讠部

讥 讥讥讥讥

[动]讽刺；挖苦：satirize; ridicule; mock; sneer at | 反唇相～ fǎnchún-xiāngjī *answer back sarcastically*

讥笑 jīxiào ridicule; jeer; sneer at; deride

击 (擊) jī　　5画　凵部

击 击击击击击

❶ [动]打；敲打：strike; knock; beat | ～鼓jīgǔ *beat the drum* / ～掌jīzhǎng *clap one's hands*

点击 diǎnjī

❷ [动]攻打：attack; strike | 拳～ quánjī *give a punch; boxing*

击败 jībài defeat; beat; vanquish

出击 chūjī	打击 dǎjī
反击 fǎnjī	攻击 gōngjī
回击 huíjī	抗击 kàngjī
射击 shèjī	突击 tūjī
袭击 xíjī	游击 yóujī

❸ [动]碰；接触：touch; bump into; get touched | 撞～zhuàngjī *ram; dash against* / 目～mùjī *see with one's own eyes; witness* / 他不小心被电～了一下。Tā bù xiǎoxīn bèi diàn jīle yīxià. *He got an electric shock due to carelessness.*

冲击 chōngjī

目击者 mùjīzhě

❹ [动]刺：stab

击剑 jījiàn fencing; swordplay

饥 (飢) jī　　5画　饣部

饥 饥饥饥饥饥

[形]饿：hungry | 又～又渴 yòu jī yòu kě *be hungry and thirsty* / ～不择食 jībùzéshí *be too hungry to be picky*

饥饿 jī'è hungry; starved

饥寒交迫 jīhán-jiāopò suffer

346

from cold and hunger

机 (機) jī　　6画 木部

机　机机机机机机

❶ [名]机器：machine | 发电~fā-diànjī *generator* / 打字~dǎzìjī *typewriter* / 收音~shōuyīnjī *radio* / 他现在已经能上~操作了。Tā xiànzài yǐjīng néng shàngjī cāozuò le. *Now he is capable of operating the machine.*

机车 jīchē locomotive; engine

机床 jīchuáng machine tool

机动 jīdòng ① flexible; expedient; mobile ② in reserve; for emergency use ③ power-driven; motorized

机构 jīgòu ① mechanism ② organization; setup

机关 jīguān ① stratagem; scheme; intrigue ② office; organ; body

机器 jīqì machine; machinery; apparatus

机枪 jīqiāng machine gun

机械 jīxiè ① machinery; machine; mechanism ② mechanical; inflexible; rigid

机油 jīyóu engine oil; machine oil

机动车 jīdòngchē vehicles

机器人 jīqìrén robot

分机 fēnjī　　　司机 sījī

死机 sǐjī　　　相机 xiàngjī

打印机 dǎyìnjī

发动机 fādòngjī

复印机 fùyìnjī

计算机 jìsuànjī

录音机 lùyīnjī

摄像机 shèxiàngjī

拖拉机 tuōlājī

洗衣机 xǐyījī

照相机 zhàoxiàngjī

❷ [形]灵巧；机敏：skilful (in hand); handy; adroit; clever; sharp

机灵 jīling clever; smart; sharp; intelligent

机智 jīzhì quick-witted; resourceful

机灵鬼 jīlingguǐ a clever person

❸ [名]特指飞机：aircraft; plane | 客~kèjī *a passenger plane* / 旅客们被要求全部离~。Lǚkèmen bèi yāoqiú quánbù lí jī. *All passengers are asked to leave the plane.* / ~上各种设备非常齐全。Jī shang gè zhǒng shèbèi fēicháng qíquán. *The plane is fully equipped.*

机场 jīchǎng airport; aerodrome

班机 bānjī　　　飞机 fēijī

❹ [名]关键的时刻；适宜的时候：chance; occasion; opportune moment | 见~行事 jiànjī-xíngshì *do as one sees fit; use* one's discretion

机会 jīhuì chance; opportunity

机遇 jīyù favourable circumstances; opportunity

乘机 chéngjī　　良机 liángjī

商机 shāngjī　　随机 suíjī

投机 tóujī　　　危机 wēijī

转机 zhuǎnjī

投机倒把 tóujī-dǎobǎ

❺ [名] 极重要而有保密性质的事情：important matter which should be kept secret | ~密 jīmì *sth. secret; secret* / ~要 jīyào *confidential*

❻ [名] 心思；念头：speculation; reflection; conjecture; idea

动机 dòngjī

◇机体 jītǐ ①organism ②fuselage

手机 shǒujī

肌 jī　　6画 月部

肌　肌肌肌肌肌肌

[名] muscle; flesh

肌肤 jīfū (formal) (human) skin and muscle

肌肉 jīròu muscle; flesh

鸡 (鷄) jī　　7画 又部

鸡　鸡鸡鸡鸡鸡鸡

[名] chicken | 我们家里养了许多 ~。Wǒmen jiāli yǎngle xǔduō jī. *We raised a lot of chickens at home.* / 他最喜欢吃 ~。Tā zuì xǐhuan chī jī. *He likes eating chicken the most.*

鸡蛋 jīdàn egg

公鸡 gōngjī

积 (積) jī　　10画 禾部

积　积积积积积积积积积积

[动] 逐渐聚集：accumulate, amass, store up little by little | ~少成多 jīshǎo-chéngduō *many a mickle makes a muckle; small things add up* / 几年来他 ~了不少钱。Jǐ nián lái tā jīle bùshǎo qián. *He has scraped together quite a lot of money over the years.* / 柜子上 ~了厚厚一层灰。Guìzi shang jīle hòuhòu yī céng huī. *A thick layer of dust collected on the cupboard.* / 垃圾越 ~越多。Lājī yuè jī yuè duō. *More and more rubbish has been stored up.*

积累 jīlěi accumulate

积蓄 jīxù ① put aside; save; accumulate ② savings

积压 jīyā keep long in stock; overstock

堆积 duījī　　公积金 gōngjījīn

◇积极 jījí ① positive ② active; energetic; vigorous

积极性 jījíxìng zeal; initiative; enthusiasm

基 jī 11画 土部

基 基基基基基基基基
基基基

❶ [名]基础；建筑物的根底部分：
foundation; base of a building
| 地～dìjī *foundation* / 墙～
qiángjī *the base of a wall*
基础 jīchǔ foundation; base;
basis

❷ [形]起始的；根本的：primary;
elementary; initial
基本 jīběn ① foundation ② basic; fundamental; elementary ③
main; essential
基层 jīcéng basic level; primary level; grassroots
基地 jīdì base
基金 jījīn fund
基因 jīyīn (biol.) gene
基本上 jīběnshàng basically; in
the main; by and large
基金会 jījīnhuì foundation
转基因 zhuǎnjīyīn
◇基督教 Jīdūjiào Christianity;
the Christian religion

激 jī 16画 氵部

激 激激激激激激激激
激激激激激激激激

❶[动]水受阻或震荡而涌起或溅起：
(of water) wash; surge; dash | ～

起浪花jīqǐ lànghuā *(of waves)*
break up into a spray

❷[动]使感情冲动：arouse; stimu-
late; excite | 用话～他 yòng
huà jī tā *stimulate him with*
words / 他被～怒了。Tā bèi jīnù
le. *He was incited to anger.*
激动 jīdòng excite; stir; agitate
激发 jīfā arouse; stimulate; set off
激励 jīlì encourage; impel; urge
激素 jīsù hormone
刺激 cìjī   感激 gǎnjī

❸[形]急剧；猛烈：rapid; sharp;
sudden; fierce; violent | ～战
jīzhàn *fierce battle*
激烈 jīliè intense; sharp; fierce;
acute
激情 jīqíng intense emotion;
fervour; passion; enthusiasm

❹[动]因受冷水刺激而得病：fall ill
from getting wet | 他被雨～病
了。Tā bèi yǔ jībìng le. *He got*
a chill from getting wet in the rain.
◇激光 jīguāng laser
激活 jīhuó (phys.) activation

及 jí 3画 丿部

及 及及及

❶ [动]达到：reach; come up to |
由表～里 yóubiǎo-jílǐ *from the*
outside to the inside; from the
surface to the centre / 力所能～
lìsuǒnéngjí *within one's power*
or ability / 水深～腰。Shuǐ

shēn jí yāo. *The water came up to the waist.; The water was waist-deep.*

及格 jígé pass a test, examination, etc.; pass

波及 bōjí 普及 pǔjí
涉及 shèjí 来不及 láibují
来得及 láidejí

❷ [动]趁着：take advantage of; avail oneself of

及时 jíshí ① timely; in time; seasonable ② promptly; without delay

及早 jízǎo at an early date; as soon as possible; before it is too late

❸ [连]连接并列的名词性成分：and | 地里种着小麦、油菜～其他作物。Dì li zhòngzhe xiǎomài, yōucài jí qítā zuòwù. *Wheat, rape and other crops are growing in the fields.*

及其 jíqí and; as well as

 吉 jí　6画 士部

吉 吉吉吉吉吉吉

[形]幸福；顺利(跟"凶 xiōng"相对)：happy; smooth (the opposite of "凶 xiōng") | ～日 jírì *the date of good luck* / 万事大～ wànshì-dàjí *all is well; everything is fine*

吉利 jílì lucky; auspicious; propitious

吉祥 jíxiáng lucky; auspicious; propitious

吉祥物 jíxiángwù mascot

凶多吉少 xiōngduō-jíshǎo

◇吉他 jítā guitar

 级(級) jí　6画 纟部

级 级级级级级级

❶ [名]等次：grade; rank; level; class | 他今年又提了一～工资。Tā jīnnián yòu tíle yī jí gōngzī. *He had another rise in salary this year.*

级别 jíbié rank; level; grade; scale

层级 céngjí 超级 chāojí
等级 děngjí 低级 dījí
高级 gāojí 阶级 jiējí
上级 shàngjí 升级 shēngjí
特级 tèjí 下级 xiàjí

工人阶级 gōngrén jiējí
无产阶级 wúchǎn jiējí
资产阶级 zīchǎn jiējí

❷ [名]年级：grade | 升～shēngjí *(of grade) go up* / 留～liújí *(of pupils) fail to go up to the next grade* / 高年～gāo niánjí *senior grade*

年级 niánjí

❸ [量]用于台阶、楼梯等：used for steps, stairs, etc. | 那台阶有十多～。Nà táijiē yǒu shí duō jí. *That flight has more than ten steps.*

极 (極) jí　　7画 木部

极 极 极 极 极 极 极

❶ [形]最高的；最终的：the utmost point; extreme; of the highest degree; ultimate｜登峰造～ dēngfēng-zàojí *reach the peak of perfection* / 他的事迹使我们～受鼓舞。Tā de shìjì shǐ wǒmen jí shòu gǔwǔ. *His deeds have encouraged us greatly.* / 他是个～聪明的孩子。Tā shì ge jí cōngmíng de háizi. *He is an extremely clever child.*

极度 jídù extremely; exceedingly; to the utmost

极端 jíduān ① extreme ② extremely; exceedingly

极力 jílì do one's utmost; spare no effort

极限 jíxiàn the limit; the maximum; the ultimate

南极 nánjí　南极洲 Nánjízhōu

太极拳 tàijíquán

❷ [副]表示最高程度：extremely; to the highest extent｜～重要 jí zhòngyào *of the utmost importance* / 冷～了 lěngjí le *extremely cold* / 高兴～了 gāoxìng jí le *extremely happy*

极其 jíqí most; extremely; exceedingly

◇ 积极 jījí

消极 xiāojí

积极性 jījíxìng

即 jí　　7画 卩部

即 即 即 即 即 即 即

❶ [动]靠近；接触：reach; be near; touch; approach｜可望而不可～ kě wàng ér bù kě jí *within sight but beyond reach*

若即若离 ruòjí-ruòlí

❷ [动]就是：in other words; namely; be; mean｜番茄～西红柿。Fānqié jí xīhóngshì. *Fanqie is tomato.*

❸ [副]表示动作在很短时间内或在某种条件下立即发生：立即，马上：used to indicate an action which takes place immediately; under a certain circumstance; promptly; at once｜两三天～可见效。Liǎng-sān tiān jí kě jiànxiào. *It's going to have an effect in a day or two.*

即将 jíjiāng (adv.) be about to; be on the point of; soon

即日 jírì (formal) ① this or that very day ② within the next few days

当即 dāngjí

❹ [副]表示在某种条件下就会有某种结果：used to indicate the result of an action prompted under a certain condition｜稍加修改，～可使用。Shāo jiā xiūgǎi, jí kě shǐyòng. *It will be applicable after some small modifications.*

◇即便 jíbiàn even; even if; even though

即使 jíshǐ even; even if; even though

jí   9画 心部

急急急急急急急急
急

❶[形]迅速而且猛烈：rapid and violent | 水流得很~。Shuǐ liú de hěn jí. *The current is swift.* / 雨下得正~。Yǔ xià de zhèng jí. *It's raining hard.*

急剧 jíjù rapid; sharp; sudden

❷[形]迫切；紧迫：pressing; urgent | 任务很~。Rènwù hěn jí. *The task is very urgent.* / 有件~事，请赶快办一办。Yǒu jiàn jíshì, qǐng gǎnkuài bànyibàn. *There is a pressing matter. It needs to be dealt with immediately.* / 他走得很~。Tā zǒu de hěn jí. *He left in a hurry.*

急救 jíjiù first aid; emergency treatment

急切 jíqiè ① eager; impatient ② in a hurry; in haste

急需 jíxū ① be badly in need of ② urgent need

加急 jiājí   紧急 jǐnjí
危急 wēijí   应急 yìngjí

❸[形]想要达到某种目的而激动不安：impatient; anxious | 别~着走。Bié jízhe zǒu. *Don't leave in such a hurry.*

急忙 jímáng in a hurry; in haste

急于 jíyú be eager; be anxious; be impatient

焦急 jiāojí   着急 zháojí

❹[形]容易发怒；急躁：irritated; annoyed; ill-tempered | ~性子 jí-xìngzi *an impetuous person* / 别人没说上几句他就~了。Biérén méi shuōshang jǐ jù tā jiù jí le. *He was annoyed after just a few words from other people.*

急躁 jízào irritable; rash

jí   10画 疒部

疾疾疾疾疾疾疾疾
疾疾

[名]病：illness | 积劳成~ jīláo-chéngjí *fall ill from constant overwork*

疾病 jíbìng disease; illness

残疾人 cánjírén

jí   12画 隹部

集集集集集集集集
集集集集

❶[动]聚在一起；会合：get together; converge

集合 jíhé gather; assemble;

muster; call together

集会 jíhuì assembly; rally; gathering; meeting

集体 jítǐ collective

集团 jítuán group; clique; circle; bloc

集训 jíxùn assemble for training

集邮 jíyóu stamp collecting; philately

集中 jízhōng concentrate; centralize; focus; amass; put together

集资 jízī raise funds; collect money; pool resources

集装箱 jízhuāngxiāng container

采集 cǎijí   筹集 chóují

汇集 huìjí   聚集 jùjí

密集 mìjí   收集 shōují

搜集 sōují   召集 zhàojí

征集 zhēngjí

❷[名]由许多单篇作品汇编成的书：collection; anthology | 歌曲~ gēqǔjí *a collection of songs* / 诗~ shījí *a collection of poems*

全集 quánjí   选集 xuǎnjí

❸[名]定期或临时聚在一起进行买卖的场所：fair; market | 赶~ gǎnjí *go to a country fair; go to market* / 这个~不大，却很热闹。Zhège jí bù dà, què hěn rènao. *This country fair is a small one, but full of life.* / 这是在~上买的。Zhè shì zài jí shang mǎi de. *I picked it up at the fair.*

集市 jíshì country fair; market

 辑 (輯) jí   13画 车部

辑 辑辑辑辑辑辑辑辑辑辑辑辑辑

[动]聚集材料编书、报等：(of books, newspaper, etc.) collect; compile; edit | 专~ zhuānjí *special edition* / 这部丛书共有十~。Zhè bù cóngshū gòng yǒu shí jí. *This collection has 10 volumes.*

编辑 biānjí

◇逻辑 luójí

籍   jí   20画 竹部

籍 籍籍籍籍籍籍籍籍籍籍籍籍籍籍籍籍籍籍籍籍

❶[名]书：book | 书~ shūjí *books*

❷[名]出生地或祖居地：birthplace or home of one's ancestors | 原~ yuánjí *ancestral home*

籍贯 jíguàn the place of one's birth or origin; native place

户籍 hùjí

 几 (幾) jǐ   2画 几部

几 几几

❶[数]询问数目的多少：how many | ~个人? Jǐ gè rén? *How*

J

J

many people? / 来~年了?Lái jǐ nián le? *How many years have you been here?*

❷ [数] 表示不定的数目：a few; some | ~本书 jǐ běn shū *several books* / 他才十几岁。Tā cái shí jǐ suì. *He is only a teenager.*

◇ 几何 jǐhé geometry
See jī.

己　　jǐ　　3画 己部

己 己 己 己

[代] 自己：oneself | 坚持~见 jiānchí jǐjiàn *stick to one's own opinion*
舍己为人 shějǐ-wèirén
损人利己 sǔnrén-lìjǐ

挤　　jǐ　　9画 扌部

挤 挤 挤 挤 挤 挤 挤 挤 挤

❶ [动] 用力推、拥：squeeze; press; push against; jostle | ~进会场 jǐjìn huìchǎng *push one's way into the meeting hall* / 人太多，~不过去。Rén tài duō, jǐ bù guòqù. *We couldn't push our way through because it was too crowded.*

❷ [动] 用力压出：squeeze sth. out | ~牙膏 jǐ yágāo *squeeze the toothpaste out* / ~牛奶 jǐ niúnǎi

milk a cow

❸ [形] 紧紧地挨在一起：packed with; crowded with | 屋里~满了人。Wūli jǐmǎnle rén. *The room is packed with people.*
拥挤 yōngjǐ

脊　　jǐ　　10画 月部

脊 脊 脊 脊 脊 脊 脊 脊 脊 脊

[名] spine; backbone | ~骨 jǐgǔ *spine*
脊梁 jǐliang back (of the human body)

计 (計)　jì　4画 讠部

计 计 计 计

❶ [动] 核算：calculate; count; check | 不~其数 bùjì-qíshù *countless; innumerable*
计较 jìjiào ① haggle over; fuss about; bother about ② argue; dispute
计算 jìsuàn ① count; compute; calculate ② consideration; planning
计算机 jìsuànjī computer
计算器 jìsuànqì calculator; counter

共计 gòngjì　　　估计 gūjì
会计 kuàijì　　　统计 tǒngjì
预计 yùjì　　　　总计 zǒngjì

倒计时 dàojìshí
会计师 kuàijìshī

❷[动]谋划；打算：plan; plot; intend｜预~yùjì budget / 估~ gūjì estimate
计划 jìhuà ① map out; plan ② project; programme
设计 shèjì　　设计师 shèjìshī

❸[名]策略；主意：tactics; scheme; idea｜妙~miàojì an excellent idea; a brilliant scheme
千方百计 qiānfāng-bǎijì

❹[名]测量有关数值的仪器：meter; gauge｜温度~wēndùjì thermometer / 血压~xuèyājì blood pressure gauge

 记(記) jì　5画 讠部

记 记记记记记

❶[动]把事物写下来：write down｜~日记 jì rìjì keep a diary / 把这些内容都~在笔记本上。Bǎ zhèxiē nèiróng dōu jì zài bǐjìběn shang. Write down all these in the notebook.
记录 jìlù ① take notes; keep the minutes; record ② minutes; notes; record ③ notetaker
记载 jìzǎi ① put down in writing; record ② record; account
记者 jìzhě reporter; correspondent; newsman; journalist
登记 dēngjì　　书记 shūjì

❷[动]把印象保持在脑子里：bear in mind｜~不清楚 jì bù qīngchu can not recall exactly / 你要~住这件事。Nǐ yào jìzhù zhè jiàn shì. You should remember this.
记得 jìde remember
记性 jìxing memory
记忆 jìyì ①remember; recall ② memory
记忆力 jìyìlì the faculty of memory; memory
惦记 diànjì　　牢记 láojì
忘记 wàngjì

❸[名]记载事物的书或文章：notes; records｜大事~dàshìjì chronicle of events
笔记 bǐjì　　日记 rìjì
传记 zhuànjì
笔记本 bǐjìběn
◇记号 jìhao mark; sign

 纪(紀) jì　6画 纟部

纪 纪纪纪纪纪纪

❶[名]制度；纪律：system; discipline｜校~xiàojì school discipline / 违法乱~wéifǎ-luànjì break the law and violate discipline
纪律 jìlǜ discipline

❷[动]记载：record; take notes｜~事 jìshì account of events
纪念 jìniàn commemorate; mark
纪要 jìyào summary of min-

utes; summary

纪录片 jìlùpiàn documentary film; documentary

纪念碑 jìniànbēi monument; memorial

纪念馆 jìniànguǎn memorial hall; museum in memory of sb.

纪念品 jìniànpǐn souvenir; keepsake; memento

纪念日 jìniànrì commemoration day

❸ [名]纪年的单位。古时以十二年为一纪;公历以一百年为一世纪: epoch; one epoch equals twelve years in ancient China; a hundred years is one century

年纪 niánjì　　　世纪 shìjì

技　　　jì　　7画 扌部

技 技技技技技技技

[名]某方面的能力；本领：ability; skill | 一~之长 yījìzhīcháng *proficiency in a particular line; professional skill*

技能 jìnéng technical ability; mastery of a skill or technique

技巧 jìqiǎo skill; technique; craftsmanship

技师 jìshī technician

技术 jìshù technology; skill; technique

技术员 jìshùyuán technician

竞技 jìngjì　　　科技 kējì

演技 yǎnjì　　　杂技 zájì

系 (繫) jì　　7画 系部

系 系系系系系系系

[动]结；扎：tie; fasten; bind; tie | ~扣子 jì kòuzi *button up* / ~鞋带 jì xiédài *do up shoelaces* / ~领带 jì lǐngdài *wear a tie*

See xì.

忌　　　jì　　7画 己部

忌 忌忌忌忌忌忌忌

❶ [动]因为别人比自己强而怨恨： be jealous of | 妒~dùjì *jealousy* / ~恨 jìhèn *envy and hate*

❷ [动]怕：fear; dread | 顾~gùjì *scruple; misgiving*

❸ [动]因为不适合或不喜欢而避免： regard certain thing as unfit and avoid it | ~口 jìkǒu *avoid certain food* / ~生冷 jì shēnglěng *avoid cold and raw food*

❹ [动]戒除：give up; quit | ~烟 jìyān *quit smoking* / ~酒 jìjiǔ *give up alcohol*

际 (際) jì　　7画 阝(左)部

际 际际际际际际际

❶ [名]交界或靠边的地方：border;

edge | 天～tiānjì *horizon* / 水～ shuǐjì *the edge of a body of water; waterside*

无边无际 wúbiān-wújì

一望无际 yīwàng-wújì

❷[名]彼此之间：between; among | 国～guójì *international* / 校～ xiàojì *interschool* / 人～关系 rénjì guānxi *interpersonal relations*

国际法 guójìfǎ

国际象棋 guójì xiàngqí

◇实际 shíjì

季 季季季季季季季季

❶[名]season | 一年分春、夏、秋、冬四～. Yī nián fēn chūn, xià, qiū, dōng sìjì. *A year is divided into four seasons, spring, summer, autumn and winter.*

季度 jìdù *a quarter (of a year)*

春季 chūnjì   冬季 dōngjì

秋季 qiūjì   四季 sìjì

夏季 xiàjì   月季 yuèjì

❷[名]一年里具有某种特征的一段时期：a period of the year featuring particular conditions of weather, temperature, etc. |

雨～yǔjì *rainy season*

季节 jìjié *season*

淡季 dànjì   赛季 sàijì

◇季军 jìjūn *third place winner in a sports competition*

剂 (劑) jì   8画 刂部

剂 剂剂剂剂剂剂剂剂

[名]配制成的药物：pharmaceutical or chemical preparation | 针～ zhēnjì *injection* / 药～yàojì *medicament; drug* / 润滑～rùnhuájì *lubricant*

兴奋剂 xīngfènjì

迹 jì   9画 辶部

迹 迹迹迹迹迹迹迹迹迹

❶[名]留下的印子：mark; trace | 血～xuèjì *blood stain* / 笔～bǐjì *handwriting*

迹象 jìxiàng sign; indication

轨迹 guǐjì   痕迹 hénjì

足迹 zújì

❷[名]前人遗留下的事物：remains; vestige | 名胜古～ míngshēnggǔjì *places of historical interest and scenic beauty*

济 (濟) jì   9画 氵部

济 济济济济济济济济济

[动]用钱或物帮助有困难的人；救助：help those in distress and peril with money or other things;

aid; help ｜ 救~jiùjì *help sb. in difficulty; succour* / 接~jiējì *help (with money, food, etc.)*

既 jì 9画 无部

既 既既既既既既既既既
既

[连]跟"且 qiě""又 yòu""也 yě"呼应，表示两种情况同时存在：used in combination with "且qiě""又yōu""也yě", meaning "and; both...and..." ｜ ~高又大jì gāo yòu dà *tall and massive* / ~快又好jì kuài yòu hǎo *both quick and well done* / ~生动又活泼jì shēngdòng yòu huópo *both lively and vigorous*

既…也… jì... yě... both...and; as well as

既…又… jì...yōu... both...and; as well as

◇既然 jìrán *since; as; now that*

继 (繼) jì 10画 纟部

继 继继继继继继继继
继继

[动]接续；连续；接替：continue; go on continuously; succeed; replace ｜ ~任jìrèn *succeed sb. in a post*

继承jìchéng ①inherit ②carry on

继续 jìxù continue; go on

相继 xiāngjì

祭 jì 11画 示部

祭 祭祭祭祭祭祭祭祭
祭祭祭

❶[动]供奉鬼神或祖先：hold a memorial ceremony for (deceased ancestors, ghosts and gods, etc.) ｜ ~神jìshén *offer a sacrifice to a god*

❷[动]对死者表示追悼：perform a memorial service for the dead ｜ ~奠 jìdiàn *hold a memorial ceremony for (the dead)*

寄 jì 11画 宀部

寄 寄寄寄寄寄寄寄寄
寄寄寄

❶[动]托付：entrust; place ｜ 这些东西~放在他那里。Zhèxiē dōngxi jìfàng zài tā nàli. *These things are left to his care.*

寄托jìtuō ① entrust to the care of sb.; leave with sb. ② place hope on; find sustenance in

❷[动]依附；靠：depend on; attach oneself to ｜ ~生jìshēng *parasitic* / ~居 jìjū *live away from home; live with another's family*

❸[动]通过邮局传递：send by post

| ～信 jìxìn *post (or mail) a letter* / ～包裹 jì bāoguǒ *send a parcel by post*
邮寄 yóujì

寂 jì 11画 宀部

寂寂寂寂寂寂寂寂寂寂寂寂

❶[形]静；没有声音：silent; quiet; soundless | ～然无声 jìrán wúshēng *quiet and still*
寂静 jìjìng quiet; still; silent

❷[形]冷清；冷落：lonely; deserted; desolate
寂寞 jìmò ① lonely; lonesome ② quiet; still; silent

绩 (績) jì 11画 纟部

绩绩绩绩绩绩绩绩绩绩绩

[名]功业；成果：achievement; merit; exploit; fruit; result | 伟大的功～ wěidà de gōngjì *great merits and achievements; great contribution*
成绩 chéngjì　　业绩 yèjì

加 jiā 5画 力部

加加加加加加

❶[动]把本来没有的添上去；安放：

add; put in; append; place; put | ～标点符号 jiā biāodiǎn fúhào *put in punctuation marks* / ～注解 jiā zhùjiě *append notes to* / 汤里～点儿盐。Tāng li jiādiǎnr yán. *Put a little salt in the soup.*
加工 jiāgōng process
加入 jiārù ① add; mix; put in ② join; accede to
加油 jiāyóu oil; refuel; lubricate
参加 cānjiā　　添加 tiānjiā

❷[动]在原有的基础上增多、扩大或提高：increase; gain; add | ～工资 jiā gōngzī *increase (raise) sb.'s wage* / 件衣服再出去。Jiā jiàn yīfu zài chūqù. *Put on more clothes before you go out.* / 我们小组又～了一个人。Wǒmen xiǎozǔ yòu jiāle yī gè rén. *One more person has been assigned to our group.*
加班 jiābān work overtime; work an extra shift
加急 jiājí urgent (telegram, post, etc.)
加紧 jiājǐn step up; speed up; intensify
加剧 jiājù aggravate; intensify; exacerbate
加强 jiāqiáng strengthen; enhance; augment; reinforce
加热 jiārè heat
加深 jiāshēn deepen
加速 jiāsù quicken; speed up; accelerate; expedite
加重 jiāzhòng make or become

heavier or more serious; aggravate

加油站 jiāyóuzhàn filling (or petrol, gas) station

附加 fùjiā 更加 gèngjiā

增加 zēngjiā

❸[动]施以某种动作：carry out a certain action or pay certain consideration｜不~考虑 bù jiā kǎolǜ *not consider certain thing at all*／~以保护 jiāyǐ bǎohù *protect; safeguard*／多~注意 duō jiā zhùyì *pay more attention*

加以 jiāyǐ *in addition; moreover*

❹[动]把两个或两个以上的数目或东西合在一起：add two or more numerals｜三个数相~sān gè shù xiāngjiā *add up three numerals*

加法 jiāfǎ (*math.*) *addition*

 (夾) jiā 6画 一部

夹 夹夹夹夹夹夹

❶[动]从两旁用力使物品不动：press from both sides; place in between｜用筷子~菜 yòng kuàizi jiā cài *pick up food with chopsticks*／手指被门~住shǒuzhǐ bèi mén jiāzhù *fingers got squeezed by the door*／鞋子~脚。Xiézi jiā jiǎo. *The shoe pinches.*

❷[动]夹在胳膊底下：carry sth. under one's armpit｜~着几本书 jiāzhe jǐ běn shū *carry several books under the armpit*／~着皮包 jiāzhe píbāo *carry a briefcase under the armpit*

❸[动]混杂；掺杂：mix; mingle; couple with｜风声~着雨声 fēngshēng jiāzhe yǔshēng *a mixture of the sounds of wind and rain*／~在人群里 jiā zài rénqún li *mingle with the crowd*

夹杂 jiāzá *be mixed up with; be mingled with*

❹[名]夹东西的器具：clip; folder｜皮~儿 píjiār *wallet*／文件~ wénjiànjiā *folder; binder*／衣~ yījiā *clothes peg*

夹子 jiāzi ①clip; tongs ②folder; wallet

◇ 夹克 jiākè *jacket*

皮夹克 píjiākè

 jiā 8画 亻部

佳 佳佳佳佳佳佳佳佳

[形]美；好：beautiful; good｜~音 jiāyīn *welcome news; good tidings*／~作jiāzuò *a fine piece of writing; an excellent work*／身体欠~shēntǐ qiàn jiā *not feel well*

最佳 zuìjiā

 jiā 10画 宀部

家 家家家家家家家家家家

❶ [名]家庭的住所：home ｜ 回~ huíjiā *go home* ／ 他的~在北京。Tā de jiā zài Běijīng. *His home is in Beijing.*

老家 lǎojiā

❷ [名]家庭：family ｜ 我~有四口人。Wǒ jiā yǒu sì kǒu rén. *There are 4 family members in my family.*

家常 jiāchǎng daily life of a family; domestic trivia

家具 jiājù furniture

家人 jiārén family member

家属 jiāshǔ family member; (family) dependant

家庭 jiātíng family; household

家务 jiāwù household duties

家乡 jiāxiāng hometown; native place

家用 jiāyòng family expenses; housekeeping money

家园 jiāyuán home; homeland

家长 jiāzhǎng head of a family; parent or guardian of a child

家政 jiāzhèng ① household management ② home economics

家族 jiāzú clan; family

家常饭 jiāchángfàn ① homely food; simple meal ② common occurrence; routine; all in a day's work

家家户户 jiājiā-hùhù each and every family; every household

家喻户晓 jiāyù-hùxiǎo widely known; known to all

当家 dāngjiā　国家 guójiā

传家宝 chuánjiābǎo

拉家常 lājiācháng

❸ [名]经营某种行业的人家或具有某种身份的人：person or family who engages in a certain profession or trade or has a certain status ｜ 酒~ jiǔjiā *wine-shop; restaurant* ／ 渔~ yújiā *fisherman's family*

独家 dújiā　商家 shāngjiā

赢家 yíngjiā　庄家 zhuāngjiā

企业家 qǐyèjiā

❹ [词尾]指掌握某种专门学识或从事某种专门活动的人：specialist in a certain field ／ 科学~ kēxuéjiā scientist ／ 文学~ wénxuéjiā a man of letters; writer

画家 huàjiā　专家 zhuānjiā

作家 zuòjiā　书法家 shūfǎjiā

艺术家 yìshùjiā

政治家 zhèngzhìjiā

资本家 zīběnjiā

❺ [名]学术流派：school of thought ｜ 儒~ Rújiā *the Confucian school*

道家 Dàojiā

❻ [形]人工饲养的（跟"野 yě"相对）：domesticated (the opposite of "野 yě")

家畜 jiāchù domestic animal; livestock

家禽 jiāqín domestic fowl; poultry

❼ [名]对人称自己的亲属中年纪大或辈分高的：used to address

family members or relatives older than oneself when talking with others | ～父 jiāfù *my father*

◇家伙 jiāhuo ① tool; utensil; weapon ② fellow; guy

老人家 lǎorénjia

嘉 jiā 14画 士部

嘉嘉嘉嘉嘉嘉嘉嘉
嘉嘉嘉嘉嘉嘉

❶[形]善；美；good; nice; beautiful

嘉宾 jiābīn distinguished guest

❷[动]夸奖；赞许：commend; praise; speak well of; speak favourably of | 精神可～ jīng-shen kějiā *the spirit is worthy of praise*

嘉奖 jiājiǎng commend; cite

◇嘉年华 jiāniánhuá carnival

颊 (頰) jiá 12画 页部

颊颊颊颊颊颊颊颊
颊颊颊颊

[名]脸的两侧眼以下的部分：cheek | 两～发红 liǎngjiá fāhóng *with rosy cheeks* / 泪水沿着她的面～流下来。Lèishuǐ yán-zhe tā de miànjiá liú xiàlai. *Tears streamed down her cheeks.*

甲 jiǎ 5画 丨部

甲甲甲甲甲

❶[名]顺序或等级的第一位：the first of the ten Heavenly Stems; the first in sequence or grade | 桂林山水～天下。Guìlín shān-shuǐ jiǎ tiānxià. *The mountains and rivers in Guilin are the best on earth.*

❷[名]动物身上有保护功用的硬壳：shell or carapace, hard protective outer covering of some animals | 龟～ guījiǎ *tortoise shell*

甲骨文 jiǎgǔwén inscriptions on bone or tortoise shells of the Shang Dynasty (c. 16th-11th centuries B.C.)

❸[名]手指和脚趾上的角质硬壳：nail

指甲 zhǐjia

❹[名]围在物体外面起保护作用的装备：protective covering wrapped round the outside of an object | 盔～ kuījiǎ *helmet*

◇甲板 jiǎbǎn deck

假 jiǎ 11画 亻部

假假假假假假假假
假假假

❶[形]虚伪的；不真实的；伪造的；

人造的（跟"真zhēn"相对）: hypocritical; sham; untrue; unreal; false; fake (the opposite of "真zhēn") | ~发jiǎfà *wig* / ~话jiǎhuà *lie; falsehood* / 这些金银首饰都是~的。Zhèxiē jīnyín shǒushi dōu shì jiǎ de. *These gold and silver jewels are not genuine.*

假冒jiǎmào pass oneself off as; palm off (a fake as genuine)

假装jiǎzhuāng pretend; feign; simulate; make believe

虚假xūjiǎ

半真半假bànzhēn-bànjiǎ

弄虚作假nòngxū-zuòjiǎ

❷ [副]姑且: for the time being

假定jiǎdìng ① suppose; assume; grant; presume ② hypothesis

假设jiǎshè ① suppose; assume; grant; presume ② hypothesis

❸ [连]如果: if

假如jiǎrú if; supposing; in case

假若jiǎruò if; supposing; in case

假使jiǎshǐ if; in case; in the event that

　　See jià.

价 (價) jià　　6画 亻部

价 价价价价价价

❶ [名]商品的价钱: price of commodity | 物~稳定 wùjià wěndìng *commodity prices remain stable*

价格 jiàgé price

价钱 jiàqian price

价位 jiàwèi marked price; price

报价 bàojià　　比价 bǐjià

标价 biāojià　　差价 chājià

代价 dàijià　　定价 dìngjià

高价 gāojià　　股价 gǔjià

讲价 jiǎngjià　　降价 jiàngjià

廉价 liánjià　　票价 piàojià

售价 shòujià　　调价 tiáojià

物价 wùjià　　造价 zàojià

涨价 zhǎngjià

讲价钱 jiǎngjiàqian

讨价还价 tǎojià-huánjià

❷ [名]价值: value | 等~交换 děngjià jiāohuàn *exchange of equal values* / 我请他对这些画估个~。Wǒ qǐng tā duì zhèxiē huà gū ge jià. *I asked him to evaluate these paintings.*

价值 jiàzhí ① value ② cost; be worth

价值观 jiàzhíguān values

评价 píngjià

身价百倍 shēnjià-bǎibèi

驾 (駕) jià　　8画 马部

驾 驾驾驾驾驾驾驾驾

❶ [动]使牲口拉（车或农具）: make an animal pull a cart or farm tool | 两匹马~着车。Liǎng pǐ mǎ jiàzhe chē. *Two horses are harnessed to the cart.*

❷ [动]操纵（车、船或飞机等）:

drive; operate｜~车 jiàchē *drive a car* / ~飞机 jià fēijī *pilot a plane*

驾驶 jiàshǐ drive; pilot

驾驶员 jiàshǐyuán driver (of a vehicle); pilot (of an aeroplane)

❸[名]对人的尊称：you (term of respect)｜大~光临dàjià guānglín *you honour us with your presence*

劳驾 láojià

架　jià　9画 木部

架架架架架架架架架

❶[名]支撑物体的构件或放置器物的用具：frame or rack used to support or place an object on｜笔~儿bǐjiàr *pen rack; pen holder* / 衣~yījià *coat hanger*

架子 jiàzi ① frame; rack; shelf; stand ② framework; skeleton; outline ③ airs; haughty manner ④ posture; stance

框架 kuàngjià　　书架 shūjià

❷[动]搭；支起：put up; pitch; prop｜~桥 jiàqiáo *build a bridge* / ~电线 jià diànxiàn *set up power lines*

❸[动]抵挡；承受：ward off; fend off; withstand｜拿我的长枪~住他的刀。Ná wǒ de cháng qiāng jiàzhù tā de dāo. *I fended off his sword with my spear.*

❹[动]劫持：kidnap; hijack; abduct

绑架 bǎngjià

❺[动]争吵；殴打：make a row; quarrel; fight

吵架 chǎojià　　打架 dǎjià

❻[量]用于某些有支柱或骨架的物体：used for machinery or things which have a stand as a support｜几百~飞机jǐ bǎi jià fēijī *several hundred planes* / 一~钢琴yī jià gāngqín *a piano*

◇摆架子 bǎijiàzi

假　jià　11画 亻部

假假假假假假假假假假假

[名]法定或经批准暂时停止工作、学习的时间：holiday or leave of absence｜病~bìngjià *sick leave* / 事~shìjià *leave of absence (to attend to personal matters)*

假期 jiàqī holiday; vacation

假日 jiàrì holiday; day off

假条 jiàtiáo application for leave

长假 chángjià　　度假 dùjià

放假 fàngjià　　寒假 hánjià

请假 qǐngjià　　暑假 shǔjià

休假 xiūjià　　节假日 jiéjiàrì

　　See jiǎ.

嫁

jià 13画 女部

嫁嫁嫁嫁嫁嫁嫁
嫁嫁嫁嫁嫁

❶[动]女子结婚（跟"娶 qǔ"相对）：(of female) marry (the opposite of "娶 qǔ") | 出~ chūjià (of a girl) marry / 她~给了一位医生。Tā jiàgěile yī wèi yīshēng. *She married a doctor.*

❷[动]转移（罪名、损失、负担等）：shift; transfer (charge, loss, burden, etc.) | ~祸于人 jiàhuò-yúrén *shift the misfortune onto sb. else; put the blame on sb. else*

尖

jiān 6画 小部

尖 尖尖尖尖尖尖

❶[形]末端细小；锐利： pointed; tip; sharp | 铅笔削~了。Qiānbǐ xiāojiān le. *The pencil is sharpened.*

尖端 jiānduān ① pointed end; acme; peak ② most advanced; sophisticated

尖锐 jiānruì ①sharp-pointed ② penetrating; incisive; sharp; keen

顶尖 dǐngjiān

❷[形]声音又高又细：high-pitched and sharp | ~嗓子 jiān sǎngzi

sharp voice / 声音非常~。Shēngyīn fēicháng jiān. *The voice is piercing.*

❸[形]感觉灵敏：(of senses) sensitive; keen; agile; acute | 眼~yǎnjiān *have sharp eyes; have a keen sight* / 耳朵~érduo jiān *have sharp ears*

◇尖子 jiānzi the best of its kind; the pick of the bunch; the cream of the crop

奸

jiān 6画 女部

奸 奸奸奸奸奸奸

❶[形]虚伪、狡猾、自私：hypocritical and treacherous; selfish | 这人很~。Zhè rén hěn jiān. *The man is very treacherous.*

❷[名]出卖国家、阶级、民族利益的人：traitor

汉奸 hànjiān

❸[动]发生不正当的男女关系 | have illicit sexual relations | 强~qiángjiān *rape*

歼（殲） **jiān** 7画 歹部

歼 歼歼歼歼歼歼歼

[动]消灭：eliminate; wipe out; annihilate | 围~wéijiān *surround and annihilate*

歼灭 jiānmiè annihilate; wipe out; destroy

坚 (堅) jiān　　7画 土部

坚 坚坚坚坚坚坚坚

❶[形] 硬；结实：hard; solid | ~
冰 jiānbīng *solid ice*
坚固 jiāngù firm; solid; sturdy;
strong; durable
坚韧 jiānrèn ① tough and ten-
sile ② firm and tenacious
坚实 jiānshí solid; substantial
坚硬 jiānyìng hard; solid
❷[形] 不动摇：unyielding; un-
shakable
坚持 jiānchí persist in; per-
severe in; uphold; stick to; adhere to
坚定 jiāndìng ① firm; staunch;
steadfast ② strengthen
坚决 jiānjué firm; resolute;
determined; resolved
坚强 jiānqiáng strong; firm;
staunch
坚信 jiānxìn firmly believe;
be firmly convinced; be fully
confident of
坚贞 jiānzhēn faithful; constant
坚贞不屈 jiānzhēn-bùqū stand
firm and unyielding

间 (間) jiān　　7画 门部

间 间间间间间间间

❶[名] 中间，两段时间或两种事物
相接的地方：space in between;
opening | 天地~ tiāndì jiān
between the sky and the earth /
相互~有差别。Xiānghù jiān
yǒu chābié. *Differences exist
between each other.*
❷[名] 一定的时间或范围：a cer-
tain time or area | 田~ tiánjiān
in the field / 晚~ wǎnjiān *in the
evening*
空间 kōngjiān　　民间 mínjiān
期间 qījiān　　人间 rénjiān
日间 rìjiān　　夜间 yèjiān
空间站 kōngjiānzhàn
时间表 shíjiānbiǎo
❸[名] 房间：room | 卫生~ wèi-
shēngjiān *toilet (room)* / 衣帽~
yīmàojiān *cloakroom*
车间 chējiān　　房间 fángjiān
❹[量] 房屋的最小单位：the small-
est unit in a building | 两~教
室 liǎng jiān jiàoshì *two class-
rooms* / 三~房子 sān jiān fángzi
three rooms
　　See jiǎn.

肩　　jiān　　8画 户部

肩 肩肩肩肩肩肩肩肩

[名] shoulder | 左~ zuǒjiān *left
shoulder* / 右~ yòujiān *right
shoulder*
肩膀 jiānbǎng shoulder

披肩 pījiān

艰 (艱) jiān 8画 又部

艰 艰 艰 艰 艰 艰 艰 艰

[形]困难：difficult; hard | ～辛
jiānxīn *hardships*

艰巨 jiānjù arduous; formidable;
onerous

艰苦 jiānkǔ arduous; difficult;
hard; tough

艰难 jiānnán difficult; hard;
arduous

艰险 jiānxiǎn hardships and
dangers; perilous

艰苦奋斗 jiānkǔ-fèndòu hard
struggle

监 (監) jiān 10画 皿部

监 监 监 监 监 监 监 监 监
监 监

❶ [动]从旁严密注视；督察：super-
vise; inspect | ～考 jiānkǎo
invigilate / ～工 jiāngōng
supervise work; supervisor

监测 jiāncè monitor

监察 jiānchá supervise; control

监督 jiāndū supervise; super-
intend; control

监禁 jiānjìn take into custody;
imprison; put in jail

监控 jiānkòng inspect and control

监视 jiānshì keep watch on;
keep a lookout over; guard

总监 zǒngjiān

❷ [名]关押犯人的处所：prison;
jail

监狱 jiānyù prison; jail

兼 jiān 10画 丷部

兼 兼 兼 兼 兼 兼 兼 兼
兼 兼

[形]同时涉及或具有几种事物：
having or involving more than
one thing | ～管 jiānguǎn *be
concurrently in charge of; look
after (another matter) at the
same time* / 品学～优 pǐnxué-
jiānyōu *(of a student) perform
well both in moral conduct and
study*

兼并 jiānbìng annex (territory,
property, etc.)

兼顾 jiāngù give consideration
to (or take account of) two or
more things

兼任 jiānrèn hold a concurrent
post

兼职 jiānzhí ① hold two or more
posts concurrently ② con-
current post; part-time job

煎 jiān 13画 灬部

煎 煎 煎 煎 煎 煎 煎 煎
煎 煎 煎 煎 煎

❶[动]把食物放在少量热油里加热使熟：fry in a small amount of oil | ~鱼 jiān yú *fry fish in shallow oil*

❷[动]用水熬煮：simmer in water; decoct | ~药 jiānyào *decoct medicinal herbs*

拣 (揀) jiǎn　8画 扌部

拣 拣拣拣拣拣拣拣拣拣

❶[动]挑选；选择：choose; select | 挑~ tiāojiǎn *pick and choose* / ~重活儿干 jiǎn zhònghuór gàn *choose the heavy work voluntarily*

❷[动]把地上的东西拿起来：collect | ~废品 jiǎn fèipǐn *pick up waste materials*

茧 (繭) jiǎn　9画 艹部

茧 茧茧茧茧茧茧茧茧 茧

❶[名]某些昆虫变蛹之前吐丝做成的壳：cocoon | 蚕~ cánjiǎn *silkworm cocoon*

❷[名]手掌脚掌因摩擦而生成的硬皮：callus | 老~ lǎojiǎn *thick callus*

柬 jiǎn　9画 一部

柬 柬柬柬柬柬柬柬柬 柬

[名]信件、请帖等：general term for letters, visiting cards, invitations | 请~ qǐngjiǎn *invitation card*

俭 (儉) jiǎn　9画 亻部

俭 俭俭俭俭俭俭俭俭 俭

[形]节省；不浪费：thrifty; frugal; economical | 勤~ qínjiǎn *frugal*

俭朴 jiǎnpǔ thrifty and simple; economical

勤工俭学 qíngōng-jiǎnxué

捡 (撿) jiǎn　10画 扌部

捡 捡捡捡捡捡捡捡捡 捡捡

[动]把地上的东西拿起来：pick up; collect | ~柴 jiǎn chái *gather firewood* / 把笔~起来 bǎ bǐ jiǎn qǐlai *pick up the pen*

检 (檢) jiǎn　11画 木部

检 检检检检检检检检 检检检

[动]查：check up; examine | ~阅 jiǎnyuè *inspect; review*

检测 jiǎncē examine and survey

检查 jiǎnchá ① check up; inspect; examine ② self-criticism

检察 jiǎnchá procuratorial work

检举 jiǎnjǔ report (an offence) to the authorities; inform against (an offender)

检讨 jiǎntǎo self-criticism

检修 jiǎnxiū examine and repair; overhaul

检验 jiǎnyàn test; examine; inspect; verify

检察官 jiǎncháguān public procurator (or prosecutor)

抽检 chōujiǎn   体检 tǐjiǎn

减 jiǎn   11画 冫部

减减减减减减减减
减减减

❶ [动] 从总体或原有的数量中去掉一部分 (跟 "增zēng" 相对): subtract; deduct (the opposite of "增zēng") | ～掉一半 jiǎndiào yī bàn *reduce by half* / 5～3是2。Wǔ jiǎn sān shì èr. *5 minus 3 is 2.*

减法 jiǎnfǎ subtraction

减免 jiǎnmiǎn ① mitigate or annul (a punishment) ② reduce or remit (taxation, etc.)

减轻 jiǎnqīng lighten; ease; alleviate; mitigate

减少 jiǎnshǎo reduce; decrease; lessen; cut down

削减 xuējiǎn

❷ [动] 降低；衰退：decrease; weaken; decline; wane | 他工作热情不～。Tā gōngzuò rèqíng bù jiǎn。 *He works as enthusiastically as before.*

减产 jiǎnchǎn reduction of output; drop in production

减低 jiǎndī reduce; lower; bring down; cut

减肥 jiǎnféi reduce weight; slim

减弱 jiǎnruò weaken; abate

减速 jiǎnsù slow down; decelerate; retard

剪 jiǎn   11画 刀部

剪剪剪剪剪剪剪剪
剪剪剪

❶ [动] 用剪刀等使东西断开：cut with scissors, shears, etc. | 把绳子～断 bǎ shéngzi jiǎnduàn *cut the rope* / 他头发～短了。Tā tóufa jiǎnduǎn le. *He has his hair cut short.*

剪彩 jiǎncǎi cut the ribbon at an opening ceremony

剪纸 jiǎnzhǐ paper-cut; scissor-cut

❷ [名] 一种用来剪断东西的用具：scissors | ～子 jiǎnzi *scissors*

剪刀 jiǎndāo scissors; shears

简 (簡) jiǎn   13画 竹部

简 简简简简简简简简简 简简简简简

❶[形]不复杂；简单（跟"繁 fán"相对）：uncomplicated; simple; simplified (the opposite of "繁 fán") | ~本 jiǎnběn *simplified version (of a book)*

简便 jiǎnbiàn simple and convenient; handy

简称 jiǎnchēng ① the abbreviated form of a name; abbreviation ②be called sth. for short

简单 jiǎndān ① simple; uncomplicated ② (usu. used in the negative) commonplace; ordinary ③ oversimplified; casual

简短 jiǎnduǎn brief; short

简洁 jiǎnjié succinct; terse; pithy

简介 jiǎnjiè introduction; synopsis; summarized account

简陋 jiǎnlòu simple and crude

简历 jiǎnlì biographical notes; résumé

简明 jiǎnmíng simple and clear; concise

简要 jiǎnyào concise and to the point; brief

简易 jiǎnyì ①simple and easy ②simply constructed; simply equipped; unsophisticated

简体字 jiǎntǐzì simplified Chinese character

❷[动]使简单；简化：simplify; make simple | 精~ jīngjiǎn retrench; reduce

简化 jiǎnhuà simplify

◇简直 jiǎnzhí simply; at all; virtually

碱   jiǎn   14画 石部

碱 碱碱碱碱碱碱碱碱碱 碱碱碱碱碱碱

[名] alkali | 烧~ shāojiǎn *alkali* / 纯~ chúnjiǎn *soda*

见 （見） jiàn   4画 见部

见 见见见见

❶ [动]看到：see; catch sight of | ~闻 jiànwén *what one sees and hears* / 眼~是实。Yǎn jiàn shì shí. *Seeing is believing.*

见证 jiànzhèng witness; testimony

见世面 jiànshìmiàn see the world; enrich one's experience

不见 bùjiàn   常见 chángjiàn

罕见 hǎnjiàn   少见 shǎojiàn

❷[动]会面：meet; call; see | 明天~。Míngtiān jiàn. *See you tomorrow.* / 他要来~你。Tā yào lái jiàn nǐ. *He'll come to see you.*

见面 jiànmiàn meet; see

会见 huìjiàn   接见 jiējiàn

再见 zàijiàn

❸ [动]接触；遇到：get in touch with; meet with | 这种药怕~光。Zhè zhǒng yào pà jiàn guāng. *This medicine cannot be exposed to light.* / 冰~热就化。Bīng jiàn rè jiù huà. *Ice melts with heat.*

❹[名]对事物的认识和看法：view; opinion | ~地 jiàndì *insight; judgment* / 主~ zhǔjiàn *one's own judgment*

见解 jiànjiě view; opinion; understanding; idea

见识 jiànshi knowledge and experience

偏见 piānjiàn　　意见 yìjiàn
预见 yùjiàn
寻短见 xúnduǎnjiàn

❺[动]看得出；显现出：show evidence of; appear to be | ~分晓 jiàn fēnxiǎo *know the outcome* / 日久~人心。Rìjiǔ jiàn rénxīn. *Time reveals a person's true colours.*

见效 jiànxiào become effective; produce the desired result

可见 kějiàn

显而易见 xiǎn'éryìjiàn

由此可见 yóucǐ-kějiàn

❻[动]指明出处或需要参看的地方：refer to; see (in written language) | ~上 jiànshàng *see above* / ~右图 jiàn yòutú *refer to the picture on the right*

❼[动]用在表示感觉、视觉、听觉、嗅觉等动词的后面，表示结果：used after some verbs, denoting senses to indicate result | 听得~ tīngdejiàn *can hear* / 看

不~ kànbujiàn *cannot see*

看见 kànjiàn　　碰见 pèngjiàn
听见 tīngjiàn　　遇见 yùjiàn

◇不见得 bùjiàndé

件　　　jiàn　　6画 亻部
········
件 件件件件件件

❶[名]指可以一一计算的事物：piece; item

案件 ànjiàn　　部件 bùjiàn
零件 língjiàn　　配件 pèijiàn
软件 ruǎnjiàn　　事件 shìjiàn
信件 xìnjiàn　　硬件 yìngjiàn
邮件 yóujiàn　　元件 yuánjiàn

❷[名]文件：document | 急~ jíjiàn *urgent document or dispatch* / 密~ mìjiàn *confidential (classified) document; secret paper*

稿件 gǎojiàn　　快件 kuàijiàn
文件 wénjiàn
证件 zhèngjiàn

❸[量]用于衣服(上衣类)、个体器物、公文、事情等：used for a jacket, article, document, matter, etc. | 一~大衣 yī jiàn dàyī *an overcoat* / 两~东西 liǎng jiàn dōngxi *two articles* / 一~艺术品 yī jiàn yìshùpǐn *a piece of artwork* / 几~公文 jǐ jiàn gōngwén *several documents* / 一~事 yī jiàn shì *a matter*

件

jiàn

间 (間) jiàn 7画 门部

间 间间间间间间间

❶[名]空隙：interval | 当～儿 dāngjiànr *in the middle; in the interval*

亲密无间 qīnmì-wújiàn

❷[动]隔开；不连接：separate; disconnect | ～断 jiànduàn *be disconnected; be interrupted*

间隔 jiàngé separate

间接 jiànjiē indirect; second-hand
See jiān.

建 jiàn 8画 廴部

建 建建建建建建建建

❶[动]修筑；修造：build; construct | 重～家园 chóngjiàn jiāyuán *rebuild one's homeland* / 学校新～了一座教学大楼。Xuéxiào xīn jiànle yī zuò jiāoxué dàlóu. *The school has newly put up a classroom building.*

建材 jiàncái construction materials

建造 jiànzào build; construct; erect

建筑 jiànzhù ① build; construct ② building; structure

建筑师 jiànzhùshī architect

重建 chóngjiàn 搭建 dājiàn

改建 gǎijiàn 扩建 kuòjiàn

兴建 xīngjiàn 修建 xiūjiàn

❷[动]设立；创立：establish; set up; found | ～校 jiàn xiào *found a school* / 这个工厂刚～起来。Zhège gōngchǎng gāng jiàn qǐlai. *The factory has just been set up.*

建交 jiànjiāo establish diplomatic relations

建立 jiànlì build; establish; set up; found

建设 jiànshè build; construct

筹建 chóujiàn 创建 chuàngjiàn

组建 zǔjiàn

❸[动] 提出自己的主张：propose; suggest

建议 jiànyì ① propose; suggest; recommend ② proposal; suggestion; recommendation

荐 (薦) jiàn 9画 艹部

荐 荐荐荐荐荐荐荐荐荐

[动]推举；介绍：elect; introduce | 举～ jǔjiàn *recommend (a person)*

推荐 tuījiàn

贱 (賤) jiàn 9画 贝部

贱 贱贱贱贱贱贱贱贱贱

❶[形]价钱低(跟"贵 guì"相对)：

cheap (the opposite of "贵
guì") | 价格~jiàgé jiàn *of
cheap price*

❷[形]地位低下：low in status |
贫~pínjiàn *poor and lowly*

剑 (劍) jiàn　9画 刂部

剑 剑剑剑剑剑剑剑剑剑
剑

[名]古代兵器，前端尖，两面有刃，
有鞘：sword | 宝~bǎojiàn
double-edged sword / 舞~wǔ
jiàn *perform a sword-dance* / 这
把~真锋利。Zhè bǎ jiàn zhēn
fēnglì. *This sword is very sharp.*

jiàn　10画 亻部

健 健健健健健健健健
健健

[形]具有活力的；强壮的：healthy;
strong | 稳~的脚步 wěnjiàn
de jiǎobù *firm steps*
健康 jiànkāng in good health;
sound; fit
健美 jiànměi strong and handsome
健全 jiànquán ① sound; per-
fect ② improve; refine; perfect
健壮 jiànzhuàng healthy and
strong
保健 bǎojiàn　　稳健 wěnjiàn
◇健身 jiànshēn take exercise;

have physical training

舰 (艦) jiàn　10画 舟部

舰 舰舰舰舰舰舰舰舰舰
舰舰

[名]大型军用船只：big ship for
military use; warship; man-of-
war | ~队 jiànduì *fleet; naval
force*
军舰 jūnjiàn　　　旗舰 qíjiàn

渐 (漸) jiàn　11画 氵部

渐 渐渐渐渐渐渐渐渐
渐渐渐

[副]慢慢地；一步步地：gradually;
by degrees; step by step | 天
气~冷。Tiānqì jiàn lěng. *The
weather is getting cold.*
渐渐 jiànjiàn gradually; by degrees; little by little
循序渐进 xúnxù-jiànjìn

践 (踐) jiàn　12画 𧾷部

践 践践践践践践践践
践践践践

❶[动]踩；踏：tread; trample; step
on
践踏 jiàntà tread on; trample
underfoot

❷[动]实行；履行：practise; carry
out; put into practice; keep | ~

约jiànyuē *keep an appointment*
实践 shíjiàn

溅(濺) jiàn 12画 氵部

溅 溅溅溅溅溅溅溅溅溅溅 溅溅溅溅

[动] 液体受冲击而向四外飞射：splash; spatter | 衣服被~湿了。Yīfu bèi jiànshī le. *The clothes were splashed.*

鉴(鑒) jiàn 13画 金部

鉴 鉴鉴鉴鉴鉴鉴鉴鉴 鉴鉴鉴鉴鉴

[动] 审察：appraise; inspect; examine
鉴别 jiànbié distinguish; differentiate; discern; identify
鉴定 jiàndìng ① appraisal ② identify
鉴赏 jiànshǎng appreciate
鉴于 jiànyú (in written) in view of; seeing that
借鉴 jièjiàn

键(鍵) jiàn 13画 钅部

键 键键键键键键键键 键键键键键

❶[名] 插门用的金属插销：bolt of a door
❷[名] 乐器或机器上可以按动的部分：(of a musical instrument or machine) key | 琴~qínjiàn *keys of a musical instrument*
键盘 jiànpán keyboard; fingerboard
◇关键 guānjiàn

箭 jiàn 15画 竹部

箭 箭箭箭箭箭箭箭箭 箭箭箭箭箭箭箭

[名] arrow | 拉弓射~lāgōng shèjiàn *pull the bow and let go the arrow*
射箭 shèjiàn
挡箭牌 dǎngjiànpái

江 jiāng 6画 氵部

江 江江江江江江

❶[名] 大河：big river | 这条~很长。Zhè tiáo jiāng hěn cháng. *The river is very long.*
黑龙江 Hēilóng Jiāng
❷[名] 指长江：referring to the Yangtze River | ~南 Jiāngnán *the Southern Yangtze region*
长江 Cháng Jiāng
珠江 Zhū Jiāng

将(將) jiāng 9画 丬部

将 将将将将将将将将 将

❶ [介]拿；用：with; by means of; by | ～功补过 jiānggōng-bǔguò *make amends for one's faults by good deeds*

将心比心 jiāngxīn-bǐxīn *compare oneself to another; feel for others*

❷ [介]similar to "把 bǎ" | ～门关上 jiāng mén guānshang *close the door* / ～药方交给他 jiāng yào-fāng jiāogěi tā *give him the prescription*

❸ [副]表示动作或情况不久就会发生；快要；就要：will; be going to; be about to | 天色～亮了。Tiānsè jiāng liàng le. *It's going to dawn.* / 火车～进站了。Huǒchē jiāng jìnzhàn le. *The train is about to pull into the station.*

将近 jiāngjìn close to; nearly; almost

将来 jiānglái future

将要 jiāngyào be going to; will; shall

即将 jíjiāng

◇将军 jiāngjūn ① general ② (in a chess game) check

姜 (薑) jiāng 9画 羊部

[名]ginger | 喝～汤可以去寒。Hē jiāngtāng kěyǐ qùhán. *Having ginger soup helps to keep out the cold.* / 做鱼要放些～。Zuò yú yào fàngxiē jiāng. *Put in some ginger while cooking fish.*

浆 (漿) jiāng 10画 水部

[名]较浓的液体：thick liquid | 泥～ níjiāng *slurry; mud* / 纸～ zhǐjiāng *paper pulp; pulp* 豆浆 dòujiāng

僵 jiāng 15画 亻部

❶ [形] (肢体) 直挺，不能活动：(of body) stiff; numb | 手脚都冻～了。Shǒujiǎo dōu dòngjiāng le. *Both feet and hands are numb with cold.*

❷ [形]事情难于处理；停滞不前：difficult to deal with; dead-locked | 闹～了 nàojiāng le *bring to a deadlock* / ～持 jiāng-chí *(of both parties) refuse to budge*

僵局 jiāngjú deadlock; impasse; stalemate

疆 jiāng 19画 弓部

jiāng

疆

疆疆疆疆疆疆疆疆疆
疆疆疆疆疆疆疆疆
疆疆疆

jiāng

❶[名]边界：boundary; border | ~
域 jiāngyù *territory; domain*
边疆 biānjiāng

❷[名]极限；止境：the limit; the
maximum; the ultimate | 万寿
无~ wànshòu-wújiāng *(in old
formal writing) (may you enjoy)
boundless longevity*

讲 (講) jiǎng   6画 讠部

讲 讲讲讲讲讲讲

❶[动]说；评说：speak; say; tell;
talk about | ~故事 jiǎng gùshi
tell a story / ~笑话 jiǎng xiàohua *crack a joke* / 有什么意见
请~出来。Yǒu shénme yìjiàn
qǐng jiǎng chūlai. *Please let us
know whatever opinion you
have.*
讲话 jiǎnghuà ① speak; talk;
address ② speech; talk
讲理 jiǎnglǐ ① reason with sb.;
argue ②listen to reason; be sensible
讲述 jiǎngshù tell about; give
an account of; narrate; relate
❷[动]就某方面来说：speaking of
sth. | ~能力，我不如你。Jiǎng
nénglì, wǒ bùrú nǐ. *In terms
of ability, I am no match for you.*

❸[动]商谈；商议：discuss; con-
sult; take counsel with; consult
with | ~条件 jiǎng tiáojiàn
*negotiate the terms; insist on the
fulfilment of certain conditions*
/ 这件事还没~妥。Zhè jiàn shì
hái méi jiǎngtuǒ. *The discussion about this matter has
not been finished yet.*
讲价 jiǎngjià ① haggle over the
price; bargain ② negotiate the
terms; insist on the fulfilment of
certain conditions
讲价钱 jiǎngjiàqian ① haggle
over the price; bargain ② negotiate the terms; insist on the
fulfilment of certain condition
❹[动]说明；解释：say; illustrate;
explain | 你把事情的经过~清
楚。Nǐ bǎ shìqing de jīngguò
jiǎng qīngchu. *You are asked
to give a full account of the
matter.* / 他反复~了好几遍，我
还是听不懂。Tā fǎnfù jiǎngle
hǎo jǐ biàn, wǒ háishì tīngbu-
dǒng. *He explained several
times, but I still could not understand what he meant.* / 这个
词有三个~法。Zhège cí yǒu
sān gè jiǎngfǎ. *This word has
three meanings.*
讲解 jiǎngjiě explain
讲课 jiǎngkè teach; lecture
讲演 jiǎngyǎn lecture; speech
讲义 jiǎngyì lecture notes

讲座 jiǎngzuò a course of lectures

听讲 tīngjiǎng 演讲 yǎnjiǎng

❺[名]注重;追求: stress; be particular about; seek after | ～排场 jiǎng páichang go in for ostentation and extravagance; go in for showy display; be ostentatious; show off / ～卫生 jiǎng wèishēng pay attention to hygiene / ～礼貌 jiǎng lǐmào maintain good manners / 不～情面 bù jiǎng qíngmiàn have no consideration for anyone's sensibilities

讲究 jiǎngjiu ① be particular about; pay attention to; stress; strive for ② exquisite; tasteful ③ careful study

奖 (獎) jiǎng　9画 大部

奖 奖奖奖奖奖奖奖奖奖

❶[动]称赞: encourage; praise; reward

过奖 guòjiǎng　嘉奖 jiājiǎng　夸奖 kuājiǎng

❷[动]为了鼓励或表扬而授予(荣誉或钱物等): encourage and reward | 老师～给他一本词典。Lǎoshī jiǎnggěi tā yī běn cídiǎn. He got a dictionary from his teacher as a reward.

奖杯 jiǎngbēi cup (as a prize)

奖金 jiǎngjīn money award; bonus; premium

奖励 jiǎnglì encourage and reward; award; reward

奖牌 jiǎngpái medal

奖品 jiǎngpǐn prize; award

奖状 jiǎngzhuàng certificate of merit; certificate of award; citation; honorary credential; diploma

奖学金 jiǎngxuéjīn scholarship

❸[名]为鼓励、表扬而给的荣誉或物品等: prize or award given as encouragement and praise | 发～fājiǎng award prizes / 获～ huòjiǎng win a prize / 一等～ yīděngjiǎng first prize / 他在体育比赛中得了～。Tā zài tǐyù bǐsài zhōng déle jiǎng. He was awarded a prize in the sports competition.

颁奖 bānjiǎng 抽奖 chōujiǎng 大奖 dàjiǎng 中奖 zhòngjiǎng

桨 (槳) jiǎng　10画 木部

桨 桨桨桨桨桨桨桨桨桨桨

[名]划船的用具: oar; scull; paddle | 划～huájiǎng rowing a boat

匠 jiǎng　6画 匚部

匠 匠匠匠匠匠匠

[名]有专门技术的手工业工人：craftsman; artisan ｜ 木～mùjiang *carpenter* / 铁～tiějiang *blacksmith* / 能工巧～nénggōng-qiǎojiàng *skillful craftsman; skilled artisan*

降 jiàng 8画 阝(左)部

降降降降降降降降降

❶[动]由高往低移动；落下(跟"升shēng"相对)：descend (the opposite of "升shēng") ｜ ～雨jiàngyǔ *rainfall; a fall of rain* / 体温～了。Tǐwēn jiàng le. *The temperature dropped.*

降临 jiànglín befall; arrive; come

降落 jiàngluò descend; land; touch down

降水 jiàngshuǐ precipitation; rain, snow, etc.

降温 jiàngwēn ① lower the temperature (as in a workshop) ② drop in temperature

下降 xiàjiàng

❷[动]使落下：make fall ｜ ～级 jiàngjí *reduce to a lower rank* / ～低价格jiàngdī jiàgé *lower the price* / 这种药可以～血压。Zhè zhǒng yào kěyǐ jiàng xuèyā. *The medicine can bring down high blood pressure.*

降低jiàngdī reduce; cut down; drop; lower

降价 jiàngjià lower the price

　　See xiáng.

酱 (醬) jiàng 13画 酉部

酱酱酱酱酱酱酱酱
酱酱酱酱酱

❶[名]豆、麦等经发酵制成的调味品：thick sauce made from fermented beans, wheat, etc. ｜ 甜面～tiánmiànjiàng *sweet sauce made of fermented flour* / 豆瓣儿～dòubànrjiàng *thick broad bean sauce*

酱油 jiàngyóu soy sauce

❷[形]像酱的糊状食品：food that looks like sauce ｜ 果～guǒjiàng *jam* / 芝麻～zhīmajiàng *sesame paste*

交 jiāo 6画 亠部

交交交交交交

❶ [动]互相交叉；连接：intersect; cross; join; connect ｜ 两条线相～。Liǎng tiáo xiàn xiāngjiāo. *Two lines cross each other.*

交叉jiāochā ①intersect; cross; criss-cross ② overlapping ③ alternate; stagger

交错jiāocuò ①interlock; criss-cross ② staggered

交点 jiāodiǎn ① point of intersection ② node

相交 xiāngjiāo

公交车 gōngjiāochē

立交桥 lìjiāoqiáo

❷[动]互相往来；互相接触：come into contact; get in touch with each other | ～朋友 jiāo péngyou *make friends* / 打～道 dǎjiāodào *come into contact with; have dealings with*

交锋 jiāofēng cross swords; engage in a battle or contest

交际 jiāojì social interaction; communication

交涉 jiāoshè negotiate; make representations; negotiate with sb. on sth.

交手 jiāoshǒu fight hand to hand; be engaged in a hand-to-hand fight; come to grips

交往 jiāowǎng ① association; ② contact; associate with; be in contact with

外交官 wàijiāoguān

❸[名]朋友；交情：friend; friendship; friendly relation | 建～ jiànjiāo *establish diplomatic relations* / 我和他没有深～。Wǒ hé tā méiyǒu shēnjiāo. *I do not have a deep friendship with him.*

❹[副]互相：mutually | ～流经验 jiāoliú jīngyàn *exchange experiences; draw on each other's experience* / ～换意见 jiāohuàn yìjiàn *exchange views; compare notes*

交换 jiāohuàn exchange; swap; interchange

交流 jiāoliú exchange; interflow; interchange

交谈 jiāotán talk with each other; converse; chat

交替 jiāotì ① supersede; replace ② alternately; by turn; in turn

交易 jiāoyì business; deal; trade; transaction

❺[动]把事物转移给有关方面：hand over; deliver; refer (the matter) to the care of the party concerned | 这事～给我办。Zhè shì jiāogěi wǒ bàn. *Leave this matter to me.* / 货已经～齐了。Huò yǐjīng jiāoqí le. *The goods have been delivered in full.*

交代 jiāodài ① turn over; hand over; transfer ② tell; leave words; order ③ explain; make clear; account for ④ confess

交付 jiāofù ① pay ② turn over; hand over; deliver; consign

交给 jiāogěi hand over sth. to sb.; turn over; deliver

交纳 jiāonà hand in

递交 dìjiāo   上交 shàngjiāo

提交 tíjiāo   移交 yíjiāo

转交 zhuǎnjiāo

◇交通 jiāotōng traffic; communications

饥寒交迫 jīhán-jiāopò

郊 jiāo 8画 阝(右)部

郊 郊郊郊郊郊郊郊郊

[名]城市周围的地区：outskirts of a city | ～外jiāowài outskirts / ～游jiāoyóu outing; excursion 郊区jiāoqū suburbs; outskirts; suburban district

浇（澆）jiāo 9画 氵部

浇 浇浇浇浇浇浇浇浇浇

❶[动]把液体倒在物体上：pour liquid on; sprinkle | ～铅字jiāo qiānzì casting type
❷[动]灌溉；把水输送到田地里：irrigate; water; lead water to the field | ～花jiāohuā water flowers / ～水jiāoshuǐ water / ～地jiāodì irrigate the fields 浇灌jiāoguàn irrigate; water

娇（嬌）jiāo 9画 女部

娇 娇娇娇娇娇娇娇娇娇

❶[形]柔嫩；美丽可爱：tender; delicate; lovely; charming | ～嫩jiāonèn tender and delicate / ～弱jiāoruò tender and fragile
❷[形]意志脆弱，不坚强：weak-willed; not strong-willed | 她什么都依赖丈夫，真太～了。Tā shēnme dōu yīlài zhàngfu, zhēn tài jiāo le. She depends on her husband for everything. She is really too weak.
娇气jiāoqì squeamish
❸[形]过分宠爱：spoil | 别太～孩子。Bié tài jiāo háizi. Don't pamper the child.
娇惯jiāoguàn pamper; coddle; spoil
娇生惯养jiāoshēng-guànyǎng grow up in soft surroundings; be pampered and spoiled

骄（驕）jiāo 9画 马部

骄 骄骄骄骄骄骄骄骄骄

[形]自高自大：conceited; proud; arrogant | 胜不～shèng bù jiāo not made dizzy with success 骄傲jiāo'ào ① arrogant; conceited ② be proud of; take pride in

胶（膠）jiāo 10画 月部

胶 胶胶胶胶胶胶胶胶胶胶

❶[名]有黏性，能粘合东西的物质：glue; gum | 万能～wànnéng-jiāo all-purpose adhesive / 鞋开～了。Xié kāijiāo le. The *shoes have come apart at the seams.*

❷[名]指橡胶：rubber | ～皮 jiāopí *rubber* / ～鞋 jiāoxié *rubber boots* / ～布 jiāobù *adhesive plaster*

橡胶 xiàngjiāo

◇胶卷 jiāojuǎn roll film; film

胶片 jiāopiàn film

jiāo　11画 攵部

教教教教教教教教
教教教

[动]传授知识、技能：teach; instruct | ～汉字 jiāo Hànzì *teach Chinese characters* / 我～历史。Wǒ jiāo lìshǐ. *I teach history.* / 我～你做。Wǒ jiāo nǐ zuò. *Let me show you how to do it.*

教书 jiāoshū teaching; education

See jiào.

jiāo　12画 木部

椒椒椒椒椒椒椒椒
椒椒椒椒

[名]指某些果实或种子有刺激性味道的植物：hot spice plants | 花～huājiāo *Chinese prickly ash* / 辣～làjiāo *chilli*

青椒 qīngjiāo

jiāo　12画 隹部

焦焦焦焦焦焦焦焦
焦焦焦焦

[形]着急；烦躁：worried; anxious; fidgety; agitated | 心～xīnjiāo *anxious; worried* / ～虑 jiāolǜ *anxious and worried*

焦急 jiāojí anxious; worried

◇焦点 jiāodiǎn ① focal point; focus ② central issue; point at issue

焦炭 jiāotàn coke

聚焦 jùjiāo

jiāo　15画 艹部

蕉蕉蕉蕉蕉蕉蕉蕉
蕉蕉蕉蕉蕉蕉蕉

See 香蕉

香蕉 xiāngjiāo

jiāo　20画 口部

嚼嚼嚼嚼嚼嚼嚼嚼
嚼嚼嚼嚼嚼嚼嚼嚼
嚼嚼嚼嚼

[动]用牙齿磨碎食物：masticate; chew; munch | ～碎 jiáosuì *chew well* / 细～慢咽 xìjiáo-mànyàn *chew carefully and swallow slowly; chew one's food well before swallowing it*

jiǎo　7画 角部

角 角角角角角角角

❶[名]horn; antler ｜ 牛~niújiǎo *ox horn* / 鹿~lùjiǎo *antler*

❷[名]物体两个边沿相接的地方：corner; the point at which two lines, surfaces, or edges meet ｜ 桌子~儿zhuōzijiǎor *the edge of a table* / 墙~儿 qiángjiǎor *a corner formed by two walls*

角落 jiǎoluò corner; nook

❸[名]几何学名词：(geog.) angle ｜ 直~zhíjiǎo *right angle* / 锐~ruìjiǎo *acute angle*

角度 jiǎodù ① angle ② point of view; angle

三角 sānjiǎo

三角洲 sānjiǎozhōu

❹[量]我国货币名。10角合人民币1元：(Chinese currency) ten *jiao* equal one *yuan*

◇豆角 dòujiǎo　　视角 shìjiǎo

狡　jiǎo　　9画 犭部

狡 狡狡狡狡狡狡狡狡狡

[形]奸猾；诡诈：crafty; foxy; cunning; deceitful; tricky; sly ｜ ~辩 jiǎobiàn *quibble*

狡猾 jiǎohuá sly; crafty; cunning; tricky

饺 (餃) jiǎo　　9画 饣部

饺 饺饺饺饺饺饺饺饺饺

[名]半圆形有馅的面食：dumpling ｜ 水~ shuǐjiǎo *dumplings* / 蒸~ zhēngjiǎo *steamed dumplings*

饺子 jiǎozi dumpling

绞 (絞) jiǎo　　9画 纟部

绞 绞绞绞绞绞绞绞绞绞

❶[动]把两股以上的条状物扭在一起：twist; wring; entangle ｜ 把几股铁丝~在一起bǎ jǐ gǔ tiěsī jiǎo zài yīqǐ *twist several strands of iron wire together*

❷[动]握住条状物的两端同时向相反方向转动，使受到挤压：wring; twist ｜ 把毛巾~干 bǎ máojīn jiǎogān *wring out wet towels*

❸[动]用绳子等捆住或套住，再用力拉紧：hang by the neck ｜ ~刑 jiǎoxíng *death by hanging; sentence to the gallows*

矫 (矯) jiǎo　　11画 矢部

矫 矫矫矫矫矫矫矫矫矫矫矫

❶[动]纠正：rectify; correct; straighten out ｜ ~形 jiǎoxíng *orthopaedics*

矫正 jiǎozhèng correct; put
right; rectify

❷[形]强壮；勇敢：strong; brave
矫健 jiǎojiàn strong and vigorous
矫捷 jiǎojié vigorous and nimble;
brisk

脚 jiǎo 11画 月部

脚脚脚脚脚脚脚脚
脚脚脚

❶[名]foot | ~底 jiǎodǐ sole / 她
的~走肿了。Tā de jiǎo zǒu-
zhǒng le. *Her feet are swollen
from walking.*
脚步 jiǎobù step; pace
绊脚石 bànjiǎoshí
大手大脚 dàshǒu-dàjiǎo

❷[名]物体的最下部：the foot or
base of sth. | 墙~qiángjiǎo *the
foot of a wall*
山脚 shānjiǎo

◇做手脚 zuòshǒujiǎo

搅 (攪) jiǎo 12画 扌部

搅搅搅搅搅搅搅搅
搅搅搅搅

❶[动]扰乱；打乱：disturb; con-
fuse; mess up | 你别把问题~混
了。Nǐ bié bǎ wèntí jiǎohùn
le. *Don't mess up the question.* /
吵闹的孩子们把我的头都~昏

了。Chǎonào de háizimen bǎ
wǒ de tóu dōu jiǎohūn le. *The
noisy children made me confused.* / 这事全让他~了。Zhè
shì quán ràng tā jiǎo le. *He
made a mess of everything.*

❷[动]拌和，使混和物均匀：stir;
mix | ~鸡蛋 jiǎo jīdàn *stir the
eggs.* / 她用小勺~咖啡。Tā yòng
xiǎo sháo jiǎo kāfēi. *She stirred
the coffee with a teaspoon.*
搅拌 jiǎobàn stir; agitate; mix

缴 (繳) jiǎo 16画 纟部

缴缴缴缴缴缴缴缴
缴缴缴缴缴缴缴缴

❶[动]交纳；交出：pay; hand over;
hand in | 上~shàngjiǎo *turn in
to higher authorities* / ~学费 jiǎo
xuéfèi *pay tuition fees* / 我每月
都去邮局~电话费。Wǒ měi yuè
dōu qù yóujú jiǎo diàn-huàfèi.
*I go to pay my telephone bill at
the post office every month.*
缴纳 jiǎonà pay; hand in

❷[动]迫使交出(武器)：capture | ~
了许多武器 jiǎo le xǔduō wǔqì
seize a lot of weapons / ~了敌
人的枪 jiǎole dírén de qiāng
disarm the enemy

叫 jiǎo 5画 口部

叫 叫叫叫叫叫

❶[动]大声呼喊：cry out ｜ 大～一声 dàjiào yī shēng *give out a loud cry; shout* / 他疼得～了起来。Tā téng de jiào le qǐlai. *He gave out a loud cry of pain.*

叫喊 jiàohǎn shout; yell; howl

叫唤 jiàohuàn cry out; call out

叫嚷 jiàorǎng shout; howl; clamour

喊叫 hǎnjiào

大喊大叫 dàhǎn-dàjiào

❷[动]动物发出声音：sound made by animals ｜ 鸟～niǎo jiào *chirping of a bird* / 鸡～jī jiào *crowing (of a cock)* / 蝉在树上不停地～。Chán zài shù shang bù tíng de jiào. *The cicadas chirped continuously in the tree.*

❸[动]名称(是)；称呼；称作：name; be called ｜ 他～什么名字? Tā jiào shénme míngzi? *What's his name?* / 我～小华。Wǒ jiào Xiǎohuá. *My name is Xiaohua.*

叫做 jiàozuò be called

❹[动]呼唤；招呼：call; summon ｜ ～他明天来。Jiào tā míngtiān lái. *Tell him to come over tomorrow.* / 请你把他～来。Qǐng nǐ bǎ tā jiàolai. *Please call him over.*

❺[动]通知人送来：tell sb. to have sth. delivered ｜ ～菜 jiào cài *order dishes (at a restaurant)*

❻[动]要求；命令；使：demand; order; make; cause ｜ ～人为难 jiào rén wéinán *make sb. feel difficult* / 公司～我马上去开会。Gōngsī jiào wǒ mǎshàng qù kāihuì. *The company told me to attend a meeting at once.*

❼[动]容许；听任：allow; permit; let ｜ 他不～我去。Tā bù jiào wǒ qù. *He forbids me to go.*

❽[介]用在句子中表示主语是受事，相当于"被bèi"：by (used to introduce the doer of an action, same as "被bèi") ｜ 他的衣服～雨淋湿了。Tā de yīfu jiào yǔ línshī le. *His clothes were soaked in the rain.* / 画儿～风刮下来了。Huàr jiào fēng guā xiàlai le. *The wind tore the picture down.* / 他的手～玻璃划破了。Tā de shǒu jiào bōli huápò le. *His hand was scratched by glass.*

 (覺) jiào　9画 见部

觉 觉觉觉觉觉觉觉觉觉

[名]睡眠：sleep ｜ 午～wǔjiào *a nap at midday* / 一～醒来yī jiào xǐnglái *awake from sleep* / 吵得

我睡不成～。Chǎo de wǒ shuì-
bùchéng jiào. *It was so noisy
that I couldn't sleep.*
睡觉 shuìjiào
　　See jué.

轿（轎）jiào　10画 车部
轿 轿轿轿轿轿轿轿轿
　　轿轿

[名]由人抬着走或由牲口驮着走的
旧式交通工具：sedan｜花～
huājiào *a sedan chair for a
bride* / 抬～táijiào *carry a sedan chair*
　轿子 jiàozi（old）sedan chair
◇轿车 jiàochē bus or car

较（較）jiào　10画 车部
较 较较较较较较较较
　　较较

❶[副]比较：comparatively｜气
温～低 qìwēn jiàodī *the temperature is quite low* / 内容～好
nèiróng jiàohǎo *the content is
quite nice*
较量 jiàoliàng measure one's
strength with; have a contest
with
　比较 bǐjiào　　　计较 jìjiào
❷[副]表示具有一定的程度：com-
paratively
❸[介]用来比较性状和程度；比：by

comparison｜工作～以前更努
力 gōngzuò jiào yǐqián gèng
nǔlì *work harder than before* /
他～以前胖多了。Tā jiào yǐ-
qián pàngduō le. *He's much
fatter than before.*

教　　jiào　11画 攵部
教 教教教教教教教教
　　教教教

❶[动]教育；指导：educate; give
instruction; direct; guide｜执～
zhíjiào *be a teacher; teach* /
指～zhǐjiào *give advice or
comments*
教材 jiàocái teaching material
教导 jiàodǎo ① instruct; teach;
give guidance ② teaching;
guidance
教练 jiàoliàn ① train; drill;
coach ② coach; instructor
教师 jiàoshī teacher; school-
teacher
教室 jiàoshì classroom
教授 jiàoshòu ① professor
② instruct; teach
教学 jiàoxué teaching; edu-
cation
教训 jiàoxùn ① lesson; moral ②
give a lesson to sb.
教养 jiàoyǎng ① bring up;
train; educate ② upbringing;
education; fine breeding
教育 jiàoyù ① education ② educate

教员 jiàoyuán teacher; instructor

教科书 jiàokēshū textbook

教练员 jiàoliànyuán coach; instructor; trainer

教师节 Jiàoshījié Teacher's Day (on September 10th in China)

教研室 jiàoyánshì teaching and research section

助教 zhùjiào

高等教育 gāoděng jiàoyù

❷[动]使；令：make; let; order; cause｜他~我别出声。Tā jiào wǒ bié chūshēng. *He instructed me to keep silent.*

教唆 jiàosuō instigate; abet; put sb. up to sth.

❸[名]宗教：religion｜佛~Fójiào *Buddhism* / 道~Dàojiào *the Taoist religion; Taoism*

教会 jiàohuì (the Christian) church

教堂 jiàotáng church; cathedral

教条 jiàotiáo dogma; doctrine; creed; tenet

基督教 Jīdūjiào

天主教 Tiānzhǔjiào

伊斯兰教 Yīsīlánjiào

See jiāo.

阶（階）jiē　6画 阝(左)部

阶 阶阶阶阶阶阶

❶[名]台阶：flight of stairs｜~梯 jiētī *steps* / 石~shíjiē *stone steps*

台阶 táijiē

❷[名]等级：(social) class; grade

阶层 jiēcéng a class of people; a social stratum; a walk of life

阶段 jiēduàn period; phase; stage

阶级 jiējí social class

工人阶级 gōngrén jiējí

无产阶级 wúchǎn jiējí

资产阶级 zīchǎn jiējí

皆 jiē　9画 比部

皆 皆皆皆皆皆皆皆皆

[副]全；都：all; each and every｜~大欢喜 jiēdàhuānxǐ *everybody is happy; to the satisfaction of all* / 人人~知 rénrén jiē zhī *everybody knows*

结（結）jiē　9画 纟部

结 结结结结结结结结结

[动]植物长出果实或种子：bear fruit or seed｜开花~果 kāihuā jiēguǒ *bloom and bear fruit* / 树上~了很多苹果。Shù shang jiēle hěn duō píngguǒ. *The apple tree bears a lot of apples.*

◇结实 jiēshi tough; strong; sturdy; robust; durable

See jié.

接 jiē 11画 扌部

接接接接接接接接
接接接

❶[动]靠近；接触：approach; get in contact with | ～地线 jiēdìxiàn (elec.) *ground wire; earth lead*

接触 jiēchù ① make contact with; contact; come into contact with; get in touch with ②touch; be exposed to

接近 jiējìn draw near; come close; approach; near to

❷[动]连接; connect; join | ～电线 jiē diànxiàn *connect wires* / 上句不～下句。Shàngjù bù jiē xiàjū. *The sentences are not connected.*

接管 jiēguǎn take over control; take over

接口 jiēkǒu (elec.) socket; jack

间接 jiànjiē　　连接 liánjiē

链接 liánjiē　　衔接 xiánjiē

直接 zhíjiē

❸[动]连续；继续：continue; go on with | ～着往下讲 jiēzhe wǎng xià jiǎng *continue or go on with one's speech*

接力 jiēlì work by relays

接连 jiēlián one after another; in quick (rapid; frequent) succession; repeatedly; continuously; on end; in a row

接着 jiēzhe ① catch; take hold of; accept ② follow; carry on; go on with; proceed; continue ③ then; shortly afterwards; thereupon

接二连三 jiē'ěr-liánsān one after another; in quick succession

❹[动] 接过别人的工作继续干：take over (duties, etc.); take up; succeed; take the place of | 谁～你的班?Shéi jiē nǐ de bān? *Who comes on duty after you?* / 主任让我～王老师的课。Zhǔrèn ràng wǒ jiē Wáng lǎoshī de kè. *The director asked me to take over Mr Wang's classes.*

接班 jiēbān take one's turn on duty; take over; carry on；replace

接替 jiētì take over; replace

❺[动]托住；承受：catch; take hold of | ～球jiēqiú *catch a ball* / 用手～住 yòng shǒu jiēzhù *catch with hands* / 他双手～过礼物。Tā shuāngshǒu jiēguo lǐwù. *He accepted the present in both hands.*

❻[动]接受；收到：accept; receive | ～到一封信 jiēdào yī fēng xìn *receive a letter* / 我不能～这笔钱。Wǒ bùnéng jiē zhè bǐ qián. *I can't accept this money.*

接到 jiēdào receive; take; accept

接纳 jiēnà admit (into an

organization)

接收 jiēshōu take over; expropriate; receive; take in

接受 jiēshòu accept; take; embrace

承接 chéngjiē

❼[动]迎接 (跟 "送 sòng" 相对): greet; meet (the opposite of "送 sòng") | ～待宾客 jiēdài bīnkè *receive guests* / 到火车站～朋友 dào huǒchēzhàn jiē péngyou *go to the railway station to meet one's friend*

接待 jiēdài receive; reception

接见 jiējiàn receive; grant an interview (audience) to

接洽 jiēqià take up a matter with; arrange (consult; discuss; negotiate with)

迎接 yíngjiē

◇接种 jiēzhòng have an inoculation; inoculate

揭 jiē 12画 扌部

揭 揭揭揭揭揭揭揭揭 揭揭揭揭

❶[动]掀起;掀开: lift; raise; uncover; open | ～被子 jiē bèizi *lift the quilt* / ～锅盖 jiē guōgài *lift the lid (of a cooking pot)* / 把这张膏药～下来。Bǎ zhè zhāng gāoyao jiē xiàlai. *Tear off the plaster.*

揭开 jiēkāi uncover; reveal; open

揭幕 jiēmù unveil (a monument, etc.); inaugurate

❷[动]使隐蔽的事物显露: expose; show up | ～短 jiēduǎn *rake up sb.'s faults, shortcomings or weaknesses* / 他的谎言被～穿了。Tā de huǎngyán bèi jiēchuān le. *His lies have been laid bare.*

揭发 jiēfā lay bare (lay open); show up; expose; unmask; bring to light

揭露 jiēlù lay bare; show up; unmask; expose; uncover; bring to light; disclose

揭示 jiēshì ① make public; announce; proclaim; promulgate ② reveal; bring to light

揭晓 jiēxiǎo announce; make known; publish

❸[动]把粘贴着的片状物取下: tear off | 把墙上的画～下来。Bǎ qiáng shang de huà jiē xiàlai. *Peel the painting off the wall.*

按揭 ànjiē

街 jiē 12画 彳部

街 街街街街街街街街 街街街街

[名]street | 上～买东西 shàng jiē mǎi dōngxi *go out shopping* / ～上非常热闹。Jiē shang fēicháng rènao. *The street is bustling.*

街道 jiēdào street; neighbour-

hood
街坊 jiēfang neighbour
街区 jiēqū residential district; neighbourhood
街头 jiētóu street; street corner
大街 dàjiē
大街小巷 dàjiē-xiǎoxiàng

节 (節) jié　5画 ⺌部

节 节节节节节

❶ [名]物体各段之间相连接的地方：length; joint｜竹~ zhújié bamboo joint
❷ [名]段落；整体中的一个部分：section; part｜~拍 jiépāi beat / 音~ yīnjié syllable
节目 jiémù programme; item (on a programme)
节奏 jiézòu rhythm
环节 huánjié　　细节 xìjié
❸ [名]节令；节日；纪念日：one of the 24 periods into which the year is divided; festival; anniversary or red-letter day｜国际劳动~ Guójì láodòngjié the International Labour Day / 春~ Chūnjié Spring Festival / 过~我一定回来。Guòjié wǒ yīdìng huílai. I am sure to come back for the coming festival.
节日 jiérì festival
重阳节 Chóngyángjié
端午节 Duānwǔjié
复活节 Fùhuójié

感恩节 Gǎn'ēnjié
国庆节 Guóqìngjié
教师节 Jiàoshījié
泼水节 Pōshuǐjié
清明节 Qīngmíngjié
圣诞节 Shèngdànjié
愚人节 Yúrénjié
元宵节 Yuánxiāojié
中秋节 Zhōngqiūjié
逢年过节 féngnián-guòjié
❹ [动]俭省；限制；约束：economize; save; limit; restrict｜~电 jiédiàn save on electricity / ~水 jiéshuǐ save water
节能 jiénéng save energy
节省 jiéshěng be thrifty; be frugal; be sparing; cut down; economize; save; use sparingly; use with thrift
节育 jiéyù birth control
节约 jiéyuē be thrifty; be frugal; be sparing; economize; save; practice thrift (austerity, economy, frugality)
节假日 jiéjiàrì festivals and holidays
❺ [名]礼仪：ceremony; rite; protocol
礼节 lǐjié
◇调节 tiáojié

劫 jié　7画 力部

劫 劫劫劫劫劫劫劫

❶ [动]强抢；掠夺：rob; plunder

劫匪 jiéfěi highwayman; robber

打劫 dǎjié

❷ [动]威逼；胁迫：coerce; compel

劫持 jiéchí ① hijack; kidnap; abduct ② hijacking

杰 jié 8画 木部

杰 杰 杰 杰 杰 杰 杰 杰

[形]突出，超乎寻常：outstanding; extraordinary

杰出 jiéchū outstanding; prominent; distinguished

杰作 jiézuò masterpiece

洁（潔）jié 9画 氵部

洁 洁 洁 洁 洁 洁 洁 洁 洁

[形]干净：clean; pure ｜纯~ chúnjié pure and clean

洁白 jiébái immaculate white; pure white; spotlessly (spotless) white

洁具 jiéjù sanitary equipment; sanitary utensils

简洁 jiǎnjié   清洁 qīngjié

结（結）jié 9画 纟部

结 结 结 结 结 结 结 结 结

❶ [动]用条状物打成扣或编织：knit ｜~毛衣 jié máoyī knit a sweater / ~网 jié wǎng weave a net

❷ [名]用条状物打成的扣：knot ｜蝴蝶~ húdié jié bowknot / 打个~ dǎ ge jié tie a knot

❸ [动]凝固；凝聚：solidify ｜~冰 jié bīng freeze; ice up / 从那时起我们~下了深厚的友谊。Cóng nàshí qǐ wǒmen jiéxiàle shēnhòu de yǒuyì. From then on a deep friendship has been built up between us.

结晶 jiéjīng ① crystallize ② crystal ③ crystallization

冻结 dòngjié

❹ [动]结合；形成某种关系：combine; couple; form a certain kind of relationship ｜~交 jiéjiāo make friends with; associate with

结构 jiégòu structure; composition; construction

结合 jiéhé ① combine; unite; integrate; link ② get married; marry; be united

结婚 jiéhūn get married

巴结 bājie   缔结 dìjié

勾结 gōujié   归结 guījié

团结 tuánjié

❺ [动]发展或进行到最后阶段，不再继续：settle; conclude ｜~账 jiézhàng settle (or square) accounts; balance the books

结果 jiéguǒ ① result; outcome; consequence ② at last; finally;

in the end

结局 jiéjú final result; outcome; ending; upshot

结论 jiélùn conclusion; verdict

结束 jiéshù end; finish; conclude; wind up; close; come to a close

结算 jiésuàn settle (close,wind up) an account

结业 jiéyè complete a course; wind up one's studies

结账 jiézhàng settle (or square) account; balance the books

终结 zhōngjié   总结 zǒngjié
See jiē.

捷   jié   11画 扌部

捷 捷捷捷捷捷捷捷 捷捷捷

[形]快;迅速: quick; fast; rapid

便捷 biànjié   快捷 kuàijié
敏捷 mǐnjié

截   jié   14画 住部

截 截截截截截截截 截截截截截截

❶[动]切断: cut; sever | ～开木料 jiékāi mùliào cut the log in parts

斩钉截铁 zhǎndīng-jiétiě

❷[动]阻挡: stop; check | ～住他 jiézhù tā stop him

拦截 lánjié

❸[动]到一定期限停止: end (close) by a specified time | 交费时间～至下午5点半。Jiāofèi shíjiān jiézhì xiàwǔ wǔ diǎn bàn. Payment of bills closes at 5:30 in the afternoon.

截止 jiézhǐ close; end

竭   jié   14画 立部

竭 竭竭竭竭竭竭竭竭 竭竭竭竭竭竭

[动]完;尽: use up; exhaust; be completely exhausted; do one's utmost | 衰～shuāijié exhaustion; prostration

竭力 jiélì do one's best (utmost); exert one's utmost strength; spare no efforts

姐   jiě   8画 女部

姐 姐姐姐姐姐姐姐姐

❶[名]同父母或同辈亲属中比自己年纪大的女子: elder sister | 表～biǎojiě cousin

姐姐 jiějie elder sister

姐妹 jiěmèi sisters

大姐 dàjiě

❷[名]称呼年轻女子: used to address a young woman of the same generation

空中小姐 kōngzhōng xiǎojiě

解

jiě　13画 角部

解解解解解解解解
解解解解解

❶[动]剖开：cut apart
解剖 jiěpōu dissect

❷[动]分开：separate; take apart |
难分难～nánfēn-nánjiě *inseparable*
解散 jiěsàn ① dismiss ② dissolve; disband
分解 fēnjiě　　溶解 róngjiě
瓦解 wǎjiě

❸[动]把捆着或系着的东西打开：
untie; undo; unfasten | ～扣子
jiě kōuzi *unbutton* / ～鞋带 jiě
xiédài *undo the shoelaces* / 他
把包装上的绳子～了下来。Tā
bǎ bāozhuāng shang de
shéngzi jiěle xiàlai. *He untied
the rope from the pack.*
解放 jiěfàng ① liberate; emancipate ② liberation; emancipation
解救 jiějiù save; rescue; deliver

❹[动]去掉；消除：dismiss; dispel
| ～约 jiěyuē *terminate an
agreement; cancel a contract* /
～渴 jiěkě *quench one's thirst* /
～乏 jiěfá *recover from fatigue*
解除 jiěchú absolve; remove;
relieve; get rid of; dismiss; annul; cancel
解雇 jiěgù fire; dismiss; discharge; give the sack
解禁 jiějìn lift a ban
解决 jiějué ① resolve; settle;
solve ② finish off; dispose of
解密 jiěmì remove the confidential state of certain information (usu. document, archive,
etc.)
和解 héjiě　　调解 tiáojiě

❺[动]说明：explain; give an account of | ～说 jiěshuō *explain
orally*
解答 jiědá ①answer; explain ②
solution
解释 jiěshì ① account for; explain; expound; interpret ② explanation; interpretation
辩解 biànjiě　　见解 jiànjiě
讲解 jiǎngjiě　　注解 zhùjiě

❻[动]明白；懂：know; understand
| 费～fèijiě *hard to understand;
obscure* / 感到不～gǎndào bùjiě *feel puzzled* / 通俗易～tōngsú
yìjiě *easy to understand*
不解 bùjiě　　理解 lǐjiě
谅解 liàngjiě　　了解 liǎojiě
误解 wùjiě

介

jiè　4画 人部

介 介介介介

❶[动]在两者中间：interpose; put
or come between | 中～zhōng-
jiè *intermediary; agent*
介入 jièrù intervene; interpose;

get involved

❷[动]使二者发生联系：introduce; make the two come into contact with each other

介词 jiècí (gram.) preposition

介绍 jièshào ① introduce; present ② recommend; suggest

简介 jiǎnjiè

◇介意 jièyì (usu. used in the negative) take offence; mind

戒 戒戒戒戒戒戒戒

jiè   7画 戈部

❶[动]防备；警惕：guard; guard against; defend | ~备 jièbèi guard against / ~心 jièxīn vigilance; wariness

戒严 jièyán cordon off an area; enforce martial law; impose a curfew

❷[动]改掉 (不良嗜好)：get rid of (a habit); kick (a habit) | ~烟 jièyān give up smoking / ~酒 jièjiǔ quit drinking

戒毒 jièdú come off drugs; drug detoxification

◇戒指 jièzhi (finger) ring

届 届届届届届届届届

jiè   8画 尸部

[量]用于定期的会议或毕业的班级等：time; session | 本~毕业生

běn jiè bìyèshēng this year's graduates; the graduating students (class) / 下一~ xià yī jiè the next / 第一~ dì-yī jiè the first

界 界界界界界界界界界 界

jiè   9画 田部

❶[名] 地区跟地区相交的地方：boundary; border | 国~ guójiè national boundary / 以河流为~ yǐ héliú wéi jiè take the river as the boundary

界定 jièdìng define; decide

界线 jièxiàn boundary

界限 jièxiàn demarcation line; dividing line; bounds; limits

边界 biānjiè

❷[名]一定的范围：scope; extent | 眼~ yǎnjiè field of vision

出界 chūjiè   境界 jìngjiè

世界 shìjiè   外界 wàijiè

租界 zūjiè   世界观 shìjièguān

❸[名]特指按职业、工作或性别等划定的范围：circles, esp. groups of people of the same profession, sex, etc. | 文艺~ wényìjiè literature and art circles / 科学~ kēxuéjiè scientific circles / 教育~ jiàoyùjiè educational circles

各界 gèjiè

诫 (誡) jiè　9画 讠部

诫 诫诫诫诫诫诫诫诫诫
诫

[动]警告；劝告：warn; advise; alarm; try to persuade｜告~gàojiè *give warning; admonish* / 劝~quànjiè *persuade*

借 (藉❸❹) jiè　10画 亻部

借 借借借借借借借借借借

❶[动]暂用别人的；借进：borrow｜~东西 jiè dōngxi *borrow sth. from others* / 我去图书馆~书。Wǒ qù túshūguǎn jiè shū. *I am going to the library to borrow books.* / 买房子的钱是向哥哥~的。Mǎi fángzi de qián shì xiàng gē-ge jiè de. *It was from my elder brother that I borrowed the money to buy the house.*

❷[动]把自己的财物给别人暂用：lend｜~给朋友一笔钱 jiègěi péngyou yī bǐ qián *lend a sum of money to a friend* / 把书~给同学 bǎ shū jiègěi tóngxué *lend books to a classmate* / 我把车~给小王了。Wǒ bǎ chē jiègěi Xiǎo Wáng le. *I lent my car to Xiao Wang.*

续借 xùjiè

❸[动]依靠；利用：depend on; make use of; take advantage of｜凭~píngjiè *rely on* / 我~这个机会向大家表示感谢。Wǒ jiè zhège jīhuì xiàng dàjiā biǎoshì gǎnxiè. *I would like to take this opportunity to thank you all.*

借鉴 jièjiàn learn a lesson from another person's experience; benefit by another person's experience; use for reference

借助 jièzhù have the aid of; draw support from; with the help of

❹[动]假托：use as a pretext｜他~故走了。Tā jiègù zǒu le. *He found an excuse and left.*

借口 jièkǒu ① use as an excuse; use as a pretext ② excuse; pretense

巾 jīn　3画 巾部

巾 巾巾巾

[名]用来擦、裹或覆盖的纺织品：a piece of cloth used for wiping, wrapping or covering things｜毛~máojīn *towel* / 围~wéijīn *scarf* / 浴~yùjīn *bath towel*

丝巾 sījīn　　纸巾 zhǐjīn
红领巾 hónglǐngjīn

斤 jīn　4画 斤部

斤 斤斤斤斤

[量]市制重量单位，合500克：unit of weight, equalling 500g ｜ 我买一~苹果。Wǒ mǎi yī jīn píngguǒ. *I'd like to buy one jin of apples.* / 这只鸡有三~重。Zhè zhī jī yǒu sān jīn zhòng. *This chicken weighs 3 jin.*

今 jīn 4画 人部

令 今今今今

[名]当前;现在：present; now ｜ ~春 jīnchūn *this spring* / ~晨 jīnchén *this morning* / 从~以后 cóng jīn yǐhòu *from now on; henceforth*

今后 jīnhòu from now on (forward, onwards); in the days to come; henceforth; hereafter; in future

今年 jīnnián this year

今日 jīnrì ① today ② present; now

今天 jīntiān ① today ② present; now

当今 dāngjīn   如今 rújīn

至今 zhìjīn

金 jīn 8画 金部

釒 金金金金金金金金

❶ [名]金属的通称，通常指金、银、铜、铁、锡等：general term for metals ｜ 五~店 wǔjīndiàn *hardware store*

金属 jīnshǔ metal

合金 héjīn   冶金 yějīn

❷ [名]钱：money ｜ 现~xiànjīn *cash* / 基~jījīn *fund* / 奖学~jiǎngxuéjīn *scholarship*

金额 jīn'é amount (sum) of money

金钱 jīnqián money

金融 jīnróng finance; banking

本金 běnjīn   定金 dìngjīn

美金 měijīn

保证金 bǎozhèngjīn

基金会 jījīnhuì

公积金 gōngjījīn

❸ [名]gold ｜ 镀~dùjīn *gild* / ~戒指 jīnjièzhi *gold ring*

金牌 jīnpái gold medal

黄金 huángjīn

❹ [形]比喻尊重、贵重：valuable ｜ ~贵 jīnguì *valuable*

❺ [形]像黄金的颜色：golden ｜ ~发 jīnfà *blonde hair*

金黄 jīnhuáng golden yellow; golden

金色 jīnsè golden

金鱼 jīnyú goldfish

金字招牌 jīnzì zhāopái a gold-lettered signboard; a vainglorious title

津 jīn 9画 氵部

津 津津津津津津津津津津

See below

津贴 jīntiē subsidy; allowance; money in addition to salary

津津有味 jīnjīn-yǒuwèi with keen pleasure

筋 jīn 12画 竹部

筋 筋筋筋筋筋筋筋筋筋筋筋筋

❶ [名]肌腱或骨头上的韧带: muscle; tendon; sinew | 扭～了 niǔjīn le *get one's sinew (tendon) sprained* / 我的腿抽～了。Wǒ de tuǐ chōujīn le. *I have a cramp in the leg.*

❷ [名]可以看见的皮下静脉血管: vein | 青～qīngjīn *blue veins* / 这条～很粗。Zhè tiáo jīn hěn cū. *This vein is rather thick.*

❸ [名]像筋的东西: things resembling a tendon | 钢～gāngjīn *reinforced steel bar* / 橡皮～儿 xiàngpíjīnr *rubber band*

◇伤脑筋 shāngnǎojīn

仅 (僅) jīn 4画 亻部

仅 仅仅仅仅

[副]单单;只: only; alone; merely | 不～bùjǐn *not only* / ～供参考 jǐngōng cānkǎo *only for reference* / 我和他～是一般的朋友。Wǒ hé tā jǐn shì yībān de péngyou. *We are just ordinary friends.*

仅仅 jǐnjǐn only; merely

尽 (儘) jǐn 6画 尸部

尽 尽尽尽尽尽尽

❶ [动]力求达到最大限度: exert to the greatest extent; try one's best | ～可能减少错误 jǐn kěnéng jiǎnshǎo cuòwù *try to avoid mistakes as much as we can* / ～着力气干 jǐnzhe lìqi gàn *work as hard as one can*

尽快 jǐnkuài as quickly (soon, early) as possible

尽量 jǐnliàng as far as possible; to the best of one's ability

尽早 jǐnzǎo as early as (one) can; as early as possible

❷ [介]把某些人或事物放在优先地位: giving priority to sb.; using sth. first | ～着老人先坐 jǐnzhe lǎorén xiān zuò *let the elderly sit down first*

◇尽管 jǐnguǎn despite; even if; even though; though; in spite of

尽管如此 jǐnguǎn rúcǐ even so

See jǐn.

紧 (緊) jǐn 10画 系部

紧 紧紧紧紧紧紧紧紧
紧紧

❶ [形]物体受到拉力或压力后呈现的状态(跟"松sōng"相对)：tight (the opposite of "松sōng") | 把绳子拉~ bǎ shéngzi lājǐn *pull the rope taut* / 这根弦太~。Zhè gēn xián tài jǐn. *The string is too tight.*

❷ [动]收束：tighten | ~一~腰带 jǐnyijǐn yāodài *tighten up the belt* / 把弦~一下 bǎ xián jǐn yīxià *fasten the string*
紧缩 jǐnsuō retrench; curtail; cut down; reduce

❸ [形]非常接近；空隙极小：very tight; very close; leaving hardly any space | 这双鞋太~了。Zhè shuāng xié tài jǐn le. *This pair of shoes is too tight for me.* / 窗户真~，拉不开。Chuānghu zhēn jǐn, lābukāi. *The window got stuck and I cannot open it.* / 他的桌子~靠着墙。Tā de zhuōzi jǐnkàozhe qiáng. *His desk is close to the wall.*
紧密 jǐnmì close together; closely

❹ [形]经济不宽裕：short of money; hard up | 手头~ shǒutóu jǐn short of money / 他的日子总是过

得很~。Tā de rìzi zǒngshì guò de hěn jǐn. *He is always in financial straits.*
紧缺 jǐnquē in short supply; badly needed

❺ [形]急迫；动作先后密切相连：urgent; pressing; taking place one after another in succession | 任务~。Rènwù jǐn. *The task is urgent.* / 风刮得很~。Fēng guā de hěn jǐn. *The wind blows hard.* / 时间很~。Shíjiān hěn jǐn. *Time is pressing.* / 问题一个~接着一个。Wèntí yī gè jǐnjiēzhe yī gè. *Problems arose one after another.*
紧急 jǐnjí urgent; pressing; critical; emergent
紧迫 jǐnpò pressing; urgent; imminent
紧张 jǐnzhāng nervous; keyed-up; tense; strained in short supply; tight
赶紧 gǎnjǐn   加紧 jiājǐn
要紧 yàojǐn   抓紧 zhuājǐn
不要紧 búyàojǐn

锦 (錦) jǐn 13画 钅部

锦 锦锦锦锦锦锦锦锦锦
锦锦锦锦锦

[名]有彩色花纹的丝织品：brocade | ~缎 jǐnduàn *brocade*
锦绣 jǐnxiù as beautiful as brocade; beautiful; splendid

◇锦标赛 jǐnbiāosài champion-
ship; contest

谨 (謹) jǐn　13画 讠部

谨 谨谨谨谨谨谨谨谨
谨谨谨谨谨

[形]小心慎重：careful; cautious
｜～记 jǐnjì *bear in mind* / ～守
诺言 jǐnshǒu nuòyán *strictly
keep one's promise*
谨慎 jǐnshèn cautious; prudent;
circumspect
严谨 yánjǐn

尽 (盡) jìn　6画 尸部

尽 尽尽尽尽尽尽

❶[动]完：exhaust; use up｜不～
bùjìn *inexhaustible* / 油快燃～
了。Yóu kuài ránjìn le. *The oil
is nearly burned up.*
无穷无尽 wúqióng-wújìn
❷[动]全部用出；竭力完成：use up;
exhaust｜～最大的努力 jìn zuì
dà de nǔlì *do one's best; exert
one's utmost effort*
尽力 jìnlì do one's best; try
one's best; exert oneself; put
forth exertion
尽情 jìnqíng to one's heart's content; as much as one likes
尽兴 jìnxìng to one's heart's
content; enjoy oneself to the full

详尽 xiángjìn
See jìn.

进 (進) jìn　7画 辶部

进 进进进进进进进

❶[动]向前移动（跟"退 tuì"相
对）：advance (the opposite of
"退 tuì")｜两国关系～了一大
步。Liǎngguó guānxi jìnle yī
dà bù. *The bilateral relations
of these two countries have
greatly improved.*
进步 jìnbù ①advance; improve;
progress ② progressive
进程 jìnchéng course; pace;
process; progress; proceed-
ing
进度 jìndù ① rate of progress
(or advance) ② planned speed;
schedule
进而 jìn'ér proceed to the next
step
进攻 jìngōng attack; assault;
offend
进化 jìnhuà evolution
进军 jìnjūn march; advance
进取 jìnqǔ be aggressive; be eager to make progress; be enter-
prising
进行 jìnxíng ① be in progress;
be underway; go on; progress
② carry on; carry out; conduct
进修 jìnxiū engage in advanced
studies; take a refresher

course

进展 jìnzhǎn ① advance; make progress; make headway ② progress; headway; advancement

进一步 jìnyībù go a step further; further

促进 cùjìn	改进 gǎijìn
冒进 màojìn	前进 qiánjìn
上进 shàngjìn	推进 tuījìn
先进 xiānjìn	增进 zēngjìn
循序渐进 xúnxù-jiànjìn	

❷ [动] 从外面到里面 (跟 "出 chū" 相对)：enter; come into; go into (the opposite of "出 chū") | 请~。Qǐngjìn. *Come in, please.* / ~大学 jìn dàxué *enter the college* / 闲人免~。Xiánrén miǎnjìn. *No admittance except on business.; Staff only.* / 火车~站了。Huǒchē jìnzhàn le. *The train is pulling in.*

进出 jìnchū ① pass in and out ② (business) turnover

进口 jìnkǒu ① enter port ② import ③ entrance

进来 jìnlái(lai) come in

进去 jìnqù(qu) go in; get in; enter

进入 jìnrù enter; get into

❸ [动] 接纳；收入：admit; receive | ~了一批货 jìnle yī pī huò *lay in a new stock of goods* / ~款 jìnkuǎn *income*

进货 jìnhuò stock (a shop) with goods; lay in a stock of

merchandise; replenish one's stock

❹ [动] 用在动词后作补语，表示动作由外到里的趋向：used as a complement after a verb to indicate "in" | 买~一批图书 mǎijìn yī pī túshū *purchase a number of books*

跑进 pǎojìn   引进 yǐnjìn

近   jìn   7画 辶部

近 近近近近近近近

❶ [形] 空间或时间距离短 (跟 "远 yuǎn" 相对)：(of time or space) near (the opposite of "远 yuǎn") | 这段路可不~啊! Zhè duàn lù kě bù jìn a! *It's a long way to go!* / 高考的日期越来越~了。Gāokǎo de rìqī yuèláiyuè jìn le. *The date of the college entrance examination is drawing near.*

近代 jìndài modern times

近来 jìnlái recently; of late; lately

近年 jìnnián in recent years

近期 jìnqī in the near future

近日 jìnrì ① recently; in the past few days ② within the next few days

近视 jìnshì ① myopia ② short-sighted

逼近 bījìn   附近 fùjìn
接近 jiējìn   就近 jiùjìn

靠近 kàojìn　　邻近 línjìn
临近 línjìn　　贴近 tiējìn
渐近 xīnjìn　　最近 zuìjìn

❷[形]关系密切：intimate; closely related | 他们的关系很～。Tāmen de guānxi hěn jìn. *They are very close.* / 两家关系挺～。Liǎng jiā guānxi tǐng jìn. *The two families are on very close terms.*

❸[动]靠近；接近：get near; amount to | 观众～万人。Guānzhōng jìn wàn rén. *There were nearly 10,000 spectators.* / 这学期已～期末了。Zhè xuéqī yǐ jìn qīmò le. *This semester is drawing to its end.*

近似 jìnsì approximate; similar
将近 jiāngjìn

劲 (勁) jìn　　7画 力部

劲 劲劲劲劲劲劲劲

❶[名]力气；力量：strength; power; might | 用～ yòngjìn *put forth strength* / 手～ shǒujìn *the strength of the hands* / 小王的～真大。Xiǎo Wáng de jìn zhēn dà. *Xiao Wang really has great strength.*

使劲 shǐjìn

❷[名]精神；情绪：vigour; strength; drive; zeal | 干得非常起～ gàn de fēicháng qǐjìn *work with unusual vigour;*

work with great zeal / 最近他学习的～儿不足。Zuìjìn tā xuéxí de jìnr bù zú. *Recently he has not put enough effort into his studies.*

劲头 jìntóu　strength; energy
干劲 gànjìn　　起劲 qǐjìn

❸[名]神情；态度：air; manner; expression | 亲热～儿 qīnrè jìnr *intimate attitude* / 瞧他那高兴～儿。Qiáo tā nà gāoxìng jìnr. *See how happy he looks.*

❹[名]兴致；趣味：interest; mood; relish; gusto | 下棋没～ xiàqí méi jìn *no interest in chess*

带劲 dàijìn

晋 (晋) jìn　　10画 日部

晋 晋晋晋晋晋晋晋晋晋晋

[动]向前进；向上升：advance; promote; ascend | ～级 jìnjí *promotion*

晋升 jìnshēng promote to a higher position

浸 jìn　　10画 氵部

浸 浸浸浸浸浸浸浸浸浸浸

❶[动]泡在液体里：soak; steep; immerse | 她把面包～在牛奶

里。Tā bǎ miànbāo jìn zài niúnǎi li. *She soaked the bread in milk.* / 衣服要～一会再洗。Yīfu yào jìn yīhuì zài xǐ. *Wash the clothes after they have soaked in water for a while.*

❷[动]液体渗入：soak; saturate | 汗水～透了他的衣服。Hànshuǐ jìntòule tā de yīfu. *He got soaked through with sweat.*

 jìn　13画 示部

禁禁禁禁禁禁禁禁
禁禁禁禁禁

❶[动]不准；制止：forbid; disallow; stop | 生产重地，严～入内。Shēngchǎn zhòngdì, yánjìn rùnèi. *Production area, entry forbidden.* / 严～吸烟。Yān-jìn xīyān. *No smoking.*
禁毒 jìndú curtail drugs
禁区 jìnqū forbidden zone; restricted zone / area
禁止 jìnzhǐ ban; forbid; prohibit
解禁 jiějìn
紫禁城 Zǐjìnchéng
❷[动]拘押：take into custody | 拘～ jūjìn *detain*
监禁 jiānjìn

 (莖) jīng　8画 艹部

茎茎茎茎茎茎茎茎

[名]stem | 花～huājīng *the stem of a flower*

 jīng　8画 亠部

京京京京京京京京

[名]中国首都北京的简称：short for Beijing | 赴～fù Jīng *go to Beijing*
京城 jīngchéng ① Beijing city ② (old) the capital of a country
京剧 jīngjù Beijing Opera
京戏 jīngxì Beijing Opera
北京 Běijīng

 (經) jīng　8画 纟部

经经经经经经经经

❶ [名]传统的权威性的著作：classics; scripture; canon | 《诗～》Shījīng *The Book of Songs* / ～书 jīngshū *Confucian classics*
经典 jīngdiǎn ① classics ② scriptures ③ classical
❷[形]长时间不变的：constant; regular
经常 jīngcháng ① day-to-day; everyday; daily ② frequently; constantly; regularly; often
经费 jīngfèi funds; outlay

❸[动]经营；治理：manage; run; engage in; rule; govern; administer

经纪 jīngjì ① manage (a business) ② manager; broker

经理 jīnglǐ ①handle ②director; manager

经商 jīngshāng engage in trade; be in business

经销 jīngxiāo sell on commission; deal in; distribute; sell

经营 jīngyíng manage; operate; run; engage in

经销商 jīngxiāoshāng dealer; franchiser

财经 cáijīng

总经理 zǒngjīnglǐ

❹[动]通过（处所、时间、动作等）：travel by way of; go via | 路～大连 lù jīng Dàlián *pass through Dalian* / ～他一说我才知道。Jīng tā yī shuō wǒ cái zhīdāo. *I learned about it after he mentioned it.*

经过 jīngguò ① pass; go by (through) ② as a result of; after; through

经历 jīnglì ①undergo; go through; pass through; experience; see ② experience

经验 jīngyàn experience

曾经 céngjīng   已经 yǐjīng

❺ [动]经受；承受：experience; undergo | ～受 jīngshòu *undergo; experience; withstand; stand; weather*

◇经济 jīngjì ① economy ② finan-cial condition; income ③ economical; economic

 惊 (驚) jīng 11画 忄部

惊 惊惊惊惊惊惊惊惊 惊惊惊

❶[动]骡马因受到突然的刺激而狂跑起来：shy; stampede | 马～了。Mǎ jīng le. *The horse shied.*

❷[动]因突然的刺激而精神紧张或恐惧不安：start; be frightened; be stupefied | 心～肉跳 xīn-jīng-ròutiào *be filled with apprehension*

惊慌 jīnghuāng alarmed; scared; panic-stricken

惊奇 jīngqí be surprised (amazed, astonished, astounded)

惊喜 jīngxǐ pleasantly surprised

惊险 jīngxiǎn alarmingly dangerous; breathtaking; thrilling

惊讶 jīngyà surprised; amazed; astonished; astounded

惊异 jīngyì surprised; amazed; astonished; astounded

吃惊 chījīng   震惊 zhènjīng

❸[动]使受惊；惊动：startle; shock; alarm | 打草～蛇 dǎcǎo-jīng-shé *beat the grass and frighten away the snake; act rashly and alert the enemy* / 孩子刚睡着，小心不要～了他。Háizi gāng shuìzháo, xiǎoxīn būyào jīngle

402

tā. *The baby has just fallen asleep. Be careful not to disturb him.*

惊动 jīngdòng startle; alarm

惊人 jīngrén alarming; surprising; astonishing; astounding; startling

睛 jīng 13画 目部

睛 睛睛睛睛睛睛睛睛睛 睛睛睛睛睛

[名]眼球；眼珠：eyeball | 画龙点~ huàlóng-diǎnjīng *bring a picture of a dragon to life by putting in the pupils of its eyes; add the touch that brings a work of art to life*

眼睛 yǎnjing

兢 jīng 14画 十部

兢 兢兢兢兢兢兢兢兢 兢兢兢兢兢兢

See below

兢兢 jīngjīng cautious and conscientious

兢兢业业 jīngjīng-yèyè cautious and conscientious; (act) with caution and focus

精 jīng 14画 米部

精 精精精精精精精精 精精精精精精

❶[名]提炼出来的东西：extract; essence | 香~xiāngjīng *flavouring essence*

酒精 jiǔjīng   味精 wèijīng

❷[名]精神；精力：spirit; mind; consciousness; energy; vigour | 聚~会神 jùjīng-huìshén *concentrate one's attention*

精力 jīnglì energy; vigour; vitality

精神 jīngshen ① spirit; mind; consciousness ②vigour; vitality

精神病 jīngshénbìng mental disease; mental disorder; psychosis

❸[形]经过提炼或挑选的：refined; purified; selected | ~盐 jīngyán *refined salt* / ~白米 jīng báimǐ *polished white rice*

精华 jīnghuá cream; choice; elite; extract; essence; essentials

精品 jīngpǐn ① fine works (of art) ② quality goods; articles of fine quality

精选 jīngxuǎn ①carefully chosen ② choice

精英 jīngyīng essence; cream; flower

❹[形]完美；最好：perfect; best | 少而~shǎo ér jīng *smaller quantity, better quality; fewer but better*

精彩 jīngcǎi brilliant; splendid; wonderful; marvellous

精益求精 jīngyìqiújīng strive for perfection; always endeavour to do sth. better

❺[形]熟练掌握某种学问或技术：having a good mastery of some knowledge or skill | 他对这方面的技术很～。Tā duì zhè fāngmiàn de jìshù hěn jīng. *He is highly proficient in this field. |* 他懂电脑，但是不～。Tā dǒng diànnǎo, dànshì bù jīng. *He knows computers in general, but isn't very proficient with them.*

精通 jīngtōng be versed in; have an excellent (a good) command (mastery) of; expert at; master well; be proficient in; be skilled in; be conversant with; have a sound (thorough) knowledge of

❻[形]细致；严密：careful; meticulous; strict; rigorous; exquisite | ～读 jīngdú *intensive reading* / 这花瓶工艺很～。Zhè huāpíng gōngyì hěn jīng. *This vase is of exquisite workmanship.*

精简 jīngjiǎn cut; reduce; retrench; simplify

精美 jīngměi exquisite; elegant

精密 jīngmì precise; accurate

精确 jīngquè precise; accurate; exact

精细 jīngxì meticulous; fine; careful

精心 jīngxīn meticulously; painstakingly; elaborately

精致 jīngzhì fine; exquisite; delicate

精打细算 jīngdǎ-xìsuàn careful and meticulous calculation

❼[形]聪明；机智：smart; clever; bright; quick-witted; resourceful | 这孩子比大人还～。Zhè háizi bǐ dàrén hái jīng. *The child is even smarter than grown-ups.*

 鲸(鯨) jīng   16画 鱼部

鲸鲸鲸鲸鲸鲸鲸鲸
鲸鲸鲸鲸鲸鲸鲸鲸

[名] whale

鲸鱼 jīngyú whale

 井 jǐng   4画 一部

井井井井

❶[名] well | 水～ shuǐjǐng *water well* / 挖～ wā jǐng *dig a well*
井底之蛙 jǐngdǐzhīwā be like a frog at the bottom of a well; a person with narrow perspective
坐井观天 zuòjǐng-guāntiān

❷[名]形状像井的东西：a well-shaped thing | 油～ yóujǐng *oil well* / 排水～ páishuǐjǐng *pumping shaft*
矿井 kuàngjǐng   天井 tiānjǐng

 颈(頸) jǐng   11画 页部

颈颈颈颈颈颈颈颈
颈颈颈

[名]neck | 脖～bójǐng neck
长颈鹿 chángjǐnglù

景 **jǐng** 12画 日部

景 景景景景景景景景
景景景景

❶ [名]情况；情形：situation; condition; circumstance | 好～不
长。Hǎojǐng bù cháng. *Good times do not last long.*
景象 jǐngxiàng scene; sight; picture
背景 bèijǐng 场景 chǎngjǐng
前景 qiánjǐng 情景 qíngjǐng
远景 yuǎnjǐng
❷ [名]风景：scene; scenery | 雪～
xuějǐng *snow scene* / 街～
jiējǐng *view of the street; scenes in the street* / 风～真好。Fēng-
jǐng zhēn hǎo. *The scenery is so beautiful.*
景点 jǐngdiǎn scenic spot
景观 jǐngguān landscape
景色 jǐngsè view; scene; scenery; landscape; prospect
景物 jǐngwù scenery
风景 fēngjǐng 盆景 pénjǐng
❸ [名]舞台或摄影棚外的景物：scenes or stage outside the film studio | 外～wàijǐng *outdoor scene; location scene*
◇景气 jǐngqì prosperity; boom

景泰蓝 jǐngtàilán cloisonné enamel; cloisonné
不景气 bùjǐngqì

警 **jǐng** 19画 言部

 警警警警警警警警
警警警警警警警警
警警警

❶ [动]提醒；告诫：remind; warn; exhort; admonish
警告 jǐnggào warn; caution; admonish
预警 yùjǐng
❷ [动]戒备；防备：guard; take precautions; be on the alert; guard against; take precautions against
警报 jǐngbào alarm; warning; alert
警戒 jǐngjiè be on the alert against; guard against; keep a close watch on
警卫 jǐngwèi (security) guard
❸ [形](对危险或异常情况)感觉敏锐：alert; vigilant | 机～jījǐng *alert; sharp-witted; vigilant* / ～
醒 jǐngxǐng *alert; watchful*
警惕 jǐngtì be on the alert; be on guard against; be vigilant; watch out for
❹ [名]警察：police | 民～mín-
jǐng *civilian police* / 交通～
jiāotōngjǐng *traffic police*
警察 jǐngchá policeman

警车 jǐngchē police car; police van

警官 jǐngguān police officer

报警 bàojǐng　巡警 xúnjǐng

净 jìng　8画 冫部

净 净净净净净净净净

❶ [形]清洁；不脏：clean; not dirty | 脸要洗～。Liǎn yào xǐjìng. *Wash your face clean.* / 玻璃擦不～。Bōli cā bù jìng. *The glass cannot be wiped clean.* 干净 gānjìng 一干二净 yīgān-èrjìng

❷ [动]使清洁：clean | ～手 jìngshǒu *clean one's hands* / ～一～桌面儿。Jìngyijìng zhuōmiànr. *Clean the top of the table.* 净化 jìnghuà purify

❸ [形]没有剩余：nothing left; completely; thoroughly | 钱用～了。Qián yòngjìng le. *The money is used up.* / 碗里的水没喝～。Wǎn li de shuǐ méi hējìng. *Not all of the water in the bowl has been drunk.*

❹ [形]纯；单纯：net; merely | ～重 jìngzhòng *net weight* / ～收入 jìngshōurù *net income*

❺ [副]表示单纯而没有别的；只：nothing but; only; merely | ～说不干 jìng shuō bù gàn *all talk, no action* / 满地～是树叶。

Mǎndì jìngshì shùyè. *There were nothing but leaves all over the ground.* / 书架上～是科技书。Shūjià shang jìngshì kējì shū. *The books on the bookshelves are exclusively on science and technology.*

竞 (競) jìng　10画 立部

竞 竞竞竞竞竞竞竞竞竞

[动]比赛；互相争胜：compete with each other | ～走 jìngzǒu *walking race* 竞标 jìngbiāo (of bidders) compete in bidding 竞技 jìngjì sports; athletics 竞赛 jìngsài contest; race; competition 竞选 jìngxuǎn enter into an election contest; campaign for (office); run for 竞争 jìngzhēng compete; contest; vie; contend 竞争力 jìngzhēnglì competitive power

竟 jìng　11画 立部

竟 竟竟竟竟竟竟竟竟竟竟

[副]表示出乎意料之外：indicating something happening unexpectedlly | 在这里～遇到多年不见的老同学。Zài zhèlǐ jìng yùdào duō nián bù jiàn de lǎo tóngxué. *Here I ran into an old schoolmate whom I had not seen for years.* / 这么大的事你～会不知道? Zhème dà de shì nǐ jìng huì bù zhīdào? *How could it be that you never heard of such an important event?*

竟然 jìngrán ① unexpectedly; to one's surprise; actually ② go so far as to; go to the length of

jìng　12画 攴部

敬敬敬敬敬敬敬敬
敬敬敬敬

❶ [动]尊重: respect; honour | ～客 jìngkè *treat the guest with respect*

敬爱 jìng'ài respect and love
敬业 jìngyè study or work diligently
敬意 jìngyì respect; tribute
敬而远之 jìng'éryuǎnzhī stay at a respectful distance from sb.
崇敬 chóngjìng　恭敬 gōngjìng
致敬 zhìjìng　　尊敬 zūnjìng

❷ [动]有礼貌地送上: present (sth.) with respect | ～茶 jìngchá *serve tea (to a guest)* / ～你一杯! Jìng nǐ yī bēi! *To your health!*

敬酒 jìngjiǔ drink (propose) a toast to

敬礼 jìnglǐ ① salute; give a salute ② extend one's greetings

静　　jìng　14画 青部

静静静静静静静静
静静静静静静

❶ [形]安定不动 (跟 "动 dòng" 相对): still; calm; motionless (the opposite of "动 dòng") | ～止 jìngzhǐ *static; motionless* / 风平浪～ fēngpíng-làngjìng *the wind has dropped and the waves have subsided (fig. calm and tranquil)*

❷ [形]不出声; 没有声音: silent; quiet; noiseless; soundless | 夜深人～ yèshēn-rénjìng *in the still of the night* / 会场里慢慢～下来。Huìchǎng li mànmàn jìng xiàlai. *The assembly hall gradually quieted down.*

静悄悄 jìngqiāoqiāo very quiet
安静 ānjìng　　寂静 jìjìng
宁静 níngjìng　幽静 yōujìng

❸ [形]安详: composed; serene; unruffled

沉静 chénjìng　　动静 dòngjìng
冷静 lěngjìng　　平静 píngjìng
镇静 zhènjìng

jìng　14画 土部

境

境境境境境境境境境
境境境境境境

❶[名]国界或地域的边界：bound-ary; border ｜ 国~guójìng national boundary
境内jìngnèi within the national territory
境外jìngwài outside the national territory
边境biānjìng 出境chūjìng
入境rùjìng

❷[名]地方；处所：place; location ｜ 仙~xiānjìng fairyland; para-dise
境界jìngjiè ① boundary ② ex-tent reached; plane attained; state; realm
环境huánjìng

❸[名]情景；状况：condition; situ-ation; circumstances ｜ 家~jiā-jìng family financial situation ｜ ~况jìngkuàng situation
境地jìngdì condition; circum-stances
处境chǔjìng 困境kùnjìng

镜 (鏡) jìng 16画 钅部

镜镜镜镜镜镜镜镜
镜镜镜镜镜镜镜镜

❶[名]mirror ｜ 圆~yuánjìng round mirror / 穿衣~chuān-yījìng dressing mirror
镜子jìngzi mirror

❷[名]利用光学原理制成的改善视力或作科学实验的器具：lens; glass ｜ 花~huājìng presby-opic glasses; reading-glasses / 望远~wàngyuǎnjìng tele-scope
镜头jìngtóu ① camera lens ② shot; scene
墨镜mòjìng 眼镜yǎnjìng
显微镜xiǎnwēijìng

纠 (糾) jiū 5画 纟部

纠纠纠纠纠

❶[动]缠绕：entangle ｜ ~缠jiū-chán get entangled
纠纷jiūfēn dispute; quarrel; is-sue; entanglement; tangle

❷[动]改正：correct; rectify ｜ ~错 jiūcuò correct errors; redress
纠正jiūzhèng amend; mend; remedy; correct; rectify; redress

究 jiū 7画 穴部

究究究究究究究

[动]深入追求；钻研：look into; seek after; study carefully; investigate ｜ 深~shēnjiū go into (a matter) seriously
讲究jiǎngjiu 研究yánjiū
追究zhuījiū
研究生yánjiūshēng
研究所yánjiūsuǒ

研究员 yánjiūyuán

◇究竟 jiūjìng ① outcome; what actually happened ② on earth ③ after all; anyway

揪　jiū　12画 扌部

揪揪揪揪揪揪揪揪揪揪揪揪

[动]紧紧抓住；抓住并用力拉：hold tight; seize with the hand | ～耳朵 jiū ěrduo *seize sb. by the ear* / ～断了绳子 jiūduànle shéngzi *tear off a rope* / 快～住他。Kuài jiūzhù tā. *Get hold of him quickly.*

九　jiǔ　2画 丿部

九 九九

[数]数目八加一的和：nine | ～成新 jiǔ chéng xīn *ninety percent new* / 三三得～。Sān sān dé jiǔ. *Three times three is nine.*

久　jiǔ　3画 丿部

久 久久久

❶[形]时间长：long; for a long time | 很～以前 hěnjiǔ yǐqián *long time ago* / 日子～了，记不得了。Rìzi jiǔ le, jìbudé le. *It's a long time ago and is not easy to recall.*

不久 bùjiǔ　　长久 chángjiǔ
持久 chíjiǔ　　永久 yǒngjiǔ
悠久 yōujiǔ　　前不久 qiánbùjiǔ

❷[形]时间的长短：length of time | 两个月之～ liǎng gè yuè zhī jiǔ *for as long as two months*
多久 duōjiǔ

灸　jiǔ　7画 火部

灸 灸灸灸灸灸灸灸

[名]中医的一种治疗方法，用燃烧的艾绒（由一种药用植物加工成的制品）熏烤一定的穴位：moxibustion (medical treatment that involves searing or smoking acupoints of the body with moxa)
针灸 zhēnjiǔ

酒　jiǔ　10画 氵部

酒酒酒酒酒酒酒酒酒酒

[名]alcoholic drink; wine; liquor; spirits | 戒～ jièjiǔ *quit drinking* / 他喜欢喝～。Tā xǐhuan hējiǔ. *He is fond of drinking.*

酒吧 jiǔbā bar; barroom
酒杯 jiǔbēi cup; goblet
酒店 jiǔdiàn wineshop
酒会 jiǔhuì cocktail party
酒精 jiǔjīng ethyl alcohol
酒楼 jiǔlóu winehouse; pub; res-

409

taurant

酒肉朋友 jiǔròu péngyou wine-and-meat friends; fair-weather friends

白酒 báijiǔ	黄酒 huángjiǔ
敬酒 jìngjiǔ	啤酒 píjiǔ
喜酒 xǐjiǔ	酗酒 xùjiǔ
葡萄酒 pútaojiǔ	

旧（舊）jiù　　5画 丨部

旧 旧 旧 旧 旧

❶[形]过去的；过时的；用过的（跟"新 xīn"相对）：past; outdated; used; second-hand; worn (the opposite of "新 xīn") | ～衣服 jiù yīfu *old clothes* / ～书 jiùshū *old books* / 这些观点大都是～的。Zhè xiē guāndiǎn dàdōu shì jiù de. *Generally speaking, these opinions are outdated.*

陈旧 chénjiù	废旧 fèijiù
破旧 pòjiù	

❷[形]原先的；以往的：former; past; bygone | ～都 jiùdū *former capital*

仍旧 réngjiù	依旧 yījiù
照旧 zhàojiù	

救 jiù　　11画 攵部

救 救 救 救 救 救 救 救 救 救 救

❶[动]帮助使灾难或危急情况消除、终止：rescue; save | ～急 jiùjí *cope with an emergency*

救济 jiùjì extend relief to; relieve the distress of

救援 jiùyuán rescue; come to sb.'s help

救灾 jiùzāi provide disaster relief; send relief to a disaster-stricken area

救助 jiùzhù help sb. in danger or difficulty

❷[动]援助，使脱离危险或免遭灾难：make sure that sb. is rescued from danger or a disaster | 病人得～了。Bìngrén déjiù le. *The patient was saved.* / 一定要把他～出来。Yīdìng yào bǎ tā jiù chūlai. *We are sure to rescue him.*

救命 jiùmìng ① save sb.'s life ② (call for other people's help in state of emergency) Help!

救护车 jiùhùchē ambulance

补救 bǔjiù	急救 jíjiù
解救 jiějiù	抢救 qiǎngjiù
挽救 wǎnjiù	营救 yíngjiù

就 jiù　　12画 丶部

就 就 就 就 就 就 就 就 就 就 就 就

❶ [动]凑近；靠近；趋向：come near; get near; move fowards | ～着灯光看书 jiùzhe dēng-guāng kànshū *read a book by the light of a lamp*

❷ [动]进行；开始从事：engage in; enter upon; undertake; go in for | ～业 jiùyè *obtain employment; get a job*

就餐 jiùcān have a meal

就医 jiùyī seek medical advice; go to a doctor

就职 jiùzhí assume office

❸ [动]趁着；借着：take advantage of; by means of; by the light of | ～着年轻，要抓紧时间好好学习。Jiùzhe niánqīng, yào zhuājǐn shíjiān hǎohǎo xuéxí. *Make good use of your time and study hard when you are young.*

就地 jiùdì on the spot

就近 jiùjìn (do or get sth.) nearby; in the neighbourhood; without having to go far

❹ [介]引进动作的对象、范围或表示行动的凭据：introducing the object, scope of an action, or the basis on which an action takes place | 大家～这个问题谈了自己的看法。Dàjiā jiù zhège wèntí tánle zìjǐ de kànfǎ. *People expressed their own views on this matter.* / ～学习成绩来说，我不如你。Jiù xuéxí chéngjì lái shuō, wǒ bùrú nǐ. *As to academic performance, I am not as good as you.*

❺ [副]表示动作行为很快要发生、已经发生或两件事紧跟着发生：indicating that an action is about to take place, has already taken place, or two actions following one after another | 我～去。Wǒ jiù qù. *I'm going right away.* / 天很快～亮了。Tiān hěn kuài jiù liàng le. *It will be dawn soon.* / 事情早～清楚了。Shìqing zǎo jiù qīngchu le. *It's already clear.* / 说干～干。Shuō gàn jiù gàn. *Let's start working at once.; Act without delay.* / 她说完～走。Tā shuōwán jiù zǒu. *She left right after saying so.*

❻ [副]表示肯定或强调的语气：expressing an affirmative or emphatic tone | 这样～好办了。Zhèyàng jiù hǎobàn le. *In this way, it will be easier.* / 不是你去，～是我去。Bùshì nǐ qù, jiùshì wǒ qù. *Either you or I will go.*

就是 jiùshì quite right; exactly; precisely

就要 jiùyào be about to; be going to; be on the point of

❼ [副]仅仅；只：used to indicate a small amount or number; merely; only; just | 他～爱看书。Tā jiù ài kànshū. *He is only fond of reading.* / ～等你一个人了。Jiù děng nǐ yī gè rén le. *You are the only one we are waiting for.* / 我～一件大衣。Wǒ jiù yī jiàn dàyī. *I have only one*

就

jiù

overcoat.

❽[副]表示承接上文，得出结论：used to link the above-mentioned and what follows, indicating a deduction | 如果他去，我～不去了。Rúguǒ tā qù, wǒ jiù bù qù le. *If he goes, I won't go.* / 只要天不下雨，运动会～一定开。Zhǐyào tiān bù xiàyǔ, yùndònghuì jiù yīdìng kāi. *The sports meet will definitely go ahead unless it rains.*

❾[连]表示假设兼让步；就是；即使：used to indicate a hypothesis and concession; even if; even though (usu. oral) | 你～不说，我也会知道。Nǐ jiù bù shuō, wǒ yě huì zhīdào. *Even if you won't tell me, I'll know in the end.*

就算 jiùsuàn even if; granted that

❿[动]副食搭配着主食或酒吃：be eaten with; go with | ～花生米下酒 jiù huāshēngmǐ xià jiǔ *have peanuts with liquor*

成就 chéngjiù   造就 zàojiù

舅   jiù   13画 臼部

舅 舅 舅 舅 舅 舅 舅 舅 舅
舅 舅 舅 舅 舅

[名]母亲的弟兄：mother's brother; uncle | 大～dàjiù *eldest uncle*
舅舅 jiùjiu mother's brother; uncle

舅妈 jiùmā (inf.) wife of mother's brother; aunt
舅母 jiùmǔ wife of mother's brother; aunt

拘   jū   8画 扌部

拘 拘 拘 拘 拘 拘 拘 拘

❶[动]逮捕；扣押：arrest; detain | ～禁 jūjìn *detain; take into custody*
拘留 jūliú ① detain; hold in custody ② detention

❷[动]约束；限制：restrain; restrict; limit; limitation | 无～无束 wú-jū-wúshù *unconstrained; free and easy*
拘束 jūshù ① restrain; restrict; tie sb. down ② constrained; ill at ease; uneasy; restrained

居   jū   8画 尸部

居 居 居 居 居 居 居 居

❶ [动]住：live; inhabit | 分～ fēnjū *live apart*
居民 jūmín resident; inhabitant
居室 jūshì bedroom
居住 jūzhù live; dwell; inhabit; reside
定居 dìngjū

❷ [名]住处：lodging; residence | 新～ xīnjū *new home; new residence* / 迁～ qiānjū *move one's home from one place to another* | 居委会 jūwěihuì neighbourhood (or residents') committee | 故居 gùjū

❸[动]处在某个位置或占有某种地位：occupy | ~中 jūzhōng *be in the middle* / ~世界首位 jū shìjiè shǒuwèi *top the world; rank first in the world*

◇居然 jūrán *incredibly; to one's surprise (disbelief); unexpectedly; go so far as to; go to the length of; have the impudence (effrontery) to*

 鞠 jū 17画 革部

鞠 鞠 鞠 鞠 鞠 鞠 鞠 鞠 鞠 鞠 鞠 鞠 鞠 鞠 鞠 鞠 鞠

See 鞠躬

鞠躬 jūgōng ① *bow* ② *in a discreet and scrupulous manner*

局 jú 7画 尸部

局 局 局 局 局 局 局 局

❶[形]拘束；狭窄：restrained; restricted; narrow; cramped | ~促 júcù *(of time) short*
局限 júxiàn limit; confine

❷[名]一部分：part; portion
局部 júbù part

❸[名]政府中按业务划分的办事机构：department in a government; bureau; office | 教育~ jiàoyùjú *education bureau* / 铁路~ tiělùjú *railway bureau* / 电话~ diànhuàjú *telephone exchange*

局长 júzhǎng director

❹[名]某些业务机构：institutions engaged in certain businesses | 书~ shūjú *publishing house; bookstore*
邮局 yóujú

❺[名]形势；情况：situation; state of affairs | 时~ shíjú *the current political situation*

局面 júmiàn aspect; situation
局势 júshì aspect; situation
布局 bùjú   大局 dàjú
格局 géjú   僵局 jiāngjú
结局 jiéjú   平局 píngjú
全局 quánjú
顾全大局 gùquán-dàjú

◇出局 chūjú

 菊 jú 11画 艹部

菊 菊 菊 菊 菊 菊 菊 菊 菊 菊 菊

[名]chrysanthemum | 赏~ shǎngjú *admire the chrysanthemum* / ~花 júhuā *chrysanthemum*

 橘 jú 16画 木部

橘 橘橘橘橘橘橘橘橘
橘橘橘橘橘橘橘

[名] tangerine

橘子 júzi tangerine

矩 jǔ   9画 矢部

矩 矩矩矩矩矩矩矩矩
矩

❶ [名] 木工画直角或方形的曲尺：carpenter's square

❷ [名] 法度；规则：rules; regulations | 守规~shǒu guīju *obey the rules*

规矩 guīju

举 (舉) jǔ   9画 丶部

举 举举举举举举举举
举

❶ [动] 往上抬；往上托：lift; raise; support | ~杯 jǔbēi *raise one's glass* / 他把孩子~到肩上。Tā bǎ háizi jǔdào jiān shang. *He lifted the child up to his shoulder.*

举重 jǔzhòng weight lifting

❷ [名] 动作；行为：act; deed; move | ~止 jǔzhǐ *bearing; manner*

举动 jǔdòng act; deed; move; action

一举 yījǔ

❸ [动] 发起；兴起：start | ~事 jǔshì *start a revolt; rise in revolt; stage an uprising*

举办 jǔbàn conduct; hold; host; run; sponsor; organize

举行 jǔxíng hold; take place; have; stage

❹ [动] 推荐；选拔：recommend; elect; choose | 大家~他做代表。Dàjiā jǔ tā zuò dàibiǎo. *We all elected him as the representative.*

选举 xuǎnjǔ

❺ [动] 提出：cite; enumerate | ~例说明 jǔlì shuōmíng *illustrate with examples* / ~出事实 jǔchū shìshí *cite the instance; illustrate with examples*

举例 jǔlì give an example; cite

检举 jiǎnjǔ   列举 lièjǔ

❻ [形] 全：whole; entire | ~国 jǔguó *the whole nation*

举世闻名 jǔshì-wénmíng be known to the whole world; world-famous; world-renowned

举世瞩目 jǔshì-zhǔmù attract worldwide attention

◇ 举人 jǔrén a successful candidate in the imperial examinations at the provincial level in the Ming and Qing dynasties

大举 dàjǔ

巨 jù   4画 匚部

巨 巨巨巨巨

[形] 大；非常大：big; huge | ~款 jùkuǎn *a very large sum of*

money / ～型 jùxíng *(of scale)*
tremendous

巨大 jùdà huge; tremendous;
gigantic

巨人 jùrén giant; colossus

巨头 jùtóu magnate; tycoon

 句
jù　　5画 勹部

句 句句句句句

❶ [名] sentence

句号 jùhào full stop; full point;
period

句子 jùzi sentence

词句 cíjù

文句 wénjù

陈述句 chénshùjù

绝句 juéjù

造句 zàojù

❷ [量]用于言语或诗文：used for
speech or lines of verse | 一～
话 yī jù huà *one sentence* / 两～
诗 liǎng jù shī *two lines of verse*
/ 我来说几。Wǒ lái shuō jǐ jù.
Let me say a few words.

 拒
jù　　7画 扌部

拒 拒拒拒拒拒拒

[动]不接受：not accept | ～不接受
jù bù jiēshòu *refuse to accept*

拒绝 jùjué refuse; reject; turn
down; decline

 具
jù　　8画 八部

 具
具具具具具具具具

❶ [名]日常生活和生产活动中使用
的器物：utensil; tool; imple-
ment | 餐～cānjù *tableware* /
雨～yǔjù *rain gear* / 文～wénjù
stationery

工具 gōngjù

洁具 jiéjù

器具 qìjù

用具 yòngjù

工具书 gōngjùshū

家具 jiājù

农具 nóngjù

玩具 wánjù

❷ [动]有：have; possess | ～有 jù-
yǒu possess; have; bear

具备 jùbèi possess; have; be
provided with

❸ [量]用于棺材、尸体和某些器物：
used for a coffin, corpse, etc. |
一～棺材 yī jù guāncai *a coffin* / 一～尸体 yī jù shītǐ *a corpse*

◇具体 jùtǐ concrete; exact;
specific; particular

俱
jù　　10画 亻部

俱 俱俱俱俱俱俱俱
俱俱

[副]全；都：all; entirely; com-
pletely | 面面～到 miànmiàn-
jùdào *attend to each and every
aspect of a matter*

◇俱乐部 jùlèbù club

 剧 (劇) jù　　10画 刂部

剧

剧剧剧剧剧剧剧剧剧
剧剧

❶ [形]厉害；猛烈：acute; severe; violent; fierce; sharp | ～痛 jùtòng *great pain* / ～变 jùbiàn *great change; dramatic change*

剧烈 jùliè acute; severe; fierce

急剧 jíjù　　　　加剧 jiājù

❷ [名]戏剧：drama; play; theatre | 京～ jīngjù *Beijing Opera*

剧本 jùběn ① drama; play ② script; scenario

剧场 jùchǎng theatre

剧目 jùmù a list of plays or operas

剧情 jùqíng the story (or plot) of a play or opera

剧团 jùtuán theatrical company; opera troupe

剧院 jùyuàn theatre

悲剧 bēijù　　　　编剧 biānjù

歌剧 gējù　　　　话剧 huàjù

喜剧 xǐjù　　　　戏剧 xìjù

越剧 yuèjù

连续剧 liánxùjù

◇恶作剧 èzuòjù

据 (據) jù　　11画 扌部

据 据据据据据据据
据据据

❶ [动]依靠；凭借：depend on; rely on

❷ [介]按照；依照：in accordance with | ～报道 jù bàodào *according to (press) reports; it is reported that ...* / 这部电影～同名小说改编。Zhè bù diànyǐng jù tóngmíng xiǎoshuō gǎibiān. *The film is adapted from a novel of the same title.*

据说 jùshuō it is said that...

据悉 jùxī it is reported that...

根据 gēnjù　　　　依据 yījù

❸ [名]可以用作证明的东西：evidence; proof; grounds | 字～ zìjù *written pledge* / 真凭实～ zhēnpíng-shíjù *genuine evidence; hard evidence*

数据 shùjù　　　　证据 zhèngjù

数据库 shùjùkù

❹ [动]占有：occupy; take by force; seize | ～为己有 jùwéijǐyǒu *take forcible possession of; appropriate*

据点 jùdiǎn strongpoint; fortified point; stronghold

占据 zhànjù

距

jù　　11画 足部

距 距距距距距距距距
距距距

❶ [动]在空间或时间上相隔：away from | 两地相～不远。Liǎng dì xiāngjù bù yuǎn. *The two places are not far from each other.* / ～今 jù jīn (*from that time*) *to present*

距离 jūlí be apart (or away) from; be at a distance from

❷ [名]相隔的长度：distance of the length｜行～hángjù *the distance between the lines*

距离 jūlí ① distance ② be apart (or away) from; be at a distance from

差距 chājù

惧(懼) jū　11画 忄部

惧 惧惧惧惧惧惧惧惧 惧惧惧

[动]害怕：fear｜～怕 jūpà *fear; dread*

恐惧 kǒngjù

锯(鋸) jū　13画 钅部

锯 锯锯锯锯锯锯锯锯 锯锯锯锯锯

❶ [名]saw｜拉～lājù *saw*／电～diànjù *electric saw*

❷ [动]用锯割开或截断：cut off with a saw｜～木头 jū mùtou *saw wood*／把竹竿～断 bǎ zhúgān jūduàn *cut up a bamboo pole with a saw*／他们正在～树。Tāmen zhèng zài jù shù. *They are cutting trees with a saw.*

聚 jū　14画 耳部

聚 聚聚聚聚聚聚聚聚 聚聚聚聚聚聚

[动]会集；集合：get together; meet together; assemble; gather｜～在一起谈天 jū zài yīqǐ tántiān *get together to have a chat*／星期天咱们找个地方～～。Xīngqītiān zánmen zhǎo ge dìfang jùjù. *Let's get together somewhere this Sunday.*

聚会 jūhuì ① get together; meet; assemble; gather ② meeting; gathering

聚集 jūjí gather; assemble; collect

聚焦 jūjiāo (phys.) focus

聚精会神 jūjīng-huìshén do sth. attentively (with attention); concentrate (centre) all one's attention on

凝聚 níngjù

捐 juān　10画 扌部

捐 捐捐捐捐捐捐捐 捐捐

❶ [动]献出或舍弃：donate; relinquish; abandon｜～棉衣 juān miányī *offer cotton-padded coats (as material assistance)*

捐款 juānkuǎn contribute (donate, subscribe) money; contribution; donation

捐献 juānxiàn contribute (to an

organization); donate; present 捐赠 juānzèng contribute (as a gift); donate; present 捐助 juānzhù offer (financial or material assistance); contribute; donate

❷ [名]税收的一种名称：taxes and levies (now usu. use "税 shuì" instead) | 车~ chējuān *tax on a vehicle* / 房~ fángjuān *tax on housing*

 (捲) juǎn　8画 已部

卷 卷卷卷卷卷卷卷卷卷

❶ [动]把东西弯转成圆筒形：roll up; coil; curl | ~行李 juǎn xíngli *roll up one's bedding (into a pack)* / ~帘子 juǎn liánzi *roll up the screen (or curtain)*
卷铺盖 juǎnpūgai to pack the bedding — dismissal from work; to get fired; to pack oneself off
卷心菜 juǎnxīncài (dial.) cabbage

❷ [动]强力裹挟带动：sweep off; carry along; swirl | 汽车一~起尘土。Qìchē juǎnqǐ chéntǔ. *A cloud of dust was raised by a passing car.* / 风~着雨点儿 fēng juǎnzhe yǔdiǎnr *the wind blowing along with rain drops*

❸ [名]弯转成圆筒形的东西：sth. rolled in a cylindrical shape |

烟~儿 yānjuǎnr *cigarette* / 纸~儿 zhǐjuǎnr *a roll of paper* / 行李~儿 xínglijuǎnr *bedroll; bedding pack*
花卷 huājuǎn

❹ [量]用于成卷儿的东西：roll; reel | 一~儿纸 yī juǎnr zhǐ *a roll of paper* / 一~布 yī juǎn bù *a roll of cloth*
See juàn.

 juàn　8画 已部

卷 卷卷卷卷卷卷卷卷卷

[名]回答试题用的纸：examination paper | 交~ jiāojuàn *hand in the examination paper* / 历史~子 lìshǐ juànzi *examination paper for history*
卷子 juànzi examination paper
试卷 shìjuàn　问卷 wènjuàn
See juǎn.

倦 juàn　10画 亻部

倦 倦倦倦倦倦倦倦倦倦倦

[形]劳累；疲乏：tired; run down; overworked; weary | 困~ kùnjuàn *tired and sleepy* / 不~地工作 bū juàn de gōngzuò *work tirelessly*
疲倦 píjuàn

绢 (絹) juàn 10画 纟部

绢 绢绢绢绢绢绢绢绢绢 绢绢

[名]一种薄而结实的丝织品：thin, hard-wearing silk

手绢 shǒujuàn

圈 juàn 11画 口部

圈 圈圈圈圈圈圈圈圈 圈圈圈

[名]饲养家畜或家禽的场所，一般有栏或围墙：pen; fold | 猪～ zhūjuàn *pigsty; pigpen* / 羊～ yángjuàn *sheepfold; sheep pen* See quān.

决 jué 6画 冫部

决 决决决决决决

❶ [动]水冲垮（堤岸）：breach; burst | ～裂 juéliè *break with* 决口 juékǒu breach; break

❷ [动]作出判断；确定：arrive at a judgement; decide; determine; resolve
决策 juécè ①make policy; make a strategic decision ② policy decision; decision of strategic importance
决定 juédìng decide; determine

决算 juésuàn final accounts
决心 juéxīn ① decide; be determined; make up one's mind ② determination; resolve; resolution
决议 juéyì resolution
裁决 cáijué　　否决 fǒujué
解决 jiějué　　判决 pànjué
判决书 pànjuéshū

❸ [动]决定最后胜负：decide the outcome (of a game, war, etc.)
决赛 juésài the final
决战 juézhàn decisive battle (engagement)
半决赛 bànjuésài

❹ [形]果断；坚定：decisive; determined; definite; firm
坚决 jiānjué
犹豫不决 yóuyù-bùjué

❺ [副]一定：definitely; certainly | ～无此事。Jué wú cǐ shì. *Definitely no such a thing has ever happened.* / 他～不会失败。Tā jué bùhuì shībài. *He'll never fail.*
决不 juébù by no means; under no circumstances

觉 (覺) jué 9画 见部

觉 觉觉觉觉觉觉觉觉 觉

❶ [动]醒悟；明白：become aware of; realize
觉悟 juéwù ① become aware;

awake; awaken ② consciousness

觉醒 juéxǐng awaken

发觉 fājué　　　　自觉 zìjué

❷[动]感到：feel ｜我～出他不高兴。Wǒ juéchu tā bù gāoxìng. *I realized he was not happy at the moment.* / 不知不～bùzhī-bùjué *unconsciously; unwittingly* / 下雪了，～出冷来了。Xiàxuě le, juéchū lěng lái le. *It's snowing, come in from the cold.*

觉察 juéchá detect; become aware of; perceive; be awake to; realize; sense

觉得 juéde ① be conscious of; be aware of; find ② feel; think; hold; be of the opinion that; in sb.'s opinion; to one's mind

不觉 bùjué　　感觉 gǎnjué

❸[名]对外界刺激的感受和辨别：sense; perception

视觉 shìjué　　　知觉 zhījué

See jiāo.

绝（絕）jué　　9画 纟部

绝 绝 绝 绝 绝 绝 绝 绝 绝 绝

❶[动]断：cut off; sever ｜掌声不～zhǎngshēng bùjué *prolonged applause*

绝望 juéwàng give up all hope; despair

绝缘 juéyuán ① insulation ② be cut off from; be isolated from

杜绝 dùjué　　　断绝 duànjué
隔绝 géjué　　　拒绝 jùjué
谢绝 xièjué
滔滔不绝 tāotāo-bùjué

❷[形]完：穷尽：finished; used up; exhausted ｜斩尽杀～zhǎnjìn-shājué *exterminate* / 方法都用～了。Fāngfǎ dōu yòngjué le. *All possible means and ways have been tried.*

❸[形]独一无二的；没有人能赶上的：unique; superb; matchless ｜叫～jiàojué *express admiration by thumping the table* / 你这个办法真～。Nǐ zhège bànfǎ zhēn jué. *Your idea is really superb.*

❹[副]最；极：extremely; most ｜～大多数 jué dà duōshù *most; the overwhelming majority* / ～好的机会 jué hǎo de jīhuì *a wonderful opportunity*

❺[副]断然；绝对：definitely; categorically; absolutely ｜～不可能 juébù kěnéng *absolutely impossible* / 你这样做，我～不同意。Nǐ zhèyàng zuò, wǒ juébù tóngyì. *In no case will I agree to your doing so.*

绝不 juébù nohow; not in the least

绝对 juéduì absolute(ly); definite(ly)

绝非 juéfēi nohow; not in the

least

◇ 绝句 juéjù *jueju*, a poem of four lines, each containing five or seven characters, with a strict tonal pattern and rhyme scheme; quatrain

 掘 jué 11画 扌部

掘 掘掘掘掘掘掘掘 掘掘掘

[动]刨；挖：dig; excavate; dig | ～土 jué tǔ *dig up the soil* / ～一口 井 jué yī kǒu jǐng *dig a well*
发掘 fājué　　　　挖掘 wājué

 军 (軍) jūn 6画 冖部

军 军军军军军军

❶[名]军队：armed forces; army; troop
军备 jūnbèi armament; arms
军队 jūnduì armed forces; army; troop
军阀 jūnfá warlord
军官 jūnguān officer
军火 jūnhuǒ munitions; arms and ammunition
军舰 jūnjiàn warship; naval vessel
军人 jūnrén soldier; serviceman
军事 jūnshì military affairs
军用 jūnyòng for military use;

military
军医 jūnyī medical officer; military surgeon
军装 jūnzhuāng military (army) uniform

裁军 cáijūn	参军 cānjūn
撤军 chèjūn	海军 hǎijūn
进军 jìnjūn	空军 kōngjūn
陆军 lùjūn	行军 xíngjūn
千军万马 qiānjūn-wànmǎ	

❷[名]军队编制单位，是师的上一级：corps (military unit, higher than a division)
军长 jūnzhǎng army commander
◇ 季军 jìjūn

 均 jūn 7画 土部

均 均均均均均均均

[形]分布或分配在各部分的数量相同：equal; even | 分布不～ fēnbù bù jūn *not equally distributed*
均衡 jūnhéng balance; equilibrium
均匀 jūnyún even
平均 píngjūn　　　人均 rénjūn

 君 jūn 7画 口部

君 君君君君君君君

❶[名]国家的最高统治者：supreme ruler; monarch; sovereign |

421

国～guójūn

君主 jūnzhǔ monarch; sovereign

❷ [名]对人的尊称：(term of respect) Mr.; Ms. | 张～ Zhāng jūn *Mr. Zhang* / 我有要事与诸～商议。Wǒ yǒu yàoshì yǔ zhūjūn shāngyì. *I have something important to discuss with all of you.*

◇伪君子 wěijūnzǐ

菌 jūn　11画 艹部

菌菌菌菌菌菌菌菌菌菌菌

[名]指细菌：bacteria

病菌 bìngjūn　　细菌 xìjūn

俊 jūn　9画 亻部

俊俊俊俊俊俊俊俊俊

❶ [名]才智出众的人：a person of outstanding talent

俊杰 jùnjié a person of outstanding talent; hero

❷ [形]相貌清秀好看：handsome; pretty in appearance | 那小姑娘真～。Nà xiǎo gūniang zhēn jùn. *That little girl is so pretty.*

英俊 yīngjùn

峻 jūn　10画 山部

峻峻峻峻峻峻峻峻峻峻

❶ [形](山)高大：(of mountains) high and big | 高山～岭 gāoshān-jùnlǐng *high mountains and lofty peaks*

❷ [形]严厉：stern; severe | 严～ yánjùn *stern*

K k

咖 kā 8画 口部

咖 咖咖咖咖咖咖咖咖

See 咖啡

咖啡 kāfēi coffee

卡 kǎ 5画 卜部

卡 卡卡卡卡卡

❶[名]指卡车，运输货物等的载重汽车：lorry; truck
卡车 kǎchē lorry; truck

❷[名]卡片：card | 优惠～yōuhuìkǎ *discount card* | 贺年～hèniánkǎ *New Year card* | 读者～dúzhěkǎ *library card*
卡片 kǎpiàn card
磁卡 cíkǎ
打卡 dǎkǎ
刷卡 shuākǎ
信用卡 xìnyòngkǎ

❸[量]热量单位卡路里的简称：short for calorie, the amount of heat needed to raise the temperature of one gram of water by one degree Celsius

◇卡通 kǎtōng ① caricature; cartoon ② animated film (or drawing)

开（開）kāi 4画 一部

开 开开开开

❶[动]打开（跟"关guān""闭bì"相对）：open (the opposite of "关guān" or "闭bì") | ～门 kāi mén *open the door* | ～抽屉 kāi chōuti *open a drawer*
开刀 kāidāo ① (inf.) perform or have an operation; operate or be operated on ② make sb. the first target of attack
开关 kāiguān switch
开口 kāikǒu open one's mouth; start to talk
开幕 kāimù ① the curtain rises ② open; inaugurate
开眼界 kāiyǎnjiè open one's eyes; widen one's view (or horizons); broaden one's mind
打开 dǎkāi   公开 gōngkāi

❷[动]解除；除掉：be released; quit; get rid of
开除 kāichú expel; discharge
开放 kāifàng ① come into bloom ② lift a ban, restriction, etc. ③ open to traffic or public use; be open (to the public)

❸[动](液体)沸腾：boil | 水～了。Shuǐ kāi le. *The water is boiling.*
开水 kāishuǐ ① boiling water ② boiled water

423

❹ [动]打通；开辟：get through; open up; hew out | ～路 kāilù *open a way* / ～矿 kāikuàng *open up a mine; exploit a mine*

开采 kāicǎi mine; extract; exploit

开发 kāifā develop; open up; exploit

开垦 kāikěn open up (reclaim) wasteland; bring under cultivation

开辟 kāipì open up; hew out; establish

开启 kāiqǐ open; start

开通 kāitōng ① remove obstacles from; dredge; clear ② open-minded; liberal; enlightened

开拓 kāituò open up; reclaim

开天辟地 kāitiān-pìdì ① when heaven was separated from earth; the creation of the world ② since the beginning of history

❺ [动]开创；设立：set up; found; start; pioneer; establish; set up | ～工厂 kāi gōngchǎng *run a factory* / ～医院 kāi yīyuàn *set up a hospital* / 这里新～了一家店。Zhèlǐ xīn kāile yī jiā diàn. *A new shop has been set up here recently.*

开办 kāibàn open; set up; establish; start; found

开创 kāichuàng start; initiate

开设 kāishè open; set up; establish

开业 kāiyè ① (of a shop, etc.) start business ② (of a lawyer, doctor, etc.) open a private practice

开张 kāizhāng ① open a business; begin doing business ② conduct the first transaction of a day's business ③ (of certain activities) begin; start

❻ [动]起始：begin; start | 这篇文章头～得好。Zhè piān wénzhāng tóu kāidehǎo. *The beginning of the article is well-written.*

开饭 kāifàn serve a meal

开工 kāigōng ① (of a factory, etc.) go into operation ② (of work on a construction project, etc.) start

开课 kāikè ① school begins ② (chiefly in college) give a course; teach a subject

开盘 kāipán (econ.) give the opening quotation (on the exchange)

开始 kāishǐ begin; start; commence

开头 kāitóu begin; start

开学 kāixué school opens; term begins

开演 kāiyǎn begin; start

开场白 kāichǎngbái ① prologue (of a play) ② opening (or introductory) remarks

❼ [动]举行（会议等）：hold / host (a meeting, etc.) | 会不～了。Huì bù kāi le. *The meeting is cancelled.* / 这个讨论会要～三天。Zhège tǎolùnhuì yào kāi sān tiān. *The symposium will last three days.*

开会 kāihuì hold a meeting

召开 zhàokāi

❽[动]发动；操纵：start; operate; control │ ～车 kāichē *drive a car* / ～动脑筋 kāidòng nǎojīn *exercise one's wits* / 火车～了。Huǒchē kāi le. *The train has started.*

开动 kāidòng start; set in motion

开枪 kāiqiāng fire with a rifle, pistol, etc.

❾[动]（合拢或连接的东西）展开；分离：spread out; unfold; separate; sever │ 花～了。Huā kāi le. *The flowers bloomed.* / 扣子～了。Kòuzi kāi le. *The button has come undone.*

开花 kāihuā ① blossom; bloom ② feel happy or smile happily

开心 kāixīn feel happy

开展 kāizhǎn develop; launch

避开 bìkāi	分开 fēnkāi
揭开 jiēkāi	离开 líkāi
撇开 piēkāi	盛开 shèngkāi
展开 zhǎnkāi	

❿[动]写出；标出（价钱）：write out; make out; mark; indicate (the price) │ ～发票 kāi fāpiào *make an invoice* / ～药方 kāi yàofāng *write out a prescription* / 介绍信～好了。Jièshàoxìn kāihǎo le. *The letter of introduction has been prepared.*

⓫[动]支付：pay │ ～工资 kāi gōngzī *pay out wages* / ～销 kāixiāo *expenses; spending*

开支 kāizhī spending; pay expenses

⓬[动]（队伍）由驻地或休息处出发：(of troops) move; set out │ 队伍～走了。Duìwu kāizǒu le. *The troops moved away.*

⓭[动]用在动词或形容词后作补语，表示动作扩大或继续下去：(used as a complement after a verb, indicating the extension or continuation of an action) open; widely │ 睁～眼 zhēngkāi yǎn *open one's eyes* / 打～窗子 dǎkāi chuāngzi *open the window* / 这话传～了。Zhè huà chuánkāi le. *These words have spread about.*

开化 kāihuà become civilized

开阔 kāikuò open; wide

开朗 kāilǎng sanguine; optimistic; outgoing

开明 kāimíng enlightened; liberal-minded

开玩笑 kāiwánxiào crack a joke; joke; make fun of

开夜车 kāiyèchē work late into the night; put in extra time at night; burn the midnight oil

◇ 开后门 kāihòumén open the "back door"; give sb. special advantage or privilege

开绿灯 kāilùdēng give the green light; give the go-ahead

K

凯（凯）kǎi　8画 几部

凯 凯凯凯凯凯凯凯

[名]军队得胜回来奏的乐曲：(of troops) triumphant strains | ~歌 kǎigē *a song of triumph* 凯旋 kǎixuán *triumphant return*

刊 kān　5画 干部

刊 刊刊刊刊刊

❶[动]刻；排印出版：carve; engrave; print; publish | ~载 kānzǎi *publish in a newspaper or magazine* / 停~tíngkān *stop publication*

刊登 kāndēng publish in a newspaper or magazine; carry

❷[名]杂志；报纸上的专栏：magazine; a regular column or feature in a newspaper | 月~ yuèkān *monthly magazine*

刊物 kānwù publication

报刊 bàokān

期刊 qīkān

周刊 zhōukān

副刊 fùkān

书刊 shūkān

看 kān　9画 手部

看 看看看看看看看看看

❶[动]照料；守护：look after; take care of; guard; defend | ~小孩 kān xiǎohái *look after the child* / ~门 kānmén *guard the entrance; serve as a doorkeeper* / ~家 kānjiā *look after the house; mind the house*

❷[动]监管：take into custody | 把他~起来 bǎ tā kān qǐlai *detain him*

　　See kàn.

勘 kān　11画 力部

勘 勘勘勘勘勘勘勘勘勘勘勘

[动]实地查看；探测：reconnoitre; prospect; survey; sound; probe | ~查 kānchá *reconnoitre; prospect*

勘探 kāntàn explore; prospect; exploration; prospecting

砍 kǎn　9画 石部

砍 砍砍砍砍砍砍砍砍砍

❶[动]用刀、斧猛劈：chop; cut (with a knife or axe) | ~柴 kǎnchái *cut firewood* / 把树枝~下来 bǎ shùzhī kǎn xiàlai *cut off branches*

❷[动]削减；取消：cut (down / off) | 这个项目被~掉了。Zhège

K

xiāngmù bèi kǎndiào le. *The project has been cancelled.*

看 kàn　9画 手部

看 看看看看看看看看
看

❶[动]使视线接触人或物：see; look at | ～书 kànshū *read (a book)* / ～电影 kàn diànyǐng *watch a film; go to the movies*
看见 kànjiàn catch sight of; see
看台 kàntái bleachers; stands
观看 guānkàn　好看 hǎokàn
难看 nánkàn　眼看 yǎnkàn

❷[动]观察并判断：observe and size up the situation | 依我～ yī wǒ kàn *in my opinion (view)* / 他～问题很全面。Tā kàn wèntí hěn quánmiàn. *He always considers things in an all-round way.*
看来 kànlái it seems; it looks as if
看中 kànzhòng take a fancy to; settle on
看起来 kànqǐlai it looks as if; it seems; it appears
看上去 kànshàngqu it appears; it seems
看样子 kànyàngzi it seems (appears); it looks as if
查看 chákàn

❸[动]看待；对待：look upon; regard; treat; approach; handle |

别把我当外人～。Bié bǎ wǒ dàng wàirén kàn. *Don't treat me as an outsider.*
看待 kàndài look upon; regard; treat
看法 kànfǎ view; a way of looking at things
看作 kànzuò look upon as; regard as
看不起 kànbuqǐ look down upon; disdain; scorn

❹[动]表示试一试：have a try | 你猜猜～。Nǐ cāicāi kàn. *Take a guess.*

❺[动]诊治：treat; attend; give medical advice | 大夫把我的病～好了。Dàifu bǎ wǒ de bìng kànhǎo le. *The doctor has cured my illness.*
看病 kànbìng ① attend; give medical advice ② see a doctor; consult a doctor

❻[动]提防；小心：mind; take care; watch out | 别跑，～摔着。Bié pǎo, kàn shuāizháo. *Don't run. Be careful not to fall.*

❼[动]访问：visit | ～朋友 kàn péngyou *visit one's friends* / 到医院里去～病人 dào yīyuàn li qù kàn bìngrén *go to the hospital to visit (or see) a patient*
看望 kànwàng call on; visit; see
See kān.

康 kāng　11画 广部

康

康康康康康康康康
康康康

[形] 身体强健：in good health | ～
乐 kānglè *happy and peaceful*
康复 kāngfù restored to health;
recovered
健康 jiànkāng

慷

kāng 14画 忄部

慷慷慷慷慷慷慷
慷慷慷慷慷

See 慷慨
慷慨 kāngkǎi *generous; fervent*

糠

kāng 17画 米部

糠糠糠糠糠糠糠
糠糠糠糠糠糠糠
糠

[名] 从稻、麦、谷子等子实上脱下来
的皮、壳：chaff; husk; bran |
米～ mǐkāng *rice bran*

扛

kāng 6画 扌部

扛扛扛扛扛扛

[动] 用肩膀担着：carry on the
shoulder | ～枪 káng qiāng
shoulder a gun / ～粮食 káng
liángshi *carry (a bag of) grain
on one's shoulder* / 这箱子太重，

我～不动。Zhè xiāngzi tài
zhòng, wǒ kángbudòng. *The
suitcase is too heavy for me to
carry.*

抗

kàng 7画 扌部

抗抗抗抗抗抗抗

❶ [动] 抵挡；抵御：resist; com-
bat; defend; guard against | ～
洪 kànghóng *fight or combat a
flood*
抗旱 kànghàn fight (combat) a
drought
抗击 kàngjī resist; beat back
抗战 kàngzhàn ① war of resistance against aggression ② War
of Resistance Against Japanese
Aggression (1937–1945)
抵抗 dǐkàng　对抗 duìkàng
反抗 fǎnkàng
❷ [动] 拒绝；不接受：refuse; defy
| ～拒 kàngjù *resist; defy* / ～命
kàngmìng *defy orders; disobey*
抗议 kàngyì protest

炕

kàng 8画 火部

炕炕炕炕炕炕炕炕

[名] 北方用砖或土坯砌成的睡觉用
的长方台，下面有洞，连通烟道，
可烧火取暖：kang, heatable bed
made of brick, clay, etc., with a
hole underneath attached to a

chimney (generally used in North China) | ～烧得真热。Kàng shāo de zhēn rè. *The kang is so warm.*

考　　　kǎo　　6画 尸部

考 考考考考考考

❶ [动] 考试：give an examination; take an examination | ～语文 kǎo yǔwén *examination in Chinese* / 数学很难～。Shùxué hěn nán kǎo. *The mathematics examination is very difficult.*
考场 kǎochǎng an examination hall or room
考取 kǎoqǔ pass an entrance examination; be admitted to school or college (after an examination)
考生 kǎoshēng a candidate for an examination; examinee
考试 kǎoshì ①take an exam ② examination; test
报考 bàokǎo　　高考 gāokǎo
❷ [动] 检查：check; inspect | ～勤 kǎoqín *check on work attendance*
考察 kǎochá ① inspect; make an on-the-spot investigation ② observe and study
考核 kǎohé exam; check; assess sb.'s proficiency
考验 kǎoyàn test; trial; ordeal

❸[动]仔细地想；研究：think over; consider; study; investigate | ～证 kǎozhèng *make textual criticism; do textual research*
考古 kǎogǔ ①engage in archaeological studies ② archaeology
考虑 kǎolǜ think over; consider
参考 cānkǎo　　思考 sīkǎo

烤　　　kǎo　　10画 火部

烤 烤烤烤烤烤烤烤烤烤烤

❶ [动] 用火把东西烘熟或烘干：bake; roast; toast | ～面包 kǎo miànbāo *toast; toast bread* / 把你的湿袜子～干。Bǎ nǐ de shī wàzi kǎogān. *Dry your wet socks by the fire.*
烤鸭 kǎoyā roast duck
❷[动]靠近火取暖：warm oneself by a fire or other sources of heat | ～手 kǎoshǒu *warm one's hands (by a fire or a heater, etc.)* / 围炉～火 wéi lú kǎohuǒ *warm oneself by a stove*

靠　　　kǎo　　15画 非部

靠 靠靠靠靠靠靠靠靠靠靠靠靠靠靠

❶ [动] (人)倚在别的人或东西上支持身体：lean against; lean on | 背～沙发 bēi kào shāfā *lean* one's back against the sofa / ~墙站着 kào qiáng zhànzhe *lean against the wall* / 孩子~在妈妈身上睡着了。Háizi kào zài māma shēnshang shuìzháo le. *The child has fallen asleep on her mother's lap.*

❷[动] 物体凭借别的东西支持而立住：lean against sth. for support | 雨伞~着椅子。Yǔsǎn kàozhe yǐzi. *The umbrella was leaning against the chair.*

❸[动] 接近；挨近：get near; come up to | 船~岸了。Chuán kào'àn le. *The ship has pulled into shore.*

靠近 kàojìn ① be close to; be near ② draw near; approach

停靠 tíngkào

❹[动] 依赖：depend on; rely on; be dependent on | 要创造幸福，全~我们自己。Yào chuàngzào xìngfú, quán kào wǒmen zìjǐ. *It all depends on ourselves if we want to bring about happiness in our lives.* / 他学习好完全是~勤奋。Tā xuéxí hǎo wánquán shì kào qínfèn. *It is hard work that enables him to excel in studying.* / 我~朋友的帮助解决了困难。Wǒ kào péngyou de bāngzhù jiějuéle kùnnan. *I overcame the difficulty with the help of my friends.* / 他~自学考上了大学。Tā kào zìxué kǎoshàngle dàxué. *He*

passed the college entrance examination by self-study.*

依靠 yīkào

❺[动] 信任；信赖：have confidence in; trust; count on; have faith in | ~得住 kàodezhù *reliable; trustworthy* / 这个人~不住。Zhège rén kàobuzhù. *This person is not trustworthy.*

可靠 kěkào

科　kē　9画 禾部

科科科科科科科科科

❶[名] 学术或业务的类别：branch of academic or vocational study | 牙~ yákē *dentistry* / 文~ wénkē *liberal arts* / 理~ lǐkē *science (as a branch of study)*

科技 kējì science and technology

科目 kēmù subject (in a curriculum); course

科普 kēpǔ popular science

科学 kēxué science; scientific knowledge

科研 kēyán scientific research

科学家 kēxuéjiā scientist

科学院 kēxuéyuàn academy of sciences

本科 běnkē　　　内科 nèikē

外科 wàikē　　　学科 xuékē

本科生 běnkēshēng

教科书 jiàokēshū

❷[名]行政机关按工作性质而分设的办事部门：department; section | 财务～cáiwùkē *finance section* / 总务～zǒngwùkē *general affairs section* 科长 kēzhǎng section chief

 棵 kē 12画 木部

棵 棵棵棵棵棵棵棵棵 棵棵棵棵

[量]用于植物等：used for plants | 一～树 yī kē shù *a tree* / 三～白菜 sān kē báicài *three heads of Chinese cabbage*

 颗（顆）kē 14画 页部

颗 颗颗颗颗颗颗颗颗 颗颗颗颗颗颗

[量]多用于圆粒状的东西：used for things small and roundish | 一～珍珠 yī kē zhēnzhū *a pearl* / 一～心 yī kē xīn *a heart*
◇颗粒 kēlì ① anything small and roundish (as a bean, pearl, etc.); pellet ② grain

 磕 kē 15画 石部

磕 磕磕磕磕磕磕磕磕 磕磕磕磕磕磕磕

❶[动]碰在硬东西上：knock against sth. hard | ～破了头 kēpòle tóu *knocked heavily and injured one's head* / 碗边～掉了一块。Wǎnbiān kēdiàole yī kuài. *The edge of the bowl was partly chipped.*
❷[动]磕打：knock sth. out of a vessel; knock out; rap | 请把烟灰～在烟灰缸里。Qǐng bǎ yānhuī kē zài yānhuīgāng li. *Please tap your ash into the ashtray.*

 壳（殼）kē 7画 士部

壳 壳壳壳壳壳壳壳

[名]坚硬的外皮：shell | 鸡蛋～儿 jīdànkér *egg shell* / 子弹～儿 zǐdànkér *bullet shell* 贝壳 bèikē

 咳 kē 9画 口部

咳 咳咳咳咳咳咳咳咳 咳

[动] cough | 病人～得很厉害。Bìngrén kē de hěn lìhai. *The patient coughed badly.* 咳嗽 késou cough See hāi.

 可 kě 5画 口部

可 可可可可可

❶ [动] 表示准许：expressing approval; may | 不置～否 bùzhìkěfǒu *neither approve nor deny*

认可 rènkě 　　　许可 xǔkě

❷ [动] 可以或能够：can or may | ～大～小 kě dà kě xiǎo *can be larger or smaller* / ～长～短 kě cháng kě duǎn *can be either longer or shorter*

可见 kějiàn it is thus clear (evident, obvious) that

可靠 kěkào reliable

可乐 kělè ① laughable; funny; amusing ② cola (a type of non-alcoholic drink)

可行 kěxíng feasible

可疑 kěyí suspicious; dubious; questionable

可以 kěyǐ ① can; may ② passable; pretty good; not bad

可想而知 kěxiǎng'érzhī you can imagine it

不可 bùkě 　　　宁可 nìngkě

不可避免 bùkě bìmiǎn

不可思议 bùkě-sīyì

大有可为 dàyǒu-kěwéi

无话可说 wúhuà-kěshuō

无可奉告 wúkěfènggào

无可奈何 wúkěnàihé

由此可见 yóucǐ-kějiàn

❸ [动] 表示值得或应该：be worth (doing); need (doing) | 这本书没什么～看的。Zhè běn shū méi

shénme kě kàn de. *The book is not worth reading in general.*

可爱 kě'ài lovely

可观 kěguān ① worth seeing ② considerable; sizable

可贵 kěguì valuable; praise-worthy; commendable

可怜 kělián ① pitiful; pitiable; poor ② have pity on; pity

可怕 kěpà fearful; frightful; terrible

可恶 kěwù hateful; abominable; detestable

可惜 kěxī it's a pity; it's too bad

可喜 kěxǐ gratifying; heartening

可笑 kěxiào laughable; ridiculous

可歌可泣 kěgē-kěqì move one to song and tears

❹ [副] 用在不同类型的句子里，加强不同的语气：used in various types of sentences to intensify the tone | 他学习～用功了。Tā xuéxí kě yònggōng le. *He studies really hard.* / 你～知道? Nǐ kě zhīdào? *Have you ever known it?* / 这话～是真的?Zhè huà kě shì zhēn de? *Is that really true?*

可不是 kěbushì isn't it so (used in a rhetorical question)

❺ [连] 可是；但是：yet; but | 大家很累，～都很愉快。Dàjiā hěn lèi, kě dōu hěn yúkuài. *Everybody was very tired and yet so happy.* / 他年纪虽小，～知道的事不少。Tā niánjì suī xiǎo, kě zhīdào de shì bù shǎo. *Young as he is, he knows a lot.*

可是 kěshì but; yet; however

❻[动] 适合；合意：suit; fit; satisfy; to the satisfaction of | ～心 kěxīn *satisfying; to the satisfaction of one's heart*

可口 kěkǒu good to eat; delicious; tasty; palatable

可巧 kěqiǎo as luck would have it; luckily

◇可能 kěnéng ① possibility ② possible

渴 kě　12画；部

渴 渴渴渴渴渴渴渴渴渴
渴渴渴渴

❶[形] 口干想喝水：thirsty (for water) | 我～了。Wǒ kě le. *I'm thirsty.* / 西瓜可以解～。Xīguā kěyǐ jiěkě. *Watermelon can quench one's thirst.*

❷[形] 迫切地：eager | ～求 kěqiú *crave for*

渴望 kěwàng thirst for; long for; yearn for

克 (剋❶) kè　7画 十部

克 克克克克克克克

❶[动]制服；抑制：overcome; overwhelm; restrain; control; check | 以柔～刚 yǐróu-kè-gāng *subdue*

toughness with softness

克服 kèfú surmount; overcome; conquer

攻克 gōngkè

❷[量] 法定质量单位，1000克为1公斤：unit of weight, 1,000 grams is equal to one kilogram | 每人每天吃8～盐就够了。Měi rén měi tiān chī bā kè yán jiù gòu le. *Each person should have eight grams of salt per day.*

◇克隆 kèlóng clone

夹克 jiākè　　皮夹克 píjiākè

巧克力 qiǎokèlì

奥林匹克 Àolínpǐkè

刻 kè　8画 刂部

刻 刻刻刻刻刻刻刻刻

❶[动]用刀子在器物上雕：carve; engrave; cut | ～图章 kè túzhāng *cut a seal*

雕刻 diāokè

❷[量] 时间单位，十五分钟为一刻：unit of time, 15 minutes; quarter of an hour | 飞机下午两点一～起飞。Fēijī xiàwǔ liǎng diǎn yī kè qǐfēi. *The plane takes off at 2:15 pm.* / 一个课时有三～钟。Yī gè kèshí yǒu sān kè zhōng. *One period lasts three quarters of an hour.*

❸[名] 短暂的时间；时候：a short time; time | 顷～ qǐngkè *in a*

moment

此刻 cǐkè　　　　立刻 lìkè

片刻 piānkè　　　时刻 shíkè

❹ [形] 形容程度极深：indicating a very high degree | 深～shēnkè *profound; penetrating*

刻苦 kèkǔ ① assiduous; hard-working; painstaking ② (of life style) simple and frugal

刻意 kèyì be painstaking; be meticulous about; sedulously strive

客 kè　9画 宀部

客 客客客客客客客客客

❶ [名] 被邀请或来访的人 (跟 "主zhǔ" 相对)：guest; visitor (the opposite of "主zhǔ") | 招待～人 zhāodài kèrén *entertain guests* / 家里来～了。Jiāli lái kè le. *There are visitors to my home.* / 晚上主人请～。Wǎn-shang zhǔrén qǐngkè. *The host will treat guests tonight.*

客人 kèrén visitors; guests

客厅 kètīng drawing room; parlour

好客 hàokè　　会客 huìkè

来客 láikè　　请客 qǐngkè

作客 zuòkè　　做客 zuòkè

❷ [名] 旅店业、交通运输业、服务行业对主顾的称呼： guest at a hotel; passenger of public transportation; customer in a service

trade

客车 kèchē ① passenger train ② bus

客户 kèhù customer

客机 kèjī passenger plane; air-liner

乘客 chéngkè　　顾客 gùkè

旅客 lǚkè　　　游客 yóukè

❸ [形] 离开人的意识而独立存在的：objective | ～体 kètǐ *object*

客观 kèguān objective

◇客气 kèqi ① polite; courteous ② modest ③ make polite remarks or act politely; be polite; be courteous

客套话 kètàohuà polite expressions of formulas

课 (課) kè　10画 讠部

课 课课课课课课课课课课

❶ [名] 有计划的分段教学：lesson | 今天没～。Jīntiān méi kè. *We don't have class today.*

课本 kèběn textbook

课程 kèchéng course; curriculum

课时 kèshí class hour; period

课堂 kètáng classroom; school-room

课题 kètí ① a theme for study or discussion ② problem; task

课文 kèwén text

课程表 kèchéngbiǎo school

timetable; class schedule

补课 bǔkè　　讲课 jiǎngkè
开课 kāikè　　旷课 kuàngkè
上课 shàngkè　　下课 xiàkè

❷[名]教学活动的时间单位：class hour; period | 上午有 4 节～。Shàngwǔ yǒu sì jié kè. *There are four periods in the morning.*
课时 kèshí lesson hour

❸[名]教学科目：subject; course | 这学期新开一门～。Zhè xuéqī xīn kāi yī mén kè. *A new subject has been set this term.* / 我选修了三门～。Wǒ xuǎnxiūle sān mén kè. *I have three elective courses.*

肯　　kěn　8画 止部

肯 肯肯肯肯肯肯肯肯

❶[动] 同意；许可：agree; consent; allow; permit | 他不～来。Tā bù kěn lái. *He is not willing to come over.* / 只要你～做就能成功。Zhǐyào nǐ kěn zuò jiù néng chénggōng. *If only you are willing to have a try, you are sure to make it.*

❷[动] 表示愿意：be willing to | 这孩子～帮助人。Zhè háizi kěn bāngzhù rén. *The child is always willing to offer help to others.* / 只要你～下功夫，就可以学会。Zhǐyào nǐ kěn xià gōngfu, jiù kěyǐ xuéhuì. *If you*

are willing to make the effort, you are sure to learn it.

◇肯定 kěndìng ① affirm; confirm; approve; regard as positive ② positive ③ definite; sure

恳（懇）kěn　10画 心部

恳 恳恳恳恳恳恳恳恳 恳恳

[形]真诚：genuine; sincere; true | ～谈 kěntán *exchange opinions sincerely*
恳切 kěnqiè earnest; sincere
恳求 kěnqiú implore; entreat; beseech
诚恳 chéngkěn　勤恳 qínkěn

啃　　kěn　11画 口部

啃 啃啃啃啃啃啃啃 啃啃啃

[动] 一点儿一点儿往下咬；也比喻刻苦地钻研：keep biting hard bit by bit; gnaw; nibble; (fig.) work hard at sth. | ～骨头 kěn gǔtou *gnaw a bone* / ～书本 kěn shūběn *delve into books*

坑　　kēng　7画 土部

坑 坑坑坑坑坑坑坑

[名] 洼下去的地方：hole; pit;

435

hollow | 水~shuǐkēng *puddle; pool* / 泥~níkēng *mud pit; mire* / 他们在挖~栽树。Tāmen zài wā kēng zāi shù. *They are digging pits to plant trees in.*

空　　　kōng　8画 穴部

空　空空空空空空空空

❶ [形] 里面没有内容或没有东西；不切实际的：empty; hollow; void; unrealistic; impractical | ~房子kōng fángzi *an empty house* / ~谈kōngtán *empty talk*
空洞 kōngdòng empty; hollow
空话 kōnghuà empty talk; hollow words
空想 kōngxiǎng daydream; an impractical idea
空心 kōngxīn hollow
空虚 kōngxū hollow; void
一场空 yīchángkōng
❷ [名] 天空：sky; heaven
空间 kōngjiān space
空军 kōngjūn air force
空中 kōngzhōng in the sky; in the air; aerial; overhead
空间站 kōngjiānzhàn space station
空中小姐 kōngzhōng xiǎojiě air hostess; stewardess
高空 gāokōng　航空 hángkōng
上空 shàngkōng　太空 tàikōng
天空 tiānkōng
◇空气 kōngqì　① air　② atmosphere
空前 kōngqián unprecedented
空调 kōngtiáo air conditioner; air conditioning
　See kòng.

孔　　　kǒng　4画 子部

孔　孔孔孔孔

[名] 洞；窟窿：cave; opening; hole | 鼻~bíkǒng *nostril* / 针~zhēnkǒng *the eye of a needle; pinprick*
◇孔雀 kǒngquè peacock
孔子 Kǒngzǐ Confucius

恐　　　kǒng　10画 心部

恐　恐恐恐恐恐恐恐恐恐恐

[动] 害怕：be afraid of; fear | 唯~完成不了任务 wéikǒng wánchéng bùliǎo rènwù *for fear that the task may not be finished*
恐怖 kǒngbù terror
恐慌 kǒnghuāng panic
恐惧 kǒngjù fear; dread; be afraid of
恐怕 kǒngpà ① fear; dread; be afraid ② perhaps; probably; maybe
争先恐后 zhēngxiān-kǒnghòu

空

kōng　8画　穴部

空 空空空空空空空空

❶ [动] 腾出来；使空：vacate; leave empty | ～一个格儿kōng yī gè gér *leave a blank space* / ～出一间房子 kōngchū yī jiān fángzi *vacate a room*

❷ [形]空缺的；没有使用的：un-occupied; vacant | ～房 kōngfáng *a vacant house (or room)* / ～地 kōngdì *vacant lot; open ground*

空白 kōngbái blank space

空缺 kōngquē ① vacant position; vacancy ② gap (in a broad sense); empty or missing part of sth.

空隙 kōngxì space; gap; interval

❸[名]未被利用的地方或时间: free time; spare time; vacant space | 有～儿再来。Yǒu kòngr zài lái. *Come over again when you're free.* / 屋子里满得连一点儿～儿都没有。Wūzi li mǎn de lián yī diǎnr kòngr dōu méiyǒu. *The room was so crowded that there was no vacant space left at all.*

空儿 kòngr unoccupied; vacant

抽空儿 chōukòngr

钻空子 zuānkòngzi

　　See kōng.

控

kòng　11画　扌部

控 控控控控控控控控控控控

❶ [动]掌握；操纵：grasp; master; know well; operate; control

控制 kòngzhì control; dominate; command

监控 jiānkòng　　失控 shīkòng

遥控 yáokòng

❷ [动]告发；揭发：report (an offender); inform against; expose; lay bare | ～告 kònggào *accuse; charge*

控诉 kòngsù accuse; denounce; make a complaint against

指控 zhǐkòng

抠 (搝) kōu　7画　扌部

抠 抠抠抠抠抠抠抠

❶ [动]用手指或细小的东西挖或掏: dig or dig out with a finger or sth. pointed | ～了个小洞 kōule ge xiǎo dòng *have dug a small hole* / 这孩子把自己的脸～破了。Zhè háizi bǎ zìjǐ de liǎn kōupò le. *The child scratched his own face.*

❷ [动]雕刻：carve; cut | 他把树根～成一件艺术品。Tā bǎ shùgēn kōuchéng yī jiàn yìshùpǐn. *He produced an artwork* out of a length of tree root.

❸[动]不必要的深究：go into (a matter) in unnecessary earnest; split hairs | ~字眼儿 kōu zì-yǎnr *find fault carefully with the choice of words* / 死~书本 sǐ kōu shūběn *pay too much attention to book knowledge; be inflexible in studying*

kǒu 3画 口部

口 口 口 口

❶ [名] 嘴：mouth | 病从~入 bìng cóng kǒu rù *illness finds its way in by the mouth; illness comes from unhealthy eating habits*

口腔 kǒuqiāng oral cavity
口味 kǒuwèi ① a person's taste ② the flavour or taste of food
开口 kāikǒu 可口 kěkǒu

❷ [名]指说话：talk, speech, utterance

口号 kǒuhào slogan; watchword
口气 kǒuqì tone; note
口试 kǒushì oral examination; oral test
口头 kǒutóu oral; orally
口语 kǒuyǔ spoken language
有口无心 yǒukǒu-wúxīn

❸[名]容器通外面的地方：opening; mouth | 碗~ wǎnkǒu *rim of a bowl* / 瓶~ píngkǒu *mouth of a bottle*

窗口 chuāngkǒu 接口 jiēkǒu

❹[名]出入通过的地方：opening; entrance; inlet; outlet; exit | 海~ hǎikǒu *seaport* / 胡同~儿 hútòngkǒur *entrance of an alley*

口岸 kǒu'àn port
出口 chūkǒu 渡口 dùkǒu
港口 gǎngkǒu 进口 jìnkǒu
路口 lùkǒu 门口 ménkǒu
入口 rùkǒu

❺[名](人体或物体表面)破裂的地方：cut; hole; opening | 衣服撕了个~儿。Yīfu sīle ge kǒur. *The clothes were torn.*

决口 juékǒu 缺口 quēkǒu
伤口 shāngkǒu

❻[量]用于人或物：measure word for family members or utensils | 一家五~ yī jiā wǔ kǒu *a family of five* / 一~锅 yī kǒu guō *a pot* / 一~井 yī kǒu jǐng *a well*

❼[量]用于口腔动作的次数：used to denote the number of oral actions | 一~水 yī kǒu shuǐ *a mouthful of water* / 一~饭 yī kǒu fàn *a mouthful of food*

一口气 yīkǒuqì
◇口袋 kǒudài pocket

kòu 6画 扌部

扣 扣 扣 扣 扣 扣

❶ [动]用圈、环一类的东西套住或

搭住：button up; buckle; do up the buttons | 把门~上bǎ mén kōushang *latch the door* / 他正在~衣服扣子。Tā zhèngzài kōu yīfu kòuzi. *He is doing up the buttons of his clothes.*

② [名]纽扣：button | 衣~儿 yī-kōur *button*

　纽扣儿 niǔkòur

③ [动]强制留下；关押：detain; keep from leaving; hold in custody | 驾驶证被~了。Jiā-shǐzhèng bèi kōu le. *The driver's licence has been taken away (by the police).* / 他被~了起来。Tā bèi kōule qǐlai. *He has been detained (or arrested).*

　扣押 kōuyā ① detain; hold in custody ② (leg.) distrain; seize

④ [动]从原数额中减去一部分：deduct; take off | ~工资 kōu gōngzī *deduct a certain amount from one's salary*

　扣除 kōuchú deduct

　回扣 huíkōu 　　折扣 zhékòu

⑤ [动]器物口朝下放或覆盖东西：place a cup, bowl, etc. upside down; cover with an inverted container | 把碗~在桌上bǎ wǎn kōu zài zhuō shang *place the bowl upside down on the table* / 把饭~上，免得凉了。Bǎ fàn kōushang, miǎn de liáng le. *Cover the bowl of rice with a lid to keep warm.*

⑥ [动]用力朝下击打（球）：smash (the ball forcefully) | ~球 kōu-qiú *smash the ball*

枯 kū 9画 木部

枯枯枯枯枯枯枯枯枯

① [形]植物等失去水分：dried up; withered | 草~了。Cǎo kū le. *The grass withered.* / 树已经~朽了。Shù yǐjīng kūxiǔ le. *The tree has dried and decayed.*

② [形]（河、井）等变干：(of river, well) dry up | 这口井~了。Zhè kǒu jǐng kū le. *The well has dried up.*

③ [形]没有趣味：uninteresting; dull
　枯燥 kūzào dry and dull; uninteresting

哭 kū 10画 犬部

哭哭哭哭哭哭哭哭哭哭

[动]因悲伤或激动而流泪(有时发出声音)：weep; cry; sob | 放声大~fàngshēng dà kū *cry loudly* / 痛~tòngkū *weep bitter tears; cry one's heart out* / 姑娘激动得~了。Gūniang jī-dòng de kū le. *The girl was so excited that she burst into tears.* 哭笑不得 kūxiào-bùdé not know whether to laugh or to cry; find sth. both funny and annoying

 窟 kū　13画 穴部

窟 窟窟窟窟窟窟窟窟窟 窟窟窟窟窟

[名]洞穴：hole; cave | 狼～lángkū wolves' den

窟窿 kūlong ① hole; cavity ② deficit; debt

苦 kǔ　8画 艹部

苦 苦苦苦苦苦苦苦苦

❶ [形]（跟"甜 tián"相对）：bitter (the opposite of "甜 tián"）| 这药很～。Zhè yào hěn kǔ. *This medicine tastes very bitter.* / 良药～口 liángyào-kǔkǒu *good medicine tastes bitter*

苦瓜 kǔguā (bot.) bitter gourd

❷ [形]难受；痛苦：suffering; pain; having a hard time | 吃～chīkǔ *bear hardships* / ～日子已经过去了。Kǔ rìzi yǐjīng guòqu le. *The hard days have gone.*

苦难 kǔnàn suffering; misery; distress

苦恼 kǔnǎo vexed; worried

艰苦 jiānkǔ　　　刻苦 kèkǔ

困苦 kùnkǔ　　　贫苦 pínkǔ

穷苦 qióngkǔ　　痛苦 tòngkǔ

辛苦 xīnkǔ

❸ [副]竭力；耐心地：with all one's might; assiduously; patiently | ～干kǔgàn *do one's utmost* / ～练基本功 kǔ liàn jīběngōng *practise basic skills very hard*

苦苦 kǔkǔ strenuously; hard; persistently

库 (庫) kù　7画 广部

库 库库库库库库库

[名]warehouse | 书～shūkù *stack room (for books)* / 这种商品～里还有很多。Zhè zhǒng shāng-pǐn kù li háiyǒu hěn duō. *We have plenty of stock of these goods.*

库存 kùcún stock; reserve

库房 kùfáng storehouse; store-room

宝库 bǎokù　　　仓库 cāngkù

水库 shuǐkù

国库券 guókùquàn

数据库 shùjùkù

裤 (褲) kù　12画 衤部

裤 裤裤裤裤裤裤裤裤 裤裤裤裤

[名]裤子：trousers; pants | 棉～miánkù *cotton-padded trousers* / 短～duǎnkù shorts

裤子 kùzi trousers; pants

内裤 nèikù　　　牛仔裤 niúzǎikù

夸 (誇) kuā　6画 大部

夸 夸夸夸夸夸夸

❶[动]说大话：exaggerate; talk big | ～口 kuākǒu boast; brag / ～张 kuāzhāng exaggerate / 不要～大 bùyào kuādà don't exaggerate; no exaggeration
夸大 kuādà exaggerate; overstate; magnify
❷[动]称赞：praise; commend; speak highly of | 人人都～他进步快。Rénrén dōu kuā tā jìnbù kuài. Everyone praised him for his rapid progress.
夸奖 kuājiǎng praise; commend; extol; compliment

垮 kuǎ　9画 土部

垮 垮垮垮垮垮垮垮垮垮

[动]倒塌：collapse; fall; break down | 房子被大水冲～了。Fángzi bèi dàshuǐ chōngkuǎ le. The flood broke down the house.

挎 kuà　9画 扌部

挎 挎挎挎挎挎挎挎挎挎

❶[动]用胳膊钩或挂住东西：carry on the arm | 他胳膊上～着篮子。Tā gēbo shang kuàzhe lánzi. He carries a basket on his arm.
❷[动]把东西挂在肩上、脖颈或腰里：sling; hang | 肩上～着一个包 jiānshang kuàzhe yī gè bāo carry a bag over one's shoulder / 他脖子上～着一个照相机。Tā bózi shang kuàzhe yī gè zhàoxiàngjī. He had a camera slung over his neck. / 他腰上～着一把剑。Tā yāoshang kuàzhe yī bǎ jiàn. He had a sword hanging at his side.

跨 kuà　13画 足部

跨 跨跨跨跨跨跨跨跨跨跨跨跨跨

❶[动]抬起一只脚向前或向左右迈（一大步）：stride forward or sideways | ～着大步 kuàzhe dàbù walk with great strides / ～进校门 kuàjìn xiàomén enter a school; enter the school gate
❷[动]两腿分在物体的两边坐着或立着：ride (a horse, etc.) astride; straddle; bestride | ～在马上 kuà zài mǎ shang mount a horse
❸[动]超越一定数量、时间或地区的界限：cut across; go beyond

| ～年度 kuǎ niándù *go beyond the year* / ～地区 kuǎ dìqū *transregional* / ～行业 kuǎ hǎngyè *across industries*
跨越 kuǎyuè stride across; leap over; cut across; span

 (會) kuǎi　6画 人部

 会会会会会会

[动]总计；合计：amount to; add up to; total
会计 kuǎijì accounting
会计师 kuǎijìshī certified accountant; chief accountant; treasurer
　　　See huì.

 (塊) kuǎi　7画 土部

块 块块块块块块块

❶[名]成团块状的东西：piece; lump; chunk | 糖～儿 tángkuǎir *hard candy (or fruit drops)*; *lump of sugar* / 土～儿 tǔkuǎir *lump of earth; clod*
❷[量]用于块状或片状的东西：measure word for a piece (cake) of sth. | 一～香皂 yī kuǎi xiāngzào *a cake of perfumed soap* / 一～手表 yī kuǎi shǒubiǎo *a wristwatch* / 一～布 yī kuǎi bù *a piece of cloth*
❸[量]用于货币，相当于"元 yuán"：used for currency as "元 yuán" | 一～钱 yī kuǎi qián *one yuan*
◇一块儿 yīkuǎir

 kuǎi　7画 忄部

快 快快快快快快快

❶[形]高兴；喜悦：happy; pleased; gratified | 拍手称～ pāishǒu-chēngkuǎi *clap and cheer*
快活 kuǎihuo happy; cheerful
快乐 kuǎilē happy; joyful; cheerful
愉快 yúkuǎi
❷[形]直爽；直截了当：plain-spoken; straightforward; forthright | 心直口～ xīnzhí-kǒukuǎi *quick in speech and straightforward in thought; open-hearted and outspoken*
爽快 shuǎngkuai
痛痛快快 tòngtōng-kuǎikuǎi
❸[形]速度高，迅速（跟"慢 màn"相对）：fast; quick; rapid; swift (the opposite of "慢 màn") | ～车 kuǎichē *express train (or bus)* / 进步很～ jìnbù hěn kuǎi *make rapid progress* / 他跑得真～。Tā pǎo de zhēn kuǎi. *He runs so fast.*
快餐 kuǎicān quick meal; snack; fast food
快递 kuǎidì express delivery
快件 kuǎijiàn express mail, package, etc.

快捷 kuàijié fast (speed); nimble (action)

快速 kuàisù fast; quick; high-speed

飞快 fēikuài 　　赶快 gǎnkuài

尽快 jǐnkuài

❹ [形]锋利（跟"钝 dùn"相对）：sharp; keen (the opposite of "钝 dùn") | 这剪刀不~。Zhè jiǎndāo bù kuài. *This pair of scissors is not sharp.*

❺ [形]反映敏捷：quick-witted; ingenious | 脑子~nǎozi kuài *quick-witted; quick-minded*

❻ [副]赶紧；从速：hurry; make haste; as soon as possible | ~上学去! Kuài shàngxué qù! *Hurry to school!* / ~回去吧! Kuài huíqu ba! *Go back immediately!* / 你~来帮我一下。Nǐ kuài lái bāng wǒ yīxià. *Come over quickly and give me a hand.*

❼ [副]将要；马上；就：about to; immediately; right away; in a moment | 天~亮了。Tiān kuài liàng le. *It will get light soon.* 他~五十岁了。Tā kuài wǔshí suì le. *He is nearly fifty years old.* / 我~毕业了。Wǒ kuài bìyè le. *I'm going to graduate soon.*

◇ 捞外快 lāowàikuài

 筷 kuài 13画 竹部

筷 筷筷筷筷筷筷筷 筷筷筷筷筷

See 筷子

筷子 kuàizi chopsticks

宽（宽） kuān 10画 宀部

宽 宽宽宽宽宽宽宽宽 宽宽

❶ [形]横向的距离大；面积大（跟"窄 zhǎi"相对）：wide; broad; roomy; spacious (the opposite of "窄zhǎi") | 这衣服太~了。Zhè yīfu tài kuān le. *These clothes are too baggy.* / 这条马路很~。Zhè tiáo mǎlù hěn kuān. *The street is very broad.*

宽敞 kuānchǎng spacious; roomy

宽大 kuāndà ① spacious; roomy ② lenient

宽度 kuāndù width; breadth

宽广 kuānguǎng broad; extensive; vast

宽阔 kuānkuò broad; wide

❷ [形]度量大；不严厉：tolerant; magnanimous; generous; lenient | ~容 kuānróng *tolerant; lenient* / ~厚 kuānhòu *tolerant and generous; honest and kind* / 从~处理 cóngkuān chǔlǐ *handle leniently; treat with leniency*

宽松 kuānsōng ① (of clothes)

loose and comfortable ② not crowded ③ feel relieved; be free from worry ④ comfortably off; ample; easy

❸ [形] 富余：well-to-do; comfortably off; well-off | 手头不～ shǒutóu bù kuān *not well-off; short of money*

 款 kuǎn 12画 欠部

款 款款款款款款款款款 款款款款

❶ [形] 诚恳；殷勤：sincere; earnest; cordial; eagerly attentive; solicitous | ～待 kuǎndài *treat cordially; entertain; receive cordially*

❷ [名] 法令、规章等分条列举的事项：section; paragraph; item | 条～tiáokuǎn *clause (in a formal document)*

❸ [名] 钱：money | 现～xiànkuǎn *cash*

拨款 bōkuǎn　存款 cúnkuǎn
贷款 dàikuǎn　罚款 fákuǎn
付款 fùkuǎn　公款 gōngkuǎn
货款 huòkuǎn　捐款 juānkuǎn
赔款 péikuǎn

◇ 款式 kuǎnshì pattern; style; design
新款 xīnkuǎn

筐 kuāng 12画 竹部

 筐 筐筐筐筐筐筐筐筐 筐筐筐筐

[名] 用竹子、柳条或荆条编成的盛东西的器具：basket; crate made of bamboo, willow twigs, etc. | 竹～zhúkuāng *bamboo basket* 箩筐 luókuāng

狂 kuáng 7画 犭部

狂 狂狂狂狂狂狂狂

❶ [形] 疯；精神失常：mad; insane; crazy; out of one's mind | 发～ fākuáng *go mad; go crazy* 狂热 kuángrè fanaticism 疯狂 fēngkuáng

❷ [形] 极端的自高自大：extremely conceited; wildly arrogant | 这个人太～了，谁也瞧不起。Zhège rén tài kuáng le, shéi yě qiáobuqǐ. *He is too conceited to look up to anyone.* 狂妄 kuángwàng wildly arrogant; frantic; presumptuous

❸ [形] 不加约束；尽情地：unbridled; wild; delirious; unrestrained | ～喜 kuángxǐ *wild with joy* / ～欢 kuánghuān *revelry; carnival* 猖狂 chāngkuáng

❹ [形] 猛烈；声势大：violently; great in strength and impetus; powerful and dynamic 狂风 kuángfēng fierce wind;

gale

旷 (曠) kuàng 7画 日部

旷 旷旷旷旷旷旷旷

[动] 耽误；荒废：delay; hold up; waste; neglect

旷工 kuànggōng stay away from work without permission

旷课 kuàngkè be absent from school without reason; cut school; cut classes; skip school

况 kuàng 7画 冫部

况 况况况况况况况

❶ [名] 情形：condition; situation | 近~ jìnkuàng *recent condition or situation*

路况 lùkuàng 情况 qíngkuàng

状况 zhuàngkuàng

❷ [连] 表示更进一层：furthermore | 何~ hékuàng *let alone; moreover*

况且 kuàngqiě moreover; besides; in addition

矿 (礦) kuàng 8画 石部

矿 矿矿矿矿矿矿矿矿

❶ [名] 埋藏在地下的有开采价值的物质：ore deposit | 铁~ tiě-kuàng *iron ore* / 煤~ méikuàng

coal ore

矿藏 kuàngcáng mineral resources (reserves); ore deposits

矿产 kuàngchǎn mineral products; minerals

矿石 kuàngshí ore

矿物 kuàngwù mineral

❷ [名] 开矿的场所或单位：mine; pit

矿工 kuànggōng miner

矿井 kuàngjǐng mine shaft (pit)

矿区 kuàngqū mining area

矿山 kuàngshān mine (with its accompanying shafts, buildings, etc.)

框 kuàng 10画 木部

框 框框框框框框框框框框

❶ [名] 嵌在墙上为安装门窗用的架子：frame; framework for installing doors or windows | 门~ ménkuàng *door frame* / 窗~ chuāngkuàng *window frame*

❷ [名] 器物周边的支架：frame as support for sth. | 画~ huà-kuàng *picture frame* / 眼镜~ yǎnjìngkuàng *rims or frames (of spectacles)*

框架 kuàngjià frame; framework

眶 kuàng 11画 目部

眶 眶眶眶眶眶眶眶眶眶眶眶

[名]眼的四周： eye socket | 眼泪夺~而出。Yǎnlèi duókuàng'ér chū. *Tears gushed.; Tears trickled from the eyes.*

眼眶 yǎnkuàng

亏 (虧) kuī 3画 一部

亏 亏亏亏

❶[动]受损失；损耗(跟"盈yíng"相对)： suffer losses; lose; wear and tear (the opposite of "盈yíng") | 经营~本 jīngyíng kuīběn *lose money in business*

亏损 kuīsǔn loss; deficit

吃亏 chīkuī   盈亏 yíngkuī

自负盈亏 zìfù yíngkuī

❷[动]欠缺，短少： lacking; deficient; short of | 理~lǐkuī *be in the wrong* / 这月钱又花~了。Zhè yuè qián yòu huākuī le. *I have run short of money again this month.*

❸[动]使吃亏；对不起：make suffer losses; fail; treat unfairly | ~心 kuīxīn *have a guilty conscience*

亏待 kuīdài treat unfairly; treat shabbily

❹[动]幸而：fortunately; luckily | ~了你提醒我，我才想起来。Kuīle nǐ tíxǐng wǒ, wǒ cái xiǎng qǐlai. *Luckily you reminded me—now I remember.*

多亏 duōkuī   幸亏 xìngkuī

❺[动]反说，表示讥讽或斥责：used to express sarcasm or reproach | 这种话~你说得出来。Zhè zhǒng huà kuī nǐ shuō de chūlái. *How could you have the nerve to say so?*

葵 kuí 12画 艹部

葵 葵葵葵葵葵葵葵葵葵葵葵葵

See 向日葵
向日葵 xiàngrìkuí

昆 kūn 8画 日部

昆 昆昆昆昆昆昆昆昆

See 昆虫
昆虫 kūnchóng insect

捆 kǔn 10画 扌部

捆 捆捆捆捆捆捆捆捆捆

[动]用绳子把东西缠紧：tie; bind; fasten sth. with ropes | ~行李

kǔn xíngli *tie up the baggage* / 你把东西～起来。Nǐ bǎ dōngxi kǔn qǐlai. *Tie up your stuff.*
捆绑 kǔnbǎng tie up (usu. a person); truss up; bind

困 (睏❶) kǔn　　7画 口部

困 困 困 困 困 困 困

❶ [形]艰难；穷苦：difficult; hard; arduous; poverty-stricken; poor | 生活～苦 shēnghuó kǔnkǔ *live in extreme poverty*
困苦 kǔnkǔ hardship; tribulation
困难 kǔnnan ① difficulty ② financial difficulty; straitened difficulty
贫困 pínkǔn
❷ [动]陷在艰难痛苦中难以摆脱：be hard pressed; be distressed | 被疾病所～ bèi jíbìng suǒ kǔn *be stricken by illness*
困惑 kǔnhuò perplexed; puzzled
困境 kǔnjìng difficult position; predicament; straits
❸ [动]控制在一定范围内；包围：confine in some space; surround; pin down | 别把小狗～在屋子里。Bié bǎ xiǎogǒu kǔn zài wūzi li. *Don't confine the puppy in the house.*
❹ [形]疲乏想睡：tired; drowsy | 孩子～了，该睡觉了。Háizi kǔn le, gāi shuìjiào le. *The child is sleepy. It's time for him to go to bed.*

扩 (擴) kuò　　6画 扌部

扩 扩 扩 扩 扩 扩 扩

[动]使（范围、规模等）增大：magnify | ～音器 kuòyīnqì *megaphone; audio amplifier* / ～大范围 kuòdà fànwéi *expand the scope*
扩充 kuòchōng expand; strengthen
扩大 kuòdà enlarge; expand; extend
扩建 kuòjiàn extend (a factory, mine, etc.)
扩散 kuòsàn spread; diffuse; proliferate
扩展 kuòzhǎn expand; spread; extend; develop
扩张 kuòzhāng expand; enlarge; extend

括 kuò　　9画 扌部

括 括 括 括 括 括 括 括 括

[动]包容：contain; include | 总～ zǒngkuò *sum up*
包括 bāokuò　　概括 gàikuò

阔 (闊) kuò　　12画 门部

447

阔

阔 阔 阔 阔 阔 阔 阔 阔
阔 阔 阔 阔

阔
kuò

❶[形]（面积）大；宽广：vast; ex-
pansive; wide | 海～天空 hǎi-
kuò-tiānkōng *as boundless as
the sea and sky; unrestrained
and far-ranging* / 广～天地
guǎngkuò tiāndì *a vast world*
广阔 guǎngkuò　开阔 kāikuò

宽阔 kuānkuò　辽阔 liáokuò
❷[形]富裕；讲排场：prosperous;
well-to-do; well off; osten-
tatious; showing off | ～气
kuòqi *luxurious; extravagant* /
你别摆～，还是节约一点好。Nǐ
bié bǎikuò, háishì jiéyuē
yīdiǎn hǎo. *Don't be so extravagant. You'd better spend
your money wisely.*

L l

 lā　8画 土部

垃 垃垃垃垃垃垃垃垃

See 垃圾

垃圾 lājī　rubbish; garbage; refuse

 lā　8画 扌部

拉 拉拉拉拉拉拉拉拉

❶ [动] pull; draw; tug; drag | ～车 lāchē *pull a cart* /东西太沉，我～不动。Dōngxi tài chén, wǒ lābudòng. *It's too heavy for me to pull it along all by myself.* / 他们手～着手边跳边唱。Tāmen shǒu lāzhe shǒu biān tiào biān chàng. *They danced and sang together hand in hand.* 拖拉机 tuōlājī

❷ [动] 用车载运：transport by vehicle; haul | ～货 lāhuò *transport goods by vehicle* /快把门口的垃圾～走。Kuài bǎ ménkǒu de lājī lāzǒu. *Quickly haul away (by vehicle) the rubbish by the door.*

❸ [动] 牵动乐器的某一部分使发声：play (a musical instrument) | ～小提琴 lā xiǎotíqín *play the violin* /～二胡 lā èrhú *play the* erhu

❹ [动] 牵累；拉扯：drag in; implicate | 一人做事一人当，不要～上别人。Yī rén zuòshì yī rén dāng, bùyào lāshang biérén. *A man should take the consequences of his own conduct without dragging in other people.*

❺ [动] 拖长；使延长：drag out; draw out; space out | ～长声音 lā cháng shēngyīn *(of voice) drawl* /～开距离 lākāi jùlí *space out; leave distances in between* / 这两个队的比分～得越来越远。Zhè liǎng gè duì de bǐfēn lā de yuèlāiyuè yuǎn. *The scores of these two teams pulled away from each other farther and farther.*

❻ [动] 联络；拉拢：draw in; win over; canvass | ～关系 lā guānxi *try to establish a relationship with sb.* /～选票 lā xuǎn-piào *canvass votes*

❼ [动] 排泄：empty the bowels | ～肚子 lā dùzi *suffer from diarrhoea; have loose bowels*

◇拉家常 lājiācháng talk about everyday matters; engage in small talk; chitchat

阿拉伯语 Ālābóyǔ

 lǎ　12画 口部

喇 喇喇喇喇喇喇喇喇喇
喇喇喇喇

See 喇叭

喇叭 lǎba ①a popular name for the *suona*, a woodwind instrument ②brass-wind instruments in general or any of these instruments

落 là　　12画 艹部

落落落落落落落落
落落落落

❶ [动] 因跟不上被丢在后面：lag behind; fall behind; drop behind | 快跟上，别～下。Kuài gēnshang, bié làxia. *Close up. Don't fall behind.* /她～了一个星期的课。Tā làle yī gè xīngqī de kè. *She has missed one week's lessons.*

❷ [动] 遗漏；忘记带走：leave out; forget to take | 这里～了两行。Zhèli làle liǎng háng. *Two lines are missing here.* / 作业本～在家里了。Zuòyèběn là zài jiāli le. *The exercise book was left at home.*

　　See luò.

腊 (臘) là　　12画 月部

腊腊腊腊腊腊腊腊
腊腊腊腊

[名] 农历十二月：the 12th lunar month

腊月 làyuè the 12th month of the lunar year; the 12th lunar month

蜡 (蠟) là　　14画 虫部

蜡蜡蜡蜡蜡蜡蜡蜡
蜡蜡蜡蜡蜡蜡

[名] wax | 涂～ túlà *apply a coat of wax* /石～ shílà *paraffin wax* 蜡烛 làzhú candle

辣 là　　14画 辛部

辣辣辣辣辣辣辣辣
辣辣辣辣辣辣辣

❶ [形] 姜、蒜、辣椒等具有的刺激性的味道：(of the taste of ginger, garlic, hot pepper, etc.) peppery; hot | 他爱吃～的东西。Tā ài chī là de dōngxi. *He likes spicy food.*
辣椒 làjiāo hot pepper

❷ [形] 凶恶；狠毒 vicious; ruthless | 心狠手～ xīnhěn-shǒulà *cruel and ruthless*

来 (來) lái　　7画 一部

来来来来来来来来

❶ [动] 从别的地方到说话人所在

的地方（跟"去qù""往wǎng"相对）：come; move toward the speaker or a particular place (the opposite of "去qù" or "往wǎng") | 家里~了客人。Jiāli láile kèrén. *We have some guests at home.* / 我~北京三年了。Wǒ lái Běijīng sān nián le. *I have been in Beijing for three years.*

来宾 láibīn guest; visitor

来访 láifǎng come to visit; come to call

来回 láihuí ① make a round trip; make a return trip; go to a place and come back ② back and forth; to and fro

来客 láikè guest; visitor

来临 láilín arrive; come; draw near; be at hand

来往 láiwǎng ①come and go ② dealings; contact; intercourse

来信 láixìn ① send a letter here ② incoming letter

来源 láiyuán ①origin; source ② come from; stem from; derive from; be from; originate from

来自 láizì come from

到来 dàolái 　　归来 guīlái

往来 wǎnglái

❷ [形] 未来的；以后的（时间）：future; coming; from now on | ~年 láinián *the coming year; next year*

将来 jiānglái 　　未来 wèilái

❸ [名] 从过去到说话时为止的一段时间；以来：indicating a period of time that extends from the past to this moment | 这一年~他的进步很大。Zhè yī nián lái tā de jìnbù hěn dà. *He has made great progress in the past year.*

本来 běnlái 　　从来 cónglái
后来 hòulái 　　近来 jìnlái
历来 lìlái 　　向来 xiànglái
以来 yǐlái 　　原来 yuánlái

❹ [动]（事情、问题等）发生，来到：happen; appear; arise | 春天就要~了。Chūntiān jiùyào lái le. *Spring is coming.* / 问题~了。Wèntí lái le. *Problems have arisen.* / 通知~得很及时。Tōngzhī lái de hěn jíshí. *The notice has arrived just in time.*

❺ [动] 用在另一个动词前，表示要做某件事：used in front of a verb, indicating an intended action | 我~试试。Wǒ lái shìshi. *Let me try.* / 我~问你。Wǒ lái wèn nǐ. *Let me ask you (a question).* / 大家~想想办法。Dàjiā lái xiǎngxiǎng bànfǎ. *Let's think of a solution.*

❻ [动] 做某个动作(代替意义具体的动词)：used as a substitute for a preceding verb | 再~一个! Zài lái yī gè! *Encore!* / 我办不了，你~吧! Wǒ bànbuliǎo, nǐ lái ba! *I cannot do it. Could you have a try?*

胡来 húlái

451

❼[动] 用在动词后，表示动作的趋向：(used after a verb, indicating motion towards the speaker) hither; (to) here | 前面开~了一辆小汽车。Qiánmiàn kāilaile yī liàng xiǎo qìchē. *Here comes a car.* / 他给我送~了许多参考资料。Tā gěi wǒ sōnglaile xǔduō cānkǎo zīliào. *He has brought me a lot of reference materials.*

出来 chūlái(lai) 带来 dàilái(lai)
过来 guòlái(lai) 回来 huílái(lai)
进来 jìnlái(lai) 起来 qǐlái(lai)
上来 shànglái(lai)
下来 xiàlái(lai)
看起来 kànqǐlái(lai)
推来推去 tuīlái-tuīqù

❽[数] 表示大概的数目：(used to indicate an estimated number) approximately; about | 十~个 shí lái gè *about ten* / 三米~长 sān mǐ lái cháng *about three metres long* / 五十一~岁 wǔshí lái suì *in one's fifties*

◇来历 láilì origin; source
来不及 láibují there is not enough time to do sth.; it is too late
来得及 láidejí be able to do sth. in time
用来 yònglái

赖 (賴) lài   13画 贝部

赖 赖 赖 赖 赖 赖 赖 赖
赖 赖 赖 赖 赖

❶[动] 倚靠：rely; depend on; lean on | 依~ yīlài *rely on; be dependent on*
信赖 xìnlài

❷[形] 不好；坏：no good; poor | ~的不要。Lài de bùyào. *Things of poor quality are not wanted.* / 这孩子字写得不~。Zhè háizi zì xiě de bùlài. *The child's handwriting is good.*

❸[动] 留在某处不肯走：hang on (at a place) | ~在那儿 lài zài nàr *hang on there* / 孩子~着不肯走。Háizi làizhe bùkěn zǒu. *The child stayed there and refused to leave.*

❹[动] 抵赖：不承认错误或不承担责任：go back on one's words; deny one's error or responsibility | 事情是你干的，你~不掉。Shìqing shì nǐ gàn de, nǐ làibudiào. *You cannot deny that it is you who did it.*

❺[动] 责怪；责备：blame; reproach | 这事不~他。Zhè shì bù lài tā. *He's not to blame for this.* / 没有证据不能乱~别人。Méiyǒu zhèngjù bùnéng luàn lài biérén. *You can not put the blame on others without evidence.*

兰 (蘭) lán   5画 丷部

452

兰 兰兰兰兰兰

[名] orchid
兰花 lánhuā orchid; sword-leaved cymbidium
玉兰 yùlán

拦 (攔) lán　　8画 扌部
拦 拦拦拦拦拦拦拦拦

[动] 不让通过；阻挡：bar; block｜不要～我。Bùyào lán wǒ. *Let me go.* / 快把那辆车～住。Kuài bǎ nà liàng chē lánzhù. *Stop that car at once.*
拦截 lánjié intercept

栏 (欄) lán　　9画 木部
栏 栏栏栏栏栏栏栏栏栏

[名] 用来遮拦的东西：fence; railing
栏杆 lángān railing; banister; balustrade
护栏 hùlán　　木栏 mùlán
◇栏目 lánmù the heading or title of a column (in a magazine, etc.)
专栏 zhuānlán

蓝 (藍) lán　　13画 艹部
蓝 蓝蓝蓝蓝蓝蓝蓝蓝
蓝蓝蓝蓝蓝

[形] blue; azure｜～墨水 lán mòshuǐ *blue ink* /～衣服 lán yīfu *blue clothes* / 她有一双美丽的～眼睛。Tā yǒu yī shuāng měilì de lán yǎnjing. *She has beautiful blue eyes.*
蓝色 lánsè blue (colour)
蓝天 lántiān blue sky
景泰蓝 jǐngtàilán

篮 (籃) lán　　16画 竹部
篮 篮篮篮篮篮篮篮篮篮
篮篮篮篮篮篮篮篮

❶ [名] 篮子：basket｜竹～ zhúlán *bamboo basket* / 花～ huālán *basket of flowers*
篮子 lánzi basket
摇篮 yáolán
❷ [名] 篮球架上的铁圈和网子：a metal hoop with net, on a frame (for playing basketball)｜球～ qiúlán *goal; basket* / 投～ tóulán *shoot towards the basket*
篮球 lánqiú basketball

览 (覽) lǎn　　9画 见部
览 览览览览览览览览
览

[动] 观看：look at｜游～ yóulán *tour; go sightseeing* / 阅～ yuèlán *read*
展览 zhǎnlǎn

博览会 bólǎnhuì
阅览室 yuèlǎnshì
展览会 zhǎnlǎnhuì

懒 (懶) lǎn　16画 忄部

懒 懒懒懒懒懒懒懒懒
懒懒懒懒懒懒懒懒

lǎn
﹨
láng

❶ [形] 不勤快；不爱劳动（跟"勤qín"相对）: lazy; indolent (the opposite of "勤qín") | 好吃懒做 hàochī-lǎnzuò be gluttonous and lazy / 这孩子真懒。Zhè háizi zhēn lǎn. *The child is so lazy.*

懒惰 lǎnduò lazy
懒骨头 lǎngǔtou (inf.) lazybones

❷ [形] 疲倦；没力气: sluggish; languid | 浑身发懒 húnshēn fālǎn *feel sluggish all over* / 伸懒腰 shēn lǎnyāo *stretch oneself*

烂 (爛) làn　9画 火部

烂 烂烂烂烂烂烂烂烂
烂

❶ [形] 某些固体物质组织破坏或水分增加后松软: mashed; soft | 肉煮得真烂。Ròu zhǔ de zhēn làn. *The meat is stewed so well (that it melts in the mouth).*

❷ [形] 腐坏: rotten or bad | 这些

橘子烂了。Zhèxiē júzi làn le. *These tangerines are rotten.* / 桃子和葡萄容易烂。Táozi hé pútao róngyì làn. *Peaches and grapes rot easily.*

腐烂 fǔlàn

❸ [形] 破碎；残破: worn-out; broken | 破铜烂铁 pòtóng làntiě *odds and ends of copper and iron* / 衣服穿烂了。Yīfu chuānlàn le. *The clothes have been worn out.*

破烂 pòlàn

❹ [形] 头绪乱: messy; disorderly | 烂摊子 làntānzi *an awful mess* / 真是一本烂账。Zhēn shì yī běn lànzhàng. *The accounts are (or the situation is) all in a mess.*

❺ [副] 表示程度极深: to a great extent; thoroughly | 台词背得烂熟 táicí bèi de lànshú *learn one's lines thoroughly*

滥 (濫) làn　13画 氵部

滥 滥滥滥滥滥滥滥滥
滥滥滥滥滥

[动] 水漫出来: overflow; flood
泛滥 fànlàn

狼 láng　10画 犭部

狼 狼狼狼狼狼狼狼狼
狼狼

[名] wolf | ～咬死了好几头羊。 Láng yǎosǐle hǎo jǐ tóu yáng. *The wolf bit several sheep to death.*

狼狈 lángbèi in a dilemma; in an awkward situation

朗 lǎng 10画 月部

朗 朗朗朗朗朗朗朗朗 朗朗

❶ [形] 明亮；光线充足：light; bright | 明～mínglǎng *bright and clear* / 开～kāilǎng ① *spacious and with plenty of light* ② *sanguine; optimistic*

晴朗 qínglǎng

❷ [形] 声音清楚、响亮：loud and clear | 学校里到处书声～～。 Xuéxiào li dàochù shūshēng lǎnglǎng. *All around the campus, one can hear students reading out loud.*

朗读 lǎngdú read aloud

朗诵 lǎngsòng recite aloud; deliver a recitation

浪 lǎng 10画 氵部

浪 浪浪浪浪浪浪浪 浪浪

❶ [名] 水波；波浪：wave; billow | 海～hǎilǎng *ocean wave* / 今天～很大，不要去游泳了。 Jīntiān lǎng hěn dà, bùyào

qù yóuyǒng le. *Don't go swimming today, the sea has turned rough.*

浪潮 lǎngcháo tide; wave

波浪 bōlǎng 冲浪 chōnglǎng

风浪 fēnglǎng

❷ [名] 像波浪一样起伏的东西：sth. resembling waves | 麦～ màilǎng *rippling wheat; billowing wheat fields* / 热～ rèlǎng *heat wave; hot wave* / 声～ shēnglǎng *sound wave; acoustic wave*

❸ [动] 放纵；不受约束：unrestrained; indulgent | 放～fànglǎng *without restraint; dissolute*

浪费 lǎngfèi waste; lavish; fritter; squander; go (run) to waste

流浪 liúlàng

◇浪漫 lǎngmàn romantic

捞 (撈) lāo 10画 扌部

捞 捞捞捞捞捞捞捞 捞捞

❶ [动] 从液体中取东西：scoop up from a liquid; fish for | ～鱼lāo yú *net fish; catch fish* / 打～ dǎlāo *get out of the water; salvage*

捕捞 bǔlāo

❷ [动] 用不正当的手段取得：get by dishonest means | ～油水 lāo yóushuǐ *reap some profit; gain some advantage*

捞外快 lāowàikuài make money (by quick or improper means)

劳 (勞) láo 7画 艹部

劳 劳劳劳劳劳劳劳

❶ [形] 辛苦；累：hard-working; tired | 辛～xīnláo pains; toil
疲劳 píláo   勤劳 qínláo

❷ [动] 费；烦劳：put sb. to the trouble of | ～您费心了。Láo nín fèixīn le. *I'm sorry to trouble you.* / ～你帮个忙。Láo nǐ bāng ge máng. *Could you please do me a favour (or give me a hand)?*
劳驾 láojià excuse me

❸ [动] 劳动：work; labour | 多～多得 duōláo-duōdé *more pay for more work*
劳动 láodòng labour; work; toil
劳务 láowù labour services
劳动力 láodònglì labour; labour force
操劳 cāoláo
按劳分配 ànláofēnpèi
不劳而获 bùláo'érhuò

❹ [名] 功绩：meritorious deed; service
功劳 gōngláo

牢 láo 7画 宀部

牢 牢牢牢牢牢牢牢

❶ [名] 监禁囚犯的地方：prison; jail | 坐～zuòláo *be in prison; be in jail* / 监～jiānláo *prison; jail*
牢房 láofáng cell; ward

❷ [形] 结实；坚固：solid; firm; fast | 记得～jìdeláo *keep firmly in mind* / 请把钉子钉得～一点儿。Qǐng bǎ dīngzi dìng de láo yīdiǎnr. *Please drive in the nail a bit more firmly.*
牢固 láogù firm; secure
牢记 láojì keep firmly in mind; remember well

◇ 牢骚 láosāo discontent; complaint; grievance

老 lǎo 6画 老部

老 老老老老老老

❶ [形] 年岁大 (跟"少shào""幼yòu"相对)：(of age) old (the opposite of "少shào" or "幼yòu") | 他已经～了。Tā yǐjīng lǎo le. *He is old now.* / 他60岁了，可一点儿也不显～。Tā liùshí suì le, kě yīdiǎnr yě bù xiǎn lǎo. *He is already 60, but doesn't look old at all.*
老伴 lǎobàn (inf.) (of an old married couple) husband or wife
老成 lǎochéng experienced and steady
老汉 lǎohàn ① old man ② (an old man calling himself) "an old fellow like me"

老化 lǎohuà aging

老年 lǎonián old age

老人 lǎorén ① old man or woman; the aged; the old ② one's aged parents or grandparents

老子 lǎozi ① father ② (usu. said in anger or for fun) (of an arrogant man) I, your father

老大妈 lǎodàmā aunty; granny

老大娘 lǎodàniang aunty; granny

老大爷 lǎodàye uncle; grandpa

老年人 lǎoniánrén old people; the old; the aged

老人家 lǎorénjia ① a respectful form of address for an old person ② parent

老太婆 lǎotàipó old woman

老太太 lǎotàitai ① old lady ② your (my, his, etc.) mother

老头儿 lǎotóur old man; old chap

老一辈 lǎoyībèi older generation

老字号 lǎozìhào old name in business; long-established shop

衰老 shuāilǎo　养老 yǎnglǎo

中老年 zhōnglǎonián

男女老少 nán-nǚ-lǎo-shào

月下老人 yuèxià lǎorén

❷ [形] 时间久的 (跟 "新 xīn" 相对): (of time) long (the opposite of "新 xīn") | ~朋友 lǎo péngyou *old friend* / ~毛病 lǎo máobìng *a chronic ailment; an inveterate habit (disease); old weakness*

古老 gǔlǎo

❸ [形] 过时的 (跟 "新 xīn" 相对): outdated; old (the opposite of "新 xīn") | ~房子 lǎo fángzi *an old house* / ~机器 lǎo jīqì *outmoded machine* / ~脑筋 lǎo nǎojīn *old way of thinking; an old fogey*

老掉牙 lǎodiàoyá very old; out of date; obsolete; antediluvian

老一套 lǎoyītào conventionality; the same old stuff; the same old story

❹ [形] 原来的：original; former | ~家 lǎojiā *native place; hometown* / ~地方 lǎo dìfang *the same old place*

❺ [形] (蔬菜) 生长时间过长或 (食物) 加工过了火候而不好吃 (跟 "嫩 nèn" 相对): overgrown; overcooked (the oppoite of "嫩 nèn") | 菠菜长 ~ 了。Bōcài zhǎnglǎo le. *The spinach is overgrown.* / 别把肉丝炒得太 ~ 了。Bié bǎ ròusī chǎo de tài lǎo le. *Don't stir-fry shredded pork too long (to avoid being overdone).*

❻ [副] 经常；一直：often; always | 这孩子 ~ 迟到。Zhè háizi lǎo chídào. *The boy is always late (for class).* / 这个人 lǎo 爱开玩笑。Zhège rén lǎo ài kāi wánxiào. *He is cracking jokes all the time.* / 他心里 ~ 想着你。Tā xīnli lǎo xiǎngzhe nǐ. *He is always*

thinking of you.
老是 lǎoshì always

❼ [副] 很；极：very; extremely | ～远 lǎoyuǎn *far away* / ～高的个子 lǎogāo de gèzi *very tall stature*

❽ [词头] 附在某些动、植物名称及姓氏、排行前面：used to precede a person's surname to indicate seniority; also used to precede certain animals and plants | ～张 Lǎo Zhāng *Lao Zhang* / ～大 Lǎo Dà *the number one; the eldest* / ～三 Lǎo Sān *the number three; the third eldest*
老板 lǎobǎn boss; master; proprietor
老公 lǎogōng (dial.) husband
老虎 lǎohǔ tiger
老婆 lǎopo wife
老师 lǎoshī teacher
老鼠 lǎoshǔ mouse; rat
老外 lǎowài ① layman; raw hand; amateurish ② foreigner
老乡 lǎoxiāng ① fellow townsman; fellow-villager ② a friendly form of address for people living in the countryside
老爷 lǎoye master; bureaucrat; lord
老百姓 lǎobǎixìng common people; ordinary people; civilians
老天爷 lǎotiānyé God; Heavens

❾ [形] 排行在最后的：youngest in seniority; the last born | ～儿子 lǎo'érzi *the youngest son* /

～舅 lǎojiù *the youngest uncle*
◇老实 lǎoshi ① honestly and sincerely ② honest; truthful; frank; playing no tricks

姥 lǎo 9画 女部

姥 姥姥姥姥姥姥姥姥姥

See below
姥姥 lǎolao (maternal) grandmother; grandma
姥爷 lǎoye (dial.) (maternal) grandfather; grandpa

涝 (澇) lào 10画 氵部

涝 涝涝涝涝涝涝涝涝涝涝

❶ [动] 庄稼因水多被淹：waterlog | 防旱防～ fánghàn fánglào *take precautions against drought and waterlogging* / 庄稼～了。Zhuāngjia lào le. *The crop fields are waterlogged.*

❷ [名] 田中积存的雨水：rain water held up in the field | 排～ páilào *drain waterlogged areas*

乐 (樂) lē 5画 丿部

乐 乐乐乐乐乐

❶ [形] 愉快：joyful; pleasant;

458

delightful | 取～qǔlè *make merry; take delight in* / 助人为～zhùrén-wéilè *feel happy in helping people*

乐观 lèguān ① optimistic ② optimism

乐趣 lèqù delight; pleasure; joy; fun; enjoyment; amusement

乐园 lèyuán paradise; playground; amusement park

欢乐 huānlè   可乐 kělè

快乐 kuàilè   享乐 xiǎnglè

娱乐 yúlè

❷ [动] 很高兴(做某事)：be glad to; find pleasure in | ～于助人 lèyú zhùrén *be glad to give help*

乐意 lèyì be willing to; be glad to; be ready to

❸ [动] 笑：laugh | 把一屋子人都逗～了 bǎ yī wūzi rén dōu dòulè le *have everyone in the room amused* / 看!宝宝～了! Kàn! bǎobao lè le. *Look! The baby is smiling!*

◇俱乐部 jùlèbù

See yuè.

了 le   2画 一部

了 了了

❶ [助] 用在动词或形容词后，表示动作或变化已经完成：used after a verb or an adjective, indicating the completion of an action or change | 买～一本书 mǎile

yī běn shū *have bought a book* / 看～一半 kànle yībàn *have read half of it* / 吃～饭再走。Chīle fàn zài zǒu. *Go after you have eaten.*

除了 chúle

❷ [助] 用在句子末尾，表示出现新情况或发生某种变化：used at the end of a sentence, indicating a change or sth. has newly appeared | 春天来～。Chūntiān lái le. *Spring has come.* / 快下雪～。Kuài xiàxuě le. *It's going to snow.* / 你已经是大学生～。Nǐ yǐjīng shì dàxuéshēng le. *Now you've become a college student.*

❸ [助] 用在句尾或句中停顿处，表示劝阻、催促、命令或感叹等语气：used at the end of a sentence, or in its middle where there is a pause, to indicate a command, request, advice or exclamation in response to a changed situation | 好～，不要说话～。Hǎo le, bùyào shuōhuà le. *Well, no more talking now.* / 我们不能再等～。Wǒmen bùnéng zài děng le. *We can't wait any longer.* / 别打架～。Bié dǎjià le. *Stop fighting!* / 太棒～! Tài bàng le! *It's great!*

See liǎo.

勒 lēi   11画 革部

了
勒
le
乚
lēi

L

459

勒 勒勒勒勒勒勒勒勒勒
勒勒勒

[动] 用绳子等捆住或套住，然后拉
紧：tie or strap sth. tight (with
a rope, etc.) | ~紧点，免得散了。
Lēijǐn diǎnr, miǎnde sǎn le.
*Tighten it up, so it won't come
loose.*

雷 lěi　　13画 雨部

雷 雷雷雷雷雷雷雷雷
雷雷雷雷雷

❶ [名] 闪电时发出的巨响：thunder
| 春~ chūnléi *spring thunder* /
一阵响~ yí zhèn xiǎngléi *a peal
of thunder* / 打~了 dǎléi le *it is
thundering*
雷雨 léiyǔ *thunderstorm*
❷ [名] 军事上用的爆炸武器：mine
| 地~ dìléi *mine* / 扫~ sǎoléi
sweep mines; demine
◇雷达 léidá *radar*

垒 (壘) lěi　　9画 土部

垒 垒垒垒垒垒垒垒垒
垒

❶ [名] 军队作防守用的墙壁或工
事：fortification or defence
works | 两军对~ liǎng jūn
duìlěi *two armies pitted against
each other*
堡垒 bǎolěi

❷ [动] 用砖、石等砌或建筑：build
by piling up bricks, stones and
earth | ~墙 lěi qiáng *build a
wall*

泪 lèi　　8画 氵部

泪 泪泪泪泪泪泪泪泪

[名] 眼泪：tear; teardrop | 流~
liúlèi *shed tears* / ~珠 lèizhū
teardrop / ~水 lèishuǐ *tear;
teardrop*
眼泪 yǎnlèi

类 (類) lèi　　9画 米部

类 类类类类类类类类
类

❶ [名] 种类；相似或相同事物的
集合：kind; type; class;
category | 这一~ zhè yí lèi *(of)
this category; (of) this kind* / 蝙
蝠和鸟不同~。Biānfú hé niǎo
bù tónglèi. *Bat and bird do not
belong to the same category.* /
这些问题请你按性质归一下~。
Zhèxiē wèntí qǐng nǐ àn
xìngzhì guī yíxià lèi. *Please
classify these questions according to their type.*
类别 lèibié *classification; category*
类型 lèixíng *type;sort;category*
大类 dàlèi　　分类 fēnlèi
另类 lìnglèi　　同类 tónglèi

种类 zhǒnglèi
诸如此类 zhūrú-cǐlèi
❷[动]相似：be similar to; resemble
类似 lèisì similar; alike; analogous; like

累　　　lèi　　11画　田部

累累累累累累累累
累累累

❶[形]疲劳：tired; weary｜我今天～了。Wǒ jīntiān lèi le. *I'm tired today.* / 我干了一天活儿，真～。Wǒ gànle yī tiān huór, zhēn lèi. *I've been working all day long, and I'm so tired now.*

❷[动]使疲劳；使劳累：tire; wear out｜～病了 lèibìng le *get ill from overwork* / ～坏了 lèihuài le *be tired out* / 别～着他。Bié lèizháo tā. *Don't tire him out.*

棱　　　léng　　12画　木部

棱棱棱棱棱棱棱棱
棱棱棱棱

❶[名] arris; sharp edge｜有～角 yǒu léngjiǎo *angular* / 窗户～上积了好些灰土。Chuānghuléng shang jīle hǎo xiē huītǔ. *A lot of dust has collected on the window edges.*

❷[名] 物体表面凸起的条状物：ridge, a long narrow raised part of any surface｜瓦～wǎléng *rows of tiles*

冷　　　lěng　　7画　冫部

冷冷冷冷冷冷冷

❶[形]温度低；感觉温度低(跟"热 rè"相对)：of low temperature; cold (the opposite of "热 rè")｜去年冬天真～。Qùnián dōngtiān zhēn lěng. *It was really cold last winter.* / 好～的水啊! Hǎo lěng de shuǐ a! *The water is so cold!*
冷却 lěngquè cooling
冷饮 lěngyǐn cold drink
冷战 lěngzhàn ① cold war ② (inf.) shiver
寒冷 hánlěng

❷[形] 不热情；意含轻蔑、讥诮：cold in manner; frosty; scornful; mocking｜不～不热 bùlěng-bùrè *neither cold nor warm* /他对我态度非常～。Tā duì wǒ tài-dù fēicháng lěng. *He is very cold to me.*
冷淡 lěngdàn cold; indifferent; frosty; icy

❸[形] 不热闹；不繁华：cheerless; desolate; not flourishing｜～清 lěngqīng *cold and cheerless; desolate; lonely; deserted* / ～落 lěngluò *unfrequented; desolate*

冷静 lěngjìng calm; cool; sober; composed

愣 lèng 12画 忄部

愣愣愣愣愣愣愣愣
愣愣愣愣

[动] 发呆：be dazed; be nonplussed | 两眼发~ liǎngyǎn fālèng *stare blankly* / 吓得他一~ xià de tā yī lèng *he was struck dumb by fear* / 听我这么说,他~住了。Tīng wǒ zhème shuō, tā lèngzhù le. *Hearing me saying that, he was bewildered.*

厘 lí 9画 厂部

厘厘厘厘厘厘厘厘
厘

[量] 法定长度单位：centi- (unit of length)
厘米 límǐ centimetre

离 (離) lí 10画 一部

离离离离离离离离
离离

❶ [动] 分开；分别：part from; separate from | 他每天书不~手。Tā měi tiān shū bù lí shǒu. *There is never a day when he doesn't have a book in his hand.* / 这孩子从来没~过家。Zhè

háizi cónglái méi lí guo jiā. *The child has never been away from home.*
离别 líbié ① leave; separate; part; bid farewell; depart ② departure; separation
离婚 líhūn divorce; break off a marriage; dissolve a marriage
离开 líkāi leave; depart from; deviate from
离去 líqù leave; away; off
离休 líxiū (of veteran cadres) retire

撤离 chèlí	分离 fēnlí
隔离 gélí	逃离 táolí
脱离 tuōlí	远离 yuǎnlí
若即若离 ruòjí-ruòlí	

❷ [动] 缺少：without; independent of | 这项工作~不了你。Zhè xiàng gōngzuò lí buliǎo nǐ. *This job cannot be done without you.*

❸ [动] 相距：be apart from | 我家~这儿很远。Wǒ jiā lí zhèr hěn yuǎn. *My home is far away from here.* / ~开学只有三天了。Lí kāixué zhǐyǒu sān tiān le. *It is only three days to the beginning of term.*
距离 jùlí

梨 lí 11画 木部

梨梨梨梨梨梨梨梨
梨梨梨

[名] pear | 这种~很甜。Zhè zhǒng lí hěn tián. *This kind of pear is very sweet.*

犁 lí 11画 牛部

犁犁犁犁犁犁犁犁犁犁犁

❶ [名] 翻土用的农具，用畜力或机器牵引：plough, a farm tool used to plough the land
❷ [动] 用犁耕地：work with a plough | ~田 lítián *plough fields*

黎 lí 15画 水部

黎黎黎黎黎黎黎黎黎黎黎黎黎黎黎

See 黎明
黎明 límíng dawn; daybreak

篱 (籬) lí 16画 竹部

篱篱篱篱篱篱篱篱篱篱篱篱篱篱篱篱

[名] bamboo or twig fence | 竹~ zhúlí *bamboo fence*
篱笆 líba fence; hedge

礼 (禮) lǐ 5画 礻部

礼礼礼礼礼

❶ [名] 为表示敬意、庆祝或纪念而举行的仪式：ceremony or rite held to show respect, express celebration or commemoration in connection with an event
礼堂 lǐtáng assembly hall; auditorium
典礼 diǎnlǐ   婚礼 hūnlǐ
葬礼 zànglǐ
❷ [名] 表示尊敬或客气的言语、行为：courtesy; manners | 失~ shīlǐ *breach of etiquette; impoliteness; discourtesy*
礼拜 lǐbài ① religious service ② week
礼节 lǐjié courtesy; etiquette; protocol; ceremony; civility; rules of politeness
礼貌 lǐmào polite; courteous; politeness; courtesy; etiquette; good manners; civility
非礼 fēilǐ   敬礼 jìnglǐ
❸ [名] 礼物：gift; present | ~轻情意重。Lǐ qīng qíngyì zhòng. *Affection outweighs gifts.*
礼品 lǐpǐn gift; present
礼物 lǐwù gift; present
送礼 sònglǐ
◇礼拜天 lǐbàitiān (inf.) Sunday

李 lǐ 7画 木部

李李李李李李李李

❶ [名] 李子树或它的果实：plum tree; plum

李子 lǐzi plum

❷ [名] 姓：a surname

里 (裏❷❸) lǐ　　7画 里部

里 里里里里里里里

❶ [量] 长度单位：unit of length
里程 lǐchéng ① mileage ②
course of development; course
里程碑 lǐchéngbēi milestone
英里 yīnglǐ　　公里 gōnglǐ
平方公里 píngfāng gōnglǐ

❷ [名] lining | 被~bèilǐ *the un-
derneath side of a quilt* / 衣服~
子 yīfu lǐzi *the lining of a garment*

❸ [名] 里边；内部（跟"外wài"
相对）：inside; in; within (the
opposite of "外wài") | 屋子~
wūzi li *inside the house* / 手~
shǒuli *in one's palm* / 箱子~面
xiāngzi lǐmian *in (or inside) the
case*
里边 lǐbian inside; in; within
里面 lǐmian inside; interior
里头 lǐtou inside; interior

❹ [名] 指处所、时间或范围：used
to indicate the limit of a place
or time
哪里 nǎli　　　那里 nàli
心里 xīnli　　　夜里 yèli
这里 zhèli

理　　　lǐ　　11画 王部

理 理理理理理理理理理理理

❶ [动] 管理；办理：manage; run;
handle | ~家 lǐjiā *keep house-
hold; manage family affairs*
理财 lǐcái manage money matters; conduct financial tran-
sactions
理赔 lǐpéi compensate; pay an
indemnity; pay reparations
理事 lǐshì member of a council;
director
理事会 lǐshìhuì executive council; board of directors
办理 bànlǐ　　　处理 chǔlǐ
代理 dàilǐ　　　管理 guǎnlǐ
护理 hùlǐ　　　料理 liàolǐ
经理 jīnglǐ　　　审理 shěnlǐ
受理 shòulǐ　　　治理 zhìlǐ
助理 zhùlǐ　　　总理 zǒnglǐ
处理器 chǔlǐqì 代理人 dàilǐrén
代理商 dàilǐshāng
总经理 zǒngjīnglǐ

❷ [动] 对别人的言语、行动表示
态度或意见：pay attention to;
make known one's position |
答~dālǐ pay attention to / 他见
了我却不~。Tā jiànle wǒ què
bù lǐ. *When he saw me, he simply ignored me.*
理睬 lǐcǎi pay attention (heed)
to; show interest in; acknowledge

❸ [动] 整理；使整齐：put in or-
der; tidy up | 把书~一~bǎ

shū lǐyílǐ *put the books in order* / 房间太乱了，该～一下了。 Fángjiān tài luàn le, gāi lǐ yīxià le. *The room is in a mess. It's time to tidy it up.*

理发 lǐfà haircut; hairdressing
理发师 lǐfàshī barber; hair-dresser

清理 qīnglǐ　　　梳理 shūlǐ
修理 xiūlǐ　　　整理 zhěnglǐ

❹ [名] 道理; 事物的规律: reason; logic | ～应如此 lǐ yīng rúcǐ *the logic (of certain matter) should be so*

理论 lǐlùn ① theory ② argue; debate
理念 lǐniàn ① belief; conviction ② idea; thought; concept
理性 lǐxìng ① rational ② the rational faculty; reason
理由 lǐyóu reason; grounds; excuse; argument; causes
理智 lǐzhì ① reason; intellect ② rational
理所当然 lǐsuǒdāngrán of course; naturally
理直气壮 lǐzhí-qìzhuàng be self-confident on the strength of one's righteousness

道理 dàolǐ　　　地理 dìlǐ
定理 dìnglǐ　　　合理 hélǐ
讲理 jiǎnglǐ　　　情理 qínglǐ
条理 tiáolǐ　　　推理 tuīlǐ
无理 wúlǐ　　　原理 yuánlǐ
真理 zhēnlǐ
合情合理 héqíng-hélǐ

岂有此理 qǐyǒu-cǐlǐ
◇理会 lǐhuì ① understand; comprehend ② take notice of; pay attention to
理解 lǐjiě ① understand; comprehend ② understanding; comprehension
理想 lǐxiǎng ideal

力 lì　　　2画 力部

力 力力

❶ [名] 力量; 能力; 体力: strength; ability; power | 身强～壮 shēnqiáng-lìzhuàng *healthy and strong; powerfully built* / 号召～ hàozhàolì *public appeal*

力度 lìdù (mus.) dynamics
力量 lìliang (physical) strength
力气 lìqi power; force; strength
力所能及 lìsuǒnéngjí within one's power (or ability)

暴力 bàolì　　　财力 cáilì
吃力 chīlì　　　大力 dàlì
得力 délì　　　电力 diànlì
动力 dònglì　　　费力 fèilì
奋力 fènlì　　　风力 fēnglì
国力 guólì　　　活力 huólì
火力 huǒlì　　　极力 jílì
接力 jiēlì　　　竭力 jiélì
尽力 jìnlì　　　精力 jīnglì
马力 mǎlì　　　耐力 nàilì
脑力 nǎolì　　　能力 nénglì
努力 nǔlì　　　气力 qìlì
潜力 qiánlì　　　权力 quánlì

力

lì

L

465

人力 rénlì
体力 tǐlì
外力 wàilì
无力 wúlì
物力 wùlì
压力 yālì
毅力 yìlì
有力 yǒulì
主力 zhǔlì
购买力 gòumǎilì
竞争力 jìngzhēnglì
劳动力 láodònglì
生产力 shēngchǎnlì
生命力 shēngmìnglì
注意力 zhùyìlì

水力 shuǐlì
听力 tīnglì
威力 wēilì
武力 wǔlì
效力 xiàolì
眼力 yǎnlì
用力 yònglì
智力 zhìlì
阻力 zǔlì
记忆力 jìyìlì

❷ [动] 尽力; 努力: do all one can; make every effort
力求 lìqiú make every effort to; do one's best to; strive to
力图 lìtú try hard to; strive to
力争 lìzhēng struggle hard to; strive to; do one's best to; make every effort to; make all efforts to
全力以赴 quánlìyǐfù
◇巧克力 qiǎokèlì

历 (歷) lì   4画 厂部

历 历历历历

❶ [动] 经过; 经历: go through; undergo; experience | ~时十年 lìshí shí nián last ten years
历程 lìchéng course
历史 lìshǐ history; personal

records
经历 jīnglì

❷ [名] 亲身经历的事: what one has experienced | 阅~yuèlì experiences
简历 jiǎnlì
学历 xuélì
来历 láilì

❸ [形] 过去的各次或各个: all previous | ~朝 lìcháo dynasties in the past
历代 lìdài successive dynasties; past dynasties
历年 lìnián ① over the years ② calendar year
历来 lìlái always; constantly
◇农历 nónglì   日历 rìlì
台历 táilì

立   lì   5画 立部

立 立立立立立

❶ [动] 站; 物体竖直放着: stand; upright; be erected | 坐~不安 zuòlì-bù'ān be fidgety; be on tenterhooks; be restless / 他~在门口跟人说话。Tā lì zài ménkǒu gēn rén shuōhuà. He stands at the gate, talking to someone.
立场 lìchǎng position; stand; standpoint
立足 lìzú ① have a foothold somewhere ② base oneself upon
挺立 tǐnglì

❷ [动] 使直立; 竖起: set or stand

sth. up; erect | ~旗杆 lì qígān *erect a flagstaff* / 先把架子~起来。Xiān bǎ jiàzi lì qǐlai. *Set up the frame first.*

❸ [动] 建立; 树立: set up; build | ~碑 lì bēi *set up (or erect) a monument* / ~功 lìgōng *make contributions; render meritorious service*

立案 lì'àn ① register; put on record ② (leg.) place a case on file for investigation and prosecution

立法 lìfǎ make (or enact) laws; legislate

成立 chénglì   创立 chuànglì
公立 gōnglì   建立 jiànlì
确立 quèlì   设立 shèlì
树立 shùlì

❹ [动] 存在; 生存: exist; live | 自~zìlì *be on one's feet*
独立 dúlì   对立 duìlì
孤立 gūlì   中立 zhōnglì
独立自主 dúlì-zìzhǔ

❺ [副] 即刻; 马上: immediately; instantaneously | ~等可取 lìděng kěqǔ *prompt (instant) service*

立即 lìjí at once; immediately; promptly

立刻 lìkè at once; immediately; right away

◇立方 lìfāng ① cube ② cubic metre; stere

立体 lìtǐ ① three-dimensional; stereoscopic ② solid

立方米 lìfāngmǐ cubic metre

立交桥 lìjiāoqiáo overpass; flyover; motorway interchange

丽 (麗) lì   7画 一部

丽 丽丽丽丽丽丽丽

[形] 好看; 漂亮: beautiful; pretty | 壮~zhuànglì *majestic; glorious* / 风和日~fēnghé-rìlì *with a breeze blowing and the sun shining; warm and sunny*
亮丽 liànglì   美丽 měilì
秀丽 xiùlì

励 (勵) lì   7画 力部

励 励励励励励励励

[动] 劝勉; 奋勉: encourage
鼓励 gǔlì   奖励 jiǎnglì
勉励 miǎnlì

利 lì   7画 禾部

利 利利利利利利利

❶ [形] 器物头尖、刃薄; 快(跟"钝 dùn"相对): sharp (the opposite of "钝 dùn") | ~刃 lìrèn *sharp edge (of sword, knife, etc.)* / ~剑 lìjiàn *a sharp sword*
锋利 fēnglì   锐利 ruìlì

❷ [形] 顺利: smooth; without a hitch | 吉~jílì *lucky; auspi-*

cious; propitious

便利 biànlì 　　不利 búlì

胜利 shènglì 　　顺利 shùnlì

❸ [动] 好处 (跟 "害 hài" 或 "弊 bì" 相对): advantage; gain (the opposite of "害hài" or "弊bì")

利弊 lìbì advantages and disadvantages; pros and cons

利害 lìhài ① advantages and disadvantages; gains and losses ② terrible; formidable

利益 lìyì interest; benefit; profit; good; gain; advantage

福利 fúlì 　　权利 quánlì

水利 shuǐlì 　　有利 yǒulì

专利 zhuānlì 　势利眼 shìlìyǎn

❹ [名] 利润; 利息: profit; interest | 薄～ bólì *a small profit* / 年～ niánlì *annual interest*

利率 lìlǜ rate of interest; interest rate

利润 lìrùn profit; gain

利息 lìxī interest

暴利 bàolì 　　红利 hónglì

谋利 móulì 　　让利 rànglì

赢利 yínglì

❺ [动] 使得到好处: do good to; benefit | ～国～民 lìguó-límín *benefit the nation and its people* / 有～条件 yǒulì tiáojiàn *beneficial conditions; advantageous factors*

利用 lìyòng use; utilize; make use of; take advantage of; avail oneself of; exploit

损人利己 sǔnrén-lìjǐ exploit others to benefit oneself

自私自利 zìsī-zìlì selfish; self-centred

 沥 (瀝) lì 　　7画 氵部

沥 沥沥沥沥沥沥沥

See 沥青

沥青 lìqīng pitch; asphalt; bitumen

 例 lì 　　8画 亻部

例 例例例例例例例例

❶ [名] 从前有过的、可以用来比照或依据的事物: example; instance | 先～xiānlì *precedent* / 照～ zhàolì *according to usual practice*

惯例 guànlì

❷ [名] 用来说明某种情况或道理的事物: case; instance | 举～ jǔlì *give an example* / 实～shílì *instance*

例如 lìrú for example; for instance; such as; e.g.

例子 lìzi example; instance; case

案例 ànlì 　　病例 bìnglì

事例 shìlì

❸ [名] 标准或规则: rule; regulation | 法～fǎlì *legal statutes* / 不在此～ bùzài cǐlì *be treated as an exception*

例外 lìwài exception; be an exception

比例 bǐlì　　　　　条例 tiáolì

隶 (隸) lì　　8画 隶部

隶　隶隶隶隶隶隶隶隶

[名] 附属于主人，没有人身自由的
人：a person in servitude; a
person subordinate to his or her
master
奴隶 núlì
◇隶书 lìshū official script, an ancient style of calligraphy current
in the Han Dynasty (206 BC—
AD 220)

荔 lì　　9画 艹部

荔　荔荔荔荔荔荔荔荔
荔

See 荔枝
荔枝 lìzhī litchi; lichee

栗 lì　　10画 西部

栗　栗栗栗栗栗栗栗栗
栗栗

See 栗子
栗子 lìzi chestnut

粒 lì　　11画 米部

粒　粒粒粒粒粒粒粒粒
粒粒粒

❶ [名] 小圆珠形或小碎块形的东
西：grain; granule; pellet | 米
儿 mǐlìr grains of rice / 豆～儿
dòulìr beans; peas
颗粒 kēlì

❷ [量] 用于粒状的东西：used for
small, grain-like things | 一～
米 yī lì mǐ a grain of rice / 两～
药丸 liǎng lì yàowán two pills
(of medicine) / 三～子弹 sān lì
zǐ-dàn three bullets
◇粒子 lìzǐ (phys.) particle

俩 (倆) liǎ　　9画 亻部

俩　俩俩俩俩俩俩俩俩
俩

❶ [数] 两个：two | 夫妇～ fūfù liǎ
both husband and wife; the
couple / ～馒头 liǎ mántou two
steamed buns / 弟兄～长得差不
多。Dìxiōng liǎ zhǎng de
chàbuduō. The two brothers
look alike.

❷ [数] 不多；几个：some; several
| 他有～钱儿。Tā yǒu liǎ
qiánr. He has some money. / 就
这么～人呀! Jiù zhème liǎ rén
ya! Only so few people!

连 (連) lián　　7画 辶部

连　连连连连连连连

❶ [动] 连接：link; join | 骨肉

相～gǔròu-xiānglián *closely linked as flesh and blood* / 天水相～tiānshuǐ xiānglián *sky and the water seem to merge* / 我们的心紧紧地～在一起。Wǒmen de xīn jǐnjǐn de lián zài yīqǐ. *Our hearts are joined together.*

连词 liáncí (gram.) conjunction
连接 liánjiē join; bind; tie; link; connect
连绵 liánmián continuous; unbroken; uninterrupted
连锁 liánsuǒ linked together
连同 liántóng together with; along with

接连 jiēlián 相连 xiānglián
接二连三 jiē'ěr-liánsān

❷ [副] 连续;一个接一个地: in succession; running; continuously | ～打三枪 lián dǎ sān qiāng *fire three shots in succession* / 我们～发了两封信催她回来。Wǒmen lián fāle liǎng fēng xìn cuī tā huílai. *We sent two letters in succession to urge her to return.*

连连 liánlián again and again; time and again; repeatedly; one after another; continuously
连年 liánnián in successive years; in consecutive years; for years running
连续 liánxù ① continuous; successive ② continuously; successively; incessantly; in succession; in a row; at (on) a stretch
连夜 liányè the same night; that very night
连续剧 liánxùjù (of TV show) serial

❸ [介] 表示包括、算上: including; counting | ～根拔 lián gēn bá *tear up by the root; uproot* / ～我一共三人。Lián wǒ yīgòng sān rén. *There are three people altogether including me.*
连滚带爬 liángǔn-dàipá roll and crawl

❹ [介] 表示强调: used for emphasis | 他～饭也没吃就走了。Tā lián fàn yě méi chī jiù zǒu le. *He left even without having his meal.* / 我～想都没想过。Wǒ lián xiǎng dōu méi xiǎngguo. *I didn't even give it a thought.*

❺ [名] 军队的编制单位: company, a military unit | 这个～共有一百二十名战士。Zhège lián gòng yǒu yībǎi èrshí míng zhànshì. *There are one hundred and twenty soldiers in this company.*

连队 liánduì company
◇连忙 liánmáng promptly; at once

怜 (憐) lián   8画 忄部

怜 怜怜怜怜怜怜怜怜

[动] 对不幸表示同情：sympathize with ｜ ～惜 liánxī *take pity on; show mercy to* / 同病相～tóngbìng-xiānglián *those who have the same illness (complaint) sympathize with each other*
可怜 kělián

帘 (簾) lián　　8画 穴部

帘 帘帘帘帘帘帘帘帘帘

[名] 用布、竹子等做的有遮蔽作用的器物：curtain; screen (made of cloth, bamboo, etc.) ｜ 竹～ zhúlián *bamboo screen* / 门～儿 ménliánr *door curtain; portiere*
窗帘 chuānglián

莲 (蓮) lián　　10画 艹部

莲 莲莲莲莲莲莲莲莲
莲莲

See 莲子
莲子 liánzǐ　lotus seed

联 (聯) lián　　12画 耳部

联 联联联联联联联联
联联联联

[动] 连合；结合在一起：ally oneself with; unite ｜ ～结 liánjié

bind; tie; join
联邦 liánbāng federation; union; commonwealth
联合 liánhé ① unite; ally; integrate; associate; combine ② alliance; union; coalition; combination ③ joint; combined; concerted
联欢 liánhuān have a get-together
联络 liánluò get in touch with; keep in touch with; communicate with; touch
联盟 liánméng alliance; union; league; coalition
联赛 liánsài (sports) league matches
联手 liánshǒu work in coordination with; cooperate with
联网 liánwǎng network
联系 liánxì ① contact; touch; integrate; relate; link ② connection; relation; communication
联想 liánxiǎng ① associate; connect ② association
联合国 Liánhéguó the United Nations
春联 chūnlián　　关联 guānlián
互联网 hùliánwǎng

廉 lián　　13画 广部

廉 廉廉廉廉廉廉廉廉
廉廉廉廉廉

❶[形] 不损公肥私；不贪污受贿：honest and clean; incorruptible | 清～qīnglián *honest and upright; free from corruption*

廉洁 liánjié honest and clean; incorrupt; incorruptible; upright

廉政 liánzhèng honest and clean government

❷[形] 便宜；价钱低：cheap; low-priced | 低～dīlián *cheap; low-priced* / 价～物美 jiàlián-wùměi *good quality and low price (of a commodity)*

廉价 liánjià cheap; low-priced; inexpensive

镰（鐮）lián　18画 钅部

镰 镰镰镰镰镰镰镰镰镰镰镰镰镰镰镰镰镰

[名] 收割庄稼和割草用的农具：sickle, a farm tool for cutting grain and grass

镰刀 liándāo sickle

脸（臉）liǎn　11画 月部

脸 脸脸脸脸脸脸脸脸脸脸脸

❶[名] 面孔：face | 圆～yuánliǎn *a round face* / 姑娘羞红了～。Gūniang xiūhóngle liǎn. *The girl blushed in shyness.*

脸盆 liǎnpén washbasin; washbowl

脸谱 liǎnpǔ types of facial makeup in operas

脸色 liǎnsè complexion; look; face; facial expression

脸皮厚 liǎnpíhòu (fig.) thick-skinned; shameless

变脸 biànliǎn

❷[名] 面子：face; reputation; prestige; feelings | 丢～diūliǎn *lose face* / 赏～shǎngliǎn *honour me (with your presence, etc.); show due respect for sb.'s feelings*

不要脸 bùyàoliǎn

❸[名] 脸上的表情：facial expression | 笑～xiàoliǎn *a smiling face* / 做鬼～zuò guǐliǎn *make grimaces (faces); make a face* / 愁眉苦～chóuméi-kǔliǎn *have a worried look; have a distressed expression*

练（練）liǎn　8画 纟部

练 练练练练练练练练

❶[动] 练习；训练：practise; train | ～操 liàncāo *drill* / ～本领 liàn běnlǐng *practise one's skills*

练兵 liànbīng troop training; training

练习 liànxí ① train; practise; drill ② exercises; drills
操练 cāoliàn 晨练 chénliàn
教练 jiàoliàn 排练 páiliàn
训练 xùnliàn
教练员 jiàoliànyuán
❷ [形] 经验多;纯熟:experienced; skilled | 老～lǎoliàn *experienced and assured* / 干～gānliàn *capable and experienced*
熟练 shúliàn

炼 (煉) liàn 9画 火部

炼 炼炼炼炼炼炼炼炼炼炼

[动] 用加热等方法使物质纯净或坚韧: temper with fire; smelt | ～钢 liàngāng *make steel; steel making* / ～铁 liàntiě *iron smelting*
炼油 liànyóu ① refine oil ② extract oil by heat ③ heat edible oil
锻炼 duànliàn 提炼 tíliàn
冶炼 yěliàn

恋 (戀) liàn 10画 心部

 恋恋恋恋恋恋恋恋恋恋

❶ [动] 不忍分离;想念不忘: long for; feel attached to | ～家 liànjiā *be reluctant to be away from home* / 留～liúliàn *be re-*
luctant to leave; cannot bear to part from (sb. or sth.)
❷ [动] 男女相爱: love between the sexes | 初～chūliàn *be in love for the first time; first love* / 失～shīliàn *be lovelorn* / 他深深地～着那个女孩儿。Tā shēnshēn de liànzhe nàge nǚháir. *He felt deeply attached to that girl.*
恋爱 liàn'ài love
恋情 liànqíng romantic love
暗恋 ànliàn

链 (鏈) liàn 12画 钅部

链 链链链链链链链链链链链链

[名] 用金属环连接而成的长条状的东西: chain | 表～儿 biǎoliànr *watch chain* / 铁～tiěliàn *iron chain; shackles*
链接 liànjiē link; links; interlinkage
链条 liàntiáo ① chain ② roller chain (of a bicycle); chain
链子 liànzi chain
手链 shǒuliàn

良 liáng 7画 丶部

 良良良良良良良

[形] 好: good; fine | ～药 liángyào *good medicine* / ～田 liángtián

473

good farmland; fertile farmland
良好 liánghǎo good; fine; desirable; favourable; well
良机 liángjī (formal) good (or golden) opportunity
良心 liángxīn conscience
良性 liángxìng (med.) benign
良种 liángzhǒng ① (fine) improved variety ② fine breed
不良 bùliáng　改良 gǎiliáng
善良 shànliáng　优良 yōuliáng

凉 liáng 10画 冫部

凉凉凉凉凉凉凉凉凉凉凉

❶ [形] 温度低：low in temperature | ～风 liángfēng cool breeze / 饭～了。Fàn liáng le. The meal's got cold. / 立秋以后天气～了。Lìqiū yǐhòu tiānqì liáng le. The weather becomes cold after liqiu (the day marking the beginning of autumn).
凉快 liángkuai ① pleasantly cool; cool and comfortable ② cool oneself; cool off; cool down
凉菜 liángcài cold dish
凉水 liángshuǐ ① cold water ② unboiled water
凉鞋 liángxié sandals
着凉 zháoliáng
❷ [形] 比喻灰心或失望：disappointed; discouraged | 听到这消息，我心里就～了。Tīngdào

zhè xiāoxi, wǒ xīnli jiù liáng le. My heart sank at the news.
凄凉 qīliáng
❸ [形] 冷落；不热闹：desolate; deserted
荒凉 huāngliáng

梁 liáng 11画 木部

梁梁梁梁梁梁梁梁梁梁梁

❶ [名] 桥：bridge | 桥～qiáoliáng bridge
❷ [名] 架在墙上或柱子上支撑房顶的横木：roof beam | 栋～dòngliáng ridgepole and beam; person of great ability
❸ [名] 物体中间高起成长条的部分：ridge | 山～shānliáng ridge (of a mountain or hill) / 鼻～bíliáng bridge of the nose
脊梁 jǐliang

量 liáng 12画 日部

量量量量量量量量量量量量

❶ [动] 用作为标准的器具确定东西的长度、重量、大小、多少等：gauge; measure | ～身高 liáng shēngāo measure sb.'s height / ～体温 liáng tǐwēn take sb.'s temperature / 用尺～布 yòng chǐ liáng bù measure a piece of cloth with a ruler

测量 cèliáng

❷ [动] 估计：estimate; reckon | 商~shāngliang consult; discuss; talk over

打量 dǎliang

See liǎng.

粮（糧）liáng 13画 米部

粮 粮粮粮粮粮粮粮粮
粮粮粮粮粮

[名] 粮食：food; grain; beans

粮食 liángshi grain; cereals; food

杂粮 záliáng

两（兩）liǎng 7画 一部

两 两两两两两两两

❶ [数] 数目"二 èr"：two | ~万 liǎng wàn twenty thousand / ~个人 liǎng gè rén two persons / ~本书 liǎng běn shū two books / ~个月 liǎng gè yuè two months / ~半儿 liǎngbànr two halves

两边 liǎngbiān ① both sides; both directions; both places ② both parties; both sides

两极 liǎngjí ① the two poles of the earth ② the two poles (of a magnet or an electric battery)

两旁 liǎngpáng both sides; either side

两口子 liǎngkǒuzi husband and wife; couple

❷ [数] 双方：both sides; the two parties | ~可 liǎngkě both or either will do / ~全其美 liǎng-quán-qí-měi satisfy both sides; satisfy rival claims

❸ [数] 表示不定的数目，和"几 jǐ"差不多：(used to indicate an uncertain number) few; some (less than ten) | 过~天再说吧。Guò liǎng tiān zài shuō ba. Let's leave it for a couple of days. / 我说~句。Wǒ shuō liǎng jù. Let me say a few words. / 他真有~下子。Tā zhēn yǒu liǎngxiàzi. He is really capable.

◇两手 liǎngshǒu dual tactics; both hands

亮 liàng 9画 一部

亮 亮亮亮亮亮亮亮亮
亮

❶ [形] 光线强；有光泽：bright; luminant; light | 这个房间非常~。Zhège fángjiān fēicháng liàng. The room gets good light. / 今晚的月光真~。Jīnwǎn de yuèguāng zhēn liàng. The moon is really bright tonight. / 地板擦得真~。Dì bǎn cā de zhēn liàng. The floor has been cleaned till it shines.

亮光 liàngguāng light

亮丽 liànglì ① brilliant; splendid; bright and beautiful ② beautiful; graceful; brilliant

明亮 míngliàng

❷ [动] 发光：give off light | 天～了。Tiān liàng le. *Day is breaking.* / 屋里～着灯。Wūli liàngzhe dēng. *Lights are on in the room.*

❸ [形] 声音响：loud and clear | 洪～hóngliàng *loud and clear; sonorous* / 她的嗓子真～。Tā de sǎngzi zhēn liàng. *She has a resonant voice.*

响亮 xiǎngliàng

◇ 亮相 liàngxiàng ① (in Beijing opera, dancing, etc.) strike a pose on the stage ② declare one's position; state one's views

---

谅 (諒) liàng 10画 讠部

谅 谅谅谅谅谅谅谅谅谅谅

[动] 原谅：forgive; understand | 体～tǐliàng *show understanding and sympathy for; make allowances for*

谅解 liàngjiě ① understanding ② forgivingness; make allowance for

原谅 yuánliàng

辆 (輛) liàng 11画 车部

辆 辆辆辆辆辆辆辆辆辆 辆辆辆

[量] 用于车：used for vehicles | 一～汽车 yī liàng qìchē *a bus (car, etc.)* / 三～卡车 sān liàng kǎchē *three trucks*

量 liàng 12画 日部

量 量量量量量量量量量 量量量量

❶ [名] 能容纳或经受的限度：capacity (for tolerance or taking food or drink) | 酒～jiǔliàng *one's capacity for liquor* / 饭～fànliàng *appetite* / 气～qìliàng *tolerance; forbearance*

胆量 dǎnliàng 尽量 jìnliàng

力量 lìliàng 能量 néngliàng

❷ [名] 数量；数目：quantity; amount | 降雨～jiàngyǔliàng *rainfall* / 水流～shuǐliúliàng *rate of flow*

量词 liàngcí (gram.) measure word; classifier

产量 chǎnliàng 大量 dàliàng

定量 dìngliàng 分量 fēnliàng

含量 hánliàng 流量 liúliàng

热量 rèliàng 容量 róngliàng

少量 shǎoliàng 数量 shùliàng

销量 xiāoliàng 质量 zhìliàng

重量 zhòngliàng

总量 zǒngliàng

❸ [动] 估计; 衡量: estimate; measure; weigh | ~力而行 liànglì'érxíng *do what one is capable of; act according to one's capability*

较量 jiàoliàng

See liàng.

 liàng 12画 日部

晾晾晾晾晾晾晾晾晾晾晾晾

[动] 把东西放在通风或阴凉的地方, 使干燥; 晒: *dry in the sun or in the air* | ~干菜 liàng gān-cài *dry vegetable in the air* / ~衣服 liàng yīfu *air clothes in the sun; hung the wash out to dry*

 (遼) liáo 5画 辶部

辽辽辽辽辽辽

[形] 远: faraway | ~远 liáoyuǎn *distant; faraway; far-off*

辽阔 liáokuò vast; extensive

 (療) liáo 7画 疒部

疗疗疗疗疗疗疗

[动] 医治: treat; cure | ~病 liáo-bìng *cure an illness; treat sb.'s*

disease / 诊~ zhěnliáo *make a diagnosis and give treatment*

疗法 liáofǎ therapy; treatment

疗效 liáoxiào treatment; curative effect

疗养 liáoyǎng recuperate; convalesce

医疗 yīliáo   治疗 zhìliáo

 liáo 11画 耳部

聊聊聊聊聊聊聊聊聊聊聊

[动] 闲谈: chitchat | ~家常 liáo jiācháng *have a small talk* / 晚饭后咱们~~。Wǎnfàn hòu zánmen liáoliao. *Let's have a chat after supper.*

聊天儿 liáotiānr chat; have a chitchat; make small talk

 liáo 15画 氵部

潦潦潦潦潦潦潦潦潦潦潦潦潦潦潦

See 潦草

潦草 liáocǎo ① (of handwriting) hasty and careless; illegible ② sloppy; slovenly

了 (瞭❸)liǎo 2画 一部

了 了了

❶ [动] 完毕; 结束：end; finish; settle; dispose of | 没完没～ méiwán-méiliǎo *endless* / 事情已经～了。Shìqing yǐjīng liǎo le. *It has already been settled.*

❷ [动] 跟 "不" 或 "得" 连用, 表示可能或不可能：used with "不" or "得", indicating possibility or impossibility | 他吃不～这样的苦。Tā chībuliǎo zhèyàng de kǔ. *He cannot endure such hardship.* / 这事你办得～。Zhè shì nǐ bàndeliǎo. *You can do it.*

❸ [形] 明白：clear about | 明～ míngliǎo *understand; be clear about* / 一目～然 yīmù-liǎorán *be clear at a glance; discern easily*

了解 liǎojiě understand; know clearly; acquaint oneself with

◇ 了不起 liǎobuqǐ amazing; terrific; extraordinary; wonderful; marvelous; excellent

See le.

料 料料料料料料料料料料

liào   10画 米部

❶ [动] 估计; 推测：suppose; expect; conjecture | 不～bùliào *unexpectedly; to one's surprise* / 他～事很准。Tā liàoshì hěn zhǔn. *He predicts things with great accuracy.*

不料 bùliào   意料 yìliào
预料 yùliào
出人意料 chūrényìliào

❷ [动] 处理; 照管：arrange; manage; take care of

料理 liàolǐ arrange; manage; attend to; take care of
照料 zhàoliào

❸ [名] 喂牲口的食物：feed | 草～cǎoliào *forage; fodder*
饲料 sìliào

❹ [名] 材料; 原料：material; raw material | 衣～yīliào *material for clothing; dress material* / 木～mùliào *timber; lumber*

材料 cáiliào   肥料 féiliào
燃料 ránliào   染料 rǎnliào
塑料 sùliào   养料 yǎngliào
油料 yóuliào   原料 yuánliào
资料 zīliào
原材料 yuáncáiliào

列 列列列列列列

liè   6画 刂部

❶ [动] 按顺序放或站; 排列：arrange; line up | ～队欢迎 lièduì huānyíng *line up to welcome sb.* / ～出数据 lièchū shùjù *tabulate data* / 他的名字～在名单上。Tā de míngzi liè zài míngdān shang. *His name is on the list.*

列举 lièjǔ enumerate; list; cite

并列 bìngliè　　陈列 chénliè
罗列 luóliè　　排列 páiliè
下列 xiàliè

❷ [名] 排成的行：row; file; rank
| 后~ hòuliè *the rear rank*
列车 lièchē train
行列 hángliè　　前列 qiánliè

❸ [量] 用于成行列的事物：used for things presented in a series or rows | 一~火车 yī liè huǒchē *a train* / 一~队伍 yī liè duìwu *a procession*

❹ [动] 安排；归入：arrange; list; include | 名~榜首 míngliè-bǎngshǒu *head the list of successful candidates*
列入 lièrù list; enter in a list; be included (incorporated) in
列席 lièxí attend (a meeting) as a nonvoting delegate

 liè　　6画 力部

劣 劣 劣 劣 劣 劣

[形] 坏；不好（跟 "优 yōu" 相对）：bad; inferior; of bad quality (the opposite of "优 yōu") | 优~ yōuliè *the good and the bad*
劣质 lièzhì of poor quality; inferior
低劣 dīliè　　恶劣 èliè

烈 liè　　10画 灬部

烈 烈 烈 烈 烈 烈 烈 烈 烈 烈

❶ [形] 强烈；猛烈：strong; violent | ~日 lièrì *burning sun; scorching sun; blazing sun*
烈火 lièhuǒ raging fire; raging flames
激烈 jīliè　　剧烈 jùliè
猛烈 měngliè　　强烈 qiángliè
轰轰烈烈 hōnghōng-lièliè
兴高采烈 xìnggāo-cǎiliè

❷ [名] 为正义事业而牺牲的人：one who sacrifices himself for a just cause | 先~ xiānliè *martyr*
烈士 lièshì martyr

猎（獵）liè　　11画 犭部

猎 猎 猎 猎 猎 猎 猎 猎 猎 猎 猎

[动] 捕捉野兽：hunt wild animals | ~兔 liè tù *hunt hare*
猎人 lièrén hunter; huntsman
猎头 liètóu headhunter (who looks for senior talents for enterprises)
打猎 dǎliè

裂 liè　　12画 衣部

裂 裂 裂 裂 裂 裂 裂 裂 裂 裂 裂 裂

[动] 破开；分开：split; crack | ~

痕 liêhén *rift; crack* / 手冻~了。Shǒu dòngliê le. *The hands are chapped by the cold.* / 这只碗~了。Zhè zhī wǎn liê le. *This bowl is cracked.*

断裂 duànliê   分裂 fēnliê

邻 (鄰) lín   7画 阝(右)部

邻 邻邻邻邻邻邻邻

❶ [名] 住处接近的人家：neighbour | 四~sìlín *one's near neighbours*

❷ [形] 靠近的；靠近：neighbouring; near | ~乡 línxiāng *neighbouring village*

邻近 línjìn be near; be close to
邻居 línjū neighbour
邻国 línguó neighbouring country

林 lín   8画 木部

林 林林林林林林林林

❶ [名] 成片的树木或竹子：forest; woods | 竹~zhúlín *bamboo forest; groves of bamboo* / 丛~cónglín *jungle*

林场 línchǎng forestry centre (including tree nursery, lumber camp, etc.); tree farm
林区 línqū forest zone; forest region; forest
森林 sēnlín   树林 shùlín

园林 yuánlín

❷ [名] 林业：forestry | 农~牧副渔 nóng-lín-mù-fù-yú *farming, forestry, animal husbandry, sideline production and fishery*
林业 línyè forestry

◇奥林匹克 Àolínpǐkè
穆斯林 mùsīlín

临 (臨) lín   9画 丨部

临 临临临临临临临临临

❶ [动] 到；来到：arrive; be present | 来~láilín *arrive; approach* / 喜事~门 xǐshì lín mén *good news (or a happy event) comes to the house*

临时 línshí temporary; provisional; for the time being; for a short time
光临 guānglín   降临 jiànglín

❷ [动] 靠近；面对着：near; approach; be faced with | 背山~水 bēishān-línshuǐ *facing the water with hills behind* / 我家房子~街。Wǒ jiā fángzi línjiē. *My house overlooks the street.*

临床 línchuáng (of a doctor) be at the sickbed providing medical services
临近 línjìn close to; close on; close by; draw close; draw near
面临 miànlín

淋 lín 11画 氵部

淋 淋淋淋淋淋淋淋淋淋淋淋

[动] 液体落在东西上或人身上：pour; water; shower | ～浴 línyù *shower; have a shower* / 他被雨～得浑身湿透了。Tā bèi yǔ lín de húnshēn shītòu le. *He was drenched by the rain.*

◇冰淇淋 bīngqílín

伶 líng 7画 亻部

伶 伶伶伶伶伶伶伶

See 伶俐

伶俐 línglì clever; bright; quick-witted

灵 (靈) líng 7画 彐部

灵 灵灵灵灵灵灵灵

❶ [名] 精神；灵魂：spirit; soul | 英～yīnglíng *spirit of the brave departed; spirit of a martyr*

灵感 línggǎn inspiration (for creative work)

灵魂 línghún soul; spirit

心灵 xīnlíng

❷ [形] 有效；能够应验：efficacious; effective | 这个办法很～。Zhège bànfǎ hěn líng. *This method works well.* / 这种药治

感冒很～。Zhè zhǒng yào zhì gǎnmào hěn líng. *This medicine is an effective treatment for a cold.*

灵通 língtōng ① having quick access to information; well-informed ② (dial.) be of use (or help)

❸ [形] 聪明；机敏：clever; quick; sharp | 心～手巧 xīnlíng-shǒuqiǎo *clever in mind and skillful in hand; clever and deft* / 耳朵很～ěrduo hěn líng *have sharp ears*

灵活 línghuó nimble; agile; quick; elastic; quick-witted; quick-minded; flexible

灵敏 língmǐn sensitive; keen; agile; acute; skillful; active; nimble

灵巧 língqiǎo dexterous; handy; nimble; skillful; ingenious; cute

机灵 jīling   机灵鬼 jīlingguǐ

铃 (鈴) líng 10画 钅部

铃 铃铃铃铃铃铃铃铃铃铃

[名] bell | 门～ménlíng *door bell* / 电～diànlíng *an electric bell* / 摇～yáolíng *ring the bell*

铃声 língshēng (bell) ring

◇马铃薯 mǎlíngshǔ

凌 líng 10画 冫部

凌 凌凌凌凌凌凌凌凌凌 凌凌

[动] 接近：approach; be near
凌晨 língchén very early in the morning; in the small hours; close on daybreak; just before daybreak (dawn)

零 líng 13画 雨部

零 零零零零零零零零 零零零零零

❶ [形] 分散的；细碎的（跟"整 zhěng"相对）：fragmentary; fractional (the opposite of "整 zhěng")｜～用 língyòng money spent on minor purchases; pocket money / ～活儿 línghuór odd jobs
零件 língjiàn part; spare parts; component parts
零钱 língqián small change; petty cash; odd change
零售 língshòu retail; sell retail; sell in small lots
零碎 língsuì ① scrappy; fragmentary; piecemeal ② fragments; fractions; odds and ends
零星 língxīng scattered; fragmentary; odd; sporadic; occasional

❷ [名] 零头；整数以外的零数：(used after a round figure to introduce the fraction) fragment;

fraction｜一年～三天 yī nián líng sān tiān one year and three days

❸ [数] 表示没有数量：zero; nil｜1 减 1 等于～。Yī jiǎn yī děngyú líng. One minus one equals zero. / 光说不做等于～。Guāng shuō bù zuò děngyú líng. Unfulfilled promises are worth nothing.
零下 língxià below zero (on a thermometer)

❹ [数] 数的空位，写作"〇"：zero sign in a sum, written as "〇"｜一九八～年 yījiǔbālíng nián 1980 / 五一二房间 wǔ líng èr fángjiān Room 502

龄（齡）líng 13画 齿部

龄 龄龄龄龄龄龄龄龄 龄龄龄龄龄

❶ [名] 岁数：age｜高～ gāolíng venerable age; over-age / 同～ tónglíng the same age
年龄 niánlíng

❷ [名] 年数：length of time; duration｜军～ jūnlíng length of military service / 工～ gōnglíng length of service; years of service; standing

岭（嶺）lǐng 8画 山部

岭 岭 岭 岭 岭 岭 岭 岭

❶ [名] 有路可通行的山峰：mountain; ridge | 翻山越~fānshān yuèlǐng *climb mountain after mountain; travel over hill and dale*

❷ [名] 高大的山脉：high mountain | 秦~Qín Lǐng *the Qinling Mountains* / 南~Nán Lǐng *the South Mountains*

领 (領) lǐng 11画 页部

领 领 领 领 领 领 领 领 领 领 领

❶ [名] 脖子：neck
领带 lǐngdài necktie; tie
红领巾 hónglǐngjīn

❷ [名] 领子：collar; neckband | 衣~yīlǐng *collar*
领子 lǐngzi collar
白领 báilǐng

❸ [名] 大纲;要点：outline; main point | 抓不住要~zhuābuzhù yàolǐng *unable to grasp the key points; fail to grasp the main points*
本领 běnlǐng 纲领 gānglǐng
要领 yàolǐng

❹ [动] 占有;管辖：have jurisdiction over; be in possession of | ~海 lǐnghǎi *territorial waters; territorial sea* / ~空 lǐngkōng *territorial sky; territorial air (space)*
领土 lǐngtǔ territory
领域 lǐngyù realm; field; sphere; domain
占领 zhànlǐng

❺ [动] 引导;带领：lead; usher | ~队 lǐngduì *lead a group; leader of a group* / 爷爷~着孩子过马路。Yéye lǐngzhe háizi guò mǎlù. *Grandpa led the child across the street.* / 她~着外宾参观了工厂。Tā lǐngzhe wàibīn cānguānle gōngchǎng. *She showed the foreign visitors round the factory.*
领先 lǐngxiān lead; walk (run, get, draw) ahead; take the lead; have a lead
带领 dàilǐng 率领 shuàilǐng

❻ [动] 接受;领取（发给的东西）：receive; get | ~情 lǐngqíng *feel grateful to sb.; appreciate the kindness*/ ~奖品 lǐng jiǎngpǐn *receive a prize*
领取 lǐngqǔ receive; draw; get

❼ [动] 了解;懂得：understand; comprehend | ~悟 lǐngwù *comprehend; grasp*
领会 lǐnghuì understand; appreciate; comprehend; grasp
领略 lǐnglüè have a taste of; understand; appreciate

◇领导 lǐngdǎo ① lead; guide ② exercise leadership ③ leader; cadre; guide; leadership
领事 lǐngshì consul
领袖 lǐngxiù leader
首领 shǒulǐng

另 另另另另另 lìng 5画 口部

[副] 之外；其他：besides; other | ～买一个 lìng mǎi yī gè *buy another one* / 我们～想办法吧。Wǒmen lìng xiǎng bànfǎ ba. *Let's try some other way.*
另类 lìnglèi ① people or things not of the mainstream; oddball; nonconformist ② alien; different from the common run; unconventional; offbeat; out of the way
另外 lìngwài besides; in addition

令 令令令令令 lìng 5画 人部

❶ [名] 上级发布的命令：order; decree | 口～kǒulìng *word of command; password* / 因违反纪律，学校～他退学。Yīn wéifǎn jìlǜ, xuéxiào lìng tā tuìxué. *As he breached the school regulations, he was ordered to leave school.*
法令 fǎlìng   命令 mìnglìng
司令 sīlìng   下令 xiàlìng
责令 zélìng   指令 zhǐlìng
司令员 sīlìngyuán
总司令 zǒngsīlìng
❷ [动] 使；让：cause sb. (to do sth.); let | ～人兴奋 lìng rén xīngfèn *exciting* / ～人怀疑 lìng rén huáiyí *cause suspicion*
◇夏令营 xiàlìngyíng

溜 溜溜溜溜溜溜溜溜溜溜溜溜溜 liū 13画 氵部

❶ [动] 在平面上滑行或向下滑动：slide; glide | ～冰 liūbīng *skating; roller-skating* / 孩子们～滑梯。Háizimen liū huátī. *Children slid down a slide.*
❷ [动] 偷偷走开：slip away | ～出房间 liūchū fángjiān *slip out of the room* / 他悄悄地～了。Tā qiāoqiāo de liū le. *He sneaked off without being noticed.*

留 留留留留留留留留留留 liú 10画 田部

❶ [动] 停在某个地方或位置；不离开：stay (remain) in a certain place or position | 他～在天津

了。Tā liú zài Tiānjīn le. *He stayed on in Tianjin.* / 你们去吧，我～下来。Nǐmen qù ba, wǒ liú xiàlai. *You may go. I'll stay.*

留恋 liúliàn be reluctant (unwilling) to leave (part); recall with nostalgia; yearn for the past

停留 tíngliú

❷ [动] 不让离开：try to retain sb. | 挽～wǎnliú *persuade sb. to stay* / 他们～我吃晚饭。Tāmen liú wǒ chī wǎnfàn. *They persuade me to stay for supper.*

拘留 jūliú

❸ [动] 保存；遗留：reserve; keep | ～饭 liú fàn *keep a portion of meal for sb.* / ～底稿 liú dǐgǎo *keep the manuscript or draft* / ～下遗产 liúxià yíchǎn *bequeath a legacy* / ～条子 liú tiáozi *leave a note* / 你给我的信我一直～着。Nǐ gěi wǒ de xìn wǒ yīzhí liúzhe. *I have kept all the letters you wrote to me.*

留念 liúniàn accept as a souvenir

留言 liúyán leave one's comments; leave a message

保留 bǎoliú   遗留 yíliú

❹ [动] 注意力集中在某方面：concentrate on sth.

留神 liúshén pay attention; be careful; take care; look out

留心 liúxīn take care; look out; pay attention; take heed; be careful; be cautious

留意 liúyì pay attention; be careful; be cautious; take care; look out

❺ [动] 特指居留外国求学：study abroad | ～日 liú Rì *study in Japan* / ～美 liú Měi *study in the United States*

留学 liúxué study abroad

留学生 liúxuéshēng student studying abroad; overseas student

流 liú 10画 氵部

流流流流流流流流流流

❶ [动] 液体移动；流动：(of liquids) flow | ～汗 liúhàn *perspire; sweat* / ～血 liúxuè *lose blood; shed blood* / 水往低处～。Shuǐ wǎng dīchù liú. *Water flows downward.*

流动 liúdòng ① flow; run ② be on the move; move from place to place; mobile; drift

流量 liúliàng volume of flow; rate of flow; flow; discharge

流水 liúshuǐ running water

流向 liúxiàng ① the direction of a current ② the direction of the flow of personnel, commodities, etc.

流水账 liúshuǐzhàng day-to-day (bookkeeping) account; current account

川流不息 chuānliú-bùxī

❷ [动] 没有固定方向地移动：move without a certain direction
流寇 liúkòu roving bandits
流浪 liúlàng roam (loaf, wander) about; rove; stroll; drift; lead a vagrant life
流露 liúlù reveal; betray; evince; manifest; show unintentionally
流氓 liúmáng ① hoodlum; villain; rogue; gangster; hooligan; scoundrel; rascal; ruffian ② immoral behaviour; hooliganism
流通 liútōng in circulation; circulate
交流 jiāoliú   轮流 lúnliú
外流 wàiliú

❸ [动] 传下来; 传播：disseminate; propagate; spread
流传 liúchuán spread; circulate; hand down; transmit; go about
流失 liúshī ① run off; be washed away ② (of students) drop out
流行 liúxíng prevalent; popular; fashionable

❹ [名] 指流水：the flowing of water
流域 liúyù valley; river basin; drainage area
潮流 cháoliú   河流 héliú
逆流 nìliú   主流 zhǔliú

❺ [动] 像水流一样移动的东西：sth. that moves like water
电流 diànliú   分流 fēnliú
气流 qìliú

❻ [形] 通顺; 畅快：fluent; easy and smooth; carefree
流畅 liúchàng (of writing) easy and smooth
流利 liúlì fluent; smooth

❼ [名] 品类; 等级：class; grade; school; rate | 一～产品 yīliú chǎnpǐn top-grade product
一流 yīliú

硫 liú 12画 石部

See 硫酸
硫酸 liúsuān sulphuric acid

榴 liú 14画 木部

See 石榴
石榴 shíliu

瘤 liú 15画 疒部

See 瘤子
瘤子 liúzi tumour

柳 liǔ 9画 木部

柳柳柳柳柳柳柳柳
柳

See 柳树
柳树 liǔshù willow

 liǔ 4画 一部

六 六六六六

[数] 数目：six | ～天 liù tiān *six days* / ～个月 liù gè yuè *six months*
五颜六色 wǔyán-liùsè

龙 (龍) **lóng** 5画 龙部

龙 龙龙龙龙龙

❶ [名] dragon | 墙上画着一条～。Qiáng shang huàzhe yī tiáo lóng. *A dragon was drawn on the wall.*
龙眼 lóngyǎn (bot.) longan
龙舟 lóngzhōu dragon boat
❷ [名] 封建时代用作帝王的象征，也指与帝王有关的东西：symbol of the emperor in feudal times (used to refer to things belonging to the emperor) | ～床 lóng-chuáng *the emperor's bed*
❸ [名] 近代古生物学上指一些巨大的爬行动物：used to refer to some big reptiles | 恐～ kǒnglóng *dinosaur*

◇龙头 lóngtóu tap; faucet; cock
黑龙江 Hēilóng Jiāng

聋 (聾) **lóng** 11画 龙部

聋 聋聋聋聋聋聋聋聋
聋聋聋

[形] 听不见或听不清声音：deaf; hard of hearing | 他耳朵～了。Tā ěrduo lóng le. *He is deaf.*

笼 (籠) **lóng** 11画 竹部

笼 笼笼笼笼笼笼笼笼
笼笼笼

See 笼子
笼子 lóngzi ① cage; coop ② basket; container
See lǒng.

隆 **lóng** 11画 阝(左)部

隆 隆隆隆隆隆隆隆隆
隆隆隆

[形] 盛大：grand; deep
隆重 lóngzhòng grand; solemn; ceremonious; elaborate
◇克隆 kèlóng

拢 (攏) **lǒng** 8画 扌部

拢 拢拢拢拢拢拢拢拢

❶[动] 合上; 使不分散、离开: hold (or gather) together; bring together; tie | ~ 紧 lǒngjǐn hold (sth.) tight / 笑得嘴都合不~了 xiào de zuǐ dōu hébulǒng le grin from ear to ear / 妈妈把孩子~在怀里。Māma bǎ hǎizi lǒng zài huáili. Mother held the baby to her bosom.

❷[动] 梳(头发): comb | 她用梳子~了~头发。Tā yòng shūzi lǒnglelǒng tóufa. She arranged her hair with a comb.

垄 (壟) lǒng　8画 龙部

垄 垄垄垄垄垄垄垄垄

See 垄断

垄断 lǒngduàn monopolize; corner

笼 (籠) lǒng　11画 竹部

笼 笼笼笼笼笼笼笼笼笼
笼笼笼

[动] 遮盖; 罩住: cover; envelop
笼罩 lǒngzhào envelop; shroud
See lóng.

楼 (樓) lóu　13画 木部

楼 楼楼楼楼楼楼楼楼
楼楼楼楼楼

❶[名] 两层或两层以上的房屋: a storeyed building | 办公 ~ bàngōnglóu office building / 高 ~ 大厦 gāolóu-dàshà tall buildings and large mansions

楼道 lóudào corridor; passageway

楼房 lóufáng a building of two or more storeys

楼梯 lóutī stair; staircase

大楼 dàlóu　　　酒楼 jiǔlóu

红楼梦 Hónglóumèng

❷[名] 楼房的某一层: storey; floor | 三~sān lóu (BrE) second floor; (AmE) third floor

搂 (摟) lóu　12画 扌部

搂 搂搂搂搂搂搂搂搂
搂搂搂搂

[动] 两臂合抱: hold in arms | ~ 着腰lǒuzhe yāo hold sb. by the waist / ~着脖子 lǒuzhe bózi hold sb. by the neck / 把孩子~在怀里 bǎ hǎizi lǒu zài huáili hold a child in one's arms

漏 lòu　14画 氵部

漏 漏漏漏漏漏漏漏漏
漏漏漏漏漏漏漏

❶[动] 从孔、缝中流出、透过或掉出: leak | 水壶~了。Shuǐhú lòu le. The kettle leaks. / 水龙头~得很厉害。Shuǐlóngtóu

488

lòu de hěn lìhai. *The faucet is leaking badly.*

漏洞 lòudòng ① leak ② flaw; hole; loophole

❷ [动] 没保守住秘密; 泄露: divulge; leak | ~了风声 lòule fēngshēng *divulge a secret; leak out information* / 走~消息 zǒulòu xiāoxi *leak out the news* / 考题千万不要~出去。Kǎotí qiānwàn bùyào lòu chūqu. *The examination questions must be kept secret.*

❸ [动] 遗落: left out; missing | ~字 lòuzì *missing words* / 这份名单把你的名字~了。Zhè fèn míngdān bǎ nǐ de míngzi lòu le. *Your name is left out in the name list.*

漏税 lòushuì tax evasion

露   lòu   21画 雨部

露 露露露露露露露露 露露露露露露露露 露露露露露

[动] 显露; 表现: show; manifest; display | ~头 lòutóu *appear; emerge* / ~馅儿 lòuxiànr *let the cat out of the bag; give the game away; spill the beans*

露面 lòumiàn show one's face; appear on public occasions; be present; show up; make an appearance; put in an appearance

露马脚 lòumǎjiǎo give oneself away; let the cat out of the bag

露一手 lòuyīshǒu make an exhibition of one's abilities or skills; show off

See lù.

炉 (爐) lú   8画 火部

炉 炉炉炉炉炉炉炉炉

[名] stove; oven; furnace
炉子 lúzi stove; oven; furnace
微波炉 wēibōlú

虏 (虜) lǔ   8画 虍部

虏 虏虏虏虏虏虏虏虏

[名] 打仗时捉住的敌人: prisoner of war; captive
俘虏 fúlǔ

鲁 (魯) lǔ   12画 鱼部

鲁 鲁鲁鲁鲁鲁鲁鲁鲁 鲁鲁鲁鲁

❶ [形] 粗野: rude; rough; boorish
粗鲁 cūlǔ

❷ [名] 山东省的别称: Lu, another name for Shandong Province

陆 (陸) lù   7画 阝(左)部

陆 陆陆陆陆陆陆陆

[名] 高出水面的土地：land | 飞机在机场着～了。Fēijī zài jīchǎng zhuólù le. *The plane has landed at the airport.* / 绝大部分鱼不能在～上生活。Jué dà bùfen yú bùnéng zài lù shang shēnghuó. *Most fish cannot survive on land.*

陆地 lùdì land; dry land

陆军 lùjūn ground force; land force; army

大陆 dàlù　　　登陆 dēnglù

着陆 zhuólù

◇陆续 lùxù one by one; one after another; continuous; in succession

录 (録) lù　　8画 彐部

录 录录录录录录录录

❶ [动] 记载；抄写：record; copy; write down | 抄～chāolù copy down / 把他讲的话笔～下来。Bǎ tā jiǎng de huà bǐlù xiàlai. *Copy down what he says.*

登录 dēnglù　　记录 jìlù

❷ [名] 记载言行或事物的文字材料：written records | 备忘～bèiwànglù memorandum / 回忆～huíyìlù reminiscences; memoirs; recollections

目录 mùlù

❸ [动] 选取；任用：select; employ | 收～shōulù employ; include

录取 lùqǔ enroll; recruit; admit

录用 lùyòng employ; take sb. on the staff

❹ [动] 用仪器记录(声音或图像)：record sounds or images with apparatuses

录像 lùxiàng video; videotape

录音 lùyīn record; recording; sound recording

录制 lùzhì record; transcribe

录像带 lùxiàngdài ① videotape ② video cassette ③ a videotape recording

录音机 lùyīnjī (tape) recorder

纪录片 jìlùpiàn

鹿 lù　　11画 鹿部

鹿 鹿鹿鹿鹿鹿鹿鹿鹿
鹿鹿鹿

[名] deer | ～的角是珍贵的药材。Lù de jiǎo shì zhēnguì de yàocái. *The deerhorn is valuable medicine.*

路 lù　　13画 足部

路 路路路路路路路路
路路路路路

❶ [名] 来往的通道：road; path | 修～xiūlù repair a road / 水～shuǐlù waterway; water route /

这是通往机场的～。Zhè shì tōngwǎng jīchǎng de lù. *This road leads to the airport.*

路灯 lùdēng street lamp; road lamp

路口 lùkǒu crossing; intersection

路况 lùkuàng road conditions (road surface, road traffic flow, etc.)

路面 lùmiàn road surface; pavement

路上 lùshang on one's way; on the way; during one's journey; en route

道路 dàolù　电路 diànlù

辅路 fǔlù　公路 gōnglù

马路 mǎlù　问路 wènlù

走路 zǒulù　走弯路 zǒuwānlù

高速公路 gāosù gōnglù

❷ [名] 路程：distance; journey | ～不远，坐车去只要10分钟。Lù bù yuǎn, zuòchē qù zhǐyào shí fēnzhōng. *It's not far, only ten minutes' drive.*

路程 lùchéng distance; journey; route

一路平安 yīlù-píng'ān

一路顺风 yīlù-shùnfēng

❸ [名] 思想或行动的方向；途径：(of thinking or action) way; means | 思～sīlù *train of thought; thinking* / 去～qùlù *the way along which one is going; outlet*

路子 lùzi way; means; approach

出路 chūlù　　　销路 xiāolù

❹ [名] 路线：route | 9～电车 jiǔ lù diànchē *No. 9 trolleybus*

路线 lùxiàn route; line

线路 xiànlù

◇路过 lùguò　pass by or through (a place)

lù　　21画 雨部

露 露 露 露 露 露 露 露 露
露 露 露 露 露 露 露 露 露
露 露 露 露 露

[动] 显露；表现出：show; reveal | ～出笑容 lùchū xiàoróng *reveal a smile* / 水面上～出几个小脑袋。Shuǐmiàn shang lùchū jǐ gè xiǎo nǎodai. *Several small heads (of children) appeared above the water's surface.*

露出 lùchū show; reveal; betray

暴露 bàolù　　　揭露 jiēlù

流露 liúlù　　　披露 pīlù

透露 tòulù　　　显露 xiǎnlù

泄露 xièlù

　　See lòu.

驴 (驢) lú　　7画 马部

驴 驴 驴 驴 驴 驴 驴

[名] donkey

毛驴 máolǘ

侣 lǚ　8画 亻部

侣 侣侣侣侣侣侣侣侣

[名] 伙伴；同伴：companion; associate | 情 ～ qínglǚ *sweetheart; lover*
伴侣 bànlǚ

旅 lǚ　10画 方部

旅 旅旅旅旅旅旅旅旅旅旅

❶ [名] 军队的编制单位：brigade (military unit)
❷ [名] 泛指军队：troops | 军 ～ jūnlǚ *army; troops*
❸ [动] 离家居留在外地：travel; stay away from home | ～居海外 lǚjū hǎiwài *live abroad*
旅店 lǚdiàn inn; hostel
旅馆 lǚguǎn hotel; hostel
旅客 lǚkè hotel guest; traveller; passenger; lodger
旅途 lǚtú journey; trip; route; on one's way; during one's trip
旅行 lǚxíng travel; journey; tour; trip; travelling
旅游 lǚyóu tour; tourism; travel; travelling
旅行社 lǚxíngshè travel service; travel agency
旅游业 lǚyóuyè tourist trade; tourism
旅游鞋 lǚyóuxié sneakers; walking shoes

铝 (鋁) lǚ　11画 钅部

铝 铝铝铝铝铝铝铝铝铝铝铝

[名] aluminium | ～锅 lǚguō *aluminium cooking pot*

屡 (屢) lǚ　12画 尸部

屡 屡屡屡屡屡屡屡屡屡屡屡屡

[副] 多次，不止一次：time and again; repeatedly | ～战～胜 lǚzhàn-lǚshèng *have fought many battles and won every one of them; score one victory after another*
屡次 lǚcì time and again; repeatedly

履 lǚ　15画 尸部

履 履履履履履履履履履履履履履履履

[动] 实行；执行：carry out; fulfil | ～约 lǚyuē *keep a promise, agreement, etc.*
履行 lǚxíng meet; fulfil; act up to; enforce; execute; carry out; observe; perform

律 lǜ　9画 彳部

律律律律律律律律律

[名] 规章;法则：rule; law; regulation ｜ 规~ guīlǜ *law; regular pattern* / 纪~ jìlǜ *discipline*
法律 fǎlǜ

◇ 律师 lǜshī *lawyer; counsel; counselor; solicitor; barrister (barrister-at-law); attorney (attorney-at-law) (American)*
自律 zìlǜ

虑 (慮) lǜ　10画 虍部

虑虑虑虑虑虑虑虑虑虑

❶ [动] 思考：consider; ponder ｜ 深思远~ shēnsī-yuǎnlǜ *deep and careful consideration*
考虑 kǎolǜ

❷ [动] 担忧：worry
顾虑 gùlǜ　　　焦虑 jiāolǜ
疑虑 yílǜ　　　忧虑 yōulǜ

率 lǜ　11画 一部

率率率率率率率率率率率

[名] 两个相关的数在一定条件下的比值：rate; ratio ｜ 升学~ shēngxuélǜ *enrolment rate* / 出

勤~ chūqínlǜ *attendance rate; attendance* / 增长~ zēngzhǎnglǜ *rate of increase; growth rate*
比率 bǐlǜ　　　概率 gàilǜ
功率 gōnglǜ　　汇率 huìlǜ
利率 lìlǜ　　　频率 pínlǜ
税率 shuìlǜ　　效率 xiàolǜ
兑换率 duìhuànlǜ
生产率 shēngchǎnlǜ
　　See shuài.

绿 (綠) lǜ　11画 纟部

绿绿绿绿绿绿绿绿绿绿绿

[形] green ｜ 红花~叶 hónghuā lǜyè *red flowers and green leaves* / 春天到了，树都~了。Chūntiān dào le, shù dōu lǜ le. *Spring has come, and all trees are turning green.*
绿茶 lǜchá green tea
绿地 lǜdì greenery patches (in a town or city)
绿化 lǜhuà make (a place) green by planting trees, flowers, etc.; afforest
绿色 lǜsè green colour
碧绿 bìlǜ　　　翠绿 cuìlǜ
开绿灯 kāilǜdēng

卵 luǎn　7画 丿部

卵卵卵卵卵卵卵

[名] ovum; egg | 鸟～niǎoluǎn bird's egg

乱 (亂) luǎn　7画 舌部

乱　乱乱乱乱乱乱乱

❶ [形] 没有秩序;没有条理：in disorder; in a mess | 次序～了 cìxù luǎn le it is out of order / 字写得太～。Zì xiě de tài luǎn. The handwriting is too messy.

乱七八糟 luànqī-bāzāo be in confusion; be in a mess; chaotic; be in extreme disorder; at sixes and sevens

混乱 hùnluàn　　杂乱 záluàn

❷ [动] 使混乱;使杂乱：cause confusion; make chaotic | 这使他～了手脚。Zhè shǐ tā luànle shǒujiǎo. It threw him into chaos.

捣乱 dǎoluàn　　扰乱 rǎoluàn

❸ [形] 动荡不安;战乱：upheaval; riot | 叛～pànluàn armed rebellion

动乱 dòngluàn

❹ [形] (心情、心绪)不安宁：(of mood) be confused and disconcerted; be troubled | 心烦意～ xīnfán-yìluàn be perturbed; be vexed / 他心里很～,不知道该说什么。Tā xīnli hěn luàn, bù zhīdào gāi shuō shénme. He was so confused that he did not know what to say.

慌乱 huāngluàn

❺ [副] 不加限制地；随便：indiscriminately; at random | ～说 luàn shuō talk nonsense / 不能在马路上～跑。Bùnéng zài mǎlù shang luànpǎo. Don't rush about on the street.

胡乱 húluàn

掠 lüè　11画 扌部

掠　掠掠掠掠掠掠掠掠
掠掠掠

[动] 抢夺：plunder; pillage | ～取 lüèqǔ seize; grab; plunder
掠夺 lüèduó take by force; plunder; pillage; sack; loot

略 lüè　11画 田部

略　略略略略略略略略
略略略

❶ [动] 抢;夺取：rob; seize
侵略 qīnlüè

❷ [名] 计谋;规划：strategy; plan | 方～fānglüè general plan / 谋～móulüè tactics; strategy
策略 cèlüè　　战略 zhànlüè

❸ [动] 简化;省去：simplify; omit; delete | ～去 lüèqù leave out
忽略 hūlüè　　省略 shěnglüè

❹ [副] 大致;稍微：briefly; a little; a bit; slightly | ～知一二

lüèzhī-yī'ěr *have only a smat-
tering of knowledge of; know
only a little about* / 粗～地计算
一下 cūlüè de jìsuàn yīxià
make a rough calculation / 请
你～等片刻。Qǐng nǐ lüèděng
piànkè. *Please wait for a while.*
略微 lüèwēi *slightly; a little;
somewhat*
◇领略 lǐnglüè

抢（搶）lūn   7画 扌部

抢 抢抢抢抢抢抢抢

[动] 用力挥动：brandish; swing
| ～拳 lūnquán *swing one's fist*

轮（輪）lún   8画 车部

轮 轮轮轮轮轮轮轮轮

❶ [名] 轮子：wheel | 车～ chēlún
wheel (of a vehicle) / 飞～儿 fēi-
lúnr *flywheel; free wheel (of a
bicycle)*
轮胎 lúntāi *tyre*
轮椅 lúnyǐ *wheelchair*
轮子 lúnzi *wheel*
齿轮 chǐlún 三轮车 sānlúnchē
❷ [动] 按次序替换：take turns
| ～班 lúnbān *in shifts; in re-
lays* / 这回～到我了。Zhè huí
lúndào wǒ le. *Now it's my turn.*
轮流 lúnliú *take turns; by turns;
in turn; in rotation; by rotation*

❸ [名] 轮船：ship; boat | 海～
hǎilún *seagoing vessel* / 巨～
jùlún *large ship*
轮船 lúnchuán *steamer; steamship; ship*
◇轮廓 lúnkuō *outline; contour;
rough sketch*

论（論）lùn   6画 讠部

论 论论论论论论

❶ [动] 分析和说明事理：discuss
and analyze; talk about; dis-
course | ～资历 lùn zīlì *as to
qualifications* / 就事～事 jiùshì-
lùnshì *confine the discussion to
certain issue; deal with a matter on its merits*
论点 lùndiǎn *argument; opinion;
view; thesis; proposition; point*
论述 lùnshù *discuss; expound;
discourse; treatment; exposition*
论文 lùnwén *paper; disserta-
tion; treatise; thesis; discourse*
论证 lùnzhèng *argue; expound;
prove; demonstrate; argument;
proof; demonstration*
辩论 biànlùn   评论 pínglùn
谈论 tánlùn   讨论 tǎolùn
推论 tuīlùn   议论 yìlùn
争论 zhēnglùn
评论员 pínglùnyuán
❷ [动] 评定：看待：decide on; judge;
evaluate | ～功行赏 lùngōng-
xíngshǎng *reward people ac-

495

cording to their contributions
一概而论 yīgài'érlùn

❸ [名] 分析、说明道理的言论或文章：dissertation, theory, or statement that analyzes or expounds the principles of something | 相对~xiāngduìlùn *theory of relativity*

结论 jiélùn   理论 lǐlùn
谬论 miùlùn   言论 yánlùn
舆论 yúlùn
唯物论 wéiwùlùn
唯心论 wéixīnlùn
◇ 无论如何 wúlùn-rúhé

啰 (囉) luō   11画 口部

啰啰啰啰啰啰啰啰
啰啰啰

See 啰唆
啰唆 luōsuo wordy; verbose; long-winded

罗 (羅) luó   8画 四部

罗 罗罗罗罗罗罗罗罗

[动] 排列;分布：display; spread out
罗列 luóliè ① spread out; arrange for display; set out; display ② list; enumerate; cite

萝 (蘿) luó   11画 艹部

萝 萝萝萝萝萝萝萝萝
萝萝萝

See below
萝卜 luóbo radish; turnip
菠萝 bōluó   胡萝卜 húluóbo

逻 (邏) luó   11画 辶部

逻 逻逻逻逻逻逻逻逻
逻逻逻

[动] 巡查：patrol; inspect
巡逻 xúnluó
◇ 逻辑 luóji logic

锣 (鑼) luó   13画 钅部

锣 锣锣锣锣锣锣锣锣
锣锣锣锣锣

[名] gong | ~鼓 luógǔ gongs and drums
敲锣打鼓 qiāoluó-dǎgǔ

箩 (籮) luó   14画 竹部

箩 箩箩箩箩箩箩箩箩
箩箩箩箩箩箩

See 箩筐
箩筐 luókuāng a large bamboo or wicker basket

骡 (騾) luó   14画 马部

骡 骡骡骡骡骡骡骡骡
骡骡骡骡骡骡

See 骡子
骡子 luózi mule

螺 luó 17画 虫部

螺 螺螺螺螺螺螺螺螺
螺螺螺螺螺螺螺
螺

See 螺丝钉
螺丝钉 luósīdīng screw

骆 (駱) luò 9画 马部

骆 骆骆骆骆骆骆骆骆
骆

See 骆驼
骆驼 luòtuo camel

落 luò 12画 艹部

落 落落落落落落落落
落落落落

❶ [动] 掉下来：fall; drop | ～泪 luòlèi *shed tears; weep* / 太阳～
山了。Tàiyáng luòshān le. *The sun has set.* / 树叶都～光了。
Shùyè dōu luòguāng le. *The leaves have all fallen.*
落地 luòdì ① fall to the ground

② (of babies) be born
散落 sànluò 脱落 tuōluò

❷ [动] 下降；使下降：descend; go down; decline
降落 jiāngluò

❸ [动] 归属：fall onto; rest with | 这个任务～到了我身上。Zhège rènwu luòdàole wǒ shēnshàng. *The task rested squarely on my shoulders.*
落实 luòshí ① fix in advance; ascertain; make sure; check ② implement; carry out; fulfil

❹ [动] 遗留在后面：lag behind; fall behind | ～伍 luòwǔ *fall behind the ranks; straggle; drop behind; drop out*
落后 luòhòu ① get behind; fall behind; lag behind ②backward; old-fashioned
落选 luòxuǎn fail to win the election; fail to be chosen; lose an election

❺ [动] 停留；留下：sojourn; stay | ～户 luòhù *settle down* / 没有地方～脚 méiyǒu dìfang luòjiǎo *have no place to stay for a time*

◇落成 luòchéng completion (of a building, monument, etc.)
部落 bùluò 角落 jiǎoluò
坐落 zuòluò
   See là.

M m

(Header left margin) 妈 麻 马

mā ~ mǎ

妈 (媽) mā 6画 女部

妈 妈妈妈妈妈妈

❶ [名] 母亲：mother | ~的话你要记着。Mā de huà nǐ yào jìzhe. *You should keep mum's words in mind.*
妈妈 māma ma; mum; mummy; mother
❷ [名] 称长一辈或年长已婚的妇女：aunt; auntie (form of address for a woman of an older generation) | 姑~ gūmā *father's sister; aunt* / 姨~ yímā *mother's sister; aunt*
大妈 dàmā   舅妈 jiùmā

麻 mā 11画 麻部

麻 麻麻麻麻麻麻麻麻麻麻麻

❶ [名] 麻类植物的统称：general term for hemp, flax, etc.
麻袋 mádài sack
❷ [形] 带细碎斑点的：pock-marked; speckled | ~脸 máliǎn *pockmarked face*
麻雀 máquè (house) sparrow

❸ [形] 部分或全部失去感觉：unable to feel anything; numb | 手发~ shǒu fāmá *feel pins and needles in one's hands* / 舌头发~ shétou fāmá *one's tongue becomes numb* / 腿压~了。Tuǐ yāmá le. *My legs became numb from the pressure.*
麻痹 mábì ① paralysis ② off one's guard; lose one's vigilance
麻木 mámù ① numb ② apathetic; insensitive; lifeless
麻醉 mázuì ① anaesthesia ② corrupt (sb.'s mind); poison
◇麻烦 máfan ① troublesome ② trouble sb.; bother

马 (馬) mǎ 3画 马部

马 马马马

[名] horse | 骑~ qímǎ *ride on a horse* / ~不停蹄 mǎbùtíngtí *doing sth. without stopping; nonstop; doing sth. with no break*
马车 mǎchē (horse-drawn) carriage；cart
马路 mǎlù road; street; avenue
马术 mǎshù horsemanship
马戏 mǎxì circus
河马 hémǎ   赛马 sàimǎ
千军万马 qiānjūn-wànmǎ
◇马达 mǎdá motor
马虎 mǎhu careless; casual
马克 mǎkè mark[former mone-

M

tary unit of Germany]; markka [former monetary unit of Finland]

马力 mǎlì horsepower

马上 mǎshàng at once; immediately; straight away; right away

马大哈 mǎdàhā ① heedless; unmindful ② scatterbrain; careless and forgetful person

马铃薯 mǎlíngshǔ potato

马马虎虎 mǎma-hūhū ① careless; casual ② not very good; just passable; so-so; fair; not so bad

马克思主义 Mǎkèsī zhǔyì Marxism

露马脚 lòumǎjiǎo

码 (碼) mǎ   8画 石部

码 码码码码码码码码

[名] 表示数目的符号：a sign or thing indicating number | 数~ shùmǎ *number* / 页~ yèmǎ *page number* / 价~ jiàmǎ *marked price* 筹码 chóumǎ   号码 hàomǎ 密码 mìmǎ

◇码头mǎtou ①wharf; dock; quay; pier ②port city; commercial and transportation centre

蚂 (螞) mǎ   9画 虫部

蚂 蚂蚂蚂蚂蚂蚂蚂蚂 蚂

See 蚂蚁

蚂蚁 mǎyǐ ant

骂 (罵) mà   9画 马部

骂 骂骂骂骂骂骂骂骂 骂

[动] 用粗话、恶意的话伤人；斥责：abuse; curse; swear; call names; reproach | ~人 màrén *swear (at people)* / 他~了孩子一顿。Tā màle háizi yī dùn. *He gave his child a scolding.*

吗 (嗎) ma   6画 口部

吗 吗吗吗吗吗吗

❶ [助] 用在句末表示疑问：used at the end of a question to indicate doubt | 他明天来~?Tā míngtiān lái ma? *Will he come tomorrow?* / 身体好些了~? Shēntǐ hǎoxiē le ma? *Do you feel better?* / 你听明白了~?Nǐ tīng míngbai le ma? *Do you understand what I say?*

❷ [助] 用在反问句末尾，表示强调、质问、责备的语气：used at the end of a rhetorical question to indicate emphasis, reproach or interrogation | 你这样做对得起父母~?Nǐ zhèyàng zuò duìdeqǐ fùmǔ ma? *Don't you realize that you will disappoint*

M

your parents by doing so? | 难道我还不懂~?Nándào wǒ hái bù dǒng ma? *You think I don't understand that?* | 你不能走快点~? Nǐ bùnéng zǒukuài diǎn ma? *Couldn't you walk a little faster?*

嘛 ma 14画 口部

嘛嘛嘛嘛嘛嘛嘛嘛嘛嘛嘛嘛嘛

❶[助] 表示事情本应如此或显而易见: indicating that sth. is obvious | 有意见就提~。Yǒu yìjiàn jiù tí ma. *Put forward your suggestions if you have any.* | 这本来就是你的错~。Zhè běnlái jiùshì nǐ de cuò ma. *Obviously it was your fault.* | 人多当然力量大~。Rén duō dāngrán lìliang dà ma. *It goes without saying that more people means greater strengh.*

❷[助]表示希望、劝阻: used to express hope or give advice | 你不要走得那么快~!Nǐ bùyào zǒu de nàme kuài ma! *Hey, don't walk so fast!*

❸[助]用在句子停顿处, 引起对下文的重视: used to form a pause in a sentence, calling the listener's attention | 大家的事~, 就得大家做。Dàjiā de shì ma, jiù děi dàjiā zuò. *Since it is the business of all of us, let's do it*

together. | 你~, 就不用亲自去了。Nǐ ma, jiù bùyòng qīnzì qù le. *As for you, there is no need to go in person.*

埋 mái 10画 土部

埋埋埋埋埋埋埋埋埋埋

[动] 用土等盖住: cover with earth; bury | 掩~ yǎnmái *bury* | ~种子 mái zhǒngzi *plant seeds* | 树根要~得深一些。Shùgēn yào mái de shēn yīxiē. *The roots of the tree should be planted deeper.*

埋伏 máifú ① lie in ambush; ambush ② hide; lie low

埋没 máimò ① cover up; bury ② neglect; stifle

埋头 máitóu immerse oneself in; be engrossed in

See mán.

买 (買) mǎi 6画 一部

买买买买买买买

[动]用钱换取东西(跟"卖mài"相对): buy (the opposite of "卖 mài") | ~书 mǎi shū *buy books* | ~彩电 mǎi cǎidiàn *buy a colour TV set*

买卖 mǎimai ① buying and selling; business; deal; transaction ②

a private shop or small business.
购买 gòumǎi　收买 shōumǎi
不买账 bùmǎizhàng
购买力 gòumǎilì

（邁）mài　6画 辶部

迈　迈迈迈迈迈迈

[动] 抬脚向前跨步：step; stride
| ~过去 mài guòqu *step over*
/ ~了一大步 màile yī dà bù
take a big stride / 向前~进xiāng
qián màijìn *stride forward*

（賣）mài　8画 十部

卖　卖卖卖卖卖卖卖卖

❶[动] 用东西换钱（跟"买 mǎi"
相对）： sell (the opposite of "买
mǎi") | ~衣服 mài yīfu *sell
clothes* / ~日用品 mài rìyòngpǐn *sell everyday goods* / 这种
商品早就~完了。Zhè zhǒng
shāngpǐn zǎo jiù màiwán le.
This product sold out long ago.
卖淫 màiyín prostitution
贩卖 fànmài　　买卖 mǎimai
拍卖 pāimài　　外卖 wàimài
专卖店 zhuānmàidiàn
❷[动] 为了自己的利益出卖国家、
民族或他人：betray (one's
country or friends)
卖国 màiguó betray one's country

出卖 chūmài
❸[动] 尽量用出：exert oneself; do
one's utmost | ~劲儿 màijìnr
*exert all one's strength; spare no
effort* / ~力气 mài lìqi *exert all
one's strength; do one's very
best; exert oneself to the utmost*
◇卖关子 màiguānzi (stop a story
at a climax to) keep the listeners
in suspense; keep people guess-
ing

　mài　9画 月部

脉　脉脉脉脉脉脉脉脉
　　脉

[名] pulse
脉搏 màibó pulse
把脉 bǎmài　　号脉 hàomài

　mán　10画 土部

埋　埋埋埋埋埋埋埋埋
　　埋埋

See 埋怨
埋怨 mányuàn blame; com-
plain; grumble
　　See mái.

馒（饅）mán　14画 饣部

馒　馒馒馒馒馒馒馒馒
　　馒馒馒馒馒馒

See 馒头

馒头 mántou steamed bun; steamed bread

瞒（瞞）mán 15画 目部

瞒 瞒瞒瞒瞒瞒瞒瞒瞒
瞒瞒瞒瞒瞒瞒瞒

[动]隐藏真实的情况，不使人知道：hide the truth from | 隐～ yǐnmán *hide a secret from people* / 这事不必～他。Zhè shì bùbì mán tā. *There is no need to keep him in the dark about this.*

满（滿）mǎn 13画 氵部

满 满满满满满满满满
满满满满满

❶[形] 里面充实；没有余地：full; filled; packed | 桶里的水已经～了。Tǒng li de shuǐ yǐjīng mǎn le. *The pail has been filled with water.* / 会场已经坐～了。Huìchǎng yǐjīng zuòmǎn le. *The assembly hall is already packed with people.*

满怀 mǎnhuái have one's heart filled with; be imbued with
饱满 bǎomǎn 充满 chōngmǎn
丰满 fēngmǎn

❷[动] 感到足够：be satisfied; be content; be contented | 心～意足 xīnmǎn-yìzú *satisfied; to one's heart's content*

满意 mǎnyì statisfied; pleased; content
满足 mǎnzú ① satisfy; meet (needs, demands) ② satisfied; content; contented
不满 bùmǎn   美满 měimǎn
圆满 yuánmǎn

❸[形] 骄傲：complacent; self-satisfied; conceited
自满 zìmǎn

❹[形] 达到一定的期限：reaching the end of a certain period of time; reaching the limit | 假期已～。Jiàqī yǐ mǎn. *The holidays are over.* / 她工作不～三年。Tā gōngzuò bùmǎn sān nián. *She has not yet worked for three years.*

满月 mǎnyuè ① full moon ② a baby's completion of its first month of life

❺[副] 整个；完全：completely; entirely; perfectly; fully | ～口答应 mǎnkǒu dāyìng *readily promise* / ～身是泥 mǎnshēn shì ní *have one's body covered with mud; muddy all over* / ～院子都是花。Mǎn yuànzi dōu shì huā. *The flowers are blooming everywhere in the yard.*

满腔 mǎnqiāng have one's bosom filled with

蔓 màn 14画 艹部

蔓蔓蔓蔓蔓蔓蔓蔓
蔓蔓蔓蔓蔓蔓

[动]滋生；扩展：spread; extend
(like weeds)
蔓延 mànyán spread; extend

màn 14画 氵部

漫漫漫漫漫漫漫漫
漫漫漫漫漫漫

[形]时间久或道路长：(of time or
distance) very long; endless
漫长 màncháng very long;
endless
漫游 mànyóu go on a pleasure
trip; roam; wander
◇漫画 mànhuà comic strip; cartoon

màn 14画 忄部

慢慢慢慢慢慢慢慢
慢慢慢慢慢慢

❶[形]速度低；迟缓（跟"快 kuài"
相对）：slow (the opposite of
"快 kuài"）：| 车子的速度很～。
Chēzi de sùdù hěn màn. The
car moves slowly. / 你读得真～!
Nǐ dú de zhēn màn! How
slowly you read! / 我的表～了 5
分钟。Wǒ de biǎo mànle wǔ
fēnzhōng. My watch is five minutes slow.
慢性 mànxìng ①chronic ②slow

(in taking effect)
缓慢 huǎnmàn

❷[形]对人没礼貌：supercilious;
rude | 傲～àomàn arrogant;
haughty
怠慢 dàimàn

忙

máng 6画 忄部

忙忙忙忙忙忙

❶[形]事情多，没有空闲（跟"闲
xián"相对）：busy (the oppo-
site of "闲 xián"）| 工作～
gōngzuò máng be busy at
work; be fully occupied / 这几天
很～。Zhè jǐ tiān hěn máng. I
am very busy these days. / 他一
个人～不过来。Tā yī gè rén
máng bù guòlái. He can't
manage all this by himself.
忙碌 mánglù be busy; bustle
about
帮忙 bāngmáng 繁忙 fánmáng
帮倒忙 bāngdàománg
不慌不忙 bùhuāng-bùmáng

❷[动]急迫；急着去做：hurry; has-
ten | 别～，再想一想。Bié máng,
zài xiǎngyixiǎng. Don't hurry.
Think it over. / 她～于家务。Tā
mángyú jiāwù. She was fully
occupied by the housework.
匆忙 cōngmáng 赶忙 gǎnmáng
慌忙 huāngmáng
急忙 jímáng 连忙 liánmáng

盲 盲盲盲盲盲盲盲盲

❶ [形] 看不见东西：blind; unable to see

盲人 mángrén a blind person

❷ [形] 对某些事物不认识或分辨不清：unable to see or make a difference between things ｜ 色～ sèmáng *colour blindness*

盲从 mángcóng follow blindly

盲目 mángmù blind

文盲 wénmáng

茫 茫茫茫茫茫茫茫茫茫

❶ [形] 十分广阔；看不到边：vast; boundless and indistinct

茫茫 mángmáng boundless and indistinct; vast

❷ [形] 不清晰；不明白：indistinct; vague; ignorant; in the dark ｜ ～无头绪 mángwútóuxù *without a clue; at a loss*

茫然 mángrán ① ignorant; in the dark; at a loss ② feel lost

猫 猫猫猫猫猫猫猫猫
猫猫猫

[名] cat

夜猫子 yèmāozi

毛 máo 4画 毛部

毛 毛毛毛毛

❶ [名] hair; feather ｜ 鸡～jīmáo *chicken feather* / 羊～yángmáo *wool* / 桃子的表面有一层～。Táozi de biǎomiàn yǒu yī céng máo. *The peach has a downy skin.*

毛笔 máobǐ brush pen

毛巾 máojīn towel

毛驴 máolǘ donkey

毛线 máoxiàn wool thread

毛衣 máoyī woollen sweater; sweater; woolly

眉毛 méimao 　羽毛 yǔmáo

羽毛球 yǔmáoqiú

一毛不拔 yīmáo-bùbá

❷ [形] 小；细微：little; small; tiny ｜ ～孩子 máoháizi *a small child; a mere child* / ～～雨 máomaoyǔ *drizzle*

❸ [量] 角，1元钱的1/10；*mao, unit of money in China, colloquial term for jiao* (1 *jiao* is equal to 1/10 *yuan*) ｜ 5～钱 wǔ máo qián *fifty cents; five mao*

❹ [名] 东西上长的霉：mildew; mould ｜ 馒头长～了。Mántou zhǎng máo le. *The buns became mouldy.*

◇毛病 máobìng defect; shortcoming; fault; mistake

矛 矛矛矛矛矛 mǎo 5画 矛部

[名]古代兵器：spear (an ancient weapon)

矛盾 máodùn ①(philosophy) paradox ② problem; conflict; contradiction ③ contradictory

自相矛盾 zìxiāng-máodùn

茂 茂茂茂茂茂茂茂茂 mào 8画 艹部

[形]草木旺盛：luxuriant; exuberant | 根深叶～ gēnshēn-yèmào deep roots and luxuriant leaves

茂密 màomì (of grass or trees) dense; thick

茂盛 màoshèng (of plants) luxuriant; exuberant; flourishing

冒 冒冒冒冒冒冒冒冒冒 mào 9画 日部

❶[动]不顾；顶着：risk; brave; disregard | ～雨 màoyǔ braving the rain; in spite of the rain

冒险 màoxiǎn take a risk; take chances

❷[形]轻率；鲁莽：rash; abrupt | ～失 màoshi rash; abrupt

冒进 màojìn premature advance; rash advance

冒失鬼 màoshiguǐ hothead; daredevil

❸[动]用假的充当真的：pass off; assume false identity | ～名 màomíng go under sb. else's name; assume another's name / ～领 màolǐng falsely claim as one's own

冒充 màochōng pretend to be (sb. or sth. else); pass (sb. or sth.) off as

冒牌 màopái fake

冒牌货 màopáihuò imitation (of a well-known trade mark); pirated goods

假冒 jiǎmào

❹[动]上升；向外透出来：emit; send out (up, forth) | ～汗 màohàn sweat / ～烟 màoyān send up smoke / ～热气 mào rèqì give off steam

贸 (贸) 贸贸贸贸贸贸贸贸贸 mào 9画 贝部

[动]交易；买卖：trade; do business with

贸易 màoyì trade

农贸市场 nóngmào shìchǎng

帽 mào 12画 巾部

M

505

帽 帽帽帽帽帽帽帽帽
帽帽帽帽

[名] hat; cap | 礼~lǐmào *top hat; bowler hat* / 军~jūnmào *service cap*

帽子 màozi ① headgear; hat; cap ② label; tag; brand

没 méi 7画 氵部

没 没没没没没没没

❶ [动] 没有；不存在：not have; there is not; without | ~时间 méi shíjiān *have no time* / ~根据 méi gēnjù *unfounded; groundless* / 他~哥哥。Tā méi gēge. *He doesn't have any elder brothers.* / 屋里~人。Wūli méi rén. *There isn't anyone in the room.*

没错 méicuò ① it is quite sure; you can rest assured ② can't go wrong

没命 méimìng ① lose one's life; die ② recklessly; desperately; like mad; for all one is worth

没关系 méiguānxi it doesn't matter; it's nothing; that's all right; never mind

没什么 méishénme it doesn't matter; it's nothing; that's all right; never mind

没事儿 méishìr ① have nothing to do; be free; be at a loose end ② it does not matter; it's nothing; that's all right; never mind

没说的 méishuōde ① really good ② there's no need to say any more about it; it goes without saying

没意思 méiyìsi ① bored ② boring; uninteresting

❷ [动] 不够；不到（某个数量等）：be less than | ~两个星期他就走了。Méi liǎng gè xīngqī tā jiù zǒu le. *He left in less than two weeks.* / ~几天她就死了。Méi jǐ tiān tā jiù sǐ le. *She died only a few days later.*

❸ [动] 不如：be not as...as | 我学习~他刻苦。Wǒ xuéxí méi tā kèkǔ. *I don't study as hard as he does.* / 这本书~那本有趣。Zhè běn shū méi nà běn yǒuqù. *This book is not as interesting as that one.*

❹ [副] 否定动作或状态已经发生；不曾：have not or did not | 商店还~开门。Shāngdiàn hái méi kāimén. *The shop hasn't opened yet.* / 大水还~退。Dà shuǐ hái méi tuì. *The flood hasn't gone yet.* / 昨天我~见到他。Zuótiān wǒ méi jiàndào tā. *I didn't see him yesterday.*

从没 cóngméi

玫 méi 8画 王部

玫玫玫玫玫玫玫玫

See 玫瑰
玫瑰 méigui rugosa rose; rose

 méi　9画　目部

眉眉眉眉眉眉眉眉
眉

[名] 眉毛：eyebrow | ～开眼笑
méikāi-yǎnxiào be all smiles;
beam with joy
眉毛 méimao eyebrow; brow
眉头 méitóu brows

 méi　11画　木部

梅梅梅梅梅梅梅梅
梅梅梅

See below
梅花 méihuā plum blossom
杨梅 yángméi

媒 méi　12画　女部
媒

媒媒媒媒媒媒媒媒
媒媒媒媒

See below
媒介 méijiè intermediary;
medium; vehicle
媒体 méitǐ media (including
newspapers, magazines, radio
and TV broadcasts and adver-
tising)

传媒 chuánméi
多媒体 duōméitǐ

 méi　13画　火部
煤

煤煤煤煤煤煤煤煤
煤煤煤煤煤

[名] coal | 采～cǎiméi cut (mine)
coal
煤矿 méikuàng coal mine;
colliery
煤气 méiqì coal gas; gas
煤炭 méitàn coal

 méi　14画　酉部
酶

酶酶酶酶酶酶酶酶
酶酶酶酶酶酶

[名] enzyme; ferment

霉 (黴❷)méi　15画　雨部
霉

霉霉霉霉霉霉霉霉
霉霉霉霉霉霉霉

❶ [动] 东西因发霉而变质：become
mildewed; go mouldy | 这些旧
衣服都发～了。Zhèxiē jiù yīfu
dōu fāméi le. These old clothes
have gone mouldy.
❷ [名] 霉菌：mould (of food,
clothes, etc.)

 měi　7画　母部

每 每每每每每每每

❶ [代] 指全体中的任何一个或一组：every; each | ～人 měi rén everyone; each person / ～回 měi huí every time / ～次 měi cì every time; each time / ～三天 měi sān tiān every three days / ～个小组 měi ge xiǎozǔ each group; every group

❷ [副] 指反复动作中的任何一次或一组：on each occasion; each time | ～逢星期日休息 měiféng xīngqīrì xiūxi have a day off every Sunday / ～六米种一棵树。Měi liù mǐ zhòng yī kē shù. One tree is planted every six metres.

美 měi 9画 羊部

美 美美美美美美美美美

❶ [形] 好看（跟"丑 chǒu"相对）：beautiful (the opposite of "丑 chǒu") | 风景～ fēngjǐng měi beautiful scenery / 姑娘长得～。Gūniang zhǎngdeměi. The girl is pretty.

美观 měiguān pleasing to the eye; beautiful; artistic

美丽 měilì beautiful

美妙 měimiào beautiful; splendid; wonderful

美女 měinǚ a beautiful woman

美人 měirén a beautiful woman; beauty

美中不足 měizhōng-bùzú a blemish in an otherwise perfect thing; some slight imperfection

健美 jiànměi   精美 jīngměi
审美 shěnměi   优美 yōuměi
赞美 zànměi

❷ [动] 使好看：beautify | ～容 měiróng improve one's looks; beautify appearance / ～发 měifà get a haircut; do sb.'s hair

美化 měihuà beautify; prettify; embellish

❸ [形] 好的；令人满意的：good; fine; satisfying | 完～ wánměi perfect / 物～价廉 wùměi-jiàlián of high quality and inexpensive; good and cheap

美德 měidé virtue; moral excellence

美好 měihǎo fine; happy; glorious

美满 měimǎn happy; perfectly satisfactory

美食 měishí good food; delicacies

美味 měiwèi ① delicious food; delicacy ② delicious; dainty

十全十美 shíquán-shíměi

❹ [名] 指美洲或美国：referring to North America or the United States

美金 měijīn American dollar; US dollar

美元 měiyuán American dollar; US dollar

美洲 Měizhōu America

南美 Nánměi

北美洲 Běiměizhōu

南美洲 Nánměizhōu

◇美术 měishù ① the fine arts; art ② painting

美术馆 měishùguǎn art gallery

 mèi 8画 女部

妹 妹妹妹妹妹妹妹妹

❶[名] 称同父母比自己年龄小的女子：younger sister of the same parents | 姐~jiěmèi *sisters; elder sister and younger sister* / 兄~xiōngmèi *older brother and younger sister*

妹妹 mèimei younger sister; sister

❷[名] 亲友中同辈而年龄比自己小的女子：younger female cousin | 表~biǎomèi *younger female cousin*

 (悶) mēn 7画 门部

闷 闷闷闷闷闷闷闷

❶[形] 空气不流通，使人不舒服：stuffy; close | 天气~热。Tiānqì mēnrè. *The weather is sultry.* / 房间里太~了，快打开窗子吧! Fáng jiān li tài mēn le, kuài dǎkāi chuāngzi ba! *It's too stuffy in the room. Open the win-*

dow right away.

❷[动] 使不透气：keep tightly closed | 饭菜~在锅里。Fàncài mēn zài guō li. *The food has been kept in the pot.* / 茶刚泡上，~一会儿再喝。Chá gāng pàoshang, mēn yīhuìr zài hē. *The tea has just been prepared. Let it brew for a while before drinking.*

See mèn.

 (門) mén 3画 门部

门 门门门

❶[名] 建筑物的出入口；设在出入口能开关的装置：entrance of a building; door; gate | 前~qiánmén *front door* / 房~fángmén *door* / 铁~tiěmén *iron gate*

门口 ménkǒu entrance; doorway

门票 ménpiào entrance ticket; admission ticket

门外汉 ménwàihàn layman; the uninitiated

车门 chēmén   出门 chūmén

大门 dàmén   对门 duìmén

开门 kāimén

鬼门关 guǐménguān

开后门 kāihòumén

天安门 Tiān'ānmén

❷[名] 器物上可以开关的部分：part of an object that can be

opened or closed | 柜～guì-mén *cabinet door* / 炉～lúmén *stove door*

❸[名]形状或作用像门的东西：switch; sth. that resembles or functions like a door | 水～shuǐmén *water valve* / 电～diānmén *electric switch* / 球～qiúmén *goal*

射门 shèmén　油门 yóumén
守门员 shǒuményuán

❹[名]事物的类别：class; category | 分～别类 fēnmén-biélèi *divide into different categories*

部门 bùmén　热门 rèmén
专门 zhuānmén
五花八门 wǔhuā-bāmén

❺[名]家庭：family | 喜事临～xǐshì-línmén *A blessing has descended upon the family.*

门当户对 méndāng-hùduì *be well-matched in social and economic status (for marriage)*

❻[量]用于炮、技术、功课等：used for artillery, skill, subjects of study | 一～炮 yī mén pào *a piece of artillery; a cannon* / 学一～技术 xué yī mén jìshù *learn a skill* / 一～功课 yī mén gōngkè *a subject; a course*

◇门诊 ménzhěn outpatient service

闷（悶）mèn　7画 门部

闷 闷闷闷闷闷闷闷闷

[形]心情不舒畅；心烦：bored; unhappy; depressed | ～～不乐 mènmèn-bùlè *depressed; in low spirits*

沉闷 chénmèn　烦闷 fánmèn
纳闷儿 nàmènr
　　See mèn.

们（們）men　5画 亻部

们 们们们们们

[词尾]用在代词和指人名词的后边，表示多数：suffix used after a personal pronoun or a noun referring to a person or living things to form a plural | 朋友～péngyoumen *friends* / 学生～xuéshengmen *students* / 工人～gōngrénmen *workers* / 孩子～háizimen *children*

你们 nǐmen　　人们 rénmen
他们 tāmen　　它们 tāmen
她们 tāmen　　我们 wǒmen
咱们 zánmen

蒙（矇）mēng　13画 艹部

蒙 蒙蒙蒙蒙蒙蒙蒙蒙
蒙蒙蒙蒙蒙

❶[动]欺骗：cheat; deceive; dupe; hoodwink | 别～人!Bié mēng rén. *Don't swindle me!* / 没人

敢～他。Méi rén gǎn mēng tā. *No one dares to deceive him.*

❷[动]胡乱猜测：make a wild guess | 不知道就是不知道, 不要乱～。Bù zhīdào jiùshì bù zhīdào, bùyào luàn mēng. *It's no good pretending to know what you don't know. Don't make wild guesses about things.* / 这回叫你～对了。Zhè huí jiào nǐ mēng duì le. *You've made a lucky guess this time.*

萌 萌萌萌萌萌萌萌萌萌萌萌 méng 11画 艹部

[动]植物发芽：(of plants) sprout; germinate; bud

萌芽 méngyá ① sprout; shoot forth; bud; germinate ② rudiment; shoot; seed; germ

猛 猛猛猛猛猛猛猛猛猛猛猛 měng 11画 犭部

❶ [形]凶暴：fierce; violent | ～兽 měngshòu *beast of prey* 凶猛 xiōngměng

❷ [形] 力量大, 气势壮：vigorous; energetic | 勇～ yǒngměng *bold and powerful* / 用力太～ yònglì tài měng *use too much strength; overexert*

oneself / 火力～ huǒlì měng *heavy gunfire*

猛烈 měngliè fierce; vigorous; violent

❸ [副] 突然：suddenly; abruptly | ～地跑了进来 měng de pǎole jìnlái *run into (a room) suddenly; break into*

猛然 měngrán suddenly; abruptly

梦 (夢) mèng 11画 夕部

梦梦梦梦梦梦梦梦梦梦梦梦

❶[名] dream | 我昨天夜里做了一个恶～。Wǒ zuótiān yèlǐ zuòle yī gè èmèng. *I had a nightmare last night.*

梦话 mènghuà ① talking in one's sleep; somniloquy ② daydream; nonsense

做梦 zuòmèng

白日梦 báirìmèng

红楼梦 Hónglóumèng

❷ [动] 做梦：have a dream | ～见 mèngjiàn *see in the dream; dream about* / ～游 mèngyóu *sleepwalk*

❸ [名] 比喻幻想：fancy; illusion

梦想 mèngxiǎng ① vain hope; wishful thinking ② vainly hope; dream of

眯 mī 11画 目部

眯 眯眯眯眯眯眯眯眯
眯眯眯

[动]眼皮微微合上：shut one's eyes slightly | ～着眼笑 mīzhe yǎn xiào *narrow one's eyes into a smile* / 在床上～一会儿 zài chuáng shang mī yīhuìr *take a short nap in bed*

弥 (彌瀰❶) mí 8画 弓部

弥 弥弥弥弥弥弥弥弥弥

❶ [形]满；遍：full; all over | ～月 míyuè *(of an infant) full month* / ～天大罪 mítiān-dàzuì *monstrous crime; heinous crime* 弥漫 mímàn fill the air; spread all over the place

❷ [动]填满：fill to capacity | ～补 míbǔ *make up; remedy; make good*

迷 mí 9画 辶部

迷 迷迷迷迷迷迷迷迷迷

❶ [动]分辨不清；失去判断能力：be confused; lose good judgement | ～了路 míle lù *have lost one's way; get lost* / ～了方向 míle fāngxiàng *lose one's bearings; get lost*

迷糊 míhu ① dazed; confused

② misted; blurred; dimmed ③ muddleheaded

迷惑 míhuò puzzle; confuse; perplex; baffle

迷失 míshī lose (one's way, etc.)

低迷 dīmí   昏迷 hūnmí

❷ [动]对某人或某事特别喜爱：be crazy about | 入～ rùmí *be fascinated; be enchanted* / 最近他～上了电脑。Zuìjìn tā mí shangle diànnǎo. *These days he is addicted to the computer.* / 他被这些书～住了。Tā bèi zhèxiē shū mízhù le. *He is fascinated by these books.*

迷信 míxìn ① superstition; blind faith ②have blind faith in; make a fetish of

❸ [名]对某种事物特别喜爱的人：fan; enthusiast | 棋～ qímí *chess fan; chess enthusiast* / 戏～ xìmí *theatre fan*

歌迷 gēmí   球迷 qiúmí

❹ [动]使人分辨不清或陶醉：fascinate; enchant | 景色～人 jǐngsè mírén *the scenery is enchanting*

迷人 mírén enchanting; captivating; attractive

谜 (謎) mí 11画 讠部

谜 谜谜谜谜谜谜谜谜谜谜谜

❶ [名]暗射事物或文字等让人猜测的言语：riddle; conundrum ｜ 猜～cāimí *guess a riddle* / 灯～dēngmí *riddle written on lanterns; lantern riddle*

谜语 míyǔ riddle; conundrum

❷ [名]比喻还没有弄明白的或难以理解的事物：(fig.) enigma; mystery; puzzle ｜ 这对我来说是个～。Zhè duì wǒ lái shuō shì ge mí. *It's a mystery to me.*

米 mǐ 6画 米部

米 米米米米米米米

❶ [名]去掉壳或皮后的种子等：shelled seed ｜ 花生～huāshēngmǐ *shelled peanut; peanut kernel*

小米 xiǎomǐ　　玉米 yùmǐ

❷ [名]稻米；大米：rice ｜ 买一袋～mǎi yī dài mǐ *buy a bag of rice*

米饭 mǐfàn cooked rice

米粉 mǐfěn ① ground rice; rice flour ② rice noodles

大米 dàmǐ　　稻米 dàomǐ

❸ [量]法定长度单位：metre (international system of unit of length)

毫米 háomǐ　　厘米 límǐ

立方米 lìfāngmǐ

秘 mì 10画 禾部

秘 秘秘秘秘秘秘秘秘秘秘

[形] 不公开的；叫人摸不透的：secret; mysterious ｜ ～方 mìfāng *secret recipe* / ～诀 mìjué *the secret (of success)*

秘密 mìmì ① secret; clandestine; confidential ② sth. secret

奥秘 àomì　　神秘 shénmì

◇秘书 mìshū secretary

文秘 wénmì

密 mì 11画 宀部

密 密密密密密密密密密密密

❶ [形]隐蔽的，不公开的：secret; confidential ｜ ～谈 mìtán *(have) a secret talk* / ～谋 mìmóu *conspire; plot*

密码 mìmǎ cipher; cipher code; secret code

机密 jīmì

❷ [名]秘密：secret

保密 bǎomì　　解密 jiěmì

秘密 mìmì

❸ [形]事物之间距离近、间隔小（跟"疏shū"相对）：close; dense; thick (the opposite of "疏shū") ｜ ～林 mìlín *thick (dense) forest* / 树长得很～。Shù zhǎng de hěn mì. *The trees grow thick.*

密度 mìdù density

密封 mìfēng ① sealed up ② seal airtight; seal hermetically

密集 mìjí concentrated; crowd-ed together

稠密 chóumì 紧密 jǐnmì

茂密 màomì 严密 yánmì

❹[形]关系近；感情好：intimate; close | ～友 mìyǒu *close friend; bosom buddy*

密切 mìqiè ① close; intimate ② (forge; establish) close links (between two parties)

亲密 qīnmì

亲密无间 qīnmì-wújiàn

❺[形] 细致：fine; meticulous | 细～ xìmì *fine and closely-woven; detailed; meticulous*

精密 jīngmì 周密 zhōumì

◇哈密瓜 hāmìguā

蜜 mì 14画 宀部

蜜蜜蜜蜜蜜蜜蜜蜜
蜜蜜蜜蜜蜜蜜

❶[名] 蜂蜜：honey | 苹果～ píngguǒmì *apple honey* / 蜜蜂在采～。Mìfēng zài cǎimì. *Bees are collecting honey.*

蜜蜂 mìfēng honeybee; bee

蜂蜜 fēngmì

❷[形] 甜美：sweet; luscious | 甜言～语 tiányán-mìyǔ *sweet talk; honeyed words* / 像～一样甜 xiàng mì yīyàng tián *as sweet as honey*

甜蜜 tiánmì

眠 mián 10画 目部

眠眠眠眠眠眠眠眠
眠眠

[动] 睡觉：sleep | 失～ shīmián *suffer from insomnia* / 安～ ānmián *sleep peacefully* / 他整夜未～。Tā zhěngyè wèi mián. *He was up all night.*

睡眠 shuìmián

棉 mián 12画 木部

棉棉棉棉棉棉棉棉
棉棉棉棉

[名] cotton | 这件衣服是纯～的。Zhè jiàn yīfu shì chúnmián de. *This garment is made of pure cotton.*

棉花 miánhua cotton

棉衣 miányī cotton-padded clothes

棉织品 miánzhīpǐn cotton goods; cotton textiles; cotton fabrics

免 miǎn 7画 丶部

免免免免免免免

❶[动]去掉；除掉：remove; dismiss; relieve | ～职 miǎnzhí *remove sb. from office; relieve sb. of his post* / ～税 miǎnshuì

514

duty free

免除 miǎnchú ① prevent; avoid ②remit; excuse; exempt; relieve

免费 miǎnfèi free of charge; free; gratis

免去 miǎnqù ① excuse sb. from sth; exempt; dispense with ② remove from office; dismiss; relieve

减免 jiǎnmiǎn

❷[动]避开：avoid; avert; escape | ～受灾害 miǎnshòu zāihài *avert a calamity (disaster)*

免得 miǎnde so as not to; so as to avoid

避免 bìmiǎn　　不免 bùmiǎn

难免 nánmiǎn　　未免 wèimiǎn

以免 yǐmiǎn

不可避免 bùkěbìmiǎn

勉 miǎn　9画 力部

勉 勉勉勉勉勉勉勉勉勉 勉

❶[动]鼓励：encourage; urge; exhort | 自～zìmiǎn *spur oneself on* / 互～hùmiǎn *encourage each other*

勉励 miǎnlì exert oneself; try hard; make a great effort

❷[动]能力不够或心里不愿意而尽力做：manage with an effort; do sth. with difficulty; strive to do what is beyond one's power

勉强 miǎnqiǎng ① manage with an effort; do with difficulty

② reluctant; grudging ③ force sb. to do sth.

面 (麵 ❼-❾) miàn 9画 面部

面 面面面面面面面面 面

❶[名] 脸：face | 笑容满～xiào-róng mǎnmiàn *have a broad smile on one's face* / 脸～liǎn-miàn *face; self-respect*

面部 miànbù face; front part of the head

面孔 miànkǒng face

面貌 miànmào ① face; features ② appearance (of things); look; aspect

面目 miànmù ① face; features; visage ②apearance (of things); look; aspect

面前 miànqián in (the) face of; in front of; before

面容 miànróng facial features; countenance; face

面对面 miànduìmiàn facing each other; face-to-face

面巾纸 miànjīnzhǐ face tissues

出面 chūmiàn　当面 dāngmiàn

对面 duìmiàn　会面 huìmiàn

见面 jiànmiàn　露面 lòumiàn

迎面 yíngmiàn

❷[动] 向着；朝着：face (a certain direction) | 背山～水 bèi shān miàn shuǐ *with hills behind and the river in front* / 这房

子～南。Zhè fángzi miàn nán. *The house faces south.*

面对 miànduì confront; face

面临 miànlín be faced with; be confronted with; be up against

❸ [名] 事物的部位或方面：side or aspect of a thing

面面俱到 miànmiàn-jùdào attend to each and every aspect; give mature consideration to all aspects

北面 běimiàn　背面 bèimiàn

表面 biǎomiàn　侧面 cèmiàn

层面 céngmiàn　东面 dōngmiàn

反面 fǎnmiàn　方面 fāngmiàn

负面 fùmiàn　后面 hòumian

里面 lǐmian　片面 piànmiàn

前面 qiánmian　全面 quánmiàn

上面 shàngmian　西面 xīmiàn

下面 xiàmian　右面 yòumiàn

正面 zhèngmiàn　左面 zuǒmiàn

单方面 dānfāngmiàn

四面八方 sìmiàn-bāfāng

一面…一面… yīmiàn...yīmiàn...

❹ [名] 物体的表面，物体外面的那一层：the external surface of sth. flat; surface; face | 镜～ jìngmiàn *surface of a mirror /* 被～儿 bèimiànr *facing of a quilt /* 水～ shuǐmiàn *surface of water*

面积 miànjī area

版面 bǎnmiàn　场面 chǎngmiàn

地面 dìmiàn　封面 fēngmiàn

海面 hǎimiàn　画面 huàmiàn

局面 júmiàn　路面 lùmiàn

平面 píngmiàn

书面 shūmiàn

❺ [量] 用于扁平或能展开的东西：used for sth. flat and thin or sth. that can be extended | 一～旗 yī miàn qí *a flag /* 一～镜子 yī miàn jìngzi *a mirror /* 一～锣 yī miàn luó *a gong*

❻ [量] 用于表示见面的次数：used to indicate the number of meetings | 见过一～ jiànguo yī miàn *have met once*

❼ [名] 粮食磨成的粉：flour | 小米～ xiǎomǐmiàn *millet flour /* 玉米～ yùmǐmiàn *maize flour; cornmeal*

面包 miànbāo bread

面粉 miànfěn wheat flour; flour

面条 miàntiáo noodles

❽ [名] 像面粉一样的东西；粉末：powder-like things | 药～儿 yàomiànr *medicine powder /* 粉笔～儿 fěnbǐmiànr *chalk powder (or dust)*

❾ [名] 面条：noodles | 挂～ guàmiàn *dried noodles /* 切～ qiēmiàn *freshly cut noodles*

◇ 面试 miànshì interview

面子 miànzi ① outer part; outside; face ② reputation; prestige; face

爱面子 àimiànzi

见世面 jiànshìmian

miáo　8画 艹部

苗 苗苗苗苗苗苗苗苗苗

❶[名]初生的植物；有时专指某些蔬菜的嫩茎、嫩叶：young plant; seedling; (sometimes) tender parts of certain vegetables | 树~shùmiáo *young trees* / 麦~儿 màimiáor *wheat seedling* / 禾苗 hémiáo

❷[名]某些初生的饲养的动物：the young of some animals | 鱼~ yúmiáo *(fish) fry* / 猪~zhūmiáo *piglet; pigling*

 描　　　miáo　11画　扌部

描 描描描描描描描描描 描描描

❶[动]照原样画或写：trace; copy | ~图样miáo túyàng *trace designs; copy designs* / 把这些字都~下来。Bǎ zhèxiē zì dōu miáo xiàlai. *Copy all these words down.*

描绘 miáohuì depict; describe; portray

描述 miáoshù describe

描写 miáoxiě describe; depict; portray

扫描 sǎomiáo

❷[动]重复地涂抹：retouch | 写毛笔字不要~。Xiě máobǐzì bùyào miáo. *Don't retouch when writing Chinese characters with a brush pen.*

 秒　　　miǎo　9画　禾部

秒 秒秒秒秒秒秒秒秒 秒

[量]计算时间的单位：second (unit of time) | 在比赛中他跑了45~。Zài bǐsài zhōng tā pǎole sìshíwǔ miǎo. *He ran the race in 45 seconds.*

 渺　　　miǎo　12画　氵部

渺 渺渺渺渺渺渺渺渺 渺渺渺渺

[形]微小：tiny; insignificant 渺小miǎoxiǎo tiny; negligible; insignificant; paltry

妙　　　miào　7画　女部

妙 妙妙妙妙妙妙妙

❶[形]美好：wonderful; fine | 这办法真~。Zhè bànfǎ zhēn miào. *It's an excellent idea.* / 这首诗真~。Zhè shǒu shī zhēn miào. *The poem is wonderful.* 美妙 měimiào

❷[形]神奇：ingenious; subtle | ~计 miàojì *brilliant scheme* / ~用 miàoyòng *magical effect* 奇妙 qímiào 巧妙 qiǎomiào 微妙 wēimiào 莫名其妙 mòmíng-qímiào

庙 (廟) miǎo　8画 广部

庙 庙庙庙庙庙庙庙庙

[名] 供祖先、神、佛及历史上名人的处所：temple; shrine | 孔~ Kǒngmiào the Confucian Temple / 龙王~lóngwángmiào the Dragon-king Temple

庙会 miǎohuì temple fair
寺庙 sìmiào

灭 (滅) miè　5画 火部

灭 灭灭灭灭灭

❶[动] 熄灭；使熄灭：extinguish; put out | ~灯 mièdēng turn off the light / 火~了。Huǒ miè le. The fire died out.
扑灭 pūmiè　　熄灭 xīmiè
❷[动] 不再存在；使不再存在：eliminate; wipe out | ~蝇 miè yíng kill flies
灭亡 mièwáng be destroyed; become extinct; die out
毁灭 huǐmiè　　歼灭 jiānmiè
消灭 xiāomiè

蔑 miè　14画 艹部

蔑 蔑蔑蔑蔑蔑蔑蔑蔑蔑蔑蔑蔑蔑蔑

[形] 小；轻微：slight; inconsider-able | 轻~qīngmiè disdain
蔑视mièshì despise; show contempt for; scorn

民 mín　5画 一部

民 民民民民民

❶[名] 人民：people | 为人~wèi rénmín for the people
民间 mínjiān ① among the people; popular; folk ②nongovernmental
民警 mínjǐng police; policeman
民意 mínyì will of the people; popular will
民众 mínzhòng masses of the people; general public; the populace
民主 mínzhǔ ① democracy; democratic rights ②democratic
民族 mínzú nation; nationality; ethnic group
便民 biànmín　村民 cūnmín
公民 gōngmín　国民 guómín
居民 jūmín　　难民 nànmín
贫民 pínmín　平民 píngmín
全民 quánmín　人民 rénmín
市民 shìmín　　网民 wǎngmín
选民 xuǎnmín　移民 yímín
灾民 zāimín
国民党 guómíndǎng
人民币 rénmínbì
殖民地 zhímíndì

殖民主义 zhímín zhǔyì

❷[名]民间：of the people; folk ｜ ～歌 míngē *folk song* / ～谣 mínyáo *folk rhyme* / ～俗 mínsú *folk custom; folkways*

❸[名]某个民族的人：member of an ethnic group ｜ 回～Huímín *the Hui people* / 藏～Zàngmín *the Zang (Tibetan) people* 少数民族 shǎoshù mínzú

❹[名]从事某种职业的人：person engaged in a certain occupation ｜ 牧～mùmín *herdsman*

民工 míngōng labourer working on a public project; farm labourer

股民 gǔmín　农民 nóngmín 渔民 yúmín

❺[名]非军人；非军事的：civilian ｜ 公～gōngmín *citizen*

民兵 mínbīng ① people's militia; militia ② militiaman

民航 mínháng civil aviation

民事 mínshì relating to civil law; civil

民用 mínyòng for civil use; civil

敏　　mǐn　11画 攵部

敏 敏 敏 敏 敏 敏 敏 敏 敏 敏 敏

[形] 灵活；反应快：quick; nimble ｜ ～锐 mǐnruì *sharp; acute* / 机～jīmǐn *alert and re-*

sourceful

敏感 mǐngǎn sensitive; susceptible

敏捷 mǐnjié quick; nimble; agile

敏锐 mǐnruì sharp; acute; keen

灵敏 língmǐn　过敏 guòmǐn

名　　míng　6画 夕部

名 名 名 名 名 名 名

❶[名]人或事物的称呼：name of a person or thing ｜ 人～rénmíng *person's name* / 地～dìmíng *name of a place* / 他～叫小华。Tā míng jiào Xiǎohuā.*His given name is Xiaohua.*

名称 míngchēng name (of a thing or organization)

名词 míngcí ① (gram.) noun; substantive ② term; phrase ③ (log.) name

名单 míngdān name list

名片 míngpiàn visiting card; business card

名字 míngzi name

报名 bàomíng　点名 diǎnmíng 更名 gēngmíng　化名 huàmíng 命名 mìngmíng　签名 qiānmíng 提名 tímíng　无名 wúmíng 姓名 xìngmíng　罪名 zuìmíng 黑名单 hēimíngdān

❷[名] 名义：name; excuse by which sth. is done ｜ 他以参加比

赛为～不来上课。Tā yǐ cānjiā bǐsài wéi míng bù lái shàngkè. *He was absent from school on the pretext of attending a competition.*

名义 míngyì ① name ② nominal; titular; in name

❸ [名] 声誉：fame; reputation | 有～ yǒumíng *well-known* / ～利 mínglì *fame and gain*

名声 míngshēng reputation; repute; renown

名誉 míngyù ① fame; reputation ② honorary

名副其实 míngfùqíshí the name matches the reality; be sth. in reality as well as in name; be worthy of the name

成名 chéngmíng

出名 chūmíng 闻名 wénmíng

知名 zhīmíng

赫赫有名 hèhè-yǒumíng

举世闻名 jǔshì-wénmíng

❹ [形] 有名的：famous; well-known | ～医 míngyī *a well-known doctor* / ～画 mínghuà *a well-known picture* / ～言 míngyán *well-known saying; maxim; aphorism*

名贵 míngguì famous and precious; rare

名牌 míngpái ①famous brand ② nameplate; name tag

名气 míngqì (inf.) reputation; fame; name

名人 míngrén famous person; eminent person; celebrity; notables

名胜 míngshèng place famous for its scenery or historical relics; scenic spot

名胜古迹 míngshèng-gǔjì places of historical interest and scenic beauty; scenic spots and historical sites

❺ [量] 用于人：used for people | 一～学生 yī míng xuésheng *a student*

◇名次 míngcì position in a name list; place in a competition

名额 míng'é the number of people assigned or allowed; quota of people

排名 páimíng

莫名其妙 mòmíng-qímiào

明 míng 8画 日部

明 明明明明明明明明

❶ [形] 亮（跟"暗 àn"相对）：bright (the opposite of "暗 àn") | 灯火通～ dēnghuǒ tōngmíng *be brightly lit; be brilliantly illuminated* / 天～了。Tiān míng le. *Day is breaking.*

明朗 mínglǎng ① bright and clear ② clear; obvious ③ forthright; bright and cheerful

明亮 míngliàng well-lit; bright

明星 míngxīng a famous performer; star

明信片 míngxìnpiàn postcard
光明 guāngmíng 黎明 límíng
透明 tòumíng 鲜明 xiānmíng
照明 zhàomíng
清明节 Qīngmíngjié
透明度 tòumíngdù

❷[形]（从当前算起的）第二（年、日）: next; immediately following in time
明年 míngnián next year
明天 míngtiān ① tomorrow ② the near future

❸[形]明白；清楚: clear; distinct | 不~ bùmíng unknown; not clear / 分~ fēnmíng distinct; sharply contrasted
明白 míngbai ①clear; plain ② unequivocal; explicit ③ understand; realize; know
明明 míngmíng (adv.) obviously; plainly; undoubtedly
明确 míngquè clear and definite; clear-cut; unequivocal
明显 míngxiǎn clear; obvious; evident; distinct
表明 biǎomíng 查明 chámíng
简明 jiǎnmíng 声明 shēngmíng
说明 shuōmíng 证明 zhèngmíng
指明 zhǐmíng 注明 zhùmíng
说明书 shuōmíngshū

❹[形]视力好；有眼光: clear-sighted; sharp-eyed | 眼~手快 yǎn-míng-shǒukuài quick of eye and deft of hand; sharp and quick
聪明 cōngming

高明 gāomíng 开明 kāimíng

鸣（鳴）míng 8画 口部

鸣 鸣鸣鸣鸣鸣鸣鸣鸣

❶[动]（鸟兽或昆虫）叫: (of birds, animals or insects) cry | 鸟~ niǎo míng cry (or singing) of birds / 鸡~ jī míng crowing of a cock / 蝉~ chán míng chirping of cicadas

❷[动]发出声响；使发出声响: make a sound; ring | 雷~ léi míng thunder / ~礼炮 míng lǐpào fire a salute
共鸣 gòngmíng

❸[动]表达（情感、意见、看法）: express (emotions, opinions, etc.); voice; air | ~谢 míngxiè express one's thanks formally / ~不平 míngbùpíng complain of unfairness; cry out against injustice
百家争鸣 bǎijiā-zhēngmíng

命 mìng 8画 人部

命 命命命命命命命命

❶[动]上级对下级发出指示: order; command | 学校~你立即返校。Xuéxiào mìng nǐ lìjí fǎnxiào. The school has ordered you to return immediately.
命令 mìnglìng order; command

任命 rènmìng

❷[名]命令；指示：order; instruction | 奉~ fèngmìng *receive orders; act under orders* / 遵~ zūnmìng *obey a command* / 随时待~ suíshí dàimìng *await orders at any time*

使命 shǐmìng

❸[名]命运：destiny; fate; lot | 算~ suànmìng *tell sb.'s fortune* / 听天由~ tīngtiān-yóumìng *submit to the will of Heaven; trust to luck; resign oneself to one's fate* / 他的~真苦。Tā de mìng zhēn kǔ. *He has a hard lot.*

命运 mìngyùn destiny; fate; lot
本命年 běnmìngnián

❹[名]生命：life | 救~ jiùmìng *save sb.'s life; Help! Help!*

命根子 mìnggēnzi one's very life; lifeblood

拼命 pīnmìng 生命 shēngmìng
寿命 shòumìng 性命 xìngmìng
要命 yàomìng 致命 zhìmìng
生命力 shēngmìnglì

❺[动] 给予或确定：assign; determine

命名 mìngmíng name (sb. or sth.)

命题 mìngtí ① assign a topic; set a question ② proposition

 (謬) miù 13画 讠部
. . . .

 谬谬谬谬谬谬谬谬
谬谬谬谬谬

[形]错误的；不合情理的：wrong; false, erroneous; mistaken | ~误 miùwù *mistake; error; falsehood*

谬论 miùlùn fallacy; false (absurd) theory; falsehood

荒谬 huāngmiù

摸 | 摸 mō 13画 扌部

摸摸摸摸摸摸摸摸
摸摸摸摸摸

❶[动]用手接触或抚摩：feel; stroke; touch | ~~多光滑 mōmo duō guānghuá *feel how smooth it is* / 我~了他的额头，觉得烫手。Wǒ mōle tā de étóu, juéde tàngshǒu. *I touched his forehead and found it very hot.*

❷[动]用手取；寻找：feel for; grope | ~鱼 mōyú *grope for fish (in water)* / 他在口袋里~出一个硬币。Tā zài kǒudai li mōchu yī gè yìngbì. *He fished out a coin from his pocket.*

摸索 mōsuǒ feel about

❸[动]试着了解；试着做：try to find out; sound out | ~底 mōdǐ *try to find out sb.'s real intention or the real situation; sound sb. out; know the real situation* /

先～清情况 xiān mōqīng qíngkuàng *try to find out the real situation first* / 我～准他的脾气了。Wǒ mōzhǔn tā de píqi le. *I've found out his temperament very well already.*

摸索 mōsuǒ *try to find out*

❹ [动] 在黑暗中行动：go in the dark; grope for | ～黑 mōhēi *grope in the dark* / ～了半夜才到家 mōle bànyè cái dào jiā *arrive at home after feeling one's way back for a long time in the night*

模 mó 14画 木部

模模模模模模模模
模模模模模模

❶ [名] 标准；规范：pattern; standard | ～范 mófàn *an exemplary person or thing; model; fine example*

模式 móshì *pattern*
模型 móxíng *model*
规模 guīmó

❷ [动] 仿效：imitate; copy | ～拟 mónǐ *imitate; simulate*

模仿 mófǎng *imitate; copy; model oneself on*

◇ 模糊 móhu ① blurred; indistinct; dim; vague ② blur; obscure; confuse; mix up

模特儿 mótèr *model*

See mú.

膜 mó 14画 月部

膜膜膜膜膜膜膜膜
膜膜膜膜膜膜

❶ [名] 人或动物体内像薄皮一样的组织：membrane | 耳～ěrmó *tympanic membrane; eardrum*

❷ [名] 像膜一样的薄皮：film; thin coating | 一层薄～yī céng bómó *a layer of thin film*

摩 mó 15画 麻部

摩摩摩摩摩摩摩摩
摩摩摩摩摩摩摩

[动] rub; scrape; touch

摩擦 mócā ① rub ② friction ③ clash (between two parties); friction

按摩 ànmó

◇ 摩托车 mótuōchē *motorcycle*
摩托艇 mótuōtǐng *motorboat*

磨 mó 16画 麻部

磨磨磨磨磨磨磨磨
磨磨磨磨磨磨磨磨

❶ [动] 用磨料磨物体使光滑、锋利：grind; polish; sharpen | ～刀 módāo *sharpen a knife* / ～剪子 mó jiǎnzi *grind (sharpen) scissors*

琢磨 zhuómó

❷ [动] 摩擦：rub; wear | 袜子～

523

破了。Wàzi mópò le. *The socks are worn out.* / 这种布耐～。Zhè zhǒng bù nài mó. *This kind of cloth is durable.* / 他手上～起了泡。Tā shǒushang móqǐle pào. *His hands were blistered from rubbing.*

磨合 móhé break in; grind in; wear in

磨嘴皮 mózuǐpí (dial.) argue pointlessly

❸ [动]消耗时间；拖延：waste time; dawdle | ～时间 mó shíjiān *dawdle; waste time*

磨洋工 móyánggōng dawdle over one's work (in a broad sense); loaf on the job; lie down on the job

❹ [动]折磨；纠缠：wear down; wear out | 这病真～人!Zhè bìng zhēn mó rén! *What a torment this illness is!* / 别老来～我!Bié lǎo lái mó wǒ! *Don't keep bothering me!* / 他不答应，你就跟他～。Tā bù dāying, nǐ jiù gēn tā mó. *If he doesn't agree, just keep on at him until he does.*

折磨 zhémó

蘑 | mó | 19画 艹部

蘑蘑蘑蘑蘑蘑蘑蘑
蘑蘑蘑蘑蘑蘑蘑
蘑蘑蘑

See 蘑菇

蘑菇 mógu mushroom

魔 | mó | 20画 麻部

魔魔魔魔魔魔魔魔
魔魔魔魔魔魔魔
魔魔魔魔

❶ [名]宗教或神话传说里的鬼怪；也比喻邪恶的坏人：evil spirit; demon; devil; monster | 恶～ èmó *evil spirit* / 病～ bìngmó *tormenting illness*

魔鬼 móguǐ devil; demon; monster

❷ [形]神秘；奇异：magic; mystic | ～力 mólì *magic power*

魔术 móshù magic; conjuring; sleight of hand

抹 | mǒ | 8画 扌部

抹抹抹抹抹抹抹抹

❶ [动]涂上：smear; put on | ～粉 mǒ fěn *put on powder* / ～药 mǒ yào *apply ointment*

❷ [动]涂掉；除去：erase; cross out | ～去零头 mǒqù língtou *wipe away the remnants* / 把这一行～了。Bǎ zhè yī háng mǒ le. *Cross out this line.*

抹杀 mǒshā blot out; obliterate

❸ [动]擦拭：wipe | ～眼泪 mǒ yǎnlèi *wipe one's eyes; weep* / ～

把脸mǒ bǎ liǎn *wipe one's face*

末　mǒ　5画　木部

末　末末末末末

❶[名]梢；尽头：tip; end ｜ ～梢 mǒshāo *tip; end*

❷[形]最后；终了：end; last stage ｜ 月～yuèmǒ *end of a month* / ～班车mǒbānchē *last train or bus; last chance* / 本世纪～běnshìjì mǒ *the end of this century* 周末 zhōumǒ

❸[名] 不是根本的、主要的事物（跟"本běn"相对）：trivial matter; trifle; the minutest detail in everything (the opposite of "本běn") ｜ 本～倒置 běnmǒ-dàozhì *take the branch for the root; put the cart before the horse*

❹[名]碎屑；细粉：powder; dust ｜ 肉～儿 ròumǒr *minced meat* / 茶叶～儿 cháyèmǒr *tea dust; broken tea leaves* / 粉笔～儿 fěnbǐmǒr *chalk powder* 粉末 fěnmǒ

陌　mǒ　8画　阝(左)部

陌　陌陌陌陌陌陌陌陌

See below

陌生 mǒshēng strange; unfamiliar

陌生人 mǒshēngrén stranger

莫　mǒ　10画　艹部

莫　莫莫莫莫莫莫莫莫莫莫莫

❶[副]不：do not; no one; nothing; none ｜ ～名其妙 mǒmíng-qímiào *be unable to make head or tail of sth.; be baffled*

❷[副]不要：no; not ｜ 闲人～入 xiánrén mǒ rù *no admittance except on business* / ～提此事 mǒ tí cǐ shì *don't mention it*

墨　mǒ　15画　黑部

墨　墨墨墨墨墨墨墨墨墨墨墨墨墨墨

❶[名]写字绘画用的黑色颜料：ink ｜ ～汁 mǒzhī *prepared Chinese ink* / 磨～mómǒ *rub an ink stick against an inkstone* / ～太稠了。Mǒ tài chóu le. *This ink is too thick.* 墨盒 mǒhé inkbox (for Chinese calligraphy or painting); ink cartridge

❷[名]泛指写字、绘画或印刷用的某种颜料：certain colour or material for painting or printing ｜ 油～yóumǒ *printing ink* / 蓝～lánmǒ *blue ink* 墨水儿 mǒshuǐr ① ink ② book

— see note; marginal index: 末 陌 莫 墨　mǒ

525

learning

❸[名]借指写的字和画的画：written words or paintings ｜ ～宝 mòbǎo *treasured scrolls of calligraphy or painting*

◇墨镜 mòjìng *sunglasses*

默 mò 16画 黑部

默 默默默默默默默默
默默默默默默默默

[动]不说话；不出声：silent; tacit; quiet ｜ ～读 mòdú *read silently* / ～记 mòjì *silently remember* / ～认 mòrèn *give tacit consent to; acquiesce to*

默默 mòmò quiet; silent
沉默 chénmò

谋 (謀) móu 11画 讠部

谋 谋谋谋谋谋谋谋谋
谋谋谋

❶[动]想主意；策划：plan; plot: ～划 móuhuà *plan; scheme*
谋杀 móushā murder
参谋 cānmóu

❷[名]主意；计策：plan; scheme ｜ 有勇无～yǒuyǒng-wúmóu *more brave than wise; bold but not crafty*
阴谋 yīnmóu

❸[动]设法找到或取得：work for; seek ｜ ～职 móuzhí *look for a*

job; apply for a post ｜ 为人民～幸福 wèi rénmín móu xìngfú *strive for the happiness of the people*

谋求 móuqiú seek; strive for; be in quest of

某 mǒu 9画 甘部

某 某某某某某某某某
某

❶[代]指不确定的或不便明确地说出来的人或事物：(of people, place, thing) certain; some ｜ ～人 mǒurén *someone; somebody; a certain person* / ～工厂 mǒu gōngchǎng *a certain factory* / ～地 mǒudì *a certain place* / ～年 mǒunián *a certain year*

某个 mǒugè certain; so-and-so
某些 mǒuxiē certain (people, places, things)

❷[代]用在姓氏后，指确定的人或自称：(used after a surname) certain person or oneself ｜ 李～Lǐ mǒu *a certain person called Li; a certain Li* / 我张～不敢不同意。Wǒ Zhāng mǒu bùgǎn bù tóngyì. *I, Zhang, dare not go against it.*

模 mú 14画 木部

模模模模模模模模
模模模模模模

[名] 形状：mould; pattern
模样 múyàng appearance; look
See mó.

母 mǔ 5画 母部

母 母母母母母母

❶[名]妈妈：mother | 家~jiāmǔ
my mother / ~女 mǔnǚ *mother
and daughter*
母亲 mǔqīn mother
母语 mǔyǔ ① mother tongue ②
parent language; native language
父母 fùmǔ
❷[名]亲属中的长辈女子：one's
female elders | 姑~gūmǔ
father's sister; aunt / 姨~yímǔ
mother's sister; aunt
伯母 bómǔ   舅母 jiùmǔ
祖母 zǔmǔ   外祖母 wàizǔmǔ
❸[形] (禽兽)雌性的(跟"公 gōng"
相对)：female (the opposite of
"公 gōng") | ~鸡 mǔjī *hen* /
~牛 mǔniú *cow*
❹[名] 最初的或能产生其他事物的
东西：origin; parent | ~校
mǔxiào *one's old school; alma
mater*
分母 fēnmǔ   声母 shēngmǔ
韵母 yùnmǔ   字母 zìmǔ

 (畝) mǔ   7画 亠部

亩 亩亩亩亩亩亩亩

[量] 我国的土地面积单位：*mu*,
Chinese unit of area | ~产量
mǔchǎnliàng *yield per* mu

姆 mǔ 8画 女部

姆 姆姆姆姆姆姆姆姆

See 保姆
保姆 bǎomǔ

木 mù 4画 木部

木 木木木木

❶[名] 树：tree | 草~cǎomù
trees and grass / 伐~fámù *fell
trees*
灌木 guànmù   树木 shùmù
❷[名] 木头；木料：wood; timber
| 松~sōngmù *pinewood*
木材 mùcái wood; timber; lumber
木匠 mùjiang carpenter
木头 mùtou (inf.) wood; log;
timber
❸ [形]身体某些部位失去知觉：
numb | 舌头~了。Shétou mù
le. *My tongue has gone numb.* /
两脚冻~了。Liǎng jiǎo
dòngmù le. *Both feet were
numb with cold.*

麻木 mámù

◇木瓜 mùguā ① (bot.) Chinese flowering quince ② (dial.) papaya

目   mù   5画目部

目 目 目 目 目 目

❶[名]眼睛：e y e｜双~失明 shuāngmù shīmíng *be blind in both eyes* /~瞪口呆mùdēng-kǒudāi *be stunned (speechless); dumbstruck*

目睹 mùdǔ see with one's own eyes; witness

目光 mùguāng ①sight; vision; view ② gaze; look

目前 mùqián at present; at the moment

目击者 mùjīzhě eyewitness; witness

目中无人 mùzhōng-wúrén consider everyone beneath one's notice; be supercilious; be overweening

盲目 mángmù   面目 miànmù
心目 xīnmù   醒目 xǐngmù
注目 zhùmù

举世瞩目 jǔshì-zhǔmù

引人注目 yǐnrén-zhǔmù

❷[名]项目，大项下分成的小项：item within a larger category｜细~xìmù *specific item; detail*

节目 jiémù   科目 kēmù
项目 xiàngmù

❸[名]目录，按一定顺序列出的内容名称：catalogue; table of contents｜价~jiàmù *price list* /剧~jùmù *a list of plays or operas* / 书~shūmù *book list*

目录 mùlù ① list; catalogue ② table of contents; contents

栏目 lánmù   曲目 qǔmù

◇目标 mùbiāo ① objective; target ② goal; aim; objective

目的 mùdì purpose; aim; goal; objective; end

目的地 mùdìdì destination

牧   mù   8画牛部

牧 牧 牧 牧 牧 牧 牧 牧

[动]放养牲畜：tend (sheep, cattle, etc.); herd｜~羊mùyáng *tend sheep* / ~童mùtóng *shepherd boy; buffalo boy*

牧场 mùchǎng grazing land; pasture; ranch

牧民 mùmín herdsman

牧区 mùqū pastoral area

牧业 mùyè animal husbandry; stock raising

畜牧 xùmù

墓   mù   13画艹部

墓 墓 墓 墓 墓 墓 墓 墓
墓 墓 墓 墓 墓

[名]埋葬死人的地方：grave; tomb

| 公～gōngmù *cemetery* / 烈
士～lièshìmù *tomb of a revolutionary martyr*
坟墓 fénmù

幕　mù　13画 艹部

幕幕幕幕幕幕幕幕
幕幕幕幕幕

❶[名] 覆盖或悬挂的大块的布、绸等；帐篷：curtain; canopy; tent | ～已经拉开，演出就要开始了。Mù yǐjīng lākāi, yǎnchū jiùyào kāishǐ le. *The curtain has been raised, and the performance is about to start.*

闭幕 bìmù　　黑幕 hēimù
揭幕 jiēmù　　开幕 kāimù
内幕 nèimù　　屏幕 píngmù
银幕 yínmù
闭幕式 bìmùshì

❷[量] 戏剧的一个段落：act of a play or an opera | 第二～dì-èr mù *the second act* / 独～剧 dúmùjù *one-act play*
序幕 xùmù

睦　mù　13画 目部

睦睦睦睦睦睦睦睦
睦睦睦睦睦

[形] 关系好；亲近：peaceful; harmonious | ～邻 mùlín *good relationship (with one's neighbour or a neighbouring country)*
和睦 hémù

慕　mù　14画 艹部

慕慕慕慕慕慕慕慕
慕慕慕慕慕慕

[动] 敬仰；喜爱：admire | 爱～àimù *admire; love; adore* / 仰～yǎngmù *look up to with admiration*
羡慕 xiànmù

穆　mù　16画 禾部

穆穆穆穆穆穆穆穆
穆穆穆穆穆穆穆穆

See 穆斯林
穆斯林 mùsīlín Moslem; Muslim

N n

ná　10画 手部

拿拿拿拿拿拿拿拿
拿拿

❶[动]用手取或握住；搬：hold; take; carry │ ～东西 ná dōngxi *take something* /～出来 ná chūlai *take out* /你把书～来。Nǐ bǎ shū nálái. *Bring the book here.*

❷[动]捕捉；夺取：seize; capture │ 这个工程两年就能～下来。Zhège gōngchéng liǎng nián jiù néng ná xiàlai. *This project can be completed in two years.*

❸[动]装出或做出（某种姿态、样子）：put on; assume │ ～架子 ná jiàzi *put on airs*

❹[动]领取；得到：get; obtain; receive │ ～工资 ná gōngzī *get one's pay* /～一等奖 ná yīděngjiǎng *get first prize*

❺[动]掌握：have a firm grasp of; be sure of │ ～主意 názhǔyi *make a decision* /这事你～得准吗？Zhè shì nǐ nádezhǔn ma? *Are you sure about it?*

❻[介]引进所凭借的工具、方法等；用：by means of; with; by │ ～水洗 ná shuǐ xǐ *wash with*

water /～尺量 ná chǐ liáng *measure with a ruler* /～眼睛看 ná yǎnjing kàn *look squarely at* /～事实来证明 ná shìshí lái zhèngmíng *prove with facts*

❼[介]引进所处理的对象：used in the same way as "把bǎ" │ 你别～我当小孩。Nǐ bié ná wǒ dāng xiǎohái. *Don't treat me like a child.* /我～你当朋友看待。Wǒ ná nǐ dāng péngyou kàndài. *I regard you as my friend.*

哪

nǎ　9画 口部

哪哪哪哪哪哪哪哪
哪

❶[代]用于疑问，要求在同类事物中确认一个：(used in questions) which, or what │ 你喜欢读～种书？Nǐ xǐhuan dú nǎ zhǒng shū? *What kind of books do you like to read?* /～本书是你的？Nǎ běn shū shì nǐ de? *Which book is yours?* /你学的是～国语言？Nǐ xué de shì nǎ guó yǔyán? *What foreign language are you studying?*

哪儿 nǎr ① where ② wherever; anywhere ③ used in rhetorical questions to express negation, same as "how could"?

哪个 nǎge ① which ② who

哪里 nǎli ① where ② wherever;

where ③ (used as a polite reply to a compliment) I'm flattered

哪怕 nǎpà even; even if; even though; no matter how

哪些 nǎxiē which ones

❷[代] 指任何一个：which | 这些衣服～一件也不合适。Zhè xiē yīfu nǎ yī jiàn yě bù héshì. *None of these dresses fits me.*

❸[代] 用于虚指，表示不确定的一个：used in statements to indicate sth. indefinite | 你～天来都行。Nǐ nǎ tiān lái dōu xíng. *You can come any time.*

❹[副] 用于反问，表示否定：used in rhetorical questions to indicate negation | ～有这样的事? Nǎ yǒu zhèyàng de shì? *Is that possible?* /～能这样马虎? Nǎ néng zhèyàng mǎhu? *How could you be so careless?*

那　nà　6画 阝(右)部

那 那那那那那那

❶[代] 指称比较远的人或事物（跟"这 zhè"相对）：that (the opposite of "这 zhè") | ～天 nà tiān *that day* /～是我的家。Nà shì wǒ de jiā. *That is my house.* /～是谁? Nà shì shéi? *Who is that?* /～本书不见了。Nà běn shū bù jiàn le. *I can't find that book.*

那边 nàbiān over there

那个 nàge that

那里 nàli that place; there

那时 nàshí at that time; then; in those days

那些 nàxiē those

那样 nàyàng of that kind; such; so

❷[代] 代替比较远的人或事物：used to replace a relatively distant person or object

❸[连] 连接上文说明结果：then; in that case | 他不来，～就得另外找人了。Tā bù lái, nà jiù děi lìngwài zhǎo rén le. *If he doesn't come, we will have to find someone else.* / 如果你喜欢，～就买吧! Rúguǒ nǐ xǐhuan, nà jiù mǎi ba! *If you like it, buy it then!*

那么 nàme ① like that; in that way ② about; or so ③ then; in that case; such being the case

纳 (納) nà　7画 纟部

纳 纳纳纳纳纳纳纳

❶[动] 放进；接受：accept; let in; admit | 出～ chūnà *receive and pay out money; cashier; teller*

采纳 cǎinà　　归纳 guīnà

接纳 jiēnà　　容纳 róngnà

吸纳 xīnà

❷[动] 交付：pay; offer

纳税 nàshuì pay taxes

交纳 jiāonà
◇纳闷儿 nāmènr feel puzzled; be perplexed; wonder
纳粹 Nàcuì Nazi

呐 na 7画 口部

呐 呐呐呐呐呐呐呐

[助] 用法同 "呢 ne"：used in the same way as "呢 ne"
❶ 表示疑问的语气：used at the end of a rhetorical question to indicate an interrogative mood | 怎么办～?Zěnme bàn na? *What should we do?* / 我错在哪儿～? Wǒ cuò zài nǎr na? *Where have I gone wrong?*
❷ 用在陈述句的末尾，表示确认事实：used at the end of an indicative sentence to indicate confirmation of a fact | 收获不小～。Shōuhuò bù xiǎo na. *You have gained a lot.* / 到车站还有好几公里～。Dào chēzhàn háiyǒu hǎo jǐ gōnglǐ na. *We have several kilometres to go to the station.*
❸ 用在陈述句的末尾，表示正在进行：used at the end of an indicative sentence to indicate that sth. is in progress | 天下着雨～。Tiān xiàzhe yǔ na. *It's raining now.* / 老吴，有人找你～。Lǎo Wū, yǒu rén zhǎo nǐ na. *Lao Wu, somebody is looking for you.*
❹ 用在句中表示停顿：used in a sentence to indicate a pause | 我骑自行车去，你们～，坐汽车去。Wǒ qí zìxíngchē qù, nǐmen na, zuò qìchē qù. *I will go there by bike and you ...go by bus.*

乃 nǎi 2画 丿部

乃 乃乃

[动] 是；就是：be | 失败～成功之母。Shībài nǎi chénggōng zhī mǔ. *Failure is the mother of success.*

奶 nǎi 5画 女部

奶 奶奶奶奶奶奶

❶ [名] 乳房：breast
❷ [名] 乳汁；乳制品：milk; dairy product | 羊～yángnǎi *sheep's milk* / ～油 nǎiyóu *cream* / 妈妈正在给孩子喂～。Māma zhèng-zài gěi háizi wèi nǎi. *The mother is breast-feeding the baby (or giving the baby milk).*
奶茶 nǎichá tea with milk
奶粉 nǎifěn milk powder; powdered milk; dried milk
奶牛 nǎiniú dairy cow; milk cow; cow

牛奶 niúnǎi

◇奶奶 nǎinai ① (paternal) grand-mother; grandma ② a respectful form of address for an old woman

耐 nài 9画 而部

耐 耐耐耐耐耐耐耐耐 耐

[动] 忍受得住；禁得起：be able to endure or bear | ～洗 nàixǐ *be durable for washing* /～穿 nàichuān *be durable for wearing* / 这种植物～寒。Zhè zhǒng zhíwù nàihán. *This plant can resist the cold.*

耐烦 nàifán patient

耐力 nàilì endurance; staying power; stamina

耐心 nàixīn patient

耐用 nàiyòng durable

忍耐 rěnnài

男 nán 7画 田部

男 男男男男男男男

[形] 男性（跟 "女 nǚ" 相对）：man; male (the opposite of "女 nǚ") | ～学生 nánxuésheng *male student; boy student* /～演员 nányǎnyuán *actor*/ 一～一女 yī nán yī nǚ *one male and one female*

男人 nánrén ① man ② menfolk

③ husband

男生 nánshēng male student; boy student; schoolboy

男士 nánshì man; gentleman

男性 nánxìng ① the male sex ② man

男友 nányǒu boyfriend

男子 nánzǐ man; male

男孩儿 nánháir ① boy ② son

男女老少 nā-nǚ-lǎo-shào men and women, old and young

南 nán 9画 十部

南 南南南南南南南 南

[名] 方向（跟 "北 běi" 相对）：south (the opposite of "北 běi") | 往～走 wǎng nán zǒu *go southwards* / 指～针 zhǐnánzhēn *compass* / 这屋子朝～。Zhè wūzi cháo nán. *The house faces south.*

南边 nánbian south

南部 nánbù southern part; south

南方 nánfāng ① south ② the southern part of the country

南海 Nánhǎi the Nanhai Sea; the South China Sea

南极 nánjí ① the South Pole; the Antarctic Pole ② the south magnetic pole

南美 Nánměi South America

南面 nánmiàn south; the south-ern side

南半球 Nánbànqiú the South-
ern Hemisphere
南极洲 Nánjízhōu the Antarc-
tic Continent; Antarctica
南美洲 Nánměizhōu South
America
东南 dōngnán　　西南 xīnán
指南 zhǐnán
◇南瓜 nánguā pumpkin; cushaw

难 (難) nán　　10画 又部

难 难难难难难难难难
难难

❶ [形] 做起来费事 (跟 "易 yì" 相
对)：difficult; hard; trouble-
some (the opposite of "易 yì") |
路~走。Lù nán zǒu. *The road
is rough.* / 题目很~。Tímù hěn
nán. *The questions are quite
difficult.* / 说起来容易，做起
来~。Shuō qǐlai róngyì, zuò
qǐlai nán. *Easier said than
done.* / 韩语并不~学。Hányǔ
bìng bù nán xué. *Korean is
not difficult to learn.*
难处 nánchǔ hard to get along
(or on) with
难处 nánchu difficulty;
trouble
难得 nándé ①hard to come by;
rare ② seldom; rarely
难点 nándiǎn a difficult point;
difficulty; a hard nut to crack
难度 nándù degree of difficulty;
difficulty
难怪 nánguài ①no wonder ②
understandable; pardonable
难关 nánguān difficulty; crisis
难堪 nánkān ①intolerable; un-
bearable ② embarrassed
难免 nánmiǎn hard to avoid
难题 nántí difficult problem;
hard nut to crack
难忘 nánwàng unforgettable;
memorable
难以 nányǐ hard to; difficult to
艰难 jiānnán　　困难 kùnnán
为难 wéinán　　疑难 yínán
出难题 chūnántí

❷ [形] 不好 (跟 "好 hǎo" 相对)：
bad (the opposite of "好 hǎo")
| ~听 nántīng *unpleasant to
the ear* / ~吃 nánchī *taste bad*
难过 nánguò ① have a hard
time ② feel sorry; feel bad; be
upset
难看 nánkàn ①ugly; unsightly
② shameful; embarrassing
难受 nánshòu ① feel unwell;
feel ill; suffer pain ② feel unhappy; feel bad
◇难道 nándào used to reinforce
a rhetorical question
　　See nàn.

难 (難) nàn　　10画 又部

难 难难难难难难难难
难难

[名]不幸的遭遇：calamity; disaster; trouble | 逃～táonàn *flee from danger; be a refugee* / 大～临头 dànàn-líntóu *be faced with imminent disaster*
难民 nànmín refugee
苦难 kǔnàn　　　遇难 yūnàn
灾难 zāinàn
　　　See nàn.

 挠 (撓) nǎo　　9画 扌部

挠 挠挠挠挠挠挠挠挠 挠

[动] 阻止：hinder; disturb
阻挠 zǔnáo

恼 (惱) nǎo　　9画 忄部

恼 恼恼恼恼恼恼恼恼 恼

❶ [动] 生气：be/get angry; annoy | 气～qìnǎo *angry; incensed* / 你别～我。Nǐ bié nǎo wǒ. *Don't be angry with me.*
恼火 nǎohuǒ annoyed; irritated; vexed
❷ [形] 烦闷; 心里不痛快：vexed; worried; unhappy
烦恼 fánnǎo　　　苦恼 kǔnǎo

脑 (腦) nǎo　　10画 月部

脑 脑脑脑脑脑脑脑脑 脑脑

❶ [名] brain | 用～过度 yòng nǎo guòdù *overtax one's brain* / 你必须自己动～。Nǐ bìxū zìjǐ dòng nǎo. *You must use your head.*
脑筋 nǎojīn ① brains; mind; head ② way of thinking; ideas
脑力 nǎolì mental power; intelligence
脑子 nǎozi brains; mind; head
大脑 dànǎo　　　电脑 diànnǎo
头脑 tóunǎo
伤脑筋 shāngnǎojīn
昏头昏脑 hūntóu-hūnnǎo
头昏脑胀 tóuhūn-nǎozhàng
❷ [名]头：head | 探头探～tàntóu-tànnǎo *pop one's head in and look about*
脑袋 nǎodai ① head ② brain; mind
首脑 shǒunǎo

闹 (鬧) nào　　8画 门部

闹 闹闹闹闹闹闹闹闹

❶ [形] 声音响而杂乱：noisy | ～市 nàoshì *busy streets; downtown area* /这里很～。Zhèli hěn nào. *It is very noisy here.*
热闹 rènao 凑热闹 còurènao
❷ [动] 吵嚷; 争吵：raise hell; make a noise; stir up trouble | 又哭

又～yǒu kū yǒu nǎo *make a tearful scene* / 他俩昨天～了一场。Tā liǎ zuótiān nǎole yī chǎng. *The two of them made a scene yesterday.*

❸[动] 搅乱; 扰乱: disturb; mess up | ～翻了天 nǎofānle tiān *make a hell of a fuss* /～事 nǎoshì *create a disturbance; make trouble*

❹[动] 发生; 发作 (不好的事情): make (sth. bad) happen | ～矛盾 nǎo máodùn *be at loggerheads* /～脾气 nǎo píqi *vent one's spleen; lose one's temper*
闹别扭 nǎobièniu be difficult with sb.; be at odds with sb.
闹笑话 nǎoxiàohua make a fool of oneself; make a stupid mistake

❺[动] 发泄 (感情): give vent (to one's anger or resentment) | ～情绪 nǎo qíngxù *be disgruntled; be in low spirits*

❻[动] 搞; 弄; 干: go in for; make | 把问题～清楚 bǎ wèntí nǎo qīngchu *get things clear in one's mind*

❼[动] 戏耍; 玩笑: do sth. for fun; joke
闹着玩儿 nǎozhewǎnr be joking

呢
ne　8画 口部

呢 呢呢呢呢呢呢呢呢

❶[助] 用在疑问句 (特指问、选择问、正反问) 的末尾, 表示疑问的语气: used at the end of a question to denote interrogation | 你问谁～? Nǐ wèn shéi ne? *Who are you asking?* / 问题出在哪儿～? Wèntí chū zài nǎr ne? *Where is the problem?; What's the matter?* / 他怎么会忘了～? Tā zěnme huì wàngle ne? *How could he forget?*

❷[助] 用在陈述句的末尾, 表示确认事实: used at the end of an indicative sentence to confirm a fact | 早着～zǎozhe ne *it is still early* / 他还没有来～。Tā hái méiyǒu lái ne. *He hasn't come yet.* / 这次学习, 收获不小～。Zhè cì xuéxí, shōuhuò bù xiǎo ne. *We have benefited a lot from this learning session.*

❸[助] 用在陈述句的末尾, 表示动作或情况正在继续: used at the end of a declarative sentence to indicate the continuation of an action or situation | 外边正下着雨～。Wàibian zhèng xiàzhe yǔ ne. *It is raining outside.* / 他正睡觉～。Tā zhèng shuìjiào ne. *He is sleeping now.*

❹[助] 用在句中表示停顿或表示对举: used in the middle of a sentence to mark a pause (oft. meaning "one way or another") | 你要是饿了～, 就自己做点儿吃

的。*Nǐ yàoshì èle ne, jiù zìjǐ zuòdiǎnr chī de.* If you are hungry, make some food for yourself. / 喜欢～，你就买；不喜欢～，就别买。*Xǐhuan ne, nǐ jiù mǎi; bù xǐhuan ne, jiù bié mǎi.* Buy it if you like it, if you don't then don't buy it.

内   nèi   4画 门部

内 内内内内

[名] 里面(跟"外wài"相对)：inside (the opposite of "外wài") | ～衣 nèiyī *underwear* / 国～ guónèi *internal; home; domestic* / 由～到外yóu nèi dào wài *from the inside to the outside*

内部 nèibù ① inside; interior; within ② inside; restricted

内存 nèicún internal memory; storage or storage capacity as of a computer

内地 nèidì inland; interior; hinterland

内阁 nèigé cabinet

内行 nèiháng ① be expert at; be adept in; know the ins and outs of ② expert; a dab hand; master

内科 nèikē (department of) internal medicine

内裤 nèikù underwear; under-clothes

内幕 nèimù what goes on behind the scenes; inside story

内容 nèiróng content; substance

内外 nèiwài ① inside and outside; domestic and foreign ② around; about

内心 nèixīn heart; innermost being

内在 nèizài inherent; intrinsic; internal; inner

内脏 nèizàng internal organs; viscera

内战 nèizhàn civil war

内政 nèizhèng internal (domestic, home) affairs

境内 jìngnèi   室内 shìnèi
以内 yǐnèi   在内 zàinèi
之内 zhīnèi

嫩   nèn   14画 女部

嫩 嫩嫩嫩嫩嫩嫩嫩嫩嫩嫩嫩嫩嫩嫩

❶ [形] 初生而柔弱的(跟"老lǎo"相对)：tender; delicate (the opposite of "老lǎo") | ～芽 nènyá *shoots* / ～叶 nènyè *tender leaves* / 孩子的小手又白又～。*Háizi de xiǎo shǒu yòu bái yòu nèn.* The child's little hands are fair and delicate.

❷ [形] 食物烹调时间短，软而好嚼

（跟"老lǎo"相对）：(of cooked food) rare; tender; underdone (the opposite of "老lǎo") | 这肉片炒得很～。Zhè ròupiàn chǎo de hěn nèn. *The stir-fried sliced meat is quite tender.* / 鸡蛋煮得～。Jīdàn zhǔdenèn. *The boiled egg is tender.*

❸ [形]（颜色）浅：light | ～黄 nènhuáng *light yellow* /这衣服颜色太～，我穿不合适。Zhè yīfu yánsè tài nèn, wǒ chuān bù héshì. *The colour of the dress is too light for me.*

能

能 néng 10画 厶部

能 能能能能能能能能能能

❶ [名] 才干; 本领：ability; capability

能力 nénglì ability; capacity; capability

本能 běnnéng 才能 cáinéng
功能 gōngnéng 技能 jìnéng
潜能 qiánnéng 全能 quánnéng
体能 tǐnéng 性能 xìngnéng
职能 zhínéng 智能 zhìnéng
多功能 duōgōngnéng
无能为力 wúnéng-wéilì

❷ [形] 有才干的：able; capable | ～人 néngrén *able person* /你真～，一个人干两个人的活。Nǐ zhēn néng, yī gè rén gàn liǎng gè rén de huó. *You are really capable! You have done the work of two.*

能手 néngshǒu dab hand; expert; master

❸ [动] 表示有能力或有条件做某事：be able to; be capable of | 他～完成任务。Tā néng wánchéng rènwù. *He is able to complete the assignment.* / 他还不～来。Tā hái bùnéng lái. *It is not convenient for him to come yet.* / 这么简单的题，你应该～做。Zhème jiǎndān de tí, nǐ yīnggāi néng zuò. *The problem is simple, you should be able to solve it.*

力所能及 lìsuǒnéngjí

❹ [动] 表示善于做某事：be good at doing sth. | 我们当中他最～写。Wǒmen dāngzhōng tā zuì néng xiě. *He is the best at writing among us.*

能干 nénggàn able; capable; competent

能歌善舞 nénggē-shànwǔ can both sing and dance; be good at singing and dancing

❺ [动] 表示有可能：can possibly
可能 kěnéng

❻ [动] 表示有某种用途：have some purpose

❼ [动] 表示情理、环境上许可：be possible; be probable

能够 nénggòu can; be able to; be capable of

只能 zhǐnéng

❸[名] 能量：energy
能量 néngliàng energy
能源 néngyuán source of energy; energy resource; energy
节能 jiénéng
太阳能 tàiyángnéng
原子能 yuánzǐnéng

 嗯 ńg 13画 口部

嗯 嗯嗯嗯嗯嗯嗯嗯嗯嗯嗯嗯嗯嗯嗯

[叹] 表示疑问：used to indicate query | ～?你说什么?Ńg? Nǐ shuō shénme? *Eh? What did you say?*

 尼 ní 5画 尸部

尼 尼尼尼尼尼

See 尼龙
尼龙 nílóng nylon

 泥 ní 8画 氵部

泥 泥泥泥泥泥泥泥泥

❶[名]土和水混合成的东西：mud; mire | 烂～lànní *slush* / 刚下过雨，地上都是～。Gāng xiàguo yǔ, dì shang dōu shì ní. *After the rain, there is mud all over the place.*
泥土 nítǔ ① earth; soil ② clay

❷[名]像泥一样的东西：substance like paste or pulp | 印～yìnní *red ink paste used for seals* / 枣～zǎoní *jujube paste* / 肉～ròuní *mince meat*
水泥 shuǐní

 拟（擬） nǐ 7画 扌部

拟 拟拟拟拟拟拟拟

❶[动] 设计；起草：draft; draw up | ～稿nǐgǎo *make a draft* /～一个计划 nǐ yī gè jìhuà *draw up a plan*
拟定 nǐdìng draw up; draft; work out

❷[动] 打算；想要：intend; plan | ～发表 nǐ fābiǎo *intend to publish* /～采用 nǐ cǎiyòng *intend to adopt* / 我校～在下周进行考试。Wǒ xiào nǐ zài xiàzhōu jìnxíng kǎoshì. *Our school is planning to hold exams next week.*
◇ 模拟 mónǐ　　虚拟xūnǐ

 你 nǐ 7画 亻部

你 你你你你你你你

❶[代] 称对方（一个人）：you (singular) | ～好。Nǐ hǎo. *How are you?* /这是～的书。Zhè shì nǐ de shū. *This is your book.* /～的歌唱得真好。Nǐ de gē chàng de zhēn hǎo. *You sing really well.*

你们 nǐmen you (plural)

❷ [代] 泛指任何人（有时实际上指"我"）：used to refer to anyone, sometimes the speaker himself / herself | ～想成功，就得努力。Nǐ xiǎng chénggōng, jiù děi nǔlì. *If you want to succeed, you have to work hard.* / ～如果骄傲自满，就不会进步。Nǐ rúguǒ jiāo'ào zìmǎn, nǐ jiù bùhuì jìnbù. *If you are proud and complacent, you will not progress.*

❸ [代] 单位间互相称呼对方：used as an address for the other party | ～方 nǐ fāng *your side; you* / 请～校选派三名学生参加。Qǐng nǐ xiào xuǎnpài sān míng xuésheng cānjiā. *Please select three pupils from your school to participate.*

逆 nì 9画 辶部

逆 逆逆逆逆逆逆逆逆 逆

❶ [动] 向反方向（活动）：counter; go against | ～风 nìfēng *go against the wind* / ～水行舟 nìshuǐ-xíngzhōu *sail against the current*

逆流 nìliú go against the current; countercurrent

❷ [形] 不顺当：adverse | ～境

nìjìng *adverse circumstances*

年 nián 6画 丿部

年 年年年年年年

❶ [名] 地球绕太阳运行一周的时间：year, the period of time the earth takes to travel once round the sun | 他离家已经20～了。Tā lí jiā yǐjīng èrshí nián le. *It has been twenty years since he left home.* / 我在这个学校学习了五～。Wǒ zài zhège xuéxiào xuéxíle wǔ nián. *I have studied at this school for five years.*

年底 niándǐ the end of the year

年度 niándù year (a yearly period fixed for a certain purpose)

年级 niánjí grade; year

年薪 niánxīn annual salary; yearly pay

年头儿 niántóur ① the beginning of a year ② year ③ years; a long time

常年 chángnián   后年 hòunián

今年 jīnnián   来年 láinián

历年 lìnián   连年 liánnián

明年 míngnián   前年 qiánnián

去年 qùnián   同年 tóngnián

往年 wǎngnián   学年 xuénián

终年 zhōngnián   周年 zhōunián

逐年 zhúnián

本命年 běnmìngnián

长年累月 chángnián-lěiyuè

❷ [名] 年纪；岁数：age | ～老

niánlǎo *old; at an old age* / ~

过六十 nián guò liùshí *over sixty (years old)*

年纪 niánjì age

年龄 niánlíng age

年青 niánqīng young

年轻 niánqīng young

年轻人 niánqīngrén young people

❸ [名]人的一生中按年龄划分的阶段：a period in one's life

成年 chéngnián

老年 lǎonián 青年 qīngnián

少年 shàonián 童年 tóngnián

晚年 wǎnnián 中年 zhōngnián

成年人 chéngniánrén

老年人 lǎoniánrén

青少年 qīng-shàonián

中老年 zhōng-lǎonián

未成年人 wèichéngniánrén

❹ [名]时期；时代：a period in history | 光绪 ~ 间 Guāngxù niánjiān *during the reign of Emperor Guangxu*

年代 niándài ① age; years; time ② a decade of a century

当年 dāngnián 近年 jìnnián

❺ [名]年节：lunar New Year; the Spring Festival | ~ 画儿 niánhuàr *New Year pictures* / ~ 货 niánhuò *purchases for the Spring Festival*

年糕 niángāo New Year cake (made of glutinous rice flour)

年夜饭 niányèfàn the lunar New Year's Eve dinner

拜年 bàinián 过年 guònián

新年 xīnnián

逢年过节 féngnián-guòjié

捻 niǎn 11画 扌部

捻捻捻捻捻捻捻捻捻捻捻

[动]用手指搓：twist sth. with the fingers | ~ 胡子 niǎn húzi *twist one's beard* / ~ 麻绳 niǎn máshéng *twist hemp strings*

撵 (撵) niǎn 15画 扌部

撵撵撵撵撵撵撵撵撵撵撵撵撵撵

[动]驱逐；赶走：drive out; oust | ~ 走 niǎnzǒu *drive sb. away* / ~ 出去 niǎn chūqu *drive sb. out*

念 niàn 8画 心部

念念念念念念念念

❶ [动]惦记；常常想：think of; miss | 妈妈一直 ~ 着你。Māma yīzhí niànzhe nǐ. *Mother misses you all the time.* / 他已离家十年，但还常常 ~ 着故乡。Tā yǐ líjiā shí nián, dàn hái chángcháng niànzhe gùxiāng. *Though he has been away from home for 10 years,* he still often misses his homeland.

悼念 dàoniàn　惦念 diànniàn
怀念 huáiniàn　纪念 jìniàn
留念 liúniàn　　思念 sīniàn
想念 xiǎngniàn
纪念碑 jìniànbēi
纪念馆 jìniànguǎn
纪念品 jìniànpǐn
纪念日 jìniànrì

❷[名] 想法或打算：thought; idea; intention | 杂～zániàn *distracting thoughts*
念头 niàntou thought; idea; intention
概念 gàiniàn　观念 guānniàn
理念 lǐniàn　　信念 xìnniàn
悬念 xuánniàn

❸[动] 读：read | ～诗 niàn shī *read a poem* / 请再～一遍。Qǐng zài niàn yī biàn. *Please read it again.* / 他激动得～不下去了。Tā jīdòng de niàn bù xiàqù le. *He was in such an excited mood that he could not read on.*
念书 niànshū read; study

❹[动] 指上学：go to school | 她已经～中学了。Tā yǐjīng niàn zhōngxué le. *She is already in secondary school.* / 小王～过大学。Xiǎo Wáng niánguo dàxué. *Xiao Wang has finished his college education already.*

娘　　niáng 10画 女部

娘　娘娘娘娘娘娘娘
娘娘

❶[名] 母亲：mother | 孩子想～。Háizi xiǎng niáng. *The child misses his mother.*

❷[名] 称长一辈或年长已婚女性：form of address for an elderly married woman | 婶～shěnniáng *aunt*
大娘 dàniáng

❸[名] 年轻女子：general term for young women
姑娘 gūniang　新娘 xīnniáng
伴娘 bànniáng

酿 (釀)　niàng 14画 酉部

酿酿酿酿酿酿酿酿
酿酿酿酿酿酿

❶[动] 通过发酵作用制造：make; brew | ～酒 niàngjiǔ *make wine* / ～造 niàngzào *make (wine, vinegar, etc.)*

❷[动] 逐渐形成：lead to; result in | ～成水灾 niàngchéng shuǐzāi *lead to flood*
酝酿 yùnniàng

❸[动] 蜜蜂做蜜：(of bees) make honey | ～蜜 niàngmì *make honey*

鸟 (鳥)　niǎo 5画 鸟部

鸟 鸟鸟鸟鸟鸟

[名] bird
候鸟 hòuniǎo

尿　　niào　7画 尸部

尿 尿尿尿尿尿尿尿

❶[名] urine ｜撒～sāniǎo *pass water*
糖尿病 tángniàobìng
❷[动] 撒尿：urinate ｜孩子～了。Háizi niào le. *The child urinated.*

捏　　niē　10画 扌部

捏 捏捏捏捏捏捏捏捏捏捏

❶[动] 用拇指和其他手指夹住：hold between fingers and thumb ｜～着一根针 niēzhe yī gēn zhēn *hold a needle* / 手里～着一张纸条 shǒuli niēzhe yī zhāng zhǐtiáo *hold a slip of paper in one's hand*
❷[动] 用手指把软东西做成一定的形状：knead with fingers ｜～泥人 niē nírén *mould clay figurines* /～饺子 niē jiǎozi *make dumplings*
❸[动] 假造；虚构：fabricate; fake; make up
捏造 niēzào fabricate; concoct; fake; trump up

您　　nín　11画 心部

您 您您您您您您您您您您您

[代] 你的尊称：respectful form of address for "你nǐ" ｜～先请。Nín xiān qǐng. *After you, please.* / 请～多多指教。Qǐng nín duōduō zhǐjiào. *Please kindly give us your advice.*

宁（寧）níng　5画 宀部

宁 宁宁宁宁宁

[形] 安宁：peaceful; tranquil
宁静 níngjìng peaceful; tranquil; quiet; calm
See nìng.

柠（檸）níng　9画 木部

柠 柠柠柠柠柠柠柠柠柠

See 柠檬
柠檬 níngméng lemon

凝　　níng　16画 冫部

凝 凝凝凝凝凝凝凝凝凝凝凝凝凝凝凝凝

❶[动] 气体变为液体或液体变为固体：congeal; condense

凝固 nínggù solidify
凝结 níngjié congeal; coagulate; curdle; condense

❷[动]聚集; 集中: fix (one's attention); concentrate | ~神 níng-shén *with fixed attention*
凝聚 níngjù (of vapour) condense; (of fluids) coagulate or curdle
凝视 níngshì gaze fixedly; stare

 拧 (擰) nǐng   8画 扌部

拧 拧拧拧拧拧拧拧拧

[动]控制住物体向里转或向外转: twist; wring | ~开瓶盖儿 nǐng-kāi pínggàir *twist the cap off a bottle* | ~螺丝钉 nǐng luósī dīng *drive a screw* /把水龙头~紧 bǎ shuǐlóngtóu nǐngjǐn *tighten up the tap*

 宁 (寧) nìng   5画 宀部

宁 宁宁宁宁宁

[副]宁可: rather; would rather | ~早勿晚。Nìng zǎo wù wǎn. *Better early than late.* /~死不屈 nìngsǐ-bùqū *would rather die than submit*
宁可 nìngkě would rather
宁肯 nìngkěn would rather
宁愿 nìngyuàn would rather

See níng.

 牛   niú   4画 牛部

牛 牛牛牛牛

[名] cow; ox; cattle | 奶~ nǎiniú *milk cow* /这头~老了。Zhè tóu niú lǎo le. *The cow is getting old.*
牛奶 niúnǎi milk
牛肉 niúròu beef
牛仔裤 niúzǎikù jeans
吹牛 chuīniú
牵牛花 qiānniúhuā

 扭   niǔ   7画 扌部

扭 扭扭扭扭扭扭扭

❶[动]拧伤（筋骨）: sprain; wrench | ~了筋 niǔle jīn *wrench sinews* /~了腰 niǔle yāo *strain one's lower back*

❷[动]掉转; 转动: turn round; move | ~过脸来 niǔguò liǎn lai *turn one's head round* /~转身 niǔzhuàn shēn *turn round*
扭转 niǔzhuàn turn back; reverse; turn round

❸[动]身体左右摇摆: roll; swing | ~秧歌 niǔ yāngge *do the yangge dance (a traditional dance of northern China)* /~着身子走路 niǔzhe shēnzi zǒu lù *walk with a swagger; strut*

N

544

◇扭曲 niǔqū twist; distort
闹别扭 nàobièniu

纽 (紐) niǔ　7画 纟部

纽 纽纽纽纽纽纽纽

See 纽扣儿
　　纽扣儿 niǔkòur button

农 (農) nóng　6画 、部

农 农农农农农农

[名] 农业: agriculture; farming |
务～wùnóng go in for agriculture; do farming
农场 nóngchǎng farm
农村 nóngcūn rural area; countryside; village
农户 nónghù peasant/farmer household
农具 nóngjù farm implements; farmtools
农历 nónglì the traditional Chinese calendar; the lunar calendar
农民 nóngmín peasant; farmer
农田 nóngtián farmland; cropland; cultivated land
农药 nóngyào agricultural chemical; farm chemical; pesticide
农业 nóngyè agriculture; farming
农产品 nóngchǎnpǐn agricultural product; farm produce

农作物 nóngzuòwù crops
农贸市场 nóngmào shìchǎng market for farm produce

浓 (濃) nóng　9画 氵部

浓 浓浓浓浓浓浓浓浓
浓

[形] 稠密; 含某种成分多 (跟 "淡
dàn" 相对): dense; thick (the opposite of "dàn") | ～烟
nóngyān dense smoke / 茶很～。Chá hěn nóng. The tea tastes strong.
浓度 nóngdù consistency; concentration; density
浓厚 nónghòu ① strong; pronounced ② dense; thick
浓缩 nóngsuō (chem.) concentrate; enrich
浓郁 nóngyù (of perfume, fragrance, etc.) strong; rich

弄 nòng　7画 廾部

弄 弄弄弄弄弄弄弄

❶[动] 手里拿着玩: play with; toy with; fool with | 不要～火
bùyào nòng huǒ don't play with fire / 小孩儿爱～沙土。Xiǎoháir ài nòng shātǔ. Children like to play with sand.
玩弄 wánnòng
❷ [动] 搞; 做; 办: do; manage;

handle ｜ ～饭吃 nòng fàn chī *prepare the meal* /把身上～干净 bǎ shēn shang nòng gānjìng *clean oneself* /别把机器～坏了。 Bié bǎ jīqì nònghuài le. *Be careful not to damage the machine.*

弄虚作假 nòngxū-zuòjiǎ *practise fraud; employ trickery; resort to deception*

❸ [动]设法取得：manage to get ｜ ～点水来 nòng diǎn shuǐ lái *fetch some water* /听说那个话剧不错，你去～几张票吧! Tīngshuō nàge huàjù bùcuò, nǐ qù nòng jǐ zhāng piào ba! *People say the play is good. Try to get several tickets.*

 nú 5画 女部

奴 奴奴奴奴奴

❶ [名]受人压迫和使唤，没有人身自由的人：slave ｜ 农～nóngnú *serf* /家～jiānú *lackey; servant* 奴隶 núlì slave

❷ [动]像对待奴隶一样：enslave; treat as a slave 奴役 núyì enslave; keep in bondage

 nǔ 7画 力部

努 努努努努努努努

[动]尽量地使出（力气）：put forth one's strength; exert oneself 努力 nǔlì make great efforts; try hard; exert oneself

 nù 9画 心部

怒 怒怒怒怒怒怒怒怒怒

❶ [形]生气：angry; furious ｜ 发～fānù *fly into a rage* /他～气冲冲地走了。 Tā nùqì chōngchōng de zǒu le. *He left in great fury.* 怒火 nùhuǒ flames of fury; fury 愤怒 fènnù 喜怒哀乐 xǐ-nù-āi-lè

❷ [形]气势强、猛烈：forceful; vigorous; dynamic ｜ ～涛 nùtāo *furious billows* / 狂风～号。 Kuángfēng nùháo. *A violent wind is howling.* / 百花～放 bǎihuā nùfàng *all the flowers are in full bloom* 怒吼 nùhǒu roar; howl

 nǔ 3画 女部

女 女女女

❶ [形]女性的（跟"男 nán"相对）：female (the opposite of "男 nán") ｜ ～士 nǔshì *lady* / ～学生 nǔxuésheng *female student* / 男～平等 nánnǔ píngděng

equality between men and women

女儿 nǚ'ér daughter

女郎 nǚláng a young woman; maiden; girl

女人 nǚrén woman; womenfolk

女生 nǚshēng female student; girl student; schoolgirl

女士 nǚshì (a polite term for a woman, married or unmarried) lady; madam

女王 nǚwáng queen

女性 nǚxìng ① the female sex ② woman

女子 nǚzǐ woman; female

女孩儿 nǚháir ① girl ② daughter

女朋友 nǚpéngyou girlfriend

妇女 fūnǚ   美女 měinǚ

少女 shàonǚ   仙女 xiānnǚ

男女老少 nán-nǚ-lǎo-shào

❷ [名] 女儿：daughter

儿女 érnǚ   闺女 guīnǚ

孙女 sūnnǚ   侄女 zhínǚ

子女 zǐnǚ

独生子女 dúshēng zǐnǚ

生儿育女 shēng'ér-yùnǚ

nuǎn 13画 日部

暖 暖暖暖暖暖暖暖暖暖 暖暖暖暖暖

[形] 不冷也不热：neither hot nor cold; warm | 春～花开 chūn-nuǎn-huākāi *flowers blossom in warm spring* | 天气～了。Tiānqì nuǎn le. *It's getting warm.*

暖和 nuǎnhuo ① (of weather; environment, etc.) warm; nice and warm ② drink some hot water to warm oneself up

暖气 nuǎnqì central heating

温暖 wēnnuǎn

---

nuó   9画 扌部

挪 挪挪挪挪挪挪挪挪挪

[动] 移动；转移：move; shift | 请您～一下。Qǐng nín nuó yīxià. *Will you move aside a little, please?* | 把桌子～到门口去。Bǎ zhuōzi nuódào ménkǒu qù. *Move the table to the door.*

O o

噢 ō　15画　口部

噢噢噢噢噢噢噢噢噢噢噢噢噢噢噢

[叹] 表示了解：used to indicate sudden realization | ～, 就是他! Ō, jiùshì tā! *Oh, it's him!* / ～, 我懂了! Ō, wǒ dǒng le. *Oh, I see.*

哦 ó　10画　口部

哦哦哦哦哦哦哦哦哦哦

[叹] 表示将信将疑：used to indicate surprise or doubt | ～, 是这样的吗? Ó, shì zhèyàng de ma? *What! Is it true?* / ～, 是那样? Ó, shì nàyàng? *Oh, just like that?*

欧 (歐) ōu　8画　欠部

欧欧欧欧欧欧欧欧欧

[名] 指欧洲：Europe | ～美 Ōu-Měi *Europe and America* / 东～ Dōng'ōu *Eastern Europe*

欧元 ōuyuán euro
欧洲 Ōuzhōu Europe

殴 (毆) ōu　8画　殳部

殴殴殴殴殴殴殴殴

[动] 打(人)：beat up; hit | 斗～ dòu'ōu *fight*
殴打 ōudǎ beat up

呕 (嘔) ǒu　7画　口部

呕呕呕呕呕呕呕

[动] 吐：vomit; throw up | 吃的东西都～出来了。Chī de dōngxi dōu ǒu chūlai le. *Everything eaten was vomited out.*
呕吐 ǒutù vomit; throw up

偶 ǒu　11画　亻部

偶偶偶偶偶偶偶偶偶偶

❶ [形] 双数的；成对的(跟"奇 jī"相对)：even (numbers)(the opposite of "奇 jī"); in pairs | ～数 ǒushù *even number*
❷ [名] 夫妻或其中一方；mate; spouse | 佳～ jiā'ǒu *happily married couple*
配偶 pèi'ǒu
❸ [副] 不是必然的；不经常的：by chance/accident | ～发事件 ǒu-

噢 哦 欧 殴 呕 偶

ō ～ ǒu

O

548

fā shìjiàn *an accident; an accidental occurrence*

偶尔 ǒu'ěr once in a while

偶然 ǒurán ① by accident ② accidental

◇偶像 ǒuxiàng image; idol

偶

ǒu

O

P p

趴 pā 9画 足部

趴 趴趴趴趴趴趴趴趴趴

❶ [动] 胸腹朝下卧倒：lie on one's stomach; lie prone | ～在地上 pā zài dìshang *lie face down on the ground*

❷ [动] 身体向前靠在物体上：bend over; lean on | 弟弟～在桌子上画画。Dìdi pā zài zhuōzi shang huàhuà. *My brother was bending over the desk, drawing a picture.* / 孩子～在妈妈肩上睡着了。Háizi pā zài māma jiān shang shuìzháo le. *With her head on her mother's shoulder, the child fell asleep.*

扒 pā 5画 扌部

扒 扒扒扒扒扒

[动] 用手或工具使东西聚拢或散开：gather up; rake up | ～土 pátǔ *gather the dirt up* /他把草～在一起。Tā bǎ cǎo pá zài yīqǐ. *He raked the grass together.*
See bā.

爬 pá 8画 爪部

爬 爬爬爬爬爬爬爬

❶ [动] 伏在地上手、脚一齐用力向前移动：crawl; creep | 蚂蚁～到洞里去了。Mǎyǐ pádào dòng li qù le. *The ants crawled into the hole.* / 这孩子才会～。Zhè háizi cái huì pā. *The baby has just learnt to crawl.*
连滚带爬 liángǔn-dàipá

❷ [动] 抓住东西往上去；攀登：climb; scramble | ～山 páshān *climb a mountain* /～楼梯 pá lóutī *climb the stairs* / 猴子会～树。Hóuzi huì páshù. *Monkeys can climb trees.*

怕 pà 8画 忄部

怕 怕怕怕怕怕怕怕怕

❶ [动] 畏惧；害怕：fear; dread | 老鼠～猫。Lǎoshǔ pà māo. *Mice are afraid of cats.* /你别～那条狗。Nǐ bié pà nà tiáo gǒu. *Don't be frightened by the dog.* / 他不～死。Tā bù pà sǐ. *He was not scared of dying.*
害怕 hàipà

❷ [动] 担心：be afraid that...; expressing doubt or supposition | ～出差错 pà chū chācuò *be afraid of any errors* / 她～把孩

子吵醒。Tā pà bǎ háizi chǎo-xǐng. *She was afraid of waking the child.* / 她~在办公室找不到他。Tā pà zài bàngōngshì zhǎobudào tā. *She worried that he might not be in his office.*

恐怕 kǒngpà

❸[副] 表示估计：used to indicate supposition, estimation or judgement | 他~是不来了。Tā pà shì bù lái le. *I'm afraid that he won't come.* / 会议~要延期了。Huìyì pà yào yánqī le. *I'm afraid the meeting needs to be postponed.* / 事情~不这么简单。Shìqing pà bù zhème jiǎndān. *I'm afraid things are not so simple.*

拍
排

拍 **pāi** 8画 扌部

拍 拍拍拍拍拍拍拍拍

❶[动] 用手掌打：pat; clap; beat | ~球 pāiqiú *bounce a ball* /~手 pāishǒu *clap one's hands* / 他~了一下我的肩膀。Tā pāile yīxià wǒ de jiānbǎng. *He patted me on my shoulder.*

❷[名] 拍打东西的用具：racket; swatter | 球~儿 qiúpāir *bat; racket* / 蝇~儿 yíngpāir *flyswatter*

拍子 pāizi ① bat; racket ② beat; time

❸[动]发出：send | ~电报 pāi

diànbào *send a telegram*

❹[动] 摄影：shoot; photograph | ~照片 pāi zhàopiān *take a picture* / 公园里正在~电影。Gōngyuán li zhèngzài pāi diànyǐng. *They are shooting a film in the park.*

拍摄 pāishè take (a picture); shoot

拍照 pāizhào take a picture

❺[动]奉承：flatter | ~马屁 pāi mǎpì *lick someone's boots; flatter* / 吹吹~~ chuīchuī-pāipāi *boast and flatter*

◇拍卖 pāimài ① auction ② selling off goods at reduced price; sale

排 **pái** 11画 扌部

排 排排排排排排排排 排排排

❶[动] 除去；消除：exclude; eject; discharge | 打开门窗，把烟气~出去。Dǎkāi ménchuāng, bǎ yānqì pái chūqu. *Open the door and windows to let out the smoke.* / 大家动手，快把污水~出去。Dàjiā dòngshǒu, kuài bǎ wūshuǐ pái chūqu. *Let's work together to drain the dirty water.*

排斥 páichì ① exclude; repel ② exclude; reject

排除 páichú get rid of; over-

P
pāi
~
pái

come; remove

排放 páifàng ① discharge; let out; drain off ② place (things) in correct order

排挤 páijǐ push out;squeeze out

❷[动] 按顺序站位或摆放：arrange; put in order | 队伍～得很整齐。Duìwu pái de hěn zhěngqí. *They lined up in good order.* | 新学期要重新～座位。Xīn xuéqī yào chóngxīn pái zuòwèi. *The students' seats will be rearranged in the new semester.*

排队 páiduì queue up

排列 páiliè arrange; put in order

排名 páimíng rank

排行榜 páihángbǎng ranking list

安排 ānpái 并排 bìngpái

❸[名] 排成的横队：row | 他坐在第一～。Tā zuò zài dì-yī pái. *He sat in the first row.*

❹[名] 军队的编制单位：platoon, a military unit | 他是我们～的新兵。Tā shì wǒmen pái de xīnbīng. *He is a new recruit to our platoon.*

排长 páizhǎng platoon leader

❺[动] 演员练习剧目：rehearse | ～戏 páixì *rehearse* / 彩～ cǎipái *dress rehearsal* /～节目 pái jiémù *have a rehearsal*

排练 páiliàn rehearse

◇排球 páiqiú volleyball

徘
徘

pái   11画 彳部

徘徘徘徘徘徘徘
徘徘徘

See 徘徊

徘徊 páihuái ① pace up and down ② hesitate; waver

牌
牌

pái   12画 片部

牌牌牌牌牌牌牌
牌牌牌牌

❶[名] 用木板或其他材料做的标志：plate; tablet | 车～chēpái *(of vehicle) number plate* / 招～ zhāopai *signboard* / 路～lùpái *sign*

牌照 páizhào licence plate; licence tag; licence certificate; licence

牌子 páizi trademark; brand

红牌 hóngpái 黄牌 huángpái

奖牌 jiǎngpái 金牌 jīnpái

铜牌 tóngpái

挡箭牌 dǎngjiànpái

❷[名] 一种娱乐用品：cards, dominoes, etc. used for entertainment or in gambling | 纸～zhǐpái *playing cards* / 扑克～pūkèpái *playing cards; poker*

❸[名] 企业为自己的产品起的名称：brand; make | 解放～汽车 jiěfàngpái qìchē *a Liberation brand truck*

冒牌 màopái　　名牌 míngpái
品牌 pǐnpái
冒牌货 màopáihuò
金字招牌 jīnzì zhāopai

派　　　pài　　9画 氵部

派 派 派 派 派 派 派 派
派

❶[名]指立场、见解或作风、习气相同的一些人：group; sect; factions within a political party; learned society or religious group, formed according to their different stands or views | 在学术观点上，他们是一～的。Zài xuéshù guāndiǎn shang, tāmen shì yī pài de. *They belong to the same academic school.*

派别 pàibié faction; school
党派 dǎngpài　　学派 xuépài
宗派 zōngpài

❷[动]派遣；分配：send; dispatch; assign; appoint | ～工作 pài gōngzuò *assign works to people* / 学校～王老师出国教汉语。Xuéxiào pài Wáng lǎoshī chūguó jiāo Hànyǔ. *The school sent Mr. Wang to teach Chinese abroad.*

派遣 pàiqiǎn send; dispatch
◇派出所 pàichūsuǒ local police station; police substation

攀　　　pān　　19画 手部

攀 攀 攀 攀 攀 攀 攀 攀
攀 攀 攀 攀 攀 攀 攀
攀 攀 攀

❶[动]抓住东西往上爬：climb; clamber | ～岩 pānyán *rock climbing* / 他～着绳子往上爬。Tā pānzhe shéngzi wǎng shàng pá. *He climbed up a rope hand over hand.*

攀登 pāndēng climb; clamber

❷[动]指跟地位高的人结亲戚或拉关系：seek connection in high places | 高～ gāopān *make friends or claim ties of kinship with sb. of a higher social position or with better qualification* / ～谈 pāntán *engage in small talk; have a chat*

盘 (盤)　pán　　11画 舟部

盘 盘 盘 盘 盘 盘 盘 盘
盘 盘 盘

❶[名]盘子：plate; dish | 托～ tuōpán *serving tray* / 茶～儿 chápánr *tea tray* / ～里放着一条鱼。Pán li fàngzhe yī tiáo yú. *There is a fish in the dish.*

盘子 pánzi tray; plate; dish
拼盘 pīnpán

❷[动]环绕；旋转：coil; twist; wind | ～绳子 pán shéngzi *coil up*

the rope / 树上~着一条蛇。Shù shang pánzhe yī tiáo shé. *A snake coiled round the tree.*

盘旋 pánxuán ① circle ② linger; stay

❸[动] 仔细查问或清点：check; examine; interrogate | ~问 pánwèn *cross-examine; interrogate* / ~货 pánhuò *make an inventory of stock on hand* / 这家店每月~一次账。Zhè jiā diàn měi yuè pán yī cì zhàng. *The shop checks its accounts once a month.*

盘点 pándiǎn check; make an inventory of

❹[量] 用于盘装的食品等：used for food on a plate | 一~菜 yī pán cài *a dish* / 两~肉 liǎng pán ròu *two plates of meat*

◇ 磁盘 cípán   存盘 cúnpán
底盘 dǐpán   光盘 guāngpán
开盘 kāipán   硬盘 yìngpán
方向盘 fāngxiàngpán

判   pàn   7画 刂部

判 判判判判判判判

❶[动] 分辨；断定：distinguish; discriminate | 评~ píngpàn *pass judgment on sth. or sb.*

判定 pàndìng judge; decide; determine

判断 pànduàn decision; judgement

批判 pīpàn

❷[动] 司法机关对案件作出决定：judge; decide | 这件案子到现在还没有~。Zhè jiàn ànzi dào xiànzài hái méiyǒu pàn. *The case has not been decided.*

判处 pànchǔ sentence; condemn

判决 pànjué decide

判刑 pànxíng pass a sentence on; sentence sb. to

判决书 pànjuéshū (leg.) court verdict; written judgment

裁判 cáipàn   审判 shěnpàn
宣判 xuānpàn
裁判员 cáipànyuán

盼   pàn   9画 目部

盼 盼盼盼盼盼盼盼盼

[动] 希望；期待：hope for; long for; expect | 妈妈~儿子平安归来。Māma pàn érzi píng'ān guīlái. *The mother is longing to see her son return safe and sound.* / 好消息终于~来了。Hǎo xiāoxi zhōngyú pànlái le. *The good news we were yearning for came at last.*

盼望 pànwàng hope for; look forward to

 pàn   9画 丶部

叛 叛叛叛叛叛叛叛叛
叛

[动]背离自己的一方，投靠敌对一方：betray; rebel against | 反～ fǎnpàn rebel

叛变 pànbiàn turn traitor
叛徒 pàntú traitor
背叛 bèipàn

畔　　　　pàn　10画 田部

畔 畔畔畔畔畔畔畔畔
畔畔

[名]旁边；附近：side; bank | 河～ hépàn river bank | 湖～húpàn shore of a lake

庞 (龐) páng　8画 广部

庞 庞庞庞庞庞庞庞庞

[形](形体或数量)极大：huge; enormous; colossal; gigantic | 数字～大 shùzì pángdà innumerable

庞大 pángdà huge; large; immense

旁　　　　páng　10画 方部

旁 旁旁旁旁旁旁旁旁
旁旁

❶[名]近侧；附近：side | 路～ lùpáng roadside | ～观

pángguān look on; be an onlooker

旁边 pángbiān side
旁听 pángtīng be a visitor at a meeting, in a school class, etc.
两旁 liǎngpáng 一旁 yīpáng

❷[形] 其他；另外：other; else | ～人pángrén others / 我还有～的话跟你说。Wǒ hǎiyǒu páng de huà gēn nǐ shuō. I have something else to tell you.

胖　　　　pàng　9画 月部

胖 胖胖胖胖胖胖胖胖
胖

[形]（人体）脂肪多；肉厚（跟"瘦shòu"相对）：fat; stout; plump (the opposite of "瘦shòu") | ～娃娃 pàng wāwa a fat baby / 这人长得真～! Zhè rén zhǎng de zhēn pàng! This person in really fat!

胖子 pàngzi fat person
肥胖 féipàng

抛　　　　pāo　7画 扌部

抛 抛抛抛抛抛抛抛

❶[动]扔；投：throw; toss; fling | ～球 pāo qiú toss a ball / 不要乱～垃圾。Bùyào luàn pāo lājī. Don't litter.

❷[动]舍弃；丢下：leave behind;

cast aside | 他跑得很快,把我们远远地~在后面。Tā pǎo de hěn kuài, bǎ wǒmen yuǎnyuǎn de pāo zài hòumian. *He ran so fast that we were left far behind.*

抛弃 pāoqì abandon; cast aside

刨 páo 7画 刂部

刨 刨刨刨刨刨刨刨刨

❶[动]挖掘:dig; excavate | ~土 pāotǔ *dig earth* / ~坑 pāo kēng *dig a pit* / 花生 pāo huāshēng *dig up peanuts* / 把那棵小树连根~起来。Bǎ nà kē xiǎoshù lián gēn pāo qǐlai. *Dig up the roots of that little tree.*

❷[动]从原有事物中除去;减去:exclude; substract | ~去他还有两人。Pāoqù tā hǎiyǒu liǎng rén. *There are two people besides him.* /~去水、电、房费,还能剩多少钱?Pāoqù shuǐ, diàn, fángfèi, hǎinéng shèng duōshao qián? *How much would be left after paying the charges for water, electricity and rent?*

跑 pǎo 12画 足部

跑 跑跑跑跑跑跑跑跑跑跑跑跑

❶[动]迅速前进:run | 快~kuài pǎo *run fast* / 他~得很快。Tā pǎo de hěn kuài. *He runs very fast.*

跑步 pǎobù run; jog
跑道 pǎodào ① runway ② track
奔跑 bēnpǎo

❷[动]为某种事而奔走:run about doing sth.; run errands | ~买卖 pǎo mǎimai *go about soliciting clients* / ~材料 pǎo cáiliào *run about buying materials* / 我终于把签证~下来了。Wǒ zhōngyú bǎ qiānzhèng pǎo xiàlai le. *I was eventually granted the visa.*

❸[动]逃走:run away; escape; flee | 别让小偷~了。Bié ràng xiǎotōu pǎo le. *Don't let the thief run away.*

逃跑 táopǎo

❹[动]漏出;挥发:leak; evaporate | ~电 pǎodiàn *leakage of electricity* / ~油 pǎoyóu *leakage of gasoline*

◇跑车 pǎochē ① racing bicycle ② (inf.) (of vehicle drivers, train conductors, etc.) be on the job

泡 pào 8画 氵部

泡 泡泡泡泡泡泡泡泡泡

❶[名]气体在液体内使液体鼓起的球状体:bubble | 水~shuǐpào *bubble* | 冒～儿 màopàor *send up bubbles* /肥皂～fēizào-pào *soap bubbles*

泡沫 pàomò foam; froth

❷[名] 像泡一样的东西：sth. puffy and soft like a bubble | 脚上起了一个～。Jiǎo shang qǐle yī gè pào *get a blister on one's foot*

灯泡 dēngpào

❸[动] 较长时间地放在液体里：steep; soak | ～茶 pàochá *make tea* / 用热水～衣服 yòng rèshuǐ pào yīfu *soak clothes in hot water*

❹[动] 故意消磨（时间）：dawdle | ～病号 pào bìnghào *avoid work on pretence of illness* / 他整天～在茶馆里。Tā zhěng-tiān pào zài cháguǎn li. *He spent the whole day in the tea house.*

炮 pào 9画 火部

炮 炮炮炮炮炮炮炮炮炮

❶[名] cannon; artillery piece | ～声把耳朵都震聋了。Pàoshēng bǎ ěrduo dōu zhènlóng le. *Deafened by the sound of the cannon.*

炮弹 pàodàn (artillery) shell

炮火 pàohuǒ artillery fire; gunfire

大炮 dàpào

❷[名] 爆竹：firecracker | 春节里我家放了很多～。Chūnjié li wǒ jiā fàngle hěn duō pào. *We let off a lot of firecrackers during the Spring Festival.*

鞭炮 biānpào

陪 péi 10画 阝(左)部

陪 陪陪陪陪陪陪陪陪陪陪

[动] 随同做伴：keep sb. company; accompany | ～客 péikè *keep a guest company* / 我～你去。Wǒ péi nǐ qù. *I'll accompany you there.* / ～我散步 péi wǒ sànbù *have a walk with me*

陪伴 péibàn accompany; keep sb. company

陪同 péitóng accompany

陪审员 péishěnyuán juror; member of the jury

培 péi 11画 土部

培 培培培培培培培培培培培

❶[动] 在根基部分加土，以保护植物或建筑物：bank up with earth; earth up | 玉米根部要多～点儿土。Yùmǐ gēnbù yào duō péi-diǎnr tǔ. *The roots of the maize plant need to be earthed up securely.*

❷[动]培养：foster; train | 人工～植人参 réngōng péizhí rénshēn *artificially cultivate ginseng*

培训 péixùn training

培养 péiyǎng ① develop; educate; train ② cultivate

培育 péiyù cultivate; breed; foster

培训班 péixùnbān training course

栽培 zāipéi

赔（賠）péi 12画 贝部

赔 赔赔赔赔赔赔赔赔赔赔赔赔

❶[动]补偿损失：make good a loss; compensate | ～他钱 péi tā qián *compensate him with money* / 损坏东西要～。Sǔnhuài dōngxi yào péi. *Damages should be compensated for.*

赔偿 péicháng compensate; pay for

赔付 péifù pay an indemnity; pay reparations

赔款 péikuǎn ① pay an indemnity; pay reparations ② indemnity; reparations

理赔 lǐpéi   索赔 suǒpéi

❷[动]经营亏损：operate at a loss | ～本 péiběn *sustain losses in business; run a business at a loss* / ～钱 péiqián *lose money in business*

❸[动]道歉；认错：make an apology; apologize | ～不是 péibùshi *apologize* /～礼道歉 péilǐ dàoqiàn *make a formal apology; apologize*

佩 pèi 8画 亻部

佩 佩佩佩佩佩佩佩佩

See 佩服

佩服 pèifú admire; think highly of; revere

配 pèi 10画 酉部

配 配配配配配配配配配配

❶[名]丈夫或妻子：husband or wife

配偶 pèi'ǒu spouse

❷[动] 按比例或标准加以调和或凑在一起：mix according to a fixed ratio; compound | ～药 pèiyào *make up a prescription* /～颜色 pèi yánsè *mix colours (on a palette); (of dressing) find the correct match of colours*

配方 pèifāng make up a prescription; formula

配套 pèitào form a complete set

搭配 dāpèi   装配 zhuāngpèi

❸[动] 有计划地分派；安排：distribute according to a plan; ap-

P

portion | ～售 pèishòu *ration* / 上级～给我们一辆汽车。Shàngjí pèigěi wǒmen yī liàng qìchē. *We were assigned a car by the higher-ups.* / 每个班都～了一台CD播放机。Měi gè bān dōu pèile yī tái CD bōfàngjī. *Each class has been provided with a CD player.*

配备 pèibèi provide; equip; fit out

分配 fēnpèi 支配 zhīpèi
按劳分配 ànláo fēnpèi

❹ [动] 把缺少的东西补上：replace what is missing or short of | ～钥匙 pèi yàoshi *duplicate a key* /～零件 pèi língjiàn *replace parts* /这套书没～齐，还缺一本。Zhè tào shū méi pèiqí, hái quē yī běn. *One book is missing from the set.*

❺ [动] 衬托；陪衬：match; harmonize with | 红花～绿叶 hónghuā pèi lǜyè *green leaves and red flowers go well together* / 这首歌很～那个舞蹈。Zhè shǒu gē hěn pèi nàge wǔdǎo. *This song goes well with that dance.*

配合 pèihé coordinate; cooperate; concert

配件 pèijiàn ① parts, fittings, or accessories ② replacement

配角 pèijué supporting role; supporting actor

配音 pèiyīn dub (a film, etc.)

匹配 pǐpèi

❻ [动] 符合；够得上；相当：agree with; deserve; be qualified | 这菜很～我的胃口。Zhè cài hěn pèi wǒ de wèikǒu. *The dish suits my taste.* /他的穿着和年龄很不相～。Tā de chuānzhuó hé niánlíng hěn bù xiāngpèi. *His clothes do not fit with his age.*

喷 (噴) pēn 12画 口部

喷 喷喷喷喷喷喷喷喷喷 喷喷喷喷

[动] (液体、气体、粉末等) 受到压力而射出：spurt; spout; gush | ～壶 pēnhú *watering can; sprinkling can* /～农药 pēn nóngyào *spray insecticide* /火山正在～发。Huǒshān zhèngzài pēnfā. *The volcano is erupting.*

喷射 pēnshè spray; spurt; jet

盆 pén 9画 皿部

盆 盆盆盆盆盆盆盆 盆

[名] 盛东西或洗东西的用具：basin; tub; pot | 花～huāpén *flower pot* / 澡～zǎopén *bathtub*

盆地 péndì basin

盆景 pénjǐng potted landscape; miniature trees and rockery

脸盆 liǎnpén

烹 pēng 11画 灬部

烹烹烹烹烹烹烹烹烹烹烹烹

[动] 煮；烧制饭菜：boil; cook in water; brew; fry quickly in hot oil and stir in sauce | ～虾 pēng xiā *quick-fried shrimp* /～制中国菜 pēngzhì Zhōngguócài *cook Chinese dishes*

烹饪 pēngrèn cooking; culinary art

烹调 pēngtiáo cook (dishes)

朋 péng 8画 月部

朋朋朋朋朋朋朋朋

[名] 彼此要好的人：friend | 亲～好友 qīnpéng-hǎoyǒu *relatives and friends*

朋友 péngyou ① friend ② boy friend or girl friend

女朋友 nǚpéngyou

酒肉朋友 jiǔròu péngyou

棚 péng 12画 木部

棚棚棚棚棚棚棚棚棚棚棚棚

[名] 简陋的房屋或竹木搭起的架子：shed; shack | 工～ gōngpéng *builders' temporary shed; work shed* /天～ tiānpéng *ceiling* /凉～ liángpéng *cool shed*

蓬 péng 13画 艹部

蓬蓬蓬蓬蓬蓬蓬蓬蓬蓬蓬蓬蓬

See 蓬勃

蓬勃 péngbó flourishing; vigorous

膨 péng 16画 月部

膨膨膨膨膨膨膨膨膨膨膨膨膨膨膨膨

[动] 胀大：inflate | ～大 péngdà *expand*

膨胀 péngzhàng expand; swell; dilate; inflate

捧 pěng 11画 扌部

捧捧捧捧捧捧捧捧捧捧捧

❶ [动] 用双手托：hold or carry in both hands | ～着一个坛子 pěngzhe yī gè tánzi *hold a jar with both hands* / 手～鲜花 Shǒu pěng xiānhuā *hold flowers in both hands* / 她～起孩子的脸。Tā pěngqǐ háizi de liǎn.

She cupped the child's face in her hands.

❷[量] 用于能用手捧的东西：handful | 一～花生 yī pěng huāshēng *two handfuls of peanuts* / 捧了两～米 pěngle liǎng pěng mǐ *scoop up two handfuls of rice*

❸[动] 奉承；替人吹嘘：flatter; boast | ～场 pěngchǎng *sing the praises of; boast* / 他被～上天了。Tā bèi pěngshang tiān le. *He was praised to the skies.*

吹捧 chuīpěng

碰 pèng 13画 石部

碰 碰碰碰碰碰碰碰 碰碰碰碰碰

❶[动]撞击：touch; bump | ～杯 pèngbēi *clink glasses; drink a toast* /～破了皮 pèngpòle pí *scratch the skin* / 那花瓶一～就碎。Nà huāpíng yī pèng jiù suì. *The vase breaks easily.*

碰壁 pèngbì *run up against a stone wall; be rebuffed*

碰撞 pèngzhuàng ① *collide; run into* ② *offend; affront* ③ *(phys.) collision; impact*

碰钉子 pèngdīngzi *meet with a rebuff; be rebuffed*

❷[动]偶然遇见：meet by chance | ～面 pèngmiàn *see each other; meet* /我在半路上～到他。Wǒ zài bànlù shang pèngdào tā. *I met him halfway.*

碰见 pèngjiàn *meet unexpectedly; run into*

❸[动]试探：take one's chance | ～运气 pèng yùnqi *try one's luck* /～机会 pèng jīhuì *take a chance*

批 pī 7画 扌部

批 批批批批批批批

❶[动] 指示；批改：write instructions or comments on a report from a subordinate; correct students' papers | ～改 pīgǎi *correct* /你的出国申请～下来了。Nǐ de chūguó shēnqǐng pī xiàlai le. *Your application to go abroad has been approved.*

批复 pīfù *give an offcial, written reply to a subordinate body*

批示 pīshì *written instructions or comments on a report, memorandum, etc. submitted by a subordinate*

批准 pīzhǔn *approve; ratify; sanction*

审批 shěnpī

❷[动] 评判；批评：judge; criticize | 挨～āi pī *be criticized*

批判 pīpàn *criticize*

批评 pīpíng *criticize*

❸[形]大量的：in batches; on a large scale | ～量购买 pīliàng gòumǎi *buy goods in batches*
批发 pīfā ① wholesale ② be authorized for dispatch
大批 dàpī
分批 fēnpī
❹[量] 用于大量货物或多数的人：batch; lot; group | 一～货yī pī huò *a batch of goods* / 一～人 yī pī rén *a group of people*

pī   8画 土部

坯坯坯坯坯坯坯坯

[名]特指土坯：unburnt brick; earthen brick; adobe | 打～dǎpī *make earthen bricks* / 脱～tuōpī *mould adobe blocks*

pī   8画 扌部

披披披披披披披披

[动]覆盖或搭在肩背上：w r a p around; drape over one's shoulders | ～着大衣 pīzhe dàyī *have an overcoat draped over one's shoulders*
披肩 pījiān ① cape ② shawl
◇披露 pīlù ① publish; announce ② reveal; show; disclose

pī   15画 刀部

劈 劈劈劈劈劈劈劈劈劈劈劈劈劈劈劈

[动]用刀斧等破开：split; chop; cleave | ～木头pī mùtou *chop wood* / 木头被～成两半。Mùtou bèi pīchéng liǎng bàn. *The piece of wood was split in two.*

pí   5画 皮部

皮 皮皮皮皮皮

❶[名]人或生物体表面的一层组织：skin; rind; peel | 树～ shùpí *bark* / 西瓜～xīguāpí *watermelon rind*
皮肤 pífū skin
磨嘴皮 mózuǐpí
❷[名]皮革或毛皮制的：made of leather or fur | ～大衣 pídàyī *leather coat*
皮草 pícǎo (dial.) furs and fur products
皮带 pídài ① leather belt ② (driving) belt
皮革 pígé leather; hide
皮球 píqiú rubber ball; flexible hollow ball
皮鞋 píxié leather shoes
皮划艇 píhuátǐng (sports) canoeing (including kayaking)
皮夹克 píjiākè leather jacket
❸[名]表面或包在外面的东西：cover; wrapper | 封～fēngpí *(paper) wrapping; cover; enve-*

lope / 饺子～儿 jiǎozipír *dumpling wrapper* / 书～儿 shūpír *book cover; jacket*

疲 pí 10画 广部

疲 疲疲疲疲疲疲疲疲疲 疲疲

[动] 劳累：tired; weary | 精～力尽 jīngpí-lìjìn *exhausted; run down*

疲惫 píbèi exhausted

疲乏 pífá weary

疲倦 píjuàn tired; fatigued

疲劳 píláo fatigued; tired

脾 pí 12画 月部

脾 脾脾脾脾脾脾脾脾 脾脾脾脾

See below

脾气 píqi temperament; disposition

发脾气 fāpíqi

匹 pǐ 4画 匚部

匹 匹匹匹匹

❶[量]用于马、骡子等：used for horses, mules, etc. | 三～马 sān pǐ mǎ *three horses*

❷[量]用于整卷的布、绸子等：roll, used for cloth or silk | 两～布

liǎng pǐ bù *two bolts of cloth*

◇匹配 pǐpèi ① (formal) mate; marry ② matching

奥林匹克 Àolínpǐkè

屁 pì 7画 尸部

屁 屁屁屁屁屁屁屁屁

[名]由肛门排出的臭气：wind from bowels | 放～ fàngpì *break wind; fart*

屁股 pìgu ① buttocks; bottom; behind; backside ② end; butt

譬 pì 20画 言部

譬 譬譬譬譬譬譬譬譬 譬譬譬譬譬譬譬譬 譬譬譬譬

[动] 打比方：example; analogy | ～喻 pìyù *metaphor*

譬如 pìrú for example; for instance; such as

偏 piān 11画 亻部

偏 偏偏偏偏偏偏偏 偏偏偏

❶ [形]歪斜（跟"正 zhèng"相对）：inclined to one side; slanting; leaning (the opposite of "正 zhèng") | 镜子挂～了。Jìngzi guàpiān le. *The mirror is lean-*

ing to one side. /这一枪打~了。 Zhè yī qiāng dǎpiān le. *The shot was off-target.*

偏差 piānchā deviation; error

❷ [形] 单独着重于一方面; 不公正: partial; prejudiced | 他的看法太~了。Tā de kànfǎ tài piān le. *His opinion is too partial.* / 是他错了，你怎么还~着他？Shì tā cuò le, nǐ zěnme hái piānzhe tā? *It's his mistake. Why do you still defend him?*

偏见 piānjiàn prejudice; bias

偏向 piānxiàng ① erroneous tendency; deviation ② be partial to

偏心眼儿 piānxīnyǎnr partiality; bias

❸ [副] 表示故意跟客观要求或客观情况相反: used to indicate contrary to expectations or anticipations | 你不让我去，我~要去。Nǐ bū ràng wǒ qù, wǒ piān yào qù. *I insist on going even though you won't allow me.*

偏偏 piānpiān wilfully; insistently; persistently

◇偏僻 piānpì remote; out-of-the-way

篇 piān 15画 竹部

篇篇篇篇篇篇篇篇篇篇篇篇篇篇

[量] 用于纸张、书页或文章等:

used for paper, book leaves, articles | 一~论文 yī piān lùnwén *a paper; a thesis* / 一~文章 yī piān wénzhāng *a piece of writing; an article*

便 piān 9画 亻部

便便便便便便便便便

See 便宜

便宜 piányi ① cheap ② petty gain ③ let sb. off lightly

See biàn.

片 piān 4画 片部

片 片片片片

❶ [形] 不全的; 零星的; 短的: odd; short; incomplete | ~断 piānduàn *part of an entirety; extract; fragment*

片刻 piānkè a short while; an instant; a moment

片面 piānmiàn one-sided; unilateral

❷ [名] 扁平而薄的东西: flat, thin piece; slice | 布~ bùpiàn *small piece of cloth* / 纸~ zhǐpiàn *small piece of paper* / 明信~ míngxìnpiàn *postcard* / 碎玻璃~suì bōlipiàn *bits and pieces of glass*

唱片 chàngpiàn

名片 míngpiàn 照片 zhàopiàn

❸[量] 用于平面薄的东西：used for sth. flat and thin | 两～药 liǎng piàn yào *two tablets* / 一～儿面包 yī piànr miànbāo *a slice of bread* / 一～枫叶 yī piàn fēngyè *a maple leaf*

❹[量] 用于地面、水面等：used for a stretch of land, a water surface, etc. | 一～草地 yī piàn cǎodì *a tract of meadow* / 一～水面 yī piàn shuǐmiàn *an expanse of water*

❺[量] 用于景象、声音、语言、心意等：used for atmosphere, scene, sound, feeling, etc. | 一～新气象 yī piàn xīn qìxiàng *a new look* / 一～漆黑 yī piàn qīhēi *a pall of darkness* / 一～真心 yī piàn zhēnxīn *in all sincerity*

◇纪录片 jìlùpiàn

 骗（騙） piàn 12画 马部
骗 骗骗骗骗骗骗骗骗骗骗骗骗

[动]用谎言或诡计使人上当：deceive; fool; hoodwink | ～人 piànrén *kid; cheat sb.* / 受～ shòupiàn *be taken in; be deceived* / 你～我。Nǐ piàn wǒ. *You're kidding me.*

骗取 piànqǔ gain sth. by cheating; cheat (or trick, swindle) sb.

out of sth.; defraud

骗子 piànzi swindler; impostor; cheat; trickster

欺骗 qīpiàn　　诈骗 zhàpiàn

 piāo 14画 氵部
漂 漂漂漂漂漂漂漂漂 漂漂漂漂漂漂

[动] 浮在液体表面；浮在水面上，随着水流、风向移动：flow; drift | 树叶在水面上～着。Shùyè zài shuǐmiàn shang piāozhe. *Leaves are floating on the water's surface.* /小船顺着水～去。Xiǎochuán shùnzhe shuǐ piāo-qù. *The boat drifted down the stream.*

漂泊 piāobó float; drift

See piǎo.

 (飄) piāo 15画 风部
飘 飘飘飘飘飘飘飘飘 飘飘飘飘飘飘飘

[动] 随风摇动或飞扬：wave to and fro; float in the air; flutter | 外面～着小雪。Wàimian piāozhe xiǎoxuě. *It was snowing lightly.* / 气球～过天空。Qìqiú piāoguo tiānkōng. *A balloon floated across the sky.*

飘扬 piāoyáng fly; wave

票 piāo 11画 覀部

票 票票票票票票票票
票票票

[名] 印的或写的作为凭证的纸片：ticket | 电影～diànyǐngpiào *movie ticket* / 买～mǎipiào *get (buy) a ticket* /车～chēpiào *(of train, bus, etc.) ticket* / 凭～入场。Píng piào rùchǎng. *Admission by ticket only.*

票房 piàofáng box office (at a theatre, stadium, etc.); booking office (at a railway station, airport, etc.)

票价 piàojià the price of a ticket; admission fee; entrance fee

彩票 cǎipiào 　钞票 chāopiào
发票 fāpiào 　　股票 gǔpiào
门票 ménpiào 　投票 tóupiào
选票 xuǎnpiào 　邮票 yóupiào
月票 yuèpiào 　　支票 zhīpiào

漂 piāo 14画 氵部

漂 漂漂漂漂漂漂漂漂
漂漂漂漂漂漂

See 漂亮
漂亮 piàoliang ① handsome; good-looking; beautiful ② remarkable; brilliant; splendid
See piāo.

撇 piē 14画 扌部

撇 撇撇撇撇撇撇撇
撇撇撇撇撇撇

❶[动] 舍弃；丢下：cast aside; throw overboard; neglect | ～开 piēkāi *leave aside; bypass* / 我们不能～下他。Wǒmen bùnéng piēxià tā. *We should not leave him alone.*

❷[动] 由液体表面舀取：skim | ～油 piēyóu *skim off the grease* / ～掉沫儿 piēdiào mòr *skim off the froth*

瞥 piē 16画 目部

瞥 瞥瞥瞥瞥瞥瞥瞥
瞥瞥瞥瞥瞥瞥瞥

[动] 很快地看一下：shoot a glance at | ～了他一眼 piēle tā yī yǎn *cast a glance at him*

拼 pīn 9画 扌部

拼 拼拼拼拼拼拼拼拼
拼

❶[动] 合在一起：piece together; join | ～图 pīntú *jigsaw puzzle* / 东～西凑 dōngpīn-xīcòu *knock together* / 把两块板子～起来。Bǎ liǎng kuài bǎnzi pīn qǐlai. *Join the two boards together.*

拼盘 pīnpán assorted cold dishes; assorted hors d'oeuvre

❷ [动] 不顾一切地干：do one's utmost; do sth. adventurously | ~到底 pīndàodǐ *fight to the bitter end*

拼搏 pīnbó struggle hard; exert one's strength to the utmost

拼命 pīnmìng exert all one's strength

贫 (貧) pín   8画 贝部

贫 贫 贫 贫 贫 贫 贫 贫

❶ [形] 穷 (跟 "富 fù" 相对)：poor; impoverished (the opposite of "富 fù") | 清~ qīngpín *poor; badly off* / 许多国家国内的~富差距很大。Xǔduō guójiā guónèi de pínfù chājù hěn dà. *In many countries there is a considerable gap between the rich and poor.*

贫乏 pínfá poor; short; lacking

贫苦 pínkǔ poor; poverty-stricken; badly off

贫困 pínkùn poor; impoverished; in straitened circumstances

贫民 pínmín poor people; pauper

贫穷 pínqióng poor; needy; impoverished

❷ [动] 缺少；不足：be lacking; be inadequate; be deficient | ~血 pínxuè *anaemia*

频 (頻) pín   13画 页部

频 频 频 频 频 频 频 频 频 频 频 频 频

[副] 多次；连续几次：frequently; repeatedly | ~~招手 pínpín zhāoshǒu *wave one's hand again and again*

频繁 pínfán frequently; often

频率 pínlǜ frequency

◇ 频道 píndào (TV) frequency channel; channel

视频 shìpín

品   pǐn   9画 口部

品 品 品 品 品 品 品 品 品

❶ [名] 物品：article; product | 赠~ zèngpǐn *gift; present* / 非卖~ fēimàipǐn *articles not for sale* / 木制~ mùzhìpǐn *wood products*

产品 chǎnpǐn   成品 chéngpǐn
出品 chūpǐn   毒品 dúpǐn
废品 fèipǐn   奖品 jiǎngpǐn
礼品 lǐpǐn   商品 shāngpǐn
食品 shípǐn   物品 wùpǐn
样品 yàngpǐn   药品 yàopǐn
用品 yòngpǐn   展品 zhǎnpǐn
制品 zhìpǐn   作品 zuòpǐn
纺织品 fǎngzhīpǐn
工艺品 gōngyìpǐn

化妆品 huàzhuāngpǐn
纪念品 jìniànpǐn
棉织品 miánzhīpǐn
农产品 nóngchǎnpǐn
日用品 rìyòngpǐn
消费品 xiāofèipǐn
畜产品 xùchǎnpǐn
艺术品 yìshùpǐn

❷[名]种类: grade; class | 上~ shàngpǐn *top grade (goods, products, etc.)* / 下~xiàpǐn *low grade (goods, products, etc.)* / 精~jīngpǐn *quality (or choice) goods; articles of fine quality*
品牌 pǐnpái brand of a product, esp. of a famous product
品种 pǐnzhǒng variety

❸[名]性质: character; quality | 人~ rénpǐn *moral quality; character*
品德 pǐndé moral character
品行 pǐnxíng conduct; behaviour
品质 pǐnzhì character; quality

❹[动] 辨别好坏: taste sth. with discrimination; sample | ~茶 pǐnchá *sample tea* / 我~出他话里的意思了。Wǒ pǐnchū tā huà li de yìsi le. *I have figured out the meaning of his words.*
品尝 pǐncháng taste; savour
◇ 小品 xiǎopǐn

聘
聘 pìn 13画 耳部
聘聘聘聘聘聘聘聘
聘聘聘聘聘

❶[动]请人担任工作: engage | ~书 pìnshū *letter of appointment* / 他被学校~为教授。Tā bèi xuéxiào pìn wéi jiàoshòu. *He was engaged as a professor by the school.* /他是从国外~来的。Tā shì cóng guówài pìnlái de. *He was recruited from abroad.*
聘请 pìnqǐng engage; invite
聘任pìnrèn engage; appoint to a position
聘用pìnyòng employ; engage; appoint to a position
应聘 yìngpìn

❷[动]订婚; 女子出嫁: be betrothed; be married off

乒
乒 pīng 6画 丿部
乒 乒乒乒乒乒乒

See 乒乓球
乒乓球 pīngpāngqiú ① table tennis; ping-pong ② table tennis ball; ping-pong ball

平
平 píng 5画 一部
平 平平平平平

❶[形]表面没有凹凸, 不倾斜: flat; even | 地面很~。Dìmiàn hěn píng.*The ground is quite even.* / 把位置摆~bǎ wèizhì bǎi-píng *put sth. level (or even)* /

把纸铺～了 bǎ zhǐ pūpíng le *smooth out the paper*

平面 píngmiàn plane

平坦 píngtǎn (of land,etc.) level; even; smooth

平原 píngyuán plain; flatlands

平整 píngzhěng ① level ② neat; smooth

❷[形]高低相等或不相上下：be on the same level; be on a par; equal | 树梢和屋顶齐～。Shùshāo hé wūdǐng qí píng. *The tree top is level with the roof of the house.*

平等 píngděng equality

平衡 pínghéng balance

平局 píngjú draw; tie

平行 píngxíng parallel

持平 chípíng

❸[形]均等; 公正：equal; fair | ～分 píngfēn *divide equally*

平均 píngjūn average

不平 bùpíng 公平 gōngpíng

❹[形]安定：calm; peaceful | 风～浪静 fēngpíng-làngjìng *the wind has subsided and the waves have calmed down* /～定 píngdìng *stable; calm down*

平安 píng'ān safe and sound

平和 pínghé gentle; mild; moderate; placid

平静 píngjìng calm; quiet; tranquil

平稳 píngwěn smooth and steady; smooth; stable

和平 hépíng   太平 tàipíng

太平洋 Tàipíngyáng

和平共处 hépíng gòngchǔ

一路平安 yīlù-píng'ān

❺[形]一般的; 通常的：common; ordinary | ～淡 píngdàn *commonplace; prosaic*

平常 píngcháng common; ordinary

平凡 píngfán ordinary; common

平民 píngmín the common people; the populace

平日 píngrì on ordinary days

平时 píngshí ① at ordinary times; in normal times ② in peacetime

◇平方 píngfāng square

平方米 píngfāngmǐ square metre (sq. m.)

平方公里 píngfāng gōnglǐ square kilometre (sq. km.)

 评 (評) píng 7画 讠部

评 评评评评评评评

[动] 议论; 判定：comment; criticize; judge; appraise; evaluate | ～理 pínglǐ *judge between right and wrong* /书～ shūpíng *book review* / 获得好～ huòdé hǎo píng *receive favourable comments; be well received* /裁判～得公正。Cáipàn píng de gōngzhèng. *The judge gives fair judgements.*

评比 píngbǐ appraise through comparison

评定 píngdìng pass judgment on; evaluate; assess

评估 pínggū assess

评价 píngjià appraise

评论 pínglùn comment on

评判 píngpàn pass judgment on; judge

评审 píngshěn examine and appraise

评选 píngxuǎn choose through public appraisal

评议 píngyì appraise sth. through discussion; deliberate (a question) in a formal meeting

评论员 pínglùnyuán commentator

点评 diǎnpíng 好评 hǎopíng 批评 pīpíng

苹 (蘋) píng 8画 艹部

苹 苹苹苹苹苹苹苹苹

See 苹果

苹果 píngguǒ apple

凭 (憑) píng 8画 几部

凭 凭凭凭凭凭凭凭凭

❶ [动] 依靠; 倚仗: lean on; depend on; rely on | 光~师傅教是不够的, 还要自己肯学。Guāng píng shīfu jiāo shì bù

gòu de, háiyào zìjǐ kěn xué. *Depending on the master's guidance is not enough. You must study hard as well.* /他~着这点儿资金办成了一家公司。Tā píngzhe zhè diǎnr zījīn bànchéngle yī jiā gōngsī. *With this little capital, he succeeded in setting up his firm.*

凭借 píngjiè rely on; depend on

❷ [介] 根据: go by; base on | ~票入场 píng piào rùchǎng *admission by ticket* /~个人的口味挑选 píng gèrén de kǒuwèi tiāoxuǎn *choose according to one's taste*

❸ [名] 证据: evidence; proof | ~据 píngjù *evidence; proof*

凭证 píngzhèng proof; evidence; certificate; voucher

文凭 wénpíng

屏 píng 9画 尸部

屏 屏屏屏屏屏屏屏屏屏

[名] 遮蔽; 遮挡: screen; shield | ~风 píngfēng *screen*

屏幕 píngmù (electron.) screen

屏障 píngzhàng protective screen

◇ 显示屏 xiǎnshìpíng

瓶 píng 10画 瓦部

瓶 瓶瓶瓶瓶瓶瓶瓶瓶
瓶瓶

[名]口小腹大的容器：bottle; vase;
jar | 花~huāpíng *flower vase*
/ 酒~jiǔpíng *wine bottle*
瓶子 píngzi bottle
瓷瓶 cípíng

萍
píng　11画 艹部
萍 萍萍萍萍萍萍萍萍萍
萍萍萍

[名]duckweed
萍水相逢 píngshuǐ-xiāngféng
(of strangers) meet by chance
like patches of drifting duck-
weed

坡
pō　8画 土部
坡 坡坡坡坡坡坡坡坡

[名]地形倾斜的地方：slope | 山~
shānpō *a mountain slope; hill-
side* / 高~gāopō *steep slope* /
上~shàngpō *an upward slope;
climb up a slope* / 下~xiàpō *a
downward slope; going down-
hill*
滑坡 huápō

泼（潑）pō　8画 氵部
 泼泼泼泼泼泼泼泼

[动]用力把液体向外倒或向外洒：
sprinkle; splash; spill | ~水
pōshuǐ *splash water*
泼水节 Pōshuǐjié the Water-
Splashing (or Water-Sprinkling)
Festival of the Dais and some
other ethnic minorities

颇（頗）pō　11画 皮部
颇 颇颇颇颇颇颇颇颇
颇颇颇

[副]很；相当地：rather; quite | ~
感兴趣 pō gǎn xìngqù *have
considerable interest*

婆
pó　11画 女部
婆 婆婆婆婆婆婆婆
婆婆婆

❶[名]称奶奶辈的或年老的妇女：
old woman | 老太~lǎotàipó
old woman

❷[名]丈夫的母亲：husband's
mother | 公~gōngpó
husband's parents /~媳 pōxí *a
woman and her daughter-in-law*
婆婆 pópo husband's mother;
mother-in-law

迫
pō　8画 辶部
迫 迫迫迫迫迫迫迫迫

571

❶[动] 强逼; 压制: compel; force; press | ～使 pòshǐ force; compel
迫害 pòhài persecute
被迫 bèipò　　　逼迫 bīpò
强迫 qiǎngpò　　压迫 yāpò
饥寒交迫 jīhán-jiāopò
❷[形] 急促; 紧急: urgent; pressing | 从容不～cōngróng-bùpò ① be at leisure and without pressure; take one's time ② calm; unhurried
迫切 pòqiè urgent; pressing
紧迫 jǐnpò

破　　pò　10画 石部

破 破破破破破破破破破破

❶[动] 损坏; 使损坏; 使分裂: break; damage; split | ～成两半 pòchéng liǎng bàn break (split) into two halves
破产 pòchǎn ①go bankrupt ② fail; fall through
破坏 pòhuài ① destroy; do damage to ②change completely ③ violate
破裂 pòliè break; split
破碎 pòsuì ① tattered; broken ②smash (break) sth. into pieces; crush
爆破 bàopò
❷[动] 除掉; 突破: get rid of; break; violate | ～格 pògé break a rule; make an exception

/ 打～纪录 dǎpò jìlù break a record
破除 pòchú do away with; get rid of; eradicate; break with
冲破 chōngpò　　打破 dǎpò
突破 tūpò
❸[动] 把整的换成零的: break (a note) | 请把这一百元的票子～开。Qǐng bǎ zhè yībǎi yuán de piàozi pòkāi. Break this one-hundred-yuan note, please.
❹[动] 使真相露出; 揭穿: lay bare; expose the truth of | ～案 pò'àn crack a criminal case / 看～kànpò see through / 说～shuōpò lay bare; reveal
破获 pòhuò crack a case and capture the criminal
❺[形] 不完整的; 破烂的: broken; torn; worn out; tattered | 衣服～了。Yīfu pò le. The clothes are worn out. / 手擦～了皮。Shǒu cāpòle pí. My hand was grazed. / 纸撕～了。Zhǐ sīpò le. The paper is torn.
破旧 pòjiù old and shabby; worn-out; dilapidated
破烂 pòlàn ①ragged; worn-out ② junk
❻[形]不好的: lousy; paltry | 我不想看那个～电影。Wǒ bù xiǎng kàn nàge pò diànyǐng. I don't want to see that lousy film.

 剖　　pōu　10画 刂部

剖 剖剖剖剖剖剖剖剖剖
剖剖

[动] 切开；破开：cut open; rip open | 把瓜～开 bǎ guā pōukāi *cut open the melon*
解剖 jiěpōu

扑 (撲) pū　　　5画 扌部

扑 扑扑扑扑扑

❶[动] 拍打：flap; flutter | 海鸥～着翅膀，飞向高空。Hǎi'ōu pūzhe chìbǎng, fēixiàng gāokōng. *The seagulls flapped their wings and flew into the sky.*
扑灭 pūmiè stamp out; extinguish

❷[动] 用力向前冲，使身体突然伏在物体上：throw oneself on or at; pounce on | 孩子～到妈妈的怀里。Háizi pūdào māma de huái li. *The child threw himself into his mother's arms.* /老虎向山羊～去。Lǎohǔ xiàng shānyáng pūqù. *The tiger sprang on the goat.*

❸[动] 将全部心力用到 (某方面)：devote oneself to (work, etc.) | 他一心～在教学上。Tā yīxīn pū zài jiàoxué shang. *He devoted himself heart and soul to teaching.*

◇扑克 pūkè ① playing cards ②

poker

铺 (鋪) pū　　　12画 钅部

铺 铺铺铺铺铺铺铺铺
铺铺铺铺

[动] 把东西展开或摊平：spread; extend; unfold | ～床 pūchuáng *make the bed* /～路面 pū lùmiàn *surface a road, etc.* /～平道路 pūpíng dàolù *pave the way*
铺盖 pūgài spread (evenly) over
铺盖 pūgai bedding; bedclothes
卷铺盖 juǎnpūgai

仆 (僕) pú　　　4画 亻部

仆 仆仆仆仆仆

[名] 指被雇到家中做杂事、供役使的人 (跟 "主 zhǔ" 相对)：servant (the opposite of "主 zhǔ") | 女～nǚpú *female servant* /男～nánpú *male servant*
仆人 púrén (domestic) servant

葡 pú　　　12画 艹部

葡 葡葡葡葡葡葡葡葡
葡葡葡葡

See below
葡萄 pútao grape
葡萄酒 pútaojiǔ grape wine;

wine
葡萄糖 pútáotáng glucose

普通话 pǔtōnghuà putonghua;
Mandarin; common speech (of
the Chinese language); standard
Chinese pronunciation
科普 kēpǔ

朴（樸）pǔ　　6画 木部

朴　朴朴朴朴朴朴

[形] 纯真的；没有经过修饰的：
simple; plain
朴实 pǔshí ① simple; plain ②
sincere and honest; guileless
朴素 pǔsù simple; plain
质朴 zhìpǔ

谱（譜）pǔ　　14画 讠部

谱　谱谱谱谱谱谱谱谱
谱谱谱谱谱谱

❶ [名] 按照事物的类别或系统编成
的表、书或画成的图形：register
or record for reference in the
form of charts, tables, lists, etc.
| 家~ jiāpǔ family tree; genea-
logical tree / 食~ shípǔ recipe;
cook book / 棋~ qípǔ chess
manual
菜谱 càipǔ　　　脸谱 liǎnpǔ

普　pǔ　　12画 日部

普　普普普普普普普普
普普普普

[形] 广泛；全面：general; universal
| ~选 pǔxuǎn general election /
阳光~照大地。Yángguāng
pǔzhào dàdì. Sunlight floods
the earth; The sun illuminates
every corner of the land. / 昨天
晚上全市~降大雨。Zuótiān
wǎnshang quánshì pǔ jiàng
dàyǔ. Last night there was
heavy rain all over the city.
普遍 pǔbiàn general; wide-
spread
普查 pǔchá general investigation
普及 pǔjí popularize; spread
普通 pǔtōng average; com-
mon; ordinary

❷ [名] 用符号记载下来的音乐作
品：music score | 歌~ gēpǔ
music of a song / 乐~ yuèpǔ
music score
❸ [动] 为歌词配曲：set to music;
compose (music) | 请把这首
诗~成歌曲。Qǐng bǎ zhè
shǒu shī pǔchéng gēqǔ.
Please set this poem to music.
谱曲 pǔqǔ set to music
❹ [名] 大致的标准；把握：sth. to
count on | 他做事有~。Tā
zuòshì yǒu pǔ. He knows what
he is doing.

瀑　pù　　18画 氵部

瀑 瀑瀑瀑瀑瀑瀑瀑瀑
瀑瀑瀑瀑瀑瀑瀑
瀑瀑

See 瀑布

瀑布 pù bù waterfall; falls; cata-
ract

Q q

七 七七

[数] 数字：seven｜一个星期~天。Yī gè xīngqī qī tiān. *A week consists of seven days.*

七嘴八舌 qīzuǐ-bāshé seven mouths and eight tongues;with everybody trying to get a word in

乱七八糟 luànqībāzāo

沏 沏沏沏沏沏沏沏

[动]（用开水）冲；泡：infuse (with boiling water)｜~茶 qīchá *make tea*

妻 妻妻妻妻妻妻妻妻

[名]男子的配偶（跟"夫 fū"相对）：wife; spouse of a man (the opposite of "夫 fū")｜未婚~ wèihūnqī *fiancee*
妻子 qīzi wife

凄 | qī 10画 冫部

凄 凄凄凄凄凄凄凄凄凄
凄凄凄

❶[形]悲伤：sad; miserable
凄惨 qīcǎn tragic; wretched

❷[形]寂寞；冷落：chilly; cold
凄凉 qīliáng desolate; bleak

期 | qī 12画 月部

期 期期期期期期期期
期期期期

❶[名]预定的时间：scheduled time｜按~完成任务 ānqī wánchéng rènwù *accomplish the task according to schedule* / 你借的书明天到~。Nǐ jiè de shū míngtiān dàoqī. *The book you borrowed is due tomorrow.*

期货 qīhuò (econ.) futures
期限 qīxiàn deadline
按期 ānqī   档期 dàngqī
到期 dàoqī   定期 dìngqī
改期 gǎiqī   过期 guòqī
任期 rènqī   限期 xiànqī
预期 yùqī   有效期 yǒuxiàoqī

❷[名]一段时间：a period of time｜短训班 6 个月一~。Duǎnxùn-bān liù gè yuè yī qī. *Each short-term training class lasts six months.*

期间 qījiān in the period of
期刊 qīkān periodical; journal

长期 chángqī　分期 fēnqī
后期 hòuqī　假期 jiàqī
近期 jìnqī　前期 qiánqī
日期 rìqī　时期 shíqī
暑期 shǔqī　同期 tóngqī
星期 xīngqī　学期 xuéqī
早期 zǎoqī　中期 zhōngqī
周期 zhōuqī
星期日 Xīngqīrì
星期天 Xīngqītiān

❸[量] 用于分期的事物：(for things scheduled by period) issue; number; session | 讲习班办了三～。Jiǎngxí bān bànle sān qī. *The study session has been held three times.* / 这杂志我读过两～。Zhè zázhì wǒ dúguo liǎng qī. *I have read two issues of this magazine.*

❹[动]等待；盼望：expect | ～盼 qīpàn *expect; look forward to*
期待 qīdài expect;hope for; await; look forward to
期望 qīwàng ① hope; expect; wish ② hope; expectation

qī　12画 欠部

欺欺欺欺欺欺欺欺
欺欺欺欺

❶[动]骗：deceive | 自～zìqī *deceive oneself*
欺骗 qīpiàn deceive; dupe

❷[动]压迫、侮辱：bully; take advantage of | ～压 qīyā oppress
欺负 qīfu bully

漆　qī　14画 氵部

漆漆漆漆漆漆漆漆
漆漆漆漆漆漆

[名]用漆树皮的黏汁或其他树脂做成的涂料：various kinds of paint, both natural and man-made
漆器 qīqì lacquerware; lacquerwork
油漆 yóuqī

◇漆黑 qīhēi as dark as night; pitch black

齐(齊) qí　6画 齐部

齐齐齐齐齐齐

❶[形] 整齐：uniform; neat | 整～的队伍 zhěngqí de duìwu *a neat procession of troops* / 书理得很～。Shū lǐ de hěn qí. *The books are put in a neat order.*
整齐 zhěngqí

❷[动] 达到一样的高度：level with; be on a level with | 草长得～人高了。Cǎo zhǎng de qí rén gāo le. *The weeds have grown so high that they are as tall as a person.*

❸[形] 同样；一致：alike; identical | ～心 qíxīn *be of one mind*

/～声歌唱 qíshēng gēchàng *sing in chorus*

❹[副] 一起；同时：simultaneously; together ｜ 大家～动手。Dàjiā qí dòngshǒu. *Everybody pitched in.*
一齐 yīqí
百花齐放 bǎihuā-qífàng

❺[形] 全；完备：all ready; all present ｜ 客人来～了。Kèrén láiqí le. *The guests are all present. /* 准备～了 zhǔnbèi qí le *everything is ready*
齐全 qíquán complete

其 qí 8画 八部

其 其 其 其 其 其 其 其

❶[代]那个；那样：that; such ｜ ～中 qízhōng among (that, those, etc.)
其次 qícì ① next; then ② secondary
其间 qíjiān ① between or among them; in it ② time; period
其实 qíshí actually
其余 qíyú the others; the rest
及其 jíqí

❷[代]他、她、它(们)的：his (her, its, their) ｜ ～父 qífù *his (or her) father*

❸[代]他、她、它(们)：he (she, it; they) ｜ 劝～努力学习 quàn qí nǔlì xuéxí *encourage him to study hard*
其他 qítā other; else

奇 qí 8画 大部

奇 奇 奇 奇 奇 奇 奇 奇

❶[形]少见的；特殊的：rare; strange; queer ｜ ～人 qírén *a unique person; legendary figure*
奇怪 qíguài peculiar; strange
奇妙 qímiào wonderful
奇特 qítè singular; unusual
奇异 qíyì strange; surprised
奇花异草 qíhuā-yìcǎo exotic flowers and rare herbs
传奇 chuánqí 好奇 hàoqí

❷[形]出人意料的：unexpected; against all expectations ｜ ～袭 qíxí *surprise attack*
奇迹 qíjì marvel; miracle
神奇 shénqí

❸[动] 觉得奇怪：be surprised; be astonished
惊奇 jīngqí

歧 qí 8画 止部

歧 歧 歧 歧 歧 歧 歧 歧

❶[形]岔(道)：fork; branch ｜ ～途 qítú *wrong road*

❷[形]不相同；不一样：divergent; different
歧视 qíshì discriminate
分歧 fēnqí

骑 (騎) qí 11画 马部

骑 骑骑骑骑骑骑骑骑
骑骑骑

[动] 两腿分开跨坐：ride; sit on the back | ～马 qímǎ *ride a horse* / ～自行车 qí zìxíngchē *ride a bicycle*

棋　　qí　　12画 木部

棋 棋棋棋棋棋棋棋棋
棋棋棋棋

[名] 文娱项目的一类：chess or any board game | 我们下一盘～吧。Wǒmen xià yī pán qí ba. *Let's play a game of chess.*
棋手 qíshǒu chess player
下棋 xiàqí
象棋 xiàngqí
国际象棋 guójì xiàngqí

旗　　qí　　14画 方部

旗 旗旗旗旗旗旗旗旗
旗旗旗旗旗旗

[名] 旗子：flag; banner | 国～ guóqí *national flag* / 升～仪式 shēng qí yíshì *flag raising ceremony*
旗号 qíhào banner; pretext
旗舰 qíjiàn flagship
旗帜 qízhì ① banner; flag; colours ② standard; colours ③ good example; model
旗子 qízi flag; banner; pennant
红旗 hóngqí

◇旗袍 qípáo a close-fitting woman's dress with high neck and slit skirt; cheongsam

乞　　qǐ　　3画 ∠部

乞 乞乞乞

[动] 向人讨取；请求：beg (for alms, etc.); supplicate | ～讨 qǐtǎo *beg; go begging*
乞求 qǐqiú beg for; invoke

岂 (豈)　　qǐ　　6画 山部

岂 岂岂岂岂岂岂

[副] 怎么；难道，表示反问：used in a rhetorical question for emphasis; where, how | ～敢 qǐgǎn *you flatter me; I don't deserve such praise (or honour)* / ～能 qǐnéng *(used to ask a rhetorical question) how could...; how can...*
岂不 qǐbù isn't that...; doesn't that...; hasn't that...; won't that...
岂有此理 qǐyǒu-cǐlǐ outrageous; absurd; who ever heard of such absurdity

企　　qǐ　　6画 人部

企 企企企企企企

[动]希望；盼望：anxiously expect; look forward to ｜ ～盼 qǐpàn hope for; long for

企图 qǐtú attempt; seek; try

企鹅 qǐ'é penguin

◇企业 qǐyè enterprise; business

企业家 qǐyèjiā entrepreneur; big businessman

 (啟) qǐ 7画 户部

启 启 启 启 启 启 启

❶[动]开导：enlighten; awaken ｜ ～蒙 qǐméng enlighten; enlightenment

启发 qǐfā enlighten; inspire

启示 qǐshì inspiration; enlightenment; revelation

❷[动]开始：start; begin

启程 qǐchéng start off on a journey

启动 qǐdòng start (a machine, etc.); switch on

开启 kāiqǐ

❸[动]陈述；说明：state; inform

启事 qǐshì notice; announcement

 qǐ 10画 走部

起 起 起 起 起 起 起 起 起 起

❶[动]由躺而坐；由坐而站：rise; get up; stand up ｜ 早睡早～

zǎoshuì zǎoqǐ *early to bed and early to rise* ｜ 他站～身。Tā zhànqǐ shēn. *He stood up.*

起床 qǐchuáng get up; get out of bed

起伏 qǐfú undulate; rise and fall

起来 qǐlái (lai) stand up

起身 qǐshēn ① get up; rise ② leave; set out; get off

掀起 xiānqǐ

❷[动]物体由下往上升：rise ｜ 皮球拍不～来了。Píqiú pāi bù qǐlái le. *The leather ball does not bounce.*

❸[动]长出：appear; grow ｜ 脚上～水泡 jiǎo shang qǐ shuǐpào *get blisters on one's feet*

❹[动]发生；开始：start; begin ｜ ～火 qǐhuǒ *fire broke out* ｜～心 qǐ yíxīn *become suspicious* ｜～作用 qǐ zuòyòng *take effect* ｜～风了。Qǐfēng le. *The wind is picking up.*

起步 qǐbù start; move

起初 qǐchū originally; at first; at the outset

起点 qǐdiǎn starting point

起飞 qǐfēi take off

起哄 qǐhòng ① gather together to create a disturbance ② (of a crowd of people) jeer; boo and hoot

起劲 qǐjìn vigorously; in high spirits

起诉 qǐsù sue; conduct a suit

起义 qǐyì uprising

起源 qǐyuán ① origin; source ② stem from; originate

发起 fāqǐ　　兴起 xīngqǐ

引起 yǐnqǐ

❺[动]拟订：draft; work out | ~稿 qǐgǎo *make (work out) a draft*

起草 qǐcǎo draft

◇起码 qǐmǎ ① minimum ② at least

不起眼 bùqǐyǎn

对不起 duìbuqǐ

对得起 duìdeqǐ

看不起 kànbuqǐ

看起来 kànqǐlai

气（氣）qì　　4画 气部

气 气气气气

❶[名] 气体；特指空气：gas; air | 打开窗子透透~。Dǎkāi chuāngzi tòutòu qì. *Open the window to let the fresh air in.* / 这球~很足。Zhè qiú qì hěn zú. *The ball is completely inflated.*

气垫 qìdiàn air cushion

气流 qìliú ①air current; airflow; airstream ② breath

气球 qìqiú balloon

气体 qìtǐ gas

气温 qìwēn air temperature; atmospheric temperature

气压 qìyā atmospheric pressure; barometric pressure

大气 dàqì　　电气 diànqì

废气 fèiqì　　空气 kōngqì

煤气 méiqì　　暖气 nuǎnqì

尾气 wěiqì　　氧气 yǎngqì

大气压 dàqìyā

水蒸气 shuǐzhēngqì

天然气 tiānránqì

❷[名]冷暖阴晴等自然现象：weather; climate | 天~tiānqì *weather*

气候 qìhòu ①climate; weather ② situation ③ successful development

气象 qìxiàng ①meteorological phenomena ② meteorology ③ atmosphere; scene

❸[名]呼吸时出入的气；气息：breath | 喘不过~来 chuǎnbuguò qì lái *lose one's breath; gasp for breath* / 上~不接下~ shàngqì bù jiē xiàqì *be out of breath; gasp for breath*

气喘 qìchuǎn asthma

气功 qìgōng breathing exercise

气力 qìlì effort

气息 qìxī ① breath ② flavour; smell

气管炎 qìguǎnyán tracheitis

力气 lìqi　　叹气 tànqì

一口气 yīkǒuqì

❹[动] 恼怒；使人发怒：get angry; be enraged; be annoyed | 又~又急 yòu qì yòu jí *both angry and worried* /他~得直哆嗦。Tā qì de zhí duōsuo. *He*

581

is trembling with rage. / 孩子被~哭了。Háizi bèi qìkū le. *The kid was enraged to tears.* / 我故意~他一下。Wǒ gùyì qì tā yīxià. *I deliberately annoyed him.; I made him angry on purpose.*

气愤 qìfèn indignation

生气 shēngqì

❺ [名] 气味: smell; odour; flavour | 香~xiāngqì *sweet smell*

气味 qìwèi ① smell; odour; flavour ② smack; taste

❻ [名] 人的精神状态: spirit; morale | 神~shénqì *manner; spirited; cocky*

气氛 qìfēn air; atmosphere

气概 qìgài lofty quality; mettle; spirit

气魄 qìpò boldness of vision; imposing manner

气色 qìsè complexion; colour

气势 qìshì momentum; imposing manner

气质 qìzhì ① temperament; disposition ② qualities; makings

服气 fúqì	口气 kǒuqì
名气 míngqì	丧气 sāngqì
泄气 xièqì	勇气 yǒngqì
语气 yǔqì	朝气 zhāoqì
争气 zhēngqì	志气 zhìqì

❼ [名] 作风; 习气: airs; manner | 官~guānqì *bureaucratic airs* / 孩子~háiziqì *childishness* / 书生~shūshēngqì *bookish*

风气 fēngqì	和气 héqì
娇气 jiāoqì	景气 jǐngqì
客气 kèqì	脾气 píqì
淘气 táoqì	正气 zhèngqì
小气鬼 xiǎoqìguǐ	
发脾气 fāpíqì	

弃 qì 7画 廾部

弃 弃弃弃弃弃弃弃

[动] 舍去; 扔掉: throw away; discard | 遗~yíqì *abandon; cast off* / ~医从文 qì yī cóng wén *abandon medicine for literature*

放弃 fàngqì 抛弃 pāoqì

汽 qì 7画 氵部

汽 汽汽汽汽汽汽汽

❶ [名] 液体或固体受热后变成的气体: vapour; steam | 蒸笼里的~正往外冒。Zhēnglóng li de qì zhèng wǎngwài mào. *The food steamer was emitting steam.* / 他刚洗过澡, 卫生间都是水~。Tā gāng xǐguo zǎo, wèishēngjiān dōu shì shuǐqì. *He has just had a bath, and the bathroom is full of steam.*

汽车 qìchē automobile; car; motor vehicle

汽水 qìshuǐ fizzy water; soft drink; soda water

❷[名]特指水蒸气：water steam
汽船 qìchuán steamship;
steamer
蒸汽 zhēngqì
◇汽油 qìyóu petrol; gasoline

砌 qì 9画 石部

砌 砌砌砌砌砌砌砌砌砌
砌

[动] 用泥灰将砖石粘合、垒起：
build by laying bricks or stones
｜～墙 qìqiáng build a wall
(with bricks, stones, etc.)

器 qì 16画 口部

器 器器器器器器器
器器器器器器器

❶[名]用具；工具：implement;
utensil; ware｜瓷～cíqì chinaware; china; porcelain / 木～
mùqì wooden furniture
器材 qìcái equipment; material
器具 qìjù utensil
器械 qìxiè ① apparatus; appliance; instrument ② weapon
电器 diànqì　　机器 jīqì
漆器 qīqì　　容器 róngqì
武器 wǔqì　　仪器 yíqì
乐器 yuèqì
处理器 chǔlǐqì 服务器 fúwùqì
核武器 héwǔqì
计算器 jìsuànqì

青铜器 qīngtóngqì
热水器 rèshuǐqì
听诊器 tīngzhěnqì
显示器 xiǎnshìqì
❷[名]指器官：organ
器官 qìguān organ

掐 qiā 11画 扌部

掐 掐掐掐掐掐掐掐
掐掐掐

❶[动]用手指甲按或用指甲刻入、
截断：pinch; nip｜不要～花儿。
Bùyào qiā huār. Don't pick the
flowers. /把香烟～了。Bǎ xiāng-
yān qiā le. Stub out the cigarette.
❷[动]用手的虎口紧紧按住：clutch
｜～脖子 qiā bózi seize sb. by
the throat; take by the throat /
他～住我的手腕不放。Tā qiā-
zhù wǒ de shǒuwàn bù fàng.
He seized me by the wrist and
wouldn't let me go.

洽 qiǎ 9画 氵部

洽 洽洽洽洽洽洽洽洽
洽

[动]接头；商量：arrange with;
consult｜接～jiēqiǎ meet to discuss
洽谈 qiǎtán consult; discuss together

恰

qià　9画 忄部

 恰恰恰恰恰恰恰恰恰

❶ [形]合适；适当：appropriate; proper

恰当 qiàdàng proper

❷ [副]正好：just; exactly ｜他来得∼是时候。Tā lái de qià shì shíhou. *He came in the nick of time.*

恰好 qiàhǎo just right

恰恰 qiàqià just; exactly; precisely

恰巧 qiàqiǎo by chance; by coincidence

恰到好处 qiàdào-hǎochù just fine

恰如其分 qiàrúqífèn appropriate

千

qiān　3画 十部

千 千千千

❶ [数]十个一百：thousand ｜成∼上万 chéngqiān-shàngwàn *tens of thousands* / 他每月工资是两∼元。Tā měiyuè gōngzī shì liǎng qiān yuán. *His monthly pay is two thousand yuan.*

千克 qiānkè kilogram (kg.)

千瓦 qiānwǎ kilowatt (kw.)

千万 qiānwàn ① ten million; millions upon millions ② be sure to

千千万万 qiānqiān-wànwàn thousands upon thousands

❷ [数]表示很多：a great number of ｜∼言万语 qiānyán-wànyǔ *thousands and thousands of words*

千变万化 qiānbiàn-wànhuà ever-changing

千方百计 qiānfāng-bǎijì in a thousand and one ways; by every possible means; by hook or by crook

千家万户 qiānjiā-wànhù innumerable households or families; every family

千军万马 qiānjūn-wànmǎ thousands upon thousands of horses and soldiers; a powerful army; a mighty force

迁 (遷)

qiān　6画 辶部

 迁 迁迁迁迁迁迁

❶ [动]（住所等）搬到别处：move ｜乔∼qiáoqiān *move to a better place; move to a new house* / 他已经∼往外地了。Tā yǐjīng qiān wǎng wàidì le. *He has moved away to another place.*

迁移 qiānyí move; remove; migrate

搬迁 bānqiān

❷ [动]改变：change ｜变∼biànqiān *change of situation;*

change

◇迁就qiānjiù yield to; accommodate oneself to

牵 (牽) qiān　9画 大部

牵 牵牵牵牵牵牵牵牵牵
牵

❶[动]拉; 领着向前: lead along; pull | 手～手 shǒu qiān shǒu *hand in hand* / 这匹马很好～。Zhè pǐ mǎ hěn hǎo qiān. *This horse can easily be led along.*
牵引 qiānyǐn tow; draw
牵制 qiānzhì check
牵牛花 qiānniúhuā (white-edged) morning glory
❷[动]连带; 关系到: involve | 他不愿意～进去。Tā bù yuànyì qiān jìnqu. *He doesn't want to get involved.*
牵扯 qiānchě involve; implicate; drag in
牵强 qiānqiǎng farfetched

铅 (鉛) qiān　10画 钅部

铅 铅铅铅铅铅铅铅铅
铅铅

❶[名]lead
铅球 qiānqiú (sports) shot
❷[名]指石墨笔心: black lead | 这种铅笔～比较粗。Zhè zhǒng qiānbǐ qiān bǐjiào cū. *The*

lead of this kind of pencil is thicker.
铅笔 qiānbǐ pencil

谦 (謙) qiān　12画 讠部

谦 谦谦谦谦谦谦谦谦
谦谦谦谦

[形]虚心; 不自满: modest; self-effacing | ～和 qiānhé *modest and amiable*
谦虚 qiānxū ① modest ② make modest remarks
谦逊 qiānxùn modest and humble

签 (簽) qiān　13画 竹部

签 签签签签签签签签
签签签签签

[动]在文件或单据上写姓名、文字或画符号: sign; autograph
签订 qiāndìng sign
签发 qiānfā sign and issue
签名 qiānmíng sign
签署 qiānshǔ sign; subscribe
签约 qiānyuē sign a treaty or agreement
签证 qiānzhèng visa
签字 qiānzì sign
标签 biāoqiān 抽签 chōuqiān

前 qiān　9画 丷部

前 前前前前前前前前前
前

❶ [名] 在正面的（跟"后 hòu"相对）: front (the opposite of "后 hòu") | ～门 qiánmén *front door* / 向～走 xiàngqián zǒu *go forward*

前边 qiánbian ①in front; ahead ② above; preceding

前方 qiánfāng ① ahead ② the front

前锋 qiánfēng ① vanguard ② (sports) forward ③ (meteorol.) front

前进 qiánjìn advance

前面 qiánmian front

前头 qiántou ① in front; at the head; ahead ② above; preceding

前往 qiánwǎng go to; leave for

前沿 qiányán (mil.) forward position

当前 dāngqián 跟前 gēnqián
面前 miànqián 目前 mùqián
眼前 yǎnqián

❷ [名] 过去的；较早的: past; before; ago | ～几年 qián jǐ nián *several years ago* / 晚饭～ wǎnfàn qián *before supper*

前辈 qiánbèi ①senior (person); elder ② the older generation

前年 qiánnián the year before last

前人 qiánrén forefathers; predecessors

前天 qiántiān the day before yesterday

前不久 qiánbùjiǔ not long ago

前所未有 qiánsuǒwèiyǒu hitherto unknown; unprecedented

大前天 dàqiántiān

❸ [名] 未来: future | 向～看 xiàngqián kàn *look ahead; look into the future*

前程 qiánchéng future

前景 qiánjǐng foreground; prospect

前途 qiántú future; prospect

❹ [名] 次序在先的（跟"后 hòu"相对）: first (the opposite of "后 hòu") | ～三名 qiánsānmíng *the first three* / 我的号码在你～面。Wǒ de hàomǎ zài nǐ qiánmian. *My queue number is in front of yours.*

前列 qiánliè front

前期 qiánqī earlier stage; early days

前提 qiántí premise

前线 qiánxiàn front

提前 tíqián

❺ [名] 指某事物产生之前: earlier; prior to | 事～ shìqián *before sth.; prior to sth.* / 下班～请务必关灯。Xiàbān qián qǐng wùbì guāndēng. *Make sure to turn off the lights before leaving the office.*

 钱 (錢) qián 10 画 钅部

钱 钱钱钱钱钱钱钱钱钱钱
钱钱

❶ [名]货币：money; currency
花钱 huāqián　金钱 jīnqián
零钱 língqián　现钱 xiànqián
压岁钱 yāsuìqián
赚钱 zhuànqián

❷ [名]费用; 款子：expense; fund;
sum ｜车~chēqián *(of bus,
taxi, etc.)fare* / 饭~fànqián
food expenses / 收到一笔~
shōudào yī bǐ qián *receive a
sum of money*
钱包 qiánbāo wallet; purse
本钱 běnqián　工钱 gōngqián
价钱 jiàqian
讲价钱 jiǎngjiàqian

❸ [名]钱财：wealth; money ｜有~
人 yǒu qián rén *wealthy
people; rich man*
钱财 qiáncái wealth; money

 钳 (鉗)　qián　10画 钅部
钳 钳钳钳钳钳钳钳钳钳
钳钳

See 钳子
钳子 qiánzi pliers; pincers; for-
ceps

 潜 (潛)　qián　15画 氵部
潜 潜潜潜潜潜潜潜潜
潜潜潜潜潜潜潜

❶ [动]隐在水面下：go under wa-
ter ｜ ~水 qiánshuǐ *dive; go under water*
潜艇 qiántǐng submarine

❷ [形] 隐藏的：hidden; latent
潜伏 qiánfú hide in concealment
潜力 qiánlì latent capacity; potential
潜能 qiánnéng (phys.) latent
energy
潜逃 qiántáo abscond
潜在 qiánzài latent; potential

浅 (淺)　qiǎn　8画 氵部
浅 浅浅浅浅浅浅浅浅

❶ [形]上下或里外之间的距离小
（跟"深shēn"相对）：shallow
(the opposite of "深 shēn")
｜ ~水 qiǎnshuǐ *shallow
(shoal) water* /这条河很~。Zhè
tiáo hé hěn qiǎn. *This is a
shallow river.*
深浅 shēnqiǎn

❷ [形]学问、见识不多：lack of ex-
perience and knowledge ｜他对
问题的认识很~。Tā duì
wèntí de rènshi hěn qiǎn. *His
understanding of the problem is
quite shallow.*

❸ [形]简明易懂：simple; easy ｜
这篇课文很~。Zhè piān
kèwén hěn qiǎn. *This text is
very easy.*

❹ [形]颜色淡：light; pale ｜ ~黄

qiǎnhuáng *pale yellow* / ~绿 qiǎnlǜ *light green*

❺ [形]感情不深：not on intimate terms | 关系~guānxi qiǎn *(in interpersonal relationships) not on familiar terms*

遣 qiǎn 13画 辶部

遣遣遣遣遣遣遣遣遣遣遣遣遣

[动]派出去；使离去：send; dispatch | ~送 qiǎnsòng *repatriate; send back*
派遣 pàiqiǎn

谴(譴) qiǎn 15画 讠部

谴谴谴谴谴谴谴谴谴谴谴谴谴谴谴

[动]责备：condemn; censure; reproach
谴责 qiǎnzé *condemn*

欠 qiàn 4画 欠部

欠欠欠欠

❶ [动]缺少；不够：lack; be not enough | ~妥 qiàntuǒ *be not proper* / 身体~佳 shēntǐ qiànjiā *be not well enough; feel unwell; under the weather* /说话~考虑 shuōhuà qiàn kǎolǜ *make a statement without due consid-*

eration

欠缺 qiànquē ① be deficient in; be short of ② shortcoming; deficiency

❷ [动]借别人的财物等没归还；应给别人的东西还没给：owe; be behind with | ~人情 qiàn rénqíng *owe sb. a debt of gratitude; be indebted to sb.* /我~他十块钱。Wǒ qiàn tā shí kuài qián. *I owe him ten yuan.*
拖欠 tuōqiàn

❸ [动]身体一部分稍稍向上移动：raise slightly a part of the body | ~脚 qiànjiǎo *slightly raise one's heels*

嵌 qiàn 12画 山部

嵌嵌嵌嵌嵌嵌嵌嵌嵌嵌嵌嵌

[动] 把较小的东西卡在较大的东西的凹陷里：inlay; embed; set | 镶~xiāngqiàn *inlay* /桌面上~着大理石。Zhuōmiàn shang qiànzhe dàlǐshí. *The surface of the desk is set with marble.*

歉 qiàn 14画 欠部

歉歉歉歉歉歉歉歉歉歉歉歉歉歉

[动]觉得对不住别人：owe sb. an apology; feel apologetic
歉意 qiànyì *apology*

抱歉 bàoqiàn　道歉 dàoqiàn

枪（槍）qiāng　8画 木部

枪 枪枪枪枪枪枪枪枪

[名]发射子弹的武器：rifle; gun; firearm

枪毙 qiāngbì execute by shooting

枪战 qiāngzhàn gun battle; shoot-out

枪支 qiāngzhī firearms

标枪 biāoqiāng　机枪 jīqiāng

开枪 kāiqiāng　手枪 shǒuqiāng

腔　qiāng　12画 月部

腔 腔腔腔腔腔腔腔腔腔
腔腔腔腔

❶[名]动物身体里或物体中的空心部分：cavity in human or animal bodies｜鼻～bíqiāng nasal cavity

口腔 kǒuqiāng　满腔 mǎnqiāng

❷[名]乐曲的调子：tune｜唱～chàngqiāng aria / 你唱走～儿了。Nǐ chàngzǒu qiāngr le. *You sang out of tune.*

❸[名]说话; 说话的声音、语气等：talk; tone; accent｜学生～xuéshēngqiāng *bookish talk; classroom tone of a student* / 北京～Běijīngqiāng *Beijing accent*

强　qiáng　12画 弓部

强 强强强强强强强强
强强强强

❶[形]健壮; 力量大（跟"弱ruò"相对）：strong; powerful (the opposite of "弱ruò")｜身体～壮 shēntǐ qiángzhuàng *strong and healthy*

强大 qiángdà big and powerful; formidable

强度 qiángdù intensity

强化 qiánghuà strengthen

强劲 qiángjìng powerful; forceful

强烈 qiángliè ① strong ② strongly

强盛 qiángshèng (of a country) powerful and prosperous

强硬 qiángyìng strong; tough; unyielding

富强 fùqiáng　加强 jiāqiáng

增强 zēngqiáng

发愤图强 fāfèn-túqiáng

❷[副]使用强力：by force｜～取 qiángqǔ take by force; extort /～令执行 qiánglìng zhíxíng *execute on a peremptory order*

强暴 qiángbào ① violent; brutal ② ferocious adversary

强盗 qiángdào robber; bandit

强奸 qiángjiān violate (a woman); rape

强行 qiángxíng force

强制 qiángzhì by force

❸[副]程度高（常用于感情或意志

方面）: great in degree (used for expressing emotions or will) | 能力很～nénglì hěn qiáng *very capable* / 责任心～zérènxīn qiáng *have a strong sense of responsibility*

坚强jiānqiáng 顽强wánqiáng

❹ [形] 优越; 好: excellent; fine | 一代比一代～。Yī dài bǐ yī dài qiáng. *Each generation surpasses the preceding one.* / 生活一年比一年～。Shēnghuó yī nián bǐ yī nián qiáng. *Life is getting better each year.*

◇ 强调 qiángdiào emphasize See qiǎng.

墙（墙） qiáng 14画 土部

墙 墙墙墙墙墙墙墙墙 墙墙墙墙墙墙

[名] wall | 围～wéiqiáng *enclosing (surrounding) wall* / 把画挂到～上。Bǎ huà guàdào qiáng shang. *Hang the picture on the wall.*

墙壁 qiángbì wall
城墙 chéngqiáng

抢（搶） qiǎng 7画 扌部

 抢抢抢抢抢抢抢

❶ [动] 把不属于自己的东西强行夺过来: rob; loot; snatch | ～球

qiǎngqiú *scramble for the ball* / 她把照片～了过去。Tā bǎ zhàopiàn qiǎngle guòqu. *She snatched the photo away.*

抢夺 qiǎngduó snatch; wrest; seize
抢劫 qiǎngjié rob

❷ [动] 争先: vie for; scramble for | ～着报名 qiǎngzhe bàomíng *vie for enrolling one's name* / ～着说话 qiǎngzhe shuōhuà *interrupt; break in; vie with each other to speak*

抢救 qiǎngjiù rescue; save; salvage

❸ [动] 抓紧时间（做）: make the best use of time | ～修qiǎngxiū *do rush repairs; rush to repair* / ～救 qiǎngjiù *rescue; save*

抢占qiǎngzhàn ① race to control; seize; grab ② unlawfully occupy

---

强 qiǎng 12画 弓部

强 强强强强强强强强 强强强强

[形] 迫使: force; compel | ～作笑脸qiǎngzuò xiàoliǎn *force a smile* /～作镇静qiǎngzuò zhènjìng *make an effort to appear composed; try hard to keep one's composure*

强迫 qiǎngpò compel
勉强 miǎnqiǎng

牵强 qiānqiǎng
See qiǎng.

悄 qiāo 10画 忄部

悄 悄悄悄悄悄悄悄悄
悄悄

See 悄悄
悄悄 qiāoqiāo quietly

锹 (鍬) qiāo 14画 钅部

锹 锹锹锹锹锹锹锹锹
锹锹锹锹锹锹

[名] spade｜他用～挖土。Tā
yòng qiāo wātǔ. *He dug the
ground with a spade.*

敲 qiāo 14画 高部

敲 敲敲敲敲敲敲敲敲
敲敲敲敲敲敲

[动]击；打：knock; beat｜～鼓
qiāogǔ *beat the drums* /～门
qiāomén *knock at the door* /～
警钟 qiāo jǐngzhōng *sound the
alarm bell* / 钟刚～过4点。
Zhōng gāng qiāoguo sì diǎn.
The clock has just struck four.
敲竹杠 qiāozhúgàng fleece;
overcharge; make sb. pay
through the nose
敲锣打鼓 qiāoluó-dǎgǔ beat
drums and gongs (in celebration

of sth.)

乔 (喬) qiāo 6画 丿部

乔 乔乔乔乔乔乔

[动] 作假：disguise
乔装 qiāozhuāng disguise;
dress up

侨 (僑) qiāo 8画 亻部

侨 侨侨侨侨侨侨侨侨

❶ [动]寄居国外：live abroad
❷ [名]寄居在国外的人：person
living abroad
侨胞 qiāobāo countrymen (nationals) residing abroad
华侨 huáqiāo

桥 (橋) qiāo 10画 木部

桥 桥桥桥桥桥桥桥桥
桥桥

[名] bridge｜木～mùqiāo *wooden
bridge* / 天～tiānqiāo *over-
bridge; platform bridge* / 船正
从～下过。Chuán zhèng cóng
qiāoxià guò. *The boat is passing under the bridge.*
桥梁 qiāoliáng bridge
立交桥 lìjiāoqiāo

瞧 qiāo 17画 目部

瞧 瞧瞧瞧瞧瞧瞧瞧瞧瞧瞧瞧瞧瞧瞧瞧瞧瞧瞧

[动]看：look; see｜~热闹 qiáo rènao *watch the excitement (fun)*｜~，他来了。Qiáo, tā lái le. *Look, here he comes.*｜你~着办吧。Nǐ qiáozhe bàn ba. *It depends on you.*

 巧 巧巧巧巧巧

qiǎo 5画 工部

❶ [形]心思灵敏；技术高明：skillful; ingenious; clever｜手~ shǒuqiǎo *deft with one's hands; dexterous*｜他很~。Tā hěn qiǎo. *He is very good with his hands.*
巧妙 qiǎomiào skillful
技巧 jìqiǎo 　灵巧 língqiǎo
心灵手巧 xīnlíng-shǒuqiǎo
❷ [形]正好(碰上机会)：just at the right time｜碰~ pèngqiǎo *by chance; by coincidence*｜你来得真~。Nǐ lái de zhēn qiǎo. *You arrived just at the right time.*｜他偏~那天不在。Tā piānqiǎo nà tiān bù zài. *As luck would have it, he was away that day.*
巧合 qiǎohé coincidence; by chance or coincidence
凑巧 còuqiǎo 　可巧 kěqiǎo
恰巧 qiàqiǎo 　正巧 zhèngqiǎo
◇ 巧克力 qiǎokèlì chocolate

翘 (翹) qiāo 12画 羽部

翘 翘翘翘翘翘翘翘翘翘 翘翘翘翘

[动]一头儿向上仰起：raise｜~起尾巴 qiàoqǐ wěiba *curl up the tail*｜木板~起来了。Mùbǎn qiào qǐlai le. *The plank bends upwards.*

切 qiē 4画 刀部

切 切切切切

[动]用刀把物体分成几部分：cut; slice｜~菜 qiēcài *cut up vegetables*｜~西瓜 qiē xīguā *cut up a watermelon*｜~成两半 qiēchéng liǎng bàn *cut into halves; cut into two*
See qiè.

茄 qié 8画 艹部

茄 茄茄茄茄茄茄茄茄茄

See below
茄子 qiézi eggplant; aubergine
番茄 fānqié

且 qiě 5画 丨部

且 且且且且且

❶ [副]表示暂时；姑且：just; for the time being (usu. written)｜~

慢 qiěmàn *wait a moment; no hurry* / 这事～放一下。Zhè shì qiě fàng yīxià. *Leave the matter for now.*

姑且 gūqiě　　暂且 zànqiě

❷ [连] 表示并列关系：also; both ... and ... | 并～bìngqiě *and; besides; moreover*

而且 érqiě

❸ [连] 尚且；表示让步：yet; still

❹ [连] 连接两个部分，表示递进关系：used to join two clauses, indicating a progressive increase | 既高～大 jì gāo qiě dà *both tall and big*

况且 kuàngqiě

切　　qiē　　4画 刀部

切 切切切切

❶ [动] 靠近；接近：near; approach; be close to | ～身利益 qiēshēn lìyì *one's immediate interests*

亲切 qīnqiè

❷ [形] 急迫：eager; anxious | 回家心～huíjiā xīnqiè *be anxious to return home; can't wait to go home*

迫切 pòqiè

❸ [动] 符合：correspond to | 不～实际 bù qiē shíjì *not correspond to reality; unrealistic; impractical* / 译文不～原意。Yìwén bù qiē yuányì. *The trans-*

lation does not match the original meaning.

切实 qièshí ① feasible ② earnestly

◇ 不顾一切 bùgù-yīqiè See qiē.

怯　　qiè　　8画 忄部

怯 怯怯怯怯怯怯怯

[形] 胆小；害怕：timid; cowardly; nervous | 胆～dǎnqiè *timid; cowardly* / ～场 qièchǎng *have stage fright*

窃（竊）qiè　　9画 穴部

窃 窃窃窃窃窃窃窃窃 窃

❶ [动] 偷：steal; pilfer | 失～ shīqiè *be stolen* / 行～xíngqiè *pratise theft; steal*

窃取 qièqǔ usurp; steal

盗窃 dàoqiè　　偷窃 tōuqiè

❷ [副] 偷偷地；暗中：secretly; furtively; stealthily | ～笑 qièxiào *laugh secretly; laugh up one's sleeve.*

窃听 qiètīng tap; intercept; eavesdrop

钦（欽）qīn　　9画 钅部

钦钦钦钦钦钦钦钦
钦

[动] 敬重：admire; respect
钦佩 qīnpèi admire; esteem

侵 qīn 9画 亻部

侵侵侵侵侵侵侵侵
侵

[动] (外来的敌人或有害的事物)进
入内部并造成危害：(of enemies
or harmful things) invade; intrude into; infringe upon
侵犯 qīnfàn invade
侵害 qīnhài encroach on; make
inroads on
侵略 qīnlüè invade
侵权 qīnquán tort; violate or
infringe upon other's lawful
rights or interests
侵入 qīnrù invade
侵蚀 qīnshí corrode; erode;
embezzle bit by bit
侵占 qīnzhàn seize; invade and
occupy
入侵 rùqīn

亲 (親) qīn 9画 立部

亲亲亲亲亲亲亲亲
亲

❶ [形] 关系密切; 感情深：close;
intimate; dear | ～如一家 qīn
rú yī jiā *close to each other as a*
family | 他俩的关系很～。Tā liǎ
de guānxi hěn qīn. *They two*
are very close.
亲爱 qīn'ài dear; beloved
亲密 qīnmì intimate
亲切 qīnqiè cordial
亲热 qīnrè intimate; warmhearted
亲密无间 qīnmì-wújiàn be on
intimate terms
乡亲 xiāngqīn

❷ [名] 父; 母; 父母：parent(s) |
双～ shuāngqīn *parents*
父亲 fùqīn   母亲 mǔqīn

❸ [形] 有血统或婚姻关系的：of
blood relation; next of kin | ～
属 qīnshǔ *relative; kinsfolk* | ～
兄弟 qīnxiōngdi *brothers with*
the same mother and father
亲戚 qīnqi relative; kinsman
亲情 qīnqíng emotional attachment among family members
亲人 qīnrén ① one's parent,
spouse, children, etc.; one's family members ②dear ones; those
dear to one
亲友 qīnyǒu relatives and
friends; kith and kin
探亲 tànqīn

❹ [动] 用嘴唇接触，表示喜爱：kiss
| 她～了～孩子的脸。Tā qīnle
qīn háizi de liǎn. *She kissed the*
child on the cheek.

❺ [副] 自己; 亲自：oneself; in
person | ～临 qīnlín (*term of*
respect) come (or present) per-
sonally

亲笔 qīnbǐ ① in one's own handwriting ②one's own handwriting

亲身 qīnshēn personal; firsthand

亲生 qīnshēng one's own (children, parent)

亲手 qīnshǒu with one's own hands; personally; oneself

亲眼 qīnyǎn with one's own eyes; personally

亲自 qīnzì in person

芹 qín 7画 艹部

芹 芹 芹 芹 芹 芹 芹

See 芹菜

芹菜 qíncài celery

琴 qín 12画 王部

琴 琴 琴 琴 琴 琴 琴 琴
琴 琴 琴 琴

[名]某些乐器的统称：general name for certain musical instruments | 弹~ tánqín *play a musical instrument* / 小提~ xiǎotíqín *violin*

风琴 fēngqín   钢琴 gāngqín
古琴 gǔqín   胡琴 húqín
扬琴 yángqín

禽 qín 12画 人部

禽 禽 禽 禽 禽 禽 禽 禽
禽 禽 禽 禽

[名]鸟类：bird | 家~ jiāqín *(domestic) fowl; poultry* / 飞~ fēiqín *bird*

勤 qín 13画 力部

勤 勤 勤 勤 勤 勤 勤 勤
勤 勤 勤 勤 勤

❶[形]努力做事；不偷懒：diligent; industrious; hardworking | ~学 qínxué *study diligently* / 要想写出好文章，就要~动笔。Yào xiǎng xiěchū hǎo wénzhāng, jiùyào qín dòngbǐ. *If you hope to compose a good essay, you have to practise more.*

勤奋 qínfèn industrious

勤俭 qínjiǎn hardworking and thrifty

勤恳 qínkěn diligent and conscientious

勤劳 qínláo industrious

勤工俭学 qíngōng-jiǎnxué part-work and part-study system; work-study programme

❷[形]次数多；经常：frequently; regularly; constantly | ~洗澡 qín xǐzǎo *bathe regularly* / 衣服要~换洗。Yīfu yào qín huànxǐ. *Clothes should be changed and washed regularly.* / 最近他来得很~。Zuìjìn tā lái de hěn qín. *Recently he has been coming very frequently.*

青 qīng 8画 青部

 青青青青青青青青

❶ [形]绿色、蓝色或黑色: green; blue or black | ~草 qīngcǎo *green grass* / ~山绿水 qīng-shān-lǜshuǐ *green hills and blue waters*

青菜 qīngcài green vegetable; green

青椒 qīngjiāo green pepper

青蛙 qīngwā frog

青铜器 qīngtóngqì bronze ware

沥青 lìqīng

万古长青 wàngǔ-chángqīng

❷ [形]年轻: young | 老中~ lǎo-zhōng-qīng *the old, the middle-aged and the young*

青春 qīngchūn young; youth

青年 qīngnián young; youth, young people

青少年 qīngshàonián teenagers; youngsters

年青 niánqīng

共青团 gòngqīngtuán

轻 (輕) qīng 9画 车部

轻 轻轻轻轻轻轻轻轻轻

❶ [形]重量小 (跟 "重 zhòng" 相对): light (the opposite of "重 zhòng") | 油比水~。Yóu bǐ shuǐ qīng. *Oil is lighter than water.* / 这块木头很~。Zhè kuài mùtou hěn qīng. *This piece of wood is very light.*

轻便 qīngbiàn light; portable

轻工业 qīnggōngyè light industry

减轻 jiǎnqīng

❷ [形]没有负担;轻松: free from burden; relaxed | ~音乐 qīng-yīnyuè *light music*

轻松 qīngsōng ① light; relaxed ② relax; ease up

❸ [形]不重要;不贵重: unimportant; inexpensive | 责任~ zérèn qīng *carry a light responsibility*

❹ [动]认为不重要;不重视: belittle; make light of | ~敌 qīngdí *take the enemy lightly*

轻视 qīngshì despise; make light of; look down on; contempt

❺ [形]不慎重;随便: easily; rashly | ~生 qīngshēng *not value one's life; commit suicide* / ~信 qīngxìn *readily believe*

轻易 qīngyì ① easily ② rashly

❻ [形]程度浅;数量少: slight; light; small in amount, number, degree, etc. | 口~ kǒuqīng *(of eating habit) light flavoured* / ~

伤qīngshāng *slightly wounded* / 他年纪还～。Tā niánjì hái qīng. *He is still young.* / 他的病很～。Tā de bìng hěn qīng. *His illness is nothing serious.*

轻微 qīngwēi slight; trifling; light

年轻 niánqīng

年轻人 niánqīngrén

❼ [形] 用力小：gentle | ～拿～放 qīng ná qīng fàng *handle with care; handle gently* | 走路脚步～些。Zǒulù jiǎobù qīng-xiē. *Walk softly.*

轻快 qīngkuài ① brisk; spry ② relaxed; lively

 (氢) qīng　9画 气部

氢氢氢氢氢氢氢氢氢

[名] hydrogen

倾 (傾) qīng　10画 亻部

倾倾倾倾倾倾倾倾倾倾

❶ [动] 不正；歪斜；向一边偏过去：incline; bend; lean to one side | 向左～xiàng zuǒ qīng *incline to the left* | 身子向前～shēnzi xiàng qián qīng *bend (lean) forward*

倾倒 qīngdǎo ① topple and fall; topple over ② greatly admire

倾倒 qīngdào tip; dump; empty; pour out

倾听 qīngtīng lend an ear to

倾销 qīngxiāo sell goods at a very low price; dump

倾斜 qīngxié tilt

❷ [动] 偏向；趋向：be partial; be prejudiced; tend to | ～心 qīngxīn *admire; adore*

倾向 qīngxiàng ① tendency; trend ② prefer

 qīng　11画 氵部

清 清清清清清清清清清清清清

❶ [形] 纯净透明；无杂质（跟"浊 zhuó"相对）：unmixed; clear; pure and clean (the opposite of "浊 zhuó") | ～水 qīngshuǐ *clear water* | 这水很～。Zhè shuǐ hěn qīng. *The water is quite clear.*

清洁 qīngjié clean

清新 qīngxīn pure and fresh; fresh

清真 qīngzhēn ① (formal) simple and unadorned; plain ② Islamic; Muslim

清真寺 qīngzhēnsì mosque

澄清 chéngqīng

❷ [动] 使纯洁；使干净：purify;

clean

清除 qīngchú clean up

清理 qīnglǐ put in order

肃清 sùqīng

❸ [形] 清楚；明白：distinct; clear | 查~事实 cháqīng shìshí *ascertain the facts* / 问~事情真相 wènqīng shìqing zhēnxiàng *clarify every detail; get to the bottom of the matter*

清楚 qīngchu ①clear ②know; be aware of; understand

清单 qīngdān detailed list; detailed account

清晰 qīngxī limpid; vivid; distinct

清醒 qīngxǐng ①clear-headed; sober ② come to; come round

清明节 Qīngmíngjié the Festival of the Pure Brightness (4, 5 or 6 April, traditionally observed as a festival for worshipping at ancestral graves)

分清 fēnqīng

❹ [动] 查点；结清：check up | ~仓 qīngcāng *check up warehouses; make an inventory of warehouses* /我欠你的债还~了。Wǒ qiàn nǐ de zhài huánqīng le. *I've cleared up the debts that I owed you.* / 他的钱还~了。Tā de qián huánqīng le. *He has cleared all his debts.*

清查 qīngchá check

◇清晨 qīngchén early morning

清早 qīngzǎo early in the morning; early morning

蜻 qīng 14画 虫部

蜻蜻蜻蜻蜻蜻蜻蜻蜻蜻蜻蜻蜻蜻

See 蜻蜓

蜻蜓 qīngtíng dragonfly

情 qíng 11画 忄部

情情情情情情情情情情情

❶ [名]外界事物所引起的心理反应：feeling, certain emotion or sensation felt in the mind caused by the outside world, such as love, hatred, happiness, displeasure, fear, etc. | 深~shēnqíng *deep affection (love)* /温~wēnqíng *tender sentiments*

情感 qínggǎn affection

情理 qínglǐ reason; sense

情绪 qíngxù ① mood; feeling ② depression

情意 qíngyì tender regards; affection; goodwill

表情 biǎoqíng 恩情 ēnqíng

感情 gǎnqíng 激情 jīqíng

恋情 liànqíng 亲情 qīnqíng

热情 rèqíng

盛情 shèngqíng

色情 sèqíng 同情 tóngqíng

无情 wúqíng 心情 xīnqíng

蜻
情

qīng
~
qíng

598

性情 xìngqíng 友情 yǒuqíng
真情 zhēnqíng
托人情 tuōrénqíng
诗情画意 shīqíng-huàyì
真情实感 zhēnqíng-shígǎn
❷[名]样子；状况：situation; circumstance｜灾～zāiqíng *the condition of a disaster* / 实～ shíqíng *actual situation; truth*
情报 qíngbào information
情节 qíngjié ① plot; story ② circumstance
情景 qíngjǐng scene; sight
情况 qíngkuàng situation; circumstance; condition
情形 qíngxíng circumstance; condition
案情 ànqíng 病情 bìngqíng
国情 guóqíng 行情 hángqíng
神情 shénqíng 事情 shìqing
详情 xiángqíng 知情 zhīqíng
酌情 zhuóqíng
❸[名]爱情：love; passion｜恋～ liànqíng *love; romantic love*
情人 qíngrén sweetheart
爱情 àiqíng
❹[名]情分；面子：favour; kindness｜求～qiúqíng *ask for a favour; plead with sb.*
人情 rénqíng 说情 shuōqíng
合情合理 héqíng-hélǐ
无情无义 wúqíng-wúyì
◇风情 fēngqíng

 晴 qíng 12画 日部
. . . .

晴 晴晴晴晴晴晴晴晴 晴晴晴晴

[形]天空中无云或云很少：fine; clear; cloudless｜天转～了。Tiān zhuǎnqíng le. *It's clearing up.* / 雨过天～。Yǔ guò tiān qíng. *The rain stopped and the sky cleared up.*
晴朗 qínglǎng fine
晴天 qíngtiān fine day; sunny day

请 (請) qǐng 10画 讠部

请 请请请请请请请请 请请

---

❶[动]要求：request; ask｜～她进来。Qǐng tā jìnlai. *Ask her in.* / 她～老师帮助她。Tā qǐng lǎoshī bāngzhù tā. *She asked her teacher for help.*
请假 qǐngjià ask for leave
请求 qǐngqiú request
请示 qǐngshì ask for (request) instructions
请愿 qǐngyuàn present a petition
申请 shēnqǐng
❷[动]邀请；聘请：invite; engage｜～医生 qǐng yīshēng *send for a doctor* /～专家作报告 qǐng zhuānjiā zuò bàogào *invite the expert to deliver a speech (or to give a lecture)* /他是从国外～来的。Tā shì cóng guówài

qǐnglái de. *He was invited from abroad.*

请柬 qǐngjiǎn invitation card

请客 qǐngkè stand treat; invite sb. to dinner; entertain guests; give a dinner party

请帖 qǐngtiě invitation card

聘请 pìnqǐng 宴请 yànqǐng

邀请 yāoqǐng

❸ [动] 敬词，用于希望对方做某事：please (term of respect used before a verb) | ～坐。Qǐngzuò. *Please be seated.* /～安静。Qǐng ānjìng. *Be quiet, please.* /～尽快回信 qǐng jǐnkuài huíxìn *please reply as soon as possible*

请教 qǐngjiào seek advice from sb.; ask sb. for advice

请问 qǐngwèn ① excuse me; please ② we should like to ask; it may be asked; one may ask

庆 (慶) qìng 6画 广部

庆 庆庆庆庆庆庆

❶ [动] 祝贺：congratulate | 欢～ huānqìng *celebrate joyously* /～丰收 qìng fēngshōu *celebrate a bumper harvest*

庆典 qìngdiǎn celebration; a ceremony to celebrate

庆贺 qìnghè celebrate

庆祝 qìngzhù celebrate

❷ [名] 值得庆贺的周年纪念日：anniversary; annual celebration

of an important event | 国～ guóqìng *National Day* / 校～ xiàoqìng *anniversary of the founding of a school*

喜庆 xǐqìng

国庆节 Guóqìngjié

穷 (窮) qióng 7画 穴部

穷 穷穷穷穷穷穷穷

❶ [形] 穷尽；完：finished; limited | 无～无尽 wúqióng-wújìn *endless; boundless*

无穷 wúqióng

层出不穷 céngchū-bùqióng

❷ [形] 贫困；缺少钱财：poor; with little or no money | 他过去很～。Tā guòqù hěn qióng. *He was poverty-stricken in the past.*

穷苦 qióngkǔ poverty-stricken; impoverished

穷人 qióngrén the poor; poor people

穷光蛋 qióngguāngdàn (inf.) pauper; poor wretch

贫穷 pínqióng

丘 qiū 5画 丿部

丘 丘丘丘丘丘

[名] 小山；土堆：mound; hillock | 沙～ shāqiū *sand dune*

丘陵 qiūlíng hills

秋 qiū 9画 禾部

秋 秋秋秋秋秋秋秋秋
秋

[名]四季中的第三季：autumn |
深～ shēnqiū *late autumn* /入～
以后，天气凉快多了。Rùqiū
yǐhòu, tiānqì liángkuai duō
le. *It gets much cooler after
autumn sets in.*

秋季 qiūjì autumn
秋收 qiūshōu autumn harvest
秋天 qiūtiān autumn
中秋节 Zhōngqiūjié

求 qiú 7画 一部

求 求求求求求求求

❶[动]探索；设法得到：seek; try
to get | ～学 qiúxué *seek knowl-
edge* /不～名 bù qiúmíng *not
seek fame*

求职 qiúzhí look for a job; apply for a job; seek a position;
hunt for a job
求助 qiúzhù turn to sb. for help;
seek help (from sb.); ask sb. for
help; resort to (sth.)

力求 lìqiú   谋求 móuqiú
寻求 xúnqiú   征求 zhēngqiú
追求 zhuīqiú

❷[动]请求：beg; request; ask
for | 我有事～你。Wǒ yǒu shì

qiú nǐ. *I have a favour to ask
you.*

求得 qiúdé seek; pursue; hunt
for

哀求 āiqiú   恳求 kěnqiú
乞求 qǐqiú   请求 qǐngqiú

❸[动]要求：aim at; strive for | ～
发展 qiú fāzhǎn *strive for development*

要求 yāoqiú
精益求精 jīngyìqiújīng

❹[动]需要：demand | 供大于～。
Gōng dàyú qiú.*The supply exceeds the demand.*

需求 xūqiú
供不应求 gōngbùyìngqiú

球 qiú 11画 王部

球 球球球球球球球球
球球球

❶[名]球形的物体：ball-like ob-
ject; sphere; globe | 气～ qì-
qiú *balloon* /雪～ xuěqiú
snowball

眼球 yǎnqiú

❷[名]球形的体育用品或球类运
动：ball used in sports or ball
game | 打垒～ dǎ lěiqiú *play
softball*

球场 qiúchǎng a ground where
ball games are played (volleyball, basketball, tennis, badminton, etc.); court; field

球队 qiúduì (ball game) team

球门 qiúmén goal; net; goalpost (football, etc.)

球迷 qiúmí (ball game) fan

球星 qiúxīng ball game star; star

球员 qiúyuán (ball) player

棒球 bàngqiú 　　　打球 dǎqiú

点球 diǎnqiú 　　　发球 fāqiú

罚球 fáqiú 　　　　篮球 lánqiú

皮球 píqiú 　　　　排球 páiqiú

铅球 qiānqiú 　　　台球 táiqiú

头球 tóuqiú 　　　　网球 wǎngqiú

足球 zúqiú

乒乓球 pīngpāngqiú

曲棍球 qūgùnqiú

羽毛球 yǔmáoqiú

高尔夫球 gāo'ěrfūqiú

❸[名]特指地球或星体：the earth or heavenly bodies in general | 环~航行 huánqiú hángxíng *sailed round the globe*

地球 dìqiú 　　　　全球 quánqiú

星球 xīngqiú 　　　月球 yuèqiú

西半球 xībànqiú

 区 （區） qū 　　4画 匚部

区 区区区区

❶[名]某个特定的地理范围：area; region; district | 风景~ fēngjǐngqū *scenic spot* / 住宅~ zhùzháiqū *residential area*

区域 qūyù region; area; district

产区 chǎnqū 　　　城区 chéngqū

郊区 jiāoqū 　　　街区 jiēqū

禁区 jìnqū 　　　　矿区 kuàngqū

林区 línqū 　　　　牧区 mùqū

山区 shānqū 　　　社区 shèqū

市区 shìqū 　　　　小区 xiǎoqū

灾区 zāiqū

❷[动]分别；划分：distinguish; classify

区别 qūbié ①distinguish ②difference

区分 qūfēn discriminate

❸[名]行政区划单位：district; region (administrative division) | 自治~ zìzhìqū *autonomous region*

地区 dìqū 　　　　特区 tèqū

◇误区 wùqū

曲 qū 　　6画 |部

曲 曲曲曲曲曲曲

[形]弯（跟"直 zhí"相对）：bent; curved (the opposite of "直 zhí") | ~尺 qūchǐ *carpenter's square*

曲线 qūxiàn curve

曲折 qūzhé ① circuitous; zigzag; winding ② complicated; intricate

曲棍球 qūgùnqiú ① field hockey; hockey ② hockey ball

扭曲 niǔqū 　　　歪曲 wāiqū

弯曲 wānqū

　　See qǔ.

 驱 （驅） qū 　　7画 马部

驱 驱驱驱驱驱驱驱

[动]赶走：drive out
　　驱逐 qūzhú drive out; expel;
　　banish
◇先驱 xiānqū

 屈　　qū　　8画 尸部
· · · · · · · · · · · · · · · ·
屈 屈屈屈屈屈屈屈屈

❶[动]服输; 妥协：yield to; sub-
　mit｜不~bùqū indomitable;
　dauntless; unyielding
　屈服 qūfú subdue; submit; yield
　坚强不屈 jiānqiáng-bùqū
❷[动]委屈; 冤枉：wrong; treat
　unjustly｜叫~ jiàoqū complain
　about being wronged
　委屈 wěiqu

 趋 (趨) qū　12画 走部
· · · · · · · · · · · · · · · ·
趋 趋趋趋趋趋趋趋趋
　　趋趋趋趋

[动]向; 朝某个方向发展：tend to-
　wards; tend to become｜他们的
　意见~于一致。Tāmen de
　yìjiàn qūyú yīzhì. They are
　reaching an agreement.
　趋势 qūshì trend; tendency;
　drift; current; tide
　趋向 qūxiàng ①tend to; incline
　to ② trend; direction

 渠　　qū　　11画 木部
渠 渠渠渠渠渠渠渠渠
　　渠渠渠

[名] 人工开凿的水道：canal;
　channel; ditch｜沟~gōuqú
　ditches｜引水~yǐnshuǐqú inlet
　channel
　渠道 qúdào ① irrigation ditch
　② medium of communication;
　channel

 曲　　qǔ　　6画 丨部
· · · · · · · · · · · · · · · ·
曲 曲曲曲曲曲曲

[名]乐曲; 歌谱：music of a song
　｜钢琴~gāngqínqǔ piano
　music｜进行~jìnxíngqǔ (of mu-
　sic) march
　曲目 qǔmù number; items of
　song or performance; repertoire
　曲子 qǔzi song; melody
　戏曲 xìqǔ
　　See qū.

 取　　qǔ　　8画 耳部
· · · · · · · · · · · · · · · ·
取 取取取取取取取取

❶[动]拿过来：take; fetch｜~行
李 qǔ xíngli collect or deliver
one's luggage｜我来~自行车。
Wǒ lái qǔ zìxíngchē. I came

to collect my bike.

夺取 duóqǔ　　　领取 lǐngqǔ
提取 tíqǔ

❷[动]得到;导致: get; seek | ～
乐 qǔlè *seek pleasure; take delight in*

取得 qǔdé gain; acquire; obtain
取胜 qǔshèng win victory;
score a success
取证 qǔzhèng collect evidence
换取 huànqǔ　　　获取 huòqǔ
进取 jìnqǔ　　　考取 kǎoqǔ
骗取 piànqǔ　　　窃取 qièqǔ
争取 zhēngqǔ　　赚取 zhuànqǔ

❸[动]采用;选用: adopt; choose;
select | 可～kěqǔ *advisable;
desirable*

取长补短 qǔcháng-bǔduǎn
learn from other's strong points
to offset one's weaknesses
采取 cǎiqǔ　　　录取 lùqǔ
听取 tīngqǔ　　　吸取 xīqǔ
选取 xuǎnqǔ

◇取代 qǔdài displace; replace;
substitute for; take over; supersede
取消 qǔxiāo cancel; call off;
abolish

娶 qǔ　11画 女部

娶娶娶娶娶娶娶娶
娶娶娶

[动]把女子接过来成婚(跟"嫁jià"
相对): marry (a woman) (the

opposite of "嫁jià") | 他还没
有～妻。Tā hái méiyǒu qǔqī.
He has not married yet.

去 qù　5画 土部

去去去去去

❶[动] 离开; 失掉: go; leave
去世 qùshì (of grown-up
people) die; pass away
去向 qùxiàng the direction in
which sb. or sth. has gone
免去 miǎnqù　　　失去 shīqù

❷[动] 除掉: get rid of; remove
| ～皮 qù pí *remove the peel or
skin* /～掉几个字 qùdiào jǐ gè
zì *cross out several characters*

❸[形] 以往的: past; former
去年 qùnián last year

❹[动] 从说话所在地到别的地方
(跟"来lái"相对): go to; leave
for (the opposite of "来lái")
| ～北京 qù Běijīng *leave for
Beijing; go to Beijing* /我们昨
天～工厂了。Wǒmen zuótiān
qù gōngchǎng le. *We went to
the factory yesterday.* /他已经～
外地了。Tā yǐjīng qù wàidì
le. *He's gone to another place.*

❺[动] 用在动词前, 表示要做某件
事: used before a verb, indicating the intention of doing sth.
| 你～问问他。Nǐ qù wènwèn
tā. *Go and ask him.* /我们自己～
想办法。Wǒmen zìjǐ qù xiǎng

bànfǎ. *We'll think of a way our-selves.*

❻[动] 用在动词后，表示人或事物随动作离开原来的地方；表示动作行为的继续：used after a verb, indicating the tendency of moving away from the speaker or the continuation of an action | 把这个给他带～。Bǎ zhège gěi tā dàiqù. *Please pass it to him.* / 蜜蜂向花丛中飞～。Mì fēng xiàng huācóng zhōng fēiqù. *Bees are flying towards the flow-ers.* / 让他说～，别理他。Ràng tā shuōqù, bié lǐ tā. *Let him talk, don't pay attention to him.*

出去 chūqù(qu)
辞去 cíqù
过去 guòqù(qu)
回去 huíqù(qu)
进去 jìnqù(qu)
上去 shàngqù(qu)
下去 xiàqù(qu)
看上去 kànshangqu

❼[动] 用在动词或动词结构后，表示去的目的：used after a verb or a verb structure, indicating "purpose" | 到厂里～看一位老朋友 dào chǎngli qù kàn yī wèi lǎopéngyou *go to the fac-tory to see an old friend*

趣　qù　15画 走部

趣 趣趣趣趣趣趣趣趣趣趣趣趣趣趣趣趣

❶[名] 兴味：bent; inclination | 没 ～ méiqù *feel snubbed*
乐趣 lèqù　　　兴趣 xìngqù
感兴趣 gǎnxìngqù

❷[形] 使人感到愉快或有兴味的：interesting; amusing; funny | ～事 qùshì *interesting episode*
趣味 qùwèi ① taste ② interest
有趣 yǒuqù

圈　quān　11画 口部

圈 圈圈圈圈圈圈圈圈圈圈圈圈

❶[名] 环形；环形物：circle; ring | 画个～儿 huà gè quānr *draw a circle* / 我到外面转了一～。Wǒ dào wàimian zhuànle yī quān. *I've been out for a walk.*
圈子 quānzi ① circle; ring ② circle; community; coterie
垫圈 diànquān

❷[名] 比较特定的范围或领域：scope; range | 他不是～里人。Tā bùshì quānlirén. *He is not an insider.; He's an outsider.*

◇圈套 quāntào snare; trap
　　See juàn.

权 (權)　quán　6画 木部

权 权权权权权权

❶[名] 权力：power; authority | 当～ dāngquán *in power* / 行

政~xíngzhèngquán *administrative power* | 有~处理这件事 yǒu quán chǔlǐ zhè jiàn shì *be entitled to handle this matter*

权力 quánlì authority; power

权限 quánxiàn jurisdiction; competence

霸权 bàquán　版权 bǎnquán

产权 chǎnquán 授权 shòuquán

债权 zhàiquán 政权 zhèngquán

职权 zhíquán　主权 zhǔquán

❷ [名] 权利：right | 表决~biǎojuéquán *right to vote* / 生存~shēngcúnquán *right for living* / 发言~fāyánquán *right to speak*

权利 quánlì right

权益 quányì rights and interests

侵权 qīnquán　人权 rénquán

特权 tèquán

所有权 suǒyǒuquán

◇权威 quánwēi authority

 全 quán 6画 人部

 全全全全全全

❶ [形] 完整；齐备：complete; entire | 人来~了吗? Rén lái-quánle ma? *Is everybody present?* / 手稿已经不~。Shǒugǎo yǐjīng bù quán. *The manuscript is no longer complete.*

安全 ānquán　健全 jiànquán

齐全 qíquán

安全带 ānquándài

安全感 ānquángǎn

安全套 ānquántào

十全十美 shíquán-shíměi

❷ [形] 全部；整个：whole; entire | ~校 quánxiào *the whole school* / ~过程 quán guòchéng *the entire proceeding* / ~世界 quán shìjiè *the whole world; all over the world*

全部 quánbù full

全程 quánchéng whole journey; whole course

全国 quánguó the whole nation (or country); nationwide; countrywide; throughout the country

全会 quánhuì plenary meeting; plenary session; plenum

全集 quánjí complete works; collected works

全局 quánjú overall situation

全力 quánlì with all one's strength

全面 quánmiàn comprehensive

全民 quánmín whole nation

全能 quánnéng (sports) all-round

全球 quánqiú the whole world

全体 quántǐ all; entire; whole

全力以赴 quánlìyǐfù go all out; spare no effort

全心全意 quánxīn-quányì put one's heart and soul into...

❸ [副] 表示没有例外；都：all; without exception | ~错了 quán cuò le *completely (all)*

wrong / ～怪我。Quán guài wǒ. *It's all my fault.* / 我们一家～去了。Wǒmen yī jiā quán qù le. *Our whole family went there together.*

全都 quándōu all; completely; without exception

完全 wánquán

泉　　　quán　9画 白部

[名] 从地下流出的水：spring | 矿～kuàngquán *mineral spring* / 喷～pēnquán *fountain* 山泉 shānquán 温泉 wēnquán

拳　　　quán　10画 手部

拳 拳拳拳拳拳拳拳拳拳拳拳

[名] fist
拳击 quánjī boxing; pugilism
拳头 quántou fist
太极拳 tàijíquán

犬　　　quán　4画 犬部

犬 犬犬犬犬

[名] 狗：dog | 猎～lièquǎn *hunting dog; hound* / 警～jǐngquǎn *police dog*

劝 (勸)　quàn　4画 又部

劝 劝劝劝劝

[动] 讲明事实和道理，使人听从：advise; persuade | ～他戒烟 quàn tā jièyān *advise him to give up smoking* / ～他休息 quàn tā xiūxi *urge him to take a rest* / 请你～～他。Qǐng nǐ quàn-quan tā. *Please try to persuade him.*
劝告 quàngào advise; persuade
劝说 quànshuō persuade
劝阻 quànzǔ dissuade

券　　　quàn　8画 刀部

券 券券券券券券券券

[名] 票据或作为凭证的纸片：certificate; ticket | 奖～jiǎngquàn *lottery ticket* / 入场～rùchǎng-quàn *admission ticket*
债券 zhàiquàn
证券 zhèngquàn
国库券 guókùquàn

缺　　　quē　10画 缶部

缺 缺缺缺缺缺缺缺缺缺缺

❶ [动] 残破：incomplete; imperfect | 残～cánquē *incomplete*

/这本书~了两页。Zhè běn shū quēle liǎng yè. *Two pages are missing from this book.*

缺口 quēkǒu ① breach; gap ② shortfall

❷[动]短少；不够：be short of; lack | ~人手 quē rénshǒu *be short of hands* /他们不~资金。Tāmen bù quē zījīn. *They are not short of funds.* /这花儿~水。Zhè huār quē shuǐ. *The flowers need watering.*

缺点 quēdiǎn shortcoming

缺乏 quēfá be short of; lack

缺少 quēshǎo lack

缺陷 quēxiàn deficiency

短缺 duǎnquē 紧缺 jǐnquē

空缺 kòngquē 欠缺 qiànquē

稀缺 xīquē

❸[动]应到而未到：be absent | 人都到齐了，一个也不~。Rén dōu dàoqí le, yī gè yě bù quē. *Everybody's here. Not even one is absent.*

缺席 quēxí absent

瘸 quéquē qué 16画 疒部

瘸瘸瘸瘸瘸瘸瘸瘸
瘸瘸瘸瘸瘸瘸瘸瘸

[形]腿脚有病，走路时不平稳：lame; limp | 他左腿~了。Tā zuǒtuǐ qué le. *His left leg is lame.* /他~着腿离开了运动场。Tā quézhe tuǐ líkāile

yùndòngchǎng. *He limped off the field.*

却 què 7画 卩部

却 却却却却却却却

❶[动]用在某些单音节动词或形容词后，表示结果，相当于"去qù"或"掉diào"：remove; get rid of (used after some monosyllabic verbs or adjectives, its meaning being similar to "去 qù" or "掉 diào") | 了~一个心愿 liǎoquè yī gè xīnyuàn *fulfil a che-rished desire*

冷却 lěngquè 忘却 wàngquè

❷[副]表示转折：but; yet | 这篇文章虽短，~很生动。Zhè piān wénzhāng suī duǎn, què hěn shēngdòng. *The essay is short, yet it's quite lively.* / 她有许多话要说，一时~说不出来。Tā yǒu xǔduō huà yào shuō, yīshí què shuō bù chūlái. *She had a lot to say, but at the time she was unable to utter a word.*

确（確）què 12画 石部

确 确确确确确确确确
确确确确

❶[形]肯定；坚定：definite; firm | 明~ míngquè *clear and definite*

确保 quèbǎo ensure

确定 quèdìng ①define ②definite

确立 quèlì establish

确认 quèrèn confirm

确信 quèxìn be convinced; be sure; firmly believe

确诊 quèzhěn make a definite diagnosis; diagnose

❷[形]符合事实的; 真实的：true; real │ ～有其事。Què yǒu qí shì. *It's true. It really happened.*

确切 quèqiè definite; exact

确实 quèshí ① indeed ② true

确凿 quèzáo conclusive; authentic; irrefutable

的确 díquè　　精确 jīngquè

正确 zhèngquè

准确 zhǔnquè

裙 qún 12画 衤部

裙 裙裙裙裙裙裙裙裙 裙裙裙裙

[名]裙子：skirt │ 连衣～liányīqún *dress; a woman's dress* / 围～

wéiqún *apron*

裙子 qúnzi skirt

群 qún 13画 羊部

群 群群群群群群群群 群群群群群

❶[名]聚集在一起的人或物：crowd; group │ 建筑～jiànzhùqún *building complex; cluster of buildings* / 人～rénqún *crowd; throng*

群体 qúntǐ colony; group

群众 qúnzhòng mass

族群 zúqún

❷[形]成群的; 众多的：in groups; in large numbers; multitudinous

群岛 qúndǎo archipelago

❸[量] 用于成群的人或物：used to indicate a crowd of people or a pile of things │ 一～人 yī qún rén *a crowd of people* / 一～羊 yī qún yáng *a flock of sheep* / 一～蜜蜂 yī qún mìfēng *a swarm of bees*

R r

然 rán 12画 灬部

然然然然然然然然
然然然然

❶ [代] 这样；那样：so, like that | 果～guǒrán *sure enough; if really*

然后 ránhòu then; after that; afterwards; later

必然 bìrán 不然 bùrán
当然 dāngrán 公然 gōngrán
固然 gùrán 既然 jìrán
竟然 jìngrán 偶然 ǒurán
仍然 réngrán 虽然 suīrán
天然 tiānrán 依然 yīrán
自然 zìrán 大自然 dàzìrán
天然气 tiānránqì
要不然 yàoburán
理所当然 lǐsuǒdāngrán

❷ [尾] 附在某些词后面，表示事物或动作的状态：suffix, attached to certain words, indicating state or an action | 显～xiǎnrán *obviously; clearly*

茫然 mángrán 猛然 měngrán
泰然 tàirán 突然 tūrán
毅然 yìrán

◇然而 rán'ér *yet; but; however; nevertheless; still*

燃 rán 16画 火部

燃燃燃燃燃燃燃燃
燃燃燃燃燃燃燃燃

❶ [动] 烧：burn | 蜡烛快～尽了。Làzhú kuài ránjìn le. *The candle is burning away.* / 火还～着。Huǒ hái ránzhe. *The fire is still burning.*

燃料 ránliào fuel
燃烧 ránshāo burn; light; kindle
燃油 rányóu fuel; liquid fuel, such as gasoline and kerosene, etc.

❷ [动] 引火点着：light | ～放花炮 ránfàng huāpào *set off firecrackers*

燃放 ránfàng set off (fireworks, etc.)
点燃 diǎnrán

染 rǎn 9画 木部

染染染染染染染
染

❶ [动] 用染料着色：dye | ～布 rǎnbù *dye cloth* / ～成黑色 rǎnchéng hēisè *dye it black*

染料 rǎnliào dyestuff; dye
印染 yìnrǎn

❷ [动] 沾上；传上：catch (a disease); acquire a bad habit | ～病 rǎnbìng *catch an illness; be infected with a disease* / 他这些

坏毛病是小时候～上的。Tā zhèxiē huài máobìng shì xiǎoshíhòu rǎnshang de. *He acquired those bad habits when he was young.*

传染 chuánrǎn 感染 gǎnrǎn
污染 wūrǎn
传染病 chuánrǎnbìng

壤 rǎng 20画 土部

壤 壤壤壤壤壤壤壤
壤壤壤壤壤壤壤
壤壤壤壤

[名] 泥土；松软的土：earth; loose surface layer of the earth ｜ 沃～ wòrǎng *fertile soil; rich soil*
土壤 tǔrǎng

嚷 rǎng 20画 口部

嚷 嚷嚷嚷嚷嚷嚷嚷
嚷嚷嚷嚷嚷嚷嚷
嚷嚷嚷嚷

[动] 大声喊叫；争吵：shout; make a noise; make an uproar ｜ 大声叫～dàshēng jiàorǎng *shout and cry* / 你别～了，孩子们都睡了。Nǐ bié rǎng le, háizimen dōu shuì le. *Stop yelling. The children are sleeping.*
叫嚷 jiàorǎng

让 (讓) rǎng 5画 讠部

让 让让让让让

❶ [动] 把方便或好处给别人：give up sth. for the benefit of sb. else; give way; give ground ｜ 礼～lǐrǎng *give precedence to sb. out of courtesy or thoughtfulness* / 谦～qiānrǎng *modestly decline*
让步 rǎngbù concede; make a concession; give in; give way; yield
让利 rǎnglì transfer part of interest or profit to sb.

❷ [动] 把东西、权力等转给别人：let sb. else have sth. ｜ 出～ chūrǎng *sell one's own things* / 我把椅子～给你坐。Wǒ bǎ yǐzi rǎnggěi nǐ zuò. *Please take my seat.*
转让 zhuǎnrǎng

❸ [动] 请人接受招待：invite; offer ｜ ～茶 rǎng chá *offer sb. tea* / ～进屋里 rǎngjìn wūlǐ *invite sb. into the room*

❹ [动] 容许；使：let; allow; make ｜ ～我想想。Rǎng wǒ xiǎngxiang. *Allow me to think it over.* / 不～他来。Bù rǎng tā lái. *Don't allow him to come.* / ～他去取。Rǎng tā qù qǔ. *Let him fetch it.*

❺ [介] 同 "被 bèi"：used in the passive voice to introduce the

doer of action, same as "被 bēi" | 这本书~别人借去了。Zhè běn shū ràng bié-rén jièqù le. *The book was lent out.* / 那个花瓶~他摔了。Nàge huāpíng ràng tā shuāi le. *The vase was broken by him.*

饶 (饒) **rǎo** 9画 饣部

饶 饶饶饶饶饶饶饶饶饶

[动] 宽恕；免除处罚：let sb. off; forgive | 请你~他这一次吧。Qǐng nǐ rǎo tā zhè yī cì ba. *Please let him off this time.*

扰 (擾) **rǎo** 7画 扌部

扰 扰扰扰扰扰扰扰

[动] 打搅；使混乱或不安宁：disturb; harass; trouble | 干~ gānrǎo *harass* / 搅~ jiǎorǎo *trouble; confuse*
扰乱 rǎoluàn *disturb; harass; create confusion*
打扰 dǎrǎo

绕 (繞) **rǎo** 9画 纟部

绕 绕绕绕绕绕绕绕绕绕

❶ [动] 缠：wind; coil | ~毛线 rǎo máoxiàn *wind woollen thread* / ~线圈 rǎo xiànquān *wind coils of wire*

❷ [动] 围着转：circle | 鸟~着树飞。Niǎo rǎozhe shū fēi. *The bird circled around the tree.* / 运动员~场行进。Yùndòngyuán rǎochǎng xíngjìn. *The athletes marched around the arena.*

❸ [动] 不从正面通过，从旁边转进去：make a detour; bypass; go round | ~行 rǎoxíng *make a detour* / ~远 rǎoyuǎn *go the long way round* / ~了一个大圈子 rǎole yī gè dǎ quānzi *make a big detour*
绕弯子 rǎowānzi (fig.) beat about the bush

惹 **rě** 12画 心部

惹 惹惹惹惹惹惹惹惹惹 惹惹惹惹

❶ [动] 招引；挑逗：invite or ask for (sth. undesirable); provoke | ~事 rěshì *make trouble* / ~祸 rěhuò *court disaster* / ~麻烦 rě máfan *ask for trouble; invite trouble* / ~人注意 rě rén zhùyì *attract attention* / 他的话把大家~得哈哈大笑。Tā de huà bǎ dàjiā rě de hāhā dà xiào. *What he said set everybody roaring with laughter.*

❷ [动] 触犯：offend; provoke;

tease | 我也不知道怎么就～着他了。Wǒ yě bù zhīdào zěnme jiù rězhe tā le. *I don't know how I offended him.* / 你到底说什么了，～他那么生气? Nǐ dàodǐ shuō shénme le, rě tā nàme shēngqì? *What was that you said to make him so angry?*

热（熱）rè 10画 灬部

热 热热热热热热热热热热

❶ [形] 温度高（跟"冷lěng"相对）: hot (the opposite of "冷lěng") | ～水 rèshuǐ *hot water* / 这里的夏天很～。Zhèli de xiàtiān hěn rè. *It's hot in summer here.* / 他～得直冒汗。Tā rè de zhí màohàn. *He was so hot that he kept sweating all the time.*

热带 rèdài torrid zone; tropics

热敷 rèfū (med.) hot compress

热量 rèliàng quantity of heat

热水器 rèshuǐqì hot water heater; geyser

火热 huǒrè   炎热 yánrè

副热带 fùrèdài

❷ [动] 使温度升高: heat | 把菜～一～bǎ cài rèyirè *heat up the dish*

热身 rèshēn warm-up

加热 jiārè

❸ [名] 生病引起的高体温: fever

| 退～tuìrè bring down (allay) a fever

发热 fārè

❹ [形] 情绪高；情意深厚: in high spirits; ardent; warm-hearted | ～心肠 rè xīncháng enthusiastic; warm-hearted

热爱 rè'ài ardent love; passionate love; deep attachment; have deep love for; love passionately; cherish a passion for

热烈 rèliè warm; enthusiastic; ardent

热情 rèqíng ① enthusiasm; zeal; warmth; ardour; fervour ② warm; fervent; enthusiastic; warm-hearted

热心 rèxīn enthusiastic; ardent; earnest; warm-hearted; zealous

狂热 kuángrè   亲热 qīnrè

❺ [形] (景象) 繁华、兴盛: crazy; fadish; lively | 旅游～lǚyóurè travel craze / 集邮～jíyóurè stamp-collecting craze

热潮 rècháo great mass fervour; upsurge

热点 rèdiǎn ① hot spot (in a certain time period); centre of attention ② (phys.) hot-spot

热门 rèmén arousing popular interest; popular

热闹 rènao ① lively; bustling with noise and excitement ② liven up; have fun ③ scene of bustle and excitement; spectacle

凑热闹 còurènao

◇ 热狗 règǒu hot dog

热线 rèxiàn ① hot line ② busy route

人 rén 2画 人部

人 人人

❶ [名] 人，人类，人们：human; human being; person; people | 街上~很多。Jiē shang rén hěn duō. *There are many people in the street.* / ~的大脑最发达。Rén de dànǎo zuì fādá. *The brain of the human being is the most developed.*

人格 réngé ① personality; character; moral quality ② human dignity

人工 réngōng ① man-made; artificial ② manual work; work done by hand; human labor ③ manpower; man-day

人家 rénjiā ① household ② family ③future husband's family

人间 rénjiān world; man's world; the world of mortals

人口 rénkǒu ① population ② number of people in a family

人类 rénlèi mankind; humanity; man; human race

人力 rénlì manpower; human power; human strength

or efforts

人们 rénmen people; men; public; they

人民 rénmín the people

人情 rénqíng ① human feelings; human sympathy; sensibility; human sentiment; feelings of humanity; way of human nature ② human relationship ③ favours asked or done

人权 rénquán human rights; rights of man

人群 rénqún crowd; throng; multitude

人身 rénshēn human body; person

人生 rénshēng life; human life

人士 rénshì personage; public figure

人事 rénshì ① personnel matters ② ways of the world; ways of the people ③ consciousness of the outside world

人数 rénshù (total) number of people

人体 réntǐ human body

人为 rénwéi artificial; man-made

人物 rénwù ① figure; personage ②person in literature; character in literature

人心 rénxīn popular feelings; public feelings; will of people; morale; emotion

人性 rénxìng ① human nature; humanity ② normal human

614

feelings; reason

人造 rénzào man-made; artificial; imitation

人质 rénzhì hostage

人行道 rénxíngdào pavement; sidewalk

人道主义 réndào zhǔyì humanitarianism

本人 běnrén	别人 biérén
动人 dòngrén	感人 gǎnrén
个人 gèrén	惊人 jīngrén
迷人 mírén	世人 shìrén
他人 tārén	诱人 yòurén
众人 zhòngrén	做人 zuòrén
机器人 jīqìrén	

出人意料 chūrén-yìliào

风土人情 fēngtǔ rénqíng

风云人物 fēngyún rénwù

夜深人静 yèshēn-rénjìng

❷ [名] 指某种人： person with a particular position, occupation, duty or role | 监护~jiānhùrén *guardian* / 领导~lǐngdǎorén *leader*

人员 rényuán personnel; staff

爱人 àirén	白人 báirén
病人 bìngrén	成人 chéngrén
此人 cǐrén	大人 dàrén
恩人 ēnrén	法人 fǎrén
犯人 fànrén	夫人 fūrén
妇人 fùrén	工人 gōngrén
古人 gǔrén	黑人 hēirén
华人 huárén	家人 jiārén
举人 jǔrén	巨人 jùrén
军人 jūnrén	客人 kèrén
老人 lǎorén	猎人 lièrén

盲人 mángrén	美人 měirén
名人 míngrén	男人 nánrén
女人 nǚrén	前人 qiánrén
亲人 qīnrén	情人 qíngrén
穷人 qióngrén	商人 shāngrén
生人 shēngrén	诗人 shīrén
文人 wénrén	新人 xīnrén
行人 xíngrén	艺人 yìrén
游人 yóurén	友人 yǒurén
猿人 yuánrén	丈人 zhàngren
证人 zhèngrén	主人 zhǔrén

被告人 bèigàorén

被害人 bèihàirén

残疾人 cánjírén

成年人 chéngniánrén

创始人 chuàngshǐrén

代理人 dàilǐrén

代言人 dàiyánrén

当事人 dāngshìrén

发言人 fāyánrén

负责人 fùzérén

候选人 hòuxuǎnrén

老年人 lǎoniánrén

老人家 lǎorénjia

陌生人 mòshēngrén

年轻人 niánqīngrén

仙人掌 xiānrénzhǎng

嫌疑人 xiányírén

愚人节 Yúrénjié

责任人 zérènrén

主持人 zhǔchírén

主人公 zhǔréngōng

主人翁 zhǔrénwēng

工人阶级 gōngrén jiējí

未成年人 wèichéngniánrén

月下老人 yuèxià lǎorén

❸[名] 指成年人：adult | 长大成~
zhǎngdà chéngrén *become a
grown-up*

❹[名] 指别人：other people;
other(s) | 助~为乐 zhùrén-
wéilè *find it a pleasure to help
others* / 找~帮忙 zhǎo rén
bāngmáng *ask for help* / 东西
被~拿走了。Dōngxi bèi rén
názǒu le. *Somebody took the
things away.*

人家 rénjia ① others; another;
everyone else ② I; me

❺[名] 每人；一般人：everyone;
people in general | 无~不知
wú rén bù zhī *everybody knows
(it)* / 一~一册 yī rén yī cè *one
copy for each*

人均 rénjūn per capita

❻[名] 指人手或人才：manpower;
hand | 我们这里需要~。Wǒ-
men zhèli xūyào rén. *We need
more hands.*

人才 réncái person of ability and
integrity; talent

用人 yòngrén　专人 zhuānrén

❼[名] 指人的品质、性格或名誉：
moral quality or character of a
given individual | 他~不错。
Tā rén bùcuò. *He is a kind person.* / 他~很老实。Tā rén hěn
lǎoshi. *He is quite honest.*

丢人 diūrén

◇人参 rénshēn ginseng (Panax
quinquefolius)

人民币 rénmínbì Renminbi
(RMB)

仁　rén　4画　亻部

仁 仁 仁 仁 仁

[形] 友爱；有同情心：benevolent;
kindhearted; humane | ~义
rényì benevolence and upright-
ness / ~厚 rénhòu honest and
kindhearted

仁慈 réncí ① benevolent; mer-
ciful; kind ② benevolence;
mercy; kindness; love; humanity

忍　rěn　7画　心部

忍 忍 忍 忍 忍 忍 忍 忍

❶[动] 抑制；忍受：bear; endure;
tolerate | ~着痛 rěngzhe
tòng *endure the pain* / 我~不
下去了。Wǒ rěn bù xiàqù le. *I
can no longer bear it.*

忍耐 rěnnài ① exercise pa-
tience; practise patience; exercise restraint; restrain oneself ②
patience; forbearance

忍受 rěnshòu bear; endure;
stand; suffer

忍不住 rěnbuzhù unable to bear
(resist); cannot help (doing sth.);
cannot stand it anymore; be all
on edge to do sth.

容忍 róngrěn

❷[动] 硬着心肠；忍心：be hard-hearted enough to │ 不~bùrěn *do not have the heart to do sth.* / ~心 rěnxīn *have the heart to*

认 (認) rèn 4画 讠部

认 认认认认

❶[动] 认识；分辨：recognize; know; make out │ ~字 rènzì *learn the words* / ~清是非 rènqīng shìfēi *make a clear distinction between right and wrong* / 我一时~不出这个人。Wǒ yīshí rènbuchū zhège rén. *I can't recognize the man for the moment.*

认得 rènde recognize; know

认为 rènwéi think; consider; hold; believe; deem; be of the opinion that; in sb.'s opinion

认识 rènshi ① know; understand; recognize ② understand; comprehend; realize ③ understanding; knowledge; cognition; cognizance

认知 rènzhī cognize; perceive

辨认 biànrèn

❷[动]表示同意；承认：admit; recognize │ ~错 rèncuò *admit a fault; offer an apology*

认定 rèndìng firmly believe; maintain; hold; conclude; decide; set one's mind on

认可 rènkě ① approve; accept; confirm ② sanction; approval; acceptance; confirmation

认同 rèntóng ① identify oneself with ② approve of; recognize

认证 rènzhèng (leg.) ① attest; legalize; authenticate ② attestation; authentication

承认 chéngrèn 否认 fǒurèn

公认 gōngrèn 确认 quèrèn

❸[动] 建立或明确某种关系：adopt; enter into a certain relationship │ ~徒弟 rèn túdì *accept sb. as one's apprentice*

◇认真 rènzhēn ① conscientious; earnest; serious ② take sth. seriously; take to heart; be in earnest

任 rèn 6画 亻部

任 任任任任任任

❶[动] 担当；承当：take up a job; accept an assignment; assume the office of │ ~课 rènkè *teach a course* / 他连~厂长。Tā liánrèn chǎngzhǎng. *He was appointed as factory director again.* / 他~教多年。Tā rènjiāo duō nián. *He has been a teacher for many years.*

任期 rènqī term of office; tenure of office

担任 dānrèn 兼任 jiānrèn

主任 zhǔrèn

班主任 bānzhǔrèn

认
任

rèn

R

617

❷ [名] 职责；职务：post ｜ 到~
dàorèn *take up the post*
任务 rènwù assignment; mis-
sion; job; task; work; duty
上任 shàngrèn　　责任 zérèn
重任 zhòngrèn
责任人 zérènrén

❸ [动] 任用：appoint; assign sb.
to a post ｜ 他被~为校长。Tā
bèi rènwéi xiàozhǎng. *He was
appointed as headmaster.*
任命 rènmìng ① commission;
designate; appoint ②appointment
任职 rènzhí hold a post; be in
office
聘任 pìnrèn　　信任 xìnrèn

❹ [动] 由着；听凭：let; allow;
give free reign to ｜ 放~ fāng-
rèn *not interfere; let alone; let
go* / 不能~其自然发展 bùnéng
rèn qí zìrán fāzhǎn *cannot let
it go without control*
任性 rènxìng capricious; willful; self-willed; wayward; head-
strong
任意 rènyì wantonly; arbitrarily;
wilfully; at will

❺ [介] 任凭；听凭：let go; go unchecked; let matters drift ｜
~你选择。Rèn nǐ xuǎnzé.
Choose as you like.

❻ [连] 不论；无论什么：no mat-
ter (how, what, etc.) ｜ ~你怎
么办，我都不过问。Rèn nǐ zěn-
mebàn, wǒ dōu bù guòwèn.
Whatever you do, I won't inter-

fere. / ~雨再大，我也要走。Rèn
yǔ zài dà, wǒ yě yào zǒu. *No
matter how hard it rains, I am
determined to leave.*
任何 rènhé any; whichever;
whatever

扔 rēng 5画 扌部
扔扔扔扔扔

❶ [动] 掷；投：throw; cast; toss ｜
~球 rēng qiú *throw a ball* / ~
石头 rēng shítou *throw the
stone* / 请把帽子~给我。Qǐng
bǎ màozi rēnggěi wǒ. *Please
toss the cap to me.*

❷ [动] 抛弃；丢掉：throw away; cast
aside ｜ 不要乱~垃圾。Bùyào
luànrēng lājī. *Don't litter.* / 把
这些破烂~了。Bǎ zhèxiē
pòlàn rēng le. *Throw this rubbish away.*

仍 réng 4画 亻部
仍仍仍仍

[副] 依然；还：still; yet ｜ ~要
努力 réngyào nǔlì *should continue to make efforts* / 他虽然病
了，~不肯放下工作。Tā suīrán
bìng le, réng bù kěn fàngxià
gōngzuò. *Although he is ill, he
refuses to put aside his work.*
仍旧 réngjiù as before; as usual;

as of old; till; yet

仍然 réngrán still; yet

rì   4画 日部

日 | 日 日 日 日

❶[名] 太阳：the sun｜～出 rì chū sunrise

日光 rìguāng sunlight; sunbeam

向日葵 xiàngrìkuí

风和日丽 fēnghé-rìlì

❷[名] 白天（跟 "夜 yè" 相对）：day; daytime (the opposite of "夜 yè")｜～班 rìbān day shift / 夏天～长夜短。Xiàtiān rìchángyèduǎn. *In summer, the days are long and the nights are short.*

日夜 rìyè day and night; round the clock

白日梦 báirìmèng

❸[名] 一昼夜；天：day｜三～后来取 sān rì hòu lái qǔ *collect it after three days*

日程 rìchéng programme; schedule; agenda on a specific day

日期 rìqī date

日子 rìzi ① date; day ② time; days ③ life; livelihood

当日 dāngrì   即日 jírì

今日 jīnrì

❹[名] 每天；一天一天：every day; day after day

日报 rìbào daily; daily paper; daily newspaper

日常 rìcháng daily; usually; ordinarily; day-to-day; everyday

日记 rìjì diary; journal

日历 rìlì calendar

日益 rìyì increasingly; day by day

日用 rìyòng ① daily expenses ② be of daily use; be of everyday use

日用品 rìyòngpǐn everyday goods; daily necessities

过日子 guòrìzi

❺[名] 指某一天或某一段时间：referring to a certain day or a certain period of time｜往～ wǎngrì *former days* / 纪念～ jìniànrì *memorial day; commemoration day*

假日 jiàrì   节日 jiérì

平日 píngrì   生日 shēngrì

早日 zǎorì

工作日 gōngzuòrì

节假日 jiéjiàrì

双休日 shuāngxiūrì

星期日 Xīngqīrì

❻[名] 指日本：Japan

日文 Rìwén Japanese (language)

日语 Rìyǔ Japanese (language)

日元 rìyuán yen

（榮）róng   9画 艹部

荣 | 荣荣荣荣荣荣荣荣荣

R

❶[形]光荣；光彩：glory; honour; brilliance; splendour

荣获 rónghuò get or win sth. as an honour

荣幸 róngxìng be honoured; have the honour of

荣誉 róngyù honour; glory; laurels; credit

光荣 guāngróng

❷[形]兴盛：prosperous; flourishing; thriving

繁荣 fánróng

欣欣向荣 xīnxīn-xiàngróng

 绒(絨) róng 9画 纟部

绒 绒绒绒绒绒绒绒绒绒

❶[名]柔软细小的毛：fine hair; down ｜ ～线 róngxiàn knitting wool / 鸭～ yāróng eiderdown

羊绒 yángróng

羽绒服 yǔróngfú

❷[名]上面有一层绒毛的纺织品：fabric with a soft nap or pile on one or both sides ｜ 丝～ sīróng velvet / 灯芯～ dēng-xīnróng corduroy

容 róng 10画 宀部

容 容容容容容容容容容 容容

❶[动]容纳；包含：hold; contain ｜ 教室小，～不下这么多人。Jiàoshì xiǎo, róngbuxià zhème duō rén. The classroom is too small to hold so many people.

容积 róngjī volume

容量 róngliàng capacity

容纳 róngnà ① hold; contain; accommodate; have a capacity of; put up ② tolerate

容器 róngqì container; vessel

内容 nèiróng

❷[动]不计较；原谅：tolerate; forgive ｜ 天理难～ tiānlǐ nán róng intolerable injustice / 不能宽～ bùnéng kuānróng cannot tolerate; cannot be forgiven

容忍 róngrěn tolerate; put up with; condone

❸[动]允许；让：permit; allow ｜ 不～解释 bù róng jiěshì not allow others to explain / 不能～他这样 bùnéng róng tā zhèyàng must forbid him to do this / 你～他讲下去。Nǐ róng tā jiǎng xiàqu. Let him go on.

容许 róngxǔ tolerate; permit; allow

❹[名]相貌：appearance; looks ｜ ～貌 róngmào looks; facial features

面容 miànróng

❺[名]脸上的神情和气色：facial expression; bearing ｜ 愁～ chóuróng worried look / 病～ bìngróng sickly look

笑容 xiàoróng

❻ [名] 事物的景象、状态：appearance or condition of sth. | 市～shìróng appearance (look) of a city

从容 cóngróng

◇容易 róngyì ① easy; facile ② easily; likely; be liable to; be apt to; be subject to; be open to

溶 róng 13画 氵部

溶溶溶溶溶溶溶溶溶
溶溶溶溶溶

[动] 物质在液体中化开：dissolve | 糖～在水中。Táng róng zài shuǐ zhōng. *Sugar dissolves in water.*

溶化 rónghuà dissolve; melt
溶解 róngjiě dissolve; melt
溶液 róngyè solution

熔 róng 14画 火部

熔熔熔熔熔熔熔熔
熔熔熔熔熔熔

[动] 固体加热到一定温度时变成液体：melt; fuse; smelt | ～锡 róngxī *melt tin*

融 róng 16画 虫部

融融融融融融融融
融融融融融融融融

❶ [动] 冰雪等受热变成水：melt; thaw | 太阳一晒，雪就开始～了。Tàiyáng yī shài, xuě jiù kāishǐ róng le. *The snow begins to thaw under the bright sunshine.*

融化 rónghuà melt; thaw

❷ [动] 几种不同的东西合为一体或调配在一起：mix; fuse; blend | 交～jiāoróng *blend; mingle*

融合 rónghé mix together; fuse; merge

融洽 róngqià harmonious; on friendly terms

柔 róu 9画 矛部

柔柔柔柔柔柔柔柔
柔

❶ [形] 软；不硬：soft; supple | ～嫩 róunèn *tender; delicate*

柔软 róuruǎn soft; lithe; yielding; pliable

❷ [形] 温和（跟 "刚gāng" 相对）：mild; gentle (the opposite of "刚 gāng")

柔道 róudào jujitsu; judo

柔和 róuhé soft; gentle; mild; amiable; tender; supple

温柔 wēnróu

揉 róu 12画 扌部

揉揉揉揉揉揉揉
揉揉揉揉

R

[动] 用手来回擦或搓：rub ｜ ～眼睛 róu yǎnjing *rub one's eyes* / ～一～腿 róuyiróu tuǐ *rub one's legs*

肉 ròu 6画 肉部

肉 肉 肉 肉 肉 肉 肉

[名] meat; flesh ｜ ～体 ròutǐ *human body; flesh*
肉丝 ròusī shredded meat (esp. pork)
骨肉 gǔròu   肌肉 jīròu
牛肉 niúròu
酒肉朋友 jiǔròu péngyou

如 rú 6画 女部

如 如 如 如 如 如

❶ [动] 按照；适合：comply with ｜ ～期完成 rúqī wánchéng *finish in time; finish as scheduled* / 不～意 bù rúyì *not in compliance with one's wish*
如意 rúyì as one wishes; to one's liking
如愿 rúyuàn have one's wish fulfilled
万事如意 wànshì-rúyì
❷ [动] 好像；同…一样：like; as; as if ｜ 湖水～镜。Húshuǐ rú jìng. *The water surface of the lake shines like a mirror.* / 坚强～钢 jiānqiáng rú gāng *as tough*

as steel
如此 rúcǐ so; such; in this way; like that; like this
如同 rútóng like; as
如下 rúxià as follows
犹如 yóurú   诸如 zhūrú
❸ [连] 如果；假如：if; in case (of); in the event of ｜ ～不满意，可以调换。Rú bù mǎnyì, kěyǐ diàohuàn. *If you're not satisfied, it can be exchanged.* / ～有事情，可来找我。Rú yǒu shìqing, kě lái zhǎo wǒ. *Come to me if you have any problems.*
假如 jiǎrú
❹ [动] 比得上；赶得上：be as good as; can compare with ｜ 自以为不～人 zì yǐwéi bùrú rén *consider oneself not as good as others*
不如 bùrú
❺ [介] 表示举例：for instance; such as ｜ 我到过很多城市，～北京、天津、上海。Wǒ dào-guo hěn duō chéngshì, rú Běijīng, Tiānjīn, Shànghǎi. *I've been to many cities, such as Beijing, Tianjin, and Shanghai.*
比如 bǐrú   例如 lìrú
譬如 pìrú
◇如何 rúhé how; what
如今 rújīn nowadays; now

乳 rǔ 8画 一部

乳 乳乳乳乳乳乳乳乳

❶ [名] 乳房：breast; mamma
乳房 rǔfáng ① breast; mamma
② udder

❷ [名] 奶汁； 像奶汁的东西：
milk; milk-like liquid ｜ 牛～
niúrǔ (cow's) milk / 豆～dòurǔ
bean milk

❸ [形] 初生的；幼小的：newborn;
(animal) sucking ｜ ～燕 rǔyàn
baby swallow / ～猪 rǔzhū piglet

入 rù 2画 入部

入 入入

❶ [动] 从外边到里边；进（跟"出
chū"相对）：go into; enter (the
opposite of "出 chū"） ｜ ～
口 rùkǒu ① enter the mouth ②
entrance; entry
入场 rùchǎng entrance; admission
入境 rùjìng enter a country
入侵 rùqīn invade; intrude;
make an incursion; make inroads
入围 rùwéi be included among
those selected; qualify
入乡随俗 rùxiāng-suísú when in
Rome do as the Romans do
步入 bùrù　　　　出入 chūrù
介入 jièrù　　　　侵入 qīnrù

深入 shēnrù　　　　输入 shūrù
投入 tóurù　　　　陷入 xiànrù
引入 yǐnrù　　　　注入 zhùrù
转入 zhuǎnrù

❷ [动] 参加：join; become a
member of ｜ ～会需要先提出
申请。Rùhuì xūyào xiān
tíchū shēnqǐng. To join the
association, you have to apply
for membership first.
入学 rùxué start school; go into
a school; enroll at a school (college); enter (join) a school (college)

◇ 入手 rùshǒu start with; begin
with; proceed from; take as the
point of departure

软 (軟) ruǎn 8画 车部

软 软软软软软软软软

❶ [形] 物体松软、不硬（跟"硬
yìng"相对）：soft; flexible;
supple; pliable (the opposite of
"硬 yìng"） ｜ 绸子比布～。
Chōuzi bǐ bù ruǎn. Silk is softer
than cloth.
软卧 ruǎnwò (of a train) soft
sleeper

❷ [形] 没力气：weak; feeble ｜
他两腿发～。Tā liǎng tuǐ
fāruǎn. His legs feel like jelly.
软弱 ruǎnruò weak; flabby;
weak-kneed

❸ [形] 容易动摇；不坚决：soft-

R

hearted; liable to change one's mind ｜ 心肠~xīncháng ruǎn *tenderhearted*

◇软件 ruǎnjiàn software
软盘 ruǎnpán floppy disc

锐（鋭）ruì 12画 钅部

锐 锐锐锐锐锐锐锐锐 锐锐锐锐

[形]（刀锋）又尖又快（跟"钝dùn"相对）: sharp; acute (the opposite of "钝dùn")
锐利 ruìlì sharp; keen; pointed
尖锐 jiānruì

瑞 ruì 13画 王部

瑞 瑞瑞瑞瑞瑞瑞瑞瑞 瑞瑞瑞瑞瑞

[形]吉祥的: propitious; opportune
瑞雪 ruìxuě timely snow; auspicious snow

若 ruò 8画 艹部

若 若若若若若若若若

❶[动] 好像;如同: like; resemble ｜ 欣喜~狂xīnxǐ-ruòkuáng *be wild with joy; go into raptures*

❷[连] 如果;假如: if ｜ ~不努力学习,就要落后。Ruò bù nǔlì xuéxí, jiùyào luòhòu. *If you*

don't study hard, you will lag behind.* ｜ 你~明天能来就更好了。Nǐ ruò míngtiān néng lái jiù gèng hǎo le. *It would be better if you can come tomorrow.*
倘若 tǎngruò　　假若 jiǎruò
◇若干 ruògān ①some; several; a few; a certain number (amount) of ② how many; how much

---

弱 ruò 10画 弓部

弱 弱弱弱弱弱弱弱弱 弱弱

❶[形] 力气小;实力差（跟"强 qiáng"相对）: weak; feeble (the opposite of "强 qiáng") ｜ ~小 ruòxiǎo *small and weak* / 由~变强 yóu ruò biàn qiáng *go from weak to strong* / 他年纪小,力气~。Tā niánjì xiǎo, lìqì ruò. *He is young and weak.*
弱点 ruòdiǎn weak point; weakness; failing; infirmity
弱势 ruòshì ① on a decline; become weak ② weak underprivileged; disadvantaged

薄弱 bóruò　　　脆弱 cuìruò
减弱 jiǎnruò　　软弱 ruǎnruò
衰弱 shuāiruò　　微弱 wēiruò
虚弱 xūruò　　　削弱 xuēruò
❷[形]年纪小: young ｜ 照顾老~ zhàogù lǎoruò *take care of the old and the young*

S s

撒 sā　15画 扌部

撒撒撒撒撒撒撒撒
撒撒撒撒撒撒撒

❶[动]放开；张开：cast; let go | ~
手 sāshǒu *let go one's hold; let
go* / ~网 sāwǎng *cast a net; lay
out a net*

❷[动]尽力使出；表现出：throw
off all restraint; let oneself go
| ~娇 sājiāo *act like a spoiled
child; act spoiled* / ~酒疯 sā
jiǔfēng *be drunk and act crazy;
be roaring drunk*

撒谎 sāhuǎng lie

洒（灑）sǎ　9画 氵部

洒洒洒洒洒洒洒洒
洒

[动]使水或其他东西分散落下：
sprinkle; spray; spill; shed | 扫
地前先~些水。Sǎodì qián
xiān sǎ xiē shuǐ. *Sprinkle some
water before sweeping the floor.*
/ 黄豆~了一地。Huángdòu
sǎle yī dì. *The soybeans are
scattered all over the ground.*

腮 sāi　13画 月部

腮腮腮腮腮腮腮腮
腮腮腮腮腮

[名]脸颊的下半部：cheek | 双手
托~ shuāngshǒu tuō sāi *cup
one's cheeks in one's hands* /
两~泛红 liǎng sāi fànhóng
there is a blush in the cheeks

塞 sāi　13画 宀部

塞塞塞塞塞塞塞塞
塞塞塞塞塞

[动]堵；填入：fill in; squeeze in;
stuff | ~住漏洞 sāizhù lòu-
dòng *fill up leaks or cracks* / 水
管~住了。Shuǐguǎn sāizhù
le. *The waterpipe is clogged up.*
/ 他用手指~住耳朵。Tā yòng
shǒuzhǐ sāizhù ěrduo. *He
plugged his ears with his fingers.*

◇活塞 huósāi

赛（賽）sài　14画 宀部

赛赛赛赛赛赛赛赛
赛赛赛赛赛赛

❶[动]比较高低或强弱：match;
contest | ~跑 sàipǎo *race* / ~
球 sàiqiú *compete in a ball game*
赛车 sàichē (sports) ① cycle

racing; motorcycle race; automobile race ② racing vehicle

赛季 sàijì season (during which matches are arranged)

赛马 sàimǎ horse racing

比赛 bǐsài	参赛 cānsài
大赛 dàsài	竞赛 jìngsài
决赛 juésài	联赛 liánsài
预赛 yùsài	
半决赛 bànjuésài	
锦标赛 jǐnbiāosài	

❷ [动] 胜过；比得上：surpass; be better than; be comparable to | 这些姑娘干活儿～过小伙子。Zhèxiē gūniang gànhuór sàiguo xiǎohuǒzi. *In work these young women can put young men to shame.* / 他的力气大得～过一头牛。Tā de lìqi dà de sàiguo yī tóu niú. *He is as strong as a horse.*

三   sān   3画 一部

三 三 三 三

❶ [数] 数目：three | ～倍 sān bèi *three times; threefold; triple* / 一天吃～顿饭 yī tiān chī sān dùn fàn *have three meals a day*

三国 Sān Guó *Three Kingdoms (220-280) (Wei, Shu and Wu)*

三角 sānjiǎo ① *triangle* ② *trigonometry*

三角洲 sānjiǎozhōu *delta*

三轮车 sānlúnchē *tricycle;* pedicab

❷ [数] 表示多数或多次：more than two; several; many | 接二连～ jiē'èr-liánsān *one after another; in quick succession* / ～思 sānsī *think carefully*

三番五次 sānfān-wǔcì *again and again*

三心二意 sānxīn-èryì *be of two minds; shilly-shally; be half-hearted*

再三 zàisān   第三者 dìsānzhě

伞 (傘)   sǎn   6画 人部

伞 伞 伞 伞 伞 伞

[名] umbrella | 雨～ yǔsǎn *umbrella* / 撑～ chēng sǎn *open an umbrella*

散   sǎn   12画 攵部

散 散 散 散 散 散 散 散 散 散 散 散

❶ [形] 零碎的；不集中的；分散的：scattered | ～装 sǎnzhuāng *be in bulk* / ～居 sǎnjū *live scattered*

散文 sǎnwén *prose*

❷ [动] 没有约束；松开；分散：come loose; fall apart | ～漫 sǎnmàn ① *undisciplined; careless and sloppy* ② *unorganized; scattered* / 松～ sōngsǎn ① *loose; shaky* ② *inattentive* /

把队伍～开 bǎ duìwu sǎnkāi *disperse the troops* / 行李～了。Xíngli sǎn le. *The luggage has come loose.*

See sǎn.

 散 sǎn 12画 攵部

散散散散散散散散 散散散散

❶[动]由聚集而分开：break up; disperse | ～会 sǎnhuì *(of a meeting) be over; break up* / 大家别走～了。Dàjiā bié zǒusǎn le. *Let's not get split up.* / 乌云～了。Wūyún sǎn le. *Dark clouds dispersed.*

散落 sǎnluò ① fall scattered ② be scattered ③ scatter and disappear

拆散 chāisǎn   分散 fēnsàn
解散 jiěsàn   疏散 shūsàn

❷[动]散布：distribute; disseminate; give out | 发～fāsǎn *diverge; diffuse* / ～传单 sǎn chuándān *give out handbills; distribute leaflets* / 公园里～着花香。Gōngyuán li sǎnzhe huāxiāng. *The flowers smell sweet in the garden.*

散布 sǎnbù ① spread; disseminate; distribute ② be scattered here and there

散发 sǎnfā ① send out ② distribute

❸[动]排遣；排除：dispel; let out | ～心 sǎnxīn *drive away one's boredom* / 请打开门窗～～烟。Qǐng dǎkai ménchuāng sànsàn yān. *Please open the door and windows to let the smoke out.*

◇散步 sǎnbù take a walk; go for a walk; go for a stroll
    See sǎn.

 桑 sāng 10画 木部

桑桑桑桑桑桑桑桑 桑桑

See 桑树
    桑树 sāngshù white mulberry; mulberry

 嗓 sǎng 13画 口部

嗓嗓嗓嗓嗓嗓嗓嗓 嗓嗓嗓嗓嗓

[名]喉咙：throat, larynx
    嗓子 sǎngzi ① throat; larynx ② voice

丧（喪）sàng 8画 十部

丧丧丧丧丧丧丧丧

[名]失去；丢掉：lose | ～命 sàngmìng *to lose one's life* / 他五岁～父。Tā wǔ suì sàngfù. *He* lost his father at five.

丧气 sàngqì feel disheartened; lose heart; become crestfallen

丧生 sàngshēng meet one's death; lose one's life; get killed

丧失 sàngshī lose; forfeit

 扫(掃) sǎo 6画 扌部

扫 扫扫扫扫扫扫

❶ [动] 用笤帚、扫帚除去尘土、垃圾等：sweep; clear away dust with broom | ～地 sǎo dì sweep the floor / ～垃圾 sǎo lājī sweep out the garbage / 把房间～干净。Bǎ fángjiān sǎo gānjìng. Clean the room.

扫除 sǎochú ① clear away; remove ② cleaning; clean up

打扫 dǎsǎo

❷ [动]除去；消除：eliminate; clear away | ～雷 sǎoléi mine sweeping / ～盲 sǎománg eliminate illiteracy

❸ [动] 迅速地左右移动：pass quickly along or over; sweep | ～射 sǎoshè strafe / 她～了我一眼。Tā sǎole wǒ yī yǎn. Her eyes swept over me.

扫描 sǎomiáo (electron.) scan

 嫂 sǎo 12画 女部

嫂 嫂嫂嫂嫂嫂嫂嫂嫂 嫂嫂嫂嫂

[名] 哥哥的妻子：elder brother's wife; sister-in-law | 兄～ xiōngsǎo elder brother and his wife / 表～ biǎosǎo elder cousin's wife

嫂子 sǎozi elder brother's wife; sister-in-law

大嫂 dàsǎo

 色 sè 6画 色部

色 色色色色色色

❶ [名] 脸上的神气、表情：look; countenance; expression | 面不改～ miànbùgǎisè (facing certain situation) the facial expression remains unchanged

脸色 liǎnsè   气色 qìsè

神色 shénsè   眼色 yǎnsè

使眼色 shǐyǎnsè

❷ [名] 景象；情景：scene; scenery | 湖光山～ húguāng-shānsè beautiful view of the lake and hills

景色 jǐngsè   夜色 yèsè

❸ [名] 颜色：colour | 红～ hóngsè red / 五颜六～ wǔyán-liùsè multicoloured; colourful

色彩 sècǎi colour; hue; tint; shade

白色 báisè   本色 běnsè

彩色 cǎisè   黑色 hēisè

黄色 huángsè   金色 jīnsè

蓝色 lánsè　　　　绿色 lǜsè
特色 tèsè　　　　天色 tiānsè
棕色 zōngsè

❹ [名] 女子的美貌：woman's beautiful looks | 姿~zīsè *(of woman) good looks*

◇色情 sèqíng pornography

森　　sēn　　12画 木部

[形] 树木多而密：full of trees
森林 sēnlín forest

杀 (殺) shā　　6画 木部

杀　杀杀杀杀杀杀

❶ [动] 使人或动物失去生命；弄死：kill; slaughter | ~鸡 shājī *kill a chicken* / ~手 shāshǒu *killer*
杀毒 shādú (computing) kill viruses
杀害 shāhài murder; kill
暗杀 ànshā　　谋杀 móushā
屠杀 túshā　　凶杀 xiōngshā
自杀 zìshā
❷ [动] 战斗：fight; go into battle | ~出去 shā chūqu *fight one's way out*
❸ [动] 减弱；消除：weaken; reduce; abate | ~价 shājià *force down the price; bargain*

❹ [副] 在动词后，表示程度深：exceedingly; extremely (used after a verb) | 气~人 qìshā rén *be extremely angry; hopping mad* / 笑~人 xiàoshā rén *absolutely ridiculous*

沙　　shā　　7画 氵部

沙　沙沙沙沙沙沙沙

❶ [名] 细碎的石粒：sand | 细~xìshā *fine sand*
沙漠 shāmò desert
沙滩 shātān sand beach
沙土 shātǔ sandy soil; sand
沙子 shāzi small grains; pellets
风沙 fēngshā
❷ [名] 像沙一样的东西：sth. granulated or powdered | 豆~dòushā *bean paste*

◇沙发 shāfā sofa; settee

纱 (紗) shā　　7画 纟部

纱　纱纱纱纱纱纱纱

❶ [名] 用棉花、麻等纺成的较松的细丝：yarn | 棉~miánshā *cotton yarn* / 纺~fǎngshā *spinning*
纱布 shābù gauze
❷ [名] 用纱制的稀疏的纺织品：gauze; sheer | ~窗 shāchuāng *window screen*

S

刹 shā 8画 刂部

刹 刹刹刹刹刹刹刹刹

[动] 止住(车、机器等); put on the brakes; stop | 把车子~住 bǎ chēzi shāzhù *brake the car, truck, etc.*

刹车 shāchē ① stop a vehicle by applying the brakes; put on the brakes ② stop a machine by cutting off the power; turn off a machine

砂 shā 9画 石部

砂 砂砂砂砂砂砂砂砂砂

[名] 细小的石粒, 同"沙shā①": sand; grit, same as "沙shā①"

傻 shǎ 13画 亻部

傻 傻傻傻傻傻傻傻傻傻傻傻傻

❶[形] 智力低下, 笨: stupid; muddle-headed | 这孩子有点儿~。 Zhè háizi yǒudiǎnr shǎ. *The boy is slow-witted.*
傻子 shǎzi fool; blockhead; simpleton
❷[形] 心眼死; 不知变通: (think or act) mechanically | ~干 shǎgàn *slave away at one's work; slog away at one's work* | ~等 shǎděng *keep waiting single-mindedly*

厦 shà 12画 厂部

厦 厦厦厦厦厦厦厦厦厦厦厦厦

[名] 高大的房子: tall building; mansion | 高楼大~ gāolóu-dàshà *tall buildings*

筛 (篩) shāi 12画 竹部

筛 筛筛筛筛筛筛筛筛筛筛筛筛

❶[名] 筛子: sieve; sifter, screen
❷[动] 用筛子分选东西: sift; sieve; screen; riddle | ~面 shāimiàn *sieve (sift) flour* / ~米 shāimǐ *sift rice* / ~煤 shāiméi *riddle coal*
筛选 shāixuǎn ① screen; sift ② select

晒 (曬) shài 10画 日部

晒 晒晒晒晒晒晒晒晒晒晒

[动] 阳光照射; 让阳光照射: (of the sun) shine upon; dry in the sun; bask | ~衣服 shài yīfu *dry clothes in the sun* / 脸~黑了。

630

Liǎn shàihēi le. *The face is tanned.* / 奶奶正在院子里~太阳。 Nǎinai zhèngzài yuànzi li shài tàiyáng. *Grandma is basking in the sun in the yard.*

山 shān 3画 山部

山 山山山

[名] hill; mountain; anything resembling a mountain | 高~ gāoshān *high mountain* / 上~ shàngshān *go up a hill* / 冰~ bīngshān *iceberg*

山地 shāndì ① mountainous region; hilly area; hilly country ② field on a hill

山顶 shāndǐng the summit (or top) of a mountain; hilltop

山峰 shānfēng peak

山冈 shāngāng low hill; hillock

山沟 shāngōu gully; ravine; (mountain) valley

山谷 shāngǔ mountain valley; ravine

山河 shānhé mountains and rivers; the land of a country

山脚 shānjiǎo foot of a hill

山岭 shānlǐng mountain ridge

山脉 shānmài mountain range; mountain chain

山区 shānqū mountainous area

山泉 shānquán mountain spring

山水 shānshuǐ ① water from a mountain ② mountains and waters; landscape ③ traditional Chinese landscape painting

山头 shāntóu ① hilltop; top of a mountain ② mountain stronghold; faction

山羊 shānyáng goat

山腰 shānyāo half way up the mountain

山珍海味 shānzhēn-hǎiwèi delicacies from land and sea; dainties of every kind

登山 dēngshān

黄山 Huáng Shān

火山 huǒshān

矿山 kuàngshān

泰山 Tài Shān

中山装 zhōngshānzhuāng

◇山药 shānyao (bot.) Chinese yam

删 shān 7画 刂部

删 删删删删删删删

[动] 去掉(某些字句或内容): delete; leave out | ~改 shāngǎi *delete and change; revise* / ~除 shānchú *delete; cross out* / 这一段可以~去。 Zhè yī duàn kěyǐ shānqù. *This paragraph can be left out.*

珊

shān　9画 王部

珊 珊 珊 珊 珊 珊 珊 珊
珊

See 珊瑚
珊瑚 shānhú coral

闪 (閃)

shǎn　5画 门部

闪 闪 闪 闪 闪

❶[动] 迅速侧身避开：dodge; duck; get out of the way ｜ ~开 shǎnkāi *get out of the way; jump aside* / ~过去 shǎn guòqu *get out of the way* / ~到 树后 shǎndào shù hòu *dodge behind a tree*

❷[动] 突然出现或时隐时现：flash; sparkle; shine ｜ ~念 shǎnniàn *flash of thought* / 窗外~过一个 人影。Chuāngwài shǎnguo yī gè rényǐng. *A shadow of a person flashed past the window.* / 远处灯光~了一下。Yuǎnchù dēngguāng shǎnle yī xià. *There was a flash of light in the distance.*

闪烁 shǎnshuò ① twinkle; glimmer; glisten ② evasive; vague; noncommittal
闪耀 shǎnyào glitter; shine; radiate

❸[名] 天空的电光：lightning ｜ 打~ dǎshǎn *lightning*

闪电 shǎndiàn lightning

❹[动] 因动作过猛而扭伤：twist; sprain ｜ ~了腰 shǎnle yāo *strain one's back*

扇

shàn　10画 户部

扇 扇 扇 扇 扇 扇 扇 扇
扇 扇

❶[名] 能摇动生风取凉的用具：fan ｜ 折~ zhéshàn *folding fan* 扇子 shànzi fan
电扇 diànshàn
电风扇 diànfēngshàn

❷[名] 指板状或片状的东西：leaf-shaped thing; panel ｜ 门~ ménshàn *door panel* / 隔~ géshàn *partition screen*

❸[量] 用于门窗等：used for doors, windows, etc. ｜ 一~门 yī shàn mén *a door* / 两~窗子 liǎng shàn chuāngzi *two windows*

善

shàn　12画 羊部

善 善 善 善 善 善 善 善
善 善 善 善

❶[形] 良好：wise; satisfactory; good ｜ ~策 shàncè *good plan* 改善 gǎishàn　　妥善 tuǒshàn 完善 wánshàn

❷[形] 善良；心地好（跟"恶è"相对）：good; virtuous (the opposite of "恶 è") | ~举 shànjǔ *philanthropic act or project* / ~事 shànshì *charitable deeds; good deeds* / ~心 shànxīn *kindheartedness*

善待 shàndài treat sb. well

善良 shànliáng good and honest; kind-hearted

善意 shànyì goodwill; good intentions

慈善 císhàn

❸ [动] 在某方面有专长：be good at; be expert in | ~于经营 shànyú jīngyíng *good at management*

善于 shànyú be good at; be adept in

能歌善舞 nénggē-shànwǔ

❹ [动] 容易：be apt to | ~变 shànbiàn *be apt to change; changeable* / ~忘 shànwàng *forgetful* / ~疑 shànyí *be apt to doubt; doubtful*

◇善后 shànhòu deal with problems resulting from an accident, etc.

擅 shàn 16画 扌部

擅擅擅擅擅擅擅擅擅擅擅擅擅擅

❶ [动] 超越权限自作主张：arrogate to oneself and do sth. beyond one's own authority | ~离岗位 shànlí gǎngwèi *leave one's*

post without permission

擅自 shànzì do sth. without authorization

❷ [动] 在某方面有专长；善于：be good at; be expert in | 不~交际 bù shàn jiāojì *be not particularly good at social interaction*

擅长 shàncháng be good at; be expert in; be skilled in

伤 (傷) shāng 6画 亻部

伤 伤伤伤伤伤伤

❶ [名] 人或其他物体受到的损害：wound; injury | 刀~ dāoshāng *knife wound* / 烫~ tàngshāng *scald* / ~好了。Shāng hǎo le. *The wound has healed.*

伤痕 shānghén scar; bruise

伤口 shāngkǒu wound; cut

伤势 shāngshì the condition of an injury or wound

伤亡 shāngwáng injuries and deaths; casualties

伤员 shāngyuán wounded personnel; the wounded

负伤 fùshāng 受伤 shòushāng

重伤 zhòngshāng

❷ [动] 损害：injure; hurt | ~感情 shāng gǎnqíng *hurt sb.'s feeling* / ~了筋骨 shāngle jīngǔ *be injured in the tendons or bones*

伤害 shānghài injure; harm; hurt

伤脑筋 shāngnǎojīn knotty; troublesome; bothersome
损伤 sǔnshāng
❸ [动] 悲哀；忧愁：be distressed | 哀~āishāng *sad; sorrowful* / ~感 shānggǎn *filled with sorrows; sentimental*
伤心 shāngxīn sad; grieved; broken-hearted
悲伤 bēishāng

商 商 商

商 shāng 11画 亠部

商商商商商商商商商
商商商

❶ [名] 商人：merchant; businessman | 布~bùshāng *cloth trader* / 富~fùshāng *rich businessman* / 批发~pīfāshāng *wholesaler*
商人 shāngrén businessman; merchant; trader
厂商 chǎngshāng
代理商 dàilǐshāng
❷ [名] 买卖货物的活动；商业：commerce; business
商标 shāngbiāo trade mark
商场 shāngchǎng department store; bazaar
商店 shāngdiàn shop; store
商机 shāngjī business opportunity
商家 shāngjiā business establishment
商品 shāngpǐn commodity;

goods; merchandise
商业 shāngyè commerce; trade; business
经商 jīngshāng 通商 tōngshāng
招商 zhāoshāng
❸ [动] 讨论；交换意见：discuss; consult | 面~miànshāng *discuss with sb. face to face; consult personally*
商量 shāngliang consult; discuss; talk over
商榷 shāngquè deliberate; discuss
商谈 shāngtán exchange views; confer; discuss; negotiate
商讨 shāngtǎo discuss; deliberate
商议 shāngyì confer; discuss
磋商 cuōshāng 协商 xiéshāng
❹ [名] 除法中的得数：quotient | 8被2除，~数是4。Bā bèi èr chú, shāngshù shì sì. *The quotient is four if eight is divided by two.*

晌

 shǎng 10画 日部

晌晌晌晌晌晌晌晌
晌晌

[名] 正午或正午前后：noon | 睡~觉 shuì shǎngjiào (dial.) *take a nap at noon*
晌午 shǎngwu midday; noon

赏

 (赏) shǎng 12画 贝部

赏 赏赏赏赏赏赏赏赏赏
赏赏赏赏

❶ [动] 赐给；奖励 (跟 "罚 fá" 相对)：reward; award (the opposite of "罚 fá") | 奖~jiǎng-shǎng *give awards* | ~罚分明 shǎngfá-fēnmíng *be fair in meting out rewards and punishments*

赏光 shǎngguāng (pol.) may I have the pleasure of your presence (used when requesting sb. to accept an invitation)

悬赏 xuánshǎng

❷ [动] 宣扬；称赞：advocate; praise
赞赏 zānshǎng

❸ [动] 观看；品味：admire; enjoy; appreciate | ~月 shǎngyuè *enjoy the bright full moon* | ~花 shǎnghuā *admire the beauty of flowers* | 雅俗共~yǎsú-gōngshǎng *suit both refined and popular tastes*

观赏 guānshǎng

鉴赏 jiānshǎng 欣赏 xīnshǎng

上 **shàng** 3画 卜部

上 上上上

❶ [名] 高处；位置在高处的 (跟 "下 xià" 相对)：in an upper position; above (the opposite of "下 xià") | 山~shān shàng *up in the mountains; hill-top* | ~身

shàngshēn *upper part of the body* | 往~看wǎngshàng kàn *look up (upward)*

上边 shàngbian above; over; on top of; on the surface of

上层 shàngcéng upper strata; upper levels

上空 shàngkōng in the sky; overhead

上面 shàngmian ① above; over; on top of; on the surface of ② above-mentioned; aforesaid; foregoing

上头 shàngtou ① above; over; on top of; on the surface ② higher authorities; higher-ups

上下 shàngxià ① high and low; one's superiors and inferiors ② from top to bottom; up and down ③ relative superiority or inferiority ④ (used after round numbers) about

上衣 shàngyī upper outer garment; jacket

上游 shàngyóu ① upper reaches (of a river) ② advanced position

❷ [形] 时间或次序在前的：preceding (in time or order) | ~一次 shàng yī cì *last time* | ~半年 shàngbànnián *the first half of the year* | ~册 shàngcè *the first volume; Volume One; Book One* | ~篇 shàngpiān *first section; first chapter*

上述 shàngshū above-mentioned; aforementioned; afore-said

上午 shàngwǔ forenoon; morning

上旬 shàngxún the first ten-day period of a month

❸ [名] 等级或质量较高的：the higher; the superior | ～品 shàngpǐn highest grade; best of all / ～策 shàngcè first choice; the best way out

上等 shàngděng first-class; first-rate; superior

上级 shàngjí higher level; higher authorities

上将 shàngjiàng general; admiral; air chief marshal

顶头上司 dǐngtóu shàngsi

❹ [动] 从低处到高处：go up; mount; board; get on | ～山 shàng shān climb up a mountain / ～楼 shàng lóu go upstairs / ～飞机 shàng fēijī board a plane

上场 shàngchǎng ① appear on the stage; enter ② (sports) enter the court or field; join in a contest

上来 shànglái(lai) come up

上去 shàngqù(qu) go up

上升 shàngshēng rise; go up; ascend

上台 shàngtái ①go up onto the platform; appear on the stage ② assume power; come (rise) to power

上涨 shàngzhǎng rise; go up

❺ [动] 去；往：go to; leave for | ～北京 shàng Běijīng leave for Beijing / 你～哪儿去了?Nǐ shàng nǎr qù le? Where did you go?

❻ [动] 达到；够 (一定的数量或程度)：be up to; be as many as | ～百人 shàng bǎi rén up to a hundred people / 老张已经～年纪了。Lǎo Zhāng yǐjīng shàng niánjì le. Old Zhang is getting on in years.

成千上万 chéngqiān-shàngwàn

❼ [动] 登载；播出：be put on record; be carried (in a publication) | ～光荣榜 shàng guāngróngbǎng enter the honour roll / 他的事迹～了电视了。Tā de shìjì shàngle diànshì le. His good deeds have been shown on TV.

上演 shàngyǎn put on the stage; perform

❽ [动] 安装；拧紧：place sth. in position; set; fix | ～螺丝 shàng luósī drive in a screw / 这块表已经～了弦。Zhè kuài biǎo yǐjīng shàngle xián. The watch has been wound up.

❾ [动] 涂；抹：apply; paint; smear | ～药 shàngyào apply ointment; apply medical liquid / ～颜色 shàng yánsè apply colour

❿ [动] 按规定的时间活动：be engaged (in work, study, etc.) at a fixed time | 下午的课不～了。

Xiàwǔ de kè bù shàng le. *Classes for this afternoon are cancelled.*

上班 shàngbān go to work; start work; be on duty

上课 shàngkè ① attend class; go to class ② conduct a class; give a lesson (lecture)

上任 shàngrèn take up an official post; assume office

上学 shàngxué go to school; attend school; be at school

⓫ [动] 用在动词后, 表示动作达到了目标或已经开始并继续下去: used after a verb to indicate achievement of one's goal or the beginning and continuity of an action | 锁～门 suǒshang mén *lock a door* / 考～大学 kǎoshang dàxué *be admitted to a college* / 她爱～了草原。Tā ài-shangle cǎoyuán. *She's fallen in love with the grasslands.*

赶上 gǎnshang

称得上 chēngdeshàng

看上去 kànshàngqu

⓬ [名] 用在名词后, 表示在物体的表面或在某事物的范围以内, 也表示某一方面: used after noun to indicate the surface or scope of sth. | 脸～liǎng shang *on the face* / 车～chē shang *in the car* / 会～huì shang *at the meeting* / 桌子～zhuōzi shang *on the table* / 报纸～bàozhǐ shang *in the newspaper* / 事实～shìshí shang *in fact; in reality; actually*

路上 lùshang 天上 tiānshàng

晚上 wǎnshang 早上 zǎoshang

◇ 上报 shàngbào report to a higher body; report to the leadership

上当 shàngdàng be taken in; be fooled; be duped

上帝 shàngdì God

上交 shàngjiāo turn over to the higher authorities; hand in

上市 shàngshì ① go (or appear) on the market ② be on the list of stockmarket

上诉 shàngsù (leg.) appeal (to a higher court)

上网 shàngwǎng access the Internet

基本上 jīběnshàng

尚 **shàng** 8画 小部

尚 尚尚尚尚尚尚尚尚

❶ [形] 崇高: lofty; high | 崇～chóngshàng *uphold; advocate*

高尚 gāoshàng

时尚 shíshàng

❷ [副] 还: still; yet | 年纪～小 niánjì shàng xiǎo *still young* / 为时～早。Wéishí shàng zǎo. *It is too early to handle this; The opportunity is not ripe yet.* / ～未解决 shàngwèi jiějué *remains*

to be settled; not resolved yet
尚未 shàngwèi *not yet*

裳 shang 14画 衣部

裳裳裳裳裳裳裳裳
裳裳裳裳裳裳

See 衣裳
衣裳 yīshang

捎 shāo 10画 扌部

捎捎捎捎捎捎捎捎
捎捎

[动] 顺便带：take along sth. to or for sb. | ～封信 shāo fēng xìn *bring a letter to sb. (on one's way to somewhere)*

烧 (燒) shāo 10画 火部

烧烧烧烧烧烧烧烧
烧烧

❶[动]使着火；着火：burn | ～煤 shāo méi *burn coal* / 你最好把那封信～了。Nǐ zuìhǎo bǎ nà fēng xìn shāo le. *You'd better burn that letter.*
烧毁 shāohuǐ *destroy by fire; burn up*
燃烧 ránshāo
❷[动] 加热使物体起变化：heat | ～水shāoshuǐ *heat up water* / 饭～熟了。Fàn shāoshú le.

The rice is done.
❸[动]一种烹调方法：stew after frying or fry after stewing | ～鸡 shāojī *roast chicken* / ～茄子 shāo qiézi *stewed aubergine* / ～羊肉shāo yángròu *stewed lamb* 红烧 hóngshāo
❹[动]体温增高：run a fever; have a high temperature | ～退了。Shāo tuì le. *The fever is down.* / 孩子的脸蛋儿～得通红。Háizi de liǎndànr shāo de tōnghóng. *The child had such a high temperature that his face became flushed.*
发烧 fāshāo   高烧 gāoshāo
◇烧饼 shāobing *sesame seed cake*

梢 shāo 11画 木部

梢梢梢梢梢梢梢梢
梢梢梢

[名] 条状物较细的一头：tip; the thin end of a twig, etc. | 树～ shùshāo *tip of a tree* / 眉～ méishāo *tip of the brow* / 辫～ biànshāo *end of a plait*

稍 shāo 12画 禾部

稍稍稍稍稍稍稍稍
稍稍稍稍

[副] 略微：a little; slightly | 这大衣～长了一点。Zhè dàyī shāo

chángle yīdiǎn. *The coat is a bit long.* / 请你～等一会儿。Qǐng nǐ shāoděng yīhuìr. *Please wait a moment; Just a moment, please.*

稍微 shāowēi a little; a bit; slightly; a trifle

勺 shāo　3画 勺部

勺 勺勺勺

[名] 用来舀东西的半球形器具: spoon; ladle | 铁～tiěsháo *iron ladle* / 饭～fànsháo *rice ladle* 勺子 sháozi ladle; scoop

少 shǎo　4画 小部

少 少少少少

❶ [形] 数量小(跟"多 duō"相对): few; little (the opposite of "多 duō") | 东西很～ dōngxi hěn shǎo *very few things* / 以～胜多 yǐshǎoshēngduō *defeat the many with the few* / 这个人说得多, 做得～。Zhège rén shuōdeduō, zuòdeshǎo. *The man talked much and did little.*

少见 shǎojiàn seldom seen; infrequent; rare

少量 shǎoliàng a small amount; a little; a few

少数 shǎoshù a small number;

few; minority

少有 shǎoyǒu rare; few and far between

少数民族 shǎoshù mínzú minority; ethnic minority

不少 bùshǎo　　多少 duōshǎo

多少 duōshao　减少 jiǎnshǎo

至少 zhìshǎo

❷ [动] 短缺; 不够原有的或应有的数目: be short; lack | ～穿一件衣服 shǎo chuān yī jiàn yīfu *not have an article of clothing* / 全体同学都来了, 一个没～。Quántǐ tóngxué dōu lái le, yī gè méi shǎo. *All the students have come and none is absent.* / 文娱活动～不了他。Wényú huódòng shǎobuliǎo tā. *He is a must for any recreational activities.*

缺少 quēshǎo

❸ [动] 丢失: lose; be missing | 屋里～了东西。Wūli shǎole dōngxi. *There is something missing from the room.* / ～了一本书。Shǎole yī běn shū. *One book is missing.*

See shào.

少 shào　4画 小部

少 少少少少

[形] 年纪轻(跟"老 lǎo"相对): young (the opposite of "老 lǎo")

| 男女老~nán-nǔ-lǎo-shǎo *men and women, old and young* / 青春年~qīngchūn niánshào *in the prime of youth; in the prime of life*

少年 shǎonián ① early youth (from about ten to sixteen) ② boy or girl in early teens; juvenile

少女 shǎonǔ young girl

少先队 shǎoxiānduì Young Pioneers

青少年 qīngshǎonián See shǎo.

哨 shǎo 10画 口部

哨 哨哨哨哨哨哨哨哨 哨哨

❶ [名] 巡逻、警戒、防守的岗位：sentry post; post | 放~ fàngshǎo *stand sentry; stand on sentry duty* / 岗~gǎngshǎo *sentry post*

哨兵 shǎobīng sentry; guard

❷ [名] 哨子：whistle | 吹~ chuīshǎo *blow a whistle*

奢 shē 11画 大部

奢 奢奢奢奢奢奢奢 奢奢奢

[形] 过多地花费钱财，追求享受(跟"俭jiǎn"相对)：luxurious;

extravagant (the opposite of "俭jiǎn") | ~华 shēhuá *luxurious*

奢侈 shēchǐ luxurious; extravagant; wasteful

舌 shé 6画 舌部

舌 舌舌舌舌舌舌

[名] tongue

舌头 shétou tongue

长舌妇 chángshéfù

大舌头 dàshétou

蛇 shé 11画 虫部

蛇 蛇蛇蛇蛇蛇蛇蛇蛇 蛇蛇蛇

[名] snake; serpent

舍 (捨) shě 8画 人部

舍 舍舍舍舍舍舍舍舍

[动] 放弃；丢下：give up; abandon | ~弃 shěqì *give up* / ~身 shěshēn *give up one's life* / ~近求远 shějìn-qiúyuǎn *seek far and wide and set aside what lies close at hand*

舍得 shěde be willing to part with; not grudge

舍不得 shěbude hate to part with or use; grudge

See shě.

设 (設) shè 6画 讠部

设 设设设设设设

❶ [动] 设立；布置：set up; arrange; found | ~宴款待 shè yàn kuǎndài *give a banquet in honour of sb.* / 总公司~在上海。Zǒnggōngsī shè zài Shànghǎi. *The headquarters are in Shanghai.*

设备 shèbèi equipment; facility
设定 shèdìng enactment
设立 shèlì establish; set up; found
设施 shèshī facility
设置 shèzhì set up; put up; install
摆设 bǎishè 创设 chuàngshè
建设 jiànshè 开设 kāishè
增设 zēngshè

❷ [动] 筹划；考虑：work out | ~了个圈套shèle ge quāntào *set a trap*

设法 shèfǎ manage; get by; try
设计 shèjì devise; design; set up
设想 shèxiǎng ① imagine; envisage; conceive; assume ②tentative plan; tentative idea ③ have consideration for
设计师 shèjìshī ① designer ② architect
假设 jiǎshè
想方设法 xiǎngfāng-shèfǎ

社 shè 7画 礻部

社 社社社社社社社

[名] 指某些团体或机构：organized body; agency; society | 报~ bàoshè *news agency* / 合作~ hézuòshè *cooperative* / 旅行~ lǚxíngshè *travel agency*

社论 shèlùn editorial; leading article; leader
社区 shèqū community
社团shètuán mass organization
社员 shèyuán member of a society, club, etc.
通讯社 tōngxùnshè
信用社 xìnyòngshè
◇社会 shèhuì society; community
社会主义 shèhuì zhǔyì socialism

舍 shè 8画 人部

舍 舍舍舍舍舍舍舍舍

[名] 居住的房屋，住所：house; hut | 宿~sùshè dormitory
See shě.

射 shè 10画 身部

射 射射射射射射射射
射射

❶ [动] 用压力、推力或弹力送出：shoot; fire | 扫~sǎoshè *strafe* / ~箭shèjiàn *shoot an arrow* / ~进一球 shèjìn yī qiú *kick the ball into the goal; score a goal*

射击 shèjī shoot
射门 shèmén (sports) shoot (at the goal)

❷ [动] 液体受压通过小孔迅速喷出：jet; spout
喷射 pēnshè   注射 zhùshè

❸ [动] 发出(光、热、电波等)：send out (light, heat, electric wave, etc.) | ~线 shèxiàn *ray* / 放~光芒fàngshè guāngmáng *radiate brilliant light*

反射 fǎnshè   放射 fàngshè
辐射 fúshè   折射 zhéshè

涉 / 涉   shè   10画 氵部

涉涉涉涉涉涉涉涉涉涉

[动] 牵连：involve | ~嫌shèxián *be suspected of being involved*
涉及 shèjí involve; relate to; touch upon
涉外shèwài concerning foreign affairs or foreign nationals
涉足 shèzú (formal) set foot in
干涉 gānshè   交涉 jiāoshè

摄 (攝) shè   13画 扌部

摄 / 摄 摄摄摄摄摄摄摄摄摄
摄摄摄摄摄

❶ [动] 吸取：absorb; assimilate | ~取 shèqǔ *absorb* / ~食 shèshí *(of animals) feed*

❷ [动] 摄影：take a photograph of; shoot | ~制shèzhì *produce (a film)* / 这个镜头可不容易~。Zhège jìngtou kě bù róngyì shè. *This scene is by no means easy to shoot.*

摄像 shèxiàng make a video recording (with a video camera or TV camera)
摄影 shèyǐng photography; shot
摄像机 shèxiàngjī camera
摄影师 shèyǐngshī photographer; cameraman
拍摄 pāishè
◇摄氏 shèshì Celsius

谁 (誰) shéi 10画 讠部

谁 / 谁 谁谁谁谁谁谁谁谁
谁谁

❶ [代] 疑问代词,询问不知道的人：interrogative pronoun, who | 你找~? Nǐ zhǎo shéi? *Who are you looking for?* / ~来啦? Shéi lái la? *Who's coming?*

❷ [代] 指代不能肯定的人：used in a supposition to indicate someone

❸[代]指代任何人：anyone; whoever | 大家看～合适就选～。Dàjiā kàn shéi héshì jiū xuǎn shéi. *Select whoever you think is suitable.* / ～都可以做。Shéi dōu kěyǐ zuò. *Anyone can do it.*

 shēn 5画 l部

申 申申申申申

[动]说明；陈述：state; express; explain | ～辩 shēnbiàn *defend oneself; explain oneself* / ～明理由 shēnmíng lǐyóu *explain one's reason for doing sth.*

申报 shēnbào ① report to a higher body ② declare sth. (to the Customs)

申请 shēnqǐng apply for; file an application

申述 shēnshù state; explain in detail

重申 chóngshēn

 shēn 7画 亻部

伸 伸伸伸伸伸伸伸

[动]舒展开：stretch; extend | ～直 shēnzhí *straighten* / 他～出头来四处望。Tā shēnchū tóu lai sìchù wàng. *He stuck out*

his head to look around.

伸手 shēnshǒu ① stretch (hold) out one's hand ② ask for help, etc.

伸展 shēnzhǎn spread; extend; stretch

延伸 yánshēn

 shēn 7画 身部

身 身身身身身身身

❶[名]身体：body | 转过～去 zhuǎnguò shēn qu *turn round one's body* / 这套衣服挺合～。Zhè tào yīfu tǐng héshēn. *This suit fits perfectly.*

身边 shēnbiān ① at (by) one's side ② (have sth.) on one; with one

身材 shēncái stature; figure

身高 shēngāo height (of a person)

身体 shēntǐ ① body ② health

身影 shēnyǐng a person's silhouette; form; figure

身子 shēnzi body

动身 dòngshēn   翻身 fānshēn

浑身 húnshēn   健身 jiànshēn

起身 qǐshēn   热身 rèshēn

人身 rénshēn   随身 suíshēn

❷[名]物体的主要部分：main part of a structure; body | 车～chēshēn *body of a car* / 船～chuánshēn *body of a*

ship / 树 ~shùshēn *trunk*

❸ [名] 自身；本人：oneself | ~临其中 shēnlínqízhōng *be personally on the scene*

本身 běnshēn　亲身 qīnshēn

自身 zìshēn

以身作则 yǐshēn-zuòzé

❹ [名] 生命；一生：life | 她舍~救孩子。Tā shěshēn jiù háizi. *She sacrificed her life to save the child.*

献身 xiànshēn　终身 zhōngshēn

❺ [名] 身份、地位：status

身份 shēnfèn status; capacity; identity; honourable position; dignity

身份证 shēnfènzhèng identity card; identification card; ID card; ID

出身 chūshēn　单身 dānshēn

❻ [量] 用于衣服：(for clothing) suit | 一~新衣服 yī shēn xīn yīfu *a new set of clothing*

呷　shēn　8画 口部

呷 呷呷呷呷呷呷呷

See 呷吟

呷吟 shēnyín groan; moan; utter moans

绅 (紳) shēn　8画 纟部

绅 绅绅绅绅绅绅绅

See 绅士

绅士 shēnshì gentleman; gentry

深　shēn　11画 氵部

深 深深深深深深深深
深深深

❶ [形] 从上到下或从外到里的距离大（跟"浅 qiǎn"相对）：deep (the opposite of "浅 qiǎn") | ~山 shēnshān *remote mountains* / 这条河很~。Zhè tiáo hé hěn shēn. *The river is very deep.* / 这个院子很~。Zhège yuànzi hěn shēn. *The yard is very deep.*

深层 shēncéng ① depth; deeper layers ② deep-going; thorough; incisive

深处 shēnchù depth; deep

深度 shēndù ① degree of depth ② advanced stage of development

深浅 shēnqiǎn depth

资深 zīshēn

根深蒂固 gēnshēn-dìgù

❷ [形] 程度高；（道理、含义等）不易理解：difficult; profound | 道理很~ dàolǐ hěn shēn *contain profound truth* / 这本书内容太~。Zhè běn shū nèiróng tài shēn. *This book is too difficult.*

深奥 shēn'ào abstruse; profound; recondite

深沉 shēnchén ① deep ② (of sound or voice) low-pitched; deep; dull ③ undemonstrative; reserved

深化 shēnhuà deepen

深重 shēnzhòng very grave; extremely serious

加深 jiāshēn

❸ [形] 深入，深刻；thoroughgoing; penetrating; profound | ～谈 shēntán *discuss thoroughly* / 印象很～yìnxiàng hěn shēn *have deep impression* / 影响很～yǐngxiǎng hěn shēn *exert a profound influence*

深刻 shēnkè deep; profound; deepgoing

深入 shēnrù ① go deep into; penetrate into ② thorough; deepgoing

深远 shēnyuǎn profound and lasting; far-reaching

❹ [形] (感情)深厚；(关系)密切：close; intimate | 交情～jiāoqing shēn *be on intimate terms* / 两人的关系很～。Liǎng rén de guānxi hěn shēn. *The two of them have a profound friendship.*

深厚 shēnhòu deep; profound; solid

深切 shēnqiè ① heartfelt; deep; profound ② keenly

深情 shēnqíng deep feeling; deep love

❺ [形] 颜色浓 (跟"浅 qiǎn"相对)：dark; deep (the opposite of "浅 qiǎn") | ～红 shēnhóng *deep red; crimson* / ～蓝 shēnlán *dark blue* / 颜色太～。Yánsè tài shēn. *The colour is too dark.*

❻ [形] 距离开始的时间久：late | ～秋 shēnqiū *late autumn* / 夜～了。Yè shēn le. *It was late at night.*

深夜 shēnyè late at night; in the small hours of the morning

夜深人静 yèshēn-rénjìng

❼ [副] 很；十分：very; greatly; deeply | ～知 shēnzhī *know very well; be fully(keenly) aware* / ～表同情 shēn biǎo tóngqíng *show deep sympathy*

深信 shēnxìn be deeply convinced; firmly believe

什 shén 4画 亻部

什 什什什什

See 什么

什么 shénme ① what ② any; every ③ something; anything ④ whatever ⑤ expressing anger, surprise, censure or negation ⑥ expressing disapproval or disagreement ⑦ things like; such as; and so on; and what not

See shí.

神 shén 9画 礻部

神神神神神神神神神

❶ [名] god; deity
神话 shénhuà myth
神仙 shénxiān supernatural being; celestial being; immortal
神州 Shénzhōu the Divine Land (a poetic name for China)

❷ [形] 特别高超、出奇的：supernatural; magical | ～医 shényī *highly skilled doctor* / ～效 shénxiào *magical effect* / 这事越说越～了。Zhè shì yuè shuō yuè shén le. *The more it is talked about, the more incredible it becomes.*
神秘 shénmì mysterious; mystical
神奇 shénqí magical; mystical; miraculous
神圣 shénshèng sacred; holy

❸ [名] 精神；精力：spirit; mind | 凝～ níngshén *concentrate (focus) one's attention* / 闭目养～ bìmù yǎngshén *close one's eyes and rest one's mind* / 聚精会～ jùjīng-huìshén *concentrate one's attention; be all attention*
出神 chūshén 精神 jīngshén 留神 liúshén

❹ [名] 人的表情和表现出的内心状态：expression; look
神气 shénqì expression; air; manner
神情 shénqíng expression; look
神色 shénsè expression; look
神态 shéntài expression; manner; bearing; mien
眼神 yǎnshén
◇神经 shénjīng nerve

审 (審) shěn 8画 宀部

审审审审审审审审

❶ [动] 仔细地观察；考查：examine; go over | ～阅 shěnyuè *examine carefully and critically* / ～稿 shěngǎo *go over a manuscript*
审查 shěnchá examine; investigate
审定 shěndìng examine and approve
审核 shěnhé verify; check
审美 shěnměi aethetics; appreciation of the beautiful
审批 shěnpī examine and approve; examine and give instructions
审视 shěnshì look closely at; examine closely
审议 shěnyì review; deliberate
评审 píngshěn

❷ [动] 讯问案件：interrogate; try | ～案 shěn'àn *try a case* / 公～

gōngshěn *put sb. on public trial* / 受 ~ shōushěn *be put on trial*

审理 shěnlǐ try; hear

审判 shěnpàn bring to trial; try

审讯 shěnxùn ① hearing ② interrogate; try

终审 zhōngshěn

陪审员 péishěnyuán

 婶 (嬸) shěn 11画 女部

婶婶婶婶婶婶婶婶婶婶

❶ [名] 叔叔的妻子：wife of father's younger brother; aunt 婶子 shěnzi wife of father's younger brother; aunt

❷ [名] 称呼与母亲平辈而年纪较小的已婚妇女：form of address for a woman younger than one's mother but of the same generation; aunt | 大 ~ 儿 dàshěnr *aunt*

 肾 (腎) shèn 8画 月部

肾肾肾肾肾肾肾肾

[名] kidney

肾炎 shènyán nephritis

 甚 shèn 9画 一部

 甚 甚甚甚甚甚甚甚甚
甚

[副] 很；极：very; extremely | ~ 好 shènhǎo *very good* / 欺人太 ~。Qīrén tài shèn. *It's going too far.*

甚至 shènzhì ① even to the extent that ② (go) so far as to; so much so that

甚至于 shènzhìyú furthermore; even to the extent that

 渗 (滲) shèn 11画 氵部

渗渗渗渗渗渗渗渗渗渗渗

[动] 液体慢慢地透入或漏出：ooze; seep | ~ 水 shènshuǐ *water oozing out* / 雪水 ~ 进地里去了。Xuěshuǐ shènjìn dìli qù le. *The melted snow seeped into the fields.*

渗透 shèntòu ① permeate; seep ② penetrate; infiltrate

慎 shèn 13画 忄部

慎慎慎慎慎慎慎慎
慎慎慎慎慎

[形] 小心：careful; cautious | 不 ~ bùshèn *careless*

慎重 shènzhòng cautious; careful; prudent; discreet

谨慎 jǐnshèn

升 shēng 4画 丿部

升 升升升升

❶ [动] 向上或向高处移动（跟"降 jiàng"相对）：move upward (the opposite of "降 jiàng") | ～旗 shēngqí *raise a flag* / 太阳从东方～起。Tàiyáng cóng dōngfāng shēngqǐ. *The sun rises in the east.*

升值 shēngzhí (econ.) ① revalue ② appreciate

上升 shàngshēng

❷ [动] （级别）提高：promote | ～级 shēngjí *go up one grade; promote one's status; escalate*

升学 shēngxué *go to a school of a higher grade; enter a higher school*

晋升 jìnshēng　提升 tíshēng

生 shēng 5画 丿部

生 生生生生生

❶ [动] 生育；出生；生长：give birth to; bear; grow | ～孩子 shēng háizi *give birth to a child* / 他～于 1950 年。Tā shēngyú yījiǔwǔlíng nián. *He was born in 1950.* / ～根 shēnggēn *take root* / ～芽 shēngyá *sprout*

生产 shēngchǎn ① produce; manufacture ② give birth to a child

生理 shēnglǐ physiology

生日 shēngrì birthday

生肖 shēngxiào any one of the names of 12 symbolic animals associated with a 12-year cycle, often used to denote the year of a person's birth (the 12 animals are: rat, ox, tiger, hare, dragon, snake, horse, sheep, monkey, cock, dog and pig)

生育 shēngyù give birth to; bear

生长 shēngzhǎng ① grow ② grow up; be brought up; put forth

生殖 shēngzhí reproduction

生产力 shēngchǎnlì productive forces

生产率 shēngchǎnlǜ productivity

生产线 shēngchǎnxiàn production line

生儿育女 shēng'ér-yùnǚ bear and raise (children)

出生 chūshēng　诞生 dànshēng

亲生 qīnshēng　野生 yěshēng

独生子女 dúshēng zǐnǚ

❷ [名] 学习的人；学生：pupil; student | 师～关系 shīshēng guānxi *teacher-student relation* / 毕业～ bìyèshēng *graduate*

考生 kǎoshēng

男生 nánshēng

女生 nǚshēng

师生 shīshēng

学生 xuésheng
招生 zhāoshēng
博士生 bóshìshēng
大学生 dàxuéshēng
留学生 liúxuéshēng
实习生 shíxíshēng
书生气 shūshēngqì
小学生 xiǎoxuéshēng
研究生 yánjiūshēng
中学生 zhōngxuéshēng

❸ [动] 产生；发生：happen; engender; get | ~疑心 shēng yíxīn *become suspicious* / 惹是～非 rěshì-shēngfēi *provoke a dispute; stir up trouble*
生病 shēngbìng fall ill
生气 shēngqì ① take offence; get angry ② vim; vitality
生效 shēngxiào go into effect; become effective
产生 chǎnshēng
天生 tiānshēng

❹ [动] 生存；活着（跟 "死 sǐ" 相对）：live; exist (the opposite of "死 sǐ") | 复～fùshēng *come back to life*
生存 shēngcún subsist; exist; live
生活 shēnghuó ① life ② live ③ livelihood ④ work (of workers, peasants, or handicraftsman)
生机 shēngjī ① lease of life ② life; vitality
生前 shēngqián before one's death; during one's lifetime
生态 shēngtài organisms' biological and life habits; modes of life and relation to their environment; ecology

❺ [形] 有生命力的；活着的：living; alive | 活～～huóshēng-shēng ① *real; living* ② *while still alive*
生动 shēngdòng lively; vivid
生物 shēngwù living thing; living being; organism
微生物 wēishēngwù

❻ [名] 生命；一辈子：existence; life | 丧～sāngshēng *lose one's life* / 逃～táoshēng *escape with one's life*
生命 shēngmìng life
生命力 shēngmìnglì life force; vitality
人生 rénshēng
卫生 wèishēng
养生 yǎngshēng
一生 yīshēng
维生素 wéishēngsù
卫生间 wèishēngjiān

❼ [名] 维持生活的手段：livelihood | 谋～móushēng *earn one's livelihood; make a living* / 以写作为～yǐ xiězuò wéi shēng *make a living by writing*
做生意 zuòshēngyi

❽ [形] 没有成熟的；没有煮熟的；没有加工的：unripe; green; raw; uncooked | ～吃 shēng chī *eat raw* / 吃～虾 chī shēng-xiā *eat raw shrimp* / ～黄瓜 shēng huángguā *uncooked cucumber* / 这西瓜是～的。Zhè xīguā shì shēng de. *This watermelon is not ripe yet.*

❾ [形] 没有加工或训练的：unprocessed; unrefined; crude | ～铁 shēngtiě *pig iron* / ～皮 shēngpí *rawhide; (untanned) hide*

❿ [形] 不熟悉：unfamiliar; unacquainted; strange | ～字 shēngzì *new words or characters* / 这孩子认～。Zhè háizi rènshēng. *The child is shy around strangers.*

生词 shēngcí new word
生人 shēngrén stranger
生疏 shēngshū ① not familiar ② out of practice;rusty ③ not as close as before
陌生 mòshēng
陌生人 mòshēngrén

⓫ [形] 生硬，勉强：stiff; mechanical | ～硬 shēngyìng ① *(of writing) not polished; crude* ② *stiff; rigid* / 我们不能～搬别人的经验。Wǒmen bùnéng shēngbān biérén de jīngyàn. *We cannot rigidly apply other people's experience.*

⓬ [副] 很：extremely; very | 手碰得～疼。Shǒu pèng de shēngténg. *I hit my hand and it was very painful.*

生怕 shēngpà for fear that; so as not to; lest

◇生意 shēngyi ① tendency to grow; life and vitality ② business; trade

好好先生 hǎohǎo xiānsheng

（聲）shēng 7画 士部

声 声声声声声声声

❶ [名] 声音：sound; voice | 风～ fēngshēng *sound of wind* / 笑～ xiàoshēng *laughter* / 脚步～ jiǎobùshēng *sound of footsteps* / 大～说话 dàshēng shuōhuà *speak in a loud voice*

声调 shēngdiào tone; intonation; accent
声音 shēngyīn sound; voice
大声 dàshēng   发声 fāshēng
歌声 gēshēng   呼声 hūshēng
铃声 língshēng
尾声 wěishēng
响声 xiǎngshēng
相声 xiàngsheng
心声 xīnshēng
噪声 zàoshēng
掌声 zhǎngshēng

❷ [动] 陈述；宣布；发出声音：make a sound; make known; state | ～张 shēngzhāng *make public* / ～称 shēngchēng *claim* / 不～不响 bùshēng-bùxiǎng *not utter a word; keep quiet*

声明 shēngmíng ① state; declare; announce ② statement; declaration

650

❸ [名] 名誉；威望：reputation | ~望 shēngwàng *popularity; reputation*

声势 shēngshì *impetus; momentum*

声誉 shēngyù *reputation; fame; prestige*

名声 míngshēng

❹ [名] 声调，音节的高低升降：tone | ~调 shēngdiào *tone* / 四~ sìshēng *the four tones (of Chinese)*

声母 shēngmǔ (phonet.) *the initial of a syllable (usu. a consonant)*

❺ [量] 用于声音发出的次数：used for frequency of utterance | 喊了一~ hǎnle yī shēng *give a shout* / 我接连叫了几~。Wǒ jiēlián jiàole jǐ shēng. *I shouted several times in succession.*

---

shēng 9画 牛部

牲牲牲牲牲牲牲牲牲

[名] 家畜：domestic animal

牲畜 shēngchù beast

牲口 shēngkou draught animal; beast of burden

牺牲 xīshēng

 (繩) shéng 11画 纟部

绳绳绳绳绳绳绳绳绳绳绳

[名] rope; cord; string | 麻~ máshéng *hemp rope* / 钢丝~ gāngsīshéng *steel cable; wire rope* / 用~子捆书 yòng shéngzi kǔn shū *tie up books with rope*

绳子 shéngzi rope

---

shěng 9画 目部

省省省省省省省省省

❶ [动] 免掉；减去：omit; leave out | ~一道工序 shěng yī dào gōngxù *eliminate one step from working procedure* / 这个句子可以~去。Zhège jùzi kěyǐ shěngqù. *This sentence can be omitted.*

省得 shěngde so as to save

省略 shěnglüè skip; be elliptic; ellipsis

❷ [动] 节约（跟"费 fèi"相对）：economize; save (the opposite of "费 fèi") | ~钱 shěngqián *save money; be economical* / ~力气 shěng lìqi *save labour* / ~时间 shěng shíjiān *save time* / ~俭吃用 shěngchī-jiǎnyòng *live frugally*

节省 jiéshěng

❸ [名] 全国一级行政区划单位 province

省会 shěnghuì provincial capital

省长 shěngzhǎng governor of a province

 圣（聖）shèng 5画 又部

圣 圣圣圣圣圣

❶ [形] 最崇高的：holy; sacred | ～地 shèngdì *holy land*
神圣 shénshèng

❷ [名] 宗教徒对所崇拜的事物的尊称：sage; saint | 《～经》Shèngjīng *the Bible* / ～灵 shènglíng *the Holy Spirit; the Holy Ghost*
圣诞 Shèngdàn ① (old) the birthday of Confucius ② Christmas (the birth of Jesus Christ)
圣诞节 Shèngdànjié Christmas (Day)

 胜（勝）shèng 9画 月部

胜 胜胜胜胜胜胜胜胜 胜

❶ [动] 胜利（跟"负fù""败bǎi"相对）：victory; conquer (the opposite of "负fù" or "败bǎi") | 取～ qǔshèng *win (victory)* / 打～仗 dǎ shèngzhàng *win a battle* / 他～了这盘棋。Tā shèng-le zhè pán qí. *He has won the chess game.*

胜负 shèngfù victory or defeat; success or failure
胜利 shènglì victory; attain the goal as planned
获胜 huòshèng
优胜 yōushèng 战胜 zhànshèng

❷ [动] 超过：surpass; be superior to | 一个～一个。Yī gè shèng yī gè. *One is better than the other.* / 你的条件～过他。Nǐ de tiáojiàn shèngguo tā. *Your qualifications are better than his.*

❸ [形] 优美的（景物或境界等）：beautiful scenery; scenic spot | ～景 shèngjǐng *wonderful scenery* / ～地 shèngdì *famous scenic spot*
名胜 míngshèng
名胜古迹 míngshèng-gǔjì

 盛 shèng 11画 皿部

盛 盛盛盛盛盛盛盛盛 盛盛盛

❶ [形] 繁荣；兴旺（跟"衰shuāi"相对）：flourishing; prosperous (the opposite of "衰shuāi") | 全～时期 quánshèng shíqī *period of full bloom* / 鲜花～开。Xiānhuā shèngkāi. *The flowers are in full bloom.*
盛开 shèngkāi be in full bloom; flourish; flower; bloom
昌盛 chāngshèng

茂盛 màoshèng
强盛 qiángshèng
旺盛 wàngshèng

❷[形]规模大；隆重：magnificent; grand | ～会 shènghuì *grand meeting* / ～况 shèngkuàng *grand occasion*

盛大 shèngdà grand; magnificent; flourishing

❸[形]普遍；广泛：popular; common; wide spread | ～传 shèngchuán *be widely known*

盛行 shèngxíng be current; be in vogue; be epidemic

❹[形]强烈；深厚：vigorous; energetic; abundant; plentiful; great; deep | 火势很～。Huǒshì hěn shèng. *The fire is raging.*

盛情 shèngqíng great kindness; boundless hospitality

◇盛产 shèngchǎn be abound in; teem with; be in season
See chéng.

剩　shèng　12画　刂部

剩 剩剩剩剩剩剩剩剩
剩剩剩剩

[动]余下；留下：be left (over); remain | ～饭 shèngfàn *leftovers* / 盘子里～下几只苹果。Pánzi li shèngxià jǐ zhī píngguǒ. *Several apples were left on the plate.* / 所～不多 suǒ shèng bù duō *there is not much left*

剩下 shèngxià be left (over); remain

剩余 shèngyú surplus; remainder

过剩 guòshèng

尸　shī　3画　尸部

尸 尸尸尸

[名]人或动物死后的身体：corpse; dead body | 死～sǐshī *dead body*

尸体 shītǐ dead body; corpse

失　shī　5画　丿部

失 失失失失失

❶[动]丢掉；失去：lose | ～物招领 shīwù zhāolǐng *lost and found* / 莫～良机 mò shī liángjī *don't let slip a good opportunity; opportunity knocks but once* / 不要～了信心。Bùyào shīle xìnxīn. *Don't lose your confidence.*

失掉 shīdiào ① lose ② miss

失控 shīkòng get out of control; get out of hand

失眠 shīmián insomnia

失去 shīqù lose; go adrift

失效 shīxiào lose efficiency; lose effectiveness; cease to be effective; be no longer in force;

become invalid

失学 shīxué be deprived of education; be obliged to discontinue one's studies

失业 shīyè lose one's job; be out of work; be unemployed

丢失 diūshī　流失 liúshī
丧失 sàngshī　损失 sǔnshī
消失 xiāoshī　遗失 yíshī

❷ [动] 找不着：miss

失踪 shīzōng be missing
迷失 míshī

❸ [动] 没有控制住：lose control of | ～手 shīshǒu *have a slip of the hand; drop accidentally; lose hold (of)* / ～足 shīzú *lose one's footing; take a wrong step in life* / ～火 shīhuǒ *catch fire; be on fire*

失败 shībài ①be defeated; lose ② fail; go to the devil

冒失鬼 màoshiguǐ

❹ [动] 没有达到(目的、愿望)：fail to achieve one's end | ～意 shīyì *frustrated; disappointed* / ～策 shīcè ① *do sth. unwise* ② *an error in tactics, etc.*

失望 shīwàng ① lose hope; lose heart ② be disappointed

❺ [动] 违背；背离：break (a promise); go back on (one's word) | ～信 shīxìn *break one's promise*

失约 shīyuē fail to keep an appointment

❻ [名] 错误：mishap; defect;

mistake | 闪～shǎnshī *mishap*

失误 shīwù error; fault

过失 guòshī

◇失事 shīshì have an accident

 师 (師) shī　6画 丨部

师 师师师师师师

❶ [名] 军队编制单位：unit of division in the troops division

❷ [名] 传授知识、技术的人：teacher; master | 我想拜您为～。Wǒ xiǎng bài nín wéi shī. *I want to be your student.*

师范 shīfàn ①teacher-training; pedagogical ② normal

师傅 shīfu master; (qualified) worker

师生 shīshēng teacher and student

师长 shīzhǎng ① teacher ② division commander

大师 dàshī　　导师 dǎoshī
教师 jiàoshī　　老师 lǎoshī
教师节 Jiàoshījié

❸ [名] 掌握专门知识、技术的人：person skilled in a certain profession | 技～ jìshī *technician* / 医～ yīshī *doctor* / 设计～ shèjìshī *designer* / 理发～ lǐfàshī *barber; hairdresser*

厨师 chúshī　　律师 lǜshī
工程师 gōngchéngshī

654

建筑师 jiànzhùshī
会计师 kuàijìshī
摄影师 shèyǐngshī

诗 (詩) shī　8画 讠部

诗 诗诗诗诗诗诗诗诗

[名] 文学体裁的一种：poetry; verse; poem | 讽刺~fěngcìshī *satiric poem (poetry)* / 散文~sǎnwénshī *prose poem (poetry)*

诗歌 shīgē poem; poetry
诗人 shīrén poet
诗情画意 shīqíng-huàyì a quality suggestive of poetry or painting; poetic charm
古体诗 gǔtǐshī

狮 (獅) shī　9画 犭部

狮 狮狮狮狮狮狮狮狮狮

See 狮子
狮子 shīzi lion

施 shī　9画 方部

施 施施施施施施施施施

❶ [动] 给予：give | ~礼 shīlǐ *make a bow; salute* / ~压 shīyā *exert pressure*

施加 shījiā exert; bring to bear on

❷ [动] 用上；加上：use; apply | ~粉 shīfěn *apply powder (on one's face, neck etc.)*

施肥 shīféi spread manure; apply fertilizer

❸ [动] 实行；施展：put into practice; carry out | 无计可~ wújì-kěshī *at one's wits' end*

施工 shīgōng carry out construction or large repairs

施行 shīxíng ① put (law, rules, regulations, etc.) into force; enforce; implement ② perform; administer; apply; dispense

施展 shīzhǎn put to good use; give free play to

措施 cuòshī 　　　设施 shèshī
实施 shíshī

湿 (濕) shī　12画 氵部

湿 湿湿湿湿湿湿湿湿湿湿湿湿

[形] 沾了水或含水分多的（跟"干 gān"相对）：wet; damp; humid (the opposite of "干 gān") | ~衣服 shī yīfu *wet clothes* / 地很~。Dì hěn shī. *The ground is wet.* / 手~了。Shǒu shī le. *My hands are wet.*

湿度 shīdù humidity
湿润 shīrùn moist

潮湿 cháoshī

十 shí　2画 十部

十 十 十

❶ [数] 数目：ten | ~倍 shí bèi
ten times; tenfold / ~岁的男孩
shí suì de nánhái *a boy of ten*

❷ [形] 表示达到顶点：topmost
十分 shí fēn very; fully; utterly;
extremely
十足 shí zú ① pure ② 100 per-
cent; out-and-out; sheer; down-
right; unadulterated
十全十美 shí quán-shí měi be
perfect in every way; be the
acme of perfection; leave nothing to be desired

什 shí　4画 亻部

什 什 什 什

❶ [数] 同 "十 shí"（多用于分数
或倍数）：same as "十 shí"
(often used in fractions or
multiples) | ~一 shí yī *one
tenth*

❷ [形] 多种的；杂样的：assorted;
varied; miscellaneous | ~物
shí wù *articles for daily use;
odds and ends* / ~锦 shí jǐn assorted (food or refreshments
such as sweets)

See shén.

石 shí　5画 石部

石 石 石 石 石 石

[名] 石头：stone; rock
石灰 shí huī lime
石头 shí tou stone; rock
宝石 bǎoshí　　化石 huàshí
矿石 kuàngshí　岩石 yánshí
钻石 zuānshí
绊脚石 bànjiǎoshí
大理石 dàlǐshí

◇ 石榴 shí liu pomegranate
石油 shí yóu oil; petroleum

时 （時）shí　7画 日部

时 时 时 时 时 时 时

❶ [名] 季节：season | 四~ sìshí
four seasons
时节 shí jié ① season ② a particular time; occasion

❷ [名] 较长的一段时间；时候：
time; times; days | 古~ gǔshí
in ancient times
时差 shí chā ① time difference
② (astron.) equation of time
时代 shí dài ① times; age; era;
epoch ② the times; our age; the
day; the present era ③ a period
in one's life; cycle
时光 shí guāng ① time ②
times; years; days

时候 shíhou time; moment
时机 shíjī opportunity; an opportune moment
时间 shíjiān time
时刻 shíkè ① a point of time; hour; moment ②constantly; always
时期 shíqī a particular period
时间表 shíjiānbiǎo timetable; schedule

此时 cǐshí　　当时 dāngshí
顿时 dùnshí　　临时 línshí
那时 nàshí　　平时 píngshí
随时 suíshí　　同时 tóngshí
一时 yīshí　　有时 yǒushí
暂时 zànshí
倒计时 dàojìshí

❸[名] 规定的时间：fixed time
按时 ànshí　　　　及时 jíshí
准时 zhǔnshí

❹[名] 小时，时间单位：hour ｜ 下午三~ xiàwǔ sān shí *three o'clock in the afternoon*
时速 shísù speed per hour
课时 kèshí　　　　小时 xiǎoshí
学时 xuéshí
小时工 xiǎoshígōng

❺[形] 当前的；现在的：present; current ｜ ~下 shíxià *at present*
时髦 shímáo fashionable; stylish
时尚 shíshàng fashion; fad
时事 shíshì current event; current affair
时装 shízhuāng fashionable dress; the latest fashion

赶时髦 gǎnshímáo
❻[副] 经常：frequently ｜ ~有出现 shíyǒu chūxiàn *occur now and then*
时常 shícháng often; frequently; every now and again
时时 shíshí often; constantly
❼[副] 有时候：sometimes ｜ ~快~慢 shí kuài shí màn *sometimes fast, sometimes slow*/ ~好~坏 shí hǎo shí huài *sometimes good, sometimes bad* / 天气~热~冷。Tiānqì shí rè shí lěng. *The weather is sometimes hot, sometimes cold.*
时而 shí'ér ① from time to time; sometimes ② now... now...; sometimes... sometimes

识 (識) shí　　7画 讠部

识 识识识识识识识

❶[动] 知道；认得：know; recognize ｜ ~字 shízì *learn to read; become literate* / ~货 shíhuò *know well about the goods; be able to tell good from bad*
识别 shíbié distinguish; discern; spot
认识 rènshi　　　相识 xiāngshí
❷[名] 知识；见解：knowledge; experience ｜ 学~ xuéshí *learning* / 见多~广 jiànduō-shí-

guǎng *have wide experience and extensive knowledge*
常识 chángshí
共识 gòngshí   见识 jiànshi
意识 yìshí   知识 zhīshi
知识分子 zhīshi fēnzǐ

实（實）shí   8画 宀部
．．．．．．．．．．．．
实 实实实实实实实实

❶ [形] 充满的；没有空隙的：full; solid | ～心球 shíxīnqiú *solid ball* / ～足 shízú *full* / 里面是～的。Lǐmian shì shí de. *It's solid inside.*
充实 chōngshí   坚实 jiānshí
结实 jiēshi

❷ [形] 真实；实在：true; real; honest | 情况属～。Qíngkuàng shǔshí. *The situation is real.* / ～有其事。Shí yǒu qí shì. *It's a fact.*
实词 shící (gram.) notional word
实话 shíhuà truth
实惠 shíhuì material benefit; substantial
实力 shílì actual strength; strength
实体 shítǐ ①substance ②entity
实物 shíwù material object
实在 shízài ①true; real; honest; dependable ② indeed; really
实质 shízhì substance; essence
诚实 chéngshí   核实 héshí
老实 lǎoshi   落实 luòshí

朴实 pǔshí   确实 quèshí
踏实 tāshi   扎实 zhāshi
真实 zhēnshí   忠实 zhōngshí
真情实感 zhēnqíng-shígǎn

❸ [名] 实际；事实：reality; fact | 失～ shīshí *inconsistent with the facts*
实际 shíjì ① reality; practice ② practical; realistic ③ real; actual; concrete
实践 shíjiàn ① practice ② put into practice
实况 shíkuàng what is actually happening
实施 shíshī put into effect; implement; carry out; effectuate
实习 shíxí practise; exercise one's skill in; do field work; intern
实现 shíxiàn realize; fulfil; carry out; bring about; come true
实行 shíxíng put into practice; carry out; practise; implement; use
实验 shíyàn experiment; test
实用 shíyòng practical; pragmatic; functional
实习生 shíxíshēng trainee
实验室 shíyànshì laboratory
其实 qíshí   事实 shìshí
属实 shǔshí   现实 xiànshí
证实 zhèngshí

拾   shí   9画 扌部
．．．．．．．．．．．．

拾 拾拾拾拾拾拾拾拾拾

❶[动]从地上拿起来；捡取：pick up (from the ground); collect | ～柴 shí chái *collect firewood* / ～麦子 shí màizi *glean wheat* / ～了一支笔 shíle yī zhī bǐ *pick up a pen*

❷[动]整理；收拾：tidy up; put in order | 把你的房间～一～。Bǎ nǐ de fángjiān shíyishí. *Tidy up your room.*

收拾 shōushi

食 shí 9画 食部

食 食食食食食食食食食

❶[名]吃的东西：meal; food | 零～ língshí *snack; between-meal nibbles* / 肉～ ròushí *meat* / 面～ miànshí *cooked wheaten food; pastry*

副食 fùshí 伙食 huǒshí
粮食 liángshi 美食 měishí
饮食 yǐnshí 主食 zhǔshí

❷[动]吃；吃饭：eat | ～肉 shí ròu *eat meat; be carnivorous* / 我们应多～蔬菜。Wǒmen yīng duō shí shūcài. *We should eat plenty of vegetables.*

食堂 shítáng *dining room; canteen*
食用 shíyòng *edible*

食欲 shíyù *appetite*

❸[形]可以食用的：edible | ～盐 shíyán *salt* / ～油 shíyóu *edible oil*

食品 shípǐn *foodstuff; food; provisions*
食物 shíwù *food; eatables; edibles*

史 shǐ 5画 丨部

史 史史史史史

[名]历史，自然或社会以往发展的过程：history | ～学 shǐxué *science of history* / 世界～ shìjièshǐ *history of the world*
史料 shǐliào *historical data; historical material*
历史 lìshǐ

使 shǐ 8画 亻部

使 使使使使使使使

❶[动]派遣；打发人办事：send; tell sb. to do sth. | 支～ zhīshǐ *order about; send away* / ～人去买火车票 shǐ rén qù mǎi huǒchēpiào *send sb. to buy railway tickets*
使命 shǐmìng *mission*

❷[动]致使；让：make; cause; enable | ～人高兴 shǐ rén gāoxìng *make one happy* / ～人信服 shǐ rén xìnfú *convince*

659

sb. / 他的学问～我佩服。Tā de xuéwen shǐ wǒ pèifú. *I admire his learning.*

促使 cùshǐ 　　　迫使 pòshǐ
致使 zhìshǐ

❸ [动] 使用：use; employ; apply | 这把刀很好～。Zhè bǎ dāo hěn hǎoshǐ. *The knife cuts well.*

使得 shǐdé ① can be used; usable ②will do; be workable; be feasible

使劲 shǐjìn exert all one's strength

使用 shǐyòng use; employ; apply

使眼色 shǐyǎnsè tip sb. the wink; wink

行使 xíngshǐ

❹ [名] 接受外交使命到外国去的人；奉命办事的官员：envoy; messenger | ～者 shǐzhě *messenger*

使馆 shǐguǎn embassy

使节 shǐjié diplomatic envoy; envoy

大使 dàshǐ 　　　天使 tiānshǐ

 始 shǐ 　8画 女部

始 始 始 始 始 始 始 始

[动] 开始；起头：start; begin | 自～至终 zìshǐ-zhìzhōng *from beginning to end; from start to finish*

始终 shǐzhōng from beginning to end; from start to finish; all along; throughout; the alpha and omega

开始 kāishǐ 　　　原始 yuánshǐ
创始人 chuàngshǐrén

 驶 (駛) shǐ 　8画 马部

驶 驶 驶 驶 驶 驶 驶 驶

[动] (车、马等) 飞快地跑；开动 (车、船等)：(of a vehicle, horse, etc.) speed; drive; sail | 急～ jíshǐ *(of vehicle) speed* / 停～ tíngshǐ *stop going*

驾驶 jiàshǐ 　　　行驶 xíngshǐ
驾驶员 jiàshǐyuán

 屎 shǐ 　9画 尸部

屎 屎 屎 屎 屎 屎 屎 屎
屎

❶ [名] 大便，粪：excrement; dung; droppings

❷ [名] 眼、耳等器官的分泌物：secretion (of the eye, ear, etc.) | 眼～ yǎnshǐ *sleep in the eyes* / 耳～ ěrshǐ *earwax*

 士 shì 　3画 士部

士 士 士

❶ [名] 对人的美称：commendable

person｜勇~yǒngshì *brave fighter*

烈士 lièshì　　　男士 nánshì
女士 nǚshì

❷[名]指从事某些工作或有某种才能的人：person engaged in a profession or trained in a certain field｜助产~zhùchǎnshì *midwife*

护士 hùshì　　　硕士 shuòshì
学士 xuéshì　　　院士 yuànshì
博士后 bóshìhòu
博士生 bóshìshēng

❸[名]军人：noncommissioned officer｜上~shàngshì *staff sergeant; sergeant first class* / 中~zhōngshì *sergeant*

士兵 shìbīng rank-and-file soldier; private

◇巴士 bāshì　　　的士 díshì

示　　　shì　　5画 示部

示 示示示示示

[动] 表明；把事物拿出来或指出来使人知道：show; notify; instruct｜~众 shìzhòng *put before the public* / 出~证件 chūshì zhèngjiàn *show one's ID card*

示范 shìfàn set an example; demonstrate
示威 shìwēi demonstrate; hold a demonstration
示意图 shìyìtú ① sketch map

② schematic diagram; schematic drawing

暗示 ànshì　　　表示 biǎoshì
出示 chūshì　　　揭示 jiēshì
批示 pīshì　　　启示 qǐshì
请示 qǐngshì　　提示 tíshì
显示 xiǎnshì　　演示 yǎnshì
预示 yùshì　　　展示 zhǎnshì
指示 zhǐshì
显示屏 xiǎnshìpíng
显示器 xiǎnshìqì

世　　　shì　　5画 一部

世 世世世世世

❶[名]一代又一代：generation｜~交 shìjiāo ① *old family friends*; ② *hereditary friendship* / 四~同堂 sìshì tóngtáng *four generations live under one roof*

世代 shìdài for generations; from generation to generation

❷[名]人的一生：lifetime; life｜一生一~yīshēng-yīshì *one's whole life; all one's life*

❸[名]时代：age; era｜当~dāngshì *at present; nowadays*

❹[名]社会；人间：world｜~人 shìrén *common people* / ~道 shìdào *manners and morals of the time* / ~上 shìshang *in the world*

世故 shìgù the ways of the world
世界 shìjiè world; field
世人 shìrén common people

世界观 shìjièguān world out-
look
在世 zàishì
见世面 jiànshìmian
◇世纪 shìjì century

 市　shì　5画 亠部

市 市市市市市

❶[名]集中做买卖的场所：market
| 菜~ càishì *food market (pro-
vide agricultural products
mainly)* / 上~ shàngshì ① *be
on the market; be in season* ②
*be listed and traded on the
stock market* / 夜~ yèshì *night
market*
市场 shìchǎng marketplace;
market; bazaar
超市 chāoshì　　股市 gǔshì
集市 jíshì
农贸市场 nóngmào shìchǎng
自由市场 zìyóu shìchǎng
❷[名]城市：city | ~容 shìróng
apearance of a city / ~区 shìqū
city proper; downtown area
市民 shìmín city resident;
townspeople; urban inhabitant;
citizenry
市长 shìzhǎng mayor
市镇 shìzhèn small towns;
towns
市中心 shìzhōngxīn city cen-
tre
城市 chéngshì　　都市 dūshì

❸[名]行政区划单位，分直辖市和
市：city; municipality | 北京~
Běijīng Shì *the City of Beijing* /
上海~ Shànghǎi Shì *the City of
Shanghai*
直辖市 zhíxiáshì municipal-
ity
❹[名]市制的度量衡单位：per-
taining to the Chinese system of
weights and measures | ~尺
shìchǐ *a unit of length, equal
to 0.33 metre* / ~斤 shìjīn *a traditional Chinese unit of weight,
equal to 0.5 kilogram or 1.102
pounds*

 式　shì　6画 弋部

式 式式式式式式

❶[名]特定的规格：pattern; form
方式 fāngshì　　格式 géshì
模式 móshì
❷[名]样子：type; style; fashion
| 样~ yàngshì *style* / 发~
fàshì *hair style*
式样 shìyàng style; type;
model
款式 kuǎnshì　　新式 xīnshì
形式 xíngshì　　中式 zhōngshì
各式各样 gèshì-gèyàng
❸[名]仪式；典礼：ceremony;
ritual | 开幕~ kāimùshì *open-
ing ceremony* / 毕业~ bìyè-
shì *graduation ceremony; com-
mencement* / 阅兵~ yuèbīng-

shì *military review*

仪式 yíshì

闭幕式 bìmùshì

❹ [名] 自然科学中表示某种规律的一组符号：formula | 分子～ fēnzǐshì *molecular formula* / 方程～ fāngchéngshì *equation*

公式 gōngshì

似 似似似似似似

See 似的

　似的 shìde as...as; seem
　　See sì.

(勢) shì 8画 力部

势 势势势势势势势

❶ [名] 在政治、经济或军事等方面的力量：power, force; influence | 人多～众 rénduō-shìzhòng *many hands provide great strength*

势力 shìlì force; power; influence

势利眼 shìlìyǎn ① snobbish attitude; snobbishness ② snob

局势 júshì

❷ [名] 事物显示出的力量：momentum; impetus | 来～很猛 láishì hěn měng *come with tremendous force*

气势 qìshì　　声势 shēngshì

❸ [名] 自然界的外表形貌：outward appearance of a natural object | 山～ shānshì *shape of a mountain* / 风～缓和了。Fēngshì huǎnhé le. *The wind is moderating.*

地势 dìshì

❹ [名] 人的姿态、样子：sign; posture; gesture

手势 shǒushì　　姿势 zīshì

❺ [名] 发展的状况或趋向：situation; state of affairs; circumstance

势必 shìbì certainly will; be bound to

趋势 qūshì　　弱势 ruòshì

伤势 shāngshì　　形势 xíngshì

优势 yōushì　　走势 zǒushì

事 shì 8画 一部

事 事事事事事事事事

❶ [名] 事情：matter; affair; thing; business | 国家大～ guójiā dàshì *state affairs* / 他有～请假。Tā yǒu shì qǐngjià. *He asked for leave to attend to private matters.*

事变 shìbiàn ① incident ② emergency; exigency ③ events; course of events

事迹 shìjì deed; achievement; thing

事件 shìjiàn incident; event; business

663

事例 shìlì example; instance
事情 shìqíng affair; matter; thing; business
事实 shìshí fact; reality
事态 shìtài state of affairs; situation
事务 shìwù work; routine; general affairs; transaction
事物 shìwù thing; object; matter
事先 shìxiān before the event; in advance
事项 shìxiàng item; matter
事业 shìyè ① cause; undertaking ② enterprise; facility
事务所 shìwùsuǒ office

碍事 àishì	本事 běnshi
差事 chāishi	此事 cǐshì
大事 dàshì	董事 dǒngshì
干事 gànshi	公事 gōngshì
故事 gùshi	军事 jūnshì
理事 lǐshì	领事 lǐngshì
没事 méishì	民事 mínshì
启事 qǐshì	人事 rénshì
时事 shíshì	外事 wàishì
往事 wǎngshì	喜事 xǐshì
心事 xīnshì	刑事 xíngshì
做事 zuòshì	

办事处 bànshìchù
董事会 dǒngshìhuì
董事长 dǒngshìzhǎng
理事会 lǐshìhuì
没事儿 méishìr
万事如意 wànshì rúyì

❷ [名] 职业；工作：job; work | 谋~móushì look for a job / 有~

大家一起做。Yǒu shì dàjiā yīqǐ zuò. *Everyone should work together on the job.*

❸ [名] 意外的灾祸：trouble; accident | 惹~rěshì *make trouble; stir up trouble* / 平安无~píng'ān wú shì *everything is safe and sound*
事故 shìgù accident; mishap
出事 chūshì   闹事 nàoshì
失事 shīshì

❹ [名] 关系或责任：responsibility; involvement | 请回去吧，没有你的~了。Qǐng huíqù ba, méiyǒu nǐ de shì le. *Please go back, this no longer involves you.* / 这件案子里有他的~。Zhè jiàn ànzi li yǒu tā de shì. *He is involved in this case.*
当事人 dāngshìrén

侍 shì   8画 亻部

侍 侍侍侍侍侍侍侍侍

[动] 陪伴；伺候：wait upon; attend upon; serve | 服~fúshì *attend* / ~奉shìfèng *wait upon*
侍候 shìhòu wait upon; look after; attend; minister to

饰 (飾) shì   8画 饣部

饰 饰饰饰饰饰饰饰饰

❶ [动] 使美观：adorn; dress up; polish | 文章需要修~一下。Wénzhāng xūyào xiūshì yīxià. *The writing needs to be polished.*

灯饰 dēngshì　　　服饰 fúshì
首饰 shǒushi
装饰 zhuāngshì

❷ [动] 掩盖（缺点或错误）：cover up
掩饰 yǎnshì

试 (試) shì　　8画 讠部

试 试试试试试试试试

❶ [动] 非正式地做：try | ~航 shìháng *trial voyage or flight; trial run* / ~~看 shìshi kàn *have a try*

试探 shìtàn probe or explore (a question)
试图 shìtú attempt to (do sth.); try to (do sth.)
试行 shìxíng try out
试验 shìyàn trial; experiment; test
试用 shìyòng try out
试制 shìzhì trial-produce; trial-manufacture
尝试 chángshì　调试 tiáoshì

❷ [动] 考：test | ~题 shìtí *examination question* / 复~ fùshì *reexamination*

试卷 shìjuàn examination paper; test paper

笔试 bǐshì　　　测试 cèshì
考试 kǎoshì　　　口试 kǒushì

视 (視) shì　　8画 礻部

视 视视视视视视视视

❶ [动] 看：look at | ~而不见 shì'érbùjiàn *look but see not; turn a blind eye to*

视点 shìdiǎn point of view; focus
视角 shìjiǎo angle of view; visual field
视觉 shìjué visual sense; vision; sense of sight
视力 shìlì vision; sight
视频 shìpín (phys.) video frequency
视线 shìxiàn view; vision
视野 shìyě vision; a field of vision
近视 jìnshì　　　凝视 níngshì
审视 shěnshì　　　透视 tòushì
正视 zhèngshì　　　注视 zhùshì
电视机 diànshìjī
电视剧 diànshìjù
电视台 diànshìtái

❷ [动] 观察；考察：inspect; watch | 巡~ xúnshì *make an inspection tour*

视察 shìchá inspect; watch; observe
监视 jiānshì

❸ [动] 看待：regard; look upon; treat | ~为知己 shìwéi zhījǐ

treat as an intimate friend; regard as an intimate friend

敌视 díshì 忽视 hūshì

蔑视 mièshì 歧视 qíshì

轻视 qīngshì 重视 zhòngshì

是 shì 9画 日部

是 是是是是是是是是是

❶ [动] 联系某种事物：used like "be" before nouns or pronouns (a) 表示等同：used to identify the subject｜他～北京大学的教授。Tā shì Běijīng Dàxué de jiàoshòu. *He is a professor at Peking University.*

(b) 表示解释或描述：used to explain or describe｜他～工人。Tā shì gōngrén. *He is a labourer.*／他～一片好心。Tā shì yī piàn hǎoxīn. *He is of good intentions.*

(c) 表示存在：used to indicate existence｜满身～汗 mǎnshēn shì hàn *be sweating all over*／山上全～树。Shān shàng quán shì shù. *The hill is all covered with trees.*

❷ [动] 跟 "的 de" 相呼应，构成 "是…的" 格式，表示强调：used with "的 de" at the end of the sentence for emphasis｜那所房子～石头造的。Nà suǒ fángzi shì shítou zào de. *That house*

is built of stone.*／我～来看她的。Wǒ shì lái kàn tā de. *I came to see her.*

❸ [动] 用于选择问句、是非问句或反问句：used in alternative, yes-no, or rhetorical questions｜你～坐轮船还～坐火车？Nǐ shì zuò lúnchuán háishi zuò huǒchē? *Are you going by ship or by train?*／你～累了吧？Nǐ shì lèile ba? *You're tired, aren't you?*／你妹妹～医生还～护士？Nǐ mèimei shì yīshēng háishi hùshi? *Is your sister a doctor or a nurse?*

还是 háishi

❹ [动] 联系相同的两个词语：used between two identical words (a) 连用两次这样的格式，表示严格区分，互不相干：used in two parallel clauses to indicate mutual exclusiveness｜敌～敌，友～友，必须分清界限。Dí shì dí, yǒu shì yǒu, bìxū fēnqīng jièxiàn. *A friend is a friend and a foe is a foe, so one must be clearly distinguished from the other.*／他～他，我～我，不是一回事儿。Tā shì tā, wǒ shì wǒ, bū shì yī huí shìr. *Don't lump us together, because we are two different people.*

(b) 单用这种格式，表示强调事物的客观性：used in a clause to indicate actuality

(c) 单用这种格式，表示让步，含

有"虽然"的意思：used in a clause of concession | 这东西好～好，就是太贵。Zhè dōngxi hǎo shì hǎo, jiùshì tài guì. *In spite of good quality, it's too expensive.* / 这桌子旧～旧，可还能用。Zhè zhuōzi jiù shì jiù, kě hái néng yòng. *Though the desk is old, it is still useful.* / 诗～好诗，就是长了点。Shī shì hǎo shī, jiùshì chángle diǎn. *It is a good poem, but a bit long.*

❺ [动] 用在名词前，表示适合：used before a noun, indicating appropriateness | 工具放得不～地方。Gōngjù fàng de bù shì dìfang. *The tools have not been put in the right place.* / 他来的真～时候。Tā lái de zhēn shì shíhou. *He came just at the right time.*

❻ [动] 用在名词前，表示只要、凡是：used before a noun, indicating each and every one of the kind | ～人总会犯错误。Shì rén zǒng huì fàn cuòwù. *Human beings are liable to error; No human being can be free from mistakes.* / ～重活，他都抢着干。Shì zhònghuó, tā dōu qiǎngzhe gàn. *When there's tough work, he is always willing to do it.*

凡是 fánshì

❼ [形] 对；正确 (跟 "非 fēi" 相对)：correct; right (the opposite of "非 fēi") | 自以为～zìyǐwéishì *consider oneself always be right* / 你说得～。Nǐ shuōdeshì. *What you said is right.*

是非 shìfēi ① right and wrong ② quarrel; dispute

❽ [动] 表示答应：used to answer in the affirmative | ～,我就来。Shì, wǒ jiù lái. *Yes, I'm coming right now.* / ～，我们一定完成任务。Shì, wǒmen yīdìng wánchéng rènwù. *Sure, we will definitely complete the task.*

◇ 可不是 kěbushì
要不是 yàobushì

适 (適) shì   9画 辶部

适 适适适适适适适适适

❶ [动] 符合：fit; be suitable; be proper | 她～于做这工作吗? Tā shìyú zuò zhè gōngzuò ma? *Is she suitable for this job?*

适当 shìdàng suitable; proper; appropriate

适合 shìhé suit; fit; be made for

适宜 shìyí suitable; fit; appropriate; favourable; applicable

适应 shìyìng suit; adapt to; adjust to; conform to

适用 shìyòng suitable; applicable

合适 héshì
❷[形] 舒服；comfortable; well |
我觉得身体不～。Wǒ juéde
shēntǐ bù shì. *I'm not feeling
well.*
舒适 shūshì

室 shì 9画 宀部

室室室室室室室室
室

❶[名] 屋子；房间：room | 教～
jiàoshì *classroom; schoolroom*
/ 卧～wòshì *bedroom* / 会客～
huìkèshì *reception room; sitting room*
室内 shìnèi indoor; interior
室外 shìwài outdoor; exterior
温室 wēnshì
办公室 bàngōngshì
更衣室 gēngyīshì
会议室 huìyìshì
实验室 shíyànshì
医务室 yīwùshì
❷[名] 机关团体内的工作单位：
room as an administrative or
working unit | 科～kēshì *ad-
ministrative or technical office*
/ 资料～zīliàoshì *reference
room* / 阅览～yuèlǎnshì *reading room*

逝 shì 10画 辶部

逝逝逝逝逝逝逝逝
逝逝

[动] 死亡：die; pass away | 病～
bìngshì *die from an illness*
逝世 shìshì pass away; demise

释（釋）shì 12画 釆部

释释释释释释释释
释释释释

❶[动] 放走：release; set free |
保～bǎoshì *release on bail*
释放 shìfàng ① set free; release ② relief; rid
❷[动] 解说；详细说明：explain;
expound | 注～zhùshì *anno-
tate* / ～义 shìyì *explain the
meaning (of a word, etc.)*
解释 jiěshì

誓 shì 14画 言部

誓誓誓誓誓誓誓誓
誓誓誓誓誓誓

❶[动] 表示决心依照所说的话去
做：swear; vow; pledge | 他～
守秘密。Tā shìshǒu mìmì. *He
was pledged to secrecy.*
誓言 shìyán oath; pledge
❷[名] 表示决心的话：oath; vow
| 他愿对他所说的一切起～。Tā
yuàn duì tā suǒshuō de yīqiè
qǐshì. *He was willing to take*

an oath on all he said.
发誓 fāshì　　宣誓 xuānshì

 shōu　6画 攵部

收 收收收收收收

❶ [动] 聚集；把东西放到适当的地方：put away; take in ｜ ～工具 shōu gōngjù *put the tools away* / ～好文件 shōuhǎo wénjiàn *put the documents away*
收藏 shōucáng collect and store up; stow
收购 shōugòu purchase; buy
收集 shōují collect; gather; cull
收买 shōumǎi ① purchase; buy in ② buy over; bribe
收拾 shōushi ① put in order; tidy; clear away; gather up ② get things ready; pack ③ repair; mend ④ settle with; punish
收缩 shōusuō ① contract; shrink ② concentrate one's forces; draw back

❷ [动] 获得 (利益) gain; profit
收入 shōurù ① income; revenue; receipts; proceeds ② take in; include
收益 shōuyì income; profit; earnings; gains
收支 shōuzhī revenue and expenditure; income and expenses

❸ [动] 收割 (农作物)：harvest; gather in ｜ ～麦子 shōu màizi *gather in the wheat*

收成 shōucheng harvest; crop
收割 shōugē reap; harvest; gather in
收获 shōuhuò ① gather in the crops; harvest; reap ② results; gains
丰收 fēngshōu　　秋收 qiūshōu

❹ [动] 收取；收回：collect ｜ ～废品 shōu fèipǐn *collect scrap* / ～水电费 shōu shuǐdiànfèi *collect charges for water and electricity* / 借出去的书，到现在还没有～齐。Jiè chūqu de shū, dào xiànzài hái méiyǒu shōuqí. *The books lent out have not all been collected yet.*
收费 shōufèi collect fees; charge
收复 shōufù recover, recapture
收回 shōuhuí ① take back; call in; regain; recall ② withdraw; countermand; retract
回收 huíshōu　　税收 shuìshōu
征收 zhēngshōu

❺ [动] 接到；接受；接纳：receive; accept ｜ ～信 shōuxìn *receive a letter* / ～礼物 shōu lǐwù *accept a gift* / 徒弟 shōu túdì *take in an apprentice* / 我刚～到一封信。Wǒ gāng shōudào yī fēng xìn. *I've just received a letter.*
收音机 shōuyīnjī radio
接收 jiēshōu　　验收 yànshōu
招收 zhāoshōu

❻ [动] 约束；控制：restrain; con-

收

shōu

669

trol | ~心 shōuxīn *get into the frame of mind for work; prepare to concentrate on serious things*

❼ [动] 结束；停止：bring to an end; stop | ~工 shōugōng *stop work for the day; knock off* | ~场 shōuchǎng *wind up; end* | ~尾 shōuwěi *bring to a conclusion; wind up*

shǒu　4画 手部

手 手 手 手

❶ [名] hand | ~拉~手 shǒu lā shǒu *hand in hand*

手臂 shǒubì arm

手工 shǒugōng ① by hand; manual ② charge for a piece of handwork

手势 shǒushì gesture; signal

手套 shǒutào glove

手艺 shǒuyì craftsmanship; workmanship; handicraft; trade; art

手指 shǒuzhǐ finger

手头紧 shǒutóujǐn be short of money; be hard up

出手 chūshǒu　　二手 èrshǒu

联手 liánshǒu　　入手 rùshǒu

携手 xiéshǒu

左右手 zuǒyòushǒu

心灵手巧 xīnlíng-shǒuqiǎo

大手大脚 dàshǒu-dàjiǎo

❷ [形] 小巧而便于携带的：handy; convenient | ~册 shǒucè

handbook

手表 shǒubiǎo wristwatch

手袋 shǒudài (usu. for woman's use) handbag

手机 shǒujī cellphone; mobile phone

手绢 shǒujuàn handkerchief

手链 shǒuliàn bracelet

手枪 shǒuqiāng pistol

手电筒 shǒudiàntǒng electric torch; flashlight

❸ [名] 指本领或手段：skill or means

手段 shǒuduàn ① means; medium; method ② trick; artifice

手法 shǒufǎ ① skill; technique ② trick; gimmick

手腕 shǒuwàn ① wrist ② trick; artifice ③ skill; finesse; tactics

大手笔 dàshǒubǐ

做手脚 zuòshǒujiǎo

❹ [名] 具有某种技能或做某种事情的人：a person doing (or good at) a certain job | 水~ shuǐshǒu *sailor* | 拖拉机~ tuōlājīshǒu *tractor driver*

对手 duìshǒu　高手 gāoshǒu

歌手 gēshǒu　　能手 néngshǒu

棋手 qíshǒu　　杀手 shāshǒu

凶手 xiōngshǒu

选手 xuǎnshǒu

助手 zhùshǒu

打下手 dǎxiàshǒu

一把手 yībǎshǒu

◇手术 shǒushù surgery

手续 shǒuxù procedure formality

得手 déshǒu

露一手 lòuyīshǒu

 守 shǒu 6画 宀部

守 守守守守守守

❶ [动] 依照;不违犯：observe;
abide by ｜ ～时 shǒushí *be on
time; be punctual* ／ ～纪律 shǒu
jìlǜ *observe discipline* ／ ～规矩
shǒu guīju *behave well*
守法 shǒufǎ abide by (observe)
the law; be law-abiding
信守 xìnshǒu   遵守 zūnshǒu

❷ [动] 保护;防卫：guard; defend
｜ ～球门 shǒu qiúmén *keep
goal* ／ ～住阵地 shǒuzhù
zhèndì *hold a position*
守卫 shǒuwèi guard; defend
保守 bǎoshǒu 防守 fángshǒu

❸ [动] 看护;守候：keep watch;
look after ｜ ～门 shǒumén *be
on duty at the door or gate;
keep goal* ／ ～了一夜 shǒule yī
yè *keep watch for the whole
night* ／ 护士～着病人。Hùshi
shǒuzhe bìngrén. *The nurse
watched over the patient.* ／ 你
在这儿～着。Nǐ zài zhèr
shǒuzhe. *You keep watch right
here.*
守候 shǒuhòu ① wait for; expect ② keep watch
守门员 shǒuményuán goal

keeper (in football, ice hockey,
etc.)

❹ [动] 挨近;靠近：be close to; be
near ｜ ～着水的地方可以养鱼。
Shǒuzhe shuǐ de dìfang kěyǐ
yǎng yú. *Places nearby the
water are suitable for breeding
fish.*

 首 shǒu 9画 首部

首 首首首首首首首首
首

❶ [名] 头：head ｜ 昂～ ángshǒu
hold one's head high ／ ～饰
shǒushì *(originally) head ornaments; jewellery*

❷ [名] 领头人;带头人：leader;
head; chief
首领 shǒulǐng chieftain; leader;
head
首脑 shǒunǎo head
首长 shǒuzhǎng leading cadre;
senior officer
为首 wéishǒu 元首 yuánshǒu

❸ [副] 最先;最早：first; earliest
｜ ～次 shǒucì *for the first time;
first*
首创 shǒuchuàng originate;
initiate; pioneer
首先 shǒuxiān ① first ② first of
all; above all

❹ [名] 最高的;第一：first; primary
首都 shǒudū capital
首席 shǒuxí ① seat of honour

② chief

首相 shǒuxiàng prime minister

首要 shǒuyào of the first importance; first; chief

❺ [量] 用于歌曲、诗词等：used for poems and songs, etc. | 一～诗 yī shǒu shī *a poem* / 一～歌 yī shǒu gē *a song*

◇ 自首 zìshǒu

寿（壽） shǒu　7画 寸部

寿 寿寿寿寿寿寿寿

[名] 生命；年岁：life; age

寿命 shǒumìng life span; life expectancy

长寿 chángshòu

受 shòu　8画 ⺈部

受 受受受受受受受受

❶ [动] 接受；得到：receive; accept | ～教育 shòu jiàoyù *receive education* / ～人委托 shòu rén wěituō *be entrusted by sb.*

受到 shòudào ① receive; accept ② suffer; be subjected to

受理 shòulǐ (leg.) accept (a case)

受益 shòuyì profit by; benefit from; be benefited

感受 gǎnshòu　接受 jiēshòu

享受 xiǎngshòu

❷ [动] 遭到（不幸或损害）：suffer;

meet with | ～风 shòufēng *catch a cold* / ～批评 shòu pīpíng *be criticized* / ～委屈 shòu wěiqu *feel wronged*

受害 shòuhài suffer injury; fall victim; be affected

受骗 shòupiàn be deceived (or fooled, cheated, taken in)

受伤 shòushāng be injured; be wounded; sustain an injury

遭受 zāoshòu

❸ [动] 忍耐：stand; endure; bear | ～不了 shòubuliǎo *cannot bear (it)* / 这么重的担子你～得住吗？Zhème zhòng de dànzi nǐ shòudezhù ma? *Can you endure such a heavy burden?*

承受 chéngshòu

授 shòu　11画 扌部

授 授授授授授授授授 授授授

❶ [动] 交给；给予：award; give; confer | ～奖 shòujiǎng *award a prize*

授权 shòuquán empower; authorize

授予 shòuyǔ confer; award; give

❷ [动] 传授；教；讲：teach; instruct | 讲～ jiǎngshòu *give lectures* / ～课 shòukè *give lessons*

传授 chuánshòu 函授 hánshòu
教授 jiāoshòu

售 shòu 11画 隹部

售 售 售 售 售 售 售 售
售 售 售

[动] 卖：sell | ~票 shòupiào *sell tickets*

售货 shòuhuò *sell goods*
售价 shòujià *selling price; price*
出售 chūshòu　发售 fāshòu
零售 língshòu　销售 xiāoshòu

兽（獸）shòu 11画 口部

兽 兽 兽 兽 兽 兽 兽 兽
兽 兽 兽

[名] 指全身生毛、有四条腿的哺乳动物：beast; animal | 走~ zǒushòu *beasts*
野兽 yěshòu

瘦 shòu 14画 疒部

瘦 瘦 瘦 瘦 瘦 瘦 瘦 瘦
瘦 瘦 瘦 瘦 瘦 瘦

❶ [形] 肌肉不丰满；脂肪少（跟"胖 pàng"相对）：thin (the opposite of "胖 pàng") | 不胖不~bù pàng bù shòu *(of human body) of moderate size*/ 身体很~shēntǐ hěn shòu *have a very thin figure*

❷ [形] 衣服鞋袜等窄小：tight | 这件衣裳穿着~了。Zhè jiàn yīshang chuānzhe shòu le. *This dress is too tight for me./* 这双鞋我穿太~了。Zhè shuāng xié wǒ chuān tài shòu le. *This pair of shoes are too tight for me.*

书（書）shū 4画 一部

书 书 书 书

❶ [动] 写字；记载：write | ~法 shūfǎ *calligraphy*
书画 shūhuà *painting and calligraphy*
书面 shūmiàn *written; in written form; in writing*
书写 shūxiě *write*
书法家 shūfǎjiā *calligrapher; calligraphist*

❷ [名] 装订成册的著作：book | 丛~cóngshū *a series of books; collection* / 新~xīnshū *new book* / 藏~cángshū ① *collect books* ② *a collection of books*
书包 shūbāo *schoolbag*
书本 shūběn *book*
书店 shūdiàn *bookshop; bookstore; bookseller's*
书房 shūfáng *study room*
书籍 shūjí *books; work; literature*
书架 shūjià *bookcase; bookshelf*
书刊 shūkān *books and periodicals*

书桌 shūzhuō desk; writing desk
书呆子 shūdāizi pedant; book-worm
书生气 shūshēngqì bookishness; a bookish mindset
读书 dúshū　　教书 jiāoshū
念书 niànshū　　图书 túshū
工具书 gōngjùshū
图书馆 túshūguǎn

❸ [名] 文件：document; paper | 说明～shuōmíngshū (a booklet of) directions; introductory pamphlet / 申请～shēnqǐngshū application form
文书 wénshū　证书 zhèngshū
判决书 pànjuéshū
通知书 tōngzhīshū

❹ [名] 信件：letter | 家～jiāshū letter from home
书信 shūxìn letter; written message

◇ 书记 shūji secretary
草书 cǎoshū　　隶书 lìshū
行书 xíngshū

叔　　　　　shū　　8画 又部

叔 叔叔叔叔叔叔叔叔

❶ [名] 父亲的弟弟：father's younger brother; uncle
叔叔 shūshu father's younger brother; uncle (a child's form of address for any young man of about one's father's age)
❷ [名] 称跟父亲平辈而年纪较小

的男子：form of address for a man of one's father's generation but younger | 表～biǎoshū father's younger male cousin / 李～Lǐ shū uncle Li

殊　　　　　shū　　10画 歹部

殊 殊殊殊殊殊殊殊殊
殊殊

[形] 特别的：different; special
特殊 tèshū

梳　　　　　shū　　11画 木部

梳 梳梳梳梳梳梳梳梳
梳梳梳

❶ [名] 整理头发的用具：comb | 木～mùshū wooden comb
梳子 shūzi comb
❷ [动] 用梳子整理头发：comb one's hair | ～头 shūtóu comb one's hair / ～辫子 shū biànzi wear one's hair in braids
梳理 shūlǐ ① (textiles) carding ② comb out (one's hair); dress (one's hair)

舒　　　　　shū　　12画 人部

舒 舒舒舒舒舒舒舒舒
舒舒舒舒

❶ [动] 宽松；伸展：stretch; loosen; relax | ～了一口气 shūle yī kǒu

qì *heave a sigh of relief*

舒展 shūzhǎn ① stretch; limber up ② unfold; extend

❷ [形] 轻松愉快: comfortable; at ease | ～坦 shūtǎn *at ease*

舒畅 shūchàng happy; entirely free from worry

舒服 shūfu ① comfortable ② be well

舒适 shūshì comfortable; cosy; snug

 疏 shū 12画 疋部

疏疏疏疏疏疏疏疏
疏疏疏疏

❶ [形] 不亲密；不熟悉: not intimate; not familiar | ～远 shūyuǎn *drift apart; alienate*

生疏 shēngshū

❷ [形] 粗心大意: careless | ～于职守 shūyú zhíshǒu *negligent of one's duties*

疏忽 shūhu carelessness; negligence; oversight

◇ 疏散 shūsàn ① sparse; scattered; dispersed ② evacuate; disperse

 输 (輸) shū 13画 车部

输输输输输输输输
输输输输输

❶ [动] 运送；传送: transport; convey

输出 shūchū send out; export; output

输入 shūrù bring in; introduce

输送 shūsòng carry; transport; convey

运输 yùnshū

❷ [动] 失败(跟"赢 yíng"相对): lose; be beaten; be defeated (the opposite of "赢 yíng") | ～了两个球 shūle liǎng gè qiú *lose two points in a match* | 他认～了。Tā rènshū le. *He admitted he was beaten.*

 蔬 shū 15画 艹部

蔬蔬蔬蔬蔬蔬蔬蔬
蔬蔬蔬蔬蔬蔬蔬

See 蔬菜

蔬菜 shūcài vegetable; greens; greenstuff

 熟 shú 15画 灬部

熟熟熟熟熟熟熟熟
熟熟熟熟熟熟熟

❶ [形] 食物加热到可吃的程度(跟"生 shēng"相对): cooked; done (the opposite of "生 shēng") | ～菜 shúcài *cooked dish; prepared food* | 米饭～了。Mǐfàn shú le. *The rice is cooked.*

❷ [形] 植物的果实完全长成(跟

"生 shēng" 相对）：ripe (the opposite of "生 shēng") | 葡萄 ~ 了。Pútao shú le. *The grapes are ripe.* / 麦子 ~ 了。Màizi shú le. *The wheat is ripe.* 成熟 chéngshú

❸ [形] 常见，知道得很清楚（跟"生 shēng" 相对）：familiar; well acquainted (the opposite of "生 shēng") | 面 ~ miànshú *look familiar* / ~ 人 shúrén *acquaintance* / 这条路我 ~。Zhè tiáo lù wǒ shú. *I know this route.* / 我们很 ~。Wǒmen hěn shú. *We are very familiar with each other.*

熟悉 shúxī know sth. or sb. well; be familiar with; have an intimate knowledge of

❹ [形] 有经验；不生疏（跟"生 shēng" 相对）：skilled; experienced; practised (the opposite of "生 shēng") | ~ 手 shúshǒu *expert hand; practised hand* / ~ 能生巧 shúnéngshēngqiǎo *practice makes perfect* / 他干这个活儿很 ~。Tā gàn zhège huór hěn shú. *He is very skilled at this.*

熟练 shúliàn skilled; practised; proficient

❺ [形] 程度深：deep; sound | ~ 睡 shúshuì *sleep soundly; be fast asleep* / 深思 ~ 虑 shēnsīshúlǜ *careful consideration*

---

shǔ　12画 日部

暑 暑暑暑暑暑暑暑暑 暑暑暑暑

[形] 炎热（跟"寒 hán"相对）：hot (the opposite of "寒 hán") | ~ 天 shǔtiān *hot summer days; dogdays* / 中 ~ zhòngshǔ *suffer heatstroke; be affected by the heat* / 寒 ~ hánshǔ ① *cold and hot* ② *winter and summer; a whole year*

暑假 shǔjià summer vacation
暑期 shǔqī summer vacation time

属（屬）shǔ　12画 尸部

属 属属属属属属属属 属属属属

❶ [动] 为某人或某方所有；归类：belong to; be possessed by; classify | 归 ~ guīshǔ *belong to; ownership*

属于 shǔyú belong to; be part of
纯属 chúnshǔ　　　附属 fùshǔ
所属 suǒshǔ　　　下属 xiàshǔ
直属 zhíshǔ

❷ [动] 是：be | ~ 实 shǔshí *be true* / 这些纯 ~ 谎言。Zhèxiē chúnshǔ huǎngyán. *These are sheer lies.*

❸ [动] 用十二属相记生年：be born

in the year of one of the 12 symbolic animals associated with a 12-year circle | ～马 shǔ mǎ *be born in the year of the horse*

属相 shǔxiang (inf.) popular name for 生肖 (shēngxiào)

❹ [名] 类别: category | 非金～ fēijīnshǔ *nonmetals*

金属 jīnshǔ

❺ [名] 亲属: family member; dependent | 军～jūnshǔ *families of army men* / 亲～qīnshǔ *relatives*

家属 jiāshǔ

 鼠 shǔ　13画 鼠部

鼠 鼠鼠鼠鼠鼠鼠鼠鼠
鼠鼠鼠鼠鼠

[名] mouse; rat

鼠标shǔbiāo mouse (of a computer)

老鼠 lǎoshǔ　　松鼠 sōngshǔ

 数 (數) shǔ　13画 攵部

数 数数数数数数数数
数数数数数

❶ [动] 查点(数目); 一个一个地计算: count | ～数 shǔ shù *count* /天上的星星～不清。Tiānshàng de xīngxing shǔbuqīng. *The stars in the sky are countless.*

倒数 dàoshǔ

❷ [动] 比较起来最突出: be particularly conspicuous by comparison | ～一～二 shǔyī-shǔ'èr *count as one of the very best* / 几个孩子中～她长得漂亮。Jǐ gè háizi zhōng shǔ tā zhǎng de piàoliang. *She is the prettiest one among those children.*

See shù.

 术 (術) shù　5画 木部

术 术术术术术

❶ [名] 方法; 手段: method; tactics | 战～zhànshù *tactics* / 法～ fǎshù *magic arts*

手术 shǒushù　　算术 suànshù

❷ [名] 技艺; 学问: art; skill; technique | 医～yīshù *medical skill; the art of healing* / 不学无～bùxuéwúshù *have neither education nor skill*

术语shùyǔ technical terms; terminology

技术 jìshù　　　马术 mǎshù

美术 měishù　　　学术 xuéshù

艺术 yìshù

技术员 jìshùyuán

美术馆 měishùguǎn

艺术家 yìshùjiā

艺术品 yìshùpǐn

束 shù 7画 一部

束 束 束 束 束 束 束

❶ [动] 捆绑；限制：bind; tie; control; restrain | 腰~皮带 yāoshù pídài *wear a belt round one's waist*

束缚 shùfù tie; bind up; fetter
结束 jiéshù　　拘束 jūshù
约束 yuēshù

❷ [量] 用于捆在一起或聚集成条状的东西：bundle; bunch; sheaf | 一~鲜花 yī shù xiānhuā *a bunch of flowers*

述 shù 8画 辶部

述 述 述 述 述 述 述 述

[动] 叙说；陈述：state; relate; narrate | 口~kǒushù *give an oral account* / 如上所~rúshàng suǒ shù *as stated (mentioned) above*

表述 biǎoshù　　陈述 chénshù
叙述 xùshù
陈述句 chénshùjù

树 (樹) shù 9画 木部

树 树 树 树 树 树 树 树 树

❶ [动] 立；建立：set up; establish; uphold | 建~jiànshù *achievement*

树立 shùlì set up; establish

❷ [名] 树木，木本植物的统称：tree | ~大根深 shùdà-gēnshēn *big trees with deep roots*

树干 shùgàn tree trunk; trunk
树林 shùlín trees; woods; bush; timber
树木 shùmù trees
柏树 bǎishù　　果树 guǒshù
槐树 huáishù　　桑树 sāngshù
松树 sōngshù　　杨树 yángshù
榆树 yúshù

竖 (竪) shù 9画 立部

竖 竖 竖 竖 竖 竖 竖 竖 竖

❶ [动] 使物体跟地面垂直：set upright; erect; stand | ~旗杆 shù qígān *erect the flagpole*

❷ [形] 跟地面垂直的（跟"横 héng"相对）：vertical; upright; perpendicular (the opposite of "横 héng") | 画一条~线 huà yī tiáo shùxiàn *draw a vertical line*

数 (數) shù 13画 攵部

数 数 数 数 数 数 数 数 数 数 数 数 数

❶ [名] 数目：number; figure | 人~

rénshù *the number of people* / 序~xùshù *ordinal number* / 这个~儿不一定很准确。Zhège shùr bù yīdìng hěn zhǔnquè. *The figure may not be accurate.*

数词shùcí (gram.) numeral

数额shù'é fixed number; amount

数据shùjù data

数量shùliàng quantity; amount

数码shùmǎ ① numeral ② number; amount ③ digital

数目shùmù number; amount

数学shùxué mathematics

数字shùzì ① numeral; figure; digit; character ② quantity

数据库shùjùkù database; data bank

数字化shùzìhuà digitalize; digitalization

半数bànshù 倍数bèishù
变数biànshù 次数cìshù
多数duōshù 少数shǎoshù
算数suànshù 岁数suìshù
无数wúshù 系数xìshù
指数zhǐshù 总数zǒngshù
大多数dàduōshù
分数线fēnshùxiàn
少数民族shǎoshù mínzú

❷ [名] 表示事物的量的基本数学概念：number | 分~fēnshù *fraction* / 自然~zìránshù *natural number*

代数dàishù 小数xiǎoshù
整数zhěngshù
小数点xiǎoshùdiǎn

❸ [数] 几；几个：several; a few | ~十种shù shí zhǒng *tens of types* / ~小时 shù xiǎoshí *several hours* / ~百人 shù bǎi rén *several hundred people*

See shǔ.

shuā　8画 刂部

刷 刷 刷 刷 刷 刷 刷 刷

❶ [名] brush
刷子 shuāzi brush
牙刷 yáshuā

❷ [动] 用刷子清除或涂抹：brush; clean | ~牙 shuāyá *brush one's teeth* / ~鞋 shuā xié *brush shoes* / ~锅 shuā guō *clean a pot*

刷新 shuāxīn ① renovate; refurbish ② outdo; surpass
印刷 yìnshuā

❸ [动] 除名；淘汰：eliminate; remove | 他在第一轮比赛中被~下来了。Tā zài dì-yī lún bǐsài zhōng bèi shuā xiàlai le. *He was knocked out in the very first round.*

◇刷卡 shuākǎ swipe a magnetic card on a card-reading machine

shuǎ　9画 而部

耍 耍 耍 耍 耍 耍 耍 耍
耍

679

❶ [动] 游戏；玩：play｜出去～～～ chūqù shuǎyishuǎ *go out to play* / 孩子们在院子里～着。Háizimen zài yuànzi li shuǎzhe. *The children are playing in the yard.*

❷ [动] 捉弄；玩弄：play tricks｜～人 shuǎrén *make fun of others; play tricks on others* / ～手段 shuǎshǒuduàn *play tricks* / 咱们被人～了。Zánmen bèn rén shuǎ le. *We have been fooled.*

❸ [动] 舞动、表演：play with; play｜～刀 shuǎ dāo *flourish a sword; give a performance of swordplay*

❹ [动] 施展；卖弄：give free play to｜～笔杆 shuǎbǐgǎn *wield a pen; be skilled in literary tricks* / ～脾气 shuǎpíqi *get into a huff*

耍花招 shuǎhuāzhāo ① display showy movements in *wushu*, etc. ② play (or get up to) tricks

衰 shuāi 10画 一部

衰衰衰衰衰衰衰衰
衰衰

[动] 由强变弱：decline; wane｜年老力～niánlǎo-lìshuāi *old and feeble*

衰老 shuāilǎo old and feeble; decrepit; senile

衰弱 shuāiruò weak; feeble; debility

衰退 shuāituì decay; fail; downturn; ruin; drop off; decline

摔 shuāi 14画 扌部

摔摔摔摔摔摔摔摔
摔摔摔摔摔摔

❶ [动] 用力往下扔：cast; throw; fling｜他把书～在地上。Tā bǎ shū shuāi zài dìshang. *He threw the book onto the ground.*

❷ [动] 从高处落下：fall off｜当心，别～下来。Dāngxīn, bié shuāi xiàlai. *Be careful not to fall off.*

❸ [动] 因掉下而破损：cause to fall and break; break｜～得粉碎 shuāi de fěnsuì *break into pieces*

❹ [动] 身体失去平衡而倒下：fall; tumble; lose one's balance｜～了一跤 shuāile yī jiāo *have tumbled over* / 他～倒了。Tā shuāidǎo le. *He fell down.*

甩 shuǎi 5画 门部

甩 甩甩甩甩甩甩

❶ [动] 挥动；抡：move back and forth; swing ｜ ～辫子 shuǎi biànzi *swing one's braid* / 他～开胳膊走路。Tā shuǎikāi gēbo zǒulù. *He walked along swinging his arms.*

❷ [动] 用力扔：throw; fling; toss ｜ ～手榴弹 shuǎi shǒuliúdàn *throw hand grenades*

❸ [动] 抛开；抛弃：leave sb. behind; throw off ｜ ～掉跟踪的人 shuǎidiào gēnzōng de rén *throw off a pursuer* / 被～在后面 bèi shuǎi zài hòumian *be left behind*

帅 (帥) shuài 5画 巾部

帅 帅帅帅帅帅

[形] 英俊；漂亮；神气：handsome; smart ｜ 他长得挺～。Tā zhǎng de tǐng shuài. *He looks handsome.*

率 shuài 11画 亠部

率 率率率率率率率率 率率率

❶ [动] 带领：lead; command ｜ ～队 shuàiduì *lead a team* / ～代表团访美 shuài dàibiǎotuán fǎng Měi *lead a delegation to* visit the US

率领 shuàilǐng lead; head; command

❷ [形] 不仔细；不慎重：rash; hasty ｜ 轻～ qīngshuài *hasty*

草率 cǎoshuài

See lǜ.

拴 shuān 9画 扌部

拴 拴拴拴拴拴拴拴拴 拴

[动] 用绳子等系住：tie; fasten ｜ 他把马～在树上。Tā bǎ mǎ shuān zài shù shang. *He tied the horse to a tree.*

双 (雙) shuāng 4画 又部

双 双双双双

❶ [形] 两个的；两种的（跟"单 dān"相对）：two; twin; both; dual (the opposite of "单 dān") ｜ 成～成对 chéngshuāngchéngduì *in pairs* / ～向交通 shuāngxiàng jiāotōng *two-way traffic*

双边 shuāngbiān bilateral

双层 shuāngcéng double-deck; having two layers; of two thicknesses

双重 shuāngchóng (usu. used for abstract things) double; dual; two-sided

681

双方 shuāngfāng both sides; the two parties

双向 shuāngxiàng two-way

双休日 shuāngxiūrì weekend; Saturday and Sunday

❷ [形] 偶数的；成倍的（跟"单 dān"相对）：even; double; twofold (the opposite of "单 dān") | ～数 shuāngshù even number / ～号座位 shuānghào zuòwèi even-numbered seat / ～份 shuāngfèn double the amount; twice as much

❸ [量] 用于成对的东西：pair | 一～鞋 yī shuāng xié a pair of shoes / 一～手 yī shuāng shǒu a pair of hands

霜 shuāng 17画 雨部

霜 霜霜霜霜霜霜霜霜
霜霜霜霜霜霜霜霜
霜

[名] frost | 地上结了一层厚厚的～。Dìshang jiéle yī céng hòuhòu de shuāng. *There was a thick layer of frost on the ground.*

爽 shuǎng 11画 大部

爽 爽爽爽爽爽爽爽爽
爽爽爽

❶ [形] 舒适痛快：cool; pleasant |

凉～liángshuǎng *nice and cool*

❷ [形] 直爽；性格开朗：frank; straightforward; | 直～zhí-shuǎng *straightforward* / 豪～hǎoshuǎng *bold and uninhibited*

爽快 shuǎngkuai ① refreshed; comfortable ② frank; outright; with alacrity

水 shuǐ 4画 水部

水 水水水水

❶ [名] 无色、无臭、无味的液体：water | 喝～hē shuǐ *drink water* / 鱼儿离不开～。Yúr líbukāi shuǐ. *Fish cannot survive without water.*

水稻 shuǐdào paddy (rice); rice

水电 shuǐdiàn water and electricity

水分 shuǐfèn ① dew; moisture content; humidity ② exaggeration

水果 shuǐguǒ fruit

水库 shuǐkù reservoir

水面 shuǐmiàn ① the surface of the water ② the area of a body of water

水土 shuǐtǔ ①water and soil ② natural environment and climate

水位 shuǐwèi water level

水灾 shuǐzāi flood; inundation

水质 shuǐzhì water quality

水准 shuǐzhǔn level; standard

水蒸气 shuǐzhēngqì steam; water vapour

淡水 dànshuǐ 　海水 hǎishuǐ

洪水 hóngshuǐ 　降水 jiàngshuǐ

开水 kāishuǐ 　凉水 liángshuǐ

流水 liúshuǐ 　缩水 suōshuǐ

跳水 tiàoshuǐ 　饮水 yǐnshuǐ

雨水 yǔshuǐ

流水账 liúshuǐzhàng

泼水节 Pōshuǐjié

热水器 rèshuǐqì

自来水 zìláishuǐ

❷ [名] 泛指江、河、湖、海（跟"陆陆 lù"相对）: a general term for rivers, lakes, seas, etc. (the opposite of "陆陆") | ～陆运输 shuǐlù yùnshū land and water transportation.

水产 shuǐchǎn aquatic product

水力 shuǐlì waterpower; hydraulic power

水利 shuǐlì ① water conservancy ② irrigation works

水平 shuǐpíng ① level; horizontal ② standard; level

水源 shuǐyuán ① source of a river; headwaters; waterhead ② source of water

山水 shānshuǐ

❸ [形] 稀汁: liquid; juice | 柠檬～níngméngshuǐ lemonade

水晶 shuǐjīng crystal; rock crystal

水泥 shuǐní cement

水仙花 shuǐxiānhuā (bot.) narcissus; daffodil

香水 xiāngshuǐ

墨水儿 mòshuǐr

汽水儿 qìshuǐr

药水儿 yàoshuǐr

税 shuì 12画 禾部

税税税税税税税税税
税税税税

[名] 国家向征税对象征收的货币或实物: tax; duty | 收～shōushuì collect taxes / ～款 shuìkuǎn tax payment

税费 shuìfèi tax payment; taxation

税率 shuìlǜ tax rate; rate of taxation; tariff rate

税收 shuìshōu tax revenue

关税 guānshuì 　漏税 lòushuì

纳税 nàshuì 　偷税 tōushuì

退税 tuìshuì

征税 zhēngshuì

睡 shuì 13画 目部

睡睡睡睡睡睡睡睡
睡睡睡睡睡

[动] 睡觉: sleep | 早～早起 zǎo shuì zǎo qǐ early to bed and early to rise / 孩子已经～了。Háizi yǐjīng shuì le. The baby is asleep.

睡觉 shuìjiào sleep

睡眠 shuìmián sleep

睡衣 shuìyī nightclothes; pyjamas

顺 (順) shūn 9画 页部

顺 顺顺顺顺顺顺顺顺顺

❶ [动] 依从：obey; yield to; act in submission to | ～从 shūncóng be obedient to; submit to/ 归～guīshūn pledge allegiance | 不能总是～着孩子。Bùnéng zǒngshì shūnzhe háizi. *You can't always give in to a child.*
孝顺 xiàoshūn

❷ [形] 方向相同（跟"逆 nì"相对）：in the direction of; along (the opposite of "逆 nì") | ～流 shūnliú *go downstream*
一帆风顺 yīfān-fēngshūn
一路顺风 yīlù-shūnfēng

❸ [形] 有条理；通畅：(of writings) smooth; readable; clear and well-written | 这篇作文写得挺～。Zhè piān zuòwén xiě de tǐng shūn. *This essay has been written very well.*
顺畅 shūnchàng smooth and easy; unhindered
通顺 tōngshūn
风调雨顺 fēngtiáo-yǔshūn

❹ [动] 使有秩序或有条理：arrange; put in order | 这段话需要～一～。Zhè duàn huà xūyào shūnyi-shūn. *This paragraph needs polishing.*

❺ [动] 适合；顺利：fall in with; suit; agree with | ～心 shūnxīn *be satisfactory* | 近来他做事很不～。Jìnlái tā zuòshì hěn bù shūn. *Things did not go his way these last few days.*
顺利 shūnlì smooth; successful; without a hitch
顺手 shūnshǒu ① smoothly; without difficulty ② conveniently; without extra trouble

❻ [介] 顺着；趁便：at one's convenience; conveniently | ～口说出来 shūnkǒu shuō chūlai *say sth. without thinking*
顺便 shūnbiàn in addition to what one is already doing; without much extra effort
顺序 shūnxù in proper order; in turn

说 (說) shuō 9画 讠部

说 说说说说说说说说说

❶ [动] 用语言来表达意思；解释：speak; talk; say; explain | ～普通话 shuō pǔtōnghuà *speak Mandarin* | 一～就明白 yī shuō jiù míngbai *make clear at once after explaining* | 你～得很对。Nǐ shuō de hěn duì. *What you said is quite true.*

说话shuōhuà ① speak; talk; say ② chat; talk ③ gossip; talk ④ (dial.) in a jiffy; in a minute; right away ⑤ a kind of story-telling popular in Tang and Song dynasties

说谎 shuōhuǎng tell a lie; lie

说明 shuōmíng ① illustration; explanation ② explain; show

说情 shuōqíng plead for mercy for sb.; intercede for sb.

说不定 shuōbudìng perhaps; maybe

说大话 shuōdàhuà brag; boast; talk big

说明书 shuōmíngshū booklet of directions; (technical) manual; synopsis (of a play or film)

说闲话 shuōxiánhuà ① gossip; grumble ② chat

传说 chuánshuō 好说 hǎoshuō

胡说 húshuō 据说 jùshuō

虽说 suīshuō 听说 tīngshuō

小说 xiǎoshuō 演说 yǎnshuō

再说 zàishuō

好说话 hǎoshuōhuà

没说的 méishuōde

❷ [名] 言论；主张：theory; teachings; doctrine | ~法 shuōfa ① way of saying a thing; wording ② statement; argument

学说 xuéshuō

❸ [动] 劝告；责备：scold; blame | 他挨~了。Tā āishuō le. *He was scolded.* / 老师~了他几句。Lǎoshī shuōle tā jǐ jù. *His teacher gave him a scolding.*

说服 shuōfú persuade; convince; prevail on; talk sb. over

劝说 quànshuō

司 sī 5画 一部

司 司 司 司 司

[动] 掌管；主持：take charge of; attend to; manage

司法 sīfǎ administration of justice; judicature

司机 sījī driver; chauffeur

司令 sīlìng commander; commanding officer

司令部 sīlìngbù headquarter; command

司令员 sīlìngyuán commander; commanding officer

公司 gōngsī 官司 guānsi

子公司 zǐgōngsī

总司令 zǒngsīlìng

顶头上司 dǐngtóu shàngsi

丝 (絲) sī 5画 一部

丝 丝 丝 丝 丝

❶ [名] 蚕吐的又细又长的东西：silk | 蚕在吐~。Cán zài tǔ sī. *Silkworms are spinning silk.* / 这是用~织成的。Zhè shì yòng sī zhīchéng de. *It is woven of (from)* silk.

丝绸 sīchóu silk cloth; silk

丝巾 sījīn silk scarf

真丝 zhēnsī

❷ [名] 像细丝的东西：something shaped as thin sticks | 铁～tiěsī *iron wire* / 肉～ròusī *shredded meat* / 铅～qiānsī *lead wire*

❸ [量] 表示极少的量：a tiny bit; trace | 一～风也没有。Yī sī fēng yě méiyǒu. *There isn't a breath of wind.* / 她脸上没有一～笑容。Tā liǎnshang méiyǒu yī sī xiàoróng. *There isn't a trace of a smile on her face.*

丝毫 sīháo the slightest amount or degree; a bit; a particle; a shred; an iota

◇ 螺丝钉 luósīdīng

私　　　　sī　　　7画　禾部

私　私私私私私私私

❶ [形] 属于个人的或为了个人的 (跟 "公gōng" 相对)：personal; private (the opposite of "公gōng") | ～事 sīshì *private affairs* / ～信sīxìn *personal letter*

私人 sīrén ① private; personal ② one's own man

私营 sīyíng privately owned; privately operated; private

私有 sīyǒu privately owned; private

私有制sīyǒuzhì private ownership (of means of production)

❷ [名] 个人；个人的事：individual (person); one's own business

隐私 yǐnsī　　　自私 zìsī

自私自利 zìsī-zìlì

❸ [形] 不公开的；不合法的：secret; illegal; illicit | ～下 sīxià *in secret* / ～货sīhuò *smuggled goods*

私自 sīzì privately; secretly; without permission

走私 zǒusī

思　　　　sī　　　9画　田部

思　思思思思思思思思
思

❶ [动] 考虑；想：think; consider | 深～shēnsī *think deeply about* / 左～右想 zuǒsī-yōuxiǎng *think from different angles*

思考sīkǎo think deeply; ponder over; reflect on

思索sīsuǒ think deeply; ponder

思维 sīwéi thought; thinking

思想sīxiǎng thought; thinking; idea; ideology

思前想后 sīqián-xiǎnghòu think over again and again

沉思 chénsī　　　构思 gòusī

不可思议 bùkě-sīyì

饮水思源 yǐnshuǐ-sīyuán

❷ [动] 想念；惦记：think of; miss;

long for | 相~xiāngsī *mutual longing between a couple*

思念 sīniàn think of; long for; miss

❸ [名] 心情；想法：train of thought; thinking; idea | ~路sīlù *train of thought* / 构~gòusī ① *work out through thinking* ② *concept*

思潮 sīcháo trend of thought; ideological trend

思绪 sīxù ① train of thought ② feeling; mood

心思 xīnsi　　意思 yìsi

没意思 méiyìsi

有意思 yǒuyìsi

不好意思 bùhǎoyìsi

◇ 马克思主义 Mǎkèsī zhǔyì

斯　　　sī　　12画 斤部

斯斯斯斯斯斯斯斯
斯斯斯斯

See below

斯文 sīwén refined; gentle

◇ 瓦斯 wǎsī

法西斯 fǎxīsī

穆斯林 mùsīlín

伊斯兰教 Yīsīlánjiào

撕　　　sī　　15画 扌部

撕撕撕撕撕撕撕撕
撕撕撕撕撕撕撕

[动] 扯开；剥开：tear; rip | ~破

sīpò *tear up* / ~开sīkāi *tear* / 把布~成两块bǎ bù sīchéng liǎng kuài *tear the cloth in half*

死　　　sǐ　　6画 歹部

死死死死死死

❶ [动] 失去生命（跟"活huó"或"生shēng"相对）：die (the opposite of "活huó" or "生shēng") | 病~bìngsǐ *die from an illness* / ~人sǐrén *dead person (body); the deceased* / 这棵白杨树枯~了。Zhè kē báiyángshù kūsǐ le. *The white poplar tree has died.*

死亡 sǐwáng death; doom

死刑 sǐxíng death penalty; death sentence; capital punishment

死者 sǐzhě the dead; the deceased; the departed

❷ [形] 拼命；不顾生命：to the death | ~守 sǐshǒu *defend to the death; defend to the last*

❸ [形] 固定；死板、不活动：fixed; rigid; inflexible | ~规矩 sǐ guīju *rigid rule* / ~脑筋 sǐ nǎojīn *one-track mind* / ~记硬背 sǐjì-yìngbèi *mechanical memorizing* / 窗户钉~了。Chuānghu dīngsǐ le. *The window has been nailed fast.*

❹ [形] 不可调和的：implacable;

deadly | 他俩是~对头。Tā liǎ shì sǐduìtou. *They two were irreconcilable enemies.*

死对头 sǐduìtou deadly enemy; irreconcilable opponent

❺[形] 不能通过的；不流通的：impassable; closed | ~胡同 sǐhútong *blind alley; dead end* / 把洞堵~ bǎ dòng dǔsǐ *plug the holes; stop up loopholes*

❻[形] 表示达到极点：extreme; to death | 笑~人 xiàosǐ rén *be terribly funny* / 高兴~了 gāoxìng sǐ le *be extremely happy* / 累~了 lèisǐ le *be dead tired; be dog-tired*

◇死机 sǐjī (of a computer) crash

四 四四四四四

[数] 数目：four | ~条腿 sì tiáo tuǐ *four legs* / 我家有~口人。Wǒ jiā yǒu sì kǒu rén. *There are four members in my family.*

四处 sìchù all around; in all directions; everywhere

四方 sìfāng ① the four directions (north, south, east, west); all sides; all quarters ② square; cubic

四季 sìjì four seasons

四声 sìshēng ① the four tones of classical Chinese pronunciation ② the four tones of modern

standard Mandarin pronunciation

四肢 sìzhī four limbs; arms and legs

四周 sìzhōu all around

四面八方 sìmiàn-bāfāng all directions; all quarters; all around; far and near

寺 寺寺寺寺寺寺

[名] 佛教庙宇：temple | ~庙 sìmiào *temple; monastery*
清真寺 qīngzhēnsì

似 sì 6画 亻部

似 似似似似似似

❶[动] 像；如同：seem; appear | 骄阳~火 jiāoyáng-sìhuǒ *the sun was scorching hot*
似笑非笑 sìxiào-fēixiào faint smile
近似 jìnsì   类似 lèisì
相似 xiāngsì

❷[副] 仿佛；好像：seemingly; as if | ~曾相识 sìcéngxiāngshí *seem to have met before*
似乎 sìhū as if; seemingly
似是而非 sìshì'érfēi apparently right but actually wrong; specious

❸[动] 表示超过：surpass | 我们

的生活一年胜～一年。Wǒmen
de shēnghuó yī nián shèngsì
yī nián. *Our life has been getting better year by year.*

See shì.

饲 (飼) sì   8画 饣部

饲 饲饲饲饲饲饲饲饲

[动] 喂养(动物)：raise; rear ｜～
鸡 sìjī *raise chickens*
饲料 sìliào forage; fodder; feed
饲养 sìyǎng raise; rear

松 (鬆❷-❹)sōng   8画 木部

松 松松松松松松松松

❶ [名] 松树：pine (tree)
松鼠 sōngshǔ squirrel
松树 sōngshù pine tree; pine
❷ [形] 不紧密；不紧张：loose;
slack ｜绳子～了。Shénzi sōng
le. *The rope has come loose.* /
鞋带～了。Xiédài sōng le. *The
shoelace has come undone.*
放松 fàngsōng 宽松 kuānsōng
轻松 qīngsōng
❸ [形] 不坚实：light and crisp ｜
这点心～脆可口。Zhè diǎnxīn
sōngcuì kěkǒu. *The pastry is
crisp and delicious.* / 土质～了。
Tǔzhì sōng le. *The soil is loose.*
❹ [动] 放开；使松：loosen; re-
lax; slacken ｜～开手 sōngkāi

shǒu *relax one's hold* / ～口气
sōng kǒu qì *pause for breath;
feel relieved* / 把绳子～一下。Bǎ
shéngzi sōng yīxià. *Slacken the
rope a bit, please.*

耸 (聳) sǒng   10画 耳部

耸 耸耸耸耸耸耸耸耸
耸耸

❶ [动] 引起注意；使人吃惊：
alarm; shock ｜～人听闻 sǒng-
réntīngwén *deliberately exaggerate to create a sensation*
❷ [动] 高高地立起：tower ｜～立
sǒnglì *tower over* / 高～入云
gāosǒng-rùyún *tower into the
clouds; reach the sky*

送 sòng   9画 辶部

送 送送送送送送送送
送

❶ [动]陪离去的人一起走：see sb.
off or out; accompany; escort
｜～客sòngkè *see the guests to
the door* / 到火车站～人 dào
huǒchēzhàn sòng rén *see sb.
off at the railway station* / ～孩
子上学 sòng háizi shàngxué
take a child to school
送行 sòngxíng ① see sb. off;
wish sb. bon voyage ② give a
send-off party

欢送 huānsòng

❷ [动] 赠给：give as a present; give ｜ ~礼物 sòng lǐ wù *give as a present* / 姐姐~我一本书。Jiějie sòng wǒ yī běn shū. *My elder sister gave me a book as a present.*

送礼 sònglǐ *give sb. a present; present a gift to sb.*

赠送 zèngsòng

❸ [动] 运去；带给：deliver; carry ｜ ~报纸 sòng bàozhǐ *deliver newspapers* / ~信 sòng xìn *deliver a letter* / 把这些东西~到他家里去。Bǎ zhèxiē dōngxi sòngdào tā jiāli qù. *Take these things to his home.*

播送 bōsòng　传送 chuánsòng
输送 shūsòng　运送 yùnsòng

诵 (誦) sòng　9画 讠部

诵诵诵诵诵诵诵诵诵

[动] 出声地念；朗读：read aloud; chant; recite ｜ ~读 sòngdú *chant (a poem, essay, etc.)*

背诵 bèisòng　朗诵 lǎngsòng

颂 (頌) sòng　10画 页部

颂颂颂颂颂颂颂颂颂颂

[动] 赞扬：praise; extol; eulogize;

laud ｜ ~扬 sòngyáng *sing sb.'s praises*

歌颂 gēsòng

搜 sōu　12画 扌部

搜搜搜搜搜搜搜搜搜搜搜

❶ [动] 搜索检查：search ｜ ~身 sōushēn *search the person; make a body search*

搜查 sōuchá *search; ransack; rummage*

搜索 sōusuǒ *search for; hunt for; scout around*

搜寻 sōuxún *search for; look for; hunt for; seek*

❷ [动] 仔细寻找：look for ｜ 仔细地~了一遍 zǐxì de sōule yī biàn *search for sth. carefully*

搜集 sōují *hunt high and low for; collect; gather*

艘 sōu　15画 舟部

艘艘艘艘艘艘艘艘
艘艘艘艘艘艘艘

[量] 用于船只：unit used for boats or ships ｜ 一~油船 yī sōu yóuchuán *an oil tanker* / 两~军舰 liǎng sōu jūnjiàn *two warships*

苏 (蘇) sū　7画 艹部

苏 苏苏苏苏苏苏苏苏

[动] 从昏迷中醒过来：come to; become conscious again | 复~ fùsū *come back to life*

苏醒 sūxǐng revive; regain consciousness; come to

俗 sú 9画 亻部

 俗俗俗俗俗俗俗俗俗

❶ [名] 社会上的风气、习惯：custom; convention | 旧~ jiùsú *old custom*

风俗 fēngsú　　　习俗 xísú
入乡随俗 rùxiāng-suísú

❷ [形] 粗俗；不高雅：vulgar | 脱~ tuōsú *free from vulgarity* / ~气 súqì *in poor taste* / 不可耐 súbùkěnài *unbearably vulgar*

庸俗 yōngsú

❸ [形] 通行的；大众的：popular; common | ~语 súyǔ *common saying; folk adage*

俗话 súhuà common saying; proverb

通俗 tōngsú

诉 (訴) sù 7画 讠部

 诉诉诉诉诉诉诉

❶ [动] 说出来让人知道；陈述：tell; relate; inform; say (what is

on one's mind) | ~苦 sùkǔ *complaint; pour out one's woes; vent one's grievances*

告诉 gàosu

❷ [动] 控告：appeal to; resort to | 上~ shàngsù *appeal to a higher court* / 起~ qǐsù *bring a suit against sb.*

诉讼 sùsòng lawsuit; litigation

败诉 bàisù　　　公诉 gōngsù
投诉 tóusù

肃 (肅) sù 8画 聿部

 肃肃肃肃肃肃肃肃

❶ [形] 严重；认真：solemn; serious

严肃 yánsù

❷ [动] 清除：eliminate; clean up

肃清 sùqīng eliminate; clean up; mop up

素 sù 10画 糸部

 素素素素素素素素素素

❶ [形] 本色；白色：unbleached and undyed; white | ~色 sùsè *plain colour*

❷ [形] 基本的；不加修饰的：native; original | ~材 sùcái *source material (for artistic composition or literature)*

素质 sùzhì ① quality ② (psychol.) diathesis

朴素 pǔsù

❸ [名] 构成事物的基本成分：basic element; element ｜ 色~sèsù pigment

激素 jīsù 要素 yàosù

因素 yīnsù 元素 yuánsù

维生素 wéishēngsù

❹ [名] 用植物制成的食品（跟 "荤 hūn" 相对）：vegetable dish (the opposite of "荤 hūn") ｜ ~食 sùshí vegetarian diet

素菜 sùcài vegetable dish

 sù 10画 辶部

速速速速速速速速速速速速速

❶ [形] 快：fast; rapid; quick; instant ｜ 火~huǒsù at top speed; posthaste ｜ 请~回信 qǐng sù huíxìn please reply as soon as possible ｜ ~去~回 sù qù sù huí go and return quickly

速成 sùchéng accelerated educational programme

速度 sùdù speed; rate; pace; tempo

快速 kuàisù 迅速 xùnsù

❷ [名] 速度：speed; velocity ｜ 风~fēngsù wind speed ｜ 光~guāngsù speed of light ｜ 车~chēsù speed of a motor vehicle

飞速 fēisù 高速 gāosù

加速 jiāsù 减速 jiǎnsù

时速 shísù

高速公路 gāosù gōnglù

 sù 11画 宀部

宿宿宿宿宿宿宿宿宿宿宿

[动] 夜里住下；过夜：put up for the night ｜ 住~zhùsù stay; get accommodation ｜ 露~lùsù sleep out in the open

宿舍 sùshè hostel; living quarters; dormitory

 sù 13画 土部

塑塑塑塑塑塑塑塑塑塑塑塑塑

[动] 用泥土或石膏等物做成人或物的形象：model; mould ｜ 泥~nísù clay sculpture ｜ ~像 sùxiàng statue

塑料 sùliào plastics

塑造 sùzào ① model; mould ② portray

雕塑 diāosù

 suān 14画 酉部

酸酸酸酸酸酸酸酸酸酸酸酸酸酸

❶ [形] 像醋的味道或气味：sour; tart; having the taste or smell of

vinegar | ～菜 suāncài *pickled Chinese cabbage* / ～葡萄 suān pútao *sour grape* / 牛奶～了。Niúnǎi suān le. *The milk has turned sour.*

❷ [形] 悲痛；难过：grieved; distressed | 心～xīnsuān *be grieved; feel sad* / 她鼻子一～，流下泪来。Tā bízi yī suān, liúxià lèi lai. *She felt a lump in her throat and began to weep.*

❸ [形] 微痛无力的感觉：ache; tingle; a feeling of slight pain and weakness | 腰～背疼 yāosuān-bèitòng *aching back; have a backache* / 我的腿都走～了。Wǒ de tuǐ dōu zǒusuān le. *My legs ache from walking.*

蒜　　suàn　13画 艹部

蒜蒜蒜蒜蒜蒜蒜蒜
蒜蒜蒜蒜蒜

[名] garlic | ～泥 suànní *mashed garlic*
大蒜 dàsuàn

算　　suàn　14画 竹部

算算算算算算算算
算算算算算算

❶ [动] 计数：calculate; reckon | ～账 suànzhàng *do accounts; make out bills* / 能写会～néng-

xiě-huìsuàn *be good at writing and calculating*

算盘 suànpán abacus; counting frame

算术 suànshù arithmetic

测算 cèsuàn	估算 gūsuàn
计算 jìsuàn	结算 jiésuàn
决算 juésuàn	演算 yǎnsuàn
预算 yùsuàn	运算 yùnsuàn
计算机 jìsuànjī	
计算器 jìsuànqì	

❷ [动] 谋划：calculate | 失～shīsuàn *miscalculate; make an unwise decision* / 暗～ànsuàn *plot against sb.* / ～计 suànji *scheme*

打算 dǎsuàn	合算 hésuàn

❸ [动] 料想；推测：guess; think; suppose | 我～他今天该动身了。Wǒ suàn tā jīntiān gāi dòngshēn le. *I suppose he'll set out today.* / 我～他今天会来。Wǒ suàn tā jīntiān huì lái. *I think he will come today.*

推算 tuīsuàn

❹ [动] 计算进去：include; count | 不要把我～在内。Bùyào bǎ wǒ suàn zài nèi. *Count me out.* / 明天比赛～我一个。Míngtiān bǐsài suàn wǒ yī ge. *Count me in for tomorrow's contest.*

❺ [动] 作为；当作：consider; regard as; count as | 这个～我的。Zhège suàn wǒ de. *This counts as mine.* / 这件事还不能～完。Zhè jiàn shì hái bùnéng suànwán. *The matter has not been finished yet.*

算是 suànshì ① count as ② at last

❻ [动] 算数；承认有效力：carry weight; count | 说话～话 shuōhuà suàn huà *what one says counts* / 他说的不～，你说才行。Tā shuō de bù suàn, nǐ shuō cái xíng. *It is not what he says but what you say that counts.*

算数 suànshù count; hold; stand

❼ [动] 作罢；不再计较：forget it; let it pass | ～了，别理他了。Suànle, bié lǐ tā le. *Forget it. Leave him alone.*

算了 suànle let it be; let it pass; that's enough; forget it

 虽 (雖) suī　　9画 口部

虽 虽 虽 虽 虽 虽 虽 虽 虽

[连] 虽然：though; although; even if | 事情～小，影响却极大。Shìqing suī xiǎo, yǐngxiǎng què jí dà. *Though it is a trifle, its influence is great.* / 这孩子年纪～小，志气却很大。Zhè háizi niánjì suī xiǎo, zhìqì què hěn dà. *Young as the boy is, his aspirations are very high.*

虽然 suīrán though; although
虽说 suīshuō though; although

 随 (隨) suí　11画 阝(左)部

随 随 随 随 随 随 随 随 随 随 随 随

❶ [动] 跟：follow | ～我来 suí wǒ lái *follow me; come along with me.* / 他～我们上了楼。Tā suí wǒmen shàngle lóu. *He followed us up the stairs.*

随后 suíhòu follow; soon after
随即 suíjí immediately; presently
随身 suíshēn (bring sth.) with oneself
随着 suízhe along with; in pace with
伴随 bànsuí　　跟随 gēnsuí
入乡随俗 rùxiāng-suísú

❷ [动] 顺从；任凭；由着：let sb. do as he likes; yield to sb.'s wish | 去不去～你。Qùbuqù suí nǐ. *Whether to go or not is up to you.; You may go or not as you wish.* / 这些东西～你挑。Zhèxiē dōngxi suí nǐ tiāo. *Choose as you please among these things.*

随便 suíbiàn ① casual; random; informal ② careless; in a slipshod way; as one wishes ③ wanton; willful; arbitrary ④ anyhow; anywhere; no matter
随机 suíjī ① (statistics) random ② (math.) stochastic
随时 suíshí ①at any time; at all times ②whenever necessary; as

the occasion demands
随意 suíyì at will; free rein
随时随地 suíshí-suídì at all times and all places
❸ [介] 顺便：by the way
随手 suíshǒu conveniently; without extra trouble

 岁 (歲) suì　6画 山部

岁 岁 岁 岁 岁 岁

❶ [名] 年：year | ～末 suìmò end of the year / 年～ niánsuì age
岁月 suìyuè years
贺岁 hèsuì　　周岁 zhōusuì
压岁钱 yāsuìqián
❷ [量] 表示年龄的单位：year (of age) | 三～的孩子 sān suì de háizi a child of three years old
岁数 suìshu age; year
万岁 wànsuì

 碎 suì　13画 石部

碎 碎 碎 碎 碎 碎 碎 碎
碎 碎 碎 碎 碎

❶ [动] 完整的东西破成零片、零块：break into pieces; smash | 碗打～了。Wǎn dǎsuì le. The bowl is broken to pieces.
粉碎 fěnsuì　　破碎 pòsuì
❷ [形] 零星；不完整：broken; fragmentary | ～布 suìbù scraps of cloth / ～玻璃 suì bōli

bits of broken glass / 琐～的事情 suǒsuì de shìqing trivial matters; trifles
零碎 língsuì
❸ [形] 说话唠叨：garrulous; gabby | 嘴～ zuǐsuì talk too much; garrulous

 隧 suì　14画 阝(左)部

隧 隧 隧 隧 隧 隧 隧 隧 隧
隧 隧 隧 隧 隧 隧

[名] 地道，在山中或地下凿成的通路：tunnel; underground passage
隧道 suìdào tunnel

 穗 suì　17画 禾部

穗 穗 穗 穗 穗 穗 穗 穗
穗 穗 穗 穗 穗 穗 穗
穗

❶ [名] 谷类植物聚生在一起的花或果实：ear of grain; spike | 麦～儿 màisuìr ear of wheat / 谷～儿 gǔsuìr ear of millet
❷ [名] 用丝线、绸布条结扎成的装饰品：tassel; fringe | 金色的～子 jīnsè de suìzi golden tassels

 孙 (孫) sūn　6画 子部

孙 孙 孙 孙 孙 孙

[名] 儿子的子女：grandchild;

grandson | 长~zhǎngsūn *son's eldest son; eldest grandson*

孙女 sūnnǚ granddaughter

孙子 sūnzi grandson

外孙 wàisūn   子孙 zǐsūn

外孙女 wàisūnnǚ

 损 (損) sǔn   10画 扌部

损 损损损损损损损损损
损损

❶ [动] 减少：decrease; lose | 增~ zēngsǔn *increase and decrease*

损耗 sǔnhào ① loss; wear and tear ② wastage; spoilage

损失 sǔnshī ① lose ② loss; wastage

亏损 kuīsǔn

❷ [动] 损害：harm; damage

损害 sǔnhài harm; damage; injure; damnify

损坏 sǔnhuài damage; breakdown; injure; spoil; break

损伤 sǔnshāng ① harm; damage; injure; lesion; hurt; impair ② loss

损人利己 sǔnrén-lìjǐ harm others to benefit oneself

笋   sǔn   10画 竹部

笋 笋笋笋笋笋笋笋笋
笋笋

[名] bamboo shoot

竹笋 zhúsǔn

 缩 (縮) suō   14画 纟部

缩 缩缩缩缩缩缩缩缩缩
缩缩缩缩缩缩

❶ [动] 由大变小或由长变短；收缩：contract; shrink | 热胀冷~ rèzhàng-lěngsuō *expand with heat and contract with cold* | 这种布下水不会~。Zhè zhǒng bù xià shuǐ búhuì suō. *This cloth doesn't shrink when washed.*

缩短 suōduǎn shorten; curtail; cut down

缩水 suōshuǐ (of cloth through wetting) shrink

缩小 suōxiǎo reduce; lessen; narrow; shrink

缩写 suōxiě ① abbreviation ② abridge

紧缩 jǐnsuō   浓缩 nóngsuō

收缩 shōusuō   压缩 yāsuō

❷ [动] 没伸开或伸开了又收回去；不伸出：draw back; withdraw; recoil | 他觉得很冷，身体~成了一团。Tā juéde hěn lěng, shēntǐ suōchéngle yī tuán. *Feeling cold, he curled himself up.*

❸ [动] 后退：withdraw; recoil | 退~tuìsuō *shrink back* | 畏~ wèisuō *flinch*

所 suǒ 8画 斤部

所 所所所所所所所所

❶ [名] 地方：place｜住~zhùsuǒ *dwelling place*

所在suǒzài ①place; location ② where

厕所 cèsuǒ　　场所 chǎngsuǒ

处所 chùsuǒ

事务所 shìwùsuǒ

公共场所 gōnggòng chǎngsuǒ

❷ [助] 用在动词前，跟动词组成名词性词组，作定语：used before a verb to form a substantive structure which functions as an attribute｜大家~提的意见很有道理。Dàjiā suǒ tí de yìjiàn hěn yǒu dàoli. *The opinions put forward by all of you are quite reasonable.*

所得 suǒdé income; earnings; gains

所属 suǒshǔ ① what is subordinate to one or under one's command ② what one belongs to or is affiliated with

所谓 suǒwèi ① what is called; what is known as ② so-called

所有权 suǒyǒuquán proprietary rights; ownership; title

所有制 suǒyǒuzhì system of ownership; ownership

无所谓 wúsuǒwèi

❸ [助] 跟"为wéi"或"被bèi"合用，表示被动：used together with "为wéi" or "被bèi" in the passive voice｜被表面现象~迷惑 bèi biǎomiàn xiànxiāng suǒ míhuò *be misled by appearances*

❹ [量] 用于房屋、学校等：for houses, schools, etc.｜一~房子 yī suǒ fángzi *a house* / 两~学校 liǎng suǒ xuéxiào *two schools* / 一~医院 yī suǒ yīyuàn *one hospital*

❺ [名] 某些机关或机构的名称：institute; office｜招待~zhāodàisuǒ *guest house* / 指挥~zhǐhuīsuǒ *command post*

诊所 zhěnsuǒ

派出所 pàichūsuǒ

托儿所 tuō'érsuǒ

研究所 yánjiūsuǒ

◇所以suǒyǐ ① so; therefore; as a result ② the reason why

所有suǒyǒu ①own; possess ② possession ③ all

索 suǒ 10画 十部

索 索索索索索索索索 索索

[动] 寻找；探求 search; look for; seek

索赔 suǒpéi claim damages; claim an indemnity

索要 suǒyào ask for; claim; demand

摸索 mōsuǒ   思索 sīsuǒ
搜索 sōusuǒ   探索 tànsuǒ
◇索性 suǒxìng might as well;
simply
线索 xiànsuǒ

锁 (鎖) suǒ 12画 钅部

 锁锁锁锁锁锁锁锁
锁锁锁锁

❶ [名] 加在门、箱、柜、抽屉等上面防止别人打开的器具：lock │门上装了一把～。Mén shang zhuāngle yī bǎ suǒ. *A lock was fixed on the door.*

❷ [动] 用锁关住：lock up │～门 suǒmén *lock the door*
锁定 suǒdìng ① keep to ② finally decide ③ follow closely

❸ [动] 封闭：block; close
封锁 fēngsuǒ
◇连锁 liánsuǒ

T t

他 tā 5画 亻部

他 他他他他他

❶ [代] 别的；另外的：something else; somewhere else | ~乡 tāxiāng *a place far away from home; an alien land*

他人 tārén another person; other people

其他 qítā

异国他乡 yìguó-tāxiāng

❷ [代] 称自己和对方以外的某个男性：(third person singular for male) he; him | ~是教师。Tā shì jiàoshī. *He is a teacher.* / ~清楚这件事。Tā qīngchu zhè jiàn shì. *He knows about this.* / ~的身体很好。Tā de shēntǐ hěn hǎo. *He is in good health.*

他们 tāmen they; them

◇ 吉他 jíta

它 tā 5画 宀部

它 它它它它它

[代] 称人以外的单个事物：(third person singular for nonhuman) it | ~是什么东西？Tā shì shén-me dōngxi? *What is it?* / 这把雨伞你把~带上。Zhè bǎ yǔsǎn nǐ bǎ tā dàishang. *Take this umbrella with you.* / 猫饿了，喂喂~吧! Māo è le, wèiwei tā ba! *The cat is hungry, give it something to eat.*

它们 tāmen they; them

她 tā 6画 女部

她 她她她她她她

❶ [代] 称自己和对方以外的某个女性：(third person singular for female) she; her | ~是我妹妹。Tā shì wǒ mèimei. *She is my younger sister.* / ~的男朋友是中学教师。Tā de nánpéngyou shì zhōngxué jiàoshī. *Her boyfriend is a middle school teacher.*

她们 tāmen they; them

❷ [代] 称自己敬爱或珍爱的事物：referring to sth. beloved | 祖国，~是一个多么值得骄傲的名字啊! Zǔguó, tā shì yī gè duōme zhíde jiāo'ào de míngzì a! *Motherland, what a name to be proud of!*

塌 tā 13画 土部

塌 塌塌塌塌塌塌塌塌塌塌塌塌塌

❶[动]倒下；陷下：crumple; give way; collapse | 墙～了。Qiáng tā le. *The wall collapsed.*
倒塌 dǎotā

❷[动]凹下：sink; slump | 他瘦得两腮都～下去了。Tā shòu de liǎngsāi dōu tā xiàqu le. *He is so thin that his cheeks are sunken.*

❸[动]安定；镇定：calm down; ease | ～下心来 tāxià xīn lai *set one's mind at ease; settle down (to work, etc.)*

踏 tā　15画　足部

踏踏踏踏踏踏踏踏踏踏踏踏踏踏

See 踏实
踏实 tāshi (inf.) ① steady and sure; dependable ②free from anxiety; having peace of mind
　　See tā.

塔 tǎ　12画　土部

塔塔塔塔塔塔塔塔塔塔塔塔

❶[名]佛教的一种多层尖顶的建筑物：a Buddhist building with many storeys and a pointed rooftop | 宝～bǎotǎ *pagoda* | 这座～共有10层。

Zhè zuò tǎ gōng yǒu shí céng. *This pagoda has 10 storeys.*

❷[名]塔形的建筑物：tower | 灯～dēngtǎ *lighthouse; beacon* / 水～shuǐtǎ *water tower* / 纪念～jìniàntǎ *memorial tower; monument* / 电视～diànshìtǎ *TV tower*

踏 tā　15画　足部

踏踏踏踏踏踏踏踏踏踏踏踏踏踏

[动]用脚踩：tread; stamp | ～着山间小路 tāzhe shānjiān xiǎolù *walk on mountain paths* / 大～步地前进 dà tàbù de qiánjìn *stride forward; advance in giant strides*
践踏 jiàntà　　糟踏 zāota
　　See tā.

台（臺）tái　5画　厶部

台台台台台台

❶[名]高而平的建筑物、设备：deck; terrace | 塔～tǎtái *bleachers* / 瞭望～liàowàngtái *observation tower; lookout tower*
看台 kàntái　　站台 zhàntái
查号台 cháhàotái
服务台 fúwùtái

❷[名]公共场所或室内外高出地面的设备：platform-like object; stage｜戏~xìtái *stage*／讲~ jiǎngtái *podium; stand (for instructor to stand on)*

台阶 táijiē ① footstep; bench ② an opportunity to extricate oneself from an awkward position

出台 chūtái　　后台 hòutái

上台 shàngtái　　舞台 wǔtái

下台 xiàtái　　压台戏 yātáixì

唱对台戏 chàng duìtáixì

❸[名]像台的东西或类似桌子的东西：stage-like or table-like object｜窗~chuāngtái *window sill*／梳妆~shūzhuāngtái *dressing table*／写字~xiězìtái *writing desk*

台历 táilì *desk calendar*

台球 táiqiú ① billiards ② billiard ball ③ (dial.) table tennis; ping-pong

吧台 bātái　　柜台 guìtái

阳台 yángtái

❹[量]用于戏剧、演出、机器、设备等：used for theatrical performances, machines, installations, etc.｜一~戏 yī tái xì *a play*／一~机器 yī tái jīqì *a machine*

◇台风 táifēng *typhoon*

电台 diàntái

电视台 diànshìtái

 tái　　8画 扌部

抬 | 抬抬抬抬抬抬抬抬

❶[动]举起；向上托：lift; raise｜~手 tái shǒu *raise one's hand*／~起头 táiqǐ tóu *raise one's head*

❷[动]多人共同用手提或用肩膀扛：(of two or more persons) carry｜把桌子~过来。Bǎ zhuō-zi tái guòlai. *Carry the desk over here.*

 tái　　4画 大部

太 | 太太太太

❶[副]表示程度极高，多用于赞叹：(usu. used with words of admiration) excessively; too; over｜~高兴了 tài gāoxìng le *extremely happy; too glad*／~感谢你了。Tài gǎnxiè nǐ le. *Thanks a lot.; Thank you so much.*／这办法~好了。Zhè bànfǎ tài hǎo le. *This idea is extremely good.*／这孩子~可爱了。Zhè háizi tài kě'ài le. *This child is too cute.*

❷[副]表示程度过分，超过一般情况或要求：used to indicate an extremely high degree, surpassing general circumstances or requirements｜人~多了。Rén tài duō le. *It's too crowded.*／水~热了。Shuǐ tài rè le. *The water is too hot.*／菜~咸了。Cài tài xián le. *The dish is too salty.*

❸[副] 用在"不"后，减弱否定程度：used after "不" to lessen some degree of negativeness | 不~好 bù tài hǎo *not very good; not good enough* / 不~满意 bù tài mǎnyì *not so satisfactory* / 今天不~热。Jīntiān bù tài rè. *It is not very hot today.* / 我不~喜欢这个人。Wǒ bù tài xǐhuan zhège rén. *I am not really fond of this person.*

◇太空 tàikōng firmament; outer space
太平 tàipíng peaceful and tranquil; having good social order and without war
太太 tàitai ① Mrs.; madame; lady ② mistress of a household ③ wife
太阳 tàiyáng ① sunshine; sunlight ② sun
太子 tàizǐ crown prince
太极拳 tàijíquán a system of physical exercises that emphasizes balance, coordination and effortlessness in movements, designed for attaining bodily or mental control and well-being and also an art of self-defence
太平洋 Tàipíngyáng the Pacific (Ocean)

 汰 tài 7画 氵部

汰 汰汰汰汰汰汰汰
[动] 除去差的，不合适的：discard; eliminate | 优胜劣~ yōushēng-liètài *survival of the fittest*
淘汰 táotài

 态 (態) tài 8画 心部

态 态态态态态态态态
[名] 形状、样子；情况：form; shape; condition | 丑~ chǒutài *ugly performance* / 仪~ yítài *carriage; personal appearance* / 事~ shìtài *state of affairs; situation*
态度 tàidu ① attitude ② manner
表态 biǎotài   心态 xīntài
形态 xíngtài   状态 zhuàngtài

 泰 tài 10画 水部

泰 泰泰泰泰泰泰泰泰泰泰
[形] 安定；平安：safe; peaceful | 国~民安 guótài-mín'ān *the country is prosperous and the people live in peace*
泰然 tàirán calm; composed; self-possessed
◇泰山 Tài Shān ① Mount Tai (in Shandong Province) ② a symbol of great weight or importance ③ (old) wife's father; father-in-law

景泰蓝 jǐngtàilán

贪（貪）tān　8画 贝部

贪 贪贪贪贪贪贪贪贪

[动] 不满足；一心追求（财物及其他东西）：be greedy for; have an insatiable desire for ｜ ～玩 tānwán *be too fond of enjoying oneself* / ～财 tāncái *be greedy for money*

贪官 tānguān corrupt officials; venal officials

摊（攤）tān　13画 扌部

摊 摊摊摊摊摊摊摊摊摊摊摊摊

❶ [动] 摆开；铺开：lay out; spread out ｜ ～开地图 tānkāi dìtú *spread out a map* / 桌子上～着几本书。Zhuōzi shang tānzhe jǐ běn shū. *Several books were spread out on the table.* / 把问题～出来 bǎ wèntí tān chūlai *make clear the problems*

❷ [动] 分派；分担：share; apportion ｜ ～派 tānpài *apportion (expenses, work, etc.)* / 分～费用 fēntān fèiyòng *share expenses*

❸ [动] 碰上；遇到：(sth. unpleasant) befall; happen to ｜ 倒霉的事儿都叫我～上了。Dǎoméi de shìr dōu jiào wǒ tānshang le.

I have run into all these misfortunes.

❹ [名] 设在路边、广场上的售货处：booth; stand ｜ 摆～儿 bǎitānr *set up a stall* / 货～儿 huòtānr *booth; stall* / 水果～儿 shuǐguǒtānr *fruit stand; fruit stall*

❺ [量] 用于摊开的液体或糊状物：used for mash-like things ｜ 一～水 yī tān shuǐ *a pool of water* / 一～泥 yī tān ní *a mud puddle*

滩（灘）tān　13画 氵部

滩 滩滩滩滩滩滩滩滩滩滩滩滩滩

[名] 水边泥沙淤积成的地方：water's edge; littoral; beach ｜ 险～ xiǎntān *perilous shoals and rapids*

海滩 hǎitān　　沙滩 shātān

瘫（癱）tān　15画 疒部

瘫 瘫瘫瘫瘫瘫瘫瘫瘫瘫瘫瘫瘫瘫瘫瘫

See 瘫痪

瘫痪 tānhuàn ① palsy; paralysis ②break down; be at a standstill

谈（談）tān　10画 讠部

谈 谈谈谈谈谈谈谈谈
谈谈

[动] 说话或讨论：talk; discuss |
面~miàntán *speak to sb. face
to face; interview* / 他俩~了很
久。Tā liǎ tánle hěn jiǔ. *The two
of them talked for a long time.*

谈话 tánhuà ① talk; chat ②
talk

谈论 tánlùn discuss; talk about

谈判 tánpàn negotiate; hold
talks

谈天 tántiān chat; make conversation

畅谈 chàngtán　访谈 fǎngtán
会谈 huìtán　　交谈 jiāotán
洽谈 qiàtán
商谈 shāngtán
叙谈 xùtán　　座谈 zuòtán
座谈会 zuòtánhuì

弹（彈）tán　11画 弓部

弹 弹弹弹弹弹弹弹弹
弹弹弹

❶[动] 用弹力发射：shoot; send
forth | ~石子儿tán shízir
catapult pebbles / 皮球~了起来。
Píqiú tánle qǐlai. *The ball
bounced up.*

反弹 fǎntán

❷[动] 用手指或东西拨弄、敲击：
play (with one's fingers or ob-
ject); beat; rap | ~钢琴 tán
gāngqín *play the piano* / ~吉

他 tán jíta *play the guitar*
◇弹性 tánxìng elasticity; resil-
ience; spring
　　See dàn.

痰 tán　13画 疒部

痰 痰痰痰痰痰痰痰痰
痰痰痰痰痰

[名] phlegm | 请不要随地吐~。
Qǐng bùyào suídì tǔtán.
Don't spit, please.

坦 tǎn　8画 土部

坦 坦坦坦坦坦坦坦坦

❶[形] 平而宽：smooth; level
平坦 píngtǎn

❷[形] 没有隐瞒，直率：straight-
forward; be upfront about sth.
| ~率 tǎnshuài *candid; frank;
straightforward*
坦白 tǎnbái ① honest; frank;
candid ② confess; make a confession
◇坦克 tǎnkè tank

毯 tǎn　12画 毛部

毯 毯毯毯毯毯毯毯
毯毯毯毯

[名] blanket; carpet | 毛~mǎo-
tǎn *woollen blanket*

毯子 tǎnzi blanket
地毯 dìtǎn

叹（嘆） tān　5画 口部

叹 叹叹叹叹叹

❶[动]叹气：sigh | 悲~bēitàn *sigh mournfully; lament* / 长~ chángtàn *long sigh*
叹气 tànqì sigh; heave a sigh
❷[动]赞美：praise; acclaim | 惊~不已jīngtàn-bùyǐ *exclaim with admiration; wonder at*
叹词 tàncí (gram.) interjection; exclamation
感叹 gǎntàn　　赞叹 zàntàn

炭　tàn　9画 山部

炭 炭炭炭炭炭炭炭炭炭

[名]木炭的通称：general term for charcoal | 烧~shāotàn *make charcoal* / 木~mùtàn *charcoal*
焦炭 jiāotàn　　煤炭 méitàn

探　tàn　11画 扌部

探 探探探探探探探探探探探

❶[动]深入寻求；试图发现（隐藏的事物或情况）：find (sth. hidden); sound; explore | ~路

tànlù *explore the way* / ~某人的口气 tàn mǒurén de kǒuqì *ascertain (find out) sb.'s opinions or feelings; sound sb. out*
探测 tàncè survey; sound; probe
探索 tànsuǒ explore; probe
探讨 tàntǎo inquire into; probe into
探险 tànxiǎn explore; make explorations; venture into the unknown
勘探 kāntàn　　试探 shìtàn
侦探 zhēntàn
❷[动]看望；访问：call on; visit | ~病号 tàn bìnghào *visit a patient*
探亲 tànqīn go home to visit one's family or go to visit one's relatives
探望 tànwàng ① call on sb. ② look about
❸[动]向前伸出（头或上身）：crane; stretch forward | ~出头 tàn chū tóu *crane one's neck* / 行驶时身体不要~出车外。Xíngshǐ shí shēntǐ bùyào tàn chū chē wài. *Don't lean out of the window while the bus is in motion.*

汤（湯） tāng　6画 氵部

汤 汤汤汤汤汤汤汤

❶[名]中药的汤剂：decoction of medicinal ingredients | 药～yàotāng *decoction* / 参～shēntāng *a decoction of ginseng*

❷[名]食物煮后所得的汁液：soup; broth | 米～mǐtāng ① *water in which rice has been cooked* ② *thin rice or millet gruel* / 肉～ròutāng *broth*

堂 tāng 11画 土部

堂 堂堂堂堂堂堂堂堂堂 堂堂堂

[名] building for a specific purpose | 教～jiàotáng *church* / 礼～lǐtáng *auditorium; assembly hall*

课堂 kètáng 食堂 shítáng

塘 tāng 13画 土部

塘 塘塘塘塘塘塘塘 塘塘塘塘塘

[名]水池：pond | 鱼～yútáng *fish pond* / 荷～hétáng *lotus pool*

池塘 chítáng

糖 tāng 16画 米部

糖 糖糖糖糖糖糖糖糖 糖糖糖糖糖糖糖糖

❶[名]食糖的总称：general term for sugar | 红～hóngtáng *brown sugar* / 绵白～miánbáitáng *refined sugar*

❷[名]糖制的食品：food made from sugar | 我请你们吃～。Wǒ qǐng nǐmen chī táng. *I'll treat you to some sweets.*

糖果 tángguǒ sweets; candy; confection

喜糖 xǐtáng

❸[名]糖类，即"碳水化合物"：carbohydrate, a kind of organic compound

糖尿病 tángniàobìng diabetes

葡萄糖 pútaotáng

倘 tǎng 10画 亻部

倘 倘倘倘倘倘倘倘倘 倘倘

[连]如果；假使：if; supposing; in case | ～不小心防备，会受损害。Tǎng bù xiǎoxīn fángbèi, huì shòu sǔnhài. *You will suffer losses if you don't take precautions.*

倘若 tǎngruò if; supposing; in case

躺 tǎng 15画 身部

躺 躺躺躺躺躺躺躺躺 躺躺躺躺躺躺躺

[动]身体平卧或物体横倒：lie; repose | ～在床上 tǎng zài

chuáng shang *lie in bed* / 咱们~下休息一会儿。Zánmen tǎngxià xiūxi yīhuìr. *Let's lie down for a rest.*

 (燙) **tàng** 10画 火部

烫 烫烫烫烫烫烫烫烫烫 烫烫

❶ [动] 被高温物体烧痛或烧伤：scald; burn | ~手 tàng shǒu *scald the hand* / 手~伤了。Shǒu tàngshāng le. *The hand is scalded.* / 小心~着! Xiǎoxīn tàngzháo! *Be careful not to get scalded!*

❷ [动] 用热的物体使另一物体温度升高或起变化：heat | ~脚 tàngjiǎo *bathe one's feet in hot water* / ~酒 tàngjiǔ *heat wine (by putting the container in hot water)*

❸ [形] 温度高：very hot; scalding | 这水太~了。Zhè shuǐ tài tàng le. *The water is too hot.*

 tàng 15画 走部

趟 趟趟趟趟趟趟趟趟 趟趟趟趟趟趟趟

[量] 表示走动的次数：used to indicate a trip or trips made | 走一~ zǒu yī tàng *go somewhere* / 他来了一~。Tā láile yī tàng. *He has come here once.*

涛 (濤) **tāo** 10画 氵部

涛 涛涛涛涛涛涛涛涛 涛涛

[名] 大浪：surging waves; billows 波涛 bōtāo

 tāo 11画 扌部

掏 掏掏掏掏掏掏掏 掏掏掏

❶ [动] 挖：dig | 他在墙上~了一个洞。Tā zài qiáng shang tāole yī gè dòng. *He made a hole in the wall.* / 井~得很深。Jǐng tāo de hěn shēn. *The well was very deep.*

❷ [动] 伸进去取；往外拿：draw out; pull out; fish out | ~钱 tāo qián *take out money* / ~出手帕 tāochū shǒupà *take out a handkerchief* 掏腰包 tāoyāobāo (inf.) ① pay out of one's own pocket ② pick sb.'s pocket

滔 **tāo** 13画 氵部

滔 滔滔滔滔滔滔滔 滔滔滔滔滔

[形] 大水弥漫：torrential | 波浪~天 bōlàng tāotiān *great waves surge to the sky*

滔滔不绝 tāotāo-bùjué pour out words in a steady flow; talk on and on in a flow of eloquence

逃 táo 9画辶部

逃逃逃逃逃逃逃逃
逃

❶ [动] 逃跑：escape; flee; run away | 他~进森林。Tā táojìn sēnlín. *He fled into a forest.*
逃离 táolí run away; escape from; flee from
逃生 táoshēng flee (or run, fly) for one's life; escape with one's life
逃脱 táotuō succeed in escaping; make good one's escape; get clear of
逃跑 táopǎo run away; flee; take flight; take to one's heels
逃走 táozǒu run away; flee; take flight; take to one's heels
潜逃 qiántáo   在逃 zàitáo
❷ [动] 躲避：evade; shirk; run away | ~难 táonàn *flee from a calamity (esp. a war); be a refugee*
逃避 táobì escape; evade; shirk
逃荒 táohuāng flee from famine; get away from a famine-stricken area

桃 táo 10画木部

桃桃桃桃桃桃桃桃
桃桃

❶ [名] 桃树：peach tree
桃花 táohuā peach blossom
❷ [名] 桃树结的果实：peach | 水蜜~ shuǐmìtáo *honey peach* | 这种~儿真甜。Zhè zhǒng táor zhēn tián. *Peaches of this kind are really sweet.*
桃子 táozi peach
杨桃 yángtáo

陶 táo 10画阝(左)部

陶陶陶陶陶陶陶陶
陶陶

[名] 用陶土烧制的器物：pottery; earthenware shaped from clay and hardened by heat | ~器 táoqì *pottery; earthenware*
陶瓷 táocí pottery and porcelain; ceramics
陶艺 táoyì craft of making ceramics; ceramics

淘 táo 11画氵部

淘淘淘淘淘淘淘淘
淘淘淘

❶ [动] 用水冲洗掉杂质：wash (things, granules such as grain) in a sieve | ~米 táomǐ *wash rice* | ~金 táojīn *wash for gold; pan*

淘汰 táotài ① weed out; dispense with ② die out

❷ [形] 顽皮：naughty; mischievous | 这孩子真~! Zhè háizi zhēn táo! *What a naughty child!*

淘气 táoqì naughty; mischievous

讨（討）tǎo　5画　讠部

讨 讨讨讨讨讨

❶ [动] 出兵攻打：launch a punitive expedition against; make war on | 征~zhēngtǎo *go on a punitive expedition*

❷ [动] 研究；商议：discuss; consult | 研~yántǎo *discuss; deliberate; research*

讨论 tǎolùn discuss; talk over

讨价还价 tǎojià-huánjià bargain; haggle

检讨 jiǎntǎo　商讨 shāngtǎo
探讨 tāntǎo

❸ [动] 索取；请求 | ~债 tǎozhài *demand the payment of a debt* | ~教 tǎojiào *ask for advice*

❹ [动] 引起；招惹：provoke; invite | ~人喜欢 tǎo rén xǐhuan *likable; lovable*

讨厌 tǎoyàn ① be a pain in the neck ② nasty

◇乞讨 qǐtǎo

套 tào　10画　大部

套 套套套套套套套套套套

❶ [名] 罩在外面的东西：cover | 书~shūtào *slipcase* / 外~wàitào *overcoat* / 椅~yǐtào *slipcover for a chair*
手套 shǒutào

❷ [动] 罩在外面：cover with; slip over; encase in | ~上床罩 tàoshang chuángzhào *cover the bed with a quilt or bedspread*/ ~上外套 tàoshang wàitào *slip on a coat*

❸ [名] 同类事物合成的一组：a set of sth.
成套 chéngtào　配套 pèitào

❹ [量] 用于成组的东西：used for series or sets of things | 一~制服 yī tào zhìfú *a suit* / 一~茶具 yī tào chájù *a tea set* / 一~课本 yī tào kèběn *a set of textbooks*
套餐 tàocān table d'hote; set meal
老一套 lǎoyītào

❺ [动] 模仿；沿用：imitate; ape | 他~用了那篇文章。Tā tàoyòng le nà piān wénzhāng. *He modelled this on that article.*
客套话 kètàohuà

❻ [动] 用绳拴系或捕捉：harness; hitch up; capture | ~车 tàochē *harness a draught animal*

to a cart

❼[动] 拉拢：try to win(sb's favour, friendship, etc.) | ～关系 tāo guānxi *try to win sb. over; woo* / ～交情 tāo jiāoqing *try to get on well with sb. (to achieve certain purpose)*

❽[动] 引出（真情实话）：coax a secret out of sb. | 他总想～我的话。Tā zǒng xiǎng tāo wǒ de huà. *He is always trying to trick me into telling the truth.* / 我已经把他的话～出来了。Wǒ yǐjīng bǎ tā de huà tāo chūlai le. *I have coaxed the secret out of him.*

特 tè 10画 牛部

特特特特特特特特特特

❶[形] 不同于一般的；独有的：special; particular; unique | ～例 tèlì *special case* / 能力～强 nénglì tè qiáng *extremely capable*

特别 tèbié ① special ② especially; specially

特产 tèchǎn special local product; specialty

特长 tècháng what one is skilled in; strong point; speciality

特点 tèdiǎn characteristic; distinguishing feature; peculiarity; trait

特定 tèdìng ① specially appointed ② specific

特级 tèjí special grade (or class); superfine

特区 tèqū special zone

特权 tèquán privilege; prerogative

特色 tèsè characteristic; distinguishing feature (quality)

特殊 tèshū special; particular; peculiar; exceptional

特务 tèwu special agent; spy

特性 tèxìng specific property; characteristic

特有 tèyǒu peculiar; characteristic

特征 tèzhēng characteristic; feature; trait

独特 dútè   奇特 qítè

❷[副] 专门；特地：specially; for a special purpose | 我～为看你而来。Wǒ tè wèi kàn nǐ ér lái. *I came here specially to see you.*

特此 tècǐ (used in a document or formal letter) hereby

特地 tèdì for a special purpose; specially

特许 tèxǔ specially permit

特意 tèyì specially

◇模特儿 mótèr

疼 téng 10画 疒部

疼疼疼疼疼疼疼疼疼疼

❶ [动] 痛：ache; pain ｜肚子~ dūzi téng *stomachache* / 腿摔~ 了 tuǐ shuāiténg le *fall and hurt a leg* / 我牙~。Wǒ yá téng. *I have a toothache.*

疼痛 téngtòng pain; ache; soreness

头疼 tóuténg

❷ [动] 关怀；喜爱：love dearly; be fond of ｜他奶奶最~他。Tā nǎinai zuì téng tā. *His grandmother dotes on him the most.*

心疼 xīnténg

（騰）**téng** 13画 月部

腾腾腾腾腾腾腾腾 腾腾腾腾腾

❶ [动] 上升：rise; move upward ｜彩色气球~空而起。Cǎisè qìqiú téngkōng ér qǐ. *Coloured balloons soared up to the sky.*

❷ [动] 跳跃；奔驰：gallop; jump; prance ｜听到这个好消息，整个学校都欢~起来。Tīngdào zhège hǎo xiāoxi, zhěnggè xuéxiào dōu huānténg qǐlai. *The good news has stirred up celebration throughout the school.*

奔腾 bēnténg

❸ [动] 上下左右翻动：toss up and down; turn from side to side

沸腾 fèiténg

瞎折腾 xiāzhēteng

❹ [动] 使空出来：make room; clear out; vacate ｜~出时间看书 téngchū shíjiān kàn shū *spare time for reading* / ~出两间房来 téngchū liǎng jiān fáng lai *vacate two rooms* / 请你~一个空位子出来。Qǐng nǐ téng yī gè kòng wèizi chūlai. *Vacate a seat, please.*

téng 18画 艹部

藤藤藤藤藤藤藤藤 藤藤藤藤藤藤藤藤 藤藤

[名] 某些植物的茎：any plant with a long, thin stem; vine; cane ｜~椅 téngyǐ *cane (rattan) chair* / 西瓜~xīguāténg *watermelon vine*

tī 15画 𧾷部

踢踢踢踢踢踢踢踢 踢踢踢踢踢踢踢

[动] 用脚撞击：kick; play (football) ｜~足球 tī zúqiú *play football* / 他一脚把门~开。Tā yī jiǎo bǎ mén tīkāi. *He kicked the door open.; He opened the door with a kick.*

tí 12画 扌部

提 提提提提提提提提
提提提提

❶ [动] 垂着手拿：carry in one's hand with the arm down | ～篮子 tí lánzi *carry a basket* / ～水桶 tí shuǐtǒng *carry a bucket* / 他手里～着两条鱼。Tā shǒuli tízhe liǎng tiáo yú. *He carried two fish in his hand.*

提包 tíbāo handbag; shopping bag; bag; valise

❷ [动] 往上或往前移：lift; raise; promote | ～价 tíjià *raise the price* / 开会日期往前～两天。Kāihuì rìqī wǎngqián tí liǎng tiān. *Move the meeting forward by two days.*

提拔 tíbá promote

提高 tígāo raise; heighten; enhance; increase; improve

提前 tíqián ① do sth. in advance or ahead of time ② shift to an earlier date; move up

提升 tíshēng ① promote ② hoist; elevate

提早 tízǎo shift to an earlier time; be earlier than planned or expected

❸ [动] 举出；指出：give; point out | ～建议 tí jiànyì *put forward a proposal; make a suggestion* / ～问题 tí wèntí *ask a question* / ～意见 tí yìjiàn *make a suggestion; make a criticism*

提案 tí'àn motion; proposal; draft resolution

提倡 tíchàng advocate; promote; encourage; recommend

提出 tíchū put forward; advance; pose; raise

提到 tídào mention; refer to; bring up

提名 tímíng nominate (for election)

提示 tíshì point out; prompt

提问 tíwèn put questions to; quiz

提醒 tíxǐng remind; warn; call attention to

提议 tíyì ① proposal; motion ② propose; suggest; move

❹ [动] 说起；谈起：talk about; mention; refer to | 别再～那件事了。Bié zài tí nà jiàn shì le. *Don't bring that up again.* / 我不愿～过去的事。Wǒ bùyuàn tí guòqù de shì. *I don't want to take up the old story.*

❺ [动] 取出；拿出来：draw; take out | ～款 tíkuǎn *draw money from a bank* / ～货 tíhuò *pick up goods; take delivery of goods*

提纲 tígāng outline

提供 tígōng provide; supply; furnish; offer

提交 tíjiāo submit (a problem) to; refer to

提炼 tíliàn extract and purify; abstract; refine

提取 tíqǔ ① draw; pick up; col-

lect ② extract; abstract
提要 tíyào precis; summary;
abstract; epitome

题 (题) tí   15画 页部

题 题题题题题题题题
题题题题题题题

❶ [名] 题目：topic; subject; title
| 借～发挥 jiètí-fāhuī *make
use of the subject under discussion to put over one's own ideas;
seize on an incident to exaggerate matters* / 离～太远 lítí tài
yuǎn *stray too far from the subject* / 出了三道～chūle sān dào
tí *set three problems (or questions)*

题目 tímù ① title; subject;
topic ② exercise problem

标题 biāotí   话题 huàtí
课题 kètí   命题 mìngtí
议题 yìtí   主题 zhǔtí
专题 zhuāntí

❷ [名]练习或考试时要求解答的问
题：problem | 试～shìtí *exam
question* / 问答～wèndátí
question-and-answer

难题 nántí   问题 wèntí
习题 xítí

◇题材 tícái subject matter; theme

蹄 tí   16画 足部

蹄 蹄蹄蹄蹄蹄蹄蹄蹄
蹄蹄蹄蹄蹄蹄蹄蹄

[名] hoof | 牛～niútí *cattle's
hooves* / 马不停～mǎbùtíngtí
without a stop; nonstop

体 (體) tǐ   7画 亻部

体 体体体体体体体

❶ [名] 人或动物的全身或身体的
一部分：body or part of the
body | 肢～zhītǐ *limbs; limbs
and trunk* / 他从小就～弱多病。
Tā cóngxiǎo jiù tǐruò-
duōbìng. *He has been weak
and ill ever since childhood.*

体操 tǐcāo gymnastics
体检 tǐjiǎn physical examination; health checkup
体力 tǐlì physical (bodily) strength; physical power
体能 tǐnéng (physical) stamina
体温 tǐwēn (body) temperature
体育 tǐyù physical culture;
sports; PE
体质 tǐzhì constitution
体重 tǐzhòng (body) weight
体育场 tǐyùchǎng stadium
体育馆 tǐyùguǎn gymnasium;
gym
人体 réntǐ   身体 shēntǐ
尸体 shītǐ   遗体 yítǐ

❷ [名] 物体：object
体积 tǐjī volume; bulk

体系 tǐxì system; setup

大体 dàtǐ 　　　导体 dǎotǐ

个体 gètǐ 　　　固体 gùtǐ

机体 jītǐ 　　　集体 jítǐ

具体 jùtǐ 　　　立体 lìtǐ

媒体 méitǐ 　　　气体 qìtǐ

全体 quántǐ 　　　群体 qúntǐ

实体 shítǐ 　　　团体 tuántǐ

物体 wùtǐ 　　　液体 yètǐ

整体 zhěngtǐ 　　　主体 zhǔtǐ

总体 zǒngtǐ

长方体 chángfāngtǐ

多媒体 duōméitǐ

正方体 zhèngfāngtǐ

❸[名] 文字的书写形式或文章的表现形式: style; form ｜字~ zìtǐ *form of a written or printed character; typeface* / 文~ wéntǐ *type of writing; literary style* / 手写~ shǒuxiětǐ *handwriting*

繁体 fántǐ 　　　古体诗 gǔtǐshī

❹[动] 亲身实践或经历 (某事): personally do or experience sth. ｜~谅 tǐliàng *show understanding and sympathy*

体会 tǐhuì know (learn) from experience; realize

体贴 tǐtiē show consideration for; give every care to

体验 tǐyàn learn through practice; learn through one's personal experience

◇体面 tǐmiàn ① honourable ② dignity ③ handsome

体现 tǐxiàn embody; incarnate; reflect; give expression to

体制 tǐzhì system (of organization); structure

屉 tì　　　8画 尸部

屉 屉屉屉屉屉屉屉屉

[名] 桌、柜等物上的抽斗: drawer ｜笼~ lóngtì *a food steamer with several trays*

抽屉 chōuti

剃 tì　　　9画 刂部

剃 剃剃剃剃剃剃剃剃 剃

[动] 用刀刮去毛发: shave; cut off (hair, beard, etc.) ｜~头 tìtóu *have one's hair cut* / ~胡须 tì húxū *have a shave*

惕 tì　　　11画 忄部

惕 惕惕惕惕惕惕惕惕 惕惕惕

[形] 小心谨慎: cautious; watchful

警惕 jǐngtì

替 tì　　　12画 日部

替 替替替替替替替替 替替替替

❶[动] 代换: take the place of;

replace | 他没来，你能～他吗？ Tā méi lái, nǐ néng tì tā ma? *He is absent. Can you take his place?*

替补 tìbǔ substitute for

替代 tìdài substitute for; replace; supersede

替换 tìhuàn replace; substitute for; displace; take the place of

替罪羊 tìzuìyáng scapegoat

代替 dàitì   顶替 dǐngtì

交替 jiāotì   接替 jiētì

❷ [介] 为；给；表示行为的对象：for | 我～你洗衣服。Wǒ tì nǐ xǐ yīfu. *Let me wash the clothes for you.* / 我真～你高兴。Wǒ zhēn tì nǐ gāoxìng. *I am really happy for you.*

天   tiān   4画 一部

天 天天天天

❶ [名] 天空：sky; heavens | 蓝～lántiān *blue sky* / 晴朗的夜晚满～星斗。Qínglǎng de yèwǎn mǎntiān xīngdǒu. *Stars studded the clear night sky.*

天地 tiāndì ① scope of operation ② universe; heaven and earth

天井 tiānjǐng ① small yard; courtyard ② skylight

天桥 tiānqiáo overline bridge; platform bridge; overhead walkway

天上 tiānshàng sky, heaven

天色 tiānsè colour of the sky; time of day as shown by the colour of the sky; weather

天文 tiānwén astronomy

天下 tiānxià ① land under heaven ② rule

天长地久 tiāncháng-dìjiǔ (of love) as enduring as the universe; everlasting and unchanging

航天 hángtiān

半边天 bànbiāntiān

❷ [名] 古人或某些宗教指自然界的主宰、神、佛、仙人或他们居住的地方：abode of gods, Buddha, or immortals

天使 tiānshǐ angel

天堂 tiāntáng paradise; heaven

天安门 Tiān'ānmén Tian An Men

天主教 Tiānzhǔjiào Catholicism

老天爷 lǎotiānyé God; Heavens

❸ [名] 自然界：nature | ～敌 tiāndí *natural enemy*

❹ [形] 自来就有的；天生的：natural; inborn; innate; inherent

天才 tiāncái genius; talent; gift; endowment

天赋 tiānfù ① inborn; innate; endowed by nature ② natural gift; talent; endowment

天然 tiānrán natural

天生 tiānshēng born; inborn; inherent; innate

天真 tiānzhēn innocent; simple

and unaffected

天然气 tiānránqì natural gas

❺[名]气候；天气：climate; weather | 雨 ~ yǔtiān *wet day* / ~ 晴了。Tiān qíng le. *It has cleared up.* / ~ 冷多了。Tiān lěng duō le. *It is much colder than before.*

天气 tiānqì weather

谈天 tántiān　　阴天 yīntiān
聊天儿 liáotiānr

❻[名]季节；时令：season

春天 chūntiān　冬天 dōngtiān
秋天 qiūtiān　　夏天 xiàtiān

❼[名]日；一昼夜的时间；有时专指白天：day (round the clock); daylight | 每 ~ měi tiān *every day* / 过两 ~ guò liǎng tiān *in two or three days*

白天 báitiān　　成天 chéngtiān
当天 dāngtiān　后天 hòutiān
今天 jīntiān　　明天 míngtiān
前天 qiántiān　整天 zhěngtiān
昨天 zuótiān
礼拜天 lǐbàitiān
星期天 Xīngqītiān

❽[形]位置在顶部或高处的：overhead | ~ 棚 tiānpéng *ceiling; awning or canopy* / ~ 桥 tiānqiáo *overline bridge; platform bridge* / ~ 窗 tiānchuāng *skylight*

天线 tiānxiàn aerial; antenna

tiān　　11画 氵部
. . . .

　添添添添添添添添
添添添

[动]增加：increase; add | ~ 人手 tiān rénshǒu *have one more hand* / ~ 菜 tiāncài *get more dishes* / 每人都 ~ 了新衣服。Měi rén dōu tiānle xīn yīfu. *Everybody has got new clothes.*

添加 tiānjiā add; increase
增添 zēngtiān
画蛇添足 huàshé-tiānzú

田　　tiān　　5画 田部
. . . .

田　田田田田田

❶[名]耕种的土地：field; paddy field (in some regions) | 种 ~ zhòngtián *till the land; farm* / 稻 ~ dàotián *rice field; paddy field*

田地 tiándì ① field; farmland ② wretched situation; plight
田间 tiānjiān field; farm
田野 tiányě field; open country
农田 nóngtián

❷[动]指蕴藏矿物的地带：zone with a workable mineral deposit

油田 yóutián

◇田径 tiánjìng track and field; athletics; track

　　tiān　　11画 舌部
. . . .

甜甜甜甜甜甜甜甜
甜甜甜

❶[形]像糖或蜜的味道：sweet; honeyed | 这西瓜真~! Zhè xīguā zhēn tián! *How sweet the watermelon is!* / 这种蜂蜜很~。Zhè zhǒng fēngmì hěn tián. *This kind of honey is very sweet.*

甜瓜 tiánguā muskmelon
甜蜜 tiánmì sweet; happy

❷[形]使人愉快；舒适：comfortable; pleasant | 这孩子睡得真~。Zhè háizi shuì de zhēn tián. *The child is sleeping soundly.* / 她嘴巴很~。Tā zuǐba hěn tián. *She says sweet (persuasive) words.*

填   tián   13画 土部

填 填填填填填填填填
填填填填填

❶[动]垫平或塞满：fill; stuff | ~坑 tián kēng *fill a pit* / 把沟~平 bǎ gōu tiánpíng *fill up gullies*

❷[动]补充：fill; replenish; supplement
填补 tiánbǔ fill (a vacancy, gap, etc.)

❸[动]填写：fill in; write | ~表格 tián biǎogé *fill in (out) a form* / ~申请书 tián shēnqǐngshū *fill in (out) an application form*

填写 tiánxiě fill in; write

     tiāo   9画 扌部

挑 挑挑挑挑挑挑挑挑
挑

❶[动]用肩担着：carry on the shoulder; shoulder | ~担子 tiāo dànzi *carry loads with a shoulder pole* / ~水 tiāoshuǐ *carry buckets of water with a shoulder pole* / ~行李 tiāo xíngli *carry luggage*
挑重担 tiāozhòngdàn shoulder a heavy responsibility or a demanding task

❷[动]选择：choose; pick out | 你帮我~一个大一点儿的。Nǐ bāng wǒ tiāo yī gè dà yīdiǎnr de. *Help me pick out a bigger one.* / 我先进去帮你~一个好位子。Wǒ xiān jìnqù bāng nǐ tiāo yī gè hǎo wèizi. *I'll go in first and reserve a good seat for you.*
挑选 tiāoxuǎn choose; select; pick out

❸[动]过分严格地批评细节：nitpick; be hypercritical; be fastidious | ~错 tiāocuò *pick fault* / ~毛病 tiāo máobìng *look for faults; pick holes*
     See tiǎo.

条 (條) tiáo 7画 夂部

条 条条条条条条条

❶ [名] 细长的东西：long narrow piece; strip; slip | 金~jīntiáo *gold bar* / 布~儿bùtiáor *a strip of cloth*

条子 tiáozi ① strip ② a brief informal note

链条 liàntiáo　面条 miàntiáo
线条 xiàntiáo　油条 yóutiáo
面条儿 miàntiáor

❷ [名] 层次；秩序：order | 有~不紊 yǒutiáo-bùwěn *in perfect order*

条理 tiáolǐ orderliness; method; proper agreement or presentation

❸ [名] 用于分立项目：used for listing | 第一~dì-yī tiáo *Article 1* / 逐~zhútiáo *item by item; point by point*

条件 tiáojiàn ① condition; factor; term ② requirement; qualification

条款 tiáokuǎn clause (in formal documents); article; provision

条例 tiáolì regulation; rule; ordinance

条文 tiáowén article; clause
条约 tiáoyuē agreement

❹ [名] 写有某种内容的不大的纸片：note | 纸~儿zhǐtiáor *a slip of paper*

便条 biàntiáo　　假条 jiàtiáo

❺ [量] 用于细长的东西：used for long and thin things | 三~鱼 sān tiáo yú *three fish*

❻ [量] 用于分项的东西：used for itemized things | 一~新闻yī tiáo xīnwén *a piece of news; an item of news* / 几~建议jǐ tiáo jiànyì *several suggestions*

调 (調) tiáo 10画 讠部

调 调调调调调调调调调调

❶ [动] 使配合得适当均匀：suit well; fit in perfectly | ~味 tiáowèi *flavour; season* / ~配 tiáopèi *mix; blend* / ~色tiáosè *mix colour*

调剂 tiáojì adjust; regulate

调价 tiáojià readjust (or modify) prices

调节 tiáojié regulate; adjust

调试 tiáoshì identify and remove defects from (a machine, computer programme, etc.); debug

调整 tiáozhěng regulate; adjust
空调 kōngtiáo　烹调 pēngtiáo
协调 xiétiáo
风调雨顺 fēngtiáo-yǔshùn

❷ [动] 使和解：mediate; arbitrate | ~整tiáozhěng *adjust; regulate*

调和 tiáohé ① mediate; reconcile ② compromise; make concessions

调解 tiáojiě mediate; make peace

❸ [动] 戏弄；挑逗：provoke; tease; tantalize | ～笑 tiáo-xiāo *make fun of; tease* / ～戏 tiáoxì *harass (a woman); make suggestive remarks (to a woman)*

调皮 tiáopí ① naughty; mischievous ② play tricks

See diāo.

挑 tiǎo 9画 扌部

挑 挑挑挑挑挑挑挑挑挑

❶ [动]用细长的东西拨：poke with a long, slender stick; pick | ～火 tiǎohuǒ *poke a fire* / ～刺 tiǎocì *pick out a splinter*

❷ [动]用竿子等的一头支起：push sth. up with a pole or stick; raise | ～起帘子来 tiǎoqǐ liánzi lai *raise the curtain* / 把旗子～起来 bǎ qízi tiǎo qǐlai *hoist the flag*

❸ [动] 挑动；引起；惹起：stir up; instigate | ～起事端 tiǎoqǐ shìduān *stir up trouble*

挑拨 tiǎobō instigate; incite; sow discord

挑衅 tiǎoxìn provoke

挑战 tiǎozhàn ① challenge to battle ② challenge to a contest

See tiāo.

跳 tiào 13画 足部

跳 跳跳跳跳跳跳跳跳跳 跳跳跳跳跳

❶ [动]两腿用力使身体离地向上或向前：jump; leap; move oneself suddenly from the ground | ～上马背 tiàoshang mǎbèi *leap on a horse* / 他高兴得直～。Tā gāoxìng de zhí tiào. *He is jumping for joy.*

跳槽 tiàocáo ① (of a horse) leave its own manger to eat at another ② throw aside one job and take on another

跳高 tiàogāo high jump

跳水 tiàoshuǐ (sports) diving

跳舞 tiàowǔ dance

跳远 tiàoyuǎn long jump; broad jump

跳跃 tiàoyuè jump; leap; bound

❷ [动]一起一伏地振动：move up and down; beat | 心～ xīntiào *heart beats; palpitation* / 眼皮～ yǎnpí tiào *twitching of the eyelids*

跳动 tiàodòng move up and down; beat; pulsate

❸ [动]越过：skip; make omissions | ～了一级 tiàole yī jí *skip a*

grade / ～过两页 tiāoguò liǎng yē *skip two pages*

贴 (貼) tiē　　9画 贝部

贴 贴贴贴贴贴贴贴贴
贴

❶[动]把片状物粘到别的东西上：paste; stick; glue; attach a thin slip on sth. by gluing | ～邮票 tiē yóupiào *stick on a stamp* / 墙上～着一张画儿。Qiáng shang tiēzhe yī zhāng huàr. *There is a picture pasted to the wall.*
张贴 zhāngtiē

❷[动]靠近；紧挨：keep close to; nestle closely to | ～着墙走 tiēzhe qiáng zǒu *edge along the wall* / ～身衣服 tiēshēn yīfu *underwear* / 孩子紧～着妈妈。Háizi jǐntiēzhe māma. *The child snuggled up to his mother.*
贴近 tiējìn press close to; nestle up against
体贴 tǐtiē

❸[动]补助：subsidize; help out financially | 父亲每月～给他一些钱。Fùqīn měi yuè tiēgěi tā yīxiē qián. *Father supports him with some money every month.*
补贴 bǔtiē　　津贴 jīntiē

❹[名]补贴，补助：allowance; subsidy

铁 (鐵) tiě　　10画 钅部

铁 铁铁铁铁铁铁铁铁
铁铁

[名]iron | 钢～ gāngtiě *iron and steel* / 废～ fèitiě *scrap iron*
铁道 tiědào railway; railroad
铁路 tiělù railway; railroad
铁饭碗 tiěfànwǎn iron rice bowl; a secure job
磁铁 cítiě

厅 (廳) tīng　　4画 厂部

厅 厅厅厅厅

❶[名]政府机关的办事部门：department of a government organization | 办公～ bàngōngtīng *general office* / 教育～ jiàoyùtīng *department of education*

❷[名]聚会或招待客人用的大房间：hall (for holding meetings, concerts, receiving guests, etc.) | 大～ dàtīng *hall* / 音乐～ yīnyuètīng *concert hall*
餐厅 cāntīng　　歌厅 gētīng
客厅 kètīng　　舞厅 wǔtīng

听 (聽) tīng　　7画 口部

听 听听听听听听听

❶ [动] 用耳朵接受声音：listen; hear | ～音乐 tīng yīnyuè *listen to music* / ～电话 tīng diànhuà *answer a telephone* / 你说什么我～不清楚。Nǐ shuō shénme wǒ tīng bù qīngchu. *What did you say? I couldn't hear you clearly.*

听见 tīngjiàn hear
听讲 tīngjiǎng listen to a talk; attend a lecture
听力 tīnglì ① hearing (ability) ② aural comprehension (in language teaching)
听说 tīngshuō be told; hear of
听写 tīngxiě dictation
听众 tīngzhòng audience
听诊器 tīngzhěnqì stethoscope
打听 dǎting   好听 hǎotīng
窃听 qiètīng   倾听 qīngtīng

❷ [动] 依从；接受：accept (sb.'s advice); heed; obey | 他～不进去批评。Tā tīng bù jìnqù pīpíng. *He would not listen to criticism.*

听话 tīnghuà heed what an elder or superior says; be obedient
听取 tīngqǔ listen to

 亭   tíng   9画 一部

亭 亭亭亭亭亭亭亭亭 亭

[名] pavilion | 凉～liángtíng *pavilion*
亭子 tíngzi pavilion
电话亭 diànhuàtíng

      tíng   11画 亻部

停 停停停停停停停停 停停停

❶ [动] 止；中断：stop; cease; halt; pause | ～办 tíngbàn *close; stop certain business* / 雨已经～了。Yǔ yǐjīng tíng le. *The rain has stopped.* / 我的表～了。Wǒ de biǎo tíng le. *My watch has stopped.*

停电 tíngdiàn ① cut off the power supply; have a power failure ② power cut; power failure; blackout
停顿 tíngdùn ① stop; halt; pause ② pause in speaking
停业 tíngyè ① stop doing business ② close a business; go out of business
停止 tíngzhǐ stop; cease; halt; suspend; call off
停滞 tíngzhì stagnate; be at a standstill; bog down
不停 bùtíng

❷ [动] 停留：stop over | 我经过天津时～了一天。Wǒ jīngguò Tiānjīn shí tíngle yī tiān. *I*

亭
停

tíng

721

stopped over at Tianjin for one day.

停泊 tíngbó anchor; berth

停留 tíngliú stay for some time; stop; remain

❸ [动] 放置：be parked | 飞机～在跑道上。Fēijī tíng zài pǎodào shang. *The plane is parked on the runway.* / 车～在外面。Chē tíng zài wàimian. *The car was parked outside.*

停车 tíngchē ① stop; pull up ② park (a car) ③ (of a machine) stall; stop working

停靠 tíngkào (of a train) stop; (of a ship) berth

停车场 tíngchēchǎng car park; parking lot; parking area

挺 **tǐng** 9画 扌部

挺挺挺挺挺挺挺挺挺

❶ [形] 直：hard and straight; erect | 笔～bǐtǐng *well-pressed* / ～直 tǐngzhí *straight*

挺拔 tǐngbá tall and straight

挺立 tǐnglì stand upright; stand firm

❷ [动] 伸直或凸出：stick out; straighten up (physically) | ～胸 tǐngxiōng *throw out one's chest; square one's shoulders* / ～着肚子 tǐngzhe dùzi *protrude one's belly* / ～起腰 tǐngqǐ

yāo *straighten up; straighten one's back*

❸ [动] 勉强支撑：endure; stand; hold out | ～过了一场大病 tǐng guole yī chǎng dà bìng *recover from a serious illness* / 他受了伤，还硬～着。Tā shōule shāng, hái yìng tǐngzhe. *Though wounded, he was still holding out.*

❹ [副] 很：very; rather; quite | ～和气 tǐng héqi *very kind; very amiable* / 这孩子～漂亮。Zhè háizi tǐng piàoliang. *The child is very pretty.* / 他学习～努力。Tā xuéxí tǐng nǔlì. *He studies very hard.*

艇 **tǐng** 12画 舟部

艇艇艇艇艇艇艇艇艇艇艇艇

[名] 轻便的小船：light boat, such as a pleasure boat | 游～ yóutǐng *yacht; pleasure boat* / 潜水～ qiánshuǐtǐng *submarine*

潜艇 qiántǐng

摩托艇 mótuōtǐng

皮划艇 píhuátǐng

通 **tōng** 10画 辶部

通通通通通通通通通通

❶[动] 没有阻碍，可以穿过；到达：open; be passable; arrive | ～车 tōngchē be open to traffic; have transport service / 四～八达 sìtōng-bādá extend in all directions / 这条公路～北京。Zhè tiáo gōnglù tōng Běijīng. This highway leads directly to Beijing.

通道 tōngdào thoroughfare; passageway; passage

通过 tōngguò ① pass through; get past ② adopt ③ by means of; through

通航 tōngháng be open to navigation or air traffic

通往 tōngwǎng lead to; go to

通行 tōngxíng ① go through; pass through ② general; current

畅通 chàngtōng　交通 jiāotōng
灵通 língtōng　　流通 liútōng
相通 xiāngtōng

❷[动] 了解；懂得：understand; know | 他～三种外语 Tā tōng sān zhǒng wàiyǔ. He knows three foreign languages. / 对围棋我一点儿也不～。Duì wéiqí wǒ yīdiǎnr yě bù tōng. I don't know how to play weiqi.

精通 jīngtōng

❸[形] 思路和文字合理：logical; coherent | 文理不～ wénlǐ bù tōng ungrammatical and incoherent (writing) / 这个句子不～。

Zhège jùzi bùtōng. This sentence doesn't make sense.

通顺 tōngshùn (of writing) clear and coherent

❹[形] 共同的；一般的：common; ordinary; general | ～病 tōngbìng general failing; common fault / ～称 tōngchēng general term

通常 tōngcháng general; usual; normal

通俗 tōngsú popular; common

通用 tōngyòng in common use; current; general

普通 pǔtōng

❺[动] 使不阻塞：be open; be capable of going through | 电话打～了。Diànhuà dǎtōng le. The call has been put through.

通风 tōngfēng ① ventilate; air ② divulge information

打通 dǎtōng　开通 kāitōng

❻[动] 相来往；连接：connect; communicate | 两个房间是～着的。Liǎng gè fángjiān shì tōngzhe de. The two rooms are connected (open into each other).

通商 tōngshāng (of nations) have trade relations

通信 tōngxìn communicate by letter; correspond

通讯 tōngxùn communication

通讯社 tōngxùnshè news agency; news (press) service

沟通 gōutōng

❼ [动] 传达；使知道：notify; tell | ～消息 tōng xiāoxi *pass the news* / ～电话 tōng diànhuà *phone sb.*

通报 tōngbào ① circulate a notice ② circular ③ give information to

通告 tōnggào ① announce ② public notice

通话 tōnghuà ① converse ② communicate by telephone

通知 tōngzhī ① notice ② notify; inform

通知书 tōngzhīshū ① notice ② (com.) advice note

◇通红 tōnghóng very red; red through and through

卡通 kǎtōng

同 tóng 6画 门部

同 同 同 同 同 同 同

❶ [动] 一样；没有差别：be the same; be similar; be alike | ～岁 tóngsuì *be of the same age* / ～感 tónggǎn *same feeling or impression*

同胞 tóngbāo ① born of the same parents ② fellow countryman; compatriot

同步 tóngbù synchronized; in step

同等 tóngděng of the same class, rank, or status; on an equal basis (footing)

同行 tóngháng of the same trade or occupation

同类 tónglèi of the same kind; similar

同年 tóngnián ① the same year ② of the same age

同期 tóngqī ① the corresponding period ② the same term, year or class (at school, etc.)

同情 tóngqíng sympathize; show sympathy for

同时 tóngshí at the same time; meanwhile; simultaneously

同样 tóngyàng same; equal; similar

同一 tóngyī same; identical

同意 tóngyì agree; consent; approve

同志 tóngzhì comrade

不同 bùtóng   认同 rèntóng

如同 rútóng   相同 xiāngtóng

赞同 zàntóng

不同寻常 bùtóng-xúncháng

大同小异 dàtóng-xiǎoyì

与此同时 yǔcǐ-tóngshí

与众不同 yǔzhòng-bùtóng

❷ [动] 一起；共同：be together; be in the same boat | ～甘苦，共患难 tóng gānkǔ, gòng huànnàn *share weal and woe; go through thick and thin together*

同伴 tóngbàn companion

同伙 tónghuǒ ① work in partnership; collude ② partner; confederate

同盟 tóngméng alliance; league

同事 tóngshì mate; colleague

同学 tóngxué ① fellow student ② study in the same school

共同 gòngtóng　合同 hétong

会同 huìtóng　连同 liántóng

陪同 péitóng　一同 yītóng

❸ [介] (a) 引进动作涉及的对象：used to introduce the object of an action | 有事～大家商量。Yǒu shì tóng dàjiā shāngliang. *Consult with everyone when problems arise.*

(b) 引进比较的对象：used to introduce the object of comparison | 他～哥哥一样聪明。Tā tóng gēge yīyàng cōngmíng. *He is as clever as his elder brother.* / 今年的气候～往年不一样。Jīnnián de qìhou tóng wǎngnián bù yīyàng. *The weather this year is different from last year.*

❹ [连] 连接名词或代词，表示并列关系：together with; same as; and | 我～你一起去吧。Wǒ tóng nǐ yīqǐ qù ba. *Let me go with you.*

铜 (銅) tóng 11画 钅部

铜铜铜铜铜铜铜铜铜铜铜

[名] copper | ～像 tóngxiàng *bronze statue* / ～茶壶 tóng

cháhú *copper teapot*

铜牌 tóngpái bronze medal; bronze

青铜器 qīngtóngqì

童 tóng 12画 立部

童童童童童童童童童童童童

[名] 小孩儿：child | ～装 tóngzhuāng *children's clothing* / 神～ shéntóng *child prodigy*

童话 tónghuà children's stories; fairy tales

童年 tóngnián childhood

儿童 értóng

统 (統) tǒng 9画 纟部

统统统统统统统统统

❶ [动] 总括；总管：all; entirely; together

统筹 tǒngchóu plan as a whole

统统 tǒngtǒng all; entirely; completely

统一 tǒngyī ① unify ② unified

统战 tǒngzhàn united front (abbr. for "统一战线 Tǒngyī zhànxiàn")

❷ [动] 管辖：be under the jurisdiction of

统治 tǒngzhì rule; dominate

总统 zǒngtǒng

❸ [名] 事物的连续关系：interconnected system; genealogy; continuum of interrelated things | 血~ xuètǒng *blood relationship*

传统 chuántǒng 系统 xìtǒng

捅 tǒng 10画 扌部

捅 捅捅捅捅捅捅捅 捅捅

❶[动]戳;刺：stab; poke | 把窗户~破了 bǎ chuānghu tǒngpò le *poke a hole in the window*

❷[动]碰;触动：touch; poke | 我用胳膊~了他一下。Wǒ yòng gēbo tǒngle tā yīxià. *I gave him a nudge.*

❸[动]揭露：expose; disclose; let out | 他把问题全~出来了。Tā bǎ wèntí quán tǒng chūlai le. *He disclosed all the issues.*

桶 tǒng 11画 木部

桶 桶桶桶桶桶桶桶 桶桶桶

[名]盛东西的用具：barrel; pail; bucket | 水~ shuǐtǒng *pail; bucket* / 汽油~ qìyóutǒng *petrol drum (tank)*

筒 tǒng 12画 竹部

筒 筒筒筒筒筒筒筒筒 筒筒筒筒

❶[名]较粗的管状物：thick tube-shaped object | 笔~ bǐtǒng *brush pot; pen holder* / 烟~ yāntong *chimney; smokestack* / 邮~ yóutǒng *pillar box; mailbox*

话筒 huàtǒng
手电筒 shǒudiàntǒng

❷[名]衣服等的筒状部分：tube-shaped part of clothing | 袖~儿 xiùtǒngr *sleeve* / 袜~儿 wàtǒngr *leg of a stocking*

长筒袜 chángtǒngwà

痛 tòng 12画 疒部

痛 痛痛痛痛痛痛痛痛 痛痛痛痛

❶[动]疼：pain; ache | 肚子~ dùzi tòng *stomach ache* / 这种药可以止~。Zhè zhǒng yào kěyǐ zhǐtòng. *This medicine is a painkiller.*

疼痛 téngtòng

❷[动]悲伤：grieve; mourn | ~心 tòngxīn *pained; grieved* / 沉~ chéntòng *deep feeling of grief*

痛苦 tòngkǔ pain; suffering; agony

悲痛 bēitòng

❸[副]尽情地;极度地;彻底地：extremely; deeply; bitterly; thoroughly | ~饮 tòngyǐn *drink one's fill* / ～恨 tōnghèn *hate bitterly; utterly detest* / ～改前非 tōnggǎi-qiánfēi *sincerely mend one's ways; put right one's past errors*

痛快 tōngkuài ① very happy; joyful ② to one's heart's content; to one's great satisfaction ③ simple and direct

痛痛快快 tōngtōng-kuàikuài ① to one's heart's content; to one's great satisfaction ② simple and direct; forthright; straightforward

 偷 tōu 11画 亻部

偷 偷偷偷偷偷偷偷偷偷偷偷

❶ [动] 暗中拿走别人的东西：steal; make off with | ～东西 tōu dōngxi *steal something* / 我的背包被人～了。Wǒ de bēibāo bèi rén tōu le. *My backpack was stolen.*

偷窃 tōuqiè steal; pilfer
偷税 tōushuì evade taxes
小偷 xiǎotōu

❷ [副] 悄悄地；趁人不备地：secretly; stealthily; on the sly | ～看 tōukàn *steal a glance; peep* / 猫～吃了主人的鱼。Māo tōuchīle zhǔrén de yú. *The cat stole and ate its master's fish.* / 他上课时～着看小说。Tā

shàngkè shí tōuzhe kàn xiǎoshuō. *He kept reading a novel furtively in class.*

偷偷 tōutōu stealthily; secretly; covertly; on the sly

❸ [动] 抽出（时间）：find (time) | ～空儿 tōukòngr *manage to find time (to do other things); snatch a moment* / ～闲 tōuxián *snatch a moment of leisure*

头 (頭) tóu 5画 丶部

头 头头头头头头

❶ [名] head | 抬～táitóu *raise one's head* / 扭过～niǔguò tóu *turn one's head around*
头部 tóubù head
头发 tóufa hair (on the human head)
头脑 tóunǎo brains; mind
头球 tóuqiú (football) header
头疼 tóuténg (have a) headache
头昏脑胀 tóuhūn-nǎozhàng feel giddy (or dizzy); feel one's head spinning
回头 huítóu　　猎头 liètóu
埋头 máitóu　　摇头 yáotóu

❷ [名] 头发或头发的式样：hair; hairstyle | 剪～jiǎntóu *(in oral) have one's hair cut* / 梳～shūtóu *comb hair*
白头 báitóu

❸ [名] 为首的；首领：chief; leader; boss | 这是我们的～儿。Zhè

727

shì wǒmen de tóur. *This is our chief (boss).*

头子 tóuzi chieftain; chief; boss
巨头 jùtóu
顶头上司 dǐngtóu shàngsi

❹ [形] 第一: first; number one | ~等 tóuděng *first-class* / ~号 tóuhào *number one; size one* / ~班 tóubān *the first shift*

❺ [形] 领头的；次序或时间居前的: first | ~羊 tóuyáng *bellwether; indicator of future trends* / ~一回 tóu yī huí *the first time* / ~两节课 tóu liǎng jié kè *the first two periods*

❻ [名] 物体的顶端或末端: top; tip; end | 针~ zhēntóu *the point of a needle* / 这个东西两~大中间小。 Zhège dōngxi liǎngtóu dà zhōngjiān xiǎo. *The object is thick at both ends and thin in the middle.*

车头 chētóu   镜头 jìngtóu
口头 kǒutóu   眉头 méitóu
山头 shāntóu   心头 xīntóu

❼ [名] 起点或终点: beginning; end | 从~说起 cóngtóu shuōqǐ *tell from the very beginning* / 从~到尾 cóngtóudàowěi *from beginning to end*

从头 cóngtóu   带头 dàitóu
街头 jiētóu   开头 kāitóu
源头 yuántóu
年头儿 niántóur

❽ [名] 物品的残余部分: remnant; remains; leftovers | 烟~儿 yān-tóur *cigarette end* / 布~儿 bùtóur *remnant of a bolt of cloth; odd bits of cloth* / 铅笔~儿 qiānbǐtóur *pencil stub*

❾ [量] 用于牲口: used for domestic animals | 一千~牛 yīqiān tóu niú *a thousand head of cattle* / 两~猪 liǎng tóu zhū *two pigs*

❿ [量] 用于形状像头的东西: used for sth. resembling a head | 一~蒜 yī tóu suàn *a bulb of garlic*

大头菜 dàtóucài

⓫ [助] 词尾，读轻声: used as a suffix, pronounced in an unstressed way | 木~ mùtou *wood* / 念~ niàntou *idea* / 甜~儿 tiántour *sweet taste; benefit* / 有听~儿 yǒu tīngtour *be worth listening to*

对头 duìtou   跟头 gēntou
骨头 gǔtou   罐头 guàntou
后头 hòutou   劲头 jìntou
里头 lǐtou   馒头 mántou
前头 qiántou   上头 shàngtou
舌头 shétou   石头 shítou
外头 wàitou   下头 xiàtou
枕头 zhěntou   指头 zhǐtou
吃苦头 chīkǔtou
出风头 chūfēngtou
懒骨头 lǎngǔtou
死对头 sǐduìtou
◇手头紧 shǒutóu jǐn

投

tóu 7画 扌部

投 投投投投投投投

❶ [动]向一定目标扔：throw; fling; cast; toss (toward a goal) | ~球 tóu qiú *shoot (at the basket)* / ~石子儿 tóu shízir *throw a cobblestone* / ~入江中 tóurù jiāng zhōng *throw into a river*
投篮 tóulán (basketball) shoot (a basket)
投掷 tóuzhì throw; hurl

❷ [动]跳进去(自杀)：(of suicidal behaviour) throw oneself into | ~河 tóuhé *drown oneself in a river* / ~火 tóuhuǒ *throw oneself into a fire*

❸ [动]放进去；送进去：drop; put in; cast | 把信~进信箱 bǎ xìn tóujìn xìnxiāng *drop a letter into a mailbox*
投产 tóuchǎn (of a factory) go into operation; put into production
投放 tóufàng ①throw in; put in ②put (money) into circulation; put (goods) on the market
投票 tóupiào vote; cast a vote
投资 tóuzī ① investment; money invested ② invest

❹ [动]相合；迎合：fit in with; agree with; cater to | 情~意合 qíngtóu-yìhé *agree in opinion; in love with each other* / 他俩脾气

相~。Tā liǎ píqi xiāngtóu. *They are very compatible.*
投机 tóujī ① congenial; agreeable ②speculate; seize a chance to seek private gain
投机倒把 tóujī-dǎobǎ buy low and sell high to make profit; engage in speculation and profiteering

❺ [动]寄送出去：send; deliver; dispatch | ~稿 tóugǎo *submit a piece of writing for publication; contribute to a newspaper or magazine*

❻ [动](光线等)射向物体：(of light) project | 树影~在草地上。Shùyǐng tóu zài cǎodì shang. *The tree casts a shadow on the grass.*

❼ [动]找上去；参加：go to; seek; join; enter | ~亲 tóuqīn *(written) seek aid and live with one's relatives*
投标 tóubiāo submit a tender; bid for
投入 tóurù throw into; put into
投诉 tóusù ① appeal ② (of a customer) complain
投降 tóuxiáng surrender; capitulate

透

tòu 10画 辶部

透 透透透透透透透透 透透

❶ [动] 穿过；通过：(of liquid, light) penetrate; pass through; lead or seep through | ～光 tōuguāng *be pervious to light* / ～气 tōuqì *ventilate* / 阳光～过窗户照进来。yángguāng tòuguò chuānghu zhào jìnlai. *Sunlight came in through the windows.*

透明 tòumíng transparent; diaphanous; lucid

透视 tòushì ① perspective ② (med.) fluoroscopy; roentgenoscopy ③ see through

透明度 tòumíngdù transparency

❷ [形] 彻底；清楚：thorough; clear; in a penetrating way | 我摸～了他的脾气。Wǒ mōtòule tā de píqi. *I have got to know him thoroughly.* / 道理讲得很～。Dàolǐ jiǎng de hěn tòu. *The reasons have been clearly explained.*

透彻 tòuchè penetrating; thorough

❸ [形] 达到充分的程度：full; complete; to the extreme; to the point of saturation | 雨下～了。Yǔ xiàtòu le. *It was drenching rain.* / 苹果还没熟～。Píngguǒ hái méi shútòu. *The apples are not fully ripe yet.*

❹ [动] 泄露；暗中说出去：tell secretly; inform on the sly | ～露风声 tòulù fēngshēng *leak confidential information* / 他给我～

了个消息。Tā gěi wǒ tòule gè xiāoxi. *He told me a piece of news secretly.*

透露 tòulù divulge; leak; disclose; reveal

❺ [动] 显露：show; appear; look | 白里～红 báilǐtòuhóng *white touched with red*

◇透支 tòuzhī ① (banking) overdraw; make an overdraft ② expenditure exceeds revenue; overspend ③ (old) draw one's salary in advance

tū   5画 | 部

凸 凸凸 凸凸 凸

[形] 高出四周 (跟 "凹āo" 相对)：protruding; raised; higher than the surrounding areas (the opposite of "凹āo") | 凹～不平 āotū bùpíng *full of bumps and holes; uneven*

tū   7画 禾部

秃 秃秃 秃秃 秃秃 秃

❶ [形] (人) 没有头发；(鸟兽) 没有毛：(of person) hairless; (of animal) having no hair | ～头 tūtóu *bald* / 这是只～尾巴狗。Zhè shì zhī tūwěiba gǒu. *It is a bare-tailed dog.* / 他的头有

点～了。Tā de tóu yǒudiǎn tū le. *He began to go bald.*

❷[形](山)没有草木；(树)没有叶子：(of mountain, tree) treeless; bare of leaves | 山是～的。Shān shì tū de. *The hills are barren; The hills are bare.*

❸[形]物体失去尖端；不锐利：blunt; pointless | 笔尖已经写～了。Bǐjiān yǐjīng xiětū le. *The point of the pencil is blunt.*

突 tū 9画 穴部

突突突突突突突突突

❶[副]忽然；出人意料：suddenly; abruptly; unexpectedly | ～变 tūbiàn *sudden change* / 人口～增 rénkǒu tūzēng *dramatic raise of the population* / 气温～降。Qìwēn tūjiàng *The temperature suddenly dropped.*

突发 tūfā happen unexpectedly; break out; outburst

突击 tūjī ① assault ② make a concentrated effort to finish a job quickly; do a crash job

突然 tūrán sudden; abrupt; unexpected

❷[动]猛冲；冲撞：charge; sprint; dash forward | ～破 tūpò *break through* / ～围 tūwéi *break out of an encirclement*

冲突 chōngtū

❸[名]高于周围：protruding; projecting; prominent | ～起 tūqǐ *rise high*

突出 tūchū ① outstanding; prominent ② stress; highlight; give prominence to

（圖） tú 8画 口部

图 图图图图图图图图图

❶[名]绘制出来的形象；图画：picture; drawing; chart | 插～ chātú *illustration* / 看～识字 kàntú shízì *learn to read with the aid of pictures* / 这张～画得太小。Zhè zhāng tú huà de tài xiǎo. *The drawing is too small.*

图案 tú'àn pattern; design

图表 túbiǎo chart; diagram; graph

图画 túhuà drawing; picture; painting

图片 túpiàn picture; photograph

图书 túshū books

图像 túxiàng picture; image

图形 túxíng graph; figure

图纸 túzhǐ blueprint; drawing

图书馆 túshūguǎn library

版图 bǎntú   地图 dìtú

❷[动]谋求；打算：plan; attempt; pursue

力图 lìtú   企图 qǐtú

试图 shìtú   妄图 wàngtú

发愤图强 fāfèn-túqiáng

❸[名]制定的计划；谋略：plan;

project｜宏～hóngtú *great plan*

意图 yìtú

 tú　10画 亻部

徒徒徒徒徒徒徒徒
徒徒

❶[名]徒弟；学生：apprentice; pupil; disciple｜学～xuétú *apprentice* / 门～méntú *pupil; disciple*

徒弟 túdì apprentice; disciple

❷[名]指某种人（含贬义）：referring to people (derog.)｜赌～dǔtú *gambler* / 不法之～bùfǎzhītú *lawless person; law breaker*

叛徒 pàntú

途　tú　10画 辶部

途途途途途途途途
途途

[名]道路：way; path; road｜～中 túzhōng *on the way*

途径 tújìng way; channel

旅途 lǚtú

（塗）tú　10画 氵部

涂涂涂涂涂涂涂涂
涂涂

❶[动]把油漆、颜料等抹在物体表面：apply paint or colour to objects｜～上颜色 túshang yánsè *apply colour* / 他在面包上～了些黄油。Tā zài miànbāo shang túle xiē huángyóu. *He spread some butter on his bread.* / 墙面～成了天蓝色。Qiángmiàn túchéngle tiānlánsè. *The walls were painted sky blue.*

❷[动]抹去：blot out; cross out｜～改 túgǎi *alter* / ～去一个字 túqù yī gè zì *cross or blot out a character*

❸[动]随意写、画：scrawl; scribble; daub｜别在墙上乱～。Bié zài qiáng shang luàn tú. *Don't scribble on the wall.* / 这孩子把我的书～乱了。Zhè háizi bǎ wǒ de shū túluàn le. *The child made a mess of my book by scribbling on it.*

 tú　11画 尸部

屠屠屠屠屠屠屠屠
屠屠屠

[动]残杀：slaughter; massacre; butcher

屠杀 túshā massacre; butcher; slaughter

土　tǔ　3画 土部

土 土土土

❶ [名] 土壤：soil; earth | ～山 tǔshān *earthen hill*
土豆 tǔdòu *potato*
土壤 tǔrǎng *soil*
尘土 chéntǔ　泥土 nítǔ
沙土 shātǔ　水土 shuǐtǔ
风土人情 fēngtǔ-rénqíng

❷ [名] 土地；国土：land; ground; territory | 故～gùtǔ *native land*
土地 tǔdì ① land; soil ② territory
本土 běntǔ　　国土 guótǔ
领土 lǐngtǔ

❸ [形] 某一地方的；本地的：local; native; indigenous | ～产 tǔchǎn *local product; be produced locally* / ～话 tǔhuà *local dialect*

❹ [形] 不合潮流：crude; rustic; unenlightened | ～气 tǔqì *rustic; countrified*

❺ [形] 民间的（跟"洋 yáng"相对）：popular; folk (the opposite of "洋 yáng") | ～专家 tǔzhuānjiā *local expert* / 这个～办法很好。Zhège tǔbànfǎ hěn hǎo. *This indigenous method is very good.*

吐 tǔ　6画 口部

吐 吐吐吐吐吐吐

❶ [动] 使东西从嘴里出来：spit; force sth. out of one's mouth | ～核儿 tǔhúr *spit out the pips* / 不要随地～痰。Bùyào suídì tǔtán. *No spitting.*

❷ [动] 说出来：say; tell; speak out | 谈～tántǔ *style of conversation* / ～露实情 tǔlù shíqíng *come out with the truth* / ～字清楚 tǔzì qīngchu *enunciate clearly*

❸ [动]（从口或缝隙里）长出或露出：put forth; send out; grow or expose from an opening or a seam | 蚕在～丝。Cán zài tǔsī. *The silkworm is spinning silk.*
　　See tù.

吐 tù　6画 口部

吐 吐吐吐吐吐吐

[动]（消化道或呼吸道里的东西）不自主地从嘴里涌出：vomit; throw up | ～血 tùxiě *spit blood; haematemesis* / 上～下泻 shàngtù-xiàxiè *suffer from vomiting and diarrhoea*
　　See tǔ.

兔 tù　8画 ⺈部

兔 兔兔兔兔兔兔兔兔

[名] rabbit; hare | 野～yětù *hare*
兔子 tùzi hare; rabbit

团 (團) tuán 6画 口部

团 团团团团团团

❶ [动] 聚集；会合：reunite; gather; assemble
团结 tuánjié unite; rally
团聚 tuánjù reunite; unite and gather
团圆 tuányuán reunion

❷ [名] 军队的编制单位，一般下辖若干营：regiment, military unit, subordinated to a division and commanding several battalions
团长 tuánzhǎng ① regimental commander ② head (chief, chairman) of a delegation, troupe, etc.

❸ [名] 工作或活动的集体：group; society; circle; collective for work or activities | 代表~dài-biǎotuán delegation / 旅行~lǚxíngtuán tour group; touring party
团队 tuánduì team; group; organization
团伙 tuánhuǒ gang; band; clique
团体 tuántǐ organization; group; team
集团 jítuán   剧团 jùtuán
社团 shètuán
乐团 yuètuán

❹ [名] 青少年的政治性组织，我国特指共产主义青年团：political organization for teenagers, referring to the Communist Youth League in China | 青年~qīng-niántuán Youth League
团员 tuányuán ① member ② member of the Communist Youth League of China; League member

❺ [量] 用于成团的东西：used for sth. shaped like a ball | 一~面 yī tuán miàn a lump of dough / 一~毛线 yī tuán máoxiàn a ball of wool / 一~碎纸yī tuán suìzhǐ a ball of paper scraps

推 tuī 11画 扌部

推 推推推推推推推推 推推推

❶ [动] 手向外用力使物体移动：push; thrust; shove | ~车 tuī chē push a cart / 把门~开 bǎ mén tuīkāi push the door open / 他把我从房间里~了出来。Tā bǎ wǒ cóng fángjiān li tuīle chūlai. He shoved me out of the room.
推出 tuīchū introduce; put out; present
推翻 tuīfān ① overthrow; overturn; topple ② cancel; reverse

❷ [动] 使事情开展：push forward; promote | 把工作向前~一步 bǎ gōngzuò xiàngqián tuī yī

734

bū *push ahead with one's work* / 又一批新产品被～上了市场。Yǒu yīpī xīn chǎnpǐn bèi tuīshàngle shìchǎng. *Another batch of new products has been put on the market.*

推动 tuīdòng push forward; promote; give impetus to

推广 tuīguǎng popularize; spread; extend

推进 tuījìn ① push on; advance ② move forward; drive on

推销 tuīxiāo promote sales; market; peddle

推行 tuīxíng carry out; pursue; practise

❸[动]把预定的时间向后延：delay; postpone; put off | 把会议～后两天 bǎ huìyì tuīhòu liǎng tiān *put off the meeting for two days*

推迟 tuīchí put off; postpone; defer

❹[动]举荐：recommend | 大家都～他当组长。Dàjiā dōu tuī tā dāng zǔzhǎng. *Everyone elected him as group leader unanimously.* / 你们～一个代表参加这个会。Nǐmen tuī yī gè dàibiǎo cānjiā zhège huì. *You are asked to recommend a delegate to attend the meeting.*

推荐 tuījiàn recommend

推选 tuīxuǎn elect; choose

❺[动]根据已知的求出或想到未知的：deduce; infer; form a judgement based on known facts | 类～lèituī *analogize; reason by analogy*

推测 tuīcè infer; conjecture; guess

推理 tuīlǐ inference; reasoning

推论 tuīlùn inference; deduction; corollary

推算 tuīsuàn calculate; reckon

❻[动]辞让；拒绝：decline; yield | ～让 tuīràng *decline* / 你问他什么，他都～说不知道。Nǐ wèn tā shénme, tā dōu tuīshuō bù zhīdào. *Whatever you ask, he always says he doesn't know.*

推辞 tuīcí decline (an appointment, invitation, etc.)

推来推去 tuīlái-tuīqù make all sorts of excuses; give the runaround

腿 tuǐ 13画 月部

腿 腿腿腿腿腿腿腿腿腿 腿腿腿腿腿

❶[名]leg | 把～抬起 bǎ tuǐ táiqǐ *raise one's leg*

大腿 dàtuǐ   小腿 xiǎotuǐ

拖后腿 tuōhòutuǐ

❷[名]器物下部像腿的东西：leg-like support beneath an object | 桌子～儿 zhuōzituǐr *legs of a table* / 我的眼镜～儿摔断了。Wǒ de yǎnjìngtuǐr shuāiduàn le.

735

The rim of my glasses got broken.

退 tuì 9画 辶部

退 退退退退退退退退退

❶ [动] 向后移动 (跟 "进jìn" 相对)：move backwards; retreat (the opposite of "进jìn") | ~敌 tuìdí *(in written) repulse the enemy* / 不进则~。Bùjìnzétuì. *Strive forward, or you'll fall behind.*

退步 tuìbù ① lag behind; retrogress ② leeway; room for manoeuvre

撤退 chètuì 倒退 dàotuì
后退 hòutuì

❷ [动] 离开；脱离：leave; quit; retire from | ~席 tuìxí *leave a banquet or a meeting* / ~学 tuìxué *quit school; drop out of school*

退出 tuìchū withdraw from; secede; quit

退休 tuìxiū retire

❸ [动] 下降；减退：decline; decrease; recede | ~色 tuìsè *(of colour) fade* / ~烧 tuìshāo *bring down a fever* / 潮水渐渐~了。Cháoshuǐ jiànjiàn tuì le. *The tide is receding little by little.*

退火 tuìhuǒ (Chin. med.) relieve inflammation or internal heat

衰退 shuāituì

❹ [动] 交还 (已收下或买下的东西)：return; refund; give back | ~钱 tuìqián *refund* / ~货 tuìhuò *return goods* / ~票 tuìpiào *return a ticket; get a refund for a ticket* / 快把这份礼~了。Kuài bǎ zhè fèn lǐ tuì le. *Return this gift right away.*

退还 tuìhuán return

退回 tuìhuí ① return; send (or give) back ② go (or turn) back

退税 tuìshuì (econ.) drawback

❺ [动] 撤销 (已定的事)：cancel; retract; break off

吞 tūn 7画 口部

吞 吞吞吞吞吞吞吞

❶ [动] 不嚼或不细嚼，整个或大块地咽下去：swallow; devour; gulp down | 狼~虎咽lángtūn-hǔyàn *gobble up; wolf down* / 孩子不小心~进去一个扣子。Háizi bù xiǎoxīn tūn jìnqu yī gè kòuzi. *The child carelessly swallowed a button.*

❷ [动] 侵占；兼并：annex; seize; take possession of | 独~dútūn *take exclusive possession of* / ~并 tūnbìng *annex; gobble up* / ~没 tūnmò *embezzle; swallow up*

屯 tún 4画 一部

屯 屯 屯 屯 屯

❶ [动] 聚集；储存：collect; gather; stock; get together; assemble | ～集 túnjí assemble; collect / ～积粮食 túnjī liángshi store up grain

❷ [动] (军队) 驻扎：station or quarter | ～兵 túnbīng station troops; quarter troops

❸ [名] 村庄：village

 托 tuō 6画 扌部

托 托 托 托 托 托

❶ [动] 用器物或手掌向上举着东西：lean against the palm; hold in the palm | ～举 tuōjǔ hold up / ～着下巴 tuōzhe xiàba cup one's chin in one's hands

❷ [动] 寄放：deposit; leave with 托儿所 tuō'érsuǒ nursery; child-care centre; creche

❸ [动] 借故推辞：plead; give as a pretext | 推～ tuītuō plead; offer as an excuse / ～故 tuōgù give a pretext; make an excuse / ～病 tuōbìng plead illness

❹ [动] 请人代办：entrust; ask | ～你买本书。Tuō nǐ mǎi běn shū. Please buy a book for me. / 她～我寄这封信 Tā tuō wǒ jì

zhè fēng xìn. *She asked me to mail this letter for her.*

托管 tuōguǎn trusteeship

托人情 tuōrénqíng ask an influential person to help arrange sth.; gain one's end through pull; seek the good offices of sb.

拜托 bàituō 寄托 jìtuō
委托 wěituō 信托 xìntuō
依托 yītuō 嘱托 zhǔtuō

◇摩托艇 mótuōtǐng

 拖 tuō 8画 扌部

拖 拖 拖 拖 拖 拖 拖 拖

❶ [动] 牵引；拉：pull; drag; tug; haul | ～车 tuōchē *trailer* / 大船后边～着一只小船。Dà-chuán hòubian tuōzhe yī zhī xiǎochuán. *The big boat tugged a small one behind it.*

拖后腿 tuōhòutuǐ hinder (or impede) sb.; hold sb. back; be a drag on sb.

拖拉机 tuōlājī tractor

❷ [动] 在身体后面垂着：trail; drag behind one's body | ～着一根长辫子 tuōzhe yī gēn cháng biànzi *wear a long pigtail* / 她的长裙～在地板上。Tā de cháng qún tuō zài dìbǎn shang. *Her long skirt dragged on the floor.*

拖鞋 tuōxié slipper

❸ [动] 延长时间：delay; postpone; drag on | ～时间 tuō shíjiān

play for time; stall (for time) / 房租他总是~着不交。Fángzū tā zǒngshì tuōzhe bù jiāo. *He is always behind with his rent.* / 会议一直~到晚上。Huìyì yīzhí tuōdǎo wǎnshang. *The meeting was prolonged into the evening.*

拖欠 tuōqiàn be behind in payment; be in arrears; default
拖延 tuōyán delay; put off; procrastinate

脱 tuō 11画 月部

脱 脱脱脱脱脱脱脱 脱脱脱

❶ [动] (皮肤、毛发等)掉下: (of skin, hair, etc.) shed; drop; lose; come or fall out | ~皮 tuōpí *shed skin* / ~毛 tuōmáo *shed; lose hair or feathers* / 爷爷的头发都~光了。Yéye de tōufa dōu tuōguāng le. *Grandpa's hair has all fallen out.*

脱落 tuōluò drop; fall off (away); come off
❷ [动] 取下; 除去(跟"穿 chuān"相对): take off; cast off (the opposite of "穿 chuān") | ~鞋 tuō xié *take off one's shoes* / ~衣服 tuō yīfu *take off one's clothes*
❸ [动] 离开: get out of; break away from | 逃~ táotuō *escape*

/ ~险 tuōxiǎn *escape danger*
脱离 tuōlí separate oneself from; break away from; be divorced from
摆脱 bǎituō

驮 (馱) tuō 6画 马部

驮 驮驮驮驮驮驮

[动] 用背负载: carry or bear on the back | ~东西 tuó dōngxi *carry things on the back* / 他~着我过了河。Tā tuózhe wǒ guòle hé. *He carried me on his back across the river.*

妥 tuǒ 7画 心部

妥 妥妥妥妥妥妥妥

❶ [形] 适当; 稳当: appropriate; proper; suitable; sound | 这样处理恐怕不~。Zhèyàng chǔlǐ kǒngpà bù tuǒ. *I'm afraid this isn't the proper way to handle the case.*

妥当 tuǒdang appropriate; proper
妥善 tuǒshàn appropriate; proper; well arranged
稳妥 wěntuǒ
❷ [形] 齐备: ready; settled; finished | 事情已办~了。Shìqing yǐ bàntuǒ le. *It has been settled.*

◇妥协 tuǒxié come to terms; compromise

椭 (橢) tuǒ　12画 木部

椭 椭椭椭椭椭椭椭椭
椭椭椭椭

[形] 长圆形：oval; ellipse
椭圆 tuǒyuán ellipse

唾 tuò　11画 口部

唾 唾唾唾唾唾唾唾唾
唾唾唾

[名] 唾液：saliva; spittle
唾沫 tuòmo saliva; spittle

W w

挖
wā　9画　扌部

挖 | 挖挖挖挖挖挖挖挖挖

[动] 用工具或用手掘；掏：dig; excavate ｜ ～土 wā tǔ *dig earth* / ～洞 wā dòng *dig a hole*
挖掘 wājué dig; excavate

蛙
wā　12画　虫部

蛙 | 蛙蛙蛙蛙蛙蛙蛙蛙蛙蛙蛙蛙

[名] 青蛙：*frog*
青蛙 qīngwā

娃
wá　9画　女部

娃 | 娃娃娃娃娃娃娃娃娃

[名] 小孩儿：baby; child ｜ 女～儿 nǚwár *baby girl; little girl*
娃娃 wáwa baby; child

瓦
wǎ　4画　瓦部

瓦 | 瓦瓦瓦瓦瓦

[名] 覆盖屋顶的建筑材料：tile ｜ ～房 wǎfáng *tile-roofed house*
瓦解 wǎjiě disintegrate; collapse; crumble
◇瓦斯 wǎsī gas

袜 (襪)
wà　10画　衤部

袜 | 袜袜袜袜袜袜袜袜袜袜

[名] socks; stockings; hose ｜ 尼龙～ nílóngwà *nylon socks*
袜子 wàzi socks; stockings; hose
长筒袜 chángtǒngwà

哇
wa　9画　口部

哇 | 哇哇哇哇哇哇哇哇哇

[助] 用在句子末尾，加重语气：used at the end of a sentence for emphasis ｜ 多好～! Duō hǎo wa! *Oh, how nice it is!* / 你别哭～。Nǐ bié kū wa. *Don't cry.*

歪
wāi　9画　一部

歪 | 歪歪歪歪歪歪歪歪歪

❶ [形] 斜；偏（跟"正 zhèng"相对）：inclined; slanting (the opposite of "正 zhèng") ｜ ～着头 wāizhe tóu *with one's head tilted to one side* / 这张画挂～

W

了。Zhè zhāng huà guàwāi le. *The picture on the wall is slanted.* / 他总是~戴着帽子。Tā zǒngshì wāidài- zhe màozi. *He always wears his hat at an angle.*

❷ [形] 不正当的；不正派的：devious, crooked ｜ ~风 wāifēng *evil tendency; unhealthy trend* 歪曲 wāiqū twist; misrepresent

---

外 wài 5画 夕部

外 外外外外外

❶ [名] (空间、处所) 外边，不在某种界限或范围之内的 (跟 "内 nèi" 或 "里 lǐ" 相对)：out; outside (the opposite of "内 nèi" or "里 lǐ") ｜ 从里向~走。Cóng lǐ xiàng wài zǒu. *Walk from the inside to the outside.* / 箱子先放在门~吧! Xiāngzi xiān fàng zài ménwài ba! *Put the suitcase outside for now.* / 请不要把头伸出车~。Qǐng bùyào bǎ tóu shēnchū chēwài. *Don't stick your head out of the window.*

外边 wàibian ① outside; out ② a place other than where one lives or works

外表 wàibiǎo outward appearance; surface

外部 wàibù ① outside; external ② exterior; surface

外出 wàichū go out

外观 wàiguān outward appearance; exterior

外行 wàiháng layman; outsider

外界 wàijiè ① external world ② outside

外科 wàikē surgical department

外力 wàilì ① outside force ② external force

外流 wàiliú outflow; drain

外卖 wàimài ① (usu. prepared by a restaurant or a food shop) takeaway ② food for takeaway

外面 wàimian outside; out

外套 wàitào ① overcoat ② loose coat; outer garment

外头 wàitou outside; out

外形 wàixíng appearance; external form; contour

外衣 wàiyī coat; jacket; outer clothing; outer garment

国外 guówài　　海外 hǎiwài
户外 hùwài　　境外 jìngwài
老外 lǎowài　　内外 nèiwài
室外 shìwài　　野外 yěwài
捞外快 lāowàikuài
门外汉 ménwàihàn

❷ [形] 特指外国的：foreign ｜ 中~合资 zhōngwài hézī *joint venture with Chinese and foreign capital* / 对~贸易 duìwài màoyì *foreign trade* / 他在一家~资企业工作。Tā zài yī jiā wàizī qǐyè gōngzuò. *He works in a foreign enterprise.*

外币 wàibì foreign currency

外宾 wàibīn foreign guest

外电 wàidiàn dispatches from foreign news agencies

外国 wàiguó foreign country

外交 wàijiāo diplomacy; foreign affairs

外汇 wàihuì foreign exchange

外事 wàishì foreign affairs; external affairs

外文 wàiwén foreign language

外语 wàiyǔ foreign language

外资 wàizī foreign capital

外国语 wàiguóyǔ foreign language

外交官 wàijiāoguān diplomat

涉外 shèwài   中外 zhōngwài

古今中外 gǔjīn-zhōngwài

❸ [形] 指自己所在地以外的：other | ~省 wàishěng *other provinces*

外地 wàidì parts of the country other than where one is; other places

❹ [形] 在一定界限之外的；另外：besides; in addition; beyond | 课~ kèwài *after class* / ~加 wàijiā *in addition to* / 此~ cǐwài *apart from this; besides this* / 计划~ jìhuà wài *unplanned*

除外 chúwài	额外 éwài
分外 fènwài	格外 géwài
例外 lìwài	另外 lìngwài
以外 yǐwài	意外 yìwài
之外 zhīwài	

❺ [形] 家庭成员中女性一方的亲戚：(relatives) of one's mother, sisters or daughters | ~孙 wàisūn *grandson; daughter's son*

外公 wàigōng (maternal) grandfather

外婆 wàipó (maternal) grandmother

外孙女 wàisūnnǚ daughter's daughter; granddaughter

外祖父 wàizǔfù (maternal) grandfather

外祖母 wàizǔmǔ (maternal) grandmother

 弯 (彎) wān 9画 弓部

弯 弯弯弯弯弯弯弯弯弯

❶ [形] 不直：curved; crooked | 树枝被雪压~了。Shùzhī bèi xuě yāwān le. *The branches are weighed down by the snow.*

弯曲 wānqū bend; meander

绕弯子 ràowānzi

走弯路 zǒuwānlù

❷ [动] 使不直：bend | ~腰 wānyāo *bend over* / ~着身子 wān zhe shēnzi *bend over (one's body)*

❸ [名] 曲折不直的部分：bend; turn | 转~抹角 zhuǎnwānmòjiǎo *beat about the bush; speak in a roundabout way* / 这条路有个~儿。Zhè tiáo lù yǒu ge wānr. *There is a bend in the*

弯

wān

W

742

road.

拐弯 guǎiwān 转弯 zhuǎnwān

湾 (灣) wān 12画 氵部

湾湾湾湾湾湾湾湾
湾湾湾湾

❶ [名] 水流弯曲的地方：bend of a river | 河～héwān *river bend*
❷ [名] 海岸向陆地凹入的地方：bay; gulf | 港～gǎngwān *gulf; bay*

豌 wān 15画 豆部

豌豌豌豌豌豌豌豌
豌豌豌豌豌豌豌

See 豌豆

豌豆 wāndòu pea

丸 wán 3画 丿部

丸 丸九丸

[量] 用于丸药：used for pill, bolus | 一～药 yī wán yào *a pill (bolus)* / 这种药一次吃三～。Zhè zhǒng yào yī cì chī sān wán. *Take three pills each time.*

完 wán 7画 宀部

完 完完完完完完完

❶ [形] 齐全；完整：intact; whole

| ～好 wánhǎo *in good condition; intact* / ～满 wánmǎn *perfect* / ～美无缺 wánměi-wúquē *perfect; flawless*

完备 wánbèi complete; perfect

完美 wánměi perfect; consummate

完全 wánquán whole

完善 wánshàn complete

完整 wánzhěng intact

❷ [动] 完成；全部做好：fulfil; complete | ～工 wángōng *complete a project; get through* / 他翻译的那部小说已经全部～稿。Tā fānyì de nà bù xiǎoshuō yǐjīng quánbù wángǎo. *He has finished translating that novel.*

完成 wánchéng complete

❸ [动] 结束：be finished; be over | 电影演～了。Diànyǐng yǎnwán le. *The movie is over.* / 鱼离开水，生命就～了。Yú líkāi shuǐ, shēngmìng jiù wán le. *A fish will die when it's taken away from water.*

完毕 wánbì finish; complete; end

完蛋 wándàn (inf.) be done for; be finished

完工 wángōng complete a project; finish doing sth.; get through

❹ [动] 用光；没有剩余：run out; use up | 信封用～了。Xìnfēng

W

yōngwán le. *The envelopes are all used up.* / 煤烧~了。Méi shāowán le. *The coal ran out.*

玩 wán 8画 王部

玩 玩玩玩玩玩玩玩玩玩

❶ [动] 不严肃认真对待；戏弄：trifle with; treat lightly │ ~世的态度 wánshì de tàidu *take a cynical attitude towards life; be cynical*

玩弄 wánnòng ① resort to; employ ② dally with ③ play with; juggle with

❷ [动] 使用（不正当的方法、手段等）：resort to (oft. foul play) │ 花招儿 wán huāzhāor *play tricks* / ~手段 wán shǒuduàn *play tricks; resort to crafty manoeuvres*

❸ [动] 游戏；做某种游戏：engage in some kinds of sports or re-creational activities │ ~足球 wán zúqiú *play football* / ~扑克 wán pūkè *play cards*

玩具 wánjù toy; plaything

玩笑 wánxiào joke

玩意儿 wányìr gadget

游玩 yóuwán

好玩儿 hǎowánr

顽 (頑) wán 10画 页部

顽 顽顽顽顽顽顽顽顽 顽顽

❶ [形] 固执；不容易开导或制伏：stubborn; obstinate │ ~抗 wánkàng *stubbornly resist*

顽固 wángù stubborn

顽强 wánqiáng indomitable; staunch

❷ [形] （小孩子）不听劝导；爱玩闹：naughty; mischievous │ ~童 wántóng *naughty child*

顽皮 wánpí naughty; mischievous

挽 wǎn 10画 扌部

挽 挽挽挽挽挽挽挽挽 挽挽

❶ [动] 拉；牵引：draw; pull │ 手~着手 shǒu wǎnzhe shǒu *arm in arm; hand in hand*

❷ [动] 向上卷：roll up │ ~起袖子干了起来 wǎnqǐ xiùzi gānle qǐlai *roll up one's sleeves and begin to work*

◇挽回 wǎnhuí retrieve; redeem

挽救 wǎnjiù save; remedy; rescue

晚 wǎn 11画 日部

晚 晚晚晚晚晚晚晚晚 晚晚晚

❶ [名] 晚上：evening; night │ 今~jīnwǎn *this evening*; to-

744

night / 从早到～cóng zǎo dào wǎn *from morning till night* / 天太～了，快睡吧! Tiān tài wǎn le, kuài shuì ba! *It's getting late. Go to bed now.*

晚报 wǎnbào evening paper

晚餐 wǎncān supper; dinner

晚饭 wǎnfàn supper; dinner

晚会 wǎnhuì evening party

晚上 wǎnshang evening; night

傍晚 bàngwǎn

当晚 dàngwǎn

夜晚 yèwǎn

昨晚 zuówǎn

❷[形] 迟；比规定的或合适的时间靠后：late | 来～了 láiwǎn le *be late for (sth.)* / 天已很～。Tiān yǐ hěn wǎn le. *It's late already.* / 你8点钟去就～了。Nǐ bā diǎn zhōng qù jiù wǎn le. *You'll be late if you leave at 8 o'clock.*

早晚 zǎowǎn

❸[形] 时间靠后的；临近终了的：late; belated | ～期 wǎnqī *later period* / ～秋 wǎnqiū *late autumn*

晚年 wǎnnián old age; one's later years

wǎn   11画 忄部

惋惋惋惋惋惋惋惋惋惋惋

[动] 痛惜；同情：regret; feel sorry for

惋惜 wǎnxī have pity for; regret; sympathize

wǎn   13画 石部

碗碗碗碗碗碗碗碗碗碗碗碗碗

[名] 盛饮食的器具：bowl | 饭～ fànwǎn *bowl (for rice)* / 茶～ cháwǎn *bowl (for tea); teacup*

铁饭碗 tiěfànwǎn

（萬） wàn   3画 一部

万万万

❶[数] 十个千：ten thousand | 一千～人 yī qiānwàn rén *ten million people* / 一～元钱 yīwàn yuán qián *ten thousand yuan*

千万 qiānwàn   亿万 yìwàn

❷[数] 很多；数量极大：large number; myriad | ～物 wànwù *myriads of objects* / ～家灯火 wànjiā dēnghuǒ *myriad twinkling lights (of a city)*

万岁 wànsuì long live

万古长青 wàngǔ-chángqīng remain fresh forever; be ever-lasting

万事如意 wànshì-rúyì all's well and propitious; everything goes as one wishes

万水千山 wànshuǐ-qiānshān ten thousand crags and torrents; the trials of a long journey

千变万化 qiānbiàn-wànhuà
千家万户 qiānjiā-wànhù
千军万马 qiānjūn-wànmǎ
千千万万 qiānqiān-wànwàn

❸[副] 表示程度极高，相当于"非常 fēicháng""绝对 juéduì"：absolutely; by all means; extremely; very, same as "非常 fēicháng""绝对 juéduì" | ~难 wànnán *extremely difficult; utterly impossible* / 千真~确 qiānzhēn-wànquè *absolutely true*

万万 wànwàn absolutely; wholly

◇万一 wànyī ① just in case; eventuality ② a very small percentage

汪 wāng 7画 氵部

汪 汪汪汪汪汪汪汪

[形] 水深而广：(of water) deep and vast
汪洋 wāngyáng vast; boundless

亡 wáng 3画 亠部

亡 亡亡亡

❶[动] 灭亡(跟"兴xīng"相对)：perish; doom (the opposite of

"兴 xīng") | ~国 wángguó *subjugate a nation*

❷[动] 死；die; perish | 伤~shāngwáng *injuries and deaths; casualties*
死亡 sǐwáng

王 wáng 4画 王部

王 王王王王

❶[名] 最高统治者；最高的爵位：king; monarch | 女~nǚwáng *queen* / 国~guówáng *king*
王朝 wángcháo ① imperial court; royal court ② dynasty
王宫 wánggōng (imperial) palace
王国 wángguó kingdom
王后 wánghòu queen consort; queen
王室 wángshì ① royal family ② imperial court; royal court
王子 wángzǐ king's son; prince
大王 dàwáng

❷[名] 首领；头目：chieftain; ringleader | 蜂~fēngwáng *queen bee; queen wasp* / 老虎是兽中之~。Lǎohǔ shì shòu zhōng zhī wáng. *The tiger is the king of the animals.*
霸王 bàwáng

网 (網) wǎng 6画 门部

网 网 网 网 网 网 网

❶ [名] 用绳、丝等结成的捕鱼或捉鸟兽的工具：net | 结~jiéwǎng *weave a net* / 渔~yúwǎng *fishnet; fishing net*

❷ [名] 形状像网的东西：sth. resembling a net | 电~diànwǎng *power grid* / 球~qiúwǎng *net (for ball games)* / 蜘蛛~zhīzhūwǎng *cobweb; spider web*

网吧 wǎngbā cybercafe; Internet bar

网络 wǎngluò ① network ② (elec.) network

网民 wǎngmín netizen

网球 wǎngqiú tennis

网页 wǎngyè web page

网友 wǎngyǒu netizen; net friends

网站 wǎngzhàn website

网址 wǎngzhǐ website address

法网 fǎwǎng

联网 liánwǎng

上网 shàngwǎng

互联网 hùliánwǎng

往 wǎng 8画 彳部

往 往 往 往 往 往 往 往

❶ [动] 去；向某处去：go | 人来人~rénlái-rénwǎng *(of people) coming and going* / 这列火车开~北京。Zhè liè huǒchē kāiwǎng Běijīng. *This train is leaving for Beijing.*

往返 wǎngfǎn ① come and go ② journey to and fro

往来 wǎnglái ① contact; dealings ② come and go

交往 jiāowǎng 来往 láiwǎng

前往 qiánwǎng 通往 tōngwǎng

向往 xiàngwǎng

❷ [介] 朝；向；表示动作的方向：in the direction of; to; towards | ~前看 wǎng qián kàn *look forward*

往后 wǎnghòu from now on; in the future

❸ [形] 从前的；过去的：past; previous

往常 wǎngcháng as usual; as one used to do

往年 wǎngnián (in) former years

往日 wǎngrì (in) former days; (in) bygone days

往事 wǎngshì past events; the past

以往 yǐwǎng

◇ 往往 wǎngwǎng often; more often than not; as usual

妄 wàng 6画 女部

妄 妄 妄 妄 妄 妄

[形] 不合实际；不近情理：absurd; rash | ～动 wàngdòng *act rashly*

妄图 wàngtú *vainly attempt; try in vain*

妄想 wàngxiǎng *vainly hope to do sth.*

狂妄 kuángwàng

忘 wàng 7画 心部

忘 忘忘忘忘忘忘忘

[动] 不记得：forget | 这件事别～了。Zhè jiàn shì bié wàng le. *Don't forget it.* / 别～了给她写信。Bié wàngle gěi tā xiěxìn. *Don't forget to write to her.* / 我把钥匙～在家里了。Wǒ bǎ yàoshi wàng zài jiāli le. *I left my keys at home.*

忘记 wàngjì *forget; overlook; neglect; dismiss from one's mind*

忘却 wàngquè *forget*

难忘 nánwàng

备忘录 bèiwànglù

旺 wàng 8画 日部

旺 旺旺旺旺旺旺旺旺

[形] 兴盛：prosperous; flourishing | ～季 wàngjì *peak period; busy season* / 火很～。Huǒ hěn wàng. *The fire is blazing.* / 花开得正～。

Huā kāi de zhèng wàng. *The flowers are in full bloom.*

旺盛 wàngshèng *vigorous; exuberant*

兴旺 xīngwàng

望 wàng 11画 王部

望 望望望望望望望望望 望望望

❶ [动] 向远处看：look over; gaze into the distance | 登高远～dēnggāo yuǎnwàng *ascend a height to enjoy a distant view* / ～不到边 wàng budào biān *boundless; vast; limitless*

望远镜 wàngyuǎnjìng *telescope*

观望 guānwàng

展望 zhǎnwàng

张望 zhāngwàng

❷ [名] 名声；声誉：reputation; prestige; expect

威望 wēiwàng

❸ [动] 盼望；希望：hope; expect | 丰收有～fēngshōu yǒuwàng *a hope of a bumper harvest* / ～准时到会。Wàng zhǔnshí dào huì. *Punctuality is required for the meeting.*

绝望 juéwàng   渴望 kěwàng

盼望 pànwàng   期望 qīwàng

失望 shīwàng   希望 xīwàng

欲望 yùwàng 愿望 yuànwàng
指望 zhǐwàng

❹[动] 探视；看望：call on; visit | 拜～bàiwàng *visit to pay one's respect*

看望 kànwàng 探望 tànwàng

危 wēi 6画 厃部

危 危危危危危危

❶[形] 不安全：dangerous | ～难 wēinàn *calamity; danger and disaster* / 转～为安 zhuǎnwēi-wēi'ān *take a turn for the better and be out of danger; pull through*

危机 wēijī crisis
危急 wēijí critical
危险 wēixiǎn danger
高危 gāowēi

❷[动] 使不安全；损害：endanger; imperil | ～及生命 wēijí shēng-mìng *endanger one's life*
危害 wēihài harm; jeopardize

威 wēi 9画 戈部

威 威威威威威威威威威

❶[名] 使人敬畏的气势或使人畏惧的力量：impressive strength; might
威风 wēifēng ① power and prestige ② imposing

威力 wēilì power; might
威望 wēiwàng reputation
威信 wēixìn prestige; popular trust
权威 quánwēi 示威 shìwēi

❷[动] 凭借威力制服或压迫：deter (threaten) by force | ～逼 wēibī *threaten by force; coerce*
威胁 wēixié bully; threaten; intimidate

微 wēi 13画 彳部

微 微微微微微微微微微 微微微微微

[形] 小；轻微：minute; tiny | 细～ xìwēi *minute; tiny* / ～风 wēi-fēng *gentle breeze* / ～生物 wēishēngwù *microorganism; microbe*

微观 wēiguān microcosmic
微妙 wēimiào delicate; subtle
微弱 wēiruò faint; feeble; weak
微小 wēixiǎo small; little
微笑 wēixiào smile
微型 wēixíng miniature; mini-
微波炉 wēibōlú microwave oven
微不足道 wēibùzúdào insignificant; inconsiderable; negligible; trivial
略微 lüèwēi 轻微 qīngwēi
稍微 shāowēi

W

为 (爲) wéi 4画 、部

为 为 为 为 为

❶ [动] 做：do; act | 我一定尽力而～。Wǒ yīdìng jìnlì'érwéi. *I will definitely try my best.*

为难 wéinán ① feel awkward ② make things difficult for

人为 rénwéi   行为 xíngwéi
大有可为 dàyǒu-kěwéi
无能为力 wúnéng-wéilì

❷ [动] 充当；担任：act as; serve as | 选他～班长 xuǎn tā wéi bānzhǎng *elect him as the monitor* / 以你～榜样 yǐ nǐ wéi bǎngyàng *take you as the model*

为首 wéishǒu with sb. as the leader; headed (led) by

称为 chēngwéi   认为 rènwéi
以为 yǐwéi   作为 zuòwéi

❸ [动] 变成；成为：become | 一分～二 yīfēnwéi'èr *divide one into two* / 变荒漠～绿洲 biàn huāngmò wéi lǜzhōu *turn the desert into an oasis*

变为 biànwéi   成为 chéngwéi

❹ [动] 是：be | 学习期限～两年。Xuéxí qīxiàn wéi liǎng nián. *The study period is two years.*

❺ [介] 被（跟"所 suǒ"搭配使用）：(used with "所 suǒ" in passive voice) | ～人所笑 wéi rén suǒ xiào *be laughed at*

◇为期 wéiqī by a definite date
为止 wéizhǐ up to; till
See wèi.

违 (違) wéi 7画 辶部

违 违 违 违 违 违 违

[动] 不遵守；不依从：disobey; violate | ～章 wéizhāng *break rules and regulations* / ～约 wéiyuē *break a contract; violate a treaty*

违背 wéibèi run counter to; go against

违法 wéifǎ break the law

违反 wéifǎn violate; run counter to; transgress; infringe

违犯 wéifàn violate; infringe; infract

围 (圍) wéi 7画 囗部

围 围 围 围 围 围 围

❶ [动] 四面拦住；环绕：enclose; surround | ～墙 wéiqiáng *enclosing wall; enclosure* / 青年人～着火跳起舞来。Qīngniánrén wéizhe huǒ tiàoqǐ wǔ lai. *Young people began to dance around the fire.* / 人们都～过来听他讲。Rénmen dōu wéi guòlai tīng tā jiǎng. *People gathered around him to listen.*

围攻 wéigōng ① besiege ② jointly attack sb.

围巾 wéijīn scarf; muffler

围棋 wéiqí a game played with black and white pieces on a board of 361 crosses; go

围绕 wéirào ① round; around ② centre on

包围 bāowéi

❷ [名] 四周：around; all round | 外～wàiwéi *periphery* / 四～都是山。Sìwéi dōushì shān. *It's encircled by mountains.*

范围 fànwéi　　周围 zhōuwéi

◇ 入围 rùwéi

　　wéi　10画 木部

桅桅桅桅桅桅桅桅桅桅

See 桅杆

桅杆 wéigān mast

唯　　wéi　11画 口部

唯唯唯唯唯唯唯唯唯唯唯

[副] 单单；只：only; alone | ～恐 wéikǒng *for fear (that)*

唯独 wéidú alone

唯一 wéiyī only

唯物论 wéiwùlùn materialism

唯心论 wéixīnlùn idealism

唯物主义 wéiwù zhǔyì materialism

唯心主义 wéixīn zhǔyì idealism

维 (維) wéi　11画 纟部

维维维维维维维维维维维

[动] 保持；保护：maintain; safeguard; preserve

维持 wéichí keep; maintain; preserve; support

维护 wéihù safeguard; uphold; upkeep; defend; keep

维修 wéixiū repair; service; maintain

维生素 wéishēngsù vitamin

伟 (偉) wěi　6画 亻部

伟伟伟伟伟伟

[形] 优异；超出寻常：great | 雄～ xióngwěi *magnificent*

伟大 wěidà great; grandeur

伪 (僞) wěi　6画 亻部

伪伪伪伪伪伪

[形] 假的（跟"真 zhēn"相对）：false; fake (the opposite of "真 zhēn") | ～装 wěizhuāng

pretend; feign

伪造 wěizào forge; fabricate; falsify

伪君子 wěijūnzǐ hypocrite

防伪 fángwěi 　　虚伪 xūwěi

尾尾尾尾尾尾尾

wěi　　7画 尸部

❶ [名] 尾巴: tail | 摇头摆 ~ yáotóu-bǎiwěi *shake the head and wag the tail; assume an air of complacency or levity*

尾巴 wěiba tail; tail-like part

❷ [名] 事物的末端: end | 船 ~ chuánwěi *stern* / 年 ~ niánwěi *end of the year* / 有头无 ~ yǒutóu-wúwěi *to leave sth. half done; to have a beginning but no end*

尾气 wěiqì tail gas

❸ [名] 主要部分以外的部分; 最后的阶段: remaining part; remnant | 这项工程该收 ~ 了。Zhè xiàng gōngchéng gāi shōuwěi le. *The remaining part of the project should be accomplished in time.*

尾声 wěishēng ① (mus.) coda ② epilogue ③ end

从头到尾 cóngtóu-dàowěi

❹ [量] 用于鱼: used for fish | 一 ~ 鱼 yī wěi yú *one fish*

委委委委委委委委

wěi　　8画 禾部

❶ [名] 请人代办: entrust; appoint | ~ 派 wěipài *appoint; delegate; designate* / ~ 以重任 wěiyǐ zhòngrèn *entrust an important task to sb.*

委托 wěituō entrust; commit

❷ [名] 委员会、委员的简称: (abbr. for 委员 wěiyuán or 委员会 wěiyuánhuì) committee member, committee | 市 ~ shìwěi *municipal Party committee* / 编 ~ biānwěi *editorial board*

委员 wěiyuán committee member

委员会 wěiyuánhuì committee; commission; council

常委 chángwěi

党委 dǎngwěi

居委会 jūwěihuì

◇委屈 wěiqu ① feel wronged; nurse a grievance ② put sb. to great inconvenience

卫 (衛) wěi　　3画 卩部

卫 卫卫卫

[动] 保护; 防守: defend; guard; protect | 护 ~ hùwèi *safeguard; protect* / 保家 ~ 国 bǎojiā-wèiguó *protect our homes and de-*

fend our country

卫生 wèishēng hygiene; health; sanitation

卫生间 wèishēngjiān toilet (room)

保卫 bǎowèi　捍卫 hànwèi

警卫 jǐngwèi　自卫 zìwèi

◇卫星 wèixīng artificial satellite

 为 (爲) wèi　4画 、部

为 为 为 为 为

❶ [介] 引进动作的受益者；给：(used to introduce the object of one's act or service) in the interest of; for | 不必～我担心。Bùbì wèi wǒ dānxīn. *No need to worry about me.* / 我真～你高兴。Wǒ zhēn wèi nǐ gāoxìng. *I am really happy for you.* / 他～这本书写了一篇序。Tā wèi zhè běn shū xiěle yī piān xù. *He wrote a preface for the book.*

❷ [介] 表示原因；目的：for the purpose of; for the sake of | ～我们合作愉快干杯! Wèi wǒmen hézuò yúkuài gānbēi! *A toast to our happy cooperation!*

为何 wèihé why; for what reason

为了 wèile for; for the sake of; in order to

为什么 wèishénme why; why (how) is it that

舍己为人 shějǐ-wèirén

See wéi.

 未 wèi　5画 一部

未 未 未 未 未 未

❶ [副] 没有(跟"已yǐ"相对)：have not; did not (the opposite of "已yǐ") | ～成年 wèichéngnián *under age; not yet of age* / 他的健康还～恢复。Tā de jiànkāng hǎiwèi huīfù. *He has not recovered yet.*

未来 wèilái ① future; tomorrow ② coming; next

未成年人 wèichéngniánrén (leg.) minor

从未 cóngwèi　尚未 shàngwèi

前所未有 qiánsuǒwèiyǒu

❷ [副] 不：no; not | ～知可否 wèizhī kěfǒu *not know whether it can be done* / ～经调查，不能下结论。Wèi jīng diàochá, bùnéng xià jiélùn. *We can't jump to conclusions without looking into the facts.*

未必 wèibì may not; not necessarily

未免 wèimiǎn rather; a bit too; truly

 位 wèi　7画 亻部

位 位 位 位 位 位 位

❶ [名] 位置；所在的地方：place;

location

位于 wèiyú locate; situate

位置 wèizhi ① seat; place ② position

部位 bùwèi　　车位 chēwèi

床位 chuángwèi

错位 cuòwèi　　单位 dānwèi

到位 dàowèi　　定位 dìngwèi

价位 jiàwèi　　水位 shuǐwèi

席位 xíwèi　　越位 yuèwèi

座位 zuòwèi

❷ [名] 职务；地位：position

地位 dìwèi　　岗位 gǎngwèi

学位 xuéwèi

❸ [量] 用于人（含敬意）：(polite form) used before people | 各～ gèwèi *everybody* / 一～朋友 yī wèi péngyou *a friend* / 家里来了几～客人。Jiāli láile jǐ wèi kèrén. *Some friends visit my home.*

诸位 zhūwèi

味 **wèi** 8画 口部

味 味味味味味味味味

❶ [名] 舌头尝东西所得到的感觉：taste; flavour | 甜～儿 tián wèir *sweet taste* / 这个菜～儿很鲜。Zhège cài wèir hěn xiān. *The dish tastes delicious.*

味道 wèidào taste; stink

味精 wèijīng monosodium glutamate; MSG

口味 kǒuwèi　　美味 měiwèi

滋味 zīwèi

津津有味 jīnjīn-yǒuwèi

❷ [名] 气味，鼻子闻东西所得到的感觉：smell; odour | 这个～儿很好闻。Zhège wèir hěn hǎowén. *It smells good.*

气味 qìwèi　　香味 xiāngwèi

❸ [名] 指某种菜肴；食品：delicacy | 美～ měiwèi *delicacy; delicious food* / 野～ yěwèi *game (as food)*

山珍海味 shānzhēn-hǎiwèi

❹ [名] 意味；情趣：interest; delight | 人情～儿很浓 rénqíng wèir hěn nóng *profound empathy* / 这书越看越有～儿。Zhè shū yuè kàn yuè yǒuwèir. *The more I read this book, the more interested I become.*

趣味 qùwèi

畏 **wèi** 9画 田部

畏 畏畏畏畏畏畏畏畏畏畏

[动] 害怕：fear | 无～ wúwèi *fearless; dauntless* / 不～艰苦 bù wèi jiānkǔ *fear no hardships*

畏惧 wèijù dread

胃 **wèi** 9画 田部

胃 胃胃胃胃胃胃胃胃胃胃

[名] stomach ｜ ~不舒服 wēi bù shūfu *have stomach ache* / 他经常~疼。 Tā jīngcháng wēiténg. *He often has stomach ache.* 胃病 wēibìng stomach trouble; gastricism

wēi 12画 口部

喂 喂喂喂喂喂喂喂喂 喂喂喂喂

❶ [动] 给动物吃东西；饲养： feed (an animal); raise ｜ ~鸡 wēi jī *feed chicken* / 牛已经~了。 Niú yǐjīng wēi le. *The cattle have been fed.*

❷ [动] 把食物送到别人的嘴里： send food into the mouth of a person ｜ ~奶 wēinǎi *breast-feed; nurse; suckle* / 给病人~饭 gěi bìngrén wēifàn *feed a patient*

❸ [叹] 招呼的声音： hello; hey ｜ ~，你是谁呀? Wēi, nǐ shì shéi ya? *Hello! Who is it?* / ~，别忘了给我来信。 Wēi, bié wàngle gěi wǒ lái xìn. *Hey, don't forget to write to me.*

wēi 15画 心部

慰 慰慰慰慰慰慰慰 慰慰慰慰慰慰

[动] 使人心情安适、平静： console; comfort ｜ ~劳 wēiláo *bring gifts or entertainment for sb.* 慰问 wēiwèn express sympathy to

安慰 ānwèi   欣慰 xīnwèi

wēn 12画 氵部

温 温温温温温温温温 温温温温

❶ [形] 不冷不热： warm; luke-warm ｜ ~水 wēnshuǐ *luke-warm water* / 夏天河水都是~的。 Xiàtiān héshuǐ dōu shì wēn de. *The river water is warm in summer.*
温带 wēndài temperate zone
温度 wēndù temperature; heat
温暖 wēnnuǎn ① warm ② warmth; kindness
温室 wēnshì hothouse; green-house; glasshouse; conservatory

❷ [动] 适当加热；使变暖： warm up ｜ ~酒 wēn jiǔ *warm up wine* / 把水~热点儿 bǎ shuǐ wēn rè diǎnr *warm up the water a little*

❸ [动] 复习： review; revise ｜ ~书 wēnshū *review a book* / ~习 wēnxí *review; brush up*

❹ [名] 温度： temperature ｜ 降~ jiàngwēn *lower the temperature*
温度计 wēndùjì thermograph;

755

thermometer

保温 bǎowēn　低温 dīwēn
高温 gāowēn　气温 qìwēn
体温 tǐwēn

❺ [形] 性情平和；宽厚：mild;
soft; tender | ～情 wēnqíng *ten-
der feeling; tender-heartedness* |
～顺 wēnshùn *docile; meek*

温和 wēnhé gentle; mild; temperate

温柔 wēnróu gentle; meek;
pleasingly affectionate

瘟 wēn 14画 疒部

瘟瘟瘟瘟瘟瘟瘟瘟
瘟瘟瘟瘟瘟瘟

[名] 急性传染病：acute contagious
diseases | ～病 wēnbìng (of
Chinese medical) seasonal fe-
vers

文 wén 4画 文部

文文文文

❶ [形] 非军事的事物（跟"武 wǔ"
相对）：civilian; civil (the op-
posite of "武 wǔ") | ～官
wénguān *civil official*

文人 wénrén man of letters;
scholar; literati

❷ [形] 柔和；不猛烈：gentle;
refined | ～弱 wénruò *gentle
and frail-looking* | ～火 wénhuǒ

slow fire; gentle heat

文雅 wényǎ elegant; refined

文竹 wénzhú (bot.) asparagus
fern (*Asparagus plumosus*)

斯文 sīwén

❸ [名] 自然界的某些规律性的现
象：certain natural phenomenon

天文 tiānwén

❹ [名] 字；文字：character; script;
writing | 外～wàiwén *foreign
language*

文句 wénjù sentences of an article

文本 wénběn text; version

文盲 wénmáng illiteracy

文字 wénzì writing; written language

德文 Déwén　俄文 Éwén
法文 Fǎwén　日文 Rìwén
语文 yǔwén　中文 Zhōngwén
白话文 báihuàwén

❺ [名] 文章；公文：literary com-
position; writing; official document

文件 wénjiàn document

文秘 wénmì secretary; secre-
tarial work; job or post related to
keeping documents and assist-
ing one's superior in handling
day-to-day affairs

文凭 wénpíng diploma

文书 wénshū ① document; of-
ficial dispatch ② copy clerk

文体 wéntǐ ① type of writing;
literary form; style ② recreation
and sports

文献 wénxiàn document; literature

文学 wénxué literature

文艺 wényì literature and art

文章 wénzhāng essay; article

文学家 wénxuéjiā writer; man of letters; literati

古文 gǔwén   课文 kèwén

论文 lùnwén   散文 sǎnwén

条文 tiáowén   杂文 záwén

征文 zhēngwén

作文 zuòwén

做文章 zuòwénzhāng

❻[名] 指社会科学：liberal arts | ～科 wénkē *arts* / ～教 wénjiào *culture and education*

❼[名] 文言：literary language; classical language

文言 wényán classical Chinese

◇文化 wénhuà ① civilization; culture ② schooling; education

文明 wénmíng ① civilized ② culture; civilization

文物 wénwù cultural relic; historical relic

闻（聞）wén   9画 门部

闻 闻 闻 闻 闻 闻 闻 闻 闻

❶[动] 听见：hear | 耳～ ěrwén *what one hears about*

闻名 wénmíng famous; renowned

举世闻名 jǔshì-wénmíng

❷[名] 听见的事情；消息：news; story | 见～ jiànwén *what one sees and hears; knowledge; information* / 奇～ qíwén *sth. unheard-of; thrilling, fantastic story* / 传～ chuánwén *hearsay*

丑闻 chǒuwén   新闻 xīnwén

❸[动] 用鼻子辨别气味：smell | 这种茶叶～起来很香。Zhè zhǒng cháyè wén qǐlai hěn xiāng. *This tea smells so fragrant.* / 你～这花多香啊! Nǐ wén zhè huā duō xiāng a! *Smell this flower and see how sweet it is!*

蚊 wén   10画 虫部

蚊 蚊 蚊 蚊 蚊 蚊 蚊 蚊 蚊 蚊

See 蚊子

蚊子 wénzi mosquito

吻 wěn   7画 口部

吻 吻 吻 吻 吻 吻 吻

❶[名] 嘴唇：lips | 接～ jiēwěn *kiss* / 亲～ qīnwěn *kiss*

❷[动] 用嘴唇接触：kiss | 母亲～着孩子的脸。Mǔqīn wěnzhe háizi de liǎn. *Mother is kissing her child's face.*

◇吻合 wěnhé ① be identical; coincide; tally ② (med.)

connect by anastomosis

稳 (穩) wěn 14画 禾部

稳 稳稳稳稳稳稳稳稳
稳稳稳稳稳稳

❶ [形] 稳固；平稳: steady; stable; firm | 船行得很～。Chuán xíng de hěn wěn. *The ship sails very steadily.* / 脚站～ jiǎo zhànwěn *stand steady; stand firm* / 把桌子放～ bǎ zhuōzi fàngwěn *set the table steady*

稳步 wěnbù with steady steps; steadily

稳当 wěndang reliable; secure; stable

稳定 wěndìng ① stabilize; steady ② stable; steady

稳固 wěngù ① firm; stable ② stabilize

稳健 wěnjiàn firm; steady

安稳 ānwěn   平稳 píngwěn

❷ [形] 妥帖；可靠: sure; certain; reliable | 这件事我拿得～。Zhè jiàn shì wǒ nádewěn. *I'm quite sure of it.*

稳妥 wěntuǒ reliable; sound; safe

问 (問) wèn 6画 门部

问 问问问问问问

❶ [动] 让人解答自己不知道或不清

楚的问题(跟 "答 dá" 相对): ask; inquire; seek information about (the opposite of "答 dá") | 不懂就～。Bù dǒng jiù wèn. *Ask for help when you meet problems.* / 我有件事要～你。Wǒ yǒu jiàn shì yào wèn nǐ. *I have something to ask you.* / 我想～你一个问题。Wǒ xiǎng wèn nǐ yī gè wèntí. *I would like to ask you a question.*

问答 wèndá question and answer

问卷 wènjuàn *questionnaire*

问路 wènlù ask the way

问题 wèntí ① problem; matter ② question; problem

反问 fǎnwèn   顾问 gùwèn
请问 qǐngwèn   提问 tíwèn
学问 xuéwen   询问 xúnwèn
疑问 yíwèn   追问 zhuīwèn

❷ [动] 关心地询问: ask after; inquire after | 前些日子他～到过你。Qiánxiē rìzi tā wèndàoguo nǐ. *He asked about you the other day.* / 我奶奶经常～起你呢! Wǒ nǎinai jīngcháng wènqǐ nǐ ne! *My grandmother often asks after you!*

问好 wènhǎo send one's regard to

问候 wènhòu extend greetings to

慰问 wèiwèn

❸ [动] 审讯；追究: interrogate;

examine | ～口供 wèn kǒu-gòng *interrogate (the accused)* / 法官正在～案子。Fǎguān zhèngzài wèn ànzi. *The judge is trying a case.*

❹ [动] 干预；管：intervene; interfere; care about | 不～bù guòwèn *not concern oneself with something*
过问 guòwèn

◇问世 wènshì be published; come out

窝（窩）wō　12画 穴部

窝窝窝窝窝窝窝窝
窝窝窝窝

❶ [名] 鸟兽、昆虫住的地方：nest | 鸟～niǎowō *bird's nest* / 鸡～jīwō *henhouse; roost* / 狗～gǒuwō *kennel; doghouse*
一窝蜂 yīwōfēng

❷ [名] 比喻坏人聚居的地方：place where evil-doers get together; lair; den | 贼～zéiwō *thieves' den*

❸ [名] 指人或物体所占的位置：place occupied by a human body or an object | 挪～儿 nuówōr *move to other place*

❹ [名] 凹进去的地方：hollow place; hollow part of the human body | 酒～jiǔwō *dimple* / 眼～yǎnwō *eye socket*

◇窝囊 wōnang ① feel vexed ②

good-for-nothing

我　wǒ　7画 丿部

我 我我我我我我我

❶ [代] 称呼自己或自己一方：I; me; we; our | ～校wǒ xiào *our school* / ～公司wǒ gōngsī *our company* / ～是学生。Wǒ shì xuésheng. *I am a student.* / 这是～的行李。Zhè shì wǒ de xíngli. *This is my luggage.*
我们 wǒmen we; us

❷ [代] 自己：self | 他的忘～精神十分可贵。Tā de wàngwǒ jīngshen shífēn kěguì. *His spirit of selflessness is very valuable.*
自我 zìwǒ

沃　wò　7画 氵部

沃 沃沃沃沃沃沃沃

[形] (土地) 肥：fertile; rich | ～土 wòtǔ *rich soil; fertile soil* / ～野 wòyě *fertile land; fertile fields*
肥沃 féiwò

卧　wò　8画 臣部

卧 卧卧卧卧卧卧卧卧

❶ [动] (人) 躺下；(动物) 趴着：lie; (of animals or birds) crouch; sit

｜～倒 wǒdǎo *lie down* ／～床
不起 wǒchuáng bùqǐ *be ill
and stay in bed* ／母鸡在窝里～
着。Mǔjī zài wō li wōzhe. *A hen
is sitting in the coop.*

❷ [动]睡觉：sleeping ｜～铺 wòpù
sleeping berth; sleeper
卧室 wòshì bedroom

◇ 软卧 ruǎnwò

握 wò 12画 扌部

握 握握握握握握握
握握握握

❶ [动]用手拿住，抓住：hold; grasp
｜孩子～着笔写字。Háizi wǒ-
zhe bǐ xiězì. *The child holds a
pen to write.* ／他把电影票～在
手里。Tā bǎ diànyǐngpiào
wǒ zài shǒuli. *He held the cinema ticket in his hand.*
握手 wòshǒu shake hands;
clasp hands

❷ [动]控制；掌握：hold; grasp
把握 bǎwò 掌握 zhǎngwò

乌 (烏) wū 4画 丿部

乌 乌乌乌乌

❶ [形]黑色：black; dark ｜～木
wūmù *ebony* ／～黑的头发 wū-
hēi de tóufa *dark hair*
乌云 wūyún black cloud; dark
cloud

❷ [名]乌鸦：crow
乌鸦 wūyā crow
乌鸦嘴 wūyāzuǐ a crow's mouth;
a hateful person whose words
will bring bad luck

◇ 乌龟 wūguī ① tortoise ② cuck-
old

污 wū 6画 氵部

污 污污污污污污

❶ [形]脏：dirty; filthy ｜～水
wūshuǐ *foul water* ／～泥 wūní
mud; mire
污点 wūdiǎn stain; spot; blemish; smirch

❷ [形]不廉洁：corrupt ｜贪官
吏 tānguān-wūlì *corrupt officials*
贪污 tānwū

❸ [动]弄脏：defile; smear ｜玷～
diànwū *stain; sully; tarnish* ／别
弄～衣服。Bié nòngwū yīfu.
Don't stain your clothes.
污染 wūrǎn pollute; contami-
nate

◇ 污蔑 wūmiè same as
诬蔑 wūmiè

巫 wū 7画 工部

巫 巫巫巫巫巫巫巫

See 巫婆
巫婆 wūpó witch; sorceress

呜（嗚）**wū** 7画 口部

呜 呜呜呜呜呜呜呜

[拟声] 模拟哭声、风声、汽笛声等：toot; hoot; zoom ｜ 火车～的一声飞驰而过。Huǒchē wū de yī shēng fēichí ér guò. *The train zoomed past.* / 轮船上的汽笛～～叫。Lúnchuán shang de qìdí wūwū jiào. *The ship's whistle kept tooting.*

呜咽 wūyè sob; whimper

诬（誣）**wū** 9画 讠部

诬 诬诬诬诬诬诬诬诬诬

[动] 无中生有说别人做了坏事：accuse falsely ｜ ～赖 wūlài *falsely incriminate* / ～陷 wūxiàn *frame a case against* / ～告 wūgào *bring a false charge against; trump up a charge against*

诬蔑 wūmiè slander; defile; sully

屋 **wū** 9画 尸部

屋 屋屋屋屋屋屋屋屋屋

❶ [名] 房子：house ｜ 房～fángwū *house; housing; building* / 书～

shūwū *studio; study; bookshop*
屋顶 wūdǐng roof; housetop
❷ [名] 房间：room ｜ 里～lǐwū *inner room* / 外～wàiwū *outer room* / 三间～sān jiān wū *three rooms*

屋子 wūzi room; house

无（無）**wú** 4画 无部

无 无无无无

❶ [动] 没有（跟"有 yǒu"相对）：not have; there is not (the opposite of "有 yǒu"）｜ 从～到有 cóng wú dào yǒu *start from scratch; grow out of nothing* / 房中～人。Fáng zhōng wú rén. *There isn't anyone in the room.*

无比 wúbǐ incomparable; un-paralleled; matchless
无偿 wúcháng free; gratis; gra-tuitous
无耻 wúchǐ shameless; brazen; impudent
无从 wúcóng have no way
无法 wúfǎ unable; incapable
无关 wúguān have nothing to do with
无理 wúlǐ unreasonable; unjus-tifiable
无力 wúlì ① lack strength; feel weak ② unable; incapable; pow-erless
无聊 wúliáo ① in extreme de-

pression; bored ② senseless; silly

无名 wúmíng ① nameless; unknown ② indefinable; indescribable

无奈 wúnài ① cannot help; have no alternative; have no choice ② (conj.) but; however

无情 wúqíng ruthless; heartless; inexorable

无穷 wúqióng infinite; endless; boundless

无数 wúshù ① innumerable; countless ② be uncertain

无线 wúxiàn wireless; radio

无限 wúxiàn infinite; limitless; boundless; immeasurable

无效 wúxiào of no avail; invalid; in vain

无形 wúxíng invisible; intangible

无疑 wúyí beyond doubt; undoubtedly

无意 wúyì ① have no intention ② inadvertently; unwillingly; accidentally

无知 wúzhī ignorant

无所谓 wúsuǒwèi indifferent

无线电 wúxiàndiàn radio

无边无际 wúbiān-wújì boundless; vast

无产阶级 wúchǎn jiējí proletariat

无话可说 wúhuà-kěshuō have nothing to say; draw down the curtain

无可奉告 wúkě-fēnggào no comment

无可奈何 wúkě-nàihé have no way out; have no alternative

无能为力 wúnéng-wéilì powerless; helpless; incapable of action

无情无义 wúqíng-wúyì show ingratitude for favour

无穷无尽 wúqióng-wújìn inexhaustible; endless

无所作为 wúsuǒzuòwéi attempt nothing and accomplish nothing; be in a state of inertia

无微不至 wúwēi-bùzhì meticulously; in every possible way

毫无 háowú

独一无二 dúyī-wú'èr

❷ [副] 不：no; not | ～须 wúxū *need not* | ～记名投票 wújìmíng tóupiào *secret ballot*

无论 wúlùn no matter what

无论如何 wúlùn-rúhé in any case; at any rate; whatever happens; at all events

❸ [副] 不论：no matter what (whether, when, where, how, etc.) | 事～大小，都有人负责。Shì wú dàxiǎo, dōu yǒu rén fùzé. *Everything, whether big or small, has been properly taken care of.*

wú 11画 木部

梧 梧梧梧梧梧梧梧梧
梧梧梧

See 梧桐

梧桐 wútóng Chinese parasol (tree)

五 五 五五五五五

[数] 数目：five | ~间房 wǔ jiān fáng *five rooms* / 三~成群 sānwǔ-chéngqún *in threes and fives; in knots*

五花八门 wǔhuā-bāmén multifarious; of a wide (or rich) variety

五颜六色 wǔyán-liùsè of various (or all) colours; multicoloured; colourful

二百五 èrbǎiwǔ

三番五次 sānfān-wǔcì

午 wǔ 4画 十部

午 午午午午

[名] 午时，即 11—13 点；特指中午 12 点：noon; midday; the period of the day from 11:00—13:00

午餐 wǔcān midday meal; lunch

午饭 wǔfàn midday meal; lunch

上午 shàngwǔ   下午 xiàwǔ
中午 zhōngwǔ
端午节 Duānwǔjié

伍 wǔ 6画 亻部

伍 伍伍伍伍伍伍伍

[名] 指军队：army | 入~rùwǔ *join the army* / 退~tuìwǔ *leave the army; be demobilized*

队伍 duìwu

武 wǔ 8画 止部

武 武武武武武武武武

❶ [名] 跟军事或强力有关的事物（跟 "文 wén" 相对）：military (the opposite of "文 wén") | 能文能~néngwén-néngwǔ *be able to wield both the pen and the gun*

武力 wǔlì force; armed might

武器 wǔqì weapon; arms

武装 wǔzhuāng ① armed forces; arms ②equip with arms

核武器 héwǔqì

❷ [名] 同搏斗有关的：of martial arts | 动~dòngwǔ *use force; start a fight; come to blows*

武术 wǔshù martial arts such as shadowboxing, swordplay, formerly cultivated for self-defence, now a form of physical exercise

侮　wǔ　9画 亻部

侮侮侮侮侮侮侮侮
侮

[动] 欺负；insult; bully | 欺～qīwǔ
bully; treat sb. high-handedly
侮辱 wǔrǔ insult

舞　wǔ　14画 夕部

舞舞舞舞舞舞舞舞
舞舞舞舞舞舞

❶[动] 跳舞：dance | 音乐声一起，
她们就～起来了。Yīn yuè
shēng yī qǐ, tāmen jiù wǔ
qǐlai le. *As soon as the music
started, they began to dance.*
歌舞 gēwǔ
能歌善舞 nénggē-shànwǔ
❷[名] 舞蹈；dance | 交谊～jiāo-
yìwǔ *social dance; ballroom
dance* | 她的～跳得真好。Tā de
wǔ tiào de zhēn hǎo. *She is
such a good dancer.*
舞蹈 wǔdǎo dance
舞会 wǔhuì dance; ball
舞台 wǔtái stage; arena
舞厅 wǔtīng ballroom; dance
hall
跳舞 tiàowǔ
芭蕾舞 bālěiwǔ
❸[动] 挥动；飘动：wave; flour-
ish; wield; brandish | ～剑
wǔjiàn *perform a sword-dance*

飞舞 fēiwǔ

勿　wù　4画 勹部

勿勿勿勿

[副] 表示禁止或劝阻；不；不要：
(indicating prohibition) do not;
never | 请～入内! Qǐng wù rù
nèi! *No entry please!* / 请～吸烟!
Qǐng wù xīyān! *No smoking
please!*

务 (務)　wù　5画 夂部

务务务务务

❶[名] 事情：affair; business |
公～gōngwù *public affairs; official business* / 医～工作者yīwù
gōngzuòzhě *medical staff*
家务 jiāwù　　　劳务 láowù
任务 rènwù　　　事务 shìwù
职务 zhíwù　　　服务器 fúwùqì
服务台 fúwùtái
公务员 gōngwùyuán
事务所 shìwùsuǒ
医务室 yīwùshì
❷[副] 必须；一定：must; be sure
to | ～请准时出席。Wù qǐng
zhǔnshí chūxí. *Be sure to be
present on time.*
务必 wùbì must; be sure to

物　wù　8画 牛部

物 物物物物物物物物

❶ [名] 东西：thing; matter ｜货～ huòwù *goods; commodity; merchandise* / 他每个周末开车出去购～。Tā měi ge zhōumò kāichē chūqù gòuwù. *He uses his car to go shopping every weekend.*

物价 wùjià price
物理 wùlǐ ① innate laws of things ② physics
物力 wùlì material resources; material
物品 wùpǐn article; goods
物体 wùtǐ body; substance; object
物质 wùzhì material
物种 wùzhǒng (boil.) species
物资 wùzī goods and materials

财物 cáiwù   产物 chǎnwù
宠物 chǒngwù   动物 dòngwù
读物 dúwù   废物 fèiwù
购物 gòuwù   景物 jǐngwù
刊物 kānwù   矿物 kuàngwù
礼物 lǐwù   生物 shēngwù
实物 shíwù   食物 shíwù
事物 shìwù   文物 wénwù
药物 yàowù   衣物 yīwù
植物 zhíwù   作物 zuòwù
博物馆 bówùguǎn
动物园 dòngwùyuán
吉祥物 jíxiángwù
微生物 wēishēngwù
植物园 zhíwùyuán

❷ [名] 内容；实质：content; substance; essence ｜空洞无～ kōngdòng-wúwù *(of talking or writing) have no content*

◇ 物业 wùyè real estate; property
风云人物 fēngyún rénwù

误（誤）wù   9画 讠部

误 误误误误误误误误误

❶ [名] 错：mistake; error ｜笔～ bǐwù *slip of the pen*
误差 wùchā error
误导 wùdǎo mislead; lead astray
误会 wùhuì misunderstand; misconstrue
误解 wùjiě ① misconception ② misread
误区 wùqū long-standing mistaken idea or concept
错误 cuòwù   失误 shīwù

❷ [动] 耽误：miss; delay ｜～事 wùshì *hold things up; delay matters* / 火车～点了。Huǒchē wùdiǎn le. *The train is late.; The train is behind schedule.*
耽误 dānwu   延误 yánwù

❸ [动] 使受损害：harm ｜～人子弟 wùrénzǐdì *(of a teacher) harm the younger generation; lead young people astray*

❹ [副] 不是故意地（造成某种不良后果）：unintentionally (cause bad results); by accident ｜～伤

wùshāng *accidentally injure; accidental injury*

恶 （恶） wù　10画 心部

恶 恶恶恶恶恶恶恶恶
恶恶

[动] 不喜欢；憎恨：loathe; dislike; hate

可恶 kěwù　　　　厌恶 yānwù
See ě; è.

悟 wù　10画 忄部

悟 悟悟悟悟悟悟悟
悟悟

[动] 了解；觉醒；领会：realize; awaken ｜ 我终于～出这个道理来。Wǒ zhōngyú wùchū zhège dàolǐ lai. *I've at last realized why it should be so.*

觉悟 juéwù

雾 （雾） wù　13画 雨部

雾 雾雾雾雾雾雾雾雾
雾雾雾雾雾

❶ [名] fog ｜ 早上有～。Zǎoshang yǒu wù. *There is fog in the morning.*

❷ [名] 雾状的东西：fine spray ｜ 烟～ yānwù *smoke; mist; smog* / 喷～器 pēnwùqì *sprayer*

X x

 西 xī 6画 西部

西 西西西西西西

❶[名] 方向，指日落的一边（跟"东 dōng"相对）：westward; westbound; west (the opposite of "东 dōng") | 往～去 wǎng xī qù *head westward* / 太阳～沉。Tàiyáng xī chén. *The sun sets in the west.* / 这条河由～向东流。Zhè tiáo hé yóu xī xiàng dōng liú. *This river flows from west to east.*

西边 xībian west
西北 xīběi ① northwest ② northwest China; the Northwest
西部 xībù the west
西方 xīfāng ① the west ② the West; the Occident
西湖 Xī Hú the West Lake, a famous lake in Hangzhou
西面 xīmian west side
西南 xīnán ① southwest ② southwest China; the Southwest
西半球 xībànqiú the Western Hemisphere

❷[名] 西洋（多指欧美）：the West; western world

西餐 xīcān western-style food
西服 xīfú western-style clothes
西药 xīyào western medicine
西医 xīyī ① western medicine (as distinguished from traditional Chinese medicine) ② doctor trained in western medicine
西装 xīzhuāng western-style clothes; suit
大西洋 Dàxīyáng
◇西瓜 xīguā watermelon
西红柿 xīhóngshì tomato

 吸 xī 6画 口部

吸 吸吸吸吸吸吸

❶[动] 把液体或气体等从口或鼻引入体内：inhale; breathe in; draw liquid or gas into the body from mouth or nose | ～了一口气 xīle yī kǒu qì *take a breath*
吸毒 xīdú take drugs; go on drugs
吸烟 xīyān smoke
呼吸 hūxī 呼吸道 hūxīdào

❷[动] 吸收：absorb; draw; suck up | ～尘器 xīchénqì *dust catcher; vacuum cleaner* / 海绵～水。Hǎimián xī shuǐ. *Sponges absorb water.*
吸纳 xīnà draw; absorb; receive
吸取 xīqǔ absorb; draw; assimilate; extract; suck
吸收 xīshōu ① absorb; suck up;

assimilate; imbibe ② recruit; enroll; admit

❸ [动] 把别的东西引到自己方向来：attract | ～铁石 xī tiě shí *magnet; lodestone* / 异性相～。 Yìxìng xiāng xī. *Opposites attract.*

吸引 xīyǐn ① attract; fascinate; appeal ② attract; draw

 希 xī 7画 巾部

希 希希希希希希希

[动] 盼望：hope | ～准时到会。 Xī zhǔnshí dào huì. *Please attend the meeting on time.*

希望 xī wàng hope; wish; expect

 牺 (犧) xī 10画 牛部

牺 牺牺牺牺牺牺牺牺 牺牺

[名] an animal of a uniform colour for sacrifice; sacrifice

牺牲 xī shēng ① an animal slaughtered for sacrifice; sacrifice ② sacrifice oneself; die a martyr's death; lay down one's life ③ sacrifice; give up; do sth. at the expense of

 息 xī 10画 心部

息 息息息息息息息息 息息

❶ [名] 呼出或吸入的气：breath | 鼻～ bíxī *breath* / 喘～ chuǎnxī *pant; gasp for breath*

气息 qìxī

❷ [动] 停止；歇：stop; cease | ～怒 xīnù *cease to be angry* / 歇～ xiēxī *have a rest* / 不～ bùxī *ceaseless* / 按时作～ ànshí zuòxī *work and rest according to the timetable*

休息 xiūxi

川流不息 chuānliú-bùxī

❸ [名] 音信；消息：news; information

消息 xiāoxi　　信息 xìnxī

◇ 有出息 yǒuchūxi

 悉 xī 11画 采部

悉 悉悉悉悉悉悉悉悉 悉悉悉

[动] 知道：know; be informed of | 获～ huòxī *learn (of an event)*

熟悉 shúxī

惜 xī 11画 忄部

惜 惜惜惜惜惜惜惜惜 惜惜惜

❶ [动] 对不幸的人或事表示同情：regret; show sympathy (to unfortunate people or things) | 痛～

tōngxī *deeply regret* / 惋~wǎnxī *feel sorry for*

可惜 kěxī

❷[动] 爱护；十分疼爱：value; cherish; treasure | 怜~liánxī *take pity on; feel pity for*

爱惜 àixī   珍惜 zhēnxī

稀   XĪ   12画 禾部

稀稀稀稀稀稀稀稀稀稀稀稀稀

❶[形] 事物之间间隔大；距离远（跟"密mì"相对）：few and far between; sparse; scattered (the opposite of "密mì") | 地广人~dìguǎng-rénxī *vast, sparsely populated area* / 头发~tóufa xī *thin hair; sparse hair*

❷[形] 事物的数量少或出现的次数少：few; rare | ~少 xīshǎo *few; rare; scarce* / 物以~为贵。Wù yǐ xī wéi guì. *Rare things are precious.*

稀缺 xīquē *in short supply; scarce; in pressing demand*

❸[形] 含水分多；浓度小（跟"稠chóu"相对）：watery or thin (the opposite of "稠chóu") | ~泥 xīní *thin mud* / 粥太~了。Zhōu tài xī le. *The gruel is too thin.*

稀饭 xīfàn *rice or millet soup; porridge*

锡 (錫)   XĪ   13画 钅部

锡锡锡锡锡锡锡锡锡锡锡锡锡

[名] tin | ~纸 xīzhǐ *tinfoil*

溪   XĪ   13画 氵部

溪溪溪溪溪溪溪溪溪溪溪溪溪

[名] 山间的小水流；小河沟：small stream; brook; rivulet | 小~xiǎoxī *small stream* / ~水 xīshuǐ *stream water*

熄   XĪ   14画 火部

熄熄熄熄熄熄熄熄熄熄熄熄熄熄

[动] 停止燃烧；灭(灯；火)：extinguish; put out; turn off (a light, fire, etc.) | ~灯 xīdēng *put out the light* / 火已经~了。Huǒ yǐjīng xī le. *The fire has gone out.*

熄灭 xīmiè *go out; die out*

膝   XĪ   15画 月部

膝膝膝膝膝膝膝膝膝膝膝膝膝膝膝

See 膝盖

膝盖 xīgài knee

 习（習）xí 3画 乙部

习 习 习 习

❶ [动] 反复地学：practise; exercise; review | 自～zìxí self-study
习题 xítí exercise (in school work)
补习 bǔxí 复习 fùxí
练习 liànxí 实习 shíxí
学习 xuéxí 演习 yǎnxí
预习 yùxí 实习生 shíxíshēng

❷ [名] 习惯：habit | 恶～èxí pernicious habit; vice | 积～jīxí old habit; deep-rooted habit
习惯 xíguàn ① habit; custom; usual practice ② be used to; be accustomed to
习俗 xísú custom; convention

 席 xí 10画 广部

席 席 席 席 席 席 席 席 席 席

❶ [名] mat | 草～cǎoxí straw mat / 凉～liángxí summer sleeping mat

❷ [名] 座位；席位：seat | 入～rùxí take one's seat / 来宾～láibīnxí guest seats
席位 xíwèi seat (at a conference, in a legislative assembly, etc.)
出席 chūxí 列席 lièxí

缺席 quēxí 首席 shǒuxí
主席 zhǔxí

❸ [名] 成桌的饭菜；酒席：banquet; feast | 酒～jiǔxí feast
宴席 yànxí

 袭（襲）xí 11画 龙部

袭 袭 袭 袭 袭 袭 袭 袭 袭 袭 袭

[动] 趁人不备，突然攻击：assault; attack | 空～kōngxí air raid / 偷～tōuxí sneak attack; stealth raid; surprise attack
袭击 xíjī make a surprise attack on; raid; attack by surprise

 媳 xí 13画 女部

媳 媳 媳 媳 媳 媳 媳 媳 媳 媳 媳 媳 媳

[名] daughter-in-law | 婆～póxí mother-in-law and daughter-in-law
媳妇 xífù ① son's wife; daughter-in-law ② the wife of a relative of the younger generation

 洗 xǐ 9画 氵部

洗 洗 洗 洗 洗 洗 洗 洗 洗

❶ [动] 用水或化学品去掉脏东西：wash; clean sth. with water,

gasoline, kerosene, etc. | ～脸
xǐ liǎn *wash one's face* / ～衣服
xǐ yīfu *wash clothes*

洗涤 xǐdí wash; cleanse

洗澡 xǐzǎo have (take) a bath;
bathe

洗衣机 xǐyījī washing machine;
washer

❷[动] 除掉：clear away; eliminate

❸[动] 冲印胶片、照片：develop
film | ～相片 xǐ xiāngpiàn
process a photo / ～胶卷 xǐ
jiāojuǎn *develop a roll of film*

❹[动] 清除：clear away; eliminate
| 清～qīngxǐ *cleanse; rinse*

喜　　　xǐ　　12画 士部

喜 喜喜喜喜喜喜喜喜
喜喜喜喜

❶ [动] 高兴；欢乐：happy; de-
lighted; pleased | 狂～kuángxǐ
wild with joy / 笑在脸上，～在
心里。Xiào zài liǎnshang, xǐ
zài xīnli. *With a smile on one's
face and joy in one's heart.*

喜悦 xǐyuè happy; joyous

喜怒哀乐 xǐ-nù-āi-lè happiness,
anger, grief and joy; the gamut
of human feelings

欢喜 huānxǐ　　　可喜 kěxǐ
欣喜 xīnxǐ

❷ [形] 令人高兴的；值得庆贺的：
happy (event); red-letter (day)

| 报～bàoxǐ *report good news*
/ 贺～hèxǐ *congratulate sb. on
a happy occasion*

喜酒 xǐjiǔ drinks offered to
guests at a wedding; wedding
feast

喜剧 xǐjù comedy

喜庆 xǐqìng ① joyous; jubilant
② a happy event or occasion

喜鹊 xǐquè magpie

喜事 xǐshì ① happy event; joyous occasion ② wedding

喜糖 xǐtáng wedding sweets (or
candies)

喜讯 xǐxùn happy news; good
news; glad tidings

恭喜 gōngxǐ

❸ [动] 爱好：like; have a propen-
sity for | ～新厌旧 xǐxīn-yànjiù
abandon the old for the new

喜爱 xǐ'ài like; love; be fond of;
be keen on

喜欢 xǐhuan ① like; love; be
fond of; be keen on ② happy;
elated; filled with joy

❹ [动] (某种生物)需要或适合于(某
种环境或某种东西)：(of ani-
mals or plants) have an incli-
nation for; agree with; require
| 植物一般都～光。Zhíwù
yībān dōu xǐ guāng. *Generally speaking, plants need
light.*

(戲) xì　　6画 又部

戏 戏戏戏戏戏戏

❶ [动] 玩耍；娱乐：play; have a good time | 儿~érxì *trifling matter*
游戏 yóuxì

❷ [名] 戏剧；杂技：drama; acrobatics | 看~kànxì *go to the theatre* / 唱~chàngxì *sing and act in a traditional opera* / 这场~演得很精彩。Zhè chǎng xì yǎn de hěn jīngcǎi. *It was a wonderful performance.*
戏剧 xìjù drama; play; theatre
戏曲 xìqǔ traditional opera
把戏 bǎxì 马戏 mǎxì
演戏 yǎnxì 地方戏 dìfāngxì
压台戏 yātáixì
唱对台戏 chàngduìtáixì

系 (係❶) xì 7画 系部

系 系系系系系系系

❶ [动] 关联；联结：relate to; rely on; have to do with | 干~gānxì *responsibility; implication* / 维~wéixì *hold together; maintain*
关系 guānxi 联系 liánxì

❷ [名] 相互有关系的人或事物：people or things with interrelationship | 派~pàixì *faction* / 直~zhíxì *directly related*
系列 xìliè series; set
系数 xìshù (math.) coefficient

系统 xìtǒng system
体系 tǐxì

❸ [名] 高等学校中按学科分的教学行政单位：any of the teaching divisions or branches of a college or university | 中文~zhōngwénxì *the Chinese department* / 化学~huàxuéxì *the department of Chemistry* / 这所大学有十多个~。Zhè suǒ dàxué yǒu shí duō ge xì. *There are more than ten departments in this university.*

See jì.

细 (細) xì 8画 纟部

细 细细细细细细细细

❶ [形] 条状物不粗或很窄 (跟 "粗 cū" 相对)：fine; thin; slender; not great in diameter (the opposite of "粗 cū") | ~铁丝 xì tiěsī *thin wire* / 她的手指又~又长。Tā de shǒuzhǐ yòu xì yòu cháng. *Her fingers are slender and long.* / 面条切得真~。Miàntiáo qiē de zhēn xì. *The noodles are thinly cut.*
粗细 cūxì

❷ [形] 微小的；small; tiny | ~雨 xìyǔ *drizzle; fine rain* / 故事里那些很~的情节我已经记不清了。Gùshi li nàxiē hěn xì de qíngjié wǒ yǐjīng jìbuqīng le. *I can't recall the details of* the story.

细节 xìjié detail; particular

细小 xìxiǎo very small; tiny; fine; trivial

❸[形] 声音小：soft; low | 嗓音~ sǎngyīn xì *a thready voice* / 小孩子说话声音很~。Xiǎoháizi shuōhuà shēngyīn hěn xì. *The child speaks in a soft voice.*

❹[形] 颗粒小：fine; in small particles | ~沙 xìshā *fine sand* / ~末 xìmò *powder*

❺[形] 精致：delicate; exquisite | 这绸子真~。Zhè chóuzi zhēn xì. *The silk fabric is so delicate.*

精细 jīngxì

❻[形] 周密；仔细；详细：meticulous; detailed | 这人的心真~。Zhè rén de xīn zhēn xì. *This is a very careful person.* / 他对这些情况问得很~。Tā duì zhèxiē qíngkuàng wèn de hěn xì. *He made detailed enquiries about these things.*

细心 xìxīn careful; attentive

细致 xìzhì careful; meticulous; painstaking

详细 xiángxì

◇细胞 xìbāo cell

细菌 xìjūn germ; bacterium

干细胞 gànxìbāo

虾 (蝦) xiā　9画 虫部

虾 虾虾虾虾虾虾虾虾虾
虾

[名] shrimp | 对~ duìxiā *prawn* / 龙~ lóngxiā *lobster*

瞎 xiā　15画 目部

瞎 瞎瞎瞎瞎瞎瞎瞎瞎
瞎瞎瞎瞎瞎瞎瞎

❶[动] 眼睛看不见东西：be blind; be sightless; be visionless | 他~了一只眼。Tā xiāle yī zhī yǎn. *He is blind in one eye.*

❷[副] 胡乱地；盲目地；没有效果地：groundlessly; futilely; blindly; to no purpose | ~说 xiāshuō *talk nonsense* / ~着急 xiā zháojí *worry to no avail* / ~操心 xiā cāoxīn *worry about sth. unnecessarily*

瞎折腾 xiāzhēteng expend one's energy on sth. to no avail

峡 (峽) xiā　9画 山部

峡 峡峡峡峡峡峡峡峡
峡

[名] 两山之间有水流的地方：gorge; canyon; narrow chasm with steep cliffs

峡谷 xiágǔ gorge; canyon

海峡 hǎixiá

狭 (狹) xiā　9画 犭部

狭 狭狭狭狭狭狭狭狭
狭

[形] 窄；不宽(跟"宽 kuān"相对)：
narrow (the opposite of "宽
kuān") | 一条～缝 yī tiáo
xiáfèng *a narrow crack*
狭隘 xiá'ài narrow; parochial;
limited
狭窄 xiázhǎi narrow; limited

霞 xiá 17画 雨部
霞

霞霞霞霞霞霞霞霞
霞霞霞霞霞霞霞
霞

[名]彩色的云：coloured cloud |
朝～zhāoxiá *rosy dawn; rosy
clouds of dawn* / 晚～wǎnxiá
glow of sunset; sunset cloud

下 xià 3画 一部

下 下下下

❶ [名] 低处的位置(跟"上 shàng"
相对)：down (the opposite of
"上 shàng") | 窗～chuāng xià
under the window / 楼～lóu xià
downstairs / 山～shān xià *at the
foot of the hill* / 往～看 wǎng
xià kàn *look down*
下巴 xiàba ①the lower jaw ②chin
下边 xiàbian below; under; underneath
下列 xiàliè listed below; following
下面 xiàmian ① below; under;
underneath ② next; following
下游 xiàyóu ①lower reaches (of
a river) ② backward position
下载 xiàzǎi download
底下 dǐxià   零下 língxià
❷ [形] 指时间或次序靠后的：next;
later; latter; late | ～星期
xiàxīngqī *next week* / ～半年
xiàbànnián *second half of a
year* / 我～次再来。Wǒ xià cì zài
lái. *I'll come again another time.*
下午 xiàwǔ afternoon
下旬 xiàxún last ten-day period
of a month
如下 rúxià   以下 yǐxià
❸ [形] 指等级低的：lower | ～等
xiàděng *inferior; low-grade*
下级 xiàjí ①lower level ②sub-
ordinate
下属 xiàshǔ subordinate
低下 dīxià   打下手 dǎxiàshǒu
❹ [动] 从高处到低处：descend;
alight; go down | ～山 xiàshān
go down a hill / ～楼 xiàlóu *descend the stairs* / ～飞机 xià fēijī
alight from a plane
下跌 xiàdiē (of water level,
prices, etc.) fall; drop
下降 xiàjiàng decline; drop; descend; fall; go down; come
down
下来 xiàlái(lai) ① down; off ②
grow; become
下去 xiàqù(qu) ① go down;

descend ② get; grow; become

下台 xiàtái ① step down ② fall out of power; fall from power; leave office ③ get out of a predicament or an embarrassing situation

❺ [动] 去；到 (某处)：go to | ~车间 xià chējiān *go to the workshop*

下乡 xiàxiāng go to the countryside

❻ [动] 发布；投递：issue; deliver; send | ~通知 xià tōngzhī *give a notice* / ~请帖 xià qǐngtiě *send an invitation*

下达 xiàdá make known; transmit to lower levels

下放 xiàfàng ① demote ② transfer (cadres,etc.) to work at the grass-roots level or to do manual labour in the countryside or in a factory

下令 xiàlìng give orders; order

❼ [动] 退出；离开：exit; leave | 从左边门儿~ cóng zuǒbian ménr xià *exit from the left door* / 五号队员~。Wǔ hào duìyuán xià. *Player no. 5 is ordered to leave the playing field.*

❽ [动] 按时结束 (工作等)：finish work (or study)

下班 xiàbān come or get off work; knock off

下课 xiàkè get out of class; finish class

❾ [动] (雨、雪等) 降；落：(of rain or snow) fall | ~雨 xiàyǔ *rain* / ~雪 xiàxuě *snow* / ~霜了。Xià-shuāng le. *It's frosty.*

❿ [动] 投入；放进：put in; cast | ~面条 xià miàntiáo *cook noodles* / ~饺子 xià jiǎozi *put dumplings in (boiling water); cook dumplings*

⓫ [动] 进行 (棋类游艺或比赛)：play (chess or games) | ~象棋 xià xiàngqí *play chess*

下棋 xiàqí play chess; have a game of chess

⓬ [动] (动物) 生产：(of animals) give birth to; lay | 鸡~蛋。Jī xià dàn. *The hens lay eggs.* / 母猫~小猫了。Mǔmāo xià xiǎomāo le. *The mother cat gave birth to a litter of kittens.*

⓭ [名] 表示属于一定的处所、范围、条件等：under (a certain circumstance); within (a certain scope) | 手~ shǒuxià *under the leadership of* / 在他的帮助~ zài tā de bāngzhù xià *with his help* / 在这种情况~ zài zhè zhǒng qíngkuàng xià *in such circumstances; in this situation*

地下 dìxià   天下 tiānxià
乡下 xiāngxia   眼下 yǎnxià
之下 zhīxià

⓮ [动] 作出 (某种结论、决定、判断等)：draw a conclusion; make a decision; make judgement | ~结论 xià jiélùn *draw a conclusion* / ~定义 xià dìngyì *give* a definition; define / 我的决心~定了。Wǒ de juéxīn xiàdìng le. *I am determined to do this.*

⑮[副]用在动词后作补语：used after a verb as a complement

(a) 表示由高处到低处：down, used to indicate downward motion | 坐~zuòxia *sit down* / 躺~tǎngxia *lie down* / 跑~山 pǎoxia shān *run down the hill*

(b) 表示有空间能容纳：used to indicate room or space | 这房间能坐~50人。Zhè fángjiān néng zuòxia wǔshí rén. *The room can hold (seat) fifty people.* / 我吃不~这么多东西。Wǒ chībuxià zhème duō dōngxi. *I can't eat all these foods.*

放下 fàngxià

(c) 表示动作的完成或结果：indicating completion or result of an action | 打~基础 dǎxia jīchǔ *have laid a foundation* / 准备~材料 zhǔnbèi xia cáiliào *get the material ready*

⑯[量]指动作的次数：indicating repetition of an action | 敲了三~儿 qiāole sān xiàr *knock three times* / 打十~儿 dǎ shí xiàr *hit sb. ten times*

一下儿 yīxiàr

◇下场 xiàchǎng an end that a person comes to (usually bad); fate

下落 xiàluò ① whereabouts ② fall; drop

下功夫 xiàgōngfu put in time and energy; concentrate one's efforts

下苦功 xiàkǔgōng concentrate one's great efforts

◇私下 sīxià

吓（嚇） xià 6画 口部

吓 吓吓吓吓吓吓

[动]害怕；使害怕：intimidate; scare; frighten | ~人 xià rén *frightening* / 他~了我一跳。Tā xiàle wǒ yī tiào. *I was frightened by him.* / 再大的困难也~不倒他。Zài dà de kùnnan yě xiàbudǎo tā. *No difficulty can scare him.*

夏 xià 10画 夂部

夏 夏夏夏夏夏夏夏夏夏夏

[名]夏季：summer | 冬暖~凉 dōngnuǎn xiàliáng *warm in winter and cool in summer*

夏季 xiàjì summer

夏天 xiàtiān summer

夏令营 xiàlìngyíng summer camp

◇华夏 Huáxià

仙 xiān 5画 亻部

仙仙仙仙仙

[名]celestial being; immortal | ~
人 xiānrén *celestial being; immortal*

仙女 xiānnǚ female celestial;
fairy maiden

仙人掌 xiānrénzhǎng (bot.)
cactus

◇水仙花 shuǐxiānhuā

先 xiān 6画 儿部

先 先先先先先先

❶ [名]靠前的时间或次序（跟"后
hòu"相对）：earlier (the opposite of"后hòu"）| 有言在~
yǒuyánzàixiān *make clear beforehand* / 争~恐后 zhēngxiān-
kǒnghòu *strive to be the first
and fear to lag behind* / 你怎么
不~告诉我？Nǐ zěnme bù xiān
gàosù wǒ? *Why didn't you tell
me earlier?*

先锋 xiānfēng vanguard; van

先后 xiānhòu ① early or late;
priority; order ② successively;
one after another

先前 xiānqián before; previously

先驱 xiānqū pioneer; forerunner; harbinger

领先 lǐngxiān   抢先 qiǎngxiān

事先 shìxiān   原先 yuánxiān

❷ [副]表示时间或次序在前(跟"后

hòu"相对）：indicating the
sequence of time or order (the
opposite of"后hòu"）| 我~
走了。Wǒ xiān zǒu le. *I'll leave
first.* / 我~说几句。Wǒ xiān
shuō jǐ jù. *Let me say a few
words first.* / 让老人~上车。
Ràng lǎorén xiān shàngchē.
Let senior citizens board first.

先进 xiānjìn advanced

首先 shǒuxiān   优先 yōuxiān

预先 yùxiān

❸ [名]祖先；上代：ancestor;
forefather | ~人 xiānrén *ancestor; forefather*

祖先 zǔxiān

◇先生 xiānsheng ① teacher ②
mister (Mr.); gentleman; sir ③
doctor

好好先生 hǎohǎo xiānsheng

纤 （纖） xiān 6画 纟部

纤 纤纤纤纤纤纤

[形]细小：fine; minute | ~弱
xiānruò *slim and fragile*

纤维 xiānwéi fibre; staple

掀 xiān 11画 扌部

掀 掀掀掀掀掀掀掀掀
掀掀掀

[动]揭起；打开：lift | ~窗帘 xiān
chuānglián *raise the curtain*

777

/ ～掉一块石板 xiāndiào yī
kuài shí bǎn *take a stone plate
away*
掀起 xiānqǐ ① lift ② surge ③
start; set off

鲜 (鮮) xiān　14画 鱼部

鲜 鲜鲜鲜鲜鲜鲜鲜鲜
鲜鲜鲜鲜鲜鲜

❶[形] 没有变质的；新鲜的：fresh
| ～肉 xiānròu *fresh meat* / ～奶
xiānnǎi *fresh milk* / ～蛋 xiāndàn
fresh egg
鲜花 xiānhuā　fresh flower;
flower
鲜血 xiānxuè　blood
保鲜 bǎoxiān　海鲜 hǎixiān
新鲜 xīnxiān
❷[形] 滋味好：tasty; delicious
| ～汤 xiāntāng *delicious soup*
/ 菜的味道真～。Cài de wèi-
dào zhēn xiān. *The dish is really delicious!*
❸[形] 明亮：bright; brightly-
coloured | 这块布颜色太～。
Zhè kuài bù yánsè tài xiān.
This cloth is too bright.
鲜红 xiānhóng　bright red; scar-
let
鲜明 xiānmíng ① bright ② distinct; distinctive
鲜艳 xiānyàn　brightly-
coloured; gaily-coloured

闲 (閑) xián　7画 门部

闲 闲闲闲闲闲闲闲

❶[形] 没有事情做；有空 (跟 "忙
máng" 相对)：not busy; idle;
unoccupied (the opposite of
"忙 máng") | 没有～工夫
méiyǒu xián gōngfu *have no
spare time* / 他现在没有事，
很～。Tā xiànzài méiyǒu shì,
hěn xián. *He has nothing to do
now.*
休闲 xiūxián
❷[形] 与正事无关的：having
nothing to do with official
business | ～谈 xiántán *chat* /
～人免进 xiánrén miǎn jìn *no
admittance except on business*
闲话 xiánhuà ① digression ②
complaint; gossip ③ talk casually about; chat about
说闲话 shuōxiánhuà

贤 (賢) xián　8画 贝部

贤 贤贤贤贤贤贤贤贤

[形] 善良：kind; virtuous
贤惠 xiánhuì (of a woman) virtuous

弦 xián　8画 弓部

. . . .

弦 弦弦弦弦弦弦弦弦

❶[名] 弓背两端之间的绳状物，用以发箭：bowstring; string; cord｜箭在～上 jiàn zài xián shàng *like an arrow on the bowstring (which can't avoid being shot)*

❷[名] 乐器上能震动发声的线：string of a musical instrument｜拨动琴～ bōdòng qínxián *pluck the string of a musical instrument*

❸[名] 钟表等的发条：spring of a watch or clock｜表～断了。Biǎoxián duàn le. *The spring of the watch is broken.* / 这只钟每天要上～。Zhè zhī zhōng měi tiān yào shàngxián. *This clock has to be wound every day.*

咸 (鹹) xián 9画 戈部

咸咸咸咸咸咸咸咸咸

[形] 像盐那样的味道：salted; salty｜～鱼 xiányú *salt fish* / ～菜 xiáncài *salted vegetables; pickle* / 这菜太～了。Zhè cài tài xián le. *The dish is too salty.*

衔 (銜) xián 11画 彳部

衔衔衔衔衔衔衔衔衔衔衔

❶[动] 用嘴含：hold in the mouth｜燕子～泥 yànzi xián ní *swallows carry bits of earth in their bills* / ～着烟斗 xiánzhe yāndǒu *have a pipe between one's teeth*

❷[动] 互相连接：link up; join 衔接 xiánjiē link up; join

嫌 xián 13画 女部

嫌嫌嫌嫌嫌嫌嫌嫌嫌嫌嫌嫌嫌

❶[动] 厌恶；不满：dislike; mind; complain｜讨人～ tǎo rén xián *be a nuisance* / ～麻烦 xián máfan *do not want to take the trouble; think sth. troublesome* / 她总～饭不好吃。Tā zǒng xián fàn bù hǎo chī. *She always complains about the food.* / 房子～小了一点儿。Fángzi xián xiǎole yīdiǎnr. *The house is a bit too small.*

❷[名] 猜疑；可疑之点：suspicion｜避～ bìxián *avoid suspicion* / 涉～ shèxián *be suspected of being involved; under suspicion* 嫌犯 xiánfàn criminal suspect 嫌疑 xiányí suspicion 嫌疑人 xiányírén (leg.) suspect

显 (顯) xiǎn 9画 日部

显显显显显显显显显显

❶ [形] 露在外面的；容易发现的：apparent; obvious; noticeable | 药的效果还不～。Yào de xiǎoguǒ hái bù xiǎn. *The effect of the medicine is not clear.*

显著 xiǎnzhù notable; marked; striking; remarkable; outstanding

显而易见 xiǎn'éryìjiàn obviously; evidently; clearly

明显 míngxiǎn

❷ [动] 露出；表现：show; display; manifest | 大～身手 dàxiǎn-shēnshǒu *display one's skill to the full* | 他很～老。Tā hěn xiǎn lǎo. *He looks older than his age.* | 他一出一副非常为难的样子。Tā xiǎnchū yī fù fēicháng wéinán de yàngzi. *He looks embarrassed.*

显得 xiǎnde look; seem; appear

显露 xiǎnlù become visible; appear; manifest itself

显示 xiǎnshì ① show; display; demonstrate; manifest ② show; indication

显现 xiǎnxiàn manifest (or reveal) oneself; appear; show

显示屏 xiǎnshìpíng monitor; screen

显示器 xiǎnshìqì monitor

显微镜 xiǎnwēijìng microscope

 (險) xiǎn 9画 阝(左)部

险 险险险险险险险险 险

❶ [形] 地势险恶不易通过；危险：(of terrain) dangerous; perilous; difficult to access | 脱离～境 tuōlí xiǎnjìng *be out of danger* | 他总爱干那些～事。Tā zǒng ài gàn nàxiē xiǎnshì. *He tends to do dangerous things.*

险些 xiǎnxiē narrowly (escape from sth. untoward); just barely; nearly

艰险 jiānxiǎn   危险 wēixiǎn

❷ [名] 危险的情况或境地：dangerous situation | 遇～ yùxiǎn *meet with danger* | 脱～ tuōxiǎn *be out of danger*

保险 bǎoxiǎn   风险 fēngxiǎn
冒险 màoxiǎn   探险 tànxiǎn
保险柜 bǎoxiǎnguì
担风险 dānfēngxiǎn

 (縣) xiàn   7画 厶部

县 县县县县县县县

[名] 行政区划单位：county (an administrative unit under the jurisdiction of a prefecture, autonomous prefecture or a central municipality)

县城 xiànchéng county seat; county town

县长 xiànzhǎng head of a county; county magistrate

(現) xiàn 8画 王部

现 | 现现现现现现现现

❶ [动] 显出；露出：show; appear; become visible | ～了原形xiànle yuánxíng *show one's true colours* / 他脸上渐渐～出了笑容。Tā liǎn shàng jiànjiān xiànchūle xiàoróng. *Gradually, a smile appeared on his face.*

现象 xiànxiàng phenomenon; appearance (of things)

表现biǎoxiàn　呈现chéngxiàn
重现chóngxiàn
出现chūxiàn　发现fāxiàn
实现shíxiàn　体现tǐxiàn
显现xiǎnxiàn　涌现yǒngxiàn
再现zàixiàn　展现zhǎnxiàn

❷ [形] 目前；此刻：at the moment of speaking; present; current; existing | ～阶段 xiàn jiēduàn *the present stage* / 病人～已出院。Bìngrén xiàn yǐ chūyuàn. *The patient has been discharged from hospital.* / 班里～有20个学生。Bān li xiànyǒu èrshí ge xuéshēng. *There are 20 students in the class.*

现代 xiàndài ① modern times; contemporary age ② modern; contemporary

现实 xiànshí ① reality; actuality; fact ② real; actual

现行 xiànxíng ① currently in effect; in force; in operation ② active

现在 xiànzài now; at present; today

现状 xiànzhuàng present situation; current situation; status quo; existing state of affairs

现代化 xiàndàihuà modernize; modernization

❸ [副] 当时；临时：impromptu; extempore | ～编～唱xiàn biān xiàn chàng *make up a song as one sings; improvise a song*

现场 xiànchǎng ① scene ② site; spot

❹ [形] 当时就有的：(merchandise or cash) on hand | ～货xiànhuò *merchandise on hand; spots*

现成 xiànchéng ready-made

现房 xiànfáng ready house

现金xiànjīn cash; ready money

现钱 xiànqián ready money; cash

现有 xiànyǒu now available; existing

 xiàn 8画 阝(左)部

限 | 限限限限限限限限

❶ [名] 指定的范围：limit; bound | 以年底为～yǐ niándǐ wéi xiàn *set the end of the year as the deadline* / 一个人的精力有～。Yī ge rén de jīnglì

X

yǒuxiàn. *There is a limit to one's energy.*

限度 xiàndù limit; limitation
限期 xiànqī ① deadline; time limit ② within a definite time; set a time limit

极限 jíxiàn   界限 jièxiàn
期限 qīxiàn   权限 quánxiàn
无限 wúxiàn   有限 yǒuxiàn

❷ [动] 规定范围：set a limit; limit; restrict | ～三天完工 xiàn sān tiān wángōng *(the project) must be completed within three days* / 人数不～ rénshù bù xiàn *There is no limit to the number of people.*

限于 xiànyú be confined to; be limited to
限制 xiànzhì limit; restrict; confine; impose restrictions on
局限 júxiàn

 (綫) xiàn   8画 纟部

线 线线线线线线线线

❶ [名] thread; string; wire; cord | 棉～ miánxiàn *cotton thread* / 丝～ sīxiàn *silk thread*

电线 diànxiàn   毛线 máoxiàn
天线 tiānxiàn   无线 wúxiàn
导火线 dǎohuǒxiàn

❷ [名] 像线的东西：sth. shaped like a line | 紫外～ zǐwàixiàn *ultraviolet ray*
线条 xiàntiáo (arts) line; con-

tour; figure

光线 guāngxiàn   视线 shìxiàn
在线 zàixiàn
生产线 shēngchǎnxiàn

❸ [名] 几何学上指点的运动轨迹 line; path of a moving point
曲线 qūxiàn   直线 zhíxiàn

❹ [名] 交通路线：transportation line | 京广～ Jīng-Guǎngxiàn *the Beijing-Guangzhou Railway (line)*
线路 xiànlù ① circuit; line ② line; route

干线 gànxiàn   航线 hángxiàn
路线 lùxiàn   热线 rèxiàn

❺ [名] 边缘交界的地方：demarcation line; boundary; dividing line | 国境～ guójìngxiàn *boundary (line) of a country* / 海岸～ hǎi'ànxiàn *coastline*

底线 dǐxiàn   防线 fángxiàn
界线 jièxiàn   前线 qiánxiàn
战线 zhànxiàn   阵线 zhènxiàn
分数线 fēnshùxiàn

❻ [名] 比喻所接近的某种边缘：(fig.) brink; verge | 生命～ shēngmìngxiàn *lifeline; lifeblood* / 死亡～ sǐwángxiàn *the verge of death*

◇线索 xiànsuǒ clue; lead
出线 chūxiàn

 (憲) xiàn   9画 宀部

宪 宪宪宪宪宪宪宪宪
宪

[名]宪法：constitution

 xiàn 10画 阝(左)部

陷 陷陷陷陷陷陷陷陷陷陷陷

❶[动]掉进(泥土等松软的物体里)：get stuck or bogged down (in mud or sth. soft and loose) | 越～越深 yuè xiàn yuè shēn *the longer it gets stuck, the deeper it sinks* / 汽车～在泥坑里。Qìchē xiànzài ní kēng li. *The car got bogged in the mud.*
陷入 xiànrù fall into; sink into; get bogged down in; be lost in

❷[动]想法子害人：frame (sb.)
陷害 xiànhài frame; make a false charge against
诬陷 wūxiàn

❸[动]物体凹进去：sink; cave in | 他两眼深～。Tā liǎng yǎn shēn xiàn. *His eyes became deeply sunken.* / 地基在下～。Dìjī zài xiàxiàn. *The foundation is sinking.*

❹[名]缺点；不完善的部分：defect; deficiency
缺陷 quēxiàn

 (餡) xiàn 11画 饣部

馅 馅馅馅馅馅馅馅馅馅馅馅

[名]filling; stuffing | 豆沙～儿 dòushāxiànr *sweetened bean paste filling*
馅儿 xiànr filling; stuffing

 xiàn 12画 羊部

羡 羡羡羡羡羡羡羡羡羡羡羡

[动]喜爱而希望得到：admire; envy
羡慕 xiànmù admire; envy

 (獻) xiàn 13画 犬部

献 献献献献献献献献献献献献

❶[动]恭敬庄重地送给：offer; present; give an object or idea to a person or an organization | ～礼 xiànlǐ *dedicate a gift* / 他们向老师～花。Tāmen xiàng lǎoshī xiànhuā. *They presented flowers to their teachers.*
献身 xiànshēn devote oneself to; dedicate oneself to; give one's life to
奉献 fèngxiàn 贡献 gòngxiàn
捐献 juānxiàn

❷[动]表现给人看：show; put on; display | ～技 xiànjì *show one's skill (in a performance)* / ～艺 xiànyì *present a performance* /

陷馅羡献

xiàn

xiàn

X

~殷勤 xiàn yīnqín *do every-thing to please sb.; curry favour*

◇文献 wénxiàn

乡 **(鄉)** xiāng 3画 →部

乡 乡 乡 乡

xiāng

❶[名] 农村：country; countryside; rural area | 城~chéngxiāng *the city and the countryside*

乡村xiāngcūn village; country-side; rural area

乡下xiāngxia village; country; countryside

乡镇 xiāngzhèn ① villages and towns ② small towns in general

下乡 xiàxiāng

❷[名] 家乡；老家：native place; home village or town | 同~tóngxiāng *fellow villager; townsman* / 还~huánxiāng *return to one's home town*

乡亲 xiāngqīn ① person from the same village or town; fellow villager or townsman ② local people; villager; folk

故乡 gùxiāng   家乡 jiāxiāng

老乡 lǎoxiāng

异国他乡 yìguó-tāxiāng

相 xiāng 9画 木部

相 相 相 相 相 相 相 相 相

❶[副] 互相；交互：each other; one another | ~识 xiāngshí *know each other* / 两地~距太远。Liǎng dì xiāngjù tài yuǎn. *The two places are too far apart.*

相爱 xiāng'ài be in love with each other

相比 xiāngbǐ compare

相差 xiāngchà differ

相处 xiāngchǔ get along (with one another)

相当 xiāngdāng ① match; bal-ance; correspond to; be equal to; be commensurate with ②quite; fairly; considerably; rather

相等 xiāngděng be equal

相对xiāngduì ①opposite; face to face ② relatively; compara-tively

相反 xiāngfǎn opposite; con-trary; adverse; reverse

相符 xiāngfú conform to; tally (agree) with; correspond to (with)

相关xiāngguān be interrelated

相互 xiānghù mutual; recipro-cal; each other

相交 xiāngjiāo ① intersect ② make friends with

相连 xiānglián be linked to-gether; be joined

相似 xiāngsì resemble; be simi-lar; be alike

相通 xiāngtōng communicate with each other; be interlinked

相同 xiāngtóng identical; the same; alike

相应 xiāngyìng corresponding; relevant

相遇 xiāngyù meet

相当于 xiāngdāngyú correspond to; be about equal to; be commensurate with

互相 hùxiāng

❷ [副] 表示动作是一方对另一方的：indicating an action done by one person to another | ~劝 xiāngquàn persuade; offer advice

相继 xiāngjì in succession; one after another

相信 xiāngxìn believe in; be convinced of; have faith in

See xiàng.

香 xiāng 9画 香部

香香香香香香香香香

❶ [形] 气味好闻（跟 "臭 chòu" 相对）：fragrant; aromatic; scented (the opposite of "臭 chòu") | 这花真~! Zhè huā zhēn xiāng! *How fragrant this flower is!*

香菜 xiāngcài coriander

香肠 xiāngcháng sausage

香菇 xiānggū shiitake mushroom

香蕉 xiāngjiāo banana

香水 xiāngshuǐ perfume; scent

香味 xiāngwèi sweet smell; fragrance; scent; perfume

香烟 xiāngyān ① cigarette ② incense smoke

香皂 xiāngzào perfumed (scented) soap; toilet soap

❷ [形] 味道好；吃东西胃口好：savoury; appetizing | 饭菜很~。Fàncài hěn xiāng. *The food is very appetizing.* / 这两天吃饭不~。Zhè liǎng tiān chīfàn bù xiāng. *I have lost my appetite these days.*

❸ [形] 睡得舒服；踏实：(of sleep) sound | 睡得正~shuì de zhèng xiāng be sleeping soundly

箱 xiāng 15画 竹部

箱箱箱箱箱箱箱箱
箱箱箱箱箱箱箱

[名] 箱子：chest; box; case; trunk | 皮~pí xiāng *leather suitcase* / 书~shūxiāng *bookcase*

箱子 xiāngzi chest; box; case; trunk

冰箱 bīngxiāng 信箱 xìnxiāng

邮箱 yóuxiāng

集装箱 jízhuāngxiāng

镶 （镶） xiāng 22画 钅部

镶镶镶镶镶镶镶镶
镶镶镶镶镶镶镶镶
镶镶镶镶镶镶

[动]把东西嵌入或在外围加边：in-lay; mount; set an object inside another object, or on the edge of it | ～牙 xiāngyá *put in a false tooth; insert an artificial tooth* / ～花边 xiāng huābiān *edge with lace*

 详 (詳) xiāng 8画 讠部

详 详详详详详详详详

[形] 细密；完备：detailed | ～谈 xiāngtán *detailed discussion* / ～情 xiāngqíng *the details of the matter*
详尽 xiāngjìn detailed and complete; exhaustive; thorough
详细 xiāngxì detailed; minute
◇端详 duānxiáng

降 xiáng 8画 阝(左)部

降 降降降降降降降降

[动]屈服：subdue; tame; vanquish | 一物～一物 yī wù xiáng yī wù *one thing subdues another*
投降 tóuxiáng
See jiàng.

 祥 xiáng 10画 礻部

祥 祥祥祥祥祥祥祥祥
祥祥

[形]吉利；幸运：auspicious; lucky | 吉～jíxiáng *auspicious* / 不～bùxiáng *ominous; inauspicious*
安祥 ānxiáng

 翔 xiáng 12画 羽部

翔 翔翔翔翔翔翔翔翔
翔翔翔翔

[动]盘旋地飞：fly; hover in the air | 滑～huáxiáng *glide*
飞翔 fēixiáng

享 xiǎng 8画 子部

享 享享享享享享享享

[动]享受；得到满足：enjoy; feel satisfaction | 坐～其成zuòxiǎng-qíchéng *sit idle and enjoy the fruits of others' work; reap where one has not sown* / 有福大家～yǒu fú dàjiā xiǎng *share joy and happiness with people*
享福 xiǎngfú enjoy a happy life; live in ease and comfort
享乐 xiǎnglè lead a life of pleasure; indulge in creature comforts
享受 xiǎngshòu ① enjoyment; treat ② enjoy
享有 xiǎngyǒu enjoy
分享 fēnxiǎng
共享 gòngxiǎng

响 (響) xiǎng 9画 口部

响 响 响 响 响 响 响 响 响

❶ [名] 声音：sound | 听不见～儿 tīngbujiàn xiǎngr *unable to hear any sound*
响声 xiǎngshēng sound; noise
反响 fǎnxiǎng　音响 yīnxiǎng

❷ [动] 发出声音：make a sound; resound; ring | 钟～了。Zhōng xiǎng le. *The clock is ringing.* / 电话铃～了。Diànhuàlíng xiǎng le. *The telephone is ringing.*
响应 xiǎngyìng respond; answer
影响 yǐngxiǎng

❸ [形] 声音大：sonorous; loud and clear | 铃声真～。Língshēng zhēn xiǎng. *The bell is really loud.* / 收音机开得太～了。Shōuyīnjī kāi de tài xiǎng le. *The radio is too loud.*
响亮 xiǎngliàng loud and clear; resounding; resonant; sonorous

想 xiǎng 13画 心部

想 想 想 想 想 想 想 想 想 想 想 想 想

❶ [动] 动脑筋；思考：think; ponder | ～办法 xiǎng bànfǎ *think of a way; try to find a way out* / ～问题 xiǎng wèntí *think over a problem* / 让我～一～。Ràng wǒ xiǎngyixiǎng. *Let me think it over.*
想法 xiǎngfǎ think of a way; do what one can; try
想象 xiǎngxiàng ① imagine; visualize; form a mental image of sth. not present ② imagination
想不到 xiǎngbudào never expect; be unexpected
想方设法 xiǎngfāng-shèfǎ do everything possible; try every means; try by hook or by crook
猜想 cāixiǎng　感想 gǎnxiǎng
构想 gòuxiǎng　幻想 huànxiǎng
回想 huíxiǎng　空想 kōngxiǎng
理想 lǐxiǎng　　联想 liánxiǎng
梦想 mèngxiǎng 设想 shèxiǎng
思想 sīxiǎng　妄想 wàngxiǎng
可想而知 kěxiǎng'érzhī

❷ [动] 估计；认为：think; presume; suppose | 我～他不会来了。Wǒ xiǎng tā bù huì lái le. *I don't think he will come.* / 我～我该走了。Wǒ xiǎng wǒ gāi zǒu le. *I'm afraid I have to leave now.*

❸ [动] 希望；打算：hope to; want to; would like to | 他～去学习。Tā xiǎng qù xuéxí. *He wants to go and study.* / 我～跟大家一块儿去。Wǒ xiǎng gēn dàjiā yīkuàir qù. *I'd like to go with all of you.* / 我不～参加这个聚会。Wǒ bù xiǎng cānjiā zhège jùhuì. *I don't want to go to the party.*

❹ [动] 惦记；怀念：miss | 我很~家。Wǒ hěn xiǎngjiā. *I am homesick.* / 我们很~你。Wǒmen hěn xiǎng nǐ. *We miss you very much.*

想念 xiǎngniàn long to see again; miss

向 (嚮) xiàng 6画 丿部

向 向向向向向向

❶ [动] 朝着；对着：face | 面~窗户 miàn xiàng chuānghu *face the window* / 这间房子~东。Zhè jiān fángzi xiàng dōng. *The house faces east.*

向往 xiàngwǎng yearn for; look forward to; be attracted toward

倾向 qīngxiàng

趋向 qūxiàng

外向型 wàixiàngxíng

欣欣向荣 xīnxīn-xiàngróng

❷ [名] 方向：direction | 风~fēngxiàng *wind direction* / 他~东站着。Tā xiàng dōng zhànzhe. *He stood facing east.* / 水~低处流。Shuǐ xiàng dīchù liú. *Water flows downhill.*

向导 xiàngdǎo guide

定向 dìngxiàng 动向 dòngxiàng

方向 fāngxiàng 流向 liúxiàng

去向 qùxiàng 转向 zhuǎnxiàng

走向 zǒuxiàng

❸ [副] 从过去到现在；从来：from past to present

向来 xiànglái always; all along

一向 yīxiàng

❹ [介] 引进动作的方向或对象：towards; in the direction of | ~前看 xiàng qián kàn *look ahead* / ~他道歉 xiàng tā dàoqiàn *apologize to him*

偏向 piānxiàng

项 (項) xiàng 9画 工部

项 项项项项项项项项项

❶ [名] 颈的后部；脖子：nape of the neck | 颈~ jǐngxiàng *neck*

项链 xiàngliàn necklace

❷ [名] 事物的门类或条目：item (for itemized things)

项目 xiàngmù item

事项 shìxiàng

❸ [量] 用于分类别、分条目的事物：used for categories and items of things | 各~工作 gèxiàng gōngzuò *various tasks* / 逐~进行讨论 zhúxiàng jìnxíng tǎolùn *discuss issues one by one*

长项 chángxiàng

单项 dānxiàng

xiàng 9画 巳部

巷 巷巷巷巷巷巷巷巷巷
巷

[名]较窄的街道：lane; alley｜大街
小~dàjiē xiǎoxiàng streets and
lanes

相 xiāng 9画 木部

相 相相相相相相相相
相

❶[名]容貌：looks; appearance｜
长~zhǎngxiàng appearance／
可怜~kěliánxiàng pitiful appearance; sorry figure
相机xiàngjī ① camera ② watch
for an opportunity
照相zhàoxiàng
❷[名]事物的外貌或情况：appear-
ance of an object
变相 biànxiàng 亮相 liàngxiàng
真相 zhēnxiàng
◇相声 xiàngsheng comic dia-
logue; crosstalk
属相 shǔxiàng
See xiāng.

象 xiàng 11画 勹部

象 象象象象象象象象
象象象

❶[名]哺乳动物：elephant｜大~
dàxiàng elephant
❷[名]形状；样子：appearance;
shape; image｜人间万~rénjiān-

wànxiàng everything under the
sun
象征xiàngzhēng ① symbolize;
signify; stand for ② symbol;
emblem; token
抽象chōuxiàng 对象duìxiàng
迹象jìxiàng 景象jǐngxiàng
气象qìxiàng 现象xiànxiàng
想象xiǎngxiàng 形象xíngxiàng
印象 yìnxiàng
◇象棋 xiàngqí Chinese chess

像 xiàng 13画 亻部

像 像像像像像像像
像像像像像

❶[动]相似：be like; resemble｜
这女孩儿~她母亲。Zhè nǚhái'r
xiàng tā mǔqīn. The girl takes
after her mother.／这个角色演得
很~。Zhège juésè yǎn de
hěn xiàng. He performed his
role very well.
❷[名]比照人物制成的图画、雕塑
等：picture, portrait, or image
made to resemble the appearance of a person｜画~huà-
xiàng portrait／塑~sùxiàng
statue
录像 lùxiàng 偶像 ǒuxiàng
摄像 shèxiàng 图像 túxiàng
肖像 xiāoxiàng 音像 yīnxiàng
影像 yǐngxiàng
录像带 lùxiàngdài
摄像机 shèxiàngjī

789

❸ [动] 似乎；好像：look as if; seem | 天～要下雪了。Tiān xiǎng yào xiàxuě le. *Looks like it's going to snow.* / 他～在想什么心事。Tā xiǎng zài xiǎng shénme xīnshì. *It seems there is something on his mind.* / 他高兴得～个孩子。Tā gāoxìng de xiàng ge háizi. *He is as cheerful as a child.*

好像 hǎoxiàng

❹ [动] 比如：be like | ～这样的事值得我们注意。Xiàng zhèyàng de shì zhídé wǒmen zhùyì. *We should pay attention to things like this.*

◇像样 xiàngyàng up to the mark; presentable; decent; sound

不像话 búxiànghuà

橡 xiàng 15画 木部
橡橡橡橡橡橡橡橡橡橡橡橡橡橡

[名] 橡胶树：rubber tree | ～树 xiàngshù *oak*

橡胶 xiàngjiāo rubber
橡皮 xiàngpí ①rubber ②eraser; rubber

削 xiāo 9画 刂部
削削削削削削削削削

[动] 用刀斜着切去物体表面：peel; pare the surface layer of an object sideways with a knife | ～铅笔 xiāo qiānbǐ *sharpen a pencil* / ～苹果皮 xiāo píngguǒpí *peel an apple*

See xuē.

消 xiāo 10画 氵部
消消消消消消消消消消

❶ [动] 消失：disappear; vanish | 雾渐渐地～了。Wù jiànjiàn de xiāo le. *The fog lifted gradually.* / 他的气～了。Tā de qì xiāo le. *He has cooled down now.*

消失 xiāoshī disappear; vanish; die away; fade away

❷ [动] 除掉；使消失：cause to disappear; eliminate; dispel | ～炎 xiāoyán *diminish or counteract inflammation*

消除 xiāochú eliminate; dispel; remove; clear up
消毒 xiāodú disinfect; sterilize
消防 xiāofáng ① fire fighting ② fire prevention and control
消化 xiāohuà digest
消灭 xiāomiè ①perish; die out; pass away ② annihilate; eliminate; abolish; exterminate; wipe out
取消 qǔxiāo

❸[动] 度过（时光）：spend (time)

| ～夏 xiāoxià *pass the summer in a leisurely way*
❹[动] 花费；用去：spend; consume; expend
消费 xiāofèi consume
消耗 xiāohào consume; use up; expend; deplete; drain
消费品 xiāofèipǐn consumer goods
消费者 xiāofèizhě consumer
◇消极 xiāojí ① negative ② passive; inactive
消息 xiāoxi ① news; information ② tidings; news

 销（銷） xiāo　12画　钅部
销销销销销销销销 销销销销

❶[动] 熔化金属：melt (metal)
销毁 xiāohuǐ destroy by melting or burning
❷[动] 除去；使不存在：cancel; annul | 注～zhùxiāo *write off; cancel*
报销 bàoxiāo　撤销 chèxiāo
❸[动]出售：sell; market | 脱～tuōxiāo *out of stock* / 试～shìxiāo *trial products in the market*
销量 xiāoliàng the quantity (of goods) sold; sales made
销路 xiāolù sale; market
销售 xiāoshòu sell; market
畅销 chàngxiāo　促销 cùxiāo

供销 gōngxiāo　经销 jīngxiāo
倾销 qīngxiāo　推销 tuīxiāo
展销 zhǎnxiāo
❹[动]消费：spend; consume | 开～kāixiāo *expenditure* / 花～huāxiāo *cost; expense*

 小 xiǎo　3画　小部
小 小小小

❶[形] 在体积、面积、范围、规模、力量、数量等方面不及一般的或不及比较的对象（跟"大dà"相对）：small; little; petty; minor (the opposite of "大dà") | ～河 xiǎohé *small river* / ～问题xiǎo wèntí *small problem* / 力气～lìqi xiǎo *weak in strength* / 声音太～。Shēng-yīn tài xiǎo. *The voice is too low.* / 风～些了。Fēng xiǎoxiē le. *The wind has dropped.* /这笔开支可不～。Zhè bǐ kāizhī kě bù xiǎo. *It's a big sum.*
小便 xiǎobiàn ① urinate; pass (or make) water; empty one's bladder ② urine ③ penis
小车 xiǎochē ① wheelbarrow; handbarrow; handcart; pushcart ② car; sedan
小吃 xiǎochī ① snacks; refreshments ② cold dishes (of western food)
小鬼 xiǎoguǐ ① imp; goblin ② little devil (term of endearment

in addressing a child)

小姐 xiǎojiě ① Miss ② young lady

小麦 xiǎomài wheat

小米 xiǎomǐ millet

小品 xiǎopǐn originally referred to the simplified version of a sutra; short, simple literary or artistic creation; essay; sketch

小腿 xiǎotuǐ shank; lower leg

小心 xiǎoxīn careful; attentive; cautious

小型 xiǎoxíng small-sized; small-scale; miniature

小学 xiǎoxué primary (elementary) school

小组 xiǎozǔ group

小孩儿 xiǎoháir child

小孩子 xiǎoháizi child

小伙子 xiǎohuǒzi lad; young fellow (chap); youngster

小朋友 xiǎopéngyou ① children ② (form of address by an adult to a child) little boy or girl; child

小提琴 xiǎotíqín violin

小学生 xiǎoxuéshēng primary school pupil

小心眼儿 xiǎoxīnyǎnr narrow-minded; petty

小心翼翼 xiǎoxīn-yìyì with great care; cautiously

从小 cóngxiǎo 大小 dàxiǎo

渺小 miǎoxiǎo 缩小 suōxiǎo

微小 wēixiǎo 细小 xìxiǎo

大同小异 dàtóng-xiǎoyì

空中小姐 kōngzhōng xiǎojiě

❷ [形] 排行最末的：last in seniority among brothers and sisters | ~儿子 xiǎo'érzi the youngest son / 他是我的~弟弟。Tā shì wǒ de xiǎodìdi. He is my youngest brother.

❸ [形] 称自己或与自己有关的人或事物；表示谦虚：oneself, or sb. or sth. related to oneself, used to express humbleness | ~弟 xiǎodì I myself / ~女 xiǎonǚ my daughter / ~店 xiǎodiàn my little shop

❹ [形] 与姓氏连用，用来称呼年纪小的人：used to prefix a surname as an address for someone who is young in age | ~张 Xiǎo Zhāng Xiao Zhang

◇小时 xiǎoshí hour

小数 xiǎoshù decimal

小说 xiǎoshuō novel; fiction

小偷 xiǎotōu petty (or sneak) thief; pilferer

小子 xiǎozi ① boy ② (derog.) bloke; fellow; guy

小气鬼 xiǎoqìguǐ miser; scrooge; a petty skinflint

小区 xiǎoqū residential area

小时工 xiǎoshígōng casual worker paid on an hourly basis (mostly hired to do household chores)

小数点 xiǎoshùdiǎn decimal point

晓(曉) xiǎo 10画 日部

晓晓晓晓晓晓晓晓晓晓晓晓晓晓

[动]明白；知道：know; be well versed in ｜ 知~zhīxiǎo know / 家喻户~jiāyù-hùxiǎo be known to every household
晓得 xiǎode know
揭晓 jiēxiǎo

孝 xiǎo 7画 尹部

孝孝孝孝孝孝孝

[动]尊敬并尽心奉养父母：filial; dutiful ｜ 尽~jìnxiǎo treat one's parents with filial piety
孝顺 xiǎoshùn show filial obedience

肖 xiǎo 7画 ⺌部

肖肖肖肖肖肖肖

[动]相似；像：be like; resemble
肖像 xiǎoxiàng portrait; portraiture

校 xiǎo 10画 木部

校校校校校校校校校校

[名]学校：school ｜ 技~jìxiǎo technical school / 夜~yèxiǎo night school / 军~jūnxiǎo military school
校徽 xiǎohuī school badge
校园 xiǎoyuán campus; school yard
校长 xiǎozhǎng ① headmaster; principal ② president; chancellor
高校 gāoxiǎo   学校 xuéxiǎo
高等学校 gāoděng xuéxiǎo

笑 xiǎo 10画 竹部

笑笑笑笑笑笑笑笑笑笑笑笑

❶[动]露出喜悦的表情；发出高兴的声音：crack a smile; smile; laugh; utter joyful sound ｜ ~容 xiǎoróng smiling expression; smile/ 小宝宝会~了。Xiǎo bǎobao huì xiǎo le. The baby smiles.
笑声 xiǎoshēng laughter
欢笑 huānxiǎo   玩笑 wánxiǎo
微笑 wēixiǎo
哭笑不得 kūxiǎobùdé
似笑非笑 sìxiǎo-fēixiǎo
❷[动]讥笑：ridicule; laugh at ｜ 我做得不好，请别~我。Wǒ zuò de bù hǎo, qǐng bié xiǎo wǒ. My work has not been done very well, please do not laugh at me.
嘲笑 cháoxiǎo   讥笑 jīxiǎo

可笑 kěxiào
❸ [形] 令人发笑的：humorous;
funny
笑话 xiàohua ① joke; jest ②
laugh at; ridicule
闹笑话 nàoxiàohua

 效 xiāo 10画 攵部

效效效效效效效效
效效

❶ [动] 模仿：imitate; follow the
example of｜仿~fǎngxiào
imitate
❷ [名] 功用；效果：effect; desired
result
效果 xiàoguǒ effect; result
效力 xiàolì ① render a service
to; serve ② effect
效率 xiàolǜ efficiency
效益 xiàoyì beneficial result;
benefit
长效 chángxiào
成效 chéngxiào 高效 gāoxiào
功效 gōngxiào 见效 jiànxiào
疗效 liáoxiào 生效 shēngxiào
失效 shīxiào 无效 wúxiào
有效 yǒuxiào

啸（嘯）xiào 11画 口部

啸啸啸啸啸啸啸
啸啸啸

[动]（人、兽、自然界等）发出长而
响亮的声音：(of a person or
animal) make a long and ring-
ing sound; whistle｜虎~hǔ-
xiào tiger growling / 一声长~
yīshēng chángxiào utter a
long and low cry
海啸 hǎixiào　呼啸 hūxiào

 些 xiē 8画 止部

些些些些些些些些

[量] 表示不定的数量：some｜看~
书 kàn xiē shū read some books
/ 快~走 kuài xiē zǒu go faster /
买~东西 mǎi xiē dōngxi do
some shopping / 前~日子 qián
xiē rìzi a few days ago
好些 hǎoxiē　某些 mǒuxiē
哪些 nǎxiē　那些 nàxiē
险些 xiǎnxiē　一些 yīxiē
有些 yǒuxiē　这些 zhèxiē

歇 xiē 13画 欠部

歇歇歇歇歇歇歇歇
歇歇歇歇歇

❶ [动] 休息：have a rest｜~一会儿
xiē yīhuìr have a short rest;
have a break; rest for a while
❷ [动] 停止：stop｜~工 xiēgōng
stop work; finish work / ~业
xiēyè close a business

协 (協) xié　　6画 十部

协 协协协协协协

❶[动] 合；共同：be in coordination with; make joint efforts | ～办 xiébàn *work together*
协定 xiédìng agreement
协会 xiéhuì association; society
协商 xiéshāng consult; talk things over
协调 xiétiáo coordinate; concert; harmonize; bring into line
协议 xiéyì ① agreement ② agree on
协作 xiézuò cooperation; coordination; combined efforts; joint efforts
❷[动] 帮助：help; assist
协助 xiézhù assist; help; give assistance

邪 xié　　6画 牙部

邪 邪邪邪邪邪邪

❶[形] 不正当；不正派：evil; heretical | ～说 xiéshuō *heresy* / 改～归正 gǎixié-guīzhèng *give up one's evil ways and return to the right path; turn over a new leaf*
❷[形] 不正常的：abnormal | ～门儿 xiéménr *strange; odd*

胁 (脅) xié　　8画 月部

胁 胁胁胁胁胁胁胁胁

[动] 强迫：coerce; force | ～迫 xiépò *force*
威胁 wēixié

挟 (挾) xié　　9画 扌部

挟 挟挟挟挟挟挟挟挟挟

[动] 威胁；强迫：coerce; force sb. to submit to one's will | 要～ yāoxié *hold sb. under duress*
挟持 xiéchí ① seize sb. on both sides by the arms ② hold sb. under duress

斜 xié　　11画 斗部

斜 斜斜斜斜斜斜斜斜斜斜斜

[形] 不正；不直：oblique; slanting; inclined | 墙～了。Qiáng xié le. *The wall has slanted.* / 桌子摆～了。Zhuōzi bǎixié le. *The table has not been set evenly.*
倾斜 qīngxié

谐 (諧) xié　　11画 讠部

谐谐谐谐谐谐谐谐谐
谐谐谐

[形]配合得好：in harmony; in accord | ～调 xiétiáo in agreement
和谐 héxié

携 xié 13画 扌部

携携携携携携携携
携携携携

[动]带着：carry; take along | 扶老～幼 fúlǎo-xiéyòu bring along the old and the young
携带 xiédài carry; take along
◇携手 xiéshǒu join hands

鞋 xié 15画 革部

鞋鞋鞋鞋鞋鞋鞋鞋
鞋鞋鞋鞋鞋鞋鞋

[名]shoes | 皮～píxié leather shoes / 拖～tuōxié slippers / 凉～liángxié sandals
鞋子 xiézi shoes
布鞋 bùxié
旅游鞋 lǚyóuxié

写（寫）xié 5画 宀部

写 写写写写写

❶[动]绘画：draw; paint | ～生 xiěshēng paint from life / ～真

xiězhēn ① portray a person ② portrait

❷[动]用笔书写；抄写：write; use a pen or brush to write characters; copy | ～毛笔字 xiě máobǐ zì write Chinese character with writing brush / ～对联 xiě duìlián write a couplet
写法 xiěfǎ ① style of writing; literary style ② style of handwriting; penmanship
抄写 chāoxiě   书写 shūxiě
填写 tiánxiě   听写 tīngxiě

❸[动]写作；创作：compose; write (an article, book, etc.) | ～诗 xiě shī write a poem / ～文章 xiě wénzhāng write an article / ～日记 xiě rìjì keep a diary
写作 xiězuò writing
编写 biānxiě   改写 gǎixiě
缩写 suōxiě

❹[动]描写：describe; depict | ～景 xiějǐng describe the scenery / ～实 xiěshí write or paint realistically
描写 miáoxiě

血 xiě 6画 血部

血 血血血血血血

[名]用于口语：blood (spoken) | 吐～tùxiě spit blood / 鼻子流了不少～。Bízi liúle bùshǎo xiě. A lot of blood flowed from the nose.

出血 chūxiě
See xuě.

泄 xiè 8画 氵部

泄 泄泄泄泄泄泄泄泄

❶[动]排出(液体、气体等): let out
(fluid or gas); discharge;
release | 排～pāixiè drain /
水～不通 shuǐxièbùtōng not
even a drop of water could
trickle through; be densely
packed (with people)

❷[动] 发泄: give vent to | ～愤
xièfèn give vent to spite / ～恨
xièhèn give vent to hatred

❸[动] 透露: leak; let out | ～密
xièmì let out a secret / ～底
xièdǐ reveal the inside story
泄漏 xièlòu let out; leak; divulge; give away
泄露 xièlòu let out; reveal

◇泄气 xièqì ① lose heart; feel
discouraged; be disheartened ②
disappointing; frustrating; pa-
thetic

泻 (瀉) xiè 8画 氵部

泻 泻泻泻泻泻泻泻泻

❶[动] 向下急流: flow swiftly;
rush down; pour out | 倾～
qīngxiè pour down; come
down in torrents / 水从楼上～下

来。Shuǐ cóng lóu shang xiè
xiàlai. Water poured down from
upstairs.

❷[动]拉肚子: have diarrhoea | ～
肚子 xiè dūzi have loose bowels
/ 上吐下～shàngtù-xiàxiè suffer
from vomiting and diarrhoea
腹泻 fùxiè

卸 xiè 9画 卩部

卸 卸卸卸卸卸卸卸卸
卸

❶[动] 把东西从运输工具上搬下来:
unload; discharge; remove the
cargo from a vehicle | ～货
xièhuò unload cargo / ～车
xièchē unload a truck
装卸 zhuāngxiè

❷[动] 从机器上取下零件: remove
parts from a machine | 拆～
chāixiè take apart / ～零件 xiè
língjiàn remove parts (from a
machine)

❸[动] 解除; 推脱: get rid of;
shirk; be relieved from one's
office | 推～责任 tuīxiè zérèn
shirk responsibility / ～下思想
包袱 xièxia sīxiǎng bāofu get
rid of the load on one's mind

屑 xiè 10画 尸部

屑 屑屑屑屑屑屑屑屑
屑屑

[名]碎末：bits; scraps｜铁～tiěxiē *scraps of iron; iron shavings*｜木～mùxiē *sawdust*｜纸～zhǐxiē *scraps of paper*｜面包～miànbāoxiè *crumbs (of bread)*

械 xiè 11画 木部

械械械械械械械械械械械

[名]工具：apparatus; tool
机械 jīxiè　　器械 qìxiè

谢（謝） xiè 12画 讠部

谢谢谢谢谢谢谢谢谢谢谢谢

❶[动]推辞；拒绝：decline｜～客 xièkè *refuse to receive any guest*
谢绝 xièjué　refuse; decline

❷[动]对人表示感激：thank｜道～ dàoxiè *thank*｜多～。Duō xiè. *Thanks a lot.*｜这点儿小事不用～了。Zhè diǎnr xiǎoshì búyòng xiè le. *It's my pleasure.*
谢谢 xièxie thanks; thank you
谢意 xièyì gratitude; thankfulness
答谢 dáxiè　　感谢 gǎnxiè

心 xīn 4画 心部

心心心心心

❶[名]心脏：heart｜我～痛。Wǒ xīn tòng. *My heart aches.*｜她激动得～怦怦跳。Tā jīdòng de xīn pēngpēng tiào. *Her heart was thumping with excitement.*
心脏 xīnzàng ① heart ② centre
心脏病 xīnzàng bìng heart disease

❷[名]大脑；思想感情：usu. referring to the heart; mind; feeling; intention｜同情～tóngqíngxīn *sympathy*｜她的话温暖了我的～。Tā de huà wēnnuǎnle wǒ de xīn. *Her words warmed my heart.*
心爱 xīn'ài love; treasure
心得 xīndé　what one has learned from work, study etc.
心里 xīnli in the heart; at heart; in (the) mind
心理 xīnlǐ psychology; mentality
心灵 xīnlíng ① clever; intelligent; quick-witted ② heart; soul; spirit
心目 xīnmù ① mood; frame of mind ② memory ③ mind's eye; mental view
心情 xīnqíng frame of mind; state of mind; mood
心声 xīnshēng heartfelt wishes; aspirations; thinking
心事 xīnshì sth. weighing on one's mind; a load on one's mind; worry

心思 xīnsi ① thought; idea ② thinking ③ state of mind; mood

心态 xīntài mentality

心疼 xīnténg ① love dearly ② feel sorry; be distressed

心头 xīntóu mind; heart

心血 xīnxuè painstaking care (effort)

心意 xīnyì ① regard; kindly feelings ② intention; purpose

心愿 xīnyuàn cherished desire; aspiration; wish; dream

心中 xīnzhōng in one's heart

心眼儿 xīnyǎnr ① heart; mind ② intention ③ intelligence; cleverness

心灵手巧 xīnlíng-shǒuqiǎo clever in mind and skillful in hand; clever and deft

心满意足 xīnmǎn-yìzú be perfectly content (or satisfied)

爱心 àixīn	安心 ānxīn
本心 běnxīn	操心 cāoxīn
称心 chènxīn	成心 chéngxīn
粗心 cūxīn	担心 dānxīn
当心 dāngxīn	恶心 ěxin
放心 fàngxīn	费心 fèixīn
甘心 gānxīn	关心 guānxīn
狠心 hěnxīn	灰心 huīxīn
精心 jīngxīn	决心 juéxīn
开心 kāixīn	留心 liúxīn
耐心 nàixīn	内心 nèixīn
热心 rèxīn	伤心 shāngxīn
细心 xìxīn	小心 xiǎoxīn
信心 xìnxīn	虚心 xūxīn
野心 yěxīn	一心 yīxīn

疑心 yíxīn	用心 yòngxīn
真心 zhēnxīn	
偏心眼儿 piānxīnyǎnr	
小心眼儿 xiǎoxīnyǎnr	
三心二意 sānxīn-èryì	
一心一意 yīxīn-yīyì	
有口无心 yǒukǒu-wúxīn	

❸ [名] 中心；中央的部分：centre; core | 手~shǒuxīn *the centre of the palm* / 圆~yuánxīn *the centre of a circle*

核心 héxīn	空心 kōngxīn
中心 zhōngxīn	
卷心菜 juǎnxīncài	
市中心 shìzhōngxīn	

◇ 点心 diǎnxin

辛 xīn   7画 辛部

辛 辛辛辛辛辛辛辛

[形] 劳苦；困难：hard; laborious | 艰~jiānxīn *hardship*

辛苦 xīnkǔ ① hard; toilsome; laborious ② work hard; go to great trouble; go through hardships

辛勤 xīnqín industrious; hardworking

艰辛 jiānxīn

 欣 xīn   8画 斤部

欣 欣欣欣欣欣欣欣欣

[形] 喜悦；快乐：glad; happy; joyful | 欢~ huānxīn *joyful* / ~喜 xīnxǐ *glad*

欣赏 xīnshǎng appreciate; enjoy; admire

欣慰 xīnwèi be gratified

锌（鋅） xīn 12画 钅部

锌锌锌锌锌锌锌锌
锌锌锌锌

[名] zinc

新 xīn 13画 斤部

新新新新新新新新
新新新新新

❶ [形] 初次出现的或刚经历到的（跟"旧 jiù"或"老 lǎo"相对）：new; fresh; up-to-date (the opposite of "旧 jiù" or "老 lǎo") | ~地方 xīn dìfang *new place* / ~气象 xīn qìxiàng *new atmosphere* / ~办法 xīn bànfǎ *new method* / ~事物 xīn shìwù *new things*

新款 xīnkuǎn of new model (or design, style)

新年 xīnnián New Year

新式 xīnshì new type; latest fashion; new-style

新闻 xīnwén news

新鲜 xīnxiān ① fresh ② news

新型 xīnxíng new type; new pattern

新秀 xīnxiù new star

新陈代谢 xīnchén-dàixiè ① metabolism ② the new superseding the old

清新 qīngxīn

❷ [形] 性质上改变得更好的；更进步的（跟"旧 jiù"相对）：new; made anew; renewed (the opposite of "旧 jiù") | ~思想 xīn sīxiǎng *new ideas* / ~产品 xīn chǎnpǐn *new products* / 面目一~ miànmù-yīxīn *take on a new look*

重新 chóngxīn

创新 chuàngxīn 革新 géxīn

更新 gēngxīn

刷新 shuāxīn

❸ [形] 还未用过的（跟"旧 jiù"相对）：brand new; unused (the opposite of "旧 jiù") | ~笔 xīn bǐ *new pen* / ~衣服 xīn yīfu *new dress* / ~房子 xīn fángzi *newly built house*

崭新 zhǎnxīn

❹ [形] 刚结婚的或结婚不久的：recently married; newly married

新房 xīnfáng bridal chamber

新婚 xīnhūn newly-married

新郎 xīnláng bridegroom

新娘 xīnniáng bride

新人 xīnrén ① people of a new type ② new personality; new talent ③ newlywed, esp. the bride

❺ [副] 最近；刚刚：newly; freshly;

recently | 书是～买的。Shū shì xīn mǎi de. *The book was newly bought.* / 他是～来的。Tā shì xīn lái de. *He's a new recruit.*

新近 xīnjìn recently; lately; in recent times

新生 xīnshēng ① newborn; newly born ② new life; rebirth; regeneration ③ new student

新兴 xīnxīng new and developing; rising; burgeoning

薪 xīn 16画 艹部

薪薪薪薪薪薪薪薪
薪薪薪薪薪薪薪薪

[名]指工资：pay; salary | 今天发～。Jīntiān fā xīn. *It's payday today.*

薪酬 xīnchóu salary; pay

薪金 xīnjīn salary; pay

薪水 xīnshuǐ salary; pay; wage

年薪 niánxīn　　月薪 yuèxīn

信 xìn 9画 亻部

信信信信信信信信
信

❶ [形]诚实；不虚伪：honest; true; real; trustworthy | 失～shīxìn *break one's promise*

信守 xìnshǒu abide by; stand by

信用 xìnyòng ① trustworthiness; credit ② credit

信誉 xìnyù prestige; credit; reputation

诚信 chéngxìn　　威信 wēixìn

❷ [名]消息：news; message; information | 报～bàoxìn *tip sb. off* / 那事儿到现在还没～儿呢。Nà shìr dào xiànzài hái méi xìnr ne. *There is no news about it yet.*

信号 xìnhào signal

信息 xìnxī information; news; message

短信 duǎnxìn

❸ [名]信件：letters; mail | 寄～jìxìn *post a letter* / 送～sòngxìn *deliver a letter* / 这是他托我带给你的～。Zhè shì tā tuō wǒ dàigěi nǐ de xìn. *He asked me to bring this letter to you.*

信封 xìnfēng envelope

信件 xìnjiàn letter; mail

信箱 xìnxiāng ① letter box; mailbox ② post-office box

电信 diànxìn　　回信 huíxìn

来信 láixìn　　书信 shūxìn

通信 tōngxìn

明信片 míngxìnpiàn

❹ [动]相信：believe; trust | ～不～由你 xìnbuxìn yóu nǐ *it depends on whether you believe it or not* / 别～他的话。Bié xìn tā de huà. *Don't believe what he says.*

信赖 xìnlài trust; count on; have

faith in

信念 xìnniàn faith; belief; conviction

信任 xìnrèn trust; have confidence in

信托 xìntuō trust; entrust

信心 xìnxīn confidence; faith

信仰 xìnyǎng faith; belief; conviction

信用卡 xìnyòngkǎ credit card

信用社 xìnyòngshè credit co-operative

坚信 jiānxìn	迷信 míxìn
确信 quèxìn	深信 shēnxìn
相信 xiāngxìn	自信 zìxìn

❺ [动] 信奉（宗教）：profess faith in; believe in | ～教 xìnjiào *profess a religion* / ～佛 xìnfó *believe in Buddhism*

❻ [动] 随意；听任：at will; at random; without plan | ～口 xìnkǒu *talk irresponsibly* / ～步 xìnbù *walk aimlessly*

◇信贷 xìndài credit

 衅 (釁) xìn 11画 血部

衅衅衅衅衅衅衅衅衅衅衅

[名] 争端：quarrel; dispute | 寻～ xúnxìn *pick a quarrel*

挑衅 tiǎoxìn

 兴 (興) xīng 6画 八部

兴 兴兴兴兴兴兴

❶ [动] 开始；发出；创办：start; begin; initiate

兴办 xīngbàn initiate; set up

兴建 xīngjiàn build; construct

兴起 xīngqǐ rise; spring up; be on the upgrade

❷ [动] 兴盛；流行：prosper; rise; prevail; become popular | 时～ shíxīng *in style; fashionable* / 现在正～这个。Xiànzài zhèng xīng zhège. *That's all the rage now.*

兴旺 xīngwàng prosperous; flourishing; thriving

复兴 fùxīng　新兴 xīnxīng

振兴 zhènxīng

◇兴奋 xīngfèn ① be excited ② excitation

兴奋剂 xīngfènjì anti-depressant; stimulant

　　See xìng.

 星 xīng 9画 日部

星 星星星星星星星星
星

❶ [名] 星星：star | 那颗～最亮。Nà kē xīng zuì liàng. *That star is the brightest.*

星辰 xīngchén stars

星球 xīngqiú celestial body; heavenly body

星星 xīngxing ① tiny spot ② star

恒星 héngxīng 火星 huǒxīng
卫星 wèixīng 行星 xíngxīng

❷[名] 细小、零碎或闪亮的东西: bit; particle | 火～儿 huǒxīngr *spark* / 油～儿 yóuxīngr *a bit of oil*

零星 língxīng

❸[名] 比喻某种突出的、有特殊作用或才能的人: (fig.) people of outstanding talent | 球～qiúxīng *ball-game star*

歌星 gēxīng 明星 míngxīng

◇星期 xīngqī ① week ② Sunday

星期天 Xīngqītiān Sunday
星期日 Xīngqīrì Sunday

 xīng 13画 月部

腥 腥腥腥腥腥腥腥腥腥腥腥腥腥

[名] 鱼虾等发出的气味: smell of fish or seafood | 鱼有～味儿。Yú yǒu xīngwèir. *Fish smells.*

 xíng 6画 刂部

刑 刑刑刑刑刑刑

❶[名] 对犯人的各种处罚: punishment; penalty; sentence | 缓～huǎnxíng *probation; suspended sentence* / 判～pànxíng *convict*

刑场 xíngchǎng execution ground

刑法 xíngfǎ corporal punishment; torture

刑事 xíngshì criminal; penal

服刑 fúxíng 死刑 sǐxíng

❷[名] 特指对犯人的体罚: corporal punishment; torture | 受～shòuxíng *be tortured* / 动～dòngxíng *subject sb. to torture*

 xíng 6画 彳部

行 行行行行行行

❶[动] 走: go; walk; travel | 人～道 rénxíngdào *pavement*

行动 xíngdòng ① move about; get about ② act; take action ③ action; behaviour; conduct

行军 xíngjūn (of troops) march

行人 xíngrén pedestrian

行驶 xíngshǐ (of a vehicle, ship, etc.) go; ply; travel

行星 xíngxīng planet

行走 xíngzǒu walk

步行 bùxíng 飞行 fēixíng

航行 hángxíng

平行 píngxíng

通行 tōngxíng 游行 yóuxíng

运行 yùnxíng

飞行员 fēixíngyuán

自行车 zìxíngchē

❷[名] 路程; 旅行: trip; journey | ～装 xíngzhuāng *outfit for a journey* / ～踪 xíngzōng *whereabouts*

行程 xíngchéng route or distance of travel

行李 xíngli luggage; baggage

旅行社 lǚxíngshè

❸ [动] 流通；推行：be current; circulate | ～销 xíngxiāo *be on sale* / 全国通～quánguó tōngxíng *circulate within the whole country*

发行 fāxíng　风行 fēngxíng

流行 liúxíng　旅行 lǚxíng

盛行 shèngxíng

送行 sòngxíng　推行 tuīxíng

❹ [动] 做；从事：do; perform; carry out | ～医 xíngyī *practise medicine* / 简便易～jiǎnbiàn yìxíng *simple and easy to do*

行动 xíngdòng ① move (or get) about ② act; take action ③ action; operation

行使 xíngshǐ exercise; perform

行政 xíngzhèng administration

横行 héngxíng　进行 jìnxíng

举行 jǔxíng　可行 kěxíng

履行 lǚxíng　施行 shīxíng

强行 qiángxíng　实行 shíxíng

试行 shìxíng　先行 xiānxíng

现行 xiànxíng　执行 zhíxíng

自行 zìxíng

❺ [名] 举止；行为：behaviour; conduct | 言～yánxíng *words and deeds* / 德～déxíng *moral conduct*

行径 xíngjìng act; action; move

行为 xíngwéi action; behaviour; conduct

品行 pǐnxíng　罪行 zuìxíng

❻ [动] 可以：be all right; will do; can be carried out; be practicable | ～，就这么办。Xíng, jiù zhème bàn. *All right. It's settled.*

不行 bùxíng

❼ [形] 能干；有本事：capable; competent | 你真～!Nǐ zhēn xíng! *You are really capable!* / 她教英语～吗?Tā jiāo Yīngyǔ xíng ma? *Is she competent to be an English teacher?*

◇ 行书 xíngshū running hand (in Chinese calligraphy)

　　See háng.

xíng　7画 彡部

形 形形形形形形形

❶ [名] 实体；生物的形体：body; entity | 无～wúxíng *intangible* / ～影不离 xíngyǐng-bùlí *inseparable like body and shadow*

❷ [名] 形状；样子：form; shape | 方～fāngxíng *square* / 三角～sānjiǎoxíng *triangle*

形容 xíngróng ① appearance; countenance ② describe

形式 xíngshì form; shape

形势 xíngshì ① terrain; topographical feature ② situation; circumstance

形态 xíngtài ① form; shape; pattern ② morphology

形象 xíngxiàng image; form;

figure

形状 xíngzhuàng form; appearance; shape

变形 biànxíng 地形 dìxíng
情形 qíngxíng 图形 túxíng
外形 wàixíng 无形 wúxíng
整形 zhěngxíng
长方形 chángfāngxíng

❸ [动] 现出；表露：appear; look ｜ ~成 xíngchéng form; take form; take shape

型 xíng 9画 土部

型 型型型型型型型型
型

❶ [名] 铸造器物用的模子：mould ｜ 模~móxíng mould

❷ [名] 式样；类别；规格：model; type; pattern ｜ 血~xuèxíng blood type / 句~jùxíng sentence pattern

型号 xínghào model; type
车型 chēxíng 大型 dàxíng
类型 lèixíng 微型 wēixíng
小型 xiǎoxíng 新型 xīnxíng
中型 zhōngxíng
◇造型 zàoxíng
重型 zhòngxíng
外向型 wàixiàngxíng

醒 xǐng 16画 酉部

醒 醒醒醒醒醒醒醒醒
醒醒醒醒醒醒醒醒

❶ [动] 从酒醉或昏迷中恢复常态：regain consciousness; sober up; come to ｜ 病人从昏迷中~过来了。Bìngrén cóng hūnmí zhōng xǐng guòlai le. *The patient has come out of a coma.*

清醒 qīngxǐng 苏醒 sūxǐng

❷ [动] 结束睡眠状态或还没睡着：be awake; wake up ｜ 孩子~了。Háizi xǐng le. *The child has woken up.* / 他还没睡~呢。Tā hái méi shuì xǐng ne. *He is still asleep.*

❸ [动] 醒悟；觉悟：come to realize (the truth, one's error, etc.); wake up to reality ｜ 猛~měngxǐng *suddenly wake up (to the truth)*

觉醒 juéxǐng 提醒 tíxǐng

◇醒目 xǐngmù (of written words or pictures) catch the eye; attract attention; be striking to the eye

兴 (興) xìng 6画 八部

兴 兴兴兴兴兴兴

[名] 对事物喜爱的情绪：mood or desire to do sth.; interest; excitement

兴趣 xìngqù interest; taste
兴高采烈 xìnggāo-cǎiliè be on top of the world; be in high spirits; be in great delight

高兴 gāoxìng
感兴趣 gǎnxìngqù
See xīng.

杏　xìng　7画 木部

杏 杏杏杏杏杏杏杏

[名] apricot | ~树 xìngshù *apricot tree*

幸　xìng　8画 土部

幸 幸幸幸幸幸幸幸幸

❶[形] 意外地（得到好处或免去灾祸）：lucky; fortunate | ~免 xìngmiǎn *escape by sheer luck; have a narrow escape*

幸好 xìnghǎo fortunately; luckily

幸亏 xìngkuī fortunately; luckily

❷[形] 幸福；幸运：happy; lucky

幸福 xìngfú ① happiness; well-being ② happy

幸运 xìngyùn fortunate; lucky

不幸 bùxìng　荣幸 róngxìng

性　xìng　8画 忄部

性 性性性性性性性性

❶[名] 性情；脾气：nature; character; disposition | 个~gèxìng *individuality* / 天~tiānxìng *nature* /

他的~子很急。Tā de xìngzi hěn jí. *He is quick-tempered.*

性格 xìnggé nature; disposition; temperament

性情 xìngqíng disposition; temperament; temper

慢性 mànxìng　任性 rènxìng

索性 suǒxìng

❷[名] 事物的性质特征：property; quality; attribute of sth. resulting from a certain element contained in it | 药~yàoxìng *medicinal properties* / 酒~jiǔxìng *alcoholic strength* / 弹~tánxìng *elasticity*

性能 xìngnéng function (of a machine,etc.); performance; property

性质 xìngzhì quality; nature; character

本性 běnxìng　秉性 bǐngxìng

党性 dǎngxìng 定性 dìngxìng

毒性 dúxìng　恶性 èxìng

个性 gèxìng　共性 gòngxìng

记性 jìxìng　理性 lǐxìng

良性 liángxìng 人性 rénxìng

特性 tèxìng

一次性 yīcìxìng

❸[词尾] 在别的词后面指性质、范围、方式等：suffix indicating a specified quality, property, scope, etc. | 积极~jījíxìng *activeness; vigorousness* / 必要~bìyàoxìng *necessity* / 社会~shèhuìxìng *social nature* / 灵活~línghuóxìng

flexibility

❹[名] 性别：sex

性别 xìngbié gender; sex

性感 xìnggǎn sex appeal; sexiness

男性 nánxìng　女性 nǚxìng

❺[名] 有关生殖或性欲的：sexual | ～器官 xìngqìguān *sexual organ* / ～行为 xìngxíngwéi *sexual behaviour; sexual intercourse*

◇性命 xìngmìng life

 姓 xìng 8画 女部

姓 姓姓姓姓姓姓姓姓

❶[名] 表明家族系统的字：surname | 他与我同～。Tā yǔ wǒ tóngxìng. *He and I have the same surname.*

姓名 xìngmíng surname and given name; full name

百姓 bǎixìng　贵姓 guìxìng

老百姓 lǎobǎixìng

❷[动] 以…为姓：one's surname is; be surnamed | 你～什么？Nǐ xìng shénme? *What's your surname?* / 我～王。Wǒ xìng Wáng. *My surname is Wang.*

 凶 xiōng 4画 凵部

凶 凶凶凶凶

❶[形] 不幸的（跟"吉 jí"相对）：inauspicious; ominous (the opposite of "吉 jí") | ～事 xiōngshì *unfortunate event (such as death, injury, accident)* / 吉～jíxiōng *good or bad luck*

❷[形] 凶恶；残暴：vicious; fierce; ferocious; brutal | 这个人长得很～。Zhège rén zhǎng de hěn xiōng. *This guy looks fierce.*

凶恶 xiōng'è fierce; ferocious; fiendish

凶狠 xiōnghěn fierce and malicious

凶猛 xiōngměng violent; ferocious

凶杀 xiōngshā homicide; murder

凶手 xiōngshǒu murderer; assassin; assailant

❸[形] 厉害：(of force, strength) violent; ferocious | 闹得很～。Nào de hěn xiōng. *What a terrible row!* / 雨来得很～。Yǔ lái de hěn xiōng. *The rain poured down torrentially.*

 兄 xiōng 5画 口部

兄 兄兄兄兄兄

❶[名] 哥哥：elder brother | 家～ jiāxiōng *my brother*

兄弟 xiōngdi ① brother ② fraternal; brotherly

弟兄 dìxiong

❷[名] 亲戚中同辈的年纪比自己大的男子：address for a male cousin older than oneself

❸[名] 对男性朋友的尊称：polite form of address between men | 老～lǎoxiōng *my dear (old) friend*

汹　xiōng　7画 氵部

汹汹汹汹汹汹汹汹

See 汹涌

汹涌 xiōngyǒng tempestuous; turbulent

胸　xiōng　10画 月部

胸胸胸胸胸胸胸胸胸胸

❶[名] thorax; chest; breast | 挺～tǐngxiōng *hold out one's chest* | 她感到～痛。Tā gǎndào xiōng tòng. *She felt an ache in her chest.*

胸部 xiōngbù thorax; chest

胸罩 xiōngzhào brassiere; bra

❷[名] 指心里(与思想、见识、气量等有关)：mind; heart (related to thinking, knowledge, experience, tolerance, etc.) | 心～xīnxiōng *breadth of mind*

胸怀 xiōnghuái mind; heart

雄　xiōng　12画 隹部

雄雄雄雄雄雄雄雄雄雄雄雄

❶[形] 公的(跟"雌cí"相对)：male (the opposite of "雌cí") | ～鸡 xiōngjī *cock; rooster*

❷[名] 强有力的人：a person having great power and influence

英雄 yīngxióng

❸[形] 强有力的：powerful | ～师 xióngshī *powerful army* | ～辩 xióngbiàn *eloquence; convincing argument*

雄厚 xiónghòu rich; solid; abundant

雄壮 xióngzhuàng full of power and grandeur; magnificent; majestic

❹[形] 有气魄的：grand; imposing | ～心 xióngxīn *great ambition*

雄伟 xióngwěi grand; imposing; magnificent

熊　xióng　14画 灬部

熊熊熊熊熊熊熊熊熊熊熊熊熊熊

[名] bear

熊猫 xióngmāo panda

休　xiū　6画 亻部

休休休休休休

[动]休息：rest | ～假 xiūjià *take a holiday*

休息 xiūxi take a rest; rest

休闲 xiūxián ① (agri.) lie fallow ② have one's leisure time

休养 xiūyǎng recuperate; convalesce

离休 líxiū　　　退休 tuìxiū

双休日 shuāngxiūrì

修 xiū　9画 亻部

修 修修修修修修修修 修

❶[动] 整理装饰使整齐美观：make neat and beautiful | ～饰 xiūshì embellish; decorate / ～指甲 xiū zhǐjia trim one's fingernails / ～剪树枝 xiūjiǎn shùzhī prune a branch

❷[动] 使破损的东西恢复原状和作用：mend; fix up; patch up | ～车 xiūchē repair one's car (or bike) / ～机器 xiū jīqì repair a machine

修订 xiūdìng revise

修复 xiūfù ① repair; restore; renovate ② repair

修改 xiūgǎi revise; modify; amend; alter

修理 xiūlǐ repair; mend; overhaul; fix

修整 xiūzhěng ① repair and maintain ② prune; trim

修正 xiūzhèng ① revise; amend; correct ② mutilate (Marxism–Leninism); revise

检修 jiǎnxiū　　　维修 wéixiū

❸[动] 兴建；建造：build; construct | ～水库 xiū shuǐkù build a reservoir / ～铁路 xiū tiělù build a railway

修建 xiūjiàn build; construct; erect

修筑 xiūzhù build; construct; put up

抢修 qiǎngxiū

❹[动] (学问、品行方面)学习和锻炼：(of learning, character or study) study; cultivate | 自～ zìxiū study by oneself / 进～ jìnxiū engage in advanced studies / 这些课我已经～完了。Zhèxiē kè wǒ yǐjīng xiūwán le. I've finished these courses.

修养 xiūyǎng ① accomplishment; training; mastery ② self-cultivation

必修 bìxiū　　　辅修 fǔxiū

选修 xuǎnxiū

羞 xiū　10画 羊部

羞 羞羞羞羞羞羞羞 羞羞

❶[形] 不光彩；不体面：shameful; disgraceful | 遮～zhēxiū conceal one's shame / ～辱 xiūrǔ shame; dishonour; humiliate

羞耻 xiūchǐ sense of shame; shame

❷[动] 难为情；不好意思：feel

embarrassed｜她～红了脸。Tā xiūhóngle liǎn. *She blushed with embarrassment.*

害羞 hàixiū

朽　　xiǔ　　6画 木部

朽 朽朽朽朽朽朽

[动]腐烂：(of wood) rot; decay｜～木 xiǔmù *rotten wood or tree*

腐朽 fǔxiǔ

秀　　xiù　　7画 禾部

秀 秀秀秀秀秀秀秀秀

❶[形] 美丽而不俗气：elegant; beautiful｜～气 xiùqi *delicate; elegant; fine* / 山清水～ shānqīngshuǐxiù *beautiful hills and waters; lovely scenery*

秀丽 xiùlì beautiful; handsome; pretty

❷[形] 特别优异的：excellent

新秀 xīnxiù　　优秀 yōuxiù

袖　　xiù　　10画 衤部

袖 袖袖袖袖袖袖袖袖 袖袖

[名]袖子：sleeve｜长～ chángxiù *long sleeves* / 这件衣服的～子太长了。Zhè jiàn yīfu de xiùzi tài cháng le. *The sleeves of the*

coat are too long.

袖子 xiùzi sleeve

领袖 lǐngxiù

绣 (繡) xiù　　10画 纟部

绣 绣绣绣绣绣绣绣绣 绣绣

[动]用彩线在织物上面织制花纹、图样：embroider｜～花儿 xiù huār *embroider; do embroidery* / ～字 xiùzì *embroider characters*

刺绣 cìxiù

锈 (銹) xiù　　12画 钅部

锈 锈锈锈锈锈锈锈锈 锈锈锈锈

❶ [名] rust｜铁～ tiěxiù *rust* / 刀生～了。Dāo shēngxiù le. *The knife has become rusty.*

❷ [动] 生锈：go rusty｜刀刃～了。Dāorèn xiù le. *The edge of the knife has become rusty.* / 锁～住了。Suǒ xiùzhù le. *The lock got rusty and could not be opened.*

嗅　　xiù　　13画 口部

嗅 嗅嗅嗅嗅嗅嗅嗅嗅 嗅嗅嗅嗅嗅

[动] 用鼻子辨别气味；闻：smell; scent; sniff | ～觉 xiùjué *sense of smell*

须 (須) xū　9画 彡部

须 须须须须须须须须须
须

[动] 应该；一定要：must; have to | ～注意身体 xū zhùyì shēntǐ *must take care of one's health*
须知 xūzhī ① one should know that; it must be understood (borne in mind) that ② points for attention; notice
必须 bìxū

虚 xū　11画 虍部

虚 虚虚虚虚虚虚虚虚
虚虚虚

❶ [形] 空（跟"实shí"相对）：empty; void (the opposite of "实shí") | 座无～席 zuòwúxūxí *all the seats have been occupied*
虚词 xūcí (gram.) function word; particle
空虚 kōngxū

❷ [形] 虚心；不自满：humble; modest
虚心 xūxīn open-minded; modest
谦虚 qiānxū

❸ [形] 体质弱：weak; in poor health | 他身体很～。Tā shēntǐ

hěn xū. *He is very weak.* | 病后他感到身体很～。Bìng hòu tā gǎndào shēntǐ hěn xū. *He has felt very weak since his illness.*
虚弱 xūruò ① in poor health; weak; debilitated ② weak; feeble

❹ [形] 假；不真实：false; sham | ～名 xūmíng *false reputation* | ～构 xūgòu *make up; fabricate*
虚假 xūjiǎ false; sham
虚拟 xūnǐ ① invented; fictitious ② suppositonal ③ digital; visual
虚伪 xūwěi sham; false; hypocritical
弄虚作假 nòngxū-zuòjiǎ

❺ [副] 徒然；白白地：in vain; uselessly | ～度年华 xūdù niánhuá *idle away one's time*

❻ [形] 勇气不足；胆怯：diffident; timid | 心里有点～ xīnli yǒudiǎn xū *feel rather diffident*

墟 xū　14画 土部

墟 墟墟墟墟墟墟墟墟
墟墟墟墟墟墟

[名] ruins; place which is now deserted
废墟 fèixū

需 xū　14画 雨部

需 需需需需需需需需
需需需需需需

[动]需要: need; want; require |
按～分配 ànxū fēnpèi distrib-
ute according to requirement
需求 xūqiú requirement; de-
mand
需要 xūyào ① need; want; require; demand ② needs; demand; requirement; want
必需 bìxū   急需 jíxū

徐   xú   10画 彳部

徐 徐徐徐徐徐徐徐徐徐
徐徐

[形]〈书〉慢慢地: slowly; gently
| ～步 xúbù walk slowly (lei-
surely)
徐徐 xúxú slowly; gently

许 (許) xǔ   6画 讠部

许 许许许许许许

❶ [动] 认可; 应允: allow; per-
mit; promise | 特～tèxǔ give
special permission
许可 xǔkě permit; allow
不许 bùxǔ   容许 róngxǔ
允许 yǔnxǔ
❷ [动] 预先答应; 给予; 献给:
promise to give sth. to or do sth.
for sb.; give a promise; dedi-
cate (oneself to one's nation) |

我～给他一笔钱。Wǒ xǔgěi tā
yī bǐ qián. I promised to give
him a sum of money.
❸ [副] 或者; 可能: maybe; per-
haps
或许 huòxǔ   也许 yěxǔ
❹ [数] 表示大约的数目或程度: in-
dicating a rough estimation | ～
久 xǔjiǔ for a long time / 少～
shǎoxǔ a little
许多 xǔduō many; much; a
great deal of; a lot of

    xù   7画 广部

序 序序序序序序序

❶ [名]排列的先后:order; sequence
| 先后有～xiānhòu yǒuxù in
good sequence; in perfect order
次序 cìxù   顺序 shùnxù
❷ [形]开头的; 在正式内容之前的:
introductory; initial | ～曲
xùqǔ prelude / ～幕xùmù prologue; prelude
序言 xùyán preface; foreword

    xù   9画 又部

叙 叙叙叙叙叙叙叙叙
叙

❶ [动] 交谈; 说: talk; chat | ～
旧 xùjiù talk about the old days
叙谈 xùtán chat; talk together

❷[动]（把事情经过）记下来或说出来：narrate; recount; relate | ～事 xùshì *narrate (in writing)* / 记～jìxù *recount*

叙述 xùshù narrate; recount; relate

畜 xù 10画 田部

[动]饲养：raise (domestic animals)

畜牧 xùmù rear livestock or poultry

畜产品 xùchǎnpǐn animal products

　　See chù.

酗 xù 11画 酉部

酗 酗酗酗酗酗酗酗酗酗酗酗酗

See 酗酒

酗酒 xùjiǔ excessive drinking

绪 (緒) xù 11画 纟部

绪 绪绪绪绪绪绪绪绪绪绪绪

[名]心情：mental or emotional state | 心～不宁 xīnxù-bùníng *be in a state of agitation*

情绪 qíngxù　　　思绪 sīxù

续 (續) xù 11画 纟部

续 续续续续续续续续续续续

❶[动]接连；连接不断：continue; be successive | 陆～lùxù *one after another*

持续 chíxù　　　继续 jìxù

连续 liánxù　　　连续剧 liánxùjù

断断续续 duànduàn-xùxù

❷[动]接在原有事物的后面或下面：continue; resume; extend; join

待～dàixù *to be continued* / 这条绳子太短了，再～上一截儿吧。Zhè tiáo shéngzi tāi duǎn le, zāi xùshang yī jiér ba. *This string is too short. Let's tie another piece to it.*

续借 xùjiè renew (a library book)

絮 xù 12画 系部

絮 絮絮絮絮絮絮絮絮絮絮絮絮

[形]话多；啰唆：long-winded; garrulous

絮叨 xùdao long-winded; garrulous; wordy

蓄 xù 13画 艹部

蓄 蓄蓄蓄蓄蓄蓄蓄蓄蓄蓄蓄蓄蓄

❶[动] 储藏；积聚：store up; save up | ～水池 xūshuǐchí *cistern; reservoir*

储蓄 chǔxù　　　积蓄 jīxù

❷[动]（心里）存有：entertain (ideas); harbour | ～意 xūyì *premeditated*

宣　xuān　9画 宀部

宣宣宣宣宣宣宣宣宣

[动]公开说出：declare; proclaim; announce | ～称 xuānchēng assert; declare; profess

宣布 xuānbù declare; proclaim; announce

宣传 xuānchuán conduct propaganda; propagate; disseminate; give publicity to

宣读 xuāndú read out (in public)

宣告 xuāngào declare; proclaim

宣判 xuānpàn (leg.) pronounce judgement

宣誓 xuānshì take an oath; swear an oath; make a vow; make a pledge

宣言 xuānyán declaration; manifesto

宣扬 xuānyáng publicise; propagate; advocate; advertise

◇宣纸 xuānzhǐ rice paper, a high quality paper originally made in Xuancheng in Anhui Province, esp. good for traditional Chinese painting and calligraphy

悬（懸）xuán　11画 心部

悬悬悬悬悬悬悬悬悬悬悬

❶[动] 吊；挂：hang | 明月高～。Míngyuè gāoxuán. *A bright moon hangs in the sky.*

悬挂 xuánguà ① hang; fly ② suspension

悬赏 xuánshǎng offer (or post) a reward

悬崖 xuányá overhanging (steep) cliff; precipice

❷[动] 无着落；没结果：unresolved; unsettled | ～案 xuán'àn *a suspended case* / 那件事还～在那儿。Nà jiàn shì hái xuán zài nàr. *The matter has not been settled yet.*

❸[动] 记挂：miss; be concerned about

悬念 xuánniàn ① be concerned about (sb. who is elsewhere) ② suspense; audience's involvement in a film or play; reader's involvement in a piece of literature

旋　xuán　11画 方部

旋 旋旋旋旋旋旋旋旋 旋旋旋

❶[动]转动：revolve; circle; spin ｜ 天~地转 tiānxuán-dìzhuǎn *the sky and earth were spinning round*

旋转 xuánzhuǎn revolve; rotate; spin

盘旋 pánxuán

❷[动]回来：return; come back

凯旋 kǎixuán

◇旋律 xuánlǜ melody

选 (選) xuǎn 9画 辶部

选 选选选选选选选选 选

❶[动]挑选：select; choose; pick ｜ 筛~ shāixuǎn *screen; sieve* / ~种 xuǎnzhǒng *seed selection* / ~派 xuǎnpài *select and send*

选拔 xuǎnbá select; choose

选定 xuǎndìng decide on; settle for

选购 xuǎngòu pick out and buy; choose from a variety of goods

选集 xuǎnjí selected works

选取 xuǎnqǔ select; choose

选手 xuǎnshǒu an athlete selected for a sports meet; (selected) contestant; player

选修 xuǎnxiū take as an elective course

选用 xuǎnyòng select and use; choose and apply

选择 xuǎnzé select; choose; opt

挑选 tiāoxuǎn

❷[动]选举：elect ｜ ~代表 xuǎn dàibiǎo *select a representative* / ~劳动模范 xuǎn láodòng mófàn *elect the model worker*

选举 xuǎnjǔ elect

选民 xuǎnmín voter; elector

选票 xuǎnpiào vote; ballot

选中 xuǎnzhòng pick on; decide on; settle on

大选 dàxuǎn　当选 dāngxuǎn

竞选 jìngxuǎn　落选 luòxuǎn

评选 píngxuǎn　推选 tuīxuǎn

候选人 hòuxuǎnrén

削 xuē 9画 刂部

削 削削削削削削削削 削

❶[动]义同"削(xiāo)"：having the same meaning as "削 xiāo"

❷[动]减少；减弱：lessen; reduce; cut down

削减 xuējiǎn cut down; reduce; slash; whittle down

削弱 xuēruò weaken; cripple

❸[动]搜刮；掠取：plunder

剥削 bōxuē

See xiāo.

靴 xuē 13画 革部

 靴靴靴靴靴靴靴靴 靴靴靴靴靴

[名]boots │ 皮~ pí xuē *leather boots* / 雨~ yǔ xuē *rubber boots* 靴子 xuēzi boots

穴 xué 5画 穴部

穴 穴穴穴穴穴

❶ [名] 岩洞；窟窿；动物的窝：cave; pits in the ground or holes in some buildings; den; nest; lair │ 虎~ hǔ xué *tiger's lair* / 在地上挖个~ zài dìshang wā ge xué *dig a hole in the ground*

❷ [名] 穴道，人体可以针灸的部位：acupuncture point

学 (學) xué 8画 子部

学 学学学学学学学学

❶ [动] 学习：learn; study │ ~文化 xué wénhuà *learn to read and write* / ~外语 xué wàiyǔ *learn a foreign language* / ~技术 xué jìshù *learn a certain skill* / 你来教，大家~。Nǐ lái jiāo, dàjiā xué. *You teach, we learn.*

学费 xuéfèi tuition fee; tuition
学历 xuélì record of formal schooling; educational background
学年 xuénián school (academic) year

学期 xuéqī school term; term; semester
学生 xuésheng ① student; pupil ② disciple; follower
学时 xuéshí class hour; period
学习 xuéxí study; learn; emulate
学校 xuéxiào school; educational institution
学业 xuéyè one's studies; school work
学员 xuéyuán student (usu. of a college or a training course)
学院 xuéyuàn college; academy; institute

教学 jiāoxué   开学 kāixué
留学 liúxué   失学 shīxué
同学 tóngxué   自学 zìxué
大学生 dàxuéshēng
留学生 liúxuéshēng
中学生 zhōngxuéshēng
高等学校 gāoděng xuéxiào

❷ [动] 模仿：emulate; imitate; mimic │ ~鸡叫 xué jī jiào *mimic the crowing of a cock* / 小男孩儿~他父亲走路。Xiǎo nánháir xué tā fùqin zǒulù. *The little boy imitates his father's way of walking.*

❸ [名] 学校：school
学制 xuézhì ① educational system ② length of schooling
办学 bànxué   大学 dàxué
放学 fàngxué   上学 shàngxué
小学 xiǎoxué   中学 zhōngxué

❹ [名] 学问；知识：learning; knowledge; scholarship │ 博~ bóxué

broad in learning

学会 xuéhuì ① learn; master ② association

学派 xuépài school of thought; school; schools formed due to different theories and views in the same field of learning

学士 xuéshì ① scholar ② a holder of the bachelor's degree; bachelor

学术 xuéshù learning; science

学说 xuéshuō theory; doctrine

学位 xuéwèi academic degree; degree

学问 xuéwèn learning; knowledge; scholarship

学者 xuézhě scholar; learned man; man of learning

科学 kēxué 奖学金 jiǎngxuéjīn

科学家 kēxuéjiā

科学院 kēxuéyuàn

❺ [名] 学科：branch of learning; discipline | 语言~ yǔyánxué *linguistics* / 天文~ tiānwénxué *astronomy*

学科 xuékē branch of learning; course; subject; discipline

法学 fǎxué 汉学 hànxué

化学 huàxué 数学 shùxué

文学 wénxué 医学 yīxué

哲学 zhéxué

文学家 wénxuéjiā

 xuě 11画 雨部

 雪雪雪雪雪雪雪雪 雪雪雪

❶ [名] snow | 积~ jīxuě *accumulated snow; snow* / 昨夜的~下得很大。Zuóyè de xuě xià de hěn dà. *It snowed heavily last night.*

雪花 xuěhuā snowflake

滑雪 huáxuě 瑞雪 ruìxuě

❷ [名] 颜色或光彩像雪的：(of colour or gloss) snow-like; snowy | ~亮 xuěliàng *bright as snow*

雪白 xuěbái snow-white; snowy white

血 xuè 6画 血部

血 血血血血血血

[名] blood | 抽~ chōuxuè *draw blood* / 流~ liúxuè *shed blood* / 验~ yànxuè *have one's blood tested*

血管 xuèguǎn blood vessel

血汗 xuèhàn blood and sweat; sweat and toil

血压 xuèyā blood pressure

血液 xuèyè blood

鲜血 xiānxuè 心血 xīnxuè

白血病 báixuèbìng

高血压 gāoxuèyā

See xiě.

 xūn 14画 灬部

熏 熏熏熏熏熏熏熏熏
熏熏熏熏熏熏

❶[动] 烟、气等接触物体，使变颜色或沾上气味：smoke; fumigate; subject things to smoke in order to change their colour or smell｜烟把墙～黑了。Yān bǎ qiáng xūnhēi le. *The wall was blackened by smoke.* / 茉莉花可以～茶叶。Mòlihuā kěyǐ xūn cháyè. *Jasmine can be used to cure tea.*

❷[动] 用烟、火熏制食物：smoke (food)｜～肉 xūn ròu *smoked meat* / ～鱼 xūn yú *smoked fish*

句 xún 6画 勹部

句 句句句句句句

[名]十天为一旬：period of ten days
上旬 shàngxún 下旬 xiàxún
中旬 zhōngxún

寻 (尋) xún 6画 ⺕部

寻 寻寻寻寻寻寻

[动]找：look for; search; seek｜～人 xúnrén *look for someone* / ～物 xúnwù *look for sth. lost* / 自～烦恼 zì xún fánnǎo *bring trouble on oneself*
寻求 xúnqiú seek; explore; go in quest of

寻找 xúnzhǎo seek; look for
寻短见 xúnduǎnjiàn commit suicide; take one's own life
搜寻 sōuxún
◇寻常 xúnchǎng ordinary; usual; common
不同寻常 bùtóng-xúnchǎng

巡 xún 6画 辶部

巡 巡巡巡巡巡巡

[动]patrol; make one's rounds; inspect
巡警 xúnjǐng policeman
巡逻 xúnluó go on patrol; walk (one's) beat

询 (詢) xún 8画 讠部

询 询询询询询询询询

[动]征求意见；打听：ask; enquire｜查～cháxún *make inquiries (about)* / 咨～zīxún *consult* / 探～tànxún *make cautious inquiries about*
询问 xúnwèn ask about; inquire

循 xún 12画 彳部

循 循循循循循循循
循循循循

[动] 依照；遵守：follow; abide by; be in line with｜～序渐进

xúnxù-jiànjìn follow in proper order and advance gradually
循环 xúnhuán circulate; cycle; circle
遵循 zūnxún

训（訓）xūn　5画 讠部

讠 训 训 训 训 训

[动]教导；斥责：talk to; instruct; admonish; teach | 受～ shòuxūn get a talking-to | 你不要～人。Nǐ bùyào xūn rén. *You'd better not tell people off without good reason.*
训练 xùnliàn train; drill
集训 jíxùn　　　教训 jiàoxùn
培训 péixùn
培训班 péixùnbān

讯（訊）xūn　5画 讠部

讯 讯 讯 讯 讯 讯

[名]消息；信息：news; message; information | 电～diànxūn *telecommunications* | 音～ yīnxūn *news (about sb.)* | 消防队闻～赶到现场。Xiāofángduì wénxūn gǎndào xiànchǎng. *As soon as they were informed, the fire brigade rushed to the scene.*
通讯 tōngxūn　　　喜讯 xǐxūn
资讯 zīxūn

迅　xūn　6画 辶部

迅 迅 迅 迅 迅 迅

[形]速度快：fast; swift | ～猛 xūn-měng *swift and violent*
迅速 xūnsù rapid; swift; speedy; prompt

Y y

压 (壓) yā　　6画 厂部

压 压压压压压压

❶[动] 从上往下用力：press; push down; bring pressure to bear on | ~平 yāpíng *flatten; even* / ~住 yāzhù *hold back; keep under control* / ~碎 yāsuì *crush into powder (small pieces)* / 乒乓球被~扁了。Pīngpāngqiú bèi yābiǎn le. *The table tennis ball was flattened.*

压力 yālì pressure; stress
压缩 yāsuō compress; condense; reduce

❷[动] 用强力制服；抑制：suppress; quell; crack down on | 以权势~人 yǐ quánshì yā rén *intimidate people by showing one's power* 他无法~住心头的怒火。Tā wúfǎ yāzhù xīntou de nùhuǒ. *He cannot hold back his rage.*

压迫 yāpò oppress
压抑 yāyì depress
压制 yāzhì suppress
镇压 zhènyā

❸[动] 搁着不动：set aside; shelve; pigeonhole | 这份公文已经~了

好久了。Zhè fèn gōngwén yǐjīng yāle hǎojiǔ le. *The document has been set aside for a long time.*

积压 jīyā

❹[名] 指压力：pressure; force applied uniformly over a surface
压岁钱 yāsuìqián money given to children as a lunar New Year gift
压台戏 yātáixì the last item on a theatrical programme

电压 diànyā　　　高压 gāoyā
气压 qìyā　　　　血压 xuèyā
高血压 gāoxuèyā

呀 yā　　7画 口部

呀 呀呀呀呀呀呀呀

[叹] 表示惊异：expressing surprise | ~，这水真凉啊!Yā, zhè shuǐ zhēn liáng a! *Wow, the water is so cold!* / ~，这怎么办!Yā, zhè zěnme bàn! *Oh, what shall we do?*

哎呀 āiyā
　See ya.

押 yā　　8画 扌部

押 押押押押押押押押

❶[动] 以财物作担保：give as security; mortgage; pawn | ~金 yājīn *cash pledge; deposit* / 这

些首饰能~多少钱?Zhèxiē shǒushi néng yā duōshǎo qiān? *How much can I get if I pawn these jewels?*

抵押 dǐyā

❷[动] 扣留,不准自由行动:detain; take into custody ｜ 看~kānyā *take into custody* / ~起来 yā qǐlai *put into jail; throw sb. into prison* / 他被~在警察局里。Tā bèi yā zài jǐngchájú li. *He is detained at a police station.*

关押 guānyā　　扣押 kòuyā

❸[动] 跟随着照料或看管:escort ｜ ~车 yāchē *escort goods on a train, truck, etc.* / ~运货物 yāyùn huòwù *transport goods under escort*

◇押韵 yāyùn *be in rhyme*

 (鴉) yā　　9画 牙部

鸦 鸦鸦鸦鸦鸦鸦鸦鸦 鸦

See below
　乌鸦 wūyā
　乌鸦嘴 wūyāzuǐ
◇鸦片 yāpiàn *opium*

鸭 (鴨) yā　　10画 鸟部

鸭 鸭鸭鸭鸭鸭鸭鸭鸭 鸭鸭

[名] duck

鸭子 yāzi duck
烤鸭 kǎoyā

 yá　　4画 牙部

牙 牙牙牙牙

❶[名]牙齿: tooth ｜ 拔~báyá *extract a tooth*
　牙齿 yáchǐ tooth
　牙膏 yágāo toothpaste
　牙刷 yáshuā toothbrush
　老掉牙 lǎodiàoyá
　咬牙切齿 yǎoyá-qièchǐ
❷[名] 形状像牙齿的东西:s t h. tooth-like ｜ 月~yuèyá *crescent*

芽 yá　　7画 艹部

芽 芽芽芽芽芽芽芽

[名] 植物的幼体,可以发育成茎、叶或花:sprout; shoot ｜ 幼~yòuyá *budlet* ｜ 麦子已经发~了。Màizi yǐjīng fāyá le. *The wheat has sprouted.*
　豆芽 dòuyá　　萌芽 méngyá

崖 yá　　11画 山部

崖 崖崖崖崖崖崖崖崖 崖崖崖

[名] 高山陡壁的边:precipice; cliff ｜ 山~shānyá *precipice*
　悬崖 xuányá

哑 (啞) yǎ 9画 口部

哑 哑哑哑哑哑哑哑哑哑
哑

❶[动]失去说话能力：lacking the power of speech; mute; dumb | 装聋作~zhuānglóng-zuòyǎ *pretend to be deaf and dumb* / 他生来就~。Tā shēnglái jiù yǎ. *He has been mute from birth.*

❷[形]发音困难或不清楚：husky; hoarse | 嗓子喊~了sǎngzi hǎnyǎ le *shout oneself hoarse*

轧 (軋) yà 5画 车部

轧 轧轧轧轧轧

❶[动]滚压：roll; run over | ~棉花 yà miánhua *gin cotton* / 把路面~平 bǎ lùmiàn yàpíng *roll the road surface flat* / 他被火车~了。Tā bèi huǒchē yà le. *He was run over by a train.*

❷[动]排挤：throw out; dispossess; disinherit | 倾~qīngyà *engage in internal strife*

亚 (亞) yà 6画 一部

亚 亚亚亚亚亚亚

[形]第二位的；次一等的：inferior; substandard
亚军 yàjūn second place
◇亚洲 Yàzhōu Asia

讶 (訝) yà 6画 讠部

讶 讶讶讶讶讶讶

[动]惊奇；诧异：be astonished; wonder
惊讶 jīngyà

呀 ya 7画 口部

呀 呀呀呀呀呀呀呀

[助]"啊"受前一个韵母 a、e、o、i、ü 的影响产生的音变，用在句末表示惊叹、强调等语气：used in place of "a" (啊) when the preceding character ends in sound a, e, i, o, or ü, used at the end of a sentence to indicate admiration, emphasis, etc. | 快来~! Kuài lái ya! *Come here, quickly!* / 马跑得真快~!Mǎ pǎo de zhēn kuài ya! *The horse is running very fast!* / 这个瓜~，甜得很。Zhège guā ya, tiándehěn. *The melon is so sweet!*
 See yā.

烟 yān 10画 火部

烟 烟烟烟烟烟烟烟烟 烟烟

❶ [名] 物质燃烧时产生的气体：smoke; fume | 冒～mǎoyān give off smoke / 满屋子都是～。Mǎn wūzi dōu shì yān. *The room was filled with smoke.*
烟囱 yāncōng chimney

❷ [名] 像烟的东西：smoke-like thing | 他一溜～儿似的跑远了。Tā yīliūyānr shìde pǎoyuǎn le. *He disappeared in a flash.*
烟雾 yānwù smog

❸ [名] 烟草；烟草制品：tobacco; cigarette
烟草 yāncǎo tobacco (plant)
烟卷儿 yānjuǎnr cigarette
抽烟 chōuyān　　吸烟 xīyān
香烟 xiāngyān

◇ 烟花 yānhuā ① (formal) a lovely spring scene ② (old) prostitution

淹 yān　11画 氵部

淹 淹淹淹淹淹淹淹淹 淹淹淹

[动] 浸没：flood; submerge | 庄稼被水～了。Zhuāngjia bèi shuǐ yān le. *The crops were flooded.*
淹没 yānmò flood out; drown

延 yán　6画 廴部

延 延延延延延延

❶ [动] 向长的方面发展：prolong; extend; protract | 蔓～mànyán spread / 绵～miányán be continuous
延长 yáncháng extend; prolong
延伸 yánshēn extend; stretch
延续 yánxù extend; continue

❷ [动] 推迟：put off; postpone | ～迟 yánchí postpone / 运动会因雨顺～。Yùndònghuì yīn yǔ shùnyán. *Because of rain, the sports meet was postponed.*
延缓 yánhuǎn delay; postpone; put off
延期 yánqī postpone; put off
延误 yánwù incur loss through delay
拖延 tuōyán

严 (嚴) yán　7画 一部

严 严严严严严严严严

❶ [形] 严格；严厉：strict; stern; severe | 我们要～把质量关。Wǒmen yào yánbǎ zhìliàng guān. *We must exercise strict control over quality.* / 你对孩子管得似乎太～了。Nǐ duì hāizi guǎn de sìhū tài yán le. *It seems that you are too strict with your children.*

严格 yángé strict; rigid; rigorous

严禁 yánjìn strictly forbid

严峻 yánjùn severe

严厉 yánlì stern; severe

严肃 yánsù solemn; serious; earnest

庄严 zhuāngyán　尊严 zūnyán

❷ [形] 厉害的；高度的：severe; heavy; extreme | ~冬 yán-dōng severe winter

严寒 yánhán severe cold; bitter cold

严重 yánzhòng serious

❸ [形] 严密；紧密：tight; close | 他的嘴很~。Tā de zuǐ hěn yán. He is tight-lipped. / 把窗户关~。Bǎ chuānghu guān-yán. Shut the window tight.

严谨 yánjǐn ① rigorous; strict; careful and precise ② compact; well-knit

严密 yánmì tight; close

戒严 jièyán

言 yán　7画 言部

言 言言言言言言言

❶ [动] 说：say; talk; speak | 断~ duànyán assert

预言 yùyán

自言自语 zìyán-zìyǔ

总而言之 zǒng'éryánzhī

❷ [名] 话：word; speech | 有~在先 yǒuyán-zàixiān make clear

beforehand / 一~不发 yīyán-bùfā not utter a word

言论 yánlùn speech

言语 yányǔ speech

传言 chuányán　发言 fāyán

留言 liúyán　　　誓言 shìyán

婉言 wǎnyán　　文言 wényán

宣言 xuānyán　　谣言 yáoyán

语言 yǔyán　　　寓言 yùyán

发言人 fāyánrén

❸ [名] 汉语的一个字：(in the Chinese language) word; character | 五~诗 wǔyánshī Chinese classical poem with five characters to a line

岩 yán　8画 山部

岩 岩岩岩岩岩岩岩岩

See 岩石

岩石 yánshí rock; stone

炎 yán　8画 火部

炎 炎炎炎炎炎炎炎炎

❶ [形] 热：hot; burning hot | ~夏 yánxià hot summer

炎热 yánrè heat

❷ [名] 炎症：inflammation | 肺~ fèiyán pneumonia

发炎 fāyán　关节炎 guānjiéyán

气管炎 qìguǎnyán

◇炎帝 Yándì also known as Shennong, a legendary ruler of

China in remote antiquity

沿 yán 8画 氵部

沿 沿 沿 沿 沿 沿 沿 沿

❶ [介] 顺着：along ｜ ～着河边走 yánzhe hébiān zǒu *walk along the river* / ～街种植了花木。 Yánjiē zhòngzhí le huāmù. *Trees and flowers were planted along the streets.*
沿岸 yán'àn along the bank
沿海 yánhǎi along the coast; coastal
沿途 yántú on the way; throughout the journey
沿着 yánzhe along; follow; (act) in accordance with
❷ [名] 边缘：edge ｜ 河～儿héyánr *bank of a river* / 床～儿chuáng- yánr *edge of a bed*
沿儿 yánr edge
前沿 qiányán

研 yán 9画 石部

研 研 研 研 研 研 研 研 研

[动] 精心思考；深入探求：research; study; look into ｜ ～讨 yántǎo *discuss*
研究 yánjiū ①research; study ② consider; discuss; deliberate
研制 yánzhì develop; research

and produce
研究生 yánjiūshēng graduate student; postgraduate
研究所 yánjiūsuǒ research institute
研究员 yánjiūyuán research fellow
科研 kēyán 钻研 zuānyán
教研室 jiàoyánshì

盐 (鹽) yán 10画 皿部

盐 盐 盐 盐 盐 盐 盐 盐 盐 盐

[名] 食盐：salt ｜ 精～jīngyán *refined salt; table salt* / 汤里再放 点儿～。Tāng li zài fàng diǎnr yán. *Put a bit more salt in the soup.*

颜 (顏) yán 15画 页部

颜 颜 颜 颜 颜 颜 颜 颜 颜 颜 颜 颜 颜 颜 颜

[名] 色彩：colour ｜ 五～六色 wǔyán-liùsè *colourful; a riot of colours*
颜色 yánsè colour; paint

衍 yǎn 9画 彳部

衍 衍 衍 衍 衍 衍 衍 衍 衍

See 敷衍

敷衍 fūyǎn

掩 yǎn 11画 扌部

掩掩掩掩掩掩掩掩 掩掩掩

❶[动] 隐藏；遮盖：cover up; hide | 她双手～面。Tā shuāngshǒu yǎn miàn. *She covered her face with her hands.*

掩盖 yǎngài cover; conceal

掩护 yǎnhù shield; screen; cover

掩饰 yǎnshì cover up; conceal; gloss over

❷[动]合上；关闭：shut; close | 请把门～上。Qǐng bǎ mén yǎnshang. *Close the door, please.*

眼 yǎn 11画 目部

眼眼眼眼眼眼眼眼 眼眼眼

[名] 眼睛，人或动物的视觉器官：eye; human or animal organ of vision | 睁开～zhēngkāi yǎn *open one's eyes* / 亲～所见 qīnyǎnsuǒjiàn *see with one's own eyes*

眼光 yǎnguāng eye; sight

眼睛 yǎnjing eye

眼镜 yǎnjìng glasses; spectacles

眼看 yǎnkàn ① in no time; very soon; in a moment ② look on passively

眼眶 yǎnkuàng eye socket; eyehole

眼泪 yǎnlèi tear

眼力 yǎnlì ① eyesight ② judgment

眼前 yǎnqián ① before one's eyes ② at the moment; at present; now

眼球 yǎnqiú eyeball

眼色 yǎnsè a meaningful glance

眼神 yǎnshén ① expression in one's eyes ② eyesight

眼下 yǎnxià at the moment; at present; now

龙眼 lóngyǎn

开眼界 kāiyǎnjiè

使眼色 shǐyǎnsè

势利眼 shìlìyǎn

◇针眼 zhēnyǎn

不起眼 bùqǐyǎn

偏心眼儿 piānxīnyǎnr

小心眼儿 xiǎoxīnyǎnr

演 yǎn 14画 氵部

演演演演演演演演 演演演演演演

❶[动]发展变化：develop; evolve | ～进 yǎnjìn *gradual progress* / ～化 yǎnhuà *evolve*

演变 yǎnbiàn develop; evolve

❷[动]当众表演技艺：perform | ～杂技 yǎn zájì *perform acrobat-*

ics / ～电影 yǎn diānyǐng *act in a film* / 这个剧～得很好。Zhège jù yǎn de hěn hǎo. *The play was performed very well.*

演唱 yǎnchàng sing
演出 yǎnchū put on a performance
演技 yǎnjì acting; stage performance
演讲 yǎnjiǎng lecture; speak; address
演示 yǎnshì demonstrate; demonstration
演说 yǎnshuō make a speech; deliver an oration
演戏 yǎnxì ① put on a play; act in a play ② playact; pretend
演员 yǎnyuán actor; actress; performer
演奏 yǎnzòu give musical performance
演唱会 yǎnchànghuì vocal concert

扮演 bànyǎn　表演 biǎoyǎn
导演 dǎoyǎn　讲演 jiǎngyǎn
开演 kāiyǎn　上演 shàngyǎn
主演 zhǔyǎn

❸[动]（按程式）练习或计算：perform mathematical calculation
演算 yǎnsuàn calculation
演习 yǎnxí manoeuvre; drill; exercise; practise

厌 (厭) yàn　6画 厂部

厌 厌厌厌厌厌厌

[动]不喜欢、嫌弃：detest; be disgusted | 这几本书早就看～了。Zhè jǐ běn shū zǎo jiù kānyàn le. *I have had enough of these books.*
厌恶 yànwù detest; be struck with abhorrence
讨厌 tǎoyàn

咽 yàn　9画 口部

咽 咽咽咽咽咽咽咽咽咽

[动]使食物等经过咽(yān)头进入食道：swallow | 细嚼慢～xìjiáo-mànyàn *chew carefully and swallow slowly* / 病人不能～东西。Bìngrén bùnéng yàn dōngxi. *The patient cannot swallow food.*

艳 (艷) yàn　10画 色部

艳 艳艳艳艳艳艳艳艳艳艳

[形]色彩鲜明夺目；美丽：gorgeous; colourful; gaudy | ～丽 yànlì *brightly-coloured and beautiful*
鲜艳 xiānyàn

宴 yàn 10画 宀部

宴宴宴宴宴宴宴宴宴宴

❶ [动] 请人吃饭喝酒；聚在一起会餐：fete; entertain sb. at a feast | 大~宾客 dà yàn bīnkè *entertain guests at a grand banquet* / 欢~huānyàn *merry feast*
宴会 yànhuì banquet
宴请 yànqǐng entertain (to dinner); fete
宴席 yànxí banquet; feast

❷ [名] 酒席：banquet | 设~shèyàn *give a banquet* / 盛~shèngyàn *grand banquet*

验（驗） yàn 10画 马部

验验验验验验验验验验

❶[动] 产生预期的效果：prove effective; produce an expected result | 灵~língyàn *efficacious* / 应~yìngyàn *come true*

❷[动] 检查；察看：inspect; examine; check | ~算 yànsuàn *verify the result of a mathematical calculation; check computations* / ~血 yànxiě *blood test*
验收 yànshōu check before acceptance; check upon delivery
验证 yànzhèng test and verify

测验 cèyàn 化验 huàyàn
检验 jiǎnyàn 考验 kǎoyàn
实验 shíyàn 试验 shìyàn
体验 tǐyàn
实验室 shíyànshì
◇经验 jīngyàn

焰 yàn 12画 火部

焰焰焰焰焰焰焰焰焰焰焰焰

[名] 火苗：flame; blaze | 气~qìyàn *arrogance*
火焰 huǒyàn

燕 yàn 16画 灬部

燕燕燕燕燕燕燕燕燕燕燕燕燕燕燕燕

[名] swallow
燕子 yànzi swallow

扬（揚） yáng 6画 扌部

扬扬扬扬扬扬

❶[动] 高举；升起：raise; hoist | ~手 yángshǒu *put up one's hand* / 飞~fēiyáng *fly upward* / ~起灰尘 yángqǐ huīchén *raise (kick up) dust*
昂扬 ángyáng 飘扬 piāoyáng

❷[动] 往上撒：throw up and scatter | 他把土~得到处都是。Tā bǎ

tǔ yáng de dàochù dōu shì.
He scattered the earth here and there.

❸ [动] 传出去：spread; make known | 颂～sòngyáng *sing sb's praises*

表扬 biǎoyáng　　发扬 fāyáng
宣扬 xuānyáng

◇扬琴 yángqín *dulcimer*

羊　　　　yáng　6画 羊部

羊 羊羊羊羊羊羊

[名] sheep; goat | 放～fàng yáng *graze sheep* / 一群～yī qún yáng *a flock of sheep*

羊绒 yángróng *cashmere*
山羊 shānyáng
替罪羊 tìzuìyáng

阳 (陽) yáng　6画 阝(左)部

阳 阳阳阳阳阳阳

❶ [名] 太阳；日光：sun | 朝～zhāo-yáng *the rising sun* / 这间屋子向～。Zhè jiān wūzi xiàng yáng. *The room faces south.*

阳光 yángguāng *sunlight; sunshine*
太阳 tàiyáng
太阳能 tàiyángnéng

❷ [名] 山或建筑物的南面：south of a mountain or building

❸ [形] 外露的；表面的：open; overt; outward | ～沟 yánggōu *open ditch*

阳台 yángtái *balcony; veranda*

◇重阳节 Chóngyángjié

杨 (楊) yáng　7画 木部

杨 杨杨杨杨杨杨杨

See below

杨梅 yángméi (bot.) *red bayberry* (*Myrica rubra*)
杨树 yángshù *poplar*
杨桃 yángtáo ① *carambola; the fruit of the carambola; star fruit* ② *another name for the fruit tree* Actinidia chinensis

洋　　　yáng　9画 氵部

洋 洋洋洋洋洋洋洋洋 洋

❶ [名] 比海更大的水域：ocean | 太平～Tàipíngyáng *the Pacific Ocean*

海洋 hǎiyáng
汪洋 wāngyáng
北冰洋 Běibīngyáng
大洋洲 Dàyángzhōu
大西洋 Dàxīyáng
印度洋 Yìndùyáng

❷ [形] 外来的；外国的：foreign | ～货 yánghuò *imported*

goods / ~房 yángfáng western-style house

洋葱 yángcōng onion

❸ [形] 现代化的（跟"土 tǔ"相对）：modern (the opposite of "土 tǔ") | 土~结合 tǔyǎngjiéhé combine traditional and modern methods

◇磨洋工 móyánggōng

 yǎng 6画 亻部

仰 仰仰仰仰仰仰

❶ [动] 脸向上；抬头向上（跟"俯 fǔ"相对）：face upward (the opposite of "俯 fǔ") | ~着睡 yǎngzhe shuì sleep on one's back / ~起头来 yǎngqǐ tóu lai raise one's head

❷ [动] 敬慕；佩服：look up to; admire; respect | 敬~jìngyǎng revere; venerate / 久~jiǔyǎng have long been looking forward to meeting sb.

信仰 xìnyǎng　瞻仰 zhānyǎng

❸ [动] 依靠；借助：rely on | ~仗 yǎngzhàng rely on; look to sb. for support

 （養）yǎng 9画 丷部

养 养养养养养养养养
养

❶[动] 饲养（动物）；培植（花草）：raise (animals); grow (plants) | ~鱼 yǎngyú breed fish / ~花儿 yǎnghuār cultivate flowers

养殖 yǎngzhí breed; cultivate

饲养 sìyǎng

❷[动] 供给维持生活必需的钱物：support; provide for | ~家 yǎngjiā support one's family / 她好不容易把这孩子~大。Tā hǎobùróngyì bǎ zhè háizi yǎngdà. She had a hard time bringing up the child.

养活 yǎnghuo support; feed

养老 yǎnglǎo ① provide for the aged (usu. one's parents) ② live out one's life in retirement

养育 yǎngyù bring up; rear

抚养 fǔyǎng　供养 gōngyǎng

❸[动] 生育：give birth to | 她~了个儿子。Tā yǎngle ge érzi. She gave birth to a boy.

❹[动] 休息；调理；滋补：rest; convalesce; recuperate one's health | ~病 yǎngbìng take rest and nourishment to regain one's health / ~身体 yǎng shēntǐ recuperate

养分 yǎngfèn nutrient

养料 yǎngliào nutriment; nourishment

养生 yǎngshēng care for life; conserve one's vital powers; preserve one's health; keep in good health

保养 bǎoyǎng　疗养 liáoyǎng
休养 xiūyǎng
❺ [动] 培养；形成；修养：form; acquire; cultivate | 他~成了爱劳动的好习惯。Tā yǎngchéngle ài láodòng de hǎo xíguàn. *He has cultivated the good habit of doing manual labour.*
养成 yǎngchéng form; cultivate; develop
培养 péiyǎng　修养 xiūyǎng

 氧 yǎng 10画 气部

氧 氧氧氧氧氧氧氧氧氧氧

[名] oxygen | 吸~ xīyǎng *inhale oxygen*
氧化 yǎnghuà oxidize; oxidate
氧气 yǎngqì oxygen
二氧化碳 èryǎnghuàtàn

 痒 (癢) yǎng 11画 疒部

痒 痒痒痒痒痒痒痒痒痒痒痒

❶ [形] 皮肤受刺激要抓搔的一种感觉：itch, an uneasy sensation on the skin | 浑身~得难受。Húnshēn yǎng de nánshòu. *It itches all over my body.*
❷ [动] 产生想做某事的愿望：be eager to do sth.

样 (樣) yǎng 10画 木部

样 样样样样样样样样样样

❶ [名] 形状：shape; form | 留心别把鞋穿走~。Liúxīn bié bǎ xié chuān zǒuyàng. *Be careful to wear your shoes in a proper way, otherwise they will lose their shape.*
样式 yàngshì pattern; type; style; form
样子 yàngzi shape
多样 duōyàng　花样 huāyàng
模样 múyàng　那样 nàyàng
式样 shìyàng　同样 tóngyàng
一样 yīyàng　怎样 zěnyàng
照样 zhàoyàng
字样 zìyàng
像样儿 xiàngyàngr
怎么样 zěnmeyàng
各式各样 gèshì-gèyàng
各种各样 gèzhǒng-gèyàng
❷ [名] 作标准的东西：model; sample | 式~ shìyàng *pattern* / 鞋~ xiéyàng *outline of a shoe* / 抽~检查 chōuyàng jiǎnchá *sample survey; random check*
样本 yàngběn ① sample book ② (print) sample; specimen
样品 yàngpǐn sample; specimen
榜样 bǎngyàng

看样子 kànyàngzi

❸ [量] 表示事物的种类：kind; type | 两~儿菜 liǎng yàngr cài *two dishes* / 四~儿东西 sì yàngr dōngxi *four things* / ~~都有 yàngyàng dōu yǒu *of all kinds; assorted*

妖 | 妖妖妖妖妖妖妖

yāo　　7画 女部

[名] goblin; demon

妖怪 yāoguài monster; bogy; goblin; demon

要 | 要要要要要要要要要

yāo　　9画 西部

[动] 求：demand; ask

要求 yāoqiú ask; demand; require; claim; request
See yào.

腰 | 腰腰腰腰腰腰腰腰腰腰腰腰腰

yāo　　13画 月部

❶ [名] waist; the small of the back | 弯~ wānyāo bend down / 他扭伤了~。Tā niǔshāngle yāo. *He sprained his back.*

腰带 yāodài belt; girdle

掏腰包 tāoyāobāo

❷ [名] 事物的中部：midde

山腰 shānyāo

邀 | 邀邀邀邀邀邀邀邀 邀邀邀邀邀邀邀邀

yāo　　16画 辶部

[动] 约请：invite; ask | 今天你是特~嘉宾。Jīntiān nǐ shì tè~ jiābīn. *You are today's honoured guest.* / 我~他来参加联欢会了。Wǒ yāo tā lái cānjiā liánhuānhuì le. *I have invited him to attend our get-together.*

邀请 yāoqǐng invite
应邀 yìngyāo

窑 | 窑窑窑窑窑窑窑窑 窑窑窑

yāo　　11画 穴部

❶ [名] 烧制砖、瓦、陶瓷等的建筑物：kiln; oven; furnace used for firing bricks, tiles, or ceramics | 砖~ zhuānyāo *brick kiln*

❷ [名] 土法生产的煤矿：coal pit that mines coal using old-fashioned methods | 煤~ méiyāo *coal pit*

（謠） yáo 12画 讠部

谣谣谣谣谣谣谣谣谣谣谣谣谣谣

[名] 没有事实根据的传说：rumour | 造～zàoyáo start a rumour / 辟～pìyáo refute a rumour

谣言 yáoyán rumour

 yáo 13画 扌部

摇摇摇摇摇摇摇摇摇摇摇摇摇

[动] 来回摆动；使来回摆动：shake; wave; rock; turn | ～头 yáotóu shake one's head / ～铃 yáolíng ring a bell / ～扇子 yáo shànzi wave a fan / 小狗～着尾巴跑了。Xiǎogǒu yáozhe wěiba pǎo le. Wagging its tail, the little dog ran off.

摇摆 yáobǎi sway; swing; rock; vacillate

摇滚 yáogǔn rock and roll; rock (music)

摇晃 yáohuàng rock; sway; shake

摇篮 yáolán cradle

摇头 yáotóu shake one's head

动摇 dòngyáo

 yáo 13画 辶部

 遥遥遥遥遥遥遥遥遥遥遥遥遥

[形] 远：distant; remote; far | ～望 yáowàng look into the distance

遥控 yáokòng remote control; telecontrol

遥远 yáoyuǎn remote; distant; faraway

 yǎo 9画 口部

咬咬咬咬咬咬咬咬咬

❶ [动] 用牙齿夹住或夹碎东西：bite; snap at; seize; pierce or cut with teeth | ～断 yǎoduàn snap and break / ～紧牙齿 yǎojǐn yáchǐ grit one's teeth / ～了口苹果 yǎole kǒu píngguǒ take a bite at the apple

咬牙切齿 yǎoyá-qièchǐ gnash one's teeth

❷ [动] 受审讯或责难时牵扯上无关或无辜的人：incriminate sb. (oft. innocent) | 反～一口 fǎnyǎo yīkǒu trump up a countercharge against one's accuser / 别乱～好人。Bié luànyǎo hǎorén. Don't implicate the innocent.

❸ [动] 读准（字音）：pronounce; articulate; be nitpicking about the use of words | ～字清楚 yǎozì qīngchu clear articula-

Y

tion / 这个字他～得很准。 Zhège zì tā yào de hěn zhǔn. *He pronounced this word correctly.*

◇山药 shānyao

药（藥）yào 9画 艹部

药 药药药药药药药药药

❶ [名]能防病、治病或消灭虫害的物品：medicine; drug; remedy | 服～fúyào *take medicine* / 这～已经见效了。Zhè yào yǐjīng jiànxiào le. *This medicine has taken effect.*

药材 yàocái medicinal material; crude drug

药店 yàodiàn drugstore; chemist's shop; pharmacy

药方 yàofāng prescription

药品 yàopǐn medicine; drug

药物 yàowù medication; medicine

药水儿 yàoshuǐr ① liquid medicine; medicinal liquid ② lotion

成药 chéngyào

农药 nóngyào 西药 xīyào

医药 yīyào 中药 zhōngyào

处方药 chǔfāngyào

❷ [名]有化学作用的物品：certain chemicals | 杀虫～shāchóngyào *insecticide; pesticide*

弹药 dànyào 火药 huǒyào

炸药 zhàyào

要 yào 9画 西部

要 要要要要要要要要要

❶ [名]主要的内容：main points; essentials | 概～gàiyào *essentials*

纲要 gāngyào 纪要 jìyào

提要 tíyào 摘要 zhāiyào

❷ [形]重要：important | 紧～jǐnyào *critical* / ～事 yàoshì *important matter*

要点 yàodiǎn essentials; key points; gist

要紧 yàojǐn important; essential

要领 yàolǐng main points; essentials

要素 yàosù essential factor; key element

次要 cìyào 简要 jiǎnyào

首要 shǒuyào 重要 zhòngyào

主要 zhǔyào

不要紧 búyàojǐn

❸ [动]希望得到或保有：want to keep | 我～这本书。Wǒ yào zhè běn shū. *I want this book.* / 这东西他还～呢！Zhè dōngxi tā hái yào ne! *He still needs it.* / 我想～一个房间。Wǒ xiǎng yào yī gè fángjiān. *I need a room.*

不要脸 búyàoliǎn

❹ [动] 索取：demand; ask for | ～钱 yào qián *ask for money* / 弟弟跟姐姐～一支钢笔。Dìdi gēn jiějie yào yī zhī gāngbǐ. *The younger brother begged his elder sister to give him a pen.*

要命 yàomìng drive sb. to his death; kill

索要 suǒyào

❺ [动] 要求；请求：ask; entreat | 他～我和他一起去学校。Tā yào wǒ hé tā yīqǐ qù xuéxiào. *He asked me to go to school with him.* / 他～我陪你去。Tā yào wǒ péi nǐ qù. *He asked me to go with you.*

❻ [动] 需要：need; take | 到那里～两个小时。Dào nàli yào liǎng gē xiǎoshí. *It takes two hours to get there.* / 这项任务～十天才能完成。Zhè xiàng rènwù yào shí tiān cáinéng wánchéng. *It will take ten days to get the work done.*

需要 xūyào

❼ [动] 应该；必须：must; should; it is necessary | ～努力学习 yào nǔlì xuéxí *should study hard* / 你说话做事都～当心。Nǐ shuōhuà zuòshì dōu yào dāngxīn. *You must be careful with your words and deeds.* / 这个箱子～马上抬走。Zhège xiāngzi yào mǎshàng táizǒu. *Carry this trunk away immediately.*

❽ [动] 准备；将要：will; be going to | 天快～黑了。Tiān kuài yào hēi le. *It is going to be dark.* / 明天他就～回来了。Míngtiān tā jiùyào huílai le. *He'll be back tomorrow.*

将要 jiāngyào

❾ [连] 如果：if; suppose; in case | 你～能来就好了。Nǐ yào néng lái jiù hǎo le. *It would be nice if you could come.* / 他～不去，我也不去。Tā yào bù qù, wǒ yě bù qù. *If he won't go, neither will I.*

要不 yàobù otherwise; or else; or

要么 yàome (conj.) or; either ... or ...

要是 yàoshi if; suppose; in case

要不然 yàoburán otherwise; or else; or

要不是 yàobushì if it were not for; but for

◇要好 yàohǎo ① be on good terms; be close friends ② eager to improve oneself; try hard to make progress

就要 jiùyào

See yāo.

钥 (鑰) yào   9画 钅部

钥 钥钥钥钥钥钥钥钥钥

See 钥匙

钥匙 yàoshi key

耀　yào　20画 小部

耀 耀耀耀耀耀耀耀耀耀耀
耀耀耀耀耀耀耀
耀耀耀耀

[动] 强光照射：shine; illuminate;
dazzle
　耀眼 yàoyǎn dazzling
　闪耀 shǎnyào　照耀 zhàoyào

爷 (爺) yé　6画 父部

爷 爷爷爷爷爷爷

[名] 祖父：grandfather
　爷爷 yéye ① (paternal) grand-
　father ② grandpa (a respectful
　form of address for an old man)
　大爷 dàye　　　姥爷 lǎoye
◇老大爷 lǎodàye
　老天爷 lǎotiānyé

也　yě　3画 乛部

也 也也也

❶[副] 表示两事相同：also; too;
either | 他～是上海人。Tā yě
shì Shànghǎirén. He is also
Shanghainese. / 你去，我～去。
Nǐ qù, wǒ yě qù. If you go, I'll
go too.
❷[副] 表示无论怎样, 后果都相同：
whether...or; no matter whether;

even if | 你不说我～知道。Nǐ
bù shuō wǒ yě zhīdào. Even
though you didn't say, I knew it
anyway. / 即使下雨, 我～要出
门。Jíshǐ xiàyǔ, wǒ yě yào
chūmén. I shall go out even if
it rains.
❸[副] 表示"甚至 shènzhì", 加强
语气：used for emphasis | 一颗
粮食～不能浪费。Yī kē liáng-
shi yě bùnéng làngfèi. We
should cherish even a single
grain. / 再冷的天我～不怕。Zài
lěng de tiān wǒ yě bù pà. I
can stand colder weather than
this.
❹[副] 表示委婉语气：used in a
hesitant or guarded way | 我
看～只好这样了。Wǒ kàn yě
zhǐhǎo zhèyàng le. We'll have
to leave it like that.
◇也许 yěxǔ perhaps; probably;
maybe

冶　yě　7画 冫部

冶 冶冶冶冶冶冶冶

[动] 熔炼 (金属)：smelt (metal)
　冶金 yějīn metallurgy
　冶炼 yěliàn smelt

野　yě　11画 里部

野 野野野野野野野野
野野野

❶ [名] 郊外：open country; the open | 旷~kuàngyě *open country*
野餐 yěcān picnic
野外 yěwài open country; field
田野 tiányě　　越野 yuèyě

❷ [形] 蛮横；粗鲁：rude; rough; uncivilized; savage | 粗~cūyě *boorish* | 这人说话太~了。Zhè rén shuōhuà tài yě le. *The man speaks too rudely.*
野蛮 yěmán barbarous; brutal; cruel; savage

❸ [形] 不受约束的：unrestrained; abandoned; unruly | 这孩子心都玩儿~了。Zhè háizi xīn dōu wánr yě le. *The child became unruly after playing.*
野心 yěxīn ambition; careerism

❹ [形] 非人工培植、饲养的（动植物）：(of animals and plants) wild; uncultivated; untamed; undomesticated | ~草 yěcǎo *weeds* | ~鸭 yěyā *wild duck*
野生 yěshēng wild
野兽 yěshòu wild beast

❺ [名] 范围；界限：limit; boundary
视野 shìyě

业（業）yě　　5画 业部

业 业业业业业

❶ [名] 学业；学习的内容或过程：schooling; course of study; study process
毕业 bìyè　　　　结业 jiéyè
作业 zuòyè
毕业生 bìyèshēng

❷ [名] 职业；所从事的工作：occupation; profession; employment | 就~jiùyè *employment* / 转~zhuǎnyè *be transferred to civilian work* / 失~shīyè *be out of a job* / 他以做木工活儿为~。Tā yǐ zuò mùgōnghuór wéi yè. *He is a carpenter by profession.*
业绩 yèjì outstanding achievement
业务 yèwù vocational work; professional work; business
业余 yèyú spare time; afterwork; amateur
创业 chuàngyè　从业 cóngyè
待业 dàiyè　　　副业 fùyè
敬业 jìngyè　　　开业 kāiyè
事业 shìyè　　　停业 tíngyè
营业 yíngyè　　　职业 zhíyè
专业 zhuānyè
专业户 zhuānyèhù

❸ [名] 职业的类别；行业：kind of occupation; line of business | 饮食~yǐnshíyè *catering trade*
工业 gōngyè　　行业 hángyè

837

林业 línyè　　　农业 nóngyè
企业 qǐyè　　　商业 shāngyè
物业 wùyè
工业化 gōngyèhuà
轻工业 qīnggōngyè
重工业 zhònggōngyè
各行各业 gèháng-gèyè

❹[名]财产：estate; property｜
家～jiāyè *family property*
业主 yèzhǔ owner (of an enterprise or estate); proprietor
产业 chǎnyè

 叶（葉）yè　　5画 口部

叶 叶叶叶叶叶

[名]叶子：leaf; foliage｜落～luòyè
fallen leaves／树～shùyè *tree leaves*
／菜～càiyè *vegetable leaves*
叶子 yèzi leaf

 页（頁）yè　　6画 页部

页 页页页页页页

[量]指书本中一张纸的一面：page;
leaf｜一～信纸 yī yè xìnzhǐ *a
piece of letter paper*／把书翻到
第5～。Bǎ shū fāndào dì-wǔ
yè. *Turn to page five, please.*
网页 wǎngyè　　　主页 zhǔyè

 夜　　yè　　8画 亠部

夜 夜夜夜夜夜夜夜夜

[名]从天黑到天亮的一段时间（跟
"日rì"或"昼zhōu"相对）：night;
evening; the time from dusk to
dawn (the opposite of "日rì"
or"昼zhōu")｜一个寒冷的冬～
yī gè hánlěng de dōngyè *one
cold winter night*／几天几～也
讲不完。Jǐ tiān jǐ yè yě jiǎng-
buwán. *It would take days to
tell the story.*
夜班 yèbān night shift
夜间 yèjiān at night
夜里 yèli at night
夜晚 yèwǎn night
夜猫子 yèmāozi (dial.) ① owl
② a person who goes to bed late;
night owl
夜深人静 yèshēn-rénjìng all is
quiet at dead of night; in late
night silence
半夜 bànyè　　　黑夜 hēiyè
连夜 liányè　　　日夜 rìyè
深夜 shēnyè　　　昼夜 zhòuyè
开夜车 kāiyèchē
年夜饭 niányèfàn

 液　　yè　　11画 氵部

液 液液液液液液液液
液液液

[名]液体：liquid; fluid; juice｜
血～xuèyè *blood*／溶～róngyè
solution

液体 yètǐ liquid

◇液晶 yèjīng liquid crystal

yī   1画 一部

一

❶[数] 数目，最小的整数：one, the smallest positive integer | ～张嘴 yī zhāng zuǐ *a mouth* / ～个人 yī gè rén *a person* / ～张桌子 yī zhāng zhuōzi *a table*

一半 yībàn one half; half

一边 yībiān ①one side ②at the same time; simultaneously

一侧 yīcè one side; side

一带 yīdài area around a particular place

一旦 yīdàn ① single day; very short time ②once; in case; now that

一度 yīdù once; on one occasion; for a time

一举 yījǔ with one action; at one stroke; at one fell swoop

一旁 yīpáng one side

一时 yīshí ① a period of time ② for a short while; temporary; momentary

一手 yīshǒu ① proficiency; skill ② trick; move ③ single-handed; all by oneself; all alone

一些 yīxiē a number of; certain; some; a few; a little

一行 yīxíng group travelling together; party

一一 yīyī one by one; one after another

一再 yīzài time and again; again and again; repeatedly

一阵 yīzhèn a burst; a fit; a peal

一部分 yībùfen a part (or section, share) of

一把手 yībǎshǒu ① party to an undertaking; member; a hand ② skilled worker ③ first in command; number one man; a person holding primary responsibility

一次性 yīcìxìng ① once only (without a second time) ② disposable

一点儿 yīdiǎnr a bit; a little

一会儿 yīhuìr ①a little while ② in a moment; presently ③ now...now...; one moment...the next...

一口气 yīkǒuqì ① one breath ② in one breath; without a break; at one go; at a stretch

一窝蜂 yīwōfēng like a swarm of bees

一帆风顺 yīfān-fēngshùn plain sailing

一分为二 yīfēn-wéi'èr one divides into two; everything has its good and bad sides; there are two sides to everything

一干二净 yīgān-èrjìng thoroughly; completely

一哄而起 yīhòng'érqǐ (of a group of people) be aroused to

participate; rush headlong into mass action

一技之长 yījìzhīcháng proficiency in a particular line (field); professional skill; speciality

一毛不拔 yīmáo-bùbá unwilling to give up even a hair; very stingy

万一 wànyī 之一 zhīyī
老一套 lǎoyītào

❷ [形] 相同；一样：same; alike | 意见不~yìjiàn bùyī *different opinions* / 大小不~dàxiǎo bùyī *different in size* / 我们都住在~个地方。Wǒmen dōu zhùzài yī gè dìfang. *We all live at the same place.*

一般 yībān ①same as; just like ② general; ordinary; common

一道 yīdào together; side by side; alongside

一概 yīgài one and all; without exception; totally; categorically

一律 yīlǜ ① same; alike; uniform ② all; without exception

一齐 yīqí at the same time; simultaneously; in unison

一起 yīqǐ ① in the same place ②together; in company ③altogether; in all

一同 yītóng together; at the same time and place

一样 yīyàng same; equal; alike; as...as...

一致 yīzhì showing no difference; identical; unanimous; consistent

一块儿 yīkuàir ① at the same place ② together

一概而论 yīgài'érlùn treat (different matters) as the same

单一 dānyī 同一 tóngyī
唯一 wéiyī

❸ [形] 全；满：whole; all; throughout | ~身汗 yī shēn hàn *sweat all over* / ~屋子人 yī wūzi rén *a room full of people*

一共 yīgòng altogether; in all; all told

一贯 yīguàn consistent; persistent; all along

一切 yīqiè all; every; everything

一身 yīshēn ①the whole body; all over the body ② a suit

一生 yīshēng all one's life; throughout one's life

一向 yīxiàng ① earlier on; lately ② consistently; all along

一直 yīzhí ① straight ② continuously; always; all along; all the way

一辈子 yībèizi all one's life; throughout one's life; as long as one lives; a lifetime

一场空 yīchǎngkōng all in vain; futile

统一 tǒngyī
不顾一切 bùgù-yīqiè

❹ [副] 表示动作、变化突然出现：indicating that an action occurs just once or lasts for a short time

840

一

yī

| 咳～声 ké yī shēng *give a cough* / 瞧～眼 qiáo yī yǎn *take a look*

一头 yītóu directly; headlong

一下 yīxià ① one time; once ② in a short while; all at once; all of a sudden

一下子 yīxiàzi suddenly; all at once

❺ [副] 跟 "就" 呼应，表示前后两件事紧接着发生：used with "就 jiù" to indicate that an action occurs immediately after another | 他～说话就笑。Tā yī shuōhuà jiù xiào. *Whenever he speaks, he smiles.* / 我～看就明白了。Wǒ yī kàn jiù míngbai le. *I understand as soon as I see it.* / 天～亮他就起床。Tiān yī liàng tā jiù qǐchuáng. *He got up as soon as the day broke.*

一…就… yī...jiù... no sooner...than...; the moment...; as soon as; once

❻ [数] 用在重叠的动词之间，表示动作是短暂的或尝试性的：used in the middle of a duplicated verb, oft. a single syllable | 看～看 kànyikàn *take a look* / 你们最好再谈～谈。Nǐmen zuìhǎo zài tányitán. *You'd better talk about it again.*

◇一定 yīdìng ① fixed; specified; definite; regular ② certainly; surely; necessarily ③ given; particular; certain

一连 yīlián in a row; in succession; running

一流 yīliú ① a kind; the same kind ② first-class; first-rate; top-notch

一心 yīxīn ① wholeheartedly; heart and soul ② of one mind; as one

一边…一边… yībiān ... yībiān ... at the same time; simultaneously

一面…一面… yīmiàn ... yīmiàn ... at the same time; simutaneously

一心一意 yīxīn-yīyì heart and soul; wholeheartedly

伊 yī 6画 亻部

伊 伊伊伊伊伊伊

See 伊斯兰教

伊斯兰教 Yīsīlánjiào Islam

衣 yī 6画 衣部

衣 衣衣衣衣衣衣

[名] 衣服：clothing; clothes | 内～ nèiyī *underwear*

衣服 yīfu clothes; clothing; dress; garment

衣裳 yīshang clothing; clothes

衣物 yīwù clothing and other articles of daily use

衬衣 chènyī   大衣 dàyī
风衣 fēngyī   毛衣 máoyī
棉衣 miányī
上衣 shàngyī   睡衣 shuìyī
外衣 wàiyī   雨衣 yǔyī
浴衣 yùyī
更衣室 gēngyīshì
洗衣机 xǐyījī

 （醫）yī   7画 匚部

医 医医医医医医医

❶ [名] 医生：doctor | 牙~ yáyī
dentist

法医 fǎyī   军医 jūnyī

❷ [动] 治疗：cure; treat | 有病应
该早~。Yǒu bìng yīnggāi
zǎo yī. *It's better to see the doctor promptly when you fall ill. /
张大夫~好了我的病。Zhāng
dàifu yīhǎole wǒ de bìng.
Doctor Zhang cured my illness.*

医疗 yīliáo treat

医生 yīshēng doctor; physi-
cian; surgeon; medical practitioner

医师 yīshī (qualified) doctor

医术 yīshù medical skill; art of
healing

医务 yīwù medical matter

医学 yīxué medical science;
medicine

医药 yīyào medicine

医院 yīyuàn hospital

医治 yīzhì cure; treat; heal

医务室 yīwùshì clinic (usu. affiliated to an organization,
school, etc.)

就医 jiùyī

❸ [名] 医学：medicine | ~术
yīshù *medical skill* / 他不喜欢
学~。Tā bù xǐhuan xué yī.
*He doesn't like to study medi-
cine.*

西医 xīyī   中医 zhōngyī

 yī   8画 亻部

依 依依依依依依依依

❶ [动] 靠；依赖：fall back on; rely
on; depend on | 孩子~在妈妈
怀里。Háizi yī zài māma huáili.
*The child held on to his mother's
bosom.*

依据 yījù ① according to; in the
light of; on the basis of; judging
by ② basis; foundation

依靠 yīkào depend on; rely on;
be dependent on

依赖 yīlài depend on; rely on;
be dependent on

依托 yītuō ① rely on; depend
on ② support; prop; backing

❷ [动] 顺从；听从：be obedient;
comply with; listen to | ~顺
yīshùn *obedience* / 这次就~你
吧!Zhè cì jiù yī nǐ ba! *I will go
along with your idea this time.*

❸ [介] 按照；根据：according to; in
the light; judging by | ~我看,

这样办可以。Yī wǒ kàn, zhèyàng bàn kěyǐ. *In my opinion, we can do it this way.*

依次 yīcì in proper order; successively

依旧 yījiù as before; still

依然 yīrán still; as before

依照 yīzhào according to; in accordance with; in accord with

 仪 (儀) yí　　5画 亻部

仪 仪仪仪仪仪

❶[名] 礼节；仪式：ceremony; rite | 礼~lǐyí *rite* / 司~sīyí *master of ceremonies*

仪式 yíshì ceremony; rite; function

❷[名] 容貌；举止：appearance; bearing | ~容 yíróng *looks* / ~态 yítài *bearing*

仪表 yíbiǎo appearance; bearing

❸[名] 科学实验用的装置、器具等：apparatus; instrument | 测距~cèjùyí *range finder*

仪器 yíqì instrument; apparatus

宜 yí　　8画 宀部

宜 宜宜宜宜宜宜宜宜

[形] 合适；适当：suitable; appropriate; fitting | 你做这样的工作很相~。Nǐ zuò zhèyàng de gōngzuō hěn xiāngyí. *It's very suitable for you to do this kind of work.*

适宜 shìyí

 姨 yí　　9画 女部

姨 姨姨姨姨姨姨姨姨姨

❶[名] 妻子的姐妹：wife's sister; sister-in-law | 大~dàyí *wife's elder sister*

姨夫 yífu the husband of one's mother's sister (or one's maternal aunt); uncle

❷[名] 母亲的姐妹：mother's sister; maternal aunt; aunt | ~母 yímǔ *aunt*

❸[名] 称年纪和自己母亲差不多的妇女：form of address for a woman who is nearly as old as one's mother

阿姨 āyí

 移 yí　　11画 禾部

移 移移移移移移移移移移移

❶[动] 变动位置；搬迁：move; remove; shift | 向后~xiàng hòu yí *move backwards* / 他把椅子~了一下。Tā bǎ yǐzi yíle yīxià. *He moved the chair.*

移动 yídōng move; shift

移民 yímín ① immigrant; emigrant; immigration ②migrate to another place or abroad

迁移 qiānyí　转移 zhuǎnyí

❷[动]改变；变更：change | 坚定不~jiāndìng-bùyí *firm and unshakable*

移交 yíjiāo ① turn over; transfer; deliver into sb.'s custody ② hand over one's job to a successor

移植 yízhí ① transplant ② (med.) transplanting; grafting

遗 (遺) yí　12画 辶部

❶[动]丢失；漏掉：lose; omit | ~忘 yíwàng *forget*

遗失 yíshī lose

❷[动]留下：leave behind

遗传 yíchuán heredity; inheritance

遗憾 yíhàn regret; pity

遗留 yíliú leave over; hand down

遗址 yízhǐ ruins; relics

❸[形]特指死者留下的：leave behind at one's death; hand down | ~像 yíxiàng *a portrait of the deceased* / ~物 yíwù *things left behind by the deceased*

遗产 yíchǎn legacy; inheritance; heritage

遗体 yítǐ remains; body of the

dead

疑 yí　14画 匕部

❶[动]不能确定；不相信：doubt; disbelieve; suspect; be not sure | 可~kěyí *suspicious*

疑惑 yíhuò have doubts

疑虑 yílǜ misgivings; doubts

疑心 yíxīn suspicion; doubt

猜疑 cāiyí　迟疑 chíyí

怀疑 huáiyí　无疑 wúyí

质疑 zhìyí

嫌疑人 xiányírén

❷[形]不能确定的；很难解决的：doubtful; uncertain | ~点 yídiǎn *questionable point*

疑难 yínán difficult; knotty

疑问 yíwèn query; question; doubt

乙 yǐ　1画 一部

❶[名]天干的第二位：second of the Ten Heavenly Stems

❷[名]第二等的：second

◇乙肝 yǐgān (med.) hepatitis B

已 yǐ　3画 已部

844

[副]表示时间的过去或事情的完成：already | 人～离开。Rén yǐ líkāi. *They have already left.* / 雨季～过。Yǔjì yǐ guò. *The rainy season is over.* / 问题～解决。Wèntí yǐ jiějué. *The problem has been solved.*

已经 yǐjīng already

早已 zǎoyǐ

◇不得已 bùdéyǐ

 以 yǐ 4画 人部

以 以以以以

❶ [介]表示凭借：用、拿：with; by means of | ～少胜多 yǐshǎo-shēngduō *defeat enemies who are greater in number*

以身作则 yǐshēn-zuòzé *set an example with one's own conduct*

❷ [介]表示方式；按照、根据：according to | ～成绩录取新生 yǐ chéngjì lùqǔ xīnshēng *enroll students according to their performance*

❸ [介]表示原因；因为、由于：because of; for | 他～学问深而出名。Tā yǐ xuéwèn shēn ér chūmíng. *He is famous for his learning.*

❹ [连]表示目的：in order to; so as to | ～待时机 yǐdài shíjī *wait for opportunities*

以便 yǐbiàn so that; in order to; so as to; with the aim of; for the purpose of

以免 yǐmiǎn in order to avoid; so as not to; lest

可以 kěyǐ

❺ [介]与其他词组合，表示时间、空间或数量的界限：used before certain localizers to indicate time, space or quantity limit | 黄河～北 Huáng Hé yǐběi *(to the) north of the Yellow River*

以后 yǐhòu after; afterwards; later; hereafter

以来 yǐlái since

以内 yǐnèi within; less than

以前 yǐqián before; formerly; previously

以上 yǐshàng ① more than; over; above ② the above; the foregoing; the above-mentioned

以外 yǐwài beyond; outside; other than; except

以往 yǐwǎng before; formerly; in the past

以下 yǐxià ① below; under ② the following

◇以及 yǐjí as well as; along with; and

以为 yǐwéi think or believe incorrectly

以至 yǐzhì ① down to; up to ② to such an extent as to...; so... that...

以致 yǐzhì so that; as a result

以至于 yǐzhìyú ① down to; up to ② to such an extent as to...;

845

so... that...

倚 yǐ 10画 亻部

倚 倚倚倚倚倚倚倚倚
倚倚

❶ [动] 靠着：lean on or aganist; rest on or against | 他~着门站着。Tā yǐzhe mén zhàn zhe. *He stood leaning against the door.*

❷ [动] 依靠；凭着：rely on; depend on; go by; base on; take as the basis | ~仗 yǐzhàng *rely on*

椅 yǐ 12画 木部

椅 椅椅椅椅椅椅椅椅
椅椅椅椅

[名] chair | 躺~tǎngyǐ *deck chair*
椅子 yǐzi chair
轮椅 lúnyǐ

亿 (億) yì 3画 亻部

亿 亿亿亿

[数] 数目，一万万：numeral, a hundred million
亿万 yìwàn hundreds of millions; millions upon millions

义 (義) yì 3画 丶部

义 义义义

❶ [名] 公正的、有利于社会大众的道理或行动：justice; righteousness | 正~zhèngyì *justice* / 道~dàoyì *morality and justice*
义务 yìwù duty; obligation
仁义 rényì
帝国主义 dìguó zhǔyì
共产主义 gòngchǎn zhǔyì
人道主义 réndào zhǔyì
官僚主义 guānliáo zhǔyì
社会主义 shèhuì zhǔyì
无情无义 wúqíng-wúyì
殖民主义 zhímín zhǔyì
资本主义 zīběn zhǔyì
马克思主义 Mǎkèsī zhǔyì

❷ [名] 意思；意义：meaning; significance | 词~cíyì *meaning of a word*
贬义 biǎnyì　　　含义 hányì
意义 yìyì

◇ 义工 yìgōng ① voluntary work; without pay ② volunteer

艺 (藝) yì 4画 艹部

艺 艺艺艺艺

❶ [名] 技能；技术：skill | 技~jìyì *skill* / 工~gōngyì *technology;*

craft
手艺 shǒuyì　　　　陶艺 táoyì
❷[名]艺术：art │ 曲~qǔyì *folk art forms*
艺人 yìrén ① actor or entertainer (in local drama, storytelling, acrobatics, etc.) ② artisan; handicraftsman
艺术 yìshù ① art ② skill; art; craft
艺术家 yìshùjiā artist
艺术品 yìshùpǐn work of art
布艺 bùyì　　　　文艺 wényì
园艺 yuányì　　　综艺 zōngyì

 忆 (憶) yì　　　4画 忄部

忆 忆忆忆忆

[动] 回想；想念：recall; recollect; remember │ 追~zhuīyì *recollect*
回忆 huíyì　　　　记忆 jìyì
记忆力 jìyìlì

 议 (議) yì　　　5画 讠部

议 议议议议议

❶ [动] 谈论；商讨：discuss; talk; exchange views on │ 这个问题，你们要好好~一~。Zhège wèntí, nǐmen yào hǎohǎo yìyiyì. *You must have a thorough discussion about the problem.*

议案 yì'àn bill; motion; proposal
议程 yìchéng agenda
议会 yìhuì parliament; legislative assembly
议论 yìlùn comment; talk; discuss
议题 yìtí item on the agenda; subject under discussion; topic for discussion
议员 yìyuán member of a legislative assembly; Member of Parliament
议定书 yìdìngshū protocol
会议 huìyì　　　　抗议 kàngyì
评议 píngyì　　　商议 shāngyì
审议 shěnyì　　　协议 xiéyì
争议 zhēngyì
会议室 huìyìshì
不可思议 bùkě-sīyì
❷ [名]意见；主张：opinion; view │ 建~jiànyì *suggest*
倡议 chàngyì　　　决议 juéyì
提议 tíyì

 亦 yì　　　6画 亠部

亦 亦亦亦亦亦亦

[副] 也（表示同样）：also; too │ ~然 yìrán *also; as the same*

 异 yì　　　6画 巳部

异 异异异异异异

❶[动]分开：separate; divorce ｜
离~líyì divorce
❷[形]不同的：different ｜ 没有~
议 méiyǒu yìyì without objection
异常 yìcháng unusual; abnormal
差异 chāyì
大同小异 dàtóng-xiǎoyì
❸[形]另外的；别的：other; another
｜ ~地 yìdì a place far away
from home; a strange land ／ ~
乡 yìxiāng foreign land
异国他乡 yìguó-tāxiāng alien
land
❹[形]新奇的；特别的：strange;
unusual; extraordinary ｜ ~味
yìwèi a peculiar smell
优异 yōuyì
奇花异草 qíhuā-yìcǎo
❺[形]觉得奇怪的；惊奇的：sur-
prising; astonishing ｜ 奇~qíyì
strange
诧异 chàyì   惊异 jīngyì

抑   yì   7画 扌部

抑 抑抑抑抑抑抑抑

[动]压；压制：press down; re-
strain; repress; curb
抑制 yìzhì restrain; control;
check
压抑 yāyì

译（譯）yì   7画 讠部

译 译译译译译译译

[动]翻译：translate; interpret ｜
口~kǒuyì interpret ／ 笔~bǐyì
translate ／ ~文 yìwén trans-
lated text
译员 yìyuán interpreter
翻译 fānyì

易   yì   8画 日部

易 易易易易易易易易

❶[动]交换；换：change; ex-
change
交易 jiāoyì   贸易 màoyì
❷[形]容易；不费力（跟“难 nán”
相对）：have no difficulty in
doing things; easy (the opposite of "难 nán") ｜ 通俗~懂
tōngsú yìdǒng easy to understand ／ 这个成绩得来不~。
Zhège chéngjì délái bùyì. It
was not easy to achieve such
success.
不易 bùyì   简易 jiǎnyì
轻易 qīngyì   容易 róngyì

益   yì   10画 皿部

益 益益益益益益益益
益益

[名]好处：benefit; profit; advantage | ～处 yìchu benefit / 利～ lìyì interest / 权～quányì rights and interests

公益 gōngyì　　受益 shòuyì
有益 yǒuyì

谊（誼）yì　　10画 讠部

谊 谊谊谊谊谊谊谊谊 谊谊

[名]交情：friendship | 情～qíng-yì friendly feelings / 深情厚～shēnqíng-hòuyì profound sentiments of friendship
友谊 yǒuyì

意　yì　　13画 音部

意 意意意意意意意意 意意意意意

❶ [名]心思；心愿：idea; wish; desire; thought | 好～hǎoyì kindness; good intention / 中～zhōng-yì be to one's liking
意见 yìjiàn ① idea; view; opinion; suggestion ② objection; differing opinion; complaint
意图 yìtú intention; intent
意向 yìxiàng intention; purpose
意愿 yìyuàn wish; desire; aspiration
意志 yìzhì will

诚意 chéngyì　创意 chuàngyì
大意 dàyì　　得意 déyì
恶意 èyì　　故意 gùyì
介意 jièyì　　刻意 kèyì
乐意 lèyì　　留意 liúyì
满意 mǎnyì　　民意 mínyì
歉意 qiànyì　　情意 qíngyì
任意 rènyì　　如意 rúyì
善意 shànyì　　随意 suíyì
特意 tèyì　　无意 wúyì
谢意 xièyì　　心意 xīnyì
用意 yòngyì　　有意 yǒuyì
愿意 yuànyì　　主意 zhǔyì
注意 zhùyì　　在意 zàiyì
注意力 zhùyìlì
三心二意 sānxīn-èryì
万事如意 wànshì-rúyì
心满意足 xīnmǎn-yìzú
一心一意 yīxīn-yīyì

❷ [名]意思；思想内容：meaning; intention | 同～tóngyì agree / 来～láiyì one's purpose in coming / ～思 yìsi meaning; idea
意识 yìshí be conscious of; awake to; realize
意义 yìyì meaning; sense
意味着 yìwèizhe signify; mean; imply
没意思 méiyìsi
示意图 shìyìtú
有意思 yǒuyìsi
不好意思 bùhǎoyìsi
诗情画意 shīqíng-huàyì

❸ [动]料想；推测：anticipate; expect | ～料 yìliào expectation; anticipation

849

意外 yìwài unexpected; unfore-
seen
出人意料 chūrén-yìliào
◇生意 shēngyi
玩意儿 wányìr
做生意 zuòshēngyi

毅 yì 15画 殳部

毅毅毅毅毅毅毅毅
毅毅毅毅毅毅毅

[形]刚强；果断：firm; resolute;
staunch | 刚~gāngyì resolute
and steadfast
毅力 yìlì willpower; will; stamina
毅然 yìrán resolutely; firmly;
determinedly

翼 yì 17画 羽部

翼翼翼翼翼翼翼翼
翼翼翼翼翼翼翼翼
翼

❶[名]翅膀：wing | 双~shuāngyì
two wings | 鸟~niǎoyì wing of
a bird
❷[名]类似翅膀一样的东西：wing-
like object | 机~jīyì wing (of
a plane)

因 yīn 6画 囗部

因 因因因因因因

[名]原因：reason; cause | 前~后
果 qiányīn-hòuguǒ cause and
effect | 事出有~shì chū yǒu
yīn there is a good reason for it
因素 yīnsù factor; element
原因 yuányīn
◇因此 yīncǐ therefore; for this
reason; consequently
因而 yīn'ér thus; as a result;
with the result that
因为 yīnwèi because; for; on account of
基因 jīyīn
转基因 zhuǎnjīyīn

阴 (陰) yīn 6画 阝(左)部

阴 阴阴阴阴阴阴

❶[形]天空被云遮住，不见或少见
阳光的(天气)：overcast; cloudy
| 多云转~duōyún zhuǎnyīn
change from cloudy to overcast
/ ~雨连绵 yīnyǔ liánmián
cloudy and drizzly for days on
end / 天~了。Tiān yīn le. It is
becoming cloudy.
阴暗 yīn'àn dark; gloomy
阴天 yīntiān overcast sky;
cloudy day
阴影 yīnyǐng shadow
❷[形]不外露的；隐藏的：hidden;
secret | ~文 yīnwén charac-
ters cut in intaglio
❸[形]不正大光明的；阴险的：in-
sidious; ulterior; tricky or at-

tempting to deceive | ～险 yīn-xiǎn *sinister*

阴谋 yīnmóu plot; scheme; conspiracy

音 yīn　9画 音部

音 音音音音音音音音音

❶ [名]声音：sound | 口～kǒuyīn *accent* / 扩～器 kuòyīnqì *loud-speaker*

音响 yīnxiǎng sound; acoustics; stereo set

音像 yīnxiàng audiovisual; sound and video recording

音乐 yīnyuè music

音乐会 yīnyuèhuì concert

音乐厅 yīnyuètīng concert hall

播音 bōyīn　　发音 fāyīn
录音 lùyīn　　配音 pèiyīn
噪音 sàngyīn　声音 shēngyīn
语音 yǔyīn
录音机 lùyīnjī
收音机 shōuyīnjī

❷ [名]消息：news | ～信 yīnxìn *news* / 佳～jiāyīn *good news*

银 (銀) yín　11画 钅部

银 银银银银银银银银银银银

❶ [名] silver
❷ [名] 钱或跟钱有关的事物：cur-

rency; money | ～币 yínbì *silver coin*

银行 yínháng bank

银子 yínzi silver; money

❸ [形] 像银子的颜色：silvercoloured | ～白色 yínbáisè *silvery white*

银河 yínhé (astron.) the Milky Way

银幕 yínmù screen; projection screen

淫 yín　11画 氵部

淫 淫淫淫淫淫淫淫淫淫淫淫

[形] 指男女关系不正当：illicit sexual relations; lewd; lascivious

淫秽 yínhuì obscene; pornographic; salacious; bawdy

卖淫 màiyín

引 yǐn　4画 弓部

引 引引引引

❶ [动] 向某个方向用力；拉：draw; pull | ～弓 yǐngōng *draw a bow*

牵引 qiānyǐn

❷ [动] 带领；引导：guide; lead | ～路 yǐnlù *lead the way*

引导 yǐndǎo guide; lead

引渡 yǐndù (leg.) extradite

引进 yǐnjìn import; introduce

引入 yǐnrù lead into; draw into
指引 zhǐyǐn

❸[动]招致；使出现：induce; attract; make appear ｜用纸～火 yòng zhǐ yǐnhuǒ *kindle a fire with paper* / 他这一句话～得大家笑起来。Tā zhè yī jù huà yǐnde dàjiā xiào qǐlai. *His remarks set everybody laughing.*
引爆 yǐnbào ignite; detonate
引发 yǐnfā initiate; touch off; spark off; trigger off
引起 yǐnqǐ give rise to; lead to; set off; touch off
引诱 yǐnyòu lure; seduce
引人注目 yǐnrén-zhùmù catch sb.'s attention
吸引 xīyǐn

❹[动]用来作证据或理由：quote; cite ｜～文 yǐnwén *quotation* ～用 yǐnyòng *quote; cite*
援引 yuányǐn

 饮 (飲) yǐn 7画 饣部

饮 饮饮饮饮饮饮饮

❶[动]喝：drink ｜～酒 yǐnjiǔ *drink wine or liquor* / 痛～ tòngyǐn *drink to one's heart's content; swig*
饮食 yǐnshí food and drink; diet
饮用 yǐnyòng drink
饮水思源 yǐnshuǐ-sīyuán think of its source when drinking water; be grateful for the source of benefit
餐饮 cānyǐn

❷[名]指饮料：beverage; drink
饮料 yǐnliào drink; beverage
冷饮 lěngyǐn

 隐 (隱) yǐn 11画 阝(左)部

隐 隐隐隐隐隐隐隐隐隐隐隐

[动] 藏起来不显露：hide from view; conceal ｜～含 yǐnhán *imply*
隐蔽 yǐnbì conceal; take over
隐藏 yǐncáng hide; conceal; remain under cover
隐患 yǐnhuàn hidden trouble; hidden danger; snake in the grass
隐瞒 yǐnmán conceal; hide; hold back
隐私 yǐnsī one's secrets; private matters one wants to hide
隐约 yǐnyuē indistinct; faint

 印 yìn 5画 卩部

印 印印印印印

❶[动]留下痕迹：print; leave marks ｜～书 yìnshū *print books* / 翻～ fānyìn *reprint*
❷[动]使文字或图像附着在纸上或器物上：engrave; print ｜～相片 yìn xiàngpiàn *print a photo* /

这部小说～了五万册。Zhè bù xiǎoshuō yìnle wǔ wàn cè. *Fifty thousand copies of the novel have been printed.*

印染 yìnrǎn printing and dyeing (of textiles)

印刷 yìnshuā print

印象 yìnxiàng impression

印章 yìnzhāng seal; signet; stamp

打印 dǎyìn 　　盗印 dàoyìn

复印 fùyìn 　　打印机 dǎyìnjī

复印机 fùyìnjī

◇印度洋 Yìndùyáng the Indian Ocean

（應）yīng　7画 广部

应 应应应应应应

[动] 表示情理上必须如此：should; ought to | 搬家～早作准备。Bānjiā yīng zǎo zuò zhǔnbèi. *Things should be prepared in advance when you plan to move house.*

应当 yīngdāng should; ought to

应该 yīnggāi should; ought to See yìng.

yīng　8画 艹部

英 英英英英英英英英

❶ [形] 才能出众的：outstanding in talent

英俊 yīngjùn ① eminently talented; brilliant ② handsome and spirited; smart

英明 yīngmíng brilliant; wise

英勇 yīngyǒng heroic; valiant; brave; gallant

❷ [名] 才能出众的人：outstanding person in talent or intelligence

英雄 yīngxióng hero; heroine

精英 jīngyīng

❸ [名] 指英国：Britain

英镑 yīngbàng pound sterling

英尺 yīngchǐ foot (a measure)

英寸 yīngcùn inch

英文 Yīngwén English (language)

英语 Yīngyǔ English (language)

（嬰）yīng　11画 女部

婴 婴婴婴婴婴婴婴婴
婴婴婴

[名] 初生的孩子：baby; infant | 育～yùyīng *nurse a baby* / 妇～ fùyīng *women and children*

婴儿 yīng'ér baby; infant

（櫻）yīng　15画 木部

樱 樱樱樱樱樱樱樱樱
樱樱樱樱樱樱樱

[名] cherry | ～桃 yīngtáo *cherry*

樱花 yīnghuā oriental cherry

鹰利 yínglì profit; gain

鹰(鷹) yīng　18画 广部

鹰鹰鹰鹰鹰鹰鹰鹰
鹰鹰鹰鹰鹰鹰鹰
鹰鹰

[名] hawk; eagle ｜ ~捕食小兽。
Yīng bǔshí xiǎoshòu. *Hawks prey on small animals.*

迎 yíng　7画 辶部

迎迎迎迎迎迎迎

❶[动]迎接：welcome; greet; go to meet ｜ ~宾 yíngbīn *greet the guest*
迎接 yíngjiē meet; welcome; greet
欢迎 huānyíng
❷[动]向着；对着：against; towards ｜ ~头赶上 yíngtóu gǎn-shàng *try hard to catch up*
迎面 yíngmiàn head-on; in one's face
◇迎合 yínghé cater to; pander to

盈 yíng　9画 皿部

盈盈盈盈盈盈盈盈
盈

[动] 有余；多出：surplus; have a surplus ｜ ~余 yíngyú *surplus*

营(營) yíng　11画 艹部

营营营营营营营营
营营营

❶[名] 军队驻扎的地方：camp; barracks ｜ 军 ~jūnyíng *barracks*
阵营 zhènyíng
❷[名] 军队的编制单位：battalion; military unit subordinate to a regiment
❸[动] 经营；管理：operate; run ｜ ~造 yíngzào *construct*
营业 yíngyè do business
国营 guóyíng　　合营 héyíng
经营 jīngyíng　　私营 sīyíng
◇营救 yíngjiù succour; rescue
营养 yíngyǎng nutrition; nourishment
夏令营 xiàlìngyíng

蝇(蠅) yíng　14画 虫部

蝇蝇蝇蝇蝇蝇蝇蝇
蝇蝇蝇蝇蝇蝇

[名]苍蝇：fly ｜ ~拍 yíngpāi *fly swatter* / 灭 ~miè yíng *kill flies*

赢(贏) yíng　17画 亠部

赢 赢赢赢赢赢赢赢赢
赢赢赢赢赢赢赢赢
赢

❶ [动]获胜(跟"输 shū"相对)：win (the opposite of "输 shū") | 这盘棋我～了。Zhè pán qí wǒ yíng le. *I've won the chess game.*

赢家 yíngjiā winner

❷ [动]获得：get; obtain | ～利 yínglì *profit*

赢得 yíngdé gain; win; obtain

影 yǐng 15画 彡部

影 影影影影影影影影
影影影影影影影

❶ [名]影子：shadow | 树～儿 shùyǐngr *shadow of a tree* / 人～儿 rényǐngr *shadow of a figure*

影子 yǐngzi shadow

阴影 yīnyǐng   踪影 zōngyǐng

❷ [名]照片；图像：picture; photo | 留～ liúyǐng *take a picture as a memento* / 合～ héyǐng *group photo* / ～集 yǐngjí *photo album*

影像 yǐngxiàng image

摄影 shèyǐng

摄影师 shèyǐngshī

❸ [名]电影：movie; film | ～院 yǐngyuàn *cinema* / ～评 yǐngpíng *film review*

影片 yǐngpiàn film; movie; picture

电影 diànyǐng

电影院 diànyǐngyuàn

◇影响 yǐngxiǎng ① influence; affect ② effect

应 (應) yìng 7画 广部

应 应应应应应应应

❶ [动]回答：answer; respond; reply | ～答 yìngdá *reply; answer*

应聘 yìngpìn accept an offer of employment

答应 dāying   反应 fǎnyìng

回应 huíyìng   响应 xiǎngyìng

照应 zhàoyìng

❷ [动]接受；满足要求：comply with; meet the demand; accept | ～邀 yìngyāo *at sb.'s invitation; on invitation; by invitation*

供不应求 gōngbùyìngqiú

❸ [动]适合：suitable | ～时 yìngshí *right; opportune; in season*

应用 yìngyòng apply; use

对应 duìyìng   适应 shìyìng

相应 xiāngyìng

❹ [动]采取措施对付、处理：deal with; cope with | ～变 yìngbiàn *adapt oneself to changes*

应酬 yìngchou have social interaction with; engage in social activities

应付 yìngfù meet; cope with;

855

deal with; handle

应急 yìngjí meet an urgent need; meet an emergency (or contingency)

See yīng.

 映 yìng 9画 日部

映 映映映映映映映映映

[动] 受照射而显出：silhouette; reflect; mirror; shine | 灯光~在墙上。Dēngguāng yìng zài qiáng shang. The light was shone on the wall. / 夕阳~红了湖水。Xīyáng yìng-hóngle húshuǐ. *The surface of the lake shone red under the setting sun.*

反映 fǎnyìng 放映 fàngyìng

硬 yìng 12画 石部

硬 硬硬硬硬硬硬硬硬 硬硬硬硬

❶[形] 坚固（跟 "软 ruǎn" 相对）：hard (the opposite of "软 ruǎn") | 感觉很~gǎnjué hěn yìng *feel hard* / 这种木料真~。Zhè zhǒng mùliào zhēn yìng. *The wood is really hard.*

硬件 yìngjiàn hardware

硬盘 yìngpán hard disk (of computer)

坚硬 jiānyìng 强硬 qiángyìng

❷[形]（性格）刚强；（意志）坚定：unyielding; firm; resolved and obstinate | ~汉子 yìnghànzi *man of iron* / 态度强~tàidu qiángyìng *take an unyielding attitude* / 这个人心肠很~。Zhè-ge rén xīncháng hěn yìng. *He is hard-hearted.*

❸[副] 勉强；不肯改变主意或做法：reluctantly; forcibly | ~撑 yìngchēng *force oneself to do sth.* / 他干不了却~要干。Tā gànbuliǎo què yìngyào gàn. *He kept on doing it tenaciously in spite of his inability.*

哟 (哟) yo 9画 口部

哟 哟哟哟哟哟哟哟哟 哟

[叹] 表示祈使：expressing an imperative tone | 大家加把劲~! Dàjiā jiā bǎ jìn yo! *Everybody, let's make a greater effort!*

拥 (擁) yōng 8画 扌部

拥 拥拥拥拥拥拥拥拥

❶[动] 抱：hold in one's arms; embrace; hug

拥抱 yōngbào embrace; hug

❷[动] 聚到一起：throng; swarm |

大家分散点，别~在一起。Dàjiā fēnsàn diǎn, bié yōng zài yīqǐ. *Don't crowd together.*

拥挤 yōngjǐ crowd; push and squeeze

❸[动]赞成并支持：support | ~戴 yōngdài *support (sb. as a leader)*

拥护 yōnghù support; uphold; endorse

◇拥有 yōngyǒu have; possess; own

 庸 yōng 11画 广部

庸庸庸庸庸庸庸庸庸庸庸

[形] 平常；不高明：inferior; not brilliant; unaccomplished | 平~píngyōng *mediocre*

庸俗 yōngsú vulgar; philistine; low

 永 yǒng 5画 、部

永永永永永

[形] 长久；久远：perpetual; forever; eternal | ~恒 yǒnghéng *eternal; perpetual* / 学习~无止境。Xuéxí yǒng wú zhǐjìng. *There is no end to learning.*

永久 yǒngjiǔ permanent; perpetual; everlasting; forever

永远 yǒngyuǎn forever; always; ever; in perpetuity

永垂不朽 yǒngchuí-bùxiǔ be immortal

 泳 yǒng 8画 氵部

泳泳泳泳泳泳泳泳

[动] 游水：swim | 蛙~wāyǒng *breast stroke* / 自由~zìyóu-yǒng *freestyle swimming*

泳装 yǒngzhuāng swimming costume; swimsuit

游泳 yóuyǒng

游泳池 yóuyǒngchí

 勇 yǒng 9画 力部

勇勇勇勇勇勇勇勇勇

[形] 有胆量：brave; valiant; courageous | ~攀高峰 yǒngpān gāofēng *be brave to scale the heights*

勇敢 yǒnggǎn brave; courageous

勇气 yǒngqì courage

勇士 yǒngshì brave and strong man; warrior

勇于 yǒngyú be brave in; be bold in; have the courage to

奋勇 fènyǒng

英勇 yīngyǒng

涌 yǒng　10画　氵部

涌 涌涌涌涌涌涌涌涌 涌涌

❶[动]水或云气向上冒出：(of water or clouds) gush; pour; surge | 一股泉水直往上～。Yī gǔ quánshuǐ zhí wǎngshang yǒng. *A spring gushes up.*

汹涌 xiōngyǒng

❷[动]像水升腾那样冒出或升起：rise; spring; well; emerge | 许多人从里面～出来。Xǔduō rén cóng lǐmian yǒng chūlai. *Many people were pouring out from inside.*

涌现 yǒngxiàn emerge in large numbers; spring up

踊 (踴) yǒng　14画　𧾷部

踊 踊踊踊踊踊踊踊踊 踊踊踊踊踊踊

[动]往上跳：leap up; jump up

踊跃 yǒngyuè leap; jump

用 yòng　5画　门部

用 用用用用用

❶[动]使用：use; employ; apply | ～脑 yòng nǎo *use one's mind* / ～机器 yòng jīqì *use machines* / 这支笔很好～。Zhè zhī bǐ hěn hǎo yòng. *This pen writes well.*

用法 yòngfǎ use; usage

用功 yònggōng hardworking; diligent; studious

用户 yònghù consumer; user

用具 yòngjù utensil; apparatus; appliance

用来 yònglái used as; apply to

用力 yònglì exert oneself; put forth one's strength

用品 yòngpǐn appliance; article

用人 yòngrén choose a person for a job; make proper use of personnel

用心 yòngxīn attentively; diligently; with concentrated attention

用意 yòngyì intention; purpose

用于 yòngyú used as; apply to

备用 bèiyòng　采用 cǎiyòng

常用 chángyòng

动用 dòngyòng　服用 fúyòng

公用 gōngyòng　家用 jiāyòng

军用 jūnyòng　利用 lìyòng

录用 lùyòng　民用 mínyòng

耐用 nàiyòng　聘用 pìnyòng

日用 rìyòng　实用 shíyòng

食用 shíyòng　使用 shǐyòng

适用 shìyòng　通用 tōngyòng

信用 xìnyòng　选用 xuǎnyòng

引用 yǐnyòng　饮用 yǐnyòng

应用 yìngyòng　运用 yùnyòng

占用 zhànyòng　专用 zhuānyòng

惯用语 guànyòngyǔ
日用品 rìyòngpǐn
信用卡 xìnyòngkǎ
信用社 xìnyòngshè
公用电话 gōngyòng diànhuà

❷[名]功效；用处：use; function | 功~gōngyòng *function* / 效~ xiàoyòng *function*

用处 yòngchu use; usage
用途 yòngtú use; purpose
没用 méiyòng　有用 yǒuyòng
作用 zuòyòng
副作用 fùzuòyòng

❸[名]花费的钱；费用：expense | 零~língyòng *pocket money* / 家~jiāyòng *family expenses*

费用 fèiyòng

❹[动]需要：need | 不~着急。Bù-yòng zháojí. *Don't worry.* / 你不~多说了。Nǐ búyòng duō shuō le. *You needn't say any more.* / 光线还够用，不~开灯。Guāngxiàn hái gòu yòng, bù-yòng kāidēng. *It's still bright. No need to put on the light.*

用不着 yòngbuzháo not need; have no use for

❺[介]表示动作凭借或使用的工具、手段等：by means of

优 (優) yōu　6画 亻部

优 优优优优优优

❶[形]好；非常好（跟"劣liè"相对）：excellent (the opposite of

"劣liè") | ~等 yōuděng *high-class; first-rate*

优点 yōudiǎn merit; strong point; advantage

优化 yōuhuà optimize

优惠 yōuhuì preferential; favourable

优良 yōuliáng fine; good; excellent

优美 yōuměi graceful; fine; exquisite

优胜 yōushèng winning; superior

优势 yōushì superiority; preponderance; dominant position

优秀 yōuxiù outstanding; excellent; splendid; fine

优雅 yōuyǎ graceful; elegant; in good taste

优异 yōuyì excellent; outstanding

优越 yōuyuè superior; advantageous

优质 yōuzhì high quality; high grade

❷[形]充足；富裕：ample; abundant; affluent | 生活~裕 shēnghuó yōuyù *lead a rich life*

❸[形]柔弱；少决断：weak; irresolute

❹[形]演员：actor; actress | 名~ míngyōu *well-known actor*

◇优先 yōuxiān priority; precedence

859

忧 (憂) yōu　7画 忄部

忧　忧忧忧忧忧忧忧忧

[动] 发愁；担心：worry about; be worried | ~闷 yōumēn *depressed*

忧虑 yōulǜ worried; anxious; concerned

忧郁 yōuyù melancholy; heavyhearted

幽 yōu　9画 山部

幽　幽幽幽幽幽幽幽幽幽

[形] 安静：quiet; tranquil | ~谷 yōugǔ *deep and secluded valley* / ~室 yōushì *secluded dwelling*

幽静 yōujìng quiet and secluded; peaceful

◇幽默 yōumò humour

悠 yōu　11画 心部

悠　悠悠悠悠悠悠悠悠悠悠悠

[形] 长久：long; longstanding | ~远 yōuyuǎn *a long time ago*

悠久 yōujiǔ long; longstanding; age-old

尤 yōu　4画 尢部

尤　尤尤尤尤

[副] 更加；格外：particularly; especially; more so; all the more | 这一点~为重要。Zhè yī diǎn yōuwéi zhòngyào. *It is especially important.*

尤其 yōuqí especially; particularly

由 yóu　5画 丨部

由　由由由由由

❶[介] 从；表示起点：from; by | ~上到下 yóu shàng dào xià *from top to bottom* / 代表团~北京出发。Dàibiǎotuán yóu Běijīng chūfā. *The delegation set off from Beijing.*

❷[介] 引进施动者，表示(某事)归(某人去做)：(done) by sb. | 这事~你作主。Zhè shì yóu nǐ zuòzhǔ. *It's up to you.* / 这个问题应该~他来解决。Zhège wèntí yīnggāi yóu tā lái jiějué. *It should be his responsibility to solve this problem.*

不由自主 bùyóu-zìzhǔ

❸[介] 表示凭借：because of; due to; owing to; on the basis of | 人体是~各种细胞组成的。Rén tǐ shì yóu gèzhǒng xìbāo zǔchéng de. *The human body is composed of various kinds of cells.*

由此可见 yóucǐ-kějiàn thus it is seen that; that proves; this shows

❹ [介] 表示方式、原因或来源：used to indicate manner, reason, or source ｜代表～选举产生。Dàibiǎo yóu xuǎnjǔ chǎnshēng. *The representative is chosen by election.*

由于 yóuyú owing to; thanks to; as a result of; due to; in virtue of

◇不由得 bùyóude

自由市场 zìyóu shìchǎng

 邮 (郵) yóu 7画 阝(右)部

邮 邮邮邮邮邮邮邮

❶ [动] 由邮局递送：post; mail ｜ ～信 yóu xìn *post a letter* / 他每月给家里～钱。Tā měi yuè gěi jiālǐ yóu qián. *He remits money to his family every month.*

邮购 yóugòu mail order

邮寄 yóujì send by post; post

❷ [名] 指邮政业务：post; mail ｜ ～费 yóufèi *postage*

邮包 yóubāo postal parcel; parcel

邮编 yóubiān postcode; zip code; zip

邮电 yóudiàn post and telecommunications

邮件 yóujiàn postal matter; post; mail

邮局 yóujú post office

邮票 yóupiào stamp; postage stamp

邮箱 yóuxiāng postbox; mailbox

邮政 yóuzhèng postal service

❸ [名] 邮票：stamp

集邮 jíyóu

 犹 (猶) yóu 7画 犭部

犹 犹犹犹犹犹犹犹

[动] 像；如同：be like; just as ｜ 虽死～生 suīsǐ-yóushēng *live on in spirit*

犹如 yóurú just as; like; as if

◇犹豫 yóuyù hesitate; be irresolute

 油 yóu 8画 氵部

油 油油油油油油油油

❶ [名] 油脂的总称：general term for oil; fat; grease ｜ 花生～huāshēngyóu *peanut oil*

油画 yóuhuà oil painting

油料 yóuliào oil-bearing

油门 yóumén ① throttle ② (inf.) accelerator

油条 yóutiáo ① long, deep-fried, twisted dough sticks, usu. served as breakfast ② sly person; old fox

邮
犹
油

yóu

油漆 yóuqī paint

黄油 huángyóu　酱油 jiàngyóu

❷ [名] 某些液态矿产品或制成品：petroleum | 煤~méiyóu kerosene

油田 yóutián oil field

柴油 cháiyóu　　机油 jīyóu

加油 jiāyóu　　炼油 liànyóu

汽油 qìyóu　　燃油 rányóu

石油 shíyóu　　原油 yuányóu

加油站 jiāyóuzhàn

◇油菜 yóucài rape

油滑 yóuhuá slippery; foxy

 铀（鈾）yóu　10画 钅部

铀 铀铀铀铀铀铀铀铀铀 铀铀

[名] uranium

游 yóu　12画 氵部

游 游游游游游游游游 游游游游

❶ [动] 闲逛；玩耍：move around; stroll; saunter; play | ~玩 yóuwán play / 他~遍了法国。Tā yóubiànle Fǎguó. He travelled all over France.

游船 yóuchuán pleasure boat

游客 yóukè visitor; tourist; excursionist; sightseer

游览 yóulǎn go sightseeing; tour; visit

游人 yóurén visitor (to a park, etc.); sightseer; tourist

游艇 yóutǐng yacht; pleasure boat

游戏 yóuxì game; recreation

导游 dǎoyóu　　旅游 lǚyóu

漫游 mànyóu

旅游鞋 lǚyóuxié

旅游业 lǚyóuyè

❷ [动] 在水里行动：swim; move in water | ~水 yóushuǐ swim / ~过河去 yóuguò hé qu swim across the river / 他一口气~了50米。Tā yīkǒuqì yóule wǔshí mǐ. He swam 50 metres in one breath.

游泳 yóuyǒng swim

游泳池 yóuyǒngchí swimming pool

❸ [名] 江河的一段：section of a river; reach

上游 shàngyóu　　下游 xiàyóu

中游 zhōngyóu

◇游击 yóujī guerrilla warfare

游行 yóuxíng parade; march; demonstration

 友 yǒu　4画 又部

友 友友友友

❶ [名] 朋友：friend | 好~hǎoyǒu good friend

友情 yǒuqíng friendly sentiments; friendship

友人 yǒurén friend

友谊 yǒuyì friendship

笔友 bǐyǒu　男友 nányǒu
朋友 péngyou　亲友 qīnyǒu
网友 wǎngyǒu　战友 zhànyǒu
女朋友 nǚpéngyou
酒肉朋友 jiǔròu péngyou

❷[形] 关系好；亲近：friendly; having friendly relations | ～好 yǒuhǎo *friendly* / ～善 yǒushàn *friendly*

友爱 yǒu'ài friendly affection; fraternal love

有　yǒu　6画 月部

有 有有有有有有

❶[动] 表示存在(跟"无wú"或"没méi"相对)：there is; exist (the opposite of "无wú" or "没méi") | ～雨 yǒu yǔ *it will rain* / ～意见 yǒu yìjiàn *have a different opinion* / 那里～十来个人。Nàli yǒu shí lái ge rén. *There are about ten people over there.*

❷[动] 表示领有或具有(跟"无wú"相对)：have; possess (the opposite of "无wú") | ～本领 yǒu běnlǐng *be capable* / 我～一个弟弟。Wǒ yǒu yī ge dìdi. *I have a younger brother.* / 他～很多书。Tā yǒu hěn duō shū. *He has many books.*

有偿 yǒucháng with compensation; compensated; paid

有关 yǒuguān have sth. to do with; have a bearing on; relate to; concern

有力 yǒulì strong; powerful; forceful; energetic; vigorous

有利 yǒulì advantageous; beneficial; favourable

有名 yǒumíng well-known; famous; celebrated

有趣 yǒuqù interesting; fascinating; amusing

有限 yǒuxiàn limited; finite

有效 yǒuxiào effective

有益 yǒuyì profitable; beneficial; useful

有意 yǒuyì ① have a mind to; be inclined ② intentionally; deliberately; purposely

有用 yǒuyòng useful

有出息 yǒuchūxi have prospects of success in life; show promise

有点儿 yǒudiǎnr ① some; a little ② somewhat; rather; a bit

有效期 yǒuxiàoqī term (or period) of validity; time of efficacy

有意思 yǒuyìsi ① significant; meaningful ② interesting; enjoyable

有助于 yǒuzhùyú contribute to; be conducive to; conduce to

有口无心 yǒukǒu-wúxīn be sharp-tongued but not malicious

有声有色 yǒushēng-yǒusè full of sound and colour; vivid and dramatic

持有 chíyǒu	独有 dúyǒu
公有 gōngyǒu	共有 gòngyǒu
固有 gùyǒu	国有 guóyǒu
还有 háiyǒu	含有 hányǒu
具有 jùyǒu	没有 méiyǒu
少有 shǎoyǒu	私有 sīyǒu
所有 suǒyǒu	特有 tèyǒu
现有 xiànyǒu	享有 xiǎngyǒu
拥有 yōngyǒu	占有 zhànyǒu

公有制 gōngyǒuzhì
私有制 sīyǒuzhì
所有权 suǒyǒuquán
所有制 suǒyǒuzhì
前所未有 qiánsuǒwèiyǒu

❸[动]表示估量或比较：indicating estimation or comparison | 水～三米多深。Shuǐ yǒu sān mǐ duō shēn. *The water is more than three metres deep.* / 他～哥哥那么高了。Tā yǒu gēge nàme gāo le. *He is as tall as his elder brother.*

❹[动]表示发生或出现：indicating occurrence or emergence | ～病了 yǒu bìng le *be ill* / 情况～了新发展。Qíngkuàng yǒule xīn fāzhǎn. *The situation has changed.*

❺[动]表示一部分：indicating a part | ～人性子急，～人性子慢。Yǒu rén xìngzi jí, yǒu rén xìng-zi màn. *Some people are hot-tempered, some people are laid-back.*

有的 yǒude some
有时 yǒushí sometimes; at times; now and then
有些 yǒuxiē ① some ② somewhat; rather
有时候 yǒushíhou sometimes; at times; now and then
有一些 yǒuyīxiē ① some ② somewhat; rather
◇有待 yǒudài remain; await
有机 yǒujī organic

又　yòu　2画 又部

又 又 又

❶[副]表示重复或继续：indicating repetition or continuation | 看了～看 kànle yòu kàn *look again and again* / 一年～一年 yī nián yòu yī nián *year after year* / 他今天～来了。Tā jīntiān yòu lái le. *He came again today.* / 他～立功了。Tā yòu lìgōng le. *He rendered meritorious service again.*

❷[副]表示几种情况或几种性质同时存在：indicating the simultaneous existence of more than one situation or property | ～快～好 yòu kuài yòu hǎo *both quick and of good quality* / ～高～大 yòu gāo yòu dà *tall and big* / 我～高兴，～担心。Wǒ yòu gāoxìng, yòu dānxīn. *I was happy and worried at the same time.*

❸[副]表示在某个范围之外有所补充：indicating an addition to a given scope | 除生活费之外，～发给 50 元钱作零用。Chú shēnghuófèi zhīwài, yòu fāgěi wǔshí yuán qián zuò língyòng. *Each of them was given 50 yuan as pocket money in addition to the daily allowance.*

❹[副]表示有矛盾的两件事：indicating two contradictory things | 他～想去，～不想去，拿不定主意。Tā yòu xiǎng qù, yòu bù xiǎng qù, nábudìng zhǔyì. *He couldn't make up his mind whether to go or not.*

❺[副]表示转折，有"可是"的意思：indicating a turning of meaning, similar to "可是kěshì" | 他想说话却～忍住了。Tā xiǎng shuōhuà què yòu rěnzhù le. *He want to speak but stopped himself.* / 我想去，～怕没时间。Wǒ xiǎng qù, yòu pà méi shíjiān. *I'd like to go, but I'm afraid I don't have time.*

❻[副]加强反问：used in a rhetorical question for emphasis | 我～不是外人，不必客气。Wǒ yòu bùshì wàirén, bùbì kèqi. *I'm not a stranger, no need for ceremony.*

 右　yòu　5画 口部

右　右 右 右 右 右

[名]（跟"左zuǒ"相对）：right (the opposite of "左zuǒ") | ～手 yòushǒu *right hand* / 向～拐弯 xiàng yòu guǎiwān *turn right*
右边 yòubian right (right-hand) side; the right
右侧 yòucè right (right-hand) side; the right
右面 yòumiàn right (right-hand) side; the right
左右 zuǒyòu
左右手 zuǒyòushǒu
◇座右铭 zuòyòumíng

 幼　yòu　5画 幺部

幼　幼 幼 幼 幼 幼

[形] 年纪小；未长成：young; under age | ～小 yòuxiǎo *immature* / ～儿 yòu'ér *infant* / 年～无知 niányòu-wúzhī *young and ignorant*
幼稚 yòuzhì childish; puerile; naive
幼儿园 yòu'éryuán kindergarten; nursery school; infant school

 诱（誘）yòu　9画 讠部

诱 诱诱诱诱诱诱诱诱诱
诱

❶ [动]引导；劝导：guide; lead; induce | ~导 yǒudǎo *guide; induce*

❷ [动]用手段引诱对方上当：lure; induce | 利~lìyòu *lure by promise of gain*

诱惑 yòuhuò entice; tempt; seduce; lure

诱人 yòurén alluring; fascinating; captivating; enchanting

引诱 yǐnyòu

于 yú 3画 一部

于 于于于

❶ [介]表示时间、处所、来源：indicating time, location or source | 写~北京 xiě yú Běijīng *written in Beijing* / 生~1949 年 shēng yú yījiǔsìjiǔ nián *be born in 1949*

❷ [介]表示对象：indicating object | 新鲜空气有利~健康。Xīnxiān kōngqì yǒulì yú jiànkāng. *Fresh air is beneficial to health.* / 这样~你自己不利。Zhèyàng yú nǐ zìjǐ bùlì. *It won't do you any good.*

对于 duìyú   用于 yòngyú
忠于 zhōngyú
有助于 yǒuzhùyú

❸ [介]表示被动：indicating passive voice

❹ [介]表示方面、原因、目的：indicating an aspect, cause or purpose | 易~了解yìyú liǎojiě *easy to understand* / 难~实行 nányú shíxíng *difficult to carry out*

便于 biànyú   敢于 gǎnyú
急于 jíyú   善于 shànyú
勇于 yǒngyú

❺ [介]表示比较：indicating comparison | 大~dàyú *more than; bigger than* / 少~shǎoyú *less than* / 今年小麦产量高~往年。Jīnnián xiǎomài chǎnliàng gāo yú wǎngnián. *The yield of wheat this year is higher than last year.*

相当于 xiāngdāngyú

◇于是 yúshì thereupon; hence; consequently; as a result

不至于 bùzhìyú
甚至于 shènzhìyú

余 (餘) yú 7画 人部

余 余余余余余余余余

❶ [动]剩下；多出来：spare; surplus | 这个月的收支结算之后，还~50 元。Zhège yuè de shōuzhī jiésuàn zhīhòu, hái yú wǔshí yuán. *After paying all the expenses for this month, there is a balance of fifty yuan left.*

余地 yúdì leeway; margin;

room; latitude

余额 yú'é ① vacancies yet to be filled ② remaining sum; balance

残余 cānyú　　多余 duōyú
富余 fùyú　　　其余 qíyú
剩余 shèngyú

❷[名] (某事、某种情况) 以外或以后 (的时间)：time beyond or after an event | 茶～饭后 chá-yú-fànhòu *over a cup of tea or after a meal; at one's leisure* | 他工作之～爱好下棋。Tā gōngzuò zhī yú àihào xiàqí. *He likes to play chess in his spare time.*

业余 yèyú

❸[数] 零头数：more than; -odd; over | 十～人 shí yú rén *more than ten people* | 五十～年 wǔshí yú nián *fifty-odd years*

 鱼 (魚) yú　　8画 鱼部

鱼　鱼鱼鱼鱼鱼鱼鱼鱼

❶[名] fish | 煎～ jiān yú *fry fish* | 湖里～很多。Hú li yú hěn duō. *There are many fish in the lake.*

金鱼 jīnyú

❷[名] 称某些水栖动物：term for some aquatic animals

鲸鱼 jīngyú

 娱 yú　　10画 女部

娱　娱娱娱娱娱娱娱娱娱娱

[形] 快乐：giving pleasure to; amusing

娱乐 yúlè amusement; entertainment; recreation

 渔 (漁) yú　　11画 氵部

渔　渔渔渔渔渔渔渔渔渔渔渔

[动] 捕鱼：catch fish

渔船 yúchuán fishing boat
渔民 yúmín fisherman; fisherfolk
渔业 yúyè fishery

 愉 yú　　12画 忄部

愉　愉愉愉愉愉愉愉愉愉愉愉愉

[形] 快乐；喜悦：pleased; happy; joyful | ～悦 yúyuè *joyful; cheerful* | 欢～ huānyú *cheerful*

愉快 yúkuài happy; joyful; cheerful

 榆 yú　　13画 木部

榆榆榆榆榆榆榆榆
榆榆榆榆榆

[名] elm

榆树 yúshù elm

愚 yú　13画 心部

愚愚愚愚愚愚愚愚
愚愚愚愚愚

[形] 傻；笨：foolish; stupid | ~笨
yúbèn *foolish* / ~人 yúrén *fool;*
simpleton
愚蠢 yúchǔn stupid; foolish;
silly
愚昧 yúmèi ignorant; fatuous
愚人节 Yúrénjié All Fools' Day
(April 1); April Fool's (or Fools')
Day

與 (與) yú　14画 八部

與與與與與與與與
與與與與與與

[形] 众多；众人的：public; popu-
lar
與论 yúlùn public opinion

与 (與) yǔ　3画 一部

与与与

❶ [介] 跟；引进比较或者动作的对
象：with, introducing the object of comparison or action

| ~人合作 yǔ rén hézuò *coop-*
erate with others / 此事~你无
关。Cǐ shì yǔ nǐ wúguān. *You*
have nothing to do with it.
与此同时 yǔcǐ-tóngshí at the
same time; meanwhile
与众不同 yǔzhòngbùtóng out
of the ordinary; different from
the common run

❷ [连] 和；或；连接并列的词或词组：
and; or (joining coordinate
words or phrases) | 生~死
shēng yǔ sǐ *life and death* / 战
争~和平 zhànzhēng yǔ hé-
píng *war and peace* / 工业~农
业 gōngyè yǔ nóngyè *indus-*
try and agriculture
◇与其 yǔqí rather than; better
than

　　See yú.

予 yǔ　4画 一部

予予予予

[动] 给：give; grant | 免~处分
miǎnyǔ chǔfèn *exempt sb. from*
punishment
予以 yǔyǐ give; grant
赋予 fùyǔ　　　授予 shòuyǔ

宇 yǔ　6画 宀部

宇宇宇宇宇宇

[名] 上下四方的所有空间：space;

universe; world

宇宙 yǔzhòu universe; cosmos

宇航员 yǔhángyuán astronaut;
spaceman; cosmonaut

羽 yǔ　6画 羽部

羽 羽 羽 羽 羽 羽 羽

[名] 鸟类的毛：feather

羽毛 yǔmáo　feather; plume

羽毛球 yǔmáoqiú badminton

羽绒服 yǔróngfú down jacket

雨 yǔ　8画 雨部

雨 雨 雨 雨 雨 雨 雨 雨

[名] rain | 刮风下～guāfēng
xiàyǔ *be windy and rainy* / ～过
天晴。Yǔguò-tiānqíng. *The
sun shines after the rain.* / 这场～
下得好大啊!Zhè chǎng yǔ xià
de hǎo dà a! *What a heavy
rain!*

雨点 yǔdiǎn raindrop

雨伞 yǔsǎn umbrella

雨水 yǔshuǐ　rainwater; rainfall

雨衣 yǔyī raincoat; waterproof

暴雨 bàoyǔ　　　风雨 fēngyǔ

降雨 jiàngyǔ　　　雷雨 léiyǔ

阵雨 zhènyǔ

风调雨顺 fēngtiáo-yǔshùn

语 (語) yǔ　9画 讠部

语 语 语 语 语 语 语 语
语

❶ [动] 说；谈论：speak; say; talk
| 低～dīyǔ *speak in a low voice*
自言自语 zìyán-zìyǔ

❷ [名] 说的话：language; tongue;
words | 甜言蜜～tiányán-
mìyǔ *honeyed words*

语调 yǔdiào intonation

语法 yǔfǎ grammar

语气 yǔqì　tone; manner of
speaking

语文 yǔwén Chinese (as a subject of study or a means of communication)

语言 yǔyán language; tongue

语音 yǔyīn phonetics

语种 yǔzhǒng languages

宾语 bīnyǔ　　　补语 bǔyǔ

成语 chéngyǔ　　德语 Déyǔ

短语 duǎnyǔ　　定语 dìngyǔ

俄语 Éyǔ　　　　法语 Fǎyǔ

国语 guóyǔ　　　汉语 Hànyǔ

口语 kǒuyǔ　　　谜语 míyǔ

母语 mǔyǔ　　　日语 Rìyǔ

术语 shùyǔ　　　外语 wàiyǔ

言语 yányǔ　　　英语 Yīngyǔ

主语 zhǔyǔ　　　状语 zhuàngyǔ

惯用语 guànyòngyǔ

外国语 wàiguóyǔ

阿拉伯语 Ālābóyǔ

与 (與) yǔ　3画 一部

与 与 与 与

[动] 参加：participate in; take part in | 参～cānyù *participate in (a conference, an activity etc.)*

与会 yùhuì attend a meeting

See yǔ.

玉 yù　5画 王部

玉 玉 玉 玉 玉 玉

❶ [名] 玉石：jade | 白～báiyù *white jade*

❷ [形] 比喻洁白、美丽或宝贵：(fig.) pure; fair; handsome; beautiful

玉兰 yùlán (bot.) magnolia (*Magnolia denudata*)

❸ [名] 称对方的身体等，表示尊敬：(pol.) your | ～体 yùtǐ *your esteemed health* / ～照 yùzhào *your portrait*

◇玉米 yùmǐ maize; corn; Indian corn

吁 (籲) yù　6画 口部

吁 吁 吁 吁 吁 吁

[动] 为某种要求而呼喊：appeal; plead; call on | ～请 yùqǐng

plead / ～求 yùqiú implore

呼吁 hūyù

郁 (鬱) yù　8画 阝(右)部

郁 郁 郁 郁 郁 郁 郁 郁

[动] 忧愁；烦闷：gloomy; melancholy; despondent | ～闷 yùmēn *gloomy; depressed*

忧郁 yōuyù

◇浓郁 nóngyù

育 yù　8画 月部

育 育 育 育 育 育 育 育

❶ [动] 生孩子：give birth to; labour

生育 shēngyù

生儿育女 shēng'ér-yùnǚ

❷ [动] 养活；培植：raise; bring up; rear | ～婴 yùyīng *nurse a baby; feed and take care of a baby* / ～苗 yùmiáo *grow seedlings*

❸ [动] 教育；培养：educate | 德～déyù *moral education* / 抚～fǔyù *foster* / 培～péiyù *cultivate*

教育 jiàoyù　　养育 yǎngyù

高等教育 gāoděng jiàoyù

狱 (獄) yù　9画 犭部

狱 狱狱狱狱狱狱狱狱
狱

[名] 监禁罪犯的场所：prison; jail |
入 ~rùyù be imprisoned; be put
in prison | 出 ~chūyù be released
from prison; come out of prison
监狱 jiānyù

浴 yù 10画 氵部
浴 浴浴浴浴浴浴浴浴浴
浴浴

[动] 洗澡：take a bath; bathe |
沐 ~mùyù have a bath; bathe |
淋 ~línyù shower
浴室 yùshì bathroom; shower
room
浴衣 yùyī bathrobe

预(預) yù 10画 页部
预 预预预预预预预预
预预

❶ [副] 事先；提前：in advance;
beforehand
预报 yùbào forecast
预备 yùbèi prepare; get ready
预测 yùcè calculate; forecast
预订 yùdìng reserve
预定 yùdìng predetermine
预防 yùfáng prevent; take precautions against
预告 yùgào ① announce in advance; herald ②advance notice

预计 yùjì calculate in advance;
estimate
预见 yùjiàn foresee; predict; anticipate; prevision
预警 yùjǐng early warning
预料 yùliào anticipate
预期 yùqī expect; anticipate
预赛 yùsài preliminary contest
预示 yùshì betoken; indicate;
presage; forebode
预算 yùsuàn budget
预习 yùxí (of students) review
lessons before class
预先 yùxiān in advance; be-
forehand
预言 yùyán prophecy; predic-
tion
预约 yùyuē make an appoint-
ment
预祝 yùzhù congratulate be-
forehand
❷ [动] 参与：participate in | 参 ~
cānyù participate in
干预 gānyù

域 yù 11画 土部
域 域域域域域域域域
域域域

[名] 在一定范围之内的地方：land
within certain boundaries;
domain | 海 ~hǎiyù sea area;
maritime space
领域 lǐngyù
区域 qūyù
流域 liúyù

机遇 jīyù

欲 yù 11画 欠部

欲欲欲欲欲欲欲欲
欲欲欲

❶ [动] 想要；希望：want; wish; yearn; long for | 随心所~ suíxīnsuǒyù *at one's will*

❷ [名] 欲望；愿望：desire; long for; wish | 求知~qiúzhīyù *thirst for knowledge*
欲望 yùwàng desire; lust
食欲 shíyù

遇 yù 12画 辶部

遇遇遇遇遇遇遇遇
遇遇遇遇

❶ [动] 偶然见到；碰到；遭到：meet; encounter | 相~xiāngyù *meet* / 百年不~bǎinián bùyù *not occur even in a hundred years*
遇到 yùdào run into; encounter; come across
遇害 yùhài be murdered
遇见 yùjiàn meet; come across
遇难 yùnàn ① die (or be killed) in an accident ② be murdered
遭遇 zāoyù

❷ [动] 对待：treat; receive
待遇 dàiyù

❸ [名] 机会：chance; opportunity | 奇~qíyù *adventure*

喻 yù 12画 口部

喻喻喻喻喻喻喻喻
喻喻喻喻

❶ [动] 明白；了解：explain; make clear; inform
不言而喻 bùyán'éryù
家喻户晓 jiāyù-hùxiǎo

❷ [动] 打比方：by analogy
比喻 bǐyù

御 (禦) yù 12画 彳部

御御御御御御御御
御御御御

[动] 抵挡；抵抗：resist; ward off; keep | ~寒 yùhán *keep out the cold*
防御 fángyù

寓 yù 12画 宀部

寓寓寓寓寓寓寓寓
寓寓寓寓

❶ [动] 居住：reside; live; inhabit | ~所 yùsuǒ *residence*
公寓 gōngyù

❷ [动] 寄托；隐含(在事物中)：imply; place; contain | ~意深刻 yùyì shēnkè *with a deep implied meaning*
寓言 yùyán fable; allegory; par-

able

yù　12画　衤部

裕 裕裕裕裕裕裕裕裕
裕裕裕裕

[形] 财物多；充足：abundant;
plentiful; affluent; ample | 家里
很宽～。Jiāli hěn kuānyù. *The
family is well off.* / 我们的时间
不充～。Wǒmen de shíjiān bù
chōngyù.*We don't have enough
time.*

富裕 fùyù

yù　13画　心部

愈 愈愈愈愈愈愈愈愈
愈愈愈愈愈

❶ [动] 病好了：heal; recover; be
cured | ～合 yùhé *heal* / 病～
bìngyù *recover from an illness*

❷ [副] 越；更加；表示程度的增加：
used reiteratively to indicate an
increase of degree | 山路～来～
陡。Shānlù yùláiyù dǒu. *The
mountain path becomes steeper
and steeper.*

（譽）yù　13画　言部

誉 誉誉誉誉誉誉誉誉
誉誉誉誉誉

[动] 名声；好名声：reputation;

fame | 荣～róngyù *honour* /
声～shēngyù *reputation*
名誉 míngyù　　信誉 xìnyù

yuān　10画　宀部

冤 冤冤冤冤冤冤冤冤
冤冤

[名] 冤枉；冤屈；仇恨：wrong; in-
justice; grievance | 申～shēn-
yuān *redress an injustice* / 鸣～
míngyuān *voice grievances* /
～家 yuānjia *enemy; foe*
冤枉 yuānwang wrong; treat
unjustly

元

yuán　4画　儿部

元 元元元元

❶ [形] 为首的：chief; principal;
leading | ～老 yuánlǎo *senior
statesman; founding father* / ～
帅 yuánshuài *marshal*
元首 yuánshǒu head of state
状元 zhuàngyuan

❷ [形] 开始的；第一：first; pri-
mary; initial | ～月 yuányuè
January / ～年 yuánnián *the
first year of an era or the reign
of an emperor*
元旦 yuándàn New Year's Day

❸ [形] 主要；基本：basic; funda-
mental | ～音 yuányīn *vowel*
元件 yuánjiàn element; com-

ponent

元素 yuánsù element; essential factor

❹ [量] 货币单位：unit of money

美元 měiyuán　欧元 ōuyuán

日元 rìyuán

◇元宵 yuánxiāo ① the night of the 15th of the 1st Chinese lunar month ② sweet dumplings made of glutinous rice flour (for the Lantern Festival)

元宵节 Yuánxiāojié the Lantern Festival (the 15th of the 1st lunar month)

 （園） yuán　7画 口部

园 园园园园园园园

❶ [名]种植蔬菜、花果、树木的地方：garden; plot | 果~guǒyuán orchard / 菜~càiyuán vegetable garden

园丁 yuándīng gardener; (usu. of a primary school) teacher

园林 yuánlín garden; park

园艺 yuányì horticulture; gardening

花园 huāyuán

植物园 zhíwùyuán

❷ [名]游览娱乐的场所：place of recreation; park | 动物~dòngwùyuán zoo

公园 gōngyuán　乐园 lèyuán

◇家园 jiāyuán

校园 xiàoyuán

幼儿园 yòu'éryuán

 （員） yuán　7画 口部

员 员员员员员员员

❶ [名]从事某种职业或担当某种任务的人：person engaged in some field of work or study | 营业~yíngyèyuán shop assistant

员工 yuángōng staff; personnel

船员 chuányuán

裁员 cáiyuán　店员 diànyuán

雇员 gùyuán　官员 guānyuán

教员 jiàoyuán　球员 qiúyuán

伤员 shāngyuán　学员 xuéyuán

演员 yǎnyuán　译员 yìyuán

职员 zhíyuán

裁判员 cáipànyuán

乘务员 chéngwùyuán

炊事员 chuīshìyuán

飞行员 fēixíngyuán

服务员 fúwùyuán

技术员 jìshùyuán

驾驶员 jiàshǐyuán

教练员 jiàoliànyuán

陪审员 péishěnyuán

评论员 pínglùnyuán

守门员 shǒuményuán

司令员 sīlìngyuán

研究员 yánjiūyuán

宇航员 yǔhángyuán

运动员 yùndòngyuán

❷ [名]指团体或组织等的成员：

member of a group or an organization

成员 chéngyuán 党员 dǎngyuán
队员 duìyuán 会员 huìyuán
社员 shèyuán 团员 tuányuán
委员 wěiyuán 议员 yìyuán
公务员 gōngwùyuán

原 yuán 10画 厂部

原原原原原原原原
原原

❶[名] 开始的；最初的 primary; original | ～稿 yuángǎo *original manuscript* / ～意 yuányì *original intention* / ～生动物 yuánshēng dòngwù *protozoan*

原本 yuánběn ① original manuscript; master copy ② the original (from which a translation is made) ③ originally; formerly
原创 yuánchuàng originate; initiate; pioneer created
原告 yuángào plaintiff; prosecutor
原理 yuánlǐ principle
原始 yuánshǐ ① primitive; prehistoric ② original; initial; firsthand
原先 yuánxiān former; original
原因 yuányīn reason; cause
❷[名] 没经加工的：unprocessed; crude; raw | ～煤 yuánméi *raw coal*
原料 yuánliào raw material
原油 yuányóu crude oil
原材料 yuáncáiliào raw and unprocessed materials

❸[形] 本来的；没有改变的：original; former | ～职 yuánzhí *former post* / ～作者 yuán zuòzhě *original author* / ～单位 yuán dānwèi *the organization one formerly belonged to* / ～计划 yuán jìhuà *original plan*

原来 yuánlái original; former
还原 huányuán

❹[动] 宽容；谅解：tolerate; pardon | ～谅 yuánliàng excuse; forgive; pardon

❺[名] 宽广平坦的地方：open country; plain; level and extensive land | ～野 yuányě *open country*

草原 cǎoyuán 高原 gāoyuán
平原 píngyuán
中原 zhōngyuán
◇原则 yuánzé principle; rule
原子 yuánzǐ atom
原子弹 yuánzǐdàn atom bomb; atomic bomb; A-bomb
原子能 yuánzǐnéng nuclear power; atomic energy

 （圆） yuán 10画 口部

25

圆 圆圆圆圆圆圆圆圆圆
圆圆

❶ [名] 圆周所包围的平面、圆圈：
circle; sphere ｜ 半～bànyuán
semicircle / 月～了。Yuē yuán
le. The moon is full.
椭圆 tuǒyuán

❷ [形] 像圆形的：round; circular;
spherical ｜ 滚～gǔnyuán round
as a ball
圆珠笔 yuánzhūbǐ ball-point
pen; ball-pen

❸ [形] 完备；周全： perfect; complete
圆满 yuánmǎn satisfactory
团圆 tuányuán

援
yuán 12画 扌部

援 援援援援援援援援
援援援援

[动] 帮助，救助：pull by hand;
hold; rescue ｜ 声～shēngyuán
support / 孤立无～gūlì-wúyuán
isolated and cut off from help
援助 yuánzhù support; aid
救援 jiùyuán　　支援 zhīyuán
◇援引 yuányǐn ① quote; cite ②
recommend or appoint one's
friends or favourites

缘 (緣) yuán 12画 纟部

缘 缘缘缘缘缘缘缘缘
缘缘缘缘

❶ [名] 原因：reason; cause ｜ ～由
yuányóu reason
缘故 yuángù reason; cause;
sake

❷ [名] 边：edge; rim; fringe ｜ 外～
wàiyuán outer edge
边缘 biānyuán
◇缘分 yuánfēn lot or luck by
which people are brought together

猿
yuán 13画 犭部

猿 猿猿猿猿猿猿猿猿
猿猿猿猿猿

[名] ape, mammal resembling a
monkey
猿人 yuánrén apeman

源
yuán 13画 氵部

源 源源源源源源源源
源源源源源

❶ [名] 水流起头的地方：source of a
river; fountainhead ｜ 发～fā-
yuán rise; originate from
源泉 yuánquán source; spring-
head
源头 yuántóu fountainhead;
source
水源 shuǐyuán

❷ [名] 来源，根源：source; origin ｜

货～huòyuán *source of goods* / 财～cáiyuán *source of income*

电源 diànyuán　根源 gēnyuán

来源 láiyuán　　能源 néngyuán

起源 qǐyuán　　资源 zīyuán

 远(遠) **yuǎn** 7画 辶部

远 远远远远远远远

❶[形]空间或时间的距离长(跟"近jìn"相对)：far away in time or space; distant; remote (the opposite of "近jìn") | 路～lù yuǎn *a long way* / 那件事离现在已经很～了。Nà jiàn shì lí xiànzài yǐjīng hěn yuǎn le. *It happened long ago.*

远程 yuǎnchéng long-range; long-distance

远大 yuǎndà high; far; great; bright

远方 yuǎnfāng distant place; far away; distance

远景 yuǎnjǐng long-range perspective; distant view; prospect; outlook; vista

远离 yuǎnlí keep away from; apart from; distance

长远 chángyuǎn

深远 shēnyuǎn　跳远 tiàoyuǎn

遥远 yáoyuǎn　永远 yǒngyuǎn

望远镜 wàngyuǎnjìng

❷[形]关系不密切：(of blood relation) distant | ～亲 yuǎnqīn

distant relative

❸[形](差别)程度大：(of difference) (by) far | 他俩的性格相差很～。Tā liǎ de xìnggé xiāngchà hěn yuǎn. *The two of them are very different in personality.*

 怨 **yuàn** 9画 心部

怨 怨怨怨怨怨怨怨怨怨

❶[名]不满；仇恨：resentment; enmity; hatred | 恩～ēnyuàn *love and hate* / 结～jiéyuàn *arouse sb.'s enmity*

❷[动]责怪：blame; complain | 这件事都～我。Zhè jiàn shì dōu yuàn wǒ. *I ought to be blamed for this.* / 他老是～天气不好。Tā lǎoshì yuàn tiānqì bù hǎo. *He is always complaining about the weather.*

抱怨 bàoyuàn　埋怨 mányuàn

 院 **yuàn** 9画 阝(左)部

院 院院院院院院院院院

❶[名]院子：courtyard | 他家屋后有个小～子。Tā jiā wū hòu yǒu ge xiǎo yuànzi. *At the back of his house, there is a small court-*

yard.

院子 yuànzi courtyard; yard; compound

❷[名]某些机关和公共场所的名称：designation for certain government organizations and public places | 电影～diànyǐngyuàn *cinema* / 科学～kēxuéyuàn *academy of sciences* / 疗养～liáoyǎngyuàn *sanatorium*

院士 yuànshì academician

院长 yuànzhǎng director; dean; chief; head; president

法院 fǎyuàn　　剧院 jùyuàn

学院 xuéyuàn 医院 yīyuàn

参议院 cānyìyuàn

国务院 guówùyuàn

众议院 zhòngyìyuàn

❸[名]指医院：referring to hospital

出院 chūyuàn　住院 zhùyuàn

 愿 (願) yuàn　14画 厂部

愿愿愿愿愿愿愿愿
愿愿愿愿愿愿

❶[名]愿望：desire; wish | 如～rúyuàn *have one's wishes fulfilled; obtain what one desires*

愿望 yuànwàng hope; will; wish

请愿 qǐngyuàn 心愿 xīnyuàn

意愿 yìyuàn　　志愿 zhìyuàn

祝愿 zhùyuàn

志愿者 zhìyuànzhě

❷[动] 肯；乐意：be willing; be ready | 他～做这个工作。Tā yuàn zuò zhège gōngzuò. *He is willing to take this job.*

愿意 yuànyì be willing

宁愿 nìngyuàn　　自愿 zìyuàn

❸[动]希望：hope; wish | 但～如此。Dàn yuàn rúcǐ. *How I wish it were true.*

约 (約) yuē　6画 纟部

约 约约约约约约

❶[动] 限制：restrict; restrain; confine

约束 yuēshù constrain; confine; restrain; bind

制约 zhìyuē

❷[动]预先说定：make an appointment | 我和他～好了。Wǒ hé tā yuēhǎo le. *I have made an appointment with him.*

约定 yuēdìng agree on; appoint; arrange

约会 yuēhuì appointment; engagement; date

预约 yùyuē

❸[名]共同遵守的条文；事先商定的事：agreement; pact; treaty; regulation that both sides agree on and should abide by

公约 gōngyuē 合约 héyuē

和约 héyuē　　签约 qiānyuē

失约 shīyuē　　条约 tiáoyuē

违约 wéiyuē

❹[动] 邀请：invite in advance; engage | ～他来 yuē tā lái *invite him to come* / 特～记者 tèyuē jìzhě *special correspondent*

❺[形] 节俭：economical; thrifty 节约 jiéyuē

❻[副] 大概；大约：about; approximately | ～五十人 yuē wǔshí rén *about fifty people* / ～一个月 yuē yī gè yuè *about a month* 大约 dàyuē

◇ 隐约 yǐnyuē

月　　　　　yuè　4画 月部

月 月 月 月 月

❶[名]月亮；月球：moon; luna | 赏～shǎngyuè *admire the bright full moon* / 新～xīnyuē *new moon*

月饼 yuèbing mooncake (esp. for the Mid-Autumn Festival)

月光 yuèguāng moonlight

月亮 yuèliang moon

月球 yuèqiú the moon

月下老人 yuèxià lǎorén ① the Old Man of the Moon (the god of marriage, who has on record in a book the marriage fates of those on earth and attaches betrothed couples with a red cord which will bind them for life)

② matchmaker

❷[名]时间单位，一年的十二分之一：month; one year being divided into 12 months | 本～běnyuè *this month* / 下个～xià ge yuè *next month*

月初 yuèchū the beginning of the month

月底 yuèdǐ the end of the month

月份 yuèfèn month

月季 yuèjì Chinese rose

月票 yuèpiào monthly ticket

月薪 yuèxīn monthly pay

腊月 làyuè　　满月 mǎnyuè

岁月 suìyuè　　正月 zhēngyuè

长年累月 chángnián-lěiyuè

乐 (樂) yuè　5画 丿部

乐 乐 乐 乐 乐 乐

[名]音乐：music | 奏～zòuyuè *play music*

乐队 yuèduì orchestra; band

乐器 yuèqì musical instrument

乐曲 yuèqǔ musical composition

乐团 yuètuán philharmonic orchestra

音乐 yīnyuè

音乐会 yīnyuèhuì

音乐厅 yīnyuè tīng

　　See lè.

阅 (閱) yuè　10画 门部

879

阅 阅阅阅阅阅阅阅阅
阅阅

❶[动]查看；视察：inspect; review | 检～军队 jiǎnyuè jūnduì inspect troops

❷[动]看：read; scan; peruse | 传～chuányuè circulate for perusal

阅读 yuèdú read; reading

阅览室 yuèlǎnshì reading room

参阅 cānyuè　　查阅 cháyuè
订阅 dìngyuè

❸[动]经历；经过：undergo; pass through | ～历 yuèlì experiences

悦 yuè 10画 忄部
悦 悦悦悦悦悦悦悦悦
悦悦

[形]高兴；愉快：joyous; happy; pleased; merry
喜悦 xǐyuè

跃（躍）yuè 11画 𧾷部
跃 跃跃跃跃跃跃跃跃
跃跃跃

[动]跳：leap; jump; bounce | ～过 yuèguò jump over / ～上马背 yuèshang mǎbèi leap onto a horse

跃进 yuèjìn make (take) a leap; leap forward

飞跃 fēiyuè　　活跃 huóyuè
跳跃 tiàoyuè　　踊跃 yǒngyuè

 yuè 12画 走部
越 越越越越越越越越
越越越越

❶[动]跨过；经过：get over; jump over | ～墙 yuèqiáng climb over a wall

越冬 yuèdōng live through (survive) the winter

越过 yuèguò cross; pass over

越位 yuèwèi (sports) offside

越野 yuèyě cross-country

穿越 chuānyuè　　跨越 kuàyuè

❷[动]超出（范围）：exceed; overstep; go beyond | ～出范围 yuèchū fànwéi overstep the bounds; exceed the limits

超越 chāoyuè

❸[形]超出或胜过一般的：better than; exceeding

优越 yōuyuè　　卓越 zhuóyuè

❹[副]表示程度加深：used to indicate the deepening of degree | 风～刮～大。Fēng yuè guā yuè dà. The wind blows harder and harder. / 条件～来～好。Tiáojiàn yuèláiyuè hǎo. The circumstances have become better and better.

越…越… yuè…yuè… the more... the more...

越来越 yuèláiyuè more and

more

◇越剧 yuèjù Shaoxing opera

晕 (暈) yūn　10画 日部

晕 晕晕晕晕晕晕晕晕
晕晕

❶[形] 头脑昏乱：dizzy; giddy |
头~tóu yūn feel dizzy / ~头转
向 yūntóu-zhuǎnxiàng con-
fused and disoriented

❷[动] 昏迷；失去知觉：faint; pass
out; lose consciousness | ~倒
yūndǎo fall into a faint / 他饿~
了。Tā èyūn le. He fainted from
hunger.

云 (雲) yún　4画 厶部

云 云云云云

[名] cloud | ~已经消散。Yún yǐ-
jīng xiāosàn. The clouds have
dissipated.
云彩 yúncai cloud
风云 fēngyún　乌云 wūyún
风云人物 fēngyún rénwù

匀 yún　4画 勹部

匀 匀匀匀匀

❶[形] 平均；均匀：even; equitable
| 分得不~fēn de bù yún be
unevenly divided / 颜色涂得不~。

Yánsè tú de bù yún. The colour
is not evenly spread.
均匀 jūnyún

❷[动] 使均匀：even up; divide
evenly | 这两份儿分得不均匀，
再~一~吧。Zhè liǎng fènr fēn
de bù jūnyún, zài yúnyiyún ba.
These two shares are not equal.
Let's even them up.

❸[动] 分出一部分给别人或用在别
处：take from sth. and give to
sb. | 我们~出一间屋子给他们
住。Wǒmen yúnchu yī jiān
wūzi gěi tāmen zhù. We gave
them a room to stay in. / 把你买
的纸~给我一些吧。Bǎ nǐ mǎi
de zhǐ yúngěi wǒ yīxiē ba.
Would you spare me some of the
paper you bought?

允 yǔn　4画 厶部

允 允允允允

[动] 答应；许可：permit; allow;
consent; grant | 应~yīngyǔn
consent
允许 yǔnxǔ allow; permit

孕 yùn　5画 子部

孕 孕孕孕孕孕

❶[动] 怀胎：be pregnant; be in the
family way | ~妇 yùnfù preg-
nant woman

孕育 yùnyù be pregnant with; breed; conceive

怀孕 huáiyùn

❷[名]胎儿：embryo; fetus

 运(運) yùn 7画 辶部

运 运运运运运运运

❶[动]移动：move; be in operation

运动 yùndòng movement; motion

运行 yùnxíng operate; move

运转 yùnzhuǎn operate

运动会 yùndònghuì games; sports meet

运动员 yùndòngyuán sportsman; athlete

奥运会 Àoyùnhuì

❷[动]搬运；运输：carry; transport; ship | ～货 yùnhuò transport cargo (or goods) / 客～kèyùn passenger transport / 请把行李～到火车站。Qǐng bǎ xíngli yùndào huǒchēzhàn. Please transport my luggage to the railway station.

运河 yùnhé canal

运输 yùnshū transport

运送 yùnsòng convey

搬运 bānyùn   航运 hángyùn

❸[动]使用：use; wield; apply | ～笔 yùnbǐ wield a pen

运算 yùnsuàn operation; calculation

运用 yùnyòng exercise; use; apply

运作 yùnzuò run; implement; carry out

❹[名]命中注定的遭遇：fortune; luck; fate | 好～hǎoyùn good luck / 不走～bù zǒuyùn be out of luck; have no luck

运气 yùnqi fortune

命运 mìngyùn

幸运 xìngyùn

 酝(醞) yùn 11画 酉部

酝 酝酝酝酝酝酝酝酝 酝酝酝

[动]酿酒：ferment; brew

酝酿 yùnniàng ① brew; ferment ② have a preliminary informal discussion; deliberate on

 韵 yùn 13画 音部

韵 韵韵韵韵韵韵韵韵 韵韵韵韵韵

[名]韵母：simple or compound vowel (of a Chinese syllable) | 声～shēngyùn

韵母 yùnmǔ (phonet.) the final of a syllable

押韵 yāyùn

 蕴(蘊) yùn 15画 艹部

蕴 蕴蕴蕴蕴蕴蕴蕴蕴
蕴蕴蕴蕴蕴蕴蕴

[动] 包藏；包含：accumulate; contain; hold in store
  蕴藏 yùncáng hold in store;
  contain

Z

杂 (雜) zá　　6画 木部

杂 杂杂杂杂杂杂

❶ [形] 多种多样的；不纯的：miscellaneous; sundry; mixed; varied | ～色 zásè *multicoloured* / ～货 záhuò *sundry goods*

杂技 zájì acrobatics

杂交 zájiāo hybridize; cross-breed

杂粮 záliáng food grains other than wheat and rice

杂乱 záluàn in a muddle (jumble, mess); mixed and disorderly; at sixes and sevens

杂文 záwén essay

杂志 zázhì magazine

杂质 zázhì impurity; contaminant

复杂 fùzá　　打杂儿 dǎzár

❷ [动] 混合在一起：mix; mingle | 米里偶尔～有沙子。Mǐ li ǒu'ěr zá yǒu shāzi. *Occasionally grains of sand can be found mixed in with the rice.*

夹杂 jiāzá

砸　　zá　　10画 石部

砸砸砸砸砸砸砸砸砸砸

❶ [动] 重物落在物体上；用重物撞击：pound; tamp; bang against sth. using a heavy thing | ～钉子 zá dīngzi *drive a nail* / 他的左脚被石头～伤了。Tā de zuǒjiǎo bèi shítou zá-shāng le. *His left foot was injured by a stone.*

❷ [动] 打坏；打破：smash; break | 碗～碎了。Wǎn zásuì le. *The bowl is smashed (broken).*

灾　　zāi　　7画 宀部

灾 灾灾灾灾灾灾灾

[名] 自然的或人为的祸害、不幸：calamity; catastrophe; disaster; misfortune | 天～ tiānzāi *natural calamities* / 受～ shòuzāi *be stricken by disaster* / 一场大～ yī chǎng dà zāi *a great calamity*

灾害 zāihài calamity; disaster

灾荒 zāihuāng famine due to crop failure

灾民 zāimín victims of a natural disaster

灾难 zāinàn suffering; calamity; disaster; catastrophe

灾区 zāiqū disaster area

旱灾 hànzāi　　火灾 huǒzāi

救灾 jiùzāi　　水灾 shuǐzāi

栽 zāi 10画 木部

栽 栽栽栽栽栽栽栽栽
栽栽

❶ [动] 种植：plant; grow | ～花 zāihuā *grow flowers* / ～树 zāishù *plant trees* / ～菜 zāicài *grow vegetables*

栽培 zāipéi grow; cultivate

❷ [动] 硬给安上（用于抽象事物）：impose sth. on sb.; force sth. on sb. | 他被～上了一个罪名。Tā bèi zāishangle yī gè zuìmíng. *A charge was fabricated against him.*

❸ [动] 摔倒；跌倒：tumble; fall; topple | ～跟头 zāigēntou *fall* / ～了一跤 zāile yī jiāo *have a fall*

载 (載) zǎi 10画 车部

载 载载载载载载载载
载载

[动] 记录；刊登：record; publish; carry | 登～dēngzǎi *publish (in newspapers or magazines)* / 刊～kānzǎi *carry in newspapers* / ～入史册 zǎirù shǐcè *be recorded in history*

记载 jìzǎi　　　下载 xiàzǎi
转载 zhuǎnzǎi
　　　　See zài.

宰 zǎi 10画 宀部

宰 宰宰宰宰宰宰宰宰
宰宰

❶ [动] 杀：slaughter; butcher | ～鸡 zǎi jī *kill chickens* / ～猪 zǎi zhū *butcher pigs*

❷ [动] 比喻向顾客索取高价：overcharge; fleece; charge more than a customer should pay | 挨～áizǎi *be overcharged* / ～人 zǎirén *rip sb. off*

再 zài 6画 一部

再 再再再再再再

❶ [副] 第二次；又一次：again; one more time | ～版 zàibǎn *second edition* / 请你～说一遍。Qǐng nǐ zài shuō yī biàn. *Please repeat your words.* / 这篇文章要～修改一遍。Zhè piān wénzhāng yào zài xiūgǎi yī biàn. *The article needs further revision.*

再次 zàicì once more; a second time; once again

再见 zàijiàn goodbye; see you again

再三 zàisān over and over again; time and again; again and again; repeatedly

再现 zàixiàn (of a past event)

reappear; be reproduced

一再 yīzài

❷ [副] 表示动作在一定时间后又将出现：used to indicate that an action will be repeated in future

再说 zàishuō put off until some time later

不再 bùzài

❸ [副] 表示一个动作将在另一个动作结束之后出现：used to indicate the occurrence of action after the completion of another | 吃完饭～看电视。Chī wán fàn zài kàn diànshì. *Have your dinner before watching TV.* / 你做完作业～玩。Nǐ zuòwán zuòyè zài wán. *Finish your homework before you go to play.*

❹ [副] 更；更加：to a greater extent or degree | ～用一点儿力 zài yòng yīdiǎnr lì *try a bit harder* / 声音～大一点儿。Shēngyīn zài dà yīdiǎnr. *Speak louder, please.* / ～冷的天我也不怕。Zài lěng de tiān wǒ yě bù pà. *I can stand colder weather than this.*

❺ [副] 表示追加补充；另外，又：used to indicate additional information; in addition; furthermore; besides | 盘里放着葡萄、鸭梨，～就是苹果。Pán li fàngzhe pútao, yālí, zài jiùshì píngguǒ. *There are grapes, pears, as well as apples on the plate.*

❻ [副] 用于让步的假设句，含有"即使"或"无论怎么"的意思：(used in the conditional sentence to show concession) even if; even though | 雨～大，我们也得去。Yǔ zài dà, wǒmen yě děi qù. *We have got to go, no matter how heavy the rain is.*

❼ [副] 表示范围的扩大：indicating the widening of scope | ～生产 zàishēngchǎn *reproduce; continuously repeat or renew production*

❽ [副] 用在否定句中，有加强语气的作用：(used in a negative sentence to strengthen the mood) | 菜已经咸得不能～咸了。Cài yǐjīng xián de bùnéng zài xián le. *The dish is too salty to eat.*

在 zài 6画 土部

在 在在在在在在

❶ [动] 存在；生存：exist; be alive | 这座房子还～。Zhè zuò fángzi hái zài. *The house is still there.* / 他祖父还～。Tā zǔfù hái zài. *His grandfather is still alive.*

在场 zàichǎng be on the scene; be on the spot; be present

在世 zàishì be living

在座 zàizuò (in a broad sense) be seated or present at a meeting or a banquet

存在 cúnzài　　　内在 nèizài

实在 shízài　　　自在 zìzài

❷ [动] (人或事物)处于某个地位或处所：indicating where a person or a thing is | 书～桌子上。Shū zài zhuōzi shang. *The book is on the table.* / 我父母～北京。Wǒ fùmǔ zài Běijīng. *My parents are in Beijing.*

在内 zàinèi included

在逃 zàitáo (leg.) has escaped; be at large

在线 zàixiàn be online (of telephone); be logged on to the Internet

在乎 zàihu care about; mind; take to heart

在意 zàiyì (usu.used in the negative) take notice of; care about; mind; take to heart

在于 zàiyú ① be determined by; depend on ② lie in; consist in

潜在 qiánzài　　　所在 suǒzài

❸ [动] 在于；取决于：lie in; depend on | 学习进步，主要～于自己努力。Xuéxí jìnbù, zhǔyào zàiyú zìjǐ nǔlì. *Progress in study depends mainly on one's own efforts.*

好在 hǎozài

❹ [副] 正在：indicating an action in progress | 会议～进行。Huìyì zài jìnxíng. *The meeting is going on.* / 我～看报。Wǒ zài kànbào. *I am reading a news-*

paper. / 雨～不停地下着。Yǔ zài bù tíng de xiàzhe. *It is raining now.*

正在 zhèngzài　　　现在 xiànzài

❺ [介] 表示动作行为的时间、地点、范围等：indicating time, place, scope, etc. | ～晚上读书 zài wǎnshang dúshū *study in the evening* / ～第二教室上课 zài dì-èr jiàoshì shàngkè *attend class in classroom 2* / ～这种条件之下 zài zhè zhǒng tiáojiàn zhīxià *under such conditions*

载 (載) zài　　　10画 车部

载载载载载载载载载载

[动] 用运输工具装运：carry; hold; be loaded with | ～客 zàikè *carry passengers* / ～货 zàihuò *carry cargo* / 满～而归 mǎnzài'érguī *return (home) with a full load*

载重 zàizhòng load; carrying capacity

超载 chāozài　　　承载 chéngzài

搭载 dāzài

See zǎi.

咱 zán　　　9画 口部

咱咱咱咱咱咱咱咱咱

❶[代]我们；we; us｜～班的同学都到齐了。Zán bān de tóngxué dōu dàoqí le. *The students in our class are all present.* / 哥哥，～看电影去吧。Gēge, zán kàn diànyǐng qù ba. *Brother, let's go to the movies.*

咱们 zánmen ① we (including both the speaker and the person or persons spoken to) ② I ③ you

❷[代]我：I; me｜～不懂。Zán bù dǒng. *I don't understand.*

攒 (攒) zǎn　19画 扌部

攒攒攒攒攒攒攒攒
攒攒攒攒攒攒攒
攒攒攒

[动] 积聚；储蓄：accumulate; hoard; save; scrape together｜他～下自己的休假时间去旅行。Tā zǎnxià zìjǐ de xiūjià shíjiān qù lǚxíng. *He has saved up his vacation to go travelling.* / 她把～的钱都买了衣服。Tā bǎ zǎn de qián dōu mǎile yīfu. *She spent all her savings on clothes.*

暂 (暫) zàn　12画 日部

暂暂暂暂暂暂暂
暂暂暂暂

---

❶[形] 不久；时间短（跟"久jiǔ"相对）：of short duration; transient; brief (the opposite of "久jiǔ")

暂时 zànshí ①temporary; transient ②temporarily; for the time being; for the moment

短暂 duǎnzàn

❷[副]暂时地；临时地：temporarily; for a short time｜～停zàntíng *suspend; time-out* / ～住zànzhù *stay temporarily (at a place)* / ～不答复zàn bù dáfù *put off replying*

暂且 zànqiě for the time being; for the moment

赞 (贊) zàn　16画 贝部

赞赞赞赞赞赞赞赞
赞赞赞赞赞赞赞赞

---

❶ [动] 帮助；支持：help; aid; assist; support

赞成 zànchéng approve of; agree with

赞同 zàntóng approve of; agree with; endorse

赞助 zànzhù support; assistance; sponsor

❷ [动] 夸奖；称颂：applaud; compliment; extol; praise

赞美 zànměi praise; eulogize

赞赏 zànshǎng appreciate; admire

赞叹 zàntàn gasp in (with) admiration; highly praise

赞扬 zānyáng speak highly of; praise; commend

称赞 chēngzàn

脏 (髒) zāng 10画 月部

脏 脏脏脏脏脏脏脏脏脏脏脏

[形] 有污垢;不干净: dirty; filthy; unclean | ～东西 zāng dōngxi *dirty things* / 衣服～了。Yīfu zāng le. *The clothes are dirty.* / 这间屋子～得很。Zhè jiān wūzi zāngdehěn. *This room is very dirty.*

See zàng.

脏 (臟) zàng 10画 月部

脏 脏脏脏脏脏脏脏脏脏脏脏

[名] 身体内部器官的名称: internal organs of the body

心脏 xīnzàng

心脏病 xīnzàngbìng

See zāng.

葬 zàng 12画 艹部

葬 葬葬葬葬葬葬葬葬葬葬葬葬

[动] 掩埋或处理死者遗体: inter; bury | 火～huǒzàng *cremation* / 埋～máizàng *bury (a dead person)* / 送～sòngzàng *escort*

a coffin to its burial ground; attend a funeral

葬礼 zànglǐ funeral; funeral rites

遭 zāo 14画 辶部

遭 遭遭遭遭遭遭遭遭遭 遭遭遭遭遭遭

[动] 碰上(多指不幸的事): meet with; suffer; encounter (in most cases sth. unfortunate) | ～难 zāonàn *suffer disaster* / ～灾 zāozāi *be hit by a natural calamity*

遭到 zāodào suffer; meet with; encounter

遭受 zāoshòu suffer; be subjected to; sustain

遭殃 zāoyāng suffer disaster

遭遇 zāoyù ① meet with; encounter; run up against ② (bitter) experience; (hard) lot

糟 zāo 17画 米部

糟 糟糟糟糟糟糟糟糟 糟糟糟糟糟糟糟 糟

❶[形] 腐烂;不结实: rotten; decayed; worn out | ～烂 zāolàn *decomposed; putrid* / 木头～了。Mùtou zāo le. *The wooden board is rotten.*

❷ [形]（事情或情况）不好：in a mess; in a wretched state | 你的工作做得一团~。Nǐ de gōngzuò zuò de yītuánzāo. *You've made a mess of your job.* / 你把事情弄~了。Nǐ bǎ shìqing nòngzāo le. *You've made a mess of the matter.* / 情况很~。Qíngkuàng hěn zāo. *The situation is dreadful.*

糟糕 zāogāo terrible

乱七八糟 luànqībāzāo

❸ [动] 损坏；破坏：spoil; ruin

糟蹋 zāota waste; ruin; spoil

凿 (鑿) zāo   12画 业部

凿凿凿凿凿凿凿凿凿凿凿凿

[动] 打孔；挖掘：bore a hole; chisel; dig | ~井 zāo jǐng *sink a well* / 墙上~了一个洞。Qiáng shang zāole yī gē dòng. *A hole was dug into the wall.*

早 zǎo   6画 日部

早早早早早早

❶ [名] 早晨：morning | 从~到晚 cóng zǎo dào wǎn *from morning till night* / 他一~就来了。Tā yīzǎo jiù lái le. *He came here early in the morning.*

早晨 zǎochen (early) morning

早点 zǎodiǎn (light) breakfast

早饭 zǎofàn breakfast

早上 zǎoshang (early) morning

早晚 zǎowǎn ① morning and evening ② sooner or later

清早 qīngzǎo

❷ [形] 时间靠前：early in time | 今年雪下得很~。Jīnnián xuě xià de hěn zǎo. *Snow came early this year.* / 他~年做过文艺工作。Tā zǎonián zuòguo wényì gōngzuò. *He was engaged in literary work in his early years.*

早期 zǎoqī early stage; early phase

❸ [形] 比某一时间靠前；较早：earlier than scheduled or planned; earlier | ~熟 zǎoshú *prematurity* / ~婚 zǎohūn *early marriage* / 你~点儿来。Nǐ zǎodiǎnr lái. *Please come early.*

早日 zǎorì at an early date; early; soon

及早 jízǎo   提早 tízǎo

❹ [副] 很久以前：a long time ago | 他~走了。Tā zǎo zǒu le. *He left long ago.* / 我~知道了。Wǒ zǎo zhīdào le. *I knew that long ago.*

早已 zǎoyǐ long ago; for a long time

❺ [形] 早晨见面时互相问候的话：used to greet each other in the morning | 老师~！Lǎoshī zǎo!

Good morning, teacher!

枣 （棗） zǎo　8画 一部

枣 枣枣枣枣枣枣枣枣

❶[名]枣树：jujube tree; jujube
❷[名]枣树的果实：date; jujube ｜
我喜欢吃红~。Wǒ xǐhuan chī
hóngzǎo. *I like red dates.*

澡 zǎo　16画 氵部

澡 澡澡澡澡澡澡澡澡
澡澡澡澡澡澡澡澡

[动]洗（身体）：wash (one's body)
｜ 擦~cāzǎo *rub oneself down
with a wet towel; bathe* ｜ ~盆
zǎopén *bathtub*
洗澡 xǐzǎo

皂 zào　7画 白部

皂 皂皂皂皂皂皂皂

[名]某些有洗涤去污作用的日用品：
soap
肥皂 féizào　　香皂 xiāngzào

灶 （竈） zào　7画 火部

灶 灶灶灶灶灶灶灶

[名]烧火做饭的设备；厨房：kitchen
range; cooking stove; kitchen ｜
炉~lúzào *kitchen range; cooking range* ｜ 煤气~méiqìzào *gas
ring; hob*

造 zào　10画 辶部

造 造造造造造造造造
造造

❶ [动]做；制作：make; build;
manufacture; create ｜ ~纸
zàozhǐ *produce paper* ｜ ~房子
zào fángzi *build a house* ｜ 他正
在~预算。Tā zhèngzài zào
yùsuàn. *He is making a budget.*
造成 zàochéng create; cause;
give rise to; bring about
造反 zàofǎn rise in rebellion;
rebel; revolt
造价 zàojià cost (of building or
manufacture)
造句 zàojù sentence making
造型 zàoxíng ① modelling;
mould-making ②model; mould
创造 chuàngzào　打造 dǎzào
改造 gǎizào　　构造 gòuzào
建造 jiànzào　　人造 rénzào
塑造 sùzào　　伪造 wěizào
制造 zhìzào　　铸造 zhùzào
创造性 chuàngzàoxìng
❷[动]虚构；瞎编：invent; cook up;
concoct ｜ ~谣zàoyáo *cook up
a story and spread it around* ｜
编~谎言 biānzào huǎngyán
fabricate lies
捏造 niēzào

◇造化 zàohuà (formal) the Creator; Nature; Creation
造化 zàohua good luck; good fortune
造就 zàojiù ① bring up; train ② achievements; attainments (usu. of young people)

噪   zào   16画 口部

噪噪噪噪噪噪噪噪
噪噪噪噪噪噪噪

[形]（声音）杂乱刺耳：noisy; piercing to the ear
噪声 zàoshēng noise
噪音 zàoyīn noise

燥   zào   17画 火部

燥燥燥燥燥燥燥
燥燥燥燥燥燥燥
燥

[形]缺少水分；干：dry; lacking water｜天气～热 tiānqì zàorè hot and dry weather
干燥 gānzào

躁   zào   20画 足部

躁躁躁躁躁躁躁躁
躁躁躁躁躁躁躁躁
躁躁躁躁

[形]不冷静；性急：rash; impetu-ous; restless; impatient｜烦～ fánzào annoyed / 暴～bàozào irritable
急躁 jízào

则 （則）zé   6画 贝部

则 则则则则则则

❶ [名]规章；条文：rule; decree; regulation｜总～zǒngzé general principles / 细～xìzé detailed rules
法则 fǎzé   规则 guīzé
原则 yuánzé

❷ [名]规范；榜样：standard; norm; example
准则 zhǔnzé
以身作则 yǐshēn-zuòzé

❸ [连]表示因果关系；就：indicating relationship between cause and effect｜不进～退 bù jìn zé tuì if you don't push forward you will fall behind / 物体热～涨，冷～缩。Wùtǐ rè zé zhàng, lěng zé suō. Objects expand when heated and contract when cooled.

❹ [连]表示两事物对比；转折：indicating contrast of one thing with another｜有的勤奋工作，有的～马马虎虎。Yǒu de qín-fèn gōngzuò, yǒu de zé mǎmahūhū. Some people are hard at work and some do their job carelessly.

否则 fǒuzé

责（責）zé　　8画 贝部

责 责责责责责责责责

❶ [动] 批评指责：criticize; accuse; blame; reproach ｜ 指~ zhǐzé censure / 斥~chìzé rebuke; denounce

责备 zébèi reproach; blame; reprove; take sb. to task

责怪 zéguài blame

责令 zélìng order; instruct; charge

谴责 qiǎnzé

❷ [名] 分内应做的事：duty; responsibility ｜ 尽~jìnzé do one's duty / 保护环境，人人有~。Bǎohù huánjìng, rénrén yǒu zé. It is up to everybody to conserve our environment.

责任 zérèn duty; responsibility

责任人 zérènrén the person who is in charge; the person who has the responsibility

责任制 zérènzhì system of job responsibility

负责 fùzé　　　负责人 fùzérén

择（擇）zé　　8画 扌部

择 择择择择择择择择

[动] 挑选：select; choose; pick ｜ ~友 zéyǒu choose friends / 饥

不~食jībùzéshí a hungry person is not choosy about his food

选择 xuǎnzé

贼（賊）zéi　　10画 贝部

贼 贼贼贼贼贼贼贼贼 贼贼

[名] 偷东西的人：thief; burglar ｜ 窃~qièzéi thief; burglar; pilferer / 盗~dàozéi robber; bandit

怎 zěn　　9画 心部

怎 怎怎怎怎怎怎怎怎 怎

[代] 怎么，表疑问：why; how ｜ ~不去上学?Zěn bùqù shàngxué? Why don't you go to school? / 你~知我来了呢?Nǐ zěn zhī wǒ láile ne? How did you know I was coming?

怎么 zěnme how; What's the matter?

怎样 zěnyàng how

怎么样 zěnmeyàng how about; what about

怎么着 zěnmezhe what about

增 zēng　　15画 土部

增 增增增增增增增增 增增增增增增增

[动]加多；添加（跟"减jiǎn"相对）：increase; add; augment (the opposite of "减jiǎn") | 倍～bēizēng *double in amount* | 今年的产量猛～。Jīnnián de chǎnliàng měngzēng. *Output for this year has increased sharply.*

增产 zēngchǎn increase production

增幅 zēngfú increasing range; increase

增加 zēngjiā increase; raise; add

增进 zēngjìn enhance; promote; further

增强 zēngqiáng strengthen; heighten; enhance

增设 zēngshè establish an additional or new (organization, unit, course, etc.)

增添 zēngtiān add; increase

增援 zēngyuán reinforce

增长 zēngzhǎng increase; rise; grow

增值 zēngzhí (econ.) ① rise (or increase) in value; appreciation; increment ② value added

递增 dìzēng

 （赠）zèng 16画 贝部

赠赠赠赠赠赠赠赠赠赠赠赠赠赠赠赠

[动]把东西无偿地送别人：give as a present; present as a gift | 捐～juānzèng *donate; make financial or other contribution* | ～阅 zèngyuè *(of books) provide for free by the publisher* | ～言 zèngyán *words of advice or encouragement given at parting* | ～品 zèngpǐn *gift*

赠送zèngsòng give as a present

 zhā 4画 扌部

扎 扎扎扎扎

❶[动]刺：prick | ～针 zhāzhēn *give an acupuncture treatment* / 轮胎被～了。Lúntāi bèi zhā le. *The tyre was punctured.*

❷[动]（军队）在某地住下：(of troops) encamp; pitch a camp somewhere and stay on | ～营 zhāyíng *pitch a camp*

驻扎 zhùzhā

◇扎啤 zhāpí draught beer

扎实 zhāshi ① sturdy; strong ② solid; sound; down-to-earth

See zhá.

 zhā 12画 氵部

渣 渣渣渣渣渣渣渣渣渣渣渣渣

❶[名]物质经过提炼或使用后所剩的部分：dregs; sediment; residue; leftover after the essence

has been taken out ｜煤～ méizhā *cinder* / 药～yàozhā *dregs of a decoction*
❷[名]碎屑：broken bits ｜面包～儿 miànbāozhār *crumbs (of bread)*

 扎 zhā 4画 扌部

扎 扎扎扎扎

See 挣扎
挣扎 zhēngzhá
See zhā.

 闸 (閘) zhā 8画 门部

闸 闸闸闸闸闸闸闸闸

❶[名]可控制水流的建筑物：floodgate; sluice gate; waterlock ｜水～shuǐzhā *sluice gate* / 河上有一道～。Hé shàng yǒu yī dāo zhā. *A floodgate was built in the river.*
❷[名]制动器的通称：general term for brakes ｜踩～cǎizhā *step on the brake* / 脚～jiǎozhā (on a bicycle) *backpedal brake; coaster brake*

炸 zhā 9画 火部

炸 炸炸炸炸炸炸炸炸炸

[动]把食物放在煮沸的油里弄熟：fry in deep fat or oil; deep fry ｜～油条 zhā yóutiáo *deep fried dough*
See zhǎ.

 眨 zhǎ 9画 目部

眨 眨眨眨眨眨眨眨眨眨

[动] (眼睛) 很快地开合：(of eyes) blink; wink ｜～眼睛 zhǎ yǎnjing *wink*

诈 (詐) zhà 7画 讠部

诈 诈诈诈诈诈诈诈

[动] 欺骗：cheat; swindle; deceive ｜欺～qīzhà *swindle* / ～取钱财 zhàqǔ qiáncái *cheat sb. out of their money; get money through fraud*
诈骗 zhàpiàn defraud; swindle

炸 zhà 9画 火部

炸 炸炸炸炸炸炸炸炸炸

❶[动]突然破裂：burst; blast; explode ｜玻璃杯～了。Bōlibēi zhà le. *The glass cup has shattered.*
炸弹 zhàdàn bomb
炸药 zhàyào explosive; dyna-

mite

爆炸 bàozhà

❷[动]用炸药、炸弹爆破：(of an object) burst; blast; explode | 桥被~断了。Qiáo bèi zhàduàn le. *The bridge was blown up.* / 那几间房子被~毁了。Nà jǐ jiān fángzi bèi zhàhuǐ le. *Those houses were destroyed in the blast.*

轰炸 hōngzhà

❸[动]发怒：fly into a rage; flare up | 他一听就气~了。Tā yī tīng jiù qìzhà le. *He flared up at the words.*

See zhā.

zhǎ　14画 木部

榨榨榨榨榨榨榨榨榨榨榨榨榨

[名]挤压出物体里的汁液：press; extract; squeeze liquid from sth. | ~油 zhàyóu *extract oil* / ~果汁 zhà guǒzhī *squeeze fruit juice*

zhāi　14画 扌部

摘摘摘摘摘摘摘摘摘摘摘摘摘摘

❶[动]采；取下：pick; pluck | ~棉花 zhāi miánhua *pick cotton* / ~帽子 zhāi màozi *take off one's*

cap / 把墙上的画~下来。Bǎ qiáng shang de huà zhāi xiàlai. *Take the picture off the wall.*

❷[动]选取：select; choose; take extracts from | ~录 zhāilù *extract* / 从书中~选一段 cóng shū zhōng zhāixuǎn yī duàn *extract a passage from a book*

摘要 zhāiyào excerpt; abstract; summary

宅　zhāi　6画 宀部

宅宅宅宅宅宅

[名]住所：residence; house; abode | ~门 zháimén *gate of a house* / ~院 zháiyuàn *a house with a courtyard*

住宅 zhùzhái

窄　zhǎi　10画 穴部

窄窄窄窄窄窄窄窄窄窄

❶[形]狭小；不宽(跟"宽 kuān"相对)：narrow (the opposite of "宽 kuān") | 路~ lù zhǎi *narrow path* / 这张床太~，睡不下两个人。Zhè zhāng chuáng tài zhǎi, shuìbuxià liǎng gè rén. *This bed is too narrow for two people.*

狭窄 xiázhǎi

❷[形](气量) 小；(心胸) 不开阔：petty-minded; narrow-minded | 气量~qìliǎng zhǎi *petty* / 这人心胸很~。Zhè rén xīnxiōng hěn zhǎi. *This person is rather narrow-minded.*

 (債) zhài 10画 亻部

债债债债债债债债债债债

[名]欠别人的钱财：debt | 借~ jièzhài *borrow money* / 欠~ qiànzhài *get into debt* / 还~ huánzhài *pay debts*
债权 zhàiquán (leg.) creditor's rights
债券 zhàiquàn bond; debenture
债务 zhàiwù debt; liabilities
负债 fùzhài   公债 gōngzhài
国债 guózhài

寨 zhài 14画 宀部

寨寨寨寨寨寨寨寨寨寨寨寨寨寨

❶[名]旧时指驻兵的地方：military camp in former times | 营~ yíngzhài *military camp*
❷[名]四周围有栅栏或围墙的村子：stockade; fence | 山~shānzhài *mountain fortress* / ~子 zhàizi *stockaded village*

 zhān 8画 氵部

沾沾沾沾沾沾沾沾

❶[动]浸湿：soak | 露水~湿了我的衣服。Lùshuǐ zhānshīle wǒ de yīfu. *Dew soaked my clothes.*
❷[动]因某种关系而得到：gain by association with sb. or sth.; benefit from some kind of relationship | ~便宜 zhān piányi *get a bargain* / 他这次也~了一些好处。Tā zhè cì yě zhānle yīxiē hǎochu. *He has made some profit from it this time.*
沾光 zhānguāng benefit from association with sb. or sth.
❸[动] 因接触而被附着上：be stained with; be soiled with | ~水 zhān shuǐ *get wet* / 裤子~上了泥。Kùzi zhānshangle ní. *The trousers were stained with mud.*
❹[动]接触；染上：touch; get into (the habit) | 脚不~地 jiǎo bù zhān dì *walk as if on wings* / ~上了坏习气 zhānshàngle huài xíqì *pick up bad habits*

 zhān 11画 米部

粘粘粘粘粘粘粘粘粘粘

❶[动] 有黏性的东西互相连结或附着在别的东西上：glue; stick; paste | 这种糖～牙。Zhè zhǒng táng zhān yá. *This kind of candy tends to stick to the teeth.* / 两张纸～在一起了。Liǎng zhāng zhǐ zhān zǎi yīqǐ le. *The two sheets of paper were glued together.*

❷[动] 用有黏性的东西使物体联结起来：glue; join or connect objects with a sticky substance | 把邮票～在信封上。Bǎ yóupiào zhān zǎi xìnfēng shang. *Stick the stamp on the envelope.*

瞻 (瞻) zhān 18画 目部

瞻 瞻瞻瞻瞻瞻瞻瞻瞻瞻瞻瞻瞻瞻瞻瞻瞻

[动] 向上或向前看：look forward; look up | ～望 zhānwàng *look forward*

瞻仰 zhānyǎng look at with reverence

斩 (斬) zhǎn 8画 车部

斩 斩斩斩斩斩斩斩斩

[动] 砍断：chop; cut; kill | ～断 zhǎnduàn *cut off*; *chop off* | ～首 zhǎnshǒu *behead*; *decapitate*

斩草除根 zhǎncǎo-chúgēn cut the weeds and dig up the roots; stamp out the source of trouble

斩钉截铁 zhǎndīng-jiétiě be resolute and decisive; categorical

 (盞) zhǎn 10画 皿部

盏 盏盏盏盏盏盏盏盏盏盏

[量] 用于灯：used for lamps | 一～灯 yī zhǎn dēng *a lamp*

 zhǎn 10画 尸部

展 展展展展展展展展展展

❶[动] 张开；放开：open up; spread out; unfold | 愁眉不～ chóuméi bù zhǎn *wear a worried frown* / 老鹰～翅高飞。Lǎoyīng zhǎnchì gāofēi. *The eagle soared into the sky.*

展开 zhǎnkāi spread out; unfold; open up

展望 zhǎnwàng ①look into the distance ②look into the future; look ahead ③forecast; prospect

发展 fāzhǎn　　进展 jìnzhǎn

开展 kāizhǎn　　扩展 kuòzhǎn

伸展 shēnzhǎn　舒展 shūzhǎn

❷[动] 陈列出来供人看：exhibit; display

展出 zhǎnchū put on display; be on show (view); exhibit
展览 zhǎnlǎn put on display; exhibit; show
展品 zhǎnpǐn exhibit; item on display
展示 zhǎnshì open up before one's eyes; reveal; show; lay bare
展现 zhǎnxiàn unfold before one's eyes; emerge; develop
展销 zhǎnxiāo display and sell
展览会 zhǎnlǎnhuì exhibition
❸[动]施行：put to good use; give full play to | 一～才华 yīzhǎn-cáihuá *display one's talents*
施展 shīzhǎn

崭 (嶄) zhǎn 11画 山部

崭崭崭崭崭崭崭崭崭崭崭

[形] outstanding; excellent
崭新 zhǎnxīn brand new; completely new

占 zhàn 5画 卜部

占占占占占

❶[动]据有；用强力取得：occupy; seize; take by force | 强～ qiǎngzhàn *forcibly occupy; seize* / 你一个人怎么可以～三个位子？Nǐ yī gè rén zěnme

kěyǐ zhàn sān gè wèizi? *How can you take up three seats by yourself?* / 做家务～了许多时间。Zuò jiāwù zhànle xǔduō shíjiān. *It takes a lot of time to do housework.*
占据 zhànjù occupy; hold
占领 zhànlǐng capture; occupy; seize
占用 zhànyòng occupy and use
占有 zhànyǒu own; possess; have
霸占 bàzhàn 抢占 qiǎngzhàn
侵占 qīnzhàn
❷[动]处于(某种地位或情况)：hold a certain status; be in a certain situation | ～优势 zhàn yōushì *hold an advantageous position* / ～上风 zhàn shàngfēng *gain the upper hand* / 赞成的～大多数。Zànchéng de zhàn dàduōshù. *Those in favour of it constitute the majority.*

战 (戰) zhàn 9画 戈部

战战战战战战战战
战

❶[动] 战争；打仗：war; fight | 宣～ xuānzhàn *declare war* / 停～ tíngzhàn *ceasefire*
战场 zhànchǎng battlefield; battleground; battlefront
战斗 zhàndòu ① fight; battle; combat; action ② militant;

fighting

战犯 zhànfàn war criminal

战国 Zhānguó the Warring States (475–221 B.C.)

战略 zhànlüè strategy

战士 zhànshì ①soldier; man ② champion; warrior; fighter

战术 zhànshù (military) tactics

战线 zhànxiàn battle line; battlefront; front

战役 zhànyì campaign; battle

战友 zhànyǒu comrade-in-arms; battle comrade

战争 zhànzhēng war; warfare

备战 bèizhàn   二战 èrzhàn

奋战 fènzhàn   决战 juézhàn

抗战 kàngzhàn   内战 nèizhàn

枪战 qiāngzhàn 作战 zuòzhàn

❷[动]泛指斗争：struggle; fight | 百~百胜 bǎizhàn-bǎishèng come out victorious in every battle; be ever-victorious

战胜 zhànshèng defeat; triumph over; vanquish; overcome

挑战 tiǎozhàn

◇ 统战 tǒngzhàn

站 zhàn 10画 立部

站 站站站站站站站站站站

❶[动]直立：stand | 警察~在十字路口指挥交通。Jǐngchá zhàn zài shízì lùkǒu zhǐhuī jiāotōng. The traffic policeman stands in the middle of the intersection directing traffic. / 大家都坐着，只他一个人~着。Dàjiā dōu zuòzhe, zhǐ tā yī gè rén zhànzhe. Everyone is seated; he is the only one standing.

站岗 zhàngǎng stand (mount) guard; be on sentry duty; stand sentry

❷[动]停下；停留：stop; halt

❸[名]供乘客上下或货物装卸用的固定停车点：station; stop; place set aside for passengers to get on or get off the bus or train, or a place for loading and unloading goods | 火车~huǒchēzhàn railway station / 终点~zhōngdiǎnzhàn terminal; terminus / 车进~了。Chē jìnzhàn le. The train is arriving at the station.

站台 zhàntái platform (in a railway station)

车站 chēzhàn

❹[名]为某种业务而设立的工作点：station or centre for rendering certain services | 气象~qìxiàngzhàn weather station / 保健~bǎojiànzhàn health centre

网站 wǎngzhàn

加油站 jiāyóuzhàn

空间站 kōngjiānzhàn

张 (張) zhāng 7画 弓部

张 张张张张张张张

❶ [动] 打开；展开；放开：open; spread; stretch; unfold | ～嘴 zhāngzuǐ *open one's mouth* / ～开翅膀 zhāngkāi chìbǎng *spread the wings*

❷ [动] 扩大；夸大：magnify; exaggerate; amplify | 夸～kuāzhāng *exaggerate; overstate* / 这件事千万别～扬出去。Zhè jiàn shì qiānwàn bié zhāngyáng chūqu. *Never let the matter out into the open.*

扩张 kuòzhāng

❸ [动] 陈设；布置：lay out; display | ～挂 zhāngguà *hang up (a picture, curtain, etc.)*

张贴 zhāngtiē *put up (a notice, poster, etc.)*

❹ [动] 看；望：look; glance | ～望 zhāngwàng *look around*

❺ [动] 商店开业：open a new shop | 开～kāizhāng *open a business; begin doing business*

❻ [量] 用于纸、画、皮子等：used for paper, leather, etc. | 一～纸 yī zhāng zhǐ *a sheet of paper* / 两～画 liǎng zhāng huà *two pictures* / 十～皮子 shí zhāng pízi *ten sheets of leather*

❼ [量] 用于床、桌子等：used for bed, desk, etc. | 一～床 yī zhāng chuáng *a bed* / 四～桌子 sì zhāng zhuōzi *four tables*

❽ [量] 用于嘴、脸：used for mouths and faces | 一～嘴 yī zhāng zuǐ *a mouth* / 一～笑脸 yī zhāng

xiàoliǎn *a smiling face*

◇慌张 huāngzhāng
主张 zhǔzhāng

章 zhāng 11画 立部

章 章章章章章章章章章章章

❶ [名] 法则；规程：written rules; regulations | 简～jiǎnzhāng *general regulations*

章程 zhāngchéng *rules; regulations; constitution*
党章 dǎngzhāng
规章 guīzhāng 违章 wéizhāng

❷ [名] 歌曲诗文的段落：(of book, poetry, song) chapter; section; division | 乐～yuèzhāng *(mus.) movement* / 篇～piānzhāng *section* / 第一～dì-yī zhāng *chapter one*

文章 wénzhāng
做文章 zuòwénzhāng

◇印章 yìnzhāng

彰 zhāng 14画 彡部

彰 彰彰彰彰彰彰彰彰彰彰彰彰彰彰

[动] 宣扬：cite; commend
表彰 biǎozhāng

长 (長) zhǎng 4画 长部

长 长长长长长

❶ [动] 发育；生长：grow; develop | 他~得很高。Tā zhǎng de hěn gāo. *He has become very tall.* / 我去年种的花~得很快。Wǒ qùnián zhōng de huā zhǎng de hěn kuài. *The flowers I planted last year are growing very fast.*

成长 chéngzhǎng
生长 shēngzhǎng

❷ [名] 领导人；负责人：chief; head; leader

班长 bānzhǎng　部长 bùzhǎng
厂长 chǎngzhǎng
队长 duìzhǎng
家长 jiāzhǎng　局长 júzhǎng
科长 kēzhǎng　排长 páizhǎng
省长 shěngzhǎng
师长 shīzhǎng　市长 shìzhǎng
首长 shǒuzhǎng
团长 tuánzhǎng
县长 xiànzhǎng
校长 xiàozhǎng
院长 yuànzhǎng
组长 zǔzhǎng
董事长 dǒngshìzhǎng

❸ [动] 增强；增进：boost; enhance; increase | ~力气 zhǎng lìqi *gain strength* / ~见识 zhǎng jiànshi *increase knowledge; gain experience* / 他学习有了~进。Tā xuéxí yǒule zhǎngjìn. *He has made progress in his studies.*

增长 zēngzhǎng
助长 zhùzhǎng
负增长 fùzēngzhǎng
See cháng.

涨（涨）zhǎng 10画 氵部

涨涨涨涨涨涨涨涨涨涨

❶ [动] 水位升高：(of water) rise; surge | 河里的水~起来了。Hé li de shuǐ zhǎng qǐlai le. *The water level of the river has risen.*

❷ [动] (价格、情绪)提高；上升：(of prices, mood) go up; become higher | 今年物价~了很多。Jīnnián wùjià zhǎngle hěn duō. *Commodity prices have gone up a lot this year.*

涨价 zhǎngjià rise in price
涨幅 zhǎngfú (of price, etc.) margin or rate of rise; rise
暴涨 bàozhǎng
高涨 gāozhǎng
上涨 shàngzhǎng

掌 zhǎng 12画 手部

掌掌掌掌掌掌掌掌掌掌掌掌

❶ [名] 手的里面：palm
掌声 zhǎngshēng clapping; applause
鼓掌 gǔzhǎng

❷[动] 把握；主管：hold in one's hand; be in charge of; control | ～舵 zhǎngduò be at the helm; steer a boat / ～权 zhǎngquán be in power

掌管 zhǎngguǎn be in charge of; administer

掌握 zhǎngwò ① grasp; master; know well ② have in hand; take into one's hands; control

❸[名] 某些动物的脚掌：bottom of certain animals' feet; pad; sole | 熊～ xióngzhǎng bear's paw / 鸭～ yāzhǎng duck's foot

◇仙人掌 xiānrénzhǎng

 zhàng 3画 一部

丈 丈丈丈

[量] 市制长度单位：unit of length, where 10 *chi* equals 1 *zhang* | 这座房子有一～多高。Zhè zuò fángzi yǒu yī zhàng duō gāo. *This house is more than one zhang in height.*

◇丈夫 zhàngfu husband
丈人 zhàngren wife's father; father-in-law

 (帳) zhàng 7画 巾部

帐 帐帐帐帐帐帐帐

[名] 用织物制成的遮蔽用的东西：curtain; tent; canopy | 蚊～

wénzhàng *mosquito net* / 营～ yíngzhàng *tent*

 (賬) zhàng 8画 贝部

账 账账账账账账账账

❶[名] 财物出入的记录：account | 记～ jìzhàng *keep accounts* / 查～ cházhàng *check accounts*

账号 zhànghào number of a bank account

账户 zhànghù account

流水账 liúshuǐzhàng

❷[名] 债：debt; credit | 欠～ qiànzhàng *be in debt* / 还～ huánzhàng *repay a debt*

账单 zhàngdān bill; check

结账 jiézhàng

◇不买账 bùmǎizhàng

胀 (脹) zhàng 8画 月部

胀 胀胀胀胀胀胀胀胀

❶[动] 体积增大：grow in size; expand; distend | 热～冷缩 rèzhàng lěngsuō *expand with heat and contract with cold*

膨胀 péngzhàng

❷[动] 身体里一种膨胀的感觉：swell; be bloated | 肿～ zhǒngzhàng *swelling* / 肚子～ dùzi zhàng *feel bloated*

障 zhàng 13画 阝(左)部

障 障障障障障障障障
障障障障

[动] 阻隔；遮挡：hinder; obstruct; impede; block

障碍 zhàng'ài ① hinder; obstruct ② barrier; block

残障 cánzhàng

招 zhāo 8画 扌部

招 招招招招招招招招

❶[动]用手势叫人或致意：beckon; gesture; wave hands｜用手一一他就来了。Yòng shǒu yī zhāo tā jiù lái le. *He followed when beckoned.*

招呼 zhāohu ① call ② hail ③ notify; tell

招手 zhāoshǒu beckon; wave

打招呼 dǎzhāohu

❷[动]用广告或通知的方式使人来：recruit; enlist; enrol (by means of ads or notices)｜~考 zhāokǎo *recruit through examinations* / ~学徒 zhāo xuétú *take on apprentices; employ or hire apprentices* / ~学生 zhāo xuésheng *enrol students*

招标 zhāobiāo invite tenders (or bids, public bidding)

招聘 zhāopìn give public notice of a vacancy to be filled; invite applications for a job

招商 zhāoshāng invite outside investment

招生 zhāoshēng enroll new students; recruit students

招收 zhāoshōu recruit; take on

金字招牌 jīnzì zhāopái

❸[动]引来(不好的事物)；惹：attract; invite; court; provoke; tease｜~苍蝇 zhāo cāngying *attract flies* / ~麻烦 zhāo máfan *invite trouble* / 别~他生气。Bié zhāo tā shēngqì. *Be careful not to infuriate him.* / 这孩子真~人喜欢。Zhè háizi zhēn zhāo rén xǐhuan. *This child is so lovely.*

❹[动]承认罪行：make a confession of one's crime; own up｜~供 zhāogòng *confess one's crime* / ~认 zhāorèn *confess one's crime; plead guilty*

◇招待 zhāodài receive (guests); entertain; serve (customers)

招待会 zhāodàihuì reception

耍花招 shuǎhuāzhāo

朝 zhāo 12画 十部

朝 朝朝朝朝朝朝朝朝
朝朝朝朝

[名] 早晨：morning｜~阳 zhāoyáng *morning sun*

朝气 zhāoqì youthful spirit; vigour; vitality

朝气蓬勃 zhāoqì-péngbó full
of youthful spirit; full of vigour
and vitality; imbued with vitality
朝三暮四 zhāosān-mùsì blow
hot and cold; change one's mind
frequently

    See chǎo.

zhāo　11画 羊部

着 着着着着着着着着
着着着

❶[动] 接触；挨到：touch; contact
| 脚不～地jiǎo bù zhāo dì
*(when running fast) the feet
seem not to touch the ground;
walks as if on wings*
❷[动] 感到；受到：feel; suffer | ～
风 zhāofēng *be affected by a
draught; become unwell from
being in a draught* / ～慌
zhāohuāng *get nervous*
着急zhāojí get worried; get excited; feel anxious
着凉 zhāoliáng catch cold;
catch a chill
❸[动]用在动词后表示动作有了结
果或达到目的：used after a verb
to indicate the result of reaching a goal or the completion of
an action | 猜～了。Cāizhāo le.
(You've) Guessed right. / 睡～
了。Shuìzhāo le. *He has fallen
asleep.* / 他买～了。Tā mǎi-
zhāo le. *He has bought it.*

用不着 yòngbuzháo
❹[动]燃烧；发光：burn; be ignited;
be lit | ～火了。Zhāohuǒ le.
It's on fire.
着火 zhāohuǒ catch fire; be on
fire

    See zhe; zhuó.

zhǎo　7画 扌部

找 找找找找找找找

❶[动] 寻回(丢失的东西)；寻求 (所
需要的东西)：look for; try to
find; seek | ～工作zhǎo gōng-
zuò *look for a job* / ～资料zhǎo
zīliào *look for reference materials* / 我的钥匙～不到了。Wǒ
de yàoshi zhǎobudào le. *I
can't find my keys.*
查找cházhǎo　寻找xúnzhǎo
❷[动] 退还多余的部分；补上不足的
部分：give change; even up;
balance | ～钱 zhǎoqián *give
change* / ～齐zhǎoqí *make uniform; make up a deficiency*

zhǎo　8画 氵部

沼 沼沼沼沼沼沼沼沼

[名]水池：pool; natural pond
沼泽 zhǎozé swamp

zhāo　5画 刀部

召 召召召召召

[动] 呼唤；叫人来：call together; summon; gather | ～唤 zhāohuàn *call* / ～她来见我 zhāo tā lái jiàn wǒ *tell her to come and see me*

召集 zhāojí call together; convene

召开 zhāokāi convene; convoke

号召 hàozhāo

兆   zhāo   6画 丿部

兆 兆兆兆兆兆兆

[数] 一百万：million

照   zhāo   13画 灬部

照 照照照照照照照照照照照照照

❶ [动] 光线照射：shine; illuminate | 阳光～耀大地。Yángguāng zhāoyào dàdì. *The sun is shining over the vast land.* / 拿手电筒～一～。Ná shǒudiàntǒng zhāoyizhāo. *Light it with your electric torch.*

照明 zhāomíng illumination; lighting

照射 zhāoshè shine; illuminate; light up; irradiate

照耀 zhāoyào shine; illuminate

❷ [动] 通知：inform; notify

照会 zhāohuì ① present (deliver or address) a note to (a government) ② note

❸ [动] 对着镜子或其他反光的东西看：reflect; mirror | ～镜子 zhāo jìngzi *look in the mirror* / 水面映～出朵朵白云。Shuǐmiàn yìngzhāo chū duǒduǒ báiyún. *White clouds are mirrored in the water.*

❹ [动] 察看；查对：compare; contrast; check

对照 duìzhāo

❺ [动] 看顾；看管：take care of; look after; attend to | ～管 zhāoguǎn *be in charge of* / 我给你～看孩子。Wǒ gěi nǐ zhāokàn háizi. *I'll look after your child.; I'll babysit your child.*

照顾 zhāogù ① give consideration to; show consideration for; make allowance(s) for ② look after; care for; attend to

照料 zhāoliào take care of; attend to

照应 zhāoying coordinate; correlate; look after; take care of

关照 guānzhāo

❻ [动] 拍摄：take a picture; film; photograph | 这张相片～得很好。Zhè zhāng xiàngpiàn zhāo de hěn hǎo. *This picture is well taken.*

照片 zhāopiàn photograph; picture

照相 zhāoxiàng take a picture;

photograph

照相机 zhàoxiàngjī camera

❼ [名] 相片：photograph; picture | 玉～yùzhào *your portrait* / 剧～jùzhào *stage photo; still* 拍照 pāizhào

❽ [名] 凭证：licence; permit | 牌～pāizhào *licence plate; number plate; driving licence* / 无～驾驶 wúzhào jiàshǐ *drive without a licence*

护照 hùzhào　　牌照 pāizhào

执照 zhízhào

❾ [介] 按着；依照：according to; in conformity with | ～事实讲 zhào shìshí jiǎng *speak out according to the facts* / ～这个样子做。Zhào zhège yàngzi zuò. *Do it according to the sample.; Handle it accordingly.* / ～你这么一说，我就放心了。Zhào nǐ zhème yī shuō, wǒ jiù fàngxīn le. *Hearing you say those things, I feel relieved.*

照常 zhàocháng as usual

照旧 zhàojiù as before; as usual

照例 zhàolì as a rule; as usual; usually

照样 zhàoyàng after a pattern or model

按照 ànzhào　　参照 cānzhào

依照 yīzhào　　遵照 zūnzhào

❿ [介] 对着；向着：in the direction; towards | ～直走 zhào zhí zǒu *go straight ahead* / ～着这个方向走 zhàozhe zhège fāngxiàng

zǒu *go in this direction*

zhào　13画 四部

罩 罩罩罩罩罩罩罩罩
罩罩罩罩罩

❶ [名] 遮在外面的东西：cover; shade; hood | 口～kǒuzhào *surgical mask* / 灯～dēngzhào *lamp shade* / 玻璃～bōlizhào *glass cover*

胸罩 xiōngzhào

❷ [动] 套在外面；覆盖：cover; envelop; wrap | 把桌子上的菜～起来。Bǎ zhuōzi shang de cài zhào qǐlai. *Cover the dishes on the table.* / 乌云～着大地。Wūyún zhàozhe dàdì. *The overcast sky hung over the earth.* / 外面起风了，你再～上一件外衣吧。Wàimian qǐfēng le, nǐ zài zhàoshang yī jiàn wàiyī ba. *The wind is rising. Put on another coat before you go.*

笼罩 lǒngzhào

zhē　7画 扌部

折 折折折折折折折

[动] 翻转：turn over; roll over | ～跟头 zhē gēntou *do a somersault*

折腾 zhēteng ① do sth. over and over again ②turn from side

907

to side; toss about

瞎折腾 xiāzhēteng
See zhé.

遮 zhē   14画 辶部

遮 遮 遮 遮 遮 遮 遮 遮
遮 遮 遮 遮 遮 遮

❶[动]挡住：hide from view; cover | ～雨 zhēyǔ *keep out rain* / 高楼～住了我们的视线。Gāolóu zhēzhùle wǒmen de shìxiàn. *Those tall buildings obstruct our view.*

❷[动]掩盖：cover up; cloak | ～丑 zhēchǒu *hide one's shame* / ～盖事实 zhēgài shìshí *cover up the fact*

折 (摺❻)zhé   7画 扌部

折 折 折 折 折 折 折

❶[动]弄断；断：break; snap | 骨～gǔzhé *fracture* / ～树枝 zhé shùzhī *break off a branch* / 桌子腿～断了。Zhuōzituǐ zhéduàn le. *A table leg was broken.*

❷[动]挫败，损伤：suffer the loss of; suffer defeat; damage | ～损 zhésǔn *suffer damage*
挫折 cuòzhé

❸[动]打折扣：discount | 打～ dǎzhé *sell at a discount*

折扣 zhékòu discount; rebate

❹[动]弯；弯曲：bend; twist; turn | ～腰 zhéyāo *bend one's back; bow in obeisance*
曲折 qūzhé   周折 zhōuzhé

❺[动]转变方向；返回：turn back; change direction | ～射 zhéshè *refraction* / 他走到半路又～回来。Tā zǒudào bànlù yòu zhé huílai. *He turned back halfway.*
转折 zhuǎnzhé

❻[动]折叠：fold | ～尺 zhéchǐ *folding rule* / ～纸 zhézhǐ *paper folding* / ～衣服 zhé yīfu *fold up clothes*

❼[动]按一定的比价或单位换算：convert into; amount to | ～价 zhéjià *evaluate in terms of money*
折合 zhéhé convert into; amount to

❽[动]信服：be deeply convinced | ～服 zhéfú *be filled with admiration*

◇折磨 zhémo cause physical or mental suffering; torment
存折 cúnzhé

哲 zhé   10画 口部

哲 哲 哲 哲 哲 哲 哲 哲
哲 哲

[形]明智；智慧超群：wise; sagacious; intelligent | ～人 zhé-

rén *philosopher*
哲学 zhéxué *philosophy*

 者 zhě 8画 耂部

者 者者者者者者者者

❶[名]用在某些词或词组后面，表示人或事物：used after certain words or phrases to indicate a class of persons or things | 强～ qiángzhě *the strong* / 老～ lǎozhě *the elderly* / 教育工作～ jiàoyù gōngzuòzhě *educator*

笔者 bǐzhě
读者 dúzhě
后者 hòuzhě
患者 huànzhě
记者 jìzhě
死者 sǐzhě
学者 xuézhě
作者 zuòzhě
第三者 dìsānzhě
目击者 mùjīzhě
消费者 xiāofèizhě
志愿者 zhìyuànzhě

❷[名]用在"二、三"等数词或"前、后"等方位词后面，指上文所说的人或事物：used with the numbers "二 èr" "三 sān" or location words "前""后", etc. to refer to people or things mentioned earlier | 前～qiánzhě *the former* / 后～hòuzhě *the latter* / 二～必居其一。Èr zhě bì jū qí yī. *It must be this one or the other.* / 三～缺一不可。Sān zhě quē yī bùkě. *Of these three things, not one is dispensable.*

 这 (這) zhè 7画 辶部

这 这这这这这这这

❶[代]指较近的人或事物 (跟 "那 nà" 相对)：indicating nearby persons or things (the opposite of "那 nà") | ～孩子 zhè háizi *this child* / ～地方 zhè dìfang *this place* / ～消息我知道了。Zhè xiāoxi wǒ zhīdao le. *I've heard the news already.*

这边 zhèbian this side; here
这个 zhège this one; this
这里 zhèli here; this place
这么 zhème so; such; this way; like this
这儿 zhèr ① here ② now; then
这些 zhèxiē these
这样 zhèyàng so; such; like this; this way
这会儿 zhèhuìr now; at the moment; at present

❷[代]泛指：used to make a general reference

❸[代]代替"这时候"：replacing "this moment" | 我～就走。Wǒ zhè jiù zǒu. *I'm leaving right now.* / 他～才知道锻炼身体的好处。Tā zhè cái zhīdao duànliàn shēntǐ de hǎochu. *Up until now he did not realize the benefit of exercise.*

着 zhe 11画 羊部

着 着着着着着着着着
着着着

❶ [助] 表示动作的持续：indicating an action in progress | 他正吃～午饭呢。Tā zhèng chīzhe wǔfàn ne. *He is having his lunch.* / 外面正下～大雨。Wàimian zhèng xiàzhe dàyǔ. *It is raining heavily outside now.*

❷ [助] 表示状态的持续：used to indicate the continuation of a state | 窗子开～。Chuāngzi kāizhe. *The window is open.* / 桌子上放～一台收音机。Zhuōzi shang fàngzhe yī tāi shōuyīnjī. *There is a radio on the table.*

❸ [助] 在动词或表示程度的形容词后加强命令或嘱咐的语气：used after a verb or an adjective to indicate a commanding or exhortative tone | 你听～! Nǐ tīngzhe. *Listen to me!*

❹ [助] 用在两个动词之间，表示动作的方式、状况等：used between two verbs to indicate the manner, condition, etc. in which an action is carried out | 顺～shùnzhe *along* / 朝～cháozhe *towards* / 为～wèizhe *for* 沿着 yánzhe 闹着玩儿 nàozhewánr

See zhǎo; zhuō.

贞 (貞) zhēn 6画 卜部

贞 贞贞贞贞贞贞

[形] 坚定不变：loyal; chaste | 坚贞 jiānzhēn *staunch and faithful* 忠贞 zhōngzhēn

针 (針) zhēn 7画 钅部

针 针针针针针针针

❶ [名] 缝衣物的用具：needle | 缝衣～féngyīzhēn *needle* 针眼 zhēnyǎn (med.) sty

❷ [名] 针形的东西：anything like a needle | 时～shízhēn *hour hand* / 别～biézhēn *pin* 指南针 zhǐnánzhēn 指针 zhǐzhēn

❸ [名] 注射用的药物：injection; shot | ～剂 zhēnjì *injection* 打针 dǎzhēn

◇ 针对 zhēnduì ① be directed against; be aimed at; counter ② in the light of; in accordance with; in connection with 针灸 zhēnjiǔ acupuncture

侦 (偵) zhēn 8画 亻部

侦 侦侦侦侦侦侦侦侦

[动] 暗中察看；探听：detect; scout;

investigate | ～查案件 zhēn-chá ànjiàn *investigate a case*
侦察zhēnchá *reconnoitre; scout*
侦探 zhēntàn *detective*

珍 zhēn 9画 王部

珍珍珍珍珍珍珍珍
珍

❶[形] 宝贵的、稀有的：precious; rare | ～品 zhēnpǐn *treasure* / ～宝 zhēnbǎo *treasure*
珍贵 zhēnguì *precious; valuable*
珍珠 zhēnzhū *pearl*
山珍海味 shānzhēn-hǎiwèi
❷[动] 看重、爱惜：value highly; cherish; treasure | ～视 zhēn-shì *treasure* / ～重身体 zhēn-zhòng shēntǐ *take care of oneself*
珍惜 zhēnxī *treasure; value; cherish*

真 zhēn 10画 十部

真真真真真真真真
真真

❶ [形] 符合事实的；正确的：true; genuine; real; correct | ～话 zhēnhuà *truth; genuine words* / 这个消息是～的。Zhège xiāoxi shì zhēn de. *This news is genuine.*

真诚 zhēnchéng *sincere*
真理 zhēnlǐ *truth*
真情 zhēnqíng ① the real (or true) situation; the facts; the actual state of affairs; truth ② true feelings; real sentiments
真实zhēnshí *true; real; authentic*
真相 zhēnxiàng *truth; fact*
真心 zhēnxīn *wholehearted; heartfelt; sincere*
真正 zhēnzhèng *genuine; true; real*
真情实感 zhēnqíng-shígǎn *true feelings and real intentions out of genuine friendship*
认真 rènzhēn   天真 tiānzhēn
半真半假 bànzhēn-bànjiǎ
❷[副] 的确；实在：really; truly; indeed | ～好 zhēn hǎo *really good* / ～冷 zhēn lěng *really cold* / 我见到你，～高兴!Wǒ jiàndào nǐ, zhēn gāoxìng! *I am really pleased to see you!* / 时间过得～快。Shíjiān guò de zhēn kuài. *How time flies!*
真是 zhēnshi *really; indeed; what a shame!*
❸ [名] 人或事物的原样：the original form of a person or thing
传真 chuánzhēn
仿真fǎngzhēn   清真qīngzhēn
传真机 chuánzhēnjī
清真寺 qīngzhēnsì
◇真丝 zhēnsī *silk; silk cloth*

诊 (診) zhěn 7画 讠部

诊 诊诊诊诊诊诊诊

[动] 检查病情 : examine (a patient) | 出~ chūzhěn *(of a doctor) make a house call* / 会~ huìzhěn *consultation (with doctor)*
诊断 zhěnduàn diagnose
诊所 zhěnsuǒ clinic; dispensary
门诊 ménzhěn 确诊 quèzhěn
听诊器 tīngzhěnqì

枕 zhěn 8画 木部

枕 枕枕枕枕枕枕枕枕

[名] 躺着时垫在头下的东西 : pillow
枕头 zhěntou pillow

阵 (陣) zhèn 6画 阝(左)部

阵 阵阵阵阵阵阵

❶ [名] 古代交战时布置的战斗队列；战时的兵力总部署 : battle array (or formation) | ~线 zhènxiàn front; ranks; alignment
阵容 zhènróng ① battle array (formation) ② lineup
阵营 zhènyíng camp
❷ [名] 战场 : battlefield; battlefront | 上~ shàngzhèn *go to battle*
阵地 zhèndì position; front
❸ [名] 指一段时间 : period of time | 这~儿 zhèzhènr *these days; recent days; recently* / 他病了一~儿。Tā bìngle yīzhènr. *He was ill at that time.*
❹ [量] 用于延续了一段时间的事情或现象 : used for an occurrence or phenomenon which continues for some time | 一~雨 yī zhèn yǔ *a spatter of rain* / 一~掌声 yī zhèn zhǎngshēng *a burst of applause*
阵雨 zhènyǔ shower
一阵 yīzhèn

振 zhèn 10画 扌部

振 振振振振振振振振振

❶ [动] 摇动；挥动 : shake; flap | ~铃 zhènlíng *ring the bell*
振荡 zhèndàng ① (phys.) vibration ② (elec.) oscillation
振动 zhèndòng vibration
❷ [动] 奋起；奋发 : boost; rise with force and spirit | ~作 zhènzuò *brace up* / 精神一~ jīngshen yī zhèn *feel one's spirits rise*
振奋 zhènfèn inspire; stimulate; excite
振兴 zhènxīng promote; develop

震 zhèn 15画 雨部

震 震震震震震震震震
震震震震震震震

❶[动]猛烈颤动：shake; shock; vibrate | ～耳 zhèn'ěr *deafening* / 鼓声～天 gǔshēng zhèn tiān *thundering drumbeats*
震荡 zhèndàng shake; shock; vibrate; quake
震动 zhèndòng shake; shock; vibrate; quake
震撼 zhènhàn shake; shock
地震 dìzhèn
❷[动]情绪过分激动：be excited; be shocked | ～怒 zhènnù *be enraged; be furious*
震惊 zhènjīng shock; amaze; astonish

镇 (鎮) zhèn 15画 钅部
镇 镇镇镇镇镇镇镇镇
镇镇镇镇镇镇镇

❶[动]压；抑制：press down; keep down | ～痛 zhèntòng *ease pain* / ～咳 zhènké *suppress a cough*
❷[形]安静；稳定：calm; stable; tranquil; at ease
镇定 zhèndìng calm; cool; composed; unruffled
镇静 zhènjìng calm; cool; composed; unruffled
❸[动]用武力守卫：keep peace by force | ～守 zhènshǒu *guard;* garrison
镇压 zhènyā suppress
❹[名]市镇，集镇：town
城镇 chéngzhèn
市镇 shìzhèn 乡镇 xiāngzhèn
❺[动]把食物、饮料等放在冰箱、冰块或冷水中使凉：cool sth. with cold water or ice | 冰～汽水 bīngzhèn qìshuǐ *iced soda* / 把西瓜放在冰水里～一～。Bǎ xīguā fàng zài bīngshuǐ li zhènyizhèn. *Put the watermelon in ice water to chill it.*
冰镇 bīngzhèn

 正 zhēng 5画 一部
正 正正正正正

[名]正月：the first month of the lunar calendar
正月 zhēngyuè the first month of the lunar year; the first moon
See zhèng.

争 zhēng 6画 ⺈部
争 争争争争争争

❶[动]抢夺；力求获得或达到：compete; contend; vie; strive | ～冠军 zhēng guànjūn *strive for the championship* / 大家～着发言。Dàjiā zhēngzhe fāyán. *People strive to be the first to express their opinions.*

争夺 zhēngduó fight (contend, scramble) for; vie with sb. for sth.; enter into rivalry with sb. over sth.

争气 zhēngqì try to make a good show; try to win credit for; try to bring credit to

争取 zhēngqǔ strive for; fight for; win over

争先恐后 zhēngxiān-kǒnghòu strive to be the first and fear to lag behind; fall over each other (one another) to do sth.

斗争 dòuzhēng

竞争 jìngzhēng

力争 lìzhēng 战争 zhànzhēng

竞争力 jìngzhēnglì

❷ [动] 争吵；争论：quarrel; wrangle; squabble; argue back and forth | 你们在～什么? Nǐmen zài zhēng shénme? *What are you arguing about?*

争吵 zhēngchǎo quarrel; wrangle; squabble

争端 zhēngduān dispute; controversial issue

争论 zhēnglùn controversy; dispute; debate; contention

争议 zhēngyì dispute; controversy

争执 zhēngzhí disagree; dispute; stick to one's position

百家争鸣 bǎijiā-zhēngmíng

征 (徵 ❸-❺) zhēng 8画 彳部

征 征征征征征征征征

❶ [动] 远行：go on a journey | ～途 zhēngtú *journey* / 远～ yuǎnzhēng *expedition*

长征 chángzhēng

❷ [动] 出兵讨伐：go on an expedition (or a campaign) | 出～ chūzhēng *set out on an expedition* / ～讨 zhēngtǎo *go on a punitive expedition*

征服 zhēngfú conquer; subjugate

❸ [动] 政府召集或收用：call up; enlist; take over (legally, by government) for public use | ～兵 zhēngbīng *draft* / ～用 zhēngyòng *requisition*

征收 zhēngshōu levy; collect; impose

❹ [动] 寻求：look for; seek | ～稿 zhēnggǎo *solicit contributions* / ～订 zhēngdìng *solicit for subscriptions*

征集 zhēngjí ① collect ② draft; call up; recruit

征求 zhēngqiú solicit; seek; ask for

征税 zhēngshuì levy (or collect) taxes; taxation

征文 zhēngwén solicit articles or essays

❺ [名] 迹象；现象：sign; portent | ～兆 zhēngzhào *sign; omen; indication*

特征 tèzhēng

象征 xiāngzhēng

挣 zhēng 9画 扌部

挣挣挣挣挣挣挣
挣

See 挣扎
挣扎 zhēngzhá struggle
See zhèng.

睁 zhēng 11画 目部

睁睁睁睁睁睁睁睁
睁睁睁

[动] 张开(眼睛)：open one's eyes | 他眼睛~不开。Tā yǎnjing zhēngbukāi. *He cannot open his eyes.*

蒸 zhēng 13画 艹部

蒸蒸蒸蒸蒸蒸蒸蒸
蒸蒸蒸蒸蒸

❶[动] 液体受热，化为气体上升：evaporate
蒸发 zhēngfā evaporate
蒸汽 zhēngqì steam
水蒸气 shuǐzhēngqì
❷[动]利用水蒸气的热力使食物变热变熟：use steam to heat or cook food | ~馒头 zhēng mántou *steam some buns*

整 zhěng 16画 攵部

整整整整整整整整
整整整整整整整整

❶[形] 有秩序；不乱：in good order; neat and tidy | 衣装不~ yīzhuāng bù zhěng *be slovenly in one's dress*
整洁 zhěngjié clean and tidy; neat; trim
整齐 zhěngqí in good order; neat; tidy
平整 píngzhěng
❷[动] 使有秩序；有条理；修理：put in order; rectify; repair; mend | ~编 zhěngbiān *reorganize (troops)* / ~治 zhěngzhì *renovate* / ~修 zhěngxiū *rebuild*
整顿 zhěngdùn rectify; consolidate; reorganize
整风 zhěngfēng rectification of incorrect styles of work
整合 zhěnghé (geol.) conformity
整理 zhěnglǐ put in order; straighten out; arrange; sort out
整形 zhěngxíng (med.) plastic
调整 tiáozhěng 修整 xiūzhěng
❸[动] 使受苦：make sb. suffer; punish; castigate | ~人 zhěngrén *(usu. with selfish purpose) punish someone* | 挨~ āizhěng *be the target of criticism or attack*

❹ [形] 完全；没有残缺或剩余（跟"零líng"相对）：whole; entire (the opposite of "零líng")｜一年~yī nián zhěng *a whole year* / ~套的书 zhěngtào de shū *a whole set of books*

整个 zhěnggè whole; entire

整数 zhěngshù ① integer; whole number ② round number (figure)

整体 zhěngtǐ whole; entirety

整天 zhěngtiān whole day; all day; all day long

整整 zhěngzhěng whole; full

完整 wánzhěng

正 zhēng 5画 一部

正 正正正正正

❶ [形] 在中间的；不偏斜：in the centre; main｜把帽子戴~。Bǎ màozi dàizhēng. *Put your cap on straight.* / 这幅画挂得不~。Zhè fú huà guà de bù zhēng. *This picture is hung at an angle.*

端正 duānzhèng

❷ [形] 合乎标准的：standard; regular

正版 zhèngbǎn legal copy; official edition

正本 zhèngběn reserved copy (of a library book)

正常 zhèngcháng normal; regular

正规 zhèngguī regular; standard

正经 zhèngjing ① standard; decent ② serious ③ really; indeed

正确 zhèngquè correct; right; proper

正式 zhèngshì formal; official; regular

真正 zhēnzhèng

❸ [形] 正直的；正当的：honest; upright; right｜公~gōngzhèng *just; fair; impartial* / ~轨 zhèngguǐ *the right path or track*

正当 zhèngdāng proper; appropriate; legitimate

正气 zhèngqì healthy atmosphere (tendency)

正视 zhèngshì face squarely; face up to; look squarely at

正义 zhèngyì ① justice ② just; righteous

❹ [动] 改去错误或偏差：make right; correct｜~音 zhèngyīn *correct one's pronunciation* / ~字 zhèngzì *correct one's words* / ~误 zhèngwù *correct errors*

改正 gǎizhèng

更正 gēngzhèng

纠正 jiūzhèng　修正 xiūzhèng

❺ [形] 基本的；主要的（跟"副fù"相对）：principal; chief (the opposite of "副fù")｜~文 zhèngwén *main body (of a book, etc.)* / ~本 zhèngběn *original document* / ~教授 zhèngjiàoshòu *full professor*

❻[形] 数学上指大于零的；物理学上指失去电子的（跟"负 fù"相对）：positive; plus (the opposite of "负 fù") | ～数 zhèngshù *positive number* / ～极 zhèngjí *positive electrode*

❼[副] 表示动作的进行，状态的持续 indicating an action in progress or the continuation of a state; be doing | ～下雪呢。Zhèng xiàxuě ne. *It is snowing.* / 铃声～响着。Língshēng zhèng xiǎngzhe. *The bell is ringing.* / 他～吃着饭呢。Tā zhèng chīzhe fàn ne. *He is having his dinner.*

正在 zhèngzài in the process of; in the course of

❽ [副] 恰好；刚好：just; right; precisely; exactly | 大小～合适 dàxiǎo zhèng héshì *just the right size* / 这～是我们的想法。Zhè zhèngshì wǒmen de xiǎngfǎ. *This is exactly what we want.* / 我～要谈这个问题。Wǒ zhèngyào tán zhège wèntí. *I'm just coming to that point.*

正当 zhèngdāng just when; just as; just the time for
　正好 zhènghǎo just in time; just right; just enough
　正巧 zhèngqiǎo just in time; in the nick of time; at the right time
◇正比 zhèngbǐ direct ratio
　正面 zhèngmiàn positive
　正方体 zhèngfāngtǐ cube

See zhēng.

 （證）zhèng　7画　讠部

证证证证证证证

❶[动] 用事实和道理来表明或推断真假：testify to; prove; demonstrate | 求～qiúzhèng *seek to prove*

证明 zhèngmíng prove; testify; bear out
证实 zhèngshí confirm; verify; bear out
保证 bǎozhèng
辨证 biànzhèng
公证 gōngzhèng
见证 jiànzhèng
论证 lùnzhèng　认证 rènzhèng
验证 yànzhèng　作证 zuòzhèng
保证金 bǎozhèngjīn
辨证法 biànzhèngfǎ

❷ [名] 凭据：evidence; proof | 许可～xǔkězhèng *permit* / 出入～chūrùzhèng *pass*

证件 zhèngjiàn credentials; papers; certificate
证据 zhèngjù evidence; proof; testimony
证券 zhèngquàn negotiable securities
证人 zhèngren witness
证书 zhèngshū certificate; credentials
签证 qiānzhèng　取证 qǔzhèng
凭证 píngzhèng

证

zhèng

917

身份证 shēngfènzhèng

郑 (鄭) zhèng 8画 阝(右)部

郑 郑郑郑郑郑郑郑郑

See 郑重
郑重 zhèngzhòng serious; solemn

政 zhèng 9画 攵部

政 政政政政政政政政
政

❶[名]政治：politics; political affairs | 参~cānzhèng *participate in governmental and political affairs*
政变 zhèngbiàn coup d'état; coup
政策 zhèngcè policy
政党 zhèngdǎng political party
政府 zhèngfǔ government
政权 zhèngquán political (state) power; regime
政坛 zhèngtán political arena
政协 zhèngxié the Chinese People's Political Consultative Conference (CPPCC)
政治 zhèngzhì politics; political affairs
政治家 zhèngzhìjiā statesman
廉政 liánzhèng 内政 nèizhèng
执政 zhízhèng
专政 zhuānzhèng

❷[名]政府部门主管的业务： administrative affairs of government | 民~mínzhèng *civil administration*
财政 cáizhèng 邮政 yóuzhèng
行政 xíngzhèng
◇家政 jiāzhèng

挣 zhēng 9画 扌部

挣 挣挣挣挣挣挣挣挣
挣

❶ [动]用力摆脱：struggle to get free | ~脱 zhēngtuō *throw off* / ~开束缚 zhēngkāi shùfù *free oneself from the bonds*
❷ [动]用劳动取得：earn; make; scrape for | ~饭吃 zhèng fàn chī *earn a living*
挣钱 zhèngqián earn (make) money
See zhēng.

症 zhèng 10画 疒部

症 症症症症症症症症
症症

[名]疾病：disease; malady; illness | 病~bìngzhèng *symptom* / 急~jízhèng *acute disease*
症状 zhèngzhuàng symptom

之 zhī 3画 丶部

之 之之之

❶ [代] 代替人或事物：used in place of a noun or pronoun ｜ ~间 zhījiān between; among

之后 zhīhòu later; after; afterwards

之类 zhīlèi and so on; and so forth; and the like

之内 zhīnèi in; within

之前 zhīqián before; prior to; ago

之上 zhīshàng over; above

之外 zhīwài besides; except; beyond

之下 zhīxià under

之一 zhīyī one of certain persons or things

之中 zhīzhōng in; in the midst of; among

❷ [代] 虚指，无义：used in certain set phrases without a definite designation

反之 fǎnzhī   总之 zǒngzhī

❸ [助] 相当于"的de"；corresponding to "的de" ｜ 父母~心 fùmǔ zhī xīn *the expectation of parents* ｜ 钟鼓~声 zhōnggǔ zhī shēng *sound of drums and bells*

支   zhī   4画 支部

支 支支支支

❶ [动] 撑；架起：prop up; put up ｜ 把伞~开 bǎ sǎn zhīkāi *put up an umbrella* ｜ 把帐篷~起来。Bǎ zhàngpeng zhī qǐlai. *Put up the tent.*

支撑 zhīchēng prop up; sustain; support

支柱 zhīzhù pillar; prop; mainstay

❷ [动] 支持：support; sustain; bear ｜ 体力不~ tǐlì bù zhī *be tired out*

支持 zhīchí ① sustain; bear ② support; back; stand by

支援 zhīyuán support; assist; help

❸ [动] 伸出；竖起：prick up; protrude ｜ ~起耳朵 zhīqǐ ěrduo *prick up one's ears*

❹ [名] 从总体分出来的部分：branch; off shoot ｜ ~流 zhīliú *tributary*

支部 zhībù branch (esp. of the Communist Party or the Communist Youth League of China)

分支 fēnzhī

❺ [动] 调度；指使：send away; order about; put sb. off ｜ ~使 zhīshǐ *order about* ｜ 把他~走。Bǎ tā zhīzǒu. *Find an excuse to put him off.*

支配 zhīpèi arrange; control; allocate; budget

❻ [动] 付出或领取（款项）：pay or withdraw (money) ｜ ~工资 zhī gōngzī *receive pay* ｜ 把钱款~给他。Bǎ qiánkuǎn zhīgěi tā. *Give him the money.*

支出 zhīchū ① pay (money); expend; disburse ② expenses; expenditure; outlay; disbursement

支付 zhīfù pay (money); defray

支票 zhīpiào check(cheque)

开支 kāizhī　　收支 shōuzhī

透支 tòuzhī

❼[量] 用于队伍等: (used for troops) detachment | 一～军队 yī zhī jūnduì *a contingent of troops*

❽[量] 用于歌曲或乐曲: used for songs or musical compositions | 三～歌 sān zhī gē *three songs* / 一～曲子 yī zhī qǔzi *a melody (tune)*

❾[量] 用于杆状的东西: used for long and thin cylindrical objects | 一～笔 yī zhī bǐ *a pen* / 一～蜡烛 yī zhī làzhú *a candle*

枪支 qiāngzhī

 (隻) zhī　5画 口部

只 只 只 只 只

❶[形] 单个的; 极少的: single; one only; very few | ～身 zhīshēn *alone; by oneself*

❷[量] 用于某些成对的东西的一个: used for one of certain paired things | 一～手套 yī zhī shǒutào *a glove* / 两～耳朵 liǎng zhī ěrduo *two ears*

❸[量] 用于动物: used for animals | 一～鸟 yī zhī niǎo *a bird* /

三～兔子 sān zhī tùzi *three rabbits*

❹[量] 用于船只: used for boats | 一～小船 yī zhī xiǎochuán *a small boat*

See zhǐ.

 zhī　5画 氵部

汁 汁 汁 汁 汁 汁

[名] 含有某种物质的液体: juice | 乳～rǔzhī *milk* / 果～guǒzhī *fruit juice*

橙汁 chéngzhī

 zhī　6画 艹部

芝 芝 芝 芝 芝 芝

See 芝麻

芝麻 zhīma sesame

 zhī　8画 木部

枝 枝 枝 枝 枝 枝 枝 枝

❶[名] 植物主干上分出来的茎条: branch; twig | 树～shùzhī *tree branch* / 柳～liǔzhī *willow branches*

❷[量] 用于带枝子的花朵: used for flowers on branches | 一～梅花 yī zhī méihuā *a spray of plum blossoms*

zhī   8画 矢部

知 知知知知知知知知

❶ [名] 知识：knowledge; intellect
| 求~qiúzhī *seek knowledge* /
无~wúzhī *ignorant*
知识 zhīshi knowledge; intellect
知识分子 zhīshi fēnzǐ intellectual; the intelligentsia
无知 wúzhī

❷ [动] 知道；了解：know; realize;
be aware of; it is known to all;
it is well-known
知道 zhīdào know; realize; be
aware of
知觉 zhījué consciousness
知名 zhīmíng well-known;
noted; celebrated; famous
知情 zhīqíng know the facts of
a case or the details of an incident; be in the know
得知 dézhī   须知 xūzhī
不知不觉 bùzhī-bùjué
可想而知 kěxiǎng'érzhī

❸ [动] 使知道；使了解：inform;
notify; tell | 告~gàozhī *tell*
通知 tōngzhī
通知书 tōngzhīshū

织 (織) zhī   8画 纟部

织 织织织织织织织织

[动] weave; knit | ~布 zhībù
weave cotton / ~毛衣 zhī máo-yī *knit a sweater*
纺织 fǎngzhī   组织 zǔzhī
纺织品 fǎngzhīpǐn
棉织品 miánzhīpǐn

zhī   10画 月部

脂 脂脂脂脂脂脂脂脂
脂脂

[名] 动、植物所含的油质：fat;
grease; tallow | 油~yóuzhī
grease / 树~shùzhī *resin*
脂肪 zhīfáng grease; fat; tallow

zhī   14画 虫部

蜘 蜘蜘蜘蜘蜘蜘蜘蜘
蜘蜘蜘蜘蜘蜘

See 蜘蛛
蜘蛛 zhīzhū spider

执 (執) zhí   6画 扌部

执 执执执执执执

❶ [动] 主持；掌管：take charge of;
direct; manage | ~教 zhíjiào
be a teacher; teach
执勤 zhíqín be on duty
执政 zhízhèng be in power; be
in office

❷ [动] 执行;从事(某种工作): carry out; observe

执法 zhífǎ enforce (execute) the law

执行 zhíxíng carry out; execute; implement

❸ [动] 坚持: determine; persist | ~著 zhízhuó be steadfast / ~意要去 zhíyì yào qù insist on going

固执 gùzhí 争执 zhēngzhí

❹ [名] 凭证: written acknowledge-ment | 回~huízhí receipt

执照 zhízhào licence; permit

直 zhí 8画 十部

直 直直直直直直直直

❶ [形] 不弯曲(跟"曲qū"相对): straight (the opposite of "曲qū") | 道路又平又~。Dàolù yòu píng yòu zhí. The roads are smooth and straight.

直径 zhíjìng diameter

直线 zhíxiàn straight line

笔直 bǐzhí

❷ [动] 使变直;伸直: straighten | ~起腰 zhíqǐ yāo straighten one's back; stand up straight

❸ [形] 跟地面垂直的;竖的(跟"横héng"相对): vertical (the opposite of "横héng") | ~立 zhílì stand upright / ~上~下 zhíshàng-zhíxià perpen-dicular

垂直 chuízhí

❹ [形] 公正的: just; upright | 正~zhèngzhí fair and honest

❺ [形] 爽快;坦率: candid; frank; straightforward | ~爽 zhíshuǎng straightforward / ~言 zhíyán speak bluntly; state one's views outright / 心~口快 xīnzhíkǒukuài be frank and outspoken

❻ [副] 一直;不转折;不间断: directly; straight; nonstop | ~视 zhíshì look straight / ~通北京 zhítōng Běijīng go non-stop to Beijing / 他冻得~哆嗦。Tā dòng de zhí duōsuo. He was so cold that he kept shivering.

直播 zhíbō ① direct seeding ② live broadcast

直达 zhídá through; nonstop

直到 zhídào ① until ② up to

直接 zhíjiē direct; immediate

直属 zhíshǔ directly under; directly subordinate (or affiliated) to

直至 zhízhì ① till; until ② up to

一直 yīzhí

◇ 简直 jiǎnzhí

侄 zhí 8画 亻部

侄 侄侄侄侄侄侄侄侄

[名] nephew; niece

直
侄

zhí

922

侄女 zhínǚ brother's daughter; niece

侄子 zhízi brother's son; nephew

值 zhí 10画 亻部

值值值值值值值值值值

❶ [动] 遇到；碰上(某种情况)：happen to | 我们到那里时适~雨季。Wǒmen dào nàli shí shìzhí yǔjì. *We happened to arrive there in the rainy season.*

❷ [动] 担任轮到的职务：be on duty; take one's turn at sth. | ~夜zhíyè *be on night duty; be on night shift* / ~日zhírì *be on duty for the day* / ~周zhízhōu *be on duty for the week*

值班 zhíbān *be on duty*

❸ [动] 货物和价钱相当：be worth; what a specific sum of money can buy | 这顶帽子~十元。Zhè dǐng màozi zhí shí yuán. *This hat costs 10 yuan.*

值得 zhíde *be worth; merit; deserve*

❹ [名] 价值，价格：value; price | 两样东西价~相等。Liǎng yàng dōngxi jiàzhí xiāngděng. *The two are of the same value.*

保值 bǎozhí   贬值 biǎnzhí
产值 chǎnzhí   价值 jiàzhí
升值 shēngzhí   增值 zēngzhí

价值观 jiàzhíguān

职 (職) zhí 11画 耳部

职职职职职职职职职职职

❶ [名] 职务：duty; job | 尽~jìnzhí *fulfil one's duty* / 失~shīzhí *neglect one's duty*

职称 zhíchēng *title of a technical or professional post (e.g. engineer, professor, researcher, etc.)*

职工 zhígōng *staff and workers*

职能 zhínéng *function*

职权 zhíquán *power (authority) of office*

职务 zhíwù *post; duty; job*

职业 zhíyè *occupation; profession; vocation*

职员 zhíyuán *office worker; staff member*

职责 zhízé *duty; obligation; responsibility*

求职 qiúzhí   任职 rènzhí
专职 zhuānzhí

❷ [名] 职位：position; post | 在~zàizhí *be in office* / 调~diàozhí *be transferred to another post* / 兼~jiānzhí *hold two or more posts concurrently; part-time job*

辞职 cízhí   公职 gōngzhí
就职 jiùzhí

植 zhí 12画 木部

植 植植植植植植植植
植植植植

❶ [动] 栽种：plant; grow ｜ ~树
zhíshù *plant trees*
移植 yízhí　　种植 zhòngzhí
❷ [名] 植物：plant
植物 zhíwù plant
植物园 zhíwùyuán botanical
garden

殖 zhí 12画 歹部

殖 殖殖殖殖殖殖殖殖
殖殖殖殖

[动] 生育：breed; multiply ｜ 增~
zēngzhí *proliferation*
殖民地 zhímíndì colony
殖民主义 zhímín zhǔyì colonialism
繁殖 fánzhí　　生殖 shēngzhí
养殖 yǎngzhí

止 zhǐ 4画 止部

止 止止止止

❶ [动] 停住；不再进行：stop; halt;
cease ｜ 闲人~步 xiánrén zhǐ-
bù *admittance for staff only*
停止 tíngzhǐ
❷ [动] 使停住；阻拦：prohibit;

check; hold back ｜ ~血 zhǐxuě
stop bleeding / ~痛 zhǐtòng *relieve pain*
防止 fángzhǐ　　禁止 jìnzhǐ
制止 zhìzhǐ　　中止 zhōngzhǐ
终止 zhōngzhǐ　　阻止 zǔzhǐ
❸ [动] 截止：end; terminate ｜ ~
于本月末 zhǐ yú běn yuè mò
finish at the end of this month
截止 jiézhǐ　　为止 wéizhǐ
❹ [副] 只有：only ｜ ~此一个 zhǐ
cǐ yī gè *just the only one*
不止 bùzhǐ

只 (衹) zhǐ 5画 口部

只 只只只只只

[副] 仅仅：only; just; merely ｜ 教
室里~我一个人。Jiàoshì li zhǐ
wǒ yī gè rén. *I am the only one
in the classroom.* / ~你一个人
去，行吗？Zhǐ nǐ yī gè rén qù,
xíng ma? *What do you think
about going there by yourself?*
只得 zhǐdé have no alternative
but to; be obliged to; have to
只顾 zhǐgù ① be absorbed in
② merely; simply
只管 zhǐguǎn ① by all means
② merely; simply
只好 zhǐhǎo have to; be forced
to
只能 zhǐnéng can not but
只是 zhǐshì ① merely; only;

just ② simply ③ however; but then
只要 zhǐyào so long as; provided
只有 zhǐyǒu only; alone
不只 bùzhǐ
See zhī.

 zhǐ 6画 匕部

旨 旨旨旨旨旨旨旨

[名] 意思；目的：purpose; aim; purport | 主~zhǔzhǐ *purport*
宗旨 zōngzhǐ

 zhǐ 7画 土部

址 址址址址址址

[名] 建筑物的地点：(of buildings) location; site | 住~zhùzhǐ *address* / 校~xiàozhǐ *location of a school*
地址 dìzhǐ   网址 wǎngzhǐ

 (紙) zhǐ 7画 纟部

纸 纸纸纸纸纸纸纸

[名] paper | 信~xìnzhǐ *letter paper* / 这~太薄了。Zhè zhǐ tài báo le. *The paper is too thin.*
纸巾 zhǐjīn paper towel; towel
纸张 zhǐzhāng paper
报纸 bàozhǐ   稿纸 gǎozhǐ

剪纸 jiǎnzhǐ   图纸 túzhǐ
宣纸 xuānzhǐ

 zhǐ 9画 扌部

指 指指指指指指指指指

❶ [名] 手指头：finger | 食~ shízhǐ *index finger*
指甲 zhǐjia fingernail
指头 zhǐtou finger
戒指 jièzhi
手指 shǒuzhǐ
大拇指 dàmǔzhǐ

❷ [动] (手指或物体的尖端) 对着：point to; point (a finger, stick, etc.) at | 用手一~yòng shǒu yī zhǐ *point at sth. with one's hand (or finger)* / 时针~着12点。Shízhēn zhǐzhe shí'èr diǎn. *The hour hand points to twelve.*
指针 zhǐzhēn indicator
指南针 zhǐnánzhēn compass; guideline
指手画脚 zhǐshǒu-huàjiǎo ① make gestures; gesticulate ② make indiscreet remarks or criticisms

❸ [动] 意思上针对：refer to; direct | 那句话不是~她的。Nà jù huà bùshì zhǐ tā de. *That remark does not refer to her.*

❹ [动] 点明：point out; indicate

(the direction); guide | ～方向 zhǐ fāngxiàng *point out the direction*

指标 zhǐbiāo target; quota; norm; index

指出 zhǐchū point out

指导 zhǐdǎo guide; direct

指点 zhǐdiǎn give directions; show how

指定 zhǐdìng appoint; assign

指挥 zhǐhuī command; direct; conduct

指教 zhǐjiào (pol.) give advice or comments

指控 zhǐkòng accuse; charge

指令 zhǐlìng ① instruct; order; direct ② instruction; order; directive

指明 zhǐmíng show clearly; demonstrate; point out

指南 zhǐnán guide; guidebook

指示 zhǐshì ① indicate; point out ② instruct ③ directive; instruction

指数 zhǐshù index number; index

指引 zhǐyǐn point (the way); guide; show

指责 zhǐzé censure; criticize; find fault with

❺ [动] 仰仗；依靠：depend on; rely on; count on; lean on | 你不应～着别人生活。Nǐ bù yīng zhǐzhe biérén shēnghuó. *You should not depend on others to survive.* / 单～着他一个人办不成

事情。Dān zhǐ zhe tā yī gè rén bànbuchéng shìqing. *We cannot count on him alone.*

指望 zhǐwàng look to; count on

 zhì　6画 至部

至 至至至至至至

❶ [动] 到：reach; to; until | 由南～北 yóu nán zhì běi *from south to north*

至今 zhìjīn up to now; so far; to this day; to date

直至 zhízhì

无微不至 wúwēibùzhì

❷ [副] 至于：so far as to; to such an extent

至于 zhìyú ① as for; as to ② go so far as to

甚至 shènzhì　　　以至 yǐzhì

不至于 bùzhìyú

甚至于 shènzhìyú

❸ [副] 最；极：very; most | ～高无上 zhìgāo-wúshàng *most lofty* / 感人～深 gǎnrén-zhìshēn *move sb. to the depths of their soul*

至多 zhìduō at (the) most

至少 zhìshǎo at (the) least

 zhì　7画 士部

志 志志志志志志志

❶[名]意愿；决心：ambition; ideal; will; aspiration ｜ 立～lìzhì *resolve; be determined*
志气 zhìqì aspiration; ambition
志愿 zhìyuàn aspiration; wish; ideal
志愿者 zhìyuànzhě volunteer
斗志 dòuzhì　同志 tóngzhì
意志 yìzhì　　壮志 zhuàngzhì
❷[名]文字记录：written or printed documents; records; annals ｜ 人物～rénwùzhì *biographical notes and data*
杂志 zázhì
❸[名]记号：mark; token; sign
标志 biāozhì

帜 (幟) zhì　8画 巾部

帜 帜帜帜帜帜帜帜帜

[名]旗子：banner; flag
旗帜 qízhì

制 (製❶) zhì　8画 刂部

制 制制制制制制制制

❶[动]制造；做：make; manufacture; produce; turn out ｜ ～版 zhìbǎn *plate making* / ～图表 zhì túbiǎo *draw a chart*
制品 zhìpǐn product; production; goods
制造 zhìzào make; manufac-

ture
制作 zhìzuò make; manufacture
复制 fùzhì　　　录制 lùzhì
试制 shìzhì　　　研制 yánzhì
❷[动]订立；规定：work out; draw up; formulate; stipulate ｜ ～服 zhìfú *uniform; livery*
制订 zhìdìng work (map) out; formulate
制定 zhìdìng lay down; draw up; formulate; draft
编制 biānzhì
❸[名]制度；准则：system; institution ｜ 体～tǐzhì *system of organization* / 全日～学校 quánrìzhì xuéxiào *full-time school*
制度 zhìdù system; institution
法制 fǎzhì　　　学制 xuézhì
专制 zhuānzhì
公有制 gōngyǒuzhì
股份制 gǔfènzhì
私有制 sīyǒuzhì
所有制 suǒyǒuzhì
责任制 zérènzhì
❹[动]约束；限定：rule; control; inhibit; restrict; limit
制裁 zhìcái sanction; punish
制约 zhìyuē restrict; condition
制止 zhìzhǐ curb; check; prevent; stop
抵制 dǐzhì　　管制 guǎnzhì
控制 kòngzhì　　牵制 qiānzhì
强制 qiángzhì　　限制 xiànzhì
压制 yāzhì　　　抑制 yìzhì

质 (質) zhì 8画 厂部

质 质质质质质质质质

❶ [名] 客观存在的实体；质地：matter or substance as it is | 铁~ tiězhì *iron* / 流~食物 liúzhì shíwù *liquid food*

地质 dìzhì　　　物质 wùzhì
杂质 zázhì
蛋白质 dànbáizhì

❷ [名] 事物的根本特性：nature; character; property; quality

质变 zhìbiàn qualitative change
本质 běnzhì　　　变质 biànzhì
品质 pǐnzhì　　　气质 qìzhì
实质 shízhì　　　水质 shuǐzhì
素质 sùzhì　　　体质 tǐzhì
性质 xìngzhì　　　资质 zīzhì

❸ [名] 质量：quality | 劣~lièzhì *poor quality* / 保~保量bǎozhì-bǎoliàng *guarantee both quality and quantity*

质量 zhìliàng quality
材质 cáizhì　　　优质 yōuzhì

❹ [形] 朴实：simple; natural; plain

质朴 zhìpǔ simple and unadorned; unaffected; plain

❺ [名] 抵押品：pawn; mortgage; pledge; guarantee

人质 rénzhì

◇质疑zhìyí call into question; query

zhì 8画 氵部

治 治治治治治治治治

❶ [动] 治理；管理：rule; govern; manage; administer | ~家 zhìjiā *manage a household* / ~国 zhìguó *govern a country*

治安 zhì'ān public order; public security
治理 zhìlǐ administer; govern
统治 tǒngzhì　　　整治 zhěngzhì
政治 zhèngzhì　　　自治 zìzhì
政治家 zhèngzhìjiā

❷ [动] 惩罚：punish; bring sb. to justice | 处~chǔzhì *punish* / 大家决定~~他。Dàjiā juédìng zhìzhì tā. *We've decided to teach him a lesson.*

❸ [动] 医疗：treat; cure; heal | ~病 zhìbìng *cure a disease*
治疗 zhìliáo treat; cure
防治 fángzhì　　　医治 yīzhì

❹ [动] 消灭(害虫)：eliminate; wipe out (pests) | ~蝗 zhìhuáng *eliminate locusts*

❺ [动] 研究（学问）：study or research | ~学 zhìxué *pursue one's studies*

 (摯) zhì 10画 手部

挚 挚挚挚挚挚挚挚挚挚挚

[形] 真诚而恳切：earnest; sincere | 真~zhēnzhì *sincere; cordial* / ~友 zhìyǒu *close friend*

诚挚 chéngzhì

致 (緻)❸ zhì 10画 至部

致 致致致致致致致致
致致

❶[动]给予；向对方表示(礼节、情义等)：extend; send; deliver (respects, good wishes, etc.) | ~意 zhìyì *give one's regards* / ~谢 zhìxiè *express one's thanks* / ~欢迎词 zhì huānyíngcí *make a welcome speech*
致词 zhìcí make a speech
致电 zhìdiàn send a telegram
致敬 zhìjìng salute; pay one's respect to; pay tribute to

❷[动]引起；使实现：bring on; incur; invite; lead to achieve; reach | ~病 zhìbìng *cause a disease*
致富 zhìfù become rich
致命 zhìmìng causing death; fatal; mortal; deadly
致使 zhìshǐ cause; result in
导致 dǎozhì   以致 yǐzhì

❸[形]精密；精细：precise; delicate
精致 jīngzhì   细致 xìzhì
◇标致 biāozhì

秩 zhì 10画 禾部

秩 秩秩秩秩秩秩秩秩
秩秩

[名]次序：order; sequence
秩序 zhìxù order; sequence

掷 (擲) zhì 11画 扌部

掷 掷掷掷掷掷掷掷掷
掷掷掷

[动]扔；投：throw; cast; fling | ~铁饼 zhì tiěbǐng *throw a discus* / ~手榴弹 zhì shǒuliúdàn *throw a grenade*

智 zhì 12画 日部

智 智智智智智智智智
智智智智

❶[名]智慧；见识：wisdom; wit; intelligence; resourcefulness; insight | ~勇双全 zhìyǒngshuāngquán *be both brave and resourceful*
智慧 zhìhuì wisdom; intelligence
智力 zhìlì intelligence
智能 zhìnéng intellectual ability
才智 cáizhì   理智 lǐzhì

❷[形]聪明，有见识：wise; knowledgeable; experienced | 明~ míngzhì *sensible*
机智 jīzhì

致
秩
掷
智

zhì

929

滞（滯） zhì　12画 氵部

滞 滞滞滞滞滞滞滞滞
滞滞滞滞

[动] 流通不畅；停留：stagnant;
motionless; sluggish ｜ ～留
zhìliú *be delayed; be detained* /
～销 zhìxiāo *unsalable; unmar-
ketable*
停滞 tíngzhì

置 zhì　13画 四部

置 置置置置置置置置
置置置置置

❶ [动] 设立；安排：place; put; set;
keep ｜ 配～pēizhì *dispose; deploy*
布置 bùzhì　处置 chǔzhì
设置 shèzhì　装置 zhuāngzhì
❷ [动] 买：buy; purchase ｜ 添～新
设备 tiānzhì xīn shèbèi *purchase some new equipment* / ～
了一些家具 zhìle yīxiē jiājù
have bought some furniture
购置 gòuzhì
❸ [动] 放：lay; put ｜ 放～fàngzhì
lay up / 搁～gēzhì *put aside* / ～
于桌上 zhì yú zhuō shang
place sth. on the table / ～之不
理 zhìzhī-bùlǐ *ignore; brush
aside*
安置 ānzhì　　　位置 wèizhì

稚 zhì　13画 禾部

稚 稚稚稚稚稚稚稚稚
稚稚稚稚稚

[形] 幼小：childish; young ｜ ～气
zhìqì *childishness*
幼稚 yòuzhì

中 zhōng　4画 丨部

中 中中中中

❶ [名] 中心：centre; middle ｜ 居～
jūzhōng *in the centre* / 正～
zhèngzhōng *right in the
middle*
中部 zhōngbù central section;
middle part
中东 Zhōngdōng Middle East
中锋 zhōngfēng (sports) centre
forward (as in football); centre
中间 zhōngjiān centre
中心 zhōngxīn centre; heart;
core; hub
中央 zhōngyāng ① centre;
middle ②central authorities (of
a state, party, etc.)
中原 zhōngyuán Central Plains
(comprising the middle and
lower reaches of the Yellow
River)
集中 jízhōng
党中央 dǎngzhōngyāng
市中心 shìzhōngxīn

❷[形] 位置在两端之间的：middle; mid | 月～yuèzhōng *in the middle of a month*

中断 zhōngduàn suspend; break off; discontinue

中介 zhōngjiè ① intermediary; medium ② broker; middleman; agent

中立 zhōnglì neutrality

中年 zhōngnián middle age

中途 zhōngtú halfway; midway

中午 zhōngwǔ noon; midday

中旬 zhōngxún the middle ten days of a month

中游 zhōngyóu ① middle reaches (of a river) ② middling; mediocre

中止 zhōngzhǐ discontinue; suspend; break off

中秋节 Zhōngqiūjié the Mid-Autumn Festival (15th day of the 8th lunar month)

途中 túzhōng

❸[名] 里面；在一定范围内：in; among; amid | 家～jiāzhōng *in the family; at home* / 空～kōngzhōng *in the air, in the sky* / 水～shuǐzhōng *in the water*

从中 cóngzhōng

当中 dāngzhōng

其中 qízhōng 心中 xīnzhōng

…之中… …zhīzhōng…

空中小姐 kōngzhōng xiǎojiě

❹[名] 表示事情正在进行：used after a verb to indicate an action in process | 讨论～ tǎolùn zhōng *being discussed* / 昏迷～hūnmí zhōng *in a state of unconsciousness* / 正在研究～zhèngzài yánjiū zhōng *be under research; be under study*

❺[名] 性质、等级在两端之间的：medium; intermediate | ～级 zhōngjí *intermediate* / ～篇 zhōngpiān *medium-length* / ～层 zhōngcéng *middle level*

中等 zhōngděng ① medium; moderate; middling ② secondary

中队 zhōngduì ① (mill.) military unit corresponding to a company; squadron ② a unit composed of several groups

中型 zhōngxíng medium-sized; middle-sized

中学 zhōngxué ① middle school ② a late Qing dynasty term for Chinese traditional learning; Chinese learning

中老年 zhōng-lǎonián the middle- and old-aged (people)

中学生 zhōngxuéshēng middle school student

❻[名] 指中国：China | 古今～外 gǔjīn-zhōngwài *ancient and modern, Chinese and foreign*

中餐 zhōngcān Chinese meal; Chinese food

中国 Zhōngguó China

中华 Zhōnghuá ① the Chinese nation ② China

中式 zhōngshì Chinese style

中文 Zhōngwén the Chinese language; Chinese

中药 zhōngyào traditional Chinese medicine

中医 zhōngyī ① traditional Chinese medical science ②doctor of traditional Chinese medicine; practitioner of Chinese medicine

❼ [动] 适于；合于：be suitable for; be fit for; be good for | ~看 zhōngkàn be pleasant to the eye / ~听 zhōngtīng be pleasant to the ear / ~用 zhōngyòng be of use

◇中山装 zhōngshānzhuāng Chinese suit; Mao suit

See zhòng.

忠 zhōng 8画 心部

忠 忠忠忠忠忠忠忠忠

[形] 赤诚无私，尽心竭力：loyal; faithful; dedicated | ~心 zhōngxīn loyalty / 尽~ jìnzhōng devote oneself heart and soul to

忠诚 zhōngchéng loyal; faithful; staunch

忠实 zhōngshí true; faithful

忠于 zhōngyú be true to; be loyal to; be faithful to; be devoted to

忠贞 zhōngzhēn loyal and steadfast

终 (終) zhōng 8画 纟部

终 终终终终终终终终

❶ [名] 最后阶段；结局（跟 "始 shǐ" 相对）：end; the last stage (the opposite of "始 shǐ") | 年~ niánzhōng end of a year

终点 zhōngdiǎn ① terminal point; destination ② finish; finishing line (of a track event)

终端 zhōngduān terminal

终结 zhōngjié end; final stage

终审 zhōngshěn (leg.) last instance; final judgement

始终 shǐzhōng 最终 zuìzhōng

❷ [动] 结束；完了：end

终止 zhōngzhǐ stop; end

❸ [形] 从开头到最后的：from beginning to end | ~日 zhōngrì whole day / ~生 zhōngshēng all one's life

终年 zhōngnián ① the age at which one dies ②all year round; throughout one's life

终身 zhōngshēn lifelong; all one's life

❹ [副] 到底；毕竟：in the end; eventually | ~将成功 zhōng jiāng chénggōng will succeed in the end

终究 zhōngjiū eventually; in the end; after all

终于 zhōngyú at last; in the end; finally

钟 (鐘) zhōng 9画 钅部

钅 钟 钟 钟 钟 钟 钟 钟 钟
钟

❶[名]金属制成的音响器具：bell, hollow metallic musical instrument made of copper or iron | 警～jǐngzhōng *alarm bell*

❷[名]计时的器具：timepiece; clock | 挂～guàzhōng *wall clock* / 闹～nàozhōng *alarm clock*
钟表 zhōngbiǎo clocks and watches; timepiece

❸[名]表示时间或时刻：time as measured by hours or minutes | 六点～liù diǎnzhōng *six o'clock* / 休息十分～xiūxi shí fēnzhōng *have a break of ten minutes*
钟点 zhōngdiǎn ①time for sth. to be done or to happen ②hour
钟头 zhōngtóu hour
钟点工 zhōngdiǎngōng casual worker paid on an hourly basis (mostly hired to do household chores)
点钟 diǎnzhōng 分钟 fēnzhōng

衷 zhōng 10画 一部

衷 衷 衷 衷 衷 衷 衷 衷
衷 衷

[名]内心：heart; inner feelings |

苦～kǔzhōng *difficulties that one is reluctant to discuss or mention* / 由～yóuzhōng *from the bottom of one's heart*
衷心 zhōngxīn heartfelt; whole-hearted; cordial
初衷 chūzhōng

肿 (腫) zhǒng 8画 月部

月 肿 肿 肿 肿 肿 肿 肿 肿

[动] swell; bloat | 消～xiāozhǒng *reduce; swelling reduce personnel* / 脚～了。Jiǎo zhǒng le. *The foot is swollen.*
肿瘤 zhǒngliú tumour

种 (種) zhǒng 9画 禾部

种 种 种 种 种 种 种 种
种

❶[名]生物传代繁殖的物质：seed; breed; strain | 选～xuǎnzhǒng *select seeds*
种子 zhǒngzi seed
良种 liángzhǒng

❷[名]人种：race | 黄～huángzhǒng *the 'yellow race'* / 白～báizhǒng *the 'white race'*
种族 zhǒngzú race

❸[名]类别：type; category | 兵～bīngzhǒng *a combat branch of an armed force; arm* / 工～

gōngzhǒng *type of work in production*

种类 zhǒnglèi kind; type; variety

种种 zhǒngzhǒng all sorts (kinds) of; a variety of

各种 gèzhǒng　品种 pǐnzhǒng

物种 wùzhǒng　语种 yǔzhǒng

各种各样 gèzhǒng-gèyàng

❹ [量] 用于人或事物的类别：kind; type; class; category; breed; species ｜ 一～动物 yī zhǒng dōngwù *a kind of animal* / 三～机器 sān zhǒng jīqì *three types of machines*

　　See zhòng.

zhōng　4画 丨部

中　中 中 中 中

❶ [动] 正好对上；恰好符合：fit exactly; hit ｜ 打～dǎzhòng *hit the target (mark)* / 你没猜～。Nǐ méi cāizhòng. *You didn't guess right.* / 你说～了。Nǐ shuōzhòng le. *You've got it.*

中标 zhòngbiāo get (or win) the bid or tender

中奖 zhòngjiǎng draw a prizewinning ticket (or win a prize) in a lottery; get the winning number in a bond

看中 kànzhòng

选中 xuǎnzhòng

❷ [动] 受到；遭到：be affected by; undergo; suffer ｜ ～毒 zhòngdú *be poisoned* / ～暑 zhòngshǔ *suffer heatstroke* / 腿上～了一枪 tuǐshang zhòngle yī qiāng *be shot in the leg*

　　See zhōng.

众 (衆) zhòng　6画 人部

众 众 众 众 众 众

❶ [名] 许多人：many people; crowd; multitude ｜ 公～gōngzhòng *the public*

众议院 zhòngyìyuàn House of Representatives; Chamber of Deputies

众所周知 zhòngsuǒzhōuzhī as everyone knows; as is known to all; it is common knowledge that

大众 dàzhòng

出众 chūzhòng

观众 guānzhòng

民众 mínzhòng

群众 qúnzhòng

听众 tīngzhòng

与众不同 yǔzhòng-bùtóng

❷ [形] 许多 (跟 "寡 guǎ" 相对)：many; numerous (the opposite of "寡 guǎ")

众多 zhòngduō multitudinous; numerous

众人 zhòngrén everybody

种 (種) zhǒng 9画 禾部

种 种种种种种种种种
种

[动] 种植：plant; grow; crop | ～树 zhǒng shù *plant trees* / ～庄稼 zhǒng zhuāngjia *grow crops*

种地 zhǒngdì cultivate the land

种植 zhǒngzhí plant; grow

播种 bōzhǒng

耕种 gēngzhòng

接种 jiēzhòng

See zhǒng.

重 zhòng 9画 丿部

重 重重重重重重重重
重

❶ [形] 分量大 (跟 "轻 qīng" 相对)：heavy; weighty; hefty (the opposite of "轻 qīng") | 这些铁块很～。Zhè xiē tiěkuài hěn zhòng. *These iron bars are very heavy.* / 这件行李～得很。Zhè jiàn xíngli zhòngdehěn. *This piece of luggage is very heavy.*

重读 zhòngdú (phonet.) stress

重伤 zhòngshāng a severe injury

重型 zhòngxíng heavy-duty; heavy

重工业 zhònggōngyè heavy industry

笨重 bènzhòng

沉重 chénzhòng

繁重 fánzhòng

挑重担 tiāozhòngdàn

❷ [名] 重量；分量：weight; heft | 加～jiāzhòng *increase weight* / 这条鱼有多～?Zhè tiáo yú yǒu duō zhòng? *How much does the fish weigh?*

重量 zhòngliàng weight

重心 zhòngxīn ① centre of gravity ② heart; core; focus

比重 bǐzhòng   举重 jǔzhòng

体重 tǐzhòng

❸ [名] 重要：important | ～任 zhòngrèn *important task* / ～地 zhòngdì *important place*

重大 zhòngdà great; weighty; major; significant

重点 zhòngdiǎn focal point; stress; emphasis

重要 zhòngyào important; significant; major

贵重 guìzhòng

❹ [动] 重视：attach importance to; lay stress on | 敬～jìngzhòng *revere* / 看～kānzhòng *value*

重视 zhòngshì attach importance to; pay attention to; think highly of; take sth. seriously; value

保重 bǎozhòng

慎重 shènzhòng

种
重

zhòng

935

注重 zhùzhòng
着重 zhuózhòng
尊重 zūnzhòng
❺[形] 程度深：deep; serious | ～病 zhòngbìng *serious illness* / ～伤 zhòngshāng *severe injury*
惨重 cǎnzhòng
加重 jiāzhòng 深重 shēnzhòng
严重 yánzhòng
❻[形] 不轻率：prudent; discreet | 慎～ shènzhòng *cautious; careful; circumspect; gingerly* / 稳～ wěnzhòng *sedate* / 自～ zìzhòng *self-respect*
从重 cóngzhòng
隆重 lóngzhòng
郑重 zhèngzhòng
庄重 zhuāngzhòng
See chóng.

zhōu   6画 舟部

舟 舟舟舟舟舟舟

[名] 船：boat | 小～ xiǎozhōu *small boat* / 轻～ qīngzhōu *light boat*
龙舟 lóngzhōu

zhōu   6画 丶部

州 州州州州州州

❶[名] 旧时的一种行政区划：prefecture; state; administrative division in former times

❷[名] 一种民族自治行政区划：ethnic autonomous region or area
◇神州 Shénzhōu

zhōu   8画 门部

周 周周周周周周周周

❶[动] 环绕；循环：surround; cycle; make a circuit; make a circle | ～转 zhōuzhuǎn ①turnover ②have enough to meet the need
周折 zhōuzhé *twists and turns; setbacks*

❷[形] 全面；普遍：all; whole | ～身 zhōushēn *the whole body* / ～游 zhōuyóu *travel* / 众所～知 zhòngsuǒzhōuzhī *as is known to all*

❸[形] 完备；完善：with no detail missing; thoughtful | ～全 zhōuquán *comprehensive* / 考虑不～ kǎolǜ bù zhōu *be not well advised; do not think through*
周到 zhōudào *attentive and satisfactory; thoughtful; considerate*
周密 zhōumì *careful; thorough*

❹[名] 圈子：circle | 圆～ yuánzhōu *circumference of a circle* / 绕校园一～ rào xiàoyuán yī zhōu *make a circuit of the campus*

❺[名] 周围：circumference

周边 zhōubiān (mech.) periphery

周围 zhōuwéi around; round; about

四周 sìzhōu

❻[名]时间的一轮: (of time) round

周年 zhōunián anniversary

周期 zhōuqī period; cycle

周岁 zhōusuì one full year of life

❼[名]星期: week | 上~shàngzhōu *last week* / 下~xiàzhōu *next week* / 这学期共二十~。Zhè xuéqī gòng èrshí zhōu. *There are twenty weeks in this term altogether.*

周报 zhōubào a weekly newspaper or periodical; weekly

周刊 zhōukān weekly publication (e.g. a magazine, a supplement to a newspaper); weekly

周末 zhōumò weekend

洲 zhōu 9画 氵部

洲 洲 洲 洲 洲 洲 洲 洲 洲

❶[名]河流中的陆地: land in a river | 沙~shāzhōu *sandbar; shoal* 三角洲 sānjiǎozhōu

❷[名]大陆及其附属岛屿的总称: continent; one of the earth's principal land masses and its surrounding islands | 亚~

Yàzhōu *Asia* / 地球上有七大~。Dìqiú shang yǒu qī dà zhōu. *There are seven continents on the earth.*

澳洲 Àozhōu   非洲 Fēizhōu
美洲 Měizhōu   欧洲 Ōuzhōu
北美洲 Běiměizhōu
大洋洲 Dàyángzhōu
南极洲 Nánjízhōu
南美洲 Nánměizhōu

粥 zhōu 12画 弓部

粥 粥 粥 粥 粥 粥 粥 粥 粥 粥 粥 粥

[名] porridge; congee; gruel | 大米~dàmǐzhōu *rice gruel* / 奶奶一天吃三顿~。Nǎinai yī tiān chī sān dùn zhōu. *Grandma has porridge three times a day.*

宙 zhōu 8画 宀部

宙 宙 宙 宙 宙 宙 宙 宙

[名]指古往今来无限的时间: time, conceived as past, present and future

宇宙 yǔzhòu

昼 (晝) zhōu 9画 尸部

昼 昼 昼 昼 昼 昼 昼 昼 昼

[名] 白天(跟"夜 yè"相对)：day; daytime; daylight (the opposite of "夜 yè") | 白~bǎizhòu daylight; day
昼夜 zhòuyè day and night; round the clock

皱 (皺) zhòu 10画 皮部

皱 皱皱皱皱皱皱皱皱皱皱

❶[名]脸上或物体上的折纹：wrinkle; furrow; rumple; crumple
皱纹 zhòuwén wrinkle; crease
❷[动]聚拢；使产生折纹：wrinkle; furrow; shrivel | ~起额头 zhòu-qǐ étóu wrinkle up one's forehead / 这料子容易~。Zhè liàozi róngyì zhòu. This cloth material creases easily.

珠 zhū 10画 王部

珠 珠珠珠珠珠珠珠珠珠珠

[名] pearl | 珍~zhēnzhū pearl / 夜明~yèmíngzhū a legendary luminescent pearl
珠宝 zhūbǎo pearls and jewel; jewelry
珠子 zhūzi ① pearl ② bead
◇珠江 Zhū Jiāng the Pearl River

圆珠笔 yuánzhūbǐ

株 zhū 10画 木部

株 株株株株株株株株株株

[量] 用于植物，相当于"棵 kē"：used for plants, equal to "棵 kē" | 一~桃树 yī zhū táoshù a peach tree

诸 (諸) zhū 10画 讠部

诸 诸诸诸诸诸诸诸诸诸诸

[代] 众；许多：all; various
诸多 zhūduō (formal) (used for abstract things) a good deal; a lot of
诸如 zhūrú such as
诸位 zhūwèi ladies and gentlemen; you; comrades
诸如此类 zhūrú-cǐlèi things like that; such; and so on; and so forth

猪 zhū 11画 犭部

猪 猪猪猪猪猪猪猪猪猪猪猪

[名] pig | 小~xiǎozhū pigling; piglet

zhú 6画 竹部

竹 竹竹竹竹竹竹

[名] bamboo | ~林 zhúlín *bamboo forest* / ~园 zhúyuán *bamboo garden*
竹笋 zhúsǔn bamboo shoots
竹子 zhúzi bamboo
文竹 wénzhú

 zhú 10画 辶部

逐 逐逐逐逐逐逐逐逐逐逐

❶ [动]赶走: drive out; expel | 被~出祖国 bèi zhúchū zǔguó *exile sb. from his country*
驱逐 qūzhú   追逐 zhuīzhú
❷ [动]挨着(次序): (of order) one by one | ~日 zhúrì *day by day* / ~字讲解 zhúzì jiǎngjiě *explain word by word* / ~个清点 zhúgè qīngdiǎn *check one by one*
逐步 zhúbù step by step; progressively
逐渐 zhújiàn gradually; by degrees
逐年 zhúnián year by year; year after year

 (燭) zhú 10画 火部

 烛烛烛烛烛烛烛烛烛烛

[名] candle | 红~hóngzhú *red candle*
蜡烛 làzhú

主 zhǔ 5画 丶部

主 主主主主主

❶ [名]拥有权力或财产的人: owner | 债~zhàizhǔ *creditor* / 业~yèzhǔ *proprietor*
主人公 zhǔréngōng leading character in a novel, etc.; hero or heroine; protagonist
主人翁 zhǔrénwēng master
得主 dézhǔ   地主 dìzhǔ
店主 diànzhǔ   公主 gōngzhǔ
雇主 gùzhǔ   君主 jūnzhǔ
❷ [名]邀请并接待客人的人(跟"宾 bīn"或"客 kè"相对): host (the opposite of "宾 bīn" or "客 kè") | 宾~bīnzhǔ *guests and host*
主场 zhǔchǎng home court; host arena
主人 zhǔrén host
东道主 dōngdàozhǔ
❸ [动]主持; 负主要责任: manage; direct; be in charge of | ~讲 zhǔjiǎng *master speaker; conduct a lecture*
主办 zhǔbàn direct; sponsor
主编 zhǔbiān ① chief editor; compiler; editor in chief ② share

the major responsibility of editorial work of (a newspaper, magazine, etc.)

主持 zhǔchí ①take charge of; host; manage; direct ② preside over; chair ③ uphold; stand for

主管 zhǔguǎn ① be responsible for; be in charge of ②person in charge; supervisor

主任 zhǔrèn director; head; chairman

主席 zhǔxí ① chairman (of a meeting); chairperson ② chairman or president (of an organization or a state)

主持人 zhǔchírén anchorperson; compere; toastmaster

民主 mínzhǔ   自主 zìzhǔ

班主任 bānzhǔrèn

不由自主 bùyóu zìzhǔ

独立自主 dúlì-zìzhǔ

❹[名] 主见；见解：hold a definite view about sth. | 有~见 yǒu zhǔjiàn *have definite views of one's own* / 我一时觉得心里没 ~。Wǒ yīshí juéde xīnli méi zhǔ. *I didn't know what to do for the moment.*

主义 zhǔyì doctrine

主意 zhǔyi decision; definite view

主张 zhǔzhāng ① advocate; stand for; maintain; hold ②view; position; stand; proposition

作主 zuòzhǔ

帝国主义 dìguó zhǔyì

共产主义 gòngchǎn zhǔyì

官僚主义 guānliáo zhǔyì

人道主义 réndào zhǔyì

社会主义 shèhuì zhǔyì

唯物主义 wéiwù zhǔyì

唯心主义 wéixīn zhǔyì

殖民主义 zhímín zhǔyì

资本主义 zīběn zhǔyì

马克思主义 Mǎkèsī zhǔyì

❺[形] 自身的；从自身出发的：subjective

主动 zhǔdòng initiative

主观 zhǔguān subjective

❻[名] 当事人：client; person or party concerned | 失~shīzhǔ *owner of lost property* / 买~ mǎizhǔ *buyer* / ~顾 zhǔgù *customer; client*

❼[名] 基督教徒对上帝、伊斯兰教徒对真主的称呼：(Christianity) God; Lord; (Islam) Allah

天主教 Tiānzhǔjiào

❽[形] 最重要的；最基本的：main; primary | 以预防为~，治疗为辅。Yǐ yùfáng wéi zhǔ, zhìliáo wéi fù. *Put prevention first, and treatment second.*

主导 zhǔdǎo leading; dominant; guiding

主角 zhǔjué leading role; lead; protagonist

主力 zhǔlì main force; main strength of an army

主流 zhǔliú ①mainstream; main current; mother current ② essential or main aspect; main

trend

主权 zhǔquán sovereign rights; sovereignty

主食 zhǔshí staple food; principal food

主题 zhǔtí theme; subject; motif

主体 zhǔtǐ ① main body; main part; principal part ② subject

主演 zhǔyǎn act the leading role (in a play or film); star

主要 zhǔyào main; chief; principal; major

主页 zhǔyè homepage

主语 zhǔyǔ (gram.) subject

主人公 zhǔréngōng leading character; hero or heroine; protagonist

拄 zhǔ　8画 扌部

拄 拄拄拄拄拄拄拄拄

[动] 用棍棒等顶住地面来支撑身体: lean on (a stick, etc.) | 拄拐棍儿 zhǔ guǎigùnr *walk with the help of a cane*

煮 zhǔ　12画 灬部

煮 煮煮煮煮煮煮煮煮
煮煮煮煮

[动] 把食物或东西放在水中加热: boil; cook; stew; heat food or other things in a container filled

with water | ~饭 zhǔfàn *cook rice* / ~面 zhǔmiàn *cook noodles* / 水~开了。Shuǐ zhǔkāi le. *The water is boiling.*

嘱 (囑) zhǔ　15画 口部

嘱 嘱嘱嘱嘱嘱嘱嘱嘱
嘱嘱嘱嘱嘱嘱嘱

[动] 吩咐，托付: enjoin; advise | 遗~ yízhǔ *will; testament*

嘱咐 zhǔfu enjoin; tell; exhort

嘱托 zhǔtuō entrust

叮嘱 dīngzhǔ

助 zhǔ　7画 力部

助 助助助助助助助

[动] 帮: help; assist; aid | ~学金 zhùxuéjīn *grant; scholarship; bursary*

助教 zhùjiào teaching assistant (of a college faculty)

助理 zhùlǐ assistant

助手 zhùshǒu assistant; helper; aide

助长 zhùzhǎng encourage; abet; foster; foment; put a premium on

帮助 bāngzhù　补助 bǔzhù

辅助 fǔzhù　互助 hùzhù

借助 jièzhù　救助 jiùzhù

捐助 juānzhù　求助 qiúzhù

协助 xiézhù　援助 yuánzhù

赞助 zànzhù　资助 zīzhù

自助 zìzhù

住 zhù　7画 亻部

住 住住住住住住住

❶[动]居住；住宿：live; reside; stay | 他家～在北京。Tā jiā zhù zài Běijīng. *His family live in Beijing.* / 他在旅馆～了一夜。Tā zài lǚguǎn zhùle yī yè. *He stayed for the night in a hotel.*

住房 zhùfáng housing; lodging
住户 zhùhù household; resident
住所 zhùsuǒ dwelling place; residence; domicile
住院 zhùyuàn be in hospital; be hospitalized
住宅 zhùzhái residence; dwelling
居住 jūzhù

❷[动]停止：stop | ～手 zhùshǒu stop; stay one's hand; hands off / 雨～了。Yǔ zhù le. *The rain has stopped.*

不住 bùzhù

❸[动]作动词的补语：used as a complement after a verb

(a) 表示停顿或静止：used to indicate "stop" | 拖～tuōzhù *pin down* / 挡～dǎngzhù *shelter* / 一句话把他问～了。Yī jù huà bǎ tā wènzhù le. *He was left speechless by the question.*

(b) 表示稳当或牢固：used to indicate a steady or firm state | 站～zhànzhù *halt* / 拿～názhù *grasp* / 记～jìzhù *keep in mind* / 把～方向盘 bǎzhù fāngxiàng-pán *hold the wheel firmly*

注 zhù　8画 氵部

注 注注注注注注注注

❶[动]灌入：pour; fill | ～入 zhùrù *pour into*; *empty into* / 大雨如～。Dàyǔ-rúzhù. *The rain is pouring down.*

注射 zhùshè inject

❷[动]（精神、目光等）集中在某一点上：concentrate; fix | 专～zhuānzhù *concentrate one's attention on*

注目 zhùmù gaze at; fix one's eyes on
注视 zhùshì look attentively at; gaze at
注意 zhùyì pay attention to; take note (notice) of
注重 zhùzhòng lay stress on; pay attention to; attach importance to
注意力 zhùyìlì attention
关注 guānzhù
引人注目 yǐnrén-zhùmù

❸[动]用文字解释字句：annotate; explain with words | 批～pīzhù *provide critical and explanatory notes for*; *annotate*

and comment on

注解 zhùjiě annotate; explain with notes

注明 zhùmíng give clear indication of

注释 zhùshì explanatory note; annotation

❹[动]登记；记载：record; register | ～销 zhùxiāo *cancel; write off*

注册 zhùcē register

◇注定 zhùdìng be doomed; be destined

 （駐）zhù　8画 马部

驻 驻驻驻驻驻驻驻驻

❶[动]停留：halt; stay

驻足 zhùzú halt; stop; go no further

❷[动]（部队）停留在（某地）；（机构）设立在（某地）：(of troops or organizations) be stationed; encamp | ～美大使 zhù Měi dà-shǐ *ambassador to the USA* / ～京记者 zhù Jīng jìzhě *resident correspondent in Beijing*

驻扎 zhùzhā (of troops) be stationed; be quartered

 zhù　9画 木部

柱 柱柱柱柱柱柱柱柱
柱

[名]柱子：post; pillar; column | 门～ménzhù *door post*

柱子 zhùzi post; upright; pillar; column

 zhù　9画 礻部

祝 祝祝祝祝祝祝祝祝
祝

[动] 表示良好的愿望：wish; express good wishes | ～你一路顺风! Zhù nǐ yīlù-shùnfēng! *Wishing you a pleasant trip!*

祝福 zhùfú blessing; benediction

祝贺 zhùhè congratulate

祝愿 zhùyuàn wish

庆祝 qìngzhù　　预祝 yùzhù

 zhù　11画 艹部

著 著著著著著著著著
著著著

❶ [形] 明显：marked; outstanding

显著 xiǎnzhù

❷ [动] 显露出：show; prove

著名 zhùmíng famous; celebrated; well-known

❸ [动] 写作：write | 编～biānzhù *compile; write* /《家》是巴金～的。Jiā shì Bā Jīn zhù de. *The Family is written by Ba Jin.*

❹ [名] 作品：work; book; writing

| 名 ~ míngzhù *famous work* / 巨 ~ jùzhù *monumental work* 著作 zhùzuò work; book; writings

铸 (鑄) zhù　12画 钅部

铸铸铸铸铸铸铸铸铸铸铸铸

[动] cast; found | 这口钟是铜~的。 Zhè kǒu zhōng shì tóng zhù de. *This bell is cast in bronze.* 铸造 zhùzào casting; founding

筑 (築) zhù　12画 竹部

筑筑筑筑筑筑筑筑筑筑筑筑

[动] 建造；修建：build; construct | ~路 zhùlù *construct a road* 建筑 jiànzhù　　修筑 xiūzhù 建筑师 jiànzhù shī

抓 zhuā　7画 扌部

抓抓抓抓抓抓抓

❶[动]聚拢手指握住：grab; seize; catch | ~一把米 zhuā yī bǎ mǐ *take a handful of rice* / ~住他的胳膊 zhuāzhù tā de gēbo *hold his arm*

❷[动]用指甲或爪在物体上划：scratch; scrape at sth. with nails

or claws | ~痒 zhuāyǎng *scratch an itch* / 猫用爪子~东西。Māo yòng zhuǎzi zhuā dōngxi. *The cat scratches things with its claws.*

❸[动]把握住；不放过：grasp; seize; hold | ~时间 zhuā shíjiān *make good use of one's time; find time (to do sth.)* 抓紧 zhuājǐn firmly grasp; pay close attention to

❹[动]加强领导；特别注意：stress; pay special attention to | ~纪律 zhuā jìlǜ *stress discipline* / ~重点 zhuā zhòngdiǎn *stress the essentials* / ~工作 zhuā gōngzuò *give special attention to work*

❺[动]捉拿；捕捉：arrest; bust; catch | 他被~起来了。Tā bèi zhuā qǐlai le. *He was arrested.* / 老鹰~住一只小鸡。Lǎoyīng zhuāzhù yī zhī xiǎojī. *The chick was snatched by an eagle.* 抓捕 zhuābǔ arrest; catch 抓获 zhuāhuò catch (a criminal, etc.); capture; seize

爪 zhuǎ　4画 爪部

爪爪爪爪

[名] 鸟兽的脚：claw; paw | 鸡~子 jīzhuǎzi *chicken's claw*

zhuāi 9画 扌部

拽 拽拽拽拽拽拽拽拽拽拽

[动] 拉：pull; drag; haul | ～紧 zhuāijǐn *taut* / 把门～开 bǎ mén zhuāikāi *pull the door open*

 (專) zhuān 4画 一部

专 专专专专

❶ [形] 集中在一个方面的；单一的：devoting one's attention to a particular person, occasion, purpose, etc.; focus on one thing; special | ～卖 zhuānmài *monopolize* / ～爱看小说 zhuān ài kàn xiǎoshuō *particularly like to read novels*

专长 zhuāncháng speciality; special skill or knowledge

专程 zhuānchéng special trip

专辑 zhuānjí ① special issue or column (of a periodical or newspaper) ② monograph; book published by an academic organization on the research into a specific topic

专家 zhuānjiā expert; specialist

专科 zhuānkē ① specialty; special field of study ② vocational school

专栏 zhuānlán special column

专门 zhuānmén special; specialized

专人 zhuānrén person specially assigned for a task or job

专题 zhuāntí special subject; special topic

专心 zhuānxīn concentrate one's attention; be absorbed in

专业 zhuānyè ① special field of study; specialized subject; specialty; discipline ② specialized trade or profession; special line

专用 zhuānyòng for a special purpose; for special use

专职 zhuānzhí ① sole duty; specific duty ② full-time

专注 zhuānzhù concentrate one's attention on; be absorbed in; devote one's mind to

专业户 zhuānyèhù specialized household (engaged in a particular economic activity)

❷ [动] 独自掌握或享有：monopolize | ～权 zhuānquán *arrogate all powers to oneself; monopolize power*

专利 zhuānlì patent

专政 zhuānzhèng dictatorship

专制 zhuānzhì ① autocracy ② autocratic; despotic

专卖店 zhuānmàidiàn franchised shop

 (磚) zhuān 9画 石部

砖砖砖砖砖砖砖砖砖
砖

❶[名] brick | 瓷~cízhuān *ceramic tile*

❷[名]形状像砖的东西：anything shaped like a brick | 茶~chá-zhuān *brick tea* / 冰~bīng-zhuān *ice cream bar*

 (轉) zhuǎn 8画 车部

转 转转转转转转转转

❶ [动]改变（方向、位置、形势、情况等）：(of orientation, position, situation, condition, etc.) turn; shift; change | ~身 zhuǎn-shēn *turn around* / 向左~xiàng zuǒ zhuǎn *turn left*/ ~眼之间 zhuǎnyǎn zhījiān *in the twinkling of an eye* / ~过脸来 zhuǎnguò liǎn lai *turn around*

转变 zhuǎnbiàn transform; change

转动 zhuǎndòng turn; move; turn round

转化 zhuǎnhuà change; transform

转换 zhuǎnhuàn change; transform

转机 zhuǎnjī a favourable turn; a turn for the better

转入 zhuǎnrù change over to; shift to; switch to

转弯 zhuǎnwān turn a corner; make a turn

转向 zhuǎnxiàng change direction; turn towards

转移 zhuǎnyí ① shift; transfer; divert ② change; transform

转折 zhuǎnzhé a turn in the course of events

转基因 zhuǎnjīyīn transgenic

好转 hǎozhuǎn 扭转 niǔzhuǎn

旋转 xuánzhuǎn

运转 yùnzhuǎn

周转 zhōuzhuǎn

❷[动] 把一方的物体、意见等带给另一方：pass on; transfer (objects, letters, opinions, etc.) | ~送 zhuǎnsòng *pass on; transfer* / 这件礼物托别人~给他。Zhè jiàn lǐwù tuō biérén zhuǎngěi tā. *Ask somebody to pass on the gift to him.* / 请你把我的意见~给他。Qǐng nǐ bǎ wǒ de yìjiàn zhuǎngěi tā. *Please let him know my views.*

转播 zhuǎnbō relay (a radio or TV broadcast)

转达 zhuǎndá pass on; convey; communicate

转告 zhuǎngào pass on (a message); communicate; transmit

转交 zhuǎnjiāo pass on; transmit

转让 zhuǎnràng transfer the ownership of sth.; make over

转载 zhuǎnzǎi reprint sth. that has been published elsewhere;

reprint

　　See zhuǎn.

传 (傳) zhuǎn　6画 亻部

传 传 传 传 传 传 传

❶[名] 记叙某人生平事迹的文字：biography | 小~xiǎozhuàn *brief biography* / 外~wàizhuàn *unauthorized biography* / 自~zìzhuàn *autobiography*
传记 zhuǎnjì biography

❷[名] 叙述历史故事的作品：story or novel relating historical events or personages |《水浒~》Shuǐhǔzhuàn *Water Margin*
　　See chuán.

转 (轉) zhuǎn　8画 车部

转 转 转 转 转 转 转 转

[动] 围绕着中心运动：turn; rotate | 轮子~得很快。Lúnzi zhuǎn de hěn kuài. *The wheel turns very quickly.*
转动 zhuǎndòng turn; revolve; rotate
　　See zhuǎn.

赚 (賺) zhuǎn　14画 贝部

赚 赚 赚 赚 赚 赚 赚 赚 赚 赚 赚 赚 赚 赚

[动] 获得利润（跟"赔péi"相对）：make a profit; gain (the opposite of "赔péi") | ~钱 zhuǎnqián *make money*
赚取 zhuǎnqǔ make (profit, advantage, etc.); gain

妆 (妝) zhuāng　6画 丬部

妆 妆 妆 妆 妆 妆 妆

[动] 修饰；打扮：apply makeup; make up | 梳~shūzhuāng *dress one's hair and apply makeup*
化妆 huàzhuāng
化妆品 huàzhuāngpǐn

庄 (莊) zhuāng　6画 广部

庄 庄 庄 庄 庄 庄 庄

❶[形] 严肃；不轻浮：serious; grave; sedate | 端~duānzhuāng *dignified; sedate*
庄严 zhuāngyán solemn; dignified; stately
庄重 zhuāngzhòng serious; grave; solemn; sedate

❷[名] 村子：village | 农~nóngzhuāng *farm*
村庄 cūnzhuāng

◇庄家 zhuāngjiā banker (in a gambling game)
庄稼 zhuāngjia crops

桩 (樁) zhuāng　10画 木部

桩 桩桩桩桩桩桩桩桩桩 桩桩

❶[名]插入地里的柱子：stake; pile | 木～mùzhuāng *wooden stake* / 桥～qiáozhuāng *bridge pier*

❷[量]用于事情，相当于"件jiàn"：(of things) piece; item | 一～小事 yī zhuāng xiǎoshì *a trifle* / 一～生意yī zhuāng shēngyì *a business; a transaction*

 (装) zhuāng 12画衣部

装 装装装装装装装装 装装装装

❶[名]衣服；特指演员的化装：outfit; clothing; costume | 春～chūnzhuāng *spring outfit* / 童～tóngzhuāng *children's wear* / 卸～xièzhuāng *remove stage makeup and costume*

服装 fúzhuāng
军装 jūnzhuāng
时装 shízhuāng
西装 xīzhuāng
泳装 yǒngzhuāng
中山装 zhōngshānzhuāng

❷[动] 装饰；打扮：dress; attire; deck out; play the part of | ～点 zhuāngdiǎn *decorate* / 他在戏里～一个老头儿。Tā zài xì li zhuāng yī gè lǎotóur. *He plays an old man in the play.*

装饰 zhuāngshì decorate; adorn; ornament; deck
装修 zhuāngxiū fit up (a house, etc.)
包装 bāozhuāng

❸[动] 做出某种假象：pretend; feign; make believe | ～睡 zhuāngshuì *pretend to be asleep* / ～听不见 zhuāng tīngbujiàn *pretend to be unable to hear* / 他～出一副可怜相。Tā zhuāngchū yī fù kěliánxiàng. *He assumed a pitiful look.*

假装 jiǎzhuāng
乔装 qiáozhuāng

❹[动] 把东西放进去；容纳：load; pack; hold; put sth. into a vessel | ～箱 zhuāngxiāng *pack a box* / ～车 zhuāngchē *load a truck* / 货运列车上～满了器材。Huòyùn lièchē shang zhuāngmǎnle qìcái. *The freight train is fully loaded with all kinds of equipment.*

装卸 zhuāngxiè ① load and unload ② assemble and disassemble
集装箱 jízhuāngxiāng

❺[动] 安装，把零件配成整体：install; fit; assemble | ～电话 zhuāng diànhuà *fit a telephone* / 机器已经～好了。Jīqì yǐjīng zhuānghǎo le. *The machine has been installed.*

装配 zhuāngpèi assemble; fit

together
装置 zhuāngzhì ①install; fit ②
installation; unit; device; plant
安装 ānzhuāng
武装 wǔzhuāng
组装 zǔzhuāng
◇装备 zhuāngbèi ①equip; fit out
② equipment; outfit

 (壯) zhuàng 6画 丬部

壮 壮壮壮壮壮壮

❶ [形] 强健有力：strong; robust ｜
他身体很～。Tā shēntǐ hěn
zhuàng. *He has a sturdy physique.*
健壮 jiànzhuàng
❷ [形] 雄伟；气势盛：magnificent;
grand ｜ ～美 zhuàngměi *grand
and beautiful*
壮观 zhuàngguān grand (mag-
nificent) sight
壮丽 zhuànglì majestic; magnificent; glorious
壮烈 zhuàngliè heroic; brave
壮志 zhuàngzhì great aspiration; lofty ideal
❸ [动] 加强：strengthen; make
better ｜ ～声势 zhuàng shēngshì *lend impetus and strength* /
～胆子 zhuàng dǎnzi *boost
somebody's courage*
壮大 zhuàngdà grow in
strength; expand; strengthen

 (狀) zhuàng 7画 丬部

状 状状状状状状状

❶ [名] 外形；形状：shape; form ｜ 奇
形怪～ qíxíng-guàizhuàng
grotesque shapes
状态 zhuàngtài state; condition;
state of affairs
形状 xíngzhuàng
❷ [名] 情况：state; situation; condition ｜ 现～ xiànzhuàng *present
state of affairs* / 病～ bìng-
zhuàng *symptom (of a disease)*
状况 zhuàngkuàng condition;
state; state of affairs
罪状 zuìzhuàng
❸ [名] 起诉书：written complaint;
plaint ｜ 诉～ sùzhuàng *plaint;
indictment* / ～纸 zhuàngzhǐ
written complaint
告状 gàozhuàng
◇状语 zhuàngyǔ (gram.) adverbial modifier; adverbial
状元 zhuàngyuan ① Number
One Scholar, title conferred on
the one who came first in the
highest imperial examination ②
the very best (in a certain field)

 zhuàng 15画 扌部

撞 撞撞撞撞撞撞撞撞
撞撞撞撞撞撞撞

❶[动]物体猛然相碰：knock; bump into; run into; strike; collide ｜ 他被自行车～倒了。Tā bèi zìxíngchē zhuàngdǎo le. *He was knocked down by a bike.* / 两辆小汽车在交叉路口相～。Liǎng liàng xiǎoqìchē zài jiāochā lùkǒu xiāngzhuàng. *Two cars collided at the junction.*

碰撞 pèngzhuàng

❷[动]偶然遇到：meet by chance; run into ｜ 这事儿让我～见了。Zhè shìr ràng wǒ zhuàngjiàn le. *I ran into it by chance.*

❸[动]试探：try ｜ ～～运气 zhuàngzhuang yùnqi *try one's luck*

幢 zhuàng 15画 巾部

幢幢幢幢幢幢幢幢
幢幢幢幢幢幢幢

[量]用于房屋：used for houses ｜ 一～楼房 yī zhuàng lóufáng *a building*

追 zhuī 9画 辶部

追追追追追追追追追

❶[动]紧跟在后面赶：chase (or run) after; pursue ｜ ～随 zhuīsuí *follow*

追捕 zhuībǔ pursue and capture

追赶 zhuīgǎn quicken one's pace to catch up; run after; pursue

追逐 zhuīzhú ① pursue; chase ② ask; quest

追踪 zhuīzōng follow the trail of; track; trace

❷[动]回顾过去：recall; reminisce ｜ ～忆 zhuīyì *recollect* / ～述往事 zhuīshù wǎngshì *recall and recount one's experiences*

追悼 zhuīdào mourn over people's death

❸[动]事后补办：retroactively; posthumously ｜ ～加 zhuījiā *add to (the original amount)* / ～认 zhuīrèn *admit or confer posthumously; recognize retroactively*

❹[动]力求达到某种目的：try hard to achieve an aim ｜ ～求 zhuīqiú seek; pursue

❺[动]特指追求异性：court; pursue (a woman) ｜ 两个小伙子都在～这位姑娘。Liǎng gè xiǎohuǒzi dōu zài zhuī zhè wèi gūniang. *Both young men are courting this girl.*

❻[动]查究：trace; look into; get to the bottom of ｜ 这件事不必再～了。Zhè jiàn shì bùbì zài zhuī le. *It is unnecessary to get to the bottom of the matter.*

追查 zhuīchá investigate; trace; find out

追究 zhuījiū look into; find out; investigate

追问 zhuīwèn question closely; make a detailed inquiry

缀 (綴) zhuì 11画 纟部

缀 缀缀缀缀缀缀缀缀缀 缀缀缀

[动] 装饰：embellish; decorate | 衣服上～满了珠子。Yīfu shang zhuìmǎnle zhūzi. *The garment is decorated with beads.*

点缀 diǎnzhuì

准 (準❶❷)zhǔn 10画 冫部

准 准准准准准准准准 准准

❶ [名] 标准：standard; norm | ～绳 zhǔnshéng *criterion* / 水～ shuǐzhǔn *standard; level* / 以这个为～ yǐ zhège wéi zhǔn *take this as the standard*

准则 zhǔnzé norm; criterion; rule

标准 biāozhǔn

标准化 biāozhǔnhuà

❷ [形] 正确无误：accurate; exact; precise | 瞄～miáozhǔn *take aim; hit the target* / 他射门很～。Tā shèmén hěn zhǔn. *He is great at scoring goals (usu. in soccer games).* / 他发音不～。Tā fāyīn bù zhǔn. *His pronunciation is not standard.*

准确 zhǔnquè accurate; exact; precise

准时 zhǔnshí punctual; on time; on schedule

❸ [动] 允许：allow; grant; permit | 不～小孩入内。Bùzhǔn xiǎohái rù nèi. *Children are not allowed in.* / 公司～他两周假。Gōngsī zhǔn tā liǎng zhōu jià. *The company grants him two weeks' leave.*

准许 zhǔnxǔ permit; allow

批准 pīzhǔn

◇准备 zhǔnbèi ① prepare; get ready ② intend; plan

 zhuō 8画 扌部

拙 拙拙拙拙拙拙拙拙

[形] 笨；不灵巧：clumsy; awkward; dull; stupid | ～劣 zhuōliè *clumsy; inferior*

笨拙 bènzhuō

 zhuō 10画 扌部

捉 捉捉捉捉捉捉捉捉 捉捉

❶[动] 握；拿：grasp; hold; clutch | ～笔 zhuōbǐ *hold a pen* / ～刀 zhuōdāo *hold a knife*

❷[动] 抓；捕：catch; capture | 活～ huózhuō *capture sb. alive* / 猫～老鼠 māo zhuō lǎoshǔ *cats*

951

catch mice / 小偷儿被～住了。 Xiǎotōur bèi zhuōzhù le. *The thief has been caught.*
捕捉 bǔzhuō

zhuō　10画　木部

桌桌桌桌桌桌桌桌
桌桌

[名] 桌子：table; desk ｜ 餐～cān-zhuō *dining table* / 书～shūzhuō *writing desk*
桌子 zhuōzi table; desk

zhuó　8画　十部

卓卓卓卓卓卓卓卓

[形] 不平凡；超出一般：eminent; outstanding; remarkable ｜ ～见 zhuójiàn *brilliant idea*
卓越 zhuóyuè excellent; remarkable; outstanding; brilliant

（濁）zhuó　9画　氵部

浊浊浊浊浊浊浊浊
浊

[形] 液体有杂质不透明：muddy; turbid; murky; impure ｜ 污～ wūzhuó *filthy*
混浊 hùnzhuó

酌

zhuó　10画　酉部

酌酌酌酌酌酌酌酌
酌酌

[动] 估量：deliberate; weigh and consider; mull over ｜ ～量 zhuó-liáng *consider; use one's judgment* / 请～情修改。Qǐng zhuó-qíng xiūgǎi. *Make alterations according to the situation.*
酌情 zhuóqíng take into consideration the circumstances; use one's discretion

啄

zhuó　11画　口部

啄啄啄啄啄啄啄啄
啄啄啄

[动] 鸟类用嘴取食物：peck; (of birds) take food with the beak ｜ ～食 zhuóshí *peck at food* / 鸡在～米。Jī zài zhuó mǐ. *The chickens are pecking at the rice.*

zhuó　11画　羊部

着着着着着着着着
着着着

❶[动] 接触；挨上：touch; contact ｜ 附～fùzhuó *attach to; adhere to* / ～陆 zhuólù *land; touch down* / 飞机已经～陆。Fēijī yǐjīng zhuólù. *The aeroplane has landed.*

❷ [动] 使接触或附在别的物体上：apply; attach; touch or contact another thing | ～笔 zhuóbǐ *set pen to paper* / ～眼 zhuóyǎn *view from the angle of* / ～色 zhuósè *colour*

着手 zhuóshǒu put one's hand to; set about

着想 zhuóxiǎng consider (the interests of sb. or sth.)

着重 zhuózhòng stress; emphasize

❸ [动] 穿：wear (clothes); dress | 身～红衣 shēn zhuó hóngyī *be dressed in red* / 穿～得体 chuān-zhuó détǐ *dress oneself appropriately*

穿着 chuānzhuó

See zháo; zhe.

咨 zī　9画 口部

咨咨咨咨咨咨咨咨咨

[动] 商量：consult; take counsel; seek advice; discuss with others

咨询 zīxún seek advice from; hold counsel with; consult

姿 zī　9画 女部

姿姿姿姿姿姿姿姿姿

[名] 体态：posture; carriage;

bearing | 舞～ wǔzī *a dancer's posture and movements*

姿势 zīshì posture; gesture

姿态 zītài ① posture; carriage ② attitude; pose

资 (資) zī　10画 贝部

资资资资资资资资资资

❶ [名] 钱财；费用：money; fund; expenses

资本 zīběn ①capital ② what is capitalized on; sth. used to one's own advantage

资产 zīchǎn property; capital fund; assets

资费 zīfèi expenses

资金 zījīn fund; capital

资本家 zīběnjiā capitalist

资本主义 zīběn zhǔyì capitalism

资产阶级 zīchǎn jiējí capitalist class; bourgeoisie

出资 chūzī　　　工资 gōngzī
合资 hézī　　　集资 jízī
投资 tóuzī　　　外资 wàizī

❷ [名] 身份、条件或经历：endowment; ability; background and experiences | ～历 zīlì *qualifications and record of service; seniority* / 师～ shīzī *teaching staff; faculty*

资格 zīgé qualifications; requirements

953

资深 zīshēn senior; having high credentials or seniority
◇资料 zīliào ① means ② data; material
资讯 zīxùn information; info
资源 zīyuán natural resources; resources
资质 zīzhì natural endowments; intelligence
资助 zīzhù aid sb. financially
物资 wùzī

滋 zī 12画 氵部
滋滋滋滋滋滋滋滋滋滋滋滋

❶ [动] 生长;繁殖: grow; multiply; propagate | ～养 zīyǎng ① nourish ② nutriment
滋长 zīzhǎng grow; develop
❷ [名] 味道: flavour; taste
滋味 zīwèi taste; flavour
◇艾滋病 àizībìng

子 zǐ 3画 子部
子子子

❶ [名] 儿子: son | 父～fùzǐ father and son / 独生～dúshēngzǐ only son
子弟 zǐdì sons and younger brothers; juniors; children
子孙 zǐsūn children and grandchildren; descendants
子女 zǐnǚ sons and daughters; children; offspring
儿子 érzi   太子 tàizǐ
王子 wángzǐ
独生子女 dúshēng zǐnǚ
❷ [名] 泛指人: generally referring to human beings
弟子 dìzǐ   老子 lǎozi
男子 nánzǐ   女子 nǚzǐ
骗子 piànzi   妻子 qīzi
小子 xiǎozi
书呆子 shūdāizi
伪君子 wěijūnzǐ
小孩子 xiǎoháizi
小伙子 xiǎohuǒzi
夜猫子 yèmāozi
不法分子 bùfǎ fènzǐ
花花公子 huāhuā gōngzǐ
知识分子 zhīshi fènzǐ
❸ [名] 卵: egg | 鱼～yúzǐ roe / 鸡～儿 jīzǐr (hen's) egg
❹ [名] 植物的子实: seed | 菜～儿 càizǐr vegetable seeds
瓜子 guāzǐ   莲子 liánzǐ
种子 zhǒngzi
❺ [名] 小而坚硬的块、粒: small hard lump or thing like a grain | 棋～儿 qízǐr chessman; piece / 石～儿 shízǐr small stone; pebble
子弹 zǐdàn bullet; cartridge
◇子公司 zǐgōngsī subsidiary company; subsidiary
案子 ànzi   杯子 bēizi
被子 bèizi   鞭子 biānzi

车子 chēzi
稻子 dāozi
架子 jiàzi
卷子 juǎnzi
裤子 kùzi
李子 lǐzi
骗子 piànzi
鞋子 xiézi
桌子 zhuōzi
爱面子 àimiànzi
摆架子 bǎijiàzi
醋坛子 cùtánzi
过日子 guòrìzi
卖关子 màiguānzi
命根子 mìnggēnzi
绕弯子 ràowānzi
钻空子 zuānkòngzi

橙子 chéngzi
分子 fēnzǐ
轿子 jiàozi
孔子 Kǒngzǐ
老子 Lǎozǐ
粒子 lìzǐ
桃子 táozi
银子 yínzi

 zǐ 5画 亻部

仔 仔仔仔仔仔

[形] 细密：careful; attentive; meticulous
仔细 zǐxì ①careful; attentive ② frugal; economical

 zǐ 12画 糸部

紫 紫紫紫紫紫紫紫紫
紫紫紫紫

[形] 红和蓝合成的颜色：purple | ~菜 zǐcài (bot.) laver
紫禁城 Zǐjìnchéng the Forbidden City (in Beijing)

 zì 6画 自部

自 自自自自自自自

❶ [代] 自己：self; oneself | ~修 zìxiū *self-study*; *study by oneself*
自卑 zìbēi feel oneself inferior to others; be self-abased
自称 zìchēng call oneself; claim to be; profess
自动 zìdòng ① voluntarily; of one's own accord ② automatic
自发 zìfā spontaneous
自费 zìfèi at one's own expense
自豪 zìháo have a proper sense of pride or dignity; be proud of sth.
自己 zìjǐ ① referring to the person mentioned earlier in the sentence ② oneself
自觉 zìjué ① (usu. used in the negative) be conscious ② on one's own initiative; conscious
自律 zìlǜ (formal) self-discipline; restrain oneself
自满 zìmǎn be complacent; be self-satisfied
自杀 zìshā commit suicide; take one's own life
自身 zìshēn self; oneself
自首 zìshǒu ① (of a criminal) voluntarily surrender oneself; confess one's crime; give oneself up ② make a political re-

cantation; surrender to the enemy

自私 zìsī be selfish; be self-centred

自卫 zìwèi self-defence; defend oneself

自我 zìwǒ self; oneself

自信 zìxìn self-confident; confident

自行 zìxíng ① by oneself ② of one's own accord

自学 zìxué study on one's own; study independently; teach oneself

自由 zìyóu ① freedom; liberty ② free; unrestrained

自愿 zìyuàn voluntary; of one's own accord; of one's own free will

自治 zìzhì autonomy; self-government

自主 zìzhǔ act on one's own; decide for oneself; keep the initiative in one's own hands

自助 zìzhù self-help; DIY; self-service

自来水 zìláishuǐ running water; tap water

自行车 zìxíngchē bicycle; bike

自治区 zìzhìqū autonomous region

自负盈亏 zìfùyíngkuī (of an enterprise) assume sole responsibility for its profits or losses

自力更生 zìlì-gēngshēng rely on one's own efforts; self-reliance

自相矛盾 zìxiāng-máodùn

contradict oneself; be self-contradictory

自言自语 zìyán-zìyǔ talk to oneself; think aloud; soliloquize

自由市场 zìyóu shìchǎng free (or open) market

独自 dúzì   各自 gèzì

亲自 qīnzì   擅自 shànzì

私自 sīzì   大自然 dàzìrán

不由自主 bùyóuzìzhǔ

独立自主 dúlì-zìzhǔ

❷[副] 自然；当然：certainly; of course; naturally ｜老王的这些意见，～有道理。Lǎo Wáng de zhèxiē yìjiàn, zì yǒu dàolǐ. *These views of Lao Wang's are certainly reasonable.*

自然 zìrán naturally; in the ordinary course of events

❸[介] 从；由：from; since ｜～小 zìxiǎo *since childhood* / ～这个月开始 zì zhège yuè kāishǐ *since this month*

自从 zìcóng since

自古 zìgǔ since ancient times; from time immemorial

自始至终 zìshǐ-zhìzhōng from start to finish; from beginning to end

出自 chūzì   来自 láizì

◇自在 zìzài free; unrestrained

字   zì   6画 宀部

字 字 字 字 字 字

宗
综
棕

❶[名]文字;记录语言的符号:word; character | 常用 ～chángyòng-zì everyday words / 这篇文章大约有 5 000 ～。Zhè piān wén-zhāng dàyuē yǒu wǔqiān zì. *This article has about 5,000 characters.*

字典 zìdiǎn dictionary

字画 zìhuà calligraphy and painting

字母 zìmǔ letters of an alphabet; letter

字样 zìyàng ① model of written characters ② printed or written words (which succinctly inform, instruct, warn, etc.)

别字 biézì   赤字 chìzì

错字 cuòzì   汉字 Hànzì

数字 shùzì   文字 wénzì

数字化 shùzìhuà

金字招牌 jīnzì zhāopai

❷人的姓名或别名:style name | 大诗人李白～太白。Dà shī rén Lǐ Bái zì Tàibái. *Famous poet Li Bai styled himself Taibai.*

字号 zìhao ① the name of a shop ② (dial.) reputation

名字 míngzi   签字 qiānzì

❸[名]字体:form of a written or printed character | 斜体～xié-tǐzì *italics* / 黑体～hēitǐzì *boldface; boldface type*

繁体字 fántǐzì

简体字 jiǎntǐzì

❹[名]字音:pronunciation of a word or character | 咬～清楚

yǎozì qīngchǔ *pronounce words clearly*

◇老字号 lǎozìhào

zōng   8画 宀部

宗 宗宗宗宗宗宗宗宗

❶ [名]派别:sect; faction; school | 正～zhèngzōng *orthodox school*

宗教 zōngjiào religion

宗派 zōngpài faction; sect

❷ [名]主要的目的和意图:principal aim; purpose

宗旨 zōngzhǐ aim; purpose

(综) zōng   11画 纟部

综 综综综综综综综综 综综综

[动]总合在一起:put together; sum up | ～述 zōngshù *summary*

综合 zōnghé ①comprehensive; multiple; composite ② synthesize

综艺 zōngyì comprehensive arts

zōng   12画 木部

棕 棕棕棕棕棕棕棕棕 棕棕棕棕

See 棕色

棕色 zōngsè brown

踪 zōng 15画 足部

踪踪踪踪踪踪踪踪
踪踪踪踪踪踪踪

[名] 脚印；痕迹：footprint; track; trace | ~影 zōngyǐng *trace; sign* / 跟 ~gēnzōng *follow the tracks of* / 失 ~shīzōng *lose the tracks of; missing*

踪迹 zōngjì trace; track
追踪 zhuīzōng

总 （總） zǒng 9画 心部

总总总总总总总总
总

❶ [动] 聚集；汇合到一起： assemble, put together; sum up | 汇 ~huìzǒng *assemble; collect; gather together* / ~起来说zǒng qǐlai shuō *to sum up*

总分 zǒngfēn total (score, marks); overall
总共 zǒnggòng in all; altogether; in the aggregate
总和 zǒnghé sum; total
总计 zǒngjì amount to; add up to; total
总结 zǒngjié ① sum up; summarize ② summary; summing up
总之 zǒngzhī ① in a word; in short ② anyway; anyhow

总而言之 zǒng'éryánzhī in short; in a word; in brief; to make a long story short

❷ [形] 全部的；全面的：overall; general; total | ~动员 zǒng dòngyuán *mobilization on an overall scale* / ~趋势zǒng qūshì *general trend* / ~的情况对我们有利。Zǒng de qíngkuàng duì wǒmen yǒulì. *The situation is favourable to us in general.*

总额 zǒng'é total
总量 zǒngliàng gross; total
总数 zǒngshù total; sum total
总体 zǒngtǐ overall; total

❸ [形] 概括全部的；主要的；为首的：chief; head; general | ~纲 zǒnggāng *general principles* / ~店 zǒngdiàn *head office (of a firm); flagship store* / ~编辑zǒngbiānjí *editor in chief*

总督 zǒngdū governor-general
总裁 zǒngcái director-general (of a political party); president (of a company); governor (of a bank)
总监zǒngjiān inspector general; chief inspector
总理 zǒnglǐ premier; prime minister
总统 zǒngtǒng president (of a republic)
总务 zǒngwù ① general affairs ② person in charge of general

affairs

总经理 zǒngjīnglǐ general manager; president

总司令 zǒngsīlìng commander in chief

❹[副]一直；一向：always; invariably｜你晚上〜看电视吗？Nǐ wǎnshang zǒng kàn diànshì ma? *Do you always watch TV in the evening?* / 他〜能找到借口。Tā zǒng néng zhǎodào jièkǒu. *He would invariably find an excuse for himself.*

总是 zǒngshì always; invariably

❺[副]毕竟，总归：after all; eventually; sooner or later｜迟做〜比不做好。Chí zuò zǒngbǐ bù zuò hǎo. *Better late than never.* / 你不要着急，问题〜会解决的。Nǐ bùyào zháojí, wèntí zǒnghuì jiějué de. *Keep calm. The problem will be settled sooner or later.*

总得 zǒngděi must; have to; be bound to

总算 zǒngsuàn ① at long last; finally; eventually ② considering everything; all things considered; on the whole

 （縱）zòng 7画 纟部

纵 纵纵纵纵纵纵纵

[形]竖；直（跟"横 héng"相对）：vertical (the opposite of "横 héng"）｜〜线 zòngxiàn *vertical line* / 排成〜队 páichéng zòngduì *stand in column formation*

纵横 zònghéng in length and breadth; vertically and horizontally

 zǒu 7画 走部

走 走走走走走走走

❶[动]跑：run｜〜奔 bēnzǒu *run; rush about; run errands; be busy running about*

逃走 táozǒu

东奔西走 dōngbēn-xīzǒu

❷[动]步行：walk; go｜行〜 xíngzǒu *walk* / 孩子会〜了。Háizi huì zǒu le. *The child has learned to walk.* / 他慢慢地〜了几步。Tā mànmàn de zǒule jǐ bù. *He slowly took a few steps.*

走道 zǒudào pavement; sidewalk; path; walk; footpath

走访 zǒufǎng ① interview; have an interview with ② pay a visit to; go and see

走廊 zǒuláng corridor; passage

走路 zǒulù ① walk; go on foot ② leave; go away

走弯路 zǒuwānlù to take a roundabout route; to take a

wrong path

竞走 jìngzǒu

❸[动]离开：leave | 他刚～。Tā gāng zǒu. *He's just left.* / 我明天要～了。Wǒ míngtiān yào zǒu le. *I am leaving tomorrow.*

出走 chūzǒu

❹[动]移动；挪动：move; drive; sail | 钟不～了。Zhōng bù zǒu le. *The clock has stopped.* / 你这着棋～坏了。Nǐ zhè zhāo qí zǒuhuài le. *You've made a bad move.*

❺[动]漏出；越过范围：leak; let out; escape | 球～气了。Qiú zǒuqì le. *The ball leaks.* / 他说～了嘴。Tā shuōzǒule zuǐ. *He made a slip of the tongue.*

走漏 zǒulòu leak out; divulge

❻[动]改变或失去原样：depart from the original; lose the original shape, flavour, etc. | 茶叶～味儿了。Cháyè zǒuwèir le. *The tea has lost its flavour.* / 衣服穿～样儿了。Yīfu chuān zǒuyàngr le. *The suit has been worn out of shape.*

❼[动]经过（某种途径行动）：go through a certain procedure | 这笔钱不～账了。Zhè bǐ qián bù zǒuzhàng le. *This sum of money need not be shown in the account.*

走私 zǒusī smuggle

走后门儿 zǒuhòuménr get in by the back door; secure advan-tages through pull or influence; get sth. done through influence

❽[动]（亲友间）往来：visit (relatives or friends) | ～亲戚 zǒu qīnqi *call on relatives* / 他们两家～得很勤。Tāmen liǎng jiā zǒu de hěn qín. *The two families visit each other very often.*

◇走狗 zǒugǒu running dog; lackey; flunky; stooge; servile follower

走势 zǒushì trend; tendency

走向 zǒuxiàng ① run; trend; alignment ② move towards; head for; be on the way to

zòu　　9画 一部

奏奏奏奏奏奏奏奏奏

[动]用乐器表演：play (a musical instrument) | 独～dúzòu *(instrumental) solo* / ～乐 zòuyuè *strike up a tune* / ～国歌 zòu guógē *play the national anthem*

伴奏 bànzòu　　演奏 yǎnzòu

zòu　　12画 扌部

揍揍揍揍揍揍揍揍揍揍揍揍

[动]打人：beat; hit; strike | 揍～

āizòu *get a thrashing* / 他被人～了一顿。Tā bèi rén zòule yī dùn. *He was beaten up by somebody.*

 租 zū 10画 禾部

租租租租租租租租租租

❶[动]出代价使用：rent; hire; charter | ～房 zūfáng *rent a house* / ～车 zūchē *rent a car*
租金 zūjīn rent; rental

❷[动]把东西借给别人，收取费用：lend sth. to others in return for rent | 转～zhuǎnzū *sublease; sublet* / 房子已经～出去了。Fángzi yǐjīng zū chūqu le. *The house has been leased out.*
租界 zūjiè concession (in former times, a tract of land in a Chinese port or city on lease to an imperialist power and put under its colonial rule); settlement
出租 chūzū 出租车 chūzūchē

❸[名]出租所收取的钱或实物：rent; rental | 收～shōuzū *collect rent* / 减～jiǎnzū *reduce rent*
房租 fángzū

足 zú 7画 足部

足足足足足足足

❶[名]脚：foot | ～迹 zújì *footmark*
足球 zúqiú ① soccer; football ② football (the ball used in playing either soccer or American football)
立足 lìzú 涉足 shèzú

❷[形]充足，足够：enough; ample; sufficient | 不～bùzú *insufficient; not enough*
足够 zúgòu enough; ample; sufficient
充足 chōngzú 满足 mǎnzú
十足 shízú
美中不足 měizhōng-bùzú

❸[动]完全可以，值得：be worthy of | 他～可以担任翻译工作。Tā zú kěyǐ dānrèn fānyì gōngzuò. *He is fully qualified as an interpreter.*
足以 zúyǐ enough; sufficient
足足 zúzú fully; as much as
微不足道 wēibùzúdào

 族 zú 11画 方部

族族族族族族族族族族族

❶[名]家族：clan | 家～jiāzú *clan; family*
贵族 guìzú

❷[名]民族，种族：nationality; race | 汉～Hànzú *the Han nationality* / 各～人民 gè zú rénmín *people of all nationalities*
族群 zúqún social and cultural

group of people bound together by a common language, religion, belief, customs, pedigree, race, history, geography and other factors; group of people with certain common features

民族 mínzú　　种族 zhǒngzú
少数民族 shǎoshù mínzú

阻 zǔ　7画 阝(左)部

阻 阻 阻 阻 阻 阻 阻

[动] 拦挡：hinder; block; obstruct | ~力 zǔlì the force of resistance

阻碍 zǔ'ài hinder; block; impede

阻挡 zǔdǎng stop; resist; obstruct

阻拦 zǔlán stop; obstruct; bar the way

阻挠 zǔnáo obstruct; thwart; stand in the way

阻止 zǔzhǐ prevent; stop; hold back

劝阻 quànzǔ

组 (組) zǔ　8画 纟部

组 组 组 组 组 组 组 组

❶ [动] 结合；构成：organize; form | 重~ chóngzǔ reorganization

组成 zǔchéng ① form; make up; compose ② formation; composition

组词 zǔcí（gram.）auxiliary word

组合 zǔhé ① make up; compose; constitute ② association; combination

组建 zǔjiàn put together (a group); form

组织 zǔzhī ① organize; form ② organization; organized system

组装 zǔzhuāng put together; assemble

改组 gǎizǔ

❷ [名] 由若干人结合成的单位：group; small unit consisting of a few people | 互助 ~ hùzhùzǔ mutual aid group

组长 zǔzhǎng group leader

小组 xiǎozǔ

祖 zǔ　9画 礻部

祖 祖 祖 祖 祖 祖 祖 祖

❶ [名] 家族中较早的上辈：ancestor; forefather

祖国 zǔguó mother country; one's country; homeland; native land

祖先 zǔxiān ancestry; ancestors; forebears; forefathers

❷ [名] 父母的上一辈：grandparents; grandfather | 外 ~ 母 wàizǔmǔ (maternal) grandmother

祖父 zǔfù (paternal) grandfather

祖母 zǔmǔ (paternal) grandmother

外祖父 wàizǔfù

See zuān.

钻（鑽）zuān　10画　钅部

钻 钻钻钻钻钻钻钻钻钻
钻钻

❶ [动] 穿孔；打眼：drill; bore ｜ ~孔 zuānkǒng *drill a hole* / 在木板上~个眼儿 zài mùbǎn shang zuān ge yǎnr *drill a hole in a wooden board*

❷ [动] 深入研究：study intensively; dig into
钻研 zuānyán study or scrutinize thoroughly

❸ [动] 穿透或进入：get into; go through; make one's way into ｜ ~山洞 zuān shāndòng *go into a mountain cave* / 孩子~到水里去了。Háizi zuāndào shuǐ li qù le. *The child dived into the water.*
钻空子 zuānkòngzi avail oneself to loopholes (in a law, contract, etc.); exploit an advantage
See zuān.

钻（鑽）zuān　10画　钅部

钻 钻钻钻钻钻钻钻钻
钻钻

[名] 钻石：diamond ｜ ~戒 zuānjiè *diamond ring*
钻石 zuānshí ① diamond ② jewel (used in a watch)

嘴　zuǐ　16画　口部

嘴 嘴嘴嘴嘴嘴嘴嘴嘴
嘴嘴嘴嘴嘴嘴嘴嘴

❶ [名] 口的通称：general term for "口 kǒu" ｜ 张~ zhāng zuǐ *open one's mouth*
嘴巴 zuǐba mouth
嘴唇 zuǐchún lip
打嘴仗 dǎzuǐzhàng
磨嘴皮 mózuǐpí
乌鸦嘴 wūyāzuǐ

❷ [名] 形状或作用像嘴的东西：anything shaped or functioning like a mouth ｜ 烟~儿 yānzuǐr *cigarette holder* / 瓶~儿 píngzuǐr *the mouth of a bottle* / 茶壶~儿 cháhúzuǐr *the spout of a teapot*

❸ [名] 指话语：speak; talk ｜ 别多~! Biè duōzuǐ! *Shut up!*
插嘴 chāzuǐ　吵嘴 chǎozuǐ

最　zuì　12画　日部

最 最最最最最最最最
最最最最

[副] 表示程度达到极点超过所有同类的东西：(indicating that a certain attribute has surpassed all people or things of the same kind) most; least; best; to the highest or lowest degree | ～大 zuì dà *the biggest* / ～快 zuì kuài *the fastest* / ～高级 zuì gāojí *the most advanced* / ～喜欢 zuì xǐhuan *like most*

最初 zuìchū initial; first

最好 zuìhǎo best; first rate

最后 zuìhòu ① final; last; ultimate ② finally; eventually

最佳 zuìjiā ① (phys.) optimum ② the best

最近 zuìjìn ① recently; lately; of late ② in the near future; soon

最终 zuìzhōng final; ultimate

 zuì 13画 四部

罪 罪 罪 罪 罪 罪 罪 罪 罪 罪 罪 罪 罪

❶[名]犯法的行为：crime; guilt | 认～rènzuì *confess one's guilt*

罪恶 zuì'è crime; evil

罪犯 zuìfàn criminal; offender; culprit

罪名 zuìmíng charge; accusation

罪行 zuìxíng crime; guilt; offence

罪状 zuìzhuàng facts about a crime; charges in an indictment

犯罪 fànzuì

替罪羊 tìzuìyáng

❷[名]苦难；痛苦：suffering; pain; hardship | 遭～zāozuì *suffer hardships* / 受～shòuzuì *endure*

suffering; suffer mental agony or physical pain; have a hard time

活受罪 huóshòuzuì

 zuì 15画 酉部

醉 醉 醉 醉 醉 醉 醉 醉 醉 醉 醉 醉 醉 醉 醉

[动]因喝酒过量而神志不清：be drunk; be intoxicated | 他喝～了。Tā hēzuì le. *He is drunk.* / 他喝得烂～。Tā hē de lànzuì. *He is dead drunk.*

麻醉 mázuì

 zūn 12画 寸部

尊 尊 尊 尊 尊 尊 尊 尊 尊 尊 尊 尊

[动] 敬重：show respect for | ～师 zūnshī *respect one's teacher*

尊称 zūnchēng a respectful form of address; honorific title

尊敬 zūnjìng respect; honour; esteem

尊严 zūnyán dignity; honour

尊重 zūnzhòng respect; value; esteem

遵 zūn 15画 辶部

遵 遵 遵 遵 遵 遵 遵 遵 遵 遵 遵 遵 遵 遵

[动] 依从；按照：abide by; obey; observe; follow; comply with | ～命 zūnmìng *obey a command; comply with one's wish* / ～医嘱 zūn yīzhǔ *follow the doctor's advice*

遵守 zūnshǒu observe; comply with; abide by

遵循 zūnxún follow; abide by; adhere to

遵照 zūnzhào obey; conform to; comply with; act in accordance with

昨 zuó 9画 日部

昨昨昨昨昨昨昨昨昨

[名] 今天的前一天：yesterday | ～晚 zuówǎn *yesterday evening; last night* / ～夜 zuóyè *last night*

昨天 zuótiān yesterday

琢 zuó 12画 王部

琢琢琢琢琢琢琢琢琢琢琢琢

See 琢磨

琢磨 zuómo turn sth. over in one's mind; ponder

左 zuǒ 5画 工部

左左左左左

[名] left | ～手 zuǒshǒu *left hand* / 汽车朝～转弯。Qìchē cháo zuǒ zhuǎnwān. *The car turned left.*

左边 zuǒbian the left; the left (left-hand) side

左侧 zuǒcè the left; left (left-hand) side

左面 zuǒmiàn the left; left (left-hand) side

左右 zuǒyòu ①the left and right sides ②about; more or less

左右手 zuǒyòushǒu right-hand man; capable assistant

作 zuò 7画 亻部

作作作作作作作

❶ [名] 进行某种活动：engage in a certain activity | ～报告 zuò bàogào *deliver a speech* / ～指示 zuò zhǐshì *give instructions* / 我已经～了最大的努力。Wǒ yǐjīng zuòle zuìdà de nǔlì. *I've already done the best I can.*

作案 zuò'àn commit a crime or an offence

作法 zuòfǎ way of doing things; practice

作风 zuòfēng style; style of work; way

作业 zuòyè ① school assignment; homework ② work; task; production; operation

作用 zuòyòng ① act on; affect ② action; function ③ effect

作战 zuòzhàn fight; conduct operations; engage in a battle

作证 zuòzhèng ① be used as evidence ② testify; give evidence; bear witness

作主 zuòzhǔ decide; take the responsibility for a decision

操作 cāozuò　炒作 chǎozuò
动作 dòngzuò　发作 fāzuò
工作 gōngzuò　合作 hézuò
协作 xiézuò　运作 yùnzuò
制作 zhìzuò　恶作剧 èzuòjù
副作用 fùzuòyòng
工作日 gōngzuòrì

❷ [动] 当作；作为：regard as; take sb. or sth. for | 他们把我当～自家人看待。Tāmen bǎ wǒ dàngzuò zìjiārén kàndài. They looked upon me as a family member.

作废 zuòfèi become invalid

作客 zuòkè (formal) sojourn; be a visitor

作为 zuòwéi ① conduct; deed; action ② regard as; look on as

称作 chēngzuò
当作 dàngzuò　看作 kànzuò
以身作则 yǐshēn-zuòzé

❸ [动] 创作；写：write; compose |

~曲 zuòqǔ compose music / ~文章 zuò wénzhāng write articles or essays / ~诗 zuòshī compose a poem

作家 zuòjiā writer

作品 zuòpǐn works (of literature and art)

作文 zuòwén write a composition

作者 zuòzhě author; writer

❹ [名] 作品：work; writings | 佳~jiāzuò an excellent work 杰作 jiézuò　　著作 zhùzuò

❺ [动] 装作：pretend; affect | 装～zhuāngzuò pretend

◇作物 zuòwù crop

农作物 nóngzuòwù

坐　　　　　zuò　　7画 土部

坐 坐坐坐坐坐坐坐

❶ [动] sit | 请～qǐngzuò Please sit down / 他～在沙发上。Tā zuò zài shāfā shang. He sits on the sofa.

❷ [动] 乘；搭（交通工具）：take; travel by | ～船 zuòchuán by ship / ～飞机 zuò fēijī by plane / ～火车 zuò huǒchē by train

乘坐 chéngzuò

❸ [动]（建筑物）背对着某一方向：(of a building) have its back towards | 这所房子～北朝南。Zhè suǒ fángzi zuòběi cháonán. This house faces south.

坐落 zuòluò (of a building) be situated; be located

❹[动]（把锅、壶等）放在（炉火上）：put (a pan, pot, kettle, etc.) on a fire | ～锅zuòguō *put a pot on the stove* / ～一壶水 zuò yī hú shuǐ *put a kettle of cold water on (a stove)*

◇坐班 zuòbān keep office hours

座

座 座座座座座座座座座座

❶ [名] 座位；位子：seat; place | 入～rùzuò *take one's seat*
座次zuòcì order of seats; seating arrangements
座谈zuòtán have an informal discussion
座位 zuòwèi seat; place
座谈会zuòtánhuì forum; symposium; informal discussion
座右铭 zuòyòumíng motto; maxim
讲座jiǎngzuò   在座zàizuò

❷ [名] 放在器物底下垫着的东西：stand; pedestal; base | 支～ zhīzuò *pedestal; support; abutment* / 钟～儿 zhōngzuòr *clock pedestal* / 花盆～儿huāpénzuòr *flowerpot stand*
座儿 zuòr seat; place

❸ [量] 用于较大的固定物体：used mostly for large and fixed

zuò   10画 广部

objects | 一～桥 yī zuò qiáo *a bridge* / 一～山 yī zuò shān *a mountain*

做

做 做做做做做做做做做做做做

zuò   11画 亻部

❶[动] 干；从事某种工作或活动：do; make; produce; manufacture; engage in manual and mental work | ～工作zuò gōngzuò *work; do the job* / ～买卖 zuò mǎimai *do business* / 你们～了一件好事。Nǐmen zuòle yī jiàn hǎoshì. *You have done a good thing.*

做操zuòcāo do gymnastics; do calisthenics; do exercises
做法 zuòfǎ way of doing or making a thing; method of work; practice
做饭 zuòfàn do the cooking; prepare a meal
做工 zuògōng do manual work; work
做梦 zuòmèng have a dream; dream
做人 zuòrén ① conduct oneself; behave ② be an upright person
做事 zuòshì ① do work; do a deed; handle affairs ② work; have a job
做鬼脸zuòguǐliǎn make a face;

pull a face

做生意 zuòshēngyi do business; carry on trade

做手脚 zuòshǒujiǎo juggle things; use an underhand trick

做文章 zuòwénzhāng ① write a composition ② make an issue of sth.; make a fuss about sth.

❷[动]制造：make | ~衣服 zuò yīfu *make clothes* / 这些工艺品都是手工~的。Zhèxiē gōngyìpǐn dōushì shǒugōng zuò de. *These handicrafts are all handmade.*

❸[动]充当：成为：be; become; act as | ~教员 zuò jiàoyuán *be a teacher* / ~翻译 zuò fānyì *act as an interpreter; do translation* / ~父母的 zuò fùmǔ de *as par-*

ents; being one's parents

做客 zuòkè be a guest; call on sb.

❹[动]结成某种关系：form or contract a relationship | ~亲戚 zuò qīnqi *(of two families) become relatives by marriage* / ~朋友 zuò péngyou *make friends with*

❺[动]用作：serve as; be used as | 树皮可以~造纸的原料。Shùpí kěyǐ zuò zàozhǐ de yuánliào. *Bark can be used as material in papermaking.* / 那间屋子现在~了库房。Nà jiān wūzi xiànzài zuòle kùfáng. *That room is used as a storeroom now.*

叫做 jiàozuò

Appendices

Commonly Used Radicals

Radical 部首	Name 名称	Example 例字	Stroke Order 笔顺
匚	匚字框	巨医	一匚
卜	上字头	占贞	丨卜
刂	立刀旁	刑刚	丿刂
冂(冂)	同字框	同周	丨冂
亻	单立人	化仇	丿亻
厂	反字旁	反后	一厂
𠂊	危字头	危争	丿𠂊
勹	包字头	包句	丿勹
几	风字头	风凤	丿几
亠	六字头	六亡	丶亠
冫	两点水	冲次	丶冫
丷	兰字头	并关	丶丷
冖	秃宝盖	写军	丶冖
讠	言字旁	订认	丶讠
凵	凶字框	凶画	凵凵
卩	单耳旁	却印	刁卩
阝	左耳旁	阳际	乛阝
阝	右耳旁	邦那	乛阝
厶	私字头	允台	乚厶
廴	建之旁	廷延	㇇廴
艹	草字头	艺节	一十艹
廾	弄字底	弃弄	一十廾
尢	尤字身	尤扰	一十尢
兀	尧字底	尧	一丆兀
扌	提手旁	扔扫	一十扌

Radical 部首	Name 名称	Example 例字	Stroke Order 笔顺
弋	式字框	式	一弋弋
囗	国字框	回困	丨冂囗
⺌	光字头	当尚	丶⺌⺌
彳	双立人	往很	丿彳彳
彡	三撇儿	形影	丿彡彡
犭	反犬旁	犯狼	丿犭犭
夂	折文儿	务复	丿夂夂
饣	食字旁	饥饭	丿饣饣
丬	将字旁	壮状	丶丬丬
忄	竖心旁	忙怀	丶忄忄
宀	宝盖儿	安完	丶冖宀
氵	三点水	汉汗	丶氵氵
辶	走之儿	进远	丶辶辶
⺕	录字头	录绿	乛⺕⺕
彐	寻字头	寻归	乛彐彐
纟	绞丝旁	红级	纟纟纟
幺	幼字旁	幻幼	幺幺幺
巛	三拐儿	巢	巛巛巛
耂	老字头	考孝	一十耂耂
小	竖心底	恭	亅小小小
攵	反文旁	故救	丿攵攵攵
爫	采字头	妥受	一爫爫爫
火	火字旁	炸炮	丶火火火
灬	四点底	煮照	丿灬灬灬
礻	示字旁	视祥	丶礻礻礻
皿	皿字底	盐监	丨口皿皿皿
钅	金字旁	钉针	丿钅钅钅钅
疒	病字旁	疮疯	丶疒疒疒疒

Radical 部首	Name 名	Example 例字	Stroke Order 笔顺
衤	衣字旁	补被	丶 ㇇ 衤 衤 衤
癶	登字头	登瞪	㇁ 夂 癶 癶 癶
虍	虎字头	虑虚	丨 ㇒ 卜 虍 虍 虍
⺮	竹字头	第策	ノ ト ᅡ ᅡ ⺮ ⺮
芈	撇尾羊	差着	丶 ソ 쓰 쓰 쓰 芈
羊	羊字头	美羔	丶 ソ 쓰 쓰 羊 羊
艮	垦字头	悬良	㇇ ㅋ ㅋ ㅌ ㅌ 艮
𧾷	足字旁	跌跑	丨 冂 口 ㅸ ㅸ ㅸ 𧾷
釆	番字头	悉释	丿 ㇇ ㇇ 平 平 釆
豸	豹字旁	豺豹	丿 ㇇ 𠂊 夕 豸 豸 豸
卓	朝字旁	韩戟	一 十 ㇕ 占 占 卓 卓 卓
隹	隹字旁	雄雌	丿 亻 亻 亻 ㅑ ㅑ 隹 隹

[Notes]

(1) Some radicals such as 山、马、日、月、厂 are not included, as these characters are separate words.

(2) The names presented for the radicals are the most frequently used names. However, other names are sometimes used.

Basic Rules for Writing Chinese Characters

Rule 规则	Example 例字	Stroke Order 笔顺
Horizontal strokes precede vertical strokes 先横后竖 .	十	一十
	丰	一二三丰
Downward strokes to the left precede those to the right 先撇后捺 .	人	丿人
	大	一ナ大
Strokes are written from the top to bottom 从上到下 .	三	一二三
	豆	一丆丆豆豆豆豆
Strokes are written from left to right 先左后右 .	环	一二千王王玎玎环环
	啊	丨口口叮叮叮叮叮叮啊
Enclosing strokes precede enclosed strokes 从外到内 .	问	丶门门问问问
Enclosed strokes precede enclosing strokes 从内到外 .	函	乛了了了丞丞函函
	延	一丆千正延延
First enclosing strokes, then enclosed strokes and finally the stroke at the bottom 先里头后封口 .	目	丨冂月月目
	回	丨冂冋冋回回
Vertical strokes in the middle precede strokes on either side 先中间后两边 .	办	乛力力办
	承	乛了了丞手承承承